WITHDRAWN
UTSA LIBRARIES

From Protest to Challenge

VOLUME 6

Published by Hoover Institution Press

VOLUME 1: Protest and Hope, 1882–1934
VOLUME 2: Hope and Challenge, 1935–1952
VOLUME 3: Challenge and Violence, 1953–1964
VOLUME 4: Political Profiles, 1882–1964

Published by Indiana University Press

VOLUME 5: Nadir and Resurgence, 1964–1979

From Protest to Challenge

A DOCUMENTARY HISTORY OF
AFRICAN POLITICS IN
SOUTH AFRICA,
1882–1990

VOLUME 6

CHALLENGE AND VICTORY, 1980–1990

Gail M. Gerhart & Clive L. Glaser

INDIANA UNIVERSITY PRESS   BLOOMINGTON & INDIANAPOLIS

This book is a publication of

Indiana University Press
601 North Morton Street
Bloomington, IN 47404-3797 USA

www.iupress.indiana.edu

Telephone orders 800-842-6796
Fax orders 812-855-7931
Orders by e-mail iuporder@indiana.edu

© 2010 by Gail M. Gerhart and Clive L. Glaser
All rights reserved

No part of this book may be reproduced or utilized in any form or by any means, electronic or mechanical, including photocopying and recording, or by any information storage and retrieval system, without permission in writing from the publisher. The Association of American University Presses' Resolution on Permissions constitutes the only exception to this prohibition.

♾The paper used in this publication meets the minimum requirements of the American National Standard for Information Sciences—Permanence of Paper for Printed Library Materials, ANSI Z39.48-1992.

Manufactured in the United States of America

Cataloging information for this series is available from the Library of Congress

ISBN for this volume 978-0-253-35422-8 (cloth : alk. paper)
LCCN for the series 72-152423

1 2 3 4 5 15 14 13 12 11 10

**Library
University of Texas
at San Antonio**

*To the
post-apartheid generation,
citizens of a new South Africa*

Contents

PREFACE xxi
ACKNOWLEDGMENTS xxv
LIST OF ACRONYMS xxix

PART 1. CHALLENGE AND VICTORY, 1980–1990

1. Reform and Repression in the Era of P. W. Botha 3
Pretoria on the Offensive 4
Debating the New Constitution 7
And What About the Black People? 12
Urban Influx Control and Squatters 17
The Homelands 22
KwaZulu and Inkatha 28
"Total Strategy" 31
The Struggle in the Courts 37

2. Internal Opposition: The Battle Joined 45
New Fronts of Resistance 46
Charterism Resurgent 47
Founding the United Democratic Front 52
Civic Associations and Local Struggles 57
Students and Politics 58
Black Workers and Trade Unions 61
White Allies 65
The Vaal Uprising of 1984 68

3. Internal Opposition: Moving Toward Deadlock 80
The First State of Emergency, 1985 82
Consumer Boycotts 84
The Formation of COSATU 86
The Second State of Emergency 90
Politics and Religion 93

Students and *Amabutho:* The Struggle for Control	98
Leadership Conflicts in the UDF	103
1987: Workers on the Offensive	106
The War for Natal	112

4. Exile and Underground Politics, 1980–1988 — 120

The African National Congress, 1980–1983	121
Building the Underground	128
Setback: the Nkomati Accord	130
Mutiny in Umkhonto we Sizwe	133
Restoring Legitimacy: the Kabwe Conference	136
On the Offensive, 1985–1988	139
International Pressure for Negotiation	145
The ANC and the Communist Party	149
The Pan Africanist Congress	152

5. Breaking the Deadlock, 1988–1990 — 164

The February 1988 Crackdown	166
Internal Opposition, 1988	168
The Mass Democratic Movement	172
Bargaining with the System	174
Talking About Talks	178
A Sea of Troubles	183
Grasping the Nettle	190

Epilogue — 207

PART 2. DOCUMENTS

1. Reform and Repression in the Era of P. W. Botha — 217

DOCUMENT 1. "For the Sake of South Africa, Free Nelson Mandela." Speech by Percy Qoboza, University of the Witwatersrand, March 20, 1980 — 217

DOCUMENT 2. "In the End, PW Must Do a Deal With Me." Article by Chief Mangosuthu Gatsha Buthelezi, *Sunday Times,* April 6, 1980 — 219

CONTENTS   IX

DOCUMENT 3. "Piet Freeman, Thebehali—and Ice to Eskimos . . . !" Article by Jon Qwelane, *Kwasa,* November 1980 — 221

DOCUMENT 4. "Botha Holds Key to Peaceful Future for South Africa." Op-ed article by Bishop Desmond Tutu, *Manchester Guardian Weekly,* October 4, 1981 — 222

DOCUMENT 5. "The Responsibility of Judges in Applying Unjust Laws in South Africa." Civil Rights League pamphlet, Cape Town, 1981? — 224

DOCUMENT 6. "South Africa: the Case Against Immigration—A Letter to Polish Catholics from the Church in South Africa." Southern African Catholic Bishops' Conference pamphlet, Pretoria, early 1982 — 228

DOCUMENT 7. Memorandum on threatened removal of Lusitania, a "black spot" in Natal, February 1982 — 233

DOCUMENT 8. Inkatha's minutes of a meeting between Piet Koornhof and an Inkatha delegation, Cape Town, May 3, 1982 — 235

DOCUMENT 9. Letter from Reverend Lesiba Matsaung to the South African Council of Churches, September 27, 1982 — 237

DOCUMENT 10. "YOU and the New PASS LAWS." Black Sash pamphlet, September 1982 — 239

DOCUMENT 11. Remarks to the President's Council by Mamoud Rajab, November 24, 1982 — 244

DOCUMENT 12. "The National Situation." Paper by Neville Alexander delivered at AZAPO annual congress, February 1983 — 248

DOCUMENT 13. Letter from Saul Mkhize to P. W. Botha about forced removal of Daggakraal, Driefontein and Ngema "black spots," March 31, 1983 — 253

DOCUMENT 14. "Solidarity with SAAWU and Our People in Ciskei." UDF flyer, Transvaal Region, October 1983 — 254

DOCUMENT 15. "NOvember 2: Why You Should Vote NO!" Black Sash leaflet, Durban, October 1983 — 256

DOCUMENT 16. "Be Not Overcome by Evil: the Response of the South African Council of Churches to the Eloff Commission." June 5, 1984 — 260

DOCUMENT 17. "New Constitution Changes Nothing." Natal Indian Congress flyer, August 1984 — 263

DOCUMENT 18. "Reform Versus Revolution." Labour Party election flyer, August 1984 — 267

DOCUMENT 19. "Uitenhage Police Station—On a Sunday Afternoon." Report by Audrey Coleman, March 17, 1985, *The Black Sash,* May 1985 — 268

DOCUMENT 20. Affidavit of James Michael Tamboer about police brutality, Port Elizabeth, September 1985 — 270

DOCUMENT 21. Affidavit of John Sakukhuna about violence in KwaNdebele, January 1986 — 274

DOCUMENT 22. "The New Influx Control." Bulletin of the National Committee Against Removals, Cape Town, April 9, 1986 — 275

DOCUMENT 23. "Crisis in Crossroads." Interview with Dr. Ivan Toms by the United States Committee of the International Defense and Aid Fund, May 1986 — 278

DOCUMENT 24. "Property Ownership: a Black Perspective." Speech by Enos Mabuza to South African Property Owners Association, Johannesburg, August 7, 1986 — 281

DOCUMENT 25. "The Future of South Africa: Violent Radicalism or Negotiated Settlement?" Speech by Chief Mangosuthu Gatsha Buthelezi to the Heritage Foundation, Washington, November 24, 1986 — 285

DOCUMENT 26. "The Provincial Legislature." KwaZulu-Natal Indaba constitutional proposals, Durban, November 28, 1986 — 286

DOCUMENT 27. Statement by "J," 16-year-old male, Mapetla, Soweto, March 1987 — 287

DOCUMENT 28. "The Fight for Oukasie." Interview with member of Brits Action Committee, *Sechaba,* May 1987 — 289

DOCUMENT 29. "Group Areas in Mayfair." ACTSTOP discussion paper, April 1989 — 294

2. Internal Opposition: The Battle Joined — 298

DOCUMENT 30. "Open Letter from Natal Indian Congress." Durban, November 1, 1981 — 298

DOCUMENT 31. "The Workers' Struggle—Where Does FOSATU Stand?" Speech by Joe Foster to second FOSATU congress, Hammanskraal, April 10, 1982 — 299

DOCUMENT 32. Report on meeting of FOSATU shop stewards council, Katlehong township, east Rand, November 14, 1982 — 302

DOCUMENT 33. "Manifesto of the Azanian People." Statement by AZAPO, June 1983 — 305

DOCUMENT 34. "Responses to State Strategy." Speech by Popo Molefe to National Union of South African Students conference, University of Cape Town, July 1983 — 306

DOCUMENT 35. "Peace in Our Day." Speech by Allan Boesak at national launch of the UDF, Mitchell's Plain, Cape Town, August 20, 1983 — 310

CONTENTS　　　　　　　　　　　　　　　　　　　　　　XI

DOCUMENT 36. "Declaration of the United Democratic Front." August 20, 1983 — 315

DOCUMENT 37. "Support the Cape Action League." *Worker-Tenant* newssheet, Cape Town, August 1983 — 317

DOCUMENT 38. Trade union statement condemning Ciskei government ban on SAAWU, September 1983 — 320

DOCUMENT 39. "Massacre at Ngoye." AZASM flyer, October 1983 — 321

DOCUMENT 40. "Don't Vote for Apartheid!" UDF flyer in Tswana and English, November 1983 — 322

DOCUMENT 41. "Towards a Just Peace in Our Land." End Conscription Campaign flyer, Durban, 1983 — 323

DOCUMENT 42. "A Brief History of the Durban Housing Action Committee (DHAC) and the Joint Rent Action Committee (JORAC)." Pamphlet, 1983? — 324

DOCUMENT 43. Report to UDF national executive committee from Cradock Residents Association, January 1984 — 330

DOCUMENT 44. "Million Signature Campaign: Briefing for Fieldworkers." UDF pamphlet, eastern Cape, March 1984 — 332

DOCUMENT 45. "3000 Say No to Increases." East Rand People's Organisation flyer, June 1984 — 336

DOCUMENT 46. "Boycott Their Apartheid Elections." Community Education Programme flyer, Korsten, Port Elizabeth, August 1984 — 336

DOCUMENT 47. "Congress Calls on Our People to Oppose Botha." Transvaal Indian Congress flyer, August 1984 — 337

DOCUMENT 48. Resolutions taken at meetings of the Vaal Civic Association, August 1984, in Sotho (with translation) — 338

DOCUMENT 49. "The Third Day of September: an Eye-witness Account of the Sebokeng Rebellion of 1984." Booklet by Johannes Rantete — 339

DOCUMENT 50. "The Anatomy of Rival Visions." Excerpt from paper by Lebamang J. Sebidi for Institute for Contextual Theology conference, Johannesburg, September 1984 — 344

DOCUMENT 51. "Stay Away!!! Monday and Tuesday the 5th and 6th November 1984." Transvaal Stayaway Committee flyer, in English and Sotho — 349

DOCUMENT 52. Report by Chemical Workers' Industrial Union on strike at SASOL, November 8, 1984 — 351

DOCUMENT 53. Annual secretarial report of the UDF, Border Region, by M. A. Stofile, November 30, 1984 — 354

DOCUMENT 54. "Composite Executive Report" of AZAPO, December 1984 — 358

DOCUMENT 55. "Bafundi Manyanani!/Students Unite!" COSAS leaflet, Grahamstown branch, early 1985?, in Xhosa and English — 363

DOCUMENT 56. Memorandum on education crisis signed by Popo Molefe for UDF and J. Khumalo for COSAS, January 21, 1985 — 364

DOCUMENT 57. Statement on hit squads by Johannesburg Democratic Action Committee, Black Sash, Detainees' Parents Support Committee, Detainees Support Committee, National Union of South African Students, Young Christian Students, and End Conscription Campaign, *The Black Sash,* August 1985 — 365

DOCUMENT 58. "What is a National Convention?" Black Sash circular by Sheena Duncan, September 17, 1985 — 366

DOCUMENT 59. "The Freedom Charter—For and Against." Article in *Arise! Vukani!,* journal of Action Youth, Johannesburg, September–October, 1985 — 369

DOCUMENT 60. Report to UDF on repression in Galeshewe township, Kimberley, 1985 — 372

DOCUMENT 61. Report for national workshop by Johannesburg Democratic Action Committee, January 1986 — 374

DOCUMENT 62. "OUT—Organisations United Against Traitors." Flyer by Woodstock civic group, Cape Town, May 1986 — 379

DOCUMENT 63. "Why I Refuse to Participate in the South African Defence Force." Court statement by Philip Wilkinson, May 1987 — 381

3. Internal Opposition: Moving Toward Deadlock — 385

DOCUMENT 64. "SOYCO's Programme of Action." Soweto Youth Congress memorandum, 1983 — 385

DOCUMENT 65. Letter from Chief Mangosuthu Gatsha Buthelezi to Oliver Tambo, September 7, 1984, reproduced in Inkatha's *Clarion Call,* volume 3, 1987 — 387

DOCUMENT 66. Program of the first annual National General Council of the UDF, Azaadville, Krugersdorp, April 5–7, 1985 — 388

DOCUMENT 67. Press statement by AZAPO on AZAPO-UDF clashes, May 21, 1985 — 397

DOCUMENT 68. "Western Cape Ablaze." University of Cape Town Student Representative Council flyer, August 29, 1985 — 398

DOCUMENT 69. "Challenge to the Church: a Theological Comment on the Political Crisis in South Africa—The Kairos Document." Pamphlet by Kairos theologians, September 1985 — 400

DOCUMENT 70. "Liberating the Classrooms." Article in *Upfront,* UDF journal, Cape Town, October 1985 — 406

DOCUMENT 71. Speech by Cyril Ramaphosa at COSATU launching conference, Durban, November 29, 1985 — 409

DOCUMENT 72. ANC intelligence report on Inkatha attacks, Durban, late 1985 — 411

DOCUMENT 73. Excerpts from cross-examination of Professor I. D. de Vries by Advocate Ismail Mahomed, *State v. Ramgobin and others,* Pietermaritzburg, December 2, 1985 — 413

DOCUMENT 74. "ONS Kersfees onder HULLE Noodtoestand/ OUR Christmas Under THEIR State of Emergency." New Unity Movement flyer, Cape Town, December 1985, in Afrikaans and English — 416

DOCUMENT 75. "Use Your Spending Power—Support Consumer Boycott." UDF flyer, Cape Town, 1985 — 419

DOCUMENT 76. "Alexandra Massacre." Funeral flyer, Alexandra township, Johannesburg, March 5, 1986 — 420

DOCUMENT 77. Funeral of ANC guerrilla Thanduxolo Mbethe, Uitenhage, March 14, 1986 — 422

DOCUMENT 78. "People's Education for People's Power." Speech by Zwelakhe Sisulu to National Education Crisis Committee conference, Durban, March 29, 1986 — 429

DOCUMENT 79. "On People's Power and People's Committees." Alexandra Action Committee discussion document, April 8, 1986 — 435

DOCUMENT 80. ANC minutes of meeting with leaders of South African Catholic Church, Lusaka, April 15–16, 1986 — 437

DOCUMENT 81. "Consumer Boycott." Northern Transvaal Consumer Boycott Committee flyer, May 1986 — 446

DOCUMENT 82. Notes on meeting with Brigadier Ernest Schnetler of the South African Police, by Mkhuseli Jack of Port Elizabeth Youth Congress, May 1986 — 447

DOCUMENT 83. "June 16: Commemorating the Dead, Learning the Lessons, Continuing the Fight." Article in Muslim Youth Movement newsletter, *Risalatuna: Our Message,* June 1986 — 448

DOCUMENT 84. "Message to the People of South Africa from the National Executive Committee of the United Democratic Front." Leaflet, July 17, 1986 — 449

DOCUMENT 85. "Remember Kinross." COSATU leaflet, September 1986 — 453

DOCUMENT 86. ANC memorandum on factionalism in the UDF, Lusaka, late 1986 — 455

DOCUMENT 87. "Will NGK Resolution Pave the Way for Clampdown on Activists?" Article in *Al-Qalam,* Durban, November 1986 — 464

DOCUMENT 88. Eyewitness account of Ama-Afrika vigilante attack by Peggy Sotyelelwa of KwaNobuhle township, Uitenhage, January 4, 1987 — 466

DOCUMENT 89. "Unite with OK Workers!" Commercial, Catering and Allied Workers' Union flyer, February 1987 — 467

DOCUMENT 90. "A Message to All Democrats." COSATU advertisement, *Weekly Mail,* May 29, 1987 — 468

DOCUMENT 91. "The SATS Strike—The Other Version." COSATU information sheet, early May 1987 — 469

DOCUMENT 92. "Down With Apartheid Elections! Stayaway!" UDF and COSATU flyer, May 1987 — 474

DOCUMENT 93. "Coping With Detention." Article in Detainees' Parents Support Committee newsletter, *Noma Siyaboshwa,* August 1987 — 475

DOCUMENT 94. "Build Solidarity With NUM Strike—Build the Living Wage Campaign." National Union of Mineworkers flyer, August 1987 — 477

DOCUMENT 95. "NACTU Briefing on Visit to PAC." National Council of Trade Unions report, Dar-es-Salaam, September 2, 1987 — 479

DOCUMENT 96. "Business and Trade Unions." Speech by Jay Naidoo to business conference, *Financial Mail,* November 27, 1987 — 481

DOCUMENT 97. "Trade Unions and Political Direction." National Union of Metalworkers (NUMSA) discussion paper, December 1987 — 485

DOCUMENT 98. Excerpts from speech by Chief Mangosuthu Gatsha Buthelezi to KwaZulu Legislative Assembly, Ulundi, March 1988 — 488

DOCUMENT 99. "Victory!!!" Announcement of strike outcome by National Union of Metalworkers (NUMSA), August 16, 1988 — 490

4. Exile and Underground Politics, 1980–1988 — 492

DOCUMENT 100. "*Inqindi* and Marxism." ANC discussion document circulated in Robben Island prison after 1978, handwritten by Ahmed Kathrada — 492

DOCUMENT 101. "Rules of Security, Defence and Code of Conduct." Umkhonto we Sizwe draft memorandum, March 1981 — 498

DOCUMENT 102. "Unity and Determination of PAC Cadres Bring About Important Changes." Article in *Ikwezi,* number 16, March 1981 — 502

CONTENTS xv

DOCUMENT 103. "We Remember March 21—Pan Africanist Congress." Underground PAC flyer, March 1981 — 505

DOCUMENT 104. "Decisions of the ANC National Executive Committee, Luanda, 2–5 December 1981." ANC memorandum — 506

DOCUMENT 105. "Background to the Tanzanian Repression of PAC and APLA." Statement by supporters of P. K. Leballo in Britain, January 16, 1982 — 510

DOCUMENT 106. Excerpts from "South Africa's Impending Socialist Revolution: Perspective of the Marxist Workers' Tendency of the African National Congress," London, March 1982 — 511

DOCUMENT 107. "Summary Report of the Discussion on Open Membership." Solomon Mahlangu Freedom College, Mazimbu, Tanzania, May 15, 1982 — 514

DOCUMENT 108. Statement by Santo, 26-year-old ANC exile who survived Maseru raid of December 9, 1982 — 518

DOCUMENT 109. Presentation by unidentified speaker to ANC seminar on women's political participation, Tanzania, 1982 — 520

DOCUMENT 110. Minutes of meeting of South African Communist Party Unit 7, Lusaka, September 15, 1983 — 522

DOCUMENT 111. "The Constitutional Proposals and the UDF." ANC memorandum, Lusaka, October 26, 1983 — 524

DOCUMENT 112. "Dawn Breaks." Broadcast by ANC's Radio Freedom, Lusaka, November 24, 1983 — 528

DOCUMENT 113. "Planning for People's War." Discussion document by Joe Slovo, Maputo, November 1983 — 530

DOCUMENT 114. Excerpt from "Decisions and Suggestions from NEC/PMC Meeting." Notes from ANC leadership discussion about impending Nkomati Accord, Lusaka, January 25, 1984 — 536

DOCUMENT 115. "Report: Commission of Inquiry into Recent Developments in the People's Republic of Angola [Stuart Commission]." Lusaka, March 1984 — 539

DOCUMENT 116. Notes on a visit to Nelson Mandela in Pollsmoor Prison, by Nicholas Bethell, January 27, 1985 — 549

DOCUMENT 117. Speech by Zindzi Mandela at Jabulani Amphitheatre, Soweto, February 10, 1985 — 553

DOCUMENT 118. "Sharpeville, Soweto and Sebokeng." Speech by John Nyati Pokela of PAC to the Special Committee Against Apartheid, United Nations, New York, March 22, 1985 — 555

DOCUMENT 119. "The Road to Freedom." Poem by Freddy Reddy, *Sechaba,* April 1985 — 558

DOCUMENT 120. Memo from Moscow Camp detachment of Umkhonto we Sizwe, Angola, early 1985 559

DOCUMENT 121. "ANC Call to the Nation: the Future is Within Our Grasp!" Underground leaflet, April 1985 561

DOCUMENT 122. "The Women's Question." Excerpt from report of Commission on Ideological and Political Work, ANC National Consultative Conference, Kabwe, Zambia, June 16–23, 1985 564

DOCUMENT 123. "Open Membership: Recommendations." ANC memorandum prepared for National Consultative Conference, Kabwe, Zambia, June 16–23, 1985 565

DOCUMENT 124. ANC National Executive Committee report, presented by Oliver Tambo to the National Consultative Conference, Kabwe, Zambia, June 16, 1985 567

DOCUMENT 125. A delegate's impressions of the ANC National Consultative Conference, Kabwe, Zambia, June 1985, *Umsebenzi,* vol. 1, no. 2, mid-1985 574

DOCUMENT 126. "Summary of Discussions Between Certain Representatives of Big Business and Opinion-Makers in South Africa and the ANC." ANC memorandum, September 14, 1985 576

DOCUMENT 127. "The Situation in South Africa: Minutes of Evidence." Testimony of Oliver Tambo and Thabo Mbeki before the Foreign Affairs Committee of the British House of Commons, October 29, 1985 580

DOCUMENT 128. Letter from Godfrey Motsepe, ANC representative in Brussels, to ANC headquarters, November 10, 1985 587

DOCUMENT 129. "A Submission on the Question of Negotiations." Internal ANC policy paper, Lusaka, November 27, 1985 589

DOCUMENT 130. "How to Master Secret Work." Article in *Umsebenzi,* vol. 1, no. 3, late 1985 592

DOCUMENT 131. ANC press statement by Thabo Mbeki on resignation of Van Zyl Slabbert from Parliament, February 7, 1986 594

DOCUMENT 132. Letter from Stanley Mabizela, ANC representative in Tanzania, to ANC president and secretary general, Lusaka, March 7, 1986 595

DOCUMENT 133. "Yes to ANC Visit." *SRC News,* University of Cape Town, March 1986 599

DOCUMENT 134. Report by Commonwealth Eminent Persons Group on meeting with ANC representatives in Lusaka, May 17, 1986 599

DOCUMENT 135. "The South African Communist Party and the Current Political Situation in the Western Cape." Study document for underground SACP members, late 1986 601

CONTENTS   XVII

DOCUMENT 136. "A Few Points on the Current State of Struggle in S.A." ANC intelligence report, mid-1987   604

DOCUMENT 137. "The Dakar Declaration." Statement by participants in IDASA conference, Dakar, July 12, 1987   608

DOCUMENT 138. Evaluation of Dakar conference by ANC participant, July 1987   610

DOCUMENT 139. "The Question of Negotiations." Statement by ANC National Executive Committee, Lusaka, October 9, 1987   614

DOCUMENT 140. "Briefing on Situation in P [Botswana]." ANC intelligence report, December 1987   617

DOCUMENT 141. "APLA selects white targets." Editorial in *Azania Combat,* no. 4, 1987   621

DOCUMENT 142. Report by "General Tobetsa" on unsuccessful mission of Umkhonto we Sizwe unit, late 1980s   623

DOCUMENT 143. ANC National Working Committee minutes, Lusaka, February 22, 1988   625

DOCUMENT 144. "The Quiet Thunder: Report on the Amsterdam Cultural Conference." Article by Mandla Langa, *Sechaba,* March 1988   631

DOCUMENT 145. "Problems Faced by Women." Discussion notes in SACP *Inner Party Bulletin,* August 1989   633

5. Breaking the Deadlock, 1988–1990   637

DOCUMENT 146. ANC report on meeting held in Henley-on-Thames, England, with three Stellenbosch academics, October 31–November 1, 1987   637

DOCUMENT 147. "The NIC and the Three Plagues." Article by Yunus Carrim, *Weekly Mail,* February 12, 1988   640

DOCUMENT 148. Church petition protesting restrictions on 17 organizations and COSATU, February 29, 1988   642

DOCUMENT 149. "Fight for Your Rights." *CWIU Flame,* no. 12, March 1988   644

DOCUMENT 150. "Azikwelwa! Stayaway! June 6, 7, 8—3 Days of United National Action." Anonymous flyer, June 1988   646

DOCUMENT 151. "Municipal Elections." UDF policy paper by Titus Mafolo, June 1988   648

DOCUMENT 152. "Municipal Elections." Southern African Catholic Bishops' Conference flyer, July 1988   652

DOCUMENT 153. "Constitutional Guidelines for a Democratic South Africa." ANC policy paper, Lusaka, August 1988   654

DOCUMENT 154. Response to the ANC "Constitutional Guidelines" by Cassim Saloojee and Firoz Cachalia of the Transvaal Indian Congress, *Weekly Mail,* October 7, 1988 ... 658

DOCUMENT 155. "Joint Statement of the South African Rugby Board, the South African Rugby Union and the African National Congress." Harare, October 16, 1988 ... 661

DOCUMENT 156. Letter from Mosiuoa Patrick Lekota to AZAPO leaders, handwritten, December 5, 1988 ... 661

DOCUMENT 157. "Keep South African Sports in Isolation." Op-ed article by Sam Ramsamy, *New York Times,* December 11, 1988 ... 663

DOCUMENT 158. "Business in Post-Apartheid S.A." Article by Kay Makan in Transvaal Indian Congress leaflet, "Face to Face With the ANC," December 1988 ... 665

DOCUMENT 159. "Campaign for a Friendly City." Port Elizabeth Action Committee flyer, early 1989 ... 667

DOCUMENT 160. Press statement by hunger strikers at Johannesburg Prison, Diepkloof, January 23, 1989 ... 668

DOCUMENT 161. "A Different Kind of Bias is Behind White Support of the ANC." Op-ed article by Thami Mazwai, *Los Angeles Times,* February 21, 1989 ... 669

DOCUMENT 162. Letter from Ahmed Kathrada to friends, handwritten, February 25, 1989 ... 671

DOCUMENT 163. Memorandum from Nelson Mandela to P. W. Botha, March 1989 ... 672

DOCUMENT 164. "Soweto Council Stalls Rent Negotiations." *Soweto People's Delegation NEWS,* April 5, 1989 ... 676

DOCUMENT 165. "The Path to Power: Programme of the South African Communist Party Adopted at the 7th Congress," Havana, April 1989 ... 679

DOCUMENT 166. "Report of PC Meeting With BN." Minutes of meeting of ANC President's Committee with Beyers Naudé, Lusaka, April 25, 1989 ... 683

DOCUMENT 167 "The Role of Local Government." Excerpt from report of Five Freedoms Forum-ANC conference, Lusaka, June 29–July 2, 1989 ... 687

DOCUMENT 168 "Jews for Social Justice." Excerpt from report of Five Freedoms Forum-ANC conference, Lusaka, June 29–July 2, 1989 ... 689

DOCUMENT 169. "Wat die Besoek aan Lusaka vir my Beteken Het (What the Lusaka Experience Meant for Me)." Excerpt by Flip Potgieter from report of Five Freedoms Forum-ANC conference, Lusaka, June 29–July 2, 1989, in Afrikaans and English ... 691

CONTENTS   XIX

DOCUMENT 170. "Negotiations for Political Settlement in SA." COSATU memorandum, June 1989 — 693

DOCUMENT 171. "Preparing Ourselves for Freedom: Culture and the ANC Constitutional Guidelines." Discussion paper by Albie Sachs, Lusaka, July 1989 — 695

DOCUMENT 172. "Negotiation—The Great Hoax." Editorial in *New Unity Movement Bulletin,* July 1989 — 699

DOCUMENT 173. Report to ANC on Women's Day meeting at Kaunda Square by Ronnie Kasrils, Lusaka, August 9, 1989 — 700

DOCUMENT 174. "Declaration of the Organisation of African Unity Ad Hoc Committee on Southern Africa on the Question of South Africa" (The Harare Declaration), August 21, 1989 — 702

DOCUMENT 175. "Apartheid is Dying—Bury It Now." Natal Indian Congress and the Durban Municipal Employees Union flyer, August 1989 — 705

DOCUMENT 176. Letter from ANC Department of Religious Affairs about visit by Zionist church leaders, Lusaka, October 5, 1989 — 706

DOCUMENT 177. "Keeper of the Keys." Interview with Archbishop Desmond Tutu by Paul Bell, *Leadership SA,* October 1989 — 706

DOCUMENT 178. Affidavit of Butana Almond Nofomela, Pretoria, handwritten, October 19, 1989 — 711

DOCUMENT 179. "Party Piece." Interview with Cyril Ramaphosa by Paul Bell, *Leadership SA,* November 1989 — 715

DOCUMENT 180. Interview with PAC chairman, Johnson Mlambo, Dar-es-Salaam, October 9, 1989, *SAPEM,* December 1989/January 1990 — 719

DOCUMENT 181. "Has Socialism Failed?" *Umsebenzi* discussion pamphlet by Joe Slovo, London, January 1990 — 721

DOCUMENT 182. Speech by Nelson Mandela on the Grand Parade, Cape Town, February 11, 1990 — 725

CHRONOLOGY   729

SOURCES   737

INDEX   755

MAPS

1. SOUTHERN AFRICA IN THE 1980s

2. SOUTH AFRICA IN THE 1980s

3. HOMELANDS AND "BLACK SPOTS," 1980s

4. CAPE TOWN, 1980s

5. DURBAN REGION, 1980s

6. PRETORIA-WITWATERSRAND-VEREENIGING REGION, 1980s

PREFACE

This volume of *From Protest to Challenge* chronicles the tumultuous decade of the South African liberation struggle that ended in February 1990 with the unbanning of restricted political organizations and the freeing of Nelson Mandela. Although another four years went by before a democratic election formally brought Mandela and the African National Congress to power, the unbannings of 1990 marked an irreversible turning point in the country's long colonial history of minority rule and legally enshrined race discrimination. The nature of South Africa's conflict changed fundamentally in the period between 1990 and 1994. Even as lethal clashes escalated between pro- and anti-ANC forces, the ruling National Party and the ANC itself, the principal adversaries, shifted their contest to conference rooms and bilateral bargaining sessions where they hammered out the details of a democratic post-apartheid constitution.

Once past the turning point of February 1990, neither the ANC nor the National Party could afford a return to the old order. Given that the powerful coalition of pro-ANC groups outweighed the National Party and its allies, both in bargaining power and voting strength, the eventual electoral outcome was not hard to foresee in 1990, despite the many uncertainties of the time. We have therefore chosen to regard the years 1990–1994 as a transitional interlude, and have periodized the struggle against apartheid and minority rule as ending in 1990—a choice that at this stage may not represent a final consensus among historians.

Readers who expect a full explanation of the South African breakthrough of 1990 will not find it here. Any comprehensive explanation would have to examine developments in international relations, broad economic and social changes in South Africa, and the internal politics of the Afrikaner ruling bloc, none of which receive more than passing mention in this volume. The focus here, as in past volumes of this series, is on the essential remaining source of causal explanations: the actions taken by Africans and their allies in the struggle for political change.

When the first volume in this series appeared in 1972, relatively little academic attention had been given to the subject of African politics in South Africa. Today the study of "struggle history" is expanding rapidly. Dozens of monographs, biographies, and autobiographies have been written, and major anthologies of historical essays have begun to appear, such as *The Road to Democracy in South Africa* series. The number of black South Africans with post-graduate degrees in history, political science, and sociology is steadily rising. Since 1990 important collections of political documents have been deposited in South African libraries, most notably the archives of the African National Congress, the Pan Africanist Congress, and AZAPO at Fort Hare University and the rich collections of archives from Robben Island and personal papers at the Mayibuye Centre at the University of the Western Cape. Readers who appreciate the value of studying history through primary sources can now move from the appetizing but tiny sample of documents reproduced here to the vast feast of archival material housed in South African, British, and American libraries, some of which is now also accessible online through websites such as www.Aluka.org and www.disa.ukzn.ac.za. All this bodes well for the future of historical scholarship in South Africa.

The first four volumes of *From Protest to Challenge,* produced by American scholars Thomas Karis, Gwendolen Carter, Sheridan Johns, and Gail Gerhart, were published by the Hoover Institution of Stanford University between 1972 and 1977. These books examined the period from the founding in 1882 of an early Transkeian political organization, *Imbumba Yama Afrika,* to the Rivonia trial of 1964. The apartheid government banned the third volume (1953–1964) from being sold in South Africa on the grounds that it contained the words of banned persons. Nevertheless, many institutions and individuals managed to acquire the entire series by one means or another. At one stage even prisoners on Robben Island were able to borrow the series from the University of South Africa library on the pretext that they needed it to complete correspondence courses.

For a decade after 1977, the authors of the original series turned their attention to other tasks. But as political conflict in South Africa reached new levels in the late 1980s, Karis and Gerhart began working on a post-Rivonia "update" series, conducting interviews whenever it was possible to obtain visas to South Africa, talking with South African exiles and visitors to the United States, and scouring libraries on three continents for documentary source material. This book follows volume 5, *Nadir and Resurgence, 1964–1979,* co-published in 1997 by Indiana University Press and UNISA Press. Clive Glaser of the University of the Witwatersrand has replaced Karis as co-author of the text chapters in this volume, and other new authors have contributed to the second edition of volume 4, *Political Profiles, 1882–1990,* now in preparation.

As our collective efforts in producing this series draw toward a close, it seems fitting to pay tribute again to those South Africans who labored and fought, sacrificed and died to create a just and democratic society in a country once so infamously blighted by racism, fear, and exploitation. They have inspired us, and millions more around the world, by their example, even as we recognize that post-apartheid reality has often fallen short of their ideals. The struggle continues.

Gail M. Gerhart
Clive L. Glaser

ACKNOWLEDGMENTS

This book has benefited from the contributions of many people, some of whom may have wondered if it would ever see the light of day. The footnotes and section on Sources acknowledge our debt to many of those who were interviewed during the research phase. Here we wish to express our thanks to others who contributed to the collection of documents, organization of the database, preparation of the manuscript, and funding of work on this volume.

David Lewis, many years ago, assembled our collection of documents from the independent trade unions in the 1980s, and E. S. Reddy contributed copies of documents from the United Nations Center Against Apartheid. Howard Barrell and Victoria Butler gave us access to their unique collections of interviews with ANC members, and Mark Swilling shared his interviews with activists in the eastern Cape. Arthur Chaskalson and David Dison facilitated the donation of a set of the documentary exhibits from *State v. Baleka* (the Delmas trial) to the Karis-Gerhart Collection. Amanda Armstrong allowed us to photocopy exhibits and testimony from *State v. Mayekiso,* and the late Raymond Tucker let us explore the historically rich piles of legal documents in his cellar. In the late 1990s J. D. De Bruyn of the Ministry of Justice in Pretoria gave us access to apartheid-era police files on restricted persons, invaluable materials which he had saved from the shredders of the old regime.

We are also grateful to other academics, lawyers, writers, and activists who generously shared documents or interview transcripts with us, including Jules Browde, Fran Buntman, Jim Cason, Judy Chalmers, Halton Cheadle, Janet Cherry, Davinder Dhillon, Walter Felgate, Julie Frederikse, Mark Gevisser, Henry Isaacs, Mkhuseli Jack, Priscilla Jana, Larry Jones, Ahmed Kathrada, Willem Kleynhans, Dirk Kotze, Tom Lodge, Brown Maaba, Gilbert Marcus,

Cedric Mayson, Ishmael Mkhabela, Kumi Naidoo, Quraish Patel, Rory Riordan, Steven Robins, John Saul, Lynda Schuster, Rupert Taylor, Ben Turok, Senti Thobejane, and Walter Wink. Azhar Cachalia, Pallo Jordan, Mac Maharaj, Johnson Mkhabela, Mukoni Ratshitanga, Raymond Suttner, and Pamela Yako responded to specific inquiries. Others who gave us collegial encouragement and backup support include Hilary Barker, Terri Barnes, Mary Benson, David Bonbright, Antony Bugg-Levine, Luli Callinicos, Elsbeth Court, Apollon Davidson, Bob Edgar, Irina Filatova, Jack Greenberg, Sophie Ledwaba, Sue Le Roux, Oyama Mabandla, Johannes Modibedi, Rory Riordan, Vladimir Shubin, and Brian Sokutu.

Locating, cataloging, organizing, duplicating, transcribing, typing, proofreading, and selectively digitizing the documents in the database of *From Protest to Challenge* were tasks performed by many dedicated students and researchers, including Emma Brown-Bernstein, Milissa Day, Timothy Gillam, Paul Gready, Claire Keeton, Moira Lubbock, Sipho Mahamba, Oupa Makhalemele, Xolani Malawana, Sebastian McKay, Phumlani Mkhize, Oupa Mokuena, Nhlanhla Ndebele, Mcebisi Ndletyana, Mone Raboroko, Temba Shabangu, Senti Thobejane, Heather Thuynsma, Goolam Vahed, Sonny Venkatrathnam, and Mary Ann Vincent.

Valuable comments on parts of the draft manuscript were made by Amanda Alexander, Azhar Cachalia, Stephen Ellmann, Mark Gevisser, Thomas Karis, Oyama Mabandla, Chris Saunders, and Graeme Simpson. Anriette Esterhuysen, Paul Germond, Mona Khalidi, Sekibakiba Lekgoathi, Zodwa Mathombisa, Part Mgadla, Sepetla Molapo, Malusi Mpumlwana, and Marinda Weideman helped with translations. Wendy Job made the maps; and Rita Potenza Roseanne at AfricanPictures.net helped with the photos. Amy Fontinelle provided expert copyediting.

The *From Protest to Challenge* series could never have been produced without the help of dozens of archivists and librarians in South Africa, the United States, and Britain. Their institutions are listed in the section on Sources. For assisting with this volume we are especially indebted to Moore Crossey, formerly of the Sterling Memorial Library at Yale, and Michele Pickover and the staff of the William Cullen Library at the University of the Witwatersrand.

We gratefully acknowledge the financial support which has made it possible to complete the last three volumes of the series. Principal funding was received from the National Endowment for the Humanities in the United States. Supplementary grants from the Ford Foundation, Rockefeller Foundation, and Andrew W. Mellon Foundation also helped sustain the project. Gerhart's work was subsidized by a Fulbright visiting professorship at the University of the Witwatersrand in 1994. The Centre for Science Development of the Human Sciences Research Council in South Africa supported Wits student interns in the mid-1990s, and an anonymous benefactor sponsored the interns who took a typing course.

Unstinting support from our spouses, Clare Loveday and the late John Gerhart, contributed hugely to our work on this volume. Most of all, we are indebted to Thomas Karis for his enormous dedication over many years to the task of recording, documenting, and dispassionately presenting the history of the struggle for democracy in South Africa. His work, his example, and his encouragement are reflected on every page of this book.

We thank the following for permission to reprint the documents listed:

Chapter 1. Document 6: "South Africa: the Case Against Immigration—A letter to Polish Catholics from the Church in South Africa," Southern African Catholic Bishops' Conference pamphlet, Pretoria, early 1982, reprinted with permission of the Southern African Catholic Bishops' Conference. Document 12: "The National Situation," paper by Neville Alexander delivered at AZAPO annual congress, February 1983, reproduced in Neville Alexander, *Sow the Wind: Contemporary Speeches* (Johannesburg: Skotaville, 1985), reprinted with permission of Neville Alexander. Document 23: "Crisis in Crossroads," interview with Dr. Ivan Toms by the United States Committee of the International Defense and Aid Fund, May 1986, reproduced in the newsletter of the U.S. Committee of IDAF, May 30, 1986, reprinted with permission of the late Ivan Toms.

Chapter 2. Document 35: "Peace in Our Day," speech by Allan Boesak at national launch of the UDF, Mitchell's Plain, Cape Town, August 20, 1983, reproduced in Allan Boesak, *Black and Reformed: Apartheid, Liberation and the Calvinist Tradition* (Maryknoll, N.Y.: Orbis Books, 1984), with final peroration from police transcripts of UDF launch, reprinted with permission of Allan Boesak. Document 49: "The Third Day of September: an Eye-witness Account of the Sebokeng Rebellion of 1984," booklet by Johannes Rantete (Johannesburg: Ravan Press, 1984), reprinted with permission of Johannes Rantete.

Chapter 3. Document 87: "Will NGK Resolution Pave the Way for Clampdown on Activists?," article in *Al-Qalam,* November 1986, reprinted with permission of *Al-Qalam.* Document 96: "Business and Trade Unions," speech by Jay Naidoo to business conference, *Financial Mail,* November 27, 1987, reprinted with permission of *Financial Mail.*

Chapter 4. Document 108: Statement by Santo, 26-year-old ANC exile who survived Maseru raid of December 9, 1982, reproduced in *Massacre at Maseru* (London: International Defence and Aid Fund, 1985), reprinted with permission of Horst Kleinschmidt. Document 134: Report by Commonwealth Eminent Persons Group on meeting with ANC representatives in Lusaka, May 17, 1986, reproduced in *Mission to South Africa: The Commonwealth Report* (Harmondsworth, UK: Commonwealth Secretariat, 1986), reprinted with permission of the Commonwealth Secretariat.

Chapter 5. Document 157: "Keep South African Sports in Isolation," op-ed article by Sam Ramsamy, *New York Times,* December 11, 1988, reprinted with permission of Sam Ramsamy. Document 161: "A Different Kind of Bias is Behind White Support of the ANC," op-ed article by Thami Mazwai, *Los Angeles Times,* February 21, 1989, reprinted with permission of Thami Mazwai. Document 171: "Preparing Ourselves for Freedom: Culture and the ANC Constitutional Guidelines," discussion paper by Albie Sachs, Lusaka, July 1989, reproduced in Albie Sachs, *Protecting Human Rights in a New South Africa* (Cape Town: Oxford University Press, 1990), reprinted with permission of Albie Sachs. Document 177: "Keeper of the Keys," interview with Archbishop Desmond Tutu by Paul Bell, *Leadership SA,* October 1989, reprinted with permission of Paul Bell. Document 179: "Party Piece," interview with Cyril Ramaphosa by Paul Bell, *Leadership SA,* November 1989, reprinted with permission of Paul Bell.

ACRONYMS

Actstop	Action Committee to Stop Evictions
AFCWU	African Food and Canning Workers' Union
AFRA	Association for Rural Advancement
ANC	African National Congress
Anti-SAIC	Anti-South African Indian Council
APC	Area Political Committee
APLA	Azanian People's Liberation Army
APMC	Area Politico-Military Committee
ASRO	Atteridgeville-Saulsville Residents Association
AWB	Afrikaner Weerstandsbeweging
AZACTU	Azanian Confederation of Trade Unions
AZANYU	Azanian Youth Unity
AZAPO	Azanian People's Organisation
AZASCO	Azanian Students Congress
AZASM	Azanian Students Movement
AZASO	Azanian Students Organisation
BAWU	Black Allied Workers' Union
BCM	black consciousness movement
BCMA	Black Consciousness Movement of Azania
BLA	Black Local Authority
CAL	Cape Action League

CAYCO	Cape Youth Congress
CBD	central business district
CCAWUSA	Commercial, Catering and Allied Workers' Union of South Africa
Cde	comrade
CDF	Conference for a Democratic Future
CODESA	Convention for a Democratic South Africa
Contralesa	Congress of Traditional Leaders of South Africa
COSAS	Congress of South African Students
COSATU	Congress of South African Trade Unions
CP	Communist Party
CP	Conservative Party
CPRC	Coloured Persons' Representative Council
CRADORA	Cradock Residents Association
CRC	Coloured Representative Council
CRIC	Community Resource and Information Centre
CUSA	Council of Unions of South Africa
CWIU	Chemical Workers' Industrial Union
Descom	Detainees Support Committee
DET	Department of Education and Training
DHAC	Durban Housing Action Committee
DP	Democratic Party
DPE	Department of Political Education
DPSC	Detainees' Parents Support Committee
ECC	End Conscription Campaign
EPG	Commonwealth Eminent Persons Group
FA	forward areas (frontline states)
FAWU	Food and Allied Workers' Union
FEDSAW	Federation of South African Women
FEDTRAW	Federation of Transvaal Women
FOSATU	Federation of South African Trade Unions
FRELIMO	Frente de Libertação de Moçambique
GAWU	General and Allied Workers' Union
GST	general sales tax
GWU	General Workers' Union
HNP	Herstigte Nasionale Party
HOD	House of Delegates
HQ	headquarters

IDAF	International Defence and Aid Fund
IDASA	Institute for a Democratic Alternative for South Africa
IFP	Inkatha Freedom Party
JCC	Joint Commuters Committee
JMC	Joint Management Centre
JODAC	Johannesburg Democratic Action Committee
JORAC	Joint Rent Action Committee
Kms	kilometers
LRA	Labour Relations Act
MACWUSA	Motor Assembly and Component Workers' Union of South Africa
MAWU	Metal and Allied Workers' Union
MDM	mass democratic movement
MK	Umkhonto we Sizwe
MP	member of Parliament
MPLA	Movimento Popular da Libertação de Angola
MSA	Muslim Students Association
MSC	Million Signature Campaign
MWASA	Media Workers Association of South Africa
MYM	Muslim Youth Movement
NACTU	National Council of Trade Unions
NAFCOC	National African Federated Chamber of Commerce
NAT	ANC department of intelligence and security
NCC	Natal Committee of Concern
NCM	National Convention Movement
NEC	National Executive Committee
NECC	National Education Crisis Committee
NEUM	Non-European Unity Movement
NEUSA	National Education Union of South Africa
NFC	National Forum Committee
NGK	Nederduitse Gereformeerde Kerk (Dutch Reformed Church)
NIC	Natal Indian Congress
NIS	National Intelligence Service
NLM	national liberation movement
NOW	Natal Organisation of Women
NP	National Party
NSC	National Statutory Council
NSMS	National Security Management System

NUM	National Union of Mineworkers
NUMSA	National Union of Metalworkers of South Africa
NUSAS	National Union of South African Students
NWC	National Working Committee
OAU	Organization of African Unity
OFS	Orange Free State
OVGWU	Orange Vaal General Workers' Union
PAC	Pan Africanist Congress
PASA	post-apartheid South Africa
PC	President's Committee of the ANC
PE	Port Elizabeth
PEBCO	Port Elizabeth Black Civic Organisation
PEDWU	Port Elizabeth Domestic Workers Union
PEWO	Port Elizabeth Women's Organisation
PEYCO	Port Elizabeth Youth Congress
PFP	Progressive Federal Party
PHQ	political headquarters
PMC	Politico-Military Council
PNAB	Port Natal Administration Board
PUR	permanent urban resident
PWV	Pretoria-Witwatersrand-Vereeniging region
RC	Revolutionary Council
RCC	Roman Catholic Church
REC	Regional Executive Committee
RENAMO	Resistência Nacional Moçambicana
RMC	Release Mandela Campaign
RPMC	Regional Politico-Military Council
RSA	Republic of South Africa
RSC	Regional Services Council
SAAWU	South African Allied Workers' Union
SABC	South African Broadcasting Corporation
SACBC	Southern African Catholic Bishops' Conference
SACC	South African Council of Churches
SACHED	South African Committee for Higher Education
SACOS	South African Council on Sport
SACP	South African Communist Party
SACTU	South African Congress of Trade Unions

SACWU	South African Chemical Workers' Union
SADCC	Southern African Development Coordination Conference
SADF	South African Defence Force
SAIC	South African Indian Congress
SAIC	South African Indian Council
SAIRR	South African Institute of Race Relations
SALDWU	South African Laundry and Drycleaning Workers' Union
SAMRAF	South African Military Refugee Aid Fund
SAP	South African Police
SARHWU	South African Railway and Harbour Workers' Union
SASDU	South African Scooter Drivers Union
SASO	South African Students' Organisation
SASOL	Suid-Afrikaanse Steenkool en Olie (South African Coal and Oil)
SATS	South African Transport Services
SAYCO	South African Youth Congress
SEIFSA	Steel and Engineering Industrial Federation of South Africa
SEYO	Sekhukhuneland Youth Organisation
SO	Senior Organ
SOMAFCO	Solomon Mahlangu Freedom College
SOYCO	Soweto Youth Congress
SPCC	Soweto Parents' Crisis Committee
SPD	Soweto People's Delegation
SRC	Student Representative Council
SSC	State Security Council
SWAPO	South West Africa People's Organisation
TAWU	Transport and Allied Workers' Union
TIC	Transvaal Indian Congress
TPA	Transvaal Provincial Administration
TRAC	Transvaal Rural Action Committee
TRC	Truth and Reconciliation Commission
TVBC	Transkei-Venda-Bophuthatswana-Ciskei ("independent" homelands)
Tvl	Transvaal
UCT	University of Cape Town
UDF	United Democratic Front
UNITA	União Nacional para a Independência Total de Angola
USSR	Union of Soviet Socialist Republics

UTP	Urban Training Project
UWCO	United Women's Congress
UWO	United Women's Organisation
UWUSA	United Workers' Union of South Africa
UYCO	Uitenhage Youth Congress
WC	[National] Working Committee of ANC
WCC	World Council of Churches
WF	Women's Front
YCS	Young Christian Students
YCW	Young Christian Workers
ZANU	Zimbabwe African National Union
ZANU (PF)	Zimbabwe African National Union (Patriotic Front)
ZAPU	Zimbabwe African People's Union

Note on exchange rates: The value of the rand fell steeply against the dollar during the 1980s. Exchange rates are taken from the graph in Francis Wilson and Mamphela Ramphele, *Uprooting Poverty: The South African Challenge* (New York: W. W. Norton and Cape Town: David Philip, 1989), p. xvii.

Part One

Challenge and Victory, 1980–1990

1. Reform and Repression in the Era of P. W. Botha

The 1980s were South Africa's decade of destiny, launched in a flurry of government policy maneuvers, swept by waves of black rebellion, and finally brought to a political deadlock that foreshadowed the collapse of white minority rule. At the decade's outset, the ruling National Party was firmly in control, still able to push back the swelling tide of black resistance in schools, factories, and urban ghettos, but by the decade's end the balance of power had decisively shifted. Despite repeated setbacks, the democratic movement had achieved unprecedented influence, leaving the dominant Afrikaner elite divided and frustrated in its perennial quest for a formula to ensure black subordination. In other times and places, an ethnic minority so dedicated to its own continued dominance might have prevailed through raw coercion and careful statecraft. At the end of the twentieth century, however, South Africa's system of racial hierarchy—apartheid—had become a forlorn anachronism. Its demise seemed only a matter of time and organizational effort on the part of its victims and opponents. As the 1980s began, no one could predict how much time, effort, and sacrifice would be required. "Freedom in our lifetime" had been the rallying cry of struggle veterans of an earlier generation that now was passing from the scene, its hopes unfulfilled. The generation coming of age in 1980 faced a state armed with more instruments of repression than ever before. No one could rule out the possibility that this generation too might fail to end minority domination.

Yet by early 1990, time, circumstances, and the tenacity of many thousands of activists had placed South Africa firmly on a path to majority rule. Hoping to reverse the political paralysis and economic decline brought on by black resistance to the policies of his predecessor, P. W. Botha, President F. W. de Klerk, within a few months of assuming national leadership in late 1989, resolved to take swift preemptive action to move the country toward a negotiated settlement. His intention was to grasp the initiative at a time when he believed that black resistance groups were weak and disorganized and, through bold maneuvers, to install a legitimate new institutional order in which whites would retain a decisive share of political power. As events unfolded after February 1990, however, de Klerk's gamble failed. Although whites retained their existing hold over most sectors of the economy, de Klerk's National Party was politically outmaneuvered by the African National Congress (ANC) during the negotiation of a post-apartheid constitution. What began as a preemptive effort to forestall democratization by means of tight control over political change instead became a decisive victory for full democratic rights and the end of all legal forms of racial discrimination.

Earlier volumes in the *From Protest to Challenge* series have chronicled the century of conflict that preceded the final decade of South Africa's liberation struggle. Our task in this volume is to illuminate how the historic transformation of the 1980s came about. Before turning our focus to the politics of resistance, however, we must first set the stage with an overview of reform and repression during the regime of Prime Minister (later State President) Pieter Willem Botha.

Pretoria on the Offensive

In January 1980 P. W. Botha had been prime minister for just over one year. He had replaced the inner circle of John Vorster, his predecessor, with his own team, and was introducing a new style of reform leadership better suited to the challenges facing the ruling National Party. The Soweto uprising of 1976–77 had alarmed whites with the prospect of ongoing social turmoil and capital flight.[1] Stability and business confidence were essential to the country's economic future, and Botha intended to guarantee these through stepped-up security measures and carefully calculated policy innovations. The worn-out dogmas of Afrikaner nationalism were fading from official party discourse, and Botha's men were replacing them with a modern language of technocratic management and political realism. Majoritarian democracy was still stubbornly ruled out, but no longer on the grounds that it was contrary to God's plan; now it was portrayed as unrealistic and impractical in South Africa's society of multiple ethnic communities. The special circumstances of South Africa did allow for a degree of liberalization, however, and Botha intended to coax his electorate down this path.

In the three decades since the National Party's accession to power, Afrikaners had worked their way up into the business elite, and many now shared the attitudes of English capital regarding labor relations and social policy. Setting aside the old fear that competition from Africans would harm white workers, Afrikaner capital now saw educational advancement by all races as essential because a crippling shortage of skills was holding back economic growth. The government had finally recognized African trade unions in 1979 because this seemed to be the only way to ensure order and predictability in labor management.² Instead of favoring rigid barriers to black advancement, *verligte* (enlightened or reformist) Afrikaners now saw wisdom in long-term strategies of co-optation: shaping the system to give the coloured and Indian minorities, and eventually an upper stratum of urbanized Africans, a secure stake as junior partners in the status quo.³ Once the legislative and institutional framework for this new dispensation was in place, and opposition to it dispelled by some combination of persuasion and force, apartheid's reformers envisioned an orderly and prosperous South Africa that would enjoy a wide legitimacy in the eyes of its citizens and the world.

The international environment presented obstacles, but also favored *verligte* plans in several ways. Because of apartheid, many countries by 1980 refused to trade or engage in cultural exchanges with South Africa, its diplomats were cold-shouldered at the United Nations, and a worldwide boycott had excluded the country's all-white teams from most international sports. These measures were economically and psychologically wounding to whites, and sports policy in particular became a heated subject of debate between *verligte* and *verkrampte* (conservative) members of the National Party. Nevertheless, one major feature in the international environment—the Cold War—offered a continuing guarantee to Pretoria that its morally repugnant system would be tolerated by the major Western powers. As long as South Africa aligned itself strategically with the West and rejected all demands made by the liberation movements on the grounds that they were communist-inspired, it could count on a measure of political support in Western capitals.⁴ The removal of this ace from the National Party's hand by late 1989 would be vital in pushing Pretoria down the road to change, but no one foresaw this development at the start of the decade.

Between 1979 and 1982 conservative governments were elected in Britain, the United States, and West Germany, creating conditions even more favorable for the Botha government. Pressures for economic sanctions eased and sympathy grew for the claim that Soviet imperialism threatened South Africa's security. The Soviet-backed ANC had established offices, training facilities, and guerrilla infiltration routes in South Africa's neighboring states during the 1970s. Early in the 1980s South Africa's security forces began a determined campaign of attacks aimed at forcing these "frontline" states to deny the ANC the use of their territories. Bombings, assassinations, kidnappings, and raids by the South African Defence Force occurred periodically in Swaziland, Lesotho, Botswana, Mozambique, Zambia, and Zimbabwe. Despite these violations of its neighbors' sovereignty, the Botha government could count on tacit support from conservative Western governments as long as South Africa's ultimate target was the ANC. In Namibia, where the Soviet-aligned South West Africa People's Organisation (SWAPO) was resisting South Africa's continued occupation, Western pressure on Pretoria to grant independence to the territory also waned once Ronald Reagan and Margaret Thatcher took office.

In Angola, which had offered sanctuary to the ANC and SWAPO and accepted military assistance from communist Cuba, South Africa staged periodic incursions and several full-scale invasions in the 1980s, hoping to

Map 1. Southern Africa in the 1980s

topple the country's pro-Soviet government or at least to force it to expel SWAPO and the ANC. To bring pressure on the Cubans to abandon Angola, the Reagan administration in 1981 introduced a "linkage" policy which made U.S. support for Namibian independence conditional on the Cubans' withdrawal from Angola. This gave the Botha government a welcome reason to portray its occupation of Namibia as part of a strategy to counteract communism throughout the region. While continuing to support the UNITA rebel movement in Angola in order to tie down the Angolan government in a constant struggle for survival, Pretoria also armed and encouraged RENAMO, an insurgent group in Mozambique. By 1984, RENAMO had caused such devastation that South Africa was able to force the Mozambican government to sign the Nkomati Accord, an agreement expelling ANC guerrillas from the country in return for a promise by Pretoria to end its support for Mozambique's rebel group.[5]

Not every move by the Botha government to dominate the frontline states was successful, however. In Zimbabwe's pre-independence election in March 1980, Pretoria poured money and logistical aid into the campaign of the politically pliable Bishop Abel Muzorewa, believing that his party could defeat the more militant Robert Mugabe. But Mugabe won decisively, and the lesson for South Africa seemed clear. Two weeks after Mugabe's victory, Percy Qoboza, a prominent black journalist addressing a mostly white audience at the University of the Witwatersrand in Johannesburg, said that, given a free choice, Africans would not accept collaborationist leaders imposed on them by whites; they wanted genuine democracy, and they were tired of waiting for it (*Document 1*).

Debating the New Constitution

Soon after the Soweto uprising of 1976–77, in a daring reform initiative, National Party planners had unveiled proposals to alter South Africa's parliamentary institutions. Until then these had included a Senate and a House of Assembly modeled on Britain's bicameral Westminster system. The Vorster government proposed in 1977 that two new houses of Parliament be created, one for coloureds and one for Indians. It was later also proposed that the country's largely symbolic state president be replaced by an executive state president who would be advised by a President's Council. The President's Council would replace the Senate and be a supercabinet chosen by the president and structured to include coloureds and Indians. The number of whites, coloureds, and Indians in the proposed tricameral Parliament and President's Council would be in a ratio of 4:2:1 so that whites would always outnumber non-whites.

Many government critics condemned the symbolic incorporation of the coloured and Indian minorities into the ruling bloc as a purely cosmetic reform. Neville Alexander, a prominent coloured intellectual, set out a radical critique of National Party plans (*Document 12*). Bishop Desmond Tutu, writing in 1981 as general secretary of the South African Council of Churches (*Document 4*), praised Botha for partially removing racial barriers but found his thinking too cautious. Many Afrikaners, on the other hand, viewed Botha's proposed reforms with alarm precisely because of his departure from old, white-supremacist assumptions. On the far right of the National Party, 16 *verkrampte* members of Parliament who found the proposals too threatening broke away in early 1982 to form the Conservative Party under the leadership of Andries Treurnicht.

Africans were left out of the plan to make Parliament more racially inclusive. Instead, they were to continue to exercise political rights in their ten ethnic "homelands." The designs of Vorster's predecessor, Hendrik Verwoerd—whose blueprint for territorial partition, or "grand apartheid," was still official policy in 1980—called for each of these homelands to eventually become an independent country. Thus, according to official policy, all Africans would sooner or later become foreigners in South Africa when their homelands (sometimes derisively called "bantustans") became independent. In 1980 this process was still unfolding, and a dense political and emotional fog hung around the issue of citizenship. The African's right to be a South African citizen was God given, Qoboza told his white university audience, expressing a widely held African view; in tampering with this right the Afrikaner was playing with fire.

Behind the scenes in the National Party, sharp debates continued about the best way to preserve and legitimize white rule and at the same time blunt the strength of African resistance. While waiting for solutions for this problem to emerge, Botha proceeded openly with that portion of the *verligte* plan that dealt with the co-optation of the coloured and Indian minorities. In October 1980, Parliament passed an act creating a 60-member President's Council to which Botha appointed 44 whites, 10 coloureds, 5 Indians, and 1 Chinese. The President's Council in 1982 approved proposals for a new constitution that would create a coloured House of Representatives and an Indian House of Delegates and would replace the office of prime minister with that of an executive state president. In November of the following year these constitutional proposals were submitted to white voters in a referendum. The Progressive Federal Party (the white parliamentary opposition) and liberal groups like the Black Sash, a white women's organization (*Document 15*), urged whites to vote "no" on the grounds that Africans were excluded from parliamentary representation. But two-thirds of whites voted "yes," handing Botha a significant political victory. Elections for the coloured and Indian houses were conducted in August 1984. Amid widespread protests by blacks, the new constitution was promulgated in September, and from January 1985 South Africa's Parliament was no longer exclusively white. The British and U.S. governments praised the changes as genuine reforms.

Botha's controversial new constitution confronted blacks with a dilemma familiar throughout South Africa's modern history: whether to accept or reject the second-class forms of political representation created for them by whites.[6] Was half a loaf better than none? Those who boycotted these government-created "dummy institutions" knew that there would always be collaborators willing to accept the salaries and privileges that came with participation. Those who participated could argue that they did so in order to keep out unprincipled opportunists and to use the institutions in pragmatic ways to harass the system, create protected public platforms for opposition views, and divert government resources to black communities. By the 1980s, when the National Party became increasingly divided on how to resist pressures for genuine democracy, pro-participation optimists even revived the much-disparaged argument that mere contact and dialogue between whites and blacks might help to win over the hearts and minds of die-hard racists in the ruling party.

The participation dilemma was not new to Indians and coloureds at the time of the 1983 constitution's promulgation.[7] Their racially segregated residential areas were administered by elected local councils that remained subordinate to white officials appointed by Pretoria. Some coloureds and Indians rejected these councils as puppet bodies, while others offered themselves as candidates to serve in them. In the 1960s, the Vorster government had also established national coloured and Indian advisory councils so that the white ministers of coloured and Indian affairs could appear to be consulting community leaders before approving legislation that affected these minorities. By the early 1980s these national advisory councils had become the focus of heated public debate.

The South African Indian Council (SAIC) began in 1968 as an appointed body of conservative Indian businessmen and professionals. To give the SAIC greater legitimacy and thus ease the way to acceptance of an Indian house of Parliament, Botha's government, after repeated delays, scheduled elections for 40 of the council's 45 seats in November 1981. This ignited a flurry of political activity as small competing Indian parties campaigned for their candidates and boycott proponents mobilized "anti-SAIC" committees in Natal and the Transvaal to urge voters to stay home. Despite mandatory voter registration the boycott was effective, with estimates of the average national turnout ranging as low as 8 percent.[8] Nevertheless, the victors took their seats, and after some political caucusing, a dominant coalition party, the National People's Party, was formed under the leadership of Amichand Rajbansi, an ambitious autocrat with a talent for translating petty patronage into political support.

Meanwhile, several members of the pre-1981 SAIC had accepted invitations to serve on the President's Council, formally entitling them to represent Indian opinion on the merits of the constitutional proposals. An Indian appointee, Mamoud Rajab, addressing the President's Council during its deliberations in 1982, projected himself as a critic of the government, maintaining that participation in the Council did not mean acceptance of Botha's policies or his constitutional proposals (*Document 11*). Nevertheless, with the exaggerated optimism characteristic of most pro-participation politicians, he urged Indians to take part in the future tricameral Parliament and to work there "for the inclusion of Africans in some form or other" in the new order.

The pro-boycott position was championed by the Natal and Transvaal Indian Congresses. They aggressively identified with African aspirations and the traditions of the ANC, with which they had been partners in the Congress Alliance of the 1950s. After a period of dormancy in the 1960s, the Natal Indian Congress (NIC) had been revived in 1971, but its outreach was limited and its leading figure, Mewa Ramgobin, was quickly banned and placed under house arrest. Radical younger activists breathed new life into the organization in the late 1970s by associating it with community grievances over housing, rents, and discrimination. By and large, however, the NIC remained an elite body, strongly influenced by middle-class professionals who called public meetings and made statements to the press while the mass of working-class Indians remained politically uninvolved. After several years of internal debate in the 1970s, during which some NIC members advocated a policy of "rejectionist participation"—running for election to the SAIC on a platform of working to destroy it from within—the organization by 1981 had settled firmly into a pro-boycott position.[9] Along with the Transvaal Indian Congress after its formal revival in 1983, the NIC under the leadership of M. J. Naidoo and George Sewpersadh took the lead in fighting the new constitution and trying to discredit Indians who participated in the President's Council and the tricameral Parliament. NIC's campaign urging Indians to boycott the parliamentary election of August 1984 (*Document 17*) was a major rallying point for the newly founded United Democratic Front (UDF) in which Indian organizers played a catalyzing role (chapters 2 and 3).

The history of the Coloured Persons' Representative Council (CPRC, later CRC) took a different course. Until 1956, literate coloured male property owners had been entitled to vote in the Cape Province, and white parties there had competed for their votes. When the National Party set up the CRC as an advisory body in 1968, many coloureds favored a return to the participatory tradition, although an articulate minority adhered to the fervent pro-boycott stand of the left-wing Unity Movement. From 1969, coloured parties competed for the 40 elected seats in the 60-member Council. By the late 1970s, Labour Party members were in the majority, first under the leadership of Sonny Leon, and from 1978 of Allan Hendrickse, a staid but shrewd Congregationalist minister from Uitenhage. The Labour Party took a "rejectionist participation" position, using the CRC as a platform to denounce apartheid and obstruct government business, eventually causing Botha to shut the Council down in 1980.[10]

The Labour Party expressed sympathy for the banned ANC, adopted much of the black consciousness movement's rhetoric, entered an alliance with the Inkatha movement of the Zulu leader, Chief Mangosuthu Gatsha Buthelezi, and in other ways attempted to project a "black," pro-African image.[11] In 1980 it declined to accept seats on the President's Council, though several of its discredited former members, including Leon, accepted appointments as individuals. But with the juggernaut of Botha's constitutional proposals rolling on, and without the CRC as a platform to keep its pronouncements in the media, Labour Party politicians began to feel politically marginalized. At its annual congress in Eshowe, Natal, in January 1983, Hendrickse announced that the party would put up candidates for the tricameral Parliament and would resume its efforts to undermine the apartheid system from within. In light of the party's relative credibility among coloureds at the time, its decision to participate significantly boosted prospects that the constitutional proposals would win wide acceptance. It was a triumph for Botha.

The Labour Party's decision to participate sent shockwaves through the pro-boycott camp, which in principle had chosen not to recognize that there

Figure 1. Supporters mob party leader Allan Hendrickse during the Labour Party's campaign for the House of Representatives in the tricameral parliament, August 1984. *Willie de Klerk/Cape Argus/africanpictures.net*

might be any tactical middle ground lying between boycott and full-blown collaboration. Several prominent Labour Party leaders resigned in protest against the decision, and the party's campaign meetings turned rowdy as protesters shouted insults and condemned Labour leaders as traitors. Sensitive to anything that could be taken as a personal slight to his own standing as a leader, Buthelezi denounced the Eshowe decision, though not because of any objection to participation in government-created institutions—after all, he himself had accepted leadership of the government-created KwaZulu homeland. Rather, Buthelezi was angered because in endorsing the tricameral Parliament, the Labour Party had ignored the agreement made by the South African Black Alliance, Inkatha's partnership with Labour and the Indian Reform Party, to oppose the constitutional proposals.

As the first election for the coloured House of Representatives approached in 1984, Hendrickse's party adopted increasingly conservative positions. It called for a five-year moratorium on foreign disinvestment and economic sanctions to give the Botha government a chance to demonstrate its commitment to reform. Bowing to the fear of African majority rule among coloureds as well as among whites, the party continued to advocate a universal franchise in a unitary state, but pointedly qualified this position by endorsing the concept of federalism and emphasizing that a unitary state was "negotiable."[12] This important dilution of its pro-African position potentially aligned Labour with the preference for federalism of the white opposition Progressive Federal Party. It also played to Botha's own vaguely articulated notion that all of southern Africa might in the future be organized as a federal or confederal "constellation of states" in which all members, including the independent homelands, would be part of a single regional economy but would retain sovereignty as separate, ethnically defined states. A Labour Party election flyer (*Document 18*) called on coloured voters in August 1984 to reject the politics of revolution associated with "left-leaning" organizations like the UDF, whose most popular coloured leader, the Reverend Allan Boesak, was dismissed as a purveyor of "hot air." Instead, the party commended top-down reform, even if the process took many years. "When the holders of power decide to reform society," the flyer declared optimistically, "then meaningful change is guaranteed."

The Labour Party swept the vote, taking 76 out of 80 elected seats in the tricameral House of Representatives. The turnout of coloured voters averaged only 17.6 percent countrywide, however, and in the militant Cape peninsula, only 4.9 percent of potential coloured voters went to the polls. Among Indians, the turnout was only 16.2 percent.[13] The Natal and Transvaal Indian Congresses claimed that the low poll was a victory for their boycott campaign. The government likewise declared victory, blamed intimidation and the hostile English press for keeping voters away, and proceeded, amid smoldering African anger, to promulgate the new constitution on September 3, 1984—the very day, as we shall see, that violent protests against higher rents erupted in the Vaal triangle south of Johannesburg.

And What About the Black People?

At the same time that the Botha government was redesigning national political institutions to dampen domestic and international criticism, it was also trying to come to grips with the challenge posed by African demands for full political rights. Africans were 74 percent of the country's population, and their rate of natural increase was higher than that of whites. Eventual capitulation to their demands could only be forestalled by finding a political divide-and-rule formula that could win acceptance at home and abroad. Verwoerd's vision of a South Africa stripped of its African citizens retained a powerful appeal among white voters generally and Afrikaners in particular. But politically articulate Africans were implacably hostile to exchanging their South African citizenship for homeland nationalities, and foreign governments had also refused to recognize the homelands as independent states.[14] Botha's attempt to repackage homeland independence as a step toward the creation of a confederal "constellation of states" had also attracted no support.

The departure from the National Party of Treurnicht and his *verkrampte* followers in 1982 strengthened the hand of Botha's reformers but still left them facing a hard choice. They could satisfy the white electorate and incur the anger of the black majority and of international opinion, or they could satisfy these critics but be defeated at the polls by more conservative politicians who were unconcerned about the government's lack of political legitimacy beyond the boundaries of its own electorate. In formulating political concessions that would win wider legitimacy without endangering their own continued grip on power, National Party strategists were willing, even eager, to allow non-whites to control their so-called "own affairs" in their segregated "own areas"—as long as the white electorate was not asked to assume too much of the financial cost, and as long as control of the country's political and economic systems at the national level, deemed by the National Party to be whites' "own affair," was not ultimately threatened.

By 1984, the new constitution had put in place coloured and Indian collaborators willing to take charge of these groups' "own affairs." Finding credible Africans to play a similar role was not as easy. "When the new dispensation for Coloureds and Indians was instituted, everybody asked: And what about political rights for the Black People?" declared *And What About the Black People?,* a National Party pamphlet issued in May 1985. The initial way forward, explained the pamphlet, was consultation through "an informal, nonstatutory forum" in which Africans could participate, "on an ad hoc basis and by invitation," on behalf of bodies or interest groups for whom they wished to speak. The end point of such consultations remained open and vague, but the ideal goal was officially "a South Africa in which every nation and population group—including the Whites—will . . . achieve fulfillment without any one of them being able to disadvantage, dominate or destroy any of the others."[15] Thus, in keeping with fundamental apartheid principles, "population groups," not individuals, were to have rights bestowed or withheld, and the ruling party, through Parliament, was to define who for this purpose constituted a group.

Getting the proposed forum off the ground depended on the willingness of prominent Africans to participate. Six months after the publication of *And What About the Black People?,* Botha said he would ask Parliament to make the forum a statutory body, one in which the incumbents would receive salaries and other benefits. Nevertheless, enthusiasm remained low, even among homeland chief ministers who were to be included *ex officio.* Cedric Phatudi of the Lebowa homeland agreed to be involved, but KwaZulu's Chief Buthelezi and KaNgwane's Enos Mabuza declined, as did Sam Motsuenyane, president of the National African Federated Chamber of Commerce. The last three said they would reject such a council—never defined as anything more than an advisory body—as long as recognized African leaders were imprisoned and their organizations banned. The Reverend Sam Buti, a well-known community leader in Alexandra township in Johannesburg, initially agreed to participate but later withdrew. Rather than fill the proposed council with political non-entities, Botha repeatedly postponed its creation in the hope that suppression of radical Africans would coax forward some prominent moderates. As late as September 1987 he put before Parliament an amended bill for the creation of a National Council to include Africans chosen through election, and publicly dangled the prospect that leaders of the banned ANC might be invited to participate were they to renounce violence. National

Party realists by this time had recognized, however, that popular resistance had rendered futile such schemes for diverting African energies into pseudo-consultative bodies.[16]

While trying to keep alive the notion of a future dispensation in which Africans might be invited to play a political role at the national level, government planners in the 1980s also had to grapple with immediate problems of control in urban areas, from which the loudest and most sustained African demands and protests emanated. Lack of consensus within the ruling party made coherent policy making difficult; once a policy was made, it was sometimes changed on short notice and was hardly ever enforced consistently by lower-level bureaucrats. As a result, Africans in urban areas came up against white authorities who wielded power in ways that were often confusing, arbitrary, and backed up by appeals to apartheid's non-negotiable but ever-changing principles.[17] White employers increasingly expressed frustration at the obstacles and uncertainties created by government policies regarding African labor mobility and urban rights.

Of all the time-honored principles of apartheid, the most discredited now was the Verwoerdian assumption that most Africans living in "white" cities were really just migrant workers—"temporary sojourners" whose true homes were in the rural areas. In 1979 the government-appointed Riekert Commission had renounced this anachronism and recommended that permanent urban residents be accepted and given more rights. Combined with more vigorous steps to relegate all other Africans to the status of homeland citizens, this recommended reform was seen by Afrikaner *verligtes* as a move toward greater industrial and political stability. The idea was that by dividing Africans into privileged permanent "insiders" and rural and migrant "outsiders," the government would be able eventually to incorporate an African upper stratum—comprising at most 15 to 20 percent of all Africans—into full citizenship, while shedding responsibility for the rest, who as aliens would fall under the administration of the independent homelands.

After the publication of the Riekert recommendations, government planners struggled to formulate legislation that could implement this strategy of selective incorporation. Eventually a set of proposals known as the Koornhof bills, named after Minister of Co-operation and Development Piet Koornhof, were placed before Parliament. First to become law was the Black Local Authorities Act of 1982. This aimed to build up the status of urban "insiders" by conferring increased power on township community councils to manage electricity, water, garbage removal, health services, and other matters deemed to be Africans' "own affairs." According to National Party thinking, these elected councils would be avenues through which permanently urbanized Africans would express themselves politically until such time as acceptable regional and national political mechanisms could be devised.

Meanwhile, it was envisaged that a step-by-step relaxation of restrictions on property ownership, job opportunities, and freedom of movement would dampen dissent and steadily persuade African "insiders" to adopt more ac-

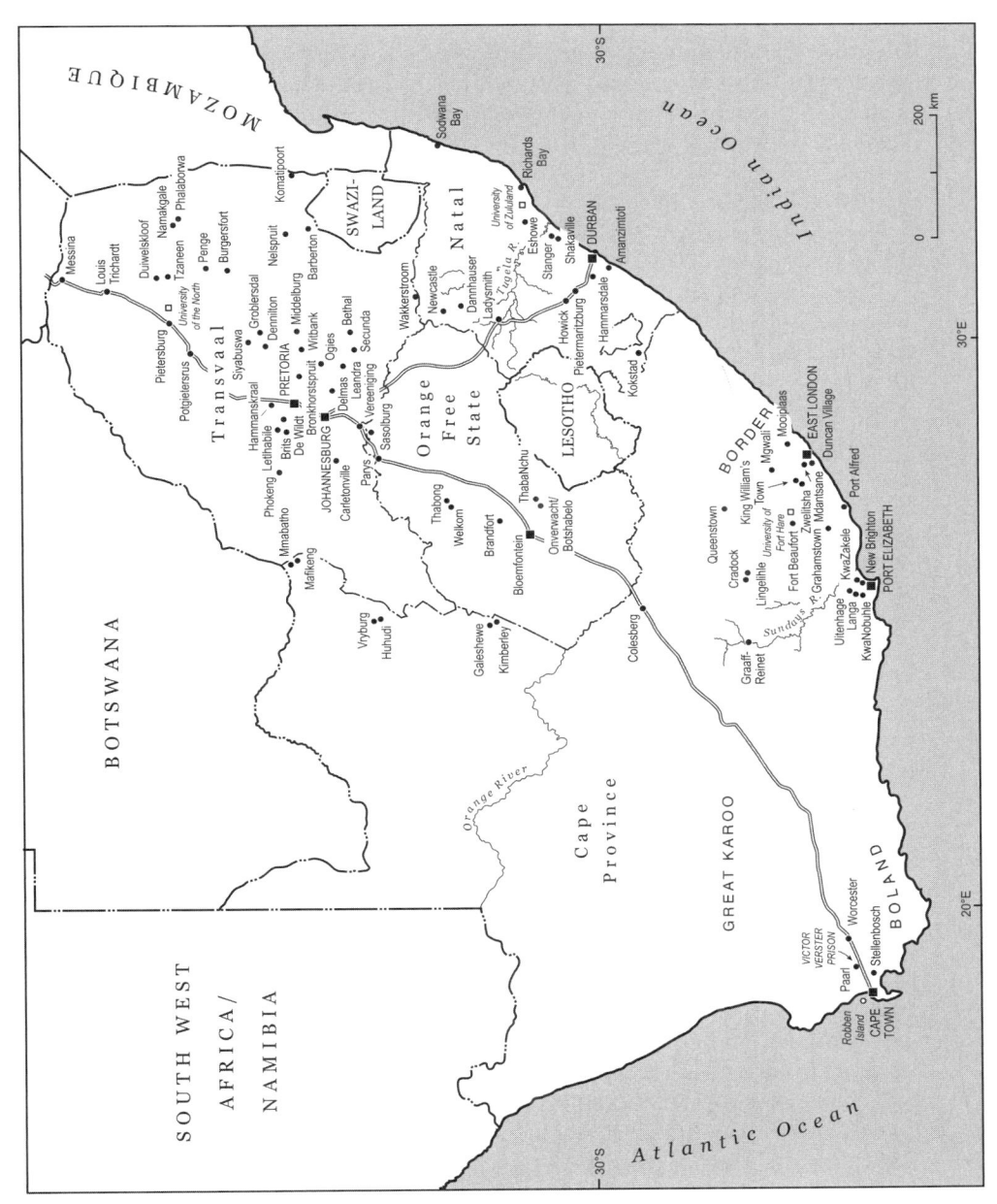

Map 2. South Africa in the 1980s

commodating attitudes toward the status quo. Liberals, both white and black, had argued along the same lines for decades. For example, Enos Mabuza, the chief minister of the Swazi homeland of KaNgwane, stressed the link between political unrest and lack of property rights in a speech in August 1986 (*Document 24*). A month before Mabuza's speech, Parliament had amended another Koornhof bill, the Black Communities Development Act, to give permanent urban residents freehold property rights in segregated African "group areas." Mabuza acknowledged this significant liberalization but urged a much broader lifting of ownership restrictions. The white businessmen who made up his audience may have agreed for the most part with Mabuza's views, but National Party strategists, constrained by a fear of alienating conservative white voters, were in no mood to rush forward.

The speed and success of reform depended in part on the willingness of whites to subsidize the cost of new housing and services in impoverished African townships—never a popular cause among white politicians, least of all in periods of economic downturn. Yet South Africa was entering just such a period of recession by mid-1982, causing stringent economic realities to overshadow optimistic reform scenarios. A brief economic boom between 1979 and 1981 had been followed by falling gold prices and growing balance-of-payments deficits that soon induced a full-blown recession. Accordingly, Koornhof's 1982 Black Local Authorities Act reaffirmed the longstanding apartheid principle that African townships were to be as financially self-sufficient as possible. Given the lack of an adequate tax base in African residential areas, this was a prescription that guaranteed trouble.

Township populations were growing, but state subsidies for municipal services remained frozen. The political costs of state parsimony proved high. Black councillors, struggling to finance meager and declining public services, had few ways to generate revenue other than to raise rents and utility fees paid by township residents. Even without taking into account the corruption of many councillors who used their positions to promote their personal business ventures, rent and utility increases alone were enough to arouse immense popular anger. Memories of protests against rent hikes in the late 1970s were still fresh in many townships. A black journalist's jocular but biting attack on David Thebehali, the head of Soweto's community council, conveyed the dislike of most ordinary people for collaborators, who were seen as public enemies rather than agents of democratic change (*Document 3*). Between 1984 and 1989 at least 11 local councillors were murdered and hundreds resigned rather than face ridicule and have their homes fire bombed by angry youths.[18] As township rebellions gathered steam nationwide in the mid-1980s, rent boycotts became a popular resistance tactic.

Undeterred, the Botha government continued until 1988 to cling to the faint hope that elected township councils would eventually win acceptance among "insider" Africans and become a mechanism for controlled political change. In 1985 a new law provided for the creation of multiracial Regional Services Councils (RSCs) that would assume responsibility for the maintenance and upgrading of urban infrastructure as well as for the provision of water, electricity, and other services in metropolitan areas. RSCs were to draw their revenues from taxes on commerce and industry, including state enterprises. Although originally designed to be run cooperatively by white, Indian, and coloured local authorities, when RSCs actually began coming into existence in 1987, the government decided to include African local authorities in their administrative decision-making processes and to authorize RSCs to redistribute resources toward infrastructural improvements in areas "where the need is greatest," namely African townships. No doubt the architects of Botha's reform tactics hoped that these daring departures from traditional apartheid would help win legitimacy for township councillors.[19] In many townships, however, especially in the southern Transvaal and eastern Cape, councils had already collapsed under the pressure of popular rebellion.

Urban Influx Control and Squatters

While working to force some Africans to accept measures that supposedly heralded their own brighter futures as political "insiders," the Botha government also made efforts in the early 1980s to implement the other half of the Riekert Commission's strategy: the political exclusion of rural and homeland "outsiders." These Africans were to be regarded as guest workers from foreign countries and systematically denied any permanent residence rights. This was the objective of the most controversial of the Koornhof bills, the Orderly Movement and Settlement of Black Persons Bill, introduced in 1982. The proposed law was designed to supplement the hated pass laws that required all adult Africans to carry pocket-sized "reference books," or passes, authorizing their presence in cities on the grounds of employment and long-term resident ("section 10") status.[20] Since many Africans succeeded in evading the pass laws, the bill aimed to tighten so-called "influx control" by shifting the burden of enforcement to employers, who were now to be liable for heavy fines or imprisonment if they gave work to "illegal" job-seekers. To further discourage African urbanization, the bill contained provisions to curb the construction of informal squatter housing: only Africans with "approved accommodation" would be eligible for section 10 status. Africans without permanent urban status might legally work in "white" cities, but only if they had permits to stay in migrant-worker hostels, or if they commuted to the city daily from a nearby homeland.

The Orderly Movement and Settlement of Black Persons Bill drew strong criticism from Africans and anti-apartheid activists of other races. In September 1982 the Black Sash published a pamphlet explaining the bill's proposed new restrictions and its harsh implications for Africans lacking section 10 status (*Document 10*). Protests also came from white conservatives who felt threatened by the changes inherent in the entire Riekert strategy. On the other hand, many white employers objected in principle to all new influx control measures, arguing that they pushed up black wages by limiting competition among job-seekers. Faced with criticism on all sides, the government withdrew the Orderly Movement bill, proposing "further study" of the matter.

Controversy over the Orderly Movement bill pointed to a serious contradiction between demographic facts and the rigid framework of apartheid planning. The Riekert Commission had stayed within the parameters of Verwoerd's grand design, accepting the premise that African urbanization could eventually be curbed by creating ethnic-based "national states" and applying strict pass controls to return unemployed migrants to these rural homelands. In reality, the townward drift of impoverished rural people could no more be stopped in South Africa than anywhere else in the late-twentieth-century world. Most opportunities for a better life lay in towns, and harsh laws and the absence of housing could do nothing to alter this fundamental truth. Unemployment and housing shortages in towns were already acute in the 1970s, but so was the economic insecurity of rural Africans as white farms became increasingly mechanized and subsistence agriculture in the homelands failed to feed burgeoning populations. Recurring drought in the 1980s accelerated the push to the cities. Even if some Africans with permanent urban status might have preferred the exclusion of urban newcomers, they were as powerless as anyone else to stem the tide.[21]

As townward movement continued, peri-urban squatter settlements that had begun to grow in the 1970s became larger and denser. These shantytowns attracted families facing intolerable crowding in existing townships as well as rural people hoping to establish a toehold in the city. Pass raids regularly forced thousands to return to rural areas, but most, usually within weeks or even days, were back in the city dodging the police again. Reflecting failing police efforts to halt urban influx, pass arrests countrywide rose from 171,000 in 1981 to 250,000 in 1984.[22] Squatters constructed houses out of wooden crates, corrugated iron, and plastic sheeting. Some found jobs in the formal sector, but many survived by engaging in informal trade and services, including driving minibus taxis, which multiplied as city populations expanded. Where homeland borders lay within an hour or two's bus ride from cities, squatter settlements of commuter workers grew up inside the homelands, becoming magnets for destitute rural families. The government preferred constructing houses or site-and-service projects in these new areas under the rubric of "homeland development" over building low-income housing in existing urban townships.[23] Subsidies and tax incentives were designed to push new industrial development outward toward these areas of decentralized urban growth, especially after the launching of Regional Services Councils in the late 1980s. Subsidizing industry to locate in out-of-the-way places was counterproductive to efficient strategies of economic growth, however, and failed to win broad support in the white business community.

A forward-looking democratic government would have started searching earlier for solutions to the problems caused by rapid urbanization, but the National Party had historically looked only to the short-term interests of white voters and relied on force to contain the dissatisfaction of everyone else. By the 1980s, however, this approach had become more and more problematic. African communities were becoming better organized at the grassroots level, and their mood was more defiant. Ever-higher levels of coercion were required to overcome popular resistance. Moreover, since the Soweto uprising, the world's media had become intent on drawing attention to South Africa's difficulties, especially to instances of violence and bloodshed. Confronted with these problems, Botha's strategists looked for new tactics better suited to the times and more in line with expectations of reform. The pressure of African urbanization made concessions unavoidable, but these could still be introduced in ways that gave white authorities maximum control over the urbanization process. To many critics, the new policy that emerged in the mid-1980s—"orderly urbanization"—looked a lot like influx control with a new name.[24] The assumptions behind the new policy were different, however. Policy makers publicly conceded that many more Africans were going to become urban; privately they recognized that creating a permanent category of "outsiders" was going to be far more difficult than Riekert had acknowledged, and that controlling the process through one-by-one pass law prosecutions had become impossible.

The publicly stated aim of "orderly urbanization" was to eliminate slums that posed health and safety hazards due to overcrowding and lack of proper sanitation. The unstated aims were to locate all African residential areas as far as possible from white neighborhoods, to prevent the maximum number of Africans from becoming permanent urban residents in "white" South Africa, and wherever possible to divide and demobilize African communities that had become highly politicized. One method of achieving these goals was simply to raze "unhealthy" townships and squatter settlements and remove their inhabitants to a nearby homeland, if one lay within a 20- to 30-mile radius. Another way to push urban dwellers toward "outsider" status without the expense of physically moving them was to redraw the boundaries of homelands to incorporate existing townships. The Durban township of Kwa-Mashu, for example, was incorporated into KwaZulu by administrative fiat in 1977. As late as 1989 the government continued to push for such incorporations in the face of stubborn African opposition.

A further option was to remove most or all the residents of crowded townships to vacant land more distant from white areas. By 1982, dozens of townships housing an estimated 730,000 people had been physically relocated, and roughly 184,000 more people lived in townships designated for future removal.[25] Since government planners had long before identified these communities as "badly situated," they had financed no improvements in them for many years, ensuring their physical deterioration into festering slums. In some relocation areas inside homeland borders, the government built houses for rent or purchase. Usually, however, relocated families were only allocated site-and-service plots and had to bear the costs of rebuilding their homes and commuting farther if they were fortunate enough to have city jobs.

Three cases of "orderly urbanization" were briefly described in a bulletin issued by the National Committee Against Removals in April 1986 (*Docu-*

ment 22): Onverwacht (later called Botshabelo), a vast site-and-service area 30 miles (48 kilometers) from Bloemfontein which the government planned to incorporate into the Southern Sotho QwaQwa homeland; Langa, a township of Uitenhage in the eastern Cape, where the first 6,000 of the 50,000 residents had already been forcibly removed to KwaNobuhle at a greater distance from white areas; and Khayelitsha, a new township on the windswept sand flats 20 miles (32 kilometers) east of Cape Town where police were forcibly relocating squatters evicted from Crossroads, a dense shantytown closer to the city. In Oukasie, a dilapidated township on the outskirts of the conservative Transvaal town of Brits, the authorities had reached a standoff in their efforts to make residents move "voluntarily" to a more remote new township likely to be incorporated into the Bophuthatswana homeland (*Document 28*).[26] These documents attest to the strong resentment among urban Africans threatened with forced removal. Although some people accepted the removals as inevitable, others fought to stay where they were and demanded that slum housing areas be upgraded rather than destroyed. Violent incidents frequently occurred, especially after the township uprising of 1984–86 gathered countrywide momentum. Squatters sometimes engaged lawyers to fight removals or homeland incorporations in court, and a handful of these challenges were successful.[27] But even when the government won in court, the obligation to publicly defend its unpopular policies imposed a political cost, as did international media reports of violent incidents.

Confrontations with squatters in the western Cape became a test of the government's ability to impose "orderly urbanization" on defiant families engaged in a harsh struggle for survival. When the Crossroads squatter settlement began growing 10 miles (16 kilometers) east of Cape Town in the late 1970s, local administrative officials tried to eliminate it by demolishing shacks and using pass raids to arrest and deport "illegals" (people without section 10 rights) to the homelands.[28] The "illegals" simply returned and rebuilt, and their numbers rapidly increased. Shack demolitions attracted wide press coverage and prompted protests by liberal whites in Cape Town who mobilized relief efforts for the victims. Turning the face of reform to apartheid's critics, Koornhof met with squatter representatives and in 1979 worked out a new dispensation that would limit the demolitions and allow inhabitants of Crossroads to apply for government houses to be built near the existing settlement.

This partial reprieve proved to be only a stop-gap solution, for reasons described in *Document 23* by Ivan Toms, a white doctor working in Crossroads. Competition to get onto the housing list became violent as newcomers hoping to get a house poured into Crossroads and squatter leaders competed for bribes to put people on the list. Demolitions soon resumed. Some "illegals" accepted an offer of removal to Khayelitsha on the Cape flats, but the majority refused to move. Meanwhile, Crossroads kept growing as new satellite shack settlements mushroomed on its western periphery, eventually pushing the total squatter population to an estimated 250,000.[29] By 1985 the Koornhof agreement had been replaced by a new decree that all residents of Crossroads would be required to move to Khayelitsha, but this too proved unenforceable.

Frustrated by "disorder" that could not be contained and appeared to feed on the growing popularity of the UDF among young Africans, police turned to a tactic that was also being tested in Natal and the eastern Cape: vigilante action, publicly characterized by the police as "black-on-black violence." During five chaotic days in May 1986, following months of rising intergenerational tension, conservative older residents from the original Old Crossroads settlement, with police connivance, were encouraged to attack radical youths and to burn down thousands of shacks belonging to families alleged to be sympathetic to the youths in the newer peripheral settlements of Nyanga Bush, Nyanga Extension, Portland Cement, and KTC. At least 60 people died in the fighting and an estimated 70,000 who were left homeless had little choice but to move to Khayelitsha.[30] In the following year Old Crossroads was declared a township under the Black Local Authorities Act and the leader of the vigilantes, Johnson Ngxobongwana, was chosen head of the town council and rewarded with the power to assign housing sites in the areas razed by the vigilantes. Thus, although the government had failed to remove all Crossroads residents to Khayelitsha, it had reduced their numbers and successfully brought them under the control of an organized collaborationist leadership.

In the meantime, the unstoppable tide of Africans migrating to Cape Town from the impoverished eastern Cape and the persistence of "illegals" in returning to the city despite repeated expulsions helped to persuade government policy makers that the pass laws had outlived their utility. White business leaders, shaken by the recession and by roiling township unrest, had long been critical of the pass system, seeing it as an obstacle both to the stabilization of an African middle class and to the free movement of surplus labor essential to create downward pressure on wages. In August 1985 the President's Council called for passes to be abolished, noting that they were not only ineffective but also harmful because they encouraged "contempt for the law and the authorities."[31] Ten months later, just as Botha was imposing a national state of emergency to crush the countrywide revolt, Parliament duly repealed the notorious pass laws.

The abolition of passes was a significant reform aimed at lowering the political temperature in the townships. Hundreds of thousands of Africans now were spared the misery of pass raids, arrests, and expulsions, and were free to seek urban employment. The new freedom did not extend to all Africans, however. Those with section 10 status retained the right to live and work in urban South Africa, although those who were citizens of the "independent" states of Transkei, Bophuthatswana, Venda, and Ciskei (TBVC) had to make individual applications to keep their permanent urban classification once the laws defining section 10 rights were repealed. But under the new dispensation, the roughly five million TBVC citizens who physically resided in the homelands, along with their descendants, became worse off. They remained classified as foreigners and were subject to restrictive immigration laws when applying to become guest workers in "white" South Africa.

The Homelands

By the early 1980s all pretense had evaporated that South Africa's ten homelands would someday become economically viable and politically sovereign entities. Yet it was impossible for the Botha regime to scrap the "grand apartheid" framework without abandoning the entire rationale for excluding Africans from political rights in "white" South Africa.[32] On the contrary, the possibility that growing domestic and international pressure might eventually compel the government to adopt a policy of selective incorporation of blacks made it all the more imperative to classify as many Africans as possible as homeland citizens—permanent outsiders. Over the course of the decade, the regime pressed forward with efforts to physically locate hundreds of thousands more people in homelands and to persuade more homeland governments to choose "independence." These efforts met with some short-term successes, but ultimately the homelands policy failed to achieve its political objectives and instead helped underscore the cruel and violent nature of the apartheid system.

The Botha government made a bold attempt to use the homelands system to denationalize its own citizens on a grand scale when it announced plans in mid-1982 to cede over 3,000 square miles (7,680 square kilometers) of South Africa to neighboring Swaziland. One area to be transferred was KaNgwane, the designated homeland for approximately 750,000 Swazi-speakers in South Africa, a majority of whom lived in areas of the Transvaal outside KaNgwane's borders. The other territory marked for transfer—on the pretext that "border adjustments" were required to satisfy Swaziland's land claims—was the Ingwavuma district of northern Natal, a remote rural area with a largely Zulu population lying between Swaziland and the coast and bordering on Mozambique to the north. Ingwavuma was part of the KwaZulu homeland, and Pretoria proposed exchanging it for other parcels of land farther south to help consolidate KwaZulu into a less fragmented territory.[33]

The real issue was not KwaZulu's consolidation, however, but Ingwavuma's location astride a guerrilla infiltration route into South Africa from politically hostile Mozambique. Pretoria's aim was to swap land and people for security, giving politically compliant Swaziland a larger population and an outlet to the sea in return for its cooperation in intercepting ANC fighters trying to enter South Africa from Mozambique. A secret agreement to this effect was concluded in February 1982 in anticipation that Pretoria would be able to deliver on its promise of territorial transfer. A side benefit to South Africa's whites was to be the loss of citizenship by Ingwavuma's estimated 135,000 African inhabitants. The proposed land deals aroused a furor of denunciations, however, both from parliamentary opposition parties and from homeland authorities in KaNgwane and KwaZulu. Speaking for the KaNgwane leadership, Enos Mabuza dared Pretoria to hold a referendum on the issue and declared that "whoever will dare swallow us by force will be doing so at the risk of the most vicious stomach upset."[34] KwaZulu leaders raised heated objections in a meeting with Koornhof in May 1982 (*Document 8*). Both homelands successfully brought court actions to halt the excisions, and the Botha government was forced to shelve its plans in late 1982.[35]

Meanwhile, failure of the Swazi land deals to effect wholesale population transfers did not interfere with the National Party's older methods of removing Africans from "white" areas. The people most easily pushed into the homelands were African farm workers living on white farms. Reduced to laborers when their rights to land were legislated away in the early part of the twentieth century, farm workers eked out a precarious sub-subsistence existence, often depending on remittances from relatives in town to make ends meet. White farmers, who in earlier generations had demanded restrictions on African land ownership in order to ensure a supply of cheap labor, now found themselves with too many laborers due to farm mechanization and natural increase in the rural population. Their response was to evict "surplus" African families, who then had little alternative but to resettle in a homeland. Even if a few able-bodied family members succeeded in finding urban jobs—not easy for rural people who usually lacked education and relevant skills—the very young, the elderly, and many women evicted from farms wound up in homeland resettlement areas, living in shacks and forbidden to keep the livestock that had previously been their main means of survival. It has been estimated that 1,129,000 Africans were evicted from white farms between 1960 and 1982, and that in the mid-1980s there were another million who still faced possible eviction.[36] To successive white governments, these were unwanted citizens who would eventually be the responsibility of other countries.

In the same 1960–82 period, approximately 139,000 additional people were uprooted as a result of consolidation programs in homelands that consisted of many separate fragments of land. A further 475,000 people were forcibly removed from so-called "black spots." These were farms located in "white" South Africa to which Africans held freehold title deeds dating from before the Natives Land Act of 1913.[37] Africans removed from these areas were often paid little or no compensation for the houses and land they were giving up; nor was any consideration given to their attachments to places where their forebears were buried. As in "badly situated" urban townships, white authorities usually harassed the people in the areas marked for removal by canceling support to their clinics, schools, roads, pension payments, and other services in order to induce "voluntary" relocation. Few rural African communities were as seemingly idyllic as Lusitania, a threatened Natal "black spot" described in *Document 7,* but almost all offered better conditions for family life and economic sustenance than the crowded, impoverished, and socially disorienting relocation sites to which evicted families were obliged to move. Many families were sent first to temporary settlements, only later to be removed again as National Party technocrats revised the plans for achieving their desired social order.

Organized resistance to these massive and socially debilitating removals was rare. Farm workers were powerless to prevent evictions, and most "black spot" communities had no alternative but to comply with removal orders. In

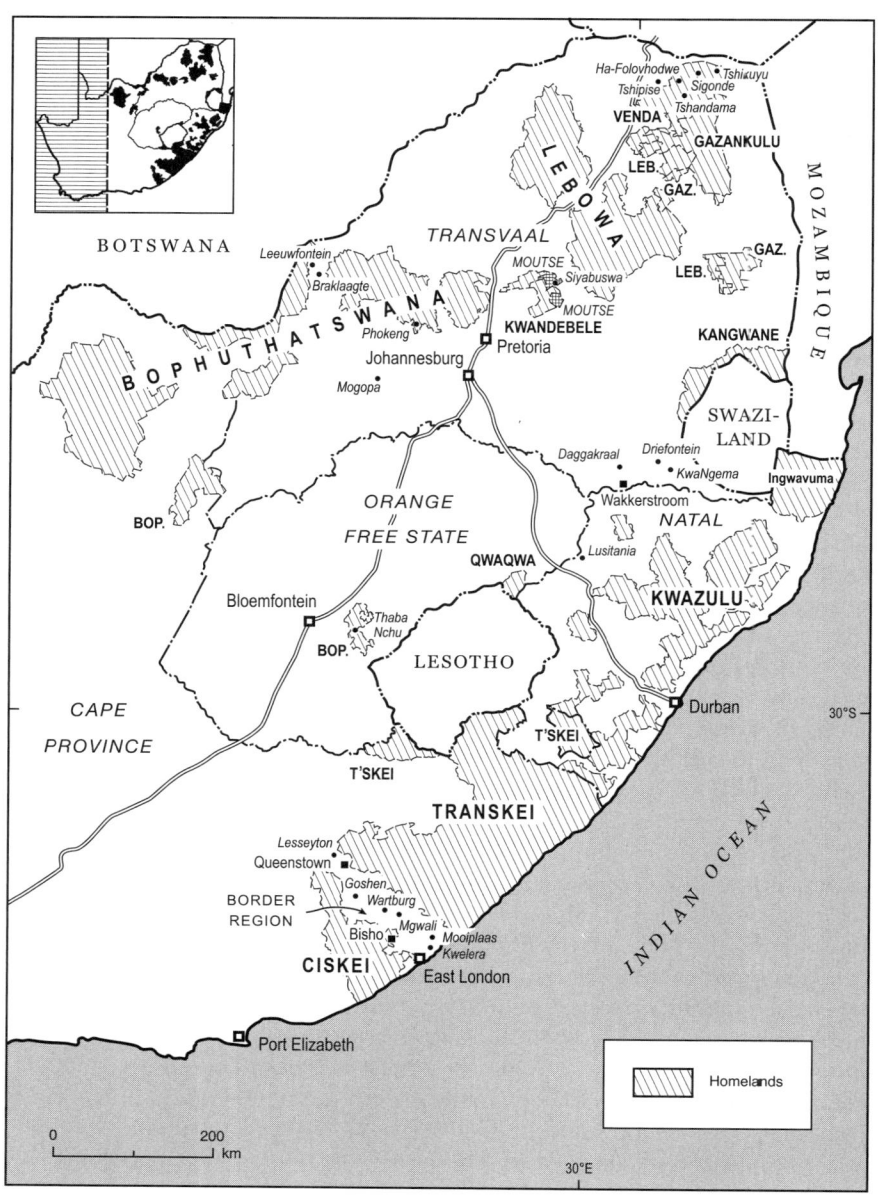

Map 3. Homelands and "Black Spots," 1980s

a handful of "black spots," however, resourceful leaders actively opposed government plans and compelled the planners to revise their thinking. Mere verbal and written protests were ineffective, but some communities contacted lawyers, newspapers, and organizations of sympathetic whites in an attempt to create legal obstacles and negative publicity for Pretoria. In Driefontein, a "black spot" near Wakkerstroom in the southeastern Transvaal, authorities temporarily halted a planned removal after community leader Saul Mkhize was shot dead by a white policeman in April 1983. The murder might have gone unnoted, and the removal carried out, but Mkhize had mounted a campaign on behalf of Driefontein and neighboring communities, and his murder and his letter to Botha sent a few days before his death (*Document 13*) received wide media publicity. Subsequent court action by neighboring KwaNgema stymied government plans to proceed with the removals, and in 1985 the two communities were granted a rare reprieve. Another bitter series of court actions undertaken by the people of Mogopa, a "black spot" near Ventersdorp in the western Transvaal, failed to stop the community's removal in 1984, but created so much unwelcome local and international publicity that Gerrit Viljoen, Koornhof's replacement as minister of co-operation and development, retreated and announced a suspension of forced removals in early 1985.[38] When removals later resumed, Viljoen tried harder to make them appear voluntary, using the time-tested method of investing authority in an appointed chief who then was rewarded for making residents obey government orders.

In the Cape Province, legal action helped reprieve the historic mission community of Mgwali and six neighboring "black spots" situated among the white farms of the Border region between the Transkei and Ciskei homelands. In preparation for cleansing the region of these Xhosa-speaking communities, the government gave Ciskei jurisdiction over them in 1981, thus delegating to the homeland the tasks of harassment and neglect aimed at inducing "voluntary" removal. Under the leadership of Wilson Fanti, an ANC veteran, the Mgwali Residents' Association challenged the government's legal right to place Mgwali under a homeland's jurisdiction, and in 1985, after a negotiated settlement, Mgwali's right to be part of South Africa was restored by court order. The neighboring "black spots" of Lesseyton, Goshen, Wartburg, Kwelera, Mooiplaas, and Hekkel were likewise reprieved, although Pretoria subsequently put new measures through Parliament to reverse the Mgwali court order and permit homelands to incorporate non-contiguous "black spots." Under this new provision the Border communities were left in suspense, but the "black spots" of Braklaagte and Leeuwfontein in the western Transvaal were placed under the authority of Bophuthatswana in 1988 despite the strenuous objections of their residents.

Government planners had scored a major success for "grand apartheid" in 1981 when the Ciskei homeland opted for full "independence," following in the footsteps of the existing "national states" of Transkei, Bophuthatswana, and Venda. Like its predecessors, Ciskei was an impoverished backwater that cooperated closely with South Africa's security services and lacked any prospect of becoming financially independent of Pretoria. The leader of its ruling party, Lennox Sebe, a former teacher and appointed chief from the Rharhabe subgroup of the Xhosa, packed his government with members of his extended family, using patronage to reward supporters and intimidation to undermine groups critical of his leadership. In 1983 he declared himself Ciskei's "Life President." As in the other three "independent" homelands, the autocratic and corrupt politics of the Ciskei government did little to bolster the legitimacy of the apartheid system and much to stir up active opposition against it.

More than a year before the Vaal uprising erupted in late 1984 and began to spill over to the rest of the country (chapter 2), the Ciskei government's unpopular policies touched off a rehearsal of the chaos to come. Because its borders had been drawn to incorporate the African townships of Mdantsane outside East London and Zwelitsha outside King William's Town, Ciskei had a relatively urbanized population compared to other homelands. When a bus-fare increase caused Mdantsane commuters to boycott homeland-owned buses in July 1983, Sebe deployed police and vigilantes to assault workers who were taking cars and trains to their jobs in East London. Violence escalated (*Document 14*), and school boycotts erupted in Mdantsane and Zwelitsha in protest over arrests of activists. ANC guerrillas fire bombed Ciskei's "consulates" in Johannesburg and Pretoria, and in early September when Sebe banned the South African Allied Workers' Union (SAAWU), the largest trade union representing East London workers, there were sympathy protests by unions countrywide. By October the official death toll had passed 90 and school attendance was down to 10 percent in Mdantsane. Popular rejection of the buses remained firm, the bus company went bankrupt, and Sebe was obliged to scale back his campaign of intimidation.

Violence even more lethal accompanied attempts to launch a fifth homeland, KwaNdebele, into independence in 1986. Under the leadership of Simon Skosana, an ambitious shopkeeper with a sixth-grade education, the small territory 65 miles (105 kilometers) northeast of Pretoria, so poor that it lacked a single hospital, was granted self-governing status in 1981 and promised full sovereignty in December 1986. Most people living there had been forcibly removed earlier from "badly situated" townships or rural "black spots" in the Transvaal, evicted from white farms, or forced out of Bophuthatswana after its independence because they were not Tswana-speakers. By the mid-1980s half a million people were crammed into what one observer described as KwaNdebele's "depressing and dreary . . . endless shanty-covered hills."[39] This impoverished population might have accepted independence passively had National Party planners not overreached in trying to make the homeland more viable by adding to it a more developed adjacent area called Moutse which fell in the Pedi-speaking homeland of Lebowa. Under the leadership of Cedric Phatudi, Lebowa had firmly refused to take independence and was run by one of the more moderate homeland governments. Moutse's 120,000 people now faced either giving up their homes to move elsewhere, or becoming part of an "independent" homeland in which they would lose their

South African citizenship and be abused by self-seeking autocrats even worse than Botha's bureaucrats.

Protests from Moutse, as well as those of the Lebowa government, went largely unheeded by Pretoria but not by Skosana and his cabinet cronies. On January 1, 1986, the day of Moutse's incorporation into KwaNdebele, in an incident emblematic of the petty tyranny of the apartheid system, vigilantes recruited by Skosana rounded up several hundred men from Moutse at dawn, old and young, trucked them to a community hall in Siyabuswa, the temporary homeland capital, and spent the day assaulting them with whips and clubs (*Document 21* is a sworn affidavit made by one of the victims). As in the Crossroads conflict, agents of "the system" were skillful in rallying conservative elders against young "comrades."[40] But the Moutse youth were not easily intimidated, and within several months violence had spread to the rest of the homeland and a full-fledged revolt was in progress. Paramount Chief David Mapoch of the Ndzundza, the largest Ndebele subgroup, openly opposed Skosana. When an estimated 25,000 people converged on Mapoch's compound for an anti-independence demonstration in May, the crowd was tear gassed from a government helicopter and police fired on protestors with birdshot and rubber bullets amidst the mayhem. In the weeks following, open warfare escalated as Skosana's Mbokodo (grinding stone) vigilantes fought youth and student activists, resulting in at least 120 deaths.[41] KwaNdebele civil servants, many of whom were not Ndebele-speakers, went on strike, school boycotts won parental approval, local white farmers spoke out against Pretoria's plans, and James Mahlangu, a son of Chief Mapoch and head of the Ndzundza tribal authority, gained popularity as a spokesman for this unusual coalition of anti-independence constituencies.

Faced with overwhelming popular opposition, the KwaNdebele legislature voted in August 1986 to rescind its earlier decision in favor of independence. Detained young activists were released and Mbokodo was condemned. A car bomb had killed government minister Piet Ntuli, the principal organizer of the vigilantes, in late July, and Skosana died of diabetes in November.[42] The victory of the anti-independence forces was short lived, however. Conservatives regrouped with Pretoria's help, and in May 1987 the homeland's legislature reversed itself, voted for independence again, and the reign of terror resumed. The Ndzundza chiefs were demoted and detained and those of the Manala subtribe of the Ndebeles promoted.

The Ndzundzas gravitated to the Congress of Traditional Leaders of South Africa (Contralesa), a new organization formed in September 1987 under the umbrella of the UDF. Contralesa spoke publicly about the role played by chiefs who had been supporters of the ANC in its early years. They challenged the National Party's assumption that hereditary rulers could easily be co-opted to serve the apartheid order. The new organization was a finger in the eye of the Botha government, but initially its strength remained untested outside KwaNdebele. More decisive in sinking KwaNdebele's ship of state was a 1988 landmark decision by South Africa's highest court invalidating the homeland's incorporation of Moutse.[43] Pretoria's answer was to draft a new law—the Alteration of Boundaries of Self-Governing Territories Bill—giving the state president the power to alter homeland borders by a process not subject to judicial review. This bill was obstructed in Parliament by the coloured and Indian houses in 1989 and never became law.

KwaZulu and Inkatha

Pretoria faced problems and opportunities of a different kind in dealing with the Zulu tribal homeland. KwaZulu was the most populous of the bantustans. Spread over the province of Natal in dozens of fragments, it was also one of the most improbable candidates for independent statehood. To coax KwaZulu toward independence, the apartheid engineers knew it would first be necessary to consolidate as many of these fragments as possible. Strong opposition by white Natal farmers to the costs and disruptions of consolidation was a problem, but equally frustrating to the government was Buthelezi's stubborn rejection of both consolidation and independence. After accepting the position of chief minister of the homeland in the early 1970s, he had repeatedly hinted at the possibility of cooperation with Pretoria's political designs, but seldom actually agreed to become a party to them. A sophisticated politician, Buthelezi was ambitious to command power as a leader beyond the confines of KwaZulu. Compared to other homeland chief ministers, he was a maverick; but from Pretoria's perspective, he was potentially a useful maverick. His public criticisms of apartheid at home and on trips abroad helped maintain his large following among blacks, and at the same time helped boost South Africa's image as a country that upheld the right of free speech. KwaZulu had self-governing status in regard to many matters; ultimately, however, its reliance on economic subsidies from Pretoria guaranteed that Buthelezi's political autonomy would always be limited.

Under Buthelezi's leadership KwaZulu was run as a one-party state in which the ruling party and the civil service overlapped heavily. Buthelezi's party, Inkatha yeNkululeko yeSizwe—the National Cultural Liberation Movement—dominated the KwaZulu legislative assembly and had a central committee of about 100 members chosen periodically at a national conference. Below this there were local party branches.[44] In practice, Inkatha was a classic top-down political machine in which Buthelezi's word was law and elections a mere formality. The slightest insubordination could cut a party member off from Buthelezi's patronage. Teachers and doctors working in the homeland could lose their jobs for refusing to join Inkatha, and party membership was a requirement for traders seeking business licenses.[45] Further to buttress his power as party leader and homeland chief minister, Buthelezi went to great lengths to project himself as the traditional leader of all Zulus, second in rank only to the Zulu king, whose power he eventually managed to limit entirely to ceremonial duties. The Zulus were famed for their military prowess during the nineteenth century when they built an empire by conquering neighboring tribes and briefly holding the invading British at bay at the battle of Isandlwana in 1879. Buthelezi frequently invoked this warrior tradition in his speeches, along with references to "the people's anger" and its potential to become "uncontrollable" if Inkatha's just demands were ignored or denigrated. Many middle-class urban Zulus were unmoved by these appeals to ethnic nationalism, but in rural areas Inkatha was able to build a strong base of support through loyal and socially conservative local chiefs and headmen—all of whose subjects were then regarded as Inkatha members. By the mid-1980s, Buthelezi was claiming that Inkatha membership exceeded one million, making it the largest African organization in South Africa's history.

When Inkatha was formed in 1975, it adopted the colors and anthem of the outlawed ANC and tried to project itself as an organization that had inherited the mantle of the country's oldest liberation movement. After 1979, when the two organizations fell out over which of them would be in the driver's seat, Buthelezi continued to pay rhetorical allegiance to the ANC as it had existed before the departure into exile of its "external mission."[46] His unspoken goal was to have Inkatha supplant the ANC, which he believed was ultimately no match for the South African government because of its distance from the main theater of struggle and its weak organization inside South Africa. Buthelezi sensed that whites would eventually feel pressure to work toward a federal or confederal solution, and when that time came, they would need black allies who could be relied upon to safeguard the rights of property owners and racial minorities. By playing his cards shrewdly, Buthelezi believed, he could position himself to be the only leader powerful enough to strike a deal on behalf of the black majority. These ambitions were evident in a speech by Buthelezi to white businessmen in early 1980 (*Document 2*). To find a way forward, he stated, the country needed "a three-way partnership between black South Africa, industrial and commercial interests, and the ruling [National] party." He implied that he alone had the courage, pragmatism, moral integrity, and mass following to push forward this process—as well as the clout to mobilize "black consumers and workers" for anti-government action if no forward movement occurred. In practice, his threats of boycotts and strikes were empty or left for implementation in the indefinite future.

Buthelezi tried to woo potential allies in order to increase his stature as a leader, but progress was slow and halting. At the time Inkatha was formed in 1975, black consciousness groups regularly denounced him as a bantustan collaborator. Because of Inkatha's reliance on appeals to Zulu nationalism, efforts to extend the movement's membership to other African language groups were short lived. Other homeland leaders could anticipate few tangible benefits from cooperation with Buthelezi, a man whose personal charm and seeming reasonableness only thinly masked a domineering personality. The South African Black Alliance, formed by Buthelezi in 1978, attracted brief support from Mabuza and the leader of the tiny QwaQwa homeland, and established formal ties between Inkatha, the coloured Labour Party, and the Indian Reform Party. The alliance crumbled, however, after Labour's decision—termed a "slap in the face" by Buthelezi—to go into the tricameral Parliament in 1983.[47]

Buthelezi was more successful in attracting white support, especially from those who were worried about the long-term economic consequences of government policies. He established cordial relations with the Progressive Federal Party and won wide support from big business, for which the Progressives were a mouthpiece in Parliament. His appeal for a partnership between Inkatha, business, and government; his opposition to foreign economic sanctions; and his belief that capitalism was a force undermining apartheid drew praise from corporate leaders, including Harry Oppenheimer of Anglo American (South Africa's largest corporation), and even from affluent Afrikaners. On trips abroad, Buthelezi met with Margaret Thatcher and Ronald Reagan and won friends in conservative business circles, where dislike of the left-leaning ANC usually outweighed distaste for apartheid. In a speech to the conservative Heritage Foundation in Washington in late 1986, Buthelezi presented himself as the proponent of negotiation in contrast to the ANC's "politics of violence" (*Document 25*). The ANC, he said, spurned the efforts of moderates to find non-violent solutions and instead was determined to shoot its way into power so that it could "establish a one-party socialist state."

Soon after the open break between the ANC and Inkatha in 1979–80, Buthelezi, in partnership with white business leaders in Natal, launched an ambitious effort to promote a model of reform which they hoped might politically transform their region and ultimately perhaps the country. For Buthelezi, this was a bold move to demonstrate that, unlike his rivals, he was a serious player "in the league above protest politics" (*Document 25*). The immediate objective was to develop a plan for what became known as the KwaNatal option, or the creation of joint administrative structures for Natal Province and the KwaZulu homeland. The Botha government was invited to participate but declined. All those involved in the exercise opposed the consolidation of KwaZulu's fragmented pieces, Buthelezi because he rejected ethnic partitioning of South Africa, and white business—particularly the powerful sugar industry—because of the severe disruption that would result from "artificially separating out the economically and demographically closely interwoven subregions of Natal and KwaZulu."[48] The participants in what became known as the Buthelezi Commission, working over several years, devised a plan for a unified provincial government with a joint executive and a single legislature. Drawing on studies of consociational political systems by Arend Lijphart and others, the commission recommended a plan in which there would be a universal franchise but ethnic groups rather than individuals would be represented in institutional structures. To ensure their participation, minorities would be given overrepresentation and various prescribed veto powers. To encourage members of all ethnic groups to outgrow their narrow identities, a group called "South African" was proposed in which any voter could opt to be represented without racial labels.[49]

When the commission announced these recommendations in 1982, the Botha government dismissed them immediately as unacceptable. Later, after nationwide black resistance mounted sharply in the mid-1980s and foreign pressures for reform increased correspondingly, the white Natal provincial government, Inkatha, the Progressives, and business, with support from moderate Natal Indians and coloureds, dusted off the Buthelezi Commission plan. A new round of talks, now called the Natal Indaba (consultation), began among the interested groups in April 1986, this time with observers present from the National Party. Before the Indaba could issue its final recommendations seven months later (*Document 26* is a description of the proposed consociational "KwaNatal" provincial legislature), Pretoria put through Parliament a measure to create a multiracial Joint Executive Authority in Natal according to its own design. Chris Heunis, the minister of constitutional development, was adamant, however, that there would be no sharing of legislative power between the white province and the black homeland. In a province where less than 8 percent of the population was white, elite consultations were permissible but democracy, even of the watered-down consociational type, was not. The Indaba proposals were shelved, and, as we shall see in chapter 3, the Botha government shifted into a different gear in its dealings with Buthelezi and Inkatha.

"Total Strategy"

The reforms of the 1980s were designed to win public support and international legitimacy for the Botha regime and to sap the will of blacks to resist the state's authority. At the same time, apartheid security chiefs—dubbed "securocrats" by the opposition press—argued that positive inducements alone could never win over or neutralize the country's radical minority of dedicated revolutionaries; it was also essential to curb resistance through a strategy of control and repression. To help justify repressive measures, the state interwove its new credo of technocratic and managerial competence with an ideology of anti-communism carried forward from earlier decades. According to this world view, reiterated endlessly for local and international audiences by Pretoria's information services, South Africa, a Christian nation upholding Western values, was a target of the Soviet Union and its allies and agents. Marxist takeovers in Mozambique and Angola had brought this "total onslaught" to South Africa's doorstep just when the exiled South African Communist Party was using the African National Congress as a front for communist penetration of South Africa.

To survive in the face of this "total onslaught" by international communism, Botha declared, South Africa had to be guided by a "total strategy." Reform was part of this strategy, but so too was war on the government's radical critics, since all such opposition furthered the aims of communism. The country's rulers were obsessed with state security—in reality, the security of their own hold on power—wrote South African Catholic leaders in a 1982 pamphlet directed at white immigrants from communist Eastern Europe (*Document 6*).[50] Since the government regarded any method of guaranteeing the regime's security as justified, the pamphlet said, repression—strikingly similar to that in the communist bloc itself—was the result: "detention without trial, the banning of people and organisations, the tapping of telephones and the opening of mail, censorship of the press, the use of informers and spies, a strong army, a security or secret police, and a special riot squad. The last three are trained to use violent methods and yield a rich crop of beaten-up victims, detainees dying or 'committing suicide' while in prison, or people simply 'disappearing.'"

As minister of defense under Vorster, Botha had overseen the development of national security policy in the 1970s, drawing on the expertise of Western counterinsurgency specialists.[51] After he became prime minister, Botha built up the State Security Council, previously a minor cabinet committee, making it into a nerve center for coordinating the police, army, and key civilian departments.[52] These departments included foreign affairs, information, and the ministry that had once been called "Bantu Affairs" but later became "Co-operation and Development." The State Security Council was charged with policy making and oversight of the National Security Management System, a pyramid of hundreds of interdepartmental committees called Joint Management Centres (JMCs). Each JMC was part of a chain of command and information gathering that stretched down to the local township level.

By the mid-1980s, this apparatus of security committees was identifying troubled townships where infrastructure projects and social programs could be introduced to ameliorate conditions and undercut local political agitators. Running parallel to this open effort to "win hearts and minds" (dubbed "WHAM" by its critics) was a second track on which the JMCs helped identify local activists so that the security police could apprehend them. Many thousands were detained without charge during the two states of emergency imposed in the mid-1980s—a partial one from July 1985 to March 1986, and a nationwide one from June 1986 until June 1990. The best-known monitoring group estimated that 25,000 people were detained in the first 12 months of the emergency that began in June 1986.[53] Most detainees belonged to affiliates of the ANC-aligned UDF or other political organizations or trade unions. Some, including children as young as 10 years old, were merely swept up during incidents of stone throwing or political vandalism.[54] Detainees were beaten and brutalized; some died as a result of torture. *Documents 19* and *20* describe the experiences of detainees in the eastern Cape, and *Document 27* is the affidavit of a teenager arrested in Soweto in March 1987. Repression was intense on the campuses of black universities, particularly the University of the North, where soldiers in armored vehicles occupied the campus from June 1986 onward.[55]

A third track of Botha's "total strategy" was a covert one in which secret units of the security forces waged a hidden war against government opponents. Their operations ranged from "dirty tricks," such as the planting of informers in opposition organizations and the distribution of disinformation leaflets announcing the "cancellation" of political events, to acts of lethal violence. Parcel bombs mailed to ANC members in exile killed Adolphus "John Dube" Mvemve, Ruth First, Jeanette Schoon, and her six-year-old daughter; a car bomb in Maputo maimed Albie Sachs; and a parcel bomb cost Michael Lapsley both his hands. Frank Chikane narrowly survived a murder attempt when a highly toxic substance was put in clothing in his suitcase on an overseas trip. Gunmen assassinated other exiled political figures including Joe Gqabi, Dulcie September, and Job "Cassius Make" Tlhabane. Many activists inside South Africa were similarly eliminated. Griffiths and Victoria Mxenge, Matthew Goniwe, Fabian Ribeiro and his wife, and David Webster were among the most prominent victims of death-squad murders in the 1980s. Deadly raids by the South African army on ANC buildings in the frontline states were carried out openly as "anti-terrorist" operations; meanwhile, bombs secretly planted by police in the offices of opposition groups inside South Africa were routinely dismissed as the work of dissident factions within opposition organizations. Official investigations of these bombings, like police investigations of the mysterious deaths of activists, invariably led nowhere.[56]

Vigilantism was another covert weapon. Attacks on government critics by armed gangs occurred in many places besides Crossroads and KwaNdebele. Sometimes the hand of the police was visible in these clashes, for example in transporting ringleaders to the sites of the attacks. At other times no direct police encouragement was evident, but their connivance was clear because victims drew no response when they appealed for police protection from the attacks. Whites read in the mainstream media about "black-on-black" violence and took little interest in who was participating or why. Africans attacking each other provided an opportunity for the state to promote the stereotyped propaganda image of South Africa as a country of multiple nationalities, each in need of its own separate area in order to avoid conflict. In reality, the spread of vigilantism was usually fanned less by ethnicity than by attitudes arising from local conflicts, often among people of the same ethnic group, reflecting antagonisms between young and old. Police were often able to capitalize on genuine grievances of older residents who had experienced intimidation or disrespect at the hands of youthful activists. In particular, migrant workers, generally less politicized than urban dwellers and deeply imbued with traditions of generational hierarchy, could be provoked into resisting the assertiveness of politicized youths. Displaced or embattled elites linked to the community councils were often ready allies in forming counteroffensive units, as were local leaders of Inkatha who commanded the loyalty of migrant Zulus living in bleak, single-sex urban hostels.

In addition to these social and political tensions, the presence of rival antigovernment organizations, some favoring the ANC and the UDF and others opposing them from an Africanist, black consciousness, or Unity Movement perspective, often led to confrontations, even where government provocateurs were not initially present—but especially when they were. Most deadly of all by the late 1980s was the rivalry between Inkatha and the ANC-backed UDF. The more credible the growing threat posed by the ANC and its allies, the more intense became the regime's efforts to weaken that alliance and to build its own coalition of black potential allies, foremost of whom had become Chief Buthelezi.

The power of religious leaders to promote or thwart government plans was another consideration that preoccupied Botha's security specialists as they pursued the "total strategy." The white NGK (Nederduitse Gereformeerde

Kerk or Dutch Reformed Church) remained staunchly in the white supremacist fold despite internal disagreements over how best to react to changing political conditions. Black clergy ministering to the segregated African, coloured, and Indian "daughter" congregations of the NGK often chafed at their inferior status, but found few ways to assert their independence. In a letter to the South African Council of Churches (SACC), an African pastor on South Africa's northern border who was being forced by the NGK to relocate to a less strategically sensitive area in 1982 expressed his frustration (*Document 9*). In contrast to the Dutch Reformed churches, the SACC, representing most other Protestant denominations, fell squarely in the anti-apartheid camp. Pressures created by the black consciousness movement in the 1970s had forced white-dominated church hierarchies to accept the gradual promotion of blacks, with the result that by the 1980s the leadership of church bodies had begun more accurately to reflect the racial composition of church membership nationwide, which was 80 percent black.[57] With leadership more attuned to black concerns, churches were cautiously moving beyond mere condemnations of injustice to calls for specific forms of action, including civil disobedience, international economic sanctions, and resistance to military conscription. The SACC was in the forefront of this growing activism.

To beat back the SACC's challenge to government policies, the Botha regime in late 1981 appointed a commission of inquiry into the organization's finances. The SACC had become a conduit for overseas donations to aid victims of apartheid after the Soweto uprising. Much of this money had been managed in informal ways to avoid government scrutiny. Auditors had chided the SACC for its failure to account properly for its funds, thus providing the government an opportunity to look for evidence of illegal actions that could justify placing restrictions on the Council. A government-appointed commission of inquiry headed by Judge C. F. Eloff investigated the SACC for more than three years, interviewing numerous witnesses. Testifying before the commission, Anglican Bishop Desmond Tutu, who had become general secretary of the SACC in 1978, and Wolfram Kistner, the head of the Council's Justice and Reconciliation division, squared off against Lieutenant-General Johann Coetzee, head of the security police, who urged that the Council be prohibited from receiving foreign funds because of its clear intention to create a revolutionary atmosphere in the country. Government witnesses denounced as tools of communism the World Council of Churches and its Program to Combat Racism, which had been giving humanitarian aid to the exiled ANC and Pan Africanist Congress (PAC) for over a decade and were also donors to the SACC. In a tart reply to the commission's final report, the SACC ridiculed Pretoria's attempts to tarnish the Council's image and warned that genuine Christians would continue to obey God rather than man (*Document 16*).

Critical international media coverage of the Eloff Commission, along with the presence of observers from foreign church bodies, served to remind the Botha government that in attacking mainstream religious leaders it was inviting worldwide disapproval. In its final report, tabled in Parliament in early 1984, the commission did not recommend placing the SACC on the government's list of organizations barred from receiving foreign funds.[58] Instead it recommended that existing laws be tightened to further criminalize the advocacy of international economic sanctions. Botha eventually decided against taking even this milder action, however, perhaps anticipating that Tutu, who was awarded the Nobel Peace Prize in late 1984, would relish a public showdown on the sanctions issue.

Despite the government's desire to avoid negative publicity internationally, banning, deportations, death threats, detention, and even torture of individual religious leaders became a feature of political life in the 1980s. Smangaliso Mkhatshwa, Frank Chikane, Simon Farisani, and others were subjected to extreme physical abuse. Over a hundred clerics and church workers were detained without charge during the second state of emergency. After the experience of the Eloff Commission, however, public statements by government spokesmen tarring anti-apartheid church leaders as hypocrites or communist dupes were largely reserved for loyal National Party audiences at election time. Meanwhile, a campaign of vilification was conducted through the publications and sermons of right-wing religious organizations, some of them financed by Pretoria.[59]

The "total onslaught" necessitated reform, according to the Botha government, but the national interest also required constraints on the mass media to prevent demoralization among whites.[60] Censorship and slanted public broadcasting had been a feature of National Party rule for many years. By the early 1980s more than a hundred laws regulated what journalists could report.[61] As repression escalated after 1984, measures to intimidate and gag opposition newspapers reached new extremes. In the early months of the 1984 Vaal uprising, the government allowed the press to cover the turmoil, proceeding from a miscalculation that "horrifying scenes in the townships would serve to justify its own increasingly desperate and drastic measures to restore law and order."[62] By early 1985 the regime had recognized its error. Police began to bar reporters from scenes of violence, invoking statutes that existed to protect the security forces from unwelcome public scrutiny. After a state of emergency was declared in 38 districts in 1985, officials claimed that the presence of TV cameras encouraged violence. Regulations were therefore issued

> prohibiting any person from photographing, filming, or recording, as well as broadcasting or distributing within or outside South Africa any film, photograph, drawing, or sound recording, of any public disturbance, disorder, riot, public violence, strike, or boycott; or any damaging of any property; or any assault on or killing of a person; or any person present at or involved in any of these activities; or any conduct of a force or member of a force with regard to the maintenance of the safety of the public . . . unless the permission of the commissioner of

the SAP [South African Police] or a commissioned officer authorised by the commissioner was given.[63]

During the more comprehensive nationwide state of emergency declared in June 1986 and renewed annually until 1990, restrictions were broadened and refined to fend off legal challenges to censorship. When the crusading *Weekly Mail* began to publish news stories containing blacked-out words, for example, a new regulation outlawed this practice. Subtler inducements created to persuade the mainstream press to practice self-censorship were superseded by tough new emergency measures. Journalists were barred from all areas where the security forces were in action. It became a serious crime, punishable by a ten-year jail sentence, to publish a "subversive statement," defined to include words furthering any objective of a banned organization, aggravating feelings of racial hostility, encouraging political resistance, or promoting foreign sanctions.[64] Dozens of journalists were detained and hundreds of foreign reporters denied entry visas to South Africa.[65] The far-from-subtle intent was not just to prevent the outside world from assessing the force of popular resistance, but also to deny this knowledge to South Africans, both white and black.

Media censorship may have dampened international criticism somewhat, but foreign pressure for economic sanctions mounted inexorably after the eruption of township revolt in late 1984, attracting thousands of anti-apartheid activists and millions of sympathizers worldwide. As well as spurring moral outrage abroad, civil unrest in South Africa undermined international business confidence. New foreign investment in South Africa waned, and the gradual exodus of multinational companies accelerated. Even without the decline in business confidence at home and abroad, South Africa's economy was already confronting a host of ills: sluggish growth, prolonged drought, rising inflation, balance-of-payments deficits, and many apartheid-induced distortions, including excessive military spending, high black unemployment combined with a shortage of skilled labor, and an overgrown and inefficient white public sector. Foreign bank loans and a spike in the gold price partially offset these problems in 1980–81, but as gold fell, a major recession loomed. Between 1982 and 1984, white business—friendly to Botha as long as he seemed intent on economic and social reform—pressured the government to step up the pace of change despite depleted state revenues. A small number of more farsighted business leaders even pressed for dialogue with exiled and imprisoned African leaders as a step toward negotiation of a political settlement.

Less than two weeks after Botha's declaration of a state of emergency in the eastern Cape and southern Transvaal in July 1985, the country was plunged into a sudden economic crisis. Political instability combined with poor economic performance had caused enough alarm among foreign creditors that a string of banks, first in the United States and then in Europe, began to call in millions of dollars of short-term loans.[66] Botha made matters worse by denouncing foreign interference in a truculent address—later dubbed the

"Rubicon" speech—at a National Party congress in Durban in August.[67] There was a sharp fall in the value of South Africa's currency (the rand), and near panic among the business and financial elite. Shrewd management of the debt crisis eventually restored stability, but the country's chronic economic problems continued to fester. Meanwhile, in September 1985, signaling an unprecedented shift in the political balance of power, the head of Anglo American and six other business and media leaders traveled to Zambia despite Botha's objections, where they met with ANC president Oliver Tambo and other top ANC leaders to talk about the future (*Document 126*).

As the township rebellion rolled on, Botha's dilemmas multiplied. A victory for the reactionary Herstigte Nasionale Party in an October 1985 by-election signaled an alarming turn to the right in white opinion.[68] Botha lifted the partial state of emergency in March 1986 to placate international bankers, but imposed a more severe countrywide emergency in June in a renewed attempt to stamp out popular revolt. This gave new ammunition to foreign anti-apartheid campaigners, who continued to pressure Western corporations and governments to adopt economic sanctions. In October 1986, U.S. activists scored a major psychological victory when the U.S. Congress passed, over a veto by President Reagan, the Comprehensive Anti-Apartheid Act, a measure prohibiting U.S. companies from making any new investments in South Africa until all apartheid laws were repealed.[69] Botha's government, which had adopted a counterrevolutionary strategy in the name of fending off a communist "total onslaught," now faced an increasingly threatening onslaught from its nominal friends. Although reform would potentially lower the pressure for sanctions, reform could not succeed without repression, and try as it might to avert the eyes of the world from its domestic conflict, Pretoria was unable to deflect the prying spotlight of the world's media.

The Struggle in the Courts

When Botha became prime minister in late 1978, the National Party had already used its three decades in power to promote its own supporters into the ranks of the all-white South African judiciary. In Natal, where English-speaking whites outnumbered Afrikaners, the provincial Supreme Court included some independent-minded jurists, but most of the country's 130 or so senior judges were conservative Afrikaners whose instincts aligned them with the "total onslaught" mentality. In any case, South Africa's judicial system gave courts no power to challenge the legality of acts of Parliament. Parliament made the laws, and the job of a judge was to apply them. South Africa's "reform" constitution of 1983, like earlier ones, contained no bill of rights to defend citizens against government abuses. At most, judges could interpret laws when their language or intent was ambiguous, bringing to bear, if they were so inclined, the preference for liberty and equality enshrined in common law. Judges were also empowered to rule on whether laws had been properly enforced or administered. Internationally, the South African judiciary enjoyed a high reputation for competence despite its unrepresentative character. At home, it was respected by most whites but regarded with ambivalence by blacks, to many of whom it was simply the punitive arm of apartheid's system of discrimination and control.[70]

For the Botha government, the courts played a dual role, helping to perpetuate white rule while also furthering the National Party's agenda of political legitimation through reform. Early in the Botha era, the government-appointed Rabie Commission reviewed the country's multiple security laws and consolidated them into a new all-purpose Internal Security Act, passed by Parliament in 1982. Judge P. J. Rabie was then named chief justice of the Supreme Court in 1983, where he was in a position to select hard-line panels of judges to sit on security cases.[71] When operatives of the underground ANC were captured, or the state brought criminal charges against people associated with the aboveground UDF and its affiliates, the resulting political trials served several ends. If successful, they branded the regime's enemies as violent, locked them away for extended periods, or sent them to the gallows. Even if a trial ended in acquittal, it tied up government opponents in long, costly, and debilitating court proceedings and intimidated other dissidents. Either way—and, ironically, particularly when skilled lawyers managed to win acquittals for political defendants—trials could demonstrate to skeptics at home and abroad that South Africa, a "civilized" country, respected judicial independence and the rule of law.[72]

Some South African critics of apartheid called for the resignation of judges on the grounds that justice could never be served in a system with so many unjust laws.[73] Others rejected this view and argued, like the authors of *Document 5*, that "between the extremes of acquiescence and resignation from the Bench [lay] a not inconsiderable area of action" in which to interpret and criticize laws, and, as experience subsequently proved, also to invalidate oppressive administrative procedures. Not many judges took this approach, however, unless pressed—or enabled—to do so by lawyers presenting aggressive rights-based arguments in well-selected test cases.

Human rights lawyers from a handful of liberal legal organizations scored some notable victories in this way. For example, the Johannesburg-based Legal Resources Centre, launched in 1979, had by the early 1980s disrupted the government's plans for tighter influx control by winning two landmark cases, *Komani v. Bantu Affairs Administration Board* and *Rikhoto v. East Rand Administration Board*. These judgments invalidated obstructive regulations facing applicants for section 10 status and contributed to the government's decision to repeal the pass laws in 1986.[74] In 1985, lawyers assisted Wendy Orr, a 24-year-old Port Elizabeth district surgeon, in obtaining an interdict against the minister of law and order in Port Elizabeth and Uitenhage to prevent assault and torture of detainees in those districts.[75] Amid many defeats and much bureaucratic foot dragging, incremental court victories of this kind ameliorated repression, emboldened grassroots resisters, and fostered, in the words of two activist lawyers, "the renascence of a civil liberties approach to statutory interpretation."[76] Following the recognition of African trade unions in 1979, advances in the framing and application of labor laws provided growing protection against the unjust treatment of workers. The Botha regime, hoping to project a reform image, sometimes refrained from introducing new laws to close the loopholes opened by anti-apartheid litigation. For example, Judge Richard Goldstone in *State v. Govender* in 1982 ruled that an Indian family living illegally in a white urban area could not be evicted unless alternative accommodations were available (*Document 29*).[77] Rather than nullifying this decision with new legislation at a time when it was trying to attract Indian and coloured support for the tricameral Parliament, the government decided to close its eyes to the growing inner-city phenomenon of racially mixed "grey areas."[78]

The real threat to Afrikaner rule was not the erosion of racial segregation but the danger that Pretoria might lose control over the extraparliamentary opposition. In the eyes of some, the occasional easing of race discrimination against Indians, coloureds, and urban African insiders, sweetened by periodic official pronouncements that apartheid was dead or dying, added credibility to promises of reform. Black resistance, however, undermined that credibility and threatened to wreck the National Party's evolving plan for restructuring South Africa into a loose confederation of states in which all citizens would fulfill their political ambitions in their "own" ethnic areas. Unless this threat could be crushed by applying the security laws when possible—but going beyond them if necessary, by fair means or foul—the National Party and white supremacy in South Africa had no future.

Notes

All conversations and interviews cited are with Thomas Karis and/or Gail Gerhart unless otherwise indicated. All conversations, interviews, and documents cited in endnotes can be found in the Karis-Gerhart Collection (hereafter KGC). The organization appearing in parentheses following each document title indicates the location of that document in the Collection. *FPTC* refers to earlier volumes in the *From Protest to Challenge* series.

1. Soweto is the complex of African townships southwest of downtown Johannesburg. See Thomas Karis and Gail Gerhart, *FPTC*, volume 5, chapter 6 on the Soweto uprising, and chapter 11 on reform moves in the late 1970s.

2. On black workers and trade unions in the 1960s and 1970s, see *FPTC*, volume 5, chapter 7.

3. The term "black" was sometimes used to denote only Africans, and sometimes to include Africans, Indians, and mixed-race coloureds. The pre-1994 South African government and some newspapers followed the former usage, but this book follows the latter. In 1985, South Africa's population was as follows:

Africans	24,901,139	(74.1%)
Coloureds	2,881,362	(8.5%)
Indians	878,300	(2.6%)
Whites	4,961,062	(14.8%)
	33,621,863	

These figures include "independent" Transkei, Bophuthatswana, Venda, and Ciskei. *South Africa Survey 2000/2001* (Johannesburg: South African Institute of Race Relations, 2001), p. 48.

4. See John Lewis Gaddis, *The Cold War* (London: Penguin, 2005).

5. After the Nkomati Accord, Pretoria secretly continued aiding RENAMO. See William Minter, *Apartheid's Contras* (London: Zed Books, 1994), conversation with Roland Hunter (October 1991) and talk by Legwaila J. Legwaila (January 1988). Pretoria was also implicated by strong circumstantial evidence in the death of Mozambican president Samora Machel in a plane crash on South African soil in October 1986. See *Truth and Reconciliation Commission of South Africa Report* (Cape Town: Truth and Reconciliation Commission, 1998) (*TRC Report*), volume 2, pp. 493–502.

6. See *FPTC,* volume 2, on African reactions to the Natives' Representative Council and urban advisory boards in the 1930s and 1940s.

7. South Africans of Indian descent live predominantly in and around the city of Durban, and mixed-race coloureds are concentrated in the western Cape. See *FPTC,* volume 5, chapter 8 on coloured and Indian politics in the 1960s and 1970s. On the 1980s, see conversations with Saths Cooper (October 1985), Don Mateman (July 1980), and Robert Schrire (November 1985).

8. Tom Lodge and Bill Nasson, *All, Here, and Now: Black Politics in South Africa in the 1980s* (New York: Ford Foundation and Foreign Policy Association, 1991), *p.* 42. *Survey of Race Relations 1981* (Johannesburg: SAIRR, 1982), p. 20, says "generally the poll was under 20%." Also see Kumi Naidoo, "Class, Consciousness and Organisation: Indian Political Resistance in Durban, South Africa, 1979–1996," Ph.D. thesis, Oxford University, 1998, p. 100.

9. The debate moved toward resolution following consultations in London between NIC activists and the ANC's Mac Maharaj in 1979. Interview by Howard Barrell with Maharaj (November 30, 1990).

10. See *FPTC,* volume 5, chapter 8.

11. Interview by Ameen Akhalwaya with Hendrickse, *Rand Daily Mail,* August 15, 1980. In the ANC's 1979 Green Book, Chris Hani described the Labour Party as a potential vehicle for mass mobilization which the ANC should infiltrate. See *FPTC,* volume 5, *Document 114.* Oliver Tambo, in speeches in 1980–81, referred to the ANC's support for "patriots" who were trying to destroy apartheid's "dummy institutions" from within.

12. Allan Hendrickse, "The Constitution (3)," *Leadership SA,* vol. 2, no. 2, 1983, p. 19.

13. Turnout figures vary depending on whether they are taken as a percentage of registered voters or all potential voters. Only slightly more than half of potential coloured voters registered, and only 31% of those actually voted, according to Richard Van der Ross, *The Rise and Decline of Apartheid* (Cape Town: Tafelberg, 1986), pp. 356–57. In the Indian House of Delegates, Rajbansi's National People's Party emerged as the majority party, and Solidarity, led by J. N. Reddy, became the official opposition.

14. Taiwan and Israel did not recognize the homelands diplomatically but permitted their citizens to do business with the four "independent" TBVC states: Transkei ("independent" from 1976), Bophuthatswana (1977), Venda (1979), and Ciskei (1981). The other homelands were Lebowa, Gazankulu, KwaZulu, KaNgwane, QwaQwa, and KwaNdebele.

15. Stoffel Van der Merwe, *And What About the Black People?* (Pretoria: National Party, 1985), pp. 1, 14, and 16.

16. "Pretoria Offers Legality to Foes," *New York Times,* September 21, 1987, reported that Stoffel Van der Merwe, a top advisor to Botha, had said a few days earlier that "the political climate was not conducive to the official plan . . . [and it] would fail if put into effect now." One state-anointed leader who agreed to serve on the proposed council was Bishop Isaac Mokoena, co-president of the short-lived and state-funded United Christian Conciliation Party

17. On policy indecision in the National Party, see Brian Pottinger, *The Imperial Presidency: P.W. Botha, the First Ten Years* (Johannesburg: Southern Book Publishers, 1988); F. W. de Klerk, *The Last Trek—A New Beginning* (London: Macmillan, 1998), pp. 101 and 106; Sheena Duncan, "Chaos in the administration of black townships," *The Black Sash,* August 1985, pp. 18–20 (KGC: Black Sash); and Fran Buntman, *Robben Island and Prisoner Resistance to Apartheid* (New York: Cambridge University Press, 2003), pp. 226–28.

18. Dozens of black police were also murdered. See Jill Wentzel, "History of Attacks on Black Local Authorities," *Spotlight,* no. 2 (Johannesburg: SAIRR, August 1991), pp. 7ff.

19. Cecil Seethal, "Restructuring the Local State in South Africa: Regional Services Councils and Crisis Resolution," *Political Geography Quarterly,* vol. 10, no. 1, 1991, pp. 8–25.

20. Under the pass laws, no African could remain in an urban area for more than 72 hours unless he or she had a valid labor contract there or qualified for section 10 rights under the 1945 Bantu (Urban Areas) Consolidation Act as amended in 1952. This act conferred rights of permanent residence in an urban area only on those Africans who (a) had resided continuously in that area since birth; (b) had worked continuously in that area for the same employer for ten years; (c) had lawfully resided continuously in that area for at least 15 years; or (d) were the wife, unmarried daughter, or minor son of a male falling under (a), (b), or (c). For a history of urban influx control, see Doug Hindson, *Pass Controls and the Urban African Proletariat in South Africa* (Johannesburg: Ravan Press, 1987).

21. *Document 12* confronts the question of how successful the regime had already been in co-opting middle-class blacks. This recurring debate is taken up in Peter Hudson and Mike Sarakinsky, "Class Interests and Politics: the Case of the Urban African Bourgeoisie," *South African Review 3* (Johannesburg: Ravan Press, 1986), and John Brewer, "Black Protest in South Africa's Crisis: A Comment on Legassick," *African Affairs,* vol. 85, no. 339, April 1986.

22. Michael Savage, "The Imposition of Pass Laws on the African Population in South Africa 1916–1984," *African Affairs,* vol. 85, no. 339, April 1986, p. 183. In 1987 the Urban Foundation estimated the number of shack-dwellers in South Africa at between 4.85 and 5.65 million, with the highest concentrations in the Durban/Pinetown and Pretoria/Witwatersrand/Vereeniging (PWV) areas. *Race Relations Survey 1988/89,* p. 162. Elsa Joubert's *The Long Journey of Poppie Nongena* (Johannesburg: Jonathan Ball, 1980), is a fictionalized account of the life of western Cape squatters.

23. The government installed water pipes (and sometimes electricity) at site-and-service projects and residents constructed their own houses. The Botha government distinguished between these "informal settlements," which were officially authorized, as cases of "orderly urbanization," and squatter settlements where residents occupied land without official permission.

24. Changing labels without changing substance was standard National Party practice. The best known renamings included changing "Natives" to "Bantus" then to "Blacks"; "apartheid" to "separate development"; "passes" to "reference books"; and the Native Affairs Department to Bantu Affairs Department, then to Department of Plural Relations, and later to Department of Co-operation and Development.

25. Surplus People Project, *Forced Removals in South Africa,* vol. 1 (Cape Town: Surplus People Project, 1983), pp. 5–7.

26. Oukasie ("Ou Lokasie" or Old Location) is described in Transvaal Rural Action Committee (TRAC), "Forced Removals Continue: Oukasie," *Work in Progress,* no. 43, August 1986 (KGC: TRAC and Alternative Media), and Richard Stengel, *January Sun: One Day, Three Lives, A South African Town* (New York: Simon & Schuster, 1990).

27. See "The Struggle in the Courts" later in this chapter. The government's attempt to incorporate Botshabelo into QwaQwa, for example, was defeated in a court case, as was Oukasie's removal. *Race Relations Survey 1988/89,* p. 89–90, and Stengel, p. 201.

28. See *FPTC,* volume 5, chapter 11.

29. *Race Relations Survey 1986, p.* 358, and Josette Cole, *Crossroads: The Politics of Reform and Repression, 1976–1986* (Johannesburg: Ravan Press, 1987). Also see interview by Steven Robins with Pippa Green (January 1988).

30. *Race Relations Survey 1986, p.* 357.

31. *Race Relations Survey 1986, p.* 336.

32. On the political evolution of the homelands see *FPTC,* volume 5, chapter 8. The term "grand apartheid" was used to distinguish territorial partition from social segregation or "petty apartheid."

33. See Ieuan Griffiths and D. C. Funnell, "The Abortive Swazi Land Deal," *African Affairs,* vol. 90, no. 358, January 1991, pp. 51–64.

34. "Let us Strive for our Rights and Privileges in South Africa, the Land of our Birth," address by Enos Mabuza in Barberton, February 6, 1982 (KGC: Homelands).

35. The suits rested on the legal obligation of Pretoria to consult homeland governments adequately before border alterations. KaNgwane's case was settled out of court. Four years later, facing nationwide rebellion, Botha's military intelligence planners advanced another imaginative but doomed scheme, Operation Katzen, aimed at "permanent normalisation of the Eastern Cape situation." The plan required unification of Transkei and Ciskei, throwing in the white land corridor between them if necessary, to create a single "Xhosa nation" under the leadership of traditionalist collaborators. See *Appendices to the Second Submission by the African National Congress to the Truth and Reconciliation Commission, 12 May 1997,* appendix 12 (KGC: ANC).

36. Surplus People Project, pp. 6–7, and Elaine Unterhalter, *Forced Removal* (London: International Defence and Aid Fund, 1987), *p.* 97.

37. Surplus People Project, *p.* 6–7. Numbers are estimates based on research by the Surplus People Project. The government's definition of "black spot" varied over time, but in 1982 the Association for Rural Advancement estimated that in Natal 102 communities had already been removed, and at least another 189 were under threat of removal. *AFRA Report 16,* April 1982 (KGC: AFRA). On the 1913 Natives Land Act, which demarcated the reserves that were later to become homelands, see *FPTC,* volume 1.

38. On Mogopa, see TRAC, *Mogopa: And Now We Have No Land,* [1987?] (KGC: TRAC), and David Goodman, *Fault Lines: Journeys into the New South Africa* (Berkeley: University of California Press, 1999), pp. 317–44.

39. TRAC, "KwaNdebele: The Struggle Against 'Independence'," in William Cobbett and Robin Cohen, eds., *Popular Struggles in South Africa* (London: Africa World Press, 1988), pp. 115–16.

40. The testimony of Ephraim Mogale to the TRC hearings, December 2, 1996 [Case JB02473] provided an insider's view of Moutse. Mogale, a Pedi-speaker and the first president of the Congress of South African Students, trained as an ANC operative in the 1970s, spent five years on Robben Island, and returned home from prison to Moutse in October 1985.

41. *Race Relations Survey 1986,* p. 657. "Introduction—the current political situation," internal UDF memo, [1986/87?], p. 13 (KGC: UDF), alludes to participation by Umkhonto we Sizwe, the ANC's military wing, in the fighting.

42. The ANC later claimed that it had assassinated Ntuli, but in the late 1990s seven South African security policemen applied to the TRC for amnesty in connection with the murder. *TRC Report,* vol. 3, p. 656. At the time, some in KwaNdebele suspected that Pretoria had disposed of Ntuli in order to make him a scapegoat for the violence, clearing the way to reopen negotiations for independence. See TRAC, "KwaNdebele," p. 131.

43. See Richard Abel, *Politics by Other Means: Law in the Struggle Against Apartheid, 1980–1994* (New York: Routledge, 1995), chapter 11.

44. Wessel de Kock, *Usuthu! Cry Peace!* (Cape Town: Open Hand Press, 1986), which casts Inkatha in a favorable light, claims on p. 184 that the central committee had 103 members. In assessing Inkatha in the 1980s, we have benefited from conversations with Ben Khoapa (October 1980), Oscar Dhlomo and Frank Mdlalose (February 1987), Joe Matthews (June 1994), and Walter Felgate (February 1998). On Inkatha in the 1970s, see *FPTC,* volume 5, chapter 9. After February 1990, Inkatha changed its name to the Inkatha Freedom Party (IFP).

45. Zulu chiefs were also required to join or face retribution. Chief Mhlabunzima Maphumulo, an anti-Inkatha chief who became president of Contralesa in 1989, was assassinated in 1991.

46. See *FPTC,* volume 5, chapter 9, and Walter Felgate, "Submission to the Truth and Reconciliation Commission: 'Conditioning Inkatha for Violence'," November 1997, pp. 53–66 (KGC: Inkatha).

47. Gatsha Buthelezi, "An Ally's Act of Betrayal," *Washington Post,* February 3, 1983. Known familiarly as "Gatsha" until the mid-1980s, Buthelezi later preferred using his given name, Mangosuthu. The ruling Dikwankwetla Party of QwaQwa, headed by Chief T. K. Mopeli, withdrew from the South African Black Alliance in 1981.

48. Daryl Glaser, "Behind the Indaba: the Making of the KwaNatal Option," *Transformation,* no. 2, 1986, p. 5.

49. For a fuller explanation of consociationalism, see Arend Lijphart, *Power-Sharing in South Africa* (Berkeley: University of California Press, 1985).

50. To address the skills shortage created by neglect of black schools, South Africa in the 1980s encouraged the immigration of workers from Eastern Europe. Janusz Walus, who assassinated Communist Party leader Chris Hani in 1993, was a glass cutter who immigrated to South Africa from Poland in 1981.

51. These experts included Americans James McCuen and Samuel P. Huntington and French General Andre Beaufre, whose relevant writings are listed in "Sources." *TRC Report,* volume 2, reviews government security strategies, as do Hilton Hamann, *Days of the Generals* (Cape Town: Zebra Press, 2001), and Philip Frankel, *Pretoria's Praetorians* (Cambridge: Cambridge University Press, 1984), chapter 2.

52. Botha, renowned for his bad temper, was not a subtle thinker, according to Van Zyl Slabbert, *The Last White Parliament* (Johannesburg: Jonathan Ball and Hans Strydom, 1985), pp. 147–48. Slabbert says Botha was "disarmingly frank about his lack of analytical ability on complicated constitutional and economic affairs, but through years of practical experience in Government [had] developed the capacity to identify a crisis with unerring accuracy. . . . His political instinct told him that to pursue the old road would deepen the crisis of Government, even if he did not know where the new road was or where it led. . . . His political philosophy is remarkably uncomplicated: if things go wrong, there must be an enemy responsible, and if they go right it is because of 'good Government.' The simplicity of the total onslaught philosophy appealed to him. . . ."

53. Estimate by the Detainees' Parents Support Committee (DPSC), *Race Relations Survey 1987/88,* p. 537. In March 1990, the DPSC estimated that at least 50,000 people had been detained in the period since 1981, according to *Race Relations Survey 1989/90,* p 175.

54. The *Annual Survey of South African Law, 1986* (Cape Town: Juta, 1987), p. 573, citing the *Star,* February 12, 1987, reported that 281 children aged 12 to 15 were in detention in early 1987. The DPSC, citing the *Star,* February 19, 1987, reported that 2 10-year-olds, 6 11-year-olds, 9 12-year-olds, 29 13-year-olds, and 86 14-year-olds had been detained since the start of the second state of emergency in June 1986.

55. "Turfloop: Campus Behind Barbed Wire," *Resister,* no. 56, June/July, 1988 (KGC: Committee on South African War Resistance).

56. On state-sponsored assassinations and other "dirty tricks," see *TRC Report,* volumes 2 and 3; Eugene De Kock, *A Long Night's Damage* (Saxonwold: Contra Press, 1998); Jacques Pauw, *In the Heart of the Whore* (Halfway House: Southern Book Publishers, 1991), and *Into the Heart of Darkness* (Johannesburg: Jonathan Ball, 1997); Patrick Laurence, *Death Squads: Apartheid's Secret Weapon* (London: Penguin Books, 1990); and Thula Bopela and Daluxolo Luthuli, *Umkhonto we Sizwe* (Alberton: Galago, 2005). According to the *Weekly Mail's* "Apartheid Barometer" of May 5, 1989, David Webster, shot dead outside his house on May 1, 1989. was the 61st assassination victim inside South Africa since 1978.

57. See *FPTC,* volume 5, chapter 3, on church-state relations in the preceding decades.

58. This threatening restriction was introduced by the Affected Organisations Act of 1974. See *FPTC,* volume 5, chapter 3, and John Dugard, *Human Rights and the South African Legal Order* (Princeton: Princeton University Press, 1978), pp. 172–73.

59. On these groups, see Charles Villa-Vicencio, "The Church: Discordant and Divided," *Africa Report,* vol. 28, no. 4, 1983; E. S. Morran and Lawrence Schlemmer, *Faith for the Fearful?* (Durban: Centre for Applied Social Sciences, University of Natal, 1984); "Christian Collaborators," *Crisis News,* no. 26, November 1988 (KGC: Western Province Council of Churches); and notes on informal talk by Larry Jones (May 1987).

60. *Survey of Race Relations 1979* (Johannesburg: SAIRR, 1980), p. 77.

61. Amanda Armstrong, "Hear No Evil . . . Media Restrictions and the State of Emergency," in Glenn Moss and Ingrid Obery, eds., *South African Review 4* (Johannesburg: Ravan Press, 1987), pp. 199–200.

62. Les De Villiers, *In Sight of Surrender: The U.S. Sanctions Campaign Against South Africa, 1946–1993* (Westport: Praeger, 1995), p. 80.

63. Quoted in *Race Relations Survey 1985,* p. 460.

64. Armstrong, pp. 202–203, and "Texts of South African Press Restrictions," *New York Times,* June 17, 1986 and "Excerpts from Rules by Pretoria," *New York Times,* December 14, 1986.

65. Jennifer Nix, *Actions against Journalists in South Africa between 1960 and 1994* (Johannesburg: Freedom of Expression Institute, 1997).

66. Laurence Harris, "South Africa's External Debt Crisis," in Bade Onimode, ed., *The IMF, the World Bank and the African Debt* (London: Zed, 1989), pp. 172–91, and Robert Massie, *Loosing the Bonds: The United States and South Africa in the Apartheid Years* (New York: Nan A. Talese, 1997), pp. 591ff.

67. Foreign minister Pik Botha later wrote that the international impact of the speech was like "a bucket of iced water in the face." Roelof (Pik) Botha, "His South African Connection," in Hans d'Orville, ed., *Leadership for Africa* (New York: Africa Leadership Foundation, 1995), p. 57.

68. Conversation with Willie Breytenbach (November 1985).

69. In the United States by October 1986, 19 states, 68 cities, and 119 colleges and universities had adopted measures to express their condemnation of apartheid, most often the sale of all stock (divestment) in companies doing business in South Africa, according to Massie, p. 621. Between January 1986 and April 1988, 114 U.S. firms withdrew from South Africa (disinvestment), including Bausch and Lomb, Coca-Cola, Exxon, Ford Motor Company, General Electric, General Motors, and IBM. See Jennifer Kibbe and David Hauck, *Leaving South Africa: the Impact of U.S. Corporate Disinvestment* (Washington: Investor Responsibility Research Center, 1988), pp. ii, 6, and 35–45. It is beyond the scope of this book to assess the full spectrum of international sanctions against South Africa or their economic impact. The extensive literature on sanctions can be accessed through the books by De Villiers, Hanlon, Hauck et al., Lipton, Massie, and Orkin listed in "Sources."

70. A system of magistrates' courts handled minor cases and a Supreme Court handled major ones, including appeals from the magistrates' courts. The Supreme Court had four provincial divisions and an Appellate Division with 15 judges, headed by a chief justice. An industrial court heard labor cases. In the Appellate Division, cases were heard by panels of 5 judges chosen by the chief justice. A single judge, sometimes sitting with several appointed assessors, usually decided other Supreme Court cases. On African attitudes toward the courts, see Stephen Ellmann, "Law and Legitimacy in South Africa," *Law and Social Inquiry*, vol. 20, no. 2, 1995.

71. The Internal Security Act defined the crimes of treason, sedition, and terrorism so broadly as to encompass many forms of non-violent advocacy of political, economic, or social change. The act *inter alia* continued to authorize banning orders, media censorship, indefinite detention without charge, severe limits on the right of assembly, and such routine intrusions as the opening of mail. The Sabotage Act of 1962, an earlier version of this act, is discussed in *FPTC*, volume 3.

72. Some of the most important political trials of the 1980s are mentioned in later chapters; Abel provides an introduction to the interplay of opposition politics and the courts in the period 1980–94; Matthew Kentridge, *An Unofficial War: Inside the Conflict in Pietermaritzburg* (Cape Town: David Philip, 1990), explains why legal action aimed at curbing Inkatha's violence was often unsuccessful or impossible.

73. See *Annual Survey of South African Law, 1983*, pp. 527–30.

74. See Abel, chapter 3.

75. *Document 20* was one of the affidavits collected in preparing this case.

76. Nicholas Haysom and Steven Kahanovitz, "Courts and the State of Emergency," in Moss and Obery, p. 190. Also see conversation with Judge John Milne (September 1986).

77. See conversation with Cassim Saloojee (October 1987).

78. Claire Pickard-Cambridge, *The Greying of Johannesburg* (Johannesburg: SAIRR, 1988), p. 19.

2. Internal Opposition: The Battle Joined

Activists involved in opposition politics at the start of the 1980s had been shaped not only by the tumult of the Soweto uprising but also by the repression that followed in its wake. On October 19, 1977, the surge of popular resistance inspired by the black consciousness movement collided with blunt counterforce when the Vorster government banned 18 student, youth, community, media, cultural, and religious organizations.[1] Dozens of office-holders in the banned organizations were jailed without charge for months, and others fled into exile. Police impounded organizational files, equipment, and bank accounts. The crackdown brought a decline in political activity for about a year but also generated intense debates among activists—including those in detention—regarding the best way forward. Experience taught many lessons, but which lessons were the most important in the new circumstances of harsher repression? Some people rejected political approaches altogether and argued that armed struggle was the only solution. Others favored a focus on building decentralized, grassroots organizations that could take up bread-and-butter issues in local communities. This approach, they believed, would draw support from ordinary people who feared overt political involvement. Many such local bodies already existed, they argued, and the deplorable living conditions in most black urban and peri-urban areas meant there was no lack of grievances around which to organize. Leadership based on mundane demands for sewers and street lights would not attract the wrath of the police, and small victories could rebuild popular confidence. Still others found this incremental approach too cautious and argued for simply reconstituting the banned organizations under new names and resuming the battle on all fronts. Repression was nothing new, they argued, and bold leadership would inspire courage and attract popular support, especially from the militant youth generation.[2]

New Fronts of Resistance

Variants of all these viewpoints found expression in the early 1980s as new opposition groups multiplied. A number of national and regional organizations adopted a highly confrontational approach, protesting against the inadequacy of political reform and pressing for more fundamental changes. They called for the release of political prisoners and denounced toothless or collaborationist bodies such as the South African Indian Council, the President's Council, homeland administrations, and community councils. In contrast, dozens and eventually hundreds of community organizations emerged to spearhead local subsistence struggles, particularly around issues of housing, rent, and transport. Student organizations and youth congresses proliferated to articulate the educational and political grievances of the young. Meanwhile, a steady trickle of would-be fighters left South Africa to enlist in the armed struggle of the exiled liberation movements or, by the middle of the decade, found ways of joining internal units of Umkhonto we Sizwe, the African National Congress's military wing (chapter 4). In addition, the independent trade union movement grew exponentially throughout the decade, transformed by the legal recognition of African unions in 1979 and an increasingly pragmatic acceptance of unionism by management.

Very few organizations tried to operate nationwide or even at a provincial level. At the start of the decade, the only national black political body was the Azanian People's Organisation (AZAPO), founded in 1978 to keep the black consciousness movement alive after the banning of its major constituent groups in the 1977 crackdown. The national Release Mandela Campaign was launched in early 1980 to focus attention on prominent political prisoners and the government's failure to recognize genuine black leaders. In 1981 a small multiracial group formed the Detainees' Parents Support Committee, which later grew into a national organization. From the late 1970s the Natal Indian Congress (NIC) became active again. Drawing on its Gandhian and Congress Alliance traditions, it supported local civic and student struggles and became an articulate mouthpiece of anti-apartheid politics.

In 1981 the government decided to hold elections for the South African Indian Council (SAIC), a powerless advisory body, and in so doing provided impetus for opposition to mobilize around an election boycott (*Document 30*). In January 1983 the Transvaal Anti-SAIC Committee converted itself into the Transvaal Indian Congress, reviving an ANC-aligned organization prominent a generation earlier. The Transvaal Anti-President's Council Committee was formed in the early 1980s to challenge that newly created apartheid institution. In 1981 two women's organizations became active. The Federation of South African Women (FEDSAW), another dormant member of the old Congress Alliance, was revived in the Transvaal, and the United Women's Organisation was launched in Cape Town. Rather than articulating grievances specific to women, these groups primarily aimed to mobilize women in opposition to Botha's reform initiatives.

One of the most pioneering of the local community organizations was the Soweto Civic Association. Set up in 1979 by prominent Sowetans, including Dr. Nthato Motlana and social worker Ellen Kuzwayo, the association attempted to articulate popular grievances and to act as an alternative representative structure to the government-backed Soweto community council.[3] Indian activists in Johannesburg formed the Action Committee to Stop Evictions (Actstop) in response to the regime's enforcement of the Group Areas Act, the apartheid law that confined race groups to segregated urban residential zones.[4] In Natal, the NIC in early 1980 helped to form the Durban Housing Action Committee (DHAC), which drew together over 20 Indian civic associations to oppose rent increases. Several residents associations also emerged in the African areas around Durban to fight rent increases during 1982 and 1983, and in April 1983 they merged to form the Joint Rent Action Committee (*Document 42*). The most striking rise of civic associations, though, occurred in the western Cape, where a dense network of efficient and articulate civic structures took shape in the coloured residential areas around Cape Town. In late 1980, 33 western Cape organizations, including church groups, trade unions, and many of these civic associations, came together to form the Cape Areas Housing Action Committee, which challenged rent increases and evictions under the Group Areas Act.[5] By early 1983, the Cape Action League (CAL), another umbrella body representing several dozen civic and community organizations, had formed, drawing together adherents of the left-wing Unity Movement tradition long influential in the western Cape.[6]

Meanwhile, young Africans, continuing a pattern begun in the heyday of the black consciousness movement, founded and joined a profusion of organizations. The Congress of South African Students (COSAS) began to organize black secondary school students in 1979. By the early 1980s it had a presence in hundreds of schools around the country. It was particularly well organized in the southern Transvaal and the eastern Cape.[7] The Azanian Students Organisation (AZASO), also established in 1979, organized black university students. COSAS and AZASO dealt primarily with educational grievances, but they also became concerned with wider township issues. From early 1982 COSAS played a key role in setting up local youth congresses to organize unemployed and non-schoolgoing youth. Within a year at least 20 local youth congresses were operating.

Charterism Resurgent

This surge of associational activity owed much to the efforts of the black consciousness movement in the 1970s to impart organizational skills, self-confidence, and determination to an angry new generation of young blacks.[8] By 1980, however, the movement's original mobilizing ideas had been widely absorbed and the movement itself had lost momentum.[9] Political theorizing based on class analysis was rapidly becoming more popular than race-based

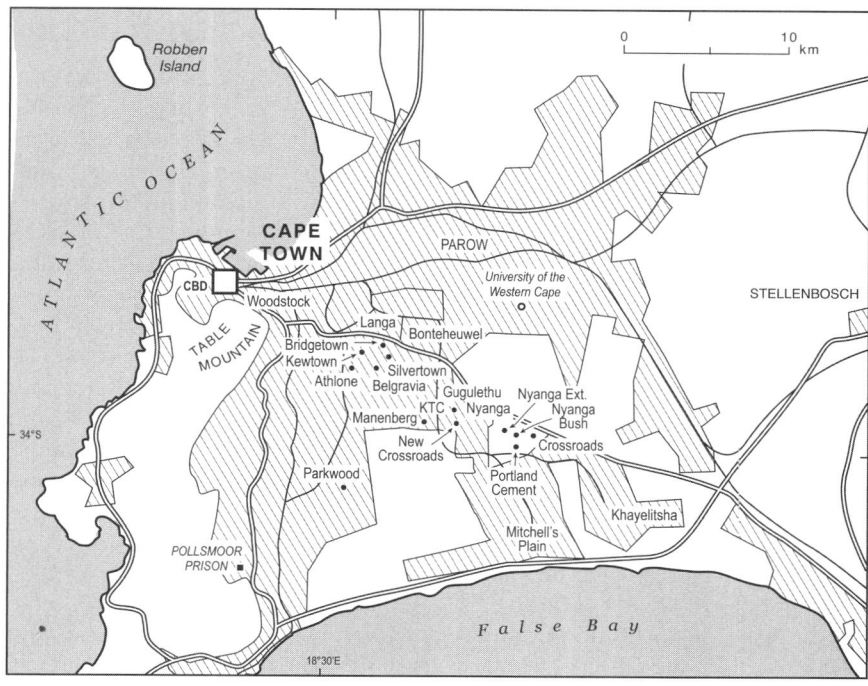

Map 4. Cape Town, 1980s

thinking among black intellectuals and activists (*Document 50*). The failure of students to forge working relationships with black workers at the time of the 1976–77 Soweto uprising was a lesson taken to heart by AZAPO, which pledged to help organize trade unions. Its progress in this regard was slow, however, and its attempts to graft the tenets of black consciousness onto a newly adopted ideology of Marxist class analysis lacked mass appeal. Nevertheless, its activists labored in the face of intense police harassment to build up a national organization. By the end of 1984, AZAPO's executive committee reported 93 functioning branches (*Document 54*). The Azanian Student Movement (AZASM), an AZAPO affiliate, was launched in 1983 to replace AZASO, the organization's original student wing, which had repudiated race-based philosophy two years earlier.

In June 1983 some 800 delegates representing 200 organizations met at Hammanskraal near Pretoria for a conference called the National Forum. The meeting was organized largely on the initiative of AZAPO, whose leaders hoped to rally opposition to the Koornhof bills and the government's constitutional proposals (chapter 1) by uniting a wide coalition of groups around a set of common principles. They intended that the National Forum would operate as a loose alliance rather than a formally constituted organization. Delegates at Hammanskraal agreed to review a draft document, a "Manifesto of the Azanian People," and report back on its acceptability at a

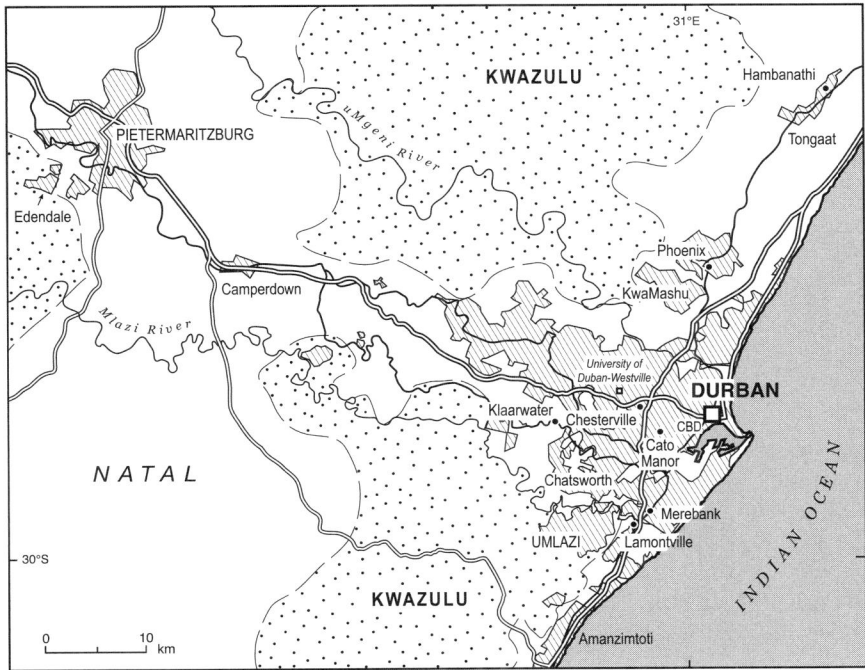

Map 5. Durban region, 1980s

future meeting.¹⁰ The National Forum convened again in July 1984 and, with minor changes, and in the absence of many of the groups represented at its first meeting, adopted the Manifesto (*Document 33*) as a declaration of common purpose.

In the tradition of the black consciousness movement, the Manifesto assailed racism, "liberal influences," and blacks who collaborated with the "system." In line with AZAPO's new adherence to Marxism, it identified the ultimate enemy as capitalism, the goal as a socialist republic, and the driving force of the liberation struggle as the black working class. In other statements by AZAPO and the National Forum coordinating committee, race-based and class-based analyses were melded into a policy line which asserted that since South African racism relegated all blacks to the lowest social class, race was therefore a "class determinant." Thus all blacks were workers, regardless of their origins or occupations, while all whites, including the "labor aristocracy" of white workers, automatically belonged to the exploiting class in South Africa's system of "racial capitalism." In this system, it was assumed, the relationship of owners and workers was that of a zero-sum game: gains by one side could only bring losses to the other. "The interests of the working class and the white capitalist ruling class can never be the same," Lybon Mabasa told AZASM's inaugural congress in July 1983; "there is no converging point for them."¹¹ However intellectually honest the leaders of AZAPO, AZASM, and their allies may have been in proclaiming their ideological radicalism, it was clear that they were also bidding for the support of other radical activists by staking out a position to the left of the growing Charterist movement.

The Charterists were supporters of the banned ANC and its 1955 manifesto, the Freedom Charter, which called for political and social rights for all on a non-racial basis and for cooperation among the regime's opponents of all classes and all races, including whites.[12] Banned in 1960 and eclipsed inside South Africa in the early 1970s by the black consciousness movement, the ANC by 1980 was in a resurgent phase. After many years of having its symbols, traditions, and leaders out of the public eye in South Africa, it had begun grabbing headlines with a growing number of sabotage attacks by its military wing, Umkhonto we Sizwe. The ANC was stronger externally than its rivals, had the largest number of skilled personnel, and was able to provide the best support for activists who were newly arrived in exile. In addition, many stalwarts from the Congress movement of the 1950s and 1960s, including Henry Fazzie, Steve Tshwete, Edgar Ngoyi, Ernest Malgas, Benson Fihla, Billy Nair, Dorothy Nyembe, and Curnick Ndlovu, were released during the late 1970s and early 1980s after serving long prison sentences and resumed political activity in their home areas.[13] Older ex-prisoners linked up with younger activists of the 1970s who had gravitated from the black consciousness movement to the Charterist camp. Among this latter group were Popo Molefe, Frank Chikane, Aubrey Mokoena, Cheryl Carolus, Valli Moosa, Patrick Lekota, and Murphy Morobe.[14] Targeting the post-Soweto generation, the exiled ANC had played a vital clandestine role in setting up COSAS, which became explicitly ANC aligned and highly influential in youth politics in the early 1980s. Lastly, the Release Mandela Campaign and the revival of FEDSAW and the Natal and Transvaal Indian Congresses raised the profile of the Charterist tradition and provided cover for a fledgling ANC underground.

To Charterists, the National Forum organizations posed unwelcome political competition. To the Forum organizations, the Charterists were opportunists trying to hijack a political following first mobilized by the black consciousness movement a decade earlier. Inevitably the rivalry of the two camps became expressed in ideological competition. For many intellectuals and activists, socialism held an almost talismanic appeal: but which camp espoused "true" socialism? The Freedom Charter proposed the nationalization of banks, mines, and monopoly industries, but stopped short of committing the ANC to socialist policies or the dismantling of capitalism. The South African Communist Party (SACP), the ANC's close ally, did advocate the dismantling of capitalism, but only as a second stage, to be achieved politically after victory in the struggle for majority rule. In the meantime, both the ANC and the SACP stood committed to building a multiclass and multiracial alliance of all South Africans opposed to apartheid.

AZAPO's founders, who were joined by several veteran black consciousness leaders released from Robben Island prison in the early 1980s, were

Figure 2. AZAPO activists protest against visiting U.S. Senator Edward Kennedy, January 1985. AZAPO viewed Kennedy as a symbol of Western imperialism despite his strong criticisms of apartheid. *Paul Weinberg/South Photographs/africanpictures.net*

well versed in arguments against working with whites since these arguments had long been a mainstay of black consciousness doctrine.[15] But they found themselves on more slippery ideological ground in trying to develop a persuasive defense for the idea of working-class leadership, a principle they saw as central in their strategy of building a student-worker alliance.[16] Searching for reinforcement, they turned to Neville Alexander, a Cape Town intellectual with roots in the ultra-left Unity Movement. Alexander in the 1970s had disparaged the black consciousness movement as theoretically misguided. With AZAPO's embrace of Marxism, however, and its invitation to the Cape Action League—Alexander's organizational home—to participate in the National Forum, he saw the possibility of gaining the mass base for his ideas that had always eluded him in the fractious intellectual circles of the Trotskyist left. Alexander, a coloured activist who had spent ten years on Robben Island for advocating sabotage, was an articulate critic of the Charterists' multiclass populism.[17] He also took strong exception to the ANC's willingness to categorize South Africa's people into race groups rather than pushing for color-blind non-racialism (or as the Azanian Manifesto expressed it, "anti-racism"). With Alexander's input, AZAPO and the National Forum gained some much-needed philosophical coherence, albeit by occupying what was to become increasingly marginal ideological terrain on the ultra left. A visit to South Africa in January 1985 by the liberal U.S. Senator Edward Kennedy—denounced by AZAPO demonstrators as an agent of imperialism—offered AZAPO an opportunity to draw media attention to its new ideological identity. Black consciousness adherents who maintained a suspicion of Marxism, and Africanists who held to the "Africa for Africans" ideology of the Pan Africanist Congress, remained loosely associated with AZAPO and the National Forum, united by their mistrust of the ANC but little else. By the late 1980s, AZAPO abandoned its effort to sustain the National Forum as a coalition of anti-Charterist groups, and it became moribund.

Founding the United Democratic Front

Two months after the National Forum's first meeting, pro-Charterist groups formally launched the United Democratic Front (UDF). Like the National Forum, the UDF was created initially as a reaction to the Koornhof bills and P. W. Botha's plan to bring the coloureds and Indians into Parliament. The Front's primary goal was to get blacks to reject the National Party's reforms and thereby to thwart the consolidation of an alliance between the government and an expanding class of conservative black collaborators. The most important early objective was thus to organize effective boycotts of elections for local councils and the tricameral Parliament. The idea of creating the UDF was first aired publicly at a conference of the Transvaal Anti-SAIC Committee in January 1983. Successive speakers called for rejection of government reforms. Reverend Allan Boesak, a leader in the coloured branch of the Dutch Reformed Church who had shot to prominence with his election as president of the World Alliance of Reformed Churches five months earlier, told the conference that progressive civic associations, church groups, trade unions, student organizations, and sports bodies should join together in a united front to expose the true purpose of the tricameral Parliament.[18]

The first half of 1983 was a period of intense organizational activity as regional UDF committees were established. Many new UDF-aligned civic associations formed during this period, although as Soweto activist Popo Molefe explained, the rate of mobilization in African areas did not keep pace with organization among Indians and coloureds (*Document 34*). In May, 32 Transvaal groups, including the Soweto Civic Association, the Transvaal Indian Congress, and the South African Allied Workers' Union (SAAWU), came together in Johannesburg to set up a regional UDF; Natal organizations did the same. In July the Western Cape UDF was officially launched. Finally, on August 20, the national UDF launch took place in Mitchell's Plain near Cape Town. The inaugural meeting was a joyous and rambling affair attended by over 1,000 delegates representing at least 400 organizations, as well as several thousand supporters and observers. High-profile figures, including Reverend Frank Chikane, Archie Gumede, and Allan Boesak (*Document 35*), spoke of popular impatience and anger. Spirited songs and chants punctuated the proceedings. As the packed meeting drew to a close, Molefe, the national UDF's newly chosen secretary general, called on the Front's affiliates to organize

Figure 3. National launch of the United Democratic Front in Mitchell's Plain, Cape Town, August 20, 1983. From left: Popo Molefe, Joe Marks (standing), Trevor Manuel. *Paul Weinberg/South Photographs/africanpictures.net*

at the grassroots level and popularize the goals of interracial cooperation, democratic participation, and political education. A declaration adopted by the conference urged democrats of all races to mobilize against the government's proposed "new deal" (*Document 36*).

The UDF claimed that its growing number of affiliated organizations had a total of at least two million supporters by October 1983.[19] Student and youth organizations constituted the largest bloc, but civic associations were also well represented. Political organizations, women's groups, religious groups, and trade unions made up the balance. More than half the original affiliates were based in the western Cape, but there was also a strong presence in the southern Transvaal and the Durban area. In other regions affiliation was initially thinly spread. All racial groups were represented, although nearly all the individual affiliates were racially homogeneous in their make-up.

Ideologically, the UDF was extremely diverse, embracing liberal humanists, social democrats, socialists and doctrinaire Marxists. What drew its adherents together was a revulsion against apartheid and an attraction to the goal of a common South African nationhood in an unfragmented, democratic state. Some UDF publications were infused with socialist rhetoric and adopted an analysis of South Africa which treated apartheid and capitalism as inseparable evils. Socialists worried about petty bourgeois domination of the Front and emphasized the importance of promoting working-class leadership. In fact, the Front's leadership, particularly at the regional level, was fairly evenly balanced between members with working-class and middle-class backgrounds, although upwardly mobile individuals predominated at all levels.[20]

The obvious overlap of the UDF's guiding principles with the ANC's ideology raised both political and legal problems for the new movement. Politically, the UDF's founders hoped to weaken the organizations associated with black consciousness, Africanism, and Trotskyism by building a coalition broad enough to attract all shades of anti-apartheid opinion. Most UDF supporters accepted the Freedom Charter as a unifying manifesto, but the Front's leadership, following the advice of the external ANC, initially avoided endorsing the Charter for fear of alienating potential supporters who were not Charterists. Legally, to further the aims of the banned ANC was a crime. This obliged the UDF strenuously to deny that it was in any way a front for the exiled or underground Congress movement. Indeed, the UDF's formation was an initiative of legal organizations operating inside South Africa, although it took place at a time when discussions about the desirability of a broad front were also taking place among underground ANC members who were aware of the main lines of strategic thinking among their exiled leaders. The ANC's 1979 policy document known as the Green Book had advanced the idea of such a united front, although in organizational terms the ANC had been able to do little to further its creation other than to commend the idea in general terms.[21] Once in existence, the Front benefited hugely from its association with the historical traditions and militant mystique of the ANC, while the ANC, after more than 20 years in exile, saw in the Front a network of activist groupings through which it could recruit new followers and extend its organizational reach inside South Africa.

As late as 1983 the ANC underground still consisted of scattered units, each with its separate lines of communication to the outside but with little or no lateral coordination and no internal cores of senior leadership even at the regional level.[22] Underground members were encouraged to join aboveground organizations and work within them to promote ANC positions. Opportunities occasionally arose for members of the underground or informal ANC supporters to travel to neighboring countries or to Europe where they could hold direct discussions with the external ANC. Thus, for example, Pravin Gordhan and several other underground Communist Party members in the Natal Indian Congress held extensive talks with Mac Maharaj and Yusuf Dadoo in London in 1979, and Cassim Saloojee, an ANC sympathizer who preferred not to have formal links with illegal organizations, met several times with ANC officials abroad after becoming treasurer of the UDF in 1983. The relationship was one of cooperation and mutual benefit in which UDF representatives welcomed advice from the exiles but did not assume a role subordinate to them. The ANC for its part welcomed the UDF's willingness to take responsibility for on-the-spot decision making in the internal struggle as well as for popularizing Congress symbols, leaders, and traditions—all without behaving (unlike Inkatha) as if it were trying to supplant the ANC.[23]

The UDF was a loose federation of organizations which coordinated rather than imposed policy on its affiliates. Its member organizations were represented in a national structure as well as in what eventually became ten regional executive committees. At the national level, 20 honorary patrons were chosen. Some became active and articulate spokespersons for the UDF, although none had executive authority. A high proportion of these patrons—including nine serving long prison sentences—were older-generation ANC stalwarts. The UDF's national executive committee consisted of three honorary presidents (Albertina Sisulu, Archie Gumede, and Oscar Mpetha, all ANC veterans), a secretary general, treasurer, publicity secretary, and regional representatives. The National General Council, an assembly of delegates from all regions, was required to convene at least once every two years to formulate UDF policy. Most of the effective day-to-day executive authority lay with the regional executive committees. These were elected by regional councils made up of delegates from local affiliates. Ultimately, affiliated organizations were free to pursue any activity they chose as long as it did not clearly contradict national UDF policy. From the later half of 1984 onward, the strength and autonomy of affiliate organizations became more significant because detentions increasingly paralyzed national and regional UDF leadership. As the UDF fought to survive at the national level, local rather than national issues came to dominate resistance politics.

Numerous activists, particularly those clustered in trade unions, were critical of the UDF. They pointed to the looseness of its organizational structures. Membership was rarely signed up, let alone paid up. Many supporters could be drawn to mass meetings, but they remained aloof from more routine activities. Decision making was left largely to high-profile leaders whose organizational mandates were often vague. Furthermore, there were unresolved contradictions in UDF membership which had disturbing implications for its structures of representation. For instance, individuals could be UDF members without necessarily belonging to an affiliated organization. In some cases, individuals had overlapping membership in two or more affiliated organizations. The least-acceptable feature of the UDF structure, as far as many trade unionists were concerned, was the equal representation of affiliates regardless of organizational strength. A group with a small and transient membership received the same representation on national and regional decision-making structures as a trade union with thousands of paid-up members. Not surprisingly, the Federation of South African Trade Unions (FOSATU) and several independent black unions decided not to affiliate with the UDF. Nevertheless, despite some acrimonious debate, they were largely sympathetic to the Front's objectives and cooperated with its national and local affiliates on several campaigns.[24]

In the National Forum camp, the emergence of the UDF generated a variety of hostile responses. Africanists and black consciousness adherents objected to the presence of the UDF's white affiliates, patrons, and office bearers, while Unity Movement partisans, including those in the Cape Action League (CAL) (*Document 37*), took issue with what they saw as the predominance of middle-class leaders who were bound eventually to betray the interests of workers. Also, while the UDF sometimes called for the government to convene a national convention, in which the masses would presumably be represented by elite spokespersons, CAL called for the election of a constituent assembly where workers by virtue of their numbers would have a decisive say in how the country would be governed. In time, with the emergence of the New Unity Movement in the mid-1980s and the spread of its publications among scattered left-wing groups, its ideas acquired a resonance among radical socialists within the UDF camp.[25] For example, an article in the magazine of Action Youth, a New Unity Movement affiliate in Johannesburg's coloured townships, critiqued the claim that the Freedom Charter was a suitable blueprint for liberation (*Document 59*).[26] In spite of such ongoing debates, however, the appeal of the Charter and the Congress movement continued to grow apace. In January 1984, even the black Media Workers Association (MWASA), a bastion of black consciousness sentiment, experienced a split as the Cape region defected to the UDF while the northern branches stood by AZAPO.[27] Several years later, black lawyers divided, with the National Association of Democratic Lawyers supporting the UDF and the Black Lawyers' Association remaining black consciousness oriented.

In November and December 1983 the UDF concentrated its attention on the black local council elections. It organized a massive boycott campaign involving house visits, public meetings, and the distribution of thousands of leaflets (for example, *Document 40*). On average about 20 percent of registered voters cast their votes in the 29 contested community councils. This represented an even smaller fraction of potential voters since many never registered. The estimated turnout of registered voters in Soweto was 10.7 percent, while in the Vaal townships of the southern Transvaal it was just under 15 percent.[28] The UDF's first major political intervention thus left the legitimacy of the community council system badly bruised. A buoyed UDF then began to organize vigorously for a boycott of the August 1984 tricameral parliamentary elections, urging the coloured and Indian communities to show solidarity with Africans by rejecting the tricameral system. CAL and AZAPO also campaigned hard for a boycott, as did the Transvaal Indian Congress (*Documents 46* and *47*). Just before the elections, more than 50 prominent opposition figures were detained under the Internal Security Act, but the state was unable to deflect the boycott campaign. It was estimated that only 17.5 percent of coloured and 15.5 percent of Indian voters turned up at the polls.[29]

Early in 1984 the UDF launched a Million Signature Campaign against the new constitution, but the effort fell short of the successes of the election boycotts. Signatures were collected door-to-door, at mass meetings, or in concentrated area blitzes (*Document 44*). Partly because of internal disagreements over tactics and uneven levels of enthusiasm among affiliates, the campaign failed to reach its target and was called off later in the year. Those who saw the UDF as too "populist" felt vindicated by the Front's inability to collect more than about 400,000 signatures. Clearly, the petition's failure exposed the fluidity of the UDF's seemingly large support base. Nevertheless, the campaign was not a complete failure since it publicized opposition views, solidified grassroots structures in some areas, and generated support for the election boycott.

Civic Associations and Local Struggles

Township grievances smoldered as the economic recession deepened from 1982 onward. As bankrupt community councils continued to raise rents in order to finance ever-more meager services, popular mobilization accelerated around issues of economic survival and illegitimate local government. Civic associations produced leaflets highlighting public anger against government-backed local councillors (*Documents 45* and *62*). Dozens of new civic associations were established in 1983–84, including the Alexandra Residents Association, the Alexandra Civic Association, the Atteridgeville-Saulsville Residents Organisation in Pretoria, and the Vaal Civic Association.[30] The most important area of growth was the eastern Cape, where clusters of UDF-affiliated organizations, consisting typically of a civic association, a youth congress, and a women's organization, established themselves in many small towns, including Grahamstown, Cradock, Graaff-Reinet, and Colesberg. Although the UDF played an important supporting role, it did not drive this new phase of community mobilization. Most of the new civic organizations were established in response to the UDF launch, but some, notably in Parys, Welkom, and Vryburg, were forged in local civil conflicts and only affiliated later with the UDF.[31] In almost all cases, though, the animating issues were intensely local, leaving the UDF no role except rhetorical support and—more so as time went on—the distribution of financial assistance.[32] UDF attempts to link local issues to broader national political questions were not always successful. In some communities, events on the ground developed a momentum well beyond national or even regional UDF control. Nevertheless, by late 1984 the UDF was able to count among its affiliates several hundred community organizations which were poised to spearhead resistance in the coming phase of struggle.

The UDF has often been credited for its contributions to a culture of grassroots political participation in South Africa, even though its component organizations varied widely in their actual adherence to democratic values and processes. The national UDF was unambiguous in its commitment to building mass-based organizations around democratic principles: leadership that was elected rather than self-appointed, collective rather than individualistic, and that could be held accountable through regular meetings, mandates, report-backs, and engagement in constructive criticism. In practice, many found these principles difficult or inconvenient to apply, especially as harassment and repression increased. Even under favorable circumstances, civic organizations were not always truly representative, even though they had more local credibility than state-supported black councils. Civic associations in small townships could achieve remarkably uniform support, but in larger, more complex urban communities, they were often dominated by particular groups or personalities. Alexandra's two civic associations made competing claims to represent the entire township. Even civic associations that were broadly popular often lacked a clear commitment to internal democracy. Their processes of recruiting members, electing leaders, making decisions, and holding leaders accountable often tended to be rather amorphous. Although some made genuine attempts to draw in a diversity of opinion and interests, many were eager to establish local hegemony and often discouraged debate or were intolerant of different points of view.[33]

The major achievement of community organizations during late 1984 and the first half of 1985 was not so much setting up democratic local structures as mobilizing for collective action. In this period efforts to defeat Pretoria's "new deal" gave way to highly localized conflicts. Politicization in the townships reached fever pitch, and residents themselves set the pace, with unemployed youths typically forming the vanguard. Townships countrywide became scenes of arson attacks on government offices and beer halls, violence against perceived collaborators, and protest actions challenging rent hikes, inferior schools, and harsh policies toward shack-dwellers. Political organizations, youth groups, and trade unions began to coordinate activities effectively. Under withering popular pressure that often included boycotts of their shops and businesses, hundreds of black local councillors resigned. This left a vacuum in local government which boosted the authority of the new "alternative" community organizations. From this time onward, political awareness in many areas was also reinforced by UDF-aligned "alternative" newspapers which began to appear monthly or more sporadically in the mid-1980s: *Grassroots, Saamstaan,* and *South* in the Cape; *The Eye* in Pretoria; *Ukusa* in Durban; *Izwi Lase Rhini* in Grahamstown; and many others. In Johannesburg, *New Nation,* a weekly newspaper funded by the Catholic Church and edited by Zwelakhe Sisulu, began appearing in 1985.[34]

Although the wave of local struggles could not be seen in isolation from the UDF, it was clear that the impetus came from the bottom up, often leaving UDF leaders unable to keep pace with events on the ground. The detention and harassment of national and regional office-holders, especially from August 1984 onward, weakened the Front's capacity to respond effectively, but this was only part of the problem. Ultimately, the UDF had been unprepared for the sheer scale and intensity of local-level mobilization. A report from the UDF executive committee in the Border region of the eastern Cape in late 1984 attests to this rapid growth (*Document 53*).[35] The UDF grappled with this issue at its April 1985 national conference, and in May leaders admitted in an internal memorandum that the UDF had largely failed to direct spontaneous militancy into ideologically coherent, disciplined, national-level political activity.[36]

Students and Politics

Under AZAPO's influence black university students experienced a political revival in 1979–80 when AZAPO's student wing, the Azanian Students Organisation (AZASO), established branches in the ethnically segregated "bush colleges" and among the growing number of black students studying at the "open," predominantly white, English-medium universities. Before the end of 1980, however, Charterists took control of AZASO and moved the organization into a strong alliance with the Congress of South African Students (COSAS). In response, AZAPO set up the black consciousness aligned AZASM, which also attracted wide support among both secondary and university students. Although relations between black consciousness and Charterist students were sometimes strained, their organizations often took similar stands on issues. When armed Inkatha supporters came onto the University of Zululand campus at Ngoye and assaulted students following an anti-Inkatha protest in October 1983, for example, both AZASO and AZASM joined in vociferously condemning the attack, which left 4 students and 1 Inkatha member dead and over 100 injured (*Document 39*).[37] For most of the decade, the deeply dissident campuses of Fort Hare, the University of the North at Turfloop, and the University of the Western Cape remained under tight control by government security forces, keeping most students' antagonisms focused firmly on the state rather than on each other.

The mobilization of secondary school students had lost momentum after the 1976–77 uprising, partly because of the imprisonment, banning, and departure of so many activists into exile, and partly because students failed to link effectively to other organizations and interest groups. COSAS, launched in June 1979, set out to regroup high school-based student organizations. Its leadership, and much of its membership, was new and determined not to repeat the mistakes of earlier organizations. Inspired and secretly financed by the ANC from exile, which after the Soweto uprising had belatedly perceived the revolutionary potential of students, COSAS from its inception worked to promote both the Freedom Charter and cooperation with groups aligned with the black consciousness movement. It established branches in every region, initially focusing on specific educational issues and dedicating itself to fight for free, compulsory, and democratic education. Its leaders were careful to establish good relations with parent and worker organizations and with other student groups. It argued that the 1976–77 uprising failed because it alienated the older generation and left students politically isolated.[38] As a Charterist organization, COSAS opposed the exclusion of sympathetic white groups and, in contrast with the black consciousness tradition, established a close working relationship with the predominantly white National Union of South African Students (NUSAS) as well as with the non-racial Young Christian Students and Young Christian Workers.

In 1980 a wave of school boycotts swept the country. Apart from dropping compulsory Afrikaans-medium instruction in African schools, the government by 1980 had done little to address the educational grievances which had sparked the uprising of 1976–77. Standards had deteriorated in many township secondary schools after the resignation of hundreds of experienced teachers in 1977. The boycotts began in February 1980 in coloured schools in the western Cape. Students demanded free and compulsory schooling and the readmission of barred students. They also objected to the assignment of uniformed white army conscripts to fill vacant teaching posts. The boycotts spread first to coloured and Indian schools in other parts of the country, and then to African schools.[39] Nationally, 77 African secondary schools were closed during early 1980.[40] The most militant flashpoint was the eastern Cape. In the western Cape, trade union and Unity Movement influences appear to have been strong, but as the boycotts spread, COSAS assumed an important leadership role. In late 1980 and early 1981, believing that the boycott tactic should be used sparingly and strategically, COSAS negotiated a suspension of the boycotts in African schools. The state needed time to respond to student demands, it was argued, and COSAS needed students in school to organize effectively.

COSAS developed an aggressive confidence between 1980 and 1983. Dozens of new branches were formed, particularly in the Transvaal and eastern Cape. In 1981, as part of efforts to popularize itself among students, it launched a national campaign around a new Education Charter, which was essentially an elaboration of the education clauses of the Freedom Charter. The organization also involved itself in practical educational support activity, such as after-school tutoring. During 1982 and 1983, it was instrumental in setting up youth congresses in Soweto, Port Elizabeth, the western Cape, and elsewhere. Despite relentless police harassment it managed to withstand the onslaught, largely because it had developed a grassroots following quickly enough to avoid dependence on a small leadership core.

Focusing and directing the rebellious energies of students was no easy task. Educational grievances persisted as the urban secondary school population, with its huge potential for political mobilization, expanded rapidly, reflecting both urban growth and industry's increasing demand for skilled workers. African secondary school enrollment rose from less than 600,000 to over one million between 1980 and 1984, yet the overcrowding and underfunding of schools did not change significantly.[41] Boycotts erupted again in early 1984, starting in the Pretoria township of Atteridgeville, in response to corrupt and inefficient marking of matriculation (university entrance) exams. The revolt was taken up in other Transvaal schools and quickly spread to the Cape. COSAS, rising in prominence as a national organization, achieved some success in generalizing student demands, thus giving the boycotts coherence and welding them into a national movement. At this stage the demands were still clearly focused around school issues: demands for an inquiry into the mishandling of matriculation exams and protests against sexual harassment by teachers, corporal punishment, age limits for enrollment, and the lack of meaningful student representation at schools.[42] *Document 55* is a boycott flyer issued by the Grahamstown branch of COSAS, and *Document 60,* a report to the UDF, describes escalating confrontations in Kimberley touched off by school boycotts.

COSAS was a key player in the formation of the UDF, to which it gave crucial muscle and credibility. At the time of the Front's formation it was the only affiliate with a genuinely national mass base. Once the UDF had been established, COSAS not only grew further but assumed an increasingly high-profile national role, especially in the context of the 1984–85 school boycott movement. COSAS and the national UDF set out joint proposals for dealing with the country's mounting education crisis at the start of the 1985 school year (*Document 56*). Significantly, in August 1985, COSAS became the first major UDF affiliate to be banned.

Black Workers and Trade Unions

The black trade union revival of the 1970s gathered momentum dramatically following the government's landmark 1979 decision to permit Africans to belong to recognized unions. Black unions began to become a political force for the first time since the suppression of the militant ANC-aligned South African Congress of Trade Unions (SACTU) in the 1960s.[43] By the early 1980s three distinctive trade union traditions had gained a foothold among black workers. First, there was a tradition which had its origins in the black consciousness movement of the 1970s and emphasized black leadership and self-reliance. Although politically cautious, these unions tended toward sympathy for either AZAPO or the Pan Africanist Congress (PAC). Second, there were unions with a shopfloor tradition which stressed building strong, factory-based organization and avoiding political alignment. A third group, often referred to as "community unions," rose to prominence in the early 1980s. These emphasized community mobilization rather than factory-floor organization. Firmly in the Charterist camp, they were eager to confront the state on political issues beyond the workplace.

The most important of the black consciousness unions were grouped under the Council of Unions of South Africa (CUSA), which formed in 1980. The established unions that affiliated to CUSA had been set up or assisted by a service organization called the Urban Training Project (UTP) in the 1970s. Ironically, the original UTP organizers, Loet Douwes Dekker and Eric Tyacke, were progressive whites who had split from the Trade Union Council of South Africa, a predominantly white trade union federation which organized black "parallel" unions.[44] CUSA was not explicitly a black consciousness federation, but it was often identified as such because of its exclusion of white officials and its emphasis on black self-reliance. Many key officials in CUSA unions, such as Cyril Ramaphosa of the National Union of Mineworkers (NUM), had a background in the black consciousness movement. Partly as a result of UTP influence during the 1970s and partly because of the self-help ethos associated with black consciousness, CUSA unions were non-ideological and initially abstained from political involvement. CUSA was initially a small federation with about 30,000 members, but NUM, its most important affiliate, grew into the single biggest union in South Africa during 1983 and 1984, giving new heft to the federation. There were several small CUSA unions which were more explicitly aligned to the black consciousness movement, such as the Black Allied Workers' Union (BAWU), but their factory organization was weak and they had little impact on the labor movement in the 1980s. However, two unions which split from BAWU, the South African Allied Workers' Union (SAAWU) and the General and Allied Workers' Union (GAWU), were to become the most forceful of the community unions during the early 1980s.[45]

The shopfloor unions were the most significant both in paid-up membership and organizational strength. By 1981 the Federation of South African Trade Unions (FOSATU), the biggest shopfloor bloc, had 95,000 tightly organized members.[46] The federation, established in 1979, advised its member unions to steer clear of politics. Its leaders argued that SACTU's demise had resulted from its overly close ties to the ANC and the underground SACP. Rather than nurturing a black labor movement, they argued, SACTU had given priority to political objectives; by involving itself in confrontational political campaigns in the late 1950s and then in the armed struggle in the 1960s, it had sacrificed labor organization and made itself vulnerable to state attack. By contrast, FOSATU was determined to maintain political independence and to build worker strength until such time as workers could set the political agenda themselves. It focused on constructing resilient shopfloor structures with accountable worker representatives and pledged itself to democratic worker control at all levels of union organization. FOSATU was also committed to establishing industrial unions (unions based in a single type of industry) rather than general unions (unions that enrolled members from diverse industries). FOSATU saw the former, which ran counter to the general unionism of the community unions, as crucial in improving worker bargaining power in each economic sector. Although the CUSA and FOSATU unions had much in common, FOSATU's tradition of non-racialism was unacceptable to CUSA. Whereas FOSATU analyzed society primarily in class terms, CUSA stressed race. CUSA saw the presence of many influential white officials in FOSATU unions as inherently contrary to the need for black self-reliance.

The rise of community unions in the early 1980s in some ways represented a revival of the SACTU tradition. Like SACTU unions, community unions such as SAAWU and GAWU were loyal to the ANC/SACP and immersed themselves in community struggles which, they argued, were inseparable from shopfloor struggles. Like most SACTU unions, they had relatively weak shopfloor structures. The community unions were quick to adopt the Freedom Charter—a symbol of support for the ANC—and to affiliate with the UDF. The shopfloor unions accused the community unions of practicing a loosely organized, top-down, unaccountable, "populist" politics, whereas the community unions criticized the shopfloor unions for overemphasizing narrow economic "workerist" issues and detaching themselves from the wider community.[47]

The government's decision to allow African unions to register sparked a heated strategic debate among trade unionists. Registration gave certain legal rights to unions but also placed obligations on them, such as making their accounts and membership information available for government inspection. The FOSATU and CUSA unions argued that the legal protection provided by registration could be used to the unions' advantage. The Cape-based General Workers' Union (GWU), which, although a general union, had a shopfloor tradition similar to that of FOSATU, argued that the industrial relations system imposed too many restrictions and would ultimately hinder rather than encourage union organization. CUSA unions registered almost immediately and so did FOSATU unions, after extensive internal debate and after extracting a concession from the government to allow racially mixed unions to register. The GWU made a strategic decision to remain unregistered, and the community unions, angrily criticizing FOSATU and CUSA for participating in "the system," also refused to register.[48]

FOSATU made some impressive gains after registering. Its membership expanded rapidly and its affiliated unions won several significant victories which in turn attracted new members. Union recognition, a key issue during 1980–81, was granted in dozens of factories. Although politically cautious, FOSATU, unlike CUSA, was militant on the shopfloor. Its affiliates were responsible for most of the dramatic growth in industrial action in the early 1980s, during which strikes cost employers over a million days of labor lost.[49] As long as FOSATU unions operated legally and restricted their activities to the shopfloor, they avoided serious state harassment. But there was growing pressure, both internally from rank-and-file members and externally from new community organizations, for FOSATU to play a greater role in struggles beyond the factories. At its 1982 congress FOSATU's general secretary, Joe Foster, gave an important keynote speech in which he accepted the need for greater political involvement but insisted that it should be on union terms. He also floated the idea of an alternative worker-controlled political movement which would avoid the dangers of a populist alliance (*Document 31*). The notion of an alternative working-class movement, periodically raised and rejected in the wider labor movement, outraged the exiled SACP, which considered itself the only legitimate representative of the South African working class.[50] From around 1982, FOSATU began cautiously to take up non-factory issues. On the East Rand, for instance, the local shop stewards council intervened in a proposed shack removal (*Document 32*), and the federation took a firm stand in opposition to the tricameral Parliament.[51] Nevertheless, FOSATU's political involvement remained sporadic until well into 1984.

In extending legal recognition to black unions, the government had intended to stabilize industrial relations and woo urban workers into collective-bargaining processes from which politics would be firmly excluded.[52] Community unions were the first to challenge this expectation and to experience tough countermeasures. SAAWU in particular bore the brunt of repression. Strong in the eastern Cape, SAAWU had a huge following in the black townships of East London. These areas fell within the jurisdiction of the nominally independent Ciskei homeland, and SAAWU soon found itself in a head-on confrontation with the government of Lennox Sebe after getting involved in the protracted bus boycott in East London's Mdantsane township (chapter 1). The Sebe regime retaliated by banning SAAWU and detaining and hounding its leaders, most notably Thozamile Gqweta and Sisa Njikelana (*Document 38*). Although SAAWU maintained a high political profile in the eastern Cape, its organizational structures suffered.

In 1983 SAAWU and the other community unions, known as the "group of seven," affiliated with the UDF. The FOSATU unions and the GWU, however, as well as several other shopfloor-oriented unions, declined the UDF's invitation to affiliate, pointing to the absence of directly accountable leadership in the UDF and the disproportionate representation given to its small affiliates. They also feared that political alignment might be divisive, particularly in Natal and the western Cape, where, respectively, Inkatha and the Unity Movement tradition remained strong. Nevertheless, the shopfloor unions were broadly sympathetic to the UDF and assured the Front that they would consider cooperation on individual campaigns.

From late 1981 a series of consultations were held in which the emerging black unions began a tentative process of establishing broader unity. The death in detention in February 1982 of Neil Aggett, a white organizer for the African Food and Canning Workers Union, drew unions from all camps closer together through joint participation in a commemorative work stoppage. All the union blocs agreed in principle that unity was desirable because it would improve the economic and political bargaining power of workers, while skills and resources could be shared more rationally. There were a number of important sticking points which prevented unity, however. CUSA refused to compromise on the demand for exclusively black leadership and criticized the presence of white officials, particularly in FOSATU and its constituent unions. The community unions wanted any prospective new federation to take an explicit political line and to adopt the Freedom Charter. They found CUSA and FOSATU's insistence on political caution and independence unacceptable. FOSATU was not prepared to compromise on the principle of industry-based unionism, yet this was threatening to the general unions because it implied that under a new federation they would be broken up into their industrial segments. FOSATU also insisted on proportional representation according to paid-up membership. This was threatening to the community unions whose membership was less stable than that of the shopfloor unions. At a union summit conference in Athlone, Cape Town, in April 1983, a committee was set up to investigate the feasibility of unity. Thereafter the union blocs hardened their positions as the group of seven joined the UDF, and FOSATU, growing in strength by the day, felt less pressure to form a new federation. Several of the smaller independent unions, seeing the advantages of unity and accepting the need for political independence and industrial unionism, moved closer to the FOSATU camp. These included the GWU; the Commercial, Catering, and Allied Workers' Union; and the African Food and Canning Workers, the oldest black union in the country and previously an affiliate of SACTU. In March 1984 the group of seven was expelled from the feasibility committee because of its refusal to accept industrial unionism, and the remaining unions made plans to form a new federation without them.

The most important development in black unionism during 1983–84 was the sudden growth of the National Union of Mineworkers. Once NUM had achieved the difficult goal of establishing a foothold in the mines, the densely populated compounds proved ideal for union recruitment. In September 1984 the union won a small wage increase in the first legal strike ever staged by Africans in the gold-mining industry.[53] Between June 1983 and the end of 1984, under the strong leadership of Cyril Ramaphosa, a law graduate who had never worked in a mine, and James Motlatsi, a miner, the union's membership grew from around 20,000 to 110,000. By then it was more than twice the size of the rest of the CUSA unions combined and was almost as big as the entire FOSATU federation which, by mid-1985, claimed 140,000 paid-up members.[54] Although this made CUSA technically the biggest black union federation, NUM became increasingly dissatisfied with its CUSA affiliation. Attracted to the organizational effectiveness and shopfloor militancy of FOSATU, and increasingly persuaded that the issue of white officials in black unions should not be a stumbling block to unity, NUM resolved in mid-1984 to join the new federation regardless of CUSA's decision.

During the political upsurge of 1984 it became impossible for the shopfloor unions to stand aloof from community issues. Throughout the country, townships were in upheaval over unpopular councils, and thousands of children were boycotting schools. As Alan Fine and Eddie Webster observe, it was daily confrontation and struggle in the townships, not "refined debate over the problems of 'populism',," which brought about workers' "decisive break with political abstentionism."[55] Unionized workers, many of whom also belonged to community organizations, began to force their unions to take a stand on township issues such as rising rents, transport costs, and the crisis in schools. COSAS, pointing to its own support of unions during consumer boycotts and strikes, called on unions to show reciprocal support. Unions started to consult with youth and community organizations and plan joint activity. Although some participants suffered victimization—most notably over 6,000 chemical workers at the government-owned SASOL plant at Secunda southeast of Johannesburg (*Document 52*)—a massive political stayaway strike in the Transvaal in November 1984, described below, became a powerful example of coordinated action. As the political differences between shopfloor and community unions increasingly blurred, obstacles to unity further receded and discussion slowly moved ahead on the formation of a broader union federation.

White Allies

In late 1983 the Botha government burnished its reformist image by winning a 66 percent "yes" vote in a whites-only referendum that asked voters if they approved of the proposed new constitution (chapter 1). The "no" vote came largely from dissident conservatives in the National Party and from supporters of Andries Treurnicht's newly formed Conservative Party, who accused Botha of "giving the country to the blacks."[56] A small portion of the "no" vote, however, came from whites who wanted to express disapproval of the exclusion of Africans in the new dispensation (*Document 15*). To the

UDF, which officially ignored the referendum, this small segment of anti-apartheid whites, plus others who had expressed their dissent by boycotting the referendum, represented a pool of potential support.

In the 1960s and 1970s, radical whites on the left—those who believed that mass action by blacks deserved support, or that capitalism was inherently evil—were rare outside the ranks of NUSAS. By the 1980s, whites on the ideological left inside South Africa may not have numbered more than a few hundred. They included students, a sprinkling of clergymen, academics, journalists and other professionals, and a few dozen white trade unionists, most of whom were veterans of the NUSAS wages commissions of the 1970s.[57] To the right of the radicals was a larger bloc of white liberals who rejected apartheid as immoral but who avoided involvement with black activists whose organizations or opinions seemed uncongenial or threatening. Lastly, in a minority among these normally passive liberals, were other whites whose beliefs or experiences made them open to active involvement.

From the efforts of these leftist and liberal whites a number of effective new groups emerged in the early 1980s, taking their places alongside older, predominantly white anti-apartheid organizations like NUSAS and the Black Sash. The Detainees' Parents Support Committee (DPSC) was formed in late 1981 by Max and Audrey Coleman whose radical son, Keith, had been detained. Parents of all races were later drawn in, and after the UDF's founding in 1983, the DPSC became one of the Front's few genuinely multiracial affiliates. Other detainee support groups like the Detention Action Committee, Descom (the Detainees Support Committee), and the Repression Monitoring Group likewise provided assistance and worked to expose government abuses. Young white men whose consciences made them question compulsory military service also began to organize. By the early 1980s, scattered groups of draft-resisters were involved in protesting conscription. In November 1983, 16 of these groups came together to launch the End Conscription Campaign (ECC).[58] *Document 41,* "Towards a Just Peace in Our Land," is an ECC manifesto that was widely reproduced. As black resistance intensified and the army deployed soldiers to help the police control township streets, the ECC gained momentum, organizing seminars, peace festivals, leaflet campaigns, public debates, and fasts. In 1984, 1,596 white draftees failed to report for induction; the following year, as more left the country rather than serve, the number rose to 7,589.[59] The security establishment, not short of conscripts but troubled by the long-term implications of the ECC's dogged campaign, gradually stepped up penalties for refusers and retaliation against ECC organizers, detaining dozens by the later part of the decade. One such detainee was Philip Wilkinson, a conscientious objector who was put on trial in 1987 for refusing to serve in the army reserve (*Document 63*).[60]

NUSAS itself, with four affiliated English-language universities plus branches on several other campuses including Afrikaans-speaking Stellenbosch, became an ally of the UDF. Although hammered by frequent detentions, riven by conflicts between different left factions, and repeatedly attacked by conservative student organizations, some of which appeared to be state funded,

NUSAS survived through the 1980s with a renewed sense of purpose, putting behind it the rejection of white students by the black consciousness movement a decade earlier. In May 1981 NUSAS initiated a new generation into protest politics with a national campaign to boycott the 20th-anniversary celebrations of the National Party's decision to declare South Africa a republic. Close working relationships were formed between NUSAS, COSAS, and AZASO.[61] NUSAS printing facilities, office space, and student artists, writers, and researchers were put at the service of other UDF organizations. After completing their studies, many NUSAS activists moved out to reinforce the wider liberal presence in white middle-class society, while a small but dedicated number remained active on the radical left. Auret van Heerden, a former president of NUSAS, built up a UDF-aligned service organization, the Community Resource and Information Centre, from which he came to lead a significant left-oriented faction within the national UDF (chapter 3).

With the UDF's launch and the approach of the white referendum in late 1983, a group of white non-student UDF sympathizers, mobilizing around the slogan "No is not enough," formed the Johannesburg Democratic Action Committee (JODAC).[62] Attracting members and developing an effective action program were not easy, as JODAC's report for a 1986 workshop attests (*Document 61*). The uphill battle to win white support for the UDF, the report concluded, reflected "the great liberal dilemma—an opposition to apartheid but a fear of majority rule." Similarly ambivalent attitudes characterized the Black Sash, which regularly protested against apartheid laws and took active measures to shield Africans from the laws' worst effects. Notwithstanding the militant stance of leading Black Sash figures including Sheena Duncan (*Document 58*), Di Bishop, Molly Blackburn, Mary Burton, and Audrey Coleman (*Document 19*), and a decision by its Natal members to affiliate with the UDF, the national Black Sash voted against affiliation.[63] For some leaders and many rank-and-file members, affiliation was too radical a step. It was no secret that most UDF supporters also were supporters of the banned ANC, an organization that condoned violence, received aid from the Soviet bloc, and called in its Freedom Charter for the nationalization of mines, banks, and monopoly industries—positions that liberals in principle opposed.

As conflict sharpened over the course of the 1980s and white opinion polarized, UDF leaders alternated between "fence-shaking" rhetoric—urging liberals to make a clear choice for or against democracy—and a pragmatic acceptance of the reality that most liberals were going to be fence-sitters for as long as white domination remained intact. Rather than join the Africanists, the Unity Movement, and AZAPO in denouncing liberal ambivalence, the UDF chose patient wooing and tactical maneuvers. In time this patience paid dividends in several ways. Importantly, it identified the UDF as a moderate political movement to which white donor bodies, both in South Africa and abroad, could quietly offer financial support. Patient maneuvering also helped gradually to erode white liberal passivity more broadly. In 1985, for example, when prominent liberals tried to launch a movement for a national convention to negotiate a solution to the country's political impasse, the UDF national executive decided to cold-shoulder the idea as impractical as long as blacks were not free to choose their real leaders to represent them in such negotiations. With this vision of change defeated, white liberals were forced to consider calling for the ANC's unbanning, for how else could the "real leaders" participate in finding a way forward?

The Vaal Uprising of 1984

On September 3, 1984, the very day South Africa's new tricameral Parliament was officially opened with pomp and ceremony, several townships in the area known as the Vaal triangle exploded into violent conflict. About 35 miles (56 kilometers) south of Johannesburg, the Vaal triangle is a heavily industrialized region encompassing the towns of Vereeniging, Sasolburg, and Vanderbijl Park. Five African townships in the area, Sebokeng, Sharpeville, Boipatong, Bophelong, and Zamdela, were administered by a black local authority called the Lekoa town council. The Vaal eruption came as a surprise to many. The area had been politically quiet since the Sharpeville massacre of March 1960 and conspicuously calm during the 1976–77 Soweto uprising. Local participation in election boycotts in 1983–84 had been lackluster. Despite the emergence of the UDF-affiliated Vaal Civic Association, links with the UDF were relatively weak in the area.[64] Economic hardship and local grievances rather than UDF initiatives galvanized the communities into action.

The economic downturn of 1981–82 had reversed a pattern of rapid industrial expansion in the Vaal triangle during the preceding decade. Real per capita income declined between 1980 and 1985 as unemployment climbed. Perhaps more significantly, income distribution widened during this period. While some managed to enrich themselves, the proportion of households with incomes below the Bureau of Market Research's designated Minimum Living Level became, according to some estimates, as high as 30 percent by 1985.[65] Rising rents took an ever-larger bite out of falling real incomes. By 1984 Vaal-area residents under the Lekoa council's authority were paying the highest average township rents in the country. The council's credibility was further eroded by its reputation for extravagant mismanagement and corruption. Many councillors had exploited their political positions to allocate business licenses and other entrepreneurial opportunities to themselves. In the context of continuing layoffs in the region's steel and chemical plants, the announcement in early August of a 16 percent rent increase, both by the Lekoa town council and the council of nearby Evaton, pushed popular frustrations beyond endurance.

Over the weeks following the announcement, residents discussed the rent increase at public meetings. The Vaal Civic Association, which had ten functioning area committees and had built credibility by fighting rent evictions, took the lead in setting up an anti-rent-hike committee. Once it become clear that the councils would not retract the rent increases, local meetings in several townships called for a rent boycott to begin. Students rallied with a call for a school boycott, and in Sharpeville, residents declared a one-day stay-away on September 3 (*Document 48*).

On September 3, bands of youths throughout the Vaal townships disrupted transport services and set up barricades to hinder access by the police. In Sharpeville and Sebokeng most of the public buildings, dozens of shops, and many homes belonging to councillors were gutted by arson attacks. The majority of workers in Sharpeville, and many from other Vaal townships, stayed away from work. For the next week the Vaal triangle was in a state of crisis and confrontation and the regional economy was severely disrupted. Police responded brutally to the uprising, using tear gas, rubber bullets, and sometimes live ammunition to disperse crowds. This further enraged and politicized residents. Angry mobs murdered several perceived collaborators, including the deputy head of the Lekoa council who had shot at people attacking his house in Sharpeville on September 3.[66] An eyewitness account by 20-year-old Johannes Rantete during the violence in Sebokeng describes the township's volatile mood (*Document 49*).

After several weeks of violence, during which at least 60 people were killed,[67] army units were dispatched to help police bring the Vaal townships under control. The use of military conscripts was a significant departure from previous government policy and set a pattern for the coming years. In a huge raid to search for pass offenders, illegal weapons, and banned literature, thousands of soldiers and police occupied Sebokeng before dawn on October 23, moving on to Sharpeville and Boipatong in the afternoon.[68] The security forces continued to hold to the belief that order could be imposed through force and intimidation, but in practice these tactics strengthened the resolve of residents to resist. Meanwhile, the presence of troops in the townships stood as a powerful symbol of the spiraling conflict as international television coverage beamed images around the world of a country's army firing on its own citizens.

The Vaal uprising soon sparked protests against collaborationist councils and high rents elsewhere. Stayaways by workers in Soweto and KwaThema on the East Rand were organized around the demand that black councillors resign. In late October, trade unionists joined youth and student leaders in Johannesburg in forming a Transvaal Stayaway Committee. The goal was to organize a regional work stoppage, partly in solidarity with the Vaal townships and partly in response to widespread popular grievances similar to those which had sparked the Vaal revolt. Approached for help by COSAS and the Soweto Youth Congress, FOSATU found itself being drawn into the political conflict by the anger of its own union members. Its representatives became key movers in the stayaway committee, whose composition indicated substantial cross-organizational and intergenerational cooperation. Convinced that the time was right for a show of strength, the committee announced a two-day general strike to begin on November 5. Members of AZAPO and the CUSA unions also endorsed the call, but the national UDF leadership, perhaps fearing violence and a new crackdown, declined to do so.[69] Never-

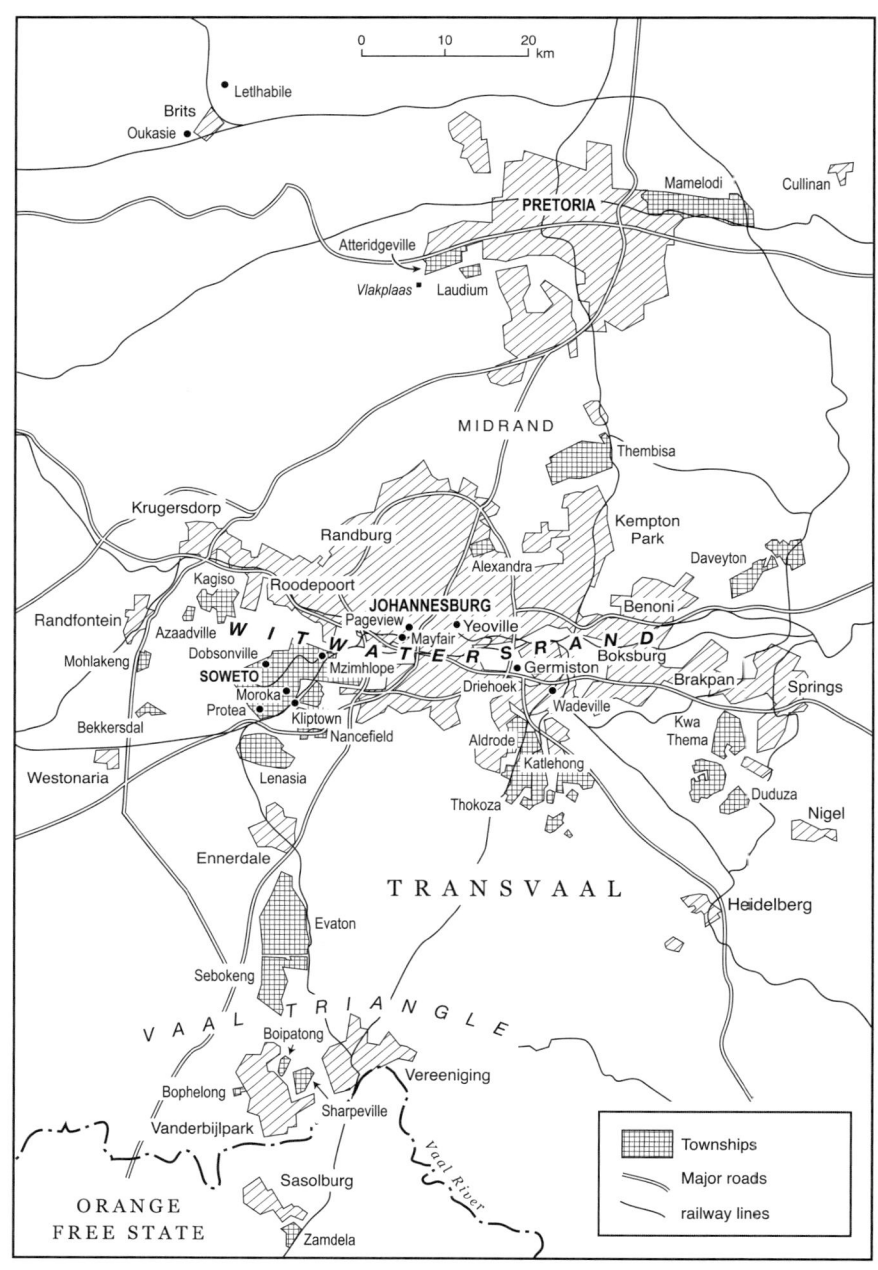

Map 6. Pretoria-Witwatersrand-Vereeniging Region, 1980s

theless, leafleting to publicize the call was intense. A Transvaal Stayaway Committee flyer (*Document 51*) enumerated some of the demands of the stayaway. Other publicity demanded the withdrawal of troops from the townships, a moratorium on bus fare as well as rent hikes, and the abolition of corporal punishment in schools. Boycotts by at least 100,000 pupils in Vaal and East Rand schools added to the tense mood of confrontation in the Transvaal from September onward.[70]

The Transvaal stayaway of November 5–6, 1984, proved startlingly successful. Strike monitors estimated that 400,000 students and between 300,000 and 800,000 workers took part.[71] The press on the first day reported "unofficial stayaway figures of 66 percent in Soweto, 85 percent on the East Rand and more than 90 percent" in the Vaal triangle,[72] as production in the Pretoria-Witwatersrand-Vereeniging (PWV) region ground to a near standstill. Migrant workers, despite their history of political caution, also participated in large numbers. Moreover, the strike held firm into the second day, revealing careful planning and close cooperation between civic organizations, the student movement, and trade unions. Unlike the UDF's cautious national leaders who could not be so easily held accountable to their ordinary members, the unions had been galvanized by worker opinion and had found the results rewarding.[73]

By late 1984 a combination of economic hardship and grassroots community organizing was also causing renewed political tremors in the eastern Cape. A school boycott in the township of Lingelihle, adjacent to the small Karoo town of Cradock, began attracting media attention during the middle of the year. The boycott had started in January after Matthew Goniwe, a popular mathematics teacher at Lingelihle High School, was transferred by the department of education to another town. Goniwe, one of the most talented political organizers in the region, was the leader of a local civic group, the Cradock Residents' Association (CRADORA). His transfer order was an undisguised attempt to weaken CRADORA (*Document 43*). Goniwe resigned his school post rather than accept the transfer, and students, supported by their parents, came out on strike. Many students were detained. Goniwe continued his political work and in August his popularity was confirmed when his detention, with two other CRADORA officials, precipitated a successful seven-day consumer boycott. CRADORA, like many other UDF-aligned civic associations, was involved in campaigns to boycott the tricameral elections, discredit collaborationist councils, and resist rent increases. In January 1985 the entire collaborationist Lingelihle town council resigned in the face of community rejection and financial impotence. By then the white Cradock municipality and local business representatives were already treating CRADORA with respect and even attempting to co-opt it into playing a more formal administrative role, moves which increased after the discredited councillors resigned.[74]

CRADORA, with its tightly organized, street-based structure, became an important model for other civic associations and made Cradock the epicenter of mobilization throughout the Karoo region. Due largely to tireless organizing by Goniwe, an underground member of the ANC and SACP, a dozen Karoo towns developed effective UDF-aligned civic associations, transforming the region into a UDF stronghold. In July 1985 Goniwe and three other CRADORA officials were mysteriously murdered in an attack widely taken by government opponents as evidence of state-sponsored death squads (*Document 57*).[75]

Meanwhile, in Port Elizabeth and Uitenhage political tensions began to rise in late 1984. Recession in the car-assembly industry had thrown the economies of these neighboring cities into crisis. Drought in the surrounding countryside had not only harmed agriculture-based industry but had accelerated urban influx. Black unemployment ran about 50 percent in the area and thousands lived in shack settlements on its urban peripheries.[76] In October the Port Elizabeth Black Civic Organization (PEBCO), which had been dormant since 1980, gained new life after recruiting two veteran ANC activists, Henry Fazzie and Edgar Ngoyi.[77] Although it was sensitive to local issues, PEBCO tended to emphasize the national struggle and its style was populist, relying on mass meetings rather than well-organized local structures.[78]

By late 1984 the Port Elizabeth and Uitenhage Youth Congresses (PEYCO and UYCO) had also grown significantly. Drawing on support from unemployed youths, PEYCO, led by the voluble and energetic Mkhuseli Jack, had developed strong neighborhood branches and was providing much of the muscle for PEBCO. UYCO had a much wider base than most youth congresses. Although its bedrock of support also came from unemployed youths, it had older members, too, and in many respects acted as Uitenhage's civic association, helping to direct public anger toward collaborationist town councillors.[79] School students were also becoming more assertive in Port Elizabeth and Uitenhage. In one of many such confrontations, thousands of students and youths erected barricades and threw stones and bricks in pitched battles with police in Port Elizabeth's KwaZakele township in late October 1984.[80] In the same month, under COSAS leadership, a school boycott was launched to demand an end to the regulation barring those over age 20 from school enrollment. The boycott, which lasted until early in the 1985 school year, had substantial parental support and was by far the most militant student action in the eastern Cape since the earlier wave of school boycotts in 1980. Intimidatory action by local police (*Document 19*) merely hardened the resolve of township activists.

Rising militancy in the eastern Cape came to an explosive climax with stayaways in Port Elizabeth and Uitenhage in March 1985. These protests did not prove to be as unifying as the November PWV strike, however. Historically, there were several distinctive points of tension and division within the black communities of Port Elizabeth and Uitenhage. First, there was a substantial coloured population which constituted roughly half of the workforce in the area. Coloureds tended to occupy more skilled positions; their standard of living was generally higher than that of Africans, and they were more shielded from the ravages of the recessionary economy. Moreover, the spatial separation of coloured and African communities was almost complete by the early 1980s. Second, there was a history of tension between local trade unions and community organizations. FOSATU and the autonomous Commercial, Catering, and Allied Workers' Union (CCAWUSA) had built up their membership and strength in the region through a cautious strategy of patient shopfloor organization. They were wary about risking hard-won gains if they engaged in confrontational politics. Whereas the trade unions represented stable employed workers, many of whom were skilled coloured artisans, the community organizations were dominated by unemployed youths from the squatter camps. There was no precedent of cooperation or consultation between the unions and the community organizations.

When PEBCO called for a stayaway on March 18 to protest job cutbacks and a fuel price rise, it quickly won support from the youth congresses. But FOSATU and CCAWUSA, which had been consulted very late, decided not to endorse the action. The unions, whose members generally mistrusted the radical unemployed youth, argued that the risks were too high, especially in a regionally isolated protest. Participation in the March 18 stayaway was uneven. About 90 percent of African workers in Port Elizabeth participated, but in Uitenhage only about a third heeded the call.[81] Coloured participation in the strike was negligible. Violent clashes broke out between bands of youths and police in Langa township outside Uitenhage. At least two protesters were killed, and the township remained tense.

In defiance of a police ban on holding funerals on March 21, the 25th anniversary of the 1960 Sharpeville massacre, several thousand people in Langa gathered that day to bury the victims of March 18. Police opened fire on a column of mourners as they marched toward the cemetery, killing at least 20 people in what became known as the Langa massacre.[82] Another stayaway was hastily arranged by UYCO and on the next day almost 100 percent of African workers in Uitenhage and Port Elizabeth stayed home. Coloured support increased but remained minimal. Although worker sympathy for the stayaways was substantial, particularly for the one in solidarity with the Langa victims, there was also an element of coercion. Many stayed home out of fear as bands of youths blocked transport routes and threatened strike breakers. Unlike in the Transvaal strike of November 1984, the stayaway tactic in Port Elizabeth/Uitenhage was not particularly successful in building black solidarity. It demonstrated that unity could be won only with careful advance consultation between organizations and between different sectional interests.[83]

The first half of the 1980s saw a rapid revival of opposition politics after the temporary downturn of 1977–78. Driven by the acute political awareness of the youth generation, the material struggles of working-class families in a recessionary economy, and the exuberant growth of black trade unions, a surge of organizational activity occurred in reaction to the hardships and indignities of everyday life under apartheid. The emergence of the UDF both inspired and was inspired by this proliferation of grassroots activity, which for the most part took place without any direct guidance from leadership at the national level. Non-Charterist groupings also rode the wave of growing

Figure 4. Desmond Tutu addresses mourners at funeral for victims of the Langa massacre, Uitenhage, March 25, 1985. Seated behind him are Black Sash members, including Molly Blackburn (without glasses). *Gideon Mendel/africanpictures.net*

public anger. Rather than relieving popular frustrations by means of constitutional changes and new measures to selectively privilege a black upper stratum of urban "insiders," the Botha government instead provoked grave unintended consequences—grassroots rebellion on a national scale. This time it was more than a spontaneous eruption of loosely allied student rebels as in 1976, although young people supplied much of the energy and raw courage of local uprisings. Now a heterogeneous countrywide movement was taking shape, made up of organized groups that were rooted in local communities, factories, schools, churches, and professional associations. Its participants came from all races, classes, generations, competing historical allegiances, and points on the ideological spectrum, but all found common ground in their rejection of National Party rule.

Notes

All conversations and interviews cited are with Thomas Karis and/or Gail Gerhart unless otherwise indicated. All conversations, interviews, and documents cited in endnotes can be found in the Karis-Gerhart Collection (hereafter KGC) unless otherwise indicated. The organization appearing in parentheses following each document title indicates the location of that document in the Collection. *FPTC* refers to earlier volumes in the *From Protest to Challenge* series.

1. See Thomas Karis and Gail Gerhart, *FPTC*, volume 5, chapter 11. All the banned organizations were black except the Christian Institute, which was predominantly white.

2. Very similar debates had taken place in the South African Students' Organisation and the Black People's Convention during the preceding years. See *FPTC*, volume 5, chapter 11.

3. See conversation with Nthato Motlana (June 1987).

4. On Actstop, see *Document 29,* conversation with Cassim Saloojee (October 1987), and *FPTC,* volume 5, chapter 11.

5. On Cape organizations, see Mizana Matiwana et al., *The Struggle for Democracy: A Study of Community Organisations in Greater Cape Town from the 1960s to 1988* (Bellville: University of the Western Cape, 1989), and Trevor Manuel, "Community Organisation," in National Union of South African Students, *Beyond Reform: The Challenge of Change,* July 1983, pp. 63–67 (KGC: NUSAS).

6. On the Unity Movement and Non-European Unity movement, see Armien Abrahams, "Cape Action League: Challenging the Clichés?" *Work in Progress,* no. 35, February 1985 (KGC: Alternative Media); Neville Alexander, "Non-collaboration in the Western Cape," in Wilmot James and Mary Simons, eds., *Class, Caste and Color: A Social and Economic History of the South African Western Cape* (New Brunswick: Transaction Publishers, 1992); Rob Davies et al., *The Struggle for South Africa: A Reference Guide to Movements, Organizations and Institutions,* volume 2 (London: Zed Books, 1984), pp. 310–14; Tom Lodge and Bill Nasson, *All, Here, and Now: Black Politics in South Africa in the 1980s* (New York: Ford Foundation and Foreign Policy Association, 1991), pp. 207–32; Bill Nasson, "The Unity Movement: Its Legacy in Historical Consciousness," *Radical History Review,* vol. 46, no. 7, January 1990; and conversations with Sonny Venkatrathnam (April 1985 and April 1988), Dullah Omar (July 1989), Zithulele Cindi (July 1989), and Saths Cooper (October 1987).

7. See interview by Tony Karon with Shepard Mati and COSAS leaders (1986?) and conversation with Mkhuseli Jack and Stone Sizani (July 1989).

8. On the black consciousness movement in the 1970s see *FPTC,* volume 5, chapters 4, 5, 6, and 11; and South African Democracy Education Trust, *The Road to Democracy in South Africa, Volume 2 [1970–80]* (Pretoria: UNISA Press, 2006), chapters 3 and 4.

9. An opinion poll of 395 urban Africans in mid-1981 found 40% supported the ANC, 21% Inkatha, 11% AZAPO, and 10% PAC. See Craig Charney, "Who Are the Black Leaders?" *Star,* September 23, 1981.

10. Changing the name of South Africa to "Azania" was first proposed in the 1960s by the PAC and was adopted by the Black People's Convention in the 1970s as part of its abortive attempt to work out an accommodation between the ANC and PAC. In 1986, long after becoming ANC aligned, AZASO stopped using "Azania," declaring it "historically irrelevant" (quoted in *Al-Qalam,* December 1986). For more background on this term, see *FPTC,* volume 5, chapter 2, note 87.

11. Lybon Mabasa, "Shaping Our Destiny," speech to AZASM conference, July 2, 1983, p. 3 (KGC: AZAPO). On AZAPO see Vincent Maphai, "The Role of Black Consciousness in the Liberation Struggle," in Ian Liebenberg et al., eds., *The Long March: The Story of the Struggle for Liberation in South Africa* (Pretoria: HAUM, 1994), and Rob Davies et al., pp. 308–10.

12. The text of the Freedom Charter is in *FPTC,* volume 3.

13. Some Congress veterans released in this period went quickly into exile, including Mac Maharaj, Kay Moonsamy, and Ebrahim Ismail Ebrahim. Tshwete, released in 1979 after a 15-year sentence, went into exile in 1985.

14. Lekota and Morobe were also ex-prisoners. Some veterans of the heyday of black consciousness, including Morobe, had long identified with the ANC in any case. Conversation with Murphy Morobe (September 1995). In a November 1990 interview, Popo Molefe told Howard Barrell that he had been in touch with underground ANC members from around 1978.

15. AZAPO's founders included Ishmael Mkhabela, Lybon Mabasa, Letsatsi Mosala, and Khehla Mthembu, who served as president in 1981–82. Saths Cooper, Pandelani Nefolovhodwe, Muntu Myeza, and Zithulele Cindi, who had been defendants in the trial of the "SASO Nine" (*State v. Cooper*) in 1975–76, completed their sentences in the early 1980s and joined the leadership of AZAPO.

16. Quraish Patel and Fr. Buti Tlhagale made early efforts to help AZAPO develop a worker-centered ideology. Conversation with Quraish Patel (July 1989).

17. Alexander's influence is reflected in the fact that even the exiled PAC, in its journal *Azania News* (September/December 1983), reproduced his essay, "The National Situation" (*Document 12*). There was longstanding antipathy between the Trotskyist (anti-Soviet) Unity Movement tradition and the pro-Soviet SACP. When Unity Movement adherents tried to take charge of the 1981 funeral of Hennie Ferris, a popular community leader in Worcester in the western Cape, for example, ANC/SACP partisans contested their right to do this and draped the coffin in an ANC flag, said to have been the first time ANC colors were publicly displayed in South Africa in a generation. Conversation with Johnny Issel (December 1989)

18. On this conference see transcript of police video, "Transvaal Anti-SAIC Congress: Selborne Hall, Johannesburg from 83-01-22 to 83-01-23" (KGC: UDF). On the genesis of the UDF see Jeremy Seekings, *The UDF: A History of the United Democratic Front in South Africa, 1983–1991* (Cape Town: David Philip, 2000), and Ineke van Kessel, *"Beyond Our Wildest Dreams": The United Democratic Front and the Transformation of South Africa* (Charlottesville: University of Virginia Press, 2000). Also see conversation with Mewa Ramgobin (July 1989) and interview by Howard Barrell with Cassim Saloojee (November 1990).

19. Letter from Archie Gumede and Oscar Mpetha to P. W. Botha, October 25, 1983. (KGC: UDF).

20. Mark Swilling, "The United Democratic Front and Township Revolt in South Africa," in William Cobbett and Robin Cohen, eds., *Popular Struggles in South Africa* (London: James Currey, 1988), pp. 96–97, and Seekings, *The UDF*, pp. 309–12.

21. Because the Green Book (*FPTC*, volume 5, chapter 10 and *Document 114*) called for a united front, Gregory Houston in *The National Liberation Struggle in South Africa: A Case Study of the United Democratic Front, 1983–1987* (Cape Town: HSRC Press, 1999), p. 27, asserts that the UDF was created through the efforts of the ANC. Govan Mbeki in *Sunset at Midday: Latshon'ilang'emini!* (Braamfontein: Nolwazi Educational Publishers, 1996), p. xi, also claims this and credits the ANC with directing and coordinating the 1984–86 uprising. Barrell, whom Houston cites, found a more tenuous and indirect relationship, arguing that "the impetus for the formation of the UDF came from a coalescence of many different forces and factors," only some of which derived from the ANC. See Howard Barrell, "The Turn to the Masses: The African National Congress' Strategic Review of 1978–79," *Journal of Southern African Studies*, vol. 18, no. 1, 1991, p. 92, and "Conscripts to Their Age: African National Congress Operational Strategy, 1976–1986," Ph.D. thesis, Oxford University, 1993, pp. 281–92. Relevant interviews by Barrell include those with Mac Maharaj (November 30, 1990), Cassim Saloojee (November 1990), Ismail Momoniat (December 1990), and Popo Molefe (November 1990). Also see conversation with Frank Chikane (June 1995). In 1996 the ANC told the TRC that despite "the identification of the UDF (and later the Mass Democratic Movement) with the ANC, they were essentially separate bodies, not direct extensions of the ANC. While broad policy was often in line with ANC positions in exile and the underground, day-to-day activities and campaigns were based on local initiatives and conditions." *African National Congress Statement to the Truth and Reconciliation Commission, August 1996*, p. 54 (KGC: ANC).

22. Interview by Howard Barrell with Ronnie Kasrils (August 1989).

23. The UDF's first publicly acknowledged consultation with the ANC took place in Stockholm in January 1986. UDF participants included Murphy Morobe, Cheryl Carolus, Valli Moosa, Hoffman Galeng, Raymond Suttner, and Makhenkesi Arnold Stofile. It is notable that when Morobe and Moosa met top ANC leaders again in Lusaka in January 1989 and were asked if they would accept leadership roles in the ANC underground, they demurred, saying they were not up to the task. See ANC "Minutes of meeting of NWC held on Wednesday 11/01/89 at 9:00 hours," p. 3 (KGC: ANC).

24. For an assessment of some of these structural problems and the disagreements between FOSATU and the UDF, see the interview with Patrick Lekota, "Lekota on UDF," *Work in Progress*, no. 30, February 1984, pp. 4–8 (KGC: Alternative Media).

25. The New Unity Movement held a preliminary meeting in December 1983, but did not elect office-bearers until April 1985, when Richard Dudley became its president. See *Muslim News*, April/May 1985.

26. For a detailed response by a Charterist to left-wing criticisms of the Freedom Charter, see Raymond Suttner, "A Political Analysis of the Freedom Charter," in "The Freedom Charter—Workshop Papers 1985," Johannesburg, January 20, 1985 (KGC: Release Mandela Campaign).

27. "The MWASA Split," *Sowetan,* February 6, 1984; "The MWASA Conflict," *Work in Progress,* no. 30, February 1984 (KGC: Alternative Media); and conversation with Joe Thloloe (September 1986). In 1987, MWASA, based in Johannesburg, voted to affiliate with the black consciousness–oriented National Council of Trade Unions ("MWASA votes to join NACTU," *Sowetan,* November 13, 1987).

28. *Survey of Race Relations 1983* (Johannesburg: SAIRR), pp. 258–59.

29. Jo-Anne Collinge, "The United Democratic Front," in South African Research Service, *South African Review 3* (Johannesburg: Ravan Press, 1986), p. 253.

30. On Alexandra local politics during this period, see Karen Jochelson, "Reform, Repression and Resistance in South Africa: A Case Study of Alexandra Township, 1979–1989," *Journal of Southern African Studies,* vol. 16, no. 1, 1990. On Atteridgeville, see interview by unidentified interviewer with UDF's Titus Mafolo (April 1986).

31. Collinge, p. 254.

32. Anthony Marx, *Lessons of Struggle* (New York: Oxford University Press, 1992), pp. 139–44.

33. On democracy in civic associations, see Janet Cherry, "Non-violent Direct Action and Civic Organisation in Port Elizabeth, 1980–1990," draft paper, Civics Project Workshop, University of the Witwatersrand, 1993, and Mark Swilling, "Civic Associations in South Africa," draft paper, April 12, 1993. Mzwanele Mayekiso, *Township Politics: Civic Struggles for a New South Africa* (New York: Monthly Review Press, 1996) offers a personal portrait of Alexandra in these years. On misleading understandings of the term "community," see Emile Boonzaier and John Sharp, eds., *South African Keywords: The Uses and Abuses of Political Concepts* (Cape Town: David Philip, 1988), pp. 29–39, as well as *Document 31.*

34. See Keyan Tomaselli and P. Eric Louw, eds., *The Alternative Press in South Africa* (London: James Currey, 1991); on *Grassroots,* see van Kessel, chapter 5.

35. Also see "Minutes of National Executive Meeting Held in Johannesburg on 10 and 11 November 1984," p. 9 (KGC: UDF).

36. Swilling, "The United Democratic Front," p. 103.

37. For conflicting accounts of the Ngoye incident see Anthea Jeffery, *The Natal Story* (Johannesburg: SAIRR, 1997), pp. 48–49 and 136–40.

38. Wantu Zenzile, "The Stormy Years of the Congress of South African Students," [1989?] (KGC: COSAS).

39. In Durban, Indian parents formed a "Committee of Ten," headed by advocate Zac Yacoob, to mediate between students and the authorities. In mid-1980, the Committee declared victory in the school boycotts and offered a detailed rationale for a policy of tactical retreat. See "We have decided to call off the boycott," [May?] 1980 (KGC: Committee of Ten, Durban). The boycott among coloured students in Cape Town is described in William Finnegan, *Crossing the Line* (Berkeley: University of California Press, 1986), part II. Also see Brian Pottinger, "The Eastern Cape Boycotts: Where Crisis has Become a Way of Life," *Frontline,* vol. 1, no. 8, March 1981.

40. See Jonathan Hyslop, "School Student Movements and State Education Policy: 1972–87," in Cobbett and Cohen, p. 188.

41. Hyslop, p. 190. By the 1980s, apart from a few mission-linked boarding schools, secondary schools for Africans were almost all located in urban areas.

42. Ibid., pp. 192–93.

43. See *FPTC,* volume 5, chapter 7.

44. On the UTP, see Donovan Lowry, *20 Years in The Labour Movement: The Urban Training Project and Change in South Africa 1971–1991* (Johannesburg: Wadmore Publishing, 1999).

45. See Marcel Golding, "Black Consciousness and Trade Unions," *South African Labour Bulletin,* vol. 10, no. 2, 1984.

46. Steven Friedman, *Building Tomorrow Today* (Johannesburg: Ravan Press, 1987), p. 243.

47. This debate continued through most of the decade. See, for example, "Errors of Workerism" and a response, *South African Labour Bulletin,* March/April 1987, pp. 51–76, which earlier appeared in a UDF journal, *Isizwe—The Nation,* November 1986 (KGC: UDF).

48. Friedman, pp. 242–47.

49. International Labor Organization, "Special Report of the Director General on the Application of the Declaration Concerning the Policy of Apartheid in South Africa" (Geneva: ILO, 1985), p. 8, and *Race Relations Survey 1987/88,* p. 667.

50. See Toussaint [Lionel Bernstein], "A Trade Union is Not a Political Party," *African Communist,* no. 93, 1983 (KGC: SACP). Moreover, declared the minutes of the SACP's Lusaka Unit 7 on September 17, 1982, "FOSATU . . . supports Solidarity [in Poland] and is therefore anti-Soviet" (Simons papers, microfilm, reel 8).

51. Interviews by Mark Swilling with Moses Mayekiso (1983?) and with Johnson Nonjeke (January 1983). The East Rand refers to the portion of the Witwatersrand ("white watershed") east of Johannesburg (map 6).

52. Friedman, chapters 7–9.

53. Friedman, pp. 365–69, and T. Dunbar Moodie, *Going for Gold: Men, Mines, and Migration* (Berkeley: University of California Press, 1994), pp. 269–72.

54. Jeremy Baskin, *Striking Back: A History of Cosatu* (Johannesburg: Ravan Press, 1991), p. 30 for NUM figure and p. 49 for FOSATU figure.

55. Alan Fine and Eddie Webster, "Transcending Traditions: Trade Unions and Political Unity" in Glenn Moss and Ingrid Obery, eds., *South African Review 5* (Johannesburg: Ravan Press, 1989), p. 259.

56. One joke making the rounds was about Conservatives who put blankets over their TVs to stop Botha from looking into their homes to see which of their possessions could be given to blacks. Conversation with Dallas Sparg (October 1985).

57. On the NUSAS wages commissions, see *FPTC,* volume 5, chapter 3 and *Document 79.*

58. Most ECC activists were supporters of the UDF, but in order to accommodate draft-resisters who were not, the ECC never became a formal UDF affiliate. See Catholic Institute for International Relations, *Out of Step* (London: CIIR, 1982), and interview by Howard Barrell with Gavin Evans (January 1991).

59. "Has the Army Invaded Your Life?" (KGC: ECC). In 1986 the government stopped releasing figures.

60. Service in a reserve unit was compulsory following a conscript's army stint. Wilkinson did military service, then became a conscientious objector on religious grounds but had his application for alternate service rejected. He was charged with refusing to report to his reserve unit, pleaded guilty, and was fined R600 ($290). Other high-profile objectors from the late 1970s onward, some of whom served prison terms, included Saul Batzofin, Charles Bester, David Bruce, Paul Dobson, Michael Evans, Glen Goosen, Peter Moll, Brett Myrdal, Billy Paddock, Richard Steele, Ivan Toms, and Charles Yeats. Michael and Gavin Evans and Laurie Nathan were among the ECC's principal organizers. See Richard Abel, *Politics by Other Means: Law in the Struggle Against Apartheid, 1980–1994* (New York: Routledge, 1995), chapter 4. Gavin Evans' autobiography, *Dancing Shoes is Dead* (London: Black Swan, 2002), provides a glimpse of white counterculture. Antiwar sentiment also affected some young Afrikaners, particularly those touched by the rock music tradition known as *voëlvry.* See Willem Pretorius, *Kerkorrel* (Cape Town: Tafelberg, 2004).

61. See excerpts from an interview with Andrew Boraine in Julie Frederikse, *The Unbreakable Thread* (Bloomington: Indiana University Press, 1990), pp. 172–74.

62. See conversation with Tom Waspe and Aneene Dawber (July 1989).

63. See Helen Zille, "UDF—Affiliate or Cooperate?" *The Black Sash,* vol. 26, no. 4, February 1984 (KGC: Black Sash), and conversation with Sheena Duncan (November 1987).

64. Jeremy Seekings, "The Origins of Political Mobilisation in the PWV Townships, 1980–84," in Cobbett and Cohen, p. 71.

65. Ibid., pp. 60–61.

66. This incident and the highly publicized trial of the "Sharpeville Six" (*State v. Sefatsa and others*), who were charged with the murder, are examined in two books: Prakash Diar, *The Sharpeville Six* (Toronto: McClelland and Stewart, 1990), and Peter Parker and Joyce Mokhesi-Parker, *In the Shadow of Sharpeville* (New York: New York University Press, 1998). Following a long series of arrests and detentions, the government in 1985 began proceedings in the case of

State v. Baleka and others (the Delmas trial), in which it tried to prove that the Vaal Civic Association and the UDF, in league with the ANC, had fomented unrest in the Vaal triangle in 1984 with a view to igniting revolutionary violence. See Rose Moss, *Shouting at the Crocodile: Popo Molefe, Patrick Lekota, and the Freeing of South Africa* (Boston: Beacon Press, 1990), and conversations with George Bizos (October 1989).

67. *Race Relations Survey 1984*, p. 71.
68. *Sowetan*, October 24, 1984.
69. Seekings, *The UDF*, p. 317.
70. *Race Relations Survey 1984*, pp. 72 and 74.
71. Seekings, *The UDF*, pp. 127–29. Also see *Financial Mail*, November 16, 1984; Labour Monitoring Group, "The November Stay-Away," *South African Labour Bulletin*, vol. 10, no. 6, May 1985; and Mark Swilling, "Stayaways, urban protest and the state," in South African Research Service, *South African Review 3*, pp. 23–31.
72. *Rand Daily Mail*, November 6, 1984.
73. From exile, the new Communist Party organ, *Umsebenzi*, in "Lessons of the Stayaway," vol. 1, no. 1, 1985, p. 10 (KGC: SACP), directed a barb at FOSATU by declaring that the stayaway had "exposed those meddlers who have been trying to stop the trade union movement from playing a part in the national liberation struggle."
74. On Cradock, see "Cradock: building a tradition of resistance," *Work in Progress*, no. 38, August 1985 (KGC: Alternative Media), and Michael Tetelman, "We Can: Black Politics in Cradock, South Africa, 1948–1985," Ph.D. thesis, Northwestern University, 1997.
75. Two official inquests into these murders failed to unmask the killers despite ample clues. Six security policemen later applied to the Truth Commission for amnesty, but their applications were denied. *Truth and Reconciliation Commission of South Africa Report* (Cape Town: Truth and Reconciliation Commission 1998) (*TRC Report*), volume 3, pp. 112–17, and volume 7, p. 129.
76. Lodge and Nasson, p. 71.
77. Fazzie, an early recruit to Umkhonto we Sizwe, was released in September 1983 after 21 years in prison; Ngoyi was released in 1981 after a 17-year sentence.
78. Three members of PEBCO's executive committee—Champion Galela, Qaqawuli Godolozi, and Sipho Hashe—disappeared while driving to meet a British diplomat at the Port Elizabeth airport in May 1985. Nine state employees later applied to the Truth Commission for amnesty in connection with the murders. Two applications were granted and the rest denied. *TRC Report*, vol. 3, p. 117, and vol. 7, pp. 120, 128, and 149.
79. See two interviews with African councillors who were forced to resign in the mid-1980s: Mark Swilling with the former mayor of Uitenhage, Mr. Tini (September 1987), and Rory Riordan and Juliette Opperman with Tamsanqa Linda, former head of the Ibhayi City Council, Port Elizabeth (July 1988). On UYCO, see interviews by Mark Swilling with Woza Made (November 1985, March 1986, and undated).
80. *IDAF Focus*, November 1984.
81. Swilling, "Stayaways, urban protest and the state," p. 32.
82. *Race Relations Survey 1985*, pp. 489–92, which summarizes the findings of the Kannemeyer Commission appointed to investigate the massacre.
83. Swilling, "Stayaways, urban protest and the state," p. 32.

3. Internal Opposition: Moving Toward Deadlock

By mid-1985 popular anger over rising rents, "gutter education," lack of houses and public services, police brutality, detentions, and scores of other grievances had reached the boiling point in black communities. Since the September 1984 eruption of violence in the Vaal triangle, township clashes had claimed several hundred lives and the toll was steadily rising. Each week's newspapers brought new accounts of protests, rioting, arson attacks, and other "unrest" incidents. School boycotts and frequent strikes by workers intensified the sense of national crisis. The presence of the United Democratic Front (UDF) and its growing number of regional and local affiliates made it possible for more people to give organized expression to their complaints, even when coordination between allied groups was poor or non-existent. Many trade unionists had modified their objections to union participation in community struggles, blurring the line between action for economic goals and demands for fundamental political change. Even as the UDF worked to focus popular action on principled, non-violent campaigns around core demands, the number of violent incidents multiplied. Foreign reactions to the violence put the government of P. W. Botha increasingly on the defensive internationally, inhibiting its ability to apply full-scale repression to crush the roiling revolt.

The UDF in early April 1985 convened the first national conference since its founding, bringing together about 300 delegates and many observers in the Indian township of Azaadville in Krugersdorp. The movement confronted both opportunities and limitations. Meeting under huge banners bearing the slogan "From Protest to Challenge, From Mobilisation to Organisation," delegates assessed the UDF's progress in its first 19 months and debated methods to improve its performance in areas of organizational weakness.[1] The program from this conference (*Document 66*), which includes the secretary general's report, candidly reviews the issues facing the Front, including the urgent need to coordinate decision making at different levels, to provide better training to activists, and to build closer relations with unaffiliated trade unions. The report points to the UDF's achievements in helping to isolate Pretoria internationally and to mobilize anti-apartheid lobbies in Europe and North America. "Even in imperialist countries," it notes, "there are people and groups who are committed to the struggle for the overthrow of apartheid." In the United States, the Free South Africa Movement had dramatically taken shape within weeks after the November 1984 re-election of conservative president Ronald Reagan. British public opinion, already shocked by televised images of township violence, had been further aroused against repression in South Africa when six UDF leaders, released from detention on a technicality in mid-September 1984, had fled into the British consulate in Durban to escape rearrest. After weeks of media publicity, five of the six had been redetained and charged with treason.[2]

Hanging over the Azaadville conference and the future of extraparliamentary opposition more broadly were Pretoria's accelerating efforts to prosecute and convict thousands of activists under laws that criminalized not only sabotage and public violence but also possession of banned literature and sometimes the mere verbal expression of dissent. Courts throughout the country processed hundreds of cases involving violent protests. Two high-profile trials that aimed at crippling the UDF and its allies began in 1985. Five of the six UDF leaders who took refuge in the Durban consulate (Mewa Ramgobin, Archie Gumede, George Sewpersadh, Paul David, and M. J. Naidoo) were charged along with 11 others with treason and furthering the aims of banned organizations in *State v. Ramgobin*. The case, which was heard over a period of eight months in Pietermaritzburg, ended in acquittal for all the accused when the state's expert witness on the UDF's alleged "revolutionary alliance" failed to stand up to sharp cross examination by defense lawyer Ismail Mahomed (*Document 73*) and the judge ruled the state's videotaped evidence inadmissible.[3] In late April 1985 Patrick Lekota and Popo Molefe, then serving respectively as publicity secretary and general secretary of the national UDF, were charged along with members of the Vaal Civic Association with treason and terrorism in *State v. Baleka,* a case where the state intended to prove that the accused had planned the Vaal uprising as part of a revolutionary conspiracy with the African National Congress (ANC). To isolate the defendants from their urban support base, the trial was held in Delmas, a small town 40 miles (64 kilometers) east of Johannesburg. The proceedings dragged on for several years as each side tried to wear the other down by bringing an endless succession of witnesses. Although the accused were released on bail after being charged, the trial drained much of their energy and curtailed their political involvement.[4]

Besides having their leaders tied down by serious legal charges, opposition groups now confronted a battery of other tactics employed by the state to crush popular resistance. One tactic used from the late 1980s into the 1990s was vigilantism, of the kind applied in Crossroads and KwaNdebele (chapter 1). Another was the use of provocateurs to foment violence between supporters of rival movements. Despite repeated attempts by church leaders to broker peace between UDF and Azanian People's Organisation (AZAPO) supporters (*Document 67*), bloody feuding left dozens of young activists dead or injured in the townships of Port Elizabeth and Johannesburg in 1985–86.[5] Leaders on both sides usually opposed the fighting but were unable to exert discipline over rank-and-file supporters. Had political tensions not created fertile conditions for conflict, provocateurs alone might have done little damage. But in the chaotic atmosphere of 1985, many young activists became convinced that victory was imminent. Tolerance for political rivals was held in disdain on both sides as each tried to position itself for the state's impending collapse. Once violence was touched off, it tended to spiral out of control as members of rival organizations and their allied youth and student groups tried to dominate particular patches of urban turf and wreak revenge on the other side. In Port Elizabeth's New Brighton township, AZAPO partisans found a safe haven in the home of black consciousness playwright and self-styled religious leader Mzwandile Maqina, whose house was located next to a police station. In time it became evident that Maqina had police backing to organize attacks on UDF supporters, obliging national AZAPO leaders to repudiate him as an ally. He later shifted his activities to an Africanist gang called Ama-Afrika, which operated as an anti-UDF vigilante force in Port Elizabeth and Uitenhage from 1986. In an eyewitness account, the wife of a UDF activist in KwaNobuhle township in Uitenhage described the destruction of her house by Ama-Afrika under the direction of local police in January 1987 (*Document 88*).[6]

The First State of Emergency, 1985

Bringing a new tool of repression into play, the government in July 1985 declared a state of emergency on the Witwatersrand and in the eastern Cape, later extending the declaration to parts of the western Cape. Security forces were given unrestrained power to arrest and interrogate, confiscate documents, prohibit gatherings, declare curfews, and restrict access to certain areas. During the emergency over 10,000 people were detained without charge, two-thirds from the eastern Cape and the majority under age 25. More than half the UDF's regional and national leaders were detained.[7] On August 28, police broke up a haphazardly organized march on Pollsmoor prison in Cape Town (*Document 68*) where several thousand protesters planned to deliver a letter of support to Nelson Mandela.[8] Twenty-eight demonstrators died in the ensuing violence. On the same day, the Congress of South African Students (COSAS), the UDF's largest affiliate, was banned. All this, however, did not significantly diminish violent confrontations in the townships, where youths continued to challenge the police and military presence, and compliant local government could not be re-established. Hundreds more died as brutal and arbitrary action by security forces provoked ever-widening resistance.

In a context of virtual civil war and driven by the slogan "make the townships ungovernable," militant and militarized youth—the so-called "comrades" or *amabutho* (warriors)—dominated local political action. Activists who pleaded for restraint and organizational discipline found themselves accused of cowardice or moderation. Ironically, the same activists urging moderation were the prime targets of state repression and harassment. The security forces, unable to comprehend the spontaneity of youth militancy, were convinced that UDF leaders were instigating violent resistance. Yet as successive layers of influential leadership were immobilized, the non-violent approach lost ground and the *amabutho* drifted further beyond organizational control.[9]

In late 1985, faced with the twin problems of escalating state repression and uncontrolled youth and encouraged by advice received from the ANC in exile, the UDF developed a strategy which became known as "people's power" (*Document 79*). In the absence of legitimate government, the strategy called for ordinary urban residents to seize control of their own lives at the grassroots level. A call to constructive action replaced the destructive goal of "ungovernability." Local activists began to set up street and area committees—"organs of people's power"—modeled on structures pioneered by Matthew Goniwe in Cradock (chapter 2). Residents of a street elected a street committee, and area committees were comprised of street committee representatives. The system had a number of benefits. First, it was highly resilient; the state could not debilitate these bottom-up structures simply by removing a layer of leadership. Second, it allowed residents to participate far more directly in political decisions. Third, it helped to bring the *amabutho* under control as undisciplined youth bands were broken down into smaller units accountable to street committees.[10]

After taking root in the Karoo, street and area structures spread quickly to Port Elizabeth and then throughout the rest of the eastern Cape during late 1985. Toward the end of the year similar structures began taking hold in Mamelodi, near Pretoria. At about the same time, street and yard committees were set up in Alexandra township on Johannesburg's northern border. This accompanied a new phase of radical resistance in Alexandra. In February 1986 a conflict later called the "six day war" broke out in the township after heavy-handed police intervention at a funeral for a local youth. For six days there were running battles between "comrades" and the security forces. At a subsequent mass funeral on March 5 (*Document 76*) the "comrades" confidently and defiantly displayed ANC and Communist Party symbols.[11] By March 1986 street committees were also forming in Naledi, a township on the western rim of Soweto, and in Atteridgeville, near Pretoria. Later they spread to other parts of the Transvaal and to small townships in the western Cape and Natal.[12] In the absence of local government, street committees often took upon themselves a variety of civic responsibilities, such as garbage collection and crime prevention. Tough action against rapists and thieves gave street committees authority and legitimacy. Where street and area committees were strong, crime rates tended to be lower and residents felt more free to walk in the streets at night.[13]

"People's courts" often sprang up in association with street committees. These courts continued traditions of community self-regulation going back to James "Sofasonke" Mpanza's "parents' courts" of the 1940s and 1950s and the *makgotla,* an urban movement of the 1970s that took its name from the customary tribunals of the Sotho and Tswana peoples. People's courts concentrated mainly on petty crimes and domestic disputes, not on political ill-discipline. It was seen as important that fines be kept within the community rather than paid to organs of the state. Initially the courts had substantial support. Women, in particular, took advantage of them to solve family quarrels. After a while, however, courts were sometimes used to settle private scores, especially once younger activists became involved. There was controversy over the use of corporal punishment, and resentment by adults who found themselves judged by youths. If older members of the community remained in charge, and if judgments remained within the parameters of what was popularly acceptable, the courts maintained support. Courts generally did not get involved in trying alleged police informers and collaborators, or in the notorious practice of "necklacing," in which alleged police informers were doused with gasoline and set alight after having tires placed around their bodies. Such murders were mostly carried out spontaneously by groups of "comrades" who had no direct accountability to a people's court.[14] In the eastern Cape, "*amabutho* tribunals," as distinct from the courts set up by street and area committees, were responsible for numerous necklacing incidents. The UDF made it clear that it did not sanction necklacing, but it did hesitate for more than a year, as did the ANC in exile, to condemn the practice outright.[15]

Consumer Boycotts

Black boycotts of white shops were an innovative political tactic that emerged during the severe repression of 1985. Its use ran parallel to the formation of street and area committees, and in some places preceded their formation. Consumer boycotts had been used by trade unions in the past to target specific employers in labor disputes. One example was the Fatti's and Moni's pasta boycott of 1979; another was the boycott of Wilson-Rowntree candy in 1981.[16] Following a widely observed "Black Christmas" in 1984, campaigns for consumer restraint were launched during subsequent Decembers, both as a gesture of mourning for victims of police violence and a reminder to whites of black buying power (*Document 74*). UDF affiliates were active in promoting the boycotts, but adherents of other political tendencies also participated.

In 1985 the consumer boycott began to be seen as a viable non-violent tactic that could be used as a broader-ranging political weapon. If black consumer spending declined, white businessmen might feel compelled to pressure local or national authorities to respond to popular demands. Like street and area committees, the tactic was first used in the eastern Cape before spreading to other regions. The first boycotts of white-owned retail shops were recorded in March 1985. Within six months they had taken hold in several dozen eastern Cape towns, with the imposition of the first state of emergency and the emotion-laden funeral of Matthew Goniwe in July both playing a catalytic role.[17] Boycott organizers made localized demands initially, including the desegregation of commercial areas, rent reductions, improved services, the withdrawal of troops from townships, and the establishment of integrated municipalities. Soon, however, the boycotts became associated with a wider UDF agenda emphasizing political demands that were explicitly national: an end to the state of emergency, the release of prisoners and detainees, and the unbanning of organizations.

The economic impact of the boycotts was uneven, but small white retailers were usually hit hardest. Local chambers of commerce, anxious to restore normal business, entered into negotiations with boycott committees. Some short-term gains, such as trading rights or improved facilities for blacks, were won and business organizations often made representations to the government to release local detainees or withdraw troops from townships. Perhaps most importantly, a high level of community solidarity was achieved in many townships. Although militant youths were difficult to control in the bigger centers, small towns experienced relatively little coercion. In August 1985 consumer boycott committees were set up in the western Cape (*Document 75*), Pretoria, and Johannesburg. The initial popular response was good, particularly in Pretoria, although the boycott experience was usually less positive in larger centers. Disagreement and confusion often prevailed regarding the demands and the duration of boycotts, consultation with non-UDF unions and community organizations was often late and halfhearted, and youths intimidated shoppers, sometimes brutally. Nevertheless, the consumer boycotts maintained pressure on white city governments, and the UDF continued to promote them. UDF groups participated in a successful union-initiated consumer boycott in Pietermaritzburg and Howick in August and September (*Document 72*).[18] By early 1986 the movement had spread outward in the Transvaal. Consumer boycott committees were set up in the West Rand township of Kagiso, on the East Rand, in Alexandra, and in the northern Transvaal (*Document 81*).

Although the UDF did not provide the original impetus for boycotts, it encouraged their spread beyond the eastern Cape and their use as an instrument for articulating national demands. Tension between local and national politics often led to paralysis, however, with national demands tending to obstruct the effectiveness of local campaigns. Chambers of commerce could make concessions on specific local demands, but their ability to influence national policy was limited. Under these circumstances, local boycott leaders were left in a quandary over whether to suspend a boycott or to press ahead in making broader demands in accordance with national strategy.[19]

Perhaps misled by the cohesiveness of small eastern Cape communities, UDF leaders elsewhere tended to underestimate the potential divisiveness of consumer boycotts. Trade unions and some of the more cautious civic associations were suspicious of the tactic because demands were too general and unrealistic, and workers, with some justification, feared exposing themselves to victimization. It was often extremely difficult for workers to avoid buying goods from white-owned stores; yet when they ignored the boycott, it was also difficult to avoid retribution from "comrades" who, due to the spatial arrangement of apartheid urban areas, were able to police township access points. Township traders, on the whole, benefited from the boycotts despite public pressure on them to keep prices low. In some areas, the state's brutal response to consumer boycotts helped to knit potentially divided communities together. In Kagiso, for instance, an initially divisive boycott gained broad support only after heavy-handed police intervention.[20]

The practical results of consumer boycotts were mixed. Some small communities made tangible socioeconomic gains, and organized business was nudged in the direction of taking a firmer political stand. More importantly, boycotts enabled the UDF to sustain resistance under highly repressive conditions. Despite their potential for divisiveness, boycotts also heightened levels of politicization and mobilization in the townships. The tactic, however, could not be sustained indefinitely, and was discontinued in most areas during the second state of emergency imposed in June 1986.

The Formation of COSATU

On the labor front, discussions continued throughout 1984 and early 1985 on the formation of a trade union superfederation. Political tensions between the shopfloor and community union traditions waned, allowing them once again to contemplate closer unity. As the political involvement of shopfloor unions deepened, they came under increasing attack from the state. This was demonstrated starkly when Andries Raditsela, Transvaal vice chairman of the Federation of South African Trade Unions (FOSATU), died of head injuries while in police custody in May 1985. At a unity summit meeting in June at Ipelegeng, Soweto, the organizing committee pushed participating unions to ratify a draft constitution for a new federation based on five key principles: "nonracialism, one union one industry, worker control, representation on the basis of paid-up membership and cooperation at national level."[21]

Both the UDF unions and a number of Africanist-oriented unions grouped under the Azanian Confederation of Trade Unions (AZACTU) sat down with FOSATU and the Council of Unions of South Africa (CUSA) in a final attempt to establish the broadest possible unity. The talks, however, did not go smoothly since most of the old sticking points remained unresolved (chapter 2). AZACTU affiliates, feeling marginalized and hostile toward the inclusion of whites, made it clear that they would not participate in the new federation. They were supported by most CUSA affiliates, but the National Union of Mineworkers (NUM) made a decisive break from CUSA and committed itself to the new federation. FOSATU, responding to internal pressures and perceiving a need to adapt to changing political conditions, was eager to incorporate the UDF unions. The "group of seven," community unions which were affiliated with the UDF, were divided about participation and made no final decision at Ipelegeng. Only after pressure from the ANC and the South African Congress of Trade Unions (SACTU) in exile, urging the UDF unions to join the federation even if it meant dissolving general unions in favor of industrial unions, did the doubters relent and climb on board the unity process.[22]

The launching conference took place in Durban at the end of November 1985. Although many disagreements remained unresolved, the conference brought together 760 delegates from 33 unions representing 460,000 workers in a massive show of solidarity.[23] It signaled the emergence of a major new force both in industrial relations and in politics. The delegates agreed to call the federation the Congress of South African Trade Unions (COSATU), satisfying the two main union camps by giving recognition to both the FOSATU and Congress traditions. Elijah Barayi, the NUM vice president, was elected COSATU's president, and FOSATU president Chris Dlamini was elected vice president. Jay Naidoo, general secretary of the Sweet, Food, and Allied Workers Union, a large FOSATU affiliate but regarded as sympathetic to the UDF bloc, was elected COSATU's general secretary, with Sydney Mufamadi, the former general secretary of the General and Allied Workers' Union, as his deputy. In opening the proceedings of this watershed conference, Cyril Ramaphosa, the mineworkers' powerful general secretary, showed no hesitation in making explicit the new federation's aims, both economic and political. "The political struggle is not only to remove the government," he declared, but also to ensure that "the wealth of the society must be shared among all those that work in this country. . . . We all agree that the struggle of workers on the shop floor cannot be separated from the wider struggle for liberation" (*Document 71*).

Although COSATU insisted that it was politically independent, two incidents, one at the post-conference rally and one shortly thereafter, indicated a clear sympathy with the ANC/UDF camp and raised fears of sectarianism. First, Barayi, in his highly publicized rally speech, made a vitriolic attack on all homeland leaders, including Chief Mangosuthu Buthelezi of KwaZulu, and proclaimed Mandela the people's "real leader." Buthelezi reacted angrily, charging that COSATU was an ANC front organization. COSATU members themselves worried about the divisiveness of the speech, especially since Inkatha maintained a significant following within many COSATU unions in Natal. Then, a few days after the conference, Jay Naidoo, on a visit to Harare to address a conference of the World Council of Churches, held an informal meeting with ANC and SACTU representatives, who expressed support for COSATU. The South African government and Inkatha saw this as further evidence of ANC-COSATU collusion, while former shopfloor unionists, true to FOSATU's tradition of democratic accountability, criticized Naidoo for linking COSATU to the ANC without a prior organizational mandate.[24]

COSATU's de facto political alignment hastened the formation of two rival trade union groups. First, Inkatha established the United Workers' Union of South Africa (UWUSA). UWUSA was set in motion in January 1986 and officially launched at a Durban rally on May 1. Established to counter COSATU's political influence in Natal, UWUSA received financial and logistical support

Figure 5. The United Workers Union of South Africa (UWUSA) is launched by Inkatha in response to the formation of the UDF-aligned Congress of South African Trade Unions (COSATU), Durban, May 1, 1986. *Omar Badsha/africanpictures.net*

from many Natal employers. Although it was able to disrupt COSATU's activities in Natal, it never achieved credibility as an organization because it was seen as an employer-friendly "sweetheart" union that failed to take up worker grievances with vigor. Nevertheless, violence and intimidation intensified in Natal during 1986 as COSATU and UWUSA fought for factory-floor supremacy. By the following year, the conflict had spread beyond workplaces and into Natal's urban townships where Inkatha hoped to reverse all advances by the ANC and its allies.

COSATU faced other competition when AZACTU and the remaining CUSA unions, fearing political isolation and rejecting COSATU's openness to whites in leadership positions, came together in late 1986 to form CUSA-AZACTU, which later changed its name to the National Council of Trade Unions (NACTU). Unlike UWUSA, most NACTU affiliates had shopfloor credibility and relatively experienced leadership, and as a result NACTU's rivalry with COSATU was rarely acrimonious or violent. NACTU, under the leadership of Phiroshaw Camay and James Mndaweni, claimed a large initial paid-up following of 248,000, but was unable to match COSATU's record of militant strike action or to stem the gradual erosion of NACTU's membership.[25] Within the federation's leadership, black consciousness partisans of AZAPO coexisted uneasily with Africanist elements loyal to the traditions of the Pan Africanist Congress (PAC). All agreed that no whites should hold leadership positions in black unions, but Africanists had no objection to black unions having white members whereas AZAPO adherents ruled this out. Africanists found it easier to contemplate cooperation with COSATU than did those with AZAPO backgrounds. In late 1987 NACTU leaders held talks with the PAC in Tanzania (*Document 95*). Over the following two years, although AZAPO partisans retained many positions of union leadership, Africanists came to dominate NACTU's national executive committee.[26] Despite their immersion in a union environment of bargaining, both groupings within NACTU rejected any suggestion that South Africa's future might lie in a negotiated political solution.

The degree of COSATU's independence from the UDF remained a hotly debated issue, but the "workerist-populist" divide narrowed, partly because the unions were already deeply enmeshed in politics by 1986, and partly because those differences that remained cut across old union loyalties. The fusion of the shopfloor and community union traditions proved to be an asset in COSATU's survival. The federation could now play a major political role, and with solid shopfloor organization as well as sheer weight of numbers, it was less vulnerable to state repression. Shopfloor unionists learned that political engagement could actually encourage union growth; yet, unlike the old community unions, COSATU had the capacity to channel new politicized membership into concrete, durable structures. The formation of COSATU fed worker militancy both because of the confidence the federation inspired and the confrontational style of its leadership. In an environment of recession that threatened jobs and inflation that eroded real wages, union membership shot up and there was an almost immediate upswing in strike activity nationally.[27]

COSATU set an aggressive tone with a campaign in 1986 to make May Day—international workers' day—a public holiday. There had been longstanding worker dissatisfaction over the choice of national holidays; most commemorated important events in Afrikaner history and ignored days of symbolic importance to the black majority. A nationwide May Day stayaway involving at least 1.5 million workers provided an early indication of COSATU's strength. Although the government delayed proclaiming May Day a holiday, most employers gave it unofficial recognition from 1986 onward.

Almost from the moment of COSATU's formation, government security forces subjected the federation to massive repression. Throughout 1986 and 1987 thousands of COSATU members and officials were detained. Many were assaulted or killed in attacks by vigilantes. Police relentlessly harassed strikers, even during legal strikes. In April 1987 COSATU House, an 11-story office building in central Johannesburg that provided offices for both the national executive and many affiliate unions, was surrounded by police and searched in a military-style operation, culminating in the detention of over 400 people and the confiscation of piles of union documents. A month later two bomb blasts virtually destroyed the federation's headquarters.[28] Several smaller COSATU offices around the country were the targets of arson attacks, burglaries, and eviction notices (*Document 90*). The tenacity and depth of COSATU's organizational structures enabled it to survive this onslaught, however, and it continued to organize strikes and political campaigns throughout its first two years of existence.

Figure 6. Chris Dlamini, vice president of COSATU, addresses a meeting of the new Food and Allied Workers' Union (FAWU), formed by merging the Food and Canning Workers' Union, the Sweet, Food and Allied Workers' Union and the Retail and Allied Workers' Union, Cape Town, May 1986. *Dave Hartman*

The Second State of Emergency

Popular resistance rode a wave of confidence during late 1985 and the first half of 1986. Pretoria, under pressure to reassure foreign lenders by restoring a climate of normalcy, lifted the state of emergency in March 1986 although it had not succeeded in subduing black defiance. Several months later, in another gesture of reform, the Botha government repealed the hated pass laws (chapter 1). Street and area committees were proliferating, consumer boycotts were spreading, and the trade union movement was stronger than ever with the formation of COSATU, the largest union confederation in South Africa's history. At a meeting of the UDF's national working committee in late May 1986, a ten-point national Program of Action was issued, urging all members to build stronger cultural, sporting, youth, and women's organizations; recruit more white allies; and promote national campaigns to release prisoners, unban organizations, and discredit homeland authorities. Although UDF leadership harbored no illusions about the government's intransigence, an optimistic belief had taken hold at the grassroots level that the end of National Party rule was in sight.

These expectations were shattered by the imposition on June 12, 1986, of a second state of emergency which proved much harsher than the first. Ringing calls from the UDF for the opposition to rally and resist (*Document 84*) were to little avail. Within six months some 25,000 activists had been detained, almost three-quarters of them from UDF affiliates. Many were held for long periods without access to their families or lawyers, and many were beaten and tortured (*Document 93*). Detentions and harassment went far beyond the leadership level. The regime seemed determined to destroy the will of township residents to participate in any form of political activity. As in the first emergency, teenagers were heavily represented among the detained, and the eastern Cape was the region most severely targeted.

Press censorship was particularly harsh, with a virtual blackout imposed on anything dealing with the "security situation." Hoping to find chinks in the regime's armor, opposition lawyers brought numerous court cases challenging the draconian emergency regulations that sanctioned censorship, indefinite detention without trial, and other abuses of power. From time to time these challenges succeeded, only to be reversed on appeal by hard-line judges in the Supreme Court's Appellate Division. When emergency security and media regulations failed altogether to stand up in court, the Botha government simply rewrote them to evade the courts' objections.[29]

In many townships the military maintained a permanent presence and the government's new National Security Management System applied its counterrevolutionary strategy of "winning hearts and minds" through local improvement projects (chapter 1). "Problem" townships such as Alexandra, Mamelodi, and Lingelihle were singled out for both repression and upgrading.[30] The UDF, as well as most other political opposition, was devastated during the second emergency. Layers of leadership were removed to such a degree that in many areas even street committees were disabled. In the East Rand town of Delmas, the marathon treason trial of Popo Molefe, Patrick Lekota, Moss Chikane, and 19 others dragged on as state prosecutors argued that township unrest proved the UDF's and AZAPO's revolutionary intent. Meanwhile, the most resilient form of resistance between 1986 and 1988, particularly in the southern Transvaal and northern Orange Free State, became the refusal of township dwellers to pay rent.

In the Vaal townships many residents had stopped paying rent since the 1984 uprising, which had initially been triggered by rent increases. There had been sporadic and isolated boycotts elsewhere during 1985. Most of the early cases evolved spontaneously, either out of disgust with local government or out of people's simple inability to pay. Responses varied; in some cases tenants continued to pay old or reduced rents, while in other cases they paid nothing at all. The authorities were slow to respond, partly because they feared conflict in an already tense political atmosphere and partly because lawyers for the boycotters sometimes found legal loopholes to ward off prosecution. Eventually, when persuasion and negotiation failed, local governments began trying to evict rent defaulters. This led to ongoing conflict and protest as communities closed ranks to protect residents served with eviction orders. Once again, state coercion served to heighten unity and resolve.[31]

After the new state of emergency was imposed, the UDF began promoting rent boycotts as part of a national strategy to pressure the government. As a tactical weapon, rent boycotts had a number of advantages over consumer boycotts. First, poverty made it difficult for residents to pay rent and many were open to an idea which eased their financial burdens. During consumer boycotts residents redirected, rather than saved, money. It was sometimes inconvenient, and usually more costly, to patronize only township shops. Rent boycotts, by contrast, actually allowed residents to spend more money on food and clothing. Second, rent boycotts put direct pressure on the state rather than on white business. Loss of rent revenues financially paralyzed local authorities, which built and owned almost all formal housing in African townships. Third, older and more conservative residents found rent boycotts more appealing because they were less public in their implementation. After Alexandra's "Six Day War," activists called simultaneously for rent and consumer boycotts in April 1986. By June, however, residents had resolved to end the consumer boycott and support only the rent boycott because the latter seemed more sustainable and was less open to the bullying tactics of local "comrades."[32]

From mid-1986 rent boycotts were often initiated with explicitly political goals. Apart from maintaining general anti-apartheid pressure, rent boycotts forced the government to acknowledge local needs, the contribution of township residents to the urban economy, and the unjust distribution of wealth and services in the cities. They became a powerful symbol of non-cooperation. According to Mark Swilling, by the end of 1986 rent boycotts had spread "to 54 townships countrywide, involving about 500,000 households and costing the state at least R40 million ($16 million) per month."[33]

A Soweto rent boycott began in June 1986. It was organized through emerging street committees in conjunction with several branches of the Soweto Civic Association. Almost from the start it involved 50 to 80 percent of households.[34] All attempts to break the strategy of non-payment failed. Government authorities tried selective evictions but street committees, some of which withstood the emergency crackdown, protected families singled out for eviction. Large numbers of residents were mobilized to block removal teams. Street committees also ensured that houses successfully cleared would not be reoccupied by other families. When residents in the White City section of Soweto resisted evictions on August 26, 1986, police opened fire, killing at least 20 people. This strengthened the resolve to boycott and made the authorities more cautious in attempting mass evictions.[35] Security forces cut off water and electricity to boycotting areas, or removed the front doors of boycotting householders. Street committees replaced doors and tried to organize basic services. The absence of services which could not be restored was borne with fortitude. In 1986 and 1987 the state attempted to enforce the payment of rent through stop-orders on wages. But employers were vehemently opposed to transferring political tensions into the workplace and putting upward pressure on wages. The trade unions also made it clear that they would resist such a tactic with all their strength. Without the cooperation of employers, stop-orders were impossible to implement, and the rent boycotts continued.[36]

Politics and Religion

The escalation of both resistance and repression created conflicting pressures on church leaders. White congregations, fearful of a radical reordering of South African society, exerted a strongly conservative influence, while black churchgoers, outnumbering whites almost four to one, looked to church leaders to articulate their aspirations for fundamental change. Within the major English-speaking churches, paternalistic white dominance had gradually given way to more racially representative leadership, but whites still disproportionately contributed to and controlled church finances.[37] Only church bodies that could raise substantial foreign funds could achieve the independence necessary to identify fully with the anti-apartheid cause. The most important of these bodies, the South African Council of Churches (SACC), after withstanding the attacks of the Eloff Commission (chapter 1), moved firmly into the forefront of resistance politics when its general secretary, Desmond Tutu, won the 1984 Nobel Peace Prize. Unequivocal in asserting the responsibility of Christians to side with the poor and oppressed, and astute in using scriptural ammunition to back up his demands for justice, Tutu became a favorite of the international media for his eloquence and wit. Government efforts to restrict him from traveling and making speeches backfired when foreign governments and churches criticized these restrictions, further bolstering his prestige.[38]

Government attacks on other outspoken churchmen, including Allan Boesak, Catholic Archbishop Denis Hurley, subsequent SACC general secretaries Beyers Naudé and Frank Chikane, and activist priests like Simon Farisani, Francois Bill, and Smangaliso Mkhatshwa, tended to create an international perception that South Africa's churches were militant institutions. More accurately, in the words of one radical cleric, "the Church [was] not an army but a battlefield" where moral questions posed by apartheid were fiercely contested, usually across a racial divide.[39] A decade after the SACC had expressed strong support for conscientious objectors in a 1974 resolution, debates still raged in its member churches over what position to take on the mounting military confrontation between the state and the exiled liberation movements.[40] If "just wars" existed—and only the strictest pacifists denied this possibility—was this such a war, and if so, on which side was God? If one condemned the use of violence by both sides (a position adopted by many white Christians), was it still right, for example, that denominational chaplains were provided to the South African Defence Force (SADF), where they wore uniforms, received weapons training, and were paid military salaries? While most whites considered this traditional practice acceptable, most blacks condemned it. Caught in the middle, church committees searched for compromise positions that would prevent members, particularly affluent whites, from resigning or defecting to the growing number of new right-wing churches.[41]

At the height of township violence in 1985 radical churchmen produced two outspoken discussion documents aimed at forcing their cautious colleagues and congregations off the political fence. The first was drafted by ministers from the Western Province Council of Churches and proposed that churches countrywide issue a "Call to Prayer for the End to Unjust Rule" on June 16, the ninth anniversary of the start of the 1976 Soweto uprising. "We have continually prayed for the authorities, that they may govern wisely and justly," it declared. "Now, in solidarity with those who suffer most, in this hour of crisis we pray that God in His grace may remove from His people the tyrannical structures of oppression and the present rulers in our country who persistently refuse to heed the cry for justice."[42] This was inviting churches to move from condemning apartheid policies to declaring the National Party government illegitimate. The SACC and several denominations agreed to circulate the document in April and May, but when June came, response at the parish level was tepid.

The second document stirred heated argument and attracted wide attention internationally. Issued in September 1985 and known as "The Kairos Document" (*Document 69*), it was produced by an ecumenical group of churchmen centered at the independent Institute for Contextual Theology in Johannesburg. Drafted principally by Catholic cleric Albert Nolan, it was eventually signed by 151 ministers and prominent lay workers. The document maintained that for churches to adopt a neutral stance toward the South African conflict was futile, because a correct reading of scripture made clear that the struggle for black liberation was just and consistent with God's will, even though violent means had become necessary for its achievement.

The Kairos Document argued that these truths had long been obscured by two false theologies. One was "State theology," which had been developed by the Dutch Reformed churches to justify Afrikaner dominance, and was not only false but heretical. Also inadequate was "Church theology," which pervaded political thinking in white, English-speaking congregations. Based on a blinkered social analysis, this held that the church could adopt a neutral and "nonviolent" position, from whence it could attempt to "reconcile" the protagonists, even if the oppressed still continued to suffer the system's injustices. What was needed, said the Kairos theologians, was a "prophetic theology" that could grasp present realities and guide Christians toward beliefs and actions that would create a just society in the future. This required a recognition of the government's illegitimacy and hence the validity of challenging apartheid laws through civil disobedience. It also required a thorough reorientation, away from the soothing of white fear and guilt and toward preaching hope and confidence to blacks.[43]

Although no church bodies officially adopted the Kairos Document, it became an important reference point during the rest of the decade in defining church debates on violence, reconciliation, civil disobedience, and other forms of political action including foreign economic sanctions, a perennial focus of controversy. By defending armed struggle as morally legitimate, the Kairos Document raised the international standing of the liberation movements and may even have pushed some passive supporters of the South African regime to reexamine their most basic assumptions. The SACC and the

Southern African Catholic Bishops' Conference (like the SACC, an umbrella body not obliged to overrepresent parish-level white opinion) moved toward open expressions of support for trade union struggles and against government attacks on COSATU.[44] The National Party government and the Dutch Reformed churches were long accustomed to battling on the terrain of religious ideology. They stepped up their campaign to depict radical clerics as agents of communist-inspired revolution, although this tactic became less effective as the Soviet Union openly retreated from its involvement in southern Africa in the late 1980s.

Links between the exiled liberation movements and international religious bodies dated from the controversial decision of the World Council of Churches (WCC) in 1970 to make annual grants to the ANC and PAC for humanitarian purposes.[45] The movements made little effort to strengthen church ties, however, until Boesak, in a startling development in 1982, succeeded in having South Africa's white Dutch Reformed churches suspended from the World Alliance of Reformed Churches. A year later the ANC sent a delegation headed by its secretary general to the Sixth Assembly of the World Council of Churches in Vancouver, where Boesak and Tutu were also present. Numerous meetings between the exiled ANC and prominent churchmen took place thereafter. Boesak visited Maputo at the Mozambique government's invitation in 1985 and was escorted during his visit by Jacob Zuma, a member of the ANC National Executive Committee.[46] The South African media took little notice of this, but widely reported the trip of Mkhatshwa and Hurley with a Catholic delegation to Lusaka in April 1986 (*Document 80*).

A WCC-sponsored conference in Harare in May 1987 became an opportunity for prominent South African clerics, including Naudé and Farid Esack, a Muslim leader from Cape Town, to meet with ANC officials. At its conclusion, the conference adopted a WCC declaration stating that liberation movements in South Africa and Namibia were fighting just wars because "the nature of the South African regime, which wages wars against its own inhabitants and neighbours, compels the movements to the use of force along with other means to end oppression."[47] The Anglican Church and the SACC both subsequently voted to endorse the WCC's declaration, provoking the Johannesburg *Financial Mail,* a mouthpiece of the white business establishment, to condemn the "repellent and specious document," and to threaten darkly that committing churches "to military opposition to the regime may be a little more than its supporters, black or white, rich or poor, have bargained for."[48] In the meantime, recognizing the enormous political value of church support, the ANC in 1987 set up a department of religious affairs to cultivate church ties.

Esack's presence in Harare was emblematic of the political awakening of South Africa's Muslims in the 1980s. Muslims, who comprise less than 2 percent of the country's population, fall into two main groups of about equal size.[49] The first are descendants of slaves and others brought during the seventeenth and eighteenth centuries to the Cape from the Dutch East Indies, Madagascar, and other points east. They were classified as "Malays," and later

Figure 7. Farid Esack, Oliver Tambo, and Beyers Naudé at a conference of the World Council of Churches in Harare, May 1987. *Learn and Teach Archive*

included in the category "coloured" under the apartheid system. The second group are descendants of Indian traders and laborers, mainly from Gujarat, who began arriving in Natal and the Transvaal in the mid-nineteenth century. Although individual Muslims were long active in opposition politics, Muslims as a religious community had never been organized around the political goal of majority rule. In the 1970s, unhappy with clerical conservatism, many younger Muslims had been mobilized by the Muslim Youth Movement (MYM) and the Muslim Students' Association (MSA) into groups for the study of progressive religious literature from India, Pakistan, and Egypt. From this modernist trend had gradually emerged a new Muslim consciousness, fed by the rising global power of oil-producing states in the Middle East and influenced by the South African black consciousness movement. In the politically charged period of the Soweto uprising, Muslim consciousness increasingly found expression in critiques of apartheid grounded in the discourse of Islamic principles and identity. This development was further spurred by the Iranian revolution of 1979. Now there was a modern state dedicated to Islamic principles; moreover, its religious zeal was overlaid with fiery anti-imperialist rhetoric. This turn of events inspired intense excitement, particularly among young coloureds in the western Cape, accelerating the formation of a Muslim subculture of political resistance.

Muslim students were in the lead when school boycotts began in Cape

Town in 1980. Some were drawn to a radical new organization called Qibla, led by Achmad Cassiem, a cerebral former PAC prisoner. Qibla preached an eclectic ideology of Africanism, socialism, and Islamic revolution, holding out a vision of South Africa purified someday under Muslim rule.[50] Similarly outside the conservative Muslim mainstream, but more attuned to South African realities, was the Call of Islam, an organization formed in 1984 by Farid Esack, Ebrahim Rasool, and others to draw Muslim support to the UDF. Downplaying the Iranian model as inappropriate to South Africa, the Call of Islam promoted goals of interfaith cooperation while encouraging Muslims to perceive the South African conflict through the prism of Islam's tenets of justice, equality, and struggle against oppression. The two older organizations, the MYM and the MSA, although not affiliated with the UDF, also encouraged their members to approach the political struggle first and foremost as Muslims (*Document 83*).

When township violence spread to Cape Town in mid-1985, demonstrations in coloured areas escalated rapidly into rioting, arson, and street fighting between the security forces and youths, some wearing the checked *kefiyyah* (head cloth) associated with the Palestine Liberation Organization and shouting *Allahu Akbar!* (God is great) from behind blazing barricades. As casualties mounted, Muslim funerals attracted large crowds of mourners and drew media attention to the surge in religious fervor. In late October, state-of-emergency regulations were extended to eight districts around Cape Town and the press was barred from reporting freely on what by that time were conditions approaching civil war.

The revolt in the western Cape eventually lost momentum, but media images of Islamic radicalism had been imprinted on the public mind, creating a new bogey. In April 1986 Botha told Parliament that violent elements in the Muslim community were planning terrorism with aid from Libya and Iran; fortunately, he assured the white public, the government was "taking the necessary counter-measures" to ensure security.[51] Six months later, a synod of the Dutch Reformed church passed a resolution asserting that Islam could not be recognized as a genuine religion. This resolution, denounced by the MYM in an article in its monthly newspaper, *Al-Qalam* (*Document 87*), set off angry reactions throughout South Africa, not least among Muslim members of the coloured and Indian houses of Parliament. Botha was forced to apologize publicly and to confirm that the country's constitution guaranteed freedom of religion.[52] Muslims were again drawn together defensively when the controversial Cassiem and six others were tried and convicted in 1988 of offenses under the Internal Security Act, including conspiracy to overthrow the state and further the aims of the PAC.[53] Issues of *Al-Qalam* were banned for opposing conscription, urging voters to boycott the municipal elections of October 1988, and siding broadly with the UDF. Repression cooled the ardor of some activists but steeled the determination of others and widely politicized a community that previously had been known for its relatively accommodating attitude toward the state.

Students and *Amabutho:* The Struggle for Control

By the time the first state of emergency was declared in July 1985, school boycotts had become entwined with wider national campaigns. COSAS together with National Forum-aligned student organizations had mobilized a boycott by nearly a million students to coincide with the August 1984 elections for the coloured and Indian houses of Parliament. The Vaal uprising and military occupation of the Vaal townships in the following months sparked further boycotts by an estimated 200,000 students, leading to the closure of 87 schools in that region alone. By October dozens of schools on the East Rand and in the eastern Cape were boycotting, primarily around demands of a national political nature. Roughly 400,000 school students in the southern Transvaal added their weight to the November 5–6 stayaway (chapter 2), helping to forge a powerful alliance between organized labor and the student movement.[54] The March 1985 stayaway in Port Elizabeth and Uitenhage proved less successful as student and youth groups failed to consult effectively with unions. Nevertheless, the school boycotts added impact to the regional stayaway.

With the imposition of the first state of emergency in 36 districts of the Transvaal and Cape, the government struck back, detaining dozens of student leaders and declaring COSAS a banned organization. The school boycott movement was too well established to fold under this kind of repression, however, and the security forces succeeded only in removing the restraining and disciplining influence of experienced leaders.[55] School boycotts continued to erupt nationwide until almost every African high school outside the relatively quiescent province of Natal was affected. Increasingly, senior primary students were drawn in as well. An eyewitness account (*Document 70*) described action by coloured students in Cape Town in August 1985. Displaying a brave if overly optimistic faith in the imminent collapse of apartheid, boycotting students were heavily involved in consumer boycotts, attacks on councillors, repelling security force interventions, and turning funerals into emotion-fraught political performances (*Document 77*).

By the end of 1985, school boycotts were losing direction and in several respects appeared to be self-defeating. First, black urban schooling had all but collapsed; thousands of students had received no schooling for months, and only 40 percent of registered final-year students in urban areas sat for matriculation exams at the year's end.[56] Students declared 1986 the "Year of No Schooling." Second, the sheer persistence of the boycotts, along with their amorphous revolutionary demands, detracted from their impact as a focused political weapon. Although boycotts placed general pressure on the state, boycotting students seemed to lose sight of specific negotiable issues. Third, the absence of students from school, especially after the banning of COSAS, created almost insurmountable organizational difficulties for the student leadership.

As the school boycotts drifted into chaos, parents, teachers, and community leaders recognized the need to intervene forcefully. The Soweto Civic Association took the lead by calling a mass meeting to discuss the crisis. Out of this meeting the Soweto Parents' Crisis Committee was established. The Committee, an alliance of UDF-aligned civic bodies, parents, and teachers, wanted a return to school but realized that students had to be offered persuasive incentives.[57] Defying legal prohibitions, the Committee sent a delegation to Harare to discuss the issue with the ANC in December 1985. On the delegation's return, at a meeting in Johannesburg attended by a wide range of community and student representatives, the Committee offered students an alternative to their widely proclaimed slogan "Liberation now, education later." The ANC was not in favor of an indefinite boycott, they reported. The alternative proposed was a policy of "People's Education for People's Power." This meant challenging the system rather than avoiding it, returning to school but maintaining pressure on education authorities to scrap biased syllabi and unfair regulations. The meeting approved the strategy and set up a new coordinating body, the National Education Crisis Committee (NECC).[58]

The NECC depended on a network of local parent-teacher-student associations. According to Eric Molobi, the NECC national coordinator, these local associations were to the NECC "what street committees are to civics and the UDF."[59] Early in 1986 the NECC arranged a series of well-attended meetings around the country to popularize the concept of "People's Education." As the new school year got underway in late January, the majority of boycotting students agreed to a conditional return to school. The NECC held its first conference two months later in Durban.[60] In an important state of the nation speech, Zwelakhe Sisulu, editor of the pro-UDF newspaper *New Nation*, cautioned students that the fall of the government was not imminent. Calling for unity, he praised the policy of People's Education and linked transformation in education to the wider national democratic struggle (*Document 78*). The return to school was not universally accepted by students since, predictably, school authorities failed to effect the changes demanded. Scattered disruptions took place throughout most of 1986 but not on the scale of the previous year.[61] At the beginning of 1987 there was a general return to school. The NECC, despite many setbacks, managed successfully to provide a measure of adult direction and coherence to what had become a meandering student revolt.

Instilling discipline and control over the political actions of unemployed township youth proved an even more difficult process than coaxing students to return to schools. At the time of its founding, COSAS had attempted to cater to the needs of a broad youth constituency, and many of its early members were school-leavers who maintained close ties with friends still in school. Gradually, however, it became clear that the interests of secondary school students diverged substantially from those of unemployed school-leavers, to whom educational issues were usually irrelevant. Starting in 1982, COSAS worked to help establish separate organizations to represent and mobilize non-schoolgoing youth. These youth congresses took shape not only in major urban areas like Soweto (SOYCO), Port Elizabeth (PEYCO), and Cape Town (CAYCO), but also in dozens of smaller cities and towns. Their organizational independence allowed COSAS to concentrate on school-based issues and develop greater organizational coherence. Meanwhile, the youth congresses played their own major role in the resistance struggles of the mid-1980s. A 1983 Soweto Youth Congress memorandum (*Document 64*) outlines SOYCO's "Programme of Action."

Youth congresses made rapid progress in organizing the huge unemployed youth constituency. By 1985 their structures often ran parallel to street and area committees. Youth-congress leadership was drawn in part from among former high-school students, many of whom had been COSAS members. Whereas students were organized in the schoolyards, unemployed youth cohered naturally in the streets. Non-schoolgoing youth lacked the political sophistication of the school students but, with time on their hands and little to lose, they became the most militant and daring element within the UDF. From 1984 onward youth-congress activists, known as "comrades," "young lions," or, when organized in quasi-military fashion, *amabutho,* played a central, often unpopular role in policing stayaways and consumer boycotts. The toyi-toyi, a high-spirited warriors' dance, became their political trademark at mass gatherings, marches, and funerals (*Document 82*).[62] Between 1985 and 1987 the "comrades" were responsible for rendering many townships temporarily off limits to state authorities—"ungovernable," in township parlance. The *amabutho's* eagerness to confront security forces and repel them from their areas was an attitude consistent with the territoriality of their street culture.

Some youth congresses kept tight control of their members and consulted thoroughly with other community representatives before taking action. But "comrades" were not always responsive to centralized leadership, particularly if their own most politically astute leaders were absent. Their activities were often spontaneous and violent, dividing communities along generational lines. Their de facto power in the townships represented a direct challenge to traditions of age hierarchy, and many older residents resented their arrogance and bullying. Often the "comrades" were very young. Researchers in the eastern Cape found that the *amabutho* were "mainly boys between 12 and 16 years old" who "had at best only a few years of primary schooling. They are unemployed, virtually illiterate, the offspring of broken or scattered families, living in packs 100 or 200 strong in what they call 'bases' on the fringes of the poorer squatter camps.... They may not have a program but they do have guns and grenades."[63] Though loyal to the UDF, they generally lacked any formal organizational links which could have made them accountable to adult leadership. Unlike participants in the school boycotts, the *amabutho* were almost exclusively male and expressed their masculinity through their militarized political activity. As the youth drifted beyond organizational control, physical prowess and street savvy superseded articulateness as necessary qualities for leadership. Young women were increasingly marginalized.[64]

Far from major urban centers, youth activism sometimes took unpredictable forms. In the mountainous Sekhukhuneland region of the Lebowa homeland in the northern Transvaal, intergenerational conflict shaped political attitudes when a regional UDF executive committee was belatedly established in February 1986. Migrant workers had brought the ideas of the ANC and the Communist Party to rural Sekhukhuneland in the 1950s, and Peter Nchabeleng, a veteran of this tradition, became the UDF regional chairman.[65] Progress was slow because most older rural villagers and migrants were respectful toward chiefs and wary of urban radicalism. Few UDF affiliates were established beyond those at the University of the North and in some of the more industrialized towns. Youth in Lebowa, however, were inspired by urban resistance and the anti-homeland message of the UDF. The Sekhukhuneland Youth Organisation (SEYO) was established in early 1986, followed by smaller local youth congresses which drew on a constituency of high-school students and school-leavers. These organizations were only sporadically in contact with UDF structures and most of the time engaged in action programs of their own devising.[66] The number of students attending high school in Lebowa had more than doubled between 1980 and 1986, but jobs for school-leavers were scarce.[67] Enraged by the corruption and collaboration they witnessed in both tribal structures and school boards, they were ripe for rebellion.

From February to April 1986 thousands of these rural "comrades" boycotted schools and attacked all institutions associated with government. Chiefs' authority was challenged, rural councillors were forced to resign or flee, policemen were assaulted, and school and government buildings were damaged and looted. For three months politically unsophisticated youths in their late teens and early twenties filled the vacuum of authority in rural Lebowa. The most disturbing aspect of their reign was witch hunting. A belief that witches were responsible for misfortune was widespread in the region, and the "comrades," as self-declared protectors of the community, resolved to root them out. Fatal lightning strikes, attributed to witches, sparked off a wave of killing. The victims were generally (though not exclusively) elderly pensioners who were perceived by jobless young men to be relatively well off. Personal jealousies and grudges intertwined with zealous political commitment in the process of sniffing out evil-doers. Parents lived in terror as they watched their children round up, abuse, and frequently burn alleged witches to death. The desirability of rooting out witches was widely accepted, but elders rejected the non-traditional methods of witch naming used by the "comrades" and the severity of punishments imposed. It was unheard of for youths to control a process which had been carefully managed for generations by chiefs.

The UDF declared witch hunting a dangerous superstition and disassociated itself from the practice entirely, but many members of SEYO remained directly involved. Forty-three alleged witches were killed in Sekhukhuneland within a matter of weeks, most of them in Nchabeleng's home area although he was one of the few leaders with the legitimacy and courage to try to persuade the witch hunters to end their campaign.[68] At least a dozen more witch killings occurred in Mpulaneng, a separate pocket of Lebowa to the east of Sekhukhuneland, where the spree continued into May.[69] The reign of the "comrades" ended between mid-April and mid-May when the SADF moved into the region to restore the tribal authorities. Order was effectively re-established at least in part because the rule of the "comrades" had become intolerable for ordinary villagers. Hundreds of politicized youths were arrested, and the rest fled into the mountains. Nchabeleng was detained by homeland police on April 11 and beaten to death within 12 hours of being arrested—presumably for refusing to admit that events in Sekhukhuneland were part of a revolutionary plot.

During the years of school boycotts (1984–86), the distinction between student and non-student youth was often blurred, as in the Sekhukhuneland violence. Away from the schoolyard for lengthy periods, many students tended to integrate into the world of the street. Under the two states of emergency, much of the student and youth-congress leadership was detained and the UDF found it increasingly difficult to impose organizational discipline on leaderless "comrades." The distinction between criminal and political activity also tended to blur. Some unemployed youths who became politically conscious also became involved in a criminal gang subculture. It was not uncommon for them to continue their criminal activities while identifying with the liberation struggle and engaging politically. During the mid-1980s these youths were often called "com-tsotsis" (a "tsotsi" is a young gangster). Politically disciplined "comrades," eager to disassociate themselves from the criminal element, were often involved in combating "com-tsotsis." Their anti-crime campaigns were important in winning support from older township residents and in cementing alliances with other community organizations.[70]

In a climate of heavy repression, the South African Youth Congress (SAYCO) was launched at a secret conference in Cape Town in late March 1987, fulfilling the UDF's longstanding goal of creating a national youth organization. In the preceding months several regional youth congresses had been established as forerunners to the formation of one overarching organization. Under emergency restrictions, organization and planning had to be highly secretive. Due to the strength of the local and regional youth organizations, however, SAYCO at its founding claimed a signed-up membership of over half a million and an informal following of two million. Under the quasi-underground leadership of a former Robben Island prisoner, Peter Mokaba, the congress immediately adopted a radical and confrontational style and rhetoric. ANC and SACP colors and symbols were brazenly displayed at meetings. The SAYCO leadership felt that the organization's sheer size would be its greatest protection.[71] In much the same way that the NECC stepped into a leadership vacuum in school politics, SAYCO hoped to regroup youth organizations and give direction to the insurrectionary youth constituency. While attempting to establish a disciplined organizational structure, SAYCO's radicalism allowed it to maintain credibility among its following. At a rhetorical level, SAYCO leaders adopted class analysis and positioned the organization close to COSATU and the SACP as symbols of worker leadership. It advocated a strong alliance between the working-class and township youth. In terms of formal alliances, however, SAYCO remained firmly within the multiclass UDF.

During 1987 and 1988 SAYCO's leadership, subjected to relentless police harassment, was forced to remain underground. Campaigns, such as the Save the Patriots Campaign which tried to stop the execution of convicted Umkhonto we Sizwe guerrillas, were conducted with a mixture of secret planning and well-publicized media events. SAYCO's membership lacked both the formality and democratic ethos of the trade union movement, and its nominally massive following remained amorphous. Its methods were ultimately populist and its survival seemed to depend on underground organizing rather than the building of multiple layers of leadership. Nevertheless, it was a potentially formidable force in the late 1980s and probably became the UDF's most influential affiliate.

Leadership Conflicts in the UDF

Despite the UDF's unprecedented success in assembling a political movement that bridged race, class, generational, regional, and ideological divisions, internal strains and conflicts plagued the Front. The need to show unity in the face of a common enemy ensured that factional disputes were seldom aired publicly or in the media. Instead, personality clashes, organizational competition, and class and racial resentments were masked behind heated policy debates or expressed in off-the-record meetings. Loyalty to the traditions and leadership of the ANC provided common ground, but also terrain that could be contested. The ANC's headquarters in Lusaka was distant and communication slow; inside South Africa, its underground networks were weak and uncoordinated. One group claiming to represent the ANC's "true" views could easily find itself confronting another also asserting that its conflicting positions were authentic ANC policy. While many in the youth and student ranks of the UDF yearned for revolutionary solutions, older activists were more likely to regard political and economic strategies of resistance as more potentially effective. The need for underground ANC members to also play active roles in legal, aboveground UDF affiliates created complex situations where tactical issues could not be publicly debated. ANC leaders sometimes tried to intervene from exile to end disputes, summoning representatives of the competing groups to confer at venues in the frontline states. Nevertheless, some of the most persistent internal conflicts were never resolved. An internal ANC memorandum compiled from intelligence reports looked at factionalism in the UDF in 1986, discussed some of the issues that divided the most tenacious or politically ambitious of these competing groupings, and commented on the "styles of work" that were said to account for the unpopularity of some activists in the eyes of rivals(*Document 86*).

One controversial grouping, labeled "the cabal" by its opponents, predated the UDF's formation. The central figures in this murkily defined group were Pravin Gordhan, Yunus Mahomed, and a small circle of energetic young Indians who became involved in the renascent Natal Indian Congress (NIC) in the late 1970s. Gordhan and Mahomed were ANC supporters who had made contact with Mac Maharaj in 1976 following his release from Robben Island and had maintained this contact after Maharaj left for exile. Experienced, dedicated, able to draw on independent resources to support their political activities, and prepared to do the patient, slogging work necessary to build strong community organizations, some of these activists moved into commanding positions in the Natal UDF from its inception. In time they formed working relationships with African UDF activists who were also in the ANC underground. Although not always in agreement on specific issues, "cabal" members appeared to share a belief in their own responsibility as a vanguard force to exercise leadership within the democratic movement. Eventually, according to *Document 86,* their alleged use of secret caucusing had provoked a backlash among other activists in Natal and beyond. Despite warnings from the external ANC about undemocratic "styles of work," accusations persisted that the UDF, in Natal if not countrywide, was being controlled by Indians, a "subjective weakness," in the words of *Document 86,* that put at risk all the achievements of the struggle.[72]

Others who entered the UDF with leadership aspirations were the key figures heading the Release Mandela Campaign (RMC), including Aubrey Mokoena, Curtis Nkondo, Jabu Ngwenya, and Winnie Mandela. Their opposition to "the cabal" assumed the tone of an African nationalist challenge to "Indian domination," introducing a volatile current into the mainstream of UDF politics. Prejudice against Indians was common among ordinary Africans, and was mirrored by the anti-African prejudices of many Indians. Although apartheid relegated Indians to second-class citizenship and the majority of Indians were poor by any measure, by the 1980s there was a relatively better-off Indian middle class that stressed education and the development of business skills by their children. Africans and Indians sometimes mixed socially but did not intermarry. Most Indians felt ambivalent at best about the possibility of African majority rule, and many took a dim view of the solidarity expressed by the Natal and Transvaal Indian Congresses (TIC) with the UDF and the ANC tradition. Ironically, the politically enlightened stance of the NIC and TIC did not necessarily shield their activists from anti-Indian attitudes among Africans in the UDF.[73] Among RMC leaders, there was strong pressure to convert what had started as a single-issue campaign into a mass membership organization for Africans that could act as a counterweight on a national level to the perceived power of "the cabal."

The RMC activists found an ally in a third grouping called "Freeway House."[74] This group drew adherents from the overwhelmingly white National Union of South African Students (NUSAS), and its pivotal figure was Auret van Heerden, who had been national president of NUSAS in the late 1970s. While still in NUSAS, van Heerden had met some leaders in the external ANC and had come to regard himself as a member of the ANC underground, even as part of its internal leadership. In 1983 he joined the Transvaal UDF's publicity secretariat and also set up a service organization called the Community Resource and Information Centre (CRIC) to assist UDF affiliates with research and staff training. A CRIC offshoot, Media and Resource Services (MARS), was established later to provide media training. An experienced fund-raiser, van Heerden used his ties with the UDF and NUSAS to generate overseas support for the activities of CRIC and MARS, which were headquartered in Freeway House, an office building adjacent to the campus of the University of the Witwatersrand in Johannesburg.

Van Heerden and his group built links with the RMC and with UDF youth and student organizations, in part by offering them office space in Freeway House and employing their activists in CRIC and MARS. Situating itself far to the ideological left, Freeway House attracted African support by attacking "the cabal"—portraying it not as a race-based caucus concerned with protecting Indian interests but as a middle-class elite group opposed to the revolutionary impulses of the working-class masses. Reaching out to radical-minded students and "workerists" in the trade unions who were unhappy about the UDF's ambivalence on socialism, van Heerden and publications under his influence promoted the goal of a rapid transition to socialism and criticized the Communist Party's two-stage doctrine that called for socialism to be given priority only after a successful democratic revolution.[75] Although the ANC favored constructive debates on tactics and ideology, to the author of *Document 86* the actions of Freeway House were less a contribution to debate than an attempt to push van Heerden's group forward as a power center within the UDF and sideline other contenders for leadership, including at times the exiled ANC itself.

African women were another UDF constituency afflicted by disunity. As trade union members, they were starting to chip away at gender discrimination by employers. As township residents, they threw their weight behind consumer, rent, and bus boycotts. Bringing them together in organized political associations was difficult, however. Working-class women with family responsibilities rarely had time to participate in political organizations. Lack of education, plus socialization into an intensely patriarchal culture, left them ill-equipped for leadership or self-assertion on the high-risk terrain of confrontation with government authorities. Local women's clubs, church groups, and self-help societies abounded, but politicizing these groups or galvanizing their members to demand an end to apartheid laws, or even improvements in schools, was usually an uphill battle for those women leaders who took up the challenge. Sometimes political or civic action groups would form, then become moribund after a few high-profile women were detained. Leaders would be elected, then fail to provide leadership; Indian, coloured, or white women would assume de facto leadership of organizations in which most members were Africans; and rivalries and resentments would fester, causing the process of building broad alliances to falter. Feminist appeals to African women to shake off male domination also gained traction only fleetingly.

In Cape Town, the United Women's Organisation (UWO), a multiracial body, was launched in 1981 by a group that included women who had been active in the 1950s in the Federation of South African Women (FEDSAW), an affiliate of the pro-ANC Congress Alliance.[76] A competing Africanist-minded group, the Women's Front, was established a year later. Both groups supported the UDF, but it took more than two years of negotiations and intervention from the exiled ANC to persuade them to merge (and become UWCO, the United Women's Congress) in 1986. Other divisions bedeviled women's groups in Natal and the eastern Cape. The long quiescent FEDSAW announced its revival in 1981, but did not succeed in establishing many durable branches outside the Transvaal, where its active members worked mainly under the banner of the Federation of Transvaal Women. Throughout the decade, ANC partisans continued to call for the countrywide resurrection of FEDSAW, but local and regional women's groups resisted the loss of their autonomy through submersion in a centralized national body. In April 1987, representatives of eight women's organizations met with little fanfare in Cape Town to create the UDF Women's Congress. The Congress, conveners assured the press, was not a centralized wing of the UDF but merely an organization bringing together all women's organizations affiliated with the UDF.[77] Like earlier efforts to mobilize women as a united political force at the national level, the Congress issued an inspiring statement of intent, then faded away.

1987: Workers on the Offensive

COSATU's main focus during 1987 was the aggressive Living Wage Campaign. From early in the year the federation began to agitate for wage increases which outpaced inflation, particularly for workers in the lower-wage categories. The campaign, which continued until 1989, inspired disputes and strikes throughout the country and in most sectors of the economy. A Commercial, Catering, and Allied Workers' Union flyer (*Document 89*) called for solidarity with striking shop workers at the OK Bazaars chain in 1987, and *Document 99* explained the outcome of a nationwide strike by the powerful National Union of Metalworkers in 1988. Many unions succeeded in negotiating real wage increases for their members between 1987 and the end of the decade. While inflation oscillated between about 12 and 15 percent annually over this period, the wages of unionized workers increased yearly by 19 to 23 percent.[78] Coupled with the Living Wage Campaign was a demand for improved health and safety standards. This was stressed most forcefully in the mining sector, still in shock after a disaster at the Kinross goldmine in September 1986 when 177 miners died in an underground fire. After the disaster the NUM coined the popular slogan "safety before profits" (*Document 85*).

Between March and June 1987 a COSATU affiliate, the South African Railway and Harbour Workers' Union (SARHWU), conducted a long and bitter struggle against the state-controlled railway company, South African Transport Services (SATS). Following the dismissal of a worker for a minor offense, the union went on strike for his reinstatement and for regulated dismissal procedures. After SATS refused to recognize SARHWU, recognition itself became the key issue in dispute. By the end of April over 20,000 workers were involved. Following a series of mass dismissals, violent clashes between workers and strike breakers, and numerous arrests and attacks on

SATS property, SATS conceded after a 12-week work stoppage. In an important victory, most of the dismissed workers, including the worker whose dismissal sparked the strike, were reinstated and the union gained de facto recognition (*Document 91*).[79]

The UDF, NECC, and COSATU called for a two-day political stayaway to coincide with the whites-only general election on May 6, 1987 (*Document 92*). The stayaway was organized as a protest against both apartheid elections and state repression. Many within the old shopfloor bloc argued against this move, fearing stepped-up exposure to police harassment, but the majority in COSATU favored a strong demonstration of resistance in the face of ongoing repression. The stayaway began the day before the white election and gathered momentum on election day. As in May 1986, about a million and a half workers responded to the call, this time for two consecutive days. They were joined by nearly a million students boycotting classes. In the early hours of May 7, the night following the stayaway, COSATU headquarters was wrecked by the bomb blasts mentioned earlier—later revealed to be the work of the police.[80]

Shaken but determined, COSATU continued its offensive, scoring a victory for its one-industry-one-union policy with the formation of a giant new amalgamated metal union, the National Union of Metalworkers of South Africa (NUMSA). Prior to the formation of NUMSA in late May 1987, COSATU unions had succeeded in establishing industrial unions in the food, transport, mining, construction, chemical, and health sectors. Mergers were rarely straightforward. Smaller unions were often anxious about being swallowed up, general unions often resisted giving up members to new sectoral unions, and political loyalties tended to cloud strategic necessities. NUMSA's creation required a year and a half of intense negotiation, but once established, its 130,796 paid-up members made it the second-largest union in COSATU after the National Union of Mineworkers.[81] The Metal and Allied Workers Union (MAWU), previously one of the core FOSATU unions, contributed just over half of NUMSA's members; the rest came from a number of smaller unions, mostly concentrated in the motor industry. In an act of solidarity and defiance, Moses Mayekiso, the former head of MAWU, in prison awaiting trial on a treason charge, was elected NUMSA's general secretary.[82] NUMSA, which provided some much-needed stability to COSATU, proved a powerful advocate of political independence, helping to balance NUM, which under the assertive leadership of Cyril Ramaphosa had adopted the Freedom Charter at its annual congress in February 1987.

COSATU held its second national conference in Johannesburg in July 1987. Fierce debate over the nature of the federation's political alliances dominated the proceedings. Having weathered the severe repression of the second state of emergency relatively successfully, COSATU found itself in a position of enormous political responsibility. The battered democratic movement looked to the unions to provide leadership. The centrality of political issues at the COSATU congress was highlighted by three invited speakers: Murphy Morobe of the national UDF executive, Peter Mokaba of SAYCO, and Frank

Figure 8. Pages from COSATU comic book popularizing the 1987 Living Wage Campaign. *Continued on the next page*

Figure 8. *Continued*

Chikane, recently elected general secretary of the South African Council of Churches—all strong ANC partisans. All three urged COSATU to form a closer alliance with the UDF.

The mineworkers, eager to make COSATU's alliance with the ANC camp more explicit, tabled a motion to adopt the Freedom Charter. The UDF, which was to hold its national conference a month later, had already declared its intention to adopt the Charter. The 260,000 mineworkers constituted roughly 35 percent of the federation's total membership and they wielded great influence. The metalworkers, in a compromise motion, called for a qualified adoption of the Charter as a document of minimum demands but called also for the drawing up of a separate workers' charter with an overtly socialist agenda. While wanting to show its support for the democratic struggle, NUMSA feared that socialist goals would be watered down and trade union independence jeopardized within a broad cross-class alliance. NUMSA's motion failed to muster support because most left-leaning unions did not want to adopt the Freedom Charter at all, whereas the UDF bloc wanted an unambivalent adoption. Ultimately, the mineworkers' motion was carried. The adoption of the Freedom Charter, however, divided COSATU; many delegates felt that they had been bulldozed into accepting NUM's position. The conference, while clarifying COSATU's political policy, concluded with a disturbing sense of dissatisfaction among many representatives. The draft of an internal NUMSA discussion paper (*Document 97*) spells out the union's critique of COSATU's decision to subordinate itself, in effect, to the political leadership of the exiled ANC, a multiclass "populist" movement not committed to socialism or the primacy of worker interests.[83] An internal ANC intelligence report (*Document 136*) offers another perspective on politics in COSATU.

International economic sanctions were a further important issue discussed at COSATU's 1987 conference. Here greater consensus prevailed. COSATU resolved that in spite of the short-term suffering which sanctions and disinvestment might cause among workers, all moves to isolate and pressure the government should be encouraged. The resolution outraged the National Party, employer bodies, and Inkatha, which all accused COSATU of being more interested in pursuing a political agenda than in serving the interests of South African workers. COSATU countered that it was acting on a clear mandate from its members, who were prepared to make economic sacrifices. COSATU also insisted that the process of disinvestment should be negotiated with workers; it was unacceptable for foreign companies to disinvest unilaterally, especially if they were simply selling off their assets to local firms.

While the COSATU conference was in progress, NUM was bracing itself for a major showdown with the mining industry. Wage negotiations between the union and the Chamber of Mines had deadlocked in May and just prior to the COSATU conference about 80 percent of NUM's membership had participated in a strike ballot in which 95 percent voted in favor of strike action.[84] Both mine owners and labor were grimly determined to test their strength. NUM, sensing its growing power, wanted to secure for mineworkers a greater slice of the huge gold-price dividend. The mining houses were flush with profits in 1987 because, while the international gold price held firm in dollar terms, the rand had declined sharply against the dollar, causing the rand value of gold to skyrocket. The mine owners felt that if they gave in to NUM wage demands, it would become increasingly difficult to curb the union's power in the future. They preferred to square up for a bruising fight sooner rather than later. After NUM declared that a strike would start on August 9, the Chamber of Mines tightened security to limit the union's ability to operate on mine premises. Mine owners announced that free food and lodging as well as pay would be withheld from striking miners. Refusing even to negotiate a strike code of conduct with the union, the Chamber made clear its intention to repel the strikers with all the means at its disposal.

By August 10, about 300,000 gold and coal miners were on strike. Well over half the strikers were employed by mining giant Anglo American and roughly a quarter by Gencor. The strike was sustained for two weeks, showing that NUM could marshal support even beyond its paid-up membership. The employers had not anticipated the tenacity of the strike, which by the second week had endured longer than any mine strike on record, but they refused to back down. Striking workers and NUM officials were subjected to ongoing harassment from both police and mine security personnel. Police raided the union's offices throughout the strike; dozens of members were arrested; supplies of food, water, and electricity were periodically cut off to hostels; and meetings and sit-ins were broken up through the use of tear gas and rubber bullets. Anglo American's management threatened workers with evictions, dismissals, and the closing down of marginal mines.

COSATU's ability to provide effective supporting action for NUM was disappointing. Affiliate unions were unable or unwilling to mount risky solidarity strikes. COSATU issued information sheets and organized support rallies but failed to achieve anything beyond symbolic solidarity (*Document 94*). Although NUM had followed legal strike procedures, theoretically protecting strikers from dismissal, the Chamber of Mines dismissed over 50,000 mineworkers during the third week, most of whom were bused back to the homelands. It was a desperate ploy by the Chamber, which decided to face the legal consequences later.

NUM, facing decimation, agreed to a wage settlement which added very little to the Chamber's original offer. About 30,000 of the dismissed workers were reinstated soon after the settlement and, after a long legal battle, a further 10,000 got their jobs back. Roughly 10,000 lost their jobs permanently, although most of these received at least some form of compensation. In many respects the strike was a defeat for both sides. The mining houses lost millions of rands through stoppages and strike damage; NUM lost thousands of members, all its reserve funds, and much of its confidence in return for minor wage gains. Eleven miners were dead and hundreds injured. Both management and labor had underestimated each other's strength and resolve, resulting in a bloody standoff. COSATU attempted to portray the settlement as a tactical retreat rather than a defeat. This was not entirely untrue, given that the union's organizational structure survived and the Chamber of Mines was left extremely wary about the prospect of another costly confrontation.

The War for Natal

The emergence of the UDF and COSATU, with their links to the outlawed ANC, presented a major obstacle to the ambitions of Chief Buthelezi, whose intention was to position himself as the future leader of South Africa (*Document 2*). Achieving his goal depended on building a powerful alliance of anti-ANC groups, both white and black. The harder it became for Inkatha to attract support from non-Zulu Africans, the more important it was for Buthelezi to solidify his claim, made frequently to foreign audiences, that he was the sole leader of the "six million" (by the late-1980s, "seven million") Zulus, the country's single largest ethnic bloc. If seeking supremacy through democratic forms of contestation was ever considered, it was quickly dismissed; instead, coercion, violence, and threats of violence became the norm. From 1984 onward, UDF supporters in Natal became targets for attack as Inkatha tried to intimidate or drive out rivals—including non-Zulus—in its home province.[85] In response, ANC and UDF partisans formed defensive units of youthful "comrades," many of whom engaged in preemptive attacks or revenge killings as violence gained momentum.

An early flashpoint was Lamontville township south of Durban, where residents had been organized by the Joint Rent Action Committee (JORAC) to protest rent increases in 1982–83 (*Document 42*). ANC traditions were deep in Natal, but historically had tended to center on provincial rather than national leaders and loyalties, a tendency that Inkatha had exploited from its inception. Lamontville was home to some independent-minded ANC veterans, including JORAC founders Msizi Dube and Mcebisi Xundu. JORAC became a UDF affiliate, inviting the ire of Buthelezi, who opposed civic associations in Natal that were not under Inkatha's patronage and control. Unlike the larger Durban townships of Umlazi and KwaMashu, which had been incorporated into the KwaZulu homeland, Lamontville remained under the authority of the local white administration board, and residents had gone to court to oppose homeland incorporation. By 1984, the level of Inkatha-UDF violence was rising in Lamontville, prompting Oliver Tambo to contact Buthelezi to urge restraint. On September 7, just as the Vaal uprising was about to propel the country into a new period of mass confrontation, Buthelezi replied to Tambo in a letter (reproduced in *Document 65*) protesting his innocence and accusing the ANC of being the aggressor.

As the Vaal revolt widened into a nationwide uprising in 1985, conflict in Natal sharpened. UDF-affiliated youth groups competed with the Inkatha Youth Brigade to recruit members, and fights erupted between armed groups, each trying to make its territory a "no go" area for its rivals. According to UDF partisans, Inkatha burned the shops of Africans and Indians in a campaign to force people to buy at white shops in defiance of the UDF-backed consumer boycott (*Document 72*). Soon after the August 1985 murder in Umlazi of UDF attorney Victoria Mxenge, a Xhosa, Inkatha vigilantes armed with spears and clubs, and accompanied by white SADF soldiers, attacked the mourners at her memorial service, killing 34 (according to the author of *Document 72*) and injuring many others.[86] Hundreds of Durban-area residents, many with no organizational loyalties, became casualties as the conflict spread, while police either failed to respond to appeals for protection or actively assisted Inkatha fighters.

When the records of Botha's State Security Council (SSC) were brought to light in the 1990s, they showed that from at least 1982 the SSC was concerned with fomenting conflict between the ANC, Inkatha, and black consciousness organizations. In September 1985, a national "contra-mobilization" program was approved by the minister of defense, Magnus Malan.[87] Based on a submission from Buthelezi outlining his needs to the director of military intelligence, the SADF recommended support for an Inkatha "paramilitary task force" for use against the UDF and ANC, while warning the SSC that special measures would be required to cover up the illegal actions that were bound to occur as a result. The proposal for what became "Operation Marion" was then cleared "at the highest level"—by the state president—in February 1986.[88] In April, special units of the SADF at a camp in Namibia's Caprivi Strip began a secret six-month training course for 200 Inkatha recruits, about 30 of whom were to constitute a "full-time offensive element."[89] The rest received weapons training but were to specialize in production of Inkatha propaganda, identification and surveillance of targets, and VIP protection.

The war for Natal intensified after the return of the Caprivi trainees in late 1986. Its new epicenter became the townships around Pietermaritzburg, particularly Edendale, which Inkatha aimed to cleanse of UDF supporters. Targets included civic associations, COSATU members, staff and students at the Federal Theological Seminary, and anyone who participated in such UDF campaigns as the "Christmas against the emergency" consumer boycott of 1986 and the stayaway protesting the white election in May 1987. Later in 1987, under the direction of local warlords, Inkatha mounted a new campaign to recruit members, attacking and burning the houses of people who refused to join. In September and October, 143 people died in the Edendale violence and hundreds more fled their homes to escape attacks.[90] In a November speech to business leaders (*Document 96*), COSATU general secretary Jay Naidoo pointed out that lawyers had obtained court interdicts naming the most notorious warlords and ordering Inkatha not to assault union members, but such measures were to little avail when the police refused to act against vigilantes.[91] The Pietermaritzburg Chamber of Commerce made earnest efforts to mediate in the conflict, but a fragile peace accord reached in late 1987 failed to hold. In the meantime, arrests and detentions of UDF and union activists continued apace while police ignored perpetrators of violence on the Inkatha side. The climate of political intolerance remained undiminished, especially after the release from Robben Island in 1988 of ANC veteran Harry Gwala who, in defiance of cautionary advice from Lusaka, threw himself with gusto into the mobilization of counterattacks against Inkatha in the Natal midlands.[92]

In early 1988 Buthelezi went before the KwaZulu Legislative Assembly to deliver his lengthy annual policy speech, from which *Document 98* is excerpted. Venting his frustration at the growing international recognition being accorded to the ANC, and perhaps at the lack of progress toward his personal goals, he unleashed an angry blast at Oliver Tambo for adopting violent tactics against the government and vaunted his own commitment to nonviolence. Later investigations revealed, however, that behind the scenes Buthelezi was bargaining with Malan for more Inkatha fighters to be trained and deployed to "swing the conflict in the townships in his favour."[93] Malan supported this in principle but shared the apprehension of top police officials that it might not be possible indefinitely to cover up the government's complicity in extrajudicial killings. The upshot was an eventual phasing out of Operation Marion and the redeployment of the Caprivi trainees into the KwaZulu police in June 1989. There, as the homeland's minister of police, Buthelezi himself became their top commander. By that time about 1,200 people had died as a result of conflict in Pietermaritzburg alone.[94] A year later, the death toll in Natal was close to 4,000 and the violence was still spreading.[95]

By early 1988 South Africa's long political conflict had reached an impasse, or what some commentators called an "unstable equilibrium."[96] The National Party government, strong when it came to wielding the instruments of repression, was politically weak. The second state of emergency had largely quelled the nationwide uprising of 1984–86 and immobilized the United Democratic Front with detentions, press censorship, and military occupation of the townships. Inkatha's collusion with Pretoria posed a challenge to the ANC and its allies. But the government had not stamped out all internal resistance, let alone created conditions in which blacks would embrace National Party concepts of reform. Collaborationist local councils were defunct or bankrupt in dozens of black townships. Despite a mood of political fatigue, most of the grassroots affiliates of the UDF and non-Charterist groupings like AZAPO remained intact. Popular political aspirations continued to focus on the opposition agenda: the end of apartheid and its "dummy institutions," the unbanning of outlawed organizations, and rapid progress toward equal political, economic, and social rights. Many looked expectantly to the exiled movements to chart a way forward.

Notes

All conversations and interviews cited are with Thomas Karis and/or Gail Gerhart unless otherwise indicated. All conversations, interviews, and documents cited in endnotes can be found in the Karis-Gerhart Collection (hereafter KGC). The organization appearing in parentheses following each document title indicates the location of that document in the Collection. *FPTC* refers to earlier volumes in the *From Protest to Challenge* series.

1. Lest readers assume that the authors have taken the title of this series from the UDF's slogan, we must point out that in this instance life imitated art. Asked during his testimony in the Delmas trial how the UDF chose this slogan, Patrick Lekota replied that it was from the title of "a book written by Karis and Carter...*From Protest to Challenge*" (testimony, *State v. Baleka and others*, p. 16,145).

2. See conversation with Mewa Ramgobin (July 1989).

3. On *State v. Ramgobin* (the Pietermaritzburg treason trial), see Fatima Meer, *Treason Trial—1985* (Durban: Madiba Publications, 1989), and press coverage (KGC: Trials). The other defendants were Albertina Sisulu, Frank Chikane, Cassim Saloojee, Professor Ismail Mohamed, Dr. Essop Jassat, Aubrey Mokoena, Curtis Nkondo, and four SAAWU leaders: Thozamile Gqweta, Sisa Njikelana, Sam Kikine, and Duze Isaac Ngcobo.

4. Conversation with George Bizos of the legal defense team (October 1989), pp. 134–52. Also see Rose Moss, *Shouting at the Crocodile: Popo Molefe, Patrick Lekota and the Freeing of South Africa* (Boston: Beacon Press, 1990).

5. On AZAPO-UDF clashes, see Rian Malan, *My Traitor's Heart* (New York: Atlantic Monthly Press, 1990), pp. 245–64.

6. On this attack by Ama-Afrika, see "Kinikini's Crude Revenge: KwaNobuhle—January 4, 1987," *Monitor,* June 1988 (Human Rights Trust); interviews by Rory Riordan with Mzwandile Maqina (January and November 1987); and *Truth and Reconciliation Commission of South Africa Report* (Cape Town: Truth and Reconciliation Commission, 1998) (*TRC Report*), vol. 2, pp. 302–306.

7. Tom Lodge and Bill Nasson, *All, Here, and Now: Black Politics in South Africa in the 1980s* (New York: Ford Foundation and Foreign Policy Association, 1991), p. 78.

8. Conversation with Johan Maree and Helen Zille (November 1985).

9. Interviews by Mark Swilling with Woza Made (November 1985), Mkhuseli Jack of PEYCO (March 1986), and *amabutho* leaders in the eastern Cape (1986?). Also see Tom Lodge and Mark Swilling, "The Year of the Amabuthu," *Africa Report,* March–April 1986, and Shaun Johnson, "'The Soldiers of Luthuli:' Youth in the Politics of Resistance in South Africa," in Shaun Johnson, ed., *South Africa: No Turning Back* (Bloomington: Indiana University Press, 1989). The generic use of *amabutho* (warriors) in this context should not be confused with the use of "amabutho" to designate groups of anti-UDF Inkatha vigilantes in Natal in the late 1980s and early 1990s.

10. Mark Swilling, "The United Democratic Front and Township Revolt in South Africa," in William Cobbett and Robin Cohen, eds., *Popular Struggles in South Africa* (London: James Currey, 1988), p. 104.

11. Karen Jochelson, "Reform, Repression and Resistance in South Africa: A Case Study of Alexandra Township, 1979–1989," *Journal of Southern African Studies,* vol. 16, no. 1, March 1990, pp. 7–9. Also see Belinda Bozzoli, *Theatres of Struggle and the End of Apartheid* (Johannesburg: Witwatersrand University Press, 2004), and on street committees, Swilling interviews with Made (1985) and *amabutho* leaders (1986?) and the document "Alexandra Action Committee," August 1989 (KGC: AAC).

12. "Building people's power," *Isizwe,* vol. 1, no. 2, March 1986 (KGC: UDF), and Swilling, "The United Democratic Front," p. 104.

13. On Alexandra and Port Elizabeth respectively, see Jochelson, p. 6, and Janet Cherry, "Non-violent Direct Action and Civic Organisation in Port Elizabeth, 1980–1990," draft discussion paper, Witwatersrand University, 1993, pp. 16–17.

14. On people's courts, see Jochelson, pp. 12–13; Lodge and Nasson, pp. 135–40; Jeremy Seekings, "People's Courts and Popular Politics," in Glenn Moss and Ingrid Obery, eds., *South African Review 5* (Johannesburg: Ravan Press, 1989); Georgina Jaffee, "Creating Mass Power: Beyond the Cannon of Mamelodi," *Work in Progress,* no. 41, April 1986 (KGC: Alternative Media); Wilfried Scharf and Baba Ngcokoto, "Images of Punishment in the People's Courts of Cape Town, 1985–7," in N. Chabani Manganyi and Andre du Toit, eds., *Political Violence and the Struggle in South Africa* (Halfway House: Southern Book Publishers, 1990), pp. 341–72; and conversation with Mpho Mashinini (October 1991).

15. During hearings of the Truth and Reconciliation Commission, commissioners criticized the ANC's failure to denounce necklacing earlier. See *TRC Report,* vol. 2, pp. 387–91, and Martin

Meredith, *Coming to Terms: South Africa's Search for Truth* (New York: Public Affairs, 1999), pp. 213–15.

16. See *FPTC,* volume 5, *Document 83.*

17. Jeremy Seekings, *The UDF* (Cape Town: David Philip, 2000), pp. 150–53, and Kirk Helliker et al., "'Asithengi': Recent Consumer Boycotts," in Glenn Moss and Ingrid Obery, eds., *South African Review 4* (Johannesburg: Ravan Press, 1987). On a consumer boycott in one small town (Port Alfred), see conversations with Dallas Sparg (October 1985), Gugile Nkwinti (July 1989), and Nkwinti's brothers (October 1985); also, in Port Elizabeth, conversations with Midlands Chamber of Industry (October 1985) and Henry Fazzie (July 1989).

18. Yunus Carrim, "Pietermaritzburg: Unions Take the Lead," *Work in Progress,* no. 39, October 1985 (Alternative Media).

19. Helliker et al., p. 47.

20. On Kagiso, see Jeremy Seekings, "From 'Quiescence' to 'People's Power': Township Politics in Kagiso, 1985–1986," *Social Dynamics,* vol. 18, no. 1, June 1992.

21. Jeremy Baskin, *Striking Back: A History of Cosatu* (Johannesburg: Ravan Press, 1991), p. 47. On "one industry, one union" (industrial unionism) see *FPTC,* volume 5, chapter 7.

22. Baskin, *p.* 48. For an ANC perspective, see Sipho Pityana, "Trade Union Unity a Matter of Urgency," *Sechaba,* November 1983 (KGC: ANC).

23. Baskin, p. 53.

24. Ibid., pp. 70–75.

25. "The Launch of CUSA-AZACTU," *Weekly Mail,* August 12, 1988, and Baskin, pp. 157–59.

26. Conversations with James Mndaweni (November 1987) and Lybon Mabasa (April 1991).

27. Baskin, pp. 77 and 86.

28. Ibid., pp. 190–92.

29. See Stephen Ellmann, *In a Time of Trouble: Law and Liberty in South Africa's State of Emergency* (Oxford: Clarendon Press, 1992) and John Dugard et al., *The Last Years of Apartheid: Civil Liberties in South Africa* (New York: Ford Foundation and Foreign Policy Association, 1991), pp. 49–54. Soon after F. W. de Klerk succeeded Botha, Chief Justice P. J. Rabie was replaced by a judicial moderate, Justice Michael Corbett.

30. Lodge and Nasson, pp. 87–92; Andrew Boraine, "Upgrading of an Oilspot [Mamelodi]," *Work in Progress,* no. 56/57, November/December 1988 (KGC: Alternative Media); Andrew Boraine, "Security Management Upgrading in the Black Townships," *Transformation,* no. 8, 1989; and Glenda Kruss, "The 1986 State of Emergency in the Western Cape," in Moss and Obery (1987).

31. See Matthew Chaskalson et al., "Rent Boycotts and the Urban Political Economy," in Moss and Obery (1987).

32. Jochelson, pp. 9–11.

33. Swilling, "The United Democratic Front," p. 105.

34. Lodge and Nasson, *p.* 95, citing a September 1986 report by the Community Research Group of the University of the Witwatersrand.

35. Khehla Shubane and Mark Swilling, "Soweto Rent Boycott: the Debate Continues," *Work in Progress,* no. 61, September/October 1989, p. 38 (KGC: Alternative Media).

36. Swilling, "The United Democratic Front," p. 106.

37. *FPTC,* volume 5, chapter 3, has an overview of church politics in the 1970s. Also see Charles Villa-Vicencio, *Trapped in Apartheid: A Socio-Theological History of the English-Speaking Churches* (Cape Town: David Philip, 1988).

38. Les De Villiers, *In Sight of Surrender: The U.S. Sanctions Campaign Against South Africa, 1946–1993* (Westport: Praeger, 1995), *p.* 81.

39. Cedric Mayson, "The Comradeship of Marx and Jesus," *African Communist,* no. 110, 1987, p. 54 (KGC: SACP). Also see Tristan A. Borer, *Challenging the State: Churches as Political Actors in South Africa, 1980–1994* (Notre Dame: University of Notre Dame Press, 1998), and conversation with Mxolisi Victor Mavi (August 1991).

40. See *Document 31* in *FPTC,* volume 5.

41. See chapter 1, note 59. On military chaplains, see Catholic Institute for International Relations, *War and Conscience in South Africa* (London: CIIR, 1982), chapter 4; "Churches and the Military: Avoiding the Issue," *Resister,* no. 41, December 1985/January 1986 (Committee on

South African War Resistance); and "Churches in Uniform—Defending Civilisation?" *Resister,* 55, April 1988.

42. "A Theological Rationale and a Call to Prayer for the End to Unjust Rule," April 16, 1985 (KGC: SACC).

43. "Kairos," a Greek word, means a time when conditions are right for the accomplishment of an important task. Moving away from the black theology of the 1970s, the Kairos Document reflects social analysis based on class, placing it closer to Latin American liberation theology. Conversation with Lebamang Sebidi (July 1989).

44. "Forging Links with Workers," *New Nation,* July 23, 1987. Other important anti-apartheid organizations with religious links included Diakonia (an umbrella organization started in 1976 by Denis Hurley for church activists in Durban), the Young Christian Students and Young Christian Workers (YCS and YCW) (offshoots of a Catholic movement founded in Belgium in the 1920s), and Koinonia (a Pretoria-based organization started in 1983 by a dissenting Dutch Reformed minister, Nico Smith, to promote interracial social contact). Several early COSAS leaders, including Shepard Mati and Lulu Johnson, came out of YCS and YCW. Conversation with Donovan Nadison (July 1989).

45. *FPTC,* volume 5, chapter 3. Grants were made through the WCC's Geneva-based Program to Combat Racism.

46. "Report on the visit of Dr. Allan Boesak [to Maputo]," March 2, 1985 (KGC: ANC).

47. Quoted in John Battersby "South African Churches Back Force by Guerillas," *New York Times,* July 4, 1987. Methodist leader Peter Storey led a minority in the SACC in opposing the Lusaka statement on the grounds that the adoption of violence was not something "compelled" by circumstances but involved willful choice.

48. *Financial Mail,* December 4, 1987.

49. Yunus Carrim, "Changing Ethnic, Racial and National Identities of Indian South Africans in the Transition to a Post-Apartheid South Africa," conference paper, University of the West Indies, Trinidad and Tobago, 1994, p. 7. Carrim says Muslims in 1994 constituted 1.4% of South Africa's population.

50. "The Revolutionary Manifesto of the Oppressed People" [1983?] (KGC: Qibla).

51. *Hansard,* House of Assembly, April 17, 1986, vol. 8, p. 3,590.

52. *Race Relations Survey 1986,* p. 325, and *Race Relations Survey 1987/88,* pp. 241–42.

53. Press coverage on *State v. Zulu and others,* 1986–88 (the Qibla trial) (KGC: Trials).

54. Jonathan Hyslop, "School Student Movements and State Education Policy: 1972–87," in Cobbett and Cohen, pp. 193–94.

55. Ibid., p. 198. Also see Colin Bundy, "'Action, Comrades, Action!' The Politics of Youth-Student Resistance in the Western Cape, 1985," in Wilmot James and Mary Simons, eds., *Class, Caste and Color: A Social and Economic History of the South African Western Cape* (New Brunswick: Transaction Publishers, 1992).

56. Hyslop, p. 199.

57. On the Soweto Parents' Crisis Committee, see interview by Mark Swilling with Mohammed Valli Moosa (early 1986).

58. On school boycotts and the NECC, see Johan Muller, "People's Education and the National Education Crisis Committee," in Moss and Obery (1987); Molefe Tsele, "Education for Democracy—a Case Study: The National Education Co-ordinating Committee (NECC)," in Klaus Nurnberger, ed., *A Democratic Vision for South Africa* (Pietermaritzburg: Encounter Publications, 1991); Helen Zille, "People's Education: The Irony and the Tragedy," *The Black Sash,* vol. 29, no. 4, February 1987 (KGC: Black Sash); and conversation with Khaya Matiso (July 1989).

59. Eric Molobi, "The NECC: Doing Battle with the DET," interviewed by Jon Campbell, *Work in Progress,* no. 45, November/December 1986, p. 19 (KGC: Alternative Media). The NECC tried to avoid ideological rivalries and did not affiliate with the UDF, but most of its leading activists were UDF supporters.

60. Choosing this venue provoked a reaction from Inkatha, which sent several busloads of supporters to assault participants trying to register for the conference. Two attackers were killed.

61. Jon Campbell, "National Education Crisis," *Work in Progress,* no. 45, November/December 1986 (KGC: Alternative Media).

62. Exchanges between the police and Mkhuseli Jack, the author of *Document 82*, are described in "The Dance the Police Don't Want Repeated," *Weekly Mail*, May 16, 1986. The toyi-toyi, invented by guerrillas in Zimbabwe's liberation war, was a regional cultural borrowing, as was use of the popular Portuguese "Viva!" and "a luta continua!" (the struggle continues).

63. Tom Lodge and Mark Swilling, "The Year of the Amabuthu," p. 5. Before his death at age 14, Stompie Seipei was the most publicized of these young warriors (chapter 5 in this volume, and *FPTC*, volume 4 second edition).

64. On gender dynamics in youth politics, see Jeremy Seekings, *Heroes or Villains?, Youth Politics in the 1980s* (Johannesburg: Ravan Press, 1993), pp. 82–85. Psychological effects of violence are discussed in Gill Straker, *Faces in the Revolution* (Cape Town: David Philip, 1992).

65. See Peter Delius, *A Lion Amongst the Cattle: Reconstruction and Resistance in the Northern Transvaal* (Johannesburg: Ravan Press, 1996), chapters 3–5 on historical links and pp. 182ff. on Nchabeleng.

66. Ineke van Kessel, *"Beyond Our Wildest Dreams": The United Democratic Front and the Transformation of South Africa* (Charlottesville: University of Virginia Press, 2000), p. 76. Also see "Northern Transvaal Region Assessment" [1986] (KGC: UDF), and "Rural Report presented to the . . . UDF on 29–30 May 1987" (KGC: UDF).

67. van Kessel, p. 88.

68. Ibid., pp. 128–29.

69. Edwin Ritchken, "Burning the Herbs: Youth Politics and Witches in Lebowa," *Work in Progress*, no. 48, July 1987 (KGC: Alternative Media), and "Leadership and Conflict in Bushbuckridge, 1978–1990," Ph.D. thesis, University of the Witwatersrand, 1995, pp. 321–22.

70. On youth politics, see Seekings, *Heroes or Villains?*, pp. 62–82, and Monique Marks, *Young Warriors* (Johannesburg: Witwatersrand University Press, 2001).

71. David Niddrie, "New National Youth Congress Launched," *Work in Progress*, no. 47, April 1987 (KGC: Alternative Media). On links between Peter Mokaba and the ANC, see interview by Victoria Butler with Jackie Selebi (February 1988).

72. Sources on "the cabal" include Seekings, *The UDF*, pp. 304–309; van Kessel, pp. 63–65; Quraish Patel, "Genesis of the Cabal," *Natal Post*, January 27, 1988; Ashwin Desai, *Arise Ye Coolies: Apartheid and the Indian, 1960–1995* (Johannesburg: Impact Africa, 1996), pp. 59–60; and Kumi Naidoo, "Class, Consciousness and Organisation: Indian Political Resistance in Durban, South Africa, 1979–1996," Ph.D. thesis, Oxford University, 1998, pp. 198–206. Also see conversations with Jerry Coovadia (June 1988), Senti Thobejane (August 1991), Omar Badsha (August 2005), interview by Dhianaraj Chetty with Yunus Mahomed (November 1990), and Anonymous, "Report and Recommendations of Commission on 'the Cabal,'" [by Govan Mbeki], 1988 (KGC: ANC).

73. At the leadership level, activists of different races often developed close working relationships that distanced them from the prejudices of people in the street. The ANC's strongest attraction for members of racial minorities was its commitment to "nonracialism"—racial equality and color blindness—even when some people in its own ranks failed to live up to these ideals. For one African's candid views on race relations in South Africa, see conversation with Mavi (August 1991). For an Indian viewpoint, see Yunus Carrim, "The Natal Indian Congress: Deciding on a New Thrust Forward," *Work in Progress*, no. 52, March 1988 (KGC: Alternative Media).

74. On Freeway House, see conversations with Auret van Heerden (July 1987) and Anriette Esterhuysen (December 1997) and interview by Howard Barrell with Gavin Evans (January 1991). Also see internal reports, "The Present Phase of Mass Democratic Struggle," late 1985? (KGC: ANC), and "Introduction—the current political situation," 1986/87? (KGC: UDF).

75. On the two-stage theory, see chapter 4, note 25.

76. On women's political roles, see Shireen Hassim, *Women's Organizations and Democracy in South Africa* (Scottsville: University of KwaZulu-Natal Press, 2006); Tessa Marcus, "The Women's Question and National Liberation in South Africa," in Maria van Diepen, ed., *The National Question in South Africa* (London: Zed, 1988); Amanda Gouws and Rhoda Kadalie, "Women in the struggle: the past and the future," in Ian Liebenberg et al., eds., *The Long March* (Pretoria: HAUM, 1994); and conversations with Ivy Gcina (July 1989), Amanda Kwadi (July 1989), and Nomboniso Gasa (March 2004).

77. "True Liberation Means the Liberation of Women," *New Nation,* August 19, 1987.
78. Baskin, pp. 252–53.
79. Ibid., pp. 171–81.
80. Eugene de Kock, *A Long Night's Damage* (Saxonwold: Contra Press, 1998), pp. 143–44; *TRC Report,* vol. 2, pp. 289–91; and Baskin, chapter 11.
81. Yunus Carrim, "COSATU: Towards Disciplined Alliances," *Work in Progress,* no. 49, September 1987, p. 11 (KGC: Alternative Media).
82. Mayekiso, a trade unionist and community leader in Johannesburg's Alexandra township, was accused with Obed Bapela and three others (in *State v. Mayekiso*) of conspiring to set up yard, street, and block committees, as well as people's courts, with a view to "seizing power" in Alexandra and rendering the area "ungovernable."
83. The critique of the ANC as a movement not committed to working-class interests or socialism was echoed by the Marxist Workers' Tendency, by the New Unity Movement, and in the academic writings of foreign left critics including Dale McKinley and Robert Fatton. This critique was rejected by ANC prisoners on Robben Island in *Document 100,* and by Thabo Mbeki in "The Fatton Thesis: A Rejoinder," *Canadian Journal of African Studies,* vol. 18, no. 3, 1984. See chapter 4, note 25.
84. Baskin, p. 227. Baskin is the main source for this account of NUM's 1987 strike.
85. Conversation with Walter Felgate (February 1998), and "Conditioning Inkatha for Violence," Felgate's submission to the TRC, November 1997 (KGC: Inkatha). For a positive view of Inkatha in this period, see conversation with Oscar Dhlomo and Frank Mdlalose (February 1987).
86. *The Sowetan,* August 16, 1985, cited in Anthea Jeffery, *The Natal Story: 16 Years of Conflict* (Johannesburg: SAIRR, 1997), p. 52, says "about 17" were killed and "more than a hundred" injured. The *TRC Report,* vol. 2, p. 461, says 14 died, but vol. 3, p. 233, says 17. *Document 128* says 36 died. The press might have been prevented from reporting on the actions of the security forces present during the attack. See Fatima Meer, *Unrest in Natal—August 1985* (Durban: Institute for Black Research, 1985), pp. 12–14, for another account of this episode.
87. *TRC Report,* vol. 2, p. 299.
88. "Submission to the Truth and Reconciliation Commission: the Caprivi Trainees" (Varney Report), August 4, 1997, pp. 12–17 (authors' copy). The report notes that F. W. de Klerk was a member of the State Security Council at this time.
89. Ibid., p. 18.
90. Baskin, pp. 332–35.
91. Police actively engaged in destroying evidence and helping culprits to disappear according to the Varney Report, p. 25, and Thula Bopela and Daluxolo Luthuli, *Umkhonto we Sizwe* (Alberton: Galago Publishing, 2005), p. 246.
92. Padraig O'Malley, *Shades of Difference: Mac Maharaj and the Struggle for South Africa* (New York: Viking, 2007), pp. 285–87.
93. Varney Report, pp. 25–30.
94. "The Role of the Police in Vigilante Violence in the Pietermaritzburg Area," April 7, 1989 (KGC: COSATU/UDF).
95. Lodge and Nasson, p. 104. Altogether 5,707 deaths from political violence countrywide in the period 1984–89 were reported to the TRC, according to the *TRC Report,* vol. 2, p. 389. Inkatha claimed over 400 of its leaders had been killed by ANC/MK/UDF members, but the TRC was able to verify only 76 of these deaths, according to the *TRC Report,* vol. 2, pp. 343–44. Members of the public reported approximately 14,000 political murders which had taken place over the full period covered by the TRC (March 1960 to December 1993). Of those the commission was able to investigate, it attributed the largest number (about 4,500) to Inkatha, the second highest (about 2,600) to the South African Police, and the third highest (about 1,300) to the ANC. Tom Lodge, *Politics in South Africa: From Mandela to Mbeki* (Bloomington: Indiana University Press, 2003), *p.* 192. On the ANC's role in the Natal violence see O'Malley, pp. 292–99, and Jeffery, chapter 4.
96. This phrase appears to have first been used in Harold Wolpe, *Race, Class and the Apartheid State* (London: James Currey, 1988), p. 105.

4. Exile and Underground Politics, 1980–1988

As the African National Congress and Pan Africanist Congress began their third decade in exile, they drew hope from widening ideological divisions inside the citadels of Afrikaner power and from South Africa's growing international isolation. At the same time, it was discouraging that their own efforts to strengthen links with political resistance inside the country and inflict military blows on the regime had registered so little progress. Unavoidably, much of exile politics was reactive: deploring Pretoria's latest maneuvers, condemning Western complicity in apartheid's evils, applauding from the sidelines each heroic new act by striking workers or rebellious students at home. For most of those involved in exile politics, life was a waiting game in which obscure functionaries drafted propaganda flyers and conference speeches in dingy offices, waited for planes in faraway airports, and struggled with boredom, homesickness, and family worries.[1] For movement leaders the challenges of exile were manifold: to win support, boost morale, build efficient administrative and military organizations, then somehow use these to topple the apartheid regime. During 20 years in exile, the Pan Africanist Congress had failed to rise to these arduous challenges, although it continued through the 1980s to try to pull itself together and improve its performance. In contrast, the ANC grew in international esteem from 1980 onward, capitalizing on the resurgence of resistance inside South Africa, although its own role in fomenting or guiding internal action was often marginal. This chapter will focus primarily on the ANC's record and the features of its organization, leadership, ideology, and political program that by the end of the decade were to elevate it to the status of a government-in-waiting.

The African National Congress, 1980–1983

When a journalist from the *New York Times* referred to the ANC in 1983 as "one of the world's least successful liberation movements," he was basing his assessment on final outcomes, not on progress shown.[2] Relative to its inauspicious beginnings in the early 1960s as a small revolutionary organization occupying a few rented rooms in London and Dar es Salaam, the exiled ANC in 20 years had vastly expanded in size and complexity. Its budget had grown from a few thousand dollars a year to three quarters of a million dollars in 1972 and $56 million in 1982, not including military operations or funds raised and passed on secretly to allied organizations inside South Africa.[3] By the early 1980s it was a major source of support for over 9,000 members,[4] operated diplomatic missions in 32 countries on five continents, had arranged scholarships for more than a thousand refugee students scattered around the world, and owned a fleet of more than 100 vehicles. It operated a farm in Zambia, and a school, the Solomon Mahlangu Freedom College (SOMAFCO), at Mazimbu near Morogoro in Tanzania. It maintained the large rural settlement of Dakawa, also near Morogoro, and across the continent it trained its guerrilla recruits in a shifting array of military camps dotted across northwestern Angola.[5] It employed mechanics, teachers, and doctors, as well as highly trained specialists in counterintelligence, sabotage, and other aspects of unconventional warfare.

The ANC's operations in the 1980s were centered in Lusaka, where the organization occupied a dozen or so modest buildings scattered across the city, including a headquarters whose run-down appearance suggested not so much neglect as a deliberate attempt to blend in with the prevailing decay of the Zambian capital. In the early 1980s, the majority of ANC National Executive Committee (NEC) members resided in Lusaka, but several lived in the capitals of other frontline states where they doubled as members of so-called senior organs that coordinated military and political work. The senior organs, located in Mozambique, Botswana, Lesotho, and London, fell under an umbrella body, the Revolutionary Council, which had been established after the ANC's 1969 consultative conference in Morogoro to oversee the ANC's guerrilla army, Umkhonto we Sizwe (MK) ("spear of the nation"), and the development of underground networks inside South Africa. The Revolutionary Council reported to the NEC, with which its membership overlapped heavily. Since the Revolutionary Council rarely met, MK's day-to-day management was overseen by its military headquarters, located in Lusaka. MK's operations in Angola were run by a regional command based in Luanda that reported to military headquarters. In between NEC meetings, which were sometimes many months apart, decisions were made by the National Working Committee, an NEC subcommittee which was the organization's most concentrated locus of power. Regional committees of active members in various ANC centers (London, Dar es Salaam, Luanda, and Maseru, for example) represented a lower level of consensus building and information sharing. In Lusaka, the offices of the president, secretary general, and treasurer general oversaw all specialized departments of the organization, which from the early 1980s included international affairs, education, health, women, youth, manpower development, and arts and culture (under the secretary general, Alfred Nzo); finance, logistics/transport, farming and other income projects, and welfare (under the treasurer general, Thomas Nkobi); and information/publicity, intelligence/security, and MK special operations (under the president, Oliver Tambo).

Much of the ANC's rising popularity inside South Africa in the early 1980s was the result of MK's campaign of "armed propaganda." ANC leaders on a study tour of Vietnam in late 1978 had taken to heart the advice of Vietnamese generals that military operations should always be designed to attract political support. MK's "special operations" unit, established in 1979, scored its first propaganda victory in June 1980 with a spectacular attack on fuel storage tanks at Sasolburg and Secunda, centers of South Africa's strategic oil-from-coal industry. Damage was estimated at over $7 million (R 5.8 million) and the attacks drew media attention around the world.[6] This was followed in 1981 by an attack with rocket launchers on Voortrekkerhoogte, an army base near Pretoria. A week before Christmas in 1982, a series of four explosions rocked Cape Town's newly constructed Koeberg nuclear power station, setting back its opening by a year at an estimated cost of $440 million (R 51 million). In all three cases the attackers escaped and no deaths were caused.[7]

Attacks by other units of MK also made an impact on the consciousness of the public, both black and white. In January 1980, three MK guerrillas took 25 customers hostage for seven hours at a bank in the white Silverton section of Pretoria, making demands that included the release of Nelson Mandela. When police stormed the bank, all three guerrillas were killed. Black Pretoria turned their burials into celebratory occasions attended by thousands of mourners. Two months later, guerrillas using rocket-launched grenades attacked a police station in Booysens, a white suburb of Johannesburg. Less-publicized attacks occurred with increasing frequency into the mid-1980s, rising from 45 in 1984 to 235 in 1987.[8] Targets included economic installations, such as rail lines and power stations, and politically symbolic buildings, such as police stations and courts. Attacks were also directed at government personnel who were seen as collaborators, including black policemen and homeland and community council officials, dozens of whom were killed or injured or had their homes fire bombed.[9] During the 1980s over 800 MK cadres were killed or captured in these attacks or in skirmishes with the police.[10] After entering South Africa, a high proportion of guerrillas abandoned their missions and became "passive deserters," either because of fear, botched organizational arrangements or a decision to simply lie low until conditions improved.[11] What the black public saw, however, was the dedication and daring of those whose attacks succeeded, or who died in gun battles with police, or, most often, those who were captured and brought to trial in cases that were covered in the press.

Behind its gratifying but exaggerated public image as a growing military force, the ANC in the early 1980s waged an ongoing struggle to build an efficient administrative apparatus that could service and utilize its expanding exile membership. The 1976–77 Soweto uprising had propelled four to five thousand new recruits into the ANC's ranks, more than doubling its previous active membership. Military training facilities had expanded, and so had the ANC's non-military bureaucracy. Increased world attention after Soweto had brought invitations from more countries to open ANC offices. Most importantly, the independence of Mozambique in 1975 and Zimbabwe in 1980 had created crucial new opportunities to shift the management of the movement's military operations to "forward areas" closer to home. Adaptation to these favorable new conditions was a continuing process, and it called for resources far exceeding those immediately available. In time, material resources were forthcoming from international supporters; much more serious was the shortfall in human resources.

The ANC's expansion in size had not been matched by an expansion of skills. Nearly all the Soweto generation recruits were in their late teens or their twenties; few had work experience, and most had not completed high school. Among older exiles, leadership was heavily concentrated in the hands of people who had left South Africa in the early 1960s, few of whom at the time of their departure had any administrative experience relevant to the running of a large and complex organization. Political refugees in the 1960s who had university degrees, or who acquired degrees in their early years of exile, normally made politics a spare-time activity and gravitated to more lucrative occupations. Between the mid-1960s and mid-1970s, although a handful of experienced ANC leaders were released from prison and made their way into exile to resume their political careers, the total outflow of political refugees from South Africa markedly subsided. Compounded together, these realities meant that the ANC entered the 1980s with serious handicaps and inefficiencies resulting from weak administration. These inefficiencies in turn were a constant catalyst to frustration and dissent among lower- and mid-level cadres, who in their expanded numbers then posed an ever-present threat to the organization's internal stability and external image.

ANC president Oliver Tambo had no illusions about the organization's administrative deficiencies, and tried to push younger members with administrative talent up the organization's bureaucratic ladders. He spoke frankly of the need for more staff training, improved planning, better reporting and coordination between departments, and tighter control over financial procedures.[12] Ultimately, however, the organization could be no stronger than the core group of its established leaders, which in the early 1980s was still dominated by Tambo's fellow exiles of the 1960s. In their fifties or sixties by the early 1980s, they had become accustomed to running the ANC in their own way. Although they were willing at times to pay lip service to the need for improved management (*Document 104*), in the end they lacked the ability or motivation to make necessary changes, especially where this might have brought in younger people who would expose their own shortcomings. Tambo's outstanding abilities, struggle credentials, and moral authority meant that he never faced credible rivals for the ANC's top position. At the NEC level, however, it was always possible that leadership shake-ups might result in splits and factions in the organization, as they had in the 1970s with the Makiwane eight.[13] This threat led Tambo to value stability above efficiency in the organization's leadership, despite the heavy cost over the 1980s in missed opportunities, disgruntlement in the lower ranks, and an organizational bias toward yes-men who owed their positions in the ANC bureaucracy less to merit than to clientelistic loyalty.[14]

Politically, the challenges facing the ANC in the early 1980s differed little from those in the previous two decades. No matter how ramshackle the vessel had become administratively, getting and keeping all passengers on board politically was still the top priority. Besides preventing schisms, this also meant doing everything possible to stunt the growth of rival movements, all with a view to establishing the ANC as the single viable alternative to the apartheid government. Second in importance was the challenge of formulating and propagating policies that could attract material and political support to the ANC from the widest possible range of constituencies inside South Africa and externally. Last, and most difficult, was the challenge of building durable and integrated underground networks of ANC leadership inside South Africa. Only if this could be achieved would the ANC be able to bring maximum pressure on the apartheid system from within and position itself optimally for the assumption of power when the moment of the system's eventual collapse arrived.

Containing the growth of rivals was a perennial concern of the ANC. The PAC, although still recognized by the Organization of African Unity (OAU) and the United Nations, was too occupied with holding its fractious external machinery together during most of the decade to score significant propaganda successes inside South Africa. Briefly more threatening to the ANC were efforts by remnants of the black consciousness movement in exile to regroup at a conference convened in London in April 1980.[15] While some black consciousness exiles believed it was their duty to work for a united front of all South African political groups, others accepted the reality of irreconcilable antagonisms between the ANC and the PAC and hoped to create a third liberation organization that could claim superior legitimacy based on its more recent contact with home. Barney Pityana, the most prominent of the black consciousness exiles, had discarded both these views by 1980 and believed the best option was for the movement to disband and encourage its adherents to join the established organizations. This view did not prevail at the 1980 conference, however, where some 54 delegates were present.[16] Instead, advocates of forming a new organization emerged in the majority, their numbers swelled by a group of leftist critics of the ANC who attacked Pityana and other ANC partisans as "bourgeois nationalists." Pityana, Ben Khoapa, and Harry Nengwekhulu declined to associate with the resulting new Black Consciousness Movement of Azania (BCMA), and without the involvement of these Biko-era veterans the BCMA soon became a minor splinter group, posing, like the PAC, no immediate challenge to the ANC's dominant position in exile politics.[17]

Most threatening to the ANC by 1980 was its increasingly open rivalry with Zulu Chief Mangosuthu Gatsha Buthelezi and his Inkatha movement. Between Inkatha's founding in 1975 and its meeting with the ANC in London in October 1979, the ANC's aim had been to maintain cordial relations in the hope that Buthelezi would continue to popularize the ANC's symbols and traditions and would tacitly permit MK fighters to enter South Africa through the northern districts of KwaZulu that bordered on Swaziland and southern Mozambique.[18] Buthelezi, interested in using other organizations rather than being used by them, and worried by the post-Soweto surge in the ANC's popularity, had set Inkatha by 1980 on a new path which he hoped would eventually enable it to supplant the ANC. The ANC's response, reluctant at first but increasingly venomous, was to attack Buthelezi as a tool of Pretoria (*Document 112,* a 1983 broadcast on the ANC's Radio Freedom, reflected this new approach) and to denounce his glorification of tribal identity as a retrograde practice utterly at odds with the broad South African nationalism championed by the ANC.[19]

The ANC's second major political task, that of formulating and propagating a coherent and appealing set of fundamental policies, had been simplified for many years by the existence of the Freedom Charter of 1955.[20] Many of the questions asked by new or prospective recruits to the ANC could be answered by reference to this resilient document which laid out a vision of a transformed post-apartheid society in which race would no longer determine social position, and the state would guarantee the provision of social services to all on an equal basis. From the late 1970s onward, apart from MK's "armed propaganda," popularizing the Charter had been the ANC's most successful political activity inside South Africa. In the 1980s, a number of policy debates centered on refinements or applications of ideas contained in the Charter.

One such debate revolved around the issue of "open membership." Should members of all races have completely equal status in the ANC, as implied in the Charter, or should leadership positions be reserved for Africans only, in order to preserve the organization's traditional identification with the struggle of the African people? For a combination of pragmatic and ideological reasons, most of the ANC's top leaders favored removing all racial restrictions on membership in the NEC. At the rank-and-file level, however, and among Africans inside South Africa, opposition to non-African leadership was assumed to be substantial. A report on a discussion of open membership by SOMAFCO students in 1982 (*Document 107*) reviews the debate against the background of the leadership's known preferences.

Another debate centered on the growing demands of women. To combat the stubbornly patriarchal culture that dominated the ANC's everyday life, Tambo favored giving new emphasis to the Charter's principle of gender equality. Progress was painfully slow, however. In 30 years of exile, only 4 of the 54 people who served on the ANC National Executive Committee were women.[21] Only among students at SOMAFCO, according to one member's assessment in 1982 (*Document 109*), had the sexist attitudes of men begun to erode; elsewhere in the organization they persisted, she lamented, firmly reinforced by the habitual submissiveness of most African women. Rank-and-file members frequently complained that male leaders used their positions to entrap and exploit women in the organization. Women in MK complained that they were not assigned combat roles or leadership positions even though their training was identical to that of men. Many post-1976 female recruits resented the dominance of conservative older women in the ANC's Women's Section for whom political participation primarily meant providing support services for men. Although the ANC's 1985 consultative conference in Zambia devoted a session to what was called "The Women's Question" (*Document 122*), its findings led to no plan of action. Even in the *African Communist,* the Communist Party's quarterly journal, doctrinally "correct" writers argued that feminism was a reformist ideology that distracted women from the higher goals of revolution and socialism.[22] Late in the decade younger women in exile were still pressing for an end to gender discrimination, drawing inspiration from the international feminist movement that by then was also spilling over into new initiatives inside South Africa (*Document 145*).[23]

Meanwhile, members of the ANC who were also South African Communist Party (SACP) members debated among themselves how far the ANC should go in advocating the goals of "scientific" socialism implied in the Freedom Charter's call for the nationalization of mines, banks, and monopoly industries. Were the aims of the ANC and the SACP not essentially the same? This was a fundamental policy question that ANC prisoners on Robben Island had argued about for years. These prison debates were summarized by Ahmed Kathrada in a handwritten document, later confiscated by prison authorities, called "*Inqindi* and Marxism" (*Document 100*).[24] Their consensus, said to have displeased left ideologues like Harry Gwala and Govan Mbeki, was that the ANC must firmly maintain its identity as a broad African nationalist movement, even though many of its members also embraced a belief in socialism.[25] The SACP itself adhered to a similar position, formulated by Michael Harmel in 1962, that rested on a theory of two-stage change: first the overthrow of white minority rule ("colonialism of a special type"), which would be removed in a "national democratic revolution" guided by African nationalist principles, then a transition to socialism by democratic means.[26] Meanwhile, many Marxists argued in the 1980s that the ANC should propagate socialist ideas as a way of laying the foundations for a future socialist order. A far-left faction calling itself the Marxist Workers' Tendency of the ANC (MWT) opposed the SACP's two-stage principle altogether and advocated an ideology derived from Leon Trotsky: immediate commitment to a worker-led revolution that would dismantle capitalism in South Africa as part of an inevitable world transition to communism (*Document 106*). Some ANC members took little interest in these ideological debates, but others avidly discussed the polemical articles alluding to such questions in the *African Communist,* the

MWT's *Inqaba ya Basebenzi,* and occasionally *Sechaba,* the ANC's monthly propaganda organ printed in East Germany and edited through the 1980s by SACP member Francis Meli.[27]

In addition to these debates about issues of fundamental principle, innumerable mundane problems also arose concerning short- or medium-term tactics. For example, amid the welter of administrative matters discussed in a December 1981 NEC memorandum (*Document 104*), two typical issues of this type are mentioned: what position to take toward church activists such as the "Beyers Naudé group" who wished to support the ANC, and how to handle a white draft-resister group (South African Military Refugee Aid Fund, or SAMRAF) wanting to do the same. Decisions on such questions were arrived at by consensus after discussions at the level of the NEC or the National Working Committee, or were delegated to the regional senior organs or to individual departments. Controversial questions such as open membership, where the active support of the rank-and-file members was sought, were thrown open for discussion in meetings of members at the regional level. In addition, decisions on a wide range of issues both political and administrative were referred to internal commissions specially appointed by the NEC. After investigation and discussion, the recommendations of these commissions would be reported to the NEC, which would accept, reject, or shelve them.[28] Significantly, as *Document 104* implies, the making of a policy decision in no way guaranteed its implementation. As in most bureaucracies, this was especially problematic if a decision ran strongly against the personal interests, inclinations, or convenience of the particular official charged with putting it into effect (for example, a tribal chauvinist told to root out tribal favoritism in his unit or department). Given the lack of resolve in the top echelons of the organization, delays, neglect, and non-compliance were just as likely to affect the carrying out of big decisions as of small ones.

Building the Underground

With the resurgence of the ANC's popularity inside South Africa in the early 1980s, it seemed realistic for the organization to step up the construction of networks of underground leadership that could gradually assume responsibility for on-the-spot planning and carrying out of ANC strategy and tactics from inside South Africa. The strategic review following the 1978 tour of Vietnam had produced an unambiguous policy in this regard: internal political work should take precedence over military action until underground construction had created a secure foundation for the safe recruiting, sheltering, and provisioning of fighters without undue reliance on external lines of supply and communication. Reports in September 1980 indicated there were then approximately 200 political cadres inside the country, but that no internal system yet existed to connect them into organized pyramids of command.[29] Instead, each individual or small cell maintained separate links with contacts in the frontline states. Hundreds, later thousands, of other political activists had no actual contact with the ANC but regarded themselves as unofficial members and tried in their community or organizational work to follow what they believed to be ANC policies and strategies.

Building coordinated networks in these circumstances called for slow and patient screening and training of cadres under the supervision of senior leaders. The experience of Chris Hani's effective underground units working out of Lesotho and the Transkei in the late 1970s showed that with effort the goal was potentially achievable.[30] Careful selection of personnel was crucial. Hard lessons had been learned in the late 1970s when overreliance on released ANC prisoners to carry out underground construction had resulted in the rearrest of Harry Gwala, Joe Mati, Martin Ramokgadi, Joe Gqabi, Elijah Loza, and other ANC figures who were under constant police surveillance. The assassination of Natal underground leader and former prisoner Griffiths Mxenge in November 1981 (*Document 178*) provided further warning that the security forces would stop at nothing to thwart the ANC's progress.

In early 1983 ANC headquarters in Lusaka replaced the ineffectual Revolutionary Council with a new body, the Politico-Military Council (PMC). The PMC was meant to correct the Revolutionary Council's overconcentration on military matters and to balance and coordinate political and military work. Regional PMCs replaced the senior organs in the front line states with the same goal. Each regional PMC was to concentrate on creating area political committees (APCs) in the portions of South Africa to which it was contiguous. By mid-1985, the PMC was able to report that the number of underground political cadres had increased to more than 500 (about 330 in cells averaging three members each, and 178 individual operatives); however, a mere two APCs had been created, neither of which was functioning well.[31] "Under a whole set of objective and subjective conditions, this task has been neglected," the report notes glumly, "even though there is an awareness of the danger that events may outstrip us." This awareness reflected a longstanding belief, all the more credible in the midst of the 1984–86 uprising, that although a prolonged war of attrition was likely, there was always a chance that the government might collapse in some swift and unanticipated way, a reversal of fortune for which the ANC should at all times be prepared.[32]

The "objective and subjective conditions" that explained the failure to create an effective underground were complex. The efficiency and ruthlessness of the security police was the most obvious reason. Dozens of trials over the course of the decade resulted in ANC political operatives being given long terms of imprisonment; others were detained, sometimes for many months, without being brought to trial.[33] Torture of detainees to extract information was routine, and led in February 1982 to the first death, highly publicized, of a white detainee, Dr. Neil Aggett, a trade union activist suspected of ANC activity. Other obstacles, psychological and practical, were of the ANC's own making. Leadership structures in the frontline states were uncoordinated and often inefficient. Promising political recruits were routinely poached by MK. Indian organizers in Natal claimed it was too difficult to find African recruits who could work with them at the APC level. Leadership in Lusaka was overstretched, inept, or bypassed by MK operatives who claimed they could not postpone their own program of cross-border attacks in order to wait for the development of proper underground reception structures that would make it possible for their fighters to be permanently based inside the country. Coordination of political and military administrations proved unworkable on any sustained basis, either inside the country or in Lusaka and the frontline states.[34]

The founding of the United Democratic Front in 1983 opened up vast new opportunities for strengthening the ANC politically inside South Africa. ANC sympathizers were drawn into UDF affiliates, and underground ANC members inside the UDF were well placed to influence its policies, principles, and symbols and to align them with those of the ANC. To safeguard the legality of the UDF, and to ensure that it was able to attract support from people who were not necessarily ANC partisans, Lusaka instructed its underground members (which included UDF secretary general Popo Molefe) not to press aggressively for open identification of the UDF with the ANC. The ANC's role was to provide strategic and tactical advice, said an ANC briefing in October 1983 (*Document 111*), not to issue directives or exercise control of the UDF. But neither was the ANC to abdicate all initiative in mass mobilization to the UDF; rather it needed to address the masses directly through propaganda that exhorted them to look to the ANC itself for revolutionary leadership—a call which the UDF as a legal organization could not make. As time went on, therefore, the result was a three-track approach: an ANC which approached mass mobilization through MK's "armed propaganda," through aboveground mass organization in the UDF, and directly through the work of its own underground, albeit an underground that only began to become coordinated inside South Africa in late 1988 through the efforts of Mac Maharaj.

Their inability to transfer any of the movement's operational leadership inside the country before 1988 did not prevent MK's external leaders from trying to improve their military performance as the ANC's popularity reached new heights in the early 1980s. Great hopes had been invested in MK at its inception 20 years earlier; it was to advance, like other guerrilla movements in the third world, from sabotage to guerrilla warfare, then to a successful full-scale war of national liberation. With the emergence of a large black industrial working class in the 1960s and 1970s, and especially after the Durban strikes of 1973, a vision of urban revolution following the Russian model gained ground in the imaginations of MK personnel who had received their military training in the Soviet bloc. The launching of the UDF seemed to create even more favorable conditions for revolutionary mass mobilization. Within a few months of the UDF's founding, Joe Slovo, MK's principal strategist, produced a discussion paper called "Planning for People's War" (*Document 113*). The paper was circulated for comments to PMC members and MK commanders, and reviewed again prior to the ANC's conference at Kabwe in June 1985. In the "narrow" sense, the paper declared, it was true that the ANC had not succeeded in building internal "revolutionary bases" in the form of APCs. But in the "broad" sense, the ANC's political base had widened immeasurably with the growth of trade unions and the UDF. In light of these advances, Slovo argued, it was time for MK to move beyond "armed propaganda" to the stage of "people's war," a new phase in which "a liberation army becomes rooted amongst the people who progressively participate actively in the armed struggle both politically and militarily, including the possibility of engaging in partial or general insurrections."

"Planning for People's War" was a romantic medley of daring themes: guerrilla warfare from secret rural bases (a goal that had perpetually eluded MK); urban commando units using weapons from secret caches and commanded by infiltrated MK soldiers; combat units recruited, trained, and armed entirely from internal sources; soldiers and policemen recruited from within government security forces to cause subversion and confusion; continued "pot boiling" sabotage attacks to impress MK's admirers and keep whites on edge; political and military operations aimed at winning over bantustan populations; stepped-up efforts to kill enemy security personnel; and heightened awareness that the situation had within it "the seeds of sudden transformation opening up the possibility of combined military and political assault on the enemy and leading to its overthrow by such combined insurrectionary forces." "Imagine the potential," wrote Slovo, if during the Soweto uprising "there had been an organized underground presence capable of giving direction and supplying a minimum of simple weaponry to quickly organized para-military units." As events transpired, an uprising on a larger scale than Soweto exploded less than a year later (chapter 2), but when it did, an ANC underground capable of mounting a coordinated response was still not in place. In the meantime, to make matters worse, a major new development was about to disrupt the forward momentum of MK.

Setback: The Nkomati Accord

The ANC's political fortunes depended heavily on the goodwill of the independent states in the southern African region. Countries on the region's outer perimeter—Zambia, Tanzania, and Angola—hosted the ANC's headquarters and its educational and military training facilities. To the south of this perimeter lay the six "frontline" countries bordering directly on South Africa. Of these six, South West Africa (later Namibia) was ruled directly by Pretoria until 1990. A second, Zimbabwe, which became independent in April 1980, adopted a reserved attitude to the ANC because of its historical alliance with Joshua Nkomo's Zimbabwe African People's Union (ZAPU), long a rival of Robert Mugabe's ruling party, the Zimbabwe African National Union (ZANU).[35] Swaziland, well disposed toward the ANC during the life of King Sobhuza II, became increasingly hostile after his death in 1982, particularly since it had by then become evident that the great majority of MK saboteurs were entering South Africa from Mozambique, using Swaziland as a corridor into Natal and the eastern Transvaal.[36] The governments of Botswana and Lesotho were sympathetic to the ANC, but refused to allow their territories to be used as military sanctuaries or staging areas for attacks on South Africa. Both, however, observed international conventions for the protection of refugees, and this created a convenient camouflage under which MK personnel could surreptitiously pass in and out of South Africa on military missions. A report by a guerrilla returning to Botswana from an unsuccessful mission (*Document 142*) provides one example of this.

The sixth border state, Mozambique, under Samora Machel's FRELIMO government, was the ANC's firmest ally. Like the ANC, FRELIMO was indebted to the Soviet bloc for military and diplomatic support. Both adhered to a nonracialism that was more ideologically rooted than the amorphous, if no less deeply felt, anti-apartheid sentiment of other black-ruled states in the region. FRELIMO, moreover, had fought a 14-year war for independence and believed in the efficacy of military solutions. With Mozambique's consent, the ANC by 1980 had made Maputo the command center for MK's campaign of attacks, with the proviso that guerrillas pass through Swaziland and not directly across Mozambique's borders with South Africa.

The Botha government, likewise inclined to military solutions, began in 1981 to test the capacity of the ANC and its host countries to withstand counterattack. In January, a convoy of South African Defence Force (SADF) vehicles crossed the Mozambique border, drove 40 miles (64 kilometers) to the Maputo suburb of Matola, and bombarded three ANC houses in a predawn raid, killing what was later officially reported as 11 ANC members and seizing a quantity of documents and equipment. Chastened by the inadequacy of their security arrangements, and stunned by the death in the raid of Montso "Obadi" Mokgabudi, third in command of MK's special operations unit, guerilla leaders tried to improve safety precautions and instill greater discipline in cadres who were sometimes dangerously careless or unruly (*Document 101*).[37] Kidnapping and assassination of ANC members in the frontline states, including the murders of Joe Gqabi in Harare in 1981 and Ruth First in Maputo in 1982, became a growing threat. SADF units in Namibia crossed into northern Botswana at will, and South African security agents entered neighboring countries freely, in Zimbabwe and Swaziland sometimes with the connivance of allies in the local security establishments. In Maseru, Lesotho, another devastating raid on ANC houses by the SADF left 42 people dead in December 1982. An ANC exile who survived the attack provides an eyewitness account in *Document 108*.

Pretoria employed an array of tactics for destabilizing the frontline states. These included economic sanctions and threats aimed at pressuring governments to expel the ANC from their territories. In Angola, Lesotho, Zimbabwe, and Mozambique, South Africa sponsored rebel movements fighting against the incumbent governments. The most tenacious of these, and the ones most heavily subsidized by Pretoria, were Jonas Savimbi's UNITA in Angola and Mozambique's RENAMO. Established in the 1970s by the Ian Smith regime in Rhodesia as a mercenary force to counteract Mozambique's support for ZANU, RENAMO turned to South Africa for sponsorship at the time of Zimbabwe's independence. FRELIMO, already faced with declining popular support in rural areas and struggling unsuccessfully to centralize control over a faltering economy, was ill equipped to dispose of RENAMO militarily. By 1982, these conditions, compounded by a severe drought and the inadequacies of Soviet aid, had brought Machel's government to the point of near collapse. Turning to Western countries for assistance, he found a surprisingly sympathetic response, but it came with conditions, particularly from Britain and the United States: Mozambique had to find a way to accommodate South Africa's demands for a non-aggression pact. These demands, shaped and refined over more than a year of meetings between Mozambican and South African officials, resulted in the signing on March 16, 1984, of the Nkomati Accord, a treaty pledging that Mozambique would end its support for the operations of MK if South Africa would cease its support for RENAMO.[38]

The ANC's close relationship with Mozambican leaders had led Tambo, Slovo, and others to discount media reports in early 1983 that FRELIMO was moving toward a deal with Pretoria. FRELIMO leaders on their part were reluctant to confront the ANC with bad news, and waited until late January 1984 before inviting Tambo and Nzo to Maputo to brief them officially on the impending treaty. The notes on a joint meeting of the ANC's national executive and the PMC on January 25 reflect the anger and shock of the ANC's leadership, as well as their lack of preparation for the shutting down of their most important military sanctuary (*Document 114*). In a "fraternal message" to FRELIMO the following week, the ANC complained that Mozambique had withheld information vital to MK's survival, and appealed to Machel to reconsider his decision and place his country once more in the vanguard of worldwide anti-imperialism.[39]

All entreaties were in vain, however, and in mid-March the ANC found itself forced to reduce its presence in Mozambique to a mere diplomatic mission with a maximum staff of ten. Over the following weeks, several hundred South African civilians and untrained recruits left Mozambique for Tanzania, while two hundred or more trained MK cadres slipped into Swaziland or through Swaziland into South Africa. Many had not completed preparations for their missions, and their failure rates were high. During several chaotic months in Swaziland, between 80 and 100 fighters were rounded up and deported, several died in gun battles with Swazi police, some were jailed for weapons possession, and four were abducted by South African agents with apparent Swazi complicity. The Swazi prime minister, who revealed in mid-April that Swaziland had also signed a non-aggression pact with South Africa, secretly, in February 1982, assumed a position of unprecedented hostility toward the ANC, calling its fighters "foreign criminals." Despite this onslaught, according to MK intelligence chief Ronnie Kasrils, more than 150 guerrillas managed to enter South Africa in the wake of Nkomati,[40] with the result that attack rates surged, temporarily challenging Pretoria's euphoric claims that the treaty would cripple ANC "terrorism."

Although the Nkomati Accord severely damaged the ANC's military capabilities, it did not destroy them altogether, and, ironically, it also represented a psychological victory for the ANC in two ways. By accentuating Pretoria's obsession with curbing MK, it gave the impression that MK was a much greater threat to white control than it actually was, thus boosting the ANC's reputation among blacks. In addition, by highlighting new obstacles to MK's penetration of South Africa's borders, the Accord created renewed momentum among ANC partisans inside the country to intensify political resistance rather than wait and hope for external deliverance.

Meanwhile, however, the setback in Mozambique was creating a momentum of its own within leadership circles in Lusaka. Hard realities were addressed at an April summit meeting of southern African heads of state with leaders of the ANC and the South West Africa People's Organisation (SWAPO) in Arusha, Tanzania. All present were steadfast in pledging political support for the goals of liberation, but Mozambique was not the only country paying a heavy price economically as a result of South Africa's campaign to impose its will on the region. Apartheid, the meeting resolved, had to be abolished by whatever means were necessary, but "leaders present . . . reiterated their strong preference for apartheid to be brought to an end by peaceful means."[41] No one in the ANC had to be reminded that Zimbabwe's liberation war had ended with a negotiated settlement after Machel informed Mugabe that he was no longer willing to sacrifice Mozambique's interests for the sake of a decisive ZANU victory on the battlefield.

Mutiny in Umkhonto we Sizwe

The Nkomati setback was made more critical by the simultaneous eruption of a mutiny by soldiers in the ANC's Angolan camps. Conditions in the camps were far from ideal. It was impossible by the late 1970s for the deployment of MK cadres into South Africa to keep pace with the intake and training of new cadres. Many recruits arrived in Angola with the expectation that they would return home after six months or a year of preparation, but discovered that the camps were full of would-be fighters who had been there for several years awaiting deployment. In the first flush of its expansion in the post-Soweto years, the ANC had focused some of its best talent on the construction and manning of the camps, but by the early 1980s many of the most able mid-level leaders had been reassigned to the new machineries in the forward areas, less-experienced South Africans had taken the place of Cuban trainers, MK headquarters had become preoccupied with other priorities, and a period of neglect and demoralization had set in.

The accidental unmasking of a spy among some highly trained cadres being prepared for deployment in early 1981 triggered a ruthless search for other agents and the discovery of a ring of spies that included two high-placed MK leaders in Angola.[42] About six months earlier, the ANC's department of national intelligence and security (NAT), long a weak branch of the organization's bureaucracy, had been placed under the direction of Mzwandile Piliso, a senior confidant of Tambo. Intense paranoia took hold as NAT expanded its staff of operatives and began to deploy them, sometimes covertly, throughout the organization, sometimes in tacit competition with the overt network of political commissars already in place whose task it was to organize political education, boost morale, and keep an eye out for political problems arising among the rank and file. In the Angolan camps, where physical conditions were harsh and frustrations endemic (*Document 119*), NAT's frequent excesses became a major grievance.[43] Desertions rose, and suicides periodically occurred. "Suspects" singled out by security personnel, sometimes for offenses no worse than smoking marijuana, drinking beer, or socializing with local village women, were beaten and incarcerated in punishment cells or at a detention facility constructed by NAT north of Quibaxe at "Camp 32," also referred to as Quatro.

In late 1982, a circular from Lusaka requested that cadres in the Angolan camps, through their commissars, compile reports giving their complaints and suggestions for improvements in the running of the ANC. The result was an outpouring of grievances that revealed, in the words of one participant at Viana Camp outside Luanda, a "generally defiant and critical mood prevailing amongst the ANC rank and file."[44] Security department operatives were severely criticized for their authoritarian heavy-handedness. Leaders were accused of high living, womanizing, and favoritism toward members of their families and language groups. The organization was charged with failure in its management of the armed struggle. Some individual cadres were bold or naive enough to submit letters alleging arbitrary actions by particular leaders. Pointing out that the ANC in exile had not held a conference since 1969, many cadres called for the convening of another conference at which members could assist in clearing the organization's leadership of dead wood. Tambo's authority was not challenged, and Chris Hani and Joe Slovo were praised as military leaders, but there was a widespread belief that these men must be ignorant of the wrongdoing and incompetence of many of those serving under them.

These complaints and demands highlighted the political and legal limbo in which the ANC found itself as an exiled organization. It was fighting for a democratic South Africa, but as a revolutionary and quasi-military organization it was not itself run democratically. Members might elect representatives to speak for them under certain circumstances, and debate was invited on contentious issues of policy, but no mechanisms existed to create accountability on the part of those at the top. Although the organization had a code of conduct, this was primarily a mechanism to discipline members, not leaders, and the protesters of 1982 appear to have made no reference to it. Legally, ANC members were not under the protection of any outside authority. Host governments did not intervene in situations where ordinary members were brutalized or killed by NAT officials, though they did offer prison facilities when host nationals had been victims of crimes committed by ANC members. Any exile who wanted to resign from the ANC faced difficulties in doing so since the local offices of the United Nations High Commissioner for Refugees would only accept responsibility for resettling individuals who could obtain written authorization from the ANC itself.[45]

In MK, which took pride in being a "people's army," there was unavoidable tension between the demands of military discipline and the belief by cadres that their leaders should be democratically answerable to them. This, Slovo later reflected, led easily to

> confusion between what, in a political organization, would be regarded as legitimate and even healthy criticism but which, in a military organization, could be characterized as insubordination and "trouble making." There was no rigid formula by which a balance between the two could be achieved. Essentially, this depended upon the sort of human relationships which developed and the attitudes of the leadership towards the rank and file. There had unfortunately been too many instances of a "yours is not to reason why" approach which, while appropriate in the heat of battle, is not always an effective method of molding or retaining the allegiance of a people's army. It was of the utmost importance to provide proper outlets for the expression of views, to avoid arrogance in relationships, and to respond with understanding to the criticisms and grievances of all cadres.[46]

The perception of many ordinary cadres that leaders led lives of luxury also posed a perennial problem. Compared to the spartan existence of military camps where a set of dominos or a guitar could be a luxury and fresh meat and vegetables a rarity, life in Lusaka or even Luanda looked opulent.[47] Those enjoying this perceived opulence might understandably be assumed to have lost their sense of urgency about advancing the struggle. Stories circulated about high officials in Lusaka involved in lucrative smuggling. Meanwhile, young protégés of top MK leaders, after being promoted to commander status, separated themselves off from the rank and file, got better food and clothing, and had opportunities to frequent Luanda, Lusaka, and Maputo, where yearnings for a better life could readily be indulged. Such "corruption," both genuine and imagined, left a sour taste in the mouths of those who remained behind to wait, perhaps forever, for their assignment to a mission home.

Partly at the request of the Luanda government, and partly in response to the problems and complaints of cadres in late 1982, MK the following year deployed a high proportion of all soldiers in the camps to units of the Angolan army fighting against UNITA in Malange province in north-central Angola. Enthusiasm for this undertaking was initially high, and MK is said to have acquitted itself well in early forays against the much better-equipped UNITA troops. Fighting was sporadic, and in time the morale of the South Africans waned, friction with Angolan commanders developed, and some casualties were suffered in ambushes. By the second week of January 1984, there was a mutinous reaction from troops ordered to return to the front. After a period of standoff between the armed mutineers and NAT operatives, the combat orders were canceled and the rebellious troops were transported to Viana Camp outside Luanda, where they hoped to explain their actions to NEC members who were in Angola at the time. The frank internal report of the Stuart Commission, an investigative body appointed by the NEC (*Docu-*

ment 115), recounts the tense events of early February during which the mutineers, their numbers augmented by soldiers from other camps converging on Viana, were eventually disarmed. Thirty-three cadres judged to be the leaders were taken into custody. The demands put by the mutineers, who elected a Committee of Ten to represent them, echoed the complaints of 1982: that the ANC's security department be curbed, that policies regarding the deployment of cadres be reviewed and explanations offered for the failure of the armed struggle, and that the ANC call a conference to elect a new NEC.[48]

At the height of the crisis, no more than 900 to 1,000 soldiers appear to have been present at Viana. All reports suggest, however, that support for the protesters and their demands was high throughout the army. In mid-May a group of the mutineers who had been transferred from Viana to Pango camp rebelled again when ordered to attend compulsory "reorientation" classes. Demanding the release of the 33, they took control of Pango by force, killing several guards. Six days later, a force of loyalists commanded by Timothy Mokoena subdued them in a pitched battle in which several died on both sides. A military tribunal condemned seven of the Pango mutineers to die by firing squad. Shortly after their execution, Ephraim Nkondo, elected chairman of the Committee of Ten at Viana in February, died in NAT's Quatro detention center, an alleged suicide. Over a decade later the ANC disclosed that between 1980 and 1984 at least 34 members of MK were executed as alleged spies, mutineers, or both.[49]

Restoring Legitimacy: The Kabwe Conference

Without publicly citing the role of the mutiny in its decision, the ANC National Executive Committee in June 1984 announced that planning would begin immediately for a national conference to be held in 1985. Preparations were exhaustive, with planning documents circulated to every region where there was an ANC presence, delegate-selection meetings held as far away as Canada and the United States, and efforts made to collect feedback from underground members in South Africa. Eighty-two written submissions were received, including many from military units in Angola and the frontline states (*Document 120* is an example). The outbreak of violent resistance in the Vaal triangle and its rapid spread across South Africa in late 1984 (chapter 2) added momentum to the preparations. For the first time, it was possible to think realistically about the ANC eventually grasping the reins of state power.

In an atmosphere of high excitement, the conference met in the Zambian town of Kabwe the week of June 16–23, 1985. About 200 elected delegates represented the regions, while about 50 others were appointed by the organizing committee.[50] Elections held on the final day returned to office all but 3 of the 22 incumbent members of the NEC and added 10 new members. The 10 included 5 non-Africans—Mac Maharaj, Aziz Pahad, Reg September, Joe Slovo, and James Stuart—who became eligible to sit on the NEC after the conference voted to adopt an unrestricted open membership policy (*Document*

123). In another notable vote, delegates ratified the expulsion of four far-left critics of the ANC belonging to the Marxist Workers' Tendency.⁵¹ A description of the conference that appeared in *Umsebenzi,* the propaganda organ of the SACP, conveys the spirit of unity and forward momentum that the organizers had successfully worked to create (*Document 125*).

Kabwe was a victory for the forces of stability within the ANC and for its generation of senior leaders, then in their sixties. Tambo, Nzo, and Nkobi were returned unopposed, and Joe Modise continued as Commander of MK. Administration of the PMC and the National Working Committee, however, passed after Kabwe primarily into the hands of the organization's younger leadership generation, people in their forties and fifties, the most influential of whom were Slovo, Maharaj, Hani, Thabo Mbeki, Pallo Jordan, Joe Nhlanhla, Simon Makana, Cassius Make, Josiah Jele, and Sizakele Sigxashe.⁵² Kabwe conferred a new legitimacy on the entire leadership, despite the belief among many young and impatient rank-and-file members that conservatism and slackness were still the norm. Loyalists at Kabwe shouted down delegates from the Angolan camps who wanted to raise complaints related to the mutiny.⁵³ No mention of the mutiny appeared in the public conference documents, and the Stuart Commission's findings were never made known to ordinary members. Kabwe delegates adopted a detailed new code of conduct and set of rules and procedures for dealing with security suspects, but reform of the security department itself was deferred for later consideration.⁵⁴ Removal from the NEC of national commissar Andrew Masondo, identified by the Stuart Commission as the person most directly responsible for the demoralization and abuse of cadres in the camps between 1981 and 1984, was the only acknowledgment of the grievances which had caused the crisis in Angola.

Kabwe did not provide a setting where complex questions of strategy and tactics could be thrashed out. Delegates representing the camps and the impatient youth generation, many of whom were dissatisfied with the ANC's military progress, had to be content for the most part with slogans about "intensifying the struggle." A conference debate on the issue of "soft targets" did, however, offer the leadership an opportunity to make a symbolic gesture toward the militants. MK had exploded a car bomb that killed 19 people, including 15 civilians, outside air-force headquarters in downtown Pretoria in May 1983. Later the ANC had backed away from operations likely to result in civilian deaths, believing it was important to woo wavering white opinion rather than to drive all whites into the extremist camp by the use of terror tactics. At Kabwe, however, the ANC caused a media stir when Tambo at a press conference on June 25 declared that as the conflict escalated, the distinction between "hard" and "soft" targets was necessarily going to disappear, even if it was not the intention of MK to attack civilians. Nevertheless, despite these dire warnings, MK in practice continued after Kabwe to aim only at what were considered military targets, merely widening the definition to include such military auxiliaries as northern Transvaal farmers who maintained defense arrangements with the SADF and who increasingly became the target of land-mine attacks in 1986. When a limpet mine killed five people in a shopping mall in Amanzimtoti south of Durban in December 1985, Tambo publicly criticized the bomber as an undisciplined cadre acting contrary to the ANC's policy of not targeting civilians.[55]

The conference adopted the rhetoric of people's war, but attempted no refinement of the ANC's broad strategic aims or the methods to be employed in achieving them. The NEC report submitted to the conference (*Document 124*) acknowledged that internal underground organization remained weak and that the construction of "mass revolutionary bases," envisioned in the theory of people's war, was still merely an idea. The conference's Commission on Internal Mobilization endorsed a new plan for the structural integration of military and political work, but in practice, as in every earlier attempt to bring military operations under the partial direction of political machineries, MK ended up going its own way.[56] The commission's recommendation that the real locus of political leadership should be transferred inside the country also seemed likely to remain an unfulfilled ideal.

The conference Commission on Strategy and Tactics reviewed the main tenets set out in "Planning for People's War;" expressed doubts, based on past experience, about the feasibility of constructing guerrilla bases in rural areas; noted the opportunities opened up by the ongoing uprising inside South Africa; then fell silent and failed to produce a final report. An animated plenary session provided an opportunity for members to question Slovo, Hani, and other commission members on some of the principles of people's war, but major ambiguities remained unaddressed. "Seizure of power" was still the ultimate goal proclaimed in ANC and SACP propaganda.[57] It was a goal that loomed large in the minds of many cadres, as it seems to have in Slovo's mind as well. But how might the actual seizing of power occur? Older visions of a guerrilla war of attrition had been superseded by dreams of a war guided by internally based "combat units" capable of assuming leadership during "partial and general insurrections" in the cities and towns. One could argue about whether insurrections could be fomented or were always spontaneous, but questions still remained about their outcome. Even if widespread turmoil in the townships, plus work stoppages building to an extended general strike, could be sustained and backed up by armed MK units—a people's war scenario sketched in "ANC Call to the Nation," a propaganda leaflet (*Document 121*) widely distributed in April 1985 shortly before Kabwe—could this necessarily produce white surrender? What of the power of the regime to strike back?

All revolutionary theories, including those taught by Soviet experts in courses on "Military and Combat Work" (MCW) for MK, agreed that powerfully armed regimes could be overthrown only if members of their armies and police had become demoralized and divided to such an extent that many would change sides in the heat of a revolutionary confrontation.[58] Applying MCW in South Africa, given intensive propaganda and successful attempts at subversion, the winning over of black policemen and homeland soldiers in substantial numbers seemed at least possible. In the case of white soldiers and police, however, this prospect was extremely remote. At best, their effectiveness might be reduced by spreading their numbers thin in response to many scattered attacks nationwide, but this also presumed wide and deep capabilities on the part of MK. Given the improbability of turning or overpowering whites in the security forces, the emphasis of MK planners in practice fell back to the pursuit of other objectives: continuing armed propaganda, accumulating small caches of smuggled and stolen weapons, and organizing combat units in which cadres trained outside the country could impart their skills to new cadres recruited and trained inside the country. By the time of Kabwe, despite continuing pressures to restrict the transit of MK fighters through the frontline states, hit-and-run bombings were being staged out of Botswana and, to a lesser extent, Zimbabwe and Swaziland. A few hundred fighters had made their way into townships, with or without benefit of underground preparations, and here and there they were forming links with amateur combat units springing up in response to police repression. In numbers, firepower, and mobility, these units were no match for the armed forces of the regime. Psychologically, however, they inspired many blacks to believe that white power could be challenged, and given time and determination, even defeated.

On the Offensive, 1985–1988

Kabwe enabled the ANC to move beyond the crises of Nkomati and the Angolan mutiny and to refocus its energies on seizing the initiative from Pretoria. By mid-1985 the Botha government was struggling to contain its own multiple crises generated by township turmoil, the growing hostility of world opinion, and the lack of strategic vision within its own ranks. Newly conscious of its vulnerability to sanctions and loan withdrawals, it seesawed between efforts to crush all opposition and to appear reformist to its foreign critics. For the ANC, determining how best to press its political advantage was not a new problem, but the complexity of the possibilities had never been greater.

Stepping up its propaganda barrage was a clear priority. Journals and pamphlets produced outside the country were smuggled into South Africa at an escalating pace, while simple leaflets and newssheets were printed and distributed by underground units inside. The ANC's Radio Freedom broadcasted for six to eight hours weekly from short-wave transmitters in Addis Ababa, Dar es Salaam, Lusaka, Luanda, and Antananarivo. Propaganda helped ensure that followers and potential supporters were familiar with official ANC policies and informed about the worldwide activities and status of the exiled movement. *Umsebenzi,* an SACP magazine circulated from 1985, aimed to popularize Marxist ideology but also to teach useful techniques of organization (*Document 130*).[59] In the late 1980s, as anti-apartheid movements in Europe and the United States gained momentum, South African musicians, writers, and artists attracted growing attention outside South Africa, throwing their weight into the war for world opinion and helping to create new interest in the ANC as a possible alternative government (*Document 144*).

Burgeoning world concern over the fate of Nelson Mandela and other life-serving political prisoners created dilemmas for Pretoria and opportunities for the ANC to publicize its leaders' martyrdom. During 1982 the government moved Mandela, Walter Sisulu, Raymond Mhlaba, Ahmed Kathrada, and Andrew Mlangeni from Robben Island to Pollsmoor maximum security prison outside Cape Town, where conditions were better but isolation from other prisoners was more extreme.[60] Seeking to shift to Mandela himself the onus for his continued imprisonment, then in its 23rd year, the government in early 1985 renewed the offer, made to him a number of times previously, that he could be released if he would renounce the ANC's policy of armed struggle. To emphasize that his imprisonment was "self-imposed" and his living conditions no worse than those in modern prisons in Europe, the government permitted Nicholas Bethell, a member of the British House of Lords and the European parliament, to interview Mandela at Pollsmoor in January 1985. Bethell duly reported on Mandela's improved living conditions and his firm refusal to reject violence (*Document 116*). Three weeks later, after verbally intimidating a warder who tried to prevent him from giving a document to one of his lawyers during a prison consultation, Mandela publicly proclaimed his unconditional loyalty to the ANC and its policies when the document was read out by his daughter, Zindzi, at a UDF rally on February 10, 1985, at Jabulani Amphitheatre in Johannesburg (*Document 117*). For the ANC, this airing of Mandela's views was a propaganda triumph; for Pretoria, it was another lesson in the slippery politics of image management.

By late 1985 the ANC had largely secured what it termed its "vanguard role" in relation to the UDF. The partnership remained fraught with tensions and uncertainties, however.[61] Unable from a distance to micromanage a large and loose organization with so many grassroots affiliates, the Lusaka leadership had to be satisfied with offering advice and guidance when this was requested. On the basis of reports from underground units and intermediary structures in the frontline states (which provided the information for memoranda such as *Document 86,* for example), political troubleshooters in Lusaka attempted to promote cooperation between fractious internal groupings, and to advance the ANC's trusted stalwarts into leadership positions while sidelining individuals whose loyalties were less certain. These interventions may have enhanced the coherence of UDF policy pronouncements and political strategizing; nevertheless, the process still left most initiative in the hands of internal activists, some of whom, contrary to Lusaka's intentions, tended to assume an autonomous role as self-appointed members of an ANC "internal leadership." Particularly worrisome in this regard, as we saw in chapter 3, was an alleged "cabal," said to be centered in the leadership of the Natal Indian Congress. According to the author of an ANC memorandum on factionalism in the UDF (*Document 86*), some members of this grouping traded on their ANC connections but refused to assist the ANC underground, discouraged

African mass mobilization, or even tried to promote the non-revolutionary scenario of a Lancaster House solution for South Africa along the lines of the British-brokered settlement reached in Zimbabwe. Advice from Lusaka was perceived to have little influence on the modus operandi of some within this grouping, which was still a source of controversy and racial recriminations within the UDF in 1990.

Also threatening, especially to the SACP, were ideological and tactical arguments raging in the trade union movement even as complex efforts to forge worker unity were bearing fruit in the formation of COSATU at the end of 1985. Following its demise in the 1960s, the South African Congress of Trade Unions (SACTU) had reestablished itself as an exile grouping in London under the SACP's wing. Its representatives attended labor conferences, published propaganda, raised funds, and liaised with the ANC in maintaining contact with SACTU stalwarts still living in South Africa.[62] We saw in chapter 2 that when independent black unions re-emerged, those grouped in the "workerist" Federation of South African Trade Unions (FOSATU) were hostile to SACTU and its "populist" tradition of prioritizing political involvement over strong shopfloor organization. Carried over into the giant new COSATU federation, the debates between "workerists" and community-oriented unionists reverberated in London and Lusaka. Committed socialists who were influential in the former FOSATU unions were known to be critical of the Soviet Union, the SACP, and SACTU. They refused to accept funds raised by SACTU and preferred seeking money directly from international unions, even from the pro-Western International Confederation of Free Trade Unions (ICFTU)—SACTU's sworn enemy.[63] Some of these same independent-minded unionists—including Moses Mayekiso, head of the powerful metal workers union (NUMSA)—also expressed skepticism about the Freedom Charter, accepting it as a minimum statement of future goals but calling for it to be supplemented by a more explicitly socialist workers' charter. Some even raised the perennial suggestion that a new workers' political organization be founded—an idea that was anathema to the SACP. Further compounding the debates over tactics and goals was the ongoing influence of the Marxist Workers' Tendency. Although its best-known proponents, all whites, had been expelled from the ANC at the Kabwe conference, its line remained the same: given the ANC's historical hegemony, the best revolutionary strategy was to bypass SACTU and the SACP and bolshevize the ANC from within. To keep conflict within tolerable bounds, the ANC tried to meet frequently with COSATU officials, encourage them to maintain a united front, and assure them that building strong shopfloor organizations and supporting the political struggle were not incompatible goals, a reality that even staunch "workerists" were coming to accept by the mid-1980s.

At the same time the ANC was battling to consolidate its dominant position among blacks inside South Africa, the organization was also turning its attention increasingly to whites. The number of whites formally recruited into the underground structures of the ANC and SACP was never large, possibly fewer than a hundred inside South Africa by the late 1980s.[64] Recognizing that few whites were ever going to join illegal organizations, the ANC aimed more broadly to encourage disillusionment with the National Party's leadership, especially among white opinion leaders. In the tactical language of the ANC, these latter whites, although not part of the "revolutionary forces" like those in the first category, could still become "forces of change." In the period of economic uncertainty and media consternation following Botha's disastrous Rubicon speech of August 1985 (chapter 1), ANC leaders in Lusaka acceded to a request made some months earlier to meet with a delegation of prominent white businessmen and editors. On September 13, at President Kenneth Kaunda's private lodge at Mfuwe in northeastern Zambia, Tambo and five other members of the NEC spoke cordially for six hours with the delegation, headed by Anglo American chairman Gavin Relly (*Document 126*). The delegation had three objectives: to become acquainted with the ANC's leaders; to hear their views on important issues including future economic policies, the role of the SACP, and the use of violence; and to find out if the ANC would lend its support to an initiative to form a National Convention Movement.

The National Convention Movement, formally launched a week later, was an attempt by the white Progressive Federal Party to build a multiracial coalition of groups to press for the holding of a national convention to hammer out a plan for South Africa's political future. The ANC and UDF saw this as an attempt to build up "moderate" leaders like Buthelezi who were friendly to big business and could occupy the middle ground between the "extremes" of the National Party and the ANC. The Relly delegation was politely rebuffed, and the Convention idea became stillborn, notwithstanding the efforts of a delegation led by Progressive Federal Party (PFP) head Van Zyl Slabbert to reopen the issue with the ANC on a visit to Lusaka in mid-October.[65] Slabbert, an Afrikaner, who later called his meeting with Mbeki, Maharaj, and others "an extraordinary revelation," had personally begun to question the value of parliamentary activity, given the country's polarizing political crisis of "the system" versus "the struggle."[66] Four months later, in a surprise move that left his party in shock, Slabbert resigned his position and his seat in Parliament, calling himself "an incurable democrat" who no longer had faith that Parliament could contribute to meaningful change.[67] The ANC in Lusaka applauded the move in a glowing press statement (*Document 131*), and also welcomed the similar resignation of the PFP's Alex Boraine six days later. The "system" was visibly cracking under the strain of popular opposition, confronting white opinion leaders with hard choices and holding out new political opportunities to the ANC.[68]

Almost overnight, the highly publicized businessmen's trek to Lusaka made it acceptable for other whites to open a dialogue with the ANC. Several had quietly held conversations with ANC leaders outside South Africa before September 1985, but now a steady, open flow of visitors to Lusaka and Harare began, despite Pretoria's bullying attempts to stem the tide. A delegation of Stellenbosch students had their passports withdrawn in October, as did a later group of church leaders which included Anglican Archbishop Philip Russell. A group of six Dutch Reformed ministers led by Reverend Nico

Figure 9. Following the July 1987 meeting in Dakar, Senegal, between the ANC and a delegation of whites that included many prominent Afrikaner intellectuals, some of the participants traveled to Burkina Faso. Here Van Zyl Slabbert and Thabo Mbeki share a joke with President Thomas Sankara (center) in Ouagadougou. *Vrye Weekblad Archive/COSATU Collection*

Smith canceled their October trek after government threats, but *Cape Times* editor Tony Heard interviewed Tambo in London and defied censorship laws by publishing the interview in early November. The National Union of South African Students organized a trek to Harare in March 1986 (*Document 133*), Catholic Church leaders went to Lusaka in April (*Document 80*), and on it went.[69] Black groups too made the pilgrimage, including a delegation from the National African Federated Chamber of Commerce (NAFCOC), and one from Inyandza, Enos Mabuza's ruling party in KaNgwane, the Swazi-speaking homeland.[70] The most highly publicized talks of all occurred in Dakar, Senegal, in July 1987. These brought together a large ANC delegation led by Mbeki with a group of about 60 whites, including 40 prominent Afrikaner intellectuals, organized by Slabbert and Boraine (*Documents 137* and *138*).[71] The returning delegates had to be spirited through the airport in Johannesburg to avoid confrontation with a chanting throng of angry right-wing Afrikaners led by Eugene Terre'blanche. As blacks increasingly rallied to the ANC, an unprecedented fracturing was taking place in white ranks.

Each group of trekkers raised its own concerns with the ANC, but four major themes predominated. First, many questioned the ANC's continued use of violent attacks, some of which were causing civilian deaths, arguing that these made the regime, and whites generally, more intransigent. Some also questioned the logic of challenging the government militarily, where its advantage was strongest, rather than concentrating all resources on the government's glaring political vulnerabilities. In response, the ANC defended violent tactics by pointing out that ultimately all violence was initiated by the government, and that without the actions of MK many whites would never have taken the ANC seriously. MK's strongest defense—that it was the main source of the ANC's emotional appeal to angry blacks—was rarely put forward publicly.[72]

Secondly, trek groups echoed the ongoing discourse in the South African media about negotiations. When and how could the government and the ANC begin to talk about a political solution? The ANC could not deny that sooner or later talks with the government would occur—even were this to happen in the improbable context of a military "seizure of power." Yet rushing into negotiations when Pretoria still clearly had the upper hand would be foolhardy. Joshua Nkomo had paid dearly for making this mistake in Rhodesia in 1978.[73] Publicly, the ANC assumed varying postures on talks at different times in the mid-1980s, sometimes listing many preconditions for its participation, and sometimes just a few, including the release of prisoners and unbanning of organizations. Rhetorically, it swung between propaganda exhorting its followers to press forward toward the "seizure of power," and diplomatic statements to trek groups and the white media that cast MK's attacks as simply part of a pressure campaign to force the government to the bargaining table.

A third issue often raised by visitors meeting the ANC was the allegedly dominant position of communists in the organization's leadership. This in turn led to the fourth and larger concern: what was the ANC's vision of a post-apartheid political and economic system? Was it a vision shaped by communist models? This was a constructive challenge to Tambo and his colleagues, who had spent most waking hours of their exile years focusing on how to destroy apartheid but not on what to put in its place. They dismissed allegations of communist domination with the argument that communists in the ANC were valued members who were loyal to the ANC's goals of democracy and non-racialism. After these goals were achieved, Tambo told the Catholic leaders (*Document 80*), members of the Communist Party would be free like any other political group to work democratically for their vision of socialism, which was not part of the ANC's political program. On questions relating to a post-apartheid political system, the ANC was undecided. Apart from supporting universal franchise, the abolition of bantustans, and a Bill of Rights that would protect individual but not "group" rights, ANC leaders had worked out no blueprint for a future political order. Their views were similarly unformed on economic systems, beyond the Freedom Charter's call for the nationalization of mines, banks, and monopoly industries and its broad demand that the country's wealth be equitably shared. Even among members of the SACP, thinking on economic questions had never gone much beyond an emotional conviction that capitalism should be abolished and workers' interests made paramount.

By the mid-1980s, however, whites who were looking for an alternative to National Party rule needed more specific details than these about the shape of a post-apartheid order before their fears and inertia could be overcome.[74] The pressure of these expectations, brought to bear through face-to-face encounters, moved the ANC by late 1985 to take its first steps in a prolonged process of studying political and economic options. Economists were not strongly represented in the ANC's ranks, but outside experts were gradually recruited to supplement the ANC's own talent. In legal affairs, the ANC could marshal significant resources, and at Tambo's initiative an internal ANC commission was appointed after Kabwe to start work on guidelines for a post-apartheid constitution.[75]

International Pressure for Negotiation

The rising tide of revolt and state repression that from late 1984 filled South Africa's streets also filled the world's television screens, provoking international opinion to a new pitch of indignation. In Europe and North America, new anti-apartheid organizations sprang up and old ones attracted new activists as universities, churches, corporate board rooms, city councils, and national parliaments became the scene of roiling debates over disinvestment, boycotts, and economic sanctions. How politicians responded to calls for or against pressure on South Africa depended on the constituencies to which they were most attuned. Conservative Prime Minister Margaret Thatcher characterized the ANC as "a typical terrorist organization," but the left-leaning Greater London Council erected a mammoth bust of Mandela outside its offices.[76] Republican President Ronald Reagan praised the South African government as a loyal ally of the United States, but liberal Republican Senator Lowell Weicker was arrested for participating in an anti-apartheid demonstration at South Africa's Washington embassy.[77] "Suddenly, like a bolt from the blue, it has dawned upon the ordinary person here that apartheid is truly akin to slavery," wrote the ANC's representative in Brussels to Alfred Nzo in late 1985 (*Document 128*). But the liberal public opinion that he saw emerging in Belgium and the Netherlands was not the only force at play. Conservative views also exerted a powerful influence in most Western countries, reflecting the strength of financial interests, racial prejudices, and a belief—assiduously cultivated by Pretoria—that the South African government was a bulwark against the spread of communism.

Just when the ANC was straining to put itself at the forefront of resistance inside South Africa, the spotlight of world attention forced it simultaneously to bring all its diplomatic skills to bear in the international arena. At an annual Commonwealth heads of government meeting in Nassau in October 1985, Thatcher fended off proposals for immediate sanctions against South Africa with a counterproposal that the Commonwealth try to bring Pretoria and the

ANC to the negotiating table through mediation. The Commonwealth Eminent Persons Group (EPG), a high-powered team co-chaired by two former heads of government, was appointed and began its mission in early 1986. Meanwhile, a week after Nassau, the ANC was invited to present testimony to the Foreign Affairs Committee of the British House of Commons. *Document 127* records Tambo's responses to the generally hostile line of questioning pursued by the committee members, who focused on the familiar issues of violence, sanctions, the ANC's commitment to nationalization, and its position on negotiations.

From 1985 onward, a faint whiff of negotiations was constantly in the air. The Botha government was under growing international pressure to demonstrate its commitment to reform or face a loss of support from the Western powers. It responded by sending out myriad signals of change, including rumors of Mandela's imminent release and offers to open talks with the ANC on condition that the movement renounce violence. Botha was hostile to what he saw as "outside interference," but agreed to permit fact-finding missions by the EPG and to allow the delegation access to Mandela, perhaps in the hope that they would prod him to abandon hard-line ANC positions. On its part, the ANC in public brushed aside the subject of negotiation on the grounds that Pretoria's professed interest in it was insincere. Wary of being caught unprepared, however, Tambo, soon after the Kabwe conference, appointed a committee to sketch out a negotiation strategy. Its report in November 1985 (*Document 129*) recommended preconditions for ANC participation and warned against any arrangements that might lure the ANC unilaterally to suspend armed struggle.[78] Once underway, the EPG's missions were regarded by the ANC as useless delaying tactics. Nevertheless, the Lusaka leadership scrutinized with interest the Group's "Possible Negotiating Concept" when presented with it on May 17, 1986 (*Document 134*). The EPG proposed that the ANC agree to "suspend" violence and negotiate a new "power-sharing" constitution if Pretoria unbanned the ANC and the PAC, released political prisoners and detainees, removed troops from the townships, "suspended" detention without trial, and provided for full freedom of expression and assembly.[79] Suspending violence was obviously more palatable than renouncing it; on the other hand, the notion of "sharing" power was unacceptable to those bent on "seizing" it. Tambo asked for ten days to consider the proposal before responding, but on May 19 the ANC saw its skepticism about the government's intentions vindicated when the South African military staged brazen attacks on ANC houses in Lusaka, Harare, and Gaborone, dramatically wrecking the Commonwealth initiative.

The more Western public opinion swung against South Africa, the more governments that had ignored African leaders for decades began to put out feelers, cautiously at first, then more aggressively, to meet and talk with the exiled liberation movements in the hope of influencing their policies. Many of these contacts were unpublicized, but some were public. In September 1986, after the EPG had collapsed and the U.S. Congress had passed the 1986 Comprehensive Anti-Apartheid Act (chapter 1), the ANC held its first official meetings with Britain's foreign minister, Sir Geoffrey Howe, and with Chester Crocker, the U.S. assistant secretary of state for Africa. Discussions with Crocker paved the way for a meeting between Tambo and U.S. Secretary of State George Shultz in Washington in January 1987, a formal recognition of the ANC's status as an important representative of black South African opinion. ANC relations with both the British and U.S. governments remained chilly, but the fact that relations existed at all was a breakthrough for the ANC and an ominous setback for Pretoria.

As the possibility of entering negotiations with the National Party became less remote, the ANC was increasingly conscious of the potential threat of rival parties being invited to join in future talks. It was safe to assume that both Pretoria and the Western powers, in order to dilute and deflect the thrust of radical opposition, would attempt at every point to push forward alternative leaders of a more moderate hue. Buthelezi was the leading candidate for this role, but PAC or black consciousness leaders were also possibilities, or even the improbable Isaac Mokoena, "bishop" of a small separatist church, whose leadership credentials were praised by Ronald Reagan at a Washington press conference in August 1986. Opinions in the ANC differed about whether to try to deter these maneuvers by persuading the United Nations and the OAU to accord the ANC the same status as SWAPO, designated by these bodies as the "sole and authentic" representative of the people of Namibia, in effect a government-in-exile. Johnny Makatini, head of the ANC department of international affairs from 1985, pursued this recognition aggressively but unsuccessfully until his death in late 1988, by which time the issue had been rendered moot by the ANC's commitment to multipartyism in its Constitutional Guidelines (*Document 153*).[80]

It was evident that long before formal negotiations could begin about a future South African constitution, the ground rules for such talks would have to be agreed upon through preliminary discussions, or "talks about talks." The earliest attempt to establish indirect contact between the ANC and the government for this purpose was an initiative by Professor Hendrik Van der Merwe of the University of Cape Town, who first traveled to Lusaka in December 1984. Van der Merwe, a Quaker who was a conflict resolution specialist, was well connected in National Party circles and had also befriended Winnie Mandela, who sometimes stayed overnight at his Cape Town home when making visits to her imprisoned husband.[81] Although the ANC's reactions to Van der Merwe were ambivalent during both his first and subsequent exploratory visits (*Document 132*), his overtures stimulated discussion about talks. They also stirred rumors among the rank and file, which the leadership was at pains to dispel lest members develop fears about the organization selling out in "secret talks." The stream of trek groups added fuel to these suspicions.

By early 1987, the lingering euphoria created by the internal uprising was still strong, but there were also grounds for unease among the ANC's rank and file and leadership alike. In South Africa, the security forces were crushing the township revolt under the cover of the state of emergency declared in June 1986. Virtually the entire UDF national leadership was in detention or on trial for treason at Delmas. Inkatha vigilantes held sway in much of Natal. Despite the ANC's continuing exhortations to township youth, surviving "combat units" had largely evaporated and street committees had been decimated (*Document 136*). The security of ANC guerrillas in transit through the frontline states was a matter of increasing worry (*Document 140*). Hundreds of MK cadres had piled up in Lusaka waiting for deployment orders that seemed to be permanently on hold. On the wider international stage, after years of relying on the Soviet Union as a staunch supporter of revolution in South Africa, the ANC had been informed by the Soviets that they now favored political solutions to all African conflicts. In a widely publicized speech in June 1986, a leading Soviet Africanist, Gleb Starushenko, had even advocated offering white South Africans guarantees against the nationalization of property,[82] a position also taken by Cuban officials in meetings with Tambo a few months earlier in Havana.[83]

For restive cadres in MK, conditioned to believe in revolutionary slogans, these were worrying developments that resurrected perennial questions about the competence and reliability of ANC leadership. At the leadership level, a gradual accommodation to new realities had begun even before the juggernaut of the second state of emergency. Tambo and Mbeki had found that the meeting with Relly and the businessmen's group at Mfuwe in September 1985 opened up prospects for new tactical alliances against the Botha government. For these two, and for many lower-ranking ANC officials not directly involved in military work, the political and diplomatic fronts now seemed to offer more promise than the armed struggle, which appeared less and less likely to produce the revolutionary outcome anticipated in the pages of *Umsebenzi*.

For Slovo, Hani, Kasrils, and others in MK who had invested years in trying to implement revolutionary plans, it was more difficult to relinquish hope that the Pretoria government might finally be brought down by "people's war." To them, the siren song of an alliance between the ANC and big capital was a trap to be avoided at all costs. As fighters, they saw talking as acceptable only as long as its function was a purely tactical one of isolating the government and narrowing its support base while the forces of people's power regrouped for the final assault. To the would-be negotiators, it seemed that although fighting still had a vital propaganda role, it was time to move beyond the unrealistic dreams of Bolshevik-style revolution and to focus instead on maneuvering the ANC into the strongest possible position to meet the South African government at the bargaining table. Completely ruling out either strategy was impossible, and the two could be seen as overlapping to some degree, so fighting and talking remained two options pursued simultaneously. Tensions persisted, with the fighters directing their frustration mainly against Mbeki, who was Tambo's protégé and the most skillful of the talkers (*Document 143*). These strains fell short of splitting the ANC into openly antagonistic factions, however. Too much was at stake, and the destinies of people in the two camps too intertwined, for the ANC to sacrifice its sense of common purpose over a tactical issue, no matter how fundamental.

The ANC and the Communist Party

The farther the talkers progressed in their efforts to woo domestic and international opinion into alignment with the ANC, the more persistently they ran up against image problems resulting from the ANC's alliance with the South African Communist Party. Would a future ANC government nationalize all large South African corporations? What about foreign companies? Would it restrict freedom of the press and religion? Would it become a client of the Soviet Union? These questions could not be deflected by reference to the slogans of the Freedom Charter, because underlying them all was a deep suspicion that the leadership of the ANC was secretly already in the hands of Communist Party members. It was well known that Eastern bloc countries were arming and training MK, and that some members of the ANC's national executive were SACP members, though the precise number was a matter of inconclusive debate among journalists, academics, and Pretoria's propaganda specialists. Might it not be in the interests of the ANC, as it was in the interests of the Western powers and the owners of productive property in South Africa, for the ANC to jettison its "communist wing" and leave its "nationalist wing" clearly in charge?

This line of argument presented the ANC with a political conundrum. It publicly rejected "all efforts to dictate to us who our allies should or should not be, and how our membership should be composed" (*Document 139*). When hard pressed (as in *Document 80*), its representatives tried to give historical explanations for the long, symbiotic relationship between the ANC and the SACP. They could try to explain that the exiled ANC had no "wings," or, since the expulsion of the Makiwane eight and the Marxist Workers' Tendency, no "factions." But what outsiders to the ANC's particular brand of revolutionary politics found hard to fathom in the end was the extent to which the views of communists and non-communists in the ANC were so heavily overlapping as to be almost indistinguishable. Communist and non-communist ANC members all came from a range of class, educational, and ethnic backgrounds, represented a variety of abilities and interests, and were less or more driven by ambition, idealism, duty, or machismo. The rejection of racial and ethnic prejudices came easily to some, and less easily to others. Some enjoyed the challenge of intellectual analysis, some did not. Some were impressed with the Soviet Union's achievements, some were not. When the prospect of negotiations loomed, some communists excelled as talkers while others remained committed to armed struggle. What united communists and non-communists alike was a rejection of racism and economic exploitation in South Africa, a common belief so strong that every difference of opinion was rendered minor by comparison.

Members of the SACP, in which membership was secret and by invitation only, were on average more intellectually inclined, more zealous in carrying out their duties, and more ideological in their outlook than most ANC members. But some party members were also ambitious careerists who joined because they saw that status came with being part of an elite, and that high-placed members could offer them patronage in the form of better assignments and postings.[84] Many in the SACP took pride in their membership because the South African government so regularly identified the party as its most dedicated enemy. Most party members in exile were not hard-line ideologues by temperament, though there were always party hacks who could turn out propaganda replete with Marxist phraseology. Some regarded party membership as a license to give vent to instinctive authoritarian ("Stalinist") tendencies, but non-communists could also be petty tyrants. Inside South Africa, where the small SACP underground had to contend at close range with both ultra leftists and the security police, hard-liners may have been more common (*Document 135*). To many SACP members, however, communism was less an ideology than an expression of emotional identification with the downtrodden, leavened for some with a vague belief that the Soviet Union was an example of what the science of human betterment could produce. That several alleged core members of the anti-revolutionary "cabal" were SACP members was testament both to the heterodoxy of thinking within the party and to the fact that communists often rose to leadership positions because of their willingness to work hard, not primarily because of their fealty to the party's ideological line.

Had the ANC sidelined its communist members as its critics demanded in the late 1980s, its prospects of defeating the Botha government would have plummeted because most of the first-string members of its team would have been removed from the field. Could it therefore be argued that communists indeed dominated the ANC as critics alleged? If the domination was one of talent and effort, the charge perhaps was true—although the minutes of a 1983 SACP unit meeting in Lusaka (*Document 110*) suggest a certain insecurity regarding the SACP-ANC relationship. Domination could take many forms. Communists brought a level of discipline to the ANC it otherwise would have lacked. They also enhanced its commitment to non-racialism and social transformation, contributed many of its best strategists, and may have helped to steer it away from the use of terrorist tactics. Ideologically, however, the ANC as an organization never committed itself to doctrinaire communist economic or political goals. Its goals remained those spelled out in the Freedom Charter and in the evolving position papers being worked over in the late 1980s by its emerging experts on "PASA"—post-apartheid South Africa. Here, had numbers and high position counted, the communists in the NEC, who made up at least three-quarters of its members after Kabwe, might have been expected to swing their weight to ensure that the ANC's vision of a future South Africa conformed to socialist principles. But this did not occur; instead, the ANC's blueprints emerged with a clear social democratic stamp. Possibly the NEC's communists were simply adhering to the party's two-stage theory which decreed that "national democratic" goals had to be reached before communists could give priority to the achievement of socialism. In the meantime, overemphasis on the armed struggle had left the SACP short of trained experts in economics. Possibly, by appointing committees of special-

Figure 10. Joe Slovo, President Samora Machel of Mozambique, and Oliver Tambo pay their respects at the funeral of Moses Mabhida, Maputo, March 29, 1986. *UWC-Robben Island Museum Mayibuye Archives*

ists to draw up the ANC's PASA blueprints, Tambo, a social democrat who was not a member of the SACP, was deliberately removing major policy decisions from the NEC's political arena, leaving it merely an advisory role, an interpretation that finds some corroboration in *Document 143*. Some combination of these factors no doubt contributed to the SACP's passivity during the PASA process, as did new uncertainties introduced by Mikhail Gorbachev's sweeping reforms in the Soviet Union and the dramatic emergence of anticommunist movements across Eastern Europe in the late 1980s.

The ANC peremptorily dismissed calls to sever its alliance with the SACP, but it did not ignore the possibility of distancing itself from the Soviet Union as a way of improving its image in the West. Vladimir Shubin, a high-ranking Soviet official who often dealt with the ANC, has described at least one occasion, in mid-1986, when Tambo explained that he could not attend a particular meeting with Kremlin officials because the ANC was trying to shed its image in the West as a Soviet client.[85] On January 8, 1987, three weeks before his meeting with Shultz, Tambo, in his address on the 75th anniversary of the ANC's founding, declared that an ANC government would guarantee a multiparty system, freedom of "speech, assembly, association, language, religion, the press, the inviolability of family life and freedom from arbitrary arrest and detention without trial." Without mentioning nationalization, he offered a new formulation of economic options, declaring that once in power, the ANC would "have to address the question of ownership, control and direction of the economy as a whole to ensure that neither the public nor the private sectors serve as a means of enriching the few at the expense of the majority."[86]

No attempt to account for the SACP's declining ideological influence in the late 1980s can ignore the powerful influence of Slovo in the SACP, or his deep personal friendship with Tambo. The two men had known each other since their years as fellow lawyers in Johannesburg in the 1950s. Since they met often and trusted each other implicitly, it would be surprising if they did not discuss their respective views about the ANC's best way forward when it faced strong pressures to distance itself from its communist allies. When Tambo argued the expediency of a tilt toward the West, Slovo was in no position to impose a veto and may also have discouraged others from trying to do so. When the group of lawyers working on the ANC's guidelines for a post-apartheid constitution produced an early draft in January 1986, it was referred to a subcommittee of the National Working Committee which included Slovo. The subcommittee criticized the draft as envisioning a system "very similar to conventional bourgeois democracy and not a framework arising from or created by a revolutionary struggle." Jack Simons, an off-and-on member of the SACP who had taught at the University of Cape Town and was the chairman of the guidelines committee, dismissed these objections angrily. Tambo backed Simons, and the drafters proceeded.[87] It would be safe to assume that such episodes did not diminish Slovo's loyalty to Tambo or to the ANC. In any case, Slovo, whose popularity in the ANC stemmed from his extrovert personality and his notoriety as Pretoria's "public enemy number one," was adept at maintaining his public persona as South Africa's leading communist, but privately was not the unswerving devotee of Stalinist orthodoxy portrayed by his critics. While his heart was with the fighters and he constantly tried to keep alive the dream of a revolutionary seizure of power, he could also see the logic of the talkers and the necessity of making tactical compromises. Like Tambo, he was aging and wanted to see the struggle end.[88]

The Pan Africanist Congress

The PAC in the 1980s was plagued by many of the same problems affecting the ANC but to a more extreme degree. It was chronically short of skilled administrators, regularly failed to implement the decisions of its own leaders, and was never able to build the basic underground political networks inside South Africa that would have been necessary to support its military ambitions. In the PAC's case, these shortcomings were exaggerated by weak leadership at the highest levels, frequent debilitating and embarrassing clashes between factions, lack of coherent ideology and strategy, and a record of lackluster diplomacy that resulted much of the time in near-empty bank accounts.

Already excluded by the governments of Mozambique, Swaziland, and Zambia from operating in their territories, the exiled PAC at the end of the 1970s also faced derecognition by Tanzania, the OAU, and the UN as a result of the divisive and inept leadership of Potlako Leballo.[89] Leballo, pressured from all sides, agreed for "health reasons" to leave Tanzania in May 1979, and the movement's central committee replaced him with an executive committee of three: Vus Make, David Sibeko, and Elias Ntloedibe. Barely six weeks later, Sibeko was shot dead in Dar es Salaam during a confrontation with Leballo loyalists from the PAC's Azanian People's Liberation Army (APLA). Make assumed caretaker leadership while the central committee tried to recruit a new chairman. When APLA cadres at the PAC's Chunya camp near Mbeya were informed in March 1980 that Make would continue heading the organization, they erupted in an angry outburst. Tanzanian troops opened fire, leaving 11 dead and over 40 wounded.[90]

It was therefore with high hopes that many members of the organization welcomed John Nyati Pokela on his arrival in Dar es Salaam from Lesotho in February 1981. Pokela, a Fort Hare contemporary of PAC founding president Robert Sobukwe, had spent 13 years on Robben Island where he was known as a conciliator. Though not a man of obvious leadership talents, he was untarnished by the PAC's record of conflict and corruption and was determined to set the organization on a new course. *Ikwezi*, a pro-PAC journal produced in Britain by Bennie Bunsee, credited the leadership change to agitation by APLA's rank and file in Tanzania (*Document 102*). Taking a contrasting view, Leballo loyalists claiming to be from the "PAC Mission to UK and Eire," in a rhetorical hodgepodge of fact and fancy, denounced Pokela's election by the central committee as part of an anti-revolutionary plot by Tanzania and conservative politicians in Zimbabwe (*Document 105*).

Pokela moved quickly to win favor with the OAU's African Liberation Committee by reversing the 1978 expulsion of Templeton Ntantala and some 60 of his followers, and even spoke positively of working for the OAU's chimerical goal of reuniting the PAC and the ANC. Hoping to improve the PAC's desperate financial situation—an underlying cause of much infighting among office-holders and misery among cadres in the organization's camps—Pokela undertook a series of diplomatic missions soon after his arrival. His dilemma was acute: without funds, APLA's ability to strike conspicuous blows inside South Africa was decidedly limited, yet a liberation movement that could strike no blows was clearly a poor investment. Because the ANC was allied with the Soviet Union, China had assisted the PAC at the height of Sino-Soviet rivalry in the 1960s and early 1970s. But China's interest waned with the gradual cooling of these tensions after Mao Zedong's death in 1976. When Deng Xiaoping began introducing capitalist-style reforms in the 1980s, Maoist groups worldwide, some of which had favored the PAC, began to lose ground. Pokela's diplomacy bore some fruit, however, when large donations were received from Nigeria and Iraq in 1982, even though the PAC's acceptance of Iraqi money provoked anger from Libya, the principal provider of military training for APLA, because Libya's Muammar Qaddafi was an ally of Iran, then at war with Iraq.[91] In Europe and North America, where the PAC's opposition to the Communist Party might have won it support among conservatives, the organization's past record of instability and mismanagement was a serious liability. The Swedish government, generous in its aid to the liberation struggle, regularly refused direct requests from the PAC lest it damage its close ties with the ANC.[92] Even if the PAC had been able to draw up plans for a school of its own along the lines of the ANC's SOMAFCO complex—an intention it expressed but never put into effect—it is unlikely that funders would have been forthcoming.[93] Despite Pokela's best efforts and some progress in improving administrative efficiency, the organizational culture of complacency, corruption, feuds, and finger-pointing persisted, perpetuating the PAC's poor public image.

Ideologically, the PAC had enjoyed an early advantage in black Africa, where its "Africa for Africans" nationalism had been more popular than the ANC's multiracialism in the 1960s.[94] The ANC's alliance with the SACP had also aroused suspicions in parts of independent Africa, giving the PAC another advantage in spite of Ntantala's promotion of Maoist ideology in the 1970s. But by the early 1980s, most African governments gave more weight to results than to philosophy. The ANC's "armed propaganda" had begun to build its worldwide reputation as a more effective movement than the PAC. Mandela's name, although not yet a household word, was far better known internationally than any names associated with the PAC. Until the PAC could claim military successes, it had nothing to trade on except its claims to past achievements. On that score, besides taking credit for the Sharpeville emergency—an unintended consequence of its 1960 anti-pass campaign—the PAC now claimed the 1976 Soweto uprising, citing state evidence in the 1978–79 trial of PAC leader Zephania Mothopeng that he had established links with the black consciousness movement and had planned and promoted revolutionary activities during the student uprising. It was a sign of the PAC's chronic weakness, both organizational and intellectual, that Pokela, invited to address the UN's Special Committee Against Apartheid in March 1985, a time when South Africa's townships were again in turmoil, chose mainly to emphasize the PAC's imagined past and not its realistic assessment of the present or future (*Document 118*).[95] Making a virtue of necessity, however, Pokela did tell his UN audience that in the PAC's view, revolution in South Africa could not be directed from the outside but would have to be "internally based"—a fall-back position that MK had also begun to accept in the post-Nkomati years.

The PAC in the 1970s had begun to arrange military training in Libya for its cadres, and trial evidence indicates that some trainees also did specialized military courses in other countries. Serious problems arose in infiltrating guerrillas back into South Africa, however. Botswana and Zimbabwe maintained formal relations with the PAC, and although officially forbidding use of their territories by guerrilla forces, were often willing to look the other way. Zambia and Mozambique, however, were openly hostile to the PAC, and this complicated access to Botswana and Zimbabwe.[96] Even Lesotho, which the PAC had used as a staging base since the 1960s, regularly expelled PAC members, especially after six were killed by the Lesotho security forces near Qacha's Nek in March 1985 while apparently participating in military operations of the rebel Lesotho Liberation Army, a force allied to the opposition Basotholand Congress Party.⁹⁷ Conceding the problem of access to South Africa's borders, PAC leaders often spoke optimistically of their progress in recruiting and training fighters inside the country, particularly in rural areas, where they sometimes asserted that violent revolution would initially begin. These fighters were on their own to acquire weapons and cash through theft from white farmers and bank robberies.⁹⁸ Security force personnel were to be their primary targets, but, declared APLA's propaganda organ, *Azania Combat*, in 1987, the "time has almost come when for every African being killed . . . a white person must be killed" (*Document 141*). Establishing the number of APLA's internally deployed recruits over the course of a decade is impossible.⁹⁹ The PAC claimed that only its urban attacks were reported in the press; other operations may statistically have been merely recorded as crimes. The PAC's top commander from 1982 on, the Chinese-trained Sabelo Gqweta "Phama," was a largely unsung leader. No attacks appear to have occurred before 1985, and, according to Major-General Herman Stadler of the South African police, PAC attacks before 1990 numbered no more than ten.¹⁰⁰ Nevertheless, official police statistics indicated that 85 of the 530 guerrillas killed or captured inside South Africa in 1987—16 percent—were from APLA.¹⁰¹

Pokela died of a heart attack in June 1985, and was succeeded by Johnson Mlambo, who, like Pokela, joined the PAC in exile after completing a long sentence on Robben Island. By the time Mlambo became PAC chairman in Dar es Salaam the Vaal uprising had grown into a nationwide revolt and world attention was focused on South Africa.¹⁰² Even if military initiatives were problematic, it was clear that the PAC's long-term political fortunes depended heavily on consolidating its support at home. Like the ANC leadership in Lusaka, Mlambo's executive in Dar es Salaam was in no position to direct the day-to-day actions of its internal allies, but was expected to play a supporting role diplomatically, financially, and strategically in pushing forward the common struggle. Unlike the ANC, which steadily rose to the challenges of coordinated political mobilization, the external PAC, while achieving some diplomatic advances, for the most part played a bystander role while Africanists in South Africa struggled to project their views against the force of government repression and the growing hegemony of the ANC and its allies.

Africanism's simple insurrectionary nationalism, as expressed in an underground PAC flyer (*Document 103*), for example, had been associated since the early 1960s with the PAC and its violent early offshoot, Poqo. Africanist philosophy—the belief that Africa belongs to and must be ruled by its indigenous people—was assumed to be what one PAC publication called "the sacred language the masses understand best."¹⁰³ Perhaps because of this assumption, PAC adherents inside South Africa were not systematic in seeking political allies; nevertheless, they occasionally found themselves making common cause with like-minded groups. After the suppression of Poqo, some Africanists found an emotional home in the black consciousness movement and later were active in AZAPO and its short-lived National Forum. Some joined the trade unions that made up AZACTU and later NACTU. The propaganda of the PAC in exile often claimed that black consciousness was an expression of Africanism (*Document 118*), but, as we saw in chapter 3, there were differences of viewpoint that in practice produced friction between the two tendencies. Africanists were open to having non-Africans, even whites, be trade union members as long as they did not assume leadership roles, while black consciousness adherents wanted all whites barred but leadership open to all "blacks" as inclusively defined. As early as 1981, Africanists in AZAPO left to form Azanian National Youth Unity (AZANYU) rather than accept Indians or coloureds in leadership positions in AZAPO. These attitudes were not evident, however, in the unusual alliance between the Muslim extremist group Qibla in the western Cape and the PAC, whose deputy military commander, Enoch Zulu, a Poqo veteran, came to trial in late 1986 with Achmad Cassiem and five others on charges of terrorism and furthering the aims of the PAC.[104]

In February 1988 when the Botha government effectively banned 18 political and labor organizations, AZAPO and its youth wing were included but no Africanist groups were on the list, perhaps because Pretoria was still taking a wait-and-see approach. Nevertheless, academic and media commentators, observing the growing presence of APLA and Africanist political sentiment, plus the new respectability that Pokela and Mlambo had brought to the exiled PAC, increasingly took the view that the PAC now constituted a potential political challenge, both to the state and to the ANC.[105] This belief—that Africanism could eventually become an effective force in South African politics—was an old assumption, ever unfulfilled, that had long haunted both the ANC and South Africa's "other" liberation movement.

Notes

All conversations and interviews cited are with Thomas Karis and/or Gail Gerhart unless otherwise indicated. All conversations, interviews, and documents cited in endnotes can be found in the Karis-Gerhart Collection (hereafter KGC). The organization appearing in parentheses following each document title indicates the location of that document in the Collection. *FPTC* refers to earlier volumes in the *From Protest to Challenge* series.

1. On exile life in this period, see Hilda Bernstein, *The Rift: The Exile Experience of South Africans* (London: Jonathan Cape, 1994); Lynda Schuster, *A Burning Hunger: One Family's Struggle Against Apartheid* (London: Jonathan Cape, 2004); and Victoria Brittain and Abdul S. Minty, eds., *Children of Resistance* (London: Kliptown Books, 1988), pp. 94–101.

2. Joseph Lelyveld, "Black Challenge to Pretoria: Rebellion, Still Puny, is Showing More Muscle," *New York Times,* October 12, 1983.

3. "Rough estimates of annual expenditure," January 5, 1972 and "Statement made by the Treasurer-General T. T. Nkobi to our Chief Representatives, Milan, March 1982" (KGC: ANC). Also see Stephen Davis, *Apartheid's Rebels* (New Haven: Yale University Press, 1987), pp. 72–74.

4. Number given to John Battersby for the period between 1976 and 1984 in interview with Chris Hani and Steve Tshwete (June 1988). Some countries that hosted ANC missions absorbed much of the cost of maintaining them, including the Scandinavian countries, the Netherlands, Austria, and countries in Eastern Europe, according to Roland Axelsson, a Swedish aid official interviewed by Victoria Butler (February 1988).

5. See Seán Morrow, Brown Maaba, and Loyiso Pulumani, *Education in Exile: SOMAFCO, the ANC School in Tanzania, 1978 to 1992* (Cape Town: HSRC Press, 2004), and Seán Morrow, "Dakawa Development Centre: An African National Congress Settlement in Tanzania, 1982–

1992," *African Affairs,* vol. 97, no. 389, 1998, pp. 497–521. On Solomon Mahlangu, see conversation with Ismail Mahomed (December 1985).

6. "Oil-Tank Glow," *Time,* June 16, 1980, at http://www.Time.com/time/magazine/article/0,9171,924227,00.htm.

7. Esther Waugh in a series on MK in the *Sunday Independent,* December 17, 24, and 31, 1995 and January 7, 14, and 21, 1996, revealed substantial information on these attacks. Joe Slovo, Aboobaker Ismail ("Rashid"), and Montso Mokgabudi ("Obadi") were the top figures in MK's special operations unit. Mokgabudi and Barney Molokoane commanded the SASOL attack, Molokoane the Voortrekkerhoogte attack; the Koeberg bomber was Rodney Wilkinson. See conversation with Aboobaker Ismail (July 2001). Between June 1980 and December 1982, the rand fell in value from US$1.20 to US$.86.

8. Police reports cited in the *Weekly Mail,* March 23, 1989, and the British *Independent,* January 9, 1990.

9. In 1982 the ANC assassinated Bartholomew Hlapane, a former ANC and SACP member who had become a state witness against Bram Fischer and others in the 1960s and 1970s. By early 1989, more than 100 anti-government activists had also died in "unsolved assassinations." *Race Relations Survey 1988/89,* pp. xxx–xxxi.

10. Howard Barrell, "Conscripts to Their Age: African National Congress Operational Strategy, 1976–1986," Ph.D. thesis, Oxford University, 1993, pp. 452–58. Barrell calculated ratios between number of attacks, number of MK casualties (deaths and captures), and number of MK weapons seized by police, and concluded that in military terms, MK's success rate was consistently low. *Document 77,* however, illustrates the power of MK's mystique.

11. Interviews by Howard Barrell with Ronnie Kasrils (September and October 1990).

12. In "President's Draft Report" to NEC meeting in Tanzania, May 1979 (KGC: ANC), for example.

13. See *FPTC,* volume 5, chapter 2 and *Documents 18* and *22.*

14. On the last of these costs, see conversation with Jabulani Nxumalo ("Mzala") (October 1990). Allegations of tribalism, a perennial feature of internal ANC politics, often centered on accusations of Zulu ethnic chauvinism or Xhosa domination. On Tambo's life and leadership, see Luli Callinicos, *Oliver Tambo: Beyond the Engeli Mountains* (Cape Town: David Philip, 2004).

15. Conversations with Ntsizi Moremi (April 1980) and Walter Felgate (February 1998).

16. *Africa Confidential,* vol. 21, no. 11, May 1980. Conversations with Geoffrey Mokoka, who said 46 delegates were present (May 1980), Ben Khoapa (October 1980 and November 1986), and Jairus Kgokong (October 1997). The Black Consciousness Movement of Azania, led by Mosibudi Mangena, existed in exile and was regarded by some as the external wing of AZAPO.

17. The South African Youth Revolutionary Council (SAYRCO), a black consciousness exile group led by Khotso Seatlholo, briefly secured financial backing in Nigeria, but collapsed when Seatlholo was captured inside South Africa in 1981. See Schuster, pp. 205–209 and 322.

18. See *FPTC,* volume 5, chapter 9.

19. On Radio Freedom, see conversation with Thami Bolani (August 1989) and interview by Victoria Butler with Don Ngubane (February 1988).

20. Reproduced in *FPTC,* volume 3.

21. They were Florence Moposho, Gertrude Shope, Ruth Mompati, and Jacqueline Sedibe. Tambo appointed several women to be diplomatic representatives of the ANC, including Mompati (London, early 1980s), Lindiwe Mabuza (Nordic countries, 1979–mid-1980s), and Dulcie September (France, 1984–88). Notable women in MK included Sedibe, Thandi Modise, Thenjiwe Mtinso, and Phila Ndwandwe.

22. See Mosadi wa Sechaba, "Women Arise and Fight for People's Power," *African Communist,* no. 98, 1984; Clara, "Feminism and the Struggle for National Liberation," *African Communist,* no. 118, 1989, and reply to "Clara" by Hilda Bernstein, no. 121, 1990 (KGC: SACP).

23. See Shireen Hassim, *Women's Organizations and Democracy in South Africa* (Scottsville: University of KwaZulu-Natal Press, 2006); Callinicos, pp. 437–44; and "Unit 4 meeting held on 12 Oct 89," minutes (Simons papers, microfilm, reel 8).

24. Despite its date (around 1979), this document, which Kathrada gave to the authors after

the publication of volume 5 of *FPTC* (1964–1979), has been included in this volume because of its historical importance.

25. Nelson Mandela refers to this debate and to the *"Inqindi"* document (without naming it) in chapter 67 of his autobiography, *Long Walk to Freedom* (Boston: Little, Brown, 1994). Also see Fran Buntman, *Robben Island and Prisoner Resistance to Apartheid* (New York: Cambridge University Press, 2003), pp. 99–102. Responding to a critic of the ANC, Thabo Mbeki wrote "[T]he ANC is not a socialist party. It has never pretended to be one . . . [and] will not become one by decree or for the purpose of pleasing its 'left' critics." "The Fatton Thesis: a Rejoinder," *Canadian Journal of African Studies,* vol. 18, no. 3, 1984, p. 609.

26. See the 1962 SACP program, "The Road to South African Freedom," reproduced in *South African Communists Speak: Documents From the History of the South African Communist Party, 1915–1980* (London: Inkululeko Publications, 1981), pp. 284–320. The doctrine of Colonialism of a Special Type ("CST") argued that racial oppression in South Africa had created a system of internal colonialism, and before class contradictions could be resolved, Africans of all classes had to be freed from this colonialism through a nationalist struggle. This theory provided what Tom Lodge and Bill Nasson in *All, Here, and Now: Black Politics in South Africa in the 1980s* (New York: Ford Foundation and Foreign Policy Association, 1991), p. 133, called a "canonical justification for the alliance of a workers' party with a [multiclass] nationalist movement"—not always a comfortable partnership for leftists who feared betrayal of the working class by petty bourgeois nationalists. For the flavor of debates over CST, see *Document 106;* Colin Bundy, "Around Which Corner? Revolutionary Theory and Contemporary South Africa," *Transformation,* no. 8, 1989; Jeremy Cronin's reply to Bundy, *Transformation,* no. 10, 1989; articles in *Africa Perspective,* no. 23, 1983; and *Social Review,* April and October 1984.

27. On the MWT, see *FPTC,* volume 5, chapter 2, n. 68. Four leaders of the MWT (Martin Legassick, David Hemson, Paula Ensor, and Rob Petersen) were suspended from the ANC in 1979 and formally expelled at the 1985 Kabwe conference (see below).

28. One example of these is "Report of the Commission of the National Executive Committee appointed to investigate the allocation and utilisation of the financial resources of the organisation in regions of the Front Line States and Forward Areas, March 1984–July 1984" (KGC: ANC). It discusses problems such as the "refugee mentality" and whether the ANC should purchase cars known to be stolen ("pipeline cars"). They do not oppose such purchases in principle "provided the methods used do not result in the embarrassment of the Organisation."

29. "Organisational Report from PHQ [Lusaka]," May 21, 1985 (KGC: ANC). A detailed 1981 document on this subject is "Problems Arising in Internal Political Work" by Barbara Hogan (KGC: ANC).

30. "Annexure D" of the Green Book, *FPTC,* volume 5, *Document 114.* Also see "Goniwe's secret work in ANC underground," *Weekly Mail,* July 2, 1993, and Tom Lodge, "The African National Congress of South Africa, 1976–1983: Guerilla War and Armed Propaganda," *Journal of Contemporary African Studies,* vol. 3, nos. 1/2, 1984, p. 175.

31. "Organisational Report from PHQ" (KGC: ANC). The report gives a breakdown of the 500: 70% male and 30% female; 72% African, 12% Indian, 6% coloured, and 10% white; no class breakdown was possible, but "the majority are youth and students."

32. The ANC had been advised by "friends in the socialist countries" that "the situation in southern Africa has the potential to develop suddenly and swiftly against the white minority regimes, especially Pretoria. They advise that we should prepare for such a contingency. The WC [national working committee] has accepted this view," Tambo wrote in "President's Draft Report" to the NEC, May 1979 (KGC: ANC). The collapse of the Shah's government in Iran earlier that year probably contributed to this judgment.

33. ANC supporters who were jailed after high-profile trials (trial dates in parentheses) included Raymond Suttner (1975), Anthony Holiday (1976), Harry Gwala (1976–77), Sibusiso Ndebele, George and Joyce Mashamba (1976–77), Jeremy Cronin and David and Sue Rabkin (1976–77), T. N. Charlimagne (1977), Joe Mati (1977), Stanley Nkosi and Kgalema Motlanthe (1977), Khehla Shubane and Rita Ndzanga (1977), Christmas Tinto (1977), Tokyo Sexwale and Martin Ramokgadi (1977–78), Mountain Qumbela (1977–78), Tim Jenkin and Stephen Lee (1978),

Mzilikazi Khumalo (1978–79), Renfrew Christie (1980), Ephraim Mogale (1980), Oscar Mpetha (1981–83), Barbara Hogan (1982), Carl Niehaus and Jansie Lourens (1983), Roland Hunter, Derek and Patricia Hanekom (1984), Regan Ntombi Shope (1984–85), Helene Passtoors (1986), M. A. Stofile (1986–88), and Andre Pienaar (1987). See press coverage (KGC: Trials).

34. This is a recurring theme in Barrell's "Conscripts to Their Age." This unpublished Ph.D. thesis is the most thorough study of the ANC's armed struggle. Barrell, a journalist, became an underground ANC member in the 1980s. Many of his points are corroborated in Padraig O'Malley, *Shades of Difference: Mac Maharaj and the Struggle for South Africa* (New York: Viking, 2007).

35. The ANC-ZAPU alliance dated from 1967. Like the ANC, ZAPU had links with the Soviet Union, whereas Mugabe's ZANU and the PAC received backing from China. Most ZAPU members were speakers of Ndebele, an Nguni language, making communication easy with South African speakers of Zulu and Xhosa. Conversation with James Stuart (April 1989).

36. On the ANC's presence in Swaziland between 1975 and 1982, see interview by Victoria Butler with Dikgang Masemola (February 1988). For a wealth of information on developments in the frontline states, see Tor Sellström, *Sweden and National Liberation in Southern Africa*, volume 2 (Uppsala: Nordiska Afrikainstitutet, 2002), especially pp. 620–97.

37. Joe Slovo's daughter, Shawn Slovo, wrote the screenplay for a Hollywood-style film about the Matola raid, *Catch a Fire* (2006).

38. The text of the Nkomati Accord is reproduced in Phyllis Johnson and David Martin, eds., *Frontline Southern Africa: Destructive Engagement* (New York: Four Walls Eight Windows, 1988), pp. 445–49. On events surrounding the accord, see Vladimir Shubin, *ANC: a View from Moscow*, (Bellville: Mayibuye Books, 1999), pp. 248–60.

39. "Fraternal message from the African National Congress to the FRELIMO Party," January 31, 1984 (KGC: ANC).

40. Ronnie Kasrils, *"Armed and Dangerous": My Undercover Struggle Against Apartheid* (Oxford: Heinemann, 1993), *p.* 226. Kasrils says over 100 cadres were deported from Swaziland at this time, while Slovo in his interview with Barrell (August 1989) puts the number at "about 80."

41. "Final Communique" of the Front Line States Summit Meeting, Arusha, Tanzania, April 29, 1984, *Sechaba*, June 1984 (KGC: ANC).

42. See *Further Submissions and Responses by the African National Congress to Questions Raised by the Commission for Truth and Reconciliation, 12 May 1997*, p. 18 (KGC: ANC), and interview by Barrell with Mac Maharaj (February 1991). *Document 101* alludes to the spy scare, and *Document 104* refers to an ANC tribunal to try the spies and decide if any should be executed. The ANC had been embarrassed in 1980 by the revelation that Craig Williamson, a police agent, had successfully infiltrated the ANC in Europe.

43. The author of *Document 119* was a psychiatrist working with the ANC in exile. Also see Brown Maaba and Seán Morrow, "Infiltration, Fear and Paranoia at Solomon Mahlangu Freedom College, 1978–1992," *War and Society*, vol. 23, no. 1, May 2005.

44. Mwezi Twala and Ed Benard, *Mbokodo: Inside MK—Mwezi Twala, a Soldier's Story* (Johannesburg: Jonathan Ball, 1994), p. 56.

45. See "Letter from ANC cadre to Ndugu Kibasa, Prime Minister's Office, Dar es Salaam, requesting refugee status," [1978?] (KGC: ANC).

46. Interview by Barrell with Slovo (1989).

47. On living conditions in Lusaka, see conversation with Penuell Maduna (early 1987).

48. Some of the mutineers pointed to an article in *African Communist*, no. 95, 1983, pp. 88–89 (KGC: SACP), in which Slovo, eulogizing J. B. Marks, recalled the 1969 Morogoro conference: "As chairman, JB was confronted by a democratically elected but at the same time very angry assembly of men and women who had lost confidence in many [ANC leaders]. . . . Morogoro asserted the right of the rank and file to have a say as to who would lead them. JB understood and sympathized with this demand, as he also understood that often resistance, under the guise of security, to the democratic process was a device used by some to hold onto the reins of power." Cited in Bandile Ketelo et al., "A Miscarriage of Democracy: the ANC Security Department in

the 1984 Mutiny in Umkhonto we Sizwe," *Searchlight South Africa,* no. 5, July 1990, pp. 88–89 (KGC: Ultraleft Organizations—Miscellaneous). The ANC eventually acted on some but not all of the Stuart Commission's recommendations.

49. *Statement to the Truth and Reconciliation Commission, August 1996,* p. 100 (KGC: ANC). In addition to Ketelo et al. and Twala and Benard, sources on the 1984 mutiny include *Appendices to the African National Congress Policy Statement to the Truth and Reconciliation Commission August 1996* (which includes *Document 115* in full and reports on two additional investigations of the mutiny made in 1992 and 1993) (KGC: ANC); *Further Submissions and Responses by the African National Congress to Questions Raised by the Commission for Truth and Reconciliation,* 12 May 1997 (KGC: ANC); Stephen Ellis, "Mbokodo: Security in ANC Camps, 1961–1990," *African Affairs,* vol. 93, no. 371, 1994, pp. 279–98; and Stephen Ellis and Tsepo Sechaba [Oyama Mabandla], *Comrades Against Apartheid* (Bloomington: Indiana University Press, 1992), chapter 6.

50. On Kabwe, see Ellis and Sechaba, pp. 148–50; Howard Barrell, "ANC Prepares for Consultative Conference," *Work in Progress,* no. 35, February 1985 (KGC: Alternative Media); and "ANC Conference: 'All For the Front'," *Work in Progress,* no. 38, August 1985 (KGC: Alternative Media); interview by Butler with Masemola (1988); and conversation with Maduna (1987).

51. See n. 25.

52. The 30 NEC members (with their ages) elected at Kabwe were: Oliver Tambo (67), Alfred Nzo (60), Thomas Nkobi (62), Stephen Dlamini (72), Ruth Mompati (67), Dan Tloome (66), Mzwai Piliso (62), Moses Mabhida (62), Reg September (62), Florence Moposho (59), Gertrude Shope (59), Joe Slovo (58), John Nkadimeng (58), Henry Makgothi (57), Joe Modise (55), Robert Manci (55?), Johnny Makatini (52), Simon Makana (50), Anthony Mongalo (50), Mac Maharaj (49), Joe Nhlanhla (49), James Stuart (49), Sizakele Sigxashe (48), Aziz Pahad (45), Chris Hani (43), Cassius Make (43), Thabo Mbeki (43), Francis Meli (43), Jacob Zuma (42), and Pallo Jordan (42). Prior to the Kabwe election, the average age of NEC members had risen every year from 1963 to 1985, but with Kabwe it fell for the first time, from 55 to 51. Between 1985 and 1990, four members died and nine others were added, returning the average age to 55 by 1990.

53. Ketelo et al., p. 59, and conversation with Mzala. After the mutiny, NAT officials tried to attribute the crisis to machinations by enemy agents, but the Stuart Commission found no evidence of this. See "Memorandum to the Leadership of ANC from the Department of National Intelligence and Security," 1991 (KGC: ANC), which argues against the appointment of the [Lewis] Skweyiya Commission, the first of two later internal ANC attempts to examine responsibility for the 1984 mutiny.

54. The conduct and management of NAT remained a vexed issue until at least 1987, and caused embarrassment to the ANC after its 1990 unbanning. The TRC found the ANC responsible for "gross abuses of human rights" in its treatment of security suspects. See *Truth and Reconciliation Commission of South Africa Report* (Cape Town: Truth and Reconciliation Commission, 1998) (*TRC Report*), vol. 2, 1998, pp. 325–66.

55. *Sechaba,* August 1986, p. 29 (KGC: ANC). On the May 1983 Pretoria bombing, see conversation with Deon Geldenhuys (July 1983).

56. Interviews by Howard Barrell with Ivan Pillay (July 1989) and Maharaj (1991).

57. For the flavor of this propaganda, see the contributions of the SACP's Jabulani Nxumalo ("Mzala") (using the pseudonyms Mzala, Khumalo Migwe, and Tebogo Kgobe) in *African Communist,* no. 82 (1980), no. 86 (1981), no. 89 (1982), no. 102 (1985), no. 117 (1989), and no. 120 (1990) (KGC: SACP) and *Sechaba,* January 1985, January 1987 and April 1987 (KGC: ANC).

58. See "MCW [Military and Combat Work], manual for MK members," [1987?] (KGC: ANC).

59. By 1985 the ANC was producing five journals: *Sechaba, Dawn* (an MK magazine), *ANC News Briefing, Mayibuye,* and *VOW* (Voice of Women). The SACP produced *African Communist* and *Umsebenzi.*

60. See Mandela, chapter 87, and Elinor Sisulu, *Walter & Albertina Sisulu: In Our Lifetime* (Cape Town: David Philip, 2002), pp. 284–85. On these five defendants in the 1964 Rivonia trial, see *FPTC,* volume 4.

61. See interview by Victoria Butler with Joel Netshitenzhe (February 1988), and chapter 5 n. 58.

62. SACTU's best-known leaders in exile were John Gaetsewe, Stephen Dlamini, Ray Alexander Simons, Archie Sibeko ("Zola Zembe"), and John Nkadimeng, who replaced Gaetsewe as general secretary in 1983. On SACTU's history, see Ken Luckhardt and Brenda Wall, *Organize or Starve! A History of the South African Congress of Trade Unions* (London: Lawrence and Wishart, 1980); Archie Sibeko, *Freedom in Our Lifetime* (Durban: Indicator Press, 1996); and interview by Victoria Butler with Eric Mtshali (February 1988).

63. See report "Manoeuvers by the ICFTU and other individuals to reverse COSATU policy," Lusaka, September 11, 1986 (KGC: ANC), and "Minutes of Emergency NWC Meeting," October 22, 1986 (KGC: ANC). *African Communist* and *Umsebenzi* periodically attacked "workerists" and "anti-Sovietism."

64. Thabo Mbeki in a 1988 press interview cited in the *Los Angeles Times*, May 10, 1988, estimated the number of white members of the ANC at "several hundreds, including those inside the country and out . . . maybe even a thousand." In Raymond Suttner's view, enumeration was impossible inside South Africa due to the blurry line between formal and informal members (email, July 8, 2007).

65. The UDF rejected the National Convention Movement, but not before several UDF leaders, speaking in their private capacities, had endorsed it. In early 1986, Jules Browde of the NCM led a delegation to Lusaka, but the ANC again refused to endorse the initiative. Other sources on these meetings include "Notes of a Meeting at Mfuwe Game Lodge, 13 September 1985" by Tony Bloom (KGC: ANC); Hugh Murray, "A Moment in History," *Leadership SA*, vol. 4, no. 3, 1985; Anthony Sampson, *Black and Gold: Tycoons, Revolutionaries and Apartheid* (London: Hodder and Stoughton, 1987), pp. 189–200; conversation with Pallo Jordan and Tom Sebina (August 1986); and interview by Rupert Taylor and Adam Habib with Van Zyl Slabbert (March 1998).

66. Interview by Taylor and Habib with Slabbert (1998).

67. *Race Relations Survey* 1986, p. 83.

68. To dedicated socialists in the labor movement, the ANC's Mfuwe meeting with big business confirmed the risks of trying to build a multiclass alliance against the government. "Once capital enjoys the status of 'fellow traveler' in the anti-apartheid struggle," socialism becomes regarded as a "divisive" issue to be left off the agenda, wrote David Lewis in "Capital, the Trade Unions, and the National Liberation Struggle," *Monthly Review*, vol. 37, no. 11, April 1986, p. 45. Thabo Mbeki is identified as the author of *Document 131* by Mark Gevisser, *Thabo Mbeki: The Dream Deferred* (Cape Town: Jonathan Ball, 2007), p. 496.

69. Karis and Gerhart were minor participants in trek discussions between New York-based ANC representatives and visiting whites. See conversations with Deon Geldenhuys (July 1983), John Kane-Berman and Neo Mnumzana (December 1985), Wynand Malan and others (December 1986), and Sampie Terreblanche (June 1987). On a trek sponsored by the Aspen Institute in early 1989, see conversation with Smangaliso Mkhatshwa (April 1989).

70. Chapter 3 described how the Soweto Parents Crisis Committee went to Harare in 1985 and returned with an authoritative ANC mandate to call off school boycotts. After his March 1986 trek, Enos Mabuza of KaNgwane made no secret of his ANC sympathies and called on other homeland leaders to give it their support. Conversation with Curtis Nkondo (May 1989) and "Report on meeting between ourselves and Comrade Jonathan of Sparrow [Enos Mabuza] held on the 21/9/86 in H[arare]" (KGC: ANC).

71. After leaving Parliament Slabbert and Boraine founded the Institute for a Democratic Alternative for South Africa (IDASA) to promote interracial dialogue. On the Dakar trek, see Max Du Preez, *Pale Native* (Cape Town: Zebra Press, 2003), pp. 148–67, and conversation with Shelagh Gastrow (July 1989).

72. Barrell in "Conscripts," pp. 465–68, argues that the ANC persisted in overemphasizing its militarily ineffectual armed struggle for several reasons: it provided important psychological compensation for the humiliation of apartheid; once launched in 1961 it could not be shut down without losing face; it verified to supporters that the ANC was "doing something" about apartheid; and because the precedents set by earlier violent revolutions, particularly the Russian revolution, weighed heavily in the strategic thinking of SACP members, whose views were adopted by the ANC for lack of more persuasive strategies of its own.

73. David Martin and Phyllis Johnson, *The Struggle for Zimbabwe* (Johannesburg: Ravan Press, 1981), pp. 227–29.

74. Afrikaners were particularly worried about the future status of Afrikaans, but the ANC had an easy answer: the Freedom Charter guaranteed all South Africans equal rights to use their own language.

75. The original members of the commission were Jack Simons (chair), Zola Skweyiya, Albie Sachs, Penuell Maduna, Kader Asmal, and Z. N. Jobodwana.

76. Thatcher used this phrase at the Commonwealth heads of government meeting in Vancouver in October 1987. The Foreign Office subsequently stated Britain's official position, which was that no solution in South Africa was possible without participation by the ANC. A similar contradiction arose in the United States in 1989 when the State Department objected to the Defense Department labeling the ANC a terrorist organization.

77. On early efforts by the U.S. State Department to establish contacts with the ANC, see conversations with Thabo Mbeki (December 1985 and May 1986), and Gevisser, pp. 487–88.

78. Gevisser, p. 533.

79. Commonwealth Group of Eminent Persons, *Mission to South Africa* (New York: Viking, 1986), pp. 103–104.

80. On deliberations preceding publication of *Document 153*, see conversation with Nathaniel Masemola (March 1988). During the Dakar trek, Afrikaner intellectual Andre Du Toit called on the ANC to accept the bona fides of those who rejected the National Party government but might not wish to identify with the ANC. ANC opinion was divided between a tradition of seeing the struggle in terms of "us versus them" and a more tolerant tradition in which diversity of opinion was accepted. ANC propaganda encouraged less-sophisticated "comrades" inside South Africa to adopt the first viewpoint, a trend that fostered violence against black rivals and laid a problematic foundation for future multiparty politics. On Du Toit's paper, see Steven Friedman's "Worm's Eye View," *Weekly Mail*, July 31, 1987. On the "sole and authentic" issue, see conversations with James Stuart (April 1989) and Aracelly Santana (December 1987), and talk by Legwaila J. Legwaila (January 1988).

81. See Hendrik W. Van der Merwe, *Peacemaking in South Africa* (Cape Town: Tafelberg, 2000), and conversation with Van der Merwe (November 1985).

82. On Starushenko see Shubin, p. 318, and conversation with Vladimir Ganchin (November 1987).

83. Shubin, p. 302 and Gevisser, pp. 537–39.

84. On rivalry in MK see Ellis and Sechaba, pp. 152–53. The SACP expanded its membership significantly in the late 1980s, according to Eddy Maloka, *The South African Communist Party in Exile 1963–1990* (Pretoria: Africa Institute of South Africa, 2002), pp. 56–57 and 61. In 1986, it had 241 members but by April 1989 there were about 609 members, of whom about 494 were in exile. Forty-nine members attended the seventh party congress in Cuba in 1989.

85. Shubin, pp. 302–303.

86. Oliver Tambo, "8 January 1987—ANC Calls for Advance to People's Power!" Speech in Lusaka (KGC: ANC).

87. "Report of the NWC Sub Committee on the Report of the Legal and Constitutional Commission," January 14, 1986 (KGC: ANC), and conversation with Albie Sachs (late 1997). See Hein Marais, *South Africa, Limits to Change* (Cape Town: University of Cape Town Press, 1998) for a retrospective analysis of the left's strategic disorientation in this period.

88. Slovo was also a key figure in Operation Vula (chapter 5). Details of Slovo's life can be found in Joe Slovo, *Slovo: The Unfinished Autobiography* (Johannesburg: Ravan Press, 1995); Gillian Slovo, *Every Secret Thing: My Family, My Country* (Boston: Little, Brown, 1997); and Gevisser.

89. On the PAC from 1964 to 1979 see *FPTC*, volume 5, chapters 2 and 10.

90. Kwandiwe Merriman Kondlo, "In the Twilight of the Azanian Revolution: The Exile History of the Pan Africanist Congress (South Africa), 1960–1990," Ph.D. thesis, Rand Afrikaans University, 2003, p. 181. Kondlo's study of the PAC in exile is a major source for this section. Henry Isaacs of the PAC in his unpublished autobiography, "Reflections of a Black South African Exile"

(1986), pp. 408–409, says four cadres died in the Chunya incident (KGC: PAC); *Document 105* says nine died.

91. Kondlo, pp. 195–96 and 216.

92. Sellström, pp. 507–12.

93. Besides the Chunya camp for APLA trainees in southern Tanzania, the PAC in the 1980s maintained a "transit and rehabilitation center" in Ruvu, Bagamoyo district, near Dar es Salaam. Conditions at Ruvu were rudimentary, and health facilities were poor for many years. By 1985, about 1,500 people lived at the settlement, according to Kondlo, chapter 5. By 1993, PAC camps in Tanzania were accommodating 2,700 people awaiting repatriation, but only "about 120 APLA soldiers were operational," according to government sources cited by Tom Lodge, "Soldiers of the Storm: A Profile of the Azanian People's Liberation Army," in Jakkie Cilliers and M. Reichardt, eds., *About Turn: The Transformation of the South African Military and Intelligence* (Midrand: Institute for Defence Policy, 1995), p. 110.

94. Mandela, chapter 48.

95. Zeph Mothopeng in later years said that many PAC members in the 1970s on Robben Island suffered from complacency because of these alleged achievements, believing that their African nationalist ideology was so intrinsically superior that working to build the organization was unnecessary. Conversation with Mothopeng (December 1989).

96. In April 1986, Greek authorities apprehended 12 Libyan-trained APLA guerrillas boarding a plane to Harare from Athens. See *Star*, February 21, 1987 and "Police dubious of PAC army claim," *Weekly Mail*, April 24, 1987.

97. The six included Thami Zani, a former leader in the Black People's Convention. On the PAC-BCP link, see conversation with Mfanasekhaya Gqobose (April 1990).

98. *TRC Report*, vol. 2, pp. 372–73, and media coverage of TRC hearings in *Business Day*, December 13, 1996, and *Cape Times*, November 24, 1998.

99. In 1994 the PAC presented approximately 6,000 APLA candidates for enlistment in the new National Defence Force, but Lodge has speculated that most of these could have been very recent recruits who had taken APLA's week-long weapons course in the Transkei or Botswana, probably after February 1990. Lodge, "Soldiers of the Storm," p. 110.

100. Interview by Howard Barrell with Herman Stadler (October 1990).

101. *Star*, July 9, 1988.

102. Poleka and Mlambo used the title of "chairman." Mothopeng, a PAC founder serving a 15-year prison sentence, was symbolically elected president in 1986.

103. *Azania News*, vol. 19, no. 7, July 1983, p. 5 (KGC: PAC). As one Africanist intellectual put it in 1989, Africanism, whatever its organizational aspects, expressed how "most" Africans felt; for proof, one had only to compare what Winnie Mandela said in the townships with what she said for foreign consumption. Conversation with Joe Thloloe (June 1989).

104. The PAC in exile sometimes defied members' presumed attitudes and appointed coloureds and Indians to leadership positions, welcoming the skills they could contribute. Gora Ebrahim and Henry Isaacs served as PAC diplomats, for example, and after 1990, Barney Desai and Patricia de Lille became PAC leaders. A handful of whites also became PAC members, including Cosmas Desmond and Dr. Costa Gazi [Gazides].

105. Tom Lodge, "Is the spirit of Robert Sobukwe rising?" *Weekly Mail*, August 5, 1988; Heribert Adam and Kogila Moodley, *The Opening of the Apartheid Mind* (Berkeley: University of California Press, 1993), p. 124; Gary van Staden, "Return of the Prodigal Son: Prospects for a Revival of the Pan Africanist Congress," *International Affairs Bulletin*, vol. 12, no. 3, 1988.

5. Breaking the Deadlock, 1988–1990

As the end of the decade approached, the National Party had not yet found a solution to black intransigence. Homeland territories and rural areas posed relatively minor problems of control. The ultimate obstacle in the way of stabilization was popular repudiation of P. W. Botha's co-optive schemes for the reshaping of African urban politics and society. Had South Africa been in a period of robust economic growth, the government might have cajoled the white electorate into supporting enough material improvements in African housing, education and employment to lower the level of mass resentment. However, the country's economy in 1988 was anything but buoyant. The debt crisis of 1985 had been temporarily alleviated, but the Reserve Bank still needed to further postpone the payment of short-term loans which had been called in by nervous foreign banks at the height of the 1984–86 uprising. Debt repayments made South Africa a net capital exporter and posed a serious obstacle to future growth, especially when added to other economic problems—the eroding value of the rand, high inflation, frequent strikes, rising military expenditures, the threat of new trade sanctions, continuing disinvestment by multinational companies, and the steady ebbing of domestic business confidence. Compounding these problems was the chronic burden of maintaining bloated state bureaucracies to administer ten ethnic homelands plus the duplicate health, education, and welfare services created for each of the four race groups in "white" areas. Ultimately, economic health depended on restoring political stability. But stability in turn required financial resources to raise African living standards and underwrite the campaign to win hearts and minds by upgrading infrastructure in the most violence-prone townships. Repressive action alone could not induce cooperation and often prompted stronger resistance.

For Botha, the options were stark. Despite broad popular rejection, he could press forward with his declared program of political reform based on continued white control thinly disguised within a system of gradually expanding group representation. Alternately, he could go all out to crush opposition and buy time to seek other paths to top-down reform. If these failed, he could accede to pressures coming from big business, foreign governments, and some members of his own inner circle to try for a durable political settlement through negotiation with genuine African leaders—a fall-back position quietly being explored by the government's National Intelligence Service under a heavy cloak of secrecy. Temperamentally more attuned to the militarists than the talkers among his close advisors, and nervous about losing white voters to the growing far-right Conservative Party, Botha chose in early 1988 to follow a course that combined the first and second options, while also permitting secret political explorations to continue.[1]

Establishing a functioning system of elected African municipal councils was central to Botha's planned reforms. These councils would provide candidates for an electoral college that in turn would choose a national advisory body of urban Africans, at various times to be called a National Forum, a "Great Indaba," or a National Statutory Council. Urban Africans had shown no interest in this cumbersome proposal, but Botha tabled a new version of it in Parliament in July 1988, clinging to the plan with a tenacity none of his underlings dared to challenge.[2] National Party optimists saw local government elections, scheduled for October 1988, as a renewed opportunity to prove the plan's viability. But to coax forward enough collaborators to be candidates, and to prevent the organized boycotts that had turned previous township elections into embarrassing fiascos, Pretoria first needed to immobilize the United Democratic Front to a degree not yet achieved under the existing state of emergency.

The February 1988 Crackdown

To ban the UDF and its affiliates outright was to invite an international outcry and possibly new economic sanctions. The government therefore took an indirect approach and issued regulations forbidding the UDF, the Azanian People's Organisation, and 16 other organizations to perform "any activities or acts whatsoever" deemed likely by the minister of law and order to promote a revolutionary climate or endanger "public safety." Henceforth all restricted organizations could exist but not lawfully engage in any political action, including the Congress of South African Trade Unions, which was warned to confine itself strictly to trade union matters. The new restrictions were promulgated with immediate effect on February 24, 1988, and individual restriction orders were also issued to 17 leading activists who were not already in detention.[3] Penalties for infringement were severe. Later in 1988, 13 organizations that had been spared in February, including the End Conscription Campaign, 7 organizations of students, and 2 of teachers, were added to the restricted list. Inkatha, as always, was left unaffected by restrictions or detentions and was free to try to expand its areas of political dominance.

Adding more weapons to his arsenal, Botha decided to tighten the curbs on fundraising by opposition groups. Media publicity during the township uprising had enabled dozens of organizations, including the UDF and many of its affiliates, to attract money directly from overseas donors or indirectly through the South African Council of Churches or the Kagiso Trust, a grant-making body funded by the European Community to assist victims of apartheid. Soon after the February crackdown, the government tabled the Promotion of Orderly Internal Politics Bill, a measure to prohibit any restricted organization, including COSATU, from receiving foreign funding. By 1988 about 95 percent of the SACC's annual budget of R15 million ($6 million) came from foreign donors.[4] A large portion of this money was passed on to other organizations for whom the SACC was a major source of funding or to the families of political prisoners and detainees. Defense lawyers in political cases were often paid with funds raised abroad by the International Defence and Aid Fund (IDAF) and transferred to South Africa by devious routes to protect the donors' anonymity.[5] Botha's bill aimed to shut down as much of this financial flow as possible.

The regime also took action to further circumscribe the opposition press. In late March 1988, under an existing regulation that enabled the minister of home affairs to suspend any publication for up to three months if, in his opinion, it systematically published material "detrimental to public order," the *New Nation,* a UDF-aligned weekly with a circulation of 60,000, was ordered to suspend publication.[6] The paper's editor, Zwelakhe Sisulu, had already been in detention without charge for more than a year. The *Weekly Mail* and the UDF-aligned *South* were shut down for a month, and at least six other opposition publications—the western Cape pro-UDF papers *Grassroots* and *Saamstaan,* the radical magazine *Work in Progress,* the pro-AZAPO *Azania Focus,* and two trade union papers, *COSATU News* and NACTU's *Izwilethu*—were warned that they faced suspension. Two other newspapers that exhorted their readers to boycott the October municipal elections, *Crisis News* and *Al-Qalam,* had the offending issues seized by police before they could be distributed.[7] Late in 1988, when a small group of dissident Afrikaner journalists applied to register a new low-budget weekly newspaper, *Vrye Weekblad,* they were forced to pay an unprecedented registration deposit of R30,000 ($12,000) although the normal charge was $4.[8]

Frustrated by his inability to silence all critical voices, Botha tightened censorship further in mid-1988. It became illegal, for example, to quote any official of a restricted organization, or to publish any information about "the success or extent of a strike . . . or the way in which the public was incited, intimidated or encouraged to join a strike."[9] Although courts in the Cape and Natal had struck down regulations introduced in 1987 to enable Pretoria to withhold subsidies from universities that refused to suppress anti-government campus demonstrations, the minister of education, F. W. de Klerk, threatened five preponderantly white universities with government retaliation in late 1988 if they permitted protests to go unchecked.[10] The National Party, still formally in control, almost seemed to be conceding that its enemies stood ready to seize the upper hand were the political playing field to be leveled. As added insurance against this eventuality, secret units within the military and police continued to receive funds to wage a "dirty war" that had been gathering momentum for more than a decade. Mysterious bombings, assassinations, and poisonings continued, as did the abduction of exiled activists from the frontline states and the deployment of armed vigilante gangs.

The February crackdown succeeded in stunning the UDF and its affiliates into a temporary silence. More than a thousand key activists languished in detention; many hundreds more were on the run or in hiding. Popo Molefe and Patrick Lekota, the UDF's national general secretary and publicity director, remained sidelined as defendants in the Delmas treason trial.[11] In December they were sentenced to lengthy jail terms. Their stand-ins, Valli Moosa and Murphy Morobe, had been in detention since mid-1987. UDF national treasurer Azhar Cachalia was among the 17 newly restricted leaders, as were two of the UDF's three co-presidents, Albertina Sisulu and Archie Gumede. The third, Oscar Mpetha, was serving a five-year prison sentence. Provincial UDF executive committees were decimated by detentions, as were the leadership ranks of dozens of local civic and youth affiliates of the UDF, down to the level of street committees. "Most of our mass organisations are facing the deepest crisis in the history of their existence," wrote the UDF's Titus Mafolo. Nevertheless, he said, here and there some had adapted to harsher conditions and had found new techniques of resistance, most notably rent boycotts, which the state was finding it difficult to combat (*Document 151*).[12] In Johannesburg, activists began spreading information about upcoming mass protests by haranguing passengers on commuter trains.

In a situation where opportunities for political maneuver were limited, the perennial question of whether to participate in government-sponsored institutions resurfaced. After Gumede in mid-1987 told a journalist that participation was being debated in UDF circles, he was rebuked by other UDF leaders, setting off a wave of media commentary that lasted for over a year. Some argued that if partisans of the UDF and its affiliated grassroots organizations stood for election to local municipal councils, or for seats in the Indian and coloured houses of Parliament in future tricameral elections, anti-apartheid forces could dominate many of these bodies. They could then use these institutions as a platform to mobilize against the government, divert state resources to community purposes, and thwart National Party plans for a docile type of black politics. The pro-participation camp also pointed out that "dummy institutions" could be wrecked by mass resignations of their anti-government members, or by rejectionist candidates who refused to take their seats after being elected. Others in the UDF, however, including the author or authors of a policy paper on municipal elections (*Document 151*), raised cogent arguments for a boycott strategy. Opponents of participation eventually prevailed, though not before the debate took on racial overtones, with Africans supporting a boycott policy and white intellectuals and some members of the alleged "cabal" supporting participation as a superior way forward for a mass movement that seemed "long on vision but short on strategy."[13] Yunus Carrim, an anti-participation leader in the Natal Indian Congress, looked at the controversy in the context of racial attitudes in Natal and the importance of NIC's alliance with the UDF in an article he wrote for the *Weekly Mail* (*Document 147*). Although democrats in the racial minority groups could debate the idea of fighting the system from within, and, he implied, had the financial resources to pursue this strategy, nothing should override the importance of aligning their politics with those of the African majority as expressed in the UDF's unbending boycott policy.[14]

Internal Opposition, 1988

After the crackdown of February 24, these strategic debates were overshadowed by the more immediate problems of functioning under conditions of tighter repression. The historic crackdowns of April 1960 and October 1977 had been followed by temporary lulls in extraparliamentary opposition during which activists fled into exile by the hundreds while the National Party consolidated its white electoral base and further developed its security apparatus. February 1988 could have brought a replay of this pattern but for several new realities unfavorable to the government. We have already seen that the regime faced mounting foreign sanctions and receding hopes that reform would improve its domestic and international image. It also faced a qualitatively different level of opposition than in earlier decades. The 1980s had seen an unprecedented buildup of new anti-government organizational activity among both blacks and whites, sometimes acting separately and sometimes jointly. The SACC was one center of this activity; the trade unions were another. As repression slowed the momentum of the UDF and other overtly political groups, activists from the churches and trade unions moved into the political vacuum created by the crackdown.

Church services were among the few remaining public forums where criticism of the government could still legally be aired. On February 29, after a well-attended multiracial service of protest at St. George's Anglican Cathedral in Cape Town, about 150 people, including many clerics, attempted to march to Parliament a short distance away to deliver a petition condemning the new restrictions (*Document 148*). Police blocked the way as the marching column emerged from the cathedral. The marchers dropped to their knees and started singing as Anglican Archbishop Desmond Tutu and Reverend Allan Boesak at the head of the procession were bundled into police vehicles. When the kneeling marchers defied an order to disperse, police routed them with blasts from a water cannon before placing them under arrest. Ultimately no legal charges were brought in connection with the cathedral protest, and black church leaders quietly continued moving toward an open alliance with the restricted organizations, even when the actions taken were illegal under the emergency regulations. Tutu, Boesak, and Frank Chikane, general secretary of the SACC, were the most prominent voices, but support for them was widespread among black clergy and also extended farther into the ranks of white clergy than in earlier years. Fewer churchmen were willing to actually defy the law themselves than to praise their fellow clergy who did. Nevertheless, the growing number who were willing through word or deed to give religious sanction to law-breaking—to go for "the jugular vein in the body politic"—reflected an ominous trend not lost on National Party strategists.[15]

In late May the SACC and the Southern African Catholic Bishops' Conference (SACBC), the highest administrative body of the Catholic church, established a joint committee to plan for a civil disobedience initiative to be known as the Standing for the Truth Campaign. Breaking laws was not new in church organizations—rules requiring publications to be submitted in advance to government censors were regularly ignored, for example—but this campaign intended to challenge Pretoria more boldly by legitimizing defiance in the eyes of the general public. In light of the importance attached to them in the government's political plans, the municipal elections scheduled for October 1988 provided an obvious focus for opposition activity, even though the emergency regulations from mid-June onward defined any call for an election boycott as a subversive act punishable by a prison sentence of up to ten years. At the SACC's annual conference in late June, 26 churchmen decided to test the government's resolve by signing a statement calling for a boycott. Literature advocating a boycott was distributed, including *Document 152*, an illegal leaflet issued by the SACBC. Early in September, Tutu made a highly publicized call for an election boycott from the pulpit of St. George's. Despite blustering threats from the minister of law and order, Adriaan Vlok, again no legal charges were brought in response to these actions. Instead, continuing the pattern at the time of the Eloff Commission (chapter 1), the police stepped up a campaign of intimidation and dirty tricks—anonymous hate calls and letters, break-ins, bombings, and other scare tactics—in an effort to contain the threat posed by clerical defiance.

The most open retaliation proposed by the government was the Orderly Internal Politics Bill, introduced in early 1988, which would have made it legal for the government to deprive the SACC of its foreign funding. In May, Beyers Naudé and Catholic Archbishop Denis Hurley accompanied Chikane to capitals in Western Europe where they worked to persuade governments to pressure Pretoria to withdraw the bill. Eventually the bill was reformulated, largely in response to European donors who argued that contributions to churches and black organizations were a substitute for imposing economic sanctions; if donations were prohibited, they said, sanctions would be the only alternative. The watered-down bill, which merely required organizations to disclose how foreign funds were used, was enacted in March 1989. Several church-related organizations declared their intention to defy the new law, and Pretoria never attempted to enforce compliance.

The government's hesitation in the face of foreign criticism and resistance by church leaders pointed to the important process of political recalculation in progress inside the National Party by the late 1980s. Eleven years earlier, following the Soweto uprising and Steve Biko's death, Prime Minister John

Vorster had brazenly flouted world opinion and staged a countrywide crackdown on black opposition, even calling an early general election in November 1977 so that he could campaign, very successfully as it turned out, on a platform of condemning "foreign interference."[16] Prominent churchmen expressed verbal outrage over state repression at the time, but the only attempt to organize a public demonstration of clerical opposition in 1977 drew a mere 12 marchers—hardly a compelling challenge.[17] By 1988, however, church hierarchies had become predominantly black, and journalists were turning to religious leaders as the political voice of the suppressed majority. Internationally prominent figures like Tutu and Boesak, and the much younger Chikane, could command the attention of powerful people and shape both the government's image abroad and its authority at home in the eyes of ordinary blacks. This was political influence that Botha could not ignore. The costs of foreign hostility and township volatility were becoming harder each year for the regime to bear; moreover, the National Party's electoral base was more alert to this reality than in the past. White voters who were impressed by *kragdadigheid* (get-tough) politics and the telling off of foreign critics had for the most part decamped to the far-right Conservative Party. National Party electoral majorities now depended on the loyalty of middle-class Afrikaners and conservative English-speaking white voters who were uneasy about international sanctions and the country's long-term economic health. Few votes at home, and no political capital in Whitehall or the White House, could be earned by jailing priests or bashing mainline churches. South Africa's political playing field was still far from level, but a perceptible shift was underway and gaining momentum from forces that were beyond Pretoria's control.

Under the repressive conditions of the state of emergency, and now the effective banning of the UDF and other mass organizations, black trade unionists also found themselves propelled into surrogate political leadership. COSATU had been placed under restrictions forbidding it to engage in political action of any kind. Yet as a federation of 13 industrial unions claiming over 900,000 paid-up members,[18] COSATU's leadership capabilities were not limited to its formal executive machinery. Long before February 1988, township grievances had become a concern of many union shop stewards (*Document 32*). Often they were organized in local groupings ("shop steward locals") drawn from unions that had once had a "workerist" orientation, as well as from "populist" unions with a long background in community activism.[19] These groupings, according to an ANC intelligence report (*Document 136*), were

> loosely defined and non-bureaucratic structures which cover one township or industrial area and tackle any issue affecting workers, including rent, Bantu education, bus fares etc. They have invited youth and students to attend their meetings and have played a coordinating role in some areas. They have continued to meet throughout the emergency and have filled some of the vacuum left by other organisations which have been smashed or hamstrung. So far they have consisted mostly of

workers and not officials. . . . [T]he Johannesburg local which consists of about 150 shop stewards . . . is very . . . innovative. An example is the initiative they took in forming street committees in Soweto. . . . The occupation of the schools and the townships by security forces makes the workplace the best forum for discussion and decision making.

Even with many leaders in detention, these grassroots networks linking experienced trade unionists with community and student activists gave COSATU a resilience and a means of organizing mass action that survived the February crackdown.[20] On March 21 and June 16, 1988, hundreds of thousands of workers took self-proclaimed holidays on the anniversaries of the 1960 Sharpeville massacre and the start of the 1976 student uprising. Most important as a demonstration of worker power was a three-day national strike called jointly by COSATU and NACTU on June 6, 7, and 8 to express popular defiance of political restrictions (*Document 150*). The stayaway was an impressive success, judged by labor historians to be the biggest in the country's history. Transportation records indicated that at least 1.9 million people stayed home on the first day, and that over the three days, absenteeism was as high as 80 percent in Johannesburg and 60 percent in the Border/East London and Pietermaritzburg/Durban areas. In the Pretoria-Witwatersrand-Vereeniging (PWV) area, steel and engineering companies reported 90 percent absenteeism over all three days, reflecting the strength of the National Union of Metalworkers (NUMSA).[21] Following a successful metalworkers' strike in August 1988 (*Document 99*), NUMSA became COSATU's fastest growing union. COSATU later acknowledged that the number of official strikes by its unions was lower in 1988 than in earlier years, but claimed that 2.5 million workers participated in the June protest, representing at least 7 million lost workdays, a mammoth cost for employers.[22]

In addition to the February crackdown, relentless police harassment, and the threat of curbs on foreign fundraising, the government's introduction of a strongly anti-union Labour Relations Act (LRA) amendment bill in late 1987 provided a further motive for trade union activism. The bill aimed to roll back many gains made by the union movement during the previous decade. It restricted the right to strike, most notably through the outlawing of sympathy strikes; it made trade unions financially liable for strike damage; and it gave employers greater freedom to lay off workers. Still reeling in the aftershock of the 1987 miners' strike and mired in internal disputes, the unions were initially slow to respond. COSATU's secretary general, Jay Naidoo, had only condemned the bill in passing when addressing businessmen in November 1987 (*Document 96*). As the implications of the pending legislation became clearer, however, COSATU and NACTU publicly rejected the new LRA and their member unions began alerting workers to its dangers. During early 1988 the bill became a focal point of union meetings and protests. Propaganda like *Document 149*, circulated by the Chemical Workers' Industrial Union, called on workers to unite against the bill. After unions had made representations to employer bodies and parliamentary committees, a few marginal changes were made to the legislation, but most worker objections were ignored when the bill came before Parliament again in May and went into effect in September.

Setbacks in fighting the Labour Relations Act added fuel to popular resentment as the crucial municipal elections of October 26, 1988, approached. Despite the clamp on open agitation by pro-boycott organizations and an expensive government advertising campaign urging voters to turn out, participation in African areas was low. Black turnout nationwide was slightly above 20 percent, although in the PWV region and in large, politicized townships elsewhere, average turnout was closer to 12 percent.[23] In addition, no voting at all occurred in 808 out of 1851 wards countrywide, either because no candidates stood for election or because there was only one candidate.[24] Among coloureds and Indians turnout was higher than among Africans, but it was Africans whom the government had hoped to coax into participation, to prove that state-backed reform could succeed once "intimidation" by radical elements was crushed. African turnout did exceed the level of participation in the local government elections of 1983, but only by a few percentage points—hardly an outcome that could support the claim of Chris Heunis, minister of constitutional development and planning, that the election demonstrated Africans' "desire to become involved in government institutions and processes" as formulated for them by Pretoria.[25]

The Mass Democratic Movement

During the township uprising, the outside world had increasingly come to regard the ANC as the voice of black South Africa in international forums, and to assume that the UDF was the ANC's de facto internal wing. Indeed, in mid-1987, after the revolt had been largely suppressed, both the UDF and COSATU, although not without a measure of internal opposition in both cases, voted at their national conferences to adopt the Freedom Charter in a symbolic gesture of loyalty to the ANC's traditions and leadership. By this stage, the ANC had also become an object of intense concern among interest groups of all sorts inside South Africa, dozens of which between 1985 and 1990 sent representatives to "meet the ANC" either in Lusaka or Harare or at venues in Europe or North America.[26] Repeated exposure to the fears, questions, and expectations of these "trek" groups pushed the ANC to confront its lack of specific plans for a post-apartheid order. At the same time, the treks created a new appreciation in Lusaka for the strategic value of the political middle ground—those South Africans of all races who were increasingly opposed to the regime but were not aligned with the ANC. Together with the United Nations, black Africa, the Eastern bloc, and anti-apartheid organizations worldwide, the ANC had been successful in isolating the Pretoria government internationally. Now, assisted by the UDF and COSATU, it turned new attention to isolating the regime at home by drawing domestic groups in the middle ground into an anti-apartheid coalition that was broader than just the ANC and its immediate allies.

This broader coalition was never formalized but by the mid-1980s had begun to be referred to in political discussions simply as "the mass democratic movement." After the February 1988 crackdown, it became convenient to refer to this vague phenomenon as "the MDM," a political formation with no headquarters, office-holders, or letterhead stationery—in short, an entity which could not be legally banned or restricted. Being in the MDM meant sharing a commitment to a future unitary, non-racial, and democratic South Africa; beyond that, it was not necessary to support any particular political views, strategies, or economic policies for a post-apartheid future. Pretoria "is trying to win over uncommitted sections of our community . . . to build a block of 'moderate' leadership," a UDF policy paper declared (*Document 151*). It will only succeed "if we fail to spread our moral and political influence to all sections of our community. . . . Our relationship with people outside our structures has been uncoordinated. We need to draw taxi-owners, sports bodies, traders and religious groups closer to the mass democratic movement." Trek participants might not be persuaded to join the ANC fold, but ground could still be gained for the MDM if, after a day or two of intense discussion, they returned home impressed, like the president of the Pietermaritzburg Chamber of Commerce (*Document 158*), that ANC leaders were "very reasonable people who were also prepared to listen to our point of view."

The door to the MDM was also open for adherents of black consciousness, Africanist, or Unity Movement groups who wanted to participate in mass actions like the three-day stayaway of June 1988, which NACTU had jointly promoted with COSATU. Lekota, awaiting sentencing in the marathon Delmas trial, appealed to two black consciousness leaders to take part in "united action" for the reception of leaders who might soon be released from Robben Island (*Document 156*), a step which could lead to future joint action.[27] Such unity efforts would later briefly bear fruit in broad participation in the December 1989 Conference for a Democratic Future.

In the important realm of sports, one major organization that ANC-aligned activists had failed to bring under their influence was the South African Council on Sport (SACOS), the principal coordinating body for anti-apartheid sports clubs nationwide. Although its members and potential members were predominantly UDF-oriented Africans, SACOS administrators were mostly coloured and Indian sportsmen who tended to neglect the needs of African township teams. By mid-1988, SACOS leaders, many with roots in the hardline boycott tradition of the Unity Movement, faced new competition from UDF activists, led by Mluleki George and Krish Naidoo, who began building an alternative sports coordinating body, the National Sports Congress. Starting in areas where the older organization was weak, the new body soon surpassed SACOS in grassroots recruitment, pulling school, university, community, and professional sports teams under the wing of the MDM with its more flexible tactics of combining boycott pressures with persuasion through dialogue with potentially supportive whites.[28] The exclusion of South Africa from international sports had steadily whittled down the resolve of whites to maintain their time-honored tradition of all-white teams (*Document 157*). To lower its direct exposure to world criticism, Pretoria had devolved most authority over sports policy to white city and town councils, schools, clubs, and professional sporting bodies. One result was the opening up of opportunities to negotiate the deracialization of sporting contacts, if blacks were prepared to seek out white allies—an approach spurned by Unity Movement adherents but embraced by the MDM.

Coaxing forward-thinking whites to move closer to the MDM became part of a sustained campaign by pro-ANC activists in 1988–89. Building on an initiative taken by Naudé, a number of white extraparliamentary political groups had met to discuss ways of influencing the white general election of May 1987. After the election, in which a majority of English-speaking whites voted for the National Party for the first time and the ineffective Progressive Federal Party lost support, momentum grew to create a political home outside of Parliament for anti-apartheid whites. Calling themselves the Five Freedoms Forum (FFF), the organizers brought together whites in UDF affiliates like the Johannesburg Democratic Action Committee (JODAC) and the Detainees' Parents Support Committee (DPSC) with those in groups not affiliated with the UDF, including the Black Sash, End Conscription Campaign, and Lawyers for Human Rights. Individuals were also invited to join the FFF as dues-paying "subscribers," a terminology adopted to avoid government restrictions on political fundraising.[29] The FFF used the issue of white emigration to launch a membership campaign around the slogan of "stay and contribute" and provided many opportunities for whites to exchange views with black activists in the MDM. In tune with the logic of Mafolo's 1988 policy paper (*Document 151*), the FFF urged whites not to boycott the controversial municipal elections but to campaign and vote for candidates who advocated non-racial democracy. Most important in influencing white opinion more broadly was a major trek to Lusaka by 114 FFF members in mid-1989 for a three-day conference with 60 ANC members. Participants were addressed by Oliver Tambo and President Kenneth Kaunda of Zambia, and were able to exchange views informally as well as in plenary sessions and small groups focused on specific issues. Excerpts from the conference report (*Documents 167, 168,* and *169*) illustrate the multiple learning processes at work in these encounters.

Bargaining with the System

After the suppression of the township revolt, many activists, both black and white, retreated from what appeared in retrospect to have been the overly ambitious goals of "people's power" and instead adopted a more incremental view of change. To some, it now seemed that the most realistic targets for collective pressure were injustices experienced at the level of local politics and individual communities. Many blacks were already applying their negotiating skills—often acquired in the trade unions—to community problems. White activists also turned to urban issues. For example, "The Role of Local

Government" (*Document 167*), an excerpt from an ANC conference report, referred to campaigns by democratic whites in a number of towns and cities to do away with the pernicious system that prevented tax revenues from "white" towns from being used to provide municipal services in black residential areas. Pretoria had finally begun to address this inequity with the introduction of Regional Services Councils in the late 1980s (chapter 1), but whites retained the upper hand in the RSCs, guaranteeing that they would be able to control any resulting redistribution. The obvious "non-racial" solution was "one city"—the merger of all areas of a municipality under a single democratic administration with a single tax base.

Local campaigners also called for "open cities" through the repeal of apartheid laws that segregated public facilities by race. A petition circulated in early 1989 by the Port Elizabeth Action Committee, a white UDF affiliate, supported a decision by the city council to desegregate public swimming pools despite a right-wing backlash (*Document 159*). After the Conservative Party won control of dozens of white town councils in the Transvaal and Orange Free State in the October 1988 municipal elections, some of the councils voted to bar blacks from public parks and other amenities that had previously been open to all. In two such towns, Boksburg on the East Rand and Carletonville, a mining town west of Johannesburg, blacks reacted by organizing consumer boycotts and hiring extra buses and taxis to drive shoppers to other towns. Both boycotts continued until late 1989 with neither town council climbing down despite the boycotts' devastating effect on local white commerce. Eventually the Transvaal Supreme Court ordered both councils to desegregate public amenities, but not before Boksburg and Carletonville had become symbols of the old-fashioned bigotry that now increasingly embarrassed new generations of cosmopolitan whites.[30]

Township rent boycotts posed a more direct threat to state finances than consumer boycotts. Starting with the protests in Sebokeng that ignited the Vaal uprising in 1984, at least 50 townships had initiated rent boycotts by 1988 in response to rent increases imposed by collaborationist local councils (chapter 3). Without rent revenues, black councillors had to beg for subsidies from white authorities in order to maintain basic municipal services such as street lights and garbage collection. When police tried to bully residents into paying rents and utility fees by evicting families or cutting off their electricity, councillors had to bear the brunt of residents' scorn.

Dozens of black civic organizations became engaged in battles to sustain rent boycotts, in the process sustaining themselves as active components of the MDM. In Soweto, a boycott that began in 1986 was still holding firm at about 80 percent participation in 1988. Lost revenue to the Transvaal provincial government from Soweto alone was over R300 million ($120 million) and rising, creating a situation of strong potential bargaining power for Africans. The Soweto Civic Association had effectively been banned in the February 1988 crackdown, but a spin-off committee of seven of its prominent members took shape later that year, calling itself the Soweto People's Delegation (SPD). The SPD, composed of Frank Chikane, Desmond Tutu, Cyril Ramaphosa,

Albertina Sisulu, Sister Bernard Ncube, Lebamang Sebidi and Ellen Kuzwayo, with the advice of an urban-planning organization called Planact, drew up a list of demands directed to the Transvaal Provincial Administration (TPA). Although the SPD's ultimate demand was "one city, one tax base," its four immediate goals were realizable in the short run, according to Planact's calculation, and were also within the power of the provincial administration to grant: cancellation of rent arrears, setting of affordable charges for electricity and water, urgent upgrading of Soweto's infrastructure, and transfer of ownership of houses to their occupants on the grounds that the cost had long since been covered by past rent payments (*Document 164*).

When approached in 1988, the TPA refused to meet the Soweto delegation and told them to take their grievances to the elected councillors. Departing from the normal practice of ignoring the "dummy" council, the SPD in December opened discussions with Soweto's official mayor and his colleagues, who had been elected by an 11.5 percent voter turnout in October. The mayor's party, Sofazonke, had told Sowetans during its election campaign that "the houses belong to the people." At the SPD's urging, he announced in early 1989 that the council would abolish rents and cancel arrears. He soon retracted his expensive promise, however, under pressure from the TPA and the government's network of Joint Management Centres, and a stalemate ensued. Directed by state security officials to find a way of ending the boycott without dealing directly with the SPD, the TPA had meanwhile drawn in representatives from Eskom, the public corporation supplying electricity to Soweto, which also had a major interest in ending the boycott. Eskom was more focused on solving its revenue problem than on cold-shouldering the de facto leaders of Soweto—"revolutionaries" according to state securocrats—so it soon bypassed both the collaborationist council and the TPA and began quiet negotiations with the SPD.

The result was a skeleton agreement to reshape Soweto service provision and move toward resolution of the SPD's other demands. Following F. W. de Klerk's election as state president and the subordination of Botha's hard-line security men to a more reform-minded cabinet, the TPA was finally authorized to meet the SPD in October 1989. A joint working committee was established and negotiations began for the cancellation of the bulk of Soweto residents' rent arrears. Although little noted for its significance at the time, this local bargaining process had already broken a major barrier to direct negotiation between high government officials and leaders of the mass democratic movement several months before de Klerk's dramatic steps forward in February 1990.[31] These developments in Soweto, a vast area of almost two million people, were also mirrored in at least 20 smaller communities. In these towns, boycotts and other forceful pressures from blacks undermined the state-supported local authorities where these still existed, creating tense standoffs with white officials and businessmen who eventually recognized that direct bargaining was the best solution. Usually the security forces intervened with repressive measures that halted the negotiating process, but often not before the affected communities had experienced small victories that reinforced their resolve to fight on.[32]

While these processes were unfolding, bargaining of a more headline-grabbing kind took place in Harare in mid-October 1988 when the ANC brought together the head of the non-racial South African Rugby Union, Ebrahim Patel, with two prominent officials from the notoriously racist world of white rugby, Danie Craven and Louis Luyt of the South African Rugby Board. The issue was South Africa's exclusion from international rugby. After several preliminary meetings in Europe, it was agreed in the Harare discussions (*Document 155*) that the first step toward resolving the problem was the creation of a single national non-racial rugby body which could take the lead in integrating the sport at every level. It was understood that the mere creation of such a body would be a necessary but not sufficient condition for South Africa's readmission to international competition. Nevertheless, Thabo Mbeki argued to journalists in Harare, it was time to recognize that change was going to be an incremental process, and that change in sports culture could encourage other changes. To reject this bargaining process was to insist that nothing about apartheid could change until everything changed, a counterproductive approach now that domestic support for the regime was demonstrably eroding.[33]

New tactical flexibility on the ANC's part was also reflected in the modification of its longstanding call for a total cultural boycott of South Africa. By the 1980s, blanket condemnation of all cultural exchanges was hindering talented black performers and artists in South Africa from winning world recognition. The irony of this became apparent when American singer Paul Simon was denounced for flouting the cultural boycott by coming to South Africa to record a portion of his *Graceland* album with local groups Ladysmith Black Mambazo and Stimela in 1986. *Graceland* became a top-selling album internationally and sparked worldwide interest in black South African music. Addressing a London audience in early 1987, Tambo observed that an alternative democratic culture of liberation was emerging to challenge apartheid culture and procedures were needed to promote the new while continuing to isolate the old. A selective boycott was a complex proposition, however, and two years passed before an official ANC position paper on the subject was issued. Passing primary responsibility to its internal allies, the ANC called for the "organisation and mobilisation . . . of the various artistic disciplines, sports codes and academics into the fold of the Mass Democratic Movement" in a cooperative relationship with the ANC.[34] Challenging the regimentation of artistic expression, the ANC's Albie Sachs caught the attention of anti-apartheid intellectuals at an ANC seminar on culture in mid-1989 with a widely discussed paper suggesting that it was time to move beyond "politically correct" art and literature lest South Africans remain "trapped in the ghettos of the apartheid imagination" (*Document 171*).

A further form of collective sparring with the state, one born of desperation, took shape in early 1989 inside Diepkloof prison in Johannesburg and soon spread to other prisons. Detainees, some held for more than two years without being charged, announced that they would undertake a hunger strike until they died or were released (*Document 160*). Twenty began refusing food on January 23, more joined a week later, and over the next two weeks several hundred more prisoners began fasting elsewhere, including at St. Alban's in Port Elizabeth, Modderbee in Benoni, as well as at prisons in Witbank, Vereeniging, Westville, Pietermaritzburg, and Cape Town. As the Diepkloof hunger strikers began to be hospitalized in the second week of February, media publicity crescendoed, support groups grew, and MDM supporters—students, lawyers, medical professionals, even prominent Americans mobilized by the TransAfrica lobby group in Washington—began holding sympathy fasts. The State Security Council ordered Vlok, the minister of law and order, to ignore the strikers. Hunger strikes by political prisoners were a recurring phenomenon, and eventually petered out; several hundred detainees had participated in them in 1988 with no significant effect.[35] The cabinet, however, which under Botha regularly deferred to the hard-line security chiefs in such matters, was being chaired in February 1989 by Chris Heunis because Botha was still recuperating from a mild stroke suffered the previous month. Asserting a newfound independence, the cabinet ordered Vlok to find a way to end the hunger strikes quickly.[36] After a lengthy meeting on February 16 between Vlok and a delegation of church leaders, Tutu informed the press that the minister had asked for two weeks to review prisoner records so that a "substantial number" of detainees could be released.[37] Within two weeks over 200 detainees had been freed; by May about 900 held under the emergency regulations had been released and the hunger strikes had ended.

Talking About Talks

In the meantime, other processes of slow-motion bargaining had been unfolding in secret while the government searched for ways to relieve the pressures for political change. As the ANC's prestige rose during the 1980s, state security experts recognized that military countermeasures alone could not suffice; political strategies would also be needed to weaken and divide African opposition. Suppressing the UDF while leaving Inkatha free to build its domestic and international support was one such strategy. Driving a wedge between what were perceived to be the ANC's communist and nationalist wings was another. With that end in view, and hoping to diminish the international notoriety of Robben Island prison, the government in 1982 had shifted five ANC men serving life sentences from Robben Island to Cape Town's Pollsmoor prison. Among the five was Nelson Mandela, South Africa's most famous prisoner and judged by the National Intelligence Service (NIS) to be the most important nationalist.[38] As long as Mandela languished in jail, he would remain an international *cause célèbre* for South Africa's critics. Nothing brought this home more clearly than a star-studded pop concert at London's Wembley Stadium in June 1988 staged to mark Mandela's 70th birthday and watched on television by millions around the world. If Mandela died in prison, his martyr status would grow; if he was released, Pretoria would win international good will. Yet to release him without forcing him first to repudiate some basic tenet of ANC policy—such as its commitment to armed struggle, its goal of majority rule, or its alliance with the Communist Party—would make the government look weak and give ammunition to Andries Treurnicht's Conservative Party. Also worrying for Botha was the possibility that Mandela's release might touch off an upsurge of uncontainable township revolt. In November 1987, 77-year-old Govan Mbeki had been released from Robben Island, purportedly for health reasons but also to test popular response. Mbeki soon began making public statements praising the ANC and the Communist Party, prompting the cautious security establishment to place him under restriction in his home city of Port Elizabeth.

After Mandela's transfer to Pollsmoor, Botha made several public calls for him to renounce violence in return for amnesty, with the results noted in the defiant rejection read out by Zindzi Mandela at a Johannesburg rally in February 1985 (*Document 117*).[39] Later in 1985 Mandela had undergone prostate surgery at Cape Town's Volks Hospital. During his recuperation, Botha's minister of justice, Kobie Coetsee, who was also responsible for prisons, paid Mandela a surprise visit. Although they merely exchanged pleasantries, Mandela was struck by Coetsee's amiable manner and optimistically concluded that the township uprising might be straining the government's confidence to the point where opportunities for talking with the ANC could open up. Mandela immediately instructed one of his lawyers, George Bizos, to go to Lusaka and assure Tambo that if approached by the government, he would adhere strictly to ANC policies.[40] After being discharged from the hospital, Mandela took heart once again when instead of being returned to the company of his ANC colleagues at Pollsmoor, he was confined alone, without explanation, in a suite of rooms in the prison's hospital section—perhaps, he believed, so that the government could approach him with complete confidentiality. Bizos in due course reported back to Mandela that Lusaka was in favor of taking advantage of any approaches from Pretoria as long as they were secret. Both sides were concerned about the high risk of public exposure: political followers could easily jump to the conclusion that their leaders were engaged in selling out to the enemy. Mandela's smuggled statement of February 1985 had been directed at calming precisely such fears.

Mandela's isolation at Pollsmoor began in late November 1985 and was followed by long intervals of silence punctuated by brief interventions from Coetsee. The pace of Coetsee's moves was constrained by Botha's determination to suppress the township uprising before considering any discussions with the ANC, lest anyone believe that violence by blacks could intimidate the government. However, to mollify foreign critics, feed Mandela's desire for freedom and encourage him to adopt more moderate views, Coetsee had his prisoner outfitted with a pinstripe suit and permitted three visits from members of the Commonwealth Eminent Persons Group in early 1986. The results were not quite what Coetsee hoped. Mandela used the opportunity to impress the visitors with his stubborn adherence to the ANC line and with his own qualities of leadership. "We were first struck by his physical authority," the mission report later stated, "by his immaculate appearance, his apparent good health and his commanding presence. In his manner he exuded authority and received the respect of all around him," including his jailers.[41] Coetsee too, who accompanied the delegation on one visit, was awed by Mandela's interaction with his guests. "I was so struck by his presence," he later recalled, "his alertness, his composure, his bearing. . . . I think that was the day I realized this could be the man."[42] But before Mandela could be released to take his place as a national leader, the government's top strategists were determined to make him drop or water down his commitment to at least one or two of the ANC's basic tenets.

In the regime's internal politics, Botha was allied with the hard-line militarists while Coetsee was closer to the "talkers." Both camps believed that the future lay down a path of negotiation, and that if government strategists played their cards right, Afrikaner power could be preserved for many years to come through a decentralized, consociational system based on the principle of group rights, much like the tricameral parliamentary system but with institutional arrangements for Africans to direct their "own affairs" and fulfill their desire for one person, one vote. If Mandela was to play a national leadership role in the future, it would first be necessary to convince him that this was the best and only option for South Africa's long-term prosperity. Most of the militarists took little interest in the political details and focused instead on the application of physical force to maintain the regime's upper hand. In their view, negotiation should take place only under circumstances where the government's superior power was unquestioned. The talkers believed that preliminary discussions with Mandela should go on even while necessary law-and-order operations were in progress, but they were constrained by Botha's preference for the militarists' view.

As a result, for almost a year and a half after the collapse of the Commonwealth mission in May 1986, Mandela's requests to meet with government officials were ignored, apart from one long conversation with Coetsee in June 1986 when Mandela was taken to the minister's residence for what Coetsee must have considered a testing of the waters. Six months later, a prison officer took Mandela for the first of many drives around Cape Town, sometimes stopping at cafés for tea and once visiting the home of a white warder. The government, Mandela believed, wanted him to see that whites were unaffected by township turmoil, and to tempt him so much with "the pleasures of small freedoms" that he "might be willing to compromise in order to have complete freedom."[43] Finally, after the uprising had been crushed and a general election in May 1987 had returned the National Party to power, Botha apparently decided it was prudent to proceed. Mandela was taken for several further meetings with Coetsee at his Cape Town home, then informed that in the year to come, a secret committee would be formed to carry the discussions forward. Coetsee would chair the committee, and Dr. Niël Barnard, head of the NIS, would be a member, as would two senior prison officials. The committee would report directly to Botha.

In late May 1988 Mandela began meeting with the committee, sometimes once a week, sometimes less frequently. Early in August he was hospitalized with incipient tuberculosis and spent the next four months being treated for the disease, during which the secret meetings continued at Cape Town's Constantiaberg Clinic. Mandela's illness could not be kept secret and led to heightened media speculation and diplomatic pressure for his release on humanitarian grounds. Botha was disdainful of these considerations, however, plowing forward with his plans for creating a National Statutory Council for Africans in which a free Mandela could eventually be invited to participate. Meanwhile Barnard, Botha's point man in the secret committee, pressed Mandela relentlessly regarding armed struggle, the ANC-SACP alliance, and the impossibility of majority rule given white fears of black domination. Mandela gave no ground on fundamental ANC positions, instead patiently explaining, over and over, the rationale for ANC policies, how they had evolved historically, and also why the ANC was committed to racial reconciliation. Little by little, as Barnard and the committee came to realize that detaching Mandela from core ANC policies was going to be impossible, they also began privately to let go of some of their own preconceived assumptions about the African struggle for democracy and to recognize that a viable negotiated settlement might be possible.

At the same time that Barnard was controlling all exchanges with Mandela, he was also monitoring a second series of secret talks taking place in Britain. In 1986, acting on a request from Tambo, a British businessman named Michael Young had undertaken to set up a channel through which the ANC could meet privately with members of the Afrikaner establishment in order to better understand their thinking.[44] Young's work began bearing fruit when the first in a series of bilateral discussions took place at an English country inn near Henley-on-Thames in October 1987. The notes taken at the meeting by one of the ANC participants (*Document 146*) indicate the broad scope of the two days of talks, presided over by Young. The Afrikaners—three Stellenbosch professors—briefed the ANC on the thinking of state securocrats in the army, police, and intelligence services. The professors reported that although the National Party, in deference to white voters, was still publicly wedded to the concept of future collaborationist bodies into which moderate Africans would be co-opted once radicals had been suppressed, the more pragmatic securocrats recognized that a mutually acceptable political solution would eventually have to be negotiated between the government and the ANC.

To effect this, the professors said, two things needed to be hammered out. First, there had to be a consensus on what preconditions were necessary before full-fledged negotiations could begin. For example, the government would probably not insist that the ANC renounce armed struggle as a precondition. National Party politicians liked to demand at election time that the ANC renounce violence, but this could instead be regarded as a bargaining point. More problematic would be the process of prisoner releases and whether the ANC could guarantee that these would not spark new turmoil. Second, before opening serious negotiations, the government needed to have as clear an understanding as possible about the "bottom line"—what kind of future political system would be mutually acceptable to both sides. On its side, the government required a future system that recognized "group rights," by which they meant, for example, the right of whites to retain full control over their own schools. What degree of future white privilege or veto power would the ANC accept?

Either before or soon after Professor Willie Esterhuyse's trip to Henley—accounts differ—he was contacted by the NIS, which had learned of his participation in Michael Young's plan through a phone tap. Esterhuyse agreed to report back to Barnard as long as he was permitted to tell Thabo Mbeki that he was doing so and that Barnard would be reporting to Botha. This meant that in February 1988 when the three professors (Esterhuyse, Sampie Terreblanche, and Willie Breytenbach) returned to Britain, and, with two new Afrikaner participants, sat down for their second meeting with the ANC (represented this time by Mbeki, Aziz Pahad, Harold Wolpe, and Tony Trew), an almost direct—but still deniable—line of communication had been opened through which the two sides could explore each other's minimum demands. At least six other secret meetings followed, most of them at Mells Park, a secluded English estate near Bath that belonged to Young's company, Consolidated Gold Fields. Jacob Zuma and Joe Nhlanhla, representing the ANC's intelligence apparatus, attended some of the meetings, as did more than a dozen additional Afrikaner opinion leaders beyond the original core group. Most important, Wimpie de Klerk, the older brother of the minister of education, F. W. de Klerk, became a participant from the third meeting in August 1988, and thereafter provided briefings to his brother, who would succeed Botha as president of South Africa the following year.

Like the highly publicized Dakar trek in 1987, these secret meetings had a quiet ripple effect on elite Afrikaner opinion, contributing to a realization, as Terreblanche later put it, that the people at the ANC's helm "were not monsters. They were reasonable, educated, civilized people; moderate leaders."[45] The ANC also gained useful knowledge about developments and disagreements inside South Africa's ruling elite. Friendships were formed and acknowledgment of a common patriotism became possible in spite of underlying fears and mistrust. Pragmatically, the secret talks enabled each side to begin shaping its positions to take into account the other's likely objections. Both came to recognize that public poses struck by the other side did not necessarily represent its true position, and each began to accept that it might ultimately not be possible to impose all its preferred solutions on the other.[46] Both gained confidence that the other side would be capable of delivering support from most of its followers once a basic agreement had been struck, but both also recognized that among their wider constituencies there were elements deeply opposed to negotiations because they believed advantages could still be gained through violence. Among Botha's hard-liners, particularly in the police and military intelligence, there were elements regularly engaged in kidnapping, assassinating, and even poisoning anti-apartheid activists—measures far in excess of the force levels required to quell township upheaval.⁴⁷ In Umkhonto we Sizwe there were still commanders as well as cadres who clung religiously to the belief that a revolutionary "seizure of power" could occur if only armed struggle were pursued more zealously.⁴⁸

A Sea of Troubles

Oliver Tambo, aging and in poor health by 1988, continued to steer the ANC's ramshackle administrative ship through rough political waters, supporting the armed struggle rhetorically even as he helped to guide the organization's clandestine dialogue with Pretoria through Mbeki at the Mells Park meetings. Minutes of the ANC National Working Committee in the late 1980s (such as *Document 143*) conveyed a sense of endemic disorder and frustration in Lusaka as decisions were reached but not implemented, communication breakdowns multiplied, and entire departments drifted while their heads were unaccountably absent. At the same time, the stream of trekkers from "home" flowed on, each requiring an appropriate response (*Document 176*). Invitations to international conferences poured in and journalists demanded interviews, putting constant pressure on the ANC to present a coherent set of policy positions to the world. Sweden made funds available for a think tank on "PASA"—post-apartheid South Africa—but for lack of expertise in its own ranks and fear of igniting divisive arguments, the ANC's progress in policy development was slow. Foreign supporters expected the ANC to spell out its future vision at a four-day international anti-apartheid conference in Arusha, Tanzania, in December 1987, but little of substance emerged.⁴⁹ One important advance came in August 1988, however, with the publication of the ANC's "Constitutional Guidelines for a Democratic South Africa" (*Document 153*), commissioned by Tambo soon after the Kabwe conference. This landmark discussion paper had gone through multiple drafts, drawing on the views of sympathetic legal experts inside and outside South Africa and taking into account the worldwide audience now scrutinizing the organization as a possible government-in-waiting. Without repudiating anything in the 1955 Freedom Charter, the Guidelines positioned the ANC as a social democratic party strongly protective of individual rights while also committed to "corrective action which guarantees a rapid and irreversible redistribution of wealth and opening up of facilities to all." Launched not as a final pronouncement but as a document for debate, the Guidelines were widely critiqued from both the right and the left, shrewdly positioning the ANC astride a broad ideological center. The Guidelines envisaged "a mixed economy combining planning and market mechanisms," said one commentary by UDF activists, but "considerable scope for debate on the precise mix remained" (*Document 154*).

Meanwhile, developments in neighboring Namibia were taking a new turn that would impact the ANC's political calculations. In early 1988 the prolonged international legal and political dispute over the territory, a de facto colony of South Africa, began moving toward resolution. After years of foot dragging, Pretoria agreed to engage in a diplomatic exercise sponsored by the Reagan administration to negotiate a withdrawal from Namibia and Angola in return for an agreement by Cuba and the Soviet Union to end their military aid to the government of Angola. Burdened by the costs of its military commitment in Angola, and under pressure from the Americans and Soviets working jointly, South Africa struck a peace deal with Cuba and Angola in December 1988.[50] SWAPO, an ally of the ANC, won a national election eleven months later, ensuring its control of a soon-to-be-independent Namibia. This outcome was positive for South African liberation groups in that it seemed likely to undermine white resistance to the logic of majority rule. On the other hand, two aspects of the brokered agreement posed serious potential threats to the ANC.

One threat was the prospect that, as in Namibia, the Botha regime in concert with foreign governments might work out a settlement over the heads of Africans who, like SWAPO, would be required to accept a solution devised for them without their participation. In Zimbabwe as well, although the Zimbabwe African National Union (ZANU) and Zimbabwe African People's Union (ZAPU) were present at the Lancaster House talks in 1979, white rule had ended on terms imposed by Britain with support from neighboring states that were suffering as a result of Robert Mugabe's determination to win an outright military victory.[51] Might the ANC also be faced with an imposed settlement in which the frontline states in effect sided with Pretoria? The governments of Botswana and Mozambique, although sympathetic to the ANC, strongly favored a negotiated settlement, and like Swaziland and Zimbabwe, actively opposed the use of their territory by guerrillas in transit. Despite Tambo's close friendship with President Kaunda, there were also serious strains in the ANC's relationship with its Zambian hosts, making expulsion from Zambia a recurring possibility.[52] And waiting in the wings was an ally of Chief Mangosuthu Buthelezi, Margaret Thatcher, who was willing to broker a Zimbabwe-style settlement if Pretoria agreed, although President George H. W. Bush in Washington, elected in late 1988, soon went on record as favoring ANC participation. Able to see which way the wind was blowing, Bush even invited a delegation from the UDF to the White House, obliging Thatcher to follow suit. The delegation, composed of Albertina Sisulu, Curnick Ndlovu, Azhar Cachalia, Sister Bernard Ncube, and Titus Mafolo, met Bush on June 30, 1989, then visited Sweden, France, and Britain, where Thatcher received them on July 12.

Potentially more threatening to the ANC was a provision in the Namibian settlement requiring the removal of MK's military camps from Angola. Lest the regime find an excuse to renege on the larger peace agreement, the ANC began shifting its guerrilla forces to distant Uganda in early 1989, knowing this retreat would be perceived as a bitter setback by many hundreds of its young cadres still hoping eventually to be deployed by MK. After the 1984 Nkomati Accord, the number of guerrilla attacks had risen every year inside South Africa, but the growing difficulty of transiting through the frontline states had resulted by 1988 in more of these attacks being carried out by fighters recruited and trained inside the country.[53] At the height of the 1984–86 uprising, a new wave of township militants—the "young lions"—began choosing exile, and many had ended up in MK's Angolan camps or stuck in the pipeline of trained cadres piling up in Zambia to await deployment. Transit obstacles (*Document 140*) were not the only problem. The ANC's inability to construct a reliable political underground meant there were too few operatives who could receive, hide and transport guerrillas after they crossed into South Africa. In addition, many of those languishing in ANC camps had been judged unfit for MK deployment. Because of its remoteness, Angola had become a dumping ground for these military rejects, and their disgruntlement was a constant source of worry in light of the ANC's calamitous experience with the camp mutinies of 1984 (chapter 4).[54] Now these angry youths, plus a portion of the fighters idling in Zambia, were to be moved north, farther from the battlefront at a time when rumors were flying about leaders working for a negotiated settlement instead of for the military "seizure of power" that all MK cadres were taught was the ANC's goal. *Document 173* conveys the resentment and frustration of young guerrillas as they confronted a member of the ANC's national executive in mid-1989. The ANC had been remarkably successful in preventing public exposure of events surrounding the 1984 mutiny. A new mutiny in the more open environments of Zambia or Uganda could have had a much more politically damaging outcome. Inside South Africa too, intergenerational conflict was always barely below the surface. When the exiled ANC talked about "ungovernability" in South Africa, one young UDF activist later recalled, "we said what they really meant was us."[55]

Alongside these threats and dysfunctions, friction between fighters and talkers inside the NEC continued, with Tambo doing what he could to encourage cooperation for common goals. Precise knowledge about the Mells Park talks was confined to a small group called the President's Committee, and periodic rumors about secret meetings in "London" irritated NEC members who were excluded (*Document 143*). Shaken by public statements of Soviet spokesmen favoring a negotiated settlement,[56] Chris Hani and Steve Tshwete, respectively MK's chief of staff and national commissar, became increasingly determined to proclaim that armed struggle still had an important role to play.[57] When at their most optimistic, they argued that history and revolutionary theory showed that even the most seemingly powerful governments—the Shah's Iran, for example—could collapse if their forces became overstretched or divided, opening the way for a well-prepared counterforce to seize power.[58]

In moments colored more by reason than by ideological faith, the fighters conceded that there was no prospect of military victory, but used practical political arguments to defend armed struggle. Any liberation movement that gave up its military capacity would be at the mercy of its enemies regardless of what kind of agreement was arrived at on paper or who won an election, they argued. Experience showed that the National Party was a thoroughly untrustworthy foe. Moreover, without MK and its fiery slogans about seizing power, the ANC's militant followers in the townships at home might fall away or turn to rival leaders inside the country. Joshua Nkomo, the father of Zimbabwe's liberation struggle and a former ANC ally, had been pushed aside by Mugabe's more militarily aggressive ZANU. In South Africa, the PAC, Unity Movement and AZAPO still had followings and were fiercely attacking anything to do with negotiation as a hoax and a sellout (*Document 172*). Chief Buthelezi was making venomous attacks on the ANC (*Document 98*) and his warlords were escalating their assaults on UDF supporters. The development of popular self-defense units had to be promoted. In these circumstances, the fighters argued, if the ANC suspended or renounced violence as the government demanded, it would be giving up its strongest weapon of self defense as well as self-promotion.

In a new departure in 1988, Hani and Tshwete argued that until whites had agreed to talk peace, MK was still needed to drive them to the negotiating table—even if this meant relaxing the ANC's policy of not attacking civilian ("soft") targets. White South Africans were still living a "sweet life," Hani told a journalist in a June 1988 interview; it was time they learned the high cost of apartheid.[59] A spate of bombings over the following months, some in white commercial areas and one that killed two whites after a rugby match at Johannesburg's Ellis Park, appeared to signal a new turn. Tambo chided the press for making news of white deaths when the violent deaths of black civilians regularly went unreported. But in a rare departure from his past practice of not removing officials who had become political liabilities, Tambo removed Tshwete as MK commissar and in August the NEC issued a statement reiterating the ANC's policy of not targeting civilians.

Just when this course correction was occurring, the ANC also began implementing a plan to overcome the underground's chronic inadequacies. The plan, Operation Vula, was first conceived in early 1986 in discussions between Tambo and four influential NEC members: Hani, Zuma, Mac Maharaj, and Joe Slovo. Two years of secret preparation had produced elaborate disguises, false documents, and cover stories to explain the disappearance from Lusaka of key actors who were to go inside South Africa. A number of foreign co-conspirators were recruited, including a Dutch airline stewardess. Armed with the latest computer technology, Maharaj and Siphiwe Nyanda, an MK commander, crossed from Swaziland into South Africa in August 1988 to begin creating a system to stockpile weapons, coordinate ANC political and military personnel, and link them with Lusaka as well as with operatives in the MDM's aboveground structures.[60] Had such an effort been made years earlier, it was reasoned, the ANC would have quickly been able to capitalize on the insurrections of 1976 and 1984 instead of merely observing them from afar. Through a system of transmitting computer-coded messages over telephone lines via modems, daily contact was established between Lusaka and Vula's gradually expanding network of underground operatives. Vula was to be overtaken by events in 1990, but by then its achievements had demonstrated that despite decades of failure the ANC was indeed capable of dramatically improving its underground organization—albeit under conditions so secret that only a handful of people in the National Executive Committee had any knowledge of it.[61]

Never abandoning hope that new circumstances might create the conditions for a long-imagined successful "people's war," Slovo set aside Moscow's declared preference for a peaceful settlement of the South African conflict and fell back on well-worn propaganda themes in drafting a major policy paper for the Communist Party's seventh congress to be held near Havana in April 1989. "The prospects of achieving a revolutionary break-through in South Africa are greater today than ever before in our history," declared "The Path to Power" (*Document 165*). "[M]ass upsurge, . . . mass defiance, escalating revolutionary combat activity, intensified international pressure, a situation of ungovernability, a deteriorating economy and growing demoralisation, division, vacillation and confusion within the power bloc" could produce a "sudden transformation. . . . The regime's grip . . . could be swiftly weakened and the stage set for a sustained national uprising leading to an insurrectionary seizure of power."[62] Three short paragraphs near the end of the lengthy document raised the possibility of a negotiated settlement. Although "The Path to Power" defiantly asserted that MK was "not engaged in a struggle whose objective is merely to generate sufficient pressure to bring the other side to the negotiating table," MK's leaders, like their militarist counterparts on the government side, could indeed foresee future talks with the enemy—but only after their own forces had established clear superiority on the ground.[63]

Thabo Mbeki, a member of the SACP Politburo, went along with the message conveyed in "The Path to Power" and agreed to present the document at the party conference in Cuba. Meanwhile, however, he and Tambo were increasingly confident that the ANC was moving toward genuine negotiations by means of the Mells Park dialogue.[64] They knew that Mandela too was pursuing this goal in his secret discussions with the government's committee, although they shared some unease about the precise content of his conversations. No one who personally knew Mandela could imagine him accepting the role of a puppet leader similar to Bishop Abel Muzorewa in Zimbabwe. On the other hand, it was conceivable that after 26 years in prison, he might be tempted to strike some kind of nefarious political bargain.

Following his stay in Constantiaberg Clinic, Mandela was moved in December 1988 to a warder's bungalow at Victor Verster prison near Paarl, a closely guarded and heavily bugged but comfortable accommodation where he was permitted to have frequent visitors (*Document 162*). At Mandela's request, Coetsee and Barnard had agreed to seek a meeting for him with Botha. To facilitate such a meeting, they proposed that Mandela put into writing the positions he had been taking in his meetings with them. In mid-January 1989, Botha suffered a mild stroke and no meeting could be scheduled, but Mandela continued to work on a memorandum for the state president. In March, he dictated the memorandum (*Document 163*) to Ismail Ayob, one of his lawyers, with instructions to take it to Lusaka. By early April copies of the memo were in the hands of both Tambo and the MDM's unofficial leadership—the so-called Crisis Committee, the core members of which were Frank Chikane, Cyril Ramaphosa, Sydney Mufamadi, Sister Bernard Ncube, Aubrey Mokoena, and Beyers Naudé.

A step closer?

Figure 11. Cartoonist's depiction of the imprisoned Mandela after news was leaked about his secret July 1989 meeting with P. W. Botha, whose nickname was "die groot krokodil." At that time, no photos of Mandela had been published in over 20 years. *By permission of the Johannesburg Star.*

When Naudé visited Lusaka in late April, Mandela's memo was discussed by the President's Committee (*Document 166*), but the memo's most controversial passage was not mentioned in the meeting's minutes:

> [t]he key to the whole situation is a negotiated settlement, and a meeting between the government and the ANC will be the first major step. . . . Two political issues will have to be addressed at such a meeting; firstly, the demand for majority rule in a unitary state, secondly, the concern of white South Africa over this demand, as well as the insistence of whites on structural guarantees that majority rule will not mean domination of the white minority by blacks. The most crucial task which will face the government and the ANC will be to reconcile these two positions. Such reconciliation will be achieved only if both parties are willing to compromise.

The ambiguity of this passage, which could be seen as offering to water down the principle of majority rule, plus rumors about Mandela's three-piece suits and "luxurious" prison accommodations, touched off a wave of anti-Mandela rumors among township and trade union activists who had not read Mandela's memo but were wary of being betrayed by the ANC's "tired" older leaders. Govan Mbeki, who had unsuccessfully challenged Mandela's leadership on Robben Island, fanned these rumors by warning MDM members to shun invitations to meet with Mandela at Victor Verster. Only a rapid exercise in damage control by Maharaj—underground with Operation Vula—averted a potential crisis of loyalties in the ANC.[65] On July 5 Mandela was taken secretly to have tea with Botha at Tuynhuys, the president's official Cape Town residence. Botha soon leaked news of the meeting to the press, producing new jitters in Lusaka and the MDM regarding Mandela's actions. Mandela, the state-run South African Broadcasting Corporation slyly proclaimed, "by identifying himself with the ideals of peaceful development" was putting "pressure on those—most notably in the ANC—who still insist on adherence to a strategy of violence."[66]

Tambo at age 71 was indeed tired, but by mid-1989 he was convinced that the only way the ANC could capture the initiative was to set out its preconditions for negotiation and win broad support for them internationally before the government could win backing for its own proposals. In early June a delegation from COSATU and the MDM came to Lusaka to consult with the ANC about this strategy. Reporting back to their members (*Document 170*), COSATU leaders stated frankly that both the ANC and the Botha regime were being pushed by foreign governments to negotiate, and that if the ANC and its allies did not respond, they might soon find themselves having to deal with the enemy on terms favorable to Pretoria. Thatcher was hoping to roll back sanctions when the Commonwealth heads of government met in October, and was scheming with Botha's heir apparent, F. W. de Klerk, to establish a negotiating forum that would persuade the world that a settlement was in sight.[67]

The pressure of deadlines spurred the ANC's diplomatic effort into high gear. When the Organization of African Unity (OAU) met in Addis Ababa in late July, the ANC urged adoption of a comprehensive document on negotiations that could win continental support. The ANC was given two weeks to submit such a document, starting from a draft that was already quietly being circulated for comment both inside and outside South Africa.[68] Using Kaunda's private jet, Tambo and a team of five younger men embarked on a diplomatic blitzkrieg in the frontline states, fine-tuning the document and incorporating the advice of experienced allies, including Tanzania's Julius Nyerere and Eduardo Dos Santos of Angola.[69] A special OAU subcommittee, meeting in Harare on August 21, 1989, accepted the document with one minor amendment and it was issued as the Harare Declaration (*Document 174*).

Devoid of the revolutionary bombast of many ANC public statements and devised to offer Pretoria achievable goals, the Harare Declaration was a masterful roadmap for the negotiation of a political settlement requiring no external mediation. It called for agreement on a set of broad constitutional principles and key measures to create a climate for negotiation, following which a "mutually binding ceasefire" could begin. The process for writing a new constitution would be a matter for negotiation, as would the transitional arrangements leading to the holding of elections. Sanctions could be lifted once a new constitution was in place. In the meantime, a program of action was proposed to maintain world support for the negotiation process. The Declaration was endorsed by the countries in the Non-Aligned Movement meeting in Belgrade in September, and in December the UN General Assembly unanimously endorsed a modified version.[70] By means of a diplomatic tour de force, the ANC had emerged as a formidable organization with an internationally acceptable vision of the road ahead. Amid the success of these efforts, however, a major setback occurred on August 9 when Tambo suffered a debilitating stroke and was forced to retire from active leadership.[71] Nzo assumed the position of acting ANC president, and Thabo Mbeki, head of the ANC's international affairs department, continued managing indirect communications with Pretoria. On-and-off peace talks between the UDF and Inkatha petered out when a proposed meeting between Tambo and Buthelezi had to be indefinitely postponed.[72]

Grasping the Nettle

Within a week of Tambo's hospitalization, a change of top leadership also occurred in the National Party. In a confrontation with his cabinet, the cantankerous Botha resigned as state president on August 14, 1989, giving way to F. W. de Klerk, who had been chosen party leader after Botha's stroke seven months earlier. A general election on September 6 then returned the National Party to power, but with a significantly reduced majority as white voters polarized, quitting the ruling party in about equal numbers for the *verkrampte* Conservative Party and the new liberal Democratic Party (an alliance of the Progressive Federal Party and earlier National Party *verligte* defectors). De Klerk was as stubbornly dedicated as his predecessor to keeping the National Party in power and whites in control. He saw Botha's reliance on the security forces as a political liability, however, and moved within a few months to dissolve the National Security Management System as well as the State Security Council, which had all but replaced the cabinet as the locus of government decision making.

De Klerk believed that negotiation was the best way forward, first to disarm international critics and then to achieve the most favorable possible political settlement for whites. Like many whites, he was confident that the majority of Africans were moderates at heart and would respond positively to honest efforts to achieve greater fairness in everyday life, even if this meant letting whites retain many forms of control. A skillful government dedicated to this goal should be able to marginalize violent extremist groups like the ANC, he believed. As he saw it, other paths into the future—Botha's policy paralysis, the Conservative Party's goal of returning to Verwoerdian-style apartheid—were doomed to fail, as was the Democratic Party's policy of one person, one vote in a federal system, a policy condemned by the National Party as white surrender. Instead, de Klerk saw the best solution as a new constitution that protected individuals through a bill of rights but was also structured to protect "group rights." This way, all groups could be represented "without domination of any group over another."

"Group rights" was a new term for the "own affairs" principle of South Africa's existing constitution, which divided all public matters into "general" affairs (for example, foreign policy, banking regulations, national roads) and "own" affairs defined as particular to racial groups (schools, cultural programs, local roads). In early 1989 the government-appointed South African Law Commission had rejected "group rights" as a valid constitutional concept, but de Klerk and his new minister of constitutional affairs, Gerrit Viljoen, brushed aside the commission's findings.[73] Borrowing from the deliberations of the Natal Indaba (chapter 1), de Klerk and Viljoen proposed instead that 1 among the 20 or more recognized "groups" or voting blocs could be a self-identified "non-racial" group composed of people who preferred not to be categorized by race or ethnicity, and who could choose to reside in racially mixed "free settlement areas."[74] Homeland governments would continue to represent African ethnic groups, despite palpable opposition to this by many of their own "citizens."[75] Thus, although liberalization—the discarding of various repressive laws and practices—could take place, and indeed was vital to restoring the confidence of foreign banks and governments, de Klerk's bottom line was not majoritarian democracy as understood elsewhere in the world. Rather, his goal remained mere "power sharing," a race-based system deemed suitable in South Africa's "special" conditions.[76] To achieve this, the National Party would need to construct a winning electoral coalition of whites and anti-ANC non-whites who were committed to a similar vision.

In their June 1989 deliberations with the ANC in Lusaka, MDM and COSATU representatives had adopted a plan to challenge the National Party with a mass campaign of civil disobedience, building on the success of the rent strikes and detainee hunger strikes. Activist church leaders had called for a similar "Standing for the Truth" campaign almost a year earlier, but had failed to generate significant popular support. Now momentum for mass action began to build, encouraged by signs that Botha's hold on power was slipping and with it the unbridled influence of the security establishment. To test the government's propaganda claims that South Africa was moving away from apartheid, black patients, backed up by demonstrators and press photographers, began seeking treatment at segregated white hospitals. Groups of black bathers descended on "white" beaches, and black pupils demonstrated against segregated schools (*Document 175*). Police broke up some of the demonstrations, beating and tear gassing protesters and foreign journalists, many of whom had obtained visas to cover the September 6 general election but found on arrival that the defiance campaign was a better story.

On August 20, the sixth anniversary of the UDF's founding, MDM leaders declared at a rally at St. George's Cathedral that the UDF was unbanning itself. A national stayaway called for September 5–6 provoked widespread police brutality resulting in at least 23 deaths. Violence was particularly marked in the western Cape where one coloured police lieutenant, Gregory Rockman— an overnight popular hero—publicly accused riot police of attacking demonstrators like "mad dogs." The opposition reaction was to escalate the defiance campaign, leading to mass marches in Cape Town, Johannesburg, Dur-

Figure 12. A march called by the mass democratic movement creates a sea of banners in central Durban, September 22, 1989. *Rafs Mayet/africanpictures.net*

ban, East London, and other urban centers in the days following the election. People of all colors and every point on the opposition spectrum participated. De Klerk won worldwide praise for allowing these post-election marches to go forward without police interference. Tutu, one of the campaign's prime movers, offered a frank appraisal of the protests and their wider political context in an October 1989 interview (*Document 177*).

De Klerk as state president was now in a position to try to control the process of change, but he also had reason to fear the heightened expectations of blacks. Thatcher was urging him to free Mandela quickly, but popular reaction to such a step was dangerously unpredictable. Even minor concessions might lead to major unanticipated consequences. Eastern Europe in late 1989 was being rocked by massive anti-government demonstrations. What if a million protesters marched on the Union Buildings in Pretoria and refused to disperse? But there was no going back, and as the annual Commonwealth heads of government meeting in October drew closer, new sanctions threats loomed. So with days to go before the Commonwealth conference, and in the midst of delicate negotiations to reschedule South Africa's debts, de Klerk in a bold gesture on October 15 freed eight high-profile prisoners: five life-serving ANC defendants from the 1964 Rivonia trial (Walter Sisulu, Ahmed Kathrada, Raymond Mhlaba, Andrew Mlangeni and Elias Motsoaledi), plus Wilton Mkwayi, Oscar Mpetha, and a life-serving PAC veteran, Jeff Masemola. African reactions were euphoric but controlled; only 70,000 people—a large number, but barely 5 percent of Soweto's population—turned out for a rally

Figure 13. F. W. de Klerk won international praise for allowing anti-apartheid marches in urban centers during September 1989, but the specter of uncontrolled mass demonstrations haunted his government. *By permission of the Johannesburg Star.*

to honor the Rivonia men at Soccer City stadium in Johannesburg on October 29. De Klerk's strategists may have concluded from this that the ANC's grassroots support was not as vast as sometimes claimed. They may also have taken heart when Cyril Ramaphosa, the popular head of the National Union of Mineworkers, made what some saw as disparaging remarks about Mandela in a magazine interview soon after the releases (*Document 179*). Perhaps an approach based on splitting the ANC and dividing it from its internal allies might yet bear fruit. Tambo's greatest achievement had been holding together the ANC and the wider Congress movement through 30 years in the wilderness. With Tambo gone and negotiations on the horizon, might leadership rivalries in the ANC now develop into openly contending factions?

A rough political road lay ahead both for the defenders of the status quo and those who challenged it. Barely a month after de Klerk's inauguration, his government was confronted with damaging revelations about illegal security force activities. In a bid to obtain a stay of execution, a black prisoner on death row in Pretoria, Butana Almond Nofomela, confessed to a lawyer that he had belonged to a police hit squad. Together they prepared an affidavit (*Document 178*) naming Nofomela's commanding officers and describing the hit squad's 1981 murder of ANC lawyer Griffiths Mxenge. An Afrikaner police captain named in the affidavit, Dirk Coetzee, fled South Africa and sought protection from the ANC in exchange for telling his story to *Vrye Weekblad*.[77] Alarmed by Coetzee's disclosures, de Klerk denied any knowledge about police crimes or responsibility for them, and used the revelations to further politically demote the security forces. Half-baked official investigations were launched to discredit Coetzee. Not until the appointment of the Goldstone Commission in late 1991 did a systematic exposure of hit squads and other illegal security-force activities finally begin.

In the meantime, however, the National Party was not alone in hoping that unsavory aspects of its past could be kept from public scrutiny as South Africa moved toward the negotiation phase of its long racial conflict. The ANC too had skeletons in its closet, most notably the execution of at least 34 alleged spies and mutineers in Angola in the early 1980s, the long detention in appalling conditions of others, and the 1989 death of ANC commander Thami Zulu under suspicious circumstances.[78] As Namibian independence approached, many victims of abuses by SWAPO in exile began to tell of their ordeals, raising the prospect of similar disclosures about the ANC. The MDM had already weathered embarrassing accusations that Winnie Mandela, Nelson Mandela's headstrong wife, had been involved in the December 1988 kidnapping and murder of Stompie Seipei, a young "comrade" she accused of being a police agent. Her own bad judgment, together with the actions of police-paid provocateurs among her gang of self-styled bodyguards, touched off a crisis in early 1989 that threatened to sully the Mandela name (*Document 166*). At the same time, tensions marred relations between MDM leaders who publicly chastised Winnie Mandela and thousands of the townships' poorest residents to whom she was a beloved champion.[79]

The startling collapse of communist rule in Eastern Europe in the last half of 1989 deeply undermined morale in the Communist Party and among trade unionists. SACP members had tended to interpret Mikhail Gorbachev's "new thinking"—which the media referred to by the shorthand terms *glasnost* and *perestroika* (openness and restructuring)—as mere tactical reform. But what could explain the sudden and massive rejection of communist leadership from Estonia to Bulgaria and the dismantling of the Berlin Wall? And would the ANC be able to prevail without support from these staunch socialist bloc allies?[80] Trying to make sense of the new situation and promote the case for democratic socialism, Slovo in January 1990 produced a pamphlet, "Has Socialism Failed?" (*Document 181*), in which he argued that to maintain "confidence in the future of socialism and its inherent moral superiority" it was vital "to subject the past of existing socialism to an unsparing critique." Influenced or not by Slovo's critique, the prestige of the SACP as a symbol of resistance remained high among young blacks inside South Africa. Once the party was unbanned, thousands applied to join, even as the Soviet Union itself was dissolving and many older party members in the ANC were quietly letting their membership lapse.

Figure 14. Pan Africanist Congress veteran Zeph Mothopeng, flanked by his wife, Urbania, and Benny Alexander, at a press conference shortly after his release from prison, Diepkloof, Soweto, November 28, 1988. Alexander, soon to be elected secretary general of the Pan Africanist Movement (PAM), later changed his name to Khoisan X. *Anna Zieminski/africanpictures.net*

In the meantime, de Klerk's release of high-profile prisoners in October 1989 had prompted opposition organizations to display banned political banners and symbols more openly inside South Africa. PAC loyalists, whose most revered senior leader, Zeph Mothopeng, had been released from prison a year earlier because of failing health, joined the increasingly fevered competition for popular support, stepping up efforts to recruit among black intellectuals, students, workers, and unemployed youth. Having established a strong foothold in NACTU by electing Africanists Patricia de Lille and Cunningham Ngcukana to the federation's executive in 1988, PAC partisans also relied on their youth organization, Azanian Youth Unity (AZANYU), to spread their message, and began courting SACOS, the anti-MDM black sports federation. By late 1989, the Pan Africanist Student Organisation had been founded, and plans were in place to create a thinly veiled internal wing of the exiled PAC, the Pan Africanist Movement (PAM). PAM was formally launched the first weekend of December at a Soweto conference. Some 600 delegates elected an executive committee headed by Clarence Makwetu, a founding member of the PAC, but dominated by Benny Alexander, an energetic young Africanist from Kimberley who became secretary general.

PAM's ideology, a melding of African nationalism and socialist rhetoric, appealed to the anti-white mindset of many blacks—"one settler, one bullet" was a popular PAM slogan—at the same time holding out to idealists the vision of a non-racial future beyond the stormy sea of revolution. Africanists debated with black consciousness advocates about whether whites should be allowed to join their organizations. AZAPO was opposed, but Africanists were not, if in rare cases, they argued, there were individual whites who psychologically had become "Africans" instead of "settlers." Neither camp displayed much tactical sense of how to take advantage of de Klerk's new openness (*Document 180*), and both adopted the same rejectionist position toward negotiations that the Unity Movement was propagating (*Document 172*). Both also complained, rather disingenuously, that their organizations faced discrimination in raising funds abroad (*Document 161*). Indeed, on that score the contrast between Africanist and black consciousness groups and UDF-aligned organizations was sharp. The latter, despite restrictions, were still able to finance over 150 paid staff, dozens of plane tickets, and office rents from a cumulative proposed annual budget of nearly R8 million ($3 million) in 1989.[81] Nevertheless, observers continued to speculate that if PAC were free to organize openly, its ability to attract followers and support would grow rapidly, an assumption lent credence because many black journalists leaned toward the philosophies of black consciousness and Africanism.

A week after the launch of PAM, the MDM convened a major meeting—the Conference for a Democratic Future (CDF)—at the University of the Witwatersrand in Johannesburg. This event, which drew over 4,000 observers and delegates representing hundreds of opposition organizations, was the culmination of a sustained effort by the MDM to build a united front inside South Africa that could eventually sit as a solid bloc to face the government at a "two-sided" negotiating table.[82] Realizing that it would be difficult for some non-Charterists to endorse the Harare Declaration, an ANC document, the CDF organizers sought simply to foster a consensus in favor of the "spirit" of the Declaration. But the composition of the conference made this an elusive goal. Inkatha was not invited, and PAM and Unity Movement groups declined to attend. AZAPO, however, put aside its reservations about negotiations and participated, bringing along representatives from the NACTU unions that were black consciousness oriented. Some senior AZAPO leaders, including Khehla Mthembu and Muntu Myeza, saw virtue in a united front, but once the conference was underway on December 9–10, the black consciousness camp balked at the presence of homeland politicians in the conference hall and at what they saw as the CDF's predetermined outcome. In the end, black consciousness delegates voted against an endorsement of the Declaration in either substance or spirit, claiming they needed more time to study the matter. The Africanists also were divided. PAM and Africanists in NACTU had boycotted the conference, but opinion was more ambivalent in the exiled PAC. Only four days after the CDF, the PAC's chief representative at the UN, Gora Ebrahim, worked through the predawn hours of December 14 with Thabo Mbeki and a committee of concerned diplomats to finalize the resolution that would be adopted later that day in the General Assembly supporting the Harare Declaration.[83]

South Africa was on the brink of historic change, advancing headlong toward a future for which few senior political leaders on either side were yet psychologically prepared. Whether particular blacks saw de Klerk's conciliatory style as a trap or an opportunity depended on their experience and expertise, plus whatever individual chemistry determined their mix of fear and hope. Just as it was common for whites to underestimate the abilities of blacks and misread their motives, blacks often held an exaggerated view of whites' skill and commitment to a common purpose. In a climate so thick with uncertainties, de Klerk might have hesitated to plunge forward. Once invested with full presidential authority, however, he was determined to seize the initiative, ward off further sanctions and international isolation, and move quickly toward the writing of a new constitution. Old propaganda about the ANC as part of a communist onslaught had lost traction with the collapse of Eastern European governments. The United States and Britain were warming to the ANC. The time had come for whites in South Africa to grapple directly with the reality of African aspirations before the scales of power tipped any further.[84] The faster he could move, de Klerk believed, the more unprepared his opponents—both on the left and the right—would be, and the less able to keep their constituencies in a state of constant mobilization. Of course, all outside attempts to dictate prescriptions to Pretoria had to be disdainfully rejected, including the Harare Declaration. Nevertheless, the declaration represented a minimal international consensus on preconditions for formal negotiations—the unbanning of organizations, freeing of prisoners, suspension of emergency restrictions and political trials, and the removal of troops from the townships—and these differed only slightly from American preconditions for repeal of the sanctions stipulated in the 1986 Comprehensive Anti-Apartheid Act. Each of these demands could be addressed in stages, and the NIS by mid-September 1989 had already begun talking secretly to the ANC about the logistics of their implementation.[85]

After dismantling the institutional power centers of Botha's security chiefs, de Klerk was ready to consult his cabinet and key administrators about the path ahead. During a three-day *bosberaad* (bush conference) in the northern Transvaal in early December, he impressed on the cabinet the necessity of accepting "the full logical consequences of power-sharing—provided there would be reasonable protection for minority rights."[86] On December 13, in time to make international headlines before the UN General Assembly session the following day, de Klerk held his first meeting with Mandela at Tuynhuys over tea. Despite de Klerk's firm rejection of majority rule and Mandela's of "group rights," each found the other's manner reassuring and came away optimistic that a deal could eventually be struck.

De Klerk retired for Christmas to his holiday home on the coast east of Cape Town where he began work on his speech for the opening of Parliament in February. Mandela was taken back to Victor Verster prison. In mid-December the appeals court in Bloemfontein overturned the convictions of Patrick Lekota, Popo Molefe, and three others in the Delmas trial, enabling them to return from Robben Island straight to active politics amid swirling rumors that Mandela would also soon be freed.[87] Walter Sisulu and the other recently released Rivonia veterans arrived in Lusaka in mid-January 1990 to confer with exiled leaders about the ANC's future course and to be welcomed by the large South African community in Zambia—including MK cadres who complained angrily to the visitors that the leadership had gone soft and placed the armed struggle on hold.[88] Facing the media in Lusaka on January 20, Chris Hani conceded there was a lull in MK attacks while the ANC took de Klerk's measure and prepared for the possibility of negotiations. Nevertheless, he said, MK had over many years inspired and attracted young blacks to the ANC, kept whites on edge, discouraged collaboration, and contributed significantly to South Africa's "present political chemistry," and there were no plans to shut it down.[89]

De Klerk knew that the world press would gather for his speech at the opening of Parliament on February 2 in the hope that Mandela's immediate release would be announced. The local press, mindful of the international public relations disaster of Botha's Rubicon speech of August 1985, would expect a judicious doling out of promises and piecemeal concessions to blunt foreign criticism. Nobody would anticipate the go-for-broke leap that de Klerk had decided to make, and the result would be massive positive publicity for the government, followed by the anti-climactic release of Mandela after a short interval. On January 31, cabinet ministers were given the speech and sworn to silence. Then, almost at the end of his address to the assembled members of the tricameral Parliament on February 2, de Klerk dropped his bombshell: to expedite the process of negotiation, with immediate effect, the ANC, PAC, Communist Party and other banned and restricted political organizations were unbanned. The release of remaining political prisoners would begin—including Mandela after "a further short passage of time"—and execution of death row prisoners would be suspended. Emergency restrictions on the media would be lifted. The effect was breathtaking and cast de Klerk briefly as a liberator rather than an embattled politician.

Nine days later, Mandela walked through the gates of Victor Verster a free man as millions worldwide watched on television. Dusk was starting to fall by the time his cavalcade could reach Cape Town's old City Hall, so dense and excited was the huge crowd awaiting his arrival. Flanked by his wife and Cyril Ramaphosa on a crowded balcony overlooking the Grand Parade, he read a militant but somber speech composed to quash rumors that his prison conversations with the government had entrapped him in a sellout (*Document 182*). "I am a loyal and disciplined member of the African National Congress," he intoned.

> I am therefore in full agreement with all of its objectives, strategies and tactics. . . . [M]y talks with the government have been aimed at normalizing the political situation in the country. We have not as yet begun discussing the basic demands of the struggle. . . . I myself . . . at no time entered into negotiations about the future of our country, except to insist on a meeting between the ANC and the government. . . . Negotiations cannot take place above the heads or behind the backs of our people.

Mandela would eventually find his feet in the slippery politics of post-February 11, 1990. His steady temperament and graceful style would provide

Figure 15. Nelson Mandela leaves Victor Verster prison near Paarl with his wife, Winnie, a free man after 27 years of imprisonment, February 11, 1990. © Reuters/CORBIS

an effective complement to the brass-tacks bargaining skills of the ANC's negotiators once serious talks got underway, even eventually winning him the confidence of many white diehards. A decisive corner had been turned in the long fight for democracy and equal rights. The anger of a mobilized majority, the force of world opinion, and the perseverance and skill of determined black leaders over a century of resistance had pushed South Africa's minority government to history's open door, and de Klerk had summoned the courage to walk through it. Immense challenges loomed ahead, but henceforth blacks and whites would face them together as one people in a new South Africa.

Notes

All conversations and interviews cited are with Thomas Karis and/or Gail Gerhart unless otherwise indicated. All conversations, interviews, and documents cited in endnotes can be found in the Karis-Gerhart Collection (hereafter KGC) unless otherwise indicated. The organization appearing in parentheses following each document title indicates the location of that document in the Collection. *FPTC* refers to earlier volumes in the *From Protest to Challenge* series.

1. The hard-liners were centered in the powerful State Security Council created in 1972 and upgraded by Botha after 1978. No firm consensus ever emerged in this body regarding long-term solutions to the political impasse.

2. The Indian and coloured houses of Parliament tried to kill Botha's proposed legislation with a filibuster, but Botha forced it through. A body called the National Forum was created in early 1989, but it collapsed for lack of credible participants.

3. See *Race Relations Survey 1987/88,* pp. 586–89. The restricted organizations were the national UDF and 14 of its affiliates: the RMC, NECC, DPSC, Detainees Support Committee, CAYCO, SAYCO, South African National Students' Congress, National Education Union of South Africa, CRADORA, Soweto Civic Association, SOYCO, PEBCO, Vaal Civic Association, and Western Cape Civic Association, plus AZAPO and the Azanian Youth Organisation. The activists restricted included Albertina Sisulu, Dorothy Zihlangu, Azhar Cachalia, Simon Gqubule, Archie Gumede, Willie Hofmeyr, Zollie Malindi, Joe Marks, Jabu Ngwenya, R. A. M. Salojee, Roseberry Sonto, Christmas Tinto, and five others. The crackdown was timed to toughen the National Party's image prior to three parliamentary by-elections in constituencies where the Conservative Party was strong. The CP won all three with increased majorities.

4. *New Nation,* March 10, 1988. The UDF had already been declared a restricted ("affected") organization in late 1986. The Natal Supreme Court reversed this ruling, but in 1988 the government was still appealing the reversal. In 1986 the European-funded Kagiso Trust, according to its director, Achmat Dangor, disbursed about R8.5 million ($3.4 million) to 48 organizations judged to be democratic, non-racial, committed to the unity of the oppressed people, and free of links to state or homeland structures. See *Weekly Mail,* May 22, 1987. Anthony Marx, *Lessons of Struggle: South African Internal Opposition, 1960–1990* (New York: Oxford University Press, 1992), p. 142, put Kagiso's annual disbursements at "roughly R30 million."

5. See Denis Herbstein, *White Lies: Canon Collins and the Secret War Against Apartheid* (Cape Town: HSRC Press, 2004); talk by Mamphela Ramphele (October 1989); and Marx, pp. 139–45, on the patronage power these funds gave to the UDF and some of the resulting controversy; also *Statement to the Truth and Reconciliation Commission August 1996,* pp. 362–64 (KGC: ANC), for a government spy's report on UDF funding.

6. Baltimore *Sun,* March 23, 1988.

7. On censorship, see *Race Relations Survey 1988/89,* pp. 548–52; Richard Abel, *Politics by Other Means: Law in the Struggle Against Apartheid, 1980–1994* (New York: Routledge, 1995), pp. 258–309; Keyan Tomaselli and P. Eric Louw, eds., *The Alternative Press in South Africa* (London: James Currey, 1991); and Christopher Merrett, *A Culture of Censorship* (Cape Town: David Philip, 1994).

8. Max Du Preez, *Pale Native* (Cape Town: Zebra Press, 2003), p. 181. Under Du Preez's editorship, *Vrye Weekblad* became an important opposition newspaper.

9. *Race Relations Survey 1988/89,* p. 548.

10. The white English-language universities of Cape Town, Natal, Witwatersrand, and Rhodes had become open to black students in the late 1970s. In the 1980s Afrikaans-medium Stellenbosch University began to admit coloured students.

11. See chapter 3.

12. *Document 151* circulated under Mafolo's name since he was one of the few UDF national leaders not in detention or under restriction at the time. According to the *Weekly Mail,* June 10, 1988, the paper was "written in his personal capacity" to avoid restrictions on the UDF.

13. Van Zyl Slabbert, quoted in the *Weekly Mail,* December 2, 1988. On "the cabal" see chapter 3.

14. On the participation debate, see Mark Swilling, "The Big What If," *Weekly Mail,* February 26, 1988; Guy Berger, "The Great Participation Debate," *Work in Progress,* no. 55, August 1988 and replies in following issue (KGC: Alternative Media); Nigel Gibson, "Why is Participation a Dirty Word in South African Politics?," *Africa Today,* vol. 37, no. 2, 1990; Jeremy Seekings, *The UDF* (Cape Town: David Philip, 2000), pp. 236–38; conversations with Jerry Coovadia (June 1988), Karl Beck (January 1988), and Ameen Akhalwaya (March 1988); and talk by Rory Riordan (February 1988).

15. This phrase is borrowed from John de Gruchy, *The Church Struggle in South Africa* (Cape Town: David Philip, 1979), p. 120.

Breaking the Deadlock, 1988–1990

16. See *FPTC,* volume 5, chapter 11.
17. Conversation with Lebamang Sebidi (July 1989).
18. COSATU in 1989 claimed 924,000 and NACTU 144,418 paid-up members. See *Race Relations Survey 1988/89,* pp. 444 and 449.
19. See chapter 2 of this volume and *FPTC,* volume 5, chapter 7.
20. According to the Centre for Applied Legal Studies at the University of the Witwatersrand, quoted in the *Weekly Mail,* June 10, 1988, of the roughly 5,000 people detained between mid-June 1987 and mid-June 1988, approximately 78% were associated with the UDF, 12.4% with COSATU, 3.4% with NACTU, 3.1% with black consciousness groups, and 3.1% with the SACC and other organizations.
21. *Race Relations Survey 1987/88,* p. 652.
22. "Unions not weary," *New Nation,* July 27, 1988. Also see Mark Bennett, comp., "Stayaway Strikes in the 1980s (Part II) June 1986–June 1988," *Indicator SA,* vol. 5, no. 3, 1988.
23. Lawrence Schlemmer, "The October Municipal Elections," *South Africa Foundation Review,* December 1988, p. 3.
24. *Race Relations Survey 1988/89,* p. 513. Also see Harry Mashabela, *Fragile Figures? The 1988 PWV Township Elections* (Johannesburg: SAIRR, 1988).
25. Quoted in Schlemmer, p. 3.
26. For a partial list see Raymond Louw, ed., *Four Days in Lusaka* (Excom: Five Freedoms Forum, 1989), pp. 160–66.
27. Lekota, Myeza, and Pandelani Nefolovhodwe had been co-accused in the "SASO Nine" trial (*State v. Cooper*) in 1975–76 and were together on Robben Island until the early 1980s.
28. Conversation with Donovan Nadison (July 1989). Also see Keith Wattrus, "Unity talks: NSC might get the ball rolling," *Democracy in Action,* December 1989 (KGC: IDASA); Kumi Naidoo, "Class, Consciousness and Organisation: Indian Political Resistance in Durban, South Africa, 1979–1996," Ph.D. thesis, Oxford University, 1998, pp. 111–12; and "Running with the ball," an interview with Dan Moyo, *New Era,* October 1989, pp. 15–17 (KGC: Alternative Media).
29. Conversation with Sheena Duncan (November 1987).
30. Harry Mashabela and Monty Narsoo, *The Boksburg Boycott* (Johannesburg: SAIRR, 1989); *Race Relations Survey 1988/89,* spp. 27–28, and *Race Relations Survey 1989/90,* pp. 12–15, 229–30, and 702–703.
31. On these events, see Steven Friedman, "The Power of Speech," *Leadership SA,* vol. 8, no. 3, May 1989; Khehla Shubane and Mark Swilling, "Soweto Rent Boycott," *Work in Progress,* no. 61, 1989 (KGC: Alternative Media); "The Greater Soweto Accord," *History in the Making,* vol. 1, no. 2, November 1990; and Mark Swilling, William Cobbett, and Roland Hunter, "Finance, electricity costs, and the rent boycott," in Mark Swilling, Richard Humphries, and Khehla Shubane, eds., *Apartheid City in Transition* (Cape Town: Oxford University Press, 1991), pp. 174–96. It should be noted that government officials had also met with local African leaders in 1986 to explore ways of ending the school boycotts. See *Document 78.*
32. Paul Hendler, *Urban Policy and Housing: Case Studies on Negotiation in PWV Townships* (Johannesburg: SAIRR, 1988); Mark Swilling, "The Extra-Parliamentary Movement: Strategies and Prospects," in Hermann Giliomee and Lawrence Schlemmer, eds., *Negotiating South Africa's Future* (Johannesburg: Southern Book Publishers, 1989); and "Local-Level Negotiations: Case Studies and Implications," 1987 (defense briefing paper, *State v. Mayekiso*). Daveyton and Tembisa in the PWV and Uitenhage, Port Alfred, Port Elizabeth, Oudtshoorn, East London, and Cradock in the Cape were among the places that experienced local-level negotiation processes in the mid- and late 1980s.
33. "Thabo, the ANC's Crown Prince Charming," *Star,* March 26, 1989; also see Mark Gevisser, *Thabo Mbeki: The Dream Deferred* (Johannesburg; Jonathan Ball, 2007), pp. 515–16.
34. "Position Paper on the Cultural and Academic Boycott adopted by the National Executive Committee of the African National Congress May 1989—Lusaka" (KGC: ANC).
35. "Hunger Strikes," *Weekly Mail,* December 23, 1988. On medical implications of detention and political fasting, see the journal *Critical Health,* no. 26, May 1989 (KGC: Alternative Media).
36. Mark Swilling in the *Star,* July 23, 1989, and as quoted in "The hunger strike has ended," *Weekly Mail,* April 21, 1989.

37. "South Africa Reportedly Planning to Release 300 Political Prisoners," *New York Times,* February 17, 1989.

38. Govan Mbeki and Harry Gwala, the most influential communists, remained on Robben Island. Fran Buntman, *Robben Island and Prisoner Resistance to Apartheid* (New York: Cambridge University Press, 2003), pp. 223–24, concludes that the government had no grand strategy in moving the five but may have believed that Mandela, if freed from the pressure of group opinion, might "agree to some form of power sharing . . . acceptable to the regime."

39. Nelson Mandela mentions earlier conditional amnesty offers in *Long Walk to Freedom* (Boston: Little, Brown, 1994), chapters 79 and 88.

40. Mandela advised Bizos to tell Coetsee that he was going to Lusaka. Bizos did so and from their conversation, concluded that Botha had approved Coetsee's hospital visit, and that the government hoped to set Mandela up as a compliant leader on the model of Bishop Abel Muzorewa of Zimbabwe. Conversation with George Bizos (April 2006). When Bizos informed Lusaka of his impending visit in mid-November 1985, Tambo was resting at a spa near Moscow. Thabo Mbeki flew to the USSR to bring Tambo back for the meeting, according to Vladimir Shubin, *The ANC: A View from Moscow* (Bellville: Mayibuye Books, 1999), p. 299. Following the Kabwe conference, a committee had been appointed to produce an ANC position paper on negotiation. This document, of which *Document 129,* dated November 27, 1985, is a summary, may not have been ready at the time of Bizos's first visit. Bizos returned to Lusaka in late February 1986, and reported back to Coetsee that there were no differences of opinion between Mandela and Lusaka regarding preconditions for negotiation.

41. Commonwealth Group of Eminent Persons, *Mission To South Africa* (New York: Viking, 1986), p. 68. On the EPG see chapter 4.

42. Allister Sparks, *Tomorrow is Another Country: The Inside Story of South Africa's Road to Change* (Sandton: Struik, 1994), p. 34.

43. Mandela, chapter 91. James Sanders, *Apartheid's Friends: The Rise and Fall of South Africa's Secret Service* (London: John Murray, 2006), pp. 238–39, sites a State Security Council memo of March 1986 recommending "a well-planned, proactive psychological action plan" to break Mandela down before his release.

44. The fullest account of these talks, despite some errors, is Robert Harvey, *The Fall of Apartheid* (Basingstoke: Palgrave Macmillan, 2001). Other accounts appear in Sparks, pp. 77–86; Patti Waldmeir, *Anatomy of a Miracle* (New York: W. W. Norton, 1997), pp. 75–80; Luli Callinicos, *Oliver Tambo* (Cape Town: David Philip, 2004), pp. 595–97; and Gevisser, chapter 33. *Document 143* also refers to these secret meetings.

45. Quoted in David Price, "How apartheid was ended—in the bar of the Compleat Angler," *Sunday Telegraph,* April 30, 2000.

46. In July 1989 Willie Breytenbach, anticipating the upcoming white general election, published a soothing essay asserting that "rapid changes of power . . . appear to be impossible in the next decade or so," and whites should expect the empowerment of Africans to involve a long transition period. W. J. Breytenbach, *The ANC: Future Prognosis* (Bellville: University of Stellenbosch Institute for Futures Research, 1989), p. 43.

47. Pretoria's security agencies and their rivalries are discussed in Mark Shaw, "Spy Meets Spy," in Steven Friedman and Doreen Atkinson, eds., *South Africa Review 7* (Johannesburg: Ravan Press, 1994), pp. 256–61; Hilton Hamann, *Days of the Generals* (Cape Town: Zebra Press, 2001), chapter 3; and Sanders. Seekings, p. 300, notes that between 1978 and 1986, the governments of Guatemala and El Salvador (with much smaller populations than South Africa), oversaw the murders of approximately 21,000 and 55,000 people respectively, aided by the indifference of world opinion. Harold Wolpe, writing before Henley, speculates that Pretoria may have reached the limits of its coercive power, closing off Latin American-style "solutions." To tip the balance decisively in the ANC's favor, Wolpe in *Race, Class and the Apartheid State* (London: James Currey, 1988), pp. 107–10, says the security forces must be stretched further by mass insurrection combined with armed struggle. He does not mention the historic changes then occurring in Eastern Europe.

48. For a summary of this position, see Mzala [Jabulani Nxumalo], "Omelettes Cannot be Made Without Breaking Eggs," *Sechaba,* June 1989, pp. 11–18 (KGC: ANC), and the articles to which he is replying.

49. Conversation of Victoria Butler with Terge Vigtel (March 1988). On PASA, see Tor Sellström, *Sweden and National Liberation in Southern Africa,* volume 2 (Uppsala: Nordiska Afrikainstitutet, 2002), pp. 794–97.

50. See Chester Crocker, *High Noon in Southern Africa* (New York: W. W. Norton, 1992). Botha hoped to defeat SWAPO by wearing down its Angolan and Cuban allies militarily, but was outbid by Fidel Castro, whose willingness to commit troops and weaponry exceeded Pretoria's. Stymied in a prolonged face-off with the Cubans at Cuito Cuanavale in southern Angola in early 1988, South Africa shifted to the diplomatic option it had earlier spurned. The deal brokered by U.S. and Soviet negotiators enabled all the combatants to claim victory. On Cuito Cuanavale, see Greg Mills and David Williams, *Seven Battles that Shaped South Africa* (Cape Town: Tafelberg, 2006), pp. 167–88; Harvey, pp. 157–58; and Hamann, chapter 5.

51. See Gevisser, p. 493. On Zimbabwe, see Michael Charlton, *The Last Colony in Africa: Diplomacy and the Independence of Rhodesia* (Oxford: Basil Blackwell, 1990), and Jeffrey Davidow, *A Peace in Southern Africa: The Lancaster House Conference on Rhodesia, 1979* (Boulder: Westview, 1984).

52. In November 1988 Tambo told the ANC national working committee that Zambia was demanding sharp reductions in the number of ANC personnel in Lusaka. He proposed moving some ANC departments to Dakawa in Tanzania, and said MK personnel would relocate to Uganda. "Minutes of meeting of NWC held on 17 November, 1988" (KGC: ANC).

53. According to police reports cited in "Apartheid Barometer," *Weekly Mail,* March 23, 1989, and the British *Independent,* January 9, 1990, the number of guerrilla ("terrorist") attacks climbed from 45 in 1984 to 136 (1985), 231 (1986), 235 (1987), and 281 (1988), then fell back to approximately 144 in 1989. Lawrence Schlemmer gives slightly different statistics in "South Africa's Futures: Probable Developments in the Medium Term," *South Africa International,* vol. 20, no. 2, October 1989, p. 63.

54. A September 1987 report, "A Matter of Great Concern," by Timothy Mokoena, MK regional commander in Angola, complained that for "almost two years we have not been allowed to send to Lusaka the comrades earmarked for [deployment] because of the congestion in Lusaka" (KGC: ANC). He said 1,440 trained cadres and 343 trainees were in Angola. All these had access to weapons, and among them were "agitators instigating for mutiny." "Minutes of meeting of NWC held on 17 November, 1988" (KGC: ANC), indicated that transfer of "plus minus 1000" soldiers from Angola to Uganda was imminent. These internal documents are probably a better indicator of MK troop levels than media reports. *Africa Confidential,* vol. 30, no. 6, March 17, 1989, for example, reported that the ANC had confirmed that "the bulk of its 6000 or so fighters from Angolan camps" would move to Uganda.

55. Conversation with Senti Thobejane, Thandeka Gqubule, and others (March 1991). Richard Rosenthal in *Mission Improbable* (Cape Town: David Philip, 1998), p. 270, says Thabo Mbeki told him in early 1989 that the ANC had to avoid any action that its angry youth constituency might construe as surrender—talking peace with Inkatha, for example.

56. See Philip Nel, "The ANC and 'Communism'," in Willie Esterhuyse and Philip Nel, eds., *The ANC and Its Leaders* (Cape Town: Tafelberg, 1990), p. 60.

57. Interview by John Battersby with Chris Hani and Steve Tshwete (June 1988).

58. Sparks, p. 101, suggests that de Klerk, pondering Mandela's release, may also have been "haunted by visions of the mass demonstrations that had followed the Ayatollah Khomeini's return to Teheran in 1979 and overwhelmed the regime of Shah Reza Pahlavi." The ANC's parallel nightmare was a scenario in which some internal black group not under its own leadership might step into such a breach and take control. This fear had played a part in the decision to create MK in 1961, and also sometimes colored the ANC's relationship with the UDF. SACP veteran Lionel Bernstein, writing to John Saul on June 8, 2001, asserted that "[i]n the late 80s, when mass popular resistance revived again inside the country led by the UDF, it led the ANC to see the UDF as an undesirable factor in the struggle for power, and to fatally undermine it as a rival focus for mass mobilisation." No specific evidence is cited (letter provided to authors by John Saul).

59. Battersby interview with Hani and Tshwete.

60. A description of what was envisaged appears in a 12-page unsigned document (probably by Maharaj), "Reflections on Perspectives for Internal Work [early 1988]" (Simons papers, microfilm, reel 8).

61. Police arrested top Vula operatives in mid-1990 and began legal proceedings against Maharaj, Nyanda, Billy Nair, Pravin Gordhan, and five others in October 1990. The trial was postponed and charges were dropped five months later. On Operation Vula, see Padraig O'Malley, *Shades of Difference: Mac Maharaj and the Struggle for South Africa* (New York: Viking, 2007), chapters 11–18; Tim Jenkin, "The Story of the Secret Underground Communications Network of Operation Vula," *Mayibuye*, vol. 6, nos. 1–6, May–October, 1995; Conny Braam, *Operation Vula* (Johannesburg: Jacana, 2004); interviews by Howard Barrell with Mac Maharaj (February 1991) and Ronnie Kasrils (October 1990), and Vula documents online at www.omalley.co.za, under "Mac Maharaj."

62. It would be wrong to assume that Slovo was merely posturing for the sake of maintaining the SACP's appeal to young radicals, though this cannot be excluded as one aspect in his thinking. In a coded message to Maharaj inside South Africa two months after the party congress in Cuba, he wrote, "Of course we cannot avoid paying attention to the pressures on negotiation. But we must in practice (not only in theory) not do so at the expense of the real thing," that is, people's war. Quoted by O'Malley, p. 318.

63. Harold Wolpe in "Aspects of the Present Situation in South Africa" (Oxford University seminar paper, September 1988) also took the position that "negotiations can happen—but not now."

64. See Gevisser's biography, chapters 30–33, for a detailed account of how Mbeki straddled the parallel tracks of ANC strategy—armed struggle and secret talks—although not without antagonizing many of his colleagues, who regarded him as manipulative and arrogant.

65. Maharaj in O'Malley, pp. 306–309 and 501–508, recounts this exercise in detail. He argues that a careful reading of *Document 163* shows that Mandela's sole purpose was to persuade the government to negotiate a settlement with the ANC, and that he proposed no specific content for such a settlement other than to reiterate the official policies of the ANC. Tambo's endorsement of this interpretation was quickly obtained and disseminated. Not surprisingly, the bait which Mandela dangled in the passage quoted also excited interest from the NIS. Among the documents apparently sent out of Victor Verster to Lusaka by Vula was a five-page portion of a letter to Mandela from Barnard's committee—"Note: English words and sentences in the text . . ." (KGC: ANC)—responding to *Document 163*. In a generally bullying tone, the letter disparaged Mandela's presentation of "obstacles to negotiation" and praised the memo's "second, shorter and more positive part [which] contains certain proposals to assist in getting over the checkmate situation now present in the RSA."

66. "Mandela Visit Called A 'Game'," *Washington Post*, July 11, 1989.

67. Stanley Uys, "ANC, UDF, COSATU plan to 'Recapture Initiative'," *Cape Argus*, July 20, 1989.

68. Vula smuggled the draft to Mandela and conveyed his comments back to Lusaka. The smuggling of documents in and out of Victor Verster inside hollowed-out book covers is described in O'Malley, pp. 304–305 and 319.

69. The team included Thabo Mbeki, Pallo Jordan, Steve Tshwete, and two lawyers, Penuell Maduna and Ngoako Ramatlhodi. See Callinicos, p. 606.

70. The clause calling for an interim government during the writing of a new constitution was deleted on Britain's insistence. United Nations, *The United Nations and Apartheid 1948–1994* (New York: United Nations, 1994), pp. 419–21, and conversations with Tebogo Mafole (January 1990) and Aracelly Santana (January 1990).

71. Tambo was hospitalized in Britain, then convalesced in Sweden, eventually recovering his speech and some of his strength, but he did not resume an active leadership role. He returned to South Africa in December 1990 and died in 1993.

72. Conversation with Oscar Dhlomo (December 1989) and "Meeting between Inkatha and UDF/COSATU Delegation, Royal Hotel, Durban," minutes, June 19 and 23, 1989 (KGC: Inkatha).

73. Gerrit Viljoen, "Open for Business," *Leadership SA*, vol. 8, no. 8, October 1989, and "Report Urges Universal Voting for South Africans," *New York Times*, March 12, 1989.

74. See "Pretoria's Masterplan: Cantons," *Front File*, August 1989, and *Washington Post*, June 30, 1989.

75. The corrupt government of the Matanzimas in the Transkei was ousted in a sequence of coups by the homeland's army in 1987, bringing to power Major-General Bantu Holomisa, who

openly expressed pro-ANC sympathies. Only the intervention of the SADF saved Lucas Mangope of Bophuthatswana from the same fate in February 1988.

76. For de Klerk's expression of this idea see his February 2, 1990, speech to Parliament, reproduced in Hassen Ebrahim, *The Soul of a Nation: Constitution-making in South Africa* (Cape Town: Oxford University Press, 1998), pp. 469–71. Note that nine years earlier, without defining the term, Desmond Tutu in *Document 4* had also defined "power sharing" as the goal.

77. "Bloedspoor van die SAP," *Vrye Weekblad,* November 17, 1989. The lawyer was Huggins "Shucks" Sefanyetso of Lawyers for Human Rights in Pretoria. *Vrye Weekblad* worked through Andre Zaaiman, an IDASA employee who was also a secret MK operative. Beyers Naudé provided money for Coetzee's plane fares. On Nofomela and Coetzee, see June Goodwin and Ben Schiff, *Heart of Whiteness* (New York: Scribner, 1995), p. 207; Jacques Pauw, *In the Heart of the Whore* (Halfway House: Southern Book Publishers, 1991), and *Into the Heart of Darkness* (Johannesburg: Jonathan Ball, 1997); Du Preez, chapter 24; and conversation with Denis Kuny (September 1990). On government "investigations" of police crimes, see Ann Eveleth, "Case Against the Prosecution," *Mail and Guardian,* August 4, 1995.

78. On the Angolan mutiny, see chapter 4. Information on events in Angola was slow to leak out. Using testimony from ANC defectors, the government in late 1986 ran a television documentary on the SABC about abuse and execution of alleged ANC dissenters. The film alluded to the 1984 Angola mutiny but offered few details. The ANC dismissed the claims as a smear. See "Dead Blacks Cited As Foes of Rebels," *New York Times,* December 19, 1986. Based on statements by dissidents, conservative U.S. Senator Jesse Helms issued a report in June 1988 on alleged ANC atrocities, but it drew little attention. The first extended account of the mutiny appeared in *Africa Confidential,* December 2, 1988. On the death in Zambia of Thami Zulu [Muziwakhe Ngwenya], see "Commission Report on the Death of Thami Zulu 1989" in *Appendices to the African National Congress Policy Statement to the TRC,* 1996 (KGC: ANC); "Meeting of the NWC held on 21/11/89 at 9:00 Hours," minutes, Lusaka (KGC: ANC); and Paul Trewhela, "The Dilemma of Albie Sachs: ANC Constitutionalism and the Death of Thami Zulu," *Searchlight South Africa,* no. 11, October 1993 (KGC: Ultraleft Organizations).

79. Among the leaders who consistently and publicly called for Winnie Mandela to be held accountable for her misdeeds were Murphy Morobe and Azhar Cachalia. See *Truth and Reconciliation Commission of South Africa Report* (Cape Town: Truth and Reconciliation Commission, 1998), vol. 2, pp. 555–82. *Document 166* considered the problems caused by her acquisition of a relatively palatial house in Diepkloof, Soweto, which had provoked bad publicity.

80. For Russian perspectives on these developments, see conversations with Vladimir Ganchin (November 1987), George Mirsky (March 1990), and Irina Filatova (March 1991).

81. Seekings, p. 245, although on p. 308 he gives figures which are lower. Foreign funds were received and redistributed to UDF affiliates through people in the MDM after the UDF in 1986 was declared an "affected" organization and thus barred from receiving foreign funds (email from Azhar Cachalia, July 18, 2007). For a discussion of UDF funding, see Marx, pp. 139–44. The World Council of Churches gave non-military support to the exiled PAC, and, according to "South Africa (5): Black consciousness," *Africa Confidential,* February 4, 1987, AZAPO's operating funds came mainly from annual grants from the SACC. It was not surprising that foreign donors, who were overwhelmingly white, felt less generous toward organizations perceived to stand for black nationalism or racial exclusivity. The exiled ANC's budget was difficult to estimate. South African journalist John Battersby claimed in "South Africa's Curbs Harden Rebels," *New York Times,* June 7, 1988, that "the congress's military operation absorbs half its estimated annual budget of $100 million, which comes mainly from contributions by foreign governments, including the Soviet Union, East Germany, Czechoslovakia, Sweden and Norway." But Eastern bloc contributions were nearly all in kind rather than cash, and the Swedes and Norwegians did not support military operations. *The Wall Street Journal,* April 18, 1988, reported Sweden's 1988 contribution as $10.2 million "in direct aid and much more indirectly," (through IDAF, for example), an amount estimated to be "one-third of the non-military budget, with another third coming from Norway, Denmark and Finland. UN organizations and anti-apartheid groups in Europe send the rest."

82. *Document 129* in late 1985 anticipates this idea, which had a long gestation period in the ANC. One objective was to counter the assertion made frequently by the National Party and

Margaret Thatcher that the ANC was "just one among many" organizations that could express black opinion.

83. On the politics of the CDF, see conversations with Joe Thloloe (December 1989), Saki Macozoma (December 1989), Aracelly Santana (January 1990), and Allan Boesak (January 1990), and talk by Gerrit Olivier (February 1990).

84. Heribert Adam and Kogila Moodley in *The Opening of the Apartheid Mind* (Berkeley: University of California Press, 1993), assessing the reasons for the February 1990 turnaround, adopt a denialist position toward the liberation movements, maintaining that the "real causes of the change" were not "the opposition's own efforts" but rather the spread of enlightenment within the Afrikaner establishment and among "corporate planners [who] had long prepared themselves for [the] historical inevitability" of negotiations (p. 52). Their rather anecdotal defense of this position raises more questions than it answers.

85. On September 12, the week of the major marches in Cape Town and Johannesburg, top operatives from NIS met for the first time directly with the ANC (Thabo Mbeki and Jacob Zuma) in Lucerne, Switzerland, to discuss how to remove obstacles to negotiation. See Sparks, chapter 9; Waldmeir, pp. 144–46; and Gevisser, pp. 546–47.

86. F. W. de Klerk, *The Last Trek: A New Beginning* (London: Macmillan, 1998), pp. 161–62. Also see Waldmeir, pp. 142–44, and Sparks, pp. 103–106.

87. The others released were Moss Chikane, Gcina Malindi, and Tom Manthata. The prosecution's ultimate failure in the Delmas trial resulted from a procedural error by the judge. No less welcome to the UDF and its allies but more indicative of the prevailing political winds was the decision of Judge P. J. Van der Walt to acquit Moses Mayekiso and others in *State v. Mayekiso* in early 1989. He ruled that the defendants' actions were a justifiable response to black "grievances and aspirations—in most cases legitimate, and [despite] the often intemperate and exaggerated language . . . liberally spiced with current political clichés, most of these citizens [are] just striving for a better South Africa." Judgment, *State v. Mayekiso and Others*, April 24, 1989 (KGC: Legal Documents).

88. Stephen Ellis and Tsepo Sechaba [Oyama Mabandla], *Comrades Against Apartheid* (Bloomington: Indiana University Press, 1992), p. 193, and Elinor Sisulu, *Walter & Albertina Sisulu: In Our Lifetime* (Cape Town: David Philip, 2002), p. 405.

89. "Chris Hani Press Conference, Lusaka, January 20, 1990," notes (by Julie Frederikse?) (SAHA Collection).

Epilogue

Between February 1990 and April 1994 South Africa traversed a tortuous path to a negotiated political settlement. Far from a "miracle," as many around the world characterized it, the settlement emerged from a tough, at times ugly, decidedly earth-bound bargaining process between political parties holding out for what they considered the best possible deal for their constituencies. Having plunged into what ironically was termed a "normalization" of politics, there was no going back for any of the major players. Restoring the apartheid political system was not an option, and all stood to gain if a mutually acceptable settlement could be negotiated. While Africanist and black consciousness political groups pondered what tactics to adopt in the emerging transitional order, the ANC and its allies prepared for what all assumed would be their dominant role in whatever formal process was established for negotiating with the government. In the meantime, thousands of private transformations took shape as prisoners released after years of incarceration struggled alongside returning exiles to rebuild lives, find livelihoods, and become reintegrated into a society that had changed dramatically during their absence.

De Klerk quickly set about demolishing the legislative foundations of apartheid in the hope that this would signal a fundamental departure from the past, build trust, and allow economic sanctions to be lifted. Afrikaners continued to desert the National Party for the Conservative Party, but de Klerk gambled that the prospect of lasting peace, the end of international isolation, and the opening up of economic, cultural, and sporting links would ultimately win whites over to the process. Inside the National Party government, the prevailing view was that once Mandela and the ANC were involved in the prosaic business of legal politics, they would lose much of their heroic aura. Moreover, if they retained their socialist rhetoric, not to mention their alliance with the South African Communist Party, the Western powers would lose sympathy with them. The ANC's initial disorganization, ideological confusion, and possible breakup into competing factions would enable the National Party to control the transition process and hold onto a substantial slice of power, or so went the most optimistic thinking within de Klerk's inner circle.[1] National Party strategy gained credibility when an all-white referendum held in March 1992 went more than two to one in favor of continuing de Klerk's reform initiatives.

The ANC had to adjust quickly from the politics of exile and illegality to open political organization. Mandela moved naturally into the vacuum left by Tambo's incapacitation, but his rather aloof, chiefly leadership style did not mesh easily with either the collegial culture of the exiled ANC leadership or the bottom-up, democratic norms characteristic of many UDF affiliates and black trade unions. Returning from exile over the course of 1990, members of the ANC National Executive Committee were even less accustomed to being answerable to a mass electoral base in the making. Jostling for position was inevitable among the exile leaders, as was rivalry between them and leading figures in the MDM who had persevered at home through the repression and violence of the 1980s. Among trade unionists, returning SACTU veterans bowed to the reality of COSATU's massive presence and dissolved the remnants of their organization. With the UDF, however, the reverse occurred. After maintaining a nominally independent existence for about a year, the UDF announced that it would formally dissolve in mid-1991. Many of its affiliates, particularly its youth organizations, simply merged into the ANC, while its non-Charterist organizations and individuals went their own way. The Natal and Transvaal Indian Congresses made a controversial decision to maintain a separate existence from the ANC. Nothing came of a recommendation by UDF leaders to convert the Front into an independent new body for the coordination and promotion of civic groups dedicated to social and economic development. Not surprisingly, the ANC's returning leaders saw no virtue in the continued existence of an independent UDF, and preferred to absorb as many of its activists as possible directly into new ANC structures at national, regional, and branch levels. Radical partisans of the UDF and its affiliates who had looked forward to a revolutionary transformation of South Africa's social order now rested their hopes in the Communist Party.

National Party hopes that disagreements would fracture the ANC/SACP/COSATU alliance failed to materialize. Inside the SACP a quiet shuffle occurred, however. The collapse of communist parties across Eastern Europe in 1989 and the melting away of Soviet support prompted half the SACP central committee members to let their memberships lapse after the party was unbanned and the time approached to make the identity of party members public.[2] In the meantime, however, thousands of township youths flocked to join the unbanned SACP, attracted by its revolutionary image and association with MK icons like Chris Hani and Joe Slovo. Along with returning MK cadres, these newcomers experienced feelings of betrayal when the ANC unilaterally announced suspension of the armed struggle in August 1990. But no rupture took place, and none occurred later, in early 1992, when Mandela and his inner circle, again without formal consultation with the ANC's allies, decided to abandon the Freedom Charter's call for nationalization—a plank that nevertheless remained solidly in the policy platform of COSATU with its million-strong membership.[3] As long as the National Party still formally retained power, the reasons for the SACP and COSATU to hold tight to the ANC's political coattails far outweighed any reasons for going it alone. By 1992, in any case, both the Communists and the trade unions were already securely represented in the ANC's own top echelons, especially COSATU following Cyril Ramaphosa's landslide election as ANC secretary general in June 1991.

The efforts of the formerly banned organizations to establish themselves as political parties took place simultaneously with preparations to negotiate a new South African constitution. During the first half of 1990 the National Party and the ANC worked to establish ground rules for negotiations. In a series of crucial meetings they haggled over the details of prisoner releases, the return of exiles, the suspension of security laws, and the monitoring of armed forces. Although not satisfied that de Klerk was doing everything possible to end the activities of death squads, the ANC agreed to suspend its armed struggle in a move to push the process forward. In spite of important disagreements, basic rapport was established between the negotiating teams. The local and international media applauded all signs of progress.

After these initial steps to level the political playing field came the first attempt to create a formal negotiating forum that would be as inclusive as possible. Although no progress could be made without bilateral agreements between the National Party and the ANC, both wanted to draw other potential allies into the process. The government tried to establish alliances with homeland leaders, Indian and coloured parliamentary parties, the white Democratic Party, and white conservatives, while the ANC also looked for allies among homeland politicians as well as among former UDF affiliates. Even the PAC was wooed by the ANC into a short-lived "patriotic front." Although the ANC and National Party were fierce political competitors, they also became dependent partners, trying to hold the middle ground against extremist groups who were, at best, suspicious and at worst, obstructionist toward the negotiation process. Even within their own ranks both parties continued to face challenges from those who still preferred military solutions.

This conflict-prone relationship was severely strained by waves of political violence that threatened to tear apart any agreements reached. In rural KwaZulu-Natal the simmering war between the ANC and Inkatha—now renamed the Inkatha Freedom Party (IFP)—escalated sharply. The fighting pitted armed gangs of Inkatha supporters against "self-defense units" of ANC youth, many of them deployed offensively in the Natal midlands by the self-styled ANC warlord, Harry Gwala. Conflict also spread to the East Rand and Vaal triangle where hostels housing migrant Zulu workers became flashpoints of violence between IFP supporters and township residents throughout the four-year transition process. Several bloody massacres resulted, most notably in Boipatong where 48 deaths resulted from an Inkatha attack in June 1992. At the same time, mysterious "third force" operatives, later revealed to be secret units within the security forces, carried out numerous brutal random attacks on black civilians, including commuter train passengers, apparently with the intent of causing voters to fear the prospect of an African-dominated government.[4]

After particularly violent flare-ups, the ANC and National Party hurled accusations at one another, the ANC charging the government with gross negligence and even complicity in these incidents and the government accusing the ANC of still being committed to a violent seizure of power. In 1991 strong evidence began confirming earlier allegations of government complicity both in death-squad murders and in Inkatha's violent offensive. Although de Klerk denied personal knowledge of these activities, they seriously damaged his credibility as an honest broker. Nor did the revelations bring any decrease in the number of politically related deaths, which continued to average several hundred per month.[5] In September 1992 a large and aggressive but unarmed crowd of ANC supporters demonstrating in Bisho against the anti-ANC bantustan government of Ciskei was attacked by the Ciskei defense force, leaving 29 people dead. Perhaps the most threatening incident in the violent backdrop to the negotiation process was Chris Hani's assassination on April 10, 1993. Hani was an immensely popular figure, particularly among militant youth, and his murder by two right-wing whites sparked angry demonstrations and rioting. Many in the ANC demanded a halt to the negotiation process, but Mandela and the ANC leadership called for calm and resolved to accelerate rather than suspend talks. A suspension, they argued, would reward the forces trying to derail the process. In the end, Hani's death brought a new urgency to negotiations as both sides realized how quickly relative political stability could unravel.

Once "talks about talks" evolved into actual negotiations, progress was slow and setbacks many. Details had to be worked out concerning the release of political prisoners and indemnity for exiles. Painstaking, stop-start, preliminary negotiations then preceded the first Convention for a Democratic South Africa (CODESA 1) which met at the World Trade Centre in Kempton Park, Johannesburg, on December 20–21, 1991. In a remarkably inclusive process, every party of significance attended. During the two-day meeting both the PAC and IFP expressed concern that the National Party and ANC were making bilateral deals and threatened to walk out. Nevertheless, a positive declaration of intent was hammered out which committed all parties to a nonracial, multiparty democracy in which elections would be based on proportional representation and the constitution, protected by an independent judiciary, would be the supreme law. Many observers expressed confidence that positive aspects of South Africa's strong legal tradition could be carried forward and augmented with the introduction of a justiciable bill of rights. Establishing a pattern for future decision making, CODESA 1 set up a system of

EPILOGUE   211

working groups and technical committees to deal with specific issues and potential stumbling blocks. These committees were mandated to develop proposals for discussion and ratification during CODESA plenary meetings.

Prior to CODESA's second round of plenary sessions in May 1992, it became clear that although the ANC and the government had found ways to compromise on many disputed issues, they were still fundamentally at odds over what had been referred to at the Mells Park talks as the "bottom line." While the ANC stood for the protection of individual rights and for rapid progress toward majority rule, the National Party was determined to delay the writing of a final constitution and in the meantime to entrench a system of "power sharing" in which "groups" would retain veto power. It also hoped to impose a federal system in which regional governments would be strong. The white right and much of the homeland leadership, including the IFP, supported these National Party positions. Both sides were adamant, and the working committee charged with reconciling the opposing positions failed to meet its May deadline. The ANC in particular was in no mood to make compromises in light of what it saw as the government's complicity in anti-ANC violence, as well as its failure to release all political prisoners, formally reincorporate the "independent" TBVC states into South Africa, and set up mechanisms to ensure the neutrality of the security forces and the highly partisan South African Broadcasting Corporation. As the ANC repeatedly declared, the National Party could not be "both player and referee" during the political transition. These significant differences led to deadlock and widespread pessimism following CODESA 2 on May 15–16, 1992.

While all parties went away to caucus and rethink, the ANC called for "rolling mass action" to pressure the National Party into accepting its demands. The ANC and COSATU called a successful one-day national strike on June 16 and followed with another massive one on August 3–4 in which several million workers participated. On the National Party side these demonstrations of strength may have caused a recalculation of the ANC's probable showing in a future election. In addition, the fury of Africans after the Boipatong massacre on June 17 had a sobering effect. On the ANC side, mass action was shelved after the deaths in Bisho on September 7, for which it bore partial responsibility. In the end, these events, plus international pressures, continuing economic decline, and important new concessions from both sides broke the deadlock of mid-1992. Also vital to the process was the personal rapport established between Roelf Meyer and Cyril Ramaphosa, respectively the heads of the National Party and ANC negotiating teams, who began meeting regularly during the period when formal negotiations were on hold.

A series of bilateral talks between the ANC and the National Party in the second half of 1992 succeeded in pushing the process forward. In late September the ANC agreed that temporary "power sharing" could occur through a transitional government of national unity (GNU). In return it demanded that Inkatha be reined in through various measures to control hostel violence. This forced the National Party to reassess its strategic alliance with the IFP, which had become an increasingly divisive issue in de Klerk's cabinet. In a critical maneuver, de Klerk defeated the pro-IFP hardliners, clearing the way for the government to seek a new tactical partnership with the ANC. Over the following few months, multiple issues were negotiated bilaterally. The National Party finally relinquished its focus on group rights and veto powers while holding to its preference for federalism. In a November position paper, the ANC set out for its followers the reasons why it would be politically necessary in an interim constitution to accept what became known as "sunset clauses"—concessions to the National Party that would be of limited duration. Besides the GNU, which would last for five years, incumbent civil servants would be given guaranteed job security or acceptable retirement packages; also, a general amnesty would be offered to civil servants or members of "armed formations" who were prepared to disclose fully the acts for which they sought amnesty. Without these short-term concessions, it was argued, there was no assurance that the country's new democracy could avoid sabotage by powerful elements from the old regime.

These developments outraged the IFP and alienated the white right, who felt excluded and regarded the National Party's concessions as unacceptable appeasement of the ANC. In late 1992 a curious new political bloc emerged, bringing conservative Afrikaners and several anti-ANC homeland leaders together. The key parties in this bloc were the IFP and the Volksfront, a new Afrikaner breakaway under the leadership of ex-army chief of staff General Constand Viljoen. Viljoen had emerged as a credible spokesman for a section of white conservatives who wanted to protect their "group rights" in an autonomous region exclusively for Afrikaners—a *volkstaat*. The two parties were drawn together by a strong attachment to ethnic identity and the desire to protect language and culture through a federal solution.

Nevertheless, once the ANC-National Party deadlock was broken, movement toward an interim constitution accelerated. All-party talks resumed at the World Trade Centre in March 1993. After the Hani assassination, in an attempt to stave off rising anger and impatience, it was agreed that national elections would be held in April 1994. This went a long way toward making the transition tangible and irreversible. By July 1993 the first draft of an interim constitution was circulated for discussion. In October the Transitional Executive Council (TEC) was established, a neutral, multiparty body that operated parallel to the government and had substantial control over large areas of state authority, especially those related to security. Agreement was reached over the creation of the Independent Electoral Commission (IEC). Provisions for the GNU were gradually hammered out, guaranteeing that the party with the second-largest vote would appoint one of two deputy presidents and all parties polling more than 5 percent would have cabinet representation based on their proportion of the vote. Though stopping short of federalism, the ANC conceded more devolved powers to an agreed nine provinces.

Viljoen and Buthelezi's conservative bloc, now called the Freedom Alliance, rejected the TEC process as well as the interim constitution, which was ratified by all other parties in November 1993 and adopted into law by Parliament. Mandela and de Klerk worked hard to draw the Freedom Alliance and IFP back into the process. Viljoen was eventually won over by the promise that a *volkstaat* would remain negotiable, and announced that his party, the Freedom Front, would participate in the election. Viljoen's participation and renunciation of violence were important because he commanded a volatile constituency which had the potential to cause major disruptions. The IFP wavered throughout late 1993 and early 1994. Buthelezi wanted a postponement of the elections but all other parties, realizing the political danger of such a move, closed ranks on this issue. Eventually the IFP, facing local and international pressure, agreed to participate seven days before the election, causing headaches for the IEC, which had to organize last-minute amendments to the ballot papers.

The election of April 26–28, 1994, was a unifying and uplifting experience for most South Africans. Voter turnout was very high—92 percent in Mandela's home region of the eastern Cape and 86 percent overall. Millions waited for hours in long lines to cast their ballots, and many polling stations experienced technical difficulties. Nevertheless, the atmosphere was peaceful for the most part, even euphoric. As expected, the ANC translated its powerful grassroots support into an overwhelming electoral victory, although its 62.6 percent of the votes put it short of the two-thirds parliamentary majority necessary to control the writing of a final constitution. The National Party, which drew substantial support from coloured and Indian voters, came second with 20.4 percent. It also captured the provincial government of the Western Cape. The IFP finished third with 10.5 percent, and despite irregularities in balloting and vote counting, was awarded control of the newly delineated province of KwaZulu-Natal. Other parties received too few votes to get cabinet representation.[6] On May 10, as air-force jets soared in a colorful display above Pretoria's Union Buildings, Nelson Mandela was inaugurated president of South Africa before a massive audience that included heads of state and dignitaries from around the world. A new era had begun.

Notes

1. On the National Party's negotiating positions at CODESA 1 and 2 and later at the multiparty talks at Kempton Park, see Steven Friedman, ed., *The Long Journey: South Africa's Quest for a Negotiated Settlement* (Johannesburg: Ravan Press, 1993) and Hassen Ebrahim, *The Soul of a Nation: Constitution-Making in South Africa* (Cape Town: Oxford University Press, 1998).

2. Raymond Suttner, "African National Congress (ANC): Attainment of Power, Post Liberation Phases and Current Crisis," unpublished draft paper, 2007, p. 30.

3. Nicoli Nattrass, "Politics and Economics in ANC Economic Policy," *African Affairs*, vol. 93, no. 372, 1994, pp. 351–54.

4. South African Military Intelligence had used this tactic in Namibia and claimed it reduced SWAPO's vote from a presumed 70% to 55% (actually 57%) in the 1989 pre-independence election, according to Allister Sparks, *Tomorrow is Another Country* (Johannesburg: Struik, 1994), pp. 153–54.

5. *Truth and Reconciliation Commission of South Africa Report* (Cape Town: Truth and Reconciliation Commission, 1998), vol. 2, p. 584, quotes an estimate that 14,000 people died in politically related violence between February 1990 and April 1994, or an average of 275 per month.

Discussion of a truth commission for South Africa began in 1992, planning meetings began in 1994, commissioners were appointed in December 1995, and public hearings started in April 1996.

6. Viljoen's Freedom Front took 2.2%, the Democratic Party 1.7%, and the PAC 1.2%. Thirteen minor parties together polled another 1.3%. See Andrew Reynolds, ed., *Election '94 South Africa* (Cape Town: David Philip, 1994), pp. 183 and 187.

Part Two

Documents

Documents have been reproduced using South African spelling and punctuation. Typographical errors have been corrected, and in some instances punctuation and spelling have been edited for the sake of clarity. Acronyms used in documents are explained by editorial insertions, or can be found in the acronyms list at the front of the book. In order to include a wide selection of materials, some documents have been abridged. Complete versions of the abridged documents can be found in the Karis-Gerhart Collection.

1. Reform and Repression in the Era of P. W. Botha

DOCUMENT 1. "For the Sake of South Africa, Free Nelson Mandela." Speech by Percy Qoboza, University of the Witwatersrand, March 20, 1980 (abridged)

Just a few years ago, standing on this very platform, I warned the people of our country that history is slowly but painfully catching up with us. I pleaded on that occasion for a realistic assessment of our national positions and urged the Government to initiate true and meaningful dialogue with the real leaders of the black community.

As if in deafening response to my call, the then Prime Minister, Mr John Vorster—may his political soul rest in peace—invited Chief Patrick Mphephu and his entire Cabinet to Cape Town! And so the pathetic tale of self-deception continued to flourish around the land.

For a few months before the Zimbabwe elections, South Africans, with the aid of their ever loyal and faithful South African Broadcasting Corporation, were being fed the palatable news that all is well in that land. They were assured by their leaders that the lovable and genial Bishop Abel Muzorewa was going to walk the free and fair elections.

In spite of warnings from us that this assumption was far from the truth and that people of Zimbabwe had other ideas, the lie continued to permeate the spirit of this nation. Instead, we were subjected to the barrage of insults and venom and accused of supporting what they usually like to describe as "terrorists". But my colleagues and I were vindicated. Bishop Muzorewa turned out to be what we said he was—a lovable and genial minister of religion. The People of Zimbabwe made their choice in what everybody accepts—with the notable and understandable exception of the SABC—that the elections were fair and free.

But for us, it is not a time for gloating. It is a time of considerable concern. . . . Just as the people of Zimbabwe had to learn the true realities of their situation, we believe that the people of this country must accept the realities of their situation. The biggest of these realities is that far too many of my people reject with increasing venom the policies imposed upon them by this society.

You must also accept that there is a frightening increase of those people who have abandoned hope for peaceful transformation of this system. Just like it happened in Zimbabwe, many have been forced by sheer frustration and hopelessness to leave the country to undergo military training around the world. In short, accept the reality that we are threatened by a far [more] dangerous conflict that would make [the] seven years the Zimbabwe conflict lasted look like a tea party. This is my fear and I am going to tell it to you straight. . . .

I beg of you today to regard our situation as a crisis situation. Do not be made comfortable at night by those of our people that Nationalists parade on your television and take their sweet words as representative of the mass of our people. Just like Zimbabwe's white community slept peacefully at night after listening to Muzorewa on TV. Please go out and listen to the voices of genuine black aspirations. Leaders approved and encouraged by Pretoria are part and parcel of a massive deception designed to distract us from true issues facing the country.

We believe that the most visible act of faith by the Government would be to release Nelson Mandela. It would give their often expressed—but never demonstrated—intention to change immense credibility. It would have the effect of immediately releasing the frightening tension in the country and create an atmosphere favourable to negotiation. Mandela stands in our midst as a giant. In spite of nearly 16 years away from public life, survey after survey portrays him as the man most blacks in our country will listen to and follow. These are the people the Government ought to be talking to.

While it is true they find comfort in talking to [homeland leaders] Matanzima and Mphephu and Sebe, the fact of the matter is those people represent only the sick elements of my community. They are men pushed down our throats by a system that has become politically bankrupt, economically insane and sociologically untenable. . . .

This decade, more than any in our history, is our final chance to solve our problems. If there is one major enemy we face, it is time. We haven't got the time to nibble away at the guerrilla warfare that is raging within the National Party. We haven't got the time to analyse the nonsensical pronouncement of John Vorster. We haven't got time to tolerate the insensitivities of Dr Andries Treurnicht. . . .

We have enough time to get Nelson Mandela out of that jail in Robben Island, and with him, enter into a serious era of negotiation to form a total national strategy that will bring peace to our land. A peace that will bring participation for all of us in the decision-making processes of our land. A peace that will, above all, bring the people of our country together in a spirit of mutual trust and freedom. Just that much time we still have. Yet it is limited.

We have to grab all of the opportunities and initiatives to bring freedom back to this land.

White South Africans have got nothing to fear. You have nothing to fear but fear itself. Your leaders told you of the damnation and collapse of Zimbabwe when the Patriotic Front took over. They have thrived over the last thirty years on that fear. They have manipulated you; they have exploited that fear to further their own interests. Well, you are witnesses to the big lies that have been going on. There is no damnation in Zimbabwe. Nothing is collapsing in Zimbabwe. Only one thing seems to be falling flat on its face—and that is the fear of white Zimbabweans as Robert Mugabe unfolds his intelligence and pushes his country into a true state of reconciliation.

Indeed the greatest demonstration of goodwill and statesmanship I have yet to see is Robert Mugabe sitting there and appointing his enemy number one, General [Peter] Walls, to be head supreme commander of his forces. It was a stroke of genius, one which many of our people dare not forget. This situation in Zimbabwe was unfortunately not arrived at so simply. It cost tens of thousands of lives. It is a stark reminder to all of us in South Africa that we must do our damnedest not to reach that stage.

In conclusion, I would like to make a strong and urgent appeal to the Government. I want to appeal to them to stop the spate of acts of intimidation they have recently engaged in, calling leaders of the black community to various police stations, asking them strange questions and generally giving them the impression they are going to be banned. Maybe they are. But I want to say to them: for the sake of this country, don't do it. We are not enemies of South Africa. We readily admit that we are consistent and unshakable enemies of injustice and deprivation. We are enemies of discrimination and exploitation. If these things form the foundations of your party philosophy, then you are quite right in regarding us as enemies.

For there is no way we can be party to humiliation. But if these things are not part and parcel of your philosophy, then we say do not regard us as enemies but as allies for justice and peace. We place a very high premium [on] individual freedom and opportunity.

And we place an even higher premium [on] our God-given right to be South Africans. It is a right that we will never be persuaded to compromise and we regard as coming from the hand of God, and not from the generosity of the National Party. So do not tamper with this right. It is one for which we are prepared to pay the ultimate price.

DOCUMENT 2. "In the End, PW Must Do a Deal With Me." Article by Chief Mangosuthu Gatsha Buthelezi, *Sunday Times*, April 6, 1980 (abridged)

Mr PW Botha has keys to white South African arsenals—but I have the key to communication with black Africa.

White South Africans cannot give content to the idea of a Southern African thrust without blacks such as myself playing a pivotal role. However economically dependent Southern African states are on our economy, the Prime Minister has not forged the warm relationships that I have with, for example, Swaziland and Lesotho and with the heads of states in Zambia, Tanzania, and Malawi. I am the only leader within South Africa, white or black, who talks openly with the leadership of the banned African National Congress-in-exile. If, therefore, Mr Botha and I cannot exercise a joint responsibility, much of the promise of these times will be eroded. Who in God's name can Mr Botha liaise with politically at this moment other than myself?

Never before has there been such fluidity at national and sub-continental level. There is hope in the air; there is recognition that we cannot go on as we have. There is, in my opinion, no prospect of the National Party returning to Verwoerdian idealism or Vorsterian political opportunism. But the challenge we face is that Mr PW Botha's Cabinet is incapable of striking out in the right direction without the backing of a three-way partnership between black South Africa, industrial and commercial interests, and the ruling party.

For me this is a bold statement. For I understand the frustration of those who despaired about dialogue and negotiation and have opted for violence. I can understand the mentality of those who talk about non-cooperation with whites and who seek a black solution for South Africa.

I have personally been subjected to tremendous pressures to abandon reason in favour of anger. When, in 1976, we faced a political eruption I was advised by many people to abandon my position. On every trip overseas I was pressurised to adopt the radical position of our South African compatriots-in-exile.

But while I was being shunned by fellow-South Africans who were whiter than I, while the Department of Information and what was then BOSS [Bureau of State Security] were actively working to diminish my hold over black South Africa, while Western governments were supporting activist black consciousness groups, while I was being denounced in international forums, I had to go on believing in calmness. Few can understand what political courage it has taken to remain both moral and pragmatic within this political babel. When you consider the utter hideousness of apartheid and the anger that exists in black minds and hearts, it takes courage for me as a black man to talk in simple terms about the possibility of a partnership between blacks, businessmen and the NP [National Party].

If I have any role in the shaping of South Africa, it is because I stand with the dispossessed and the disenfranchised. Those who compartmentalise urban and rural blacks and who see my legitimate concerns as stopping at the Tugela River are victims of a political absurdity. As a leader with the largest ever constituency in black South Africa, I am closely in touch with both the rural and the urban black. I fight for a voice for the voiceless; I seek fundamental human rights.

My people are the people of the ghettos. They continue to be threatened with starvation and unemployment. I say bluntly that unless the resources of the country are redirected to alleviate the lot of the poor, we will eventually have that bloodshed which none of us wants. . . .

Free enterprise must show real genius to survive the present situation in order to create a good future. The free enterprise system has more to offer South Africa than anything else, but then it must be enlightened. For too long it has been the willing handmaiden to sectional white interests. . . . Few realize how, as a black man in a black situation, my insistence that responsible investment in South Africa must be encouraged has been a political disadvantage. When no businessmen assisted Inkatha, when other black organisations were receiving thousands of rands in foreign aid, when in international forums I was attacked as a sell-out, I stood firm on the need for investment to create jobs for black people. I preferred to remain poor and unassisted, to retain my integrity, at the cost of being pilloried by radicals.

Inkatha has suffered a degree of isolation because of this stand, and Inkatha now requires open recognition that, practically speaking, it is the only black group which can be constructively involved in the future. But if I reject violence and the Government still refuses to admit blacks to constitutional South Africa, I will have no option but to mobilise the black consumers and workers of this country to support my drive for reform.

I ask South Africa's businessmen, unashamedly and simply, to put their full weight behind Inkatha.

Document 3. "Piet Freeman, Thebehali—and Ice to Eskimos. . . !" Article by Jon Qwelane, *Kwasa,* November 1980

I have seen dozens of cranks in my life. Cranks who would carry coals to Newcastle, sell French fries to the French, market refrigerators to Iceland and even sell ice blocks to Eskimos. The height of absurdity was reached last month when the paramount chief of Soweto gave freedom to a free man.

A lot of things have been said and written about [Soweto mayor] David Thebehali, but instead of disproving things, he goes all out to confirm them. Otherwise how does one explain Thebehali's action in giving the "freedom" of Soweto to Co-operation and Development boss Piet Koornhof? It goes without saying that Thebehali, in giving the freedom of the ghetto to Dr Koornhof, was dispensing with a commodity he himself does not have.

I can only guess at the motives which prompted Thebehali to make so momentous a decision. I can think of only two. The first, and most obvious, was for personal recognition. Thebehali knew that by giving Piet Freeman his dues he would go down in history as the only black man giving white people their freedom. In other words, he would be known as the only servant to give freedom to his masters. Even the Guinness Book of Records would not ignore such a momentous achievement.

I strongly suspect that the other reason why Piet Freeman became a citizen of Soweto was because of his good disposition towards Thebehali. They are known to have a very good working relationship.

In his welcome to Piet Freeman on the sacred day of his baptism as a bona fide resident of Soweto, Piet was told by Thebehali that "the people of Soweto regard you as their redeemer." Which is the other reason for the freedom award. As far as I know, the only resident of Soweto to be redeemed by Piet Freeman was Thebehali himself. Piet bought him a toy car to use on his "mayoral" rounds of Soweto, and for his efforts won himself the citizenship of the back streets.

Not that the freedom affair went off smoothly. There was a shortage of councillors to welcome Piet when he arrived in Soweto to grab his goodies. But that was no problem for the enterprising Thebehali, who grabbed a council messenger and a driver and tossed two gowns and in an instant he had ready-made councillors.

Piet's freedom came at a very awkward moment, which strengthens my belief that the award was made out of gratitude. He had just agreed to shelve elections which would surely have seen "Mr Six Percent" booted from office because of his bad handling of the rents issue.

Talking about rents brings to mind the increases and evictions. While Thebehali's township superintendents were serving people with eviction orders, they conveniently overlooked the fact that he himself was in heavy arrears and did nothing about it. He must be chortling with relief now that black newsmen have gone on strike. The man simply suffers an indescribable allergy [to] the media fellows, and sometimes makes a dash for it when they confront him.

As for Piet Freeman, well, that's another one. He promises the people of Soweto their freedom, and ends up grabbing it for himself. While he goes about serenely enjoying his freedom of the ghetto, one wonders whether they did not forget to issue him with a reference book [pass] as well. Perhaps Pretoria is still processing a citizenship certificate for him for [an] as yet unspecified homeland.

DOCUMENT 4. "Botha Holds Key to Peaceful Future for South Africa." Op-ed article by Bishop Desmond Tutu, *Manchester Guardian Weekly,* October 4, 1981

After all the buffeting that blacks have taken in over 30 years of apartheid rule, you would think that by now they would have become seasoned cynics. Former prime minister John Vorster proclaimed that he wanted just six months to transform the political face of South Africa. Roelof (Pik) Botha, who was at that time his ambassador at the United Nations, declared with a great flourish that South Africa was moving away from discrimination based on race. And what happened? Nothing more than the sort of intransigence that caused the 1976 uprisings and the orgy of bannings and detentions without trial capped by the death in detention of Steve Biko.

And yet when P. W. Botha came on the scene as prime minister, hopes began to rise again. Here was a man who appeared quite decisive and who knew white South Africa must adapt or die. He was speaking in a way that we had not expected to hear from a Nationalist prime minister. He seemed to have set his sights on reform and realized he would need new allies, hence his successful overtures to the private sector. Botha also knew that the traditional supporters of his party would be appalled at having to give up so much of white privilege. A survey showed that 60 percent of the blacks thought Botha was doing a good job as prime minister. That is how high hopes were flying.

Nearly two years have since passed, and there has been little more than reformist rhetoric, which has not yet been translated into reality. Botha has made a valiant effort to streamline government bureaucracy, but he has also been concentrating power more and more in his hands. He is increasingly seeking to bypass government, as witness his abolition of the senate and a new scheme for nominating parliamentarians. He deserves credit for the advent of the President's Council, which represents revolutionary thinking on the part of the Nationalists, in that it says other races (excluding blacks) would join whites in determining the future of South Africa, constitutional or otherwise. Having got so far, however, he greatly weakened this potentially revolutionary move by providing for a nominated rather than an elected membership.

Even after this setback, many people hoped against hope that change, real fundamental change, which has to do with political power-sharing, still might happen. Others, however, were beginning to suspect that Botha was going to be hoisted on the petard of Afrikaner unity, to believe that he, like all his predecessors, did not want to have the dubious honor of going down in history as the man who split the Nationalist Party and so also Afrikanerdom.

The prime minister was, for instance, humiliated by Andries Treurnicht, the archconservative leader of the Transvaal Nationalist Party, on the question of whether schoolboys of different races could play rugby together. Treurnicht declared in public, contradicting the prime minister, that it would not happen. Botha learned that if he took this momentous issue to the party caucus he would lose to Treurnicht. And so he backed down.

For various reasons, Botha decided to call an election some two years before he needed to. Perhaps he wanted his own mandate from the people. Perhaps he hoped to wipe the floor with the right wing and so be rid of it forever. And he might have done both these things had he gone boldly for a reformist platform. Unfortunately he retreated into the lager [circled wagons] of well-tried traditional Afrikaner policies, and predictably this time he lost to both the right and the left. He was not conservative enough for the right and not reformist enough for the left (if these terms mean anything in South Africa). If he were bright, he would realize that he has been relieved of the albatross of Afrikaner unity. It no longer exists.

I have spent time on Botha because he holds the key to a peaceful future for South Africa. The indisputable point is that we who are oppressed will be free. That is not in question. The logic of history, even Afrikaner history, dictates that this is so. All that the whites can do is decide whether they want freedom to come reasonably peacefully or through bloodshed and armed struggle. Those are the only options available.

Botha can play a decisive role by opting for a bold policy of change. Anything else will fail. He can never satisfy the right wing. So he should go all out to win the world and the rest of South Africa by opting for political power-sharing.

Unrest, in the schools and on the labor front, is endemic in our country and will continue to be so until political power-sharing becomes a reality. More and more blacks are becoming disillusioned as those of us calling for change by peaceful means have our credibility eroded by the authorities' often brutal and excessive action. Calls for peaceful change are being answered by tear gas, police dogs, bullets, detention without trial and banning orders. The authorities are growing in intransigence; belatedly Botha wants to demonstrate that he is tough and cannot be trifled with.

He is too late because he has not come to terms with the determination bordering on recklessness of black youth who openly flaunt the emblems of the outlawed African National Congress. He cannot control the militancy of black labor unions.

Finally, a word about foreign corporations in South Africa. Multinational corporations are not yet involved in the business of helping to destroy apartheid. They have done some good things for their employees, but all within the framework of apartheid, and really no more than what a good employer should have been doing. Ultimately their efforts are improvements and not changes. They are making apartheid more comfortable rather than dismantling it.

The international community must make up its mind whether it wants to see a peaceful resolution of the South African crisis. If it does, then let it apply pressure (diplomatic, political, but above all, economic) on the South African government to persuade it to go to the negotiating table with the authentic leaders of all sections of the South African population before it is too late. Maybe it is too late, judging from the conduct of the Reagan administration. If so, then what Mr. Vorster called the alternative too ghastly to contemplate is upon us. But hope springs eternal.

DOCUMENT 5. "The Responsibility of Judges in Applying Unjust Laws in South Africa." Civil Rights League pamphlet, Cape Town, 1981? (abridged)

In all the painful clash of the forces and counterforces for change, is there any hope that the voice of the Judiciary may at last be raised in an attempt to influence the Legislature to amend or repeal laws which make it impossible for judges to carry out the terms of their oath of office, namely to administer justice?

JUDGE'S OATH
(Supreme Court Act No. 59 of 1959)
"I (full name) do hereby swear [or] solemnly and sincerely affirm and declare that I will, in my capacity as judge of the Supreme Court of South Africa,

administer justice to all persons alike without fear, favour or prejudice, and, as the circumstances of any particular case may require, in accordance with the law and customs of the Republic of South Africa." (Emphasis added)

It is true that in our Parliamentary system, judges cannot challenge the creation of law, which is the prerogative of Parliament. And no judge can refuse to apply the existing law, however inconsistent it may be with any concept of justice. Yet there is an undeniable tension between the narrow test of validity, based on procedural formalities (the law has been passed by the requisite majority in Parliament, has been signed by the State President, and published in the Government Gazette) and the Christian basis of the Constitution.

THE CONSTITUTION not only acknowledges the sovereignty and guidance of God, but specifically declares that "we are conscious of our responsibility towards God and man." (Republic of South Africa Constitution Act No. 32 of 1961). Daily in Parliament legislators pray ". . . that we may, as in Thy presence, treat and consider all matters that shall come under our deliberation, in so just and faithful a manner as to promote Thy honour and glory. . . ."

RESPONSIBILITY OF JUDGES
What then is the responsibility of judges, when a succession of statutes has limited or removed the inherent jurisdiction of the Supreme Court, or when they are called upon to apply such blatantly unjust laws as the pass laws (which govern only certain people, because of their race, namely Africans) or the Group Areas and Mixed Marriages Acts, or Security laws which provide for banning and incommunicado detention without due process?

THE MEMORY OF NUREMBERG
Gustave Radbruch, prominent German jurist, "was compelled by the experience of the Nazi Holocaust to argue that there is a stage at which a law ceases to be a law, when it sinks below a minimum level of humanity or justice. He contended that
- "positivism with its creed of *law is law* rendered the German legal profession defenceless against statutes of an arbitrary and criminal content," and declared:
- "when laws consciously deny the will to achieve justice, for instance if they grant or retract human rights from people according to arbitrary caprice, such laws are devoid of validity, and the people owe them no obedience and even lawyers must then find the courage to deny them the nature of law." (1)

Commenting on the South African situation, a professor of law has written: "It is almost as if the courts have invoked the contempt power to protect them from the memory of Nuremberg, to spare them the agony of deciding, or even considering, at what point a law ceases to be a law on account of its immoral content and at what point confrontation or resignation becomes the lot of the judge." (2)

DETENTION INCOMMUNICADO

Section 6 of the Terrorism Act epitomises the erosion of the Rule of Law in South Africa.

- It provides for indefinite detention without trial for the purpose of interrogation.
- The Minister of Police is not obliged to give details about such detainees.
- The definition of terrorism is so wide that someone who cannot remotely be viewed as a terrorist can be held.
- The acceptance in court as valid evidence of statements made by people who have been kept in solitary confinement persists—in spite of widespread consensus that such imprisonment is a form of torture in itself. In no sense can people kept in such conditions be said to be making free statements. Such a detainee has no right of access to his own lawyer or doctor, channels that would serve to curb possible unlawful methods of interrogation. The judiciary should regard this type of evidence with profound suspicion and misgiving and be aware of the unjust nature of the pre-trial interrogation permitted under our Security laws.

BANNING UNDER THE INTERNAL SECURITY ACT

The system of restriction and house arrest orders is inherently unjust.

- Such restriction orders are based on secret reports made by Security Police, and this evidence is not tested in court.
- The Minister of Justice makes his decision in private. Justice is not *seen* to be done.
- There is no appeal to the courts from the Minister's decisions, save on the ground of his bona fides, an almost impossible case to prove.
- The banned person himself has no knowledge of the contents of information placed before the Minister, and is effectively silenced and prevented from defending himself, while the courts have no power to review the Minister's decision.
- When and if a banned person is charged with a consequent offence of having broken the restriction orders, the court has no knowledge of the grounds on which the person has already been banned.

The courts are, in effect, compelled to reinforce this administrative punishment without having any knowledge of the grounds on which it was imposed. Thus in cases involving banned people, it is impossible for judges to administer justice in terms of their oath, because a vital area of justice has already been excluded from the jurisdiction of the courts.

WHAT JUDGES COULD DO

"The only generalisation in which I shall indulge is that if one participates in a system that distorts justice, truisms about the limited functions of a judge will not necessarily save one's soul." (3)

Should judges not find ways of coming together to consider the implications of what to many is a manifest contradiction between the terms of their oath and their present hearing of cases under the above legislation? Parliament is sovereign, and judges hold office to enforce and uphold a system created by that body. But increasingly the bulk of the population now regard the legal order as "oppression" and a growing number of lawyers overseas and of law students in South Africa, consider that the legal profession here is "collaborating with and lending respectability to a fundamentally illegitimate process." (4)

The Legislature has placed the Judiciary in an increasingly intolerable position. But between the extremes of acquiesence and resignation from the Bench lies a not inconsiderable area of action which judges could take.

- There is nothing to prevent a judge in a judgment from drawing attention to the unjust consequences of the application of a law, and indeed some have done this, to their credit. More judges could follow this example. They should firmly reject any criticism that such judgments bring them into the political arena. Indeed the matter is much more fundamental than party politics.
- Just as evidence revealing criminal behaviour on the part of individuals or officials is sometimes referred by judges to the Attorney General for his consideration, so the unjust consequences of any law should be referred by judges to the appropriate Cabinet Minister for his consideration.
- Possibly only after discussion of these matters between brother judges has resulted in some approach to the Judge President of each Division, and from them to the Chief Justice, will a degree of support be established for some stronger approach to the Prime Minister.

Unanimity about the occasion or justification for resignation is hardly likely to be achieved in present circumstances, but it is contended that the situation is a deteriorating one, and the prime concern is that future generations of South Africans should retain respect for the Rule of Law and the value of an independent judiciary. Resignations on grounds of conscience may, looked at retrospectively, then be seen as the sparks which kept alight a fundamental belief in the best traditions of our Western legal heritage.

1. Dugard, Prof. John: *Human Rights and the South African Legal Order.* Princeton University Press, Princeton, New Jersey, [1978], p. 399.
2. Ibid. (commenting on the test enunciated for contempt of court in case against Prof. Barend Van Niekerk), p. 300.
3. Kentridge, Advocate Sydney: "The Pathology of a Legal System: Criminal Justice in South Africa," *University of Pennsylvania Law Review*, Vol. 128, no. 44, [1980].
4. Didcott, Justice J. M. at Inaugural Meeting of Lawyers for Human Rights, reported in *Argus* editorial, 23rd June 1980. . . .

DOCUMENT 6. "South Africa: the Case Against Immigration—A Letter to Polish Catholics from the Church in South Africa." Southern African Catholic Bishops' Conference pamphlet, Pretoria, early 1982 (abridged)

Our sympathy with Poland

Catholics in South Africa have during the past two years followed closely the events in Poland. We regret the repressive measures taken against all the movements endeavouring to bring about significant change. We protest against the cruel clampdown on Solidarity last year, and we offer our sympathy to those who felt constrained to leave Poland at this time because of grave economic problems there or intolerable political repression by the communist government and its military forces.

Our government in South Africa, along with others, has been quick to offer hospitality to the numerous Polish refugees. At present 50-60 Polish citizens, skilled workers and their families, are arriving in South Africa each week. This stream is expected to continue for the rest of this year.

A warning to prospective immigrants

We would like to warn prospective Polish immigrants about the situation and help those who are already here to understand what is happening in this country and the role they will be expected to play here.

We can easily imagine the reactions of young Polish immigrants at their first encounter with a country so different from their own. We guess that their first impression will be one of astonishment if not of admiration at the sight of an apparently affluent, well-ordered country teeming with happy and carefree people. . . . It is not our intention to destroy this first—admittedly over-optimistic—impression of South Africa . . . [but] we would like to provide some guidelines which would help new and prospective immigrants in their quest for truth, a quest that is particularly difficult in a country where truth is so carefully removed from the sight of white people.

The church opposes the ideology of the state

We also wish to spare them the unpleasant shock of suddenly discovering that the Catholic Church is in acute opposition to the dominant ideology of the state. Such a shock might not only be very unpleasant and disturbing, but might provoke a reaction of protest, if not of rebellion, against the church. Being new to this situation it would be difficult to understand the church's condemnatory attitude towards the state, which professes to be an anti-communist bastion and guardian of the "white man's paradise"—as some recent Polish immigrants were reported to have described South Africa. Why, the Polish immigrant may ask, should the church oppose the state? Is the church doctrinally opposed to a state which provides its inhabitants with material comfort? Are we, Polish immigrants, coming from a country where the church battled against the state, back at square one?

The answer to these questions is in the affirmative: the Catholic Church, together with almost all other Christian denominations, condemns the racist ideology of the National Party of South Africa. There are at least three good reasons for this stand. The first is doctrinal, the second pastoral and the third pragmatic. Doctrinally, Christians are bound to believe that God created all people in his own image. This God-given dignity is to be respected in everyone, and there are no superior or inferior versions of God's image in mankind. Therefore racialism, which makes some superior to others, is doctrinally nothing but a heresy.

The pastoral aspect of the church's stand against racialism is twofold. Firstly, more than 80 percent of the Catholic population is black. If the church were to defend the economic and political monopoly of power held by whites, it would irrevocably alienate the majority of the faithful, thus greatly compromising the future of Christianity throughout South Africa. . . .

The pragmatic argument is based on historical precedent. Whenever the doctrine of racialism has raised its ugly head, it led inevitably to the exploitation of the allegedly inferior, and in its more extreme form to mass extermination of peoples, as shown by the actions of the Nazi regime of forty years ago. There is therefore for the church no possibility of compromise with an ideology which, although it presents itself in Christian guise, is no less incompatible with Christianity than communism is. . . .

The National Security State

As the claims and expectations of blacks have grown with their growing awareness of their situation, the oppression against them has grown systematically more ruthless and efficient. The only alternative, viz black and white sharing their common heritage in South Africa on an equitable basis worked out by negotiation between equals, is totally unacceptable to many due to their racial prejudice about the purity and superiority of the white race.

With this doomsday vision vividly inscribed into the consciousness of the white inhabitants, the whole political game to which the ruling party has now been reduced is how to defer it, even for a decade, or two, possibly even beyond the life expectancy of the present ruling class. To achieve this the resources and energies of the whole white population need to be mobilised. For the effort must be total.

A project of such magnitude needs however an additional motivation, if only to overcome the built-in resistance of a basically Christian society whose collective conscience might not be prepared to stomach oppression of an intensity stretching beyond a certain threshold of decency. In the ideology of the National Security State the government has found the motivating force it needs. So during the last decade or so it has introduced this ideology slowly and methodically into all reaches of government and social life.

The antecedents of this new ideology are not savoury. It was first formulated and applied in a number of Latin American countries. There the social set-up is similar to South Africa in that a small affluent elite rule over vast

numbers of people held in poverty and ignorance. The leading ideas of the National Security ideology are as follows:
- The state is absolute. It must control and determine everything in the life of the nation. It cannot be controlled, dictated to or influenced by anything outside it, not even the church.
- The enemy of the state is seen as communism. According to the geopolitics of this ideology, the world is divided into two camps, the West and the East. The West is the free world and the East is the one and only enemy, thus anything and everything—whether religious, cultural or overtly political—that appears to threaten the supremacy of the state is labelled "communist". The state is threatened not only by external enemies but also by internal enemies; in fact, every citizen is a potential enemy because any one of them could be a communist.
- Consequently the state is understood to be facing a total onslaught. It can be attacked and undermined militarily, economically, culturally and psychologically.
- This means that the state is involved in a total war. There is no peace and the state cannot act as if there were peace. War is continuous and the state must develop a total strategy to combat the enemy. This strategy is called "total" because it includes military, economic, political, cultural, psychological and even religious strategies. The effect of such an approach to life is that people are made insecure and so put on a warlike footing; their lowest instincts are continually played upon so that they see everything that disturbs their position as a threat.
- The highest goal or aim of the state is therefore its own security and survival. Any and every means can be employed and justified so long as it is deemed necessary for reasons of state security. And, conversely, anything that threatens the security of the state must be destroyed and eliminated. It should be noted here that the National Security State does not see its highest aim as the welfare of all its peoples or as the service of the people, but as its own survival and security. To put this another way, the security in question is not that of the people, but of the state.
- Because any means can be used to ensure the security of the state, we find most of the following in every National Security State today: detention without trial, the banning of people and organisations, the tapping of telephones and the opening of mail, censorship of the press, the use of informers and spies, a strong army, a security or secret police, and a special riot squad. The last three are trained to use violent methods and yield a rich crop of beaten-up victims, detainees dying or "committing suicide" while in prison, or people simply "disappearing". These are familiar phenomena in *every* totalitarian state, but the special feature in this ideology is that it is all justified in the name of security.

It is noticeable how South African legislation over the last fifteen years has not been concerned with apartheid, but with security. In the last two general elections the National Party slogans have not been apartheid ones, but "security" and "survival". The ideological language of the National Security State became more explicit when P. W. Botha became prime minister: "total onslaught", "total war", "total strategy", "national aims", "national survival", etc. There is also a Council of National Security [State Security Council] which includes the military and which can veto the decision of any other government department. Every other National Security State has a similar council. . . .

Some dangerous illusions

Polish immigrants coming from a communist country know from personal experience what it is like to live in an unjust society. They rejected with indignation the appropriation of privileges by members of the Communist Party. They found it insufferable on moral grounds. There is therefore no valid reason why they should accept it as normal and equitable that South African whites should appropriate privileges to the detriment of others. They might observe that in communist Poland membership of the Communist Party depended—at least theoretically, though not in practice—on certain specific qualities such as integrity, concern, energy, initiative and honesty. Such is not the case in South Africa, where status and privilege depends solely on the colour of one's skin.

Migration from Poland to South Africa can be summed up as a transition from being under-privileged into membership of a privileged class. This change imposes grave obligations on the immigrant. Before concluding these guidelines, we think it necessary to warn Polish immigrants about a number of pitfalls which they might easily fall into.

• The trap of seduction: The contrast between the living standards of Poland and South Africa is of such magnitude that it might easily result in a dangerous intoxication with material possessions and pleasures. One's hierarchy of values could easily be shifted in favour of material achievements. This, coupled with a relative deprivation of spiritual, cultural and artistic nourishment, could lead people to adopt an attitude of unbalanced and gross materialism. . . .

• The trap of misunderstanding black attitudes and taking on the prevalent white attitudes: It is important to realise that many blacks view immigrants with suspicion and animosity. The reasons are easy to find. There is a large pool of unemployed black people in South Africa, more than 2 million. Furthermore, the majority of blacks work at menial, unskilled and uninteresting jobs for little pay. But the new immigrant is given on arrival a good, relatively well paid job, often in a supervisory capacity over blacks.

In the field of education immigrants have opportunities denied to blacks. Their education system is neither free nor compulsory, and has been deliberately designed to be inferior so that less than one percent of blacks receive a tertiary education. The result is an insufficient number of blacks able to take on existing skilled jobs, and so it becomes necessary to encourage European immigrants to take them. The children of immigrants can enter the free white educational system, where R724 [$650] per capita is spent on them annually compared with less than R70 for a black child.

Immigrants too are provided with accommodation and are free to move from one city to another, and to return or buy housing there. But blacks are allowed to live only in certain demarcated areas, where housing is grossly inadequate and overcrowded. They are not allowed to move freely from city to city in search of work or housing. Many in fact are forced to share houses, so that 12 or more are crowded into three rooms and a kitchen.

Immigrants also have an advantage over black South Africans in that they can become citizens after two years' residence and so acquire the right to vote. No black person has the right of South African citizenship, and they may only belong to the so called "homelands". At present more and more black people are losing what little rights they have in South Africa. They are becoming stateless persons, refusing to recognise the homeland to which they have been arbitrarily assigned.

In recent years the African National Congress, the banned organisation which is receiving increasing black support, has singled out certain strategic installations for sabotage. These include the SASOL oil plants and several power stations. Polish people are often being employed in these places as well as in factories manufacturing steel for armaments and in the mines. All these installations have a strategic importance in maintaining the present political system. So Polish immigrants working there will be regarded by the liberation movements as aiding the repressive South African regime, and being against their legitimate aspirations.

We hope that those sobering facts will help immigrants understand why many blacks do not welcome them in South Africa, and why you may encounter antagonism in your workplace. We would like to add, however, that black people generally are warm and friendly when treated as equals.

- The trap of accepting South Africa as a country in all respects normal: This view, which many immigrants adopt, is demonstrably false. South Africa is not a normal country. If it were it would be run for the benefit of its people. But the present government does not regard the black inhabitants as a potential source of its wealth. They are expendable. Illiteracy is rife. Diseases based on malnutrition and poor sanitation are ravaging the population. The immigration of white technicians from foreign countries is indispensable for providing skills which the state refuses to impart to its own black citizens. The result is that whites live in a non-competitive society with abnormally high salaries.

We have tried very briefly to give an idea of the issues involved in emigrating to South Africa. Undoubtedly there are many attractive features about South Africa, and these are widely known. We do not wish to deny them, but think it only fair to explain the other side. We hope that both prospective and newly arrived immigrants will weigh them carefully. If you are already here or decide to come, please keep yourselves informed about the real struggle that is going on in our country. Keep in contact with us and take note of what our bishops are teaching.

Document 7. Memorandum on threatened removal of Lusitania, a "black spot" in Natal, February 1982

MEMORANDUM OF LUSITANIA SYNDICATE

INTRODUCTION: Lusitania is a black-owned farm in a white district—a "Black-spot" in the centre of white farmers as described by the now said government. It is some 8 km from Cundycleugh and 13 km near Collins Pass (on the border of the Orange Free State and Natal) in the district of Klip-River, the magisterial district of Ladysmith, Natal.

The land is approximately 1165 ha [hectares] in area, well watered, with the Sundays River running through one end of this property on the East, as well as a stream in the centre of our commonage which enters the Sundays River which we use for our stock to drink, as well as irrigation for our homes. It is also well grassed and relatively free from soil erosion. This property also has a lot of water-fountains [springs] here and there all over the land and on the mountain-side. This water we use for our food and drinking consumption and it is very clean water. We are a very peaceful rural community. There is also a big natural forest on the mountain-side with all different indigenous trees of many kinds; wild animals, big and small, enjoy their life here i.e. Buck, birds, snakes, snails etc.

All kinds of fruit trees grow very well at this place, e.g. orchards of oranges, lemons, nartjies [tangerines], peaches, plums, pears, apricots, grapes, guavas, etc., and we use these for our family consumption and supply our nearest fruit-shops and supermarkets, as well as some farmers near us come and buy these fruits. There is a main road from Ladysmith to Newcastle on the boundary of our commonage and family freehold lands. This road goes through our place. It is easy for us to go to Ladysmith, Newcastle and Dannhauser with the value of this road.

HISTORY: The farm was bought from Mr Chomerald Marais by 20 (twenty) landowners shortly after the Anglo-Boer War of 1899-1902, at a Public-Auction at Ladysmith, Klip River District, and was surveyed amongst the twenty. It was then sub-divided into a commonage on the mountain side, and family Freehold lands on the eastern side. On these freehold lands each of the twenty landowners has his own Title Deed. The commonage is approximately 380 ha, and the twenty each have equal shares in this commonage. Lusitania has its general Title Deed of which the landowners are the rightful heirs, with approximately 40 ha to each holder.

The first buyers were Ndabambi, Mavuso and Mtitinyane Mahlambi. The Syndicate had a Chief Trustee and two other Trustees. Up to now this place is still under 3 Trustees and their 6 Committee members. The last of our fathers died in December 1972, Rev. Eliam Hadebe. On the death of our fathers, some willed to their sons, and a few sold their shares, now bringing the total number to twenty-eight landowners. We also have tenants at this place, approximately eighty households, with an additional eleven at the commonage. This brings the total to one hundred and nineteen kraals [livestock pens] and families at this farm, who will suffer if removed.

HISTORY OF RESETTLEMENT: In 1964 the Bantu Affairs Commissioner for Natal invited us to a meeting, where we were called a "Black-spot" which in terms of Departmental policy will have to be eliminated in due course. In the very same year the Government Officials visited Lusitania to inform us we were to be counted and the Deeds of Transfer should be made straight, to the heirs amongst everybody at Lusitania. Since then we have heard nothing from the Officials but we know the plan is to remove us, along with Matiwane's Kop etc. We discussed this and agree that we do not want to be moved.

TENANTS' LAND: Tenants have an average quarter ha residential plot for growing their crops. No tenants are self-supporting on their land, but their agricultural lands add to income derived from wage employment. Their standard of living is high.

IMPROVEMENTS: There is mixture of concrete block, wattle and daub huts and stone houses. There is a school building, concrete Dipping tanks and domesticated wattle and Gum trees as well as Palm trees etc. All households have put in other improvements i.e. fencing, toilets, cattle kraals, fruit trees. As well we have sub-divided our Commonage for grazing. It has been fenced very well, with the graveyard on the same commonage. The value of improvements runs to many thousands of rands.

CROPS: All of us grow some products, the main crop being maize, plus kaffir-corn, potatoes, beans etc. We make a good living from our land; some of us do not have to work in town.

LIVESTOCK: There is no limit to the number of cattle. Tenants' cattle varies from 1 to 5 head of cattle, plus goats, horses, pigs and as many poultry as he is able to keep. Total numbers of stock are as follows: cattle 278, 6 horses, 352 goats, 16 sheep, 16 pigs and approximately 800 poultry. Our stock is usually sold to Sales camps, stock brokers and speculators at reasonable prices.

EMPLOYMENT: Most people who are working are working in town while some are working outside the district. Many are farm labourers or waiters, domestic servants, commercial workers etc. Many of the women and girls work casual or seasonal employment on neighbouring farms.

SCHOOLS: There is a school (Lower and Higher Primary) up to Standard 5 with 7 teachers and 380 to 400 children. The community is already building and has raised some funds for another continuation (Big Building) for Standard 7, 8, and 9 as they wished. They have donated money every season to raise school-funds. We have our church and want to build a clinic.

CONCLUSION: We are all well to do here and the place is healthy, with daily transport from Lusitania to Ladysmith. We have lived here for almost 83 years, with our tenants, without quarrels and frictions. You could hardly see a Police van coming in for cases at Lusitania. There are no shebeens [bars] and we are peacefully settled. We are friendly with the farmers surrounding us. We are their Fire Brigades, casual workers and seasonal workers. During harvesting season and in destroying unrequired wattle forests we are useful to them and they are useful to us. The owners do not stay on most of the white farms surrounding Lusitania, except for one or two. In most cases these farms are used for their stock grazing, and cultivation for crops and hays in feeding their stocks. There are rich farmers surrounding us, who do not want us to be removed from this place.

We pray we should not be removed from our Lusitania Syndicate.

Lusitania Committee
c/o Lusitania H. P. [Higher Primary] School
P. 0. Box 860
LADYSMITH
3370

DOCUMENT 8. Inkatha's minutes of a meeting between Piet Koornhof and an Inkatha delegation, Cape Town, May 3, 1982 (abridged)

R.S.A. Delegation . . . [Minister for Co-operation and Development P.G.J. Koornhof; the deputy ministers for development and co-operation; the Commissioner-General; the chairman of the Consolidation Committee; director-general for Co-operation and Development; two staff persons]

KwaZulu Delegation . . . [Chief Minister M. G. Buthelezi; Alpheus Zulu, Speaker; Oscar Dhlomo, Minister for Education and Culture; Frank Mdlalose, Minister for the Interior; E.S.E. Ngubane, Secretary to the Chief Minister]

The meeting had been called by Dr. Koornhof, who would not disclose what it would all be about in advance. . . .

Dr. Koornhof. He welcomed the delegation from KwaZulu under the leadership of the Honourable Chief Minister. He then made the following points.
1. He wanted to discuss a very important issue. He thanked the delegation from KwaZulu for having come at so short a notice. When the issue was put, he was sure it would be clear why such a short notice was made, and why it was kept so secret.
2. At the last occasion of a meeting such as this was, the Honourable Chief Minister had indicated that there was a rumour about negotiations going on between R.S.A. and Swaziland on Ingwavuma. . . .

A week ago [Minister of Foreign Affairs] Mr. R. F. Botha discussed the matter concerning Swaziland border adjustments with His Majesty King Sobhuza II. . . . The Republican Government realised that to have any area or piece of land earmarked for KwaZulu being incorporated into Swaziland was a very sensitive issue so far as KwaZulu and the Honourable Chief Minister were concerned. It had been then proposed that such discussion be on the basis of adequate compensation on the basis of complete equitability. . . .

The Honourable Chief Minister. "Do you mean you want to excise the whole of Ingwavuma and give it to Swaziland?"

Dr. Koornhof. Pointed at the areas involved.

The Honourable Chief Minister. "But people there are not Swazis! Land there has never been Swaziland territory". . . .

Dr. Koornhof. Nothing has been finalised. The R.S.A. Government had decided to settle the issue only with co-operation from KwaZulu. They were now looking at the possibility of satisfying the Swazis by offering KwaZulu land of similar or better value. . . .

Dr. Zulu. He wanted to understand reasons for all this so that he could be enabled to explain to the people back home. . . .

The Honourable Chief Minister. . . . if the Afrikaners wanted to force issues at the point of the gun, he had no alternative but to say "SO BE IT!" and he would not be responsible for the consequences. . . . The Honourable Minister and his Deputies could explain their proposal to the KwaZulu Legislative Assembly Caucus, for example. It must be remembered, however, that King Dingane's remains are interred in the Nyawo area now wanted by the Swazis. One wondered if the Afrikaner out of revenge against King Dingane that they detested and loathed following the death of Piet Retief were not in fact revenging against King Dingane and the Zulus in this manner. . . . He advised that for the sake of consistency the Republic should shed off the Orange Free State to Lesotho. . . . KwaZulu people were not children and could not be so easily deceived. . . .

Dr. Koornhof. "Can we not discuss this peacefully?" . . . The Swazis had taken the issue to the United Nations some time ago. They claimed that Swazi chiefs and Swazi people lived in this area and wanted to pay allegiance to the Swazi Monarch. In terms of International Law, an independent state should if possible have access to the sea. Swazis have asked for this.

The Honourable Chief Minister. This was strange reasoning when one considered that in South Africa all beaches were precluded to Blacks. The whole coastal line was confined to Whites only. Are we now being deprived of even that bit of coastline in KwaZulu to placate the Swazis?

Mr. van der Walt. Wanted to interpolate.

The Honourable Chief Minister. He stated he did not want to hear any more from Mr. Van der Walt.

Dr. Koornhof. Appealed to have this resolved amicably. At this juncture, Mr. Van der Walt packed his papers and zipped his satchel and muttered a few words to Dr. Koornhof in Afrikaans. Dr. Koornhof, however, instructed him to stay on and not leave.

The Honourable Chief Minister. "Let us be honest. There is nothing that can be discussed amicably on this issue."

Dr. Koornhof. Indicated that he accepted the Chief Minister's idea of addressing the Caucus himself possibly with others.

Dr. Zulu. He believed that Dr. Koornhof had great respect for KwaZulu people and would not like him to talk to the people as he [Dr. Zulu] felt this issue was not really discussable.

The Honourable Chief Minister. "In fact it is a dirty deal!" We do not want to dirty our hands with it.

Mr. Wentzel. You mean it is too drastic?

Dr. Zulu. There would be nothing that could be put before the Caucus as a basis for discussion.

Dr. Koornhof. A point could be found as a basis for discussion, e.g. Sodwana Bay—a straight line could be drawn to the sea to show how Swaziland could attain access to the sea. "Would this not be discussable?"

KwaZulu Delegation said "NO!"

[The discussion continued. Koornhof had not known the location of King Dingane's remains. Dr. Zulu reconsidered, agreeing that Koornhof's coming to the Caucus would be helpful. But, he added, Swazis despised Zulus and treated Buthelezi as rubbish. Agreed: as Buthelezi suggested, he and Koornhof would each prepare a short statement indicating that the matter was placed before the Zulu King and Assembly.]

Document 9. Letter from Reverend Lesiba Matsaung to the South African Council of Churches, September 27, 1982

N.G.K.
Box 83
Messina 0900
27.9.1982

The Secretary
South African Council of Churches
P. O. Box 31190
Braamfontein 2001

Financial Assistance and Job on Part-Time Basis

Dear Brethren,
We are faced with a double problem.
1. Withdrawal of subsidy
2. Re-settlement

1. I am now looking out beyond the boundaries of the N.G. Kerk [Dutch Reformed Church] institutions for financial assistance as the only alternative to remedy this situation. We shall be glad if you can approach other friends for our sake in this regard.

The Secretary of Broederkring [NGK ministers' association] (Dr. Mabusela of Mamelodi) and Rev. S. Nkoane of St. Mary's Cathedral—JHB [Jchannesburg] advised me to consult you personally in regard to this problem, but it became impossible because of travelling expenses. We shall be glad if even your representative can visit us in order to have an empathy of what we experience.

Since 1980-1982 there are some months when we did not receive our salaries, and Broederkring now and then helped us out of this problem. This year the pressure mounted very badly as the N. G. Kerk did cut their subsidy from us. They say my presence here is undesirable because it is next to the borders of S. Africa with Zimbabwe, Botswana and Mozambique. They wish that I can be replaced by a white missionary.

Now they publicly pressurize me alone (we are 3 servants: myself, evangelist and lay-preacher).

For the last 2 MONTHS I did not receive my salary. Broederkring says they are now working beyond their Budget and are unable to assist. Therefore I am now compelled to look for financial assistance beyond the borders of N. G. Kerk institutions. Unless I find help somewhere or anywhere or somehow, by DECEMBER I will have to leave Messina in search for a new job.

I am even looking for a job as a Tent-making priest i.e. part-time minister, working for another institution or company while I still remain a minister in this congregation i.e. on part-time basis.

Many of my people in the Northern Transvaal are worried with having to leave Messina [since] at this moment the morale of the People in the Struggle for our Liberation will go down.

It is not my wish that I may leave N. Tvl at this time but because of this kind of pressure I will be forced to.

2. At present there is a re-settlement scheme going on started by the Venda and S. African government removing many of the people from next [to] the borders of Zimbabwe into the interior of Venda Homeland next to the Nwanedzi area, 92 kms from Messina and 44 kms from their place of removal.

Madimbo village (72 families) is already removed three weeks ago. Sigonde, Gumbu, Tshengelani, Tshikuyu, Mutele Bend and many others are to follow. These people are loaded to their new places by the lorries of the soldiers. They are put in pre-fabricated zinc shanty rooms—hot when hot, cold when cold. There is no resistance by these poor families.

Our team visits the place now and then, only to lament at the sufferings caused by Apartheid policy with its consequences of human degradation. The place is sandy and we leave our car (van) few meters and walk on foot before we reach the people (shanty rooms).

We have been evangelizing Malonga-vlakte, Mutele, Folovhodwe and Tshipise (38 villages) since 1977 in Tshandama and Dzanani areas and have started a congregation there—and we have erected the evangelist's parsonage by the end of last month.

But because of this cut in the subsidy our CONTACT with these suffering brothers and sisters is becoming reduced day by day, and I fear that unless these people are both materially and spiritually assisted, the lives of many may continue to deteriorate more and more.

We have consulted the N. Tvl Council of Churches but they cannot form a quorum to discuss their matters and are thus unable to assist.

The place is dusty, no clinic, poor transport, they shop at Messina and Louis Trichardt—more than 100 kms from their dumping places.

Many have lost their family members already at these new places. Unless there is help from somewhere and somehow, these people will continue to face unassisted struggle for their survival.

We therefore hereby do appeal to you and to all out brothers in the Lord Jesus Christ for assistance to help our fellow Christians. Hoping that my appeal will meet your sympathetic response, I shall be glad if our problem can receive your favourable consideration.

Yours in Christ,
Rev. Lesiba E. Matsaung

DOCUMENT 10. "YOU and the New PASS LAWS." Black Sash pamphlet, September 1982 (abridged)

Chapter I: CITIZENSHIP

In 1978 Dr Connie Mulder who was Minister of Bantu Administration and Development at that time told Parliament that if the National Party's policy was taken to its logical conclusion the day will come when *"THERE WILL NOT BE ONE BLACK MAN WITH SOUTH AFRICAN CITIZENSHIP"*.

This policy has not been changed and Black South Africans are having their citizenship taken away from them very quickly as different homelands become independent. . . .

It is very important that people in the homelands which have not yet taken independence *understand* what independence means.

- If you are a foreigner in South Africa you cannot claim a share in political power. You will *never have a vote* in the central government. . . .
- If you are a foreigner in South Africa . . . *you cannot claim a share in the land and wealth* of South Africa. . . .
- If you are a foreigner in South Africa you do not belong here. You *can be deported* if you do things which the South African Government does not like.
- You have *no right to have a South African passport* if you want to travel.
- You are an alien in the land of your birth. . . .

Chapter II: INFLUX CONTROL AND THE NEW PASS LAWS

54% of the total Black population of South Africa lives in the homelands. That means that 54 people out of every 100 Black people live inside the homelands. 46 people out of every 100 live outside the homelands. Of this 46 people, 21 people are on the "White" farms and only 25 out of every 100 Black people are living in the "White" towns. SO:-

- Many more people live in the homelands and in rural areas than live in town.
- The Government is moving tens of thousands of people from the White areas into the homelands. Between 1960 and 1980, 2 million Black people were resettled into the homelands.

- More are being resettled all the time because it is Government policy that as many Black people as possible should live in the homelands.
- Influx control and the pass laws try to *keep people* who come from the homelands and the rural areas *out of town*.

JOBS

The Government's policy is to give jobs and housing only to Black people who have legal rights to stay in town so homeland and rural people are not allowed to come to town to look for work. The only way in which a homeland person can get work is to wait at the Labour Bureau in his home area until jobs are offered by the labour officer. Now fewer and fewer jobs are offered because the Administration Boards do not want to allow employers to recruit workers from the homelands. Because of this more and more people in the homelands have no jobs and have no hope of getting a job legally.

HOMELANDS

People in the homelands are very poor. Many have no fields to plough and no land to grow mealies [corn] and vegetables. They cannot feed their children if they do not find a job and earn some money but jobs in the homelands are scarce.

Because of this many thousands of people go from the homelands to the towns without a permit to find a job. They are often arrested and sent to prison but they still stay in town illegally because only in town can they find ways of earning money. They have been able to stay in town because influx control has not worked very well and many people manage to hide from the police.

It is more difficult to find a job now if a person cannot be registered because in 1979 Dr. Koornhof increased the fine which can be imposed on the employer of an unregistered worker from R100 to R500 [$450]. Many people lost their jobs because of this.

Now it is going to be worse. The Government has written a new law called the *Orderly Movement and Settlement of Black Persons Bill*. This is *not* the Law yet. It still has to be passed by Parliament but it may be law by the middle of 1984 if we cannot persuade the Government to throw it away.

If it does become law it will make it impossible for a Black person to stay in town without a permit. *The Bill says that no Black person may be in town at night between 10 p.m. and 5 a.m. the following morning unless he is authorised (has a permit) to be there AND also has approved accommodation.*

A Black person will be able to visit town during the day and will be safe from arrest if he has his Reference Book or Homeland Travel document with him. BUT he may not work or look for work unless he has a permit and he must leave the town by 10 p.m. at night unless he is given a permit to stay for the night.

Black people who are found anywhere in town at night—either in the streets *or in a house* in a Black or White suburb will be arrested if they do not have a permit to be there. Inspectors will be allowed to enter any house or workplace at any time of day or night without a warrant to search for illegal people.

THE PUNISHMENTS

The most serious thing about this new system of influx control is the severe punishments which will be given if it becomes the law. Anyone, Black or White, who *allows* any Black person to stay in their house at night without a permit can be fined R500 or be sent to prison for 6 months. They can then also be fined an extra R20 for every day during which the illegal person goes on staying with them.

Any Black person who is found anywhere in town between 10 p.m. and 5 a.m. without a permit can also be fined R500 or be sent to prison for 6 months plus the extra R20 per day fine.

A Black person found working without a permit or found looking for work without a permit can be fined R500 or sent to prison for 6 months plus the extra R20 per day. Anyone who gives work to an unregistered Black person can be fined *R5 000* or be sent to prison for 12 months.

The people who come to town from the rural areas without a permit will suffer very much in the future because no one will want to help them by letting them stay overnight. They will not have shelter and will be forced to leave town and go to a homeland area. Then how will their children have food?

SQUATTERS—"THE BUSH PEOPLE"

People who settle on any land such as the people of Crossroads or the Nyanga Site can be removed by the police *without trial* if the Minister of Co-Operation and Development thinks that they are trying to organise to have the laws changed. If the Minister orders such a removal by notice in the Government Gazette the *people can be moved to any place* decided on by the Director General. If such an order is made the *people cannot go to Court* to try to prevent the removal.

PEOPLE ON WHITE FARMS

People who live on the White farms will also have to have a permit to stay there and to work on the farms but there will not be much change for them under the new law.

PEOPLE WHO LIVE IN TOWN

People who live in the towns will have less rights than they do now.
- Under the present law people who have lived in one town ever since they were born can have a Section 10 (1)(a) qualification.
- People who have been registered in one job in one town for ten full years or who have had a permit to live in one town for fifteen full years can have a Section 10 (1)(b) qualification.

- These people have a legal right to stay in town which means that they can appeal to the Supreme Court if the Labour Officer orders them to leave town. They have these legal rights even if they do not have a proper place to stay (approved accommodation).

Under the new law Section 10 is taken away altogether but a new group of people who can stay in urban areas is made. These people will be called Permanent Urban Residents (PURs).

They will have legal rights to be in town but will *lose those rights if they lose their accommodation.*

WHO WILL BE ABLE TO STAY IN TOWN BETWEEN 10 p.m. AND 5 a.m. UNDER THE NEW LAW?
1. "PERMANENT URBAN RESIDENTS"

"Permanent Urban Resident" will be the new "qualification". PURs will be allowed to stay in town *if they have approved accommodation.* These people will be like the people who have Section 10 qualifications now. *They will be able to work where they want to work* (except that the Coloured Labour Preference policy will still make it more difficult for Black people in the Western Cape). *They will be able to buy a house. They will be able to have their wives and children and aged parents to stay with them.* Permanent Urban Residents will be the following people:

(a) Section 10 disappears altogether but *people who have 10 (1)(a) or (b) now* will be Permanent Urban Residents under the new law.

(b) *A person who owns a house under 99 year leasehold* in a Black township will be a Permanent Urban Resident provided he is a *South African citizen* or a *citizen of an independent homeland.*

(c) *People who are South African citizens* who have been legally living in a town for ten full years can apply to be Permanent Urban Residents. Because this says *South African citizens only* it means that *people from Transkei, Ciskei, Bophuthatswana and Venda cannot apply after they have been in town for ten years.* People who come to town from independent homelands after this Bill is law will *never* be able to be PURs.

(We think that contract workers will also not be allowed to apply. We are not sure about this yet and we hope we are wrong but the Government's policy is to prevent migrant workers from getting urban qualifications).

(d) *People who were born in town* who are South African citizens or *citizens of independent homelands* will also be Permanent Urban Residents only if *both* their parents are Permanent Urban Residents. Many people cannot prove that both parents are Permanent Urban Residents. Many people have a mother who qualifies to be in town but their father is a contract worker. Many other people do not know their fathers. These people will not be PURs even if they were born in town because they will not be able to prove that *both* their parents were PURs.

Other people whose mothers or fathers come to town after the new law from *independent homelands will not be PURs* even if they are born in town because their mother or father cannot be a PUR *because they are foreign and were not born in town.*

2. DEPENDENTS OF PERMANENT URBAN RESIDENTS

Dependents of Permanent Urban Residents will also be allowed to stay in town between 10 p.m. and 5 a.m. A dependent is a wife or unmarried child, or parent or grandparent who is too old or sick to work, or a disabled adult child who cannot work.

If the Permanent Urban Resident dies his dependents will be allowed to stay in the town until they become Permanent Urban Residents themselves. They will become Permanent Urban Residents if they were born in town and both mother and father were Permanent Urban Residents, or if they inherit the father's house, or if they are South African citizens and have lived in the town for ten full years. Dependents who come from independent homelands will never be PURs unless they inherit the father's 99 year leasehold house.

3. VISITORS

Visitors can stay in town between 10 p.m. and 5 a.m. if they get a permit to stay immediately they arrive. This permit will only be given to them if they have approved accommodation. *No one can have a visitor's permit for more than a total of 14 days in any one year.* . . .

COMMUTERS

People who live in a homeland and travel to work in the White areas each day are called *commuters.*

MIGRANTS

Migrants are people whose homeland is a long way from the place where they work. They will need a permit to work *and* a permit to stay in an urban area at night. Because recruitment from the homelands is being cut back there will be fewer migrants in the future and there will be more and more unemployed people in the homelands. . . .

PASSES

Black people will still have to *produce a pass or certificate* showing that they can stay in town if it is demanded by a policeman. *THE PASS LAWS WILL STILL BE IN FORCE* and will be much worse than they are now for everybody but especially for homeland people.

Chapter III: WHAT CAN WE DO ABOUT IT?

Apartheid is a policy which is planned to push Black people away.

The resettlement programme of the S.A. Government takes them from where they are living and dumps them into the homelands.

Influx control and the pass laws lock them up in the homelands and prevent them from coming back to the White areas to earn a living.

The Citizenship laws make Black people into foreigners in their own country so that they cannot claim political power.

Apartheid has not changed even if members of the Government tell us that change is happening. Apartheid is becoming worse all the time and many thousands of people are suffering because of it. We can only do something to bring about real change and to get rid of Apartheid if we are prepared to work very hard to change it.
- We can change things *if we know how the system works* so use this booklet to teach yourself and to teach other people.
- Have a *study group* to work on these issues.
- Decide to *tell one other person* about these things every day.
- Ask your Trade Union, Civic Association, Political Party, Church Minister, Church Women's or Men's Groups, Housewives' League, or any other organisation you belong to, to study the laws and *to call meetings of members* about it.
- *Write to Dr. Koornhof at P.O. Box 15, Cape Town 8000* to tell him what you think about these things. You can also write to the Prime Minister or any other Member of Parliament at the same address.
- *Talk to people who live in the homelands* about it. Can they find a way to talk to their Chiefs and homeland Governments about it?
- *Ask your Church Minister*, or Bishop, or Moderator or other representative to talk about it at Church Synods or Assemblies.
- *Talk to your fellow workers* about it and then go together to your employer to tell him what you think about it. *Ask your employer to tell* the Chamber of Commerce or the Chamber of Industries about it and to ask the Government to change the laws.
- *Teach everyone you know* about it and discuss it with them so that you can decide what else you can do to change things.

If we have knowledge we can make plans as to how we can make change happen. These things must all be changed if we are to live together in South Africa peacefully and with justice.

Document 11. Remarks to the President's Council by Mamoud Rajab, November 24, 1982 (abridged)

Mr. Chairman, allow me first of all to associate myself with the many words of congratulations that have been heaped on both Dr. [Stoffel] Van der Merwe and his Constitutional Committee [of the President's Council], for compiling a Report in the manner in which it is presented and in the time that was available for its compilation.

I find in it many things that appeal to me and yet others that do not. I am attracted more by the spirit of the reform contained therein than by the detailed manner in which this report performs the crucial task of advising the Government on ways and means of satisfying the legitimate aspirations and expectations of the different population groups to participate effectively in those decision-making processes affecting their interests, which would contribute towards a peaceful and a better future for all in our fatherland and within a stable, effective and orderly society in South Africa.

Any discussion on South Africa today is characterized by the word "change" and commentators argue that South Africa is changing, but retrogressively; or that South Africa is static; or that South Africa is changing for the better but slowly and in many ways cosmetically. My own humble view is that South Africa's politics and way of life are certainly changing. More than that, I believe this change to be real, genuine and positive. I submit that the Report before this House is clear and ample evidence of this fact, despite whatever limitations each one of us may see in it.

In that regard, we have justified the existence of this Council to the extent that when we made our original proposals even our critics were forced to admit that a new page had been opened in South Africa's constitutional history and that for the first time communities other than White had worked together on the constitution-making process which was to give South Africa its new perspective.

The Prime Minister and his party, therefore, have to be congratulated too, for their courage in breaking the log-jam in South African politics by adopting the concept of power-sharing, even though it has resulted in the traumatic experience of yet another historic split in Afrikanerdom.

It is against this background, and the fact that we are a reform-oriented, forward-looking, and policy-advisory body that my criticisms of the recommendations have to be viewed; and despite them, I believe that, nevertheless, all of us are committed to build on the proposals before us in the spirit of constructive engagement. . . .

The President's Council should lead and not be led. But now I find that the Constitutional Committee has accepted a number of guidelines laid down by the National Party Federal Congress instead of formulating its own independent outlook. In particular I point out that in its original proposals this Committee did not make specific recommendations with respect to the legislative functions but it did conclude that South Africa's circumstances called for a single legislative authority while provision would be made in the constitution for matters essentially of interest to the particular community concerned. I understood this to mean advocating a single chamber and, therefore, I am disappointed to note that the Constitutional Committee has now accepted a three-chambered parliament.

A three-chambered parliament and voting on a communal instead of a common roll, and despite the practical advantages one may see in them, is anathema to the Indian community. I disagree with the Constitutional Committee for not recommending the incorporation of a comprehensive bill of rights. I feel that the objections raised are not really valid. If Bophuthatswana could have readily included such a bill of rights, why not we? In the United States, rights safeguarded in the constitution have served the interests of democracy to a large extent, and I believe that the image of our country would be greatly improved by such a step, especially as most countries who are vociferous in their criticisms of South Africa are sadly lacking in the safeguarding of any elementary human rights at all. . . .

However, to my mind the most glaring deficiency of the recommendations is the almost total exclusion of Africans in some form or other from the new Constitutional Dispensation. Despite the fact that the original Commission of Inquiry was clearly called into being to investigate the Government's constitutional proposals for Whites, Coloureds and Indians, that Commission concluded that all population groups should be involved in the process of consultation and deliberation; and among its recommendations was one relating to the establishment of a Council for Black South African citizens. This recommendation was accepted by the Government and provision was made for it, that any Committee of the President's Council could deliberate with the Black Council or any of its committees.

Because of the refusal of Black leaders to support the establishment of the suggested Black Council it has not come into being and, therefore, the Constitutional Committee has not put forward any substantive proposals for Africans. By adopting this stance, to my mind, the Constitutional Committee is shirking its duty, and its responsibility to South Africa. The President's Council should have taken cognisance of the reasons for the refusal of Black leaders to support a Black Council and I believe it should therefore have made recommendations to somehow overcome this difficulty.

I believe that the exclusion of Africans will cause grave concern to the Coloured and Indian communities. These communities do not wish to be regarded as having "betrayed" the African people or to be seen as "ganging-up" with Whites against Africans. While full regard has to be taken of the Government's difficulties with the White electorate, what must not be overlooked is the massive attacks that will be made on the present constitutional proposals, both inside and outside the country, especially from all internal and external African leaders and, in particular, the attacks from the ANC and the Russian dominated part of the world.

Most Africans will see in our proposals an attempt to strengthen the "White laager" [circled wagons] against them. While not personally agreeing that this is our objective, it becomes essential as soon as possible to allay the suspicions of Africans in this country by bringing them into the new dispensation in some form or other as soon as possible as I believe that time is not on our side, so as not to allow our enemies to make political capital out of our proposals.

Unless such steps are taken to move forward rapidly from the present point of departure the plans, which in my mind are there as a breakthrough, may well turn into its opposite namely increased White-Black polarisation. . . . With all humility, I feel that our present proposals will not give South Africa the long-term stability that it needs for the full exploitation of its economic and its political potential because, in the first place, for any proposal to succeed, we have to win over the hearts and minds of the population as a whole and with African opposition to the new dispensation there is little hope for this being realised.

Secondly, and highly important, I believe that where there is economic integration, political integration must follow. Since 1933 South Africa has been undergoing an industrial revolution which is expanding so rapidly that Whites can no longer fill the ever-expanding economic requirements. The situation has become so critical that it is realised today that our whole educational system has to be restructured on the basis of a single body, making available to all population groups eventually the same standards of education. In the future Africans will predominate in every aspect of our system. It has been estimated that by the year 2000 for every White matriculant [high school graduate] there will be three African ones. Today about 37% of the African people are urbanised, while over 90% of Indians and Whites live in urban areas and over 80% of the Coloured population do the some. By the year 2000 it is estimated that 75% of the African population will be urbanised.

In view of the aforegoing, and particularly in view of the ever-increasing terrorist attacks, particularly in Natal from where I come, can we win over the hearts and minds of the African people by our proposals? Consider in this regard what our Prime Minister had to say the other day when he pointed out that Whites were in a minority in the Police Force. He stressed that Black policemen could not be expected to be loyal if they were denied a public platform, and he further reinforced his argument by explaining that 40% of the forces deployed in South West Africa/Namibia were African or Coloured. He said: "Do we want those people to help us fight off the communists? If they are going to stand by us then the Government must act in such a way as to keep them on its side".

Consider also the recent figures disclosed by the Stellenbosch University Bureau for Economic Research, that growth in the self-governing homelands over five years was almost nil and that the per capita income in these places compares less than favourably with some of the poorest countries in Africa. The answer of decentralisation, which involves private enterprise participation, according to Mr. Harry Oppenheimer, is uncertain.

I wish now to address myself to the Indian and Coloured communities who have, thus far in their struggle for democratic rights in this country, engaged themselves in what I call "protest politics" and have adopted generally a "holier than thou" attitude. We all of us know that there is a time and a place for this strategy. I believe sincerely that time is now past. We are in an era of "negotiation politics" and unless we accept the challenge of the new proposals that are before us, and become involved in them, we might never have an opportunity of making our contribution to a peaceful and a better South Africa for all of us. Boycottism is a negative method of trying to influence people, whereas participation is a positive one; and participation does not mean acceptance.

To sum up: I believe that the present constitutional proposals, despite their weaknesses, are a definite breakthrough for the future of South Africa. I disagree with the segregated nature of the proposals and with the exclusion of some form of African participation. Nevertheless, I call on the Indian and Coloured people to participate in the parliamentary structures that will be offered and to work at the same time for the inclusion of Africans in some form or other in the political structures that will have to be fashioned for South Africa.

Thank you.

Document 12. "The National Situation." Paper by Neville Alexander delivered at AZAPO annual congress, February 1983 (abridged)

We meet at one of the most important moments in the history of this country. For reasons which I shall expound in more detail presently, the rulers of South Africa are faced with the most severe crisis that their system of racial capitalism has yet had to contend with. A complete realignment of political forces involving a major shift in the direction of national affairs is being undertaken in order to salvage the system that guarantees for white South Africa perpetual domination of the black working people. . . .

The Crisis of the Rulers

Let us consider some relevant aspects of the rulers' position. . . . The decisive importance of the manufacturing industry, the increasing prominence of transnational corporations, the importance of foreign trade for the South African economy: these and many other developments have rendered the economy vulnerable to the ebb and flow of world capitalism. . . .

First, adequate numbers of skilled people can no longer be imported from abroad. This means that more and more black people (those classified Black, Coloured and Indian) have to be trained to occupy skilled positions. Usually, this can only be done by kicking upstairs the white worker occupants of the job category concerned. They are graced with the title of supervisor or junior manager and remunerated accordingly in return for shutting up and forgetting about their holy cow of job reservation. Usually, also, the former job category is diluted or subdivided so that two or more so-called semi-skilled black workers producing much more efficiently than the pampered and sheltered skilled white worker of yesterday, earn relatively speaking only a fraction of his or her wages.

This process coupled with the overall expansion of the economy has led to a fundamental alteration in the relative strategic importance of white and black workers within the system of South African economy. Previously, white workers had the power to cripple the economy because of their virtual monopolisation of productive skills. Today, increasingly it is the black workers who are acquiring this strategic leverage. The white workers, on the other hand, are becoming more and more dispensable as a class. We shall see presently what the political implications of this development are.

A second consequence of the qualitative change in the economic life of South Africa is the fact that it is becoming increasingly difficult to lessen the effects of unemployment and underemployment by turning on and off the tap of migrant labour as in the past. The proletarianisation and urbanisation of the black people cannot be halted or even braked. They have to be treated as a modern labour force as in any other comparable industrialised country. Imagine for a moment what chaos would ensue if the road haulage drivers and the drivers of delivery vans and trucks in Johannesburg alone were to refuse to drive their vehicles for a few days! The dilemma for the rulers in this connection is how to reconcile the iron laws of capitalist development with the bantustan/apartheid strategy designed for an earlier phase of that development. Koornhof's Bills have in this context a historic character similar to the notorious segregatory Hertzog Bills of fifty years ago.

From within the system, pressures are building up such that it can no longer be run in the same way as before. The acquisition of productive skills and strategic leverage as well as the dramatic increase in their purchasing power have imparted to the black workers and their children a self confidence and a historic optimism that makes them demand ever more insistently their human rights to equality and liberty. Daily, in factories, in mines and even on many white-owned farms they prove that they are not the simple moronic labour units of Verwoerdian mythology but normal flesh-and-blood human beings who are becoming ever more conscious of their historic mission to liberate the entire population of South Africa. A whites-only government cannot represent this surging mass of humanity nor can it hope to repress them forever. Hence the political and social crisis of the ruling class. . . .

Enlightened Despotism

For historical reasons, the capitalist system in South Africa is administered today by the National Party moulded in the image of the likes of the Bothas, the De Klerks, Malans and Heunis. These people, representatives in the main of the Afrikaans-speaking bourgeoisie, have chosen the so-called verligte [enlightened] option, one which has been called a twentieth-century system of enlightened despotism. What exactly are they trying to do in Southern Africa?

Let us look at the domestic situation first. They claim that they want "to move away from discrimination based on colour". They claim that they are carrying out the historic mission of the Afrikaner volk [people] which is, in their view, to afford each of the so-called peoples of South Africa its god-given right of self-determination. The grand design in which their projected reforms, that is adaptations, of the apartheid system, will eventuate is a "confederation of sovereign independent Southern African states". "Nations" rather than the "races" of yesteryear are the social entities which have to be manipulated and accommodated in their ethnic utopia.

Decoded, this means simply that the bantustans, whether allegedly "independent" or not, are to be brought together with the Republic of South Africa at the top through their respective elites (consisting of bourgeois and aspiring bourgeois politicians) while the labouring people at the bottom, the vast majority of the people, are to be trapped in a divisive and debilitating ethnic consciousness. In this way, the South African state is to be remoulded. Sixty years after the compromise of 1924, which led to the co-option of the white working class, a new alliance is being forged to broaden the base of the South African state and thus to strengthen it. Just as the Rand Revolt of 1922 signaled to the ruling classes the urgency of the times, so the Soweto uprising of 1976 signaled to the National Party the lateness of the hour.

Consequently, the alliance with the white workers is to be downgraded in importance. Instead, the junior partners in the new alliance are to be the black middle class and their political representatives whether or not they are at present collaborating in the political institutions created by the South African state. . . . Already the bantustan misleaders, of whom the Sebe brothers are only the most vulgar and brutal specimens, are showing that a small section of black people in South Africa are prepared to imprison and perhaps even to kill other black people for the maintenance of the apartheid status quo. Let us have no illusions: the vulgarity of the bantustan leadership should not make us forget that there are other more subtle ways in which a middle class can be tied hand and foot to an oppressive system. The virtual neutralisation of our teachers as political animals through salary increases, fringe benefits and the threat of dismissals should be a salutary reminder to all of us that middle-class people can be trapped systemically unless there is an overwhelming countervailing force towards which they can gravitate. . . .

The political problem for the National Party is that of persuading the white workers to accept their historical demotion without allowing the black working class to fill the resultant power vacuum. They know that certain laws have to be altered in order to meet the needs of economic development; they know that some black faces have to appear to have a semblance of real power along lines similar to the bantustans, the right to tax "their own people", to imprison them, to promote individuals and groups through the control of patronage, and so forth. These are, as it were, derived rights which, though they are not bogus, are nonetheless revocable by instances other than those that elected the incumbents to their positions of "power".

Now the majority of whites, especially the white workers, are intransigently and paternalistically opposed to any such "concession", however illusory it might be. Their racism and their fears of losing their privileged position have made them into an historical road-block, an obstruction to even the modicum of reform which the theorists of the ruling class acknowledge to be necessary for salvaging the system. Parliament represents these people. Consequently, the white parliament has become a brake on progress as defined by Botha, Heunis and company. Parliament, therefore, has to be stripped of this power of blocking "reform" and, if necessary, it should be eliminated altogether. How is this to be done? By means of a multifaceted strategy which is now being carefully orchestrated in the guise of the National Party's amended version of the President's Council's proposals. An elaborate, but completely transparent charade is taking place before our eyes. All the actors in it, let me stress, are fully aware of the fact that it is no more than a charade. [David]

Curry, [Allan] Hendrickse and their likes are not only selling out as they have been doing since 1969, they *know* that they are doing just that.

Through the Executive Presidency proposed by the President's Council, a systematic disempowerment of parliament is being undertaken. Until they are certain that they have the measure of their ultra-right critics the Botha regime will not wish or dare to transform the so-called white chamber of the proposed tricameral parliament into the dummy parliament which is its destiny. The significant point is, however, that dummy representation is now becoming the norm for the whites also. . . .

It is as well to understand that the tricameral parliament and all the other fancy concessions made in the President's Council proposals are meant in the short term to accustom the white electorate to the idea of what is called the "sharing of power", i.e. elite-level co-operation for the continued domination and exploitation of the overwhelming majority of the black population. Even if the oppressed people were to reject the scheme 100%, Botha and company would still have succeeded in their main intention, namely, to get the white voters to accept the idea of "consociation".

President's Council Proposals and the Koornhof Bills

This raises a fundamental question. Most people view the so-called new dispensation in the ethnic terms in which the government and its agencies have promoted and marketed it. They speak as though this is a matter affecting the "Whites", the "Coloureds" and the "Indians". But in reality, we are faced with a completely different picture once we analyse the process as a whole.

The Koornhof Bills, in particular the Orderly Movement and Settlement of Black Persons Bill, and the proposals of the President's Council are part and parcel of a single strategy. The Koornhof Bills are designed to formalise and entrench the division between so-called permanent urban blacks and so-called rural or homelands blacks. Millions of people are to be locked up in arid and desperate so-called homelands to become commuters and contract workers in the white paradise of South Africa as and when required. Riekert's influx control, pass-law regulations will make sure that few if any escape the net. "Permanent Urban Blacks" will eventually get freehold rights in their locations, bogus undercapitalised local authorities (so-called municipalities) and finally a fourth chamber in the super-dummy parliament through which they will again be linked up in the confederation with their so-called rural kith and kin. Botha cannot sell this line to his voters at present but this is the logic of his position. In other words, what is happening to "Coloureds" and "Indians" today will be happening to "Permanent Urban blacks" tomorrow. The civilised coloured policy of today is the pilot scheme for the civilised black policy of tomorrow. The rulers obviously hope that by eliminating the left, they will provide time and space for a collaborationist and accommodationist middle-class leadership to emerge in all these sectors of the oppressed people who will be able to keep the system going in its amended form.

The President's Council proposals seem to exclude African people from the so-called central parliament. In a superficial and formal sense, this is true. For us this is not a point of discussion. Once one rejects the ethnic basis of those proposals, it dare not be an objection to them that they exclude this or that group as an "ethnic group". It is time that we put a stop to this nonsensical discussion, which is premised on the correctness of the idea that only the National Party, with its ethnic preconceptions can bring about change in South Africa. This is the point of departure of the Progressive Federal Party (PFP) and of other liberal organizations.

We who believe that the black working people are the source of all fundamental change in our society, reject that kind of reasoning as a liberal trap into which, unfortunately, many have already fallen. To put it clearly: we reject the so-called new dispensation not because statutory "Blacks" are excluded from the so-called parliament but because it is a bogus concession of ethnic or racial representation in a kitchen parliament which in no sense can satisfy the demand of the oppressed people for *nothing less than full democratic rights*. It is high time that we stop giving the impression that the PFP, Inkatha and other such groupings are a part of the national liberation movement by using their system-bound arguments to articulate our rejection of and protest against apartheid measures. To talk about "the coloured people" having sold the African people down the river because a few venal political pygmies have now formally "gone inside" into their master's kitchen, without insisting that "Blacks" be included, is to fall into the trap of playing ethnic politics as defined by the rulers and as advertised in every ruling-class newspaper in the country. Moreover, it does the Labour Party the incomprehensible honour of suggesting that it represents the "Coloured" people. Anyone who knows the situation on the ground, knows also that the Labour Party has no grassroots support in any metropolitan area and only sporadic support in certain dorps [small towns] on the platteland [in the countryside]. Even there, indeed, the people who support them do so in the mistaken belief that the Labour Party is an anti-apartheid party which, clearly, it is not. . . .

To conclude, these are some of the steps which we have to take immediately:

We have to oppose the Koornhof-President's Council new dispensation with all the force and ingenuity at our command. The scheme must be made to fail. We must show that it has no significant support among any section of the oppressed people.

As against their "new dispensation", we have to insist on our primary demand for the convention of a constituent assembly elected on the basis of one person one vote, at which democratically elected representatives of the nation will decide on a new constitution for Azania. The constituent assembly will not be a gathering of representatives of so-called ethnic groups. It is also not going to be convened by the present government. It is a goal for which we shall have to struggle in the years ahead with even greater dedication than before.

We have to build up a national united front of all people's organizations in order to fight for full democratic rights for all and an end to the system of racial capitalism. Such a front must not be an alliance of ethnically defined organizations but an alliance of workers, community, students, youth, sports and other organizations of the people. Ambivalent and opportunist elements such as white and black organizations of liberals who are not committed to the total liberation of the people of Azania, those who are merely concerned with the elimination of superficial aspects of apartheid, must be excluded from such an alliance of organizations. . . .

Document 13. Letter from Saul Mkhize to P. W. Botha about forced removal of Daggakraal, Driefontein and Ngema "black spots," March 31, 1983

RE-SETTLEMENT OF THE RESIDENTS OF DAGGAKRAAL, DRIEFONTEIN, NGEMA (DISTRICT OF WAKKERSTROOM)

Please accept my apologies for deeming to write to you direct, but, the matter being urgent, I felt it my duty to approach you in this manner.

I write to you for only one reason—your help on behalf of the people of Daggakraal, Driefontein and Ngema.

Your help is needed, because we are being forced to move from our properties by the Department of Co-operation and Development. Dr Koornhof has been known to say "There will be no forced removal of black people from black areas", and yet here we are, without any real discussion, being told by his department that we will move, like it or not.

This is not humanitarian or, in God's name, proper.

There are many reasons for my statements above and that is why I write to you.

I wish to ask that you personally arrange, with due notice to myself and my Council of Directors of Driefontein, duly elected by the landowners of Driefontein on 26 December, 1982, at a meeting specially convened to elect representatives to negotiate about the removal, for a meeting with Dr Koornhof to discuss this whole matter.

The committee of Daggakraal and Ngema, who are in a similar predicament, would like to join us at such a meeting.

May I say that we do not wish to discuss our removal, which seems to be a fait accompli by the Department of Co-operation and Development but:
1. Why we should consider leaving our homelands at all?
2. Why we should give up our legally owned property?
3. What reasons have the Department for even thinking that we are prepared to allow them to intimidate us into such a move?
4. In view of the lack of co-operation from the Department why should they expect our co-operation?

These are only a few of the items we must discuss but, in order to do so, we need a fully representative team from the Department of Development and Co-operation, including Dr Koornhof, in order to sort out this entire matter of what we consider a completely unnecessary upheaval of these well-settled, well-adjusted and happy communities.

Your Honour, we have suffered for many years due to the uncertainty of our position. We have heard rumours, we have been told to obey, but we have never been properly informed or had proper discussions regarding the "why's" and "wherefores" of our situation. In God's name, your Honour, is this merciful? Are these the actions of a Man of God, such as I know you are.

At present, our people are hungry and short of water. Our boreholes are dry and we wish to arrange to have new boreholes, but how can we do this under the present circumstances. We are, as all South Africans are, a proud people and all we ask is to remain so. We do not wish to be rebellious in any way but only to continue to live our lives out in our own environment.

We have formed a good community. We have inter-married with other tribes. We have been, and hope to continue to be, self-supporting and of benefit to the entire community, both through the land and factories in our area and also by contributing to the work-force very badly needed in places such as Johannesburg.

All that we ask is that we have a reasonable and full discussion with a duly appointed body, by someone such as yourself, to talk to us. We know we must listen but we must also have every opportunity to talk and to explain our position.

Your Honour, I beseech you to help us in this matter and to act on our behalf. We need your help and we ask for it now.

Yours, very sincerely,
SAUL MKHIZE

Document 14. "Solidarity with SAAWU and Our People in Ciskei." UDF flyer, Transvaal Region, October 1983

"An injury to one is an injury to all!" The truth of these words is shown by the call of twelve organisations to support the people in the Ciskei bantustan.

The organisations are:
1. UDF (United Democratic Front)
2. Saawu (South African Allied Workers Union)
3. Cusa (Council of Unions of South Africa)
4. Fosatu (Federation of South African Trade Unions)
5. Ccawusa (Commercial, Catering and Allied Workers Union)
6. AFCWU (African, Food and Canning Workers Union)
7. Sacwu (SA Chemical Workers Union)
8. Gawu (General and Allied Workers Union)
9. Saldwu (SA Laundry and Drycleaning Workers Union)
10. Sasdu (South African Scooter Drivers Union)
11. OVGWU (Orange Vaal General Workers Union)
12. Descom (Detainees Support Committee)

These groups have come together in an ad hoc committee to condemn [Lennox] Sebe's "government" for banning Saawu and attacking the people in the Ciskei bantustan.

WHAT IS GOING ON IN CISKEI?

Two months ago, the Ciskei Transport Corporation raised bus fares by 11% in Mdantsane, Ciskei.

But half the residents in Mdantsane are without jobs. They could not pay, so they began boycotting the buses. They used trains instead.

The Ciskei police are trying to force the people to use the buses. Police and soldiers sit on the trains. Road blocks stop cars and taxis. Vigilantes from Sebe's Ciskei National Independence Party pull people out and beat them.

One week into the boycott, police and soldiers used their guns. When the people at Fort Jackson station refused to use the buses, Sebe's boys opened fire.

Eye witnesses say 90 people were killed and several hundred injured.

Residents elected a Committee of Ten to co-ordinate the boycott. Sebe detained eight of the ten, but the boycott went on. The CTC [Ciskei Transport Corporation] is losing millions of rand.

THE PRESENT CRISIS

The Ciskei regime is now doing all in its power to break the boycott.
- *They have banned Saawu in Ciskei.*

They fear Saawu's principle that "only the working class, in alliance with other progressive minded sections of the community, can build a happy life for all South Africans, a life free from unemployment, insecurity and poverty, free from racial hatred and oppression."

- *They have detained more than 800 people.*

Their jails are so full that they are holding people in the Sisa Dukasa stadium. Widespread reports of torture, rape and assault have come from people kept there.

- *They have detained more than 15 union leaders.*
  Among these held are:
  SAAWU: Sisa Njikelana, Bonile Tulima, Eric Mntonga, Godfrey Shiba, Gardmer Mambushe, Boyce Melitafa, Yure Mdyogolo, Shepherd Mayekiso, Derick Smoko, Cameron Mzimane, Lulamile Qumane
  AFCWU: Bonisile Norushe, Dlaki Vani
  GWU: David Thandani
  TAWU: (Transport and Allied Workers Union): 3 organisers

- While the Saawu offices are being raided every couple of days by the South African security police their president Thozamile Gqweta went into hiding.
- Students in Mdantsane and Duncan Village are boycotting classes in sup-

port of their parents and to call for the release of fellow students who have been detained.
- The Ciskei police are conducting house to house searches looking for Saawu T-shirts, membership cards, political books and newspapers. During these searches residents are detained and beaten.
- All attempts to force the people of Mdantsane to end the bus boycott have failed. The banning of Saawu and the detention of its leaders and members have not decreased the popularity of the organisation.
- Ciskei police are visiting families of breadwinners who are in detention to check whether they have paid the rent and harassing them generally.

"Machine guns and detentions are not the solution to the boycott. Our people are still not riding buses…our principles and pride provide us with the determination we are displaying today"—Saawu president, Thozamile Gqweta

The UDF, Saawu, Gawu, AFCWU, Fosatu, Cusa, Ccawusa, Sacwu, Saldwu, Josdu, OVGWU, Descom call on all workers to support the people of Mdantsane by:
- Telling fellow workers, friends and members of the community about the banning of Saawu and the harassment and detention of all union officials and membership in the Eastern Cape and the people of Mdantsane generally.
- Collecting money in their union or community organisations for the Detainees Support Committee in East London.

"AN INJURY TO ONE IS AN INJURY TO ALL!"

Document 15. "NOvember 2: Why You Should Vote NO!" Black Sash leaflet, Durban, October 1983

The Black Sash has a long and proud history of saying "NO" in South Africa. We first said "NO" when the government removed the Coloured people from the voter's roll by a series of constitutional tricks in 1956. Since then, we have said "NO" to
- The banning of organisations and individuals by Ministerial decree.
- The detention, prosecution and imprisonment of political and community leaders under so-called security legislation passed by a parliament which represents a minority of South Africans.
- The removal and resettlement of millions of people in the name of apartheid.
- The influx control laws, which divide families and force productive farmers off the land and into wage labour; which allow people to be "endorsed out" to the impoverished bantustans when their labour is no longer required for the white economy.
- The establishment of so-called "independent homelands", which deprive the majority of South Africans of citizenship in the land of their birth.

Now we are saying "NO" to the government's Constitutional Bill—and this is why.

MYTH

PEOPLE should vote "YES" because the proposed new constitution is the basis for political change and reform in South Africa.

FACTS

The Constitution Bill entrenches apartheid and racial divisions The new constitution cannot exist without race classification. This is fundamental to the new local authority and parliamentary structures.

- 70 percent of the South African population is excluded from any say in a government which will make decisions affecting their lives. Clause 93 of the proposed Constitution Bill says: "The control and administration of Black affairs shall vest in the President... He could declare any Black person to be a non-South African citizen, or unlawfully resident in a white area."
- Parliament will be divided into three racially segregated houses.
- There will be three racial Councils of Ministers. The Councils will be in charge of Departments whose work affects one race group only. They will have no power to change the apartheid laws.
- Clause 89 of the Bill ensures that all discriminatory laws will remain in force.
- The Group Areas Act which forces people to live in racially segregated areas is the cornerstone of the new constitution. The system cannot work unless different race groups live in separate areas.
- The Population Registration Act which demands that all South Africans be registered and classified according to their race is entrenched in the proposed new constitution.

COMMENT

"Reform", "Power-sharing", "a step in the right direction". All these terms disguise the true nature of the proposed constitution, which is to entrench racial segregation and the power of the ruling Nationalist Party.

This is not a "new beginning" for the people of South Africa but the "final solution" of the architects of apartheid.

MYTH

By allowing Indians and Coloured people to participate in government, the proposed constitution is a "step in the right direction" and therefore it should be supported.

FACTS

The Indian and Coloured representatives elected to their separate parliaments will effectively have NO power at all. They will not be participating in the government of the country.

- Only the President's Council can make law and here the whites (25 chosen by the all-powerful white President and 20 chosen by the majority party in the white parliament) will outnumber the Indians (5 chosen by the Indian parliament) and Coloureds (10 chosen by the Coloured parliament).
- The White dominated President's Council will decide what matters will be dealt with by the parliaments.
- If any dispute arises between the three parliaments it will be settled by the white dominated President's Council.
- There is no possibility of an Indian or a Coloured person being elected President. He or she will be chosen by an electoral college of 50 whites, 25 Coloureds and 13 Indians.
- Government of the country will be in the hands of the white President and the Cabinet which will be appointed by the President and whose members do not have to be elected members of Parliament.
- The white President will decide which decisions of parliament are referred to the President's Council for a binding decision.
- The white President has the final say over what can be decided in the parliaments— whether the matter is an "own" affair in which case it will be dealt with by the parliament for one race only, or whether it is a "general" affair in which case it will be dealt with by all three parliaments. Remember, if there is any dispute here, the white dominated President's Council will settle it. The white President's decision on this is final and there is no appeal to the courts.
- The white President is able to amend any law and to regulate its application or interpretation without reference to parliament.

COMMENT

A surprising number of influential English-speaking people, including important businessmen and editors of major newspapers are supporting a "yes" vote because they claim that the proposed constitution is a move towards political reform. How can this proposed constitution, which moves away from democracy and towards strengthening the structures of apartheid, be better than the present situation? The political situation in South Africa is more fluid than it has been for a long time. The signs of Government floundering are our best hope for real change in the future.

MYTH

A "yes" vote is necessary to support P. W. Botha against the right wing. If there is a majority NO vote in the referendum P. W. Botha and his government will amend the Constitution Bill in such a way as to placate the right wing.

FACTS

- The present government's position is not at stake in this referendum. P. W. Botha has said that if he loses the referendum he will not resign as Prime Minister.

- The Conservative Party and the Herstigte Nasionale Party are not in a position to win any election at the moment.

COMMENT
- *South Africans who sincerely want to do away with repressive and racist legislation will vote NO in the referendum.*
- *People of conscience and integrity will vote 'NO'*
- *The official opposition is campaigning for a NO vote. It will be impossible for political analysts and commentators to maintain that the NO vote comes only from the C.P. and the H.N.P.*

MYTH
Abstention is the moral solution for people who do not accept the constitution but who do not wish to risk being associated with white party politics.

FACT
Abstention will not be counted at the polling stations. If there is a resounding NO vote from liberals, progressives and conscientious South Africans there is no risk of that NO vote being seen simply as a reflection of party political intentions.

MYTH
A qualified "yes" is the best solution.

FACT
There is no such thing as a "qualified yes" in this referendum. If you vote "yes" you vote for the proposed new constitution as a whole.

ARE LIBERAL BELIEFS AND OPPOSITION TO APARTHEID AMONG WHITE ENGLISH-SPEAKING SOUTH AFRICANS JUST ANOTHER MYTH?
Have we found it convenient to hide behind Apartheid and Afrikaner-dominated government? Do we only pretend to care about democracy while we take good care of our privileged life-style?

IS P. W. BOTHA CALLING OUR BLUFF?
If you vote "yes" on NOvember 2
- You align yourself with the Nationalist Government and with apartheid
- You accept the possibility of dictatorship
- You are prepared to tell the majority of South Africans that you do not want them to participate in government; that you do not care about democracy
- You are not a discerning consumer. You are buying a badly designed and untested product.

CALL P. W. BOTHA'S BLUFF
VOTE NO IN NOvember

DOCUMENT 16. "Be Not Overcome by Evil: the Response of the South African Council of Churches to the Eloff Commission." June 5, 1984 (abridged)

We, representing the member churches of the South African Council of Churches, believe the Government's primary motive in establishing the Eloff Commission was to discredit the Council of Churches and bring it into line with the policies of the Government. . . .

The facts surrounding the formation of the Eloff Commission and the manner in which it conducted its duties fuel the suspicion that it was nothing more than a political manoeuvre, part of a strategy to discredit the Council, to cast doubt upon the validity of its theology, to isolate some of its office bearers, casting them in the roles of the real culprits, and to justify its plans to silence the prophetic voices in the Church. The Council does not dispute the State's right to have its own political interests or its right to investigate financial irregularities, even in a Church body, but here we are dealing with an attempt to exploit the situation for political gain, regardless of whether its actions are in conflict with the justice demanded by God. It is not the Council that possesses an illicit interest in politics, but the State that is interfering in the work of a religious body for its own political purposes.

Theology

In its report the Commission seems to have assumed the policy that it was not competent to pass judgement on theological matters. On page 145 the report says, "No state can take it upon itself to decide what the theology of the Church should be and the question, if ever it is to be settled, is to be resolved by theologians, not by a government, and not by this commission". . . .

Having recognised its incompetence in this area, the Commission nevertheless repeatedly pronounces judgement upon the Council's theological position. At first it approaches this area "with diffidence" because of "differing theological perspectives" . . . but by the end of the report this early reluctance is forgotten. Eventually . . . it recommends that the Government control the Council's funds in order to ensure that they are used for "only truly spiritual purposes."

The Commission developed a narrow theology of its own, one in which spiritual matters are seen as a purely private transaction between God and the individual.

In its view it is the Government that must decide how far the work of the Holy Spirit may be allowed to extend. If a spiritual relationship spills over into the odd private act of charity, it can be presumed that this will be acceptable to the Commission. Public acts of charity that might affect the status quo are seen as not being "in the national interest."

Clearly this is a theology that is useful to the Commission and to its mentors in the Government. Its only discernible flaw is that no scriptural grounds are advanced in its support. It relies entirely upon a secularly perceived and parochially motivated view of the national interest. It is not in the national interest to allow the Holy Spirit to have an influence on public affairs or to allow the churches to apply the word of God to Government policies. Black theology is condemned simply because it has the potential of disturbing the political status quo. It is not the Word of God but the will of the Government that is of supreme importance here.

Politics

The Commission has chosen to see signs in the evidence that the Council has specific political objectives, mounts political campaigns, plans strategies of resistance and undertakes secret operations. In a South African context these are serious allegations. One of the accusations is that the Council orchestrates a campaign of "massive psychological warfare" against South Africa. The evidence for this astonishing allegation is drawn from a single letter, written not by a member of the Council, but to the Council from an outsider in Germany.

We repeat what the Council has said before. The SACC has no political policy, no political ideology, no political blueprint for the future and it does not mount any official political campaigns, nor does it undertake political games with the government or engage in political manoeuvres. All the statements and actions of the Council and its member churches that touch upon politics are motivated by the Word of God. Criticism of injustice in public affairs has always been part of the prophetic role of the Church. Prophecy is not politics. Prophecy does not have a political objective. The aim and objective of prophecy is that the people may turn back from their sinful ways and that the nation may experience something of God's justice and peace.

That all prophetic statements and actions are misconstrued as being political strategies is not surprising when we realize that the Commission itself has judged everything from the point of view of the Government's political interests.

If concern for the disadvantaged is politics then the Council pleads guilty. If caring for the poor and downtrodden is not in the national interest, then the Council has no defence. If the law of the Government is above the commandment of God, only then is the Eloff Commission exonerated without question.

The so-called National Interest

Every aspect of SACC activities has been judged according to only one criterion. This is not the Gospel of Jesus Christ but the *national interest* as perceived by the Government. That the Commission's view of what constitutes the national interest will be a limited and biased one can be seen from its very composition. In passing judgement on an organisation, the membership of which is largely black, it included no black member in its ranks. As the RAND DAILY MAIL pointed out in its edition of February the 18th: "The Commission saw things through white eyes." Mr Dave Dalling, the Member of Parliament for Sandton, enlarged this perception. "The entire report is couched in the language and ideology of the National Party," he said. And in case the reader of the report is not sure of what Nationalist ideology consists, one of the commissioners, Prof. P. Oosthuizen, has inserted a long account of government policy. He explains that only the present government can act in the national interest because any alternative government would dominate and have sectional interests. A government elected by all the people to govern in the interests of all the people is regarded as impossible. . . .

Here is the ultimate fallacy to be found in the Commission's report. It is not the true national interest that is being safeguarded. It is rather the sectional interest of a privileged minority, in the defence of which the Commission is acting. It is not the SACC that is acting in defiance of the national interest, but the Government itself. . . .

The Council and its member churches
. . . [T]he Commission tries to show that the Council does not enjoy the support of its member churches. Its only evidence to support this contention is the fact that ninety seven percent of the Council's funding comes from overseas. . . .

The truth of the matter is that the majority of the Christians who belong to our churches are black and that their economic circumstances make it very difficult for them to support their own churches, let alone the Council. That the majority of the Council's money comes from overseas proves only the poverty suffered by most of our people.

That some kind of political plot has been devised by one or two staff members is ridiculous. The Council has an elaborate system of accountability and cannot be manipulated by one official, nor will it allow itself to be manipulated by the State.

The tension between the SACC and the State is not based upon the activities of a few agitators, but upon the very serious grievances of many millions of Black South Africans.

Is the Church above the law?
Despite its interesting use of logic, its contradictions, misrepresentations and sectional attitudes the Commission is still a wonder of restraint and objectivity when compared to the Minister of Law and Order. "No church is above the law," he said in the Parliamentary debate on the Eloff Report. It is not unreasonable to ask which law he is referring to. The unjust laws of apartheid or just laws that are made in the interest of all the people? In accordance with Romans 13:1-7 the churches will give full respect and obedience to all laws that are just and fair. But in accordance with Romans 12:1 the Church will not adapt itself to any unjust laws, nor will it alter one jot or tittle of the Word of God in order to suit "the pattern of this present world."

His words leave every Christian before a choice. Here the Council's decision is clear. We must heed the admonition found in the Acts of the Apostles, chapter five, verse twenty nine, and obey God rather than man. In replying to the Minister's warning the churches cannot avoid exercising their own duty to warn the Minister and his supporters that they will have to account for every action, not to the Council, nor any church, but to God Himself.

Conclusion

The Eloff Commission tries to prove that the SACC destabilises and undermines the South African state, but the Christian faith places the Council under an obligation to resist evil and oppression by evildoers who legalise a system of injustice. For such a state this resistance is dangerous. The Gospel is always subversive of injustice and evil. Opposition to such evil and oppression is part of the church's vocation from God for the healing of human relationships in state and society. In doing this the Council and its member bodies are concerned not only for the victims of oppression, but also for the liberation of the oppressors from the fear by which they are obsessed. . . .

Document 17. "New Constitution Changes Nothing." Natal Indian Congress flyer, August 1984 (abridged)

It is only fair that all people in South Africa should have an equal say in the way the country is run. But in South Africa we know that only Whites are allowed to vote for the city councils and Government. Indian, Coloured and African people are forced to accept things like high rents, low wages, inferior education, high food prices, which are decided for us because we don't have a say.

But Black people have not accepted all these problems sitting down. We have always struggled and asked to have equal rights. Since 1948 when the Nationalist party started ruling South Africa a lot of bad things have happened. The group areas act, the homeland policy, job reservation and other unjust laws have been passed.

The Government has since then offered us dummy bodies (like the SAIC [South African Indian Council]) which we rejected. People then formed their own organisations to fight for equal rights for all people in other areas.

Trade unions have fought for workers, students gone on boycotts to fight for their rights. All these bodies have demanded that all people living in South Africa should have equal rights. Also people in other countries have put pressure on the Government to do away with apartheid.

This has forced the Government to make changes and now they are offering us a new deal. Before we accept it we need to look carefully at what is being offered.

THE NEW PLAN

The Indian people will have to vote for an Indian parliament, the Coloured people for a Coloured parliament and the same for Whites. *The African people, who make up the majority of the country are totally left out from the plan.*

There will be 3 separate parliaments, but they will be different in size. For every 4 Whites in parliament there will be only 2 Coloured and 1 Indian. *This means Whites will even have more votes than Indians and Coloureds put together. Even if the Indians and Coloureds unite there will be 4 Whites against 3 Black people.*

The President will be chosen by the parliaments. Because Whites have more votes the President will be White (maybe P. W. Botha). He will have a lot of power. *He will hand pick all the ministers, e.g. minister of health, minister of community development and others.* We know he will choose people that will agree with him.

The President's Council, which will help the President run the country is also controlled by Whites. Of the 60 people in this body, 25 will be chosen by the President, [and] there will be 20 Whites and only 10 Coloureds and 5 Indians [elected]. *This means 45 Whites against the 15 Coloureds and Indians put together. Again we will have no say, because Whites will have more votes.*

This problem of more Whites than Coloureds and Indians put together means that we will still have no say. Whites will still control the country and make the laws. Things like money for houses, education, hospitals, etc. will be decided by them. Our problems would not be solved by this new plan.

This plan shows clearly how the government is trying to divide us, by bringing in the coloureds and Indians but leaving out the African people. So we find we are brought into the government, but it is planned in such a way that we still don't have any say.

SOME QUESTIONS YOU MAY HAVE

There are a number of issues connected with the new constitution which have caused many of us many an anxious moment. We in the NIC have thought about each of these questions very carefully. We would like to share our answers with you.

1) *Does the New Constitution make things better for our people?* We have had white majority party rule under the old constitution and this position remains the same. All important matters such as finance, defence, educational policy and social welfare policy will, in the final analysis depend on the will of the white majority party. Those Indian stooges who participate will be outvoted at every turn. Worse still they will be doing nothing more than carrying out white majority policy in the Indian Parliament.

2) *Can we use the New Constitution to work towards democracy?* Totally outvoted and unable to make any changes in regard to policy the Indian community will not be able to contribute towards democracy. Those who say that we can use the new constitution have been unable to show how this can be done especially when we can be outvoted at every turn.

3) *Is it about time that we stopped being boycottist?* The NIC will not boycott any proposal which has real possibilities of achieving democracy. If the govt. continues to make useless proposals such as the SAIC and the New Constitution, we have no choice but to reject them. We do not apologise for rejecting a worthless constitution.

4) *Will we achieve peace in SA by accepting the new constitution?* Some say that the only way to peace in S.A. is to accept the new constitution. What are the facts? If the Indian community accepts the constitution will we not be voting for and actively supporting the total exclusion of the African people? Will

this not lead to greater division, suspicion, hatred and violence between our communities? This cannot lead to peace.

5) *What is the Alternative?* The only way to bring about peace in S.A. is to reject the new constitution. In this way we will begin to develop love and brotherhood between all the people of S.A. We must form our own organisations which express the rejection of the Constitution for all the world to hear. We must in addition build our unity and make bridges between all the people of our country. The NIC calls upon you to join us in our struggle to achieve truth, justice and equal rights for all people.

6) *Are there any disadvantages to our accepting the New Constitution?* If we accept the Constitution we will:
a) Cause division between the Indian and African people.
b) Show to the world that we accept apartheid.
c) Ruin any chance that we and our children might have of living in a peaceful S.A.
d) Take full responsibility for violent removals of African people and for all the unjust legislation in this country.
e) Join the white oppressor and help him to carry out his unjustified policy.
f) Be forcing our children to the border to defend apartheid [through military conscription].

CONGRESS—VOICE OF THE PEOPLE

The Natal Indian Congress has always been an integral part of our people's proud and brave history. Under Congress leadership our people have refused to be fooled by the Government's numerous efforts to sell us dummy institutions and divide our people from our African and Coloured brothers and sisters.

Under the guidance of the Freedom Charter since 1955, Congress has with the support of the Indian community continued to struggle against division and destruction. The Charter, which is the living voice of our people, provides for peace, housing and security for all, the right of the people to govern and a more even distribution of resources. The Charter guarantees all of us our rights to our culture, religion and heritage.

The new constitution is a move away from true democracy, peace and justice. It has been introduced precisely to kill the demands of our people.

The Congress therefore rejects the new constitution and calls upon every South African, rich and poor, young and old, to join us in this struggle.

The NIC is affiliated to the United Democratic Front (UDF) which consists of more than 600 organisations from all over the country; workers, businessmen, students, men and women alike.

All the people of South Africa will reject the Constitution through the UDF. The UDF has launched the Million Signature Campaign in which one million people will sign the declaration and say NO to apartheid.

JOIN A MILLION PEOPLE
SIGN THE DECLARATION . . .

Figure 16. UDF flyer urging western Cape coloureds to boycott the first tricameral parliamentary elections in August 1984. The puppeteer is P. W. Botha.

Document 18. "Reform Versus Revolution." Labour Party election flyer, August 1984

The Labour Party of South Africa has come down firmly on the side of Reform as the only sure road to a fully democratic society in South Africa.

This means that the Party rejects revolution which seeks to bring about change by the violent overthrow of all the existing institutions of society, such as parliament, the courts of law, the private ownership of property and even the Church.

In their place the men of violence want to enforce a dictatorship of a single party, such as the communist party dictatorships of Russia and other eastern bloc countries. The single party dictatorships that now flourish in Africa and to which Mugabe of Zimbabwe is swiftly moving by wiping out all opposition, is what is in store for South Africa if violence triumphs.

The Labour Party believes in freedom of speech and the press: the right to hold and express an independent point of view. This freedom does not exist under a communist dictatorship. The Labour Party believes in the right of every citizen to vote for the party of his choice and to be voted for. This basic principle of democracy does not exist under a communist dictatorship. Freedom of association which gives people the right to form and join trade unions is what the Labour Party also stands for, but which is also non-existent under communism.

Solidarity, the trade union of the people of Poland, is still struggling to exist as a free association in a country which is supposed to be a workers' paradise.

Violence and revolution is therefore NOT an alternative method of bringing about meaningful change and democracy. What it does bring about is dictatorship and greater oppression and continued use of violence to keep the dictatorship in power.

In any event, all possibility of a revolutionary overthrow of the present system in South Africa is out of the question. The military defeat of the ANC and the loss of its bases in Southern Africa, together with the Nkomati peace accord between South Africa and Mozambique have clearly shown that the leaders of the Black States in this region prefer to solve problems by peaceful negotiation. It is also true that no revolution ever achieved the goals it set, namely, Liberty, Brotherhood and Equality. All of them ushered in new and greater tyrannies than the old.

The Labour Party also warns against those who, while claiming not to be supporters of violence, by their words and actions help to create an atmosphere that could easily lead to violence.

For example, when Allan Boesak, patron of the U.D.F. gets up on a platform and demands: "We want all our rights here and now!" everyone knows that his words are empty rhetoric—hot air. But they inflame the youth, the most idealistic, the most vulnerable and the most susceptible to ideas that seem to offer instant solutions to social problems.

When the U.D.F. and other left-leaning organisations call upon the people to boycott the forthcoming elections, this call to boycott can lead to attempts by misguided young idealists to use violence in order to intimidate voters into staying away from the polls. In this way they hope to claim a successful boycott.

On the other hand, the leader of the Labour Party, the Rev. Allan Hendrickse, says: "Peaceful negotiation is the only way to solve South Africa's problems. Violence is committing suicide in fact. The Labour Party does not expect change to take place overnight. The Coloured people must look at the realities of the situation and use reason to determine their strategies."

To our youth the Labour Party says: There is no glory in sacrificing life and liberty in a false cause. There is honour in striving to improve the lot of your fellowman by peaceful means. This is the true commitment to the cause of freedom. Anything else is a selfish desire to boost your own ego.

What then is Reform? It is a process of change started by those in power (change from the top) as opposed to revolution—inciting people to class violence (change from the bottom). When the holders of power decide to reform society, then meaningful change is guaranteed.

The classical model of political reform is the United Kingdom of Great Britain. While across the English Channel, France chose the road of the Guillotine, Britain went in for including its people into the decision making process of government by gradually giving the vote to wider and wider layers of its citizens. While the process of change was spread over many years and every achievement had to be strenuously negotiated, they were genuine and lasting. Perhaps the greatest achievement of peaceful reform was the freeing of the slaves in Britain and throughout its dominions.

Today, South Africa stands on the threshold of a similar process of reform of all aspects of society—social, economic and political. But reform must be worked at by every group in the country. The government, by introducing a new constitution which puts an end to exclusive White rule in South Africa, has unlocked the door to vast opportunities. It is for all of us now to take up the challenge of helping to reform South African society into one in which all its citizens will be free from domination, from poverty and backwardness.

The Labour Party therefore calls upon the people, including the youth, to turn their back on boycotts and confrontation and to throw in their weight behind the Labour Party. The Party calls upon the people to turn out in their masses at the polling booths on election day, 22 August 1984 and, by voting for the Labour Party candidates, make sure that political, social and economic reform will become a reality.

DOCUMENT 19. "Uitenhage Police Station—On a Sunday Afternoon." Report by Audrey Coleman, March 17, 1985, *The Black Sash,* May 1985 (abridged)

On Friday night, the day after [a Black Sash] conference began [in Port Elizabeth], I was dining in a restaurant when I received a call from Molly Blackburn to come immediately to attend to a serious matter.

Molly had a highly-respected member of Uitenhage's KwaNobuhle black township with her. He had just been released from Port Elizabeth's Rooihell prison where he had been charged with public violence. He was extremely upset by his experiences in prison. He had seen as many as 100 children in prison. They were being abused, mainly by older prisoners and had complained to him that they were very scared. . . . [Black Sash officials contacted prison officials and several lawyers].

The only success we had was in getting permission for parents to visit their children—if we could find the parents. We returned to conference and the man from the KwaNobuhle community went to try to contact the parents. He promised to phone us on Sunday at lunch time. That call on Sunday was another urgent call for help. He asked us to come to Uitenhage immediately as another group of parents feared for the safety of their children.

It was decided that nine delegates should leave conference to go with Molly to Uitenhage. We met the parents outside the Post Office. They had a list of names of nine children who had been arrested. We went to what we thought was the charge office to try to locate the children. The officer in charge told us that we should go to the building next door.

We went out of that building, through a gate in the grounds to the building next door. The parents were with us. We came to a double door, Molly knocked and walked in. I was right behind her. I heard her shout "Good God, what is happening here?" There in front of us was a black man in plain clothes with a long quirt in his hand. He had just brought it down on a young man lying on the floor, manacled to the leg of a table. His hands were manacled behind him and he was lying awkwardly with his head askew against the leg of the table. Blood was running down the side of his face and his lip was severely bruised. He seemed to be in great pain.

The man assaulting him immediately ran out of the room. I looked around and saw another man sitting behind a desk eating. He went on eating throughout the entire episode while we were there.

We asked the young man on the floor whether he'd been charged and for what. He said he hadn't been charged with anything. His name was Norman Kona. Just then a white sergeant came into the room, also dressed in plain clothes. He identified himself as Sergeant Nel. He showed no surprise at the fact that someone was lying manacled to the table, bleeding. He shouted at us to get out of the room. Molly refused, demanding to see the station commander. The man refused to fetch him and an argument raged. I then spoke to three men sitting on a bench. They too had not been charged. They had been arrested early that morning and said they had all been assaulted. . . .

Back in the charge office, Molly, Di [Bishop] and the others had discovered that the names of the four young men had not even been entered in the charge book, nor were the police able to establish who was responsible for the four men. . . .

In the meantime Molly had been arguing with Sergeant Nel. He decided to avoid the whole issue by taking the four young men away. Molly followed them to the police cells. Then another white policeman came into the room where the rest of us were still waiting. He came in to pick up a R1 rifle that was lying abandoned on the desk. He reeked of liquor. As he picked up the rifle he dropped a magazine of bullets, just missing Gille de Vlieg's toes. He too started shouting at us, demanding to know what we were doing there. A few minutes later Colonel Pretorius arrived. He agreed to "do something about" the reeking sergeant and then took all nine of us plus the parents to his office. . . . We told the colonel what we had seen that afternoon. He agreed to come to the cells with us to find the four young men. . . .

When we got to the cells Molly went in with the colonel. Molly came out and told us that the four men we were looking for were not there. We took Colonel Pretorius to the charge office where we had witnessed the assault and showed him the blood on the floor. We were amazed by the attitude of these officers. At no time did they ask to see the man who had assaulted the young man. They told us that they could not find the young men. Their movement into or out of the police cells had not been recorded. The officers were unperturbed by this.

Some of our party went to the hospital to look for the men. After half an hour we returned to the police station where we were told that the young men had been taken away in a van and the police would not be able to contact the van as it had no radio. We never found the men and eventually left the police station.

For us, the whole episode was breathtaking. There was not even a pretence of bringing wrong-doers to book. There was a latent sense of violence—police walking in and out with guns. They seemed angry that we should dare to question what was happening in a police station.

After we got back to Johannesburg, Molly Blackburn phoned to tell us that Norman Kona had come to the Black Sash to make a statement. He had actually been released at 11 on Sunday night. He had been in a room near where we were had consulted with Colonel Pretorius. So when we were told the young men had been taken away, this was a total lie. Norman had been taken across the road to a doctor. He was returned to the officers who made him sign a statement in which he had had to swear that he would not claim damages for assault against any of the officers otherwise he would not have been released.

We came away from our national conference in Port Elizabeth with a very real sense that the Eastern Cape was in total crisis. When Thursday [March 21] dawned, the day of the [Uitenhage] massacre, we were not surprised. We had come to realise from our experiences that police were capable of this type of action.

DOCUMENT 20. Affidavit of James Michael Tamboer about police brutality, Port Elizabeth, September 1985

I, the undersigned, JAMES MICHAEL TAMBOER do hereby make oath and say:

1. I am an adult male, employed as an assembler at General Motors and residing at 206 Herrington Street, Arcadia, Port Elizabeth.

2. At 3.30 a.m. on the morning of 22 July 1985 I was arrested at home by Lt Strydom of the security police and several other policemen whose names are unknown to me. I was woken up by a loud knocking at the front door. I opened the door and a Lt Strydom and five other policemen, two of whom were black and three white, came into the house.
3. They immediately began searching the whole house waking up my three sisters, my younger brother and my mother. Lt Strydom assaulted me, striking me on the jaw and in the ribs with his fist. During the search I was assaulted on a number of occasions by the other policemen. I was hit in the stomach and slapped on the face. I gave them no cause to do so.
4. They told me to come with them and frightened my mother by telling her that she would not see me again. I followed the police outside. There were three motor vehicles and a land rover. There was a white policeman in the driver's seat of the land rover. He was asked whether he recognized me. He said he did and that I had attended the funeral at Cradock wearing a cap. I denied that I was in Cradock. The policemen then went back into the house to search for the cap. They did not find one. I was then told to get into one of the cars, a yellow Mazda. Inside the car I was again assaulted by striking me in the ribs with their elbows. In the car they accused me of instigating the strike at Ford and General Motors. I denied that I had instigated the strike. I was not even present at the strike in my department on 11 July 1985 over short-time. I am a member of National Automobile and Allied Workers Union and was in fact conducting shop steward elections in another part of the factory.
5. The black policeman sitting next to me grabbed me by the throat and choked me. The bruise marks are still on my neck.
6. We went to Algoa Park Police Station. I was told to get out of the car and join the other detainees who were then getting out of the land rover. I recognized Dennis Neer, Vusumzi George, Henry Fazzie and Eric Mapuma. We were told to go to the charge office. In the charge office we joined other detainees including Reverend [de Villiers Nteteleli] Soga and Pindile Manele. We waited in a queue while policemen took the particulars from each of us by hitting our toes with their rifle butts. While we were waiting, Reverend Soga and Henry Fazzie, who is an old man, were called outside. I did not see or hear anything outside but when they came back Henry Fazzie was bleeding from the mouth. We asked them what happened and they told us that they had been assaulted.
7. After our names were taken we remained in the charge office until we were transferred to St. Alban's [prison]. Particulars were once again taken and we were told to undress. A sergeant then looked at each of us and then noted any marks on our bodies in a register. He also asked us if we had any illnesses. I saw Dennis Neer, he had sjambok [whip] marks on his back. I also saw Themba Duze—he had several sjambok marks on his neck. These they told me had been inflicted on arrest. On my first day in detention I went on a sick parade since I had pains in my stomach and my chest.

8. We were then taken to the cells. I was locked up in a cell, together with approximately 20 to 25 detainees. I can remember Fikile Fukile, Eric Mapuma, Vusumzi George, Reverend Soga, Zolile Peter, and Pindile Manele being there. As the days went by more and more detainees were placed in our cell.
9. The new inmates included [elementary school] scholars and [secondary school] students. They appeared to have been badly assaulted, some had been beaten all over. There was still blood seeping from some of their wounds. They told us that they had been assaulted by the police. The following morning they received medical treatment—they left the cells and some returned with their wounds bandaged.
10. Each day we were taken into the prison yard for exercise. The other detainees were exercised at the same time. At exercise time we spoke to each other.
11. Every day a prison official would come and read out a list of the detainees to go to Louis Le Grange Building, where the Security Police have their local office.
12. I remember seeing Dennis Neer at exercise time on the day his name was called to go to Louis Le Grange. His name was called while we were exercising. He was in good health. At supper time I was detailed with several others by the prison wardens to dish up the food for the detainees. While waiting to collect the dishes to return to the kitchen I saw Dennis Neer and others return from Louis Le Grange. His jaw was swollen, his wrists were swollen with handcuff marks and he had red abrasions behind the knees. He was walking very slowly and was clearly in pain.
13. I spoke to Dennis and asked him what had happened. He told me that they had given him the "helicopter". This is effected by placing a stick behind the knees and then handcuffing the hands underneath the stick and on the front of the shins so as to lock the victim into a permanent crouch. The victim is then suspended on the stick which is held up between two tables. The victim is then "spun" with a kick and hence the name "helicopter".
14. I saw Dennis Neer the next day and the swelling had become worse. I did not see him for a day or so after that. When I saw him again, he told me that he had been to hospital.
15. I also remember seeing Ihron Rensburg come from Louis Le Grange Building. He was with Percy Smith, Ashwell Balfour and Andre Zakay. Ihron's nose was blue and swollen. He told me that he had been hit on the nose and that he had lost a great deal of blood from the nose injury. Percy Smith had red marks on the right hand side of his neck. They all complained of having been assaulted while being interrogated by the security police and in particular by a coloured policeman called "Billy Flemmer".
16. Ihron Rensburg was also sent to hospital as a result of the assault.
17. On Thursday or Friday of the first week while I was serving food in the afternoon, I noticed an old man coming in with some other detainees. I

discovered later that his name is Wilson Tini and that he is about 72 years old. He had just been arrested. Wilson had only one arm.

18. During the second week I was called to Louis Le Grange for interrogation together with Vusumzi George, Michael Xego, Alex Rala and some students. We were all transported to Louis Le Grange and taken upstairs. Xego and Rala were immediately taken by two white policemen into a room down the passage, and we went down to the 5th floor and were taken into an office. Lt Strydom and Warrant Office Coetzee called for Vusumzi George. We heard screaming and crying and some time later Lt Strydom came into the room with Vusumzi George. Vusumzi George's face was reddish and puffy. Strydom asked me: "Het jy gehoor hoe lekker sing die man" [Did you hear how nicely the man sang?] I said : "Ek het hom gehoor huil" [I heard him weep]. Strydom said "Hy het nie gehull nie, hy het gesing" [He was not crying, he was singing]. Then Strydom left.

19. A black plain clothed policeman called "Tungata" came into the room and asked Vusumzi to which organization he belonged. Vusumzi said that he belong to MACWUSA (Motor and Allied Component Workers Union of SA). He then asked why he was burning people. Vusumzi denied burning people. Tungata slapped him in the face and told him to stop talking "shit". He took his arm and twisted it behind his back. Vusumzi screamed in pain. They then told him to hold a chair in the air and while Vusumzi was in that position Tungata kicked him. A white policeman and a coloured policeman called "Billy Flemmer" came into the office. The white policeman held Vusumzi's legs and Tungata held his arms while a third policeman rolled Vusumzi's neck. Vusumzi cried out in pain and begged him to stop. They asked questions and when he denied anything, they would prod him with the stick.

20. I was then called to Lt Strydom's office which was on the 7th floor. When I left Vusumzi was still being assaulted. As I walked down the passage I saw someone in a room suspended on a stick as a "helicopter". I could not see who it was. Strydom told me to write out a statement on my involvement in the union. I was hit twice by Strydom with an orange sjambok and then sent back to the 5th floor to write my statement in an exercise book, which Strydom gave to me.

21. One white policeman and one coloured policemen then asked me who I was. I told them. They then told me to sit on the floor. The white policeman held my hands behind my back while Billy walked on my ankles. It was very painful. I told Billy that I had been instructed by Strydom to write in the exercise book. He replied "Jy laat die mense strike terwyl die ander mense sonder werk sit" [You are letting these people strike while other people don't have work]. He then put his hand against my forehead and banged the back of my head hard against the wall twice. He said "Sit daar jou striker" [Sit there, you striker]. I still have headaches from these blows. The white and coloured policemen then left. Tungata was in the meantime interrogating one of the students. He wanted to know why a

student had burnt Tungata's relative to death. The student denied having done so. Tungata then told the student to lie on the floor. Tungata took his two legs in his hands and stamped on the student's genitals. Rala and Xego then came back. They were dazed. Their faces were puffy and red. They claimed that they had been tortured. We were then returned to St Alban's. I did not lay a complaint of the assaults on me since I did not know that this could be done.

I certify that the Deponent has acknowledged that he knows and understands the contents of this Affidavit which was signed and sworn to before me at Port Elizabeth on this the 23RD day of SEPTEMBER 1985 and that the provisions of the Regulations contained in Government Notice R1258 of 21 July 1972, (as amended) have been complied with.

Vanessa Jacinta Brereton
Commissioner of Oaths
Practising Attorney
545 Main Street, North End
Port Elizabeth
Rep. of South Africa

Document 21. Affidavit of John Sakukhuna about violence in KwaNdebele, January 1986

I, John Sakukhuna, P.O. Box 330, Moteti, Dennilton, plot number 225 state:

1. That I was attacked at 6 am on January 1, 1986.
2. I was at my home and heard noises outside. The people outside said I must open the door. They then smashed it down with an axe.
3. I knew they were Ndebele. They had white crosses on their foreheads and were speaking siNdebele. There was a mob of people.
4. They started beating me with assegais [spears]. I was sjambokked [whipped] on the back and chopped on the head with an axe. My whole face was covered with blood. They just said "kill the animals". They had a slogan called Mmbokoto [grinding stone]. They didn't use any names, they just shouted Mmbokoto.
5. I was put in a bakkie [pick-up truck]. There were [a] few other injured people in the bakkie. Then the bakkie went up to the main road on the way to Bundu Inn. We were taken off the bakkie and put on a big truck. The truck was tightly packed with people.
6. We were taken to the Siyabuswa Community Hall. At the hall I saw S. S. Skosana, [Piet] Ntuli, the Minister of Interior, and Mr Kundu, the Minister of Education. I know them because I was a watchman at the commis-

sioner's office in Mothuntshona and [used] to open the gate for the above mentioned.
7. In the hall we were divided into groups.
8. We were then taken to a smaller hall. The old men were separated from the young ones. The old men were spoken to by Skosana. He told us that we must not let our kids burn his cars. He then said that he is now going to deal severely with the young ones.
9. I saw the young ones being stripped. Water and soap was then thrown onto the floor. The young men were then beaten with sjamboks. They were being made to jump up and down like frogs. Skosana was instructing the people to hit the young men. The other ministers were also giving encouragement. All the ministers were carrying guns.
10. There were four policemen watching, three in uniform who were black policemen and one plain clothes white policeman. I knew he was a policeman because he had a gun and was with the other policemen. The policemen didn't do anything, they just stood watching.
11. Skosana asked the old men "Why are you refusing me my land [Moutse] which was given to me in 1981. I want my land, Your chance is over. I'm banning all the meetings in the district".
12. We spent the night at the hall. We were given no food. They brought us back the next morning, the 2nd of January.
13. I went to the hospital on the 2nd of January, the morning I got back home. I was discharged from hospital on the 16th of January. My most serious injury that I got from the vigilantes was a stab wound in the chest. This was from an assegai. My head was chopped and my back was sjambokked. I was treated by Dr Kruger in the Philadelphia Hospital.

DOCUMENT 22. "The New Influx Control." Bulletin of the National Committee Against Removals, Cape Town, April 9, 1986 (abridged)

THE PRESIDENT'S COUNCIL REPORT
In September 1985 the President's Council report on "urbanisation" was made public. The report said that influx control must go. At the opening of parliament PW Botha said that South Africa no longer *needs* influx control. He said that [it] is out of date, expensive to administer and it discriminates against blacks. Both PW Botha and the President's Council report said that South Africa needs "orderly urbanisation". The President's Council report said that "orderly urbanisation" is:
"the process of urbanisation ordered and directed mainly by indirect forms of control, but also by direct means."

Direct and indirect controls are nothing new. "Orderly urbanisation" is not new either. We used to have "closer settlements" in rural areas and "emergency camps" in urban areas. Those same shanty towns are now called "site and service". All this is part of "orderly urbanisation".

SLUM & SQUATTER CONTROL

The President's Council listed a number of laws and regulations which we have *now* which can be used to control people, for example, the Prevention of Illegal Squatting Act, the Slums Act, zoning and health regulations.

The number of people allowed into an urban area will be controlled by how much land is set aside for people. The report said that land for site and service schemes should be provided. But when these areas are full, people will not be able to squat or double up in housing elsewhere, because the Illegal Squatting and the Slums Acts will stop them. The people will not be able to live where they choose, even if they could afford it, because of the Group Areas Act. . . .

RENT

Another economic control they already use in many areas is rent. In townships like Huhudi at Vryburg or Galeshewe at Kimberley the government tried to move the people to the bantustans but the people resisted. Then the government increased the rent so much that many people could not afford to live in their houses. Only those people with good jobs could afford to stay. When the residents did not pay rent, the evictions started. This is a back-door way of forcing people to move. It is also a way of keeping poor people out of urban areas.

OTHER CONTROLS

In this short summary, we have not mentioned detailed controls such as the labour, township and housing regulations or the labour bureaux system. Influx control is control over *presence in an urban* or "prescribed" area, *place of residence* and *place of employment*. If the government seriously wants to scrap influx control, it will have to scrap ALL these controls. We should watch carefully to see what they plan to do because scrapping some of these controls might sound good but they will then keep some controls and they may want to introduce other new controls. This is what they tried to do with the Koornhof Bills in 1983.

For example, if they scrap section 10 of the Urban Areas Act and they do not introduce other protections, *ALL AFRICANS* will be in the urban areas illegally! At the moment all African people are supposed to be living and working in the bantustans. Only those with Section 10 are allowed to live and work in "white" areas. So unless they scrap the whole bantustan system, they will always have a place to send those people they do not want in urban areas.

WHAT WILL "ORDERLY URBANISATION" LOOK LIKE?

ONVERWACHT—The President's Council report says that *Onverwacht* is a good example of "orderly urbanisation". Onverwacht is a huge rural slum

50 km from Bloemfontein built out of sight from the national road. There are about 300,000 people living there. It has more people than Bloemfontein. Most people were moved from the farms and the locations of the OFS. It started in 1979 when Sotho-speaking people were thrown out of ThabaNchu when Bophuthatswana took "independence". Now there are many non-Sothos living there but the area has been promised to QwaQwa [homeland]. People have to build their own houses on small plots. They have bucket toilets, communal taps, schools and some clinics. There are a handful of jobs, so most people have to commute to Bloemfontein to look for work. This is the biggest site and service scheme in South Africa. People have no land. They are not allowed to keep stock. Life is hard but the people are fighting. Many families do not have plots. So last year hundreds of people took the law into their own hands and settled on some land. They are still there.

LANGA—There are other places where "orderly urbanisation" is already in practice. Kabah at *Langa* near Uitenhage is another example. People have lived here for years but in October 1985 6000 people were told to move because they had not obtained permission from the Town Council to build their houses. The real reason is that the white area is very close to Kabah and the residents are afraid. The officials say the people must move to the site and service scheme at KwaNobuhle. Serviced sites cost R19.50 [$8.40] per month. The people cannot afford that. They know they will be evicted if they do not pay. They will end up back at Langa. They will be poorer because they will have to start to build their houses again. The community refuses to move and demands that Langa should be upgraded.

KHAYELITSHA—In the Western Cape, the site and service scheme at *Khayelitsha* is another example. The people of Crossroads have struggled to remain in Cape Town for over ten years now. The government tried to divide them and find new ways of getting rid of them, but they could not. Crossroads grew and grew. Last year a removals squad arrived to move the "legals" from Crossroads to Khayelitsha. The people fought back. 18 people died and the government had to give in to their demands. But the government did not give up. It said "illegals" could have 18 month permits IF they moved to the site and service scheme. Many people refused. They said they want full rights to be in Cape Town and they wanted Crossroads upgraded. They refused to move anywhere. Others moved to Khayelitsha because they felt they had no choice. They are desperate for a place to stay.

As we have seen "orderly urbanisation" is thus a name for the updated and modern form of influx control using many of the old ways of controlling people. We believe planning and some control is necessary in any country. But in South Africa the planning and development is not in the interests of the majority of the people because the government does not represent all the people. . . .

DOCUMENT 23. "Crisis in Crossroads." Interview with Dr. Ivan Toms by the United States Committee of the International Defense and Aid Fund, May 1986

What is the background to the fighting going on in Crossroads?

Crossroads has been there since 1975, and in 1978 the Crossroads Executive Committee was democratically elected by the people. Black Sash supervised that. The committee was 16 people, and they selected Mr. [Johnson] Ngxobongwana as chairperson. They negotiated well on behalf of the community, and actually negotiated the [Minister Piet] Koornhof deal, which said that the government would give them proper township housing and special Section 10 rights to be in the city.

Then the government did a survey of Crossroads. A lot of people were left off that survey, on purpose. They said there were only 22,800 people there when there were probably at least 30,000 at that time. The Executive Committee was given the right to check if a person was really there or not. That was very open to corruption. People on the committee, especially Mr. Ngxobongwana, could get fifty rand [$60 in 1979] a throw from somebody, because a pass is so important to a black person in the city in order to get a proper job.

Mr. Ngxobongwana was in jail for awhile, under investigation for fraud, and the vice-chairperson ran the committee and saw the possibility of getting money. After Ngxobongwana came out the committee split half-and-half between the vice-chairperson, Mr. [Oliver] Memani, and Mr. Ngxobongwana. Around '82 Ngxobongwana's group attacked the Memani group, set their shacks alight and stood around with pangas [machetes] so you either got burned to death or pangaed to death, and forced all the Memani supporters out of Crossroads. You have to remember that Memani is no better than Ngxobongwana. It's just the problem of corruption, of poor people having to deal with the potential of getting a lot of money.

In '83 the shacks had become very crowded and people made a decision to start building plastic shelters. The state's response was to come out with riot police and Administration Board officials and systematically pull down everyone's shelter. Day in and day out, this went on for three weeks in a row. Ultimately the women decided to hold onto the sticks [used to support the shelters]. They were sick and tired of having to cut these sticks every night in the forest. That constituted a riot. The police response was to bring in police dogs, tear gas, sneeze machines, and to use rubber bullets. We had a person with a fractured skull from that. This was done in winter, which in Cape Town is the rainy time, so it was cold and rainy.

Last year the government was planning to forcibly move people from Crossroads to Khayelitsha, which is further out. Khayelitsha is a security solution, not a housing solution. The government's idea was to move *all* blacks in Cape Town to Khayelitsha, even those who were in proper township housing in Langa and Gugulethu and Nyanga. Khayelitsha is 32 kilometers from Cape Town, far away from the whites, with a military establishment in one corner of it, very nice straight roads down the middle, and one access road that can be closed off. Khayelitsha has houses of 28 square meters—that's two rooms and a toilet—and very badly produced, some just precast housing. They leak and the sand comes in. The two rooms are just too small. Five thousand units have been built.

In February [1986] we found that a demolition squad of non-Xhosa-speaking blacks had been brought in from the Transvaal to move the people of Crossroads. At this time Ngxobongwana was in jail, and the community decided not to go to work that morning, because while the men were at work the women and children could be moved. Some of the trucks that came in to pick up the workers were stoned, and then the police cordoned off the whole of Crossroads. The only way we got in as doctors was by parking on the highway and walking through the bush. The police moved in to restore law and order, so-called, and in two days we at the clinic treated 198 injuries and had five deaths. Overall in those two days the police killed 18 young people from Crossroads.

That was about the time that the Cape Youth Congress group, which was very democratic and linked to the UDF, became quite strong. Ngxobongwana came out of jail and was very critical of the youth, saying they shouldn't have attacked the police. The youth started to expose the corruption which had been there for a long time, and actually criticized him publicly, at Langa. Then Ngxobongwana banned the youth group from the meeting and tried to set up a black consciousness youth group in its place, even though he was chairperson of the Western Cape Civic Association, which was linked to the UDF. He basically turned his colors.

Of course all these conflicts have been fueled by the police. Many times we had a Warrant Officer Barnard come around. He's a really dangerous guy. He's always been the one organizing the conservative blacks in Crossroads to attack the more progressive people. The latest thing is that Ngxobongwana's group attacked the Nyanga Bush group and New Crossroads, at the periphery of Crossroads, because they were harboring the Comrades: the youth. They've systematically burned down all the shacks of these groups. There are now about 40,000 people homeless from that. There's definite police involvement in this. Barnard has been seen coming in with the vigilantes or conservative folk from Old Crossroads, organizing them, and basically saying, "Attack here."

Is this sanctioned from higher up?

Oh, I'm sure. Now that the area has been burnt out, the government is saying they won't allow the people back. It's saying those people must move to Khayelitsha. This has been their overall desire. They're now bulldozing that area, and bulldozing a big road along the edge of it for military vehicles to travel up and down. Even the Urban Foundation, which had worked out an upgrading scheme for Crossroads to put in roads where there naturally are roads now, and move only a few shacks, are refusing to supervise this upgrading for the government, because the government won't allow these other people [in the peripheral areas] back.

The government has found a very clever solution to bad press internationally by using so-called black vigilantes, who are often off-duty policemen or mercenaries, to systematically attack the progressive leadership. This can then be put out in the press as "black on black violence." But actually it can be very carefully and clearly directed. It's quite a clever move, to say the least.

What role does your clinic play in this situation?
The clinic sees its role to try to encourage democracy and community participation. The patients elect the bulk of the clinic committee at an annual general meeting each year. The committee controls the budget, appoints staff, and decides the long-term goals. The more mundane things are decided at a staff meeting once a week. The clinic staff is now 29, with five white and the rest blacks. We have a rotating chairperson and anybody can put anything on the agenda. Each person has one vote, so the doctor has one vote and the baby-weigher has one vote. Our present thrust is to try to develop a community health worker program. We also have a printing press on which we print a little newspaper. This would usually carry a news item on the front, with health issues on the two middle pages and community news on the back.

In 1979, before I started the clinic, I approached the government—the Day Hospitals organization in Cape Town—and asked if they had any intention of putting up a facility in Crossroads. They said no, it was a temporary phenomenon and would go away. Six years later there are now 120,000 to 200,000 people in Crossroads, with an average of 70 new cases of tuberculosis every month.

We built the original clinic for $1,700 and opened in June 1980. At that stage, officially, the government was going to have cleared Crossroads by the end of 1981, so it was in a sense built for an 18-month emergency need. Six years later we've got ten medical consulting rooms, five dental consulting rooms, a classroom, a treatment area for dressing, injections, burns, etc., a legal advice office, and a printing room.

Thirteen percent of the children attending the clinic are malnourished, versus between 36% and 50% in the "homelands." The infant mortality rate in Crossroads was 51 per thousand in 1984—I think it may have dropped to 38 last year—but in a place like Ciskei it's estimated at something like 170 per thousand. So your child actually stands about a four times greater chance to live if you bring him to Crossroads. Even without a pass, you borrow the money, get on a bus, and come to Crossroads. That's the reality.

We saw over 500 injuries from police and army shootings over the last year, most of them from birdshot and buckshot. The advice of the surgeon was to leave the pellets in. We give the patients a high dose of intramuscular penicillin and something for pain, and send them off with mercurochrome or Methiolate to apply twice a day. If the wounds get septic we give them a stronger antibiotic. Some we've had coming back with pain, and then we've had to try to take out some of the pellets.

The police and army raided the clinic in November last year with sixty troops and riot police, surrounded the clinic with submachine guns and rifles and forced their way in. They wanted information about patients who had been shot and about the staff, which we refused to give them. They also threatened to burn down the clinic—implied that it could burn down very easily.

As a clinic we are supportive of the Comrades, and a number of our staff are members. At the moment four of our staff can't go to work because they fear for their lives. Geographically we are situated right in the middle of Ngxobongwana's area of control. The Comrades themselves have done some stupid things. I think necklacing is a horrible way to kill somebody; there's no way I could feel comfortable with the whole idea. But let's not be too critical. What happened in the West, after areas like France were liberated from Hitler's Germany, was that many collaborators were just shot. These people are collaborators, they're security police, they're informers. Many times, especially at the beginning, they were given the option of what they should do. Community councillors were told, "Resign or else we're going to attack you." There was one lovely story, I think in Cradock, where a councillor publicly resigned and the youth went home with him and ceremoniously took off the metal guards that the government had put on his windows. He was now accepted back into the community. You see the same thing with the mayor of Alexandra, Reverend Sam Buti, who's just resigned and been welcomed back by the UDF and the youth. Remember, these are often 18-year-old kids making decisions, because the leadership has been detained under the state of emergency or tied up in treason trials.

Document 24. "Property Ownership: a Black Perspective." Speech by Enos Mabuza to South African Property Owners Association, Johannesburg, August 7, 1986 (abridged)

It is a great pity that the two American speakers who were scheduled to address this convention decided to withdraw from the programme as they were not prepared to travel to our country during a State of Emergency.

Although I regard it as a singular privilege to have been asked as a late replacement to address you, I am conscious of the fact that my presence and participation in this convention is both incidental and co-incidental. It is incidental in the sense that had the American speakers not withdrawn, there would have been no Black speaker on your programme, and it is coincidental in the sense that had I not met the President of the South African Property Owners Association (SAPOA), Mr Roland Walker, at a luncheon about a month back, it is improbable that I would have been invited to participate at this convention.

The topics on which the various speakers have been addressing this convention relate directly or indirectly to property ownership. According to the SAPOA brochure, its members have property portfolios which are worth over R14-billion [$5.6 billion].

The following questions arise: How many Black members does SAPOA have, and what is their stake in the R14-billion property portfolios? The answers to both questions are probably in the negative and the reason is not difficult to find. The accumulation of discriminatory legislation over the years has militated against Blacks who have found themselves denied the right of access to and a stake in the property market.

Land ownership and finance go hand-in-hand with property ownership. Without the necessary finance, one cannot own land on which to develop property. With regard to Black people, it has not been the lack of capital which has militated against their desire to purchase and own land on which they could farm or develop property, but it has been laws such as the Natives' Land Act of 1913, the Bantu Trust and Land Act of 1936, the Urban Areas Consolidation Act of 1945 and the Group Areas Act of 1950.

From a historical perspective, the size, location and fragmentation of the homelands were the products of the conquest, annexations of and concessions on land which was previously owned by the Africans. The first point of conflict between the Blacks and White settlers was land. Blacks were gradually and systematically pushed to so-called native reserves which provided dormitories for families of migrant labourers. Although prior to 1913, Blacks were still in a favourable position with regard to the acquisition of land outside the native reserves especially in Natal and the Cape Province, land continued to be taken away from them and given to Whites either as a form of punishment for rebellion or as a means of rewarding co-operative Whites.

The passing of the Natives' Land Act of 1913 which was originally known as the Pass and Squatters Bill, secured most of the land for White ownership and development while only nine million hectares were reserved for African tribal ownership. The Act made no provision for the Africans to own land as individuals in the reserves, the rationale being that Africans were not to be economically independent, but it was expected of them to work on White farms or mines. According to those who passed the Act, it was purported to have been done for the protection of the Black people. Blacks, however, did not regard it as protection, but as deprivation. Indeed, they had been deprived of a right which they had hitherto enjoyed.

The Act was clearly not motivated by the need to create a territorial basis for a just, even if segregated, society. It was a response to the expressed interests of White farmers who constituted the dominant group in South African politics at the time and had to be rewarded with access to supplies of cheap labour. It was intended to minimize competition by denying Blacks the right to purchase land and the opportunity to become shareholders on White-owned land.

It is also common cause that much of the land that was reserved for Africans was and is of deficient quality. From a Black perspective at the time and up to today, the effect of the Native Land Act was to dispossess and reduce the Black to a veritable bondsman.

Although the 1936 Natives Trust and Land Act provided for the acquisition of more land for the native reserves, it also entailed the fact that the African people would, in keeping with the Bantustan policy, be confined to 13 percent of the land in the entire country. It also led to the rigorous enforcement of anti-squatter laws, forced removals and the end of sharecropping on White farms.

In the homelands, chiefs control the distribution of land and in many cases, this system does not make an allowance for efficient farmers to add to their holdings nor does it discourage ineffective land use. The granting of unlimited land for communal grazing has served as an impediment to proper stock breeding methods and the commercial sale thereof. Above all, the lack of private ownership has made it impossible for capable Black farmers to put up their land as security for financial loans. While loans can be granted on certain cash crops whose output and market prices can be predicted, co-operative and agricultural banks find it difficult to make loans which cannot be secured by mortgages on land. The homeland farmer has therefore had no way of securing the land or the credit he needs, nor of making a commercial success through the growing of crops or the raising of livestock.

Initially, the resistance to the need to change the communal land tenure system came from the South African Government because of its belief that this system was an important means of preserving African culture and of ensuring the maintenance of the administrative and political positions of chiefs. In spite of the commendable land ownership reforms that have been recently announced by Government, it will be a daunting task to convince some of the chiefs to appreciate the advantages which land tenure reforms will bring about for their tribal areas and their people.

Some chiefs have clung to the belief that the authority and respect which they should command depends on the number of subjects they have in their respective tribal areas. The more people they have, the greater will be their authority and respectability. In the process, some chiefs have allowed people who have been evicted from White-owned farms to settle indiscriminately in their areas without consideration of the pressure that is being brought to bear on non-renewable natural resources. . . .

Prior to the introduction of the 99-year leasehold in urban areas, which has since been substituted by freehold rights, Blacks were regarded as temporary sojourners in urban areas. Sprawling townships of four-roomed matchbox houses were established next to the big developing cities such as Johannesburg. Because of the obnoxious laws which I have already mentioned, our people could purchase neither the land nor the houses in which they live.

For years on end, Black leaders and organisations brought to the attention of the rulers of our country the need to change the laws which made Blacks fourth-class citizens in the land of their birth and denied them the right to own property and to engage in prosperous trade in the townships and the cities which they had helped develop. They wanted a change in the policies which had for generations led to their frustration and persecution under discriminatory laws which no just, let alone Christian, society could countenance. They wanted more contented communities to emerge to replace the truculent populations of the township ghettos with their high rate of violent crime. They wanted to be recognised as South African citizens, indeed as people of worth with human rights and obligations and not the outcasts and objects of bureaucratic manipulation and paternalistic charity that they were made to be.

Since the 1976 Soweto uprisings and especially during the current unrest, we have been reaping the fruits of the denial of equal opportunities to Blacks with regard to property rights. Township shopping complexes and administrative buildings, which have been seen as part of the "system" and oppression, have been attacked and destroyed. The properties of some of the Blacks who are regarded as belonging to the bourgeoisie have also been the targets of attacks because of the belief that when it comes to the crunch, these Blacks will side with the oppressor in order to safeguard their property. Because of the luxury and comfort in which the Black bourgeoisie live, it is also believed that they will be reluctant to join the struggle for equal political rights and a share in the economy.

Had Blacks been allowed to own land and develop property both in the urban and homeland areas, the chances are remote that these would have been attacked and reduced to rubble during times of unrest. Our people, including the youth, would have regarded these properties as their own, and worthy of preservation and protection. There would have been no need for the classical class distinction between the peasants and the bourgeoisie amongst our people.

Thousands if not millions of Blacks who live in urban townships are accommodated in matchbox houses for which they have to pay monthly rentals. There has recently been a campaign in some of these townships not to pay the rentals and the Black Local Authorities have threatened the occupants with eviction. The situation may become chaotic and the possibility exists that some of these townships may not just become "ungovernable" but also unserviceable.

The simple solution to all this shoddy mess is property ownership. Government and Local Authorities should embark on a programme to sell all these houses and the land to present occupants at a nominal price worked out on a slide-rule basis and with due regard to the financial income of each family. The pride of being the owner of a piece of land and of a home, no matter how modest, and the security which this ownership of property gives to one's family will not only engender the desire and the will to improve and protect such property, but will also inculcate respect for other people's as well as public property. . . .

Black townships and residential areas, be they in the urban areas or homelands, should not be developed as separate entities. They should be integrated into and developed as part of the adjacent metropolitan areas. Soweto should be developed as part of Johannesburg. Atteridgeville and Mamelodi should be developed as part of Pretoria. Instead of the mind boggling Regional Services Councils, local authorities should merge and share the responsibilities of administering a greater and nonracial metropolitan area. . . .

Property gives a sense of security to its owner and it can only be regarded as secure as the security of the country. I, however, make bold to state that, without the loyal response and patriotism of Blacks, all the security laws in our country's statute book and the military ware of the Defence Force can never make South Africa a safe and prosperous country.

Let us therefore work together for a new partnership of all the population groups of our land. The partnership should be unfettered by racial prejudice, and should be bound by the common bonds of human dignity, government by consent of the governed and equality before the law. The unconditional access of Blacks to the property markets of our country will, in itself, be a tangible contribution towards this partnership and to the creation of a truly just society.

DOCUMENT 25. "The Future of South Africa: Violent Radicalism or Negotiated Settlement?" Speech by Chief Mangosuthu Gatsha Buthelezi to the Heritage Foundation, Washington, November 24, 1986 (abridged)

The idiom of the American media and the content of American debate on South Africa indicates to me that people in the United States just have not grasped the extent to which the politics of negotiation is under siege in South Africa. . . . They fail to see that the ANC has now smelt blood and is driving in for what they think will be the final kill, and they are totally convinced that they will be a government returned from exile to establish a one-party socialist State in South Africa. They see negotiation as something that will rob them of that final reward of their revolutionary endeavors. . . . They are not interested in negotiating for an open general election from which they will be able to compete as equals. They are not interested in negotiating the kind of constitution which must necessarily be finalized before such an election could be held. Those are the facts of the matter. They see themselves as a government in a future one-party state, and they envisage themselves evolving a constitution once they are in that position. . . .

Let me say rather bluntly that black South Africa has the choice between the politics of negotiation and the politics of violence. If the choice is for the politics of negotiation, then it must ultimately be negotiations with the ruling National Party government. The politics of negotiation from the black side involves driving the South African government to the negotiating table. This will not be done by only mounting confrontation and conflict. It must also be done by undermining the basis of the government's own power.

The politics of negotiation must make even deeper incursions into the seat of power. This is possible, and it is happening. The power of the government is no longer monolithic. The total solidarity of Afrikaner support, which forms the guts of government power, is beginning to fragment. Government power has always rested in South Africa on the total control of the country's institutional life. This is no longer happening. Big business is not under government control. They are challenging the government. The trade union movement is not under government control. It is challenging the government. The government is being challenged even by its own first and second tier levels of government in white society. . . .

The same black ferment that produced June 16, 1976, produced Inkatha. . . . Inkatha is in fact the largest political organisation ever to have been formed in the history of South Africa. Inkatha plays in the league above protest politics. It has entered constituency politics as the only base from which mass black power can be mobilized in favor of the politics of negotiation. Inkatha actually engages the State. That engagement is a far more effective confrontation with the State than violent street-corner protest. We engage the State in KwaZulu and thump the State there.

We engaged the State in the Ingwavuma crisis, and we thumped the State there. We have thumped the State in the Special Cabinet Committee, and we now employ our massive power to fold our arms while we watch the State President squirm in his desperate need for a massive black constituency before his National Council can even begin to achieve anything. We employ our power to say: Mr. State President, unshackle black democracy first and then we will join you. We say to the State President: Release Dr. Nelson Mandela, Mr. Zeph Mothopeng, and other political prisoners and then we will join you. We say to the State President: Declare the death sentence on the Tricameral Parliament and then we will join you. We engage the State in this confrontation between mass black power and mass State power.

Document 26. "The Provincial Legislature." KwaZulu-Natal Indaba constitutional proposals, Durban, November 28, 1986 (abridged)

I. GENERAL

1. Size: There shall be a two chamber legislature consisting of a first chamber of 100 members and a second chamber of 50 members.

2. Elected: All members of the legislature shall be elected.

3. Qualifications: Voting will be by universal adult suffrage for all South African citizens resident in the Province in accordance with the Provincial Electoral Act, the qualifying age being 18 years old.

4. Proportional representation: A system of proportional representation will be adopted for elections.

5. Legislative powers/matters: The legislature will exercise legislative powers in respect of all the matters referred to under V below.

II. THE FIRST CHAMBER

The first chamber will consist of 100 members elected using a system of multi-member, constituency based proportional representation.

III. THE SECOND CHAMBER

1. Composition: The second chamber will consist of 50 members composed of representatives of the following groups:
   - the African background group (10 members)
   - the Afrikaans background group (10 members)
   - the Asian background group (10 members)
   - the English background group (10 members)
   - the South African group (10 members)

2. Voters: Save in the case of the South African group, a voter in a second chamber election must belong to the group whose candidates he intends voting for.

IV. PROCEDURES . . .

5. To become law, all legislation, including money bills, must be passed by both the first and the second chamber, subject to the following provisos:
   (i) In the case of legislation which affects the religious, language, cultural or other rights of the members of a background group or the South African group, such legislation will require in addition to majorities in both chambers, a majority of the representatives of that group in the second chamber.
   (ii) The second chamber will determine by a simple majority whether or not a bill falls into the category requiring such a special majority as set out in (i) above.
   (iii) Should a majority of members of the affected group be dissatisfied with a negative decision by the second chamber in terms of (ii) above, they shall have the right to cast a suspensive veto on the bill concerned until such time as the Supreme Court has ruled on the issue.
   (iv) In determining whether a bill requires a special majority as set out in (i) above, the second chamber and the Court, when asked to rule on the matter, shall determine whether the bill can reasonably be expected to affect the rights of the group concerned: Provided that the passing of such a special majority vote shall not adversely affect the rights of any other group. . . .

DOCUMENT 27. Statement by "J," 16-year-old male, Mapetla, Soweto, March 1987

1. On 16.3.87 at about midnight the South African Defence Force (SADF) arrived and knocked on the door. My grandmother opened the door. There were many SADF. They were in uniform. They searched the house. It took them some time before they decided who they wanted. While searching the house they broke two doors and they were drunk.
2. They went outside and then two of them came back and asked for J, which is my nickname. I think there was someone who pointed me out.

3. They went up to my brother, A, who is 17 years old and took him outside. A torch was shone on my brother and C, a member of SOSCO [Soweto Students' Congress], said "no he is not J". My brother was brought back. I was next. I was taken out and the torch was shone on me. I was identified by C. They then began assaulting me, kicking me and hitting me with the rifle butts. There were approximately 5 SADF. I went back to the house as I was ordered to dress. I then went out to the casspir [armored vehicle] and was pushed into it.

4. When I entered the casspir I saw two of my friends, C and I, already in it. They then drove off. On the way a captain told me I was going to point out other members. I said I know their faces but I don't know where they live. The captain then took two wires from a soldier sitting next to him. He wound the wires around my two little fingers. He had a box on the floor. I saw him turn the handle. I felt as if electricity was going up my arm and all over my body. This was done for about twenty minutes, with him switching the current on and off. I screamed every time they switched on the current. As he was shocking me, he told me I was going to have to point out "Congress members" and "Umkonto we Sizwe" members. I said I didn't know anything about "Umkonto". I asked him what "Umkonto" is. He told me it was someone who combats the society and then kills himself. I told him it was the first time I had heard of this organisation.

5. We were then driven to another house. The SADF got out of the casspir and went into the house. C had told them where to go. They went into the house and brought out M. I saw them assaulting M in the same way as I had been assaulted with the rifle butts and kicking. I still had the wire on me. They took it off me and put it onto M. They then took a school bag (canvas) and put it over my head. I heard M screaming.

6. They then drove around picking up and shocking the other victims. They picked up eleven people in all; with C pointing out the people.

7. We were finally driven to a shop where they stopped. This was in Mapetla. The soldiers got out. There were two other casspirs. We were then divided. In the casspir I was taken to, there were three others—two were girls, about eighteen. I was tied with a rope hands behind my back, around my neck and around my legs. This was done to two of us—me and C. Two of the other casspirs left. The casspir I was in stood there for approximately thirty minutes. It then moved to Protea police station.

8. I was untied and told to move into the police station. In the charge room there was a white man in plain clothes. On his table I saw books that belonged to me. He asked my name, address. He asked who is the owner of these books. I said they were my school books. There was a big MK written on the book. He accused me of being a member of the MK. I said "no". He asked me if I was a member of SOSCO. I said I was. I went to another office and stayed there until the morning. I was not given anything to eat or drink.

9. In the morning the South African Police (SAP), told me to go to his office. In the office he asked me to become an informer and they would give me money. I said "yes". They then let me go. He told me the meeting point at Midway Station on Friday 3.30 pm. I didn't go there.
10. On the following Tuesday he came to look for me. I was not at home. He asked where I was and he was told by my grandmother and aunt they didn't know where I was. He told them he would come back. I haven't stayed at home since then.
11. I asked C why he had agreed to point his friends out. He said it was because he had been assaulted and shocked and was frightened.
12. On last Friday 27.3.87 I got sick. I had sores in my throat and felt dizzy all the time. The doctor gave me tablets and I feel a bit better.

DOCUMENT 28. "The Fight for Oukasie." Interview with member of Brits Action Committee, *Sechaba,* May 1987

When was the Action Committee formed?

The Action Committee was formed in December 1985. The problem was that the so-called community council called a meeting and told the people that the township was going to be moved by the end of that year. The people decided to hold another meeting the next day, a Sunday, and at that meeting it was decided to form a committee that will fight this removal. We were elected in that meeting. Since then we have been struggling to talk to the government, explaining that moving us now will cause more hardship in the future. And there is no reason for us to get moved. Anyway, the new place [Letlhabile] is going to be the same as where we are. The only difference is that there will be flush toilets. But it will cause more hardship because at a later stage, when everybody has been moved, it is going to be incorporated in Bophuthatswana, because the border of Bophuthatswana is only about 300 metres away from the township.

The way the bantustans are being run, basically the people lose their human rights in the homelands. They do not have a right to form a trade union, they do not have a right to meetings at all. There is more brutality in Bophuthatswana. People are being silenced.

How many are you on the Action Committee?

The Action Committee has 12 members. We got some other people from the youth organisation, the women's committee and the parents' organisation. The Action Committee is the superior body. There are smaller organisations which are affiliated to us.

Besides fighting the removals what do you do?

The other aspects we are dealing with is the social life of the people, the welfare of the people I would say. We realised that the police were doing very little about the thuggery in the township. We decided that we should try to do away with the people who harass us. The street committees were the ones who, every time there is a problem, try to solve the problem on their own, to try and talk to whoever is involved [thugs] and to resolve the problem that has arisen.

On the other hand we are looking at promoting better education in the township. We have been having problems. There was a school whose roof was taken away by a storm. The school committee went to the authorities telling them that we would like them to repair the school. The government was not prepared to repair the school. They said that they have already budgeted so they were not going to repair that school. Anyway we attacked them in the media, for they are trying to get the people disillusioned so that they move. It is very easy, if the schools can be closed down.

What they were doing was encouraging or trying to get politics into education in the township. By so doing they wanted to have the schools moved out to the new township. Because of the attacks we made on them through the media and the support from the public, later they said they would repair the school and it is functioning again.

What is the main reason why they want to move Oukasie ["Old Location"]?

What Chris Heunis, the Minister [of constitutional development and planning], said was that it was impossible to upgrade the township and secondly that the place itself is a health hazard. I do not know where he got his facts. We decided last year in March to consult engineers to come and make a survey of the township, to look into the feasibility of upgrading the township. They came up with the response that it would cost only about R3 million [$1.2 million] to upgrade the township. In a week we will have another expert on community health who is going to make a study of the health of the township for the past five years. What we have been told is that Oukasie is not worse than other places. It is just the same as the other places which are not threatened with removal. The only difference with Oukasie is that we are at the doorstep of Whites, conservative Whites, the Afrikaners. That is basically the main reason behind it all. We will try to attack Heunis on the two reasons that he gave for the removal.

The first one is already out of the question because we have already shown that R3 million is nothing compared to the R4 million they spent on the [government-sponsored "pop music"] "peace song". The upgrading is not the problem. He cannot come and tell us that the township is a health hazard. We are living there. One other thing that is interesting is that there was the outbreak of cholera which swept throughout South Africa. But there was no case of cholera in our township.

If one tells me that the bucket system [for removal of human feces] is out of fashion, then what about Alexandra, what about Mphupheleli in Natal with the bucket system? It's a new township with a bucket system. There is nothing like a health hazard. Then it means that all the people who are using the bucket system definitely do not have to do that.

The other thing is that when this year started, the kids went to the crèche [day-care center] as usual. When they got there, they were told that the crèche was closed. We went to the local administration manager and asked him. He told us that it was agreed some time last year by the crèche committee and the community councillors that it would be closed. We talked a lot and later he agreed we could use the building and the equipment, but the funding would depend on us. And right now we have been looking around to find some sponsors, we have some, not enough, but at least we keep the place running. The South African Council of Churches is being very helpful in that. Well, we have funds to run the crèche for five to six months.

But then there were attacks on the government on the issue of the school and the crèche. On one Friday afternoon the Security Branch police came to me and told me that the captain wanted to talk to me. And when I was there, I was told by the captain that if I do not keep my mouth shut they are going to take me to Central Prison because I am causing too many problems for them. But then there was nothing to worry about because the job was already done.

Were there people arrested in Oukasie under the emergency?

Yes, a lot of people were arrested. Among them were trade unionists and some members of the Action Committee. In fact it was on the eve of [Mrs] Modimoeng's funeral. Modimoeng is a trade unionist and a supporter of the Action Committee. A hand grenade was thrown into his house and his wife was killed in that attack. On the eve of the funeral, that was on the 11th of June [1986], during the night, the police came and arrested many people. For the whole of that day, I was one of the those who tried to negotiate with them for they had too many restrictions on the funeral. There should not be anyone in the streets, there should not be chanting or any singing of freedom songs and that kind of thing. The committee, together with our legal adviser, went to see the police. We talked it over, and there was some arrangement. But they arrested most of the people that night.

The next day, during the funeral, we were told not to march, everyone was to get into cars. Because there was a lot of people at the funeral, close to 30 000 I would say, there was no way we could have enough transport to carry so many people. There were lots of police, some of them on horseback. There was nothing to do anyway. The people had their march, irrespective of what the police would say.

Do you have any idea of who killed Modimoeng's wife?

The police claimed they were investigating. Modimoeng said he saw two Whites and two Blacks.

How is your Action Committee functioning under the emergency?

It is very difficult. We are really having a difficulty. The Brits police are the worst you can ever find in that area. The churches have been helpful. We actually meet at churches. We meet at prayer meetings right now. Anything we would like to deliver to the people we do in the churches. We are living in difficult times. One cannot sleep in the same place twice. I only sleep in my place once a week, when no one expects me to be there. It is far better during the day, as people can see, but when it's night time everyone's life is in danger. Anything can happen. We have seen too many attacks. My house was petrol-bombed twice. And many of the activists' houses have been petrol-bombed.

Who do you think is launching these attacks?
Although we do not know who is doing it, we do not have opposition in our community. The community relies on us. They really trust us. One can easily judge from what is happening why are only activists the ones whose houses have been attacked? It means opposition, and the only opposition we have is the apartheid regime.

What do you think will happen next?
I think that this thing calls for someone's guts. I think that as long as the majority stay in Oukasie there is nothing that the regime can do. But if they can continue with their tactics of intimidating people then they are going to succeed. Even if they remain in the minority there are those people who have decided that under no circumstances are they going to be moved. Only over their dead bodies will they be moved.

How many people have already moved to this new township?
At present we have about 6 000 people who have moved to the new township. In Oukasie we have about 10 000 resisting the removal. Anyway, in some cases I do not blame the people who moved. Some of the people are old people who believe that once the White man says you must move you must move. Some people were threatened, more especially the municipal workers. They were taken on tour by bus and told to choose plots. Whoever did not want to choose a plot was threatened with dismissal. Thirdly, it was very hard to stay in the old location because every night there were shootings, explosions, the police coming in. So some people felt their lives were at stake now and had to move. Fourthly, some other people [moved] because of high unemployment. We have about 50% unemployment because some other factories have left, running away from the unions. Brits is one of the most organised areas. The factories are running away and the people become unemployed.

Whoever had a house was promised about R2 000 [$900] for his four-roomed house, could easily take that R2 000 hoping to take that money to use while he looks for work in order to build a proper house, which will never work.

What kind of buildings are in the new township?
There is a toilet built with corrugated iron, which is a flush toilet, and a thatched house of about nine square metres which is loaned while one is supposedly building a proper house.

What is the situation? Do you pay rent or is it cheaper to stay at Letlhabile after all?

At first when you get to Letlhabile, they claim that you buy at a freehold price of R52.80 for 300 square metres. It is impossible for anyone to buy land for that amount. It shows that they are cheating. Some people moved there because they were told it would be their [own] place. After the R52.80 you pay something between R6 to R7 for the services which are water and garbage collection. But now the question comes back to us, because out in the old location [Oukasie] we have built our own houses. The only services which they offer to us is a communal tap which is 100 metres from the house and night soil collection which is also done twice a week. And we have to pay R22 a month for these services which are not up to standard. This shows that this thing is a kind of bribery to get people attracted to that place.

When we discuss this with the people who are staying at Letlhabile, I always ask them, "Gentlemen, I don't blame you for going to Letlhabile, but let us face facts and let us discuss this openly. You are not the ones who are responsible for ending up at Letlhabile. The government has not been doing anything about this issue and we ourselves have been quiet. Let us work together because we are all Black brothers, we all know who is our enemy." At first they agreed they would show me the title deeds which I wanted to take and get to the title deeds office to check whether whoever has this land is actually registered in the deeds office. Suddenly all of them vanished, they do not want to give me the title deeds they claim to have. Fortunately, I personally had seen in one of the Afrikaans newspapers, *Die Beeld*, that people are buying plots at a very low price. What is happening is that they don't actually have freehold rights in that place. If they want to have freehold rights they have got to pay more, thousands more. This is a fact. There is no one who has got freehold rights in Letlhabile.

Given the fact that you are underground, how do you organise?

One of the most powerful sectors in the organisation is the women. The women are playing an important role. We were stopped from burying our dead in the township. The Roman Catholic church which is adjoining the township has been helpful by giving us some land to use for awhile to bury our dead there. We tried to talk to the government about that and they said there is nothing they can do. The women were becoming impatient. A week before I left, the women had been going to the administration office every day for a week asking for land to bury our dead.

The other thing is that most of the people, most of the street committee members were arrested. We have some other guys who have been sentenced to three years, others have been kept [in detention] under the emergency. One of them is a young guy, the security police have asked him to say that one of his friends is a member of the ANC. Anyway because of understanding that this guy is fighting through lawyers, they want to release him on condition that he will be a [state] witness [but he is refusing].

Document 29. "Group Areas in Mayfair." Actstop discussion paper, April 1989

HISTORY

The history of Indian residence in Mayfair [Johannesburg] can be traced back to the late 1970s and is related to the forced removal of people from Pageview. Some people evicted from Pageview decided to move into areas like Mayfair rather than go to Lenasia. The construction of the Oriental Plaza in 1973/4, after the forced removal of people to Lenasia, also led to the gradual return of people to the city. Some of the returning people moved into Mayfair to be close to their businesses. People either purchased homes through nominees or rented at exorbitant prices. People also came to Johannesburg from Natal in search of work. Mayfair was also the destination of some of these people. All these factors led to the gradual movement of Indian people into Mayfair before 1982.

GOVERNMENT REACTION UNTIL 1982 AND PEOPLE'S RESISTANCE

The Nationalist government reacted in its usual repressive manner against the movement of so-called "illegal" people into Mayfair. This reaction was the eviction of our people in terms of the Group Areas Act. The police started to prosecute literally hundreds of people and evictions became the order of the day. Resistance on the part of our people started with the eviction of a Mrs. Sylvia Naidoo and her family in 1978. Mrs. Naidoo had a history of resistance in Pageview and this manifested itself in Mayfair. The Naidoo family did not move away when evicted. They decided they had a moral right to stay where they choose and thus camped on the pavement outside the house from which they were evicted. The community rallied around the family and many residents camped with them. Mrs. Naidoo then approached prominent community members with a view to fighting the oppression of the state. This led to the formation of Actstop [Action Committee to Stop Evictions] with Cassim Saloojee as chairperson. Actstop secured the services of a string of lawyers who defended people prosecuted in terms of the Group Areas Act. The lawyers defended these people *pro deo* [free]. Hundreds of cases were defended over a period of four years. The *Star* of July 1982 reported that 570 cases were pending at that time.

This resistance in the face of state repression led to victory in November 1982. A Mrs. Govender was evicted and her case was heard before Justice [Richard] Goldstone on 30 November 1982. The judge ruled that conviction in terms of the Group Areas Act does NOT entail automatic eviction. He stated in his judgement that alternative accommodation in a group area pertaining to the defendant must be provided before eviction. This judgement was a water-shed in group area legislation. Its effect was to put a stop to state evictions because areas designated for black people were all saturated. The resistance of our people in Mayfair and other areas thus resulted in a serious erosion of the government's repressive policies.

THE POSITION SINCE 1982

The victory of people's resistance in Mayfair opened the way for thousands of black people to move into the inner-city areas of Johannesburg. The government was powerless to act against black people because of the *Govender* judgement. Our people began to purchase homes from low-income whites who were only too willing to make massive profits on their dilapidated properties. These homes were renovated or rebuilt at considerable cost and a viable community began to take root. The community began to thrive and the face of Mayfair changed from a dilapidated area to one where property values rose to be amongst the highest on the Witwatersrand. This made a mockery of anti-integrationist claims that property values drop when an area becomes integrated. Relations between residents were good and incidents were few.

This settled atmosphere was shattered in May 1987 when the Conservative Party made significant gains in the "white" elections. Suddenly, latent right-wing minority groupings in Mayfair-West and Homestead Park started demanding the eviction of settled people who had done so much to improve the area. The government was powerless to accede to these demands since the *Govender* judgement still applied. This inability to act on the part of government led to the right-wing racists taking the law into their own hands. Families were forcibly prevented from moving into homes bought or rented. Some who had already moved in were harassed and intimidated.

This rise in white racism led to the revival of Actstop. The Mayfair branch of Actstop was launched at a public meeting and Cassim Saloojee was elected chairperson. The organisation immediately started acting on 2 fronts. Groups were formed in various parts of Mayfair, Mayfair-West and Homestead Park. These groups established communication networks to facilitate getting people together in support of anybody who was harassed or intimidated. Groups of residents started helping people move in and rendered support in other ways. On another front Actstop began campaigning against the government's intention to introduce the Group Areas Amendment Bill. This bill was formulated to overcome the *Govender* judgement, thus enabling the state to override a Supreme Court judgement and begin evicting so-called "illegal" people again. The bill was also an attempt to pacify the right-wing faction that was demanding the implementation of the Group Areas Act. Fierce resistance to the bill from Actstop, TIC [Transvaal Indian Congress] and other organisations forced the government to scrap the bill. Members of Actstop, many of whom are also TIC activists, then concentrated on organising the community against right-wing terror in Mayfair-West and Homestead Park. The "Dayal" incident in Gothard Street brought the reality of right-wing violence and naked racism to the attention of all of S. Africa. This incident, though unfortunate and painful to the Dayal family, galvanised our people in Mayfair, Mayfair-West and Homestead Park. We united under Actstop and succeeded in repelling further right-wing attacks. It is interesting to note, at this stage, that no police action has been taken against the people who were responsible for the violent actions and unlawful acts in the "Dayal" incident.

The galvanising of our community since this incident has resulted in the focus being broadened to include facilities and amenities in the area. We are now asserting our right to live where we choose. This means the articulation of demands for adequate education facilities, sports facilities and other normal community needs. Our people are now demanding, through Actstop, the rights of any normal settled community. We want adequate schooling for our children; we want adequate sport and recreation facilities. In line with this, Actstop has demanded that all schools, as well as recreation and sports facilities in the area, be opened for the use of ALL the residents, irrespective of race. We are also demanding that schools being used for other purposes, like training of post office employees and use by the defence force, be returned to the community for education purposes. It is important to note that we are not simply making these demands by word of mouth. Numerous examples of affirmative action by our people clearly show that resistance has not been stifled:

- a picnic was held at the public park in Homestead Park. This park was usually the domain of right-wing whites. The picnic, attended by people of all races, was proof of inter-racial harmony and showed the determination of our people to use all facilities.
- we went to the "white" swimming pool for a swim. Although the city council emptied the pool on that day in an attempt to pull the rug from under our feet, our action made the point of our active resistance to a racist law.
- the Grosvenor Recreation Centre was also used by our people who played tennis there.

These positive actions indicate the determination of our people in Mayfair, Mayfair-West and Homestead Park to resist attempts by the state to deprive us, and our children, of basic amenities and facilities. The positive action is channeled through Actstop, as well as the TIC, and will manifest itself whenever there is discrimination against residents.

In looking at the current group area situation in Mayfair and surrounding areas, it is necessary to consider the Free Settlement Areas Act. This act is the government's response to the movement of black people to the inner-city areas. The Free Settlement Areas Act provides for the "opening-up" of certain areas for occupation by ALL race groups. The State President, Minister of Constitutional Development, Minister of Housing in House of Delegates or Representatives, local city council or a township developer can ask a Free Settlement Areas Board to investigate an area with a view to declaring it a free settlement area. The Free Settlement Areas Board is constituted by the Minister of Constitutional Development. The so-called "legal" residents only of an area would be consulted about such an investigation. Therefore, if Mayfair-West is investigated, only the white residents would be consulted. The board would also consult people in adjoining areas and take into consideration the effect of its decision on those areas.

The government considers this act to be part of its reform process and a watering-down of the Group Areas Act. However, we know better. The government HAD to act because they are forced to do so by people's struggle.

The resistance of people and our valiant struggle against repressive laws has already "opened-up" areas like Hillbrow, Joubert Park and Mayfair. The fact that Mayfair is proposed to be one of the areas to be investigated is NOT through the magnanimity of the government. The area is being proposed for investigation because the struggle of our people and their supporters has left the government no choice but to legalise a de facto situation. The activities of organisations like Actstop and TIC in areas like Mayfair are the manifestation of the struggles of our people. It is this resistance that forces any remotely positive moves by the state.

While the Free Settlement Areas Act will "open" certain areas and thus remove the threat of the Group Areas Act from these areas, we must look at the many negative aspects of the act as well. We must also re-emphasise that our demand still remains the total scrapping of the Group Areas Act. In order to explain some of the negative aspects of the act, let us look at Mayfair, Mayfair-West and Homestead Park in particular:

- We will have no say in the investigation of these areas, if such investigation is commissioned; only the white residents will be consulted.
- Mayfair-West and Homestead Park will still remain "whites only" areas.
- Mayfair, if declared a free settlement area, could become overcrowded as more people would move in.
- right-wing pressure could increase in Mayfair-West and Homestead Park if only Mayfair is declared a free settlement area. White racists will feel more justified in their racist acts.
- the Free Settlement Areas Act does not do away with the Group Areas Act and is still racist.

It is the moral responsibility of all concerned and progressive residents of Mayfair, Mayfair-West and Homestead Park to resist and organise against the Free Settlement Areas Act because of these negative aspects. We can not be satisfied if only the area we may be staying in is "opened-up" while our brothers and sisters in other areas still suffer the inhumanity of the Group Areas Act. We must re-emphasise our demand that nothing short of the total scrapping of the Group Areas Act will adequately begin to address the problems of housing in South Africa.

The history of group areas in Mayfair is rich with examples of the resistance of our people. Today Actstop and TIC are embedded in the black community of Mayfair, Mayfair-West and Homestead Park. The role played by these organisations in uniting people and spearheading resistance must be continued and strengthened. History has demonstrated that only our struggle and resistance brings victories. We need to organise ourselves and strengthen Actstop and TIC; since these organisations can only be as strong (or weak) as the people in the area. We must not rest until the Group Areas Act is no more and the Separate Amenities Act is scrapped.

We are here to stay and we WILL demand ALL the needs of a normal community.

2. Internal Opposition: The Battle Joined

DOCUMENT 30. "Open Letter from Natal Indian Congress." Durban, November 1, 1981

DEAR FRIENDS,

We were in your area on Saturday to talk to you about the SAIC [SA Indian Council] elections and explain to you why we think you should not vote.

We thank you for your kind reception and support. We were encouraged that our people are not bluffed, and understand clearly that the SAIC is a useless body.

There are a number of Candidates standing for election in your area. We think it is our duty to tell you about the bad behaviour of some of them. In particular Rajbansi, Thaver and Baig.

While we were visiting each family so that you could hear both sides before deciding whether to vote, these people interfered with us.

This is what happened:

1. Many of our cars were held up in front of Rajbansi's house on Road 602, by a gang of about 30 people;
2. They tore the posters and banners off our cars;
3. They swore at all of us—men and women;
4. They man-handled Congress women, including Mrs Naicker of Croftdene; and tried to force them out of the car;
5. They assaulted Congress executive members. Dr Jerry Coovadia was pulled out of his car. Another member had his beard pulled;
6. Advocate Zac Yacoob, a blind member of the NIC executive, was sworn at and roughed up;

7. Mr MJ Naidoo, the chairman of the Anti-SAIC Committee, was insulted and shouted at.

The main actors in this disgraceful incident were the following SAIC candidates —
    G. THAVER M. BAIG A. RAJBANSI MRS RAJBANSI*
        *LAC[Local Affairs Committee] Member

This same Rajbansi who lied about NIC on T.V.

You might ask why we are telling you all this?
  We believe that you must know that these are the types who are standing for the SAIC in your area.

HOW CAN THEY CLAIM TO BE LEADERS OF THE INDIAN COMMUNITY?
  The Indian Community's future is at stake.
  It cannot be entrusted to irresponsible people like these.
  Let us show our disgust with this kind of behaviour and this kind of people.

Congress asks that we DO NOT VOTE ON NOVEMBER 4, and says:
  You cannot be charged if you refuse to vote.
  You won't lose your pensions if you refuse to vote.
  It is your right not to vote.

Yours in service
MJ NAIDOO

Document 31. "The Workers' Struggle—Where Does FOSATU Stand?" Speech by Joe Foster to second FOSATU congress, Hammanskraal, April 10, 1982 (abridged)

INTRODUCTION
  Three years ago, almost to the day, we met in this very same place to form FOSATU. Today we have set as our theme "The Workers' Struggle", in a serious attempt to further clarify where we as worker representatives see FOSATU to stand in this great struggle. . . .
  All the great and successful popular movements [worldwide] have had as their aim the overthrow of oppressive—most often colonial—regimes. But these movements cannot and have not in themselves been able to deal with the particular and fundamental problem of workers. Their task is to remove regimes that are regarded as illegitimate and unacceptable by the majority.
  It is, therefore, essential that workers must strive to build their own powerful and effective organisation even whilst they are part of the wider popular struggle. This organisation is necessary to protect and further worker interests

and to ensure that the popular movement is not hijacked by elements who will in the end have no option but to turn against their worker supporters. . . .

FOSATU'S OBJECTIVE

From what has been said we believe that FOSATU must set itself the task of giving leadership and direction to the building of a working class movement. Our efforts so far have equipped us to do this. Our organisation is nationally based, located in the major industries and the militancy of our members has generally developed a politically aware and self-critical leadership.

FOSATU as a trade union federation will clearly not constitute the working class movement nor would this place FOSATU in opposition to the wider political struggle or its major liberation movement.

FOSATU's task will be to build the effective organisational base for workers to play a major political role as workers. Our task will be to create an identity, confidence and political presence for worker organisation. The conditions are favourable for this task and its necessity is absolute. . . .

Structure:

The structure of an organisation should be such that it correctly locates worker strength and makes best use of that strength.

FOSATU's experience in this has been very important. Our organisation is built up from the factory floor. As a result the base of the organisation is located where workers have most power and authority and that is where production takes place. This also has the effect of democratising our structures since worker representatives always participate from a position of strength and authority in the organisation. By stressing factory bargaining we involve our Shop Stewards in central activities and through this they gain experience as worker leadership. It could be said that they do battle every day. . . .

At the union level FOSATU has attempted to build broad industrial unions on a national basis. . . . We must accept that it will take many years to organise all workers and at present that should not be our aim. Our present aim must be to locate our organisation strategically. . . . Geographically we must clearly aim to be a national presence both as FOSATU and as the affiliates. Our organisation should be able to dominate major industrial areas. By doing this we create the major means whereby worker organisation can play a significant if not dominant role in the communities that surround these industrial areas. . . .

Worker leadership:

Here we must be immediately clear that we are not talking about leadership in the sense that it is usually discussed which is in terms of individuals and "great men". This view of leadership is not what is important for a worker organisation. What we are interested in is the elected representatives of workers and the officials they appoint to work within the organisation. . . . Probably most important. . . is the development of a sense of when to advance and when to retreat. These skills are not easily learnt and not easily replaced. So worker leadership cannot be wasted by opportunistic and overly adventuristic actions. . . .

Working Class Identity. . . .

In a very important way the building of effective trade unions does create a worker identity. However, there is the danger that the unions become preoccupied with their members and ignore workers generally. By establishing a clear political direction we can avoid this.

One answer that is often proposed is to be more involved in community activities. That FOSATU should be involved in community activities is correct since our members form the major part of those communities. However, as we have argued above we must do so from an organisational base if we are truly to be an effective worker presence.

Without this base it is more likely that we will destroy a clear worker identity since workers will be entirely swamped by the powerful tradition of popular politics. . . .

It is also the case that there has emerged into our political debate an empty and misleading political category called the community. All communities are composed of different interest groups and for a worker organisation to ally itself with every community group or action would be suicide for worker organisation. Under the surface of unity, community politics is partisan and divided. FOSATU cannot possibly ally itself to all the political groups that are contesting this arena. Neither can it ally itself with particular groups. Both paths will destroy the unity of its own worker organisation.

This simple political fact is the reason for one of our founding resolutions. It has nothing to do with not wanting to be involved in politics. Our whole existence is political and we welcome that. Our concern is with the very essence of politics and that is the relation between the major classes in South Africa being capital and labour. . . .

UNITY IN THE LABOUR MOVEMENT. . . .

At present there is a very great momentum to unity in the labour movement and we have to carefully consider and analyse what is happening. The first point to understand is that all the unions involved in the talks are relatively weak in relation to their potential—some appallingly so. . . .

The bulk of the present leadership has no clear conception of the needs of worker struggle or of a worker dominated society. There is all too often a contradiction between the political position and organisational practice. Radical political positions are adopted but the organisational practice makes little headway into the power of capital nor is it effectively democratic. . . .

As a consequence of these factors it is not possible for people to draw any distinction between worker struggle and popular struggle let alone understand the relation between the two in South Africa. The unity talks are therefore conceived of as being within the wider popular struggle and as another area where anti-State unity can be achieved. A formal unity rather than a working unity against capital is therefore seen as the prime object.

There are broadly speaking three forms of unity open to the union movement at present. . . .

- "Ad hoc unity": this is what has occurred at present where unity is issue located and attempts to take a common stand.
- "United front unity": here the organisations remain autonomous but they set up a permanent platform of contact. . . .
- "Disciplined unity": this requires common political purpose, binding policy on affiliates and close working links based on specific organisational structures. . . . Clearly by unity we should strive for "disciplined unity" since it is only such unity that can possibly meet our objective. . . .

Document 32. Report on meeting of FOSATU shop stewards council, Katlehong township, east Rand, November 14, 1982

Katlehong Local

The closing of 1982 local general meeting comprising two areas, Germiston/Wadeville and Alrode forming the Katlehong Shop Steward Council was held on the 14th November 1982 at D. H. Williams [community hall].

Agenda of the meeting:
1. The Katlehong local worker struggle in 1982—success and failures.
2. The intimidation Act and other laws affecting workers in S.A.

The Katlehong local workers struggle in 1982—successes and failures:
a) The organisation expanded very fast through the participation of the workers themselves in organising other workers. Through the formation of good structures like the Shop Steward Council which was formed in 1981. Membership now is more than 10,000. Today only Fosatu is truly existing as effective worker organisation.
b) Education of members through locally organised seminars to stabilize and build worker leaders. One speaker said, "We believe in a clear shop floor organisation which is clear [about] what it needs. To do that then you have to organise, unite, stabilise, mobilise, educate and fight."
c) The Shop Steward Council formation. This created unity right across the factories, and workers began to identify themselves against the enemy. It was then able to fight the common issues in a position of power. These in many cases were won e.g. during the wave of strikes. There were regular meetings of the committee to give advice and direction to the struggle. e.g. National Springs, Litemaster etc. One speaker said, "As workers struggling against the powerful system with structures like SEIFSA [Steel and Engineering Industrial Federation of SA], we must form our own structures that will make things easy to communicate."
d) Fosatu acquired a breeding ground—everybody is singing Fosatu in the area.

e) There are more than five signed full procedural agreements where workers themselves have fought to win some rights to channel their grievances, to have a say in their day-to-day lives and a control of their working environment. The factories are: Dresser SA; Henred Fruhauf in Wadeville; Henred Fruhauf in Driehoek; Litemaster and another steel company in Wadeville and more than ten informal agreements like Scaw Metals; Fry's Metals; TMF etc. One speaker said, "This [has] taught us to face the employers and negotiate instead of somebody negotiating for us."

Difficulties:
a) Over expansion of the organisation which created big demands and great expectations from the fledgling organisation.
b) Wave of strikes—workers in this area got many grievances and faced with tough employers. When workers tried to raise their grievances they answered by fighting instead of talking. That [created] conflicts and this escalated to strikes. We had had more than twenty strikes. Some of our members lost their jobs in this battle. One speaker said, "As workers we learned something, that we have to fight very hard to move the enemy, we have to fight in a position of power to win issues".
c) Recession—the recession has caused us a great harm. More than 1,000 of our members in the area lost their jobs. The meeting condemned the stubbornness of the employers to just dismiss the workers when things are bad. "We condemn this because the recession is caused by the employers and the consequences are suffered by us. When they build factories, they pretend to be doing that for the good of workers. When things go astray from making profits, they cut the costs on workers instead of on profits," one worker said. "This is going to cause us to lose our houses and starvation because we depend entirely on this meagre wage for our living. We've got no savings. Where are we going to stay, what are we going to eat?" said one urban worker. The workers coming from rural areas said that there is drought and if there isn't any rain they won't have means to plough their land. This is increasing the number of people that are dying of starvation and famine in these areas, like Transkei.

The local meeting also condemned the attitude of the employers refusing to negotiate retrenchment procedures with the workers. "This is bad, in fact it teaches us that the employers are not interested [in] us but [in] our labour that is creating profits. They know what they want, they've got no mercy. It teaches us to know the characteristics of the employers and to know what we want, and how cruel the system is."

New Intimidation Act of 1982:
The issue was raised because of the report from Litemaster where seven workers were arrested under this act, and were bailed by R2,100 in all. The meeting seriously condemned the Act and it was felt that the Act is designed

to break the solidarity and power of the workers, by inflicting fear to the workers. A resolution was passed that all workers should unite to fight this law. The issue should be taken to Fosatu Regional Congress and Central Congress to formulate some ways and avenues of fighting the evil act. It was also decided that Fosatu should contact other organisations to [make] this fight a reality and unite all the workers. It was also resolved that Fosatu should contact the employers to fight the Act also if they feel they care about the welfare of workers.

Influx Control: New Pass Laws.

It was discussed that there is a new law proposed called the *Orderly Movement and Settlement of Black Persons Bill*. The law was condemned as being aimed at depriving workers of their rights to have shelter, to have political power and citizenship in their land of birth. It was said that the bill will be to oppress the workers. We belong to South Africa, then we are full citizens of S.A. We have built S.A. to what it is now. There were many laws created by employers to make our labour to be cheap, like pass laws. They didn't work. The bill is worse than anything, "even a pig can't tolerate such a law," one worker said. It was resolved all workers organisations should unite to fight the bill. To be thrown away "through our power". The privileges and wealth created by our labour must be enjoyed by all of us, not just few people. It was vowed that the time has come that we workers should fight for our rights to have shelter and food for our children.

"We do not belong to the homeland, we belong to where we choose to belong, no employer or employer agent is going to tell us where we belong, this is our land. We shall fight for our rights, we are starting now and forever," said one worker.

The homeland system was criticized as created by employer agents to create cheap labour and to control workers. "We are human-beings, the employers want us to stay without our families for twelve months and see them only three weeks but they are with theirs every hour. We are no longer going to tolerate this. We want our families to be where we are. We want shelter and [food] for them, that is all," said one worker. It was decided that this be taken to the Shop Steward Council. The demolishing of Natalspruit and Thokoza shacks was condemned and attacked heavily. Those shacks are our shelters. They are demolishing them without giving us alternative accommodation. The resolution was made that all workers in Wadeville-Germiston and Alrode should fight to stop the demolishing of worker shelters. It was resolved that the employers in the area should be approached to stop the action.

It was also resolved that some other possible avenues should be [tried] to fight this. The meeting decided unanimously to unite all the workers (rural and urban) in the area to protect their houses. It was decided that no more shelter should be demolished. "The employers are pushing us to go to the hostels, we are not going to do that, we want family life and accommodation. The employers should help us in this problem. We cannot go back to the homelands or to hostel-life. They have broken our old way of living, they must accept our existence."

A main resolution was made that all workers through their Shop Steward in these areas should approach their own managements about all the grievances affecting family life in Natalspruit and Thokoza and also about the evil acts raised in the meeting. The employers must make their stand clear on these.

It was also resolved that seminars should be held with the workers discussing the dangers of the problems raised.

Document 33. "Manifesto of the Azanian People." Statement by AZAPO, June 1983

Our struggle for national liberation is directed against the system of racism and capitalism which holds the people of Azania in bondage for the benefit of the small minority of the population, i.e. the capitalists and their allies, the white workers and the reactionary sections of the middle classes. The struggle against Apartheid is no more than the point of departure for our liberatory efforts. The black working class inspired by revolutionary consciousness is the driving force of our struggle for national self-determination in a unitary Azania. They alone can end the system as it stands today because they alone have nothing at all to lose. They have a world to gain in a democratic, anti-racist and socialist Azania, where the interests of the workers shall be paramount through the worker control of the means of production, distribution and exchange. In a socialist Azania the land and all that belongs to it shall be wholly owned and controlled by the Azanian people. The usage of the land and all that accrues to it shall be aimed at ending all exploitation. It is the historic task of the black working class and its organisations to mobilise the oppressed and exploited people in order to put an end to the system of oppression and exploitation by the white ruling class.

OUR PRINCIPLES

Successful conduct of the national liberation struggle depends on the firm basis of principle whereby we will ensure that the liberation struggle will not be turned against our people by treacherous and opportunistic "leaders" and liberal influences. The most important of these principles are:
- Anti-racism, anti-imperialism and anti-sexism.
- Anti-collaboration with the ruling class and their allies and political instruments.
- Independent working-class organisations, free from bourgeois influences.

OUR RIGHTS

In accordance with these principles the following rights shall be entrenched in Azania:

- the right to work.
- state provision of free and compulsory education for all. Education shall be geared towards liberating the Azanian people from all forms of oppression, exploitation and ignorance.
- state provision of adequate and decent housing for all.
- state provision of free health, legal, recreational and other community services that will respond positively to the needs of the people.

OUR PLEDGES

In order to bring into effect these rights of the Azanian people we pledge ourselves to struggle tirelessly for:
- The abolition of all laws, institutions and attitudes that discriminate against our people on the basis of colour, sex, religion, language or class.
- The re-integration of the bantustan human dumping grounds into a unitary Azania.
- The formation of trade unions that will heighten revolutionary worker consciousness.
- The development of one national culture informed by socialist values.
- The eradication of specific and multiple oppression of black women in our country.

DOCUMENT 34. "Responses to State Strategy." Speech by Popo Molefe to National Union of South African Students conference, University of Cape Town, July 1983 (abridged)

For me it is a great honour this evening to be invited to address this historic conference. My task is to look at our responses, as progressives, to the present reform initiatives of the state.

We shall never understand the present reforms unless we go back and understand fully how they have come about. We cannot hope to respond effectively unless we do so, and therefore let us look at the South Africa we see before us today and the situation of racial capitalism. . . .

[From the arrival of the Europeans in the 17th century through the period of industrialisation, the white capitalist class consolidated its oppression of Africans through the migrant labour system and job reservation for whites. In recent years new strategies have been utilised to stem insurgency by the black working class, from the creation of bantustans and the Black Local Authorities Act, to the President's Council, which aims to obstruct the democratic movement among coloureds and Indians.]

Having looked at the Reform Package of Botha and Koornhof and their contradictions . . . we need to look at forms of resistance that have emerged. And I think these could, for the sake of argument and logic, be crystalised into two categories:

1. the popular political, which represents mass mobilisation of the oppressed masses around issues which affect them as a whole, and

2. local first level organisation of grassroots which concerns itself primarily with immediate problems of particular groups in particular points in time.

We have a long and proud tradition of popular political struggle, mass struggle culminating in the wide and large scale repression of the early sixties which left us with ten years of political dormancy. We then have another problematic decade of the seventies where we see a resurgence of political struggle which never effectively established a mass base with the particular exception of 1976 where it does constitute mass mobilisation but not necessarily mass mobilisation of a particular constructive sort. During this period, mass mobilisation was very difficult to channel strategically and even more difficult to consolidate organisationally.

Towards the end of the seventies, we see in 1978 to 1979 for the first time in a number of years the emergence of first-level grassroots organisation which represents among organisers and activists a realisation that mass political struggle has to be based and founded upon the first-level grassroots organisations which have the ability to address that which is essential, real and vital to them. And on the basis of that to teach them the skills of organisation and democracy, to give them the confidence that through their united mass action they can intervene and change their lives on no matter how small a scale. It is through practical involvement that the people get the best education of struggle, the education that exposes them to the magnitude of their own power. Also, through the involvement by themselves are they in a position to completely or relatively unmask the enemy.

From that base of first-level grassroots organisation, we can start to build progressively more political forms of organisation—a process which would culminate in the development of a national democratic struggle, through a more or less coherent national democratic movement.

The first level grassroots organisation has proved particularly difficult in the African areas with a few exceptions like the Diepkloof Civic Association in Soweto and the Krugersdorp Residents Organisation. However, we have seen it develop fairly well in the so-called coloured and Indian areas around issues like housing, rent and transport. But we have seen very little of it developing in African areas. We attribute this to a number of reasons. The history of the struggle in different areas varies considerably. We might find that the coloureds and Indians have far more affinity with formal structures given the higher preponderance of teachers, lawyers, doctors and other professional people in these communities. On the other hand, in the African areas, given the relatively smaller proportion of professional people and the relative absence of indigenous intelligentsia, we see less of a natural drift towards committees or formal styles of organisation. I must not be misconstrued as saying that grassroots organisations must be dominated by the intelligentsia and professional people, but rather to be understood as saying their presence plays a vital role because of their skills.

In the Indian and coloured areas we have a far lower level of repression than that which has characterised the African areas in recent years and as such the committee style, formal organisation is less vulnerable to state repression and reprisals than the case would be in the African areas. These are just two of the factors that influence forms of organisation in the African areas on the one hand and the coloured, Indian and white democratic communities on the other.

Another factor would be the local conditions under which people live where we might find in the African areas quantitatively greater degrees of material deprivation, material oppression, which again have implications on the way people organise. At the immediate level is the relative scarcity of resources for organisations to draw on. Also in the sense that people who already are struggling for survival may find it difficult to concern themselves with other struggles, whereas people who have more or less overcome the struggle for survival have more time and inclination to engage in other struggles.

Another factor is one that I have already referred to—namely, higher levels of repression which have a lot of Africans feeling that the only viable form of struggle is military forms of struggle, an experience which lends itself to recruiting for the liberation army rather than to recruiting people for small-scale, relatively reformist community work. . . .

These are factors amongst others which influenced different forms of organisations. I think particularly in the light of the Constitutional Proposals that these differences need to be highlighted, because I think that with the United Democratic Front seemingly dominated by the Indian and coloured community organisations and also noting that these organisations dominate the progressive movement, the focus of the UDF may be on the tri-cameral parliament simply because that is the aspect of the government and the ruling class reform initiatives which seek to co-opt the coloured and Indian communities into the tri-cameral parliament. To do this would mean that measures used to disorganise and discipline the workers are [not] given an adequate focus yet, are not even being adequately understood at the abstract and conceptual levels, and that we have not adequately identified what those measures are, those control measures. Unless we start getting actively involved in African areas or at least unless the Africans take up issues relevant to their day-to-day lives in their own areas, that is, educating the community on the implications of the Koornhof Bills, linking this up with high rental problems, spiralling electricity bills, food prices, housing shortage, our role in the UDF campaign will be very minimal if not nil. Our campaign should, in fact, go beyond reforms and challenge the entire "total strategy."

It is going to be very important for us to ensure that the control measures that are being mobilised against the African working class are given a much higher prominence. In the long run this is going to be very important. We think the actual objective of the government and the ruling class initiative is still greater control of the African working class. We repeat what we asserted before—the tri-cameral parliament is more than a racial divide and rule tactic. It is a tactic of which the overall strategy is to control the working class.

Of course, one of its tactics involves the co-option of the petty bourgeoisie, but it is against the working class that its objectives are ultimately directed. It is therefore on the organisation of the working class and on the working class counter-offensive that we must focus and direct our energies.

We already attempted to show different problems influencing forms of organisation in the African areas, but that does not mean organisation is impossible and that people—activists—must sit on their laurels using these problems as excuses or scapegoats. In Namibia people still manage to organise under harsh security conditions—conditions of virtual martial law. In Mozambique before independence, oppression and repression were the worst in the African continent. So that harsh conditions do sometimes serve as an inspiration. The higher degree of material deprivation in the African areas engender a series of contradictions. It is these contradictions which provide potential for organisation in the African areas. Of vital importance is the ability of the activists to identify specific burning issues and then to go on mobilising the people around those issues. This has been possible in the African areas like Soweto, Mohlakeng and Krugersdorp where we saw since the beginning of the decade of the eighties greater mobilisation around rent, boycotts of community councils, etc. These were always preceded by pamphleteering followed by mass meetings. But these campaigns could not be used to organise and to consolidate structures. So that the problem has always been how to organise and how to keep these people as active members of the organisations.

In Soweto, Krugersdorp and Vryburg activists in first-level grassroots organisation have since stopped relying on public meetings as ways of organising, mobilising and consolidating the organisations. Whilst at one level meetings are called to rouse the masses and to expose a specific evil in the community, other methods are used to consolidate organisations. These include amongst others:

- house meetings with sub-committees planning and chairing these meetings
- house-to-house campaigns where people are told about a specific problem and if they show concern are then invited to house meetings or asked to join a grassroots organisation
- meetings are called where representatives from various locations (in the case of Soweto) gather to share problems experienced in their areas and together they formulate strategies
- informal discussions are organised where trade unionists, students, ordinary people and prominent personalities are invited to discuss the situation in that locality and also the activities of community organisations in the area in question.
- teams of organisers go house-to-house with a set of questions relating to the problems of the residents. The information collected is then used to determine if a particular issue when discussed in a public meeting would elicit positive response and whether it is necessary to call a meeting on that issue. Here we are simply showing that there is work done in the African areas but

the pace is very slow. This position of organisations in the African areas is an indication that mobilisation around the PC [President's Council] proposals at the level of first-level grassroots organisations is a non-starter.

I am convinced that the formation of the UDF is correct both strategically and tactically. However, it is important that our approach at the level of the UDF be much more practical and realistic. We need to accept the fact that our organisations—first-level grassroots organisations which form the bone and flesh of the UDF—are at different stages of development. Unions, students, women's and community groups are still trying to organise, mobilise and educate in the particular constituencies. The strategic and tactical dynamics which prevail in each constituency vary greatly, so do the strategies and tactics of the different organisations. There is, therefore, no uniform strategy that they can adopt at any one time. With regard to the UDF we cannot expect them to take up the same issue under the banner of the UDF excepting those communities directly affected by the tri-cameral parliament, such as the Indian and coloured communities.

Some of the organisations might want to focus on the Koornhof Bills, the "Genocide Bill", whilst others may want to focus on the constitutional proposals. We need to allow them this flexibility both in terms of which aspects of UDF and in terms of the way in which they take up that aspect, and the definition that they give to it.

This is important because campaigns should actually constitute the next phase of organisation. They have actually got to pick up from where those first-level organisations leave off. In other words trade unions and community organisations [are involved in] mobilisation and education. But those struggles need to be taken further and those campaigns offer us a way of broadening the issue out, of defining it in a broader context, a more political context, and of consequently extending the process of organisation, mobilisation and education. But only if we make its starting point the end point of first-level organisation. We begin it at the level of national democratic struggle because if we do, there would not be too wide a gap between where our first-level organisations leave off and our campaigns begin.

In conclusion, chairperson and the house, let us express our hope that resolutions and deliberations of this historic conference will contribute extensively to the consolidation of the unity of the democratic movement in South Africa.

Document 35. "Peace in Our Day." Speech by Allan Boesak at national launch of the UDF, Mitchell's Plain, Cape Town, August 20, 1983 (abridged)

We have arrived at a historic moment. We have now brought together under the aegis of the United Democratic Front the broadest and most significant coalition of groups and organisations struggling against apartheid, racism, and injustice in South Africa since the early 1950s. We have been able to create a unity among freedom-loving persons that this country has not seen for many a year.

I am particularly happy to note that this meeting is not merely a gathering of isolated individuals. No, we represent organisations deeply rooted in the struggle for justice, deeply rooted in the heart of our people. Indeed, I believe we are standing at the birth of what could become the greatest and most significant popular movement in more than a quarter of a century.

We are here to say that the constitutional proposals of the government are inadequate, and that they do not express the will of the vast majority of South Africans. But more than that, we are here to say that what we are working for is one, undivided South Africa that shall belong to all its people: an open democracy from which no South African shall be excluded; a society in which the human dignity of all shall be respected. We are here to say that there are rights that are neither conferred by nor derived from the state; you have to go back beyond the dim mist of eternity to understand their origin: they are God-given. And we are not here to beg for those rights; we are here to claim them.

In a sense, the formation of the United Democratic Front both highlights and symbolizes the crisis that apartheid and its supporters have created for themselves. . . . After more than three decades of apartheid, the supporters of apartheid expected humble submission to the harsh rule of totalitarianism and racial supremacy. Instead, they are finding persons who are ready to fight this evil system at every level of society.

After more than twenty years of apartheid education, the supporters of apartheid expected to see totally brainwashed, perfect little *hotnotjies* and *kaffertjies* [little coloureds and Africans] who knew their place in the world. Instead they are finding the most politically conscious generation of young persons determined to struggle for a better future. . . . After the tragic happenings of the 1970s—the banning of our organisations and of so many of those who struggled for justice, the torture and death of so many in detention, the merciless killing of our children on the streets of the nation—the supporters of apartheid expected surrender. Instead, here we are at this historic occasion telling South Africa and the world: we are struggling for our human dignity and for the future of our children! We will never give up!

Those in power in this country have made the fundamental mistake of all totalitarian regimes that depend not on the loyalty of the people but on the power of the gun: they have not reckoned with the determination of a people to be free. Those in power depend on propaganda, deceit, and coercion. They have forgotten that no lie can live forever, and that the fear of the gun is always overcome by the longing for freedom. They have forgotten that you can kill the body but you cannot kill the spirit and the determination of a people. . . .

We must also ask the question: What is positive about the new constitutional proposals of the government? In order that there should be no misunderstanding, let me, as clearly and briefly as possible, repeat the reasons why we reject these proposals:

1) Racism, so embedded in South African society, is once again written into the constitution. All over the world, persons are beginning to recognize that racism is politically untenable, sociologically unsound, and morally unacceptable. In this country, however, the doctrine of racial supremacy, although condemned by most churches in South Africa as heresy and idolatry, is once again enshrined in the constitution as the basis upon which to build the further development of our society and the nurturing of human relationships.

2) All the basic laws, those that are the very pillars of apartheid, and without which the system cannot survive—laws concerning mixed marriages, groups areas, racial classification, separate and unequal education—remain untouched and unchanged by the new proposals.

3) The homelands policy, which is surely the most immoral and objectionable aspect of the apartheid policies of the government, forms the basis of the willful exclusion of 80 percent of our nation from the new political deal. Indeed, in the words of the President's Council, the homelands policy is to be regarded as "irreversible." So our black African brothers and sisters will be driven even further into the wilderness of homeland politics. Millions will have to find their political rights in the sham independence of those bush republics. Millions more will continue to lose their South African citizenship, and millions more will be removed forcibly from their homes into resettlement camps.

4) Clearly the oppression will continue; the brutal breakup of black family life will not end. The apartheid line is not at all abolished; it is simply shifted so as to include the so-called coloureds and Indians who are willing to cooperate with the government. . . .

To be sure, the new proposals will make apartheid less blatant in some ways. It will be modernised and streamlined, and in its new multicoloured cloak it will be less conspicuous and less offensive to some. Nonetheless, it will still be there. Apartheid, we must remember, is a thoroughly evil system, and, as such, it cannot be modified, modernised, or streamlined. It has to be eradicated irrevocably. We must continue, therefore, to struggle until that glorious day dawns when apartheid will exist no more.

To those who ask why we are not satisfied and when we shall be satisfied, we must say in clear, patient terms: we shall not be satisfied as long as injustice reigns supreme on the throne of our land. We shall not be satisfied as long as those who rule us are not inspired by justice, but dictated to by fear, greed, and racism. We shall not be satisfied until South Africa is once again one, undivided country, a democracy where there will be meaningful participation in a democratic process of government for all the people. We shall not be satisfied until the wealth and riches of this country are shared by all. We shall not be satisfied until justice rolls down like a waterfall and righteousness like a mighty stream.

There is another important question—namely, that of whites and blacks working together. This has been mentioned as a reason why the United Democratic Front has been so severely attacked by some and why some blacks have refused to cooperate with it. These persons tell us that whites cannot play a meaningful role in the struggle for justice in this country because they are always, by definition, the oppressor. Because the oppression of our people wears a white face, because the laws are made under a system created and maintained by whites, the blacks who attack the United Democratic Front say that there can be no cooperation between whites and blacks until all of this is changed.

To those who think this way I should like to say that I understand the way they feel. We have seen with our own eyes the brutalisation of our people at the hands of whites. We have seen police brutality. We have experienced the viciousness and the violence of apartheid. We have been trampled on for so long. For so long we have been dehumanised.

On the other hand we must remember that apartheid does not have the support of *all* whites. There are some who have struggled with us, who have gone to jail, who have been tortured and banned. There have been whites who died in the struggle for justice. We, therefore, must not allow our anger over apartheid to become the basis for blind hatred of *all* whites. Let us not build our struggle upon hatred; let us not hope for revenge. Let us, even now, seek to lay the foundations for reconciliation between whites and blacks in this country by working together, praying together, struggling together for justice.

The nature and the quality of our struggle for liberation cannot be determined by one's skin colour but rather by one's commitment to justice, peace, and human liberation. In the final analysis, judgment will be made not in terms of whiteness or blackness, whatever the ideological content of those words may be today, but in terms of the persistent faithfulness to which we are called in this struggle.

The very fact that we are talking about the constitutional proposals reveals already the paradox in this argument. The government has been pushing ahead with these proposals precisely because they have been supported and accepted by some persons from the black community who think that the short-term economic gains and the semblance of political power are more important than the total liberation of all South Africans. So our struggle is not only against the white government and its plans, but also against those in the black community who through their collaboration give credibility to these plans. . . .

We are doing what we are doing, *not* because we are white or black, but because what we are doing is right. We shall continue so to do until justice and peace embrace, and South Africa becomes the nation it is meant to be.

In the meantime brothers and sisters, let me, as I have done before, remind you of three little words that I think we ought to hold onto as we continue the struggle. And these are three little words that express so eloquently our seriousness in the struggle. You do not need to have a vast vocabulary to understand them. You do not need a philosophical [perspective] to grasp them. They are just three little words and the first word is the word "ALL." We mean all of our rights. Not just some rights, we want not just a few token handouts here and there that the government sees fit to give. We want all of our rights. We want all of South Africa's people to have their rights, not just a selected few, not just a few so-called coloureds and Indians, after they have been made honorary Whites.

We want all of our rights for all South Africa's people including those whose citizenship has already been shipped away by this government.

The second word is the word "HERE." We want all of our rights and we want them here in a united and undivided South Africa. I can hear the government saying that some of us must find our rights with Mr. Mphephu and Mr. Matanzima and Mr. Mangope in the homelands. And there was a time when we could hear voices telling us "You cannot be free in South Africa, so emigrate to Canada and the United States and England and Australia." But in this country we are saying something else now. We are saying that we want our rights in this country which is the country of our birth, and we do not want them in the impoverished homelands, we do not want them in our separate little group areas, we want them here in this land which one day we shall once again call our own.

The third word is the word "NOW." We want all of our rights and we want them here and we want them now.

We have been waiting for too long. We have been struggling for too long and now I hear people admonishing us saying, "You are in too much of a hurry; can't you see that the government is making progress, there are changes on the way?" And they are saying that we must be a little patient and that we must cool off. But I fear that if we keep on cooling off we may end up in a deep freeze. The world knows that we have been patient. We have waited for many years. We have pleaded, we have tried, we have petitioned for so long, we have been jailed and exiled and killed for so long now. But we are saying today: "Now is the time!"

And as we struggle let us remember that change does not roll in on the wheels of inevitability. It comes through the tireless efforts and hard work of those who are willing to take the risk of fighting for freedom, democracy and human dignity.

As we struggle on, let us continue to sing that wonderful hymn of freedom: *Nkosi Sikilel' iAfrika* [God Bless Africa]! I know that today we are singing that hymn with tears in our eyes. We are singing it while we are bowed down by the weight of oppression and battered by the winds of injustice. We are singing it while our elderly languish in resettlement camps, and our children are dying of hunger in the "homelands." We are singing it now while we suffer under the brutality of apartheid, and while the blood of our children is calling to God from the streets of our nation.

We must, however, work for the day when we shall sing it as *free* black South Africans! We shall sing it on that day when our children will no longer be judged by the colour of their skin but by the humanness of their character. We shall sing it on that day when even here in this country, in Johannesburg and Cape Town, in Port Elizabeth and Durban, the sanctity of marriage and family life will be respected, and no law will sunder what God has joined together. We shall sing it on that day when in this rich land no child will die of hunger and no infant will die an untimely death; when our elderly will close their eyes in peace, and the wrinkled stomachs of our children will be filled with food just as their lives will be filled with meaning. We shall sing it when here, in South Africa, whites and blacks will have learned to love one another and work together in building a truly good and beautiful land.

With this faith we shall be able to give justice and peace their rightful place on the throne of our land. With this faith, we shall be able to see beyond the darkness of our present into the bright and glittering daylight of our future. With this faith we shall be able to speed the day when all South African children will embrace each other and sing with new meaning:

>God bless Africa!
>Guide her rulers!
>Bless her children!
>Give her peace!
>O, give her peace!

DOCUMENT 36. "Declaration of the United Democratic Front." August 20, 1983

We, the freedom loving people of South Africa, say with one voice to the whole world that we
- cherish the vision of a united, democratic South Africa based on the will of the people,
- will strive for the unity of all people through united action against the evils of apartheid, economic and all other forms of exploitation.

And, in our march to a free and just South Africa, we are guided by these noble ideals
- we stand for the creation of a true democracy in which all South Africans will participate in the government of our country;
- we stand for a single non-racial, unfragmented South Africa. A South Africa free of bantustans and Group Areas;
- we say, all forms of oppression and exploitation must end.

In accordance with these noble ideals, and on the 20th day of August 1983 at Rocklands Civic Centre, Mitchell's Plain, we join hands as trade union, community, women's, students', religious, sporting and other organisations to say no to Apartheid.

We say NO to the Republic of South Africa Constitution Bill—a bill which will create yet another undemocratic constitution in the country of our birth;
We say NO to the Koornhof Bills which will deprive more and more African people of their birthright;
We say YES to the birth of the United Democratic Front on this historic day;

We know that
- this government is determined to break the unity of our people; that our people will face greater hardships, that our people living in racially segregated and relocated areas will be cut off from the wealth they produce in the cities. That rents and other basic charges will increase. And, that our living standards will fall;
- that working people will be divided, race from race; urban from rural, employed from unemployed, men from women. Low wages, poor working conditions, attacks on our trade unions will continue;
- students will continue to suffer under unequal education, created to supply a reservoir of cheap labour. Ethnic control and unequal facilities will remain. Apartheid will still be felt in our classrooms;
- the religious and cultural life of our people will be harmed. The sins of apartheid will continue to be stamped on the culture and religions of our people;
- the oppression and exploitation of women will continue. Women will suffer greater hardships under the new pass laws. Women will be divided from their children and families. Poverty and malnutrition will continue to disrupt family life. The brunt of apartheid will still be carried by our families;
- non-racial sport will suffer. There will be less money for the building of sports facilities. And forced separation will deal non-racial sport a further blow. We know that apartheid will continue;
- that white domination and exploitation will continue; that forced removals, the Group Areas Act and the Bantustans will remain.

We know that there will not be an end to the unequal distribution of the land, wealth and resources of the country. That the migratory labour system will live on to destroy family life.

We know that the government will always use false leaders to become its junior partners and to control us. Our lives will still be filled with fears of harassment, bannings, detentions and death. Mindful of the fact that the new Constitutional proposals and Koornhof measures will further entrench apartheid and white domination,

We commit ourselves to uniting all our people wherever they may be in the cities and countryside, the factories and mines, schools, colleges and universities, housing and sports fields, churches, mosques and temples, to fight for our freedom.

We therefore resolve to stand shoulder to shoulder in our common struggle and commit ourselves to *work together to*
- organise and mobilise all community, worker, student, women, religious, sporting and other organisations under the banner of the United Democratic Front;
- consult our people regularly and honestly and bravely and strive to represent their views and aspirations;
- educate all about the coming dangers and the need for unity;
- build and strengthen all organisations of the people;

Figure 17. Policeman photographs demonstrators at a rally of the Natal Indian Congress and the UDF protesting the proposed tricameral parliament, Durban City Hall, November 1983. *Paul Weinberg/South Photographs/africanpictures.net*

- unite in action against these Bills and other day-to-day problems affecting our people.

And now therefore
    We pledge to come together in the United Democratic Front and fight side by side against the Government's constitutional proposals and the Koornhof bills.

DOCUMENT 37. "Support the Cape Action League." *Worker-Tenant* newssheet, Cape Town, August 1983

Since the government announced its New Constitution, there have been three responses to these proposals from the ranks of the exploited and oppressed. These responses reflect the interests of various classes.
- *The Labour Party*—representing the upper sections of the Middle class, have decided to accept the New constitution. They can no longer wait for a bigger stake in the system of exploitation and oppression. They side openly with the government against the working class.

WORKERS MUST CRUSH THE SELL-OUT LABOUR PARTY AND THE MANAGEMENT COMMITTEES THROUGH WHICH THEY WORK WITH THE GOVERNMENT!
- *UDF*—representing the radical sections of the Middle class. They reject the New Constitution but their rallying call is "Let us build unity and oppose

apartheid." They want apartheid out of the way but say very little about exploitation. They form the leadership of workers' organisations and their main aim is to win the support of workers for their Middle class demands.

- *CAPE ACTION LEAGUE* (CAL) represents the interests of the *working class*. They say that *workers* must lead the struggle against exploitation and oppression. They say that the only way workers can do so is by building *independent workers organisations* free from the influence of the bosses, the state and the Middle class!

BBSK [Bokmakierie, Bridgetown, Silvertown, and Kewtown Action Committee], Manenberg and Parkwood actively support the Cape Action League. We believe that by strengthening CAL we can both defend and further the interests of all workers!

REMOVAL OF APARTHEID NOT ENOUGH—EXPLOITATION MUST BE ABOLISHED

UDF puts the struggle against apartheid before the struggle of workers against exploitation. If apartheid is removed but exploitation remains, the lot of workers will not be much better. For as long as exploitation continues—workers earning low wages and living in miserable conditions—there can be no freedom. WORKERS MUST HAVE DIRECT CONTROL OVER THE RUNNING OF ALL ASPECTS OF THEIR LIVES.

UDF says the people must govern.

CAHAC [Cape Areas Housing Action Committee] *Speaks* says, "We, the people, want a country in which we can share in the wealth". We all produce riches and wealth. "Who is the people"? The bosses, the workers or the Middle class? The Middle class uses "people" to mean the working class led by this Middle class. The Middle class hides behind this term "the people" so that *they* can get a share in the wealth—so that *they* can govern!

BUILD A STRONG WORKERS' UNITED FRONT

UDF is a Peoples Front. It includes workers organisations and organisations such as the Traders Association and NUSAS whose historical tradition and class position drive them to seek middle class compromises with the bosses and the state. The People's Front betrays the interests of workers into the hands of the bosses.

UDF is led by the radical Middle class. The Middle class finds itself between the bosses and the workers. They either side with the bosses or the workers. In struggle they will tend to choose the middle road—seeking compromises and piecemeal solutions. Where they occupy leadership positions in workers' organisations they often betray the interests of the working class in order to look after their own.

CAL feels that workers must win the support of the lower sections of the middle class. But we can only do this once we have built independent working class organisations—once we clear our organisations of middle class traits. *Workers must rid their organisations of the middle class leadership which betrays their interests!*

CAL CALLS FOR A UNITED FRONT OF WORKERS ORGANISATIONS—BY WORKERS THEMSELVES!

Only in this way can we consistently further the struggle of workers! And guard against our struggle being betrayed by the middle class and hijacked by the bosses!

WHO WILL DRAW UP A NEW CONSTITUTION?

UDF demands that a NATIONAL CONVENTION is convened—which is called by the existing government and will consist of representatives of all "Racial/National" groups who will sit down together and bargain a new constitution. Only after this will elections be held. In this way the middle class and the bosses can form an alliance against the workers. CAL demands a CONSTITUENT ASSEMBLY which is democratically elected on the basis of one person, one vote. The Constituent Assembly is not called by the government but by workers themselves. The constituent Assembly will then draw up the New Constitution. In this way workers can have a decisive say in how South Africa is to be governed.

WORKERS UNITE TO:-
- SUPPORT AND STRENGTHEN CAPE ACTION LEAGUE!
- REJECT THE PEOPLES FRONT - UDF.
- RID UDF OF ITS MIDDLE CLASS LEADERSHIP, SO THAT WORKERS' ORGANISATIONS IN UDF CAN FORM PART OF A *WORKERS UNITED FRONT*.

WORKERS DEMAND: A DEMOCRATICALLY ELECTED CONSTITUENT ASSEMBLY.
REJECT:
- ETHNIC PRESIDENT'S COUNCIL PROPOSALS.
- MIDDLE CLASS NATIONAL CONVENTION.

UDF LAUNCHING

This weekend will attract thousands of people from all over the country to Mitchell's Plain, to the national launching of the UDF. It will be a historic occasion. Yet another betrayal of the interests of the exploited and oppressed. Yet another setback in their struggle.

Despite all the supporting press coverage, banners, posters and stickers, a ground-swell of opposition is growing. The WCYL [Western Cape Youth League] is part of this trend which sees the UDF for what it is—a massive fraud.

No doubt we will be accused of breaking unity. After all, the banners scream "Apartheid divides...UDF unites." To this reply that we too stand for unity, but before we unite we must divide, we must distinguish between those *genuinely* fighting in the interests of the exploited and oppressed and those against this.

In a society such as ours the major conflict to which all others must be subordinated is that between the ruling class and the working class. Whereas the working class slaves to earn measly wages which prevent it from living a socially meaningful existence, the bosses who pay them reap the profits. It is in this context that Apartheid divides the oppressed workers into a number of racial groups to bolster their exploitation by paying some little and others even less. In so doing it cleverly ensures that the workers fight amongst one another for the measly scraps dished out to them and do not fight against their common enemy, the bosses. To resolutely fight against the ruling class all organisations of the [workers must unite.]

Document 38. Trade union statement condemning Ciskei government ban on SAAWU, September 1983

African Food and Canning Workers Union
Black and Allied Workers Union
Commercial Catering and Allied Workers Union of South Africa
Cape Town Municipal Workers Association
Council of Unions of South Africa
Food and Canning Workers Union
Federation of South African Trade Unions
General Workers Union
Motor Assemblies and Component Workers Union of South Africa
Media Workers Association of South Africa
Orange Vaal General Workers Union

We as trade unions deplore in the strongest terms the banning of the South African Allied Workers Union by the so-called authorities. We reject utterly the explanation by the "Ciskei Government" that SAAWU engages in activities which endanger "National or Public Safety." The facts are that the people of Mdantsane are boycotting buses because the bus company partly owned by the "Ciskei Government" is profiteering at their expense. Since the "Ciskei Government" tried to force people onto the buses by beating and shooting innocent people, the people are more determined than ever to continue the boycott. On several occasions both the South African and so-called Ciskeian authorities have tried to blame the trade unions for the boycott. Recently they detained officials of SAAWU, GWU and AFCWU. Now they want to make the whole of SAAWU the scapegoat, however the boycott continues. This banning is the most serious attack on the trade union movement since the banning of union leaders in 1976. Never before has a workers' organisation itself been declared illegal. Neither the SA government nor employers should think they can distance themselves from these actions. The complicity of the South African government is clearly shown by the SAP [SA Police] arresting our officials and handing them over to the Ciskei. Actions of employers such as Pick and Pay who have entered into an agreement with the "Ciskei Government" have greatly angered people. There can be no talk of reform in the labour laws and the constitution while worker organisations are suppressed. We as trade unions will stand by SAAWU and will discuss what form of action to take to prevent this banning from taking effect.

DOCUMENT 39. *"Massacre at Ngoye."* **AZASM flyer, October 1983**

That blood-thirsty, collaborationist ethnic chief has done it again—this time at the University of Zululand.

Last Saturday's cowardly and barbaric attack on unarmed students at Ngoye should be condemned by all those who profess to uphold the principles of academic freedom—and DEMOCRACY.

BACKGROUND

For quite some time now that ethnic-based organisation Inkatha has, by force and intimidation, suppressed any opposition to Gatsha [Buthelezi] at Ngoye.

A democratic student organisation had to either operate underground or face the wrath of kierie [club]-wielding thugs on campus, or operate clandestinely.

As Chancellor the "Chief" feels he has got every right to be on campus, at anytime. He could even bring his whole ill-trained, blood-thirsty and undisciplined army with him if he feels like it. "Whether students are preparing for exams or not, I GATSHA, will hold a rally on Campus."

Students at Ngoye had on several occasions demonstrated their intolerance for a supporter and defender of the system.

BUILD-UP

On August 12 a meeting that was to have been addressed by Inkatha Secretary-General, Oscar Dhlomo, was disrupted by angry students.

MASSACRE

Last Saturday while Ngoye students were within their right protesting against the disturbing and distracting presence of a collaborationist Zulu impi [warrior brigade] on their campus 17 bus loads of battle song chanting thugs, including women, attacked unarmed and defenceless students, using an array of weapons including kieries, spears, sticks, and iron rods.

The fact that a lecturer at that university was leading the onslaught against the students is deplorable to say the least. Yet that bespectacled Zulu chief blames instigators for opposition against his sell-out tactics. That is a smokescreen, Chief.

WE SAY

This cowardly, barbaric and unprovoked attack by that remote-controlled, ill-disciplined barbaric and blood-thirsty ethnic impi has no place in any society.

While the circumstances are presently not conducive for Ngoye students to prepare themselves both mentally and physically for the exams, we call for courage and calm in the face of this unprovoked and unwarranted provocation.

We pledge solidarity with the students of Ngoye.

Our heartfelt sympathy and condolences to the friends and families of the students who lost life and limb in this barbaric attack.

We wish those in hospital a speedy recovery.

We call upon all black people to observe the period starting from the fourth (4th) to the seventh (7th) November as a period of mourning.

Should we allow this oppressor to be on [the] rampage? A THOUSAND TIMES NO!!!

DOWN WITH PUPPETS: FORWARD TO A FREE, DEMOCRATIC, ANTI-RACIST WORKER REPUBLIC OF AZANIA.

Document 40. "Don't Vote for Apartheid!" UDF flyer in Tswana and English, November 1983

Le seka la tlhopa (boutela) APARTHEID
LE SEKA LA BOUTELA MAKGOTLA A GA KOORNHOF

Ke eng se se dirwang ke mmuso?
O dira melao e meswa. Mmuso o bitsa mongwe wa melao e meswa e Molao wa Bantsho wa Puso ya Selegae (Black Local Authorities Act). Ba re bolelela gore molao o o tla re naya tetla ya go bua ka mokgwa oo morafe wa rona o buswang ka teng.

Mmuso o re:
- Makgotla a maswa a teropo a tla tsaya manno a makgotla a merafe (Community Councils.)
- Makgotla a maswa jaanong a tla dira ditiro dingwe tsa Lekgotla la Tsamaiso—jaaka go thuba mekgoro le go atisa madi tshelete ya khiro kgotsa rente.
- Gore ba kgone go dira tiro e, makgotla a a tla tshwanela go nna le tshelete ya one.
- Re tshwanetse go boutela batho go tsena mo makgotleng a.

Mme jaanong molao wa puso ya selegae o bolela eng?
- Makgotla a tla nna ka fa tlase ga Koornhof mme ga a kitla a nna le thata.
- A tshwana le makgotla a merafe, mme fela a na le leina le leswa.
- Ba ka se kgone go rarabolola mathata a rona a go nna le mantlo, mesele e e thibaneng, dirente tse di kwa godimo mathata a thoro (transport).
- Makgotla a a tla bona tshelete mo go rona—ka go oketsa rente le go re fa ditshupamolato (accounts) tsa metsi le dipone tse di kwa godimo.
- Makgotla a a tla thusa fela ka go thatafatsa kgethololo (apartheid).

RE GANANA LE KGETHOLOLO!
GA RE KITLA RE BOUTELA MAKGOTLA A MASWA A!
GO BOUTELA MAKGOTLA A GO TSHWANA LE GO BOUTELA KGETHOLOLO!

E tlhagisitswe ke United Democratic Front (TVL Region). The United Democratic Front e na le dithulaganyo tse di 400 mo tirong ya yona ya go nna kgatlanong le dipolane tse dintshwa tsa mmuso.

EMANG UDF MO NOKENG KA LENANEO LA YONE LA TIRO KGATLANONG LE DIPOLANE TSE DINTSHWA TSA MMUSO

[Reverse side:]

DON'T VOTE FOR KOORNHOF'S COUNCILS

What is the Government doing?
It is making new plans. The government calls one of these new plans the Black Local Authorities Act. They tell us that this law will give us a say in how our community is run.
The government says:
- A new town council will take the place of every community council.
- The new council will now do some of the Administration Board's work—like breaking down shacks and increasing rents.
- To do this work the council must get its own money. They will get it from us.

But what does the Local Authorities Act mean?
- The council will be under Koornhof and will have no power.
- They are the same as the community councils but only have a new name.
- They cannot solve our housing problems, blocked drains, high rents or transport problems.
- The councils will get their money from us, by putting the rents up, giving us high water and light accounts and even raising dog tax.
- The councils will only help make Apartheid strong.

WE SAY NO TO APARTHEID!
WE WILL NOT VOTE FOR THESE NEW COUNCILS!
A VOTE FOR THE COUNCIL IS A VOTE FOR APARTHEID!

Issued by the United Democratic Front (Transvaal Region). The United Democratic Front has 400 organisations in opposing the government's new plans. Support the UDF's programme of action against the government's new plans.

Document 41. "Towards a Just Peace in Our Land." End Conscription Campaign flyer, Durban, 1983

A Declaration to End Conscription
We live in an unjust society where basic human rights are denied to the majority of the people.

We live in an unequal society where the land and wealth are owned by the minority.

We live in a society in a state of civil war, where brother is called on to fight brother.

We call for an end to conscription.
Young men are conscripted to maintain the illegal occupation of Namibia, and to wage unjust war against foreign countries.

Young men are conscripted to assist in the implementation and defence of apartheid policies.

Young men who refuse to serve are faced with the choice of a life of exile or a possible six years in prison.

We call for an end to conscription.
We believe that the financial cost of the war increases the poverty of our country, and that money should rather be used in the interests of peace.

We believe that the extension of conscription to Coloured and Indian youth will increase conflict and further divide our country.

WE BELIEVE THAT IT IS THE MORAL RIGHT OF SOUTH AFRICANS TO EXERCISE FREEDOM OF CONSCIENCE AND TO CHOOSE NOT TO SERVE IN THE SADF [SA Defence Force].

WE CALL FOR AN END TO CONSCRIPTION
WE CALL FOR A JUST PEACE IN OUR LAND

Document 42. "A Brief History of the Durban Housing Action Committee (DHAC) and the Joint Rent Action Committee (JORAC)." Pamphlet, 1983? (abridged)

INTRODUCTION
All human beings require certain basic things in order to live. These are: food to eat; housing for shelter, and clothes for comfort. If any of these essentials is not available, life becomes intolerable and survival critical. That, unfortunately, is the reality of the majority in our country. Being poor means having less to eat, little to wear and places to live which are inadequate, unhealthy and uncomfortable. This despite the fact that they provide the labour which contributes directly to the wealth of the country. It therefore becomes necessary for people to struggle for a share in what is rightfully theirs. . . .

FORMATION OF THE DURBAN HOUSING ACTION COMMITTEE

The late 1970's saw the re-emergence of community struggles around high rents, high transport costs, housing problems and bad living conditions. In many of the areas civic organisations were formed to take up these struggles. Many areas also saw the resurgence of activity by community organisations that had been in existence for some time. The most significant feature of these organisations was that they were rooted in the communities that they represented and worked as a whole with their communities.

By 1980, many of these organisations and communities had been through many campaigns and had fought many struggles. But, in the context of Durban, they were all organisations in different parts of Durban waging independent struggles. With the announcement of rent increases in January 1980 by the Durban City Council for all townships it controlled—the time had come for all these organisations to come together and take united action against a common problem.

It was the Natal Indian Congress (NIC) that took the initiative to bring the various communities together. On the 29th of March 1980 the NIC convened a meeting to discuss the rental increases, rates [property taxes] and housing problems. This resulted in the formation of the Durban Housing Action Committee—made up of over twenty organisations from seven different parts of Durban. The meeting elected Mr D.K. Singh as the Chairman and Mr Virgil Bonhomme and Mr Pravin Gordhan as joint secretaries.

The areas represented on DHAC include: Chatsworth, Newlands East, Phoenix, Merebank, Cato Manor, Asherville and Sydenham Heights.

THE RENT CAMPAIGN 1980-1981

The issue that warranted DHAC's immediate attention, once it was formed, was the proposed rental increases in Durban's municipal housing schemes. Although the struggles against high rentals reached their most intense phase in 1980, the Phoenix, Newlands East and Sydenham Heights communities had been protesting against high rentals from the very inception of these housing schemes. The responses if any from the Community Development and the Durban City Council to these protests were always meaningless and indicated their non-cooperation and uncaring attitude to problems faced by the Black communities.

15% increase: This attitude of the authorities led them to decide in January 1980 that the City Council was not prepared to pay for the losses incurred in running the housing schemes, from the rates fund. "To recover these losses of about R1.4 million, the rents must go up." "The tenants must pay." "The ratepayer is not prepared to subsidise the tenant." This decision affected all tenants Black and White and in the Black communities this initiated the first stage of linking up of communities, which was going to result in shattering the arrogance and confidence of the authorities.

Communities respond: DHAC's strength is and has always been the support it receives from the communities and it is with this backing that the increases were rejected. City Council had to recognise DHAC as the representatives of the people—and was also forced to postpone the increases.

Government changes policy: In response to country-wide resistance to high rentals the Department of Community Development formulated a new rent structure. This was to be implemented from the 1st October and the Durban City Council chose this time to re-introduce their increases.

October Boycotts: Negotiations and discussions with the authorities seemed to make no impact on them, and the community organisations responded by mobilising their people for confrontation with the Council. 90% of the residents of Phoenix, Newlands East and Sydenham Heights withheld their rents asking for a positive response to their demands.

The Demands: The demands of the people were simple: (i) they wanted the Council to stop the increases (ii) government to subsidise housing so that rents could be brought down to a level that people could afford.

Council Response: During negotiations DHAC demanded an immediate moratorium on the increases of four months, while negotiations took place. In the face of the overwhelming effective boycott of rentals the Council conceded a four month moratorium and created a Working Committee to investigate housing problems.

March Boycott: The four months moratorium and the Working Committee meetings in that period brought no substantial relief to tenants. The Council was extremely slow deliberately in supplying meaningful reduction of rentals.

The Newlands East Residents Association, Phoenix Rent Action Committee [PRAC] and the Sydenham Heights Tenants Association, in consultation with residents of the respective areas decided to launch a second boycott in view of the totally inadequate response of both the Durban City Council and the Department of Community Development to the residents' demand and the massive increase in rates.

Except for a meeting between PRAC and the Department of Internal Affairs there had been no positive response from the authorities.

Instead the Council began to intimidate residents by cutting off electricity of a few tenants. Recognising the hardships that would be caused to residents if more of them had their electricity cut off, organisations decided to call off the boycott. To show the extent of support for DHAC, the demands made by the residents, the rejection of the Council and the LACs [Local Affairs Committees], the people of Newlands East, Phoenix and Sydenham Heights switched their lights off at 8 p.m. on l0th April 1981, for two hours. "Candle Light Night" was a massive success—over 95% of all tenants had switched their lights off. . . .

The fundamental change required to bring really substantial relief to tenants will require greater unity of all people, affected or unaffected, and more effective means of forcing the authorities to recognise the problem and provide the relief required. . . .

A BRIEF HISTORY OF THE JOINT RENT ACTION COMMITTEE (JORAC). . . .

The struggle for low rents in townships under PNAB [Port Natal Administration Board] is a struggle for survival for the majority of residents and hostel inmates in these areas.

Should the rents go up many will have little left from their low wages many earn for their families and dependents. Unemployment, low wages, retrenchment and short time made worse by the ever increasing price of basic foodstuffs, education and clothing have left many people desperate.

Another source of tension is the shortage of houses which is responsible for many inconveniences. The situation is made worse by the neglect of houses that are there and the insensitive demolition of the people's alternative housing such as shacks.

RENT INCREASES FOR MAY 1983

It is in this atmosphere that the authorities, without proper consultation, sought to increase rentals by between 25 and 72 percent.

Some areas affected by the rent increases, such as Lamontville, Klaarwater and Chesterville, had just been hit by a bus fare increase. When, through a concerted effort expressed by the Joint Commuters Committee [JCC], the residents could not stop the bus fare increases, many chose to walk rather than pay.

However the rent increases presented a different story. Residents saw themselves evicted from their homes for failing to pay increased rents. Others saw their already diminished standard of living being worsened. Many also saw the increases as a trick to drive them out of towns and thus losing their urban rights.

FAILURE OF THE COMMUNITY COUNCILS TO RESPOND TO THE RENT INCREASES

In the eyes of the residents the Community Councils and Advisory Boards had failed them at a critical time. Some councillors and Board Members had hardly called meetings to hear people's views. These Councillors who tried anything were simply brushed aside and told that the issue is nonnegotiable. In fact in a letter to a daily newspaper the PNAB Chief Director said Councillors and Advisory Board members had accepted the rent increases because they understood the PNAB's bankruptcy.

BACKGROUND TO COMMUNITIES

KLAARWATER

In Klaarwater the people had already formed a Residents Association controlled by the residents themselves. It is this body which took up the rents issue and had already sent two petitions and several protest letters to [Minister of Co-operation and Development] Dr. Piet Koornhof and to PNAB. Klaarwater Residents Association (KLARA) was also investigating the possibility of legal action against PNAB.

HAMBANATI

Hambanati Residents Association, also independent, had already written several protest letters to Koornhof and PNAB. The women's wing of the Association had also marched to the Township Office demanding the expulsion of a clerk whom they accused of improper conduct. Several meetings had also been held to discuss the rent issue and people resolved not to pay the increases.

LAMONTVILLE

In Lamontville, residents also realising the ineffectiveness of Community Councillors elected a Rent Action Committee. The residents also felt they were not going to pay the increases. The Lamontville Rent Action Committee, working with Halayo—a youth organisation—launched a petition seeking Koornhof's intervention and stopping of increases.

SHAKAVILLE

Shakaville has the most desperate residents in all the PNAB areas. Stanger has the fewest job opportunities and the jobs that residents have are the lowest paying. The conditions of maintenance in the area are the worst. People still use the bucket system [for removal of human feces]. There are few communal taps in the streets for residents. There's no créche [day-care center]. Some houses are threatening to fall apart. Residents there are not yet organised into an independent structure. They are still represented by an Advisory Board. During *UKUSA's* [Durban alternative newspaper's] visit there people simply said "asinalutho" [we have nothing].

HOSTELS

Also around the hostels, especially Glebelands, residents were refused permission to hold meetings. But they rallied around and collected money for the legal action they had decided upon. They also elected an independent committee.

FORMATION OF THE JOINT RENT ACTION COMMITTEE

Following rent protest meetings held in Lamontville and in Hambanati, the Lamontville Rent Action Committee met with the Hambanati Residents Association on the 8 April 1983 at the Ecumenical Centre Trust where the Joint Rent Action Committee was launched.

The formation of JORAC followed a realisation by these bodies that joint action would be the best way to struggle against the tariff increases intended for May 1. . . .

THE RENT CAMPAIGN

i. The Inconsiderate PNAB: PNAB was adamant that there was going to be no discussion as to whether rents go up or not. PNAB was saying that it was the job of Community Councillors and Advisory Board members to persuade people to pay increases in rentals because, according to PNAB, the Community Councillors and Advisory Board members were covering the townships.

ii. The Campaign: Because of the urgency of the situation, JORAC's immediate task was to seek Koornhof's intervention. A memorandum summing up people's main grievances and demands was posted to the Minister of Co-operation and Development. Copies of this memo plus protest letters were sent to PNAB as well.

In order to enlist support for the campaign JORAC also sent copies of the memorandum plus letters asking for support to organisations such as DHAC, Diakonia, Black Sash and others. Other such memorandums and letters were sent to eight opposition party MP's asking them to raise it in Parliament, which they did.

The community's big turnout at meetings called by JORAC showed clearly who they supported. JORAC also took a decision to take the matter to court.

iii. The Killing of Msizi Dube: It was after this decision was taken later that night, after the meeting [on April 25, 1983], that one of the founder members of JORAC from Lamontville, Msizi H. Dube, was assassinated.

This killing affected the campaign dramatically. Dube was one of the most outspoken opponents of the increases and consistent critic of the PNAB and community councillors although he was a Councillor himself. His killing was considered by residents as an attempt to thwart their opposition to the increases. The immediate reaction of the Lamontville Community after the killing was to burn down a D.T.M.B. bus, [and] all the Beer Halls including the Bottle Store. The Township Office itself became a target of repeated stoning.

The chairperson of the Ningizimu Community Council was particularly the subject of a sustained stoning and burning attack. He finally left the township. His ward committee members who allegedly helped him to keep angry attackers at bay with bullets also had their houses burned down. They too finally left the township. In Chesterville as well as in Klaarwater the Township Offices and bottle stores were stoned and set alight.

iv. Police Action: Police went into the areas and particularly in Lamontville where they used teargas and rubber bullets among other things in an attempt to protect those who were being attacked because of their suspected involvement in the chairperson's protection and in the Dube killing.

One Bekani Manganyela was killed during the attack on the Chairperson's house, allegedly shot by the police in Chesterville while outside his home. Police denied they shot him. The funerals were some of the biggest of their kind in Durban. People carried banners reading "Forward JORAC and JCC", "Koornhof stop the increases".

v. JORAC Meets Koornhof: These developments plus the pressure of support enlisted by JORAC for the campaign finally brought Koornhof to Durban to discuss the matter with JORAC.

The meeting ended with Koornhof only agreeing to suspend the rent increases until August 1. Koornhof and PNAB also agreed to make money immediately available for maintenance. The police who were present at the meeting also promised to bring Dube's killers to book as soon as possible.

JORAC also undertook to encourage people to attend meetings called by PNAB.

vi. Community's Response to Postponement of Increases: But following a number of report back meetings in the areas affected residents unanimously rejected increases. The residents demanded the scrapping of increases. The money for maintenance was described as hopelessly inadequate.

Even at a few meetings that have been held and addressed by PNAB Officials, the response has been the same—"Asinamali" [we have no money] and also that "we don't see what we would be paying for".

vii. No Response from PNAB and DC&D: PNAB and the Dept. of Co-operation and Development has, however, not responded to the community's call to scrap increases.

Document 43. Report to UDF national executive committee from Cradock Residents Association, January 1984

The Cradock Residents Association (CRADORA) exploded onto the civic scene with a big bang on the 4 October 1983. The actual formation of Cradora was the culmination of a relentless struggle by the residents of the township, which started when a meeting was called on the 25 August 1983 to protest the high rentals in the township.

The struggle initially manifested itself as a loose formation of people who were brought together by a common problem, the rent problem. Under the determined and resolute leadership of an interim committee, the unfolding of the struggle went beyond the confines of a specific problem. The particular civic issues were seen to be interwoven with, in fact to be emanating from the general problem of exploitation in our country.

The phenomenal growth of Cradora went far beyond the expectations of those who oppose people's struggles. Clearly, the enemy underestimated the stamina of the residents. When all indications were that the organisation was gathering strength from day to day, the establishment unleashed an all-out campaign to destroy it. The leadership, particularly the chairman, comrade [Matthew] Goniwe, became the targets of the security police. Activists received visits at their homes and places of employment. Many people reported the attempts of the security police to use them as informers. But harassment by the security police only served to give the organisation credibility, most particularly in the eyes of the youth.

When harassment by the security police did not achieve the required results, thousands of pamphlets were strewn all over the township on two different occasions. Even this venture was counter-productive. The anonymous smear pamphlets served to unite the residents against a common enemy. The authors of the smear pamphlets inadvertently helped to advertise the movement.

The growth of the movement necessitated the decentralisation of meetings to various church halls. The security police responded by approaching the church authorities of the churches in question. Consequently, one church after another denied us use of their halls. The minister of the only church open to us, the Church of Ascension, tried to deny us the hall and escape with his dignity unscathed. Where all along we were allowed to use the church gratis, he demanded that we pay R2 a day retrospectively to our first meeting.

As if this was not enough, we were subsequently told that the Church Council, which boasts a security policeman and a councillor in its membership, had decided that we will never use the hall again until we pay R15 a night and R7,50 a day retrospectively to our first meeting. We were told we owe R165 [$115]. The person responsible for the hall, an active member of Cradora and a member of the Church Council, was kicked out of his duty for maintaining that there was absolutely no reason why we should be expected to pay for the hall.

On the 29 November 1983 our chairman, comrade Goniwe, who was at the time acting principal of Sam Xhallie Secondary School, received a letter from the circuit office at Graaff Reinet transferring him to Nqweba High School at Graaff Reinet as acting head of Department, with effect from the 1st January 1984. The news of the transfer was received with great shock by the community. Meetings were held to discuss the transfer. Letters were written and deputations led to various departmental authorities.

The situation is so emotion-charged, the youth association, Cradoya, has resolved to call for a school boycott if all attempts to reason with those responsible fail. Presently, a combined effort is being made by Cradora and Cradoya to circulate a petition which will be sent to the department.

There is only one aim in transferring comrade Goniwe, to wit, to frustrate the growth of Cradora. Since all other means exploded in the face of the enemy, the transfer of comrade Goniwe, who the enemy sees as the power behind the awakening in Cradock, was the only option left. Comrade Goniwe has, correctly, decided to defy the transfer. He didn't report for duty on the opening. In fact, he has decided to stay in Cradock and continue to organise the people. This is another victory for the people. Comrade Goniwe has effectively demonstrated the need to subordinate personal aggrandizement to national issues.

From last Friday, the 13 January, the security police embarked on another form of harassment and intimidation. On that Friday, the organiser of Cradora, comrade [Mbulelo] Goniwe (Jnr), was taken by security police from his place of employment. He was interrogated and released after a specimen of his writing and photograph were taken. The following morning at 4 o'clock, the secretary of the organisation, comrade Nqikashe, and two members of Cradoya, comrades Frans and Jacobs, were detained. They were also released after an interrogation which was accompanied by their writings and photographs being taken.

Cradora fervently wishes to ask the UDF for whatever kind of assistance it can offer in its efforts to have the transfer rescinded. We further wish to ask for a loan of R1000 which we promise to repay before the end of March. Following a decision which was taken at our first rent meeting on the 25 August, contributions of R5 per household were collected towards meeting the costs of taking the matter to court. We managed to collect a sum of R2,500. Whilst we enjoy the overwhelming support of the community, we feel that it will be impolitic to ask for money from the people until the court case is resolved one way or the other. The required loan will be used as capital which will be used to, amongst others, buy Cradora skippers [T-shirts] which will be sold to generate interest for the organisation.

Compiled by:
Mbulelo T. Goniwe (organiser)

Document 44. "Million Signature Campaign: Briefing for Fieldworkers." UDF pamphlet, eastern Cape, March 1984 (abridged)

Go to the people,
Live with them,
Learn from them,
Love them—
Start with what they know,
build on what they have—
..... but of the best leaders,
when their task is accomplished,
their work is done,
the people all remark:
"We have done it ourselves."

INTRODUCTION

Over the coming months we, the activists, will be going to the people to collect 1 000 000 signatures for the UDF declaration. We will be speaking to the people in their homes, at churches, in the streets, bus ranks, wherever people are to be found.

It is important that we have adequate information on the topics we are going to be discussing, i.e. the UDF, Constitution, and the Koornhof Bills (and why we reject the latter two). Very important also is that we use the correct approach when speaking to the people. . . .

Read through this briefing and discuss the ideas in here before going into the field. Remember that when we are out in the people's houses, we are carrying the name of the UDF and its policies and principles. *CARRY IT WELL.*

THE MILLION SIGNATURE CAMPAIGN

The reasons for the million signature campaign are spelt out clearly in the 5 objectives of the campaign.
1. to collect a million signatures to show that we will never accept Apartheid.
2. to popularise and show the support the UDF has.
3. to educate our people about the UDF, Constitution and Koornhof Bills.

4. to show a clear rejection of the Constitution and Koornhof Bills and support for a non-racial democratic South Africa.
5. to use the campaign to popularise and build our local organisations.

The campaign will be conducted by all UDF affiliates in SA over the next 4 months.

THE HOUSE VISIT
WHY?
• Because we need to reach all the people in our community, even if we have to go to their homes. Not all people will come to meetings.
• We need to educate people about UDF, the Constitution and Koornhof Bills. This can best be done in a small group or one to one discussion in which we can clarify any misunderstandings, answer any questions and give people individual attention which has the maximum impact.
• We need to learn about our people. We need to find out about their problems, about how they feel about various issues, their willingness to take part in activity, their level of understanding about the political situation in the country. All this we can only do by speaking to people individually, asking questions and listening carefully when they speak.

HOW?
There are various approaches to conducting a house-visit. The approach we use will depend on who we are speaking to, what are the issues affecting that community (e.g. election, Koornhof bills), other conditions such as the history of work, amount of work done in that area. This must be considered when working out the approach to a house-visit in your area.
However there are some basic points that we can keep in mind. Here is described a particular model, which must be modified for your area.
Let us assume that a pair of you are working in a particular street in the township.

STEPS FOR THE HOUSE-VISIT
Our first step is to knock on the door.
Greet the person answering the door, Good evening, I am _____, from the (name of local org.) or I am from the UDF.
I wonder if I could take up a few minutes of your time, or any similar statement, without mentioning politics or such words. *GETTING INTO THE HOUSE IS VERY IMPORTANT.*

Once you are in or have the person willing to listen, attempt to draw in other members of the family into the discussion. This can be done by asking if there are other people at home, as the matter you want to discuss affects everybody.
Once you have the maximum number of people, explain your purpose.
You are a member of an organisation affiliated to the UDF. You and others are going on a door to door campaign to discuss _____. This may

differ from area to area, e.g. you are discussing the constitution. The UDF is _____, give a brief explanation, and at present it is conducting a campaign to collect a million signatures.

At this point ask a few questions, or enquire as to whether the person knows of the UDF, or about the constitution, Koornhof bills. This must be done carefully, not in any way frightening the person, or in an abrupt manner. ASK GENTLY. e.g. Have you heard of the UDF and constitution? What do you know about it?

The answer you receive would allow you to assess how much the person knows, and how much you need to explain.

If you need to explain, use the knowledge in the earlier pages. *DO NOT GIVE A LONG SPEECH, EXPLAIN BRIEFLY, MAKE SURE THE PERSON IS FOLLOWING WHAT YOU ARE SAYING.*

Encourage discussion, get the people to talk. This can be done by asking the right type of question. How long have you been living here. Are you happy with the way the township is, what do you feel about it, are some ways of getting people to talk.

Answer all questions—if possible. If you are unable to, take down the address and tell the person you would get someone else to visit them.

At the correct time give an explanation of the signature campaign, and why it is important for people to sign.

If person is antagonistic, disagrees with you, try to persuade them gently, if this does not work, thank them and leave. *DO NOT BE PROVOKED INTO ARGUMENTS, ANGER OR VIOLENCE. DISCIPLINE IS IMPORTANT.*

If the person is supportive but scared, then explain that the UDF is a legal organisation, the campaign is legal, millions will be signing, the forms are not going to be handed to the government, etc. *BE PATIENT.*

If the person you meet is very interested, spend more time, ask if he is prepared to join or help in some way. *WATCH OUT FOR VOLUNTEERS.*

Before you leave the home, ask if there is any other information they would like to have, make sure that you have explained all the important issues to the people. *ENSURE THAT PERSON IS ADEQUATELY INFORMED AND HAS UNDERSTOOD WHAT YOU HAVE SAID.*

GET THE MAXIMUM NUMBER OF SIGNATURES OF PEOPLE OVER THE AGE OF 16 BEFORE YOU LEAVE.

Your last message to the people, tell them to continue to support the local organisation and the UDF. They can do this by reading all the newsletters that will be distributed, coming to meetings, talking to friends and taking an active part in your campaigns.

Ask them to read and discuss the newsletter that you leave with them. Thank them warmly.

While in the house, make a note (mental) of the way people respond, the questions they ask, problems they talk about, their attitude towards you, the local organisation and the UDF.

THIS FORMAT MUST BE MODIFIED TO MEET YOUR NEEDS

but remember

- DRESS NEATLY—APPEARANCE IS IMPORTANT
- BE POLITE—PEOPLE ARE DOING YOU A FAVOUR AND NOT THE OTHER WAY AROUND
- ALLOW PEOPLE TO TALK, ABOUT THEIR PROBLEMS ETC. LISTEN AND *LEARN*
- DO NOT ARGUE WITH PEOPLE. IF THEY DISAGREE WITH YOU, TRY PERSUASION, IF IT FAILS THANK THE PERSON AND LEAVE
- SPEAK IN LANGUAGE PEOPLE WILL UNDERSTAND, NO NEED TO IMPRESS PEOPLE WITH BIG WORDS. SPEAK IN A WAY THEY UNDERSTAND
- SIGNATURES ARE NOT THE ONLY IMPORTANT THING, EDUCATE AND LEARN
- LOOK OUT FOR VOLUNTEERS
- WORK HARD—THERE IS NO EASY WAY

YOU ARE NOW READY FOR THE HOUSE VISIT. TRY IT, LEARN FROM EACH VISIT. USE WHAT YOU LEARN IN THE NEXT VISIT.

QUESTIONS YOU MAY BE ASKED
   There will be some questions that may arise during your discussions with the people. PREPARE YOURSELF WELL TO ANSWER THEM.
   Some of these questions may be difficult, discuss these with the committee so that we have the best answer and also that all of us use the same approach to such questions.
   To this document must be added issues that are specific to your community.

Some of the questions one can be asked:
-Why doesn't the UDF participate in the constitution?
-What do we expect to achieve by boycotting everything?
-Is it not illegal to boycott?
-In Indian and Coloured areas, the fears people have about majority rule. Won't South Africa be another Uganda, etc.
-It is illegal to fight the govt., if I sign the police will take me away, and similar questions.
-Why does UDF not join Inkatha, why are they fighting amongst each other? And many similar questions.

WE MUST BE ARMED WITH ALL THE NECESSARY INFORMATION, WITH THE ANSWERS TO DIFFICULT QUESTIONS. We must remember that our approach to people is important.

ONCE WE ARE CONFIDENT THAT WE CAN HANDLE THE HOUSE-VISIT... GO FOR IT....

Document 45. "3000 Say No to Increases." East Rand People's Organisation flyer, June 1984

More than 3000 people gathered at the Lionel Kent Centre on the 28/06/84 to show that they are against the increases of rents, bus fares, créche [day-care center], bioscope [cinema] and burial fees proposed by the Daveyton Town Council. The meeting was organised by the East Rand People's Organisation (Erapo).

They came to discuss how they themselves felt about the increases and what to do about it. Speaker after speaker condemned the increases as unfair, especially now that the unemployment rate is high and the cost of living and general sales tax (GST) are continuously rising.

Speakers from the floor pointed that:
1. The town council cannot own land and build houses but can only let (rent) houses and collect rentals.
2. It has no control over education and health.
3. It has no money to run Daveyton efficiently.
4. The apartheid minister of co-operation and development, [Piet] Koornhof, has complete control over all Town Councils.

The people therefore resolved:
1. To reject all the proposed increases. This means that they will only pay the old site and house rental.
2. To reject the Town Council and call upon all councillors to resign.
3. To mandate Erapo to co-ordinate the struggle against all the increases.

Erapo calls upon the Daveyton community [to] discuss the resolutions with friends and neighbours adopted by the 3000 people. Make sure everyone supports it. United we shall overcome!

WE THE PEOPLE DEMAND RENTS WE CAN AFFORD
ONE CITY ONE TOWN COUNCIL.

Document 46. "Boycott Their Apartheid Elections." Community Education Programme flyer, Korsten, Port Elizabeth, August 1984

Designed to:
—DIVIDE AND RULE THE OPPRESSED
—MAINTAIN WHITE BAASSKAP [DOMINATION]
—IMPRISON US IN GROUP AREAS AND HOMELANDS
—DRAFT US INTO THEIR ARMY
—DISINHERIT US FROM THE LAND OF OUR BIRTH

- *Do you understand how the new parliament will work?*

It is important we understand *why* the rulers have planned this new deal. It is going to affect our future and the future of our children. So we must know *exactly why* we reject it.

There will be THREE HOUSES OF PARLIAMENT: A House of Assembly for whites which will make all the laws of the country and TWO PUPPET PARLIAMENTS, one each for the Coloureds and the Indians. These will be the old SAIC (South African Indian Council) and CRC (Coloured Representative Council) in new buildings. These will be toothless bodies unable to change any of the oppressive laws in this country. Millions of Africans will be enslaved in the Homelands to serve as reservoirs of cheap labour. Under Koornhof Bills they intend to regulate our movement, work and life.

- *Will our children now have to do military duty?*
The oppressors are going to say that the "Coloureds" and "Indians" now have the right to vote. So they must go and defend their "rights" on the border. In fact, what they are asking us is that *we* defend apartheid and exploitation.

- *Why is the Labour Party, Reform Party and other stooges participating?*
They will earn R4000 [$2600] per month. They are not interested in the struggles of the people, but only their pockets. They will again work the instruments of oppression. We must boycott these traitors.

- *Who will have to pay for these elections and this new government?*
Already the people are burdened by increases in basic foodstuffs, rents and rates. Yet further increases will be made to pay for this new fraud.

- *What do we demand? What do we strive for?*
ONE Parliament in which all South Africans will be represented on a non-racial basis. The *full franchise for* ALL. One undivided South Africa, free from apartheid, oppression and exploitation of the workers.

- *WHAT MUST WE DO?*
BOYCOTT ANY ELECTIONS OR OPINION POLLS OF THE RULERS.
WE BOYCOTTED C.R.C. OUT OF EXISTENCE,
LET US DO THE SAME WITH THIS APARTHEID CONSTITUTION.
LET IT BE BORN DEAD.
LET US UNITE NOW FOR FREEDOM!

Document 47. "Congress Calls on Our People to Oppose Botha." Transvaal Indian Congress flyer, August 1984

DON'T VOTE IN AUGUST
ATTEND CONGRESS MEETING
WEDNESDAY, 15th AUGUST
8 p.m. at the Seva Samaj Hall, Laudium
SPEAKERS: ·CAS SALOOJEE (TIC) ·M. J. NAIDOO (NIC) ·POPO MOLEFE (UDF)

DON'T BELIEVE THEIR EMPTY PROMISES!
Abramjee, Billy Padayachy, Chinsamy Reddy and A. Ismail are standing for the Apartheid Elections. They want you to vote for them so that they can earn R48,000 every year. BUT DO THEY CARE FOR YOUR FUTURE? During the SAIC [SA Indian Council] Elections, promises were also made. Once again, none of the promises will be kept.

Whites will be in the majority, Indians and Coloureds in Parliament WON'T be able to:
- Scrap the Group Areas Act
- Prevent military conscription
- Stop African oppression
- Stop G.S.T. [General Sales Tax], get more houses and relevant education.

CONGRESS DEMANDS TO KNOW:
- Why are candidates helping Apartheid by trying to divide Hindus, Muslims and Tamils?
- Why do they remain silent on the use of armed police, harassments and police intimidation?
- Why is Abramjee not willing to face the public and answer to the housing scandal as exposed in the Sunday Express, 22nd July 1984.

WHAT WILL WE ACHIEVE BY REFUSING TO VOTE?
We will show Botha and his puppets
- That we are not fooled. We know that they are not giving us full & equal rights.
- That we will never be used against Africans.
- That we refuse to give them the right to send our children to the army. We will show the world that Botha and his puppets do not represent us.

Congress challenges all the candidates to attend the Congress meeting to answer the above and other questions. Also to answer why are they betraying our people by participating in the Apartheid Elections.

DO NOT GIVE CREDIBILITY TO P. W. BOTHA AND HIS STOOGES BY VOTING!
A VOTE FOR THEM IS A VOTE TO STRENGTHEN APARTHEID!
A VOTE FOR THEM IS A VOTE TO MAKE P. W. BOTHA YOUR PRESIDENT!

REMEMBER, YOU ARE NOT BREAKING THE LAW
IF YOU DON'T VOTE.
DON'T VOTE IN THE AUGUST ELECTIONS.

Document 48. Resolutions taken at meetings of the Vaal Civic Association, August 1984, in Sotho (with translation)

DIQETO TSA BAAHI, BANA, BATSWADI LE BASEBETSI–VAAL TRIANGLE
Diqeto tsa baahi, bana, batswadi le basebetsi dikopanong kgweding yona ena e hodimo kgahlanong le nyollo ya dirente, tefello tsa metsi, motlakase

le ho ntshuwa ka matlong ke banna/basadi ba di-khanselara, ke hore ka mantaha ka di 3 September, 1984. Ho sebe ngwana kapa mosebetsi ya yang mosebetsing kapa sekolong ka mantaha wa di 3 September, 1984. Hona ke tshupo le ho totobatsa hore di-khanselara di tlohe ditulong (di risaene/resign), hang hang, hobane di tlisetsa baahi ditshotleho, mathata le dillo feela. Qeto e nngwe ke hore dikgwebo kaofela di kwalwe dihora tse mashome a mabedi le metso e mene (24 hours).

Translation:

RESOLUTIONS OF RESIDENTS, CHILDREN, PARENTS AND WORKERS–VAAL TRIANGLE

Resolutions of residents, children, parents and workers at the meeting held during this month against the increases of rents, payments of water, electricity and the eviction from houses of men and women by councillors on Monday, 3 September 1984. No children or worker must go to school or work on Monday, 3 September 1984. This is to show that all the councillors must resign at once because they bring only poverty, difficulties and grievances. Another resolution is all businesses must be closed for twenty-four hours (24 hours).

Document 49. "The Third Day of September: an Eye-witness Account of the Sebokeng Rebellion of 1984." Booklet by Johannes Rantete (abridged)

Rising Rents the True Source of Turbulence

Can it be denied that the riots of Sebokeng were part and parcel of the fight for liberty by the black South Africans? Although the motive was to strike against the rising rents, the course taken by the rebellion was so horrible that even the police could not withstand it. This I say because there was no roof of the business buildings that remained tall after the strikes except the well-planned Mphatlalatsane hall, Perm building, and various churches.

In Zone 11, all the shops were burnt down. The rent office, the bottle-store and the beerhall were burnt. Three houses were burnt. One councillor was killed. Several cars were burnt, including a brand-new Honda Ballade. The petrol station and the soft-drink cash-and-carry wholesale were also attacked. The roadhouse cafe was broken into and goods were taken away.

Tarred and untarred roads in this zone were blocked with stones, boxes, and anything else that was easy to carry. The Sebokeng Post Office was attacked and burnt, not surprisingly.

All the shops in Zone 12 were burnt down, too. The rent office, the bottle-store, the beerhall, a doctor's surgery and the house of a councillor were destroyed by fire. The tarred roads in this zone were blocked with stones and pelted with bottles and burning objects to hamper the passing of cars—especially police vehicles.

Zone 13, where there are more shops, was the first to come under attack.

Not a single shop kept its original shape. Everything was ashes. Here again the rent office was attacked, but the library and two clinics were spared. A house near the shopping centre was burnt. Roads used by buses were pelted with stones and broken bottles. . . .

The strikes took four days and afterwards 31 people were dead. More than 50 were injured and about 8 policemen, while 37 were arrested. The police used teargas and rubber bullets to disperse the rioting crowds. Many people were injured and some killed, and the count of police victims will probably never be known, because of news clampdowns.

Some of the victims of the strikes can be identified. The Zone 11 councillor, Mr. James Mofokeng, was killed. Councillor Caesar Motjeane was killed after shooting two youths, and on his corpse read the placard, "Away with rentals! Asinamali! [we have no money]" Ntombi Majola (12) was killed. Nomthanazo Mphutheni was hurt. Evaton's deputy mayor, Mr "Dutch" Diphoko, died in the Sebokeng hospital on Tuesday. Evaton's mayor, Mr Sam Rabotapi, had to remain homeless after his house was burnt down. His gown was worn by an elderly woman who danced down the streets and called herself the first [woman?] mayor. On Monday the Sharpeville councillor, Mr Sam Dlamini, was killed by an angry mob. The boy Wisey Mnisi of Zone 12 was gunned to death. The boy Stevenson Motsamai (13) of Modishi Primary School went missing after the riots.

I Was in the Midst of All the Horrors

Some weeks before the 'Bloody Monday' of 3 September approached, protests against the rent increase of R5.95 ($3.60) took place at various places in the Vaal Triangle. Churches and organisations warned the council time and again, but their words fell on deaf ears. The warning was even published in newspapers that the councillors should resign as they were never elected by the people. The call for their resignation was a clear rejection of the government's new system of implementing the black town councils which the people didn't ask for.

Days went by and nothing was said by the council in connection with the rents. During the last few days of August, residents in the Vaal Triangle were informed that on Monday, the third day of September, no one should go to work as it would be the day of protest against the rent hikes. Early on the morning of Friday 31 August pamphlets were distributed by the town council warning residents that if they didn't go to work on Monday they would lose their jobs and lose their houses, and in turn the future of their children would be doomed. Those pamphlets didn't have any influence on people. Saturday and Sunday came and passed. Then came the greatest day in the history of Sebokeng, the day of protest, the day of deaths, the day of arrests and the day of teargas and smoke. This day is historically named 'Bloody Monday.'

As a resident of Sebokeng I was also concerned by the events that were to take place, but was hindered by my parents to remain within the yard. In all my born days I had never found myself amidst a striking crowd, and thus the hindrance laid on me by my parents was as painful as the heart of a divorced man. I multiplied two by two to get an easy outlet from the yard. Thus, by doing so, I secured my curiosity which is the first thing a newsman should have.

I rolled down the street to the Zone 12 stores together with two friends whom I shall call Siphiwe and Xolile. None of the shops was open and people could be seen standing in groups here and there. The main topic was the rent hikes that had hit the whole of the Vaal. We turned back and joined a tarred street which we followed as far as the second bus stop. While walking, I could really feel that something was wrong with the atmosphere, and assured myself that something sad was going to eventuate. When we arrived at the bus stop, no vehicle could be seen or heard. When I looked down the road I found that it was blocked with stones. Then we met certain guys whom Siphiwe knows.

Those guys seemed to be members of a certain organisation which I can't tell at the moment. They told us that they had stopped all the VTC (Vaal Triangle Corporation) buses, and that people who boarded had been klapped [punched] and chased away. Buses were not damaged but kindly told to withdraw from service. From the bus stop we bent down towards the Roman Catholic church near the Sebokeng post office. There was a group of people standing near the post office, all of them staring up in the Vereeniging direction.

I ran to see what might be happening up there in the highway. My eyes sighted a huge crowd along the highway, and another crowd in the highway. When the crowd in the highway approached I realised that it was a white man driving a new blue car escorted by four men, while those others who swarmed around were calling out that the car must be stoned. Truly, it had already been stoned, and its windows were broken, all except the front one. After the white man passed, many people ran down the road to Zone 13's shopping centre. We used the other street to join the crowd behind a church building.

While we stood there, the police vehicles arrived. Three of them passed down the highway and the last truck turned down to Zone 13 where a number of people had run. This police truck was carrying black police. We followed down the road. The police truck went to stop next to a bottlestore near the shops. A huge crowd approached the truck from the nearby surrounding houses to which they had fled when the convoy passed. I remained hidden behind the fence and watched an interesting drama I would hardly forget in my lifetime.

As the crowd approached, the police jumped out holding some glass-like plastics which they used as shields against the stone-throwing mobs. The police could not withstand such stone-throwing, and the trucks drove off. Some police, seeing that the truck was going, ran for their lives and two of the plastic shields were thrown away. The mob lifted the shields aloft and began to sing. Meanwhile, some people entered the bottlestore and ran out with beers. Others, seeing the beers, crowded into the bottlestore and crates of beers were taken away. The moment the people crowded the open space, two police vehicles arrived and teargas was fired.

Because it was my first time, I didn't know what teargas was or how it worked. When others ran and hid behind the houses I remained at the gate. A white cop fired a rubber bullet which fell some distance away from me. You know, curiosity sometimes leads to some simple traps. I went and picked up that piece of black rubber and smelt it. I really can't tell what happened when I threw the rubber away. I became dizzy and lost my strength, and then some pains struck at my eyes. I ran to the water tap and cleansed my eyes with a handkerchief. By doing so I weakened the strength of the teargas. Because I didn't know, I thought the piece of rubber I had picked up was the cause of my dizziness. This was false, as I later learnt that teargas had been fired across the street and spread on the wind towards where I was standing.

After some three minutes the people returned to the streets again, most of them now having handkerchiefs in their hands. Still the police vans drove up and down, and teargas was fired here and there. The people then adopted a system of pouring water on every pellet of teargas fired. This system became the shield of the strikers, and the police could do nothing further. They drove off to other zones, thus giving the people in this zone a chance to run towards the shop buildings. . . .

Meanwhile strikes were also on in nearby Evaton, in Zone 7, and in other townships. By the time Bloody Monday was over more than twenty people had died and many more were injured.

On Tuesday 4 September the strikes continued. Helicopters droned overhead early in the morning and people crowded the streets again. The thing that made the strikes continue was the presence of the helicopters, dropping teargas here and there. This annoyed the people and brought them into the streets again. On this day all the shops in Zone 11 suffered the destruction by fire. . . .

How Did the Eye of the Government View the Riots?
The Minister of Law and Order, Mr Louis Le Grange, visited all the townships torn by the riots in the Vaal. He was accompanied by other cabinet ministers like Mr F W De Klerk (Minister of Internal Affairs), General Magnus Malan (Minister of Defence) and Dr Gerrit Viljoen (Minister of Education and Training). Mr Le Grange denied that it was the proposed rent increase that had led to the violence which swept through the Vaal Triangle. He blamed certain forces and organisations for the riots, but he didn't mention which were responsible. It is a simple fact of life that the demands and grievances of the black majority are never met by the government. It really was the rent hikes that led to the unrest. People showed their deepest concern by rioting, but the Minister of Law and Order dismissed that motive, being unable to feel how rent increases affect the people.

It seems as if the Minister's denial of the cause of the strikes is a plan not to meet the demands of the people concerned. The increase in rents would have driven many families away from their houses. Black families are really experiencing some hardships. Things are becoming worse and worse for them. The GST [General Sales Tax] has been increased. The majority are being paid less. Many people are being retrenched from their work, thus increasing already high unemployment. To worsen the matter, the Lekoa Town Council decided to increase the rents by R5.95 which is really too much for this community. The normal rent paid, excluding water and electricity, is already R39.30 [$24].

In Sharpeville a delegation of residents led by Rev Ben Photolo demanded the following from the Lekoa Town Council:
- All rents to be decreased to R30 a month;
- The release of all the people detained or arrested during the unrest;
- All members of the Town Council to resign.

A Sharpeville rector of the St Cyprian's Anglican church, Rev Tebogo Moselane, is the figure who has been blamed for the eruption of strikes across the whole of the Vaal Triangle. He was blamed for giving the anti-rent organisations his church in which to hold their services. Rev Moselane reappeared from his hiding place after allegations that he had been detained. He is a thorn in the flesh of the authorities and remains fearless of any mishaps that may confront him. He really is a good leader.

The statement released by the Lekoa mayor, Mr Mahlatsi, that they have been forced to increase rents because the council has paid R1.9 million from the accumulated funds to subsidise rents, is understandable, but the council failed to look carefully enough at the misfortune this would bring to the communities. Councillors are wealthy and do not pay rents, thus they ignore the fact that the hikes will do more harm to the families of the poor people.

The mayor showed us how brave he is by going on to say that he is popular with the people, and that he will make personal contact with the residents so that he can restore peace and stability. Something amazing, in view of this, is why he left his home and sought refuge outside the township he governs. . . .

[Rioting continued in the face of official intransigence.] At last the anger of the people reached the [bus companies]. Buses were attacked and windows broken. The youths swarmed aboard the buses and drivers were forced to drive them where they wished. Any motorist passing on the road had to raise his hand to show his support for what they called "black power." He who failed to do so had the windows of his car broken.

When the schools reopened on 26 September no student in the Vaal area was seen in the school yards, nor seen wearing a school uniform. What was the cause of their staying away, whereas the strikes were simmering down? It remained hard for me to understand until the following day when I made an enquiry of some of the students. The answer from one of them had this ring to it: 'It will be too difficult for us to go to school when some of our mates are languishing in jail for unspecified infringements.'

This response revealed the strong national solidarity that exists among our students. My own nerves went tough as I learnt again that blacks have something to boast of. I felt confident that if the treasure (nationalism) of the blacks is well secured, then no hail nor storm will uproot it from its basic core of indefinite depth.

As the days went by, students marched to police headquarters to seek for an answer on the rent hikes and request that their friends be released. Unfortunately their request was not met, and thus the schools remained empty throughout the following days. The boycotting of the schools must be ascribed to the council for its failure to respond to the students and its delay in coming to an agreement with the residents. The weakness of the council was that it failed to notice that the strength of the riots lay in the hands of the students. . .

DOCUMENT 50. "The Anatomy of Rival Visions." Excerpt from paper by Lebamang J. Sebidi for Institute for Contextual Theology conference, Johannesburg, September 1984

That there is a struggle, a conflict, in South Africa, nobody can deny. . . . Conflict, red-hot and acrimonious, exists in this country and stares every South African in the face. [At the same time, raging controversy exists] about *how one can best characterise and analyse the exact nature of this conflict.* And it is important to realise that this controversy is not spawned by South Africans' puerile and inane desire to indulge in mere academic palaver or logic chopping. No, South Africans are engaged in this debate because they suddenly realise that there must be something disastrously wrong for a people to struggle along for well over three hundred years and yet have very little to show by way of tangible and lasting results at the end of that gruesome period. There must be something very ineffectual with regard to the way they go about the struggle, their chosen strategies and tactics, and, perhaps, this lack of effectiveness may be due to poor, careless and inaccurate analysis of their problem. Strategies and tactics, it must be remembered, are derivatives. Good, effective strategies, like good, effective medical prescriptions, are those which are based on painstaking and accurate social analysis, diagnosis, in medical parlance.

This controversy about how best one can understand the root causes of the South African socio-political problems, analyse them and gain deeper insights into the present situation, and thereby be in a position to evolve correct and effective strategies for change in South Africa's Apartheid society, gained particular ascendancy in the beginning of the 1970s, probably occasioned by the publication of the Oxford History of South Africa in 1971, which epitomised the liberal interpretation and analysis of South African society. The attack on the liberal interpretation of South African history came fast and furious. For instance, Harrison M. Wright says that:

> In 1972 alone four influential reviews (of *The Oxford History of South Africa*) by four South African historians living abroad—Martin Legassick, Shula Marks, Stanley Trapido, and Anthony Atmore—directly challenged the assumptions, the interpretations, and the social values of the liberal historians. . . .

Indeed, ever since that time the two opposing kinds of socio-political analysis, which can be roughly termed the Liberal and the Radical paradigms, have openly fought it out in the country's debating arenas. And as it was stated earlier on in this paper, this controversy between these two paradigms split black opposition into two seemingly irreconcilable and mutually exclusive camps. The now well known obstreperous RACE-CLASS debate had begun in earnest. Furious and unremitting it was.

There were those who were fully persuaded that "race" provided them with an adequate explanatory key to the understanding of the peculiarities inherent in the South African scene, while others rejected this approach and opted, just as strongly, for the adoption of a "class" analysis of the South African situation. The basic problem, the class-analysts intoned, was not so much who should sit on the "park benches", but who should enjoy the largest share of the "goodies". The controversy, as we know, often presented its participants with an EITHER/OR, clear-cut dichotomy between these two opposing views, with the protagonists on each side refusing to accept even the slightest possibility of a *tertium quid* [third option].

THE TWO PARADIGMS IN SILHOUETTE

In this section we shall give a general outline of each of the two paradigms and see how the insights yielded by each position would apply to our so-called four phases of the black struggle. This is crucial because a good paradigm ought to be always open to empirical correction.

The Race-Analysts' Position

What do the race-analysts say in general? For them the basic ingredient in the South African three hundred year conflict is "race". The primacy of *racial ideology* or politico-racial factors they say, should be obvious to any unbiased analyst of the South African problematic. This is their point of departure. And it is this which leads them to reject what they term the nonracial myth of proletarian unity between South Africa's black workers and white workers. The basic polarisation is not between "classes" but between groups that are segmented on the basis of pigmentation. Pigmentocracy, therefore, is the name of the South African game. The whole wide world knows that. Interests are polarised on the basis of race, not class or economics. It is for this reason that the high-priest and architect of racism in South Africa, Dr. H. F. Verwoerd, could feelingly argue that he would rather remain white and poor, than rich and mixed. . . . The proponents of the race-analysis approach point to such sentiments as being affirmations of the primacy of "race" in South Africa's social formation. For them "race" is the unmistakable criterion of differential incorporation into the South African social system. And it is this differential incorporation which determines what size [piece] of the economic cake one is entitled to; it is not the size of the economic cake that determines the nature of this incorporation; otherwise financial heavy-weights like our own E. T. Tshabalala, Habakuk Shikwane, Sam Motsuenyane, etc., would be enjoying full franchise and parliamentary rights on the same par with South

Africa's white oligarchy. They do not. The South African situation, therefore, seems to indicate that it is rather the ideology of "class consciousness"—and not that of "race-consciousness"—which is false, erroneous, twisted consciousness, an inverted image of the South African reality. Race is still a valid analytical concept to use for the understanding of South Africa's core problems, this approach argues.

The protagonists of the race-analysis approach do not see how the struggle of the people, at least at this stage, could be anything but a *nationalistic struggle*. They point to the obvious fact that in this country the so-called "non-whites" are oppressed, excluded, discriminated against as a *black nation*, and not as a class. And, therefore, the proper response to this blatant and obvious national oppression is some form of *"nationalism"*—not *classism*. Nationalism at this present stage is still the only rallying cry which has the potential to rouse the oppressed African masses to join the struggle and substitute genuine democracy for an oppressive pigmentocracy.

Another point, the situation in South Africa has an unmistakable colonial character. Some would like to describe it as "internal colonialism". However, this designation does not alter the basic picture. The basic picture is colonial: a white settler community lording it over a black indigenous community. Colonialism is by definition *collective exploitation and oppression* of a whole people—not classes of people. Colonialism is not the *selective exploitation and oppression* of certain strata of people, but that of the indigenous people as a totality. Such an oppression gives rise, not to a *class consciousness*, but to a *national or race consciousness*. Thus national oppression not only transcends class, but it also turns it into an irrelevant, strategically weak, variable in the people's struggle.

Ours is therefore a fundamentally *Black versus White* struggle, the race-analysts argue. The 1922 Rand miners' strike is regarded, within this paradigm, as a classic example of lack of "natural" homogeneity between the interests of white workers and those of black workers. In this 1922 strike white workers unequivocally perceived their interests as being antagonistic to the interests of black workers. White labour and white capital would finally forge a perfect alliance against the subordinated black workers. The predominant factor here was not the so-called "objective material conditions" or "one's relationship to the forces of production," but the ideological force of racism.

It is this failure of working class solidarity between members of different races which is regarded by race-analysts as being decisive in their decision to carry on the struggle solely on the basis of black solidarity. There is no other realistic formula for change in South Africa, they argue.

The following words [of Steve Biko] are an inference drawn from the above analysis:

> What blacks are doing is merely to respond to a situation in which they find themselves the objects of white racism. . . . We are collectively segregated against—what can be more logical than for us to respond as a group? When workers come together under the auspices of a trade

union to strive for the betterment of their conditions, nobody expresses surprise in the Western world. It is the done thing. Nobody accuses them of separatist tendencies. Teachers fight their battles, garbage men do the same, nobody acts as a trustee for another. Somehow, however, when blacks want to do their thing the liberal establishment seems to detect an anomaly. . . . The liberals must understand that the days of the Noble Savage are gone; that blacks do not need a go-between in this struggle for their own emancipation. . . .

Let the blacks do their thing, on an exclusively black vantage point. This is the clarion cry of this camp.

The Class-Analysts' Position

Class analysts inveigh against what they see as the superficiality of the race-analysis of the South African situation. They feel that race-analysis arbitrarily isolates the South African struggle not only from struggle against world capitalist exploitation, but also from liberating currents that have been a longstanding feature along the borders of this country. To de-internationalise the struggle in South Africa is to cling to a truncated, myopic view of that struggle. It is to be inexcusably unrealistic about the people's struggle.

South Africa, they argue, is part of the oppressive and exploitative capitalist world. This country is not peripheral to Reaganomics. It is part of the heartbeat of this monster. Reagan's "constructive engagement" approach and the heavy presence of international corporations, IBM, Siemens, Mobil, etc., in our economy, is sufficient evidence of the fact that the profile of the *real enemy* is much broader than that which is suggested within the race-analysis purview. And if the *real enemy* is broader, perhaps, by the same token, the *victims'* profile should be broadened to include people who are, *prima facie*, excluded in the narrow profile provided by the race-analysis picture.

Race analysts are reminded, over and over again, that the international subsidiaries operating in this country are part and parcel of the oppressive and exploitative machinery that grinds workers, regardless of their colour, for what the workers can produce to feed the already over-fed affluent, capitalist minority. Now, to employ colour or race as a primary criterion in a liberatory struggle is to, automatically, alienate black South Africans, many of whom are workers, from the rest of the worker world. Given the existential set-up in South Africa today, it would be naive in the extreme to imagine that the struggle could be successfully waged internally without a massive dose of external cooperation from the non-black workers of the world. This is not merely to reject the criterion of "race" for the sake of an ephemeral, passing theory, but it is an attempt to put aside the superficiality of a political-racial analysis in favour of an approach that ferrets out the causal-rootage of the South African conflict.

Racism, they say, lacks an independent explanatory power of analysis. Racial prejudice is either *inborn* or *acquired*. If it is inborn or innate, then there is very little that one can do about it. Such inborn-ness of racism would certainly call for acquiescence, not militant involvement on the part of the victims. But the very history of South Africa furnishes us with ample evidence that racism is not an innate factor in man: the origin of the so-called "Cape Coloured," the declassification of, first, the Japanese, and now Chinese, the existence of legislation to prohibit "mixed" sexual relations and marriages, etc., etc. All these phenomena point to the fact that there is nothing inherent in man which naturally orients him antipathetically to members of other races who manifest different skin-coloration. Racism is not innate. Thank God this is so, because if it were innate, it would never be eradicated!

So racism does exist. But it exists as a social, not natural, construct. It is a socially acquired habit, the source or origin of which is something other than itself. White people do not discriminate against black people simply because, innately, they do not like "blackness" in colour. Such a theory would easily break down in the face of the numerous experiences such as [prostitution] at Sun City, Swaziland Spa, Lesotho Hilton, etc. Racism is an acquired habit, and because it is acquired, it can be de-learned through force of circumstances. Radical analysis often locates these circumstances in the *"competition-for-scarce-resources"*. This is the pulse-beat of the South African conflict: economic interests. Racism is, therefore, a function of capitalist exploitation and serves to legitimate the status of those who own the means of production and the position of their functionaries. As such "race" is not a peculiarly South African problem.

South African Blacks are oppressed not primarily because they show a different skin-colour, but because, basically, their economic interests are antithetical to those who are the economically dominant class. So whilst the conflict manifests itself in forms that are racial, its origin is decidedly nonracial. Its origin is a collective attempt to protect group-interests: the land, water, pasture, and later the mines, manufacturing industry and commerce. It is, therefore, not *race relations* that one should study and focus on, but *class-relations*. In short, the "face" of the problem is racial, but its essence is nonracial. [Eugene] Genovese summed it up neatly:

> . . . race relations are at bottom a class question into which the race question intrudes—and gives it a special force and form, but does not constitute its essence. . . .

To asses the explanatory power of race as a tool of social analysis, it might help to look at the treatment of Whites by other Whites in other countries, e.g. the Jews in Nazi Germany. It was not the colour of their skin, the shape of their noses, the texture of their hair that was the central motive behind the inhuman treatment meted out to them but the position the Jews held in Germany's economy at the time.

For the class-analysis approach racial conflicts are simply epiphenomena of much deeper conflicts—class conflicts. And classes are by definition determined by their relationship to the means of production. Economic—not racial—criteria are used in this analytic approach. The basic, structural polarisation is not between *Black and White*, but that between *Labour and Capital*. It is this latter polarisation that has international repercussions or implications: workers are workers, everywhere. Capitalists are capitalists, everywhere. Their colour or race is peripheral and incidental to these pivotal categories, "Labour" and "Capital". This stand, class-analysts argue, is both theoretically and pragmatically correct. It is a stand fraught with ideological, strategic and tactical implications for the struggle of the oppressed masses in this country.

According to this analysis, a nationalist liberation movement, which is easily countenanced by a race-analysis approach, is by definition a bourgeois movement. It is bourgeois because, as in the South African case, every black man, simply by reason of his blackness, would belong to the movement, regardless of his class position. The fact that he may be a rabid, exploitative capitalist would not seriously affect his participation in the national liberation movement. It is rather the wrong kind of colour or race that would throw one right out of the liberation movement. For instance, in a national liberation movement an E. T. Tshabalala [businessman] and a Joseph Mavi [trade unionist] can march cheek by jowl, shoulder to shoulder, completely oblivious of their deeply polarised interests. Such a movement cannot but be bourgeois—and somehow reactionary.

It is this sort of *reductio ad absurdum* which clearly shows the inadequacies and oversimplifications of the race-analysis approach.

Thus whilst class-analysts would not be averse towards "working together with progressive whites in the liberation struggle," the race-analysts would be wary of "collaboration with whites—whether progressive or reactionary." By reason of the racial category to which they belong, they are basically part of the "problem", and not the "solution", in this country.

The two paradigms are painfully at daggers drawn.

DOCUMENT 51. "Stay Away!!! Monday and Tuesday the 5th and 6th November 1984." Transvaal Stayaway Committee flyer, in English and Sotho

STAY AWAY!!!
MONDAY AND TUESDAY THE 5TH AND 6TH NOVEMBER 1984

Your sweat and toil has brought guns and hippos [armored vehicles]. It has invited the police and the army to be in our houses, hostels and compounds. It has made masters to be proud and arrogant. It has made the Government undermine our integrity, dignity and respect as People of South Africa.

Your sweat, toil and energy has been abused for ages and centuries. For decades and generations. Blood of your children has been shed in vain and shame.

Rise, you the oppressed and the down-trodden. Wake-up, you the oppressed and the exploited. Stand up, you the deceived and the fooled.

- You students stand firm in the demands for SRCs [student representative councils], abolition of age limit laws, release of detained leaders, and an end to sexual abuse by teachers in schools.
- You Residents stand firm on your resistance against high rent, electricity and water bills.
- You Taxi-owners stand up to fight a ten Rand fee (R10) imposed on you by the Council.
- You in hostels and compounds, protest against high rentals in those terrible conditions.
- You workers, stand up to support your fellow colleagues dismissed from work.
- Lastly, you Business owners close your shops and join forces with people on the march to freedom.

The stay-away is nobody but you only. The call is not for organisations but for the people as a whole. For the sweat and toil is ours as a people. It is ours as a nation. It is ours as the workers. It is ours as students.

"Workers of the Country Unite for you have nothing to lose but your chains"

POWER TO THE PEOPLE!!

HADIPALANGWE
MONDAY AND TUESDAY THE 5TH AND 6TH NOVEMBER 1984

Ka Mantaha le labobedi wa di 5 le di 6 November 1984, basebetsi ba Transvaal kaofela ba kopwa ho bontsha kopano, le matla ka ho dula hae. Ma-Afrika, bana ba thari entsho ha re duleng hae re supentsheng maburu le baditjhaba hore MATLA a rona re ka a sebedisa ka mokgwa oo re o ratang. Ha re supentsheng Bo-Tshabalala, Tom Boya, Bo-Mahlatsi hore re tennwe ke bona.

Ho na jwale DIRENTE le METLAKASE di dulelletse ho nyoloha, empa meputso ya rona ha e nyolohe. Batho ba bo rona ha ba fumane mesebetsi mme ba sebetsang bona ba tebelwa mehla ena mesebetshing ya bona.

Bana ba rona hona jwale ha ba sa kena sekolo. Ba tebelwa ka melao e mengata-ngata. Ha bana ba rona ba re ba batla di-SRC (Student Rep. Councils) ba bitsetswa masole le mapolesa ho tla ba thunya le ho ba bolaya.

Re bone se etsahetseng Sebokeng, Boipatong, Sharpeville, Evaton le Soweto ha Maburu a ne a bolaya batho ba bo rona ka sehloho, mme bongata bo sa tshwerwe hona jwale. A re emeng ka maoto Ma-Afrika. A re lwantsheng Maburu le di-Councillors, Bo-Tshabalala, Tom Boya, bo-Mahlatsi. A re fediseng di-Councillors! A re ripitleng Maburu! A re ntsheng di-Hippo makeisheneng a rona!

Basebetsi are emeng le bana ba rona dillong tsa bona! A re tlamaneng re be ngata e le nngwe! A re lwaneleng tokoloho ya rona.

AMANDLA NGAWETHU!!
MATLA! KE A RONA!!
POWER TO THE PEOPLE!!
EACH ONE TEACH ONE!!

Translation:

STAYAWAY
Monday and Tuesday the 5th and 6th November 1984

On Monday and Tuesday the 5th and 6th of November 1984, all the workers of the Transvaal are asked to demonstrate solidarity and power by staying at home. Children of Africa, let's stay at home and show the Boers and the international community that we can use our POWER as we choose. Let us show those [councillors] Tshabalalas, Tom Boya, those Mahlatsis that we are tired of them.

There are now increases in RENT and ELECTRICITY, but our incomes do not increase. Many among us are without work and those who work are constantly laid off from their work.

Our children are at this time not going to school. They are prevented by many and various laws. When our children try to establish SRCs the soldiers and police are called to shoot them and kill them.

We have seen what has happened in Sebokeng, Boipatong, Sharpeville, Evaton and Soweto when the Boers killed our people treacherously, and many are imprisoned. Let us stand up, Africans. Let us fight the Boers and the Councillors, those Tsabalalas, Tom Boya, those Mahlatsis. Let us do away with the Councillors! Let us annihilate the Boers! Let us drive out the hippos [armored vehicles] from our locations [townships]!

Workers, let us stand with our children at their schools! Let us stand together as one! Let us fight for our freedom.

Issued by:
Transvaal Stay-away Committee composed of organisations from the following areas: Soweto, Krugersdorp, Randfontein, Germiston, Alexandra, Kempton Park, Pretoria, Boksburg, Benoni, Brakpan, Springs, Pietersburg, Heidelberg, Vaal, Bronkhorstspruit, Leandra, Middelberg, Nigel, Potgietersrus, Delmas and Bethal

AN INJURY TO ONE IS AN INJURY TO ALL
A DISMISSAL TO ONE IS A DISMISSAL TO ALL

Document 52. Report by Chemical Workers' Industrial Union on strike at SASOL, November 8, 1984

INTRODUCTION

On 6th November 1984 Sasol Ltd. dismissed 6500 workers for their participation in the 2 day Transvaal Regional stay away. The following day they fled from army and Police Units and thousands were bused back to the human dumping grounds in the bantustans.

THE COMPANY

Sasol Limited is controlled by 11 Directors of whom 4 are appointed by the Minister of Mineral & Energy Affairs, 3 by Industrial Development Corporation (a state body) and 4 by the Sasol Board.

A complete range of liquid fuels are manufactured from Coal. Pipeline gas, fertilizer petrochemicals and petroleum feedstocks are also produced.

THE UNION

The Chemical Workers' Industrial Union is a broad based industrial union operating nationally with 13 500 paid up members. It is a non-racial registered union affiliated to the Federation of South African Trade Unions (FOSATU).

It was clear from the outset that Sasol would resist the Union. Despite restrictions on access to the hostels where the majority are barracked the Union recruited a majority of the 6 500 workers and as a result Sasol became a reluctant partner in a relationship with CWIU.

The Union won stop-order facilities, [was] granted access to hostels, negotiating rights and had recently elected shop stewards.

BACKGROUND TO THE DISMISSALS

As membership grew workers became increasingly militant. Over the past 3 months several issues had arisen and several long, wrangling meetings held with Management. Over this period workers had twice wanted to take direct action: a bus boycott and a strike. On both occasions being well aware of possible consequences of mass action at this early stage of organization, the Union held them back and negotiated on the issues with Management.

However, although the Union had managed to negotiate an increased bus subsidy for workers, they were still very dissatisfied with the bus service as a whole. When the United Transport Bus Company refused to meet with the Union, workers took a decision to commence a bus boycott on 5 November 1984. This would involve an hour's walk to the plant for most workers.

Whilst this was taking place in Secunda, the Transvaal Region of FOSATU decided to support the call for a 2 day stayaway to support students demands and protest against events in the townships.

Sasol workers were given an exemption from the call because of the nature of the Sasol plant i.e. state project. However, given the pent up anger and frustration of the Sasol workers at this stage, they insisted on observing the stayaway and then to follow it with a bus boycott on return to work. On 5th November over 90% of workers stayed away. In the hostel complex the stayaway was 100%.

EVENTS LEADING TO DISMISSALS

MONDAY 5TH NOVEMBER

1. Workers stayed peacefully in the hostels and houses. A large contingent of police/army vehicles stationed themselves at the hostel gates and in the township.

2. At 6 p.m. on the 5th helicopters flew over the hostels and dropped thousands of pamphlets on workers. The pamphlets threatened workers with dismissal if they did not return to work the next day by 10.00 a.m. This angered workers.
3. Shop stewards and organizers held an all night meeting. It was finally agreed that a general meeting would be held early in the morning and that the Union would recommend a return to work.

TUESDAY 6TH NOVEMBER
4. The general meeting of 6000 workers took place in the hostel grounds at 6 a.m. (the Union had persuaded Management to allow the meeting and to keep the police and army out of it). During a break in the meeting, whilst shop stewards were holding a caucus, two "hippos" (huge armoured vehicles) drove into the hostel grounds into the assembled workers. Shop stewards managed to prevent any violence, but the meeting broke up with workers now determined to continue with the stay away.
5. Following this a meeting between the Union and the Management was arranged. Union representatives awaited the Management. Whilst this was happening the build up of police/army increased substantially ("a sneeze machine" now being included in the hardware).
6. At approximately noon, Management phoned and stated that it was no longer prepared to have any dealings with the CWIU, as the employees had been dismissed. Workers remained calm as Management announced the dismissals over the public address system.

WEDNESDAY 7TH NOVEMBER
7. At about 5 a.m. on Wednesday morning, workers started to walk to work (one hour's walk). Approximately 5000 workers marched on the plant, accompanied by "hippos," "landrovers" etc. They were turned away and marched back to the hostels.
8. They then gathered inside the hostel complex for a general meeting (illegal). The meeting took decisions:
   - not collect their pay which management said would be ready that morning.
   - to remain in their accommodation despite the 6 p.m. ultimatum.
9. As the meeting was dispersing, the army/police with their "hippos" and landrovers moved in. They drove around the hostel blocks, telling workers that even if they did not collect their pay, they would have to leave the hostels.
10. In one incident four "hippos" and four landrovers charged the hostel block where shop stewards and organisers were meeting. The Shop Stewards fled for their lives, jumping out of second floor windows. T. Mothupi, an organiser, was captured and detained under the security laws. He was interrogated and then released that night.
11. In such massive show of force by the army workers were scattered and had to leave the hostels. Some sought refuge in the township, others just

fled. Most collected their pay and got into the buses Sasol had standing by, under the control of the "hippos".

By evening a mere 200 out of the 6500 workforce remained in eMbalenhle.

The Sasol II and III plants in Secunda are the pride and joy of most whites patriotic to the Pretoria regime. It is for them a symbol of South Africa's independence; South Africa's homegrown answer to the oil embargo; it represents the wonder of modern science, new technology and hope for the future. When the sale of Sasol shares on the stock market was announced they were rapidly oversubscribed. The stature of its symbolic value is matched only by the massive security installations, double electric fences, dogs, guntowers, giving one a sense of the Berlin wall. It is officially declared a "National Key Point", subject to special security laws.

Sasol's workers do not share this gleaming futuristic image. For them it means danger, arduous working conditions, barrack-like hostels, racial oppression, rumours of men killed in accidents during the night and whisked away, and generally a very repressive environment.

The Union believes that Sasol, aware of its image in South Africa, just could not tolerate the idea of its workers participating in a stay away and making a political protest from their plants. They just could not let it pass unpunished. It also provided them with an excellent opportunity to rid themselves of the Union. Their massive command of resources, police, army, political influence allowed them to accomplish extraordinary feats, like intimidating and paying off and repatriating nearly 6000 migrant workers in an afternoon; keeping a massive plant idle and sustaining massive losses while a new workforce is recruited in the homelands, security screened and trained.

No doubt part of the training will be the suggestion that a union-free plant would be much better than a unionised plant.

Document 53. Annual secretarial report of the UDF, Border Region, by M. A. Stofile, November 30, 1984 (abridged)

Preamble

The first year of the existence of UDF in this region has seen a lot of developments some of which were positive progressive steps and inevitably some negative. It is however clear that the birth of this massive collection of the various forces opposed to the unsanctioned rule of the present minority regime has been an invaluable blessing to the advancement of the cause of liberation of our oppressed masses throughout the country. . . .

Circumstances

The situation within the ranks of the oppressor at the time of the inception of UDF have been adequately outlined in the report of the secretariat to the UDF NGC [National General Council] in Port Elizabeth. All that is of importance here would be to point [out] the various aspects mentioned there insofar as they apply to our region as well as point [out] those particular aspects that are peculiar to our region only.

It is a well known fact that repression in this area has always been excessive. . . .

To enumerate a few of the obstacles placed in the way of the democratic movement in this area the following are worth noting:
- Denial of venues for meetings;
- Detention and questioning activists;
- Banning of meetings;
- Attacks on people involved in campaigns;
- Waylaying of people coming from meetings and confiscation of materials;
- Searches in homes of members and their offices;
- The ban on all meetings of more than 20 people in the Ciskei.

To sum it up there is no difference here between a banned and not banned organisation. All activity can be disrupted in whatever manner [seems] suitable by the maintainers of the status quo.

On the other hand all support, physically and ideologically, has been afforded those who stand in the ranks of our opposition. In the course of events it has become very clear who is on whose side. The tendencies of those who claim to be representing the aspirations of Coloured and Indian communities have shown a remarkable resemblance [to] the tactics of those whom we have always pointed out as their bosses. Their half-hearted denial of collaboration with the system has been shown to be the lie we have always known it to be.

The Democratic Drive

Despite all the forces against the efforts of the people in their drive towards liberation, there has been a consistent perseverance by the toiling masses of our strife-torn country. This did not escape this region.

We saw our people going through one campaign after the other, hardly stopping to mourn or moan. We have witnessed their determination at Mgwali, Mooiplaas, Duncan Village and other places steadfastly poised against removals. We have seen them at Duncan Village and Mdantsane fighting commuter struggles. We were witness to the same strength shown at the factories in a fight for workers' rights. We have witnessed the valiant fight in our places of learning for a democratic system of education. We are not blind to the efforts of residents of Fort Beaufort for civic rights. Indeed all aspects of life can and do not escape the attention of democratic loving masses of our country. . . .

Analysis

A lot has been gained in the time-period covered by this report. We have seen the UDF-Border grow from the six organisations that affiliated at its launch in Grahamstown on the 15th of October 1983 to a staggering 30. This was made possible in the initial stages by the recruitment and mobilisation drive that the region engaged in immediately after its inception. The rest was the result of activities during the course of the Million Signature Campaign and the anti-election campaign.

In an area which, up until the time of our campaigns, has had a very apathetic Coloured and Indian community for some years now, we can safely say the percentage poll that was realised during the Rajbansi-Hendrickse masquerade is favourably comparable with the political trend throughout the country. This result is not out of apathy at all as the attendance by these communities, especially the coloured comrades, in people's gatherings has increased out of all thinkable proportions. In these communities UDF has roused people who had gone to slumber since the end of the Black Consciousness era in this region.

In all, through our affiliated organisations, we have inter-action and the co-operation of no less than 100 000 people. This is without including the thousands who find themselves in a situation where they cannot overtly declare their support for the forces of democracy due to the height of repression in their areas.

The winds of democracy and liberation are indeed sweeping the dusty, famine-ravished tracts of land wherever our masses, sweltering in the heat of oppression, are to be found. One can therefore ask in the light of the above information, what is the level of success in campaigns of the UDF. Indeed this is no difficult question and a justifiable one.

We have, as previously stated, engaged in several campaigns with differing degrees of success. The first of these is the recruitment drive and the mobilisation and organisation of unorganised communities. The recruitment of organisations was a commendable success. We cannot dwell too much on the belaboured actions of certain mischievous, disgruntled individuals, who in their search for power and personal aggrandizement have deliberately sought to set the masses against the course of liberation by posing as the reference section of the liberation library. In fact, like the useless encyclopedias they resemble, with old and inaccurate information they have been left to rot in the archives of mischief-making and reactionarism while the people are following the truths as laid bare by the realities of their situation.

The Million Signature Campaign is one sad fact in the story of our region. Despite all attempts to achieve the opposite the committee charged with this responsibility totally negated all the efforts of the various activists in our area-units. It is a sad fact there can be no certainty today as to how many people actually put their names to be counted as aligning themselves with UDF against the common enemy. More than this, this can have the negative effect of discouraging people in future from freely entrusting us their confidence as they might not know what eventually became of their names.

With the failure of the Million Signature Campaign was also another failure which would have been the natural by-product of the success of the MSC, the formation of new structures where these did not exist.

Another failure has been in the area of removals. Despite the setting up of a committee to see to this aspect there has been no noticeable movement in this area. This might be due in part to the fact that the two secretaries in the region, who were also part of the committee, are full-time employees and as such some distance from the main areas where this evil manifests itself. However this cannot be much of a reason and viable alternatives need to be explored.

The women failed totally to meet the challenge posed to them by the fact that this is their year. Instead of taking up the front ranks they have effectively shrunk into total oblivion. This is due mostly to the petty divisions that have been sown amongst them. Now that there are moves to create more unity amongst them we hope this will mean a unity of purpose and not just unity for the name's sake. We hope that the wave of disinformation that is going on amongst the youth will not affect their year as the women's has been affected.

Truly the gains experienced by this region have been due mostly to the activities of individuals entrusted with various responsibilities rather than the large committees that have been formed from time-to-time. This then underlies the need to seriously consider the possibility of a full-time organiser in the region.

There is a great lack of the full application of the democratic processes in this region. There are very few, if any, activities by the affiliated organisations. This then makes one believe that there is very little feedback done to the masses who cannot get to be present in certain forums like the RGC [Regional General Council]. This is a sad state of affairs indeed as we need the mass-participation of all rather than the contriving of some geniuses.

The Future

We shall in future have to concentrate on the active strength of the affiliates and have the greater stress of activity there. This is even more preferable in view of the difficulties experienced in securing venues for big regional activities which have unfortunately been the main source of inspiration in the region. Organisations cannot be allowed to be submerged into the activities of the UDF because of the very nature of the Front. They need to be clearly visible with a definite line of emphasis and action.

Besides we must at all times maintain the base of the struggle which should at all times be the masses of our people. The bulk of our activity should for this reason be borne by them.

In electing our executive we should at all times strive to ensure that the people elected will be in a position to meet the responsibilities that go with the various portfolios into which we elect them. People who are already overburdened with work elsewhere, no matter how good they are, will find it impossible to perform as we expect them to and this is to the detriment of the Front. They can if necessary be called upon by the executive or RGC to perform certain tasks from time to time.

I hope then that this shall serve as a guide in our deliberations today and as a reference for the future. . . .

Document 54. "Composite Executive Report" of AZAPO, December 1984 (abridged)

CENTRAL COMMITTEE

At the fourth Congress of the Azanian People's Organisation held at Patidar Hall in Lenasia the following comrades were elected into the Central Committee:

President	: Cde [comrade] Lybon Mabasa
Deputy President	: Cde Saths Cooper
Cape Vice President	: Cde Peter Jones
Natal Vice President	: Cde Imrann Moosa
Orange Free State Vice President	: Cde Fikile Qithi
Transvaal Vice President	: Cde Hlaku Rachidi
Secretary General	: Cde Sefako Nyaka
Projects Co-ordinator	: Cde Zithulele Cindi
Publicity Secretary	: Cde Muntu Myeza
National Organiser	: Cde Thabo Ndabeni

Comrade Sefako Nyaka resigned as Secretary General at the end of April 1984 and Cde George Wauchope was subsequently co-opted as Administrative secretary.

In the height of the successful anti-election campaign spearheaded by the organisation, Cde Muntu Myeza was detained under Section 28 of the Internal Security Act in August 1984 and was replaced by Cde Ish Mkhabela.

In a concerted effort to embarrass and discredit the organisation in general and the President in particular two charges of alleged robbery and car theft have been formulated against the President. He has appeared a number of times but the cases have not been heard. The organisation has never at any stage doubted the credibility of the President and are positive that he will be vindicated.

SECRETARIATS

The following Secretariats were disbanded because they were non-functional: Community Development, Culture, Education, Legal Affairs, Research and Resources, Women's Affairs and Religious Affairs. Regions were requested to suggest one name for each of the above Secretariats to the Projects Co-ordinator who in turn would make recommendations to the Central Committee for the appointments.

The Health Secretariat under the leadership of Cde [Abubakr] Asvat has embarked mainly on preventative health work in

1) Brandfort: 500 people were examined, 50 cases of high blood pressure were referred for treatment, and children were referred to Pelonomi Hospital because of deformities.

2) Mzimhlophe Hostel: 150 people were seen, one positive case of cancer referred to hospital. Of the 75 children seen the majority had cardiac problems. Of the 50 people whose eyes were tested 3 had defective vision.
3) Bekkersdal: Of the 250 people who were examined 10 cases of high blood pressure were detected. From the 30 eye tests that were taken 1 had defective vision.
4) The Vaal Triangle: this area was visited five times during the uprisings and 50 cases were treated for injuries due to bullets, rubber bullets, birdshot, truncheons, sjamboks [whips] and the inhalation of teargas. Cdes [Joe] Veriava and Asvat also submitted affidavits about the behaviour of police during the unrests to the South African Catholics Bishops Conference (SACBC) whose report is the talk of the town presently.
5) Asbestos Mining Industry: Two visits were made to detect the effects of asbestos mining industry on the health of the population working and residing on the mines and the environs.
6) The Health Handbook, a publication of the Secretariat, is in circulation.

Labour:

- No Unions were formed but the existing ones viz. Black Allied Mining and Construction Workers (BAMCWU), Black Allied General Workers Union (BLAGWU), Black Electrical and Electronics Workers Union (BEEWU) and the Insurance and Assurance Workers Union of South Africa (IAWUSA) were consolidated. The Farm Workers Association has recently been launched. . . .
- BAMCWU: Has been involved in four strikes this year viz:

1) Montrose Chrome Mine: Here workers struck over wages and the recognition of their Union. A declaration of intent was signed between the Union and management, and an agreement will be signed next year.
2) Durban Roodepoort Deep Gold Mine: When workers struck over wages and the recognition of their Union, the management called police and five workers were detained. They are currently facing charges under the Intimidation Act and the Union has also been barred from entering the mine premises.
3) Pan African Shopfitters: The strike was over the dismissal of a colleague, and management agreed to reinstate him and to negotiate with the Union on all working conditions.
4) Penge Asbestos Mine: Workers struck over wages and the recognition of BAMCWU. None of their demands were met and they were subsequently dismissed, and ordered off the premises. The workers rejected the dismissal notices and management applied for and won an eviction order in the Pretoria Supreme Court, and the Union has to pay the costs.

Subsequent to the dismissal of the Penge Asbestos Mine workers the Union conducted research on the effects of asbestos dust on the health of the workers. Results have shown negligence of both capital and state of the workers health hence BAMCWU to launch the National Anti-Asbestos Campaign. Support has been received from many national and international labour and community organisations.

A Weekend long seminar for "Women at Work" was held in Port Elizabeth by the Insurance and Assurance Workers Union of S.A. . . .

BRANCHES & REGIONS

Although the organisation has concentrated in stabilising and consolidating the existing regions and branches instead of forming new ones, nine new branches have been formed to increase the number of branches from 84 last year to ninety three (93) this year.

HARASSMENT

The organisation is still continuing to withstand the yoke of direct harassment and intimidation from the security police. It is not possible to single out any incident but the few incidents cited indicate the type of hurdles the organisation has come across and overcome.

1) Frank Talk: On 10 March 1984 the security police confiscated every single copy of the first issue of *Frank Talk*. On 17 March 1984, an interdict was sought in the Durban Supreme Court before Mr Justice Didcott for the immediate return of the copies which were seized. . . . Copies of Volume 1 Number 1 of *Frank Talk* were returned. This case was a prelude to things to befall AZAPO. . . .

2) The Raids: On the morning of the 22nd May, 1984 all offices of [the] organisation throughout the country, and most homes of the members of the organisation were raided by the Security Police. These raids rendered the organisation ineffective in that all documents, cabinets, typewriters, printing paper, pencils etc. were confiscated. The excuse for this inconvenience was that AZAPO was promoting the aims and objectives of a banned organisation, but in the case of *AZAPO v Control Magistrate (Durban) and the Minister of Law and Order*, judgement was passed in our favour and the police were ordered to return all the documents and the goods seized during the raids to AZAPO. . . .

3) June 16, 1984: Northern Transvaal: The Northern Transvaal Region was supposed to hold a commemoration service at Nemakgale. The service was banned two hours before the scheduled time and two hundred (200) people were arrested for failing to produce reference books.

4) The Anti-Election Campaign: AZAPO's members were terribly harassed before, during and after the tricameral parliamentary elections. A résumé of the activities follows:

• On the 1st August 1984 Cdes Windsor Maraba, Saki Maluleka and Rachi Rasethaba were arrested by camouflage police at Westernburg in the Northern Transvaal for putting up anti-election posters, and were taken to the Pietersburg police station where they were interrogated by the security police. . . . They appeared [in court] on the 31st August, 1984, were found guilty and were charged R30.

• On Monday, August 6, 1984 Cde Jerry Waaja was confronted by two whites travelling in a white Toyota Hi-Lux combi [van] whilst putting up posters. They confiscated the posters, sprayed his eyes with a spray gun and he regained his sight after two minutes. . . .

- On the 8th August, 1984 Cdes Phambili Ntloko and Mncedisi Mbilini were arrested in Queenstown and their lawyers were informed that they would be released without being charged. However, on the 10th, a list detailing the clothing they needed was given to their relatives, which was an indication that they were being held under security legislation. They appeared in court on the 13th and were acquitted on the charge of possessing banned literature, which happened to be the edition of *Frank Talk* referred to [above]. They were kept in custody and appeared again the following day and were charged for defacing public property. They are out on R100 bail and are still reporting daily between 7h00 and 17h00. This is a very blatant case of harassment where comrades have to report daily just for putting up anti-election posters. Obviously they are being chastised for the disgracefully low percentage poll. [Similar incidents occurred in Durban and Johannesburg]. . . .
- There was a national swoop on the morning of the 22nd August, 1984, the day of the "coloured" elections. Amongst the comrades detained were Cdes Saths Cooper (Deputy President), Peter Jones (Cape Vice President), Muntu Myeza (Public Secretary), Haroon Patel (Lenasia Chairperson), Glenda Constant (former chairperson of Johannesburg Central), Shabeer Randera (former President) and Ahmed Patel (a member of the Lenasia branch). The first four comrades were detained under Section 28 of the Internal Security Act whilst the remaining three were released after a day in detention. Cdes Saths Cooper and Peter Jones were released after three weeks of incarceration and Cdes Muntu Myeza and Haroon Patel were released last Monday just in time for Congress. We welcome the comrades back into our unnatural civilisation.

From the foregoing it is clear that AZAPO played a very vital role during the anti-election campaign. Although the liberal press tried to underplay the prominent and splendid performance the organisation displayed in turning the tricameral elections into a fiasco, they could not resist putting a picture with the caption "Ek hou my stem vir 'n vry Azania" [I cast my vote for a free Azania] in their front page. It is quite clear to everyone that only AZAPO can use such a slogan.

- The Vaal Triangle unrests: Cde Oupa Hlomuka, the branch chairperson of Sebokeng, was arrested during the Vaal Triangle unrests and charged with public violence. He was acquitted on that charge and accused of murder. He is an awaiting trial prisoner under Section 29 of the Internal Security Act. Cde Geoffrey Moselane had his house teargassed, and had to take refuge elsewhere because many attempts were made on his life. He returned to his house when things quietened a bit only to be detained under Section 29 of the Internal Security Act.
- Soweto Unrests: The Azanian Students Movement, (Azasm) our sister organisation, was also affected by the harassment that befell the Black Consciousness Movement as a whole. Six of its leaders viz. Cdes Thami Mcerwa, George Ngwenya, Sipho Ligojolo, Nhlanhla Sambo, Gladstone Mkhwanazi and Martin Ngcobo were detained in October, 1984 under Section 29 of the Internal Security Act. Cde Martin Ngcobo has been released, and the rest are still in detention.
- Banning of meetings: The Steve Biko commemoration services were

banned in the Northern and Southern Transvaal regions. In the Northern Transvaal thirty-seven comrades most of them members of Azasm, appeared on the 28th September, 1984 and on the 5th October, 1984, on a charge of public violence. . . .

DIPLOMATIC OFFENSIVE

Cde Imrann Moosa, the Natal Vice President, followed up the avenues opened by the President last year by addressing a conference organised by the United Nations Special Committee Against Apartheid on 19 June 1984. This evoked some angry protest from organisations that had arrogated unto themselves the role of "sole and authentic" custodians of the liberation struggle. Little did they realise that they were protesting against the voice of the only overt, authentic political movement operating inside the country. They feared that the international world would get a current horse's mouth view of what is happening inside the country. The lie that AZAPO and the National Forum etc. belong to them was exposed.

He also addressed an African Street Carnival organised by the [U.S.] National Black United Front (NBUF). He was interviewed by numerous radio and TV stations as well as newspapers and magazines in Washington, New York, Detroit, Chicago, Toronto and London. This diplomatic offensive must be sustained vigorously in order to put our viewpoint in its proper perspective and to clear up the rubble and the disinformation campaign that is waged against us.

PROJECTION INTO THE FUTURE

The major thrust of AZAPO next year will be on education. Much as we contend that "no just and equitable system of education can thrive and function in an unjust and exploitative society", we believe that the Black Community must be equipped and be well prepared for the hardships and challenges that lie ahead.

The Education Secretariat will be restructured to incorporate the Black Students Study Project (BSSP) and Education for Liberation (Ed Lib). It will then focus on tuition schemes, political education, adult education and literacy programmes, and education in trade unionism, to help workers to understand the economy and their place in it, as well as the role of trade unions and political organisations. A seminar will be held over the Easter weekend to put this into perspective.

Another thrust will be on theology and sports because it is to these facets that the masses address themselves almost to idolatry. The other secretariats will continue with the good work they are doing and those that were non-functional will be revamped.

CONCLUSION

From the foregoing it is clear that the organisation has stoically withstood the attacks that were geared against it, and has also done a lot of good work. The road ahead is stormy and thorny, and we must tread on it like the true revolutionaries that we are. It is for this reason that in the coming year we are determined to RESIST all evil measures that will be meted against us, DEFEND ourselves against any attack on our rights and dignity, and ADVANCE the cause towards anti-racist, socialist, workers' Republic of AZANIA.

ONE AZANIA—ONE NATION!

DOCUMENT 55. "Bafundi Manyanani!/Students Unite!" COSAS leaflet, Grahamstown branch, early 1985?, in Xhosa and English

BAFUNDI MANYANANI!

Bafundi bezwe lakowethu, namhlanje sipethe umcimbi oyimfuno yabo bonke abafundi abacinezelweyo oyi SRC. I-SRC esiyibona njengeyona mfuno yethu bafundi, engumthetheleli wethu ekupheliseni icorporal punishment ukubethwa kwesifazana ngabafundi, ukunqongophala kwee textbooks kunye nothotho lwemfuno zethu ezaziwayo ngabasemagunyeni koko besimfamekisa. Izolo ingxuba kaxaka ibe ise Vaal, Soweto, Sebokeng, eBhayi kunye neendawo ezininzi zeli lizwe. Abafundi babonile ukuba alikho elinye ithuba lokulwa koko leli. Amangomso asa esihogweni.

Thina bafundi baseRhini sele siwuthathile umgama ekuzameni ukuba sifumane umlomo ongowethu oyi SRC. Njengenxalenye yabafundi bezwe lakuthi lonke, kulilungelo nemfuneko ke ukuba sihlasele kanye ngeli xesha sesiqalisile ukulwa singabisayeka. Namhlanje uRhulumente wezidlova, phantsi kwephiko lobugqwirha obuyi Department of Education and Training uzama ukusinika iPRC [Pupils Representative Council] esingazifuniyo ezo zizinto ezicacisayo mhlophe ukuba urhulumente sele esoyisakala. Igazi lase Vaal, Thabong, Cradock, Attridgeville likhwaza nakuthi ukuba sizimanye nabafundi bezinye iindawo.

Ngoku apha eRhini ingcuka ezizibiza ukuba ngamapolisa zizama ukuchwechwa zigrogrisa abanye bethu ukuba zifuna ukwazi ngeengcinga zethu, kanti ke iingcinga zethu zinye qha sifuna iSRC, loonto ayifihlwa. Kwakhona kukho ooqhimgqoshe abazama ukuphanzisa iimfuno zabafundi ukuba bangake balwele iimfuno zabo ne-SRC. Nokuba bangacikoza bathini inyani yona inye, siyayifuna iSRC yaye indlela yokwenza simanyelwe inye kukurhoxa kuphela esikolweni.

Abo bathi sizakubhala, umbuzo sibhala ntoni yaye sibhala nje ezimeko besizilwa ingaba ziphelile na yaye siyakusoloko siphi kukuthi sifuna ilungelo lethu siqhathwe ngokubhala apho kusika uthotho lwethu. Asiqali ukubhala, yaye asigqibelisi iSRC mayilwelwe.

STUDENTS UNITE!

Students of our country today we are handling the demand of all students who are oppressed, which is SRC [student representative councils]. The SRC which we students see as our [way of] negotiation to bring to an end corporal punishment. The assaulting of female students by [male] students. The shortage of textbooks. Lots of our demands which are known to the authorities but are ignored.

Yesterday the trouble was at Vaal, Soweto, Sebokeng, Port Elizabeth and many other places of this country. The students had seen that there is no other time to fight than this time. Procrastination is a thief of time.

We the students of Grahamstown had already started the struggle with other students of our country to get SRC. It is our right to attack at this time as we have already started fighting, let us not stop.

Today the dictator government under the witchcraft [evil] wing of the Department of Education and Training is trying to give us PRC [pupils representative councils, controlled by school administrations] which is not wanted by us. All those things show that the government is weakening. The blood of Vaal, Thabong, Cradock, Atteridgeville calls upon us to unite with students of other places.

Here in Grahamstown wolves who call themselves policemen are trying to threaten some of us, are trying to know our views. Our views are to get the SRC, that is no secret. There are those who are persuading the students not to demand the SRC. They can say what they like, we want the SRC.

There is only one way to do to let the authorities listen to us, that is boycott. Those who say we are going to write the examinations, what are we going to write?

Are those conditions which we were fighting for ended? We are always cheated when we make our demands. We are told to write. We are not starting to write. We are not writing for the first time nor for the last. Let us fight for the SRC.

UNITE IN ACTION FOR A DEMOCRATIC EDUCATION.
FORWARD WITH THE SRC DEMAND.
EACH ONE TEACH ONE

Document 56. Memorandum on education crisis signed by Popo Molefe for UDF and J. Khumalo for COSAS, January 21, 1985

PROPOSALS FOR DISCUSSION ON EDUCATION CRISIS

On January 17, 1985 four representatives of the Congress of South African Students comprising two N.E.C. [national executive committee] and two R.E.C. [regional executive committee] members, met with the National and Regional Secretaries of the UDF at the latter organisation's offices in Johannesburg to assess the state of Education.

The following observations were made:
1. That there was general confusion as students did not know whether to go back to school or not.
2. That whilst some students had gone back to school, many were still out on boycott e.g. P.E. [Port Elizabeth], Fort Beaufort, Cradock, Lamontville, Uitenhage registering almost 100% boycott. The Vaal, Soweto and Pretoria

have relatively higher numbers of students at school but not all students have gone back.
3. That the Congress of the SA Students has not been able to make a national call of any kind because of a variety of problems manifesting themselves differently in different regions and localities. Although the overall demands are as previously stated by COSAS, there are other problems such as unfair dismissal and/or suspension of teachers and students. We have here in mind the situation in Cradock and Lamontville where teachers have been arbitrarily dismissed. Here students and parents are determined that there will be no going back until the teachers are re-instated.
4. That although earlier on the D.E.T. [Department of Education and Training] seemed willing to resolve the crisis, it seems like they are returning to their all time intransigence. This means that they may not resolve the crisis even in the short term.
5. That although some students have gone back to school the potential for another school boycott and violence [on] a larger scale will be a great one if D.E.T. does not meet the demands of the students.
6. That the students are on the threshold of victory and that this should not be allowed to slip out of our hands.
7. That there is a need to expand the campaign by involving other forces such as the churches, unions, prominent personalities like Bishop Tutu, Allan Boesak, Archbishop Hurley, SACC [SA Council of Churches], SACBC [Southern African Catholic Bishops' Conference], etc. and to provide a clear direction in this regard.
8. That there is a need for an assessment of possible involvement in the Education Charter Campaign by the Parents Committees.
9. That there is need [for] a serious assessment of the attempts by the D.E.T. to set up Parents Liaison Committees and the possibility of replacing same with democratic structures of parents.

The UDF and COSAS urge you to discuss the above questions and to come out with practical suggestions as soon as possible. The most concrete and crucial question facing us is, precisely How can we intensify the campaign in the event of the D.E.T. refusing to meet the students' demands?

It shall be appreciated if the matter can receive your urgent attention.

DOCUMENT 57. Statement on hit squads by Johannesburg Democratic Action Committee, Black Sash, Detainees' Parents Support Committee, Detainees Support Committee, National Union of South African Students, Young Christian Students, and End Conscription Campaign, *The Black Sash,* August 1985

The deaths of Matthew Goniwe, Fort Calata, Sparrow Mkhonto and Sicelo Mhlawuli appear to be the latest in a series of attacks on democratic organisations and their leaders.

According to DPSC information, already 27 UDF leaders and supporters have disappeared without trace and are still missing. There have been at least 11 political assassinations. The existence of two hit-squads who had a list of 20 community leaders as their targets has been exposed in the press.

Last month seven Duduza Cosas leaders were blown up by hand grenades in mysterious circumstances. According to the South Africa Council of Churches, Duduza residents believe the police were responsible.

Commenting on the situation generally, Dr Beyers Naude, general secretary of the SACC, has said: "I find in the community a deep-seated suspicion that those responsible were the police or hit squads supported and protected by the police.

"We have to face the fact that we are in a situation where unless something drastic steers us in another direction, increasingly such disappearances, murders, and killings will become the order of the day.

"It will only be human to expect that there is going to be retaliation. What is happening in the black community cannot remain in the black community for all time. It will spill over into the white community."

Document 58. "What is a National Convention?" Black Sash circular by Sheena Duncan, September 17, 1985

The Black Sash has repeatedly called for a National Convention in resolutions of its National Conferences and, on a Regional level, in statements and demonstrations. It seems necessary at this time to state what we mean by National Convention.

A National Convention in South Africa must be a meeting of representatives of *all* the people in the country, gathering together on an equal basis to thrash out a mutually acceptable constitution for the future. It would not be a *National* Convention were representatives of any group or any political conviction or policy to be excluded. Therefore in South Africa a necessary preliminary to a National Convention would be the unbanning of all banned organisations, the release of political prisoners and detainees, and the free return of exiles.

The Black Sash would not support any attempt to bring together groups in the "moderate centre" in a pretence of meeting as a National Convention. Nor would we support any Convention at which the representatives were chosen and invited to be present by the Government. Representatives must be chosen by the people in their various constituencies. The present ruling party would be only one of the many constituents of a National Convention, not in control of it. (It seems likely that in the bitterly divided South African society an outside moderator would have to be invited to preside over the meetings of the Convention).

The very nature of a National Convention is essentially a coming together of people with diametrically opposed views and policies to hammer out through hard bargaining from positions of strength some constitutional framework broadly acceptable to all of them within which public affairs can be conducted in the future.

Mechanisms for constitutional change

We have to find a mechanism for moving from where we are now to a just and democratic future. Now that the government has accepted the principle of South African citizenship for all black people, including those living within the independent homelands, political rights are an inevitable corollary. Minister [Chris] Heunis and the South African Ambassador designate to Washington [Herbert Beukes] have stated this.

The present South African Constitution offers no mechanisms for transformation to democracy. Based as it is on Race Classification, Group Areas and the exclusion of the black majority it is not open to real change or any kind of acceptable reform. No possible permutations and combinations of those parties represented in the tricameral Parliament with the legislative and administrative structures set up for black people could be acceptable to the majority of the people.

It is possible that an attempt will be made by the present government, through the President's Council, in consultation with government selected black leaders, to introduce yet another new Constitution. It is impossible that such a process could bring us to an acceptable democracy. Whatever its details such a Constitution would be imposed on the people from above. Mr. [Ian] Smith tried it in Rhodesia with Bishop [Abel] Muzorewa. Such an attempt could only prolong our agony and worsen conflict in this country.

Some political leaders have rejected all negotiation and say there is nothing to be discussed but the hand over of power. It is unrealistic to think that change in South Africa can, in the foreseeable future, be brought about by the violent overthrow of the government or by coup by armed liberation forces. The power of the State is enormous and the current dreadful repression is only a fraction of the armed force which could and would be unleashed in response to such a challenge. We are in grave danger of moving into a kind of Lebanon conflict which could go on and on for many decades and which would offer little hope of justice and democracy at the end of the misery of killing and wounding, burning and disintegration.

If one sits down and tries to analyse in practical terms what mechanism can move us into that just and democratic future for which we have worked it is difficult to visualise any other way but some kind of meeting together of all the interest groups who are in conflict with each other now. Whether that meeting is called National Convention or Lancaster House or whatever is immaterial. It will not be an easy process and it will inevitably be a lengthy one. No one will get everything they want but it has to be attempted.

The Convention Alliance

Dr. Van Zyl Slabbert has proposed the formation of a Convention Alliance to pressurise for and promote the idea of a National Convention. He has specifically rejected the idea that any Convention could take place under conditions of a state of emergency. He said "I am simply saying that those who are in favour of it (a national convention) should come together and demonstrate their commitment to getting rid of apartheid completely and substituting it with one constitution with one citizenship in one individual country."

On this basis I have supported the idea of a Convention Alliance. I would not be in favour of it were the alliance to make any attempt to set up a mini-convention or to try to wield the constituents in the alliance into a power block seeking to impose solutions on the wider majority. I do not believe that this is what Dr. Slabbert has in mind.

He has said "A Convention Alliance does not mean that all who participate in it share the same policy, or belong to the same party, or necessarily have the same detailed plan for South Africa. In other words, it does not seek to compromise its members, or its supporters in terms of policy, principles, programme of action, or personalities and leaders of their individual organisations and movements".

There is considerable opposition to entering into the Convention Alliance. From conversations I have had it seems that this opposition is *not* an opposition to the idea of a National Convention. There is a very small minority of people who seem to hold to the "overthrow or nothing" theory. The majority of those who do not wish to enter the Convention Alliance are certainly not rejecting it because they believe in violent solutions. Many of them agree that a National Convention is the way forward and are prepared to work hard for it in their own constituencies but they do not wish to be part of any "alliance" with people to whose policies and principles and actions they are diametrically opposed.

This is a major difficulty for some. I myself believe that the Alliance has a specific task and that it will inevitably be composed of antagonistic interest groups just as will a National Convention. I do not experience problems with the idea of an alliance but if it is going to be a major problem within the Black Sash we will have to debate it at our next Conference. With that in mind all Regions should have discussions with their members so that delegates come well prepared to Durban in March.

One person one vote

My opinion on this is constantly being asked at the moment. I stand firmly behind our long ago Conference resolution declaring that we are unequivocally in favour of a universal franchise. I don't myself think this is really a point of conflict in South Africa. Even the National Party has said the vote is essential for everyone. Mr. [Prime Minister John] Vorster used to claim that the ruling party recognised the principle of one-man-one-vote and that everyone in South Africa has a vote! What the conflict is about is what kind of constitutional structure we will build upon the foundation of the universal franchise.

I don't think it is necessary for the Black Sash to produce constitutional blue prints. We would not be represented at a National Convention anyway. Our constituency is too small and insignificant. Our task will be to measure other people's proposals against the yardsticks of justice and democracy and to nag and push from the sidelines a system which guarantees the Rule of Law and the democratic rights of the poor and marginalised people. I expect we shall have to go on fighting for that to the end of our lives.

DOCUMENT 59. "The Freedom Charter—For and Against." Article in *Arise! Vukani!,* journal of Action Youth, Johannesburg, September–October, 1985

The Freedom Charter is a very important document in South Africa. Many people believe that the demands in the Charter can bring about a society free of oppression and exploitation. Others among the oppressed doubt this. Some people are of the opinion that the Charter does not address issues such as class exploitation and is not an adequate programme for ending all oppression and exploitation.

Unfortunately, a debate among the oppressed on the Charter is almost always conducted in an emotional, sometimes even physical manner. Some adherents of the Charter have been accused of elevating the document into gospel, where criticism is seen as sacrilege. In Action Youth, we hold that comradely debate among those involved in the struggle should be encouraged, and is both healthy and necessary.

In March this year a group of organisations issued a statement commemorating the 30th anniversary of the Charter. They said, "Nothing short of the demands in this document (the Charter) will satisfy the people." The argument put by the state in 1956 that the Charter was a communist document was overturned [both in the treason trial of 1956-61 and] last year. A former Chief Justice of South Africa, Mr. Justice Rumpff, could find no truth in this argument. In dismissing the prosecution case [in 1961], he said the Charter was a moderate document and that it is now legal to distribute the document.

Recently a debate was held between an executive member of UDF and an organiser from MAWU [Metal and Allied Workers' Union], an affiliate of FOSATU. Generally, the speaker from MAWU felt that the Charter cannot satisfy the aspirations of the majority in South Africa—the workers. We print below a part of the debate and then Action Youth's own assessment of the Charter.

1) *What sort of document is the Charter?*

Executive member of UDF: The Charter is a popular document, it keeps with democratic principles and represents the aspirations of the majority of the people. The Charter expresses both anti-imperialist and anti-capitalist sentiments as can be seen from the clause on nationalisation.

Organiser for MAWU: The Charter is a popular document but the domination of the middle class can clearly be seen. The Charter makes important demands like "freedom of speech," but these are limited as they do not address the primary conflict in society—the conflict between capital and labour. The

Charter talks for the "people" but are there not different class interests among these "people"? The Charter is not anti-capitalist as the clause on nationalisation does not equate [to] socialism. Production relations are not addressed.

2) Of what relevance are the demands of the Charter to the working class?

UDF: The Charter has relevance for the working class in every respect. When the Charter was drawn up, the South African Congress of Trade Unions existed. We must understand that in South Africa, capitalism has taken on a racist form. Black people are oppressed as a nation and as a class. The clause in the Charter "The people shall govern" therefore shows that working class interests are primary. The Charter embodies working class interests, not petit-bourgeois interests, because it is anti-imperialist.

MAWU: Some demands in the Charter are relevant to the working class but they are limited. Organisations like the UDF which support the Charter are dominated by the middle class, and cannot ensure the liberation of the working people.

3) What role has the working class to implement the demands in the Charter?

UDF: In South Africa, the working class is in the majority. The central role of the working class must be fought for. Because of repression, the Charter had to be couched in a certain manner. The Charter is representative of all the strata in South Africa.

MAWU: Bourgeois democratic rights are addressed in the Charter but not working class emancipation. Capitalism is the problem—the Charter does not address this. With the Charter, working class dominance is not guaranteed.

4) Are class alliances in the Charter still viable?

[UDF:] Class alliances are important. The working class cannot hope to take the struggle up alone. We must broaden our base and include the black middle class. For example, the Western Cape Traders Association must be included in the struggle. They are denied certain opportunities by apartheid.

MAWU: Alliances are vital but the working class must establish its hegemony.

5) Is a future society envisaged in the Charter compatible with capitalism?

UDF: Because of the nationalisation clause, the Charter is not compatible with capitalism. The Charter is not a socialist document, but neither is it a capitalist document. Society is in a state of transition and the Charter reflects this. It is adventuristic to talk of a single stage to socialism and this is not in the interest of the working class.

MAWU: The Charter can be accommodated by capitalism. At best it is social democratic, but not socialist. Nationalisation clause does not equate [to] socialism. In Britain, for example, key sectors of the economy are nationalised but one cannot say Britain is socialist.

After these questions a general discussion followed, the better part of which focused on Poland and Solidarity—the workers movement there. The

UDF spokesperson referred to Solidarity as "undermining elements" that have to be "dealt with." In answer to this, we refer readers to a speech delivered by FOSATU General Secretary, Joe Foster, to the FOSATU Congress in April 1982. He said, "Solidarity was not struggling to restore capitalism in Poland; its struggle was to establish more democratic worker control".

A Critique

The first problem we have with the Freedom Charter is its ambiguity—that is, it can be interpreted differently by different people. For instance, the clause "The people shall govern" and the clause dealing with the nationalisation of banks, mines and the land has been taken to mean that the society envisaged by the Charter is anti-capitalist.* But as the comrade from MAWU pointed out, nationalisation or state control of sections of the economy does not equal socialism. Many countries have nationalised key aspects of their economies but the sufferings of the workers continue. Workers still don't have control over decisions. The position of workers in Britain and Poland shows that even though the state in these countries control much of the economy, the workers still lead miserable lives. A respected leader [Mandela] who supports the Charter, stated the following when writing about those clauses: "It is true that in demanding the nationalisation of the banks, the gold mines and the land, the Charter strikes a fatal blow at the financial and gold mining monopolies and farming interests. *The breaking up and democratisation of these monopolies will open up fresh fields for the development of a prosperous Non-European bourgeois class. For the first time in the history of this country the Non-European bourgeoisie will have the opportunity to own in their own name and right mines and factories, and trade and private enterprise will boom [and] flourish as never before.*"

So what we see here is a denial that the Charter implies the overthrow of capitalism. In fact, it is positively interpreted as a programme of *reforming capitalism*.

The second major problem with the Charter is that it accepts the government-imposed criteria of "national groups" and "races". The supporters of the Charter agree that there are four "nations" or "races" in South Africa—so-called "Coloureds," "Africans," "Indians," and "Whites." We believe this is dangerous for many reasons. Firstly, this kind of thinking plays into the hands of the government and collaborators like Hendrickse, Buthelezi and Rajbansi. These sellouts claim to represent different "nations" and we are giving them an opportunity to do this. It is true that many ordinary people see themselves as "indian," "zulu," etc. and it is easier to organise people in this manner because of geographical separation. But divisions have been forced onto our people for a reason: in order for the state to maintain easy control. It might be more difficult to organise across colour boundaries, but it is necessary. We must fight divisions in the process of struggle and not wait for after the revolution. We have to build a single nation under the leadership of the

---

*The Freedom Charter did not advocate nationalization of land.

working class. Failure to realise this will result in a situation where opportunistic "leaders" like Gatsha Buthelezi manipulate "ethnic symbols" for their own reason. What happened in Inanda where so-called "Zulu" workers were pitted against so-called "Indian" workers for the benefit of Gatsha and Rajbansi, teaches us the dangers of the concepts "national groups" and "races". It is difficult to see any difference between the "national groups" envisaged in the Charter and the "national groups" of today's apartheid structures. Certainly the development of "own languages, folk cultures and customs" (Charter clause) ties in neatly with what the National Party has implemented.

Thirdly, there is no attempt in the Charter to explain how working-class leadership of the struggle is compatible with the idea of several "nations" each consisting of antagonistic classes. Among the so-called "Indian national group" for instance, there are different classes. A minority in this group are businessmen, even big businessmen, but the vast majority are working people. The interests of these working people are more in line with the interests of so-called "African" and "Coloured" working people, and not with the businessmen in question. The Charter does not explain this.

Some people who support the Charter call themselves socialists but believe that we must first unite people against apartheid (the first stage), and then fight for socialism (the second stage). We in Action Youth oppose attempts to separate the struggle for democracy and the struggle for workers' power. A great deal has been written and said concerning the "democratic" way the Charter was adopted. Yet none other than Chief Albert Luthuli, then president of the ANC, mentioned in his autobiography that the Charter was never circulated for amendments to affiliates of the Congress Alliance. The man who chaired the meeting which adopted the document, Dr. Wilson Conco, actually said that he saw the document for the first time at Kliptown (where the Charter was adopted). The various congresses which made up the Congress Alliance had exactly the same vote. In other words, the miniscule white Congress of Democrats had the same vote as the ANC. This is not our idea of democracy!

Instead of the Freedom Charter, we stand by a socialist programme which reflects the class struggle and will act as a guide in our fight to end both class exploitation and national oppression.

Document 60. Report to UDF on repression in Galeshewe township, Kimberley, 1985

During the 1980 school boycotts, five students were charged and convicted under the terrorism act. They were sentenced to ten years imprisonment. Towards the end of 1984 the Appeal Court confirmed the conviction but reduced the sentence to five years imprisonment. This factor, as it will appear later on in the report, was one of the main factors in the unrest.

On the 30th January 1985 the students decided at a mass meeting held at

St. Boniface to boycott classes in solidarity with these five students. The boycott was to last for two weeks. On that day thirty-three students were arrested and detained. Twenty of them were charged and fined R50 [$25] each and the remaining thirteen were released. Of the twenty that were charged, the majority of them were either expelled or suspended from classes. This led to a further boycott on or about the 7th February 1985.

On the 26th February 1985 one hundred students were detained and charged with the offence of trespassing on school premises. The female students were fined R10 each and the male students received seven cuts [strokes with switch] each. None of the above persons are represented in court.

On the 20th March 1985, a shop belonging to the mayor and trucks belonging to a furniture company were burned and the buses in the township were stoned. This led to the appearance of 19 people in court on the following day who were charged with public violence. This case has been remanded to the 22nd April 1985. All the accused in this matter are represented by Priscilla Jana.

On the 21st March 1985 the students marched to commemorate the Sharpeville shootings. Thirteen students were detained and charged. All the accused are presently in custody and the case has been remanded to the 3rd June 1985.

On the 26th March 1985, nine students were arrested and charged with public violence. They are presently in custody.

On the 30th March 1985, soldiers were deployed in the township. They were withdrawn on the 1st April 1985. On the 1st April 1985 the house of the school inspector and the deputy mayor was burned. Some students were charged with the offence of public violence in connection with this.

On the 9th April 1985 two bakery vans and a truck belonging to a Coca-Cola company were looted. The soldiers were redeployed in the townships. They were about two hundred in number and heavily armed.

On the 10th April 1985 the high schools and secondary schools were closed after the Easter holiday. On the 11th April 1985 Thomas Morebudi, fourteen years of age, was shot dead. Circumstances surrounding his shooting are still not very clear. Initially the police refused the mother permission to identify the body. On the 14th April 1985 I spoke to the mother of Thomas Morebudi and attended on the Security Police at Kimberley to enquire about the post-mortem and inquest. On the same day I also attended on the Kimberley hospital to visit two scholars Patrick Diedricks and Leon Nkoane. When I reached the hospital I was informed that Patrick Diedricks was removed a few minutes earlier by the Security Police.

The casualty [at] least thus far is that three people have lost their lives and approximately one hundred people have been assaulted. [Of] the three deceased persons, two of them have been buried in mysterious circumstances. According to reports it is alleged that the Security police had entered into a certain agreement with the parents to have these children buried. I tried to speak to the parents of the deceased children but from reports it appears that they would not be interested in re-opening this case.

STUDENTS' GRIEVANCES
1. Democratic SRCs.
2. Shortage of text books.
3. Abolition of corporal punishment.
4. Putting a stop to sexual harassment of female students by teachers.
5. Extra recreational facilities for St. Boniface High School.
6. Those who failed matric [university entrance exams] should be allowed to attend classes and write the exams on the following year.

An important factor is that there is a great degree of confusion as to which students are being represented legally and those students that are not being represented. According to reports from students some have already appeared in court without legal representation.

ATTITUDE OF CHURCHES
The general consensus is that the churches are reluctant to help the students. According to reports it appears that the Community Councillors are applying tremendous pressure on the churches. It is suggested that the SACC get in touch with the church ministers in the area to resolve this problem.

REACTION OF PARENTS
In the main, parents are very angry with the present situation in the township. Their anger is further aggravated by the presence of soldiers. It appears that the parents are on the side of students. But a lack of a parents organisation does not afford the parents an opportunity of expressing their support.

PEOPLE DETAINED LAST WEEK
[Nine students, ages 15 to 20, are listed with their addresses and mothers' names.]

A whole lot of people are appearing in court without legal representation and it is also not clear who represents who. There is tremendous organisational work to be done.

DOCUMENT 61. Report for national workshop by Johannesburg Democratic Action Committee, January 1986 (abridged)

Jodac was established in August 1983. Presently we have an active membership of about 135 and about twice as many active supporters.

Before Jodac, a disparate, divided and unorganised white left community existed in Johannesburg which had its origins in the student movement, universities, ad-hoc political groups that worked on the Anti-Republic Day campaign in 1981 and on [the 1979 consumer boycott of] Fattis and Monis and other worker support committees and detainee support committees. There were other committed whites in service groups and in the trade unions. The white left community had no single reference point or defined relationship to the progressive movement.

When UDF began there was a great deal of interest among white democrats and many attended the UDF launch. On their return, a number of meetings were arranged to discuss the implications of the launch of the UDF for white democrats. With these discussions taking place on the eve of the [November 1983] white referendum, it was felt that an organised white UDF response was needed as a matter of urgency and therefore Jodac was set up. We held our first public meeting and distributed media around the slogan: "No is not enough". Members were also very active in publicising and fundraising for victims of Ciskei repression during the bus boycott in Mdantsane.

When Jodac began our important features were:
- We were comprised primarily of activists who mostly knew each other.
- We were isolated from our community.
- The role of democratic whites was unclear. Amongst some people there was a fear that we were setting up "another Congress of Democrats" and as a result very clear and limited aims and objects were set out: to oppose the new constitution and Koornhof bills. . . .

1984 was a year of lessons. At the AGM [annual general meeting] at the end of the year, we were able to define more clearly the role, tasks, and direction of Jodac. We identified our role as having two dimensions: providing progressive political leadership in the white community and building our organisation to achieve this. . . .

To systematically begin to increase our membership we decided to set up a "Membership" standing committee whose task would be the systematic recruitment and integration of new members. It worked successfully and 1985 saw increasing numbers of "really new faces" in our organisation.

In the first few months of 1985 we used our Programme of Action a bit like a mechanical checklist of issues that needed to be taken up. While police were massacring people in Uitenhage and the townships were going up in flames, we were building structures and planning activities. We were not responding to the tempo of struggle.

As a result a debate emerged in Jodac about whether we were responding adequately to township struggles. We criticised ourselves for not being able to add to the resistance and provide non-racial solidarity. However, more seriously, we were also out of touch with our community and so we consistently underestimated the extent to which the township violence and the declining economic situation were shaking their security and outlook and thus the potential to mobilise and organise whites. Without realising what it meant, we would be constantly surprised at the good attendance of meetings despite poor advertising.

Intervention in the white community

On reflection, our initial conception of ourselves was one of "acting on our community". For example we decided to focus on the campaign to celebrate the 30th anniversary of the Freedom Charter as our major campaign to educate ourselves and to "broaden an understanding and acceptance of the Freedom Charter in our community". We did not consider where the white community was "at" but what we thought could be good for them.

We spent a lot of time defining the different constituencies in the white community i.e. the Black Sash, liberals, the so-called "Rockey Street" constituency i.e. young punks [in Yeoville, Johannesburg], women, churches and the non-Jodac left. This exercise was very useful because we began realising the complexities of our community and the importance of targeting specific constituencies.

We then organised a debate about "political alternatives" for the liberals, a cultural evening which included an Afrikaner orientation, a concert for the Rockey Streeters and intended debate with the non-Jodac left. These events were successful in that they were politicising although not necessarily winning support for the Freedom Charter. But we did not confront the growing anxieties of white South Africa about issues like violence. We were also faced with the problem of where to take people from there. . . .

Concerned Citizens began after the Black Sash called a meeting of white groups to respond to the [1985] State of Emergency. The groups which attended and later became part of Concerned Citizens were: Black Sash, Jodac, PFP [Progressive Federal Party], Nusas [National Union of SA Students], DPSC [Detainees' Parents Support Committee] and HAP [Human Awareness Programme].

The aims of Concerned Citizens were to channel the concern being expressed by increasing numbers of whites into protest action and to educate whites about the inevitability of majority rule—and in fact the desirability of majority rule to achieve lasting peace.

Both Nusas and Jodac debated participating with the PFP. After consultation with the UDF, we decided to go for it because:

• We felt that at that time we were too weak and vulnerable to go it alone.
• The PFP's constituency was also ours and we needed to make inroads into it.
• To withdraw from Concerned Citizens because of the PFP would alienate us from the Black Sash with whom it is very important to have good relations.
• The nature of CC did not prevent us from attacking the PFP and furthering the UDF.

In evaluating Concerned Citizens we perhaps reached more people than [had] we gone it "alone". But possibly it was the political climate coupled with the non-threatening slogan of CC that drew people to our meetings. The Concerned Citizens concept is definitely a successful one in our community although we are presently questioning whether we may have lost the "Concerned Citizens moment". With the clampdown on information and events like [MK's bombing in] Amanzimtoti, the concern and flux may be hardening.

The central problem of Concerned Citizens was the same as of the Freedom Charter campaign: how does one move from mobilisation to organisation. Let us look at this issue in more detail.

From mobilisation to organisation

At our public events and at events such as the Free People's Concert, we have always staffed tables with "What is Jodac" forms and encouraged people to join Jodac. People who fill in these forms are invited to new members meetings and forums where Jodac and UDF are explained and discussions are held on topical issues. People are then encouraged to pay subs and join branches or sub-committees.

In 1985 we recruited about 40 new members. More and more of our members do not come from a university background or have previous organisational experience. However our membership remains predominantly young and soon become activists if they are not already. People do not join just because they want to identify with us.

We have not resolved the problem of how to recruit hundreds of people into Jodac. And should all "concerned citizens type people" be recruited into Jodac or should we be thinking of a broader structure like a "Concerned Citizens action group" for such people. What should our response be to the people who have joined newly established groups such as "Jews for Social Justice" and "Artists against Apartheid"?. . .

Action

The issue of action was first realised when we debated how to respond to the increasing tempo of struggle. We needed to think of "creative action", we said. It was at the time of [trade unionist] Andries Raditsela's death and on the day of his funeral we held placard demonstrations, handed out pamphlets and stretched banners across bridges. These kind of activities were repeated on Republic Day, and to protest the assassination of Matthew Goniwe. Members have also placed dummies in central town and organised street theatre to protest against the Gaborone Raid [June 14, 1985] and on June 16th. . . . A "Run for Peace" was suggested which would be a protest action in which people would not feel scared to participate. As it happened the run was banned and about 200 people who came through the police "roadblocks" defied the ban. . . .

Relationship to UDF

UDF is Jodac's primary political reference point. In the Transvaal, UDF went through a process of restructuring so as to improve its internal democracy and political effectiveness. However these developments were severely impeded by intense repression crystalising in the [1985] state of emergency. Since the emergency as Jodac's membership has grown, UDF has become more and more of a distant reality. Its normal structures have stopped functioning and its public profile is mostly restricted to press releases and occasional pamphlets. How and when UDF will be able to operate openly again is not easy to predict.

New forms of organisation and activity still need to be developed to continue the struggle under present conditions. Jodac needs to be part of that process and presently we are looking at creative ways to work with UDF affiliates in the Johannesburg area. . . .

In the white community the image of the UDF has been tarnished by the constant linking of the UDF to violence. Our role is to put forward a clear understanding of violence, re-establish the primacy of mass based politics and rebuild the credibility of the UDF as the positive alternative which could bring about lasting peace. Formally the relation to UDF happens through two representatives at the UDF General Council and two observers at a Johannesburg Area Committee comprising all UDF affiliates in the Johannesburg area. This structure has not functioned since the Emergency. . . .

Johannesburg, being as large as it is, has a very wide and complex political spectrum. We are only beginning to develop an understanding of that part of the Johannesburg population which we could call our "constituency". . . .

Liberals:	Who may or may not identify with the PFP and have both conservative and progressive tendencies.
"Rockey Streeters":	Consists mainly of young people who are jollers [party-goers] but jollers who often rebel against the "system."
Afrikaans people:	There is a growing number of Afrikaans speaking people to the left of the PFP, who are looking for alternative forums of involvement.
Other left-wing people:	There is an unorganised grouping of people who are influenced by a "workerist" political tendency.
Church people:	Increasing numbers of white church goers are being influenced by progressive moves in their churches. They are also developing progressive organisation.

Concerned Citizens derived support from these sectors. Within these sectors, one could identify target groups. For example the Black Sash liberals rather than the SAIRR [SA Institute of Race Relations] liberals . . . [who] are Inkatha supporters. They make a few interventions in the white community with their newsletter and occasional forums on topical issues. At the moment they tend to be in line with the politics of big business. . . . [Fourteen other organizations are listed.]

Jodac has close working relations with all white UDF affiliates but works with them mainly in the UDF area committee (which includes black groups). Anti-apartheid feeling is growing in Johannesburg. This includes a dissatisfaction with PFP politics. However it is also characterised by flux and confusion and to some extent reflects the great liberal dilemma—an opposition to apartheid but a fear of majority rule.

Although it is difficult at this stage to really assess the strength and impact of the NCM [National Convention Movement] in the white area, it is with this disillusioned constituency that it could have most effect. The fear of township violence has also created confusion. People tend to look at the "politics of negotiation" as a viable alternative. The confusion has been made worse by the clampdown on the press from reporting township struggles.

The ongoing crisis, the political flux and lack of information all provide openings for ideological intervention, mobilisation and action.

DOCUMENT 62. "OUT—Organisations United Against Traitors." Flyer by Woodstock civic group, Cape Town, May 1986

LIGHTS OUT! EVERY WEDNESDAY 9 PM - 10 PM

PLACE CANDLES IN YOUR FRONT WINDOWS TO SHOW YOUR REJECTION OF THE MPs

Last year all over the Western Cape people united against the State of Emergency by burning candles. Let us unite and show our rejection of these MPs [Members of Parliament in the coloured House of Representatives] by having a candlelight protest every Wednesday night. Let each family put out their lights between 9 p.m. and 10 p.m. and burn candles.

WHY IS ALL THIS HAPPENING?

In 1984 the people in this area rejected the tricameral parliament with [the] lowest poll recorded in the country. Now the government is trying to force these rejected puppets on us by building their houses in our area.

If we allow them to build these houses:
- Marsden Rd residents face eviction,
- Schools in the area will be closed,
- Our only sports field, "the Greens," will be taken away from us,
- Police barracks will be built in our area.

We *MUST* reject them as we did in 1984!
We *MUST NOT* allow these houses to be built!

WE HAVE SHOWN OUR REJECTION!

In February 1986 organisations in the area formed OUT (Organisations United Against Traitors). We launched a campaign to show our opposition to the building of houses and to stop these traitors from moving into our area. OUT has held two successful Fun Runs and a Public Meeting. Two weeks ago students from Walmer Junior, Salt River, Vista, Kensington and Trafalgar protested on the land and succeeded in driving the bulldozers away.

RESIDENTS MARCH

On Saturday the residents successfully marched against the building of the houses in Walmer Estate. About 200 people holding placards saying "We rejected them in '84, we reject them now," and "MPs OUT—leave our schools alone", marched down the Main Road. On the way back, the people's march was stopped by two vans filled with armed police. They tried to take away our placards and ordered us to disperse.

WE BUILD A PEOPLE'S PARK

On Sunday morning residents from the area gathered on the building site to build a People's Park. They came with spades, plants, swings, etc. to build a much needed play park for the area. We started by building a volleyball court and started playing. But we were viciously prevented by a truck load of police armed with teargas, batons and guns. They declared our volleyball game an illegal gathering. They prevented us from using public open space that belongs to us and should be available for our use.

Why are the police reacting so strongly to our actions? Because they want to force the puppets on us. They do not want us to take control, they want to control us.

HOW TO STOP THEM

Many of us feel helpless that the police and government are too strong and we are too weak. We have power. Our greatest strength is our *UNITY* and our combined action. Our united action in 1984 was a blow to the tricameral parliament. United action has destroyed community councils in other areas.

WE SHALL BUILD A PEOPLE'S PARK

Residents, workers, students, we must occupy the land they want to build the houses on. We must make that area into a park that the whole community can use. From now on the "Greens" and land that has been cleared shall be our park. We must use this land for our sport and other open air activities, with or without permission.

HAVE YOU SIGNED THE OBJECTION FORM?

OUT is collecting signatures from residents to show how strongly we reject the building of these houses. *SIGN THE PETITION.*
- Let us unite and build our People's Park
- Let us unite and hold our candlelight demonstrations
- Let us unite and sign the petition
- Let us unite in any action needed to prevent these traitors from violating our land

PUPPETS ON STAGE NOT IN OUR AREA.
OUT!

Document 63. "Why I Refuse to Participate in the South African Defence Force." Court statement by Philip Wilkinson, May 1987

I am a Christian, brought up in the beliefs of the Catholic Church. I am committed to peace and to working for a better future for all South Africans. I abhor violence and have consciously not used violence myself since my childhood. I have been brought up to respect all people, regardless of their colour, sex, religion or status. I believe that all armies legitimise the use of violence and dehumanise the "enemy."

The SADF [SA Defence Force] defends apartheid, which in terms of my Christian understanding is a heresy. For me to participate in the SADF would therefore be a betrayal of all that I know to be good and just. The Bible and the teachings of the Catholic Church call on me to identify with the suffering and the oppressed. As a Christian, I must therefore involve myself in the community around me.

It is this concern for peace and for justice that has led me to work at the Port Elizabeth Crisis Information Centre, a centre which helps people who have been hurt by security force actions, for example, detention, harassment and assault. The centre helps trace missing people by phoning police stations, prisons, hospitals and mortuaries. It also requests permits for families to visit loved ones in detention, from the security police.

My work therefore brings me into daily contact with victims of apartheid and has confirmed my belief that service in the SADF is not national service. It serves only the ruling minority. National Service under the present system should rather involve defying this government and working for a better one.

The SADF commits crimes against humanity as long as it defends the universally condemned system of apartheid. Apartheid has been legalised, reformed and enforced to give power to a minority over a majority of South Africans. This power is used not only to ensure the vast wealth of our land is held in a few hands but also to deprive millions of people of their basic human rights.

The SADF is one of the most powerful tools in the hands of the present-day rulers. This is demonstrated by its repressive actions both in Namibia and South Africa. The South African occupation of Namibia is illegal. This has resulted in death for thousands of her combatants whilst greedy governments, multi-nationals [corporations] and individuals rape Namibia's resources and exploit her people.

A report by the South African Catholic Bishops' Conference concludes that there is universal consensus—with South Africa being the only dissenting voice—that South Africa has no right to be in Namibia. The atrocities of the security forces are described in these words:

They break into homes, beat up residents, shoot people, steal and kill cattle and often pillage stores and tea rooms. When the tracks of SWAPO [South West Africa People's Organisation] guerillas are discovered by the security forces the

Figure 18. On August 3, 1988, 143 young whites simultaneously announced their refusal to serve in the South African Defence Force. Andre Zaaiman, a former infantry captain and anti-conscription activist, addresses the Cape Town members of the group. *Eric Miller/africanpictures.net*

local people are in danger. Harsh measures are intensified. People are blindfolded, taken from their homes and left beaten up and even dead by the roadside. Women are often raped. It is not unknown for a detachment to break into a home and while Black soldiers keep watch over the family, White soldiers select the best-looking girls and take them into the veld [fields] *to rape them. There is no redress because reporting irregularities or atrocities to commanders is considered a dangerous or fruitless exercise.*

Back in South Africa, SADF troops have been responsible for brutally repressing resistance to apartheid. Troops have been used to harass, detain, maim and kill South Africans. They have cordoned off whole townships for days at a time, slowing down residents' movements while passes and I.D. books are checked. At the same time other troops go on house-to-house searches—smashing windows, breaking down doors, destroying personal property, stealing possessions and insulting and assaulting occupants. Troops have also been used to remove forcibly whole, productive and thriving communities into resettlement camps situated in dusty and barren wastelands.

My understanding of the role of the SADF in the townships is again supported by my church. In their report on unrest in the Eastern Cape, the Catholic Priests' Council says:

"Then there are the SAP [SA Police] and now the SADF who are there under the guise of restoring law and order but because of their behaviour and meth-

ods, often aggravate the situation and are themselves the cause of much distraction, loss of life, abuse and assaults on people."

Only dictatorial, minority or fascist governments will find the need to rule by force in order to keep power. By the same token, only an undemocratic government such as ours will find it necessary to declare a national state of emergency to suppress the protests of the voteless majority. This emergency enables the government to continue providing gutter education, poor housing and inadequate health services.

The use of troops in the townships is a desperate attempt to address political problems with military power. This government should have learnt by now that the people's legitimate grievances must be addressed before we can have peace in our land. They could start by allowing our exiles to come back home, by releasing all political prisoners and detainees, by withdrawing all discriminatory laws and by negotiating with the popular and respected leadership. Shooting and detaining people willy-nilly is no solution for our country.

It is brutally obvious that the SADF's main task is to prop up a political system that is based on the denial of full political rights to the majority of South Africans.

My decision to refuse to fight in the SADF is not one I have taken lightly. I realise many people will see me as a cheeky youngster who is looking for trouble or as a victim of "communist propaganda," pressurised by various organisations into an extreme position. This is not the case.

My own experiences—such as attending non-racial Catholic Schools, spending two years in a racist army, visiting the townships and working for prejudiced bosses—have led me to this position.

For all of us there comes a point when we can no longer compromise. A situation becomes so difficult to live with that we have to stand up for what we believe in—no matter what the cost to ourselves and our loved ones. I have reached that point with military service. I cannot justify going into the SADF politically, morally, or theologically. I suspect the government has also found it increasingly difficult to justify conscription and has therefore restricted public debate on the subject.

Thousands of young, white men are being forced to defend a system they do not support, when they would rather be living peacefully with their families. I cannot condemn these unwilling soldiers, for I was once one of them. I know [well] the pain that these reluctant conscripts go through. I can only advise them to act as morally as they can under the circumstances and to join the End Conscription Campaign. By doing that they would take forward its call for all conscripts to have the right to alternative service and the right to refuse to fight in the townships and Namibia.

Your worship, I have stated my reasons for refusing to be conscripted into the SADF clearly and honestly. If this court should choose to punish me on account of them, so be it. I have in my heart an absolute conviction that what I am doing is right. I will not sacrifice my life or lend my body to the defence of apartheid. Apartheid is a crime against humanity and many of those leading its armed forces are its foremost criminals. I can foresee the day when those responsible for calling me up are themselves on trial for their crimes.

As I stand before you, I stand for peace and I stand for justice. I stand here in the spirit of the South Africa we have yet to build.

3. Internal Opposition: Moving Toward Deadlock

DOCUMENT 64. "SOYCO's Programme of Action." Soweto Youth Congress memorandum, 1983

PROBLEMS OF THE YOUTH:
  Scattered all over the ghetto.
  Unemployed.
  Drop-out from school or varsity.
  Over indulgence in drinking.
  Smoking dagga [marijuana] and taking drugs.
  Involved in criminal offences.
  Many are illiterate because of financial problems.
  Poverty and hunger.

THE PURPOSE OF OUR PROGRAMME OF ACTION:
- To strengthen SOYCO by establishing branches.
- The main aim is to have 12 strong branches after six months.

How do we strengthen the branches?
- By organising seminars, workshops and group discussions.
- By holding study groups and offering literacy classes.
- By offering extra tuition to students.
- By taking care of the aged and pensioners.
- By visiting families of detained members and advising them of legal channels.
- By morally and physically helping families of the deceased members or relatives.
- By offering strict disciplinary lessons to all SOYCO members.

- By organising bursaries for needy members.
- By playing a supportive role in struggles waged by trade unions, student organisations, women's organisations, political organisations and church organisations.
- Ensurance of proper co-ordination in all the struggles waged by all sections of the population.
- To instill in the youth that spirit of loyalty and respect for the time tested leadership.
- To make sure that everybody strives for the ultimate achievement of the minimum demands stated in the Freedom Charter.
- To make sure that all the people of South Africa achieve both social and national emancipation.
- To follow all the campaigns and programmes of National nature under the auspices of the United Democratic Front and the Release Mandela Campaign.
- To root out and destroy all the reactionary and counter-revolutionary elements throughout the country and the world.
- To actively support a move towards regional and National co-ordination and consolidation of the Youth structures.
- To make a principled alliance with all the progressive forces striving towards non-racialism as embraced within the ever democratic document; the beacon of the people's liberation; the FREEDOM CHARTER.
- By organising fund raising projects like film shows, gumbas [parties], jumble sales, concerts, dramas and poetry shows, picnics, outings and youth camps.
- By organising inter-sports games with other youth clubs not antagonistic to our aims and objectives.
- By making regular visits to our members and from time to time investigating trouble-torn families within our areas.

All the above-mentioned activities will gradually involve the youth in active participation especially in a venture to solve their day to day problems. This will once more ensure mass-mobilisation and mass-action. For this will develop them from a low political profile to a high one. Such will ensure a thorough understanding of a non-racial democratic struggle towards the achievement of a National Democratic country.

A. SHORT-TERM OBJECTIVES:
- Expand our membership.
- Mobilise our membership.
- Ensure Unity in Action.
- To apply flexibility of tactics in challenging the enemy.

B. LONG-TERM OBJECTIVES
- To convert the youth into responsible disciplined positions of leadership.
- To ensure continuity and development in terms of unity, mass-participation and mass-action.

Document 65. Letter from Chief Mangosuthu Gatsha Buthelezi to Oliver Tambo, September 7, 1984, reproduced in Inkatha's *Clarion Call*, volume 3, 1987 (abridged)

Dear Brother,

I am writing to you in response to your telegram of concern about violence in Lamontville. You quite rightly call it "fratricidal" but by now you will have learnt that my meeting in Lamontville, attended by at least 15,000 people, was entirely peaceful, and I know of no single act of violence.

I am writing in the sincere hope that you will hear me when I say that Inkatha does not get involved in fratricidal violence against fellow black South Africans. Inkatha is genuinely and deeply committed to non-violence in the circumstances in which we find ourselves today. . . .

It is a simple truth that ever since we Black South Africans sent you and your colleagues out into the world to establish a Mission there to support the struggle at home, there has been a growing tendency of your Mission in Exile to encourage violence. The Mission in Exile, in repeated messages to the world, has hailed acts of Black/Black violence as heroic. In the 1976-78 period, when Blacks were killing Blacks, it was I who had to go to Soweto to stop violence there from becoming fratricidal. While I was doing so, the Mission in Exile was encouraging violence. I know of no statement during that period in which you or any one of your colleagues expressed disgust when Black militants, and even school children, turned to killing other blacks. I heard no condemnation which came from you and your colleagues when young people were encouraged to attempt to kill me at Robert Sobukwe's funeral at Graaff-Reinet. . . .

The Mission in Exile has publicly and internationally acclaimed the UDF. UDF elements together with AZASO and AZAPO, even now continue to perpetrate acts of violence against their fellow Blacks in Inkatha. It is these same elements who tried to engineer a Black/Black confrontation in Lamontville on the 1st September when I went there. . . .

Your colleagues have already declared war on KwaZulu and on Inkatha. Should your concern about fratricidal violence not direct you towards putting your own house in order first? In this part of South Africa, we come from warrior stock and there is a resilient determination in KwaZulu and in Inkatha which even the full might of the State will never be able to flatten. Do your colleagues really think they can flatten us on the way to their envisaged victory?

These are fundamentally important things which we should not be writing about. We should be talking about them face to face and for the sake of South Africa, I am still prepared to forget the past and to bring some of my people with me to meet you and your people. I make this statement not because I need to see you to bolster my own position. I make it for the sake of the struggle, firmly believing that a time may come when Black/Black reconciliation could only take place after we have gone through the traumatic experience of a civil war situation and its aftermath. Black South Africa has never been unified; you know this as well as I do, and the myth that the ANC is alive and well in the hearts and minds of the people, and that the ANC has achieved the unification of the people, are myths of potent danger. Neither you nor I have succeeded in uniting South Africa, but I have succeeded in uniting a million and more people in close political unity. Is this not a building block for national unity?

With my warmest regard to you and your colleagues,
Yours in the struggle for liberation,

MANGOSUTHU G. BUTHELEZI

DOCUMENT 66. Program of the first annual National General Council of the UDF, Azaadville, Krugersdorp, April 5–7, 1985 (abridged)

FROM PROTEST TO CHALLENGE—
FROM MOBILISATION TO ORGANISATION
UDF NATIONAL EXECUTIVE COMMITTEE

Chairperson	Curnick Ndlovu
General Secretary	Popo Molefe
Publicity Secretary	Mosiuoa Lekota
Treasurer	Azhar Cachalia
Other Members	Steve Tshwete
	Zollie Malindi
	Mcebisi Xundu
	Edgar Ngoyi
	Makhenkesi Stofile
	Yunus Mahomed
	Trevor Manuel
	Mohammed Valli [Moosa]
	Derrick Swartz
	Jomo Khasu
	Titus Mafolo
	Oliver Mohapi

UDF REGIONAL EXECUTIVE COMMITTEES

TRANSVAAL

President	:	Albertina Sisulu
Vice President	:	Samson Ndou
Vice President	:	RAM Salojee
Vice President	:	[Prof.] Ismail Mohamed
General Secretary	:	Mohammed Valli [Moosa]
General Secretary	:	Paul Mashatile
Minute Secretary	:	Eddie Makue
Publicity Secretary	:	Sydney Mufamadi
Rural Secretary	:	Murphy Morobe
Media Officer	:	Mzwakhe Mbuli

DOCUMENTS FOR CHAPTER 3   389

Education Officer	:	Raymond Suttner
Youth Portfolio	:	Dan Montsitsi
Student Portfolio	:	Mathews Sathekge
Labour Portfolio	:	Paul Maseko
Women's Portfolio	:	Amanda Kwadi
Civic Portfolio	:	Arthur Mkhwanazi
Treasurer	:	Azhar Cachalia
Treasurer	:	Titus Mafolo

NATAL

President	:	Archie Gumede
Chairman	:	Rev. M. Xundu
Vice Chairman	:	Billy Nair
Secretary	:	Yunus Mahomed
Publicity Secretary	:	Lechesa Tsenoli
Treasurer	:	Victoria Mxenge
NIC	:	Jerry Coovadia
NCC	:	Sandy Africa
RMC	:	Russell Mphanga
Youth	:	Ndaba
Students	:	Ronnie
DHAC	:	Virgil Bonhomme
JORAC	:	Ian Mkhize
NOW	:	Nosizwe
Diakonia	:	Paddy Kearney
Unions	:	Themba Nxumalo

WESTERN CAPE

President	:	Zollie Malindi
Vice President	:	Wilfred Rhodes
Vice President	:	Christmas Tinto
Secretary	:	Trevor Manuel
Secretary	:	Miranda Qwanyashe
Secretary	:	Ebrahim Rasool
Publicity Secretary	:	Zoliswa Kota
Treasurer	:	Joe Adams
Fund Raiser	:	Goolam Abubaker
Additional Member	:	Mildred Lesia
Additional Member	:	Mountain Qumbela
Additional Member	:	Graeme Bloch
Additional Member	:	Rev. Syd Luckett
Education & Training	:	Jeremy Cronin

BORDER

President	:	Steve Tshwete
Vice President	:	Nqola
Vice President	:	Sonwabo Nqoyi

Secretary	:	Rev. M. Stofile
Publicity Secretary	:	Andrew Hendricks
Treasurer	:	Hintsa Siwisa
Additional Member	:	Lucille Meyer
Assistant Treasurer	:	T. Botha
Organiser	:	Humphrey Moxhegwana
Additional Member	:	Yure Mdyogolo

EASTERN CAPE

President	:	E. Ngoyi
Vice President	:	H. Fazzie
General Secretary	:	D. Swartz
Publicity Secretary	:	S. Sizani
Recording Secretary	:	M. Ndube
Organiser	:	M. Goniwe
Treasurer	:	Vacant

STATEMENT OF THE UDF GENERAL COUNCIL

This meeting of more than 300 committed and enthusiastic delegates, representing millions of people throughout the country on this Easter weekend in Azaadville is ample proof and eloquent testimony to the strength and resilience of the UDF as a mass organisation.

Meeting in the context of state repression unparalleled in the past twenty five years and on the basis of overwhelming popular support throughout the country, the UDF continues to represent and articulate the genuine needs and demands of all democratic South Africans. . . .

We also meet at a time of unequalled world-wide support from ordinary men and women, organisations in all countries committed to the elimination of racism, and of most governments throughout the world. Against this massive show of international solidarity, the right wing Reagan/Thatcher/Kohl axis and their allies continue to bolster the apartheid regime.

Oppressed and democratic South Africans demand that these imperialist powers support the forces of justice and democracy. They must abandon their traditional role in backing the oppressive and undemocratic governments purely for motives of greed and profit. Their international duty is to support the just struggle of the South African people for peace, justice and freedom.

We take the opportunity during this period of grave crises, when the progressive forces are being threatened on all fronts, to caution those individuals and organisations who differ with us to desist from attacking the UDF and fragmenting the ranks of the oppressed and instead to emphasise the points of common concern.

We call on them to be mindful that the state is arming its agents, seeking to strengthen its support and broaden its base by co-opting the Hendrickses, Rajbansis, the Sebes and the Buthelezis, and it therefore becomes the historic duty of all those who oppose apartheid to foster unity. . . .

We therefore make the following immediate demands as the beginning of

a process of transition from the prevailing oppressive and exploitative order to a democratic state:
1. the immediate scrapping of the 1913 and 1936 Land Acts and all Group Areas Laws, and an end to any form of forced removals
2. the dissolution of the bantustans and the ending of the migratory labour system
3. the scrapping of the tri-cameral parliament and all other puppet bodies created under the Black Local Authorities Act and other instruments of racist rule
4. a unified and democratic education system
5. the repeal of the pass laws and all other restrictions on freedom of movement
6. the right of workers to freely organise in trade unions, to collectively bargain and the right to strike without being penalised, the right to security of employment, housing, social welfare, pensions and maternity benefits, as laid down in the United Nations Human Rights Covenants and the Charters of the International Labour Organisation
7. the release of all political prisoners, the unbanning of banned individuals and organisations, the return of exiles and the lifting of all restrictions on freedom of speech and assembly
8. the disbanding of the SADF [SA Defence Force], Koevoet [SADF force in Namibia], the SAP [SA Police] and all other repressive apparatuses
9. the scrapping of all barbaric "security" laws which violate the fundamental freedoms set out in the Universal Declaration of Human Rights.

SECRETARIAL REPORT

This National General Council takes place after we have just completed the first phase of our campaign against the so-called new dispensation in particular and apartheid as a whole. Although we were successful in mobilising the masses to reject the government's schemes, the Nationalists are going ahead with the tri-cameral and Black Local Authorities scheme. This means that our broad Front must move to the second phase of challenging this new dispensation because it has no democratic approval of the people. In this regard the theme of our conference, "Protest to Challenge—Mobilisation to Organisation" is indeed relevant. . . .

BUILDING AND BROADENING THE FRONT

We launched the Front with only three constituted regions. Today we have five fully constituted regions and four regions which are growing into fully fledged structures. The demand for the UDF to reach out to areas such as Northern Natal, Orange Free State and Northern Transvaal in the form of solid structures is growing louder by the day. It will be important for this conference to make provision for the executive to meet these requests of the people.

Whilst it is true that the state feels the presence and work of the Front acutely, it is also true that the UDF is still not able to employ its full strength against the government policies. A number of reasons account for this:

Decision Making

Decision making constitutes an important element of our work in that every decision taken must advance our struggle. Because of the broad nature of our Front, having a number of structures and affiliates, decision making requires a great deal of time. At times this has meant that the Front has been unable to provide a lead on some issues, for example the current education crisis. Since it is essential that we are able to lead our people in every struggle they fight, we must find a way of taking quick decisions whilst maintaining maximum unity. In this regard it may be necessary to devolve powers to regions thus enabling them to take decisions timeously on matters which are specific to them and need immediate implementation. The successful stay-aways in the Transvaal and Eastern Cape are cases in point.

Co-ordinating the work of the Front

One of the important aspects of the Front is co-ordination. With our present structures and the rate at which the Front has expanded and continues to expand, we have not been co-ordinating effectively, especially where the state attacks us as it is doing at present. We need to restructure the Front in such a way that it can respond quickly and effectively to emergencies such as sudden detentions which are similar to those of last August and early this year. . . .

Relations with unaffiliated organisations

At the inception of the Front a number of organisations, especially some unions, were sceptical of the potential of the UDF. . . .

Relations between the Front and unaffiliated trade unions have improved since the national launch. In the campaign against the new constitution [and tricameral] elections, trade unions such as Fosatu [Federation of SA Trade Unions], GWU [General Workers' Union], African Food and Canning Workers' Union and Cape Town Municipal Workers Union joined forces with the Front in regions such as the Western and Eastern Cape. Similarly in the Transvaal Stay-away last year, most unions joined forces with the UDF in making that campaign the success that it ultimately became. Unfortunately this spirit of growing unity has not yet taken root or concrete form in other regions. In the recent stay-away in P.E. [Port Elizabeth] a decidedly negative response was received from local union branches in spite of determined consultations by our Eastern Cape affiliates with unions there. We must continue to pursue the path of unity with the unions as a matter of priority.

A significant development was our establishment of bilateral relations with the South African Council on Sport in Durban last year. Presently we are seeking consultation and co-operation with SACOS on the coming New Zealand Rugby tour, if it should take place. Joint protest and boycott of the tour will help to register our people's opposition to this sell-out tour.

INTERNATIONAL RELATIONS

Since its inception our Front has been able to generate huge support on the international plane. Virtually all anti-apartheid forces have rallied to the support of the Front. Most progressive Western governments have generally protested apartheid, especially the continued exclusion of the majority of South Africans from the government of this country. Except for the U.S. and Great Britain, all the member countries in the UN General Assembly voted in support of a resolution condemning the new constitution.

Anti-apartheid organisations throughout the world have firmly supported the Front since inception. Indeed, those governments which have stood up against South Africa have done so largely because of the strength of anti-apartheid movements in those countries. In this regard we must single out the Swedish Labour Movement which was the first to acknowledge the contribution of the UDF to the struggle for freedom by awarding the Front the Let Live Prize on 27 July 1984. The prize was received by Comrades Murphy Morobe and Cassim Saloojee. Subsequent to this, a number of organisations in Sweden produced booklets and posters on the UDF and these were widely distributed. Progressives in countries such as the Netherlands, in Great Britain and elsewhere in continental Europe, rose up to the occasion as they pressured their governments to support the anti-apartheid cause. The most dramatic work was that performed by the British AAM [Anti-Apartheid Movement] and, early this year, the "Free South Africa Movement" [in the U.S.] who successfully pressured these governments to vote in favour of the call for the unconditional release of Nelson Mandela and other political prisoners; the release of UDF leaders who are charged with treason and the condemnation of murder of our people in Crossroads who were resisting forced removals.

At this stage we wish to draw attention to the fact that in our approach to international relations, our comrades must realise that there is a difference between administrations of those countries and the progressive forces therein. Reagan supports apartheid by way of constructive engagement, but it does not follow that all American people are behind constructive engagement. The activities of the "Free South Africa Movement" and the anti-apartheid congressional lobby headed by [U.S. Senator] Edward Kennedy clearly demonstrate this point. Even in imperialist countries, there are people and groups who are committed to the struggle for the overthrow of apartheid. . . .

REPRESSION
From its inception the UDF has witnessed a conscious decision by the state to undermine the work of the Front and to isolate it from the people. To this end various methods were adopted ranging from disinformation to naked vicious repression.

Disinformation
Several bogus pamphlets were distributed country-wide during most of 1984. Disinformation about the Front and its activities has also been spread through various forms of media.

Ban on Meetings
Several meetings of the UDF and its affiliates have been banned. Currently, meetings of the Front and 28 of its affiliates are banned in 18 magisterial districts. 16 of these districts are in the Eastern Cape and 2 are in the Transvaal.

In addition, all meetings, anywhere in the country, called to discuss a stay-at-home, are banned.

Denial of venues to the UDF

Premises controlled by Development boards are denied to the UDF for the purpose of meetings. Priests who have made their churches available for UDF meetings are threatened with withdrawal of lease rights.

Rural areas and Bantustans

In the Ciskei, hundreds of our people were tortured by [Lennox] Sebe during the bus boycott in 1983. Several UDF leaders and activists continue to be victims of Sebe's barbaric legal system. 38 UDF officials and members of its affiliates are currently detained in Ciskei, as well as SAAWU [SA Allied Workers' Union] being banned there.

In Bophuthatswana several of our supporters and activists have been dismissed from their jobs or transferred to areas where organising would be difficult for them.

In KwaZulu the UDF affiliates, Cosas and Azasco, are banned. In [October] 1983, four student supporters of the UDF were killed by the Inkatha impis [warrior brigades] in a desperate attempt to coerce support for Buthelezi. Leading officials of the Front, including Comrade Archie Gumede suffered assaults at the hands of Inkatha. The list of incidents of repression in this Bantustan is too long to quote.

In the Transkei the UDF is banned.

Detentions and the Treason Trial

By August last year the state methods of attempting to suppress the UDF and the support it had gained, yielded no results. On the eve of the elections for the House of Delegates, the state detained key officials of the UDF and its affiliates. This swoop culminated in trumped up treason charges. On February 19, more than one hundred houses of UDF activists and all the UDF offices countrywide were raided and all documents confiscated. An additional eight key officials of the UDF and its affiliates were charged with treason.

In October last year in a speech to the Transvaal Congress of the NP [National Party], [minister Louis] Le Grange threatened to take drastic action against the UDF for what he labeled "ANC Front work." Clearly the state was preparing white public opinion for the treason trial. . . .

Instances of General Repression

Two homes of leading UDF activists were burnt down in Welkom; the shop of a key UDF activist was vandalised and burnt; 5 homes of our activists in Soweto were petrol bombed; a comrade's brother was killed when their home was petrol bombed by a Uitenhage councillor; comrade Kratshi was shot dead by police in his home; a leading UDF activist in Graaff-Reinet was assaulted and later knocked down by a police car, and yet police refused to accept charges of assault which he brought up against them. In East London shots were fired at the house of a UDF activist. In P.E. the house of the general secretary of PEBCO [Port Elizabeth Black Civic Organisation] and that of the president of PEWO [Port Elizabeth Women's Organisation] were petrol bombed and burnt to the ground, and another comrade's uncle was shot dead at point blank range when he opened the door to persons suspected by local people to be police.

On the morning of the 21st of March, the *Citizen* carried a front page story in which General [Johann] Coetzee of the SA Police stated that he would take action to protect police because police were now being killed by people. At 10.00 am that same morning, police and army personnel opened fire with R1 rifles and shotguns. The full extent of the Langa massacre is yet to be established but our information clearly shows that by now more than 100 people have already been killed in and around Uitenhage.

What is the meaning of all this? It is that the state, or at least some arm of the state, has taken a deliberate decision to employ terrorist methods against our activists, organisations and Front because the UDF won the political battle against the government. It is important that this conference understands this point thoroughly and carries it back to our organisations and members. In this regard we have already been ushered into the period of Koevoet atrocities as witnessed in the Namibian struggle. . . .

In the face of these ominous signs a special task before this conference is to examine a style of work that will enable the Front to survive the hard times ahead.

EVALUATIONS OF CAMPAIGNS IN BRIEF

Generally all our campaigns have been successful. We achieved unprecedented levels of mobilisation for each one of our campaigns. But there are certain subjective weaknesses which must be pointed out.

Black Local Authorities

After a successful campaign against the BLA, our affiliates failed to assert their legitimacy at a local level. Subsequent to raising the level of awareness and generating excitement, our affiliates did not mobilise the masses effectively. In many areas in the townships, organisations trail behind the masses thus making it difficult for a disciplined mass action to take place. More often there is a spontaneity of actions in the townships. . . .

Million Signature Campaign

Most of the objectives of the MSC were achieved, however we need to make certain criticisms. Lack of thorough planning in the campaign was glaring. The campaign was launched when some affiliates were not ready to take it on. The campaign was launched at a crucial time in terms of the anti-election campaign, however when the decision to embark on the MSC was taken, it was hoped that the MSC would merge with the Anti-election campaign. Instead there was a definite shift of concentration from the MSC to the preparations for the anti-election work. This made it difficult for the smooth running of the MSC campaign. . . .

Training of Activists

Quite often activists had to go into the field without sufficient understanding of what was expected of them, or even the ability to answer questions raised by the masses. Very often such inabilities are demoralising. . . .

CHALLENGES FACING THE FRONT

In the last 19 months of our existence major gains were made at the level of building the Front and increasing our capacity to mobilise our people. We can call a mass meeting any time and fill Fun City or the Jabulani Amphitheatre, but now the question that we musk ask ourselves is, "What are the challenges facing the UDF today?" The key questions facing us are:

The transformation of mass support to active participation in the day to day activities of our organisations: we must deepen our organisation. Out of the mobilised mass support our current organisations must develop the cohesive structures capable of analysing their own situation and dealing with any challenge at any time of the day. Our affiliates must develop the capacity to identify and to address the needs of the masses of our people. We must increase mass participation in our organisations. Skills must not be limited to a few people, but rather spread and shared. The level of cadreship and leadership must be enhanced. . . .

In the Tri-cameral parliament, the differences between the junior partners and their seniors continue to sharpen. When the Uitenhage massacre was debated, almost all the junior partners called for the resignation of fascist Le Grange. If they did not do so, it would have been glaringly clear that they were pawns on the chessboard of the Nationalist Party. It must be further clear that this call arises out of the fear for the deepening of their isolation from even those who voted for them. We must continue to discredit and isolate these reactionaries.

In the townships, the Black Local Authorities are inoperative. They are no longer able to dictate to the masses, and already over 50 of the councillors have resigned countrywide. Some townships like Cradock and Uitenhage have no local government structures. Now our task is to extend our struggle beyond these apartheid structures and set up our alternative structures which will force the authorities to heed the popular demands of the people. We must set up projects to meet some of the practical needs of our people without compromising our principles. For example, advice offices, mobile clinics, etc., could be set up.

It must be our priority to strengthen our links with the unions. Our work must address issues of a working class nature such as unemployment, high food prices, GST [General Sales Tax] etc. We are a Front which organises a constituency whose greater portion is poor, unemployed or dumped in rural areas and Bantustans to starve. With its recent increase in GST, the state has declared war on their standards of living. . . .

The rural areas remain our priority areas, especially the Bantustans. Our thrust must be towards penetrating these far flung communities and setting up organisations. This is not going to be an easy task, we know that repression is heavy in the Bantustans. It often makes it extremely difficult to organise openly on a UDF ticket.

We must find the correct tactics and strategies which accord with the conditions we find in the Bantustans. The migrant workers living in hostels and elsewhere must also be organised. These people provide a vital link with the rural communities. The skills that they learn and the political consciousness they develop can be transferred to the next of kins, friends and acquaintances in these areas. The extent to which we mobilise and organise the migrants will determine the pace of organisation of rural communities. The work done directly in rural areas and the organisation of migrants complement each other.

The Need for Consolidation

It is generally accepted that we have achieved unprecedented levels of mobilisation and organisation since the time of the Congress Alliance [of the 1950s], yet we must acknowledge the fact that in some regions such as the OFS [Orange Free State] and the Northern Cape, very little progress was made. We started organising for the UDF in these regions as early as November 1983 but to date there exist no General Councils. Effectively this means that organisations may not take common decisions, neither is there anything that binds these organisations together. Only interim committees can take decisions, and their decisions cannot be tested by way of a democratic process. . . .

CONCLUSION

The campaigns of the UDF over the last 19 months showed very clearly that the conditions in our country today demand that we deal with issues far beyond the limited objectives set out at the time of the formation of the Front. Our conference theme, "Protest to Challenge—Mobilisation to Organisation" and the keynote address accentuate this imperative. . . .

Our affiliates in all regions must understand fully the implications of this conference's decisions. All of us have a duty to build our people's Front. This calls for hard work in all our structures. Forward to Freedom—Our Victory is Certain.

DOCUMENT 67. Press statement by AZAPO on AZAPO-UDF clashes, May 21, 1985

AZAPO welcomed and appreciated the peace initiatives by the clergy in the resolution of the conflict between the UDF and us. We welcomed the invitation with an open mind to engage ourselves positively and constructively [with] these peace moves.

To our dismay, at Regina Mundi [Soweto church] we were placed in an invidious position of having to share a platform with Inkatha. This was contrary to earlier assurances from the clergy that this would not happen. However, our reconciliatory sign of statesmanship and honest commitment to peace dictated that we participate.

The most disheartening is the news we received from our branches in the Eastern Cape to the effect that supporters of the UDF, wearing T-shirts and chanting UDF slogans attacked a vehicle carrying our members. This occurred at the gates of the Dan Qeqe stadium [in Port Elizabeth], immediately after the "Amen" to the peace efforts was sealed. Earlier on, a twelve year old member of AZASM was abducted during the prayer meeting. We have not heard of his whereabouts since. In the ensuing conflict, three of our comrades, Nelson Joyi, Nyamezeli Makasi and Sandisile Dywili were stabbed and subsequently admitted to Livingstone Hospital. Sandisile Dywili is in a critical condition. It was very noticeable that the leadership of the UDF did not control their members.

The chairman of the region, Cde. Mbuzeli Dukumbana, narrowly escaped death after his abduction. He was taken to Red House, and two tyres doused with petrol were put around his neck and feet. An approaching vehicle shone its lights and his UDF T-shirt wearing prospective murderers fled. He then managed to undo the tyres and ran towards this approaching vehicle. To his surprise it was a casspir [armored vehicle] carrying SADF [SA Defence Force] armed men. When these cops/soldiers saw his AZAPO T-shirt, they chased him back, saying to him that "the UDF has a right and duty to kill every AZAPO member."

These types of political crimes are an insult to the efforts of the clergy and all the thousands who had gathered in good faith in support of the peace initiative and the restoration of harmony in our strife torn community. This indeed is an insult to our struggle. AZAPO calls on all responsible leaders of our community to join it in condemning this infantile political banditry committed in the name of the liberation struggle. We echo the concern expressed by the clergy that the internecine fights and the struggle for territorial influence and hegemonic ambitions will only subvert and retard the liberation struggle.

The system is very unhappy that peace talks between AZAPO and UDF are in good progress. It is sad and to be regretted that certain elements within the Black community are hell bent on pleasing the system by their actions.

AZAPO is now finding it difficult to hold back its membership from defending their lives, families and property. AZAPO cannot be held responsible for whatever its members will be forced to do in their defence.

In spite of all these, AZAPO believes that the leadership of the UDF is sincere in their efforts to restore peace.

Document 68. "Western Cape Ablaze." University of Cape Town Student Representative Council flyer, August 29, 1985

South Africa enters its sixth week of the State of Emergency. Opposition to apartheid continues to grow in a wide range of areas across the country.

The Western Cape is no exception. Cape Town, along with Durban, is not an Emergency area and is able to actively protest against the State of Emergency.

Yesterday's proposed march to Pollsmoor [prison] was to bring together as many people as possible to deliver a message to Nelson Mandela. There have been many marches and protests over the last weeks and this large united action would have consolidated the Western Cape response.

This was not to materialise. By Friday night, many Western Cape UDF leaders had been detained. On Tuesday afternoon Dr. Allan Boesak, the major force behind the march, was picked up in Bellville and is being held in Pretoria.

From early yesterday morning, army and police sealed off the access to Athlone Stadium, the central meeting place for the march. Casspirs [armored vehicles] with troops lined Klipfontein Road. Quirt wielding riot police baton charged every group of people in sight.

About 4000 students marched from Hewett College. They were stopped but had agreed to sit down peacefully. Police baton charged them, chasing students back into the college with quirts and teargas. It is alleged that about 2000 students were trapped in the Hewett College hall and police filled the hall with teargas.

Pitched battles occurred all over the Peninsula, in Guguletu, where four people were killed, in Belgravia, Silvertown, Athlone and many other areas. At UCT [University of Cape Town] over 2000 students and lecturers marched peacefully down Woolsack Drive but were stopped and made to turn back. At about 4 pm, about 1000 students and staff picketed on De Waal Drive while large numbers of riot police lined the opposite side of the freeway. Traffic was stopped a number of times as the police prepared to baton charge. A number of confrontations occurred.

A group of seven organisational leaders including Nic Boraine, NUSAS [National Union of SA Students] Secretary General, Viv McMenamin, UCT SRC Projects Officer, and three UCT academics, Dr. Caroline White, Prof. Charles Villa-Vicencio and Dr. Robin Borland were arrested near Pollsmoor prison in a last attempt to take the letter to Nelson Mandela. Large amounts of riot police, a casspir and police vehicles converged on the scene surrounding the seven who had linked arms to march peacefully the short distance to the prison. They were then arrested.

The army and police seem unable to quell the increasing protest actions by the people of South Africa. The government has little room in which to manoeuvre. Throughout the black communities people continue to make this country ungovernable.

But it is not only blacks who are dissatisfied with the government. More and more whites are feeling the need to express their abhorrence [of] apartheid. They are unwilling to live in a society whose government does not represent the majority of the people, where the popular leaders are jailed and assassinated, where legitimate organisations are crushed.

And it is important for the white community to widen those cracks of opposition within their ranks, to make people realise that a peaceful, democratic future does not lie with the Botha government. This government continues to rule through the force of the army and police. This violence is being used to crush all peaceful opposition to apartheid. The Botha government must realise that the people of South Africa are being left with no legal channels through which to express themselves peacefully.

Yesterday saw many protest actions occurring all over the Peninsula, succeeding in overstretching the strength of army and police. But more importantly showing the Western Cape's widespread response to the State of Emergency.

Document 69. "Challenge to the Church: a Theological Comment on the Political Crisis in South Africa—The Kairos Document." Pamphlet by Kairos theologians, September 1985 (abridged)

THE MOMENT OF TRUTH

The time has come. The moment of truth has arrived. South Africa has been plunged into a crisis that is shaking the foundations and there is every indication that the crisis has only just begun and that it will deepen and become even more threatening in the months to come. It is the KAIROS or moment of truth not only for apartheid but also for the Church.

We as a group of theologians have been trying to understand the theological significance of this moment in our history. It is serious, very serious. For very many Christians in South Africa this is the KAIROS, the moment of grace and opportunity, the favourable time in which God issues a challenge to decisive action. It is a dangerous time because, if this opportunity is missed, and allowed to pass by, the loss for the Church, for the Gospel and for all the people of South Africa will be immeasurable. Jesus wept over Jerusalem. He wept over the tragedy of the destruction of the city and the massacre of the people that was imminent, "and all because you did not recognise your opportunity (KAIROS) when God offered it" (Lk 19:44)....

What the present crisis shows up, although many of us have known it all along, is that *the Church is divided*. More and more people are now saying that there are in fact two Churches in South Africa—a White Church and a Black Church. Even within the same denomination there are in fact two Churches. In the life and death conflict between different social forces that has come to a head in South Africa today, there are Christians (or at least people who profess to be Christians) on both sides of the conflict—and some who are trying to sit on the fence!

Does this prove that Christian faith has no real meaning or relevance for our times? Does it show that the Bible can be used for any purpose at all? Such problems would be critical enough for the Church in any circumstances but when we also come to see that the conflict in South Africa is between the oppressor and the oppressed, the crisis for the church as an institution becomes much more acute. Both oppressor and oppressed claim loyalty to the same Church. They are both baptised in the same baptism and participate together in the breaking of the same bread, the same body and blood of Christ. There we sit in the same Church while outside Christian policemen and soldiers are beating up and killing Christian children or torturing Christian prisoners to death while yet other Christians stand by and weakly plead for peace.

The Church is divided and its day of judgement has come.

The moment of truth has compelled us to analyse more carefully the different theologies in our Churches and to speak out more clearly and boldly about the real significance of these theologies. We have been able to isolate three theologies and we have chosen to call them "State Theology", "Church Theology", and "Prophetic Theology". In our thoroughgoing criticism of the first and second theologies we do not wish to mince our words. The situation is too critical for that.

CRITIQUE OF STATE THEOLOGY

The South African apartheid state has a theology of its own and we have chosen to call it "State Theology". "State Theology" is simply the theological justification of the status quo. . . .

Law and Order

The State makes use of the concept of law and order to maintain the status quo which it depicts as "normal". But this *law* is the unjust and discriminatory laws of apartheid and this *order* is the organised and institutionalised disorder of oppression. Anyone who wishes to change this law and this order is made to feel that they are lawless and disorderly. In other words they are made to feel guilty of sin.

It is indeed the duty of the State to maintain law and order, but it has no divine mandate to maintain any kind of law and order. Something does not become moral and just simply because the State has declared it to be a law and the organisation of a society is not a just and right order simply because it has been instituted by the State. We cannot accept any kind of law and any kind of order. The concern of Christians is that we should have in our country a just law and a right order. . . .

The Threat of Communism

We all know how the South African State makes use of the label "communist". Anything that threatens the status quo is labeled "communist". Anyone who opposes the State and especially anyone who rejects its theology is simply dismissed as a "communist". . . .

The God of the State

The State in its oppression of the people makes use again and again of the name of God. Military chaplains use it to encourage the South African Defence Force, police chaplains use it to strengthen policemen and cabinet ministers use it in their propaganda speeches. But perhaps the most revealing of all is the blasphemous use of God's holy name in the preamble to the new apartheid constitution.

In humble submission to Almighty God, who controls the destinies of nations and the history of peoples; who gathered our forebears together from many lands and gave them this their own; who has guided them from generation to generation; who has wondrously delivered them from the dangers that beset them.

This god is an idol. It is as mischievous, sinister and evil as any of the idols that the prophets of Israel had to contend with. Here we have a god who is historically on the side of the white settlers, who dispossesses black people of their land and who gives the major part of the land to his "chosen people". . . .

The oppressive South African regime will always be particularly abhorrent to Christians precisely because it makes use of Christianity to justify its evil ways. As Christians we simply cannot tolerate this blasphemous use of God's name and God's Word. "State Theology" is not only heretical, it is blasphemous. Christians who are trying to remain faithful to the God of the Bible are even more horrified when they see that there are Churches, like the White Dutch Reformed Churches and other groups of Christians, who actually subscribe to this heretical theology. "State Theology" needs its own prophets and it manages to find them from the ranks of those who profess to be ministers of God's Word in some of our Churches. What is particularly tragic for a Christian is to see the number of people who are fooled and confused by these false prophets and their heretical theology.

CRITIQUE OF "CHURCH THEOLOGY"

We have analysed the statements that are made from time-to-time by the so-called "English-speaking" Churches. We have looked at what Church leaders tend to say in their speeches and press statements about the apartheid regime and the present crisis. What we found running through all these pronouncements is a series of inter-related theological assumptions. These we have chosen to call "Church Theology". . . .

In a limited, guarded and cautious way this theology is critical of apartheid. Its criticism, however, is superficial and counter-productive because instead of engaging in an in-depth analysis of the signs of our times, it relies upon a few stock ideas derived from Christian tradition and then uncritically and repeatedly applies them to our situation. The stock ideas used by almost all these Church leaders that we would like to examine here are: reconciliation (or peace), justice and non-violence.

Reconciliation

"Church Theology" takes "reconciliation" as the key to problem resolution. It talks about the need for reconciliation between white and black, or between all South Africans. "Church Theology" often describes the Christian stance in the following way: "We must be fair. We must listen to both sides of the story. If the two sides can only meet to talk and negotiate they will sort out their differences and misunderstandings, and the conflict will be resolved." On the face of it this may sound very Christian. But is it?

The fallacy here is that "Reconciliation" has been made into an absolute principle that must be applied in all cases of conflict or dissension. But not all cases of conflict are the same. We can imagine a private quarrel between two people or two groups whose differences are based upon misunderstandings. In such cases it would be appropriate to talk and negotiate to sort out the misunderstandings and to reconcile the two sides. But there are other conflicts in which one side is right and the other wrong. There are conflicts where one side is a fully armed and violent oppressor while the other side is defenceless and oppressed. There are conflicts that can only be described as the struggle between justice and injustice, good and evil, God and the devil. To speak of reconciling these two is not only a mistaken application of the Christian idea of reconciliation, it is a total betrayal of all that Christian faith has ever meant. Nowhere in the Bible or in Christian tradition has it ever been suggested that we ought to try to reconcile good and evil, God and the devil. . . .

Justice

It would be quite wrong to give the impression that "Church Theology" in South Africa is not particularly concerned about the need for justice. There have been some very strong and very sincere demands for justice. But the question we need to ask here, the very serious theological question is: What kind of justice? An examination of Church statements and pronouncements gives the distinct impression that the justice that is envisaged is *the justice of reform*, that is to say, a justice that is determined by the oppressor, by the white minority and that is offered to the people as a kind of concession. . . .

Why then does "Church Theology" appeal to the top rather than to the people who are suffering? Why does this theology not demand that the oppressed stand up for their rights and wage a struggle against their oppressors? Why does it not tell them that it is *their* duty to work for justice and to change the unjust structures? Perhaps the answer to these questions is that appeals from the "top" in the Church tend very easily to be appeals to the "top" in society. An appeal to the conscience of those who perpetuate the system of injustice must be made. But real change and true justice can only come from below, from the people—most of whom are Christians.

Non-Violence

The stance of "Church Theology" on non-violence, expressed as a blanket condemnation of all that is *called* violence, has not only been unable to curb the violence of our situation, it has actually, although unwittingly, been a major contributing factor in the recent escalation of State violence. . . . [Violence by the state is assumed to be legitimate, whereas acts of self-defence by people in the townships, which are defined by the state and the media as "violence," are condemned.]

In practice what one calls "violence" and what one calls "self-defence" seems to depend upon which side one is on. To call all physical force "violence" is to try to be neutral and to refuse to make a judgement about who is right and who is wrong. The attempt to remain neutral in this kind of conflict is futile. Neutrality enables the status quo of oppression (and therefore violence) to continue. It is a way of giving tacit support to the oppressor. . . .

TOWARDS A PROPHETIC THEOLOGY

Our present KAIROS calls for a response from Christians that is biblical, spiritual, pastoral and, above all, prophetic. It is not enough in these circumstances to repeat generalised Christian principles. We need a bold and incisive response that is prophetic because it speaks to the particular circumstances of this crisis, a response that does not give the impression of sitting on the fence but is clearly and unambiguously taking a stand.

Social Analysis

The first task of a prophetic theology for our times would be an attempt at social analysis or what Jesus would call "reading the signs of the times" (Mt 16:3) or "interpreting this KAIROS" (Lk 12:56). It is not possible to do this in any detail in this document but we must start with at least the broad outlines of an analysis of the conflict in which we find ourselves.

It would be quite wrong to see the present conflict as simply a racial war. The racial component is there but we are not dealing with two equal races or nations each with their own selfish group interests. The situation we are dealing with here is one of oppression. The conflict is between an oppressor and the oppressed. The conflict is between two irreconcilable *causes* or *interests* in which the one is just and the other is unjust.

On the one hand we have the interests of those who benefit from the status quo and who are determined to maintain it at any cost, even at the cost of millions of lives. . . .

On the other hand we have those who do not benefit in any way from the system the way it is now. They are treated as mere labour units, paid starvation wages, separated from their families by migratory labour, moved about like cattle and dumped in homelands to starve—and all for the benefit of a privileged minority. . . .

This is our situation of civil war or revolution. The one side is committed to maintaining the system at all costs and the other side is committed to changing it at all costs. There are two conflicting projects here and no compromise is possible. Either we have full and equal justice for all or we don't. . . .

Tyranny in the Christian Tradition

There is a long Christian tradition relating to oppression, but the word that has been used most frequently to describe this particular form of sinfulness is the word "tyranny". According to this tradition once it is established beyond doubt that a particular ruler is a tyrant or that a particular regime is tyrannical, it forfeits the moral right to govern and the people acquire the right to resist and to find the means to protect their own interests against injustice and oppression. In other words a tyrannical regime has no *moral legitimacy*. It may be the *de facto* government and it may even be recognised by other governments and therefore be the *de jure* or legal government. But if it is a tyrannical regime, it is, from a moral and a theological point of view, *illegitimate*.

There are indeed some differences of opinion in the Christian tradition about the means that might be used to replace a tyrant *but* there has not been any doubt about our Christian duty to refuse to co-operate with tyranny and to do whatever we can to remove it. . . .

To say that the State or the regime is the enemy of God is not to say that all those who support the system are aware of this. On the whole they simply do not know what they are doing. Many people have been blinded by the regime's propaganda. They are frequently quite ignorant of the consequences of their stance. However, such blindness does not make the State any less tyrannical or any less of an enemy of the people and an enemy of God. . . .

CHALLENGE TO ACTION

God Sides with the Oppressed

To say that the Church must now take sides unequivocally and consistently with the poor and the oppressed is to overlook the fact that the majority of Christians in South Africa have already done so. By far the greater part of the Church in South Africa *is* poor and oppressed. . . .

As far as the present crisis is concerned, there is only one way forward to Church unity and that is for those Christians who find themselves on the side of the oppressor or sitting on the fence, to cross over to the other side to be united in faith and action with those who are oppressed. Unity and reconciliation within the Church itself is only possible around God and Jesus Christ who are to be found on the side of the poor and the oppressed. . . .

Civil Disobedience

Once it is established that the present regime has no moral legitimacy and is in fact a tyrannical regime certain things follow for the Church and its activities. In the first place *the Church cannot collaborate with tyranny*. It cannot or should not do anything that appears to give legitimacy to a morally illegitimate regime. Secondly, the Church should not only pray for a change of government, it should also mobilise its members in every parish to begin to think and work and plan for a change of government in South Africa. We must begin to look ahead and begin working now with firm hope and faith for a better future. And finally the moral illegitimacy of the apartheid regime means that the Church will have to be involved at times in *civil disobedience*. A Church that takes its responsibilities seriously in these circumstances will sometimes have to confront and disobey the State in order to obey God.

Moral Guidance

The people look to the Church, especially in the midst of our present crisis, for moral guidance. In order to provide this the Church must first make its stand absolutely clear and never tire of explaining and dialoguing about it. It must then help people to understand their rights and their duties. There must be no misunderstanding about the *moral* duty of all who are oppressed to resist oppression and to struggle for liberation and justice. . . .

CONCLUSION

As we said in the beginning, there is nothing final about this document. Our hope is that it will stimulate discussion, debate, reflection and prayer, but, above all, that it will lead to action. . . .

We, as theologians (both lay and professional), have been greatly challenged by our own reflections, our exchange of ideas and our discoveries as we met together in smaller and larger groups to prepare this document or to suggest amendments to it. We are convinced that this challenge comes from God and that it is addressed to all of us. We see the present crisis of KAIROS as indeed a divine visitation.

And finally we [would] also like to call upon our Christian brothers and sisters throughout the world to give us the necessary support in this regard so that the daily loss of so many young lives may be brought to a speedy end.

[Signed by 151 church leaders and lay workers]

DOCUMENT 70. "Liberating the Classrooms." Article in *Upfront*, UDF journal, Cape Town, October 1985

I have been asked, as a teacher at a "coloured" school in the Western Cape, to give an insider's story of events at schools during the past few weeks. These weeks have transformed the thinking of possibly hundreds of thousands of students, parents and teachers in the Cape. In their defiance our students have tasted freedom and experienced an unprecedented unity. I doubt whether things can ever be the same again.

The boycotts began with the Cradock funeral and the declaration of the State of Emergency. In Mitchell's Plain, Bonteheuwel and Manenberg students reacted first, boycotting "normal" classes and holding awareness programs and attending rallies. The State reacted by sjambokking [whipping] students at Spine Road Secondary School in Mitchell's Plain which set off solidarity actions throughout the Western Cape. Reports of these beatings and the news of the Emergency coupled with the disturbing coverage of police informers meeting gory deaths were the catalysts that thrust aside "normal" school. Our students' anger, fear and anguish for their future came to the surface and we were bombarded with questions and tried to answer as best we could. It was not enough. The Student Representative Council was compelled to take a lead and coordinating structures between many schools in the Western Cape were set up. In our region mandates for a one-day class boycott followed by a stayaway for students to attend a rally at UCT [University of Cape Town] were called for.

I sat in on several of the discussions subsequently held in all classes to determine this mandate. Because of the depth of the discussion in these classes it became obvious to me that much informal debate had already taken place on the streets or in the playgrounds. The self-discipline exercised at our normally unruly "ghetto" school during this discussion impressed upon me the seriousness with which our students regarded the situation and their involvement. It must be understood that the authority within the school cannot prevent student action of this nature without provoking much resentment. Our community is a poor one made much poorer under the recent recession and our students feel the need to understand their situation; they can no longer tolerate attempts to hide the truth from them, particularly in the wake of the discredited Tricameral set-up.

When the votes were taken after the class discussions, 21 classes voted for action and 8 against. I found no evidence of bad feeling towards those who voted against and they were allowed then and since then to proceed to normal classes. Any talk of intimidation is nonsense. The SRC [Student Representative Council] on the first day conducted discussions with boycotting students, crammed into 6 classrooms, explaining and answering questions as best they could. Again we were surprised at the level of self-discipline exercised. The day concluded with a short march around the school. As teachers we got a glimpse of the political sympathies existing and emerging: "Mandela is behind us, we shall not be moved!" they sang, and "Viva Cosas! [Congress of SA Students] Viva UDF! Viva ANC!" they chanted. Much of the sloganizing was at first [new to] the mass of the student body but what was quite clear was the complete failure of the State media to sway student attitudes against popular leadership and organisation. On the following day several students attended a rally at UCT where they were tear gassed, fuelling the anger of the whole school on their return.

Normal classes were resumed until the following Wednesday when more boycotts were called for in solidarity with condemned ANC guerrilla Benjamin Moloise and the impending Mineworkers' strike in the Transvaal. Again votes were taken and 90% of the school took part in social awareness programs over the next three days.

A very significant rally of over one thousand teachers took place that Thursday. It was decided that teachers would refuse to teach normal classes and would assist the students in their programs for two days of the following week (19 & 20 August) to show their solidarity. Our staff met to discuss this action. Several teachers thought that we were too vulnerable to State victimisation, so no decision was reached.

On Monday [August 19th], eighteen of our teachers met and decided to take action regardless and joined the students in defiance of new threats from the department. The students were overjoyed by this stand that their teachers had taken. On the next day a staff meeting was held where these eighteen teachers persuaded the rest of the staff to join them. The successful arguments were that we, as teachers, could no longer permit students to undertake a common struggle alone and especially that we could best protect them from reckless action and police brutality by showing our support

Figure 19. High-school students walk past their school as soldiers patrol the townships during school boycotts, Cape Town, 1985. *Dave Hartman/IDAF*

for them. Subsequent events proved this to be correct, enabling us to prevent a week later what could have been a blood-bath. We learnt the next day that at 53 schools similar action had been taken by other teachers.

At our school the Tuesday ended off with the teachers issuing a public statement of solidarity with the students and the entire school holding hands and singing "We are the World", one of the songs of the boycotts. That evening at a scheduled PTA [parent teacher association] meeting which was well attended and which included students, parents were asked to endorse our statement of solidarity, which they did unanimously. Once again students, teachers and now parents joined hands in singing "We are the World". Included in this statement of solidarity was an offer to the students to incorporate an hour of social awareness classes into the normal school day if students returned to classes. This was accepted but subsequent actions by the State, notably by the police, upset this solution.

It was during the following week after the attempted march on Pollsmoor was brutally prevented that events really unfolded. Throughout the Western Cape students had been holding peaceful mass rallies at different schools, sometimes planned but often spontaneous. There were several in our area, often attended by as many as 3000 students. The police successfully dispersed these rallies by phoning through and threatening physical action. But on the one Tuesday students refused to disperse, angered that they could be controlled by the "enemy" by telephone. The threat was repeated and the teachers managed to persuade only the youngest students to go home.

Half an hour later two Casspirs [armored vehicles] containing about 15 heavily armed policemen arrived. This resulted in the students becoming extremely agitated. They armed themselves with planks from the backs of their desks, tied hankies around their faces for the teargas and got ready, naively, to defend themselves for when the Casspirs crashed through the fence. A five minute warning was given and the teachers took up a desperate position between students and the police. With 50 seconds to go the police were persuaded to withdraw for 5 minutes and we managed to convince the students that planks were ineffective against police weapons. While they were reluctantly dispersing the Casspirs raced up and down provocatively with the effect that within half an hour burning barricades were set up in the area in defiance. A tragedy on the school grounds had been averted but once students were out of our charge on the streets we had no influence over them. I personally counted the remains of 16 barricades in our area the following morning. At our school we were relatively lucky that day. In many areas students were gassed, beaten and shot after similar peaceful gatherings.

Three days later the State closed the schools, sending the students back onto the streets.

DOCUMENT 71. Speech by Cyril Ramaphosa at COSATU launching conference, Durban, November 29, 1985 (abridged)

Workers' political strength depends upon building strong and militant organisation in the workplace. We also have to realise that organised workers are not representative of the working class as a whole but are its most effective weapon. Therefore, for workers it is important that organisation on the shop floor be strengthened and in this way we will be able to contribute to the struggle of the working class as a whole and to the struggle of the oppressed people in this country.

It is also important to draw people into a programme for the restructuring of society in order to make sure that the wealth of our society is democratically controlled and shared by its people. It is important to realise that the political struggle is not only to remove the government. We must also eliminate unemployment, improve education, improve health facilities and the wealth of the society must be shared among all those that work in this country. It is important that the politics of the working class eventually becomes the politics of all the oppressed people of this country. . . .

The formation of this Congress represents a tremendous victory for the working class. Never before has it been so powerful and so poised to make a mark in society. We are all living in urgent times, therefore it is urgent to make it clear to the South African government, employers and all sections of society where the working class, united under the banner of COSATU, will stand.

The reforms that have been proposed by the government and employers are not offering any solution. The rand is continuing to drop, there is high inflation and the cost of living is rising every day. While all this is happening the people in the country are continuing to resist. Confrontation with the police has become a daily thing. Some of the townships have become completely ungovernable. The government has clearly demonstrated that it is not in control of this country and PW Botha has failed to point the direction. It is time that the working class tell him to lay down his powers and let the legitimate leaders of the country take over the seat he now occupies.

We have seen in the past four years that organisations of the oppressed have grown stronger. And at the same time we have seen trade unions growing stronger as well. We have seen trade unions not only broaden their areas of struggle on the shop floor, we have also seen them contribute to community struggles.

However, the pace of these struggles has been determined by people in the community. As trade unions we have always thought that our main area of activity was on the shop floor—the struggle against the bosses. But we have always recognised that industrial issues are political. Workers have long realised when they are paid lower wages that it is a political issue. But what is difficult is how to make the link between economic and political issues.

We all agree that the struggle of workers on the shop floor cannot be separated from the wider struggle for liberation. The important question we have to ask ourselves is how is COSATU going to contribute to the struggle for our liberation. As unions we have sought to develop a consciousness among workers, not only of racial oppression but also of their exploitation as a working class.

As unions we have influenced the wider political struggle. Our struggles on the shop floor have widened the space for struggles in the community. Through interaction with community organisations, we have developed the principle of worker controlled democratic organisation. But our main political task as workers is to develop organisation among workers as well as a strong worker leadership. We have, as unions, to act decisively to ensure that we, as workers, lead the struggle.

Our most urgent task is to develop a unity among workers. We would wish COSATU to give firm political direction for workers. If workers are to lead the struggle for liberation we have to win the confidence of other sectors of society. But if we are to get into alliances with other progressive organisations, it must be on terms that are favourable to us as workers.

To make sure we establish alliances which are progressive, we must be strong and united. And it is COSATU that is going to unite us under one banner. To do this we have to give concrete expression to the five basic principles on which COSATU was formed. All these principles must be put into practice in order to build a stronger unity and enable us to better participate in the struggle for liberation.

When we do plunge into political activity, we must make sure that the unions under COSATU have a strong shopfloor base not only to take on the employers but the state as well. Our role in the political struggle will depend on our organisational strength.

We must meet with progressive political organisations. We have to work in co-operation with them on realistic campaigns. We must not shy away and pretend they do not exist.

We have to pay particular attention to worker education and our role in the political struggle. We must encourage a healthy exchange between our Congress and other progressive organisations.

In the next few days we will be considering resolutions which will point the direction that COSATU will take. We will be putting our heads together not only to make sure that we reach Pretoria but also to make a better life for us workers in this country. What we have to make clear is that a giant has risen and will confront all that stand in its way. . . .

Document 72. ANC intelligence report on Inkatha attacks, Durban, late 1985

The Inanda/Phoenix conflict in Durban in August 1985 was not an Indo/African clash, as it was made out to be. This was a deliberate attempt by the system with the aid of Inkatha and the Amabutho [vigilantes] to stop the economic boycott taking off in Natal. The economic boycott in the Eastern Cape and North Western Cape (Port Elizabeth, East London, Uitenhage, Cradock, Steynberg, Middleburg, Jamesville) was very successful. Many many businesses were going insolvent. In Natal, BTR Sarmcol fired 950 workers. The workers called on the community for support. One of the actions was an economic boycott of white businesses in the Harwick [Howick] and Pietermaritzburg towns. This was tremendously successful with Maritzburg being described by the media as a ghost town and the Mayor of [Howick] saying that the boycott had destroyed [Howick].

FOSATU organised a meeting of organisations to discuss the boycott in Durban. The Inyanda Chamber of Commerce initially decided to participate but pulled out on instructions from Inkatha. The boycott started off successfully in Pinetown. This was when the clash occurred. Shabalala, an Inkatha lieutenant in the Lindelani/Bambai/Inanda area attacked the Indian businesses in this area, looting and burning the buildings. Then they moved into KwaMashu. If this was an Indo/African clash, why burn down the houses and businesses of people staying in KwaMashu? Inkatha then called off the boycott saying that people must buy in the white shops, because there were no provisions in the townships and that the UDF wanted people to starve. They also took advantage of this unrest to kill many of our community activists and union organisers (10 union workers, 3 from NFW—National Federation of Workers). These people were dragged out of their houses and slaughtered in front of their wives and children. One union organiser from Lamontville begged not to be killed in sight of his children. The Amabutho [vigilantes] then dragged him to the top of a hill end slaughtered him there. His family fetched his body mutilated badly some hours later.

[A]bout ten houses were burnt down in KwaMashu (Mbatha, Ngobese, Mbuli, Khubeka, Bheka, Dlamini, Mbongi among them). Diakonia and Black Sash have about 120 sworn affidavits and statements from people in KwaMashu about Inkatha violence and police and SADF complicity in it. Police were seen looting shops. In one incident, the SADF and the Amabutho stopped a van delivering cold meat, chased the driver away, overturned the van and sat down eating polony, vienna sausages and other looted products. The rest they shared amongst themselves and drove away.

One afternoon at about 2 pm, I got a phone call saying that Ngobese's house was burning and the Amabutho were then burning the Kubhekas' home. I telephoned the police and fire brigade. They never went. I then appealed to a journalist I knew to go and see the incident. He and reporters from *Ilanga* were assaulted by police when they arrived there. The SADF were standing by watching. When Mr Ngobese objected about the destruction of his home, he was killed there by the Amabutho. No arrests have been made. When the impi [warrior brigade] finished, they got into their bus, waved to the police and SADF and drove to another section to do their dirty work.

The Amabutho wear white head cloths and cry "Usuthu" when they attack. In one morning at about 6 am, they attacked the home of Rev. Wesley Mabuza. They accused him of being a supporter of the UDF and allowing the youth to meet in his church. They dragged him out of the house in his pyjamas and frog marched him up and down the street insisting he chants "UDF is a dog, Mandela is a dog". They took him to the top of the street where Mandla Shabalala (an Inkatha man from Lindelani) was standing with about 150 heavily armed men. They made lots of accusations and Shabalala said he was to be killed right there. He was only saved by the appeal of one or two people in the group, who belonged to his church. They gave him an hour to pack his things and leave KwaMashu, saying he must come to the stadium on Sunday to confess his guilt, ask forgiveness and swear loyalty. He left Durban immediately and is now a wanted man and cannot return because they say he tricked them and did not appear at the stadium. They also attacked the home of Rev M Xundu in Lamontville. He has also left Durban. They also burnt down the Methodist Church of Rev Masondo in Lamontville as this is a big church where we have all our meetings. Inkatha has also threatened the life of Rev Shabalala in Clermont, Aubrey Nyembezi also of Clermont objected to the proposed inclusion of Clermont into KwaZulu. His house was also burnt.

At a memorial service for Mrs Nonyamezelo [Victoria] Mxenge at the Umlazi Cinema on a Wednesday before the Saturday of her burial, 34 people were killed and many more were injured. 16 people died by the spears of the Amabutho and the rest were killed by bullets of the SADF. Just after 9 pm when the meeting was finishing (attended by about 5000 people), six bus loads of Amabutho arrived chanting "usuthu" and heavily armed. The people barricaded themselves inside. The SADF then climbed through the roof of the cinema and threw tear gas amongst the people. Fortunately, Amabutho were gathered only at one door of the cinema, otherwise many more people would have been killed. People rushed out through all the exits and were shot as they ran away. Diakonia and Black Sash also have statements on this incident taken from victims in hospital and by members of the deceased families. Winnington Sabelo then gave an order that all UDF supporters must be out of the township and only cars with KwaZulu registration would be allowed in. He also warned Archbishop [Denis] Hurley not to come to the township as he would be killed and all Diakonia members who lived in the township must get out or be killed.

Durban is definitely being subjected to a reign of terror by Inkatha and the targets are the youth and community activists and trade union organisers. All this makes organising very difficult in the townships. My comrades will narrate many many more horrifying incidents by Inkatha as they live in the affected townships and are subjected to these attacks almost daily.

DOCUMENT 73. Excerpts from cross-examination of Professor I. D. de Vries by Advocate Ismail Mahomed, *State v. Ramgobin and others*, Pietermaritzburg, December 2, 1985

Mr Mahomed: Did you read the constitution of the NIC [Natal Indian Congress]? —— I've got it, yes. But that itself, it's nothing reflecting violence in itself.

And the constitution of the TIC [Transvaal Indian Congress], did you read it? —— Yes, I read it.

It says nothing about violence? —— No, true.

It is silent? —— Pardon?

Is it silent on the question of violence? —— Ja, I don't know now whether that's a legal term but the point is it's not propagated.

Is it silent? —— Yes. No, I mean it doesn't mention violence.

Is it silent on whether violence is good or bad? —— Well perhaps silent should be translated.

Is dit stilswyend op die punt op geweld? —— Ja, soos ek kan onthou. Wenslik is of nie. (Yes, as far as I can remember it is)

Milne, J P: The witness has said it says nothing about violence.

Mr Mahomed: It says nothing about violence, that's right? —— If I can remember correctly. I've been going through these things more than a year ago.

I want to put it to you, do you know when Transvaal Indian Congress got revived? —— 1983.

And there was no Transvaal Indian Congress for something like 23 years, do you know that? —— Well the way you put it, as I said, from my literature, they were dormant.

They were dormant. And you say they were silent. I put it to you that the constitution of the Transvaal Indian Congress has the following paragraphs. Its aims and objects. It says:

(a) To strive non-violently for a united democratic non-racial South Africa on the basis of universal adult suffrage.

Is that being silent? —— Well you see that's why I asked for a translation of the word silent. Because what I meant on silent, what I understood by that, was that they do not propagate violence.

In fact they propagate the opposite of violence. —— But I mean that was the idea which I wanted to create in my answer.

Okay. Now you know about this? —— Yes, I've said I've read it.

Why did you not say in your report that the Transvaal Indian Congress was opposed to violence? Why did you not say that in your report? —— Because Mr Mahomed, as I've indicated a hundred times already, that I have indicated one will have to look at the specific facts which includes—. One will have to look at the constitution; one will have to look at the pamphlet; one will have, since it exists, I suppose video material and technical recordings. But I am not, as a witness now, to express an—, to make an interpretation.

But you are so keen to tell us that [Yusuf] Dadoo committed the Congress to a policy of violence and you didn't think it was your duty to say that the Congress itself expressed itself in favour of nonviolence? You didn't think that was your duty to the Court? —— No, perhaps I don't understand it correctly, but there was no bad intent by my side. I have spelt it out that one will have to look at it. . . .

Oh yes, you went through those [police] videos and you quoted, you remarked from time to time on the videos about revolutionary symbols and who was what, but you never told the Court that the Transvaal Indian Congress has adopted a deliberate policy of nonviolence in 1983? You didn't think that was important to tell us? —— Well Mr Mahomed, I understand the point you're making but then it clearly was a misunderstanding right from the beginning as to my duty as an expert witness.

All right, you had that constitution before you? —— Yes.

Right, now you will agree . . . the very first clause says: Aims and objects: To strive non-violently for a united democratic non-racial South Africa. The second says: To promote the cause of all oppressed people of South Africa. (3) To resist all social, political and economic discrimination based on race, colour, sex or creed. (4) To promote peace, understanding and goodwill among all the people of South Africa. (5) To co-operate with other organisations striving for democracy. (6) To strive for equal economic, political, social and educational freedom for all the inhabitants of South Africa.

Do you recognise those objects? [witness nods] I'm afraid you'll have to say yes. —— Sorry, yes.

Now this is as dignified and as peaceful a document as you would find in all countries outside South Africa? —— I won't dispute that.

This is nothing particularly strange or radical about the idea that everybody should have equal rights, outside this country? —— No, I mean (voice drops).

Now let's talk about the Natal Indian Congress. Is there anything in the constitution of the Natal Indian Congress which can support the idea that the Congress supports violence? —— No, as far as I know.

Did you have that constitution before you? —— Yes.

Did you know it when you gave evidence? —— Yes.

Now let me read to you from the Natal Indian Congress constitution and that will be [Exhibit] F812 eventually. That says in paragraph (3c) objects: To promote peace, understanding and goodwill among people of all races in South

Africa (d) To co-operate with all organisations irrespective of race that are striving for democracy by non-violent methods. Do you know that? —— Yes.

You knew that? —— Of course.

Milne, J P: May I just ask a question. You expected those documents to be put before the Court? —— Yes M'Lord.

Why is it that you didn't say well, Dr Dadoo says this which seems to indicate that the Congress movement is committed to violent activity or to the support of violence, but the constitutions of the organisations themselves say something different? . . .

Mr Mahomed: I'm putting to you a very simple question. To this day, as you stand in the witness box, you are in no position to express any opinion to the Court as to whether the TIC and the NIC are revolutionary organisations. —— As I understand you now, I won't say it.

You are not in a position to? —— As I stand here. I might be in a position within 2 weeks.

In 2 weeks. How long have you been consulted by the State? —— well everything wasn't given to me as I say (intervention).

When were you first consulted by the State? —— Well, I think September 1983.

September 1983 and to this day you still haven't formed an opinion as to whether the TIC and the NIC are revolutionary organisations? —— Mr Mahomed, but you don't know what the consultations were about. They started out with some documents asking me something about SAAWU and SACTU.

Yes! —— And months later they came with something on the UDF, and months later they came with something on the TIC and the NIC. You see I didn't receive everything at the beginning. I've just indicated, I received the final transcript which they said I can now start reading, which you and Counsel for the State has sort of already preliminarily altered, 2 weeks before I got into the witness box.

So do I understand that now in the middle of cross-examination you are going to qualify yourself for the first time in order to be able to express an opinion on whether the TIC and the NIC are revolutionary organisations? Do I understand that to be so? —— But just remember Mr Mahomed (intervention).

No, that's a simple question.

Milne, J P: Have you got an opinion as to whether they are, or are not, an expert opinion? —— M'Lord, I think I'm quite capable to express an opinion but it will involve——. I mean, as Mr Mahomed has put, I have to base my opinion on facts and that means I've got to quote the transcripts, I've got to quote the pamphlets, and unless I base myself, I'm not going to express an opinion.

But is it a question of having previously formed an opinion based on detailed materials and that you now have forgotten the details, or that you have not yet formed an opinion? Which is it?—— I think I, to be quite honest, I haven't yet formed an opinion M'Lord.

DOCUMENT 74. "ONS Kersfees onder HULLE Noodtoestand/OUR Christmas Under THEIR State of Emergency." New Unity Movement flyer, Cape Town, December 1985, in Afrikaans and English

Kersfees is 'n tyd waar tydens mense jaarliks seënwense aan mekaar toewens. Families kom byeen om plesierig en gelukkig saam met mekaar te wees. So was dit voorheen. Die Kersfees van 1985 is vir ons as verdruktes en uitgebuites, verskillend. Oor die lengte en breedte van die Republiek van Suid-Afrika is daar vele families wat dié Kersfees sonder hulle vaders, moeders, seuns en dogters sal wees. Sommige is òf onwettiglik in aanhouding, òf deur die polisie òf militere magte gruwelik vermink òf doodgeskiet. Ons salueer almal wat 'n onverbiddellike stryd teen die vrede en onchristelike minderheidsregering gestry het. Ons wil ons eenheid en solidariteit aan hulle bewys deur hierdie 1985 Kersfees nie op die gewone wyse te vier nie.

GESTAPO MAGTE

Op 21 Julie 1985 is 'n formele noodtoestand oor verskeie dele van ons land verklaar. 'n Groot verskeidenheid van Gestapo Magte en indemniteite is aan die polisie en militêre magte verleen, wat tot die volgende aanleiding gegee het:

- Onskuldige mans, vrouens en kindertjies is gesjambok, gekasty, getraangas, geskiet, vermink en doodgeskiet.
- Honderde is gruwelik aangerand en gemartel.
- Meer as 6000 persone is aangehou.
- Militêre magte met Casspirs en Buffels het die woongebiede binnegeval.
- Ons organisasies, ons leierskap en ons vergaderings is deur HULLE wette stilgemaak.
- Ons protes teen bedrog-eksamens en riool-onderwys (gutter education) is deur HULLE beantwoord met skorsing, ontslag en verplasing van leerkragte.
- Studente is geforseer om by semi-militêre depots onder bedreiging met 'n vuurwapen, afgewaterde eksamens af te lê.
- Mense wat die verbruikersboikot ondersteun, word gedreig.
- Vakbondlede in hulle eis om 'n bestaanbare loon, word gemuilband.
- Sportadministrateurs, in hulle stryd teen rassisme in sport en teen 'n skandelike, geldsugtige Apartheids-Australiese krieketspan en hulle trawante, is in aanhouding geprop.
- Duisende mense word daagliks gearresteer, omdat hulle nie in besit van 'n duiwelse "Dompas" is nie.
- Bloedbad en slagtings: Ons mag nooit die bloedbad en slagtings van Langa-Sharpeville, Soweto, Uitenhage, Mitchell's Plain, Athlone en Mamelodi vergeet nie!!

DIE VLAM VAN VRYHEID BRAND VOORT!!

Selfs ons vreedsame kerslig-optogte word wreedaardig en met gruwelike geweld uitgedoof. *Hulle* mislukking is en sal altyd wees, *hulle* onvermoë om die brandende lig van vryheid in ons hart en gees uit te doof!

OUERS, WERKERS EN KINDERS VAN ONS LAND:
ONS MOET DIE STRYD TOT ALGEHELE VRYHEID VOER!
DUS, LAAT ONS, ONS SOLIDARITEIT MET ONS MEDE-STRYDERS BEWYS DEUR:
• Ons te weerhou van onnodige en buitensporige Kersfees-partytjies, Kersfees-geskenke en Kersfees-etes.
• Te dink aan ons mede-kamerade wat dié Kersfees onwettiglik agter slot-en-grendel ingehok sit. Hulle het net die boodskap van ONS vryheid verkondig.
• Morele en materiële steun en bystand aan ONS kamerade se families te betoon.
• Ons organisasies—in diens van ONS vryheid op te bou en te versterk.
• Die algehele verwerping van DUMMY-RADE deur die beleid van NIE-SAMEWERKING (NON-COLLABORATION) daagliks uit te leef en toe te pas.
• Die isolering en afhokking van alle quislings, verraaiers, verklikkers (informers) en agente van die Herrenvolk.
• Die lampe van kennis en vryheid brandend te hou. Ouers, studente en leerkragte moet gelyktydig OPVOED en BEVRY.
• Die opbou van 'n ONVERDEELDE, NIE-RASSISTIESE, DEMOKRATIESE Suid-Afrika vry van politieke verdrukking en ekonomiese uitbuiting.

AN INJURY TO ONE IS AN INJURY TO ALL!!
A VICTORY TO ONE IS A VICTORY TO ALL!!
EEN SUID-AFRIKA—EEN NASIE!!
MENSE WAT VERENIGD STAAN, WORD NIMMER NOOIT VERSLAAN!!
ABANTU BEBANYE ABASOZE BOYISWE!!
A LUTA CONTINUA—DIE STRYD GAAN VOORT!!

Every year at *Christmas*, people wish one another peace and goodwill. It has always been a time when families come together to celebrate and be joyful. The Christmas of 1985 is very *different*. Many families throughout South Africa will spend their Christmas without their sons, daughters, mothers and fathers, who were either detained or shot down by the police and military because of their courageous struggle against this cruel and unchristian minority government. THUS, AS A SHOW OF SOLIDARITY WE WILL NOT CELEBRATE IN THE USUAL WAY.

GESTAPO POWERS
Ever since 21 July 1985, a formal state of emergency has been declared in various parts of our country. Wide-ranging "Gestapo powers" and indemnities were given to the police and military, leading to the following:
• Innocent men, women and children were whipped, sjambokked [whipped], gassed, shot at, maimed and killed.
• Many were brutally assaulted and tortured.
• Over 6 000 persons were detained.

- Troops with Casspirs and Buffels [armored vehicles] invaded townships and spread terror amongst the people.
- Our organisations, our leaderships and our meetings were silenced by *THEIR* laws.
- Our protest against fraudulent exams was answered by suspensions, transfers and sacking of teachers.
- Students were forced to write exams at gunpoint.
- People who told their friends where to shop were harassed.
- Trade Union workers were victimised for coming out in defence of a living wage.
- Our Non-racial sports administrators were persecuted and detained for opposing the shameful Australian cricket mercenaries and supporters of apartheid sport.
- Thousands of our people have been and continue to be arrested for not being in possession of the despicable "dompas" [pass].
- Massacres: Can we ever forget Langa-Sharpeville? Soweto? Uitenhage? Mitchell's Plain? Athlone? Mamelodi?

THE FLAME OF FREEDOM BURNS!!!

Even our peaceful candlelight protests have been attacked with brute force. But what they failed in and what they will always fail to do is to put out the flame of freedom in our hearts and minds.

PARENTS, WORKERS, CHILDREN OF OUR COUNTRY
YOU MUST TAKE THE STRUGGLE FURTHER...TO VICTORY!
SO, LET US SHOW OUR SOLIDARITY TO OUR FELLOW FIGHTERS FOR FREEDOM BY:

- NOT SPENDING on Christmas gifts, costly meals and extravagant parties.
- REMEMBERING those locked up in jails because they spoke for *OUR* freedom and by giving moral and material assistance to their families.
- STRENGTHENING AND BUILDING up of our people's organisations.
- REJECTING DUMMY COUNCILS through the policy of non-collaboration.
- ISOLATING and BOYCOTTING collaborators, traitors, informers and other agents of the ruling class.
- KEEPING THE LAMP OF LEARNING ALIVE. Parents, students and teachers must *educate and liberate simultaneously.*
- BUILDING ONE UNITED, non-racial, democratic South Africa free from political oppression and economic exploitation

AN INJURY TO ONE IS AN INJURY TO ALL!!
A VICTORY TO ONE IS A VICTORY TO ALL!!
ONE SOUTH AFRICA—ONE NATION!!
A PEOPLE UNITED WILL NEVER BE DEFEATED!!
ABANTU BEBANYE ABASOZE BOYISWE!!
A LUTA CONTINUA—THE STRUGGLE CONTINUES!!

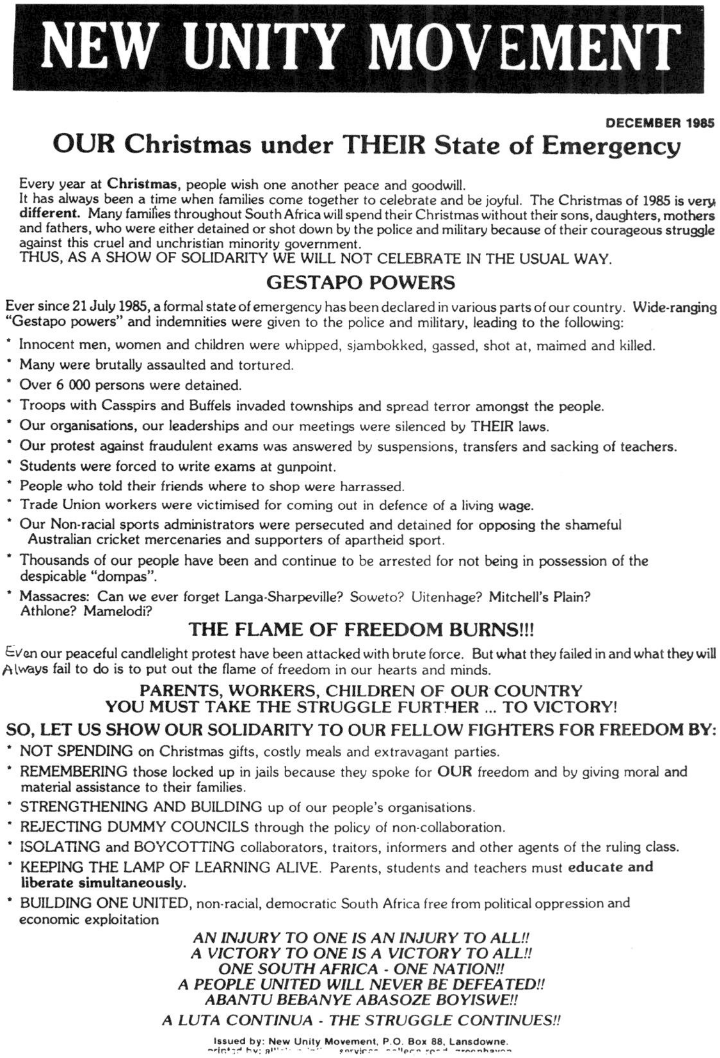

NEW UNITY MOVEMENT

DECEMBER 1985

OUR Christmas under THEIR State of Emergency

Every year at **Christmas**, people wish one another peace and goodwill.
It has always been a time when families come together to celebrate and be joyful. The Christmas of 1985 is very **different**. Many families throughout South Africa will spend their Christmas without their sons, daughters, mothers and fathers, who were either detained or shot down by the police and military because of their courageous struggle against this cruel and unchristian minority government.
THUS, AS A SHOW OF SOLIDARITY WE WILL NOT CELEBRATE IN THE USUAL WAY.

GESTAPO POWERS

Ever since 21 July 1985, a formal state of emergency has been declared in various parts of our country. Wide-ranging "Gestapo powers" and indemnities were given to the police and military, leading to the following:

* Innocent men, women and children were whipped, sjambokked, gassed, shot at, maimed and killed.
* Many were brutally assaulted and tortured.
* Over 6 000 persons were detained.
* Troops with Casspirs and Buffels invaded townships and spread terror amongst the people.
* Our organisations, our leaderships and our meetings were silenced by THEIR laws.
* Our protest against fraudulent exams was answered by suspensions, transfers and sacking of teachers.
* Students were forced to write exams at gunpoint.
* People who told their friends where to shop were harrassed.
* Trade Union workers were victimised for coming out in defence of a living wage.
* Our Non-racial sports administrators were persecuted and detained for opposing the shameful Australian cricket mercenaries and supporters of apartheid sport.
* Thousands of our people have been and continue to be arrested for not being in possession of the despicable "dompas".
* Massacres: Can we ever forget Langa-Sharpeville? Soweto? Uitenhage? Mitchell's Plain? Athlone? Mamelodi?

THE FLAME OF FREEDOM BURNS!!!

Even our peaceful candlelight protest have been attacked with brute force. But what they failed in and what they will Always fail to do is to put out the flame of freedom in our hearts and minds.

**PARENTS, WORKERS, CHILDREN OF OUR COUNTRY
YOU MUST TAKE THE STRUGGLE FURTHER ... TO VICTORY!**

SO, LET US SHOW OUR SOLIDARITY TO OUR FELLOW FIGHTERS FOR FREEDOM BY:

* NOT SPENDING on Christmas gifts, costly meals and extravagant parties.
* REMEMBERING those locked up in jails because they spoke for OUR freedom and by giving moral and material assistance to their families.
* STRENGTHENING AND BUILDING up of our people's organisations.
* REJECTING DUMMY COUNCILS through the policy of non-collaboration.
* ISOLATING and BOYCOTTING collaborators, traitors, informers and other agents of the ruling class.
* KEEPING THE LAMP OF LEARNING ALIVE. Parents, students and teachers must **educate and liberate simultaneously.**
* BUILDING ONE UNITED, non-racial, democratic South Africa free from political oppression and economic exploitation

*AN INJURY TO ONE IS AN INJURY TO ALL!!
A VICTORY TO ONE IS A VICTORY TO ALL!!
ONE SOUTH AFRICA - ONE NATION!!
A PEOPLE UNITED WILL NEVER BE DEFEATED!!
ABANTU BEBANYE ABASOZE BOYISWE!!
A LUTA CONTINUA - THE STRUGGLE CONTINUES!!*

Issued by: New Unity Movement, P.O. Box 88, Lansdowne.

Figure 20. "OUR Christmas under THEIR State of Emergency," a 1985 flyer issued by the New Unity Movement during the first state of emergency, calls on people in the western Cape to observe a consumer boycott during the holidays.

Document 75. "Use Your Spending Power—Support Consumer Boycott." UDF flyer, Cape Town, 1985

All over South Africa, people are saying: "The consumer boycott continues. We will not buy from white shops until our demands are met."

The bosses and Botha's government are beginning to shake with fear as they see the power of the people. In tiny dorpies [hamlets] in the Karoo, white shopkeepers have been rushing to the people with offers of full representation on the town council. In towns in the Eastern Cape, bosses have negotiated to have soldiers removed from the townships. In Cape Town, we have seen how the anger of the people forced [minister Louis] Le Grange to open the doors of Pollsmoor and release many of the detainees. All over the message has been clear—only united action will win our demands.

We must use this power to win more of our demands. Only last week, the price of bread went up. The government says it cannot afford to subsidise the bread any more.

But we say, you can afford to spend R7 on each rubber bullet that you use to injure our children. You can afford to spend millions of rands on teargas, casspirs [armored vehicles] and soldiers. You are prepared to spend more money on killing our children than on feeding them.

We must use our spending power to put an end to this. We must use our spending power to say that we want:

- An end to soldiers and casspirs in our streets
- The release of all our leaders and the unbanning of our organisations
- An end to price increases and a living wage
- The vote for everyone in one united South Africa.

We must also not be fooled by the fancy words the bosses can say. When [supermarket owner] Raymond Ackerman and his friends say they condemn what is happening, we must say that that is not enough. You can do more. When they bring their prices down for a few days or have sales, we must say that is not enough. We will wait until all your prices are low enough for us to afford and they stay low. We refuse to support those who keep apartheid alive and keep us poor in the land of our birth.

FORWARD THE CONSUMER BOYCOTT!

Document 76. "Alexandra Massacre." Funeral flyer, Alexandra township, Johannesburg, March 5, 1986

Mass Funeral of the Seventeen Victims in the Alexandra Massacre

For many years the black people of South Africa have struggled for political rights in the land of their birth in order to share the wealth and have a say in the formation of the laws which govern them. Now the new generation of blacks have emerged more desperate and determined than ever to reverse the tide of history. The demands have moved from educational reforms to direct political representation.

The government has responded to these demands by bullets, detention, torture, and prison sentences. It has captured the leaders and banned organisations. Pretoria's assassination squad invaded Alexandra and murdered children, students, youths and parents. The forces of Pretoria's racist regime continue to shoot our people as their first answer to all who say NO to apartheid. SADF [SA Defence Force] and SAP [SA Police] are continuously opening fire without any provocation. Our comrades whom we have already buried with bullet wounds in their bodies, bear witness to this truth.

The youth is now acting under severe political conditions of repression. This situation demands fundamental change of the whole system. Its reforms are hollow and contradictory hence the people are rejecting them. Now its acts of repression, STATE OF EMERGENCY has exacerbated the situation and inflames feelings of anger and suspicion. The brutality, stupidity and intractability of the government response to political unrest and economic morass has mobilised more and more people into protest action.

Our people want FREEDOM now. They want to govern themselves and determine the destiny of their country TODAY not TOMORROW. They have lost patience with all ideas that their liberation can be postponed for any reason whatsoever. They have measured the purpose of life by no other standard than that it should have been spent in the struggle for the liberation of our country. They have therefore SHED ALL FEAR OF DEATH because the word TO LIVE has acquired the same meaning as the words TO BE FREE.

MAATLA KE A RONA!!!
ALL POWER TO THE PEOPLE!!!
AMANDLA NGAWETHU!!!

STREET COMMITTEES

Street committees are formed in order to bring peace amongst the residents of Alex. To forget about our past differences and to prepare ourselves for the future.

Yard committee:
The people of the yard should come together and be united, forget about tribalism and form a yard committee. After that they must elect two representatives to represent them in the block committee.

Block committee:
This committee is made up of representatives from the yards and problems that are not solved by the block committee are referred to the street committee.

Street committee:
This is composed of four representatives from the block committee. If problems are more than the street committee can solve, they are taken up to the action committee.

Action committee:
It is made up of two representatives from all the streets of Alex. It is this committee that is responsible for action in Alex.

Phase two and one area Committee:
These are the committees that are to be formed by the residents of these two areas. Each and every area must have four reps to represent them in the action committee.

UNITE AND MOVE FORWARD FOR THE PEOPLE'S POWER!

THE VICTIMS OF THE ALEXANDRA MASSACRE

1. HLAPHOLOSA, OWEN
2. HLAPHOLOSA, COLIN
3. LEDWABA, NONO LUCY
4. MATELONG, OSBORNE
5. MALUKA, JACOB
6. MEYERS, JOSEPH
7. SITHOLE, JABULANE SAM
8. MOSAKA, REUBEN
9. MTHEMBU, JERRY
10. NKOSI, MHLABA
11. SITHOLE, STEPHEN
12. WILLIAMS, NEIL
13. RADEBE, ALFRED
14. MADALANI, BONGANI
15. HLUBI, JOHANNA
16. STOLT, STEPHEN
17. TSHABALALA, MEISIE
18. MOSUE, SOLOMON
19. RAMOHOIDITSANE, AMOS

Document 77. Funeral of ANC guerrilla Thanduxolo Mbethe, Uitenhage, March 14, 1986

[The church is packed to absolute capacity. People stand singing with their hands in salute. COSATU banners are up. There are political T-shirts all over, and a banner that says "go well comrade Thanduxolo Mbethe—your blood will water the tree of liberation that will grow". *Notes by Mark Swilling, researcher who tape-recorded the event*]

Song [in Xhosa]:
Nobody can stop us!
Crowd: We are the future!!
Nobody can stop us!
Crowd: We are the future!!

Song [in Xhosa]:
Look, there is Tambo (repeated 3 times)
There he comes from Zimbabwe
This burden is heavy
Look, there is Tambo (repeated 3 times)
There he comes from Zimbabwe (repeated 2 times)

M.C.: Viva Mandela viva!!
Crowd: Viva!!
M.C.: Amandla!! [Power]
Crowd: Awethu!! [is ours]
M.C.: iAfrika!!
Crowd: Mayibuye!! [Let it come back]

[The shouting of these slogans is done as the coffin is coming into the church. It is held high with clenched fists and is put down in front.]

The Priest: Glory be to God. This body which is here today is the shadow of God. I am the first and the last. Our children are being shot everyday, but we will shoot their children too.

Speaker: We feel grieved to have lost this courageous and brave proletarian, but comrades let it be known to everyone that we shall take from where this comrade left [off] to a free nonracial South Africa. We shall strive to heighten the insurgent activities, and this is the only means to achieve peace and stability in our country. We shall [imitate?] this comrade if need be for total abolition of all forms of exploitation [unintelligible] and for crushing the spirit of individualism and aggrandisement and power by individual groups and classes, to eradicate all forms of materialism for a free egalitarian society. Comrades, let the death of comrade Thanduxolo serve as a motivation factor and let us rededicate ourselves to the struggle for a free South Africa. Amandla!!

Crowd: Awethu!!

Song [in Xhosa]:
Mandela, Mandela (repeated 3 times)
Mandela bring freedom in this land of Africa (repeated 3 times)

Poet:
Our mothers are weeping
Our fathers are weeping
They are crying against imperialists
They are crying against their suffering as workers
Our mothers are crying for their sons, who are being shot as students by the SA minority regime

Our mothers are crying, demanding their sons and daughters in prison
Our mothers are crying for those who died, killed by this fascist regime
Comrades, remember the cry of Namibian mothers, when they cried for their sons and daughters who have been doomed by the SA regime
They were crying, shouting: Come guerrilla, come SWAPO
Comrades, remember in [1982] in the Lesotho raid when the Comrades were burying their compatriots, they were singing
Over the river we shall go and catch their sons

Speaker: Comrades, compatriots, I am proud today. Thanduxolo Mbethe is a freedom lover, he is a freedom fighter. My countrymen, I call this murder and I remember the Sharpeville Massacre. I wonder why in the land of our birth must we suffer like this. They refuse an education, they want to poison our minds. We are prepared to die; our blood will water the tree of liberation. Comrades, I am saying forward ever. [*Crowd:* Forward ever!!]

Comrades this is the time to sacrifice, it is the time to go forward, it is the time for Umkhonto we Sizwe which was formed in 1961. Comrades we know that this year is the year of the MK. We know that Oliver Tambo is the leader of the people. He was voted for by the people for the people."

Crowd: Viva!!
Speaker: Mayibuye!!
Crowd: iAfrica!!

Speaker 3: Comrades; Thanduxolo Mbethe left the country to go and join the ANC. Today Thanduxolo is here; Thanduxolo has fallen, comrades. But there is only one thing, comrades; his blood is going to water the tree of liberation. The ANC was formed in 1912, in 1950 [1955] the Freedom Charter was drawn.

The Charter said the doors of learning and culture shall be open. Years went by with Mandela and Sisulu peacefully negotiating with the government, but the SA government refused to listen. In Tanzania the Congress decided that it should have an educational policy because the people must learn, and must know that education is not a privilege but a right. The South African government must understand one thing, that when we say the doors of learning and culture shall be open we mean that the government shall serve the needs of the people.

The establishment of Solomon Mahlangu Freedom College in Tanzania in 1978 means today our comrades at Solomon Mahlangu are learned. All the schools in South Africa must be named after our leaders. We don't want Bantu education, we demand a people's education. Today our schools are closed. The government is demanding that our parents must report to the inspectors why the schools are closed. We can't report to these criminals. From the people's education we are moving to people's power, and we are going to rename one school as Thanduxolo High School. We are also demanding that soldiers must be removed from our schools, because they are turning our schools into police stations.

Comrades, we must never be divided. Our demands are there and they have not been met. The State of Emergency must not divide because our demands have not been met. A decade has gone since this generation of students have witnessed and participated in the struggle for a non-racial education in South Africa. This has gone by accompanied by numerous clashes between the students of the oppressed population in this country and the group of criminals and gangs who have employed ruthlessness against the revolting students. The confrontation has turned out to be an endless one, despite all the repressive measures used against the students. Our people have been tear gassed, baton charged, brutally killed; but all that has failed in subjugating the youth. Instead it has infused in us a greater militancy.

That is why we are here today saying we are proud of *Amabutho* [militarized UDF youth]. We are very proud of *Amabutho* as a people's army, and we are engaged in a battle in our streets. The most interesting part of it all is that the government has failed to break us. I heard that there are roadblocks all over but today I see thousands of people here. It means they have failed and they are going to fail.

During all this period of confrontation, our parents who are fortunately workers in this country, have been left out in the struggle because they disapprove of our militancy. Gone is the time of moderation and meekness. Time has come for our parents not to stand by and watch coldly as their children are dying. Our parents must also realise that the slogan "education before liberation" is nothing else than the first big step into the hands of the oppressive regime.

The government is also progressing and becoming even more sophisticated. We must therefore not play into the hands of the system. The unity of the working class shall never be crushed. This must be clear to the imperialists and the capitalists. Comrades, there is one thing that you must never forget—I am talking to students and parents. Non-involvement in the political struggle on the part of the oppressed students is something that the oppressors hold dear to their hearts. There is no way we can accommodate people who are standing on [the] fence in our struggle. It is better to die fighting than to live the miserable life of a slave.

Unban COSAS Unban!!

Crowd: Unban!!
Speaker 4: Viva ANC Viva!!
Crowd: Viva!!
Speaker: Viva the spirit of Umkhonto we Sizwe Viva!!
Crowd: Viva!!
Speaker: Viva the spirit of Oliver Tambo Viva!!
Crowd: Viva!!
Speaker: Viva the spirit of Nelson Mandela viva!!
Crowd: Viva!!
Speaker: Amandla!!
Crowd: Awethu!!

Speaker: Ngawethu!!
Crowd: Amandla!!
Speaker: Viva to you comrade Thanduxolo!!
Crowd: Viva!!

Speaker 4: I thank you all in the name of the [mothers], the domestic workers union of Port Elizabeth (PEDWU). This union is fighting for the right of domestic workers to be recognised as workers in South Africa. The domestic worker leaves early in the morning to work for the white man and they come back in the evening to look after their children and husbands and the wages they get is peanuts. We are pledging all domestic workers to stand up and fight for a decent wage and better working conditions. We also don't get our maternity leave pay. When the white man first came to South Africa the domestic workers looked after them and their children, and yet the conditions of the domestic workers are still worse and they refuse to recognise us as workers.

So stand up domestic workers and fight. Time is running out, workers. We demand our pension pay, maternity leave and better wages. We are tired of being slaves. There is a mother here in PE who worked for a certain family for 18 years. When she asked for a raise she was [treated] as a dog. For 18 years this woman has been paid twenty-six rand. So I am asking all domestic workers to join the UDF and fight for their rights and better working conditions!

Viva the spirit of no surrender viva!!

Crowd: Viva!!

Speaker 5: Viva ANC viva!!
Crowd: Viva!!
Speaker 5: We are the future!!
Crowd: Nobody can suffer!!
Speaker 5: We are the future!!

Mike [Odolo?], Vice President of PEYCO [PE Youth Congress]: Comrades, I am requesting that people should listen. Last week Saturday we lost comrade Moses Mabhida. I want you to know that Moses Mabhida is remembered all over the world. Even in Robben Island the comrades have gathered today to commemorate his death. Moses Mabhida is a tried and tested revolutionary for the South African struggle. AMANDLA!! [*Crowd:* Awethu!!] Parents, before we start today. Because Moses Mabhida represents the most conscious sector of the working class today, and the South African Communist Party today is a true alliance of the people because it represents the true aspirations of the working class. Comrades, in respect for Moses Mabhida, I am requesting all of us to stand up and observe a moment of silence. Despite his departure the struggle continues. AMANDLA!!

Crowd: Awethu!!
Speaker: You can sit down. Long live the South African Communist Party, long live!!
Crowd: Long live!!
Speaker: Long live the alliance of the ANC and SACP, long live!!

Speaker: Comrades, today is a historic day in the struggle for liberation in South Africa. The people's organisation, the ANC and its military wing of Umkhonto we Sizwe, is here today. Comrade Thanduxolo has fallen. He has left his AK-47 which we must pick up and continue with the struggle. When the people attend these meetings they must listen to the direction which is given. The leaders, [Mkhuseli] Jack and [Henry] Fazzie who are not here today, we don't believe that the banning of Jack and Fazzie is going to stop the struggle. Political organisations are united. Surely they don't believe that we are going to stop the consumer boycott. When the consumer boycott was started women wearing white dresses led the boycott. We know that we are going to win.

We know that we are going to push for their unbanning. We are not divided, it is the whites who are. They must unban Jack and Fazzie because they aren't the ones who are to blame for the boycotts. We are the ones, the people who are here in this hall today. The ANC believes that blood must be shed. We don't hurt anyone but they hurt us. We are only defending ourselves. When they say you must not go to town it is for your own good, because they are going to "hit the bird with the tree". If you are in town you are going to be caught in the crossfire.

If you don't listen to the streets and area committee, where are you going to get the message from? People are urged to listen to their street committees. The March stayaway is on the 16th, 17th and 18th. People must observe the call for the stayaway. We are a force to be reckoned with. The forthcoming stayaway on Monday, people must listen to their street committees for direction and instructions. There are going to be no more meetings, but only street committee meetings. This is an effort to stop the government from infiltrating our organisations.

Song [in Xhosa]:
Shoot guerilla shoot (repeated 3 times)
Shoot, shoot (repeated many times)

Speaker: Viva NEUSA [National Education Union of SA] Viva!!
Crowd: Viva!!
Speaker: Down with Botha regime down!!
Crowd: Down!!
Speaker: Amandla!!
Crowd: Awethu!!

NEUSA Speaker: I greet you all in the name of NEUSA. NEUSA is a teachers' organisation. Teachers are a guiding force in our community. We are holding the light to the future of our children and our job is the most difficult. We are supposed to show the black man the way. Parents send their kids to us for guidance, but we are told to teach these kids that the white man is superior. We as teachers know the truth. As shepherds of this flock we must not lead our children astray, but we must insist on the people's education. NEUSA stands for a democratic education that is going to serve the needs of the people. NEUSA stands for an education system that knows no colour; an education that is free of apartheid. We teach what the people want, and the cheque we get at the end of the month comes from the people not from the government. Today I am calling for unity amongst the people: let there be no black sheep among white sheep. This wagon of our struggle is moving. Teachers are urged to release the handbrakes of this wagon. The government is saying we must prepare the children to be workers of tomorrow. It is saying we must not teach politics. Teachers must teach what the people want and not what the government wants, because we must produce the leaders of tomorrow. We won't teach politics but we will teach the truth.

Song [in Xhosa]:
We will fight for our land South Africa
We will leave our parents
We will go to Angola to train
We will fight for our land (repeated several times)

The M.C.: This man who is lying here is a man of truth. One day [foreigners] came here, and asked to be accepted in our house. The government is saying it is the ANC who made the Freedom Charter but I am saying it is the people who made the Freedom Charter. Our children leave our country to go and train to come back and take the country. Thanduxolo went for training, then he came back and served the people until he died. The world is on fire. They say that they are going to keep Mkhuseli Jack and Henry Fazzie for five years; they say that for five years they must not talk. If they shoot all our children, then the women must take the AK-47 and shoot back. Women must join PEWO [PE Women's Organisation]. I know that there are people [informers] who are going to take what I have been saying to the Le Grange building [security police headquarters]. Amandla!!

Crowd: Awethu!!

[One person, believed to be an informer, was singled out by singing and shouting with everyone pointing their fingers and whistling.]

Song [in Xhosa]:
Shoot workers shoot
Come, workers, come, come through Umkhonto we Sizwe
Shoot, shoot with a bazooka (repeated several times)

Speaker: Today we are marching towards a nonracial and a free democratic South Africa. I greet you in the name of the struggle for total liberation, not only in South Africa but the world over. Comrades, I am addressing myself to the workers. The people shall be free to form trade unions, to elect officers. The state shall recognise the right and existence of unions. There shall be a 40 hour working week, the miners, the domestics, and the civil servants shall have a right to a pay raise as any other person. These are the demands of the people. The time has come for action.

Document 78. "People's Education for People's Power." Speech by Zwelakhe Sisulu to National Education Crisis Committee conference, Durban, March 29, 1986 (abridged)

Friends, Comrades, I welcome you to this historic gathering, a meeting of people from all over the country, from every province, from big and small towns, rural and urban areas. We gather here as a meeting of people drawn from all walks of life, from all sections of the people: students, teachers, parents, workers, community and political leaders. We bring together all sections of the oppressed community and all who detest apartheid. We have tried to ensure representation of all political tendencies and all sections of our population, black and white. . . .

THE CURRENT SITUATION

We stand today at a crossroads in our struggle for national liberation. We hold the future in our hands. The decisions we take at this conference will be truly historic, in the sense that they will help determine whether we go forward to progress and peace, or whether the racists push us backwards and reverse some of the gains that we have made, towards barbarism and chaos. . . .

This moment has a number of important features:
- the state has lost the initiative to the people. It is no longer in control of events.
- the masses themselves recognise that the moment is decisive, and are calling for action.
- the people are united around a set of fundamental demands, and are prepared to take action on these demands.

Having said this, I want to strike a note of caution. It is important that we don't misrecognise the moment, or understand it to be something which it is not. We are not poised for the immediate transfer of power to the people. The belief that this is so could lead to serious errors and defeats. We are, however, poised to enter a phase which can lead to a transfer of power. What we are seeking to do is to decisively shift the balance of forces in our favour. To do this we have to adopt the appropriate strategies and tactics, we have to understand our strengths and weaknesses, as well as that of the enemy, that is, the forces of apartheid reaction.

Having said this, let us describe some of the main features of the current situation. The government introduced the state of emergency because it was losing political control. It hoped that the emergency would achieve two objectives: firstly, to stop the advances of the democratic movement, and to destroy the people's organisations which were taking control in various parts of the country. Secondly, it aimed to reinstitute the puppet bodies in the townships which had been destroyed since the Vaal uprising ten months previously. Through this two-pronged attack it hoped to regain control, regain the initiative, and impose its apartheid reforms on the people.

In fact, the state failed hopelessly in these objectives. Its brutal actions, and atrocities committed by the SADF [SA Defence Force] and SAP [SA Police], only angered the people more and mobilised them in ever growing numbers. Puppet structures, instead of being restored, came under more widespread attack. In a number of areas people's organisations strengthened their structures and become more rooted in the masses. Struggle began to be waged in all corners of the country and new organisations sprang up daily. Where youth had previously waged the struggle alone, whole communities now involved themselves in united action against the regime.

Despite the heavy blows against our leaders and organisations, there was a real strengthening of the democratic forces, the people's camp; and a weakening of the forces of apartheid, the enemy camp. Let us first look at the situation in the enemy camp. When the regime declared the emergency, all sections of the white ruling bloc supported it, in the belief that the resistance of the people would be crushed, paving the way for a Buthelezi-Muzorewa option. Barely one month later this appearance of unity had crumbled. Mass resistance had spread and taken new forms. The regime stood more isolated than ever before at the international level; and the economic crisis reached new proportions with the loss of investor confidence in the stability of the South African regime.

This situation brought home to its allies that the regime was no longer able to rule in the old way. The people heightened contradictions within the ruling bloc by strategies such as the consumer boycott. The regime became increasingly divided and unable to act as greater pressure built up, locally and internationally, to meet the people's demands. The divisions reached right into the cabinet itself, as sections of the government differed with each other on the correct way to deal with the situation. The SPCC [Soweto Parents' Crisis Committee] initiative created public divisions between the SADF and SAP on the one hand, and DET [Department of Education and Training] on the other, something which previously would have been unthinkable.

The initiative passed into the hands of the people. The ANC, in particular, became seen as the primary actor on the South African stage. Not only the people, but sections of the white ruling bloc, began to look to the ANC to provide an indication of future direction.

Doubts among whites in the ability of Parliament to provide a solution to the country's problems reached a peak with the resignation of Van Zyl Slabbert. Politically, therefore, the regime had become totally isolated, both locally and internationally. Morally, it had been exposed as totally bankrupt and without any legitimate right to rule. Economically, it faced its worst crisis ever.

It was in this context that they lifted the state of emergency. They did not do this from a position of strength. The people forced them to lift the emergency. They are trying to gain a breathing space before launching a new offensive against the people. . . .

Advances of the People

When the emergency was declared [in July 1985], a situation of ungovernability existed mainly in two areas, the Eastern Cape and the East Rand. By the beginning of this year the situation was very different. Ungovernability had not only extended to far more areas. The people had actually begun to govern themselves in a number of townships.

The period of the emergency saw very important advances made by the people. Confronted by the terror of the SADF and SAP, the people, under the leadership of their organisations, closed ranks. Structures were built which would survive the period of the emergency and beyond it. In a number of townships, the area was split up into zones, blocks and areas, each of which would have its own committee, and some townships developed street committees.

As a result, in many cases our organisations matured and grew under the guns of the SADF. Action taken against the leadership didn't result in the collapse of our organisations. Not only did our organisations grow in strength, they often took over the running of the townships. So we saw the emergence of zones of People's Power in a number of townships. . . .

Greater involvement of parents gave rise in turn to initiatives such as that of the SPCC. This development wasn't confined to education, however. Parents and workers began to take a more active involvement in all issues concerning the community. There was a general recognition in the democratic movement that it was a major challenge to consolidate and accelerate this process. There was also a recognition that serious obstacles existed which had to be tackled. Our youth organisations began to play an important role in trying to channel the militancy of unorganised youth into disciplined action, responsive and accountable to the whole community.

Complementing this was the development of a close relationship between the trade unions and the rest of the democratic movement. The formation of COSATU was of particular importance in this regard, since it took a strong stand supporting trade union involvement in community and political issues.

In terms of developing the struggle nationally, we made our most significant advance in the last months of the emergency. For the first time in decades, our people took up the struggle in the rural areas. People in a number of bantustan areas challenged the so-called tribal authorities, and in some instances even replaced these bantustan sellouts with people's village councils. Areas which the enemy could previously rely on as zones of subservience and passivity were now being turned into zones of struggle. In the midst of the emergency our people waged campaigns against these puppets in seven of the nine bantustans. Of course, the majority of our people in the rural areas have yet to challenge their oppressors. But the significance of these developments should not be underestimated. Every day this process is being furthered as more and more people in the rural areas take up the cudgels of freedom. . . .

FORWARD TO PEOPLE'S POWER

Why do we use the slogan "Forward to People's Power"? Firstly it indicates that our people are now seeing the day when the people of South Africa shall have the power, when the people shall govern all aspects of their lives, as *achievable reality* which we are working towards.

Secondly, it expresses the growing trend for our people to move towards realising people's power *now*, in the process of struggle, before actual liberation. By this we mean that people are beginning to exert control over their own lives in different ways. In some townships and schools people are beginning to govern themselves, despite being under racist rule. . . .

We must stress that there is an important distinction between ungovernability and people's power. In a situation of ungovernability the *government* doesn't have control. But nor do the people. While they have broken the shackles of direct government rule the people haven't yet managed to control and direct the situation. There is a power vacuum. In a situation of people's power the *people* are starting to exercise control.

An important difference between ungovernability and people's power is that no matter how ungovernable a township is, unless the people are organised, the gains made through ungovernability can be rolled back by state repression. Because there is no organised centre of people's power, the people are relatively defenceless and vulnerable. Removal of our leadership in such situations can enable the state to reimpose control. We saw, for example, the setbacks experienced by our people in the Vaal and East Rand. Despite heroic struggles and sustained ungovernability, the state through its vicious action was able to reverse some of the gains made in these areas. Where, however, people's power has advanced, not even the most vicious repression has been able to decisively reverse our people's advances. If anything, their repressive actions serve to deepen people's power in these zones and unite the people against the occupying forces. In the Eastern Cape people's power forced the SADF out of the townships, if only temporarily. . . .

PEOPLE'S EDUCATION FOR PEOPLE'S POWER

The struggle for People's Education is no longer a struggle of the students alone. It has become a struggle of the whole community with the involvement of all sections of the community. This is not something which has happened in the school sphere alone; it reflects a new level of development in the struggle as a whole. . . .

In the few short months since the December conference, we have already seen some of the things People's Power can achieve in our education struggle. We have also seen that the state will do anything it can to reverse these gains and turn them into defeats. In hundreds of schools students have established democratic SRCs [Student Representative Councils], but the state is doing everything it can to frustrate and crush them. The state has conceded our demand for free text books, but tries to wriggle out of this by saying there aren't enough. Also, many detainees, student leaders, are being released, but then excluded from schools. These are only a few examples which show the kind of enemy we face. . . .

Another area where we are demonstrating the possibilities of people's power is through the school committees. The December Conference took a resolution to replace statutory parents' committees with progressive parent, teacher, student structures. Although these government committees continue in name, they have been rendered unworkable in many parts of the country. Our democratic people's committees have been established and are preparing to take more and more control over the running of the schools. They are the ones who are putting forward the [elementary school] pupil's demands and negotiating with the school principals. The government committees are now being ignored. In effect they are falling away. In some areas their members have abandoned them and joined the people's committees.

Even the regional directors of education are meeting with the people's committees. And finally, of course, the central government has been forced to recognise the people's crisis committees by meeting with representatives of the NECC [National Education Crisis Committee]. Therefore the government-appointed bodies are being replaced at local, regional and national level by bodies of the people. This is a substantial achievement, since what the government has enforced for decades are now being replaced by the people in a period of three short months. . . .

We cannot afford to allow any section of the community to be used against the struggles of our people. Let us use the heroic example of Matthew Goniwe as an inspiration to our teachers! Let us organise a fighting alliance between teachers, students and parents that will be unbreakable!

What do we mean when we say we want people's education? We are agreed that we don't want Bantu Education but we must be clear about *what* we want in its place. We must also be clear as to *how* we are going to achieve this.

We are no longer demanding the same education as whites, since this is education for domination. People's education means education at the service of the people as a whole, education that liberates, education that puts the people in command of their lives.

We are not prepared to accept any "alternative" to Bantu Education which is imposed on the people from above. This includes American or other imperialist alternatives designed to safeguard their selfish interests in the country, by promoting elitist and divisive ideas and values which will ensure foreign monopoly exploitation continues.

Another type of "alternative school" we reject is the one which gives students from a more wealthy background avenues to opt out of the struggle, such as commercially-run schools which are springing up.

To be acceptable, every initiative must come from the people themselves, must be accountable to the people and must advance the broad mass of students, not just a select few. In effect this means taking over the schools, transforming them from institutions of oppression into zones of progress and people's power. Of course this is a long-term process, a process of struggle, which can only ultimately be secured by total liberation. But we have already begun this process. . . . The campaign to draw up an Education Charter is an important part in this process of shaping People's Education, since it will articulate the type of education people want in a democratic South Africa. . . .

STRUGGLES IN THE COMMUNITIES . . .

It is not for me to pre-empt the decisions of this conference. What might be useful, however, is for me to outline some of the strategies and tactics that our people have adopted and are using at present in their struggles against the enemy. It is important that we assess these and understand how best they can further some of the gains that we have made and how they can increase the crisis and disarray in the ranks of the enemy. . . .

In many townships, community councillors have been forced to resign. We have noted that popular structures have often been erected to replace them. . . .

In many townships, especially in the Transvaal, successful rent boycotts have been instituted. Some of these have been sustained for more than two years. The value of rent boycotts is that they strike at the material basis of Black Local Authorities, while simultaneously relieving some of the economic pressures on the masses. . . . Amongst our people, unemployment has reached a record figure and continues to increase. GST [General Sales Tax] continues to impose a heavy burden. In this situation, the people, by refusing to pay rent, transfer part of the burden to the system. . . .

One of the key forms of struggle employed in recent years has been the consumer boycott. The weapon's potency lies in the fact that it requires the organisation of the entire community in order to be effective. To sustain it requires strong, deeply-rooted organisational structures. . . . Where organisation has been weaker the consumer boycott has been less successful [and] . . . young people, often well-meaning, have tended to apply force instead of political education to persuade the community to support the boycott. This has had the effect of alienating some people from the struggle.

Another dramatic and often-utilised weapon is the stayaway. Where it is based on strong organisation, it is powerful and builds unity not only within the community, but also between community and trade union organisations.

Where such organisation is not present, where such stayaways are not adequately prepared, they tend to produce, as with consumer boycotts, intimidation instead of persuasion, disunity instead of growing unity of the people. The adequate preparation for such a tactic requires careful discussion amongst all sections of the community, including hostel dwellers, and especially between community and worker organisations. Only then is this weapon powerful and effective.

A crucial demand of the entire African people remains the abolition of the pass system. Sensing the continued popular anger and militancy, Comrade [Elijah] Barayi, president of COSATU, made a call at the launch of the trade union federation, for the burning of the badges of slavery. Should such a call be implemented it is likely to capture popular imagination, to involve every section of the African community and enjoy the support of all democrats. . . .

We also need to examine ways of making inroads into the white community. To break the stranglehold that apartheid education has on the minds of white children, we must show their parents that apartheid education provides no future for their children, or any of South Africa's children. . . .

There are still areas where students are fighting the education struggle without the support of their parents or teachers. There are still areas where the struggle is led by the youth and the students and older members of the community are left behind or alienated. There are still sections of the teaching profession who side with the apartheid government and promote its will. . . .

We must remember that the enemy is not sleeping while we plan our activities. We know that it openly attacks us. But it does not only operate outside our ranks. It also operates from within our ranks. From within, the enemy takes advantage of any sign of indiscipline, any disunity, every sign of weakness. It does this in order to confuse our people, to increase disunity, and sow chaos in our ranks. . . .

Our task is not only to build democratic organisations, but to build these in such a way that they can withstand the harassment of the apartheid government. We know that our greatest strength lies in the power of the people, in our mass based committees in the schools, streets and factories; in our co-ordinated strength in our national organisations, such as NECC.

Long live the struggle for democratic, people's education!
Long live the united popular struggle against apartheid!
Forward to a free, democratic people's South Africa!
Amandla Ngawethu! Power to the People!

DOCUMENT 79. "On People's Power and People's Committees." Alexandra Action Committee discussion document, April 8, 1986

The State of Emergency and the constant banning of meetings has as its aim the suppression of the legitimate resistance of the people against all injustices.

Through these measures, the Botha regime had hoped to crush and stifle people's organisations, isolate activists from their communities and give the all needed period of respite to its puppet bodies—the Community Councils, the Bantustan regimes, etc. to reorganise and reclaim most of their lost ground and power. These measures have not succeeded. But it would be deceiving the people and telling lies to say because these measures were not successful all was well and perfect.

During the Emergency and the denial of the right of free association the following ugly aspects were noted in some areas:
1) Activists did not organise sufficiently
2) There was no accountability to the people
3) Organisational structures broke down
4) Activists were isolated from the communities
5) Rumour, lack of direction and communication became the order of the day.
6) Opportunists and undisciplined elements hijacked the struggles of the people for their own selfish ends.

If our organisations were thoroughly rooted, not just in words but in deed, in the people, some of these negative aspects could have been avoided.

It is never too late to rectify our mistakes. Sometimes we learn after bitter experiences. The State of Emergency and the almost permanent ban on meetings laid the basis for these bitter experiences. We have also mentioned that the people have frustrated the efforts of the Botha regime to impose puppet structures and programmes on them. In other words the people have made Apartheid unworkable. But we must hasten to add that we ought not to wait for the Botha government to dictate the pace and content of "change". *We have to start building alternative organs of People's Power in our townships and villages to give practical effect and content to the slogan: "FORWARD TO PEOPLE'S POWER."*

People's power means exactly what it says—the power of the people. It means also the involvement of every household, every resident in decision making about the matters which concern him/her in his/her own area.

Let's not talk and wait for DEMOCRACY, let's practise it without delay.

The most practical way in which we can start building structures which reflect people's power in action is through street and block committees.

Every street elects its chairperson and committee members to take care of the day to day common affairs of all the people living in that particular street and to execute decisions arrived at through full participation by every resident of the street.

Five streets shall constitute a block and the chairpersons of the five street committees shall constitute the Block Committee which shall elect its own chairperson.

The Block Committees of a particular township shall constitute an area committee which shall affiliate to a wider civic body.

This approach ensures that our organisations are rooted in the masses.

SOME ADVANTAGES OF HAVING PEOPLE'S COMMITTEES
a) They facilitate communication among residents.
b) They serve as alternatives to public meetings which get banned time and again.
c) They reduce "activists" to the level of the people.

d) They deny undisciplined elements the chance to harass the residents.
e) They ensure that our organisations are mass based and reflect the will of the people and not just that of the activists.

THE IMMEDIATE TASKS OF ORGANISERS
The immediate task of the organisers of People's committees should be to:
a) Identify all progressive individuals in every street.
b) Bring them together to discuss the concept and ways of implementing People's Power through the above mentioned committees.
c) Plan strategies of approaching the residents in house to house campaigns.
d) Organisers should work in the streets in which they live.
e) Encourage the formation of youth, women, student and civic groups.
f) Arrange for house meetings.

Since 1986 is very likely to be an explosive year and a time when the people's will is put to the utmost test, the urgency with which this programme should be implemented cannot be over emphasised.

Document 80. ANC minutes of meeting with leaders of South African Catholic Church, Lusaka, April 15–16, 1986 (abridged)

ANC Delegation: President OR Tambo, J Nkadimeng, T Mbeki, M Maharaj, R Mompati, S Tshwete, Peter Ramokoa [Joel Netshitenzhe]

RCC Delegation: Archbishop Denis Hurley, Fr. Smangaliso Mkhatshwa, Bishop Wilfrid Napier (Kokstad), Bishop Manuset Biyase (Eshowe).

OPENING REMARKS:
President OR Tambo: It's a great privilege for me to welcome the RCC [Roman Catholic Church] delegation. The ANC decided in 1985 that the turmoil in SA today marks a great stride towards victory, and we need to sacrifice to free ourselves. The present build up of conflict is unprecedented and it marks the beginning of the end. In this regard we seek to get all opponents of apartheid to close ranks and shorten the period of struggle, to bring relief quickest without refraining from sacrifice.

The ANC started the process of consultation with various forces opposed to the regime and high on the list were church leaders. SA is a Christian society, and our people are drawn to the church by, among other [things], that they believe the church understands the system and their suffering. We place faith in the credibility of the church, in its concern for our people, the hungry. . . . [The] RCC under the leadership of His Grace has contributed and continues to contribute to the democratic effort. This meeting is also a continuation of others, e.g. the one in 1984. It is one of the meetings we intend to hold with religious leaders, and we include the Moslem community. The primary purpose is to seek common understanding: The ANC never reaches the end of its analysis, and we always gain from such meetings. . . .

Archbishop Hurley: I thank you for your welcome. We are convinced that the ANC has played, is playing and will play an important role in SA. The role of the Church has been low key. It has not been concerned with tangible achievements. I should confess that the church has no tangible programme, and also that churches have to learn and are trying to learn. . . .

Tambo: This whole exercise creates the possibility of movement into the white community; it calls attention to the ANC as a movement worthy of approach by all forces interested in the ending of apartheid. . . . There are questions that recur in many of the meetings, all of them related to the system that is to replace apartheid: nationalisation of monopoly capital, whether or not whites will be swamped, our relations with the SACP [SA Communist Party], etc. We would like the views of the RCC delegation on these questions including the issue of economic sanctions. It should be emphasised that the principal source of the change in the attitudes of whites is the struggle of the oppressed people—the mass revolt, armed struggle and its dimensions—and the increasing isolation of the regime. . . .

Maharaj: It's true that Pretoria is a powerful state, but even the white community has started to question Botha's ability to lead them and hold back the forces of change. The issue is not to avoid or prevent violence; rather it is how to act decisively to minimise the violence: how to mount a united general offensive. Botha must not be given a chance; rather we must marshal our forces together to shorten the term of struggle.

To weaken Botha's base, there are three main directions of action—to weaken the state, to sow division within the white community and to activise democrats within this community, e.g. the ECC [End Conscription Campaign] campaign in which the RCC is involved. . . . The key point is to work for the isolation of the racist regime and thus minimise the loss of life. Many struggles are underway and our programme for the year includes: 1986 as Year of People's Action—we emphasise the role of armed struggle as central; that it has raised the morale of the people and generated a high level of struggle. On the education front there are many positive developments in which we have made a decisive input.

The question that arises in struggle, as was posed by the RCC delegation, is what are the effects of intensification—what about the massacres it generates. Around this revolves the issue of controlling the mass actions, giving effective leadership and heightening the spirit of fearlessness that we have generated, and not to dampen it. On the issue of "black-on-black violence", it is clear that one contingent is the regime, using the experience of the Latin American dictatorships, and dressing its campaign in such ruses as "black vs. black". It is a serious and dangerous maneouvre, especially in Natal where GB [Gatsha Buthelezi] has a social base—dangerous also for the future. On GB, the reality is that it's not us who are driving him away, as the PFP [Progressive Federal Party] intimated. He is acting on the side of the enemy.

The ANC has issued many calls to the people and all of them have been taken up. It's not that we control each and every event. People respect the ANC and they consult us on crisis after crisis. One important development is the emergence of mass combat units. We were forced to take up arms, and these arms serve a political purpose. Now we are moving beyond the stage where people were mere supportive spectators to that where they are fighting back as full participants. The fact is, if we want to minimise the violence, we have to launch an offensive to weaken the regime. There are other campaigns, e.g. the anti-pass campaign which should be intensified despite Botha's pronouncements, the RMC [Release Mandela Campaign], etc.

Napier: The isolation of the regime is not only to the left, but also to the right, especially small businessmen and the farming community. They complain also about Botha economic policies which they associate with the reform programme. In the Eastern Cape police, commanding positions are in the hands of HNP [Herstigte Nasionale Party], Conservative Party, etc. There is also the problem of violence which antagonises the fence-sitters: incidents such as Toti [an MK bombing which killed 6 civilians at Amanzimtoti, Natal, in December 1985] tip the balance in favour of the rightist forces. . . .

Mkhatshwa: Nico Smith says that conservative Afrikaners are saying that the government must stop the unrest by using the iron fist.

Tambo: Several years ago we were told that if we pushed too hard, this would have the effect of driving whites into the laager [circled wagons]. We were advised to scale down the struggle and concentrate on persuading whites. It could well happen that intensification leads to the laager; but our experience is that when you sustain struggle, the laager breaks up as a result. There are attempts now to mobilise into the laager by the Conservative Party, AWB [Afrikaner Weerstandsbeweging], etc: many whites could see the Conservative Party as their salvation; but the fact is that it can't solve the problems.

There is opposition from the right, but it weakens the enemy. Even if they overthrew Botha, the situation would be worse for all of them because the forces of change are mounting. Actions such as sanctions can be effective because nobody in his right mind could prefer destruction of the economy to changing the system. AWB intransigence will persist but we must try to explain our policies to all these people, and the church should play an important role in this regard. How do we stop their fear? Should we relax pace? Of course not. We must intensify and try to prevent the worst excesses of conflict, but we must be ready to bleed. We need to spread the struggle throughout the country—that's what we are trying to do.

On the method of necklacing, I've not got used to that, but what made people think of it, of this brutal manner! It's the measure of bitterness resulting from the regime's brutal actions. How should people feel if one among them is informing the enemy about their plans and activities, leading to loss of life! They are forced to respond in this manner. We'll outgrow it as we become more organised. It has had its positive effects: e.g. many townships are absolutely disciplined; there is law and order of the right kind. We are growing out of conflict in which lives are lost unnecessarily, and going on to disciplined actions.

With Toti, trouble lies in ANC policy of selective sabotage. . . . After adoption of armed struggle we pursued the policy of selective sabotage for many years. We were perhaps too patient. How many whites have died as a result of ANC actions, compared to Africans murdered by the regime—about 20 white non-soldiers; compare this to African civilians—thousands!

When 42 were killed in Maseru [by SADF raid in 1982], 86% of whites were for it; and at the funeral I said whites would have to start burying their dead. The problem is that it would seem the term "civilian" applies only to whites, not in reference to the SADF [SA Defence Force] killing and maiming African children. Of course whites are not used to actions of this nature. . . .

Hurley: There are other fears among whites: land reform—whether they will lose their farms; on nationalisation—who will run the complicated industries; on the civil service—where will it be from since most of them today are conservative.

Nkadimeng: There is merit in the question. . . . [But we] cannot say that we should not take over because skilled workers will run away. We should take over and prepare people for the jobs. Besides, SA has a developed black proletariat which is in fact running the industries even if they are not officially recognised as such, for e.g. in the mines. There can be no argument about land redistribution, taking into account the present disparity. . . .

Maharaj: We also have to learn from the mistakes of other countries; and our basic priority is to control the heights of the economy and ensure increased production. We need to have confidence in people's power. We stand by the Freedom Charter and all problems will be solved in the context of people's power. On the civil service it should be noted that many of them were poorly educated when they started: they were "poor whites" and today they are in full control. Within the ANC we have been trying to train our people in all the necessary skills.

Netshitenzhe: This question should be seen also in the context of actions that should be undertaken today. In our discussion with NUSAS [National Union of SA Students] they also asked about whether or not their skills as white students will be useful after liberation. And the issue is if they want their skills to be useful they should start now preparing for the future. They should for e.g., participate in the struggle for alternative education, an education that is geared to serve the people. They have to participate in community projects as doctors, etc. There are progressive groups in various faculties, for example at Wits [University of the Witwatersrand],which pursue this objective. One example is PLANACT, an association of architects and town planners which exposed the regime's scheme to "upgrade" Langa township in the E Cape—they prepared their own blueprint for genuine upgrading. Now by acting in various ways with the people, the students and skilled personnel will ensure that they will fit better in the future SA. This has to be done in action. . . .

Tambo: We have to be realistic: the ANC can't set out to destroy the economy—it's in the interest of our people that, at the instance of liberation, we have a strong economy. We had never paid enough attention to the question of details of the post-apartheid system; we are engaged in the struggle to liberate the country. But now it has come to our notice that these issues need to be addressed quite seriously. This year and in the future we shall be tackling all these questions about post-apartheid needs. We need manpower to do that: including people inside the country who will assist in research and other related tasks. On the nature of the future economy it should be said that everything will be decided in a democratic manner.

Napier: Do you consider the meetings that you have had as preliminary, building up to final negotiations?

Maharaj: Negotiations can only be conducted with a political power, not with organisations or individuals. Our meetings are part of the process of narrowing PW's [Botha's] support base.

Mbeki: Our people have said that if anybody wants to negotiate about the future of the country they should go to the ANC, to the leaders in exile and those in prison. [But] we as ANC will not do anything apart and hidden from the masses. We shall not negotiate on their behalf, but as part of them. . . .

Tambo: Since we are about to break I would like to leave the meeting with a thought: the need for us to unite the people against apartheid and try to reach across to the white population. One form is the ECC, and the RCC is deeply involved. Perhaps we should go beyond this and call for peace in the region; that there would not be a need for a vast army if peaceful conditions obtained on the subcontinent. We should mobilise against the involvement of SA troops in the neighbouring countries; raise the question with the white community and explain why the SADF is in Angola for example. It should give rise to protest within SA i.e., add a new dimension to the ECC—and this will be welcomed by the Frontline states.

Biyase: Problem is that it is linked to the image of the ANC. Whites argue that "terrorists" are in these countries and SADF has the right to punish them.

Tambo: The issue is what do they want in Angola. In Botswana the regime pressurised that the CR [Chief Representative of ANC] should leave though he was in no way related to any internal work; and the Batswana said to us that they could not protect him—this partly because there are no protests within SA against this bully, the SA regime. Protests within SA will help to strengthen the resistance of these countries to SA pressure. . . .

[following day]

Tambo: To start off we should clarify the question of ANC links with the SACP. The ANC has lived side by side with the CP for decades. At the point the Party was formed, some members of the ANC joined the CP, and this happened throughout the years membership has overlapped—even within the NEC [National Executive Committee]. The two organisations exist as separate bodies, each with its own programme and objectives. . . .

In the 1950s under the leadership of [Albert] Luthuli we were all united by our opposition to the regime, united in the Congress movement with mutual loyalties. Whatever earlier divisions were there vanished. With the adoption of the Freedom Charter by the Congress of the People, CP members accepted the document as their guide. Under Chief Luthuli—a great leader with an appeal even among whites—senior members like Moses Kotane were close to him; Kotane was his confidant. Kotane was a firm supporter and defender of ANC policy; he was perhaps the longest serving member of the NEC when he died. He defended the unity between the ANC and the CP.

We have a situation in which CP members fully understand, and are completely loyal to, the ANC; they accept the ANC as a leader of the struggle at this stage—perhaps a rare situation compared to other countries. I've been on the NEC since 1949 and I've never understood what is meant by the allegation that the CP controls the ANC. That does not exist—in fact who would control Luthuli, Mandela and other leaders of the ANC? PAC says we are controlled by whites—who would control these leaders, political giants in their own right! We are absolutely united as ANC. And there has been no change in ANC policy except in response to the changing situation. There is the claim that 19 members of the NEC are CP. Even if it were true, does it mean these 19 are not members of the ANC—all of them elected at our Conference because of their standing as ANC!

When independence comes, we shall all implement the Freedom Charter. In that SA, people will have the right to form and exist in different formations: there will be the SACP, the ANC and others. (Botha decided the other day that the ANC wants a one-party state.) The CP will pursue its objective of a socialist state. Many in the ANC believe in a socialist system, but we are bound in this national body, the ANC, and it does not call for socialism: we'll do what the Freedom Charter and the will of the people dictate. Perhaps at the end of the day that will be socialism. Our own assessment is that the ANC membership is not disposed to capitalism, but we shall not thrust socialism down the throats of the people; it has to be worked for. We have to adopt short-term and long-term solutions.

Successive presidents of the ANC found the CP there and they left it there. The fears about communism are a result of the South African regime's propaganda. At the 1956-61 Treason Trial the state concluded that the FC [Freedom Charter] was not a communist document, but the charges persist even today. Our people are not worried. Those the regime attacks most are made very popular.

The SU [Soviet Union] and other socialist countries support our struggle. I came out of the country in 1960 and first went there in 1963. We explained our situation; they asked questions and offered us assistance in all spheres including food and scholarships. They also gave us weapons because we can't pay for them; some African countries do give us weapons after buying them themselves. We have been to Sweden and other Nordic countries and they give us assistance in various spheres, Holland, etc. In Italy we enjoy the support of different parties, and I've met the Pope twice. In the US and other western countries it's not governments that support us.

There is no domination; the SU supports our views about our situation. We have just had a delegation to the PRC [People's Republic of China] and they will certainly respond to our requests. The socialist countries support us politically too, and at our request they have been involved in many political campaigns; they all do not have links with SA.

It is only now that the US administration has approached the ANC; the UK has held 2 meetings with the ANC. In the FRG [Federal Republic of Germany] we met the Foreign Minister for the first time. Not that all these governments support us—they are merely acknowledging the reality within SA. Yet they complain about SU support for our struggle. We should further emphasise that there are no strings attached. They don't give what we don't ask for.

Biyase: When they talk about influence, it sounds as if their concern is the SU, that it also sells its ideology, as for e.g., in Mozambique and Angola. I was also inclined to differentiate between SACP and the CPs in communist countries. The [SA] government has in mind world communism.

Napier: The idea is that people believe that there is no CP outside SU influence. They also say that Slovo is a dominant thinker in the ANC.

Mkhatshwa: It is said that this can be proved now by the presence of the "red flag" at mass funerals.

Maharaj: On Robben Island we had a quiz competition, and I described the contents of one book which vehemently condemns imperialism written in 1906 by a South African. Many people would say it was written by a communist, but it was written by Jan Smuts.

Mkhatshwa: I think Christians are wary of communism because Christianity has always identified with capitalism, as brother and sister. Communism is referred to as godless, as atheist. . . .

Tambo: About the red flag at funerals and meetings: Many CP members are in SA and if they hoist the red flag in protest actions, people say it's part of the front of fighters, it's also the target of the regime's repression. This development frightens Pretoria. But there has always been a CP in SA, and its members are acting.

Christians tend to shy away from communism; they see it as godless; there are very few who are also communists. This is partly due to the fact that for a long time the world has been capitalist, and when communism emerged it was attacked. Christianity has been part of capitalism in attacking communism. One could ask: apart from the propaganda aspect and so-called "godlessness", is there nothing in common between Christianity and socialism and communism; is there no basis to stand together against a common evil? One does find communists whose lives are wholly Christian: people who are kind, selfless, sensitive to injustice, ready to die for the other person—marvelous human beings except that they don't believe in God.

Hurley: One problem is the socialist countries themselves where you find an elite and dictatorships—this contrasts with what the president says about the SACP. This makes it difficult to work with Marxists—they don't believe in God; they propagate class warfare which history has disproved, for example, in W[estern] Europe CPs are disappearing because their dogmatic faith is not being realised, and there is a closer coming together of SD [social democrats] and CPs.

Tambo: One does not know what will happen when we take over but I'm talking of the CP I know. The system of apartheid perhaps makes them different; perhaps it is the quality of their leadership. I'm not setting out to explain what the CP is all about—but how we see it as ANC; how I see it as a Christian. I would speak as such anywhere. I have as president of the ANC enjoyed unquestioned loyalty of communists and non-communists.

Mompati: The communist label is used by the regime in an attempt to frighten our people. After the ANC NCC [National Consultative Conference at Kabwe] *Africa Confidential* described me as a moderate, and later changed to "radical communist". As far as I'm concerned—communist or not—the parable of the good Samaritan appeals to me. The basic question is how to break down barriers created by the regime and move forward in struggle.

Tshwete: ANC leads the democratic struggle in SA, and the regime uses anti-communism to try and destroy the ANC and isolate it from the people. . . . The Church in SA has a tradition of struggle; unlike in Czarist Russia, it has always been an ally of the democratic movement. . . . At this critical hour the church must resist the temptation to be drawn out of the struggle; to forget about oppression. The real anti-Christ in SA today is Botha.

Napier: One problem which creates psychological barriers among priests is the fact of the suppression of the church under communism—there are some priests in SA from East Germany who talk of their practical experience of suppression. In Africa there have been problems, e.g. in Mozambique and Ethiopia: because of the 20-year contracts they are forced to give their fish and coffee to the SU. The SU has no pure generosity. The church needs to be assured of your independence.

Mkhatshwa: In confirming the above I would like to point out that the vast majority of blacks do not have such problems. I think we should discuss practical issues: the programme of action.

Agree that press conference to be at the airport at 13.30 hrs.

Hurley: On the role of the church: The church leadership has occasionally made prophetic statements, but the question is how to relate such pronouncements to the actual situation. Today there are only two options open: either accept the system or accept the policies of the ANC. It's difficult to find anything else. We only need realism in the implementation of the idea of identification with the ANC: we need to plan and to explain to the people and educate them. . . .

Tambo: On the role of the church: To the majority of the people, the broad perspectives of the ANC are accepted and the question is how to bring an end to the system: not so much the detail on white fears, communism, etc, but how to destroy apartheid. Mass actions have been directed at frustrating and resisting the system as a united irresistible force. There is now the decision for a one-week stay-at-home in the Tvl [Transvaal], an example of what will happen if the people's demands are not acceded to. In general the church needs to support mass actions, to be with the people—this could help even to limit the violence. For 1986 there are many campaigns such as the consumer boycott, and the church has to encourage participation by its constituency, and find ways of participating as a church.

Hurley: We need a great deal of communication with the membership, and actual application of our decisions.

Napier: We need information from the activists themselves, in order to play our role. In areas such as Queenstown there is consultation between organisations and the church; there are established links with the UDF.

Biyase: The Tvl is active, but the problem is lack of contact between activists and the church; there is also the problem within the church of lack of co-ordination.

Netshitenzhe: With the situation in Natal, peculiar as it is, what are the experiences of the church and what are the possible actions that it can undertake?

Biyase: In Natal the majority of church members are Inkatha and they are very sensitive. We have from time to time allowed trade unions and other organisations to use our facilities; but now we are threatened with violence, and the question is what to do! One cannot advise people to invite retribution.

Mbeki: The fundamental problem is that people cannot stop struggling. And if Gatsha [Buthelezi] attacks them because they say apartheid is bad, then the conflict will simply escalate. There is now the problem between Gatsha and the trade union movement, the situation in Lamontville where the regime has come to his aid in attacking the people, etc. The church has to address this question.

Hurley: We'll make this issue an item on the agenda at our next meeting.

Mompati: [The Amanzimtoti bomber, Andrew] Zondo is to hang, and we believe the church can play an important role in the campaign to stop the judicial murder. We might disagree with his actions but we all know the cause.

Hurley: It will be very difficult because whites, and especially the families of the Toti victims, are very bitter.

CLOSING REMARKS:

President Tambo: We are moving to a close, perhaps an adjournment, of what was a very useful meeting. We covered a lot of ground on many difficult questions. The issues raised helped to focus our own minds on many areas. There is the question of violence in the townships—the extent and forms of violence—but people's violence cannot be equated with the violence of the regime. There is violence in Natal by the so-called *amabutho*, and Diakonia [a Catholic organization] is assembling affidavits. In general there are many elements of the situation that need correction. The discussion has placed importance on the need to act and to correct errors without stopping the struggle.

We discussed the question of communism, and it was helpful to know where problems lie. We shall continue to reflect on all the questions. We learnt a great deal about the fears of whites and we shall further look into them and find ways and means of allaying those fears that can be allayed. The communiqué talks about constant communication and this should be realised. We have gained immensely from your contributions and the whole exercise has been intended at uniting our people for freedom.

Archbishop Hurley: You gained very little, but we have gained a lot. It's for us a critical moment: the church is trying to find its way forward. Since 1984 the future is no more an abstract issue; it has become very tangible. We need to make a choice for justice and peace. We hope to be able to convey not just the formulations and exposé but the actual atmosphere. We shall try to have a proper report back,

Napier: This type of contact has been very useful. . . .

Biyase: We are thankful for the knowledge we have gained—we have been helped to learn. There is absolute need for future contact.

Mkhatshwa: All I can say is: Come back home!

Prayer by ARCHBISHOP HURLEY

Document 81. "Consumer Boycott." Northern Transvaal Consumer Boycott Committee flyer, May 1986

CONSUMER BOYCOTT

we don't buy in town   ga re reke toropong

TARGET TOWNS

Duivelskloof		Burgerfort
Phalaborwa		Potgietersrust
Tzaneen	Pietersburg	Groblersdal

DEMANDS   DEMANDS   DEMANDS

1. Stop police detentions, beatings and killings.
2. Resignation of police, councillors and Bantustan MPs.
3. An end to the bombings of activists' homes.
4. The release of all political detainees and prisoners.
5. Reduction of bus fares and rent payments.
6. Reinstatement of all dismissed workers.
7. Recognition of democratically elected SRC's [Student Representative Councils] and Trade Unions.
8. Provision of free books for all students.

BOYCOTT TARGETS
Town and all shops and buses belonging to police and Bantustan MPs

DURATION
To be reviewed after two months.
Date of launch 3 May.

we have the buying power

Document 82. Notes on meeting with Brigadier Ernest Schnetler of the South African Police, by Mkhuseli Jack of Port Elizabeth Youth Congress, May 1986

Q: Did you break your promise [about the dancing]?

A: Not so. The issue of toyi-toyi dance was mentioned by Brigadier Schnetler in passing—he said as an aside to the main issue of keeping the police and the youth apart, that he did not like the toyi-toyi dance. The fact that he is now claiming this trivial issue to be central to our agreement, we can only see as an effort to save face—perhaps there are those in the police and in the government who do not favour violence-free funerals, who instead favour police brutality. Perhaps it is these evil forces he is trying to appease in raising the issue of toyi-toyi.

Q: But isn't the toyi-toyi a militant, warlike dance?

A: Yes, but we see it as a product of apartheid, created by sheer circumstances of sustained brutality directed by the armed forces against our people young and old, men, women and children. However we see the toyi-toyi as a non-violent alternative letting off of steam. After all, dancing was always a way of alleviating social stress and strain. Take the "*Tiekie-draai,* the *Boere jol* [folk dancing]," where the Afrikaners will meet to hold dances. There they express solidarity and unity with their people, through the occasion marked with dance. We see no differences.

Finally we say, Saturday's funeral was the first in weeks not to be characterised by more deaths. The cycle of violence was broken and Brigadier Schnetler ought to be congratulated for making a contribution to peace in Port Elizabeth. We hope his action sets an example to the armed forces country-wide. We rejoice in the fact that a mere social dance is the latest issue of contention, not more unnecessary and tragic deaths.

Q: Will you be putting a stop to the toyi-toyi dance?

A: We Africans will never relinquish our traditions at the behest of the apartheid regime. Toyi-toyi is as African as big funerals. In fact, we will encourage toyi-toyi as an alternative to urban, violent anarchy which would result if the youth were not busy dancing the toyi-toyi. The authorities of apartheid have steadily and stolidly been eroding our rights since they assumed power in the beginning of the century; our rights to move freely, live freely, to vote, to have meetings and to organize in the land of our birth. Lately even our rights to bury our dead have been restricted, rudely disrupted and banned. The latest rumours that our rights to dance are to be banned would be supremely ludicrous if they weren't so real and hurtful. Nobody can seriously expect us to passively concur with this type of legislation.

Document 83. "June 16: Commemorating the Dead, Learning the Lessons, Continuing the Fight." Article in Muslim Youth Movement newsletter, *Risalatuna: Our Message,* June 1986

On June 16th we commemorate the brutal killing of our fellow oppressed students. We commemorate but we reflect and evaluate as well. Those struggling on the basis of Islam to establish Adl (justice) and Qist (equity) as ordained by Allah must learn from the struggles of the past. The Prophet has said *"The believer is never stung twice from the same hole."* Allah says, *"Travel through the earth and see what was the end of those before you..."* (30 verse 42). In order to establish the just system Islam demands, means consistent Jihad (struggle) and avoidance of adventurism; it demands that we evaluate our mistakes and gains and avoid sentimental dreaming; it demands planned action as opposed to sporadic emotional outbursts.

So what do we learn from the revolt of 1976, when hundreds were brutally killed and maimed?

COMMITMENT AND SACRIFICE

First, that the desire for change may exist but it must be practically and actually demonstrated. In that process the forces of Taghut (oppression) and Dhulm (evil) will have to be encountered. Commitment to the eternal cause of Islam must therefore be enhanced in our lives in order to fearlessly face the forces of Taghut. Anything less than commitment to a cause worthy of dying for, is useless.

Islam demands that we do not fight except for the Islamic cause and in the Islamic cause. By the brave example of the Soweto youth, Muslim youth and elders should learn that "freedom isn't free"; that the justice of Islam demands our lives and lifelong devotion. Allah commands, *"O you who believe, Enter into Islam wholeheartedly and completely"* (2, verse 208).

MUNAFIQUN/COLLABORATORS

Initially the revolt revolved around the issue of Afrikaans as a language of instruction. Soon the entire Apartheid system and its supporters became the objects of attack. State security forces with far superior strength persistently repressed the revolt. At one stage the police had the active co-operation of a small section of the Soweto inhabitants. A Munafiq (collaborationist) group always exists though not always exposing itself. The destructive actions of "witdoeke" [white headbands] in Crossroads, the Mbokotho [grinding stone] in KwaNdebele and "The A-Team" in Chesterville (in Natal) currently should prove to us the value of the Quranic instructions to deal decisively with munafiqun before they destroy the ranks of the Mustadaffin [oppressed]. But the Taghuti Apartheid forces used their system to break a stayaway. They employed Zulu-speaking migrant workers to strike out at any supporters of the stayaway. Although subjected to the same Taghuti oppression the migrants were set up against their fellow workers and their children. But the divisive tactics did not break the stayaway. Being hard against munafiqun is an Allah-ordained duty of each one in the just cause of the Mustadaffin and Islam. The response of the ruling Taghuti forces after the revolt was to find new collaborators, to modernise the system of collaboration and attempt to further divide the ranks of the Mustadaffin. Management committees, Community Councils, the Tricameral Circus and the new Black Capitalist elite have been opposed by the Mustadaffin but the death of these institutions and exposure of those who operate these institutions must be hastened. Until they do publicly repent and practically change their direction these munafiqun are our enemies, no different from the vicious Taghut whose lackeys they are. They live with blood on their hands.

DISCIPLINE AND COLLECTIVE ACTION

The Islamic struggle is based on disciplined action, collective struggle and commitment to build an Islamic society radically different from the present Racist Capitalist order. Undisciplined action, individualism and personality cults and "reform" have no place in the Islamic view of struggle. Allah says, *"And strive in the Cause of Allah as you ought to strive (with discipline and sacrifice)"* (22 verse 78). The pressures of Apartheid oppression certainly create the conditions for members of the Mustadaffin to unleash their anger at every time and place the system is identified. But such frustration can never lead to liberation even when collectively expressed and sustained. In Soweto resistance was clearly under student leadership. When workers returned from work on June 16th they were caught in the midst of the first day of pitched battle between the armed forces of the State and the students. This event and similar types of incidents forced the parents and workers to support the students. Only later in the unwinding of the revolt did students realise the importance and value of enlisting strong involvement by the broader community. It may at times seem to students that the road to revolution is short and a few more knocks against the system will end it. We should at all times ward against this type of thinking which is so prevalent today. *It is only by developing action in all sections of the Mustadaffin, conducting genuine Shura (consultation) with the Mustadaffin and enhancing our Imam* [leader] *with the Islamic ideals of adl and qist that we will destroy Apartheid. In doing this we will be honouring the heroes of 1976.* Allahu Akbar! [God is great]

Document 84. "Message to the People of South Africa from the National Executive Committee of the United Democratic Front." Leaflet, July 17, 1986

A call to the people of South Africa!

The civil war in our country is intensifying. Apartheid and the Nationalist Party are in decay. Yet in its death throes, the system's brutalisation is intensifying. The emergency is the new form of apartheid rule.

We call on all South Africans to unite and participate actively to end the State of Emergency. Unity in action must be our rallying cry. Together as workers, youth, students, parents, in towns and in villages we must speak with one voice. We will not allow the emergency to destroy us.

One month into the emergency, and thousands—some say as many as 5000—of our people have been detained. Striking workers are arrested. The townships are occupied by the SADF [SA Defence Force] and SAP [SA Police]. The entire population of KwaNdebele is under house arrest. Schools are being turned into fortresses.

Our organisations are not allowed to hold meetings or issue statements. Through curbs on the media the government is attempting to mask the terror it sows among our people.

The stubborn refusal of the regime to accede to the just demands of the people together with the people's refusal to continue being ruled in the old way, has made the crisis irreversible. The regime can no longer enforce its unjust laws and their so-called reforms have been exposed as mere attempts by the ruling minority to perpetuate its domination.

The state hopes, through the emergency, to re-establish its rule over our people in the only way they have—increasing repression. And they hope that the control of information by the Bureau of Information will assist this process by attempting to confuse and divide our people.

The activities of vigilantes and death squads have increased—operating behind the cover of troops and casspirs [armored vehicles] and under conditions of total secrecy. Their actions are then projected as "black on black violence" in order to discredit the democratic movement and demoralise our people.

We exposed and opposed councillors, members of the tricameral parliament and Gatsha Buthelezi as Botha's pawns in his reform game. Now, the government wants to eradicate the democratic movement so that their pawns can have free rein to participate in new dummy bodies such as the Regional Services Councils and the National Statutory Council.

The UDF says:
To the white community:
The time for you to shed your prejudices and selfishness is now. Going back to the "laager" [circled wagons] is tantamount to signing a one-way ticket to oblivion.

Join other white democrats and be part of our struggle for the creation of a greater South Africanism where race or colour shall not be a criterion for judging a person's worth.

To the business community:
Throughout the decades you have benefited from apartheid. Now you say: "Apartheid must go". This is not enough. More business leaders must follow those who have called for the unbanning of the ANC and the release of Mandela.

There is no more room for double talk and crocodile tears. You who control the economy must apply pressure on the government. Our people are demanding that you refuse to pay taxes unless the government meets our demands.

We call on you now to get the government to lift the restrictions on freedom of association and the press and release all detainees.

To councillors and members of the houses of representatives and delegates and bantustan parliaments:

Resign and join the people! Your ship is sinking. The bulldozing through the President's Council of [minister Louis] Le Grange's two amendments to the security laws exposes yet again the futility of the tricameral exercise.

Your presence in dummy structures only gives the Nationalists ammunition and credibility to attempt to further divide our people.

To Inkatha members:

Should you not be asking your leader, Gatsha Buthelezi, a few questions?
- Why does Buthelezi find it easy to attack the UDF, Cosatu and the ANC in almost the same way as the government? Why does he attack them more than he attacks the government?
- When the rest of South Africa was banned from commemorating June 16 or holding open air meetings, why was Inkatha allowed?
- Why is Buthelezi quoted almost daily by the SABC [SA Broadcasting Corporation]?
- Why does Inkatha start another trade union federation instead of joining forces with the biggest and most powerful federation?

Buthelezi is becoming another [Abel] Muzorewa. He is clearly undermining the democratic movement and attempting to sow divisions among our people. Do not allow yourselves to be used against your own brothers and sisters.

To the churches:

The system of apartheid has been declared a heresy. Yet there are sections of the church who turn a blind eye to the sufferings of our people.

Now is the time for the churches to give active support to the righteous struggle of our people. Follow the lead of the Kairos document and let the church be seen to side with the poor and downtrodden. Make your venues and resources available to the people.

To the international community:

Democratic governments and freedom loving people all over the world are calling for economic sanctions yet we note with concern that the Thatcher, Reagan and Kohl governments continue to remain willing accomplices in the crimes of apartheid.

Whilst we welcome constructive assistance, we cannot countenance—at this advanced stage—attempts by foreign governments or persons to undermine our struggle and thus prolong the suffering of our people.

When the day of liberation comes, the people of South Africa will know who are their enemies and who are their friends.

Stronger pressure against the minority regime must be applied now! Your support will go a long way towards the early destruction of apartheid.

The UDF calls on the struggling people of South Africa:

Workers!

It is your labour which keeps the economy going. It is also your collective might that will defend your unions against the emergency. Continue to put pressure on the bosses and defend Cosatu and the whole democratic movement.

Residents!

Highly successful campaigns against high rents are being waged in many parts of the country because people are refusing to be governed by puppets they never elected and are refusing to allow their money to be used to run the apartheid system.

Continue the campaigns against high rents and bad conditions. Through democratic structures continue to take greater control over the areas which affect our lives.

The government is shrouding our townships in a veil of secrecy. We cannot allow this to continue.

People in the rural areas!

Heroic struggles are being waged against the bantustan tyrants and in KwaNdebele against independence.

Demand the resignation of all undemocratic tribal authorities and MPs [members of Parliament] and continue to build democratic village councils as alternatives. We must not allow KwaNdebele independence to go ahead.

Students and teachers!

The government is trying desperately to transform the schools from zones of struggle and freedom to zones of subservience and control. Do not allow this to happen.

Continue the campaign for a people's education so that out of this chaos the seeds of a new and better society will emerge.

Parents and youth!

Strong bonds have been forged in the last year between youth and parents through joint struggles, in the street committees and in parents/teachers/student associations. The state is trying to sow divisions between old and young, parents and youth and between hostel dwellers and residents. Do not allow this to happen. Continue to build unity.

Women and mothers:

There can be no freedom without your liberation as women. Rise and assert yourself. Defend and build a decent future for your children.

Our struggle for freedom cannot be stopped by the Botha government's militarism. Our people are simply demanding the democratic transfer of power from the minority to the people as a whole. The birth of a new South Africa can only begin with:

- The unconditional release of Nelson Mandela and all other political prisoners and detainees.
- The unbanning of the ANC and all other banned organisations.
- The repeal of security legislation.
- The withdrawal of troops from our townships.
- The creation of conditions for the democratic exercise of our right to free speech, assembly and organisation.
- The dismantling of all apartheid laws, in particular the 1913 and 1936 Land Acts, the Group Areas Act and the Population Registration Act.

Nothing is going to destroy the will of our people to rid themselves of the yoke of apartheid oppression and exploitation. And the people are determined to continue building people's power in our communities, factories and schools—at whatever cost. The possibilities of freedom and democracy are no longer dim and distant. Victory is certain!

Document 85. "Remember Kinross." COSATU leaflet, September 1986

HEALTH BEFORE PROFITS
HEALTH AND SAFETY UNDER WORKER CONTROL

We remember the 16th of September 1986. On that day 177 workers died at Kinross. Two hundred and sixty six were injured. Our comrades died in darkness breathing toxic fumes.

HOW DID THE DISASTER HAPPEN?

At Kinross the tunnel walls were lined with a special plaster-polyurethane. Polyurethane is known to be dangerous. British and American mines stopped using it many years ago. It was banned because it catches fire easily and gives off poisonous gasses when alight.

The Kinross management was warned about the dangers of polyurethane. They ignored the warning and did not remove the tunnel lining.

On the 16th September 1986, the fire started when a welder tried to repair a broken railway line on level 15. He used a damaged gas cylinder. This cylinder had been inspected by the mine but their inspection procedure was so bad [that] no fault was detected.

When the welder lit the gas torch the cylinder started to flame. The welder panicked and ran away. A worker tried to put the fire out but management had not put a fire extinguisher on site. The fire was too fierce to die. It swept through level 15.

The fumes of the fire killed and injured our comrades on levels 14 and 15. There was no alarm to warn them of the danger.

KINROSS PROVES THAT MANAGEMENT CANNOT BE TRUSTED WITH SAFETY!
MANAGEMENT CANNOT BE TRUSTED WITH OUR LIVES!
SAFETY IS WORKERS BUSINESS!
ORGANISE ......OR DIE!

WHAT KINROSS MEANS
On the 16th of September a fire at Kinross Mine killed 177 workers and injured 266 others.

A worker said " Our legs turned to jelly. I had to walk in the darkness holding the walls. I could feel my chest burning so bad, I couldn't breathe."

The Kinross fire stopped production for less than a week. But for many families the destruction caused by the fire will last forever.

Children have lost their fathers and wives have lost their husbands. In many cases they lost their only breadwinner.

KINROSS REMINDS US OF BITTER THINGS:
- The dangers in the mines
- The hardship suffered by the families of our fallen comrades.

BUT KINROSS SHOULD ALSO MOTIVATE US:
Kinross demands that we organise for a safer workplace. Mine accidents must be stopped.

We demand the right to elect union safety stewards. These stewards will give us the voice to take our demands forward to the negotiating table.

FORWARD WITH UNION SAFETY COMMITTEES!

ORGANISE FOR SAFETY
The mine inspectors and management will not keep workers safe.

THE INSPECTORS SILENCED THE UNION AT THE KINROSS INQUIRY!
The NUM [National Union of Mineworkers] was not allowed to participate. It could not ask questions or give evidence. The union was not allowed to defend the rights of its members. It was not allowed to represent mineworkers' interests. MANAGEMENT WAS NOT PUNISHED FOR KINROSS!

BUT MANAGEMENT HAD MADE MANY MISTAKES. IT HAD:
- inspected welding equipment badly
- used a substance known to be a fire hazard underground
- put a faulty gas cylinder underground
- not put fire extinguishers at the place of welding
- not put an alarm into the mine to warn workers of a serious danger

WHAT CAN WORKERS DO?
- build strong safety committees
- elect union safety stewards

- demand that management recognise union safety structures
- struggle for the right to attend and participate in inquiries
- struggle for a just system of compensation for injured workers

ONLY STRONG ORGANISATION CAN STOP
TRAGEDIES LIKE KINROSS!

Document 86. ANC memorandum on factionalism in the UDF, Lusaka, late 1986 (abridged)

INTRODUCTION

Over the past two years the all round crisis of the apartheid regime has deepened, and the ruling class is incapable of extricating itself from it. Central in this development is the mass revolt of the people, of which the intensification of armed struggle forms an integral part. The ANC underground had/has been at the head of this process, guiding the people in the greatest wave of mass mobilisation and organisation ever witnessed in S.A. The emergence of the UDF was a result of painstaking work on the ground. It was at the same time a catalyst to further organisation and mobilisation around the central question of political power as well as other issues affecting the people in their daily lives. In the 3 years of its existence, the UDF, including its affiliates, has spread the message of organisation and action to virtually all areas of the country. Hundreds of grassroots structures have been formed even in the rural areas and the momentum, guided by the vanguard movement—of struggle—has led to a situation of ungovernability and emergence of rudimentary organs of power. We have, broadly speaking, entered a new phase of struggle.

The declaration of the two states of emergency by the regime—within one year—constitutes an admission of this reality. The mass democratic movement has been heavily affected by the regime's acts of repression in particular under the latest emergency which is the worst ever. However, popular organisations are recovering and activists are steadily mastering semi-legal methods of operation. The situation varies from region to region. . . . But the general direction is towards reconstruction of the structures to ensure continuation of work even under the most trying conditions. Many difficulties are being experienced, but these we viewed as the unavoidable hurdles the democratic movement has to overcome.

However, there are problems of a subjective nature which have plagued the mass democratic movement for years, and have tended to subtract from the achievements made. These have flared up from time to time, under different forms and guises, sometimes reaching acute proportions. . . . But, as all activists agree, the subjective weaknesses of the mass democratic movement and the in-fighting have never been as obvious as *now*. This is made the more alarming by the fact that the democratic movement as a whole is under attack and it can ill afford such internal schisms and subjective mistakes. The movement has been called upon to intervene strongly and decisively.

BACKGROUND TO PROBLEMS IN THE UDF

1. In the mid and late 1970s, the movement was grappling with the tasks of reviving the underground and putting it on a serious operational footing. Related to this task was the effort to start, sustain as well as intensify mass and armed actions in all parts of the country. With regard to the effort of underground reconstruction and mass mobilisation, a lot of emphasis was put on the establishment of cores composed of old stalwarts, "former BCM [black consciousness movement]" activists and other operatives from student and other circles. These were initially constituted into study groups covering mainly the Transvaal and Natal. (Eastern and Western Cape did feature but had their own specifics). . . .

2. Viewed against the backdrop of the results achieved in the direction of reviving the underground, legal "Congress" organisation and mass action, the formation of the core(s) was a necessary and productive effort. Many breakthroughs were made then, which can doubtlessly be considered as the foundation to the present phase of revolt. Yet certain inbuilt problems could be identified:

- The formation of a leadership core implied (at least in the minds of some of the members) the emergence of an ANC internal leadership, directing all aspects of struggle on behalf of the movement-in-exile. Some of the individuals continue up to this day to conceive of themselves as such.
- Emphasis on this form had the danger of allowing the development of "an elite" which, if so inclined, could monopolize Congress and even serve as a brake on the qualitative and quantitative growth of the underground.
- While the core(s) and other units considered themselves Congress, they were not disciplined underground structures of the movement, strictly accountable to it and receiving, where necessary, binding directives from it. According to the reports cited above: "many people inside . . . [have] not been put in structures of the movement, within a system ensuring proper command and control".

3. The break-up of the initial core according to regions, the lines of communication established for each and lack of centralised uniform servicing introduced new and more serious problems. Briefings from the various areas were not the same and individuals/groups started to pay allegiance to the areas/individuals servicing them. A competitive spirit was one direct result of this phenomenon. Considering the constitution of the conflicting caucuses today, it could as well be asserted that these were carried over, from this period, into the mass democratic movement.

- During 1980-82 many successes were scored in the direction of consolidating political awareness, mass organisation and united action: Freedom Charter, Release Mandela, Anti-SAIC campaigns, the school boycotts, [boycotts] against ghetto councils etc. The extent of action varied from region to region and with the school boycotts, for e.g., regions flared up at different times. The problems of caucuses did not manifest themselves seriously partly because the "caucuses" were not as developed as today, and there was no national organisation of the nature of the UDF where all democrats belonged. However, within Natal, differences of approach came to the fore: the militant students in the Indian schools clashed with the PG [Pravin Gordhan] grouping on many questions of tactics. Since [then], the tempo of the 1980 student actions has been lost.

4. Towards and during the formation of the UDF nationally, the following issues had a bearing on present-day related problems:
- The fact that the UDF found itself focusing (for good reason or bad) on the issue of tri-cameral elections removed the spotlight from the struggles in the African areas. At the same time the actions were campaign oriented and thus relegated organisation to the background.
- The revival/formation of the NIC/TIC contributed a great deal in the organisation and galvanisation of the Indian areas and putting Congress on the map. These organisations went into the UDF as organised political units and thus tended to overshadow other affiliates. The fact that some of the leaders belonged to identifiable caucuses did not help matters.
- For a long time the movement did not pay enough attention to the "Coloured" areas. We contented ourselves with the positions of the Labour Party and relatively ignored the militant grassroots structures and leaders. Various influences found fertile ground among the youth and other sections, especially in the Western Cape, and "popular figures", such as Johnny Issel, developed without movement influence.
- In the Border region the personality problems among leading operatives slowed down the formation of unified structures.
- During the process towards the formation of the UDF, many organisational and political questions had to be resolved e.g. Freedom Charter, attitude to referendum, regional representation in national structures, presidents and patrons etc. Even at this period, positions tended to be taken on the basis of the caucus groups.
- Already the struggle for the control of resources had become acute e.g. Freeway House desperately wanted the office of National Treasury. [Auret van Heerden] had been going around collecting funds ostensibly for the UDF, however the resources were used to establish spheres of control especially among youth organisations.

This brief and cursory review of the problems prior to the formation of the UDF is an attempt to demonstrate that the schisms existing today have a very long history. To heal them, we must understand them in this context, so as to start at the root causes.

GROUPINGS WITHIN THE UDF:
1. Since its launch, the UDF has had to contend with problems of differences among various individuals and groupings. Certain identifiable centres have been consolidated over the years and they do not see eye to eye on

virtually all the thorny questions which the front has to tackle from time to time. In practically all instances, positions are taken rigidly on the basis of group identification. More often than not, the problems are not of a serious strategic/ideological nature but a reflection of personality differences. Yet the more intense they become, the more they have a bearing on the fundamental issues and the more they weaken the democratic movement as a whole. There are many leaders, especially the stalwarts who have risen above the groupings, but they are deliberately clubbed together with one caucus or another, damned for being "soft" on others etc.

THE CABAL
  "...the view was expressed that Archie [Gumede] and Paul [David] were part of the cabal in Natal who manipulated individuals to gain control over organisations even in Transvaal and the Cape. MJ [Naidoo] and Mewa [Ramgobin] were mainly responsible for identifying members of the Cabal as including Pravin Gordhan, Paul, Archie, Farouk Meer, Zac Yacoob, Yunus Mahomed and Billy Nair as he was in a weak position with no grassroots base because of years in prison. Private discussions among such people as Essop [Jassat], Cassim [Saloojee], Ismail, Aubrey [Mokoena], Curtis [Nkondo], Thozamile [Gqweta], Sam Isaac confirmed the view that this Cabal, in collaboration with others in Tvl and Cape, would screw up (slander) those in other organisations the Cabal failed to manipulate or incorporate. . . . Albertina [Sisulu], while trying to seek reconciliation and unity between the women's groupings mentioned also expressed fears that many of the problems stem from the role of Yunus and Zac. Frank [Chikane] always seeks to unite the divided groups but is closely associated with some of the people in the Cabal but says he will not align himself with any group." [source not identified]

- Positions they hold:
The Cabal is not a politically homogeneous group:
—Some advocate non-violence or underplay armed struggle and undermine the importance of underground work in an attempt to preserve the legality of their organisations, even to the extent of cautioning comrades against underground work/involvement.
—Some advocate an autonomous internal ANC and view themselves as the internal ANC leadership.
—There is also a group which has been identified as the "Lancaster House grouping".
—The Cabal does not pay enough attention to the working class. This reflects the lack of grassroots organisation and social composition and ideological leanings of most Natal UDF and NIC leaders. Hence have an "elitist" approach.

- The Cabal is criticised for:
   i) Politically . . . [they have] been accused of adopting a reformist or go-slow approach on certain issues in contradiction to the popular mood and demands of the concrete situation e.g. silence on Inkatha's Hambanathi kill-

ings and a general failure to deal forcefully with Inkatha which is seen as due to the fact that many Cabal members own shops and are scared to jeopardise their markets in the African townships.

ii) Organisationally and in relation to resources:
—Decision-making and policy determined in an undemocratic manner e.g. claims that Providence has embargoed ANC propaganda with which it does not agree.
—Bad style of work.
—Organisational sectarianism, do not widen their circle. . . .

3. FREEWAY HOUSE
[This grouping has been at odds with the End Conscription Campaign and the Johannesburg Democratic Action Committee]. . . . The AvH group has always been bent on trying to split the UDF and different tactics have been used.
• The creation of an evaluation committee in the Tvl region to look into the work of the regional office and to expose how inefficient it was and if possible replace the staff with the AvH people.
• They criticised the national UDF for getting the best cadres from its affiliates into the national and regional leadership. They termed this the weakening of the affiliates instead of strengthening them.
• The AvH group failed to secure positions of influence in the UDF; they then refused to stand for nomination to UDF structures and tried to [win] influence in rural areas e.g. N. Tvl.
• The AvH group has tried to win over the RMC [Release Mandela Campaign] (Tvl) as an ally both in the UDF and against the TIC/NIC, much as they do not agree on everything i.e. ideology and funding.
• Auret is known to have discouraged people from consulting with the ANC, because the external leadership is "irrelevant and out of touch with the situation at home." He was pushing for internal leadership as represented by his group.
• Auret is opposed to the theory of colonialism of a special type; he has produced documents reproduced and distributed from CRIC [Community Resource and Information Centre] offices expounding a theory of racial capitalism.
• When the movement made a "Call to the Nation" the AvH grouping distorted it. They alleged that because of the militancy at home the UDF was no more suitable for the situation. He is said to be thinking about "insurrectionary situation", armed "mobile units", and "people's committees".

Criticism against the group:
Organisationally
• The group is criticised for withholding funds and resources and using them to manipulate other groups and rope them into their influence. The creation of Freeway House was seen as such a strategy and there is general complaints about Freeway House. "The TIC/NIC have undertaken to destroy the Freeway House at all costs."

- While they claim to serve the mass democratic movement they are not accountable to any of the structures.

Politically
- Critics of CRIC see their commitment to a public socialist position based on "class analysis" as inopportune and damaging the future evolution of the UDF as a tactical weapon in the hands of progressive forces.
- The critics see an insistence on "townships as the centre" and class analysis as a convenient device to co-opt African led groups like RMC which have such an antipathy [to] Indian and NIC/TIC leadership.

4. THE RMC

RMC started as a campaign body but there have been attempts by people like Aubrey [Mokoena] to transform it into an organisation, for instance the issuing of membership cards and payment of membership fees. The leadership is made up of people like:
-Aubrey Mokoena
-Jabu Ngwenya
-Tiego Moseneke
-Tshidiso Matone
-Winnie Mandela
-Curtis Nkondo.

The view on the need for the formation of an African organisation is propounded mainly by this grouping.

Aubrey has been in the forefront of attacks against the Cabal. Once he was called to the REC [Regional Executive Committee] of the Tvl UDF to account for a statement he allegedly made attacking the TIC for being a Cabal controlled body. This happened as a sequel to the Release Mandela rally which was organised by the Natal REC [of] UDF after the PMB [Pietermaritzburg] treason trial, which Aubrey did not attend.

Winnie has associated actively with the RMC leadership and its positions. She has refused to work in structures e.g. FEDTRAW [Federation of Transvaal Women] where she can account. Oscar Mpetha forced the RMC down the throats of the people in the W. Cape. They were not consulted on the setting up of a branch and RMC has become a centre for divisive activities in the region. His activities during the attempts to unite UWO [United Women's Organisation] and WF [Women's Front] were not helpful. Incidentally the UWCO [United Women's Congress] (W. Cape) recently proposed Winnie as president of the national women's organisation when it is formed. FEDTRAW proposed Ma Sisulu. Our briefing was that prominent figures could be made patrons and presidents be chosen from other activists. . . .

POLITICO ORGANISATIONAL PROBLEMS, MANIFESTATION TODAY:
1. The first group of questions relate to the strategic perspectives of struggle. In this regard they do reflect an ideological struggle which cannot be dis-

DOCUMENTS FOR CHAPTER 3   461

missed out of hand. However, the labeling that ensues from such debates (nationalists/workerists) is in the strict political sense inaccurate. Above all, matters are not pursued in friendly democratic debate, each section is first to retreat into its encampment.

a) The Freeway House opposed two-stage theory in favour of "racial capitalism" and socialist revolution. However, it shifts positions when publicly confronted by the movement e.g. after the Harare Nusas [National Union of South African Students] meeting.

b) Challenged on the questions of accountability they claim to be responsible to UDF leaders in the E. Cape as the "left" of the mass democratic movement. Incidentally some activists say that [Matthew] Goniwe had stated that if he happened to be killed his coffin should be draped in the red flag. This in no way contradicts movement and united front policies but when questionable groupings such as Freeway House parasite on the good work of activists such as Goniwe they introduce debates at a level which can easily be exploited by the enemy.

c) Some members of the Cabal are said to be in favour of and actively working towards a Lancaster-type solution. This, it is claimed, is shown by their position re: the referendum question, wariness in dealing with people's committees, fear to "provoke" state repression, attitudes to u/g [underground] work etc. It is also claimed that some have started serious studies of the Lancaster House agreement [on Zimbabwe's independence] and how it can be applied to our situation.

d) Discussion on the national convention was also reduced to these acrimonious debates. Movement briefing—UDF could call for it but not make it a campaign—helped resolve it.

2. With the intensification of the mass revolt and its transformation into people's war, the legal movement faces the question of how to relate to this without jeopardising its legality. Some of the individuals, especially in the Cabal, do drag their feet when it comes to decisive mass actions.

a) Ineffective response to the Vaal triangle ('84) uprisings. Instead, the Consulate affair became central. Transvaal stay-away did not receive active support of UDF—including necessary resources. The 1985 Day of Prayer aborted because UDF did not follow up on joint UDF, SACC etc decision taken much earlier.

b) Areas where ungovernability has been achieved e.g. Alexandra, N. Transvaal, E. Cape do not receive sufficient funds from UDF Head Office. Even Peter Nchabeleng funeral was not financed. This is characterized as a deliberate act, and Mohammed Valli [Moosa] (Cabal) is said to be the culprit.

c) At the TIC Conference Dr Jassat et al came strongly against youth forming self-defence units—if they engage in any form of violence they would have to move out of the TIC.

3. [Undermining ANC leadership]

a) There is a tendency within Cabal to emphasize legal at the expense of

underground work. Yet they consider themselves as the "Internal ANC" and want to control whatever U/G structures exist. In some instances, it is claimed they even go to the extent of blocking ANC literature from circulation if the contents challenge their positions.
b) The Freeway House grouping has campaigned against any contact with the FAs [forward areas, i.e. ANC personnel in frontline states]. Floating "security problems" they then advise activists to report to them.

4. A number of political and organisational questions have confronted the UDF in the process of growth.
- African political organisation (Ref RMC). This arises also in the context of the existence of NIC/TIC, the fact that there is no central "Congress Organisation" which would be the core of the UDF etc. Our briefings have not been decisive, though the issue has died down. Related to this was the question of converting the UDF into a political organisation.
- Policy decisions are taken at national level with minimal consultation with the regions. As a result decisions are sometimes taken by one grouping. Under conditions of repression this becomes more obvious. It is claimed that in some instances, the Cabal deliberately does not invite leaders such as Ma Sisulu to NEC [National Executive Committee] meetings in order to impose its decisions.
- In Natal the existence of the Cabal and lack of resolute African leadership has weakened the organisational thrust of the UDF. In the Indian areas, grassroots structures are either weak or non-existent: the Cabal concentrates on building caucus groups who claim control of townships and suburbs. They would then prevent anybody else from organising. On the other hand, the African leadership has not engaged in active organisation in their areas. They point an accusing finger at the Cabal—"its domination" that "the Cabal-dominated UDF REC [regional executive committee] does not take up African issues", "lack of resources" etc—while they do not do much to correct the situation in the African townships. . . .

5. The problems in the UDF have affected the youth and women's organisations to differing extents. . . . Within youth organisations the decisions resulted in the stalling of the process towards the national youth organisation for the whole of 1985. Two groupings emerged around Dan Montsitsi (supported by Cabal) and Deacon Mathe (Freeway House).
- Within Nusas the two groupings are now fighting for the control of Nusas head office in 1987. At Wits they had to field opposing candidates.

6. Conflict around these and other issues has come to a head. Even though some of the problems have long been resolved e.g. referendum and National Convention, the groupings refer to them to show the "reactionary nature" of their opponents. It is quite evident that the enemy is fully aware of the conflict and it has encouraged and used these differences for its own ends. Agents infiltrated into the mass democratic movement simply have to identify

with one or other grouping to gain acceptance as "genuine democrats/lefties". In some instances, the regime trains its repression on one grouping in order to promote it, or to weaken it. Some detainees are persuaded to give information on other groupings or urged to be co-operative "so that they can be released before the other grouping takes the upper hand". What is encouraging is that all groupings now recognise the dangers resulting from such caucuses and have called for urgent movement [ANC] intervention.

OUR SHORTCOMINGS
1. The problems in the mass democratic movement reflect the weaknesses in the underground. We are not able to make timely interventions, and the FA's [forward areas, i.e. personnel in frontline states] occasionally give conflicting briefings to the operatives e.g. referendum issue.
2. Most of the leadership of the mass democratic movement considers itself Congress but they do not belong to movement structures to which they can account and be given collective assistance.
3. Our discussions with the leadership of the mass democratic movement tend to be suggestive: we do not assert our positions clearly and unambiguously. In some cases when we meet forces who belong to one of the groupings we merely accept their briefings without question, and leave them to go back and continue their activities with assumed movement approval.
4. Tracing the history of some of the caucus groups it emerges that the problems were worsened by the fact that we have tended to take sides— encouraging one grouping or the other. We have not harmonised our views on the mass democratic movement.
5. Some of the problems have long been identified and solutions proposed but there has been no follow-up. Where decisions have been taken we take too long to implement them.
6. Many meetings have been held with groups and individuals e.g. Stockholm UDF meeting, London with [Jonty] Joffe and [Andrew] Boraine, Harare meeting with Natal African leadership, but there has not been feedback to the PMC [Politico-Military Council] and other relevant structures. In the absence of such reports, PMC is unable to prepare briefings to the FA's which have to reply to questions from activists and to properly service units to which some of the people we meet belong.
7. Our input has been reactive partly because the leadership is far away from the theatre of struggle.
8. Since the dissolution of PHQ [political headquarters], political work has not received sufficient attention. The PMC Secretariat was supposed to direct the struggle on a day to day basis but the members are rarely at HQ.
9. The calibre and capacity of RPMC's [regional PMCs] differ from FA to FA, affecting their political input.
10. Creation and development of underground structures is not systematic. While the idea of bodies of leadership (APMC's) [area PMCs] was adopted

more than a year ago, this is being systematically implemented only in some areas of the country.

MOVEMENT INTERVENTION:
In addition to resolving the problems cited above, we should:
1. Meet the various groupings together and separately.
2. Issue a public call for unity.
3. Work towards establishment of disciplined ANC leadership cores within the mass democratic movement. This should not be misinterpreted for "ANC internal leadership": Only politico-military units which would include selected cadres from the legal movement can exercise overall leadership in the Areas, Districts, Cities etc.

Document 87. "Will NGK Resolution Pave the Way for Clampdown on Activists?" Article in *Al-Qalam,* Durban, November 1986

In recent years the Muslims of South Africa have come to play a more active role in the struggle for freedom and justice. Significant milestones have been the death (martyrdom) of Imam Abdullah Haroon in detention and the scale of Muslim involvement in the 1985 uprisings. Muslims have increasingly come to see Islam as a vehicle for the promotion and establishment of freedom and justice and the eradication of oppression and exploitation.

This resurgence of Muslims in taking up their role alongside their fellow oppressed has alarmed the apartheid regime. President P.W. Botha's speech in parliament in May 1986 confirmed that he had instructed his security and intelligence services to take the necessary counter measures *(against Muslim activists)*.

Ideology of freedom
It is in this context that the proposals adopted by the Ned Geref Kerk (NGK) [Nederduitse Gereformeerde Kerk or Dutch Reformed Church] at its recent general synod should be seen and responded to. On 23 October 1986 the commission's report on Islam by Prof. D. Crafford was tabled and discussed. Thereafter the following proposals were adopted by the general synod of the NGK:
• Islam is a false religion and a great threat to Christianity in South Africa, Africa and the world at large.
• Church members and officials should "witness to the Gospel of Jesus Christ in all areas of life as the only answer to the onslaught of Islam".
• Concern was expressed that many young black and coloured people, particularly after 1976, had begun embracing Islam as an ideology which furthered the freedom struggle.
• Islam was recognised as a minority religion in South Africa.
• It warned Muslims that radical involvement in revolutionary action and the incitement of people to acts of terror would seriously harm the relation-

ship between Muslims and most Christians in South Africa and endanger the peaceful co-existence of the religions.

Loving co-existence
The following conciliatory recommendations (which were in direct contradiction to the proposals accepted) were only noted:
• The point of departure for the Church should be a loving co-existence with Muslims rather than enmity and confrontation;
• A call for better understanding of the religious convictions of both groups; and
• A warning against "watering down" the Christian truth for the sake of dialogue.

The question which arises is, why is there such a divergence between the proposals accepted (which called for an intensification of the evangelical crusade against Muslims) and those only noted (which are of a more conciliatory nature, prompting love, peace and co-existence)?

This answer can be found with Dominee [Reverend] Stoffel Colyn, Chaplain general of the South African Police, whose role was to use the church effectively as part of an overall strategy of the government's security services to counter the threat Islam poses to the apartheid regime. It was Dominee Colyn who opposed the report's conciliatory guidelines and argued that Islam was a threat and the church could not co-operate with it. He thus played a pivotal role in aligning the NGK's resolutions with that of the security services. Whether Dominee Colyn was instructed or not by the South African Police or security services is immaterial. What is apparent is that his actions reflect the concerns and interests of the State. Judging by Dominee Colyn's remarks, the threat posed by Islam is quite clearly Muslims' participation in the struggle in South Africa which the report terms "radical" and "revolutionary".

Continue struggle for justice
Islam commands that when a Muslim sees a wrong, he changes it with his hand, and if unable to, he speaks out against it, and if unable to, he hates it in his heart and this is the weakest form of belief.

It is precisely this command by Islam for active participation in eradicating oppression and injustice which gives Islam the universal appeal it has. And it is precisely this which has sent shivers down Dominee Colyn's spine. There can be no greater encouragement given to Muslims to continue the struggle to eliminate injustice and oppression. They should take this opportunity of rededicating themselves to this struggle and follow in the footsteps of those finding themselves in the prisons of apartheid.

There can be no doubt that both Muslims and Christians who oppose injustice and uphold the brotherhood of man will reject the NGK's proposals outright. The unity between Muslims and Christians which has been won by their joint participation in the struggle against apartheid should be guarded with due sanctity.

And nearest among them in love to the believer will thou find those who say "we are Christians" (Qur'an: 5:85).

DOCUMENT 88. Eyewitness account of Ama-Afrika vigilante attack by Peggy Sotyelelwa of KwaNobuhle township, Uitenhage, January 4, 1987

My husband Sipho is on a UDF Area Committee. He has been in hiding for some time now. At about 9.00 am on Sunday 4th January a van with about 8 people in it arrived at my house—I was at the front fence. The van's registration number was CCN 44680. I was asked "Where's Sotyelelwa's house?" and didn't reply. However one of the group pointed out my house, and the group jumped out of the van.

They broke every pane of glass in the house. One of my children, a girl of 15, began crying, and only the pleas of my other children, claiming as they did that my daughter was not Sotyelelwa's child, saved her from attack.

The group went inside. They took out my 6 piece lounge suite, the room divider, TV, generator, Hi-fi, double-bed, base, mattress, headboard, tank for the fridge, children's beds, mattresses and headboards, all my linen, curtains, blankets, sheets, lamps and ornaments. They chopped these up with axes, and the furniture they could not remove, i.e., wardrobes and the fridge, they smashed up inside with axes. They drank coldrink from my fridge. They removed all of my husband's clothing, but not mine, and made a pile of all of our smashed belongings on the pavement outside.

Then a blue SABTA HiAce Taxi CCN 76993 arrived, as well as a Red Citi Golf, CCN 83127. I recorded all of these registration numbers shortly afterwards. This group took the paraffin from my primus stove, and poured it over my smashed belongings, and lit them.

My neighbour, Miss Pamela of 20 Relu Street, who is 26 years old, recognized, from the white van, K- S-, M- V- and W- M-. They told her to "Go inside—you mustn't look at us."

As the fire caught, so they all left. 5 minutes later, a hippo [armored vehicle] number 85 (I think the registration number began BDZ 465) arrived with a SAP [SA Police] landrover S21B. They left immediately. Thereafter a second hippo arrived with 2 white SAP and 1 black municipal policemen in it. The white policemen emerged. I had meanwhile hidden next door, and watched through a window.

The white policeman radioed "This is Comrade Sotyelelwa's house 18 Relu Street." He asked the black policeman if this was correct, had it confirmed, and they left. This was at 9.30—it all took just half an hour.

That afternoon a beige Sierra containing three black policemen arrived. I was again watching from the window of 20 Relu Street. One of the black policemen, whom I know, is J- N-. He shouted out: "HA-HA, SIYIFUMENE LE RUBBISH YENKUNKUMA, JONGALE UKUBANTLE KWENDLU YAKHE KWAKUNJE NAJUTHI KWIZINDLU ZETHU." Which translates as: "Ha-Ha,

Figure 21. Vigilantes attack UDF "comrades" at the funeral of Chief Ampie Mayisa, Leandra, East Rand, January 1986. *Paul Weinberg/South Photographs/africanpictures.net*

we've got this rubbish. Look how beautiful is his house. It looks beautiful like our houses." (The reference is to the fact that all black policemen who used to live in KwaNobuhle have had their homes burnt).

Then they left. The police, I understood, returned on Monday 5th, but I was not there.

DOCUMENT 89. "Unite with OK Workers!" Commercial, Catering and Allied Workers' Union flyer, February 1987

The OK workers strike continues!
11,000 workers have been on strike for over 50 days already.

OK WORKERS DEMAND A LIVING WAGE!
  In this strike, workers have faced terrible harassment by police and SADF [SA Defence Force] who have been working with OK management. About 1,000 OK workers have been arrested already. This includes 161 workers who have been detained under the state of emergency regulations.

Some of the workers have been detained for over 7 weeks now.
  Yet the strike continues. Workers are united and determined that they must get a living wage—no matter how long the strike may last. The employers'

hardline attitude cannot break the strike. The police cannot break the strike. Even the SADF cannot break the strike.

WE SAY: NO SURRENDER .... NO RETREAT
FORWARD TO A LIVING WAGE FOR ALL WORKERS

COSATU members have taken action to support the OK strike. Thousands of FAWU [Food and Allied Workers' Union] members have already stopped delivering goods to OK Bazaars.

Hundreds and thousands of consumers have stopped buying at OK in solidarity with the strike.

CCAWUSA worker supporters have organised shoppers' demonstrations in solidarity with the strike.

We call on the workers and community to join with OK Bazaars workers in saying:
"I don't buy at OK Bazaars!"
"I don't supply to OK Bazaars!"

FORWARD WITH THE STRUGGLE OF OK BAZAARS WORKERS FOR A LIVING WAGE
AN INJURY TO ONE IS AN INJURY TO ALL

Document 90. "A Message to All Democrats." COSATU advertisement, *Weekly Mail,* May 29, 1987

Our people are experiencing an attack on all forms of democracy. Many of you are already victims of the National Party's intolerance of opposition. The attack on Cosatu is part of the co-ordinated campaign to stamp out the voice of democracy.

Democratic Organisation

We are today the largest national democratic organisation that is still able to operate openly. Most other mass-based organisations have been driven underground by repression.

In Cosatu
- we have 750 000 paid-up members in 21 affiliates
- representatives are elected—irrespective of race, sex or religion—in factories, mines and shops organised under the banner of the federation
- representatives negotiate wages and working conditions. They also speak out on community issues and the wider political aspirations of their constituencies
- these representatives are subject to recall at any time and operate on the basis of reports and mandates
- the policies of Cosatu derive from these mandates that are carried democratically through our structures

Propaganda Campaign

Yet our organisation is the victim of a vicious propaganda war by the SABC [SA Broadcasting Corporation] and others who want you to believe that Cosatu is a clique of violent criminals.

The government believes that if the public can be persuaded to doubt Cosatu's legitimacy, then repressive legislation and actions against us will appear justified. In this climate of hostility, the work of shadowy bombers and arsonists—who have already struck—will continue with impunity. No public outcry will follow and the news blackout will hide all the details.

"Hands Off Cosatu" Campaign

Cosatu has launched a "Hands Off Cosatu" campaign. As a legitimate, representative trade union federation we demand our right to:
- speak freely without intimidation
- meet freely without harassment
- organise freely without victimisation
- campaign for a living wage and release of our members in detention
- campaign for a stake in a unitary, non-racial South Africa.

We say further:
- if demanding a living wage is a "communist plot" then millions of workers and unemployed in South Africa are communists
- if demanding the release of detained people is subversive, then millions of South Africans are "subversives".

We call on all democrats:
- contact Cosatu offices and get our side of the story
- build mass support for the "HANDS OFF COSATU" CAMPAIGN
- spread the facts to all our people
- encourage friends and family who are workers to join Cosatu affiliates.

We believe that unless we build and defend democratic organisations in South Africa, whether in Cosatu or the communities where we live, the people in our country will become increasingly polarized and there will be spiralling conflict, chaos and violence.

Defend democracy, support the
"Hands Off Cosatu" Campaign

Document 91. "The SATS Strike—The Other Version." COSATU information sheet, early May 1987

During the past few days, when we have been listening to the radio or viewing the TV or reading the commercial newspapers, the SATS [SA Transport Services] strike has been "high on the agenda." We all know that the TV, radios and most commercial newspapers are controlled by the ruling class and therefore it's not surprising if they report against the working class. This pamphlet is therefore being circulated primarily to tell the other side of the story so that you may judge for yourself what the facts are. This is only a short summary of the chronological events. For more information please consult a local COSATU office which has a more complete dossier of the events.

THE BACKGROUND TO THE STRIKE

Andrew Nedzamba, a SATS worker, was fired on Thursday 12th March 1987. He had arrived late at the City Deep Depot to cash in the money. The cashier had knocked off and gone home. Nedzamba had gone home with the takings so as to submit the money on the next working day. On cashing in on the next working day, Nedzamba was accused of having failed to cash in on time and was then taken for a disciplinary action despite his explanation that he could not have done otherwise. He had understood it to be common procedure to pay in on the next working day if the driver returned to the depot after the cashier had gone home. Nedzamba was fired. And thus a long string of events was set into motion.

FELLOW WORKERS TAKE SOLIDARITY ACTION

On the 13th March 1987 about 600 SATS workers struck in protest against Comrade Nedzamba's unfair dismissal. Worker representatives began negotiations with SATS management immediately. The negotiations continued with the grievance unresolved until, by the 19th, the strike had spread to other depots involving 2500 workers according to SATS, and 6000 workers according to SARHWU [SA Railway and Harbour Workers' Union].

THE STRIKE SPREADS

On 23rd March the government published a Special Government Gazette empowering the dismissal of all striking workers. This angered the workers even more and the strike spread to most depots on the Witwatersrand.

At a Johannesburg depot about 250 striking workers were dispersed by the police with teargas and as a result the negotiations broke down on the 24th, paving the way for the strike to spread to Vereeniging.

At this stage COSATU felt deeply concerned and urged SATS to resolve the dispute lest it degenerate into violent conflict.

In its display of blatant intransigence, SATS management said that the escalation of the strike was the work of a small group of SARHWU members who were intimidating non-strikers. By this time the strike coverage in the media was intensive and there was obvious cause for concern in all responsible circles.

It was at this juncture, on the 27th March, that COSATU called on the business sector to intervene with a view to resolving the dispute. COSATU suggested to the employer organizations that they persuade SATS to agree to independent mediation. By this time the strike had spread to 23 depots! Far from heeding the call, SATS management accused SARHWU of taking advantage of the strike situation for the purpose of inciting the workers. The strike continued and then took a new turn. SATS, the police and the Minister of Transport Affairs were to act together.

POLICE INTERVENTION ON BEHALF OF SATS

On Saturday 28th the police, armed to the teeth with rifles and teargas, sealed off COSATU House where 400 workers were meeting to work out their proposals for the resolution of the dispute.

The whole situation had now degenerated into police activity and violence. One worker was arrested and two injured at Meyerton/Kliprivier Station on March 30. In Soweto a SATS worker was shot and his house burnt on 31 March, according to the Bureau of Information. To this incident SATS issued a pamphlet addressed to workers saying that it (SATS) had no control over the actions of the security forces.

The spate of arrests spread to Springs and Nancefield. When, on April 1, SATS threatened to dismiss the striking workers en masse, COSATU and the UDF had no option but to pledge solidarity support with the strikers in the light of SATS' attitude towards the dispute.

But [Minister of Transport] Eli Louw, under whose portfolio SATS falls, explained the COSATU/UDF pledge in a different light—"they were taking the crisis out of the schools and townships to the workplace." Now that the boss had entered the scene, things became much tougher. Hopes of negotiations being resumed collapsed, and they did not take place.

SATS INTRANSIGENCE—VIOLENCE ESCALATES

Negotiations scheduled for Wednesday April 8th did not take place because SATS refused to allow SARHWU representatives to attend. Instead, 305 strikers were arrested at Ogies under the Emergency regulations and on the same day there was a bomb blast on the railway line which disrupted the passenger services.

When the negotiations collapsed on Thursday 9th, COSATU offered to mediate in the dispute BUT SATS REJECTED THE OFFER! The dispute was to take yet another new turn—this time in the form of discrediting COSATU.

THE SMEAR CAMPAIGN

The three main actors in the propaganda campaign to discredit COSATU have been the SABC [SA Broadcasting Corporation], the police and certain sections of the press.

On Monday 15 March, the *Citizen* newspaper did not hesitate to "report" that SATS' "Non strikers beaten up at COSATU Head Quarters" and the police were quick to say they had sworn affidavits and photos to that effect.

On the 16th April, SATS embarked on an intensive advertising campaign in the major papers under the theme: "Judge for yourself." COSATU was badly smeared without any justification. This smear campaign went on until SATS Director General, Grove, issued a press statement saying that SARHWU, COSATU and the ANC were linked together. He also told foreign newspapers that COSATU was affiliated to the ANC.

The SABC's morning commentator of the 21st April also wanted to be counted. He added a grain of salt on Grove's vendetta by saying the strike had "degenerated into an outright campaign of intimidation and terrorism conducted against the public, railway workers and service itself." This elaborate smear campaign was rapidly gaining momentum on the eve of the brutal police onslaught on SARHWU and COSATU. Was the campaign an ingenious act of paving a way for a showdown with SARHWU and COSATU?

POLICE MOVE INTO ACTION

On 22 April the police broke up a meeting of SARHWU workers in the Germiston offices. Without any warning the police opened fire and three SARHWU workers were shot dead.

A short while later three more workers were killed in a clash with the police near Doornfontein Station.

On the same day at about 3 o'clock a contingent of police invaded COSATU House and [it] was besieged on and off for the next five days. A worker was killed in the course of the siege. A wide range of excesses was reported to have been committed by the police, including vicious assaults on people in COSATU House, and extensive damage to the building and equipment. Damage was estimated at more than R53 000 [$24,000]. This was followed by the mass dismissal of about 16 000 workers.

THE SABC REJOICES

Just on the heels of the mass dismissals, the Bureau of Information claimed that police had captured 3 suspected ANC terrorists in COSATU House. For some reasons best known to the Bureau, the statement was withdrawn shortly after the release of this statement. Later the three "terrorists" were released with no charges laid against them. However the SABC continued to use this unsubstantiated allegation for several weeks.

Again on the 29th April, COSATU House was sealed off, raided and several arrests were made. The SABC TV rushed to the studio to tell the public that the raid was a sequel to the discovery of four bodies of people who had been killed by "necklacing" the day before. They went further to suggest that they were killed at COSATU House and then driven to the spot where they were burnt! They did not report that COSATU had, from the early stages of the dispute, warned against the danger of violence being a possibility and had in fact condemned the violence when it eventually surfaced. COSATU and SARHWU denials of this received little coverage.

COUNTRYWIDE CLAMPDOWN

It would seem that the forces of repression had now done enough groundwork and time was now ripe to act decisively against COSATU.

May Day rallies countrywide were either banned or had restrictions imposed on them. Reactionary forces attacked COSATU members in Pietermaritzburg and elsewhere. A number of COSATU offices around the country, and those of union-supporting organisations like SACHED [SA Committee for Higher Education] were vandalised and some completely destroyed and many COSATU officials and shop stewards were arrested.

On Thursday, 7th May two huge bombs rocked COSATU House, rendering the building unsafe for occupation.

Not unexpectedly, the SABC suggested that the bombs were of Soviet origin and it pointed out that 3 suspected ANC terrorists had been arrested at COSATU House during the previous raid—implying that COSATU had harboured terrorists to sabotage their own building.

As if this vendetta by the SABC was not enough, its morning "comment" of May 12 referred to COSATU as being openly murderous and it encouraged management to refuse to negotiate with the unions. COSATU is looking into taking legal action in this regard.

But who between SATS and SARHWU/COSATU is really the guilty party? It's your turn to JUDGE FOR YOURSELF.

JUDGE FOR YOURSELF

On April 16, SATS embarked on an advertising campaign in major newspapers under the slogan "Judge for yourself." It is not easy, if not impossible, to judge without sufficient facts in hand or if such "facts" have been blatantly distorted. Below we are giving you extracts from correspondence/communication between SATS and SARHWU through their lawyers. We hope this may assist you in your judgement.

MARCH 13, 1987: SARHWU's lawyers, instructed by SARHWU, phone SATS to ask for access to City Deep depot in order to try to resolve dispute. SARHWU claims it has overwhelming majority here. SATS' Regional Manager replies "I don't see any positive contribution being possible from SARHWU." SATS says the work stoppage has been resolved, most of the employees are back at work and it hopes the remainder will be back soon.

MARCH 13, 1987 12:46: SARHWU's lawyers, instructed by SARHWU, send telex to SATS requesting access of SARHWU representatives to the workforce so as to advise them to return to work. No reply from SATS.

MARCH 18, 1987 11:43: SARHWU'S lawyers, instructed by SARHWU, send telex to SATS offering assistance in resolving the dispute and getting workers to return to work. No reply from SATS.

MARCH 18, 1987 12:00: SARHWU's lawyers, instructed by SARHWU, send telegram to SATS noting that workers at Kazeme [Kaserne depot] have joined in the work stoppage and once again offer to resolve the dispute and request access to members to do so. No reply from SATS.

MARCH 18, 1987 16:03: SARHWU's lawyers, instructed by SARHWU, send telex to SATS detailing the spread of the stoppage and reiterating SARHWU's preparedness to assist in resolving the dispute and requesting a meeting with management. No reply from SATS.

MARCH 18, 1987 after 16:03: SARHWU's lawyers, instructed by SARHWU, telephone SATS management asking them to meet with SARHWU. SATS refuse to meet with SARHWU saying that they are not recognised by the Minister of Transport Affairs.

MARCH 19, 1987 10:11: SARHWU's attorneys, instructed by SARHWU, send an urgent telegram to SATS suggesting that an independent mediator and/or an arbitration be set up in an attempt to resolve the dispute. In addition, SARHWU indicates that since many of the people on strike are its members, it believes it can play a constructive role in resolving the dispute and expresses its willingness to negotiate with management. No reply from SATS. Further communication on the same date also meets with no response from SATS.

MARCH 24, 1987: SARHWU's attorneys, instructed by SARHWU, send letter to SATS calling for a meeting to discuss the dispute and expressing SARHWU's willingness to meet and negotiate with SATS so as to resolve the dispute as quickly as possible and suggesting that the dispute concerning Andrew Nedzamba's dismissal be referred to independent arbitration.

MARCH 25, 1987: SARHWU's lawyers send a telex requesting an urgent reply to letter of March 24, 1987.

MARCH 26, 1987: The State Attorney replies, with the first written reply from SATS to these nine letters, stating that SATS is unwilling to negotiate with SARHWU.

MARCH 26,1987: SARHWU attorneys reply to letter from the State Attorney repeating SARHWU's proposal for mediation and arbitration.

APRIL 1, 1987: SATS sends letter rejecting these proposals.

APRIL 7, 1987: SARHWU addresses a telex to the Minister of Transport and General Manager of SATS, calling for a ballot to determine which union enjoys the majority of support at SATS, following from a statement by the Minister of Transport that SATS will negotiate with the union representing the majority of its workers. No reply from SATS.

APRIL 10, 1987: SARHWU's attorneys once again write to the State Attorney requesting an urgent meeting.

APRIL 15, 1987: SARHWU's attorneys, instructed by SARHWU, send letter to the State Attorney placing on record that SARHWU abhors violence and that it will do everything in its power to ensure that none occurs. At the same time it asks SATS to withdraw its statements linking SARHWU with unlawful acts (intimidation) and violence, which statements had been published in the press and on television. No response from SATS.

Numerous letters relating to the dispute concerning Andrew Nedzamba's dismissal and the possible resolution of this have passed between the parties' legal representatives, but to date no agreement has been reached.

Now you can judge.

Document 92. "Down With Apartheid Elections! Stayaway!" UDF and COSATU flyer, May 1987

STAY AT HOME ON MAY 5 & 6

The UDF, COSATU, and the democratic movement has called on all our people for TWO DAYS OF NATIONAL PROTEST on May 5 & 6

WE THE FREEDOM LOVING PEOPLE OF SOUTH AFRICA
SUPPORT THIS CALL.
WE DEMAND

- SCRAP THE RACIST PARLIAMENT
- UNBAN THE ANC AND RELEASE POLITICAL PRISONERS
- END THE STATE OF EMERGENCY
- HANDS OFF THE UDF AND COSATU
- TROOPS OUT OF THE TOWNSHIPS

STAY AT HOME ON MAY 6!
Let us organise the biggest stayaway in our history

WE APPEAL TO OUR PEOPLE
1. NO ONE TO WORK
2. NO SCHOOLING
3. ALL SHOPS TO CLOSE
4. NO SHOPPING IN TOWN
5. NO BUSES OR TAXIS TO TOWN ON MAY 5 & 6

(Only health workers and journalists are allowed to work. Health workers must please wear their uniforms and journalists carry their identity cards)

LET US SHAKE UP BOTHA AND HIS NATS [National Party]!
LET US SHOW HIM WE'VE HAD ENOUGH!

THE TIME HAS COME TO END MINORITY RULE
THE TIME HAS COME TO PUT AN END TO BOTHA'S DICTATORSHIP
VERY IMPORTANT: *all the above must be observed in a disciplined way. Our youth must take responsibility to ensure that the stayaway call is explained to our people before [election day] May 6.*

We demand one person, one vote
Hands off the UDF and COSATU
STAY AT HOME MAY 5 & 6

Document 93. "Coping With Detention." Article in Detainees' Parents Support Committee newsletter, *Noma Siyaboshwa*, August 1987

It is important to be prepared for detention—or to be as prepared as possible. But how do you prepare for something as unpredictable as this?

One way is to learn from the experiences of others, to look at what happens to them. A group of university researchers recently did just that, and what they found can be very useful information for anyone who feels they face the possibility of being detained. Although the researchers did their study before the imposition of the State of Emergency in 1986, their findings are still a very good indicator. In all, the researchers spoke to 176 ex-detainees. From what they said, it is possible to build the "most likely" situation leading to your detention, and the "most likely" situations you will find yourself in.

Actual Arrest

Your arrest is likely to be unexpected, and you are likely to have little warning. Only one out of every five of the detainees had received previous visits from the security police. You are most likely to be picked up at home, and there will probably be between one and five security policemen.

The most dangerous time is between midnight and 6.00 am—particularly between 3.00 am and 6.00 am. You will probably be taken by car to either a police station (as 53% of the detainees were) or security police offices. The security police will be aggressive, too—only 30% of the detainees said they acted "calmly".

Inside

You will probably have a window in your cell, but be unable to turn off the light switch. Clean clothes are possible, but not likely—only half seem to get through. The same applies to food parcels. Sleeping conditions are generally poor, and you will get little or no exercise.

One thing you probably will get is medical attention, even though this may be poor. Only 30% of the detainees said they had received "sound" medical attention.

Interrogation

Teams seemed to be used quite rarely, and usually only 2 or 3 people will interrogate you. Sessions will probably last between 5 and 8 hours, and there will be at least 2 or 3 sessions—although there could be as many as 11. Apart from this contact with the security police, you are unlikely to see many other people during your time inside. Magistrates or doctors are your most likely visitors, although you may see the occasional uniformed policeman.

You might, of course, see other detainees. But there is also a 30% chance that you won't see anyone but the people who interrogate you.

Torture

According to the ex-detainees, you are highly likely to be tortured—both physically and psychologically. Only 17% of the detainees said there was no torture at all, either of the body or the mind. And the younger you are, the higher your chances of being hurt.

The most likely form of torture is beatings, followed by forced standing (experienced by every second detainee) and being forced to sit, crouch or lie in strange positions. Other forms of torture include a bag over the head, electric shocks, strangulation and the use of cold water.

If you escape physical torture, you are unlikely to escape mental torture.

The researchers found that every single ex-detainee they spoke to had experienced some kind of psychological torture.

There are 4 kinds:
- Distorting or confusing the situation by making false accusations against you.
- Trying to weaken you mentally, either by putting you in solitary or interrogating you for hours on end.
- Using "psychological terror tactics"—threatening to kill you, or your family, making you watch others being tortured, and that kind of thing.
- Trying to humiliate you.

The researchers point out: "All this may be considered as cruel treatment".

Health

You can accept that your health is going to suffer while you're inside.

Your main problem will probably be sleeping although you're also likely to experience headaches, weight loss, and have problems concentrating. Your health problems don't end when you're released, either. Many ex-detainees reported problems after their releases, such as getting tired easily (45%), difficulty relating to family and feelings of aggression.

Conclusion

As we said earlier, it is impossible to be fully prepared for detention. But, from the remarks above, you now have a clearer idea of what to expect.

Finally, some advice from one of the ex-detainees questioned for this survey:

"I think the greatest thing that would stand you in good stead in detention is to be fully aware of your rights under different sections [of the security laws]; to be fully prepared for the lines of questioning and how you are going to relate them to the actual work you're involved in, and to understand the way the security police work—their team approach, what pleases them, what are likely tactics to be used, and how you should survive—and to respond in order to survive under these difficult situations".

Document 94. "Build Solidarity With NUM Strike—Build the Living Wage Campaign." National Union of Mineworkers flyer, August 1987

Over half COSATU's membership is on strike for a living wage!

In the mining, chemical, metal, public sector, construction, municipal, transport, food, textile and farm sectors hundreds and thousands of workers are right now striking for a living wage.

Workers—we are in the middle of the biggest strike wave ever in the history of our struggle! In our hundreds and thousands we are uniting and fighting together for a living wage for all workers. We are organising in COSATU to fight starvation by demanding our right to a living wage—to a decent life for ourselves and our children!

At the front of our struggle are the most oppressed and exploited comrades of us all—the militant miners of the NUM. In the biggest wage strike ever, 350,000 gold and coal miners from 50 mines have been striking for ten days now for a living wage.

NUM Demands

The miners are demanding:

—*30% increase in wages.* Workers on gold mines earn R238 [$107] a month minimum and on coal mines R225 for working a 48 hour week—mostly deep underground. The bosses are offering increases between 15% and 23.5%.

—*30 days leave.* At the moment leave is between 14 days and 28 days. Is this enough time to see your family in one year? Is this a decent life?

—*June 16 as a paid holiday.* This day is ours. The day of our youth. The day of our future. Why should we only have bosses holidays? What about our own days?

—*Danger pay.* Miners do the most dangerous work. Every year more than 600 workers die in the gold mines alone. And thousands are seriously injured. Workers have the right in this situation to demand danger pay.

—*Better death benefit.* Miners' families only get two years earnings if a miner dies. Two years for a life! No—all of our lives are priceless. Our families are totally dependent on our earnings. After two years our families will be doomed to starvation.

The NUM strike so far

The miners' strike is presently as solid as the rock our comrades break up every day miles underground. The bosses and their mine security and the police have tried to crush it. They have:

- forced some workers to work at gunpoint
- caused injuries—some very serious—to over 300 workers in clashes with mine security and police
- threatened to close one mine and two shafts affecting thousands and thousands of jobs
- arrested or detained hundreds of workers and shaft stewards
- put out fake pamphlets to try and confuse workers and discredit the NUM
- raided NUM offices

But despite all these attacks and intimidation, they haven't been able to break COSATU's gold—the mine workers.

Solidarity with NUM, Build living wage campaign

The mining houses control the economy of our country. They have stood firm in the face of the just demands of mineworkers and millions of other workers in the factories they own.

The miners have also stood firm. And so is every worker in COSATU. Because the miners are the heart of COSATU's living wage campaign. A victory for the NUM is a victory for every worker. That is why the miners need the active support of every worker.

The COSATU National Living Wage Co-ordinating Committee calls on all workers to build the maximum solidarity with the miners' strike by:
- linking your own struggle for a living wage to the struggle of the miners
- discussing the miners' strike and what kind of support and solidarity you can bring to strengthen it at every meeting of workers
- inviting comrades from the NUM to come and address your meetings about the progress of the strike and the support you need
- collecting money for the NUM's Relief Fund to assist the strikers
- putting pressure on your bosses to telex the mine bosses to meet the just demands of the miners
- raising the issue of the miners' strike at every meeting you have with bosses and making it clear you stand side by side with them
- co-ordinating your own action for a living wage so that it can be united with the NUM struggle and so give each other greater strength
- giving a mandate to your leaders about what kind of solidarity action you will be prepared to take to support the miners and strengthen COSATU's campaign for a living wage
- writing to the newspapers in support of the living wage struggle

Comrades—Now is the hour. Now is the time to drive forward for a living wage. Now is the time to unite and fight for a living wage. Now is the time to build the maximum unity in action for a living wage.

UNITE AND FIGHT FOR A LIVING WAGE

DOCUMENT 95. "NACTU Briefing on Visit to PAC." National Council of Trade Unions report, Dar es Salaam, September 2, 1987

A five-person delegation of NACTU visited Dar Es Salaam, Tanzania from 26 to 29 August 1987 at the invitation of JUWATA [Tanzanian Workers' Association].

During the visit the delegation briefed JUWATA and other concerned local and international officials on the current internal situation in Apartheid South Africa, the role of NACTU and the importance of the struggle of the workers.

Whilst in Tanzania, the NACTU delegation, led by its President, James Mndaweni, held formal discussion with senior members of the Central Committee of the Pan Africanist Congress of Azania (PAC), led by the Chairman, Cde Johnson P. Mlambo.

The NACTU delegation briefed the PAC on the intensification of the total resistance against the apartheid regime, especially in the townships and the rural areas. The implications of the State of Emergency, now in its second year, was thoroughly examined. Concern was raised over the continued detention of children by the minority regime.

This exchange was particularly important in the light of the expected further press curbs recently announced by the regime.

The meeting also noted with grave concern the continued detention of many trade union leaders and activists within NACTU and other trade unions.

The two delegations voiced their deep concern over the continued repression and killings by the police and defence force, and its impact on the oppressed and exploited majority.

The NACTU delegation explained its principles and policies adopted at the inaugural conference on 4-5 October 1986, such as the aspect of democratic worker control and unity, commitment to the national liberation struggle, principled relations with national and international organisations; continued commitment of NACTU to a comprehensive sanctions programme as long as the racist capitalist minority regime exists.

These principles and policies are appreciated by PAC, given the concrete conditions prevailing in the country. The basic principles and policies of the PAC on national liberation and self-determination were explained and appreciated by the NACTU delegation, namely, the establishment of a genuine non-racial/anti-racist democratic society based on the rule of majority through one person one vote and the guarantee of individual rights as opposed to group rights.

This was explained on the principled understanding that:
1. Apartheid cannot be reformed, it must be eradicated;
2. The initiators and custodians for change is the exploited, oppressed and dispossessed majority;
3. The use of all forms of struggle at the disposal of the oppressed majority;
4. The introduction of the East/West conflict into our situation should be strongly resisted.

An intense, but cordial dialogue over issues of common concern occurred over many hours. Issues that were discussed related to the form and content of the struggle.

Both parties agreed that the only acceptable method of liberation was a principled non-collaborationist stand as manifested in the rejection of all the puppet institutions and strategies of the racist regime to maintain and perpetuate its hegemony.

The participants strongly condemned the so-called "Black on Black violence" including the "necklacing" [murder of alleged collaborators]. It was agreed that this method is now used by both the oppressor as well as those forces wishing to impose undemocratically their ideological will on others.

This initial but historic dialogue has paved the way for further substantive ongoing consultations with the specific aim of finding agreed democratic solutions to all the problems besetting our motherland.

The NACTU delegation confirmed its objective of pursuing dialogue with all liberatory organisations consistent with its principle of non-affiliation to political organisations. The PAC, on its part, encouraged NACTU to pursue its task of uniting the Azanian workers on liberatory principles.

Document 96. "Business and Trade Unions." Speech by Jay Naidoo to business conference, *Financial Mail,* November 27, 1987 (abridged)

Some people may not like what I say, but . . . what I have to say does reflect what my constituency—our membership—feels on the issues we've been asked to speak on today. I've taken the liberty of talking on the relationship between business and labour in the context of the current crisis that faces us today. It is the severest crisis we have gone through in our history. It is not just for you as businessmen a purely economic crisis, but it is a very deep-rooted political and ideological crisis as well. . . . [Good relations between unions and management are only possible if there is a common understanding that South African society needs to be fundamentally restructured. Apartheid arose historically from the needs of capital to control labour in the mines. Now business tends to shy away from today's political imperative: to rid South Africa of fundamental economic injustices.]

Statistics show the highly monopolised economy in South Africa. Small businesses have been ruthlessly wiped out during periods of recession. Our "living wage" campaign was an attempt by the labour movement to redress the questions or the issues of wealth redistribution. Yet what we saw was the massive attack on our campaign, including allegations made by the state in court statements, that it is a communist plot. This was followed up by the banning of our meetings and confiscation of our union material. . . .

We have also seen, in this period when we were under very intensive attack, that employers have remained conspicuously silent, particularly earlier this year when the government launched a sophisticated smear campaign against us. And clearly this was designed to create a climate under which further attacks could be made against us without the hindrance of a public outcry. . . .

But what alternative is given to us? We have to contend with rising inflation, a hopelessly inadequate social security system, mass unemployment and retrenchment, and we are simply asked to accept this without you being compelled in any way to disclose your profitability [and] without us being involved in any way in any form of economic planning.

Now clearly these things affect the whole structure of collective bargaining. . . . The collective bargaining structures we believe have failed to address the issue of the redistribution of wealth. Yet this is an issue which is of vital interest not only to our members, but to our people as a whole.

The way in which this has been done makes it very clear that business has the ability to adjust to wage pressures. And secondly we believe that the role of apartheid to intervene in what are industrial and labour disputes, is also a contributory factor. In July we saw a legal strike planned by metal workers in this country illegalised overnight after months of negotiation.

In the strike by mineworkers—a legal strike—for a living wage, we saw state repression and the ability of management to dismiss 40 000 striking mineworkers, striking over wages that were at a minimum of R228-R230 [$100] a month. Striking for an increase of 30% that would not even have amounted to R60 [$26] per month!

Now these experiences do not—as some of the spokesmen for big business put it—show groups with different interests and different racial and social backgrounds arriving at a mutual resolution of serious conflicts in negotiations. It rather shows us that business is not reluctant to use the full power of state repression to suppress our demands. We regard this repression as very short-sighted. It is short-sighted because the hard-line attitudes adopted can only increase instability and polarisation and further undermine the apparent impartiality of the law in the eyes of workers as a group.

The proposed amendments to the Labour Relations Act, which will severely restrict our ability to organise and take legal strike action, must be seen in the same light. They are attempts to reverse the precedent set in unfair labour practices, to give management the power to refuse to deal [with] majority unions. To make the unions targets of damages claims will seriously threaten the credibility of the labour relations structures that we have painfully built up over the last 10 years.

In this context, offering such options as share ownership is not going to resolve the credibility crisis that business faces in the country. Employee share options are not an alternative to our primary demands, particularly where such options are implemented without proper consultation with our unions, or [are] offered on an individual basis to workers. The collapse of the stock market underlines our reservation [about] these shares that are being offered on such a small scale to workers. . . .

In this context one must also say that we don't believe that there are any blueprints for the future. What we embrace is a commitment to build a nonracial democracy in the future, and a willingness to negotiate the terms with those who share this objective.

There must have been a lot of reflection on our adoption of the Freedom Charter. But what must be seen is that the trade union federation is not a political party, but will link [to] those programmes of political parties that most adequately address the needs and the aspirations of our members. This is the context in which we have adopted the Freedom Charter.

Now the challenge of building democracy: the political solutions that have been raised, either by business or by the state, are not sophisticated. In fact, some of the initiatives in the political area have been frankly positively backward. We therefore call on you to reassess the role that you are playing in the [State] Security Council and the Joint Management Councils (JMC), and the close collaboration with right-wing elements and shadowy military and security personnel. [Do not] consolidate what in our eyes is an alliance with such forces, with an undemocratic government that is hostile to the interests of the majority, and has put a number of our respected leaders in detention or imprisonment at Pollsmoor or on Robben Island. It is destructive to any credibility you might want to develop with us as a trade union movement or with black workers more broadly.

Another issue of our concern is the support that many businessmen give to the tricameral system, which has deepened the resentment that our people feel—our members feel—towards the political system in South Africa. The implementation of the system with your support and against the better advice of the trade unions and the democratic movement as a whole has been primarily responsible for the increased instability experienced since 1984.

Most recently we have seen that business is prepared to forge ahead with the KwaZulu-Natal Indaba which we view as undemocratic, because it focuses and lodges itself on a regional solution based on similar principles as offered by the tricameral system. You have brushed aside the trade unions and the democratic movement and forged ahead with this scheme. The danger of the business sector's involvement in undemocratic ventures—particularly at a time when the majority of our leaders are in jail or in detention or in exile—is that [it results in our] rejection not only of that political system, but of the whole system of capitalism. . . .

The growing violence against our organisation in Natal is evidence of this. We have refused to believe that it's purely black-on-black violence. It relates to the whole question of who claims political supremacy in Natal, and [to] what we have seen with the growth of the trade union movement, with the growth of the community-based organisation, and a democratic alternative offered.

And what we are seeing is that in fact the violence is aimed at crushing that democratic alternative. And very often, like I've said, it's been alleged that it's black-on-black violence. Or it's a conflict between opposing political groups. It seems to be immaterial that we've brought numerous court applications against high-ranking officials, particularly of Inkatha, to refrain from intimidating or assaulting our members. We do not deny that some of our members have become embroiled in this violence, but there is no leading Cosatu or UDF person that has been found guilty of involvement in violent intimidation. Therefore, what we have said is that we condemn the violence and we condemn forced recruitment. And we believe our membership is voluntary and our membership and recognition depend on agreements we negotiate with yourselves. And it cannot be alleged that we as Cosatu are forcing people to join us.

Recently in Pietermaritzburg we have released a memorandum on the violence in the area and it's become clear to us that the main perpetrators of violence are the people that we have termed "warlords"—people who blatantly commit violence. We have collected and documented evidence of this. We have presented this to the courts, but what we see is that people—the police particularly—are not prepared to take action against those who perpetrate criminal activity even though there are eye-witness accounts. We believe it is mainly because those people represent the conservative force in that community.

Now we are committed to achieving a cessation of violence in Pietermaritzburg, but what we argue is that the issue that confronts us is not the signing of a formal peace agreement, but the creation of conditions that are conducive to the implementation of such a peace agreement. And that is that those individuals that are identified in documented and attested statements of committing violent acts must be prosecuted. We must have the police taking action against them. And it's not by pumping more troops and more policemen into the townships that we are going to resolve that crisis. We have also said that Cosatu and the UDF are prepared to publicly condemn forced recruitment, and we are saying that what we must do is support the principle of the freedom of association and the freedom of expression.

This brings us to another area for which the labour movement has been condemned—sanctions. Our support for sanctions is another strategy that we are condemned for, but let us look at what alternatives you have presented to us as the labour movement. We are saying that all democratic South Africans are perturbed by the spectre of escalating and uncontrolled violence in the country. We look in horror at the lives that are wasted both as a result of political violence in our townships and on our borders. But we believe that business has the power to influence the state to end repression and move towards a peace that is based [on] democracy and an end to poverty. However, what we detect is a reluctance by business to use their considerable clout to bring this government to its senses.

You seem very eager in our view to wash your hands of responsibility regarding apartheid, but you are unwilling to act. The plea for sanctions is a very urgent message that people are sending to business: that the majority of workers and people in our country refuse to accept that they must endure the pain and suffering and the indignity of apartheid indefinitely. We see supporting sanctions and disinvestment as a means of driving that message home, particularly to those employers who are still comfortable with apartheid. We know that as soon as your interests are affected, you will sit up and take stock of it. We see that decisive economic pressure could help to break the present logjam and compel you to actively pressurise this government to move towards a nonracial democracy.

If you oppose sanctions and disinvestment then it is up to you to put forward a viable alternative to us that can end the political impasse that is grinding our country to a halt.

In the last year we have seen a spate of determined and sustained attacks on our democratic rights. The government has spent this year stripping away the democratic rights of trade unions, of universities, of the media. The answer to the widespread condemnation of army occupation of the townships has been to declare the state of emergency, and to tighten restrictions. The passive response of the liberal community we believe is convincing the government that they can move with impunity to further strip away our rights.

Ironically, every time they attack democracy, it is a broader attack on the South African population which is affected as much as the democratic movement or the labour movement. It is therefore very difficult for us to understand why there is still such substantial support in your ranks for the leadership of a government which is systematically diminishing democratic rights and concentrating more and more power in its own hands.

Now, what can business do to protect democracy and salvage the damaged image that you suffer at the moment? Your response, we contend, will concretely shape the future relationship between yourselves and us as a labour movement, and this in turn will shape the future of our country.

DOCUMENT 97. "Trade Unions and Political Direction." National Union of Metalworkers (NUMSA) discussion paper, December 1987 (abridged)

The aim of this paper is to address the question: "WHAT SHOULD BE THE POLITICAL DIRECTION OF OUR UNION IN THE CURRENT SOUTH AFRICAN SITUATION?"

The full answer to this question however will have to come through discussion and debate at all levels of our organisation. This paper only aims to begin that debate. . . .

COSATU DIRECTION

When COSATU was formed at the end of 1985 the office bearers felt that it was important for COSATU to be very much involved in the political struggle in our country. They argued that the members of COSATU themselves were pushing the political struggle and strongly supported political organisations especially the UDF and ANC. They said that if COSATU was not respected politically by all groups then it would be ignored and members would lose faith in the organisation. We believe these beliefs of the COSATU leadership were largely correct.

The COSATU leadership therefore decided to make a lot of public political statements in the newspapers, at meeting, at funerals etc. Soon afterwards they went to meet the ANC and issued a communique saying that COSATU was committed to struggling for a non-racial South Africa under the leadership of the ANC. Here we believe that the COSATU leadership made some mistakes because:

i) they did not get mandates from the unions and their members to say many of the things in the newspapers and at meetings and at funerals.
ii) they should have got a very clear mandate to meet the ANC and should not have issued a statement until they had fully discussed their meeting inside COSATU first.
iii) they should not have agreed to COSATU struggling under the leader-

ship of the ANC. They should have made it clear that COSATU, in terms of its own policies, would struggle together with other progressive organisations but independently under its own leadership.

By themselves these mistakes may not appear to be very great but they have certainly created other problems for the Federation. For example:
i) those within the Federation who supported the ANC believed that since COSATU was now operating under the leadership of the ANC there was no room for the other workers who did not fully support the ANC. Workers who expressed different views were threatened and invitations to meet other political organisations were refused.
ii) some unions expected that it was not necessary to get full and proper mandates on all issues from workers and COSATU made some bad errors like the July 14th Stay-Away.
iii) many strong personal attacks were made against people like [Chief M. G.] Buthelezi, which created many problems for unionists and members in Natal when there were in fact better ways to fight Inkatha and UWUSA [United Workers' Union of SA].

As a result of these problems (and other problems as well) COSATU was not able to consolidate itself as an organisation. Most regions are not operating properly. Also COSATU has not learnt to campaign effectively and operate independently and to analyse its mistakes openly and constructively. The question may be raised as to why the COSATU leadership made these mistakes. This paper will not try and answer that question but it is clearly something for members to discuss if they wish.

What we believe is important is for us to learn from those mistakes and to push COSATU also to learn from their mistakes because we are a part of the Federation and we are certainly committed to seeing it survive and grow to be [the] most effective Federation this country has ever seen.

THE ROAD FORWARD
There can surely be no question of the fact that workers in the trade unions (the organised working class) must be part of the national liberation struggle. If we were not actively part of this struggle then we would not be properly representing the aspirations of our members who want an end to apartheid, who want the right to vote, who want the equal rights etc.

But we should ask two further questions:-
i) do our members want more than just an end to apartheid—are they in fact calling for socialism?
ii) do our members want their trade unions to be put under the control of any political party?

If our members are calling for socialism and if they wish their trade unions to maintain their independence (which we believe is the case) then we have a duty to follow those instructions. This means firstly that we must start building for socialism and secondly that we must establish the independence of COSATU within the national liberation struggle.

1. Building for socialism

If it is really our aim to build socialism in South Africa then we have to start building now. It is not a task we can leave to some date in the future—socialism cannot be established overnight. We have to ensure that we build up democratic trade unions and democratic community organisations which have the full support of the people. These organisations can then be our vehicles to socialism.

In building these organisations though, we must be sure that they are based on proper socialist principles like democracy, working class leadership, mass participation and worker control. Organisations which are undemocratic, outside of workers' control or just inactive [are] usually of little value to the struggle for socialism. If policies are just dictated from on top then organisations will be weak and can just be used by anybody.

2. Establishing independence and unity

Our responsibility in the struggle is to unite with other progressive groups wherever this is possible, but we should be careful about exactly what kind of unity we are trying to build and what is the basis of that unity. We believe that unity must be built out of action not on the basis of big press conferences and vague promises.

When we unite with other organisations it should be in order to carry out campaigns to win rights for the working class and thereby for other oppressed groups as well. Our members right down to the shop floor should participate in these campaigns and struggle for their rights.

When we decide to unite with other organisations to push any campaign we should be sure that the campaign will take us further along the road to socialism. *We should be clear that the groups we are campaigning with accept that socialism is the goal which must be achieved under the leadership of the working class.*

We should be free to choose which groups we wish to unite with and which we wish to reject. No other organisation should be allowed to dictate to us whom our allies should be. If we adopt this *programme of action* which involves building democratic mass based trade unions and community organisations and participating in the national liberation struggle with other organisations on the basis of UNITY IN ACTION, INDEPENDENCE OF ORGANISATIONS AND A COMMITMENT TO SOCIALISM then it is clear that our members must begin to define what they mean by socialism.

This is the responsibility of the working class. A document drawn up by workers spelling out what socialism is would not have to replace other charters like the Freedom Charter. It would simply express what the working class [is] aiming to achieve under socialism.

A working class programme is called for in the COSATU resolutions. But it cannot be imposed from above. It must develop out of the struggles and experiences of workers themselves.

THIS IS AN IMMEDIATE TASK.

Document 98. Excerpts from speech by Chief Mangosuthu Gatsha Buthelezi to KwaZulu Legislative Assembly, Ulundi, March 1988

Mr. Speaker, Honourable Members, in looking at the current political situation, I have drawn attention to certain aspects of Black and White politics and it is against the background of the remarks that I have already made that I now turn my attention to the African National Congress. I am not going to indulge in party political rhetoric. I am not going to make polemical statements. The time has come for me to address some very fundamental issues and Mr. Speaker, Honourable Members, I am not going to talk about the ANC. I am going to address Mr. Oliver Tambo. . . .

Mr. Tambo and senior members of his Executive have been outside South Africa now for nearly 28 years. For that period of time he has not had the advantage that Inkatha's and KwaZulu's democratic structure gives me. . . . I know how difficult it was for Mr. Tambo to establish any kind of base abroad. I speak to him man to man with a sympathetic understanding of how difficult his role has been and how Godforsaken he must have felt when he went out into the world as a nobody. . . .

I have never ever for one moment doubted that . . . we will have a multi-party democracy. I know that you and your lieutenants are totally preoccupied with returning to South Africa as a government returned from exile. I know that you can only achieve this if you bring about the circumstances in which the people are robbed of their sovereignty and a one-party state can be foisted on them. . . .

You and your colleagues in your collective wisdom decided to attempt to make the armed struggle the primary means of bringing about radical change. Mr. Tambo, were you yourself in South Africa, you would have been deeply shocked by any political leader who tried to tackle the military might of Pretoria and failed and then turned to planting bombs in public places. We in South Africa are shocked by the ANC's attacks on soft targets. We are shocked by the politics of violent intimidation. . . . I am addressing you as a brother in the struggle who has lost his way out there in the outside world and who stands in the real danger of being finally alienated in the land of his birth.

If there was anything I could do to help bring you back home, I would do it. The attacks that you and your organization make against my honour are, however, so offensive to people at the grass root level who support me in their masses that I am beginning to doubt that the people will ever permit me to bring you in from the cold. . . .

Who are you, Mr. Tambo, and who is any one of your colleagues, or who are you collectively, to dictate to millions of South Africans here on the ground in this country that non-participation must be raised as a principle? You are not elected to office by the masses as I am. You are not answerable to the masses as I am answerable to them each and every year when I stand before Inkatha's Annual General Conference to be held accountable and to be judged. I tell you now, Mr. Tambo, that the people themselves in their millions refuse to be obeisant to your demands to elevate non-participation to the level of principle. If we don't fight apartheid where it is strangling us, we will be strangled. . . .

Surely you have by now seen that what Inkatha has done has already altered the course of history in South Africa. Were it not for my participatory opposition to apartheid and if . . . I had sanctimoniously stepped aside and allowed Pretoria to make KwaZulu a so-called independent state, there would by now have been a confederation of Southern African states which would have included Swaziland. We would all be facing a totally different ball game and the clocks would have been set back to Vorster's or Verwoerd's time. I have done more to stamp on the government's homeland policy than anything you have ever been able to do. . . .

It is because you have none of the real action which is moving this country forward that you want to destroy everything that those who are succeeding have done. . . . I sympathize with your plight. I sympathize with the fact that you cannot exercise true African-style leadership in your own organisation. . . .

You talk very pretentiously about the ANC being the country's vanguard movement. . . . You have at your disposal a multi-million dollar propaganda machine. On my side I only have the pennies that come out of the pockets of the poorest of the poor. . . .

No Black leader in South Africa has a stronger or longer track record than mine when it comes to commitments to non-violent tactics and strategies. . . . Your organization attacks Inkatha brutally and threatens the lives of ordinary people and I respond in self-defence. . . .

I throw down the gauntlet, Mr. Tambo, and tell you that if you really want a fight you have got it. . . . Inkatha is the largest Black political organisation ever to have emerged in the history of the country. . . .

You will never ever succeed if you make Black unity a question of total and blind allegiance to your organisation. I have a very powerful advantage over you and that is that I do not attempt to do this. I have potential working partners in South Africa which you have ensured that you do not have. History will work its course in South Africa and the alliances that Inkatha is developing are alliances that will stand the test of history. Inkatha is allied to forces working for change which are there in their own right. The ANC Mission in Exile has to create those forces one at a time.

Mr. Tambo, if you have your way a decade or perhaps two or three decades hence, this country will still remain locked in that equilibrium of violence which neither the government of the day nor revolutionaries of the day can escape. Break out of the sterility of being locked into a situation in which equal force constantly meets equal force.

DOCUMENT 99. "Victory!!!" Announcement of strike outcome by National Union of Metalworkers (NUMSA), August 16, 1988

The joint strike committees today decided to call NUMSA members to return to work. All locals are asked to convene meetings of the Shop Stewards Council tonight to discuss this. General meetings of workers should be held tomorrow, so that there can be a return to work by Thursday. Although we did not force SEIFSA [Steel and Engineering Industrial Federation of SA] to move on money, SEIFSA gave us things which will make us much stronger in the future.

- The strike damaged SEIFSA's ability to control its members—more than 120 SEIFSA companies settled higher than SEIFSA's offer.
- SEIFSA has had to agree that NUMSA is the main union in the Industrial Council—Not the CMBU [Confederation of Metal and Building Unions].
- Our strike is the only national industrial strike which has taken place in 1988. It shows that the heavy political repression has not intimidated our members.
- The moves which SEIFSA has made have exposed the other unions, especially the CMBU as the sell-outs which they are.
- Many more workers will join NUMSA now. We should aim for at least 40,000 new members by the end of the year.
- Our organization and structures have been strengthened in this struggle.
- The wage structure of the whole industry has been changed—many companies are now paying more than R4-00 [$1.60] per hour minimum because of the supplementary bargaining.

And we have won these things with very few casualties! Because of careful planning and strategies, it was hard for management to attack us—and SEIFSA has agreed to pressurise the few companies which dismissed workers.

This is what SEIFSA has agreed (full details were sent to your local by telex)

1. 1 May and 16 June swapped for other holidays.
2. Back-dating of the SEIFSA increase to 1st July,
3. Compulsory stop order facilities—management can't block our stop orders anymore,
4. Wage anomalies to be eliminated by 1991,
5. Arbitration and full information of any alleged racial discrimination,
6. Attendance bonus: 1 day's pay for 180 shifts;
   2 day's pay for 235 shifts;
   (Authorised absence or illness, and short time qualify as full shifts)

7. SEIFSA agrees to change the collective bargaining system and to recognise NUMSA as the major union,
8. SEIFSA will support SACCOLA [SA Coordinating Committee on Labour Affairs] if it calls on its members not to use the bad clauses of the LRA [Labour Relations Act],
9. SEIFSA will push companies to reinstate workers who were dismissed or locked out for the legal strike.

There will be a meeting of the Industrial Council on Thursday to finalise this agreement—but there will be no problem because SEIFSA has already agreed.

Members must go back to work peacefully. We must now go forward to build NUMSA to 200,000 members.

AMANDLA AWETHU!!!!! [Power is ours]

4. Exile and Underground Politics, 1980–1988

DOCUMENT 100. *"Inqindi and Marxism."* ANC discussion document circulated in Robben Island prison after 1978, handwritten by Ahmed Kathrada (abridged)

Inqindi *("fist" in Zulu and Xhosa) refers to the ANC. ANC leaders in the prison's "B section" sent an earlier draft to prisoners in the general section, then collectively produced the document below after receiving their responses.*

INTRODUCTION

The polemics arising from "Inqindi-Marxism" constitute an important milestone in our political education and enlightenment. It certainly was timely. The two basic aims of "Inqindi-Marxism" were to encourage comrades to study Marxism, and to remind them of the distinction between a national struggle and a class struggle. We were happy to note that both viewpoints that were sparked off by "Inqindi-Marxism" rely on the dialectical method. They try to tackle the problem scientifically and at grass roots—something unique in a broad national movement.

The polemic is also evidence of the dynamic nature of the FC [Freedom Charter], which is capable of being interpreted in the light of the developing situation. Neither critics nor supporters of "Inqindi-Marxism" suggest that FC has become outmoded. On the contrary, some even claim that it envisages a "pd" [people's democracy] with a dictatorship of the proletariat. That is significant and shows that FC is flexible to allow for different interpretations in accordance with changing conditions.

However, it must be emphasised that such flexibility of interpretation will be influenced strictly by concrete conditions, and will enable the policy of *Inqindi* to keep pace with the developing situation.

There was a time when the political work of the CM [Congress Movement] concentrated almost entirely on day to day issues. Naturally we will always give attention to bread and butter questions. Our success or failure will depend largely on the effectiveness with which we tackle such problems. But in the light of developments in our country, on our borders from the Atlantic to the Indian oceans, and in the world at large, we naturally expect theoretical discussions on some central political problems to dominate our work more and more. Recent political developments have created a ferment in our own ranks, which must be fully encouraged and utilised through organised and individual political discussions. There is a quest for scientific knowledge for the understanding of the economic basis of class conflicts, for fundamental solutions which have been tested by revolutionary movements in other parts of the world. This ferment requires us to gear ourselves for such theoretical discussions and be ready to facilitate them in every possible way.

We concede that some of the formulations in Inqindi-M were obscure, misleading, or otherwise wrong. We also mistakenly assumed that our interpretation [in the leaders' "B" section] of the FC was the same as that of comrades in other sections, and that we all accepted the basic differences between the policies and ultimate objectives of the CM and CP [Communist Party]. For this reason we did not sufficiently elaborate our statements. All this may have contributed to the polemics.

Some of us have not seen the CP Program for 15 years, and again we concede that our recollection of the actual words used in that document was wrong; that the actual expression employed is "national democracy" and not "bourgeois democratic republic" as stated in Inqindi-M. We humbly apologise.

It is important for our people to know that Inqindi-M is not the product of any individual, but of all the comrades here [in "B" section]. It was drafted by the secretariat at the request of the HO [High Organ], discussed and unanimously approved by the latter. There was not a single dissentient when it was read out to the rest of our comrades. We must, however, point out that subsequent discussions showed that when it was first read out, comrades did not pay attention as seriously as they did when they received your comments [from the general section]. This document represents their considered views.

In this connection, we wish to remind you that we have already commended comrades Δ and Ø and for their timely actions which forestalled the threat of serious misunderstanding in our ranks. Their efforts restored the comradely atmosphere in which important internal discussions can be fruitfully conducted. We also wish to congratulate comrades holding differing viewpoints for their valuable contributions. The standard was high and each viewpoint was well argued. It is the quality of those contributions that led us to observe that this polemic constitutes an important milestone in our education.

The sharply differing viewpoints that emerged emphasise the inconvenience, and even harm that is caused to our work by our isolation from one another. Had we been housed together, and discussing daily, some of the differences would have been either avoided or easily smoothed out. Experience inside and outside prison has always shown that the closeness of the bonds of unity among CM members, and the serious way they always apply themselves to problems, have not only helped the Congress to correct its mistakes and to assess the position in the light of new knowledge, but has also helped to further weld us together. The alertness of comrades, their profound knowledge, their constructive ideas and suggestions have enabled the CM to correctly interpret the aspirations of the people, and to make a far greater impact on the masses than any other organisation in the NLM [National Liberation Movement].

We would welcome further comments from comrades who still wish to add their views. However, it must be appreciated that we are conducting this discussion under very difficult conditions. It is undesirable, on security grounds, for correspondence to pile up, and to drag on the discussion indefinitely.

It must be borne in mind that the views expressed in the final document should not be interpreted as an expression of criticism against any particular person or persons holding certain viewpoints.

SUMMARIES OF DIFFERENT VIEWPOINTS

SUMMARY OF INQINDI-M

Hereunder are the salient points. Others, not mentioned here, will be found [in] other sections of this document.

"Inqindi-Marxism" welcomes the deep interest shown by our comrades in Marxism and the study of this doctrine as set out in the Communist Manifesto. It describes the Bolshevik Revolution and the introduction of scientific socialism in the Soviet Union as a milestone of a new kind in human history. It points out that here at home the CPSA [Communist Party of South Africa] has systematically spread Marxist ideas within the CM for 57 years, that right from the beginning the CP accepted ANC, SAIC [SA Indian Congress] and APO [the coloured African People's Organisation] as the true voices of Black nationalism in the country.

It continues "But speaking purely as Congressites, we expect all our members to specialise first and foremost on the history of the Congresses and be able to speak authoritatively on our policy. We also expect them to have more than a general knowledge of the history and policy of the other sections of the CM, the power structure in the country and the political situation in the ruling class."

But the document warns that the growing interest in the study of Marxism and the 57 year old heritage of joint campaigning by the CM and CP should not be allowed to obscure the basic differences between the policies of the two organisations. ANC and the other Congresses are neither Marxist organisations nor C[ommunist]-fronts. They are national organisations which lead the struggle against racial oppression and not against capitalism. The FC, not Marxism, is the policy of CM.

Inqindi-M adds that the democratic changes envisaged will create the ideal conditions for the CP to pursue the struggle for a socialist SA. Until then the FC will continue to serve the dual purpose of being the basic policy of the CM, and the foundation on which the alliance between the Congresses and the CP rests. It ends by stressing that the failure of the enemy to check our advance is a measure of the unbreakable bond between the CM and CP, and the correctness of the policy of the CM.

SUMMARY OF VIEWPOINTS DIFFERING WITH INQINDI-M

Several contributions criticise the views expressed in Inqindi-M. However, all of them welcome the suggestion that the comrades should be encouraged to study Marxism. One of them adds that the study of Marxism will help comrades not to confuse Inqindi for the CP and CP for Inqindi. It further suggests that all political lectures should be centralised so as to avoid a multiplicity of interpretations, particularly in fundamental matters.

The general theme of these comments is that the source of the eagerness of our youth for Marxism must be sought in the fundamental changes that have taken place in the industrial, commercial and agricultural sectors during the last decade in which supermarkets and even hypermarkets [giant supermarkets] have taken over. Gone are the days of the small and middle entrepreneurs. Their place is now taken over by monopoly chain stores. The peasantry has been destroyed by the advent of border industries and that class has now given place to the rural proletariat, while the middle class is now bought off by the big monopolies. Even the majority of whites are not only removed from the ownership of industry and financial houses, but from commerce and agriculture as well. As a result the majority of the people of SA now reject capitalism, while the preponderance of the working class in the CM has resulted in a leftward shift in [thinking?]

The present period differs from that of 1955 when our policy was one of non-violence and when it was hoped that freedom might be attained through peaceful means. In support of this argument reliance is placed among other things on a 1964 publication (Z) in which OR [Oliver Reginald Tambo] is alleged to have told the author that our real aim then was to sit down with Verwoerd and discuss reforms.

The argument goes on to say that after Kliptown [site of the Congress of the People in 1955], a powerful people's army embracing all national groups in the country emerged. It is said that on several occasions OR has declared that Inqindi is fighting for seizure of political power. According to this view the people's struggle in Angola and Mozambique culminated in the social struggle which forced the MPLA and FRELIMO to form Marxist governments as the only alternative. The struggle of the people of Zimbabwe and Namibia has reached such a stage. Hence they also talk of the seizure of power and the formation of Marxist states.

It is also said that when the FC was adopted, Communism was still unpopular in the African states and that African nationalism was the most attractive ideology. It would thus have been tactically and diplomatically wrong for either Inqindi or CP to have declared the FC as a step towards a people's democracy (PD). But it is argued that today things have changed. The CP committed itself to the realisation of democracy in this country under the leadership of Inqindi, and that the FC would establish PD. According to this view "the foundation of capitalism would still be there, and such a democracy would, therefore, be a bourgeois democracy (BD) in character but transitory in content."

Apartheid is veiled fascism and threatens all democratic values. Hence the struggle ceases to be merely a national struggle and becomes a social struggle that demands the participation of all social groups. "Therefore it is clear that the issue is that of a PD versus apartheid."

In further support of the contention that the FC fights for a PD and not for a BD, reliance is placed on the special issue of Sechaba (v 3 no 7, July 1969) which stated "on the wake of a victorious revolution a Democratic People's republic shall be proclaimed."

On the nature of the SA we are fighting for, the statement adds: "And comrades we contend that with our liberation movement comprised of the working class majority, and with the CP in its ambit, we are more prepared than just to establish a PD Rep. but to introduce socialism (S) right away. We are obviously in a much better advantage than Frelimo, MPLA, PF [Patriotic Front of Zimbabwe] and SWAPO because we have a strong CP. . . ."

Finally, the view that in addition to the CM there are other sections of the liberation movement in this country is challenged. It is said that according to comrade [ANC secretary general Alfred] Nzo Inqindi does not recognise Impama [Pan Africanist Congress, symbolized by the open palm] as a LM [Liberation Movement], that Inqindi policy is, and has always been, to accept individuals from Impama who wanted to join Inqindi as individuals and not as a movement. It is also said that OR maintained that Inqindi recognised the BPC [Black People's Convention] as a progressive political organisation but not as part of the NLM. They were also welcomed to join as individuals. . . .

THE CONTENT OF OUR REVOLUTION . . .

Both the CM and CP have consistently advocated the principle that the liberation of the African people is the main content of the struggle against white domination, and for a free democratic South Africa. . . .

Recognition of African nationalism as the driving force of our struggle does not mean that we in any way belittle the role played by the Coloured and Indian communities and the white democrats, all of whom have fought gallantly alongside the African people. But the concrete realities of our situation have shown that the maximum efforts of these communities, without the participation of the African masses, can hardly make a dent in the armoury of white domination. Even if Coloureds and Indians are granted equal status with the whites—which is advocated by elements in the ruling class—this does not mean that Africans will be liberated. True liberation and freedom can only come when the masses of African people are freed. It is in this sense that the SA revolution is regarded as basically an African revolution.

Comrades have made the point that Inqindi has been transformed from a purely "African liberation movement" to simply "liberation movement of SA". Once Inqindi decided to throw open its doors to other population groups, it would be incongruous to present it still as an exclusively African organisation. It is correct that, in the light of the present situation in our country, where the forces of change cut across racial lines, and where the efforts of all revolutionaries require it to be properly coordinated, the struggle should be conducted under the leadership of one central non-racial organisation: Inqindi is this organisation. . . .

The role of African nationalism is to unite Africans in the struggle against national oppression. It is because the spirit of nationalism is deeply rooted among us that our people have emphatically rejected separate development.

Inqindi has always stood for a progressive nationalism. After opening its doors to all, that nationalism will become even more tempered and broad. But it would be a mistake to over-emphasise the importance of African nationalism. Unlike Marxism, which guides a CP before and after the taking of power, the role of African nationalism is limited to the pre-liberation phase of the struggle. It cannot be used to reshape society after liberation, nor for the purpose of developing a new mode of production different from capitalism or socialism, as some political organisations claim. . . .

CONCLUSION

The most urgent task before Inqindi is to rally the masses behind the revolution. When that goal has been reached then, and only then, can we rightly and confidently claim that the days of white supremacy are numbered. Throughout its long history Inqindi has successfully parried the most vicious enemy blows, rallied its forces, and [gone] on the offensive many a time. In spite of great odds that offensive is still in progress, and our men are fighting the enemy on several fronts. Despite our undoubted success in resisting and isolating the enemy, the persistence of racial discrimination and oppression is a painful reminder that we still have a long way to go in the task of mobilising our people fully behind the struggle. We are duty bound to harness all forces which will enable us to accomplish our aims.

In order to be able to fully harness the people's patriotism, we should first be clear on our priorities. We can only grasp the nature of our struggle if we thoroughly study the history of our country and people and their struggle. This can only serve to enlighten us on the tasks that lie ahead and the manner in which those tasks could best be tackled with understanding, confidence and determination.

Naturally, our history is part of the history of the whole of mankind and is influenced by more or less the same factors. We study the struggles of revolutionary movements in other parts of the world because their experiences illuminate our problems and make us see the way forward more clearly. It is for this reason that we have repeatedly encouraged our members to study Marxism and the history of major revolutions of the world as part of the study of our own history. If we firmly grasp its principles and are fully conversant with the peculiarities of our situation, Marxism will operate like a bright searchlight in a dark tunnel.

DOCUMENT 101. "Rules of Security, Defence and Code of Conduct." Umkhonto we Sizwe draft memorandum, March 1981 (abridged)

Introduction: LET US DEFEND OUR ANC AND OUR PEOPLE!

1. Comrades we are passing through challenging but dangerous times. The whole future of our liberation movement and our people's struggle is at stake. As our struggle grows in strength and scope so the enemy becomes more desperate and dangerous. In response to our revolutionary blows and the rising militancy of our people the enemy answers with increased counter-revolutionary violence and activity. The Matola raid, and many other incidents, are a dramatic illustration of this new, higher level of struggle.
2. This is the nature of Revolution. Marx has said that Revolution advances by giving rise to a more united and determined counter-revolution. As the revolutionary struggle develops so counter-revolution seeks more powerful methods to defend its interests. This in turn compels the revolutionaries to find more effective methods of coming back to the attack. . . .
7. Comrades, where there is bad discipline and poor behaviour we play into the enemy's hands. We weaken our movement. We create contradictions between our movement and our friends and hosts. We create conditions in which the traitors and infiltrators can work more easily and do more damage. Indiscipline helps to lower our standards of vigilance and security. It endangers our lives.
8. Comrades, we are witnessing the way in which FRELIMO is dealing with their own problem of indiscipline, corruption and treachery. They have learnt the lesson of Matola. They are showing a revolutionary response to the counter-revolutionary blow of the enemy.
9. We too, who have lost 11 brave comrades at Matola, must clearly show that we have learnt the lesson of that attack. Otherwise our comrades will have died in vain. . . .

RULES OF ACCOMMODATION, SECURITY, DEFENCE AND BEHAVIOUR
FARMHOUSE [Maputo] *3.3.81*

ACCOMMODATION
a. Commander and members of machinery [MK leadership] to have separate accommodation, i.e. secret command HQ of machinery.
b. Couriers also to be separately accommodated.

c. As soon as it is clear that the enemy might have information concerning the address of operational residences these must be changed.

Operatives
a. House for operatives. Numbers must be limited. Not more than 7 unless specifically approved.
b. The house must have a Commander and Commissar who are permanent plus the unit who are undergoing preparation for home. Additional numbers must be specifically approved by the Working group of the Senior Organ.
c. Requisition of personnel by the machinery must be in accordance with practical planning so as to avoid unnecessary build up of personnel.
d. In order to maintain secrecy of accommodation, no visitors are permitted other than the officials connected with the work.
e. Rules of conspiracy must govern the way in which officials visit the accommodation and the way in which all work is conducted on the premises. Known ANC vehicles not to be parked outside the residence.
f. Particular care must be taken in the way in which cadres relate to neighbours in order to conceal our ANC connection and the kind of work taking place on the premises.
g. Special effort must be taken by the machinery to limit the knowledge of comrades being prepared for home concerning the area in which they live. Comrades must be confined to their residence as much as possible, particularly during the day. The machinery must organise methods of external relaxation, medical treatment etc. in keeping with the security requirements. No comrade may leave the residence unless on officially organised excursion or business.
h. No documents or records of a sensitive nature to be kept at the place where operatives are housed. These to be kept under totally safe and secure conditions.
i. Each residence to maintain a daily visitors book recording time of visits and departures. To be inspected by relevant authority on weekly basis and then removed.
j. No logistics deliveries to be made direct from ANC stores. Arrangements to be organised through the relevant authority.
k. Residences of operatives going home to be dispersed from one another. . . .

CONTROL OF MOVEMENT
1. Since our area is an operational area the movement of all personnel—in and out—must be under the strict control of the SO [senior organ] working in conjunction with the office.
2. No person should be accepted in this area without clear reason. . . .
6. Legal movement between Farmyard [Swaziland?] and Farmhouse [Maputo] must be strictly controlled by the SO in conjunction with the office. A record of this movement must be kept giving reasons for the journeys. People with passports must first ask permission from the appropriate authority—the office or SO. The Secretary or Chairman of the SO to clear people with pass-

ports with the office. No individual can make an illegal crossing without permission of the department concerned. . . .

INT [Intelligence] *AND SENIOR ORGAN RELATIONSHIP*
1. Written report featuring important items relating to the security of our personnel, whether here or in Farmyard or Farmlands [SA], to be presented to Working Group every Monday—if Working Group not meeting then such report to be submitted to the Secretary of the SO.
2. Certain data of a crucial nature to be made known to the SO immediately.
3. Lines of communication between Farmyard and Farmhouse concerning such information must be dynamic. SO to make sure that these means of communication reach the required standards of effectiveness.
4. Urgent information that relates to our various departments or residences etc. must be handed over as soon as possible to the relevant departments or residences. At the same time relevant INT and Security information in the hands of these departments must be promptly passed on to the INT section.
5. Captured agents in the hands of INT must be open to interview by the departments under which they have been operating with the permission of the SO. INT should consult with the department concerned on the line of interrogation to be pursued. . . .

DEFENCE SYSTEM:
1. Preamble
a. It cannot be stressed sufficiently that security of our residences depends in the first place on depriving the enemy of information concerning the residence and thus maintaining its secrecy.
b. Secondly the security of our residences are provided by maintaining an organised system of vigilance so as to provide advanced warning of any enemy manoeuvres. . . .
7. Residences must be adequately armed. As a principle there should be sufficient weapons to allow for the arming of each comrade. Commander and Commissar should each have a pistol. A residence occupied by 7 comrades should be allocated 4 AKs [machine guns] and 3 other automatic weapons. In addition each comrade should be armed with 2 hand grenades—defensive and offensive, and knives for hand-to-hand fighting. Sufficient ammunition and magazines to be provided.
8. Commander to organise suitable armoury—concealed in some way—to store weapons when not in use, but easily accessible at times of emergency. However, every comrade to be issued with his weapon at night. Commander to maintain strict control over weapons. Inspection to take place weekly.
9. Where possible fortification of residence to be organised by building sand bagged firing positions and bomb shelters, hiding places, escape tunnels and escape routes—in such a way as not to arouse curiosity of neighbours. Alarm systems. . . .

13. A system of communication and co-ordination between the residence and the local police and soldiers to be worked out as to:
a. avoid being tricked by Boers [Afrikaners] posing as Frelimo
b. support and collaboration in event of attack
c. evacuation of and assistance for wounded. . . .

CODE OF BEHAVIOUR: T/Q [Mozambique-Swaziland] *AREA*
1. All cadres are expected to conduct themselves in a revolutionary manner. This means that their behaviour must reflect the ideals of the ANC and bring credit to the name of the ANC.
2. All cadres to behave in a courteous and modest manner to civilians and local authority in the TQ area. . . .
5. The consumption of alcohol in a bar or public place where alcohol is exclusively served is forbidden.
6. The consumption of alcohol at an embassy function, wedding or with a meal in a restaurant, must be taken moderately. The excessive consumption of alcohol at these places is forbidden.
7. In Q area all operatives engaged in internal work are to totally refrain from consuming liquor.
8. In Q area operatives are forbidden to enter public places where liquor is exclusively consumed eg bars or hotel bars.
9. Any cadres who has the duty and responsibility of driving a movement car is prohibited from drinking prior to driving or during driving. This cannot be tolerated.
10. The smoking of dagga [marijuana] and taking of any form of drugs is strictly forbidden.
11. The negligent handling of our cars, and dangerous driving, is prohibited and liable to punishment.
12. The frequenting of the Diplomatic Shop in Maputo must be limited. ANC cadres must not be seen purchasing liquor. The spending of foreign currency in T area must be explained and accounted for.
13. Threatening behaviour, abusive language, assault, the sexual abuse of women, sexual malpractice in our movement and in relation to the local population, is forbidden and is a punishable offence.
14. Any form of theft, whether from comrades, the organisation, local population or host country is punishable.
15. Orders given by the appropriate officers of the organisation must be promptly and courteously obeyed. The defiance of such orders, the refusal to carry out orders is a punishable offence.
16. Great care must be taken in the handling and control of weapons. Weapons are for self-protection, guard duty and to combat the enemy. No cadre is permitted to carry a weapon in public unless permission has been granted by the higher authority. Cadres returning to T from the operational area are to hand their weapons back to their commanders. Weapons are not to be handled in a careless manner or to threaten innocent persons or in any way

that might endanger the peace, create controversy or adversely effect the name of the movement.

17. Any behaviour that brings the name of our movement into disrepute is counter revolutionary and will be punished.

TRIBUNAL

Contravention of this code of conduct, cases of indiscipline, will be brought before a tribunal. The tribunal is set up by the Senior Organ and is empowered to hear the case brought before it, and to pass judgement and sentence.

Document 102. "Unity and Determination of PAC Cadres Bring About Important Changes." Article in *Ikwezi,* number 16, March 1981 (abridged)

Radical and important changes at the last meeting of the Central Committee of the Pan Africanist Congress of Azania held in January last shows that the organization is well on its way towards re-organisation and re-structuring that portends well for its future. Among the major changes was the election of John Pokela as chairman. He is a founder member of the PAC and a close colleague of Sobukwe. He came out of the country to assume this important position.

An event of great significance was the return of the T. M. Ntantala group that formed the APRP [African People's Revolutionary Party] after their expulsion from the PAC at the Arusha Conference, to the fold of the PAC. The return of the former APRP members means the recognition of the Arusha Conference for the farce that it was. It is to be hoped that the talents and abilities of these members and particularly its leading elements will be properly deployed.

Another significant decision was the appointment of a six man Committee to attend to the preparations for the next PAC conference. This will ensure that there will be a properly constituted PAC conference for the first time in the history of the movement in exile which will reflect the genuine interests of the organisation and its rank and file. Three members of the cadre forces are on the Committee. This is also of great importance as for the first time a proper relationship is being established between the leadership and the cadre forces, based on unity, trust and confidence. In one bold stroke the PAC has made qualitative advances.

The PAC cadre forces must be congratulated for these very significant changes. It was their resolute struggle against Leballo and his clique that cleared the way for these changes. . . .

The main problem of the PAC lay with certain opportunist elements within the Central Committee and the cadre shafts were directed mainly against these elements in an effort to get a PAC leadership that is not only accountable to the rank and file but is also worthy of the name revolutionary in terms of prosecuting the struggle on the highest levels. The cadre movement has its roots in the influx of youth into the organisation following the Soweto uprising. They challenged and galvanised the old leadership, and while a section of it was temporarily deceived by Leballo's rhetoric, another section pursued the struggle on a much more mature level. They were able to learn from the mistakes of their colleagues and it was mainly through their instrumentality that Leballo was removed from the leadership of the PAC and finally expelled. . . .

The movement is sincerely concerned in seeing the PAC led by a responsible leadership so that it can also move ahead with its tasks at this crucial stage of the struggle. It is only natural that they are bound to make mistakes, taking into account their youthfulness. But thus far they have shown considerable political skill and maturity. They certainly have shown that they are not to be messed around. The courage and determination of the cadre forces has now paved the way for all those sincere and genuine elements in the PAC to return to the organisation and participate in its reorganisation. . . .

What are some of the major characteristics of Leballoism that afflicted the PAC for 20 years and almost destroyed it? Pre-eminently it was organised disorganisation and an anarchistic style of work. The greater the chaos and disarray the happier were the Leballoists which suited them very well. Under the cover of revolutionary rhetoric this ad hoc style of work maintained them in power. It also protected their particular cliquism where people were promoted onto the Central Committee because they were good lackeys. . . .

Struggle Between Left and Right

The drawing up a PAC Political Programme also poses some key problems as the history of the PAC-in-exile shows that there has always been a two-line struggle between Left and Right in the organisation with the Right invariably winning out, mainly because the Left always lacked an effective strategy and policies which in any case can be the only guarantee of their success in any situation. The history of the PAC is the history of most nationalist organisations in the Third World. At the outset most national liberation organisations start off from a nationalist position. But experience and political development soon moves them towards radical left positions. This has also been the experience of the PAC. The struggle between Left and Right inside the PAC took place over the "New Road to Revolution", a document that defined the Azanian struggle from a rigorous Marxist viewpoint. The Right eventually scored a victory (which has now turned out to be a Pyrrhic victory) over the Left at the [1978] Arusha Conference which led to the expulsion of a section of the PAC. . . . The facts of the two line struggle also reveals that the right wing elements have been involved with imperialist forces centering around the question of monies. On the leadership level the PAC has always had a problem with the narrowly nationalistic anti-communist types. It is from this point of view that the Basic Documents need to be updated in terms of giving a more precise definition to the relationship between race (the national struggle) and class. . . . [A]ny PAC Programme has not only to take up correct ideological positions but it must also be able to make a correct analysis of the situation and formulate correct tactics and strategy for the political and military struggle.

Democratic Centralism in PAC

The organised disorganisation also prevented the proper functioning of democratic centralism in both its aspects—centralism and democracy. The lack of centralism meant that there were no overall policies guiding the work of the PAC, so that the part was not related to the whole. This encouraged a situation of personal empire building where the prestige of the organisation and its resources were used more to build a particular individual rather than meeting the objective needs of the struggle and revolution. Representatives abroad were particularly guilty of this. In future all work undertaken on behalf of the PAC must be made accountable to the Central Committee and the rank and file members.

The question of democracy within the PAC is in itself a very serious question and one which is not always easy to achieve under the difficult conditions of exile since the organisation is cut off from its mass base. The question is just how are the C.C. members of the movement going to be made accountable to the rank and file. Who comprises the rank and file in exile. And equally important, how can the leadership indeed reflect the mass base, so that there is no contradiction and divorce between the leadership and the rank and file as has been all these years and which has been the principal cause of the revolutionary decline of the PAC-in-exile. There are of course a large number of PAC members abroad but many of them have atrophied over the years, many are of dubious political character, and there are no meaningful branches abroad. There is also the significant question of the quality of the leadership. The one significant base from which democracy can be imposed and the quality of the leadership maintained is the cadre base in Dar es Salaam. Almost invariably the cadre forces are closer to the needs of the struggle and the revolution than the leadership.

Need for New Constitutional Guidances

Related to the kind of Leballoist organised disorganisation is the important issue of constitutional guidances for the work of the PAC-in-exile, a point which was made by the cadre document. Obviously the old constitution as embodied in the Basic Documents, while befitting the internal conditions, restricts the work of the exile movement. Without proper constitutional guidances all manner of arbitrary actions can be taken and disruption caused as was the wont of Leballo in his exercise of Clause 14b.

These are some of the problems to which we feel the PAC must urgently address itself as it begins the process of re-organisation and re-structuring involving the entire PAC membership.

Document 103. "We Remember March 21—Pan Africanist Congress." Underground PAC flyer, March 1981

Revolutionary Greetings

Your heroic determination, your sacrifices, your courage are breaking the chains of slavery. You are the makers of Azania Revolution.

Workers and Peasants Unite

Africans Unite

Be an Africanist – Be an Africanist in Revolution – Be a Freedom Fighter

Our Aims

i) To wage an armed struggle for the complete liberation of Azania.
ii) To destroy the present fascist Pretoria regime. To replays it with the African Democratic Socialist State or Government.
iii) To destroy capitalism, tribalism, settlerism and colonialism.

Ma-Afrika war is the only answer to brutal oppression!!!
United We Stand, Unite We Win.
Amandla Ngawethu–Africa for Africans
One Africa, One Nation
Socialism is Justice

March 21 1960 - March 21 1981

21 years of bloodshed and brutality. The brutality continues to today.

From more than 90 who died in 1960, with 69 in Sharpeville, to the hundreds who died in 1976 Africa's cry for total liberation from the conquerors continues.

The path of bloodshed is soaked, with the deaths of Mangaliso Sobukwe, Steve Biko, Mapetla Mohapi, and the hundreds that have died.

The racist's path of bloodshed, vying with Nazi Germany's trail of inhumanity, will be brought to a shocking halt, with victory on our side.

March 21, 1960 was the day when Sobukwe (may his soul rest in peace) led the Pan Africanist Congress in protest against the inhuman pass laws.

The reply from the conquerors was bullets. The bullets still fly today. Every cry for justice we make is met with bullets.

March 21, 1960 shook South Africa to its foundations. The next event in our bloodsoaked but glorious march to freedom will be Mother Africa's final regurgitation of the racists from her sacred land—Azania.

When PAC threw the gauntlet down, many responded, some died, some wavered, some sold out. This pattern continues.

The time has now come for you to decide, are you with the people, or against them.

The focal point in 1960 was Sharpeville, the focal point tomorrow will be the entire country.

The call will come, be ready for it.

THE STRUGGLE CONTINUES

DOCUMENT 104. "Decisions of the ANC National Executive Committee, Luanda, 2–5 December 1981." ANC memorandum

SPECIAL SESSION:
1. Leaders should correct one another or other comrades in good time. This will assist comrades; delays in this respect destroy comrades.
2. Heads of Departments should submit reports regularly at interval of three months. These will be available to all NEC members for study and information.
3. Promotion of young comrades done too quickly. Promotion or appointments should be on merits.
4. All allegations against leaders must be seriously considered and those that are found to be true must be corrected.
5. There must be accountability of all members of various departments to make sure that each member is briefed about work of others.
6. NEC and Working Committee (WC) must ensure implementation of decisions.
7. NEC/WC should respond to RC [Revolutionary Council] reports and communications.
8. Headquarters [Lusaka] should ensure the presence of a core of NEC members constituting the WC at all times at Headquarters.
9. Leaders should go to the forward areas and meet people from home. RC is instructed to arrange a programme of visits by NEC members.
10. NEC should define the task of each member of the Committee in order to avoid accumulation of tasks on a few comrades.
11. NEC members stationed in the forward areas to brief NEC/WC regularly on their work with SO [senior organ] and the home-front.
12. The NEC/WC should discuss at great length the Craig Williamson allegations of infiltrating ANC. All relevant reports on the issue to be made available to NEC/WC for study and discussion. Comrade Mzwai [Piliso] to collect information. Time limit end of February 1982.
13. NEC should always remain a cohesive body united [and] respecting and implementing its own decisions. Administrative Secretary to bring to NEC/WC non-implementation of decisions.
14. ANC has one leadership which includes leaders who are at home and abroad.
15. Question on open membership is to be thrown open for discussion within ANC ranks both inside and outside the country. Comrade Secretary-General to report back in six months time.
16. The relevance or otherwise of the RC. If changes are necessary then proper preparation should be made. WC should prepare very carefully for such a discussion.
17. Comrade Florence Mophosho to report on departments' shortage of personnel. Comrade to report back end of December 1981. JJ [Josiah Jele] volunteered to assist her.

18. Leaders—WC to report back to ordinary members on the numerous allegations raised.
19. NEC/WC to study the question of elections and to decide how to handle this question.
20. RC must look into the question of how the old comrades are to be rehabilitated. This applies to those who are unemployed.

21. *TRIBALISM*
    (a) ANC should root out tribalism out of its vocabulary even as a word. We should use such positive words as nationalities. NEC noted that tribalism exists outside South Africa and is being used.
    (b) ANC should educate its members to the dangers of tribalism.
    (c) Need to learn the various languages spoken by South African people.
    (d) ANC should study the phenomenon of tribalism and its various manifestations. We should work out the strategy of destroying it.

22. *REVIEW COMMITTEE:* NEC decided on the need to have a tribunal to look at cases after investigations. The Review Committee then will look at cases that have ultimate [death] sentence. There will be cases that are referred to it by *Tribunal*.
    (a) RC instructed to recommend the composition of the tribunal to the WC.
    (b) All cases below the ultimate sentence will be handled and completed by Tribunal.
    (c) Tribunal to work out a system of sentences for the various crimes.
    (d) In the meantime it is decided that the Review Committee should handle the work of both the tribunal and Review Committee.

23. *AWARDS COMMITTEE*
    (a) The Awards Committee should be a national one. Its members are not necessarily NEC members.
    (b) *Sub-Committee*: President, Secretary-General, T. More [Joe Modise], JP [John Pule Motshabi] and Jack Simons. Convenor JP.

24. *Mazimbu*:
    (a) National Commissar to look into the question of Assistant to Arthur in Mazimbu [Solomon Mahlangu Freedom College].
    (b) The Treasury to look into the question of vacations for the children.
    (c) On staffing: SG [Secretary General] should create an organ for finding teachers for Mazimbu.
    (d) Dakawa: National Commissar to go to Dakawa [non-military settlement] for the opening of the place.

25. *Conference of Youth*: WC to arrange without delay the Conference of the youth in order to reconstitute the Youth Section and create a strong Youth Secretariat.

26. *SECURITY SITUATION:*
    (a) Need to develop new places like T [Mozambique] to handle infiltrators. This to be handled by RC and NAT [ANC security department].
    (b) NAT to handle question of car-smuggling and Economic Sabotage. Time limit—Report not later than March.

27. *FINANCE COMMITTEE*
    (a) TG [Treasurer General] with Economists at Headquarters: TG directed to convene meeting with Economists at Headquarters like Thabo [Mbeki], Nkokheli [Simon Makana], [Joe] Nhlanhla, Magapatona, Siza [Sigxashe] to discuss ways and means to handle Treasury.
    (b) *Commission on TQ* [Mozambique-Swaziland] *Funds*: The ANC delegation led by SG is directed to look into the question of Funds. The same delegation to call Chris [Hani] or Lehlohonolo [Lambert Moloi] to sort out Island's [Lesotho's] funds.

28. *WOMEN'S SECTION*:
    (a) The Women's Section to be headed by a member of the NEC.
    (b) Comrade Gertrude Shope co-opted into the NEC.
    (c) WC to work out the tasks of the Women's Section.

29. *Committee of 5 on NEC work*: To report back in March.
30. WC to meet SACTU [SA Congress of Trade Unions] Tuesday the 7th to discuss collaboration and funds.

31. *ON 70TH ANNIVERSARY*
    (a) International support of the ANC on the 70th Anniversary should feed on internal support and work done.
    (b) Agreed to JK [?] invitation of Rev. [James] Calata and Selby Msimang—Founding Fathers of ANC to USA.
    (c) Films: ANC agreed to Films on Camps for Archives
    (d) ANC [to] accept offer of GDR [German Democratic Republic] in principle but the timing to be worked out.

BN [Beyers Naude] *GROUP:*
32. NEC directed WC to discuss whole question of BN Group with all documents collected. Also to hold joint discussion with RC.
33. SO in London reporting to RC Headquarters.

DOCUMENTS FOR CHAPTER 4   509

CHURCH FRONT: The church sub-committee of WC to report to WC on the Church front and Church Conference held in Lusaka. Also matter to be discussed jointly by WC and RC. Deadline 3rd week of December.

34. Sub-committee of WC on personnel of offices to report to WC.
35. WC to settle question of Rep in P [Botswana] and number of persons allowed. SACTU's needs to be accommodated.
36. President to meet KK [Kenneth Kaunda, Zambian president] on ANC Headquarters.
37. Materials of ANC to be evacuated out.
38. Need for dispersal of cadres in view of security situation. NAT to work out contingency plans.
39. *Madagascar:* NEC agreed on exchange to save six condemned comrades. Matter to be handled with Government not lawyer. WC to send delegation very urgently.

40. *GENERAL:*
    Review Committee to decide sentence on Bocibo, Joel Klaas and Wellington, etc., case.
41. *SAMRAF:* London Resistance Group to assist and handle SAMRAF [SA Military Refugee Aid Fund].
42. *Derecognition of PAC:* Jele and [Johnny] Makatini to work out strategy of derecognition of PAC. This to be tabled before WC for consideration.
43. Every session of NEC must discuss an internal Report of RC.
44. NEC/WC to recall some senior comrades inside for internal work outside. Not all but some.
45. RC to recruit people specifically like workers and peasants. RC to report within three months.
46. International Department to have young comrades in offices understudying Chief Reps. Training on the job. Report within three months.
47. Radio stations to be manned by people at leadership level.
48. *Contributions by Working ANC members:*
    (a) Working members of the ANC should contribute monthly to ANC [financially]. This to be fixed.
    (b) ANC reserves the right to call out of jobs for fulltime work working ANC members.
49. RC Headquarters should have a uniform system of briefing forward areas so that the SO's should brief people from home in the same voice.
50. Our people should be informed about members of the NEC.
51. Propaganda inside should use cassettes more frequently.
52. *On Joe Nhlanhla:*
    (a) Joe Nhlanhla co-opted into the NEC.
    (b) Joe Nhlanhla remains Administrative-Secretary.
53. RC with NAT to work out contingency plans for protecting Residences and Camps. SO's to do the same.

DOCUMENT 105. "Background to the Tanzanian Repression of PAC and APLA." Statement by supporters of P. K. Leballo in Britain, January 16, 1982

The Tanzanian Government of Julius Nyerere has been attempting to coerce PAC, and APLA [Azanian People's Liberation Army] for the last three years for a number of reasons. Firstly there is the personal animosity for Leballo felt by Nyerere himself. Secondly there are American imperialist pressures which offer money for political meddling on their behalf and thirdly there is a fear of the nature of PAC itself.

Ever since Leballo came to lead the PAC in exile he has been under attack from bourgeois colleagues in PAC and their sympathisers because he is not a graduate and appeals mostly to ordinary people throughout the continent. He despises alcohol and socialising and is considered an embarrassment by the self-styled sophisticated intellectual leaders who pass themselves off as the true leaders of Africa. His outspokenness against totalitarianism and the cynical use of peasants, workers and guerrilla forces to place bourgeoisie in power who then terminate all constitutional methods through which they can be removed, has caused Leballo to be disliked in many quarters where African leaders have acquired wealth and luxury, or, like Nyerere, an intellectual monopoly and unchallenged domain where entire populations can be manipulated in social experimentation with hideous results. Leballo earned (ironically) great displeasure for saving Nyerere [in 1970] from the [Oscar] Kambona plot and also for criticising the recognition of "South Africa" as a sovereign state.

When [Henry] Kissinger proposed that Tanzania should be paid off in order to put pressure on liberation movements to enter detente and dialogue, Leballo fiercely resisted. The Zimbabwe movements were forced to enter discussions with their enemies and eventually took over a country which they hardly controlled. Tanzania was tottering on the brink of financial collapse and appeased Kissinger by curbing liberation movements through its control of the OAU Liberation Committee and funds, and by talking of "giving South Africa five years in which to change," a slogan renewed on its expiry last year. The Americans wanted a reformist or diplomat as PAC leader. On the death of [Robert] Sobukwe in restriction, Leballo was elected PAC leader in 1978 at Arusha. The Americans, Tanzanians and the SACP-ANC backed [David] Sibeko, the PAC UN representative and bon viveur. The Tanzanians threatened Leballo when he objected to PAC arms being taken by the Tanzanian People's Defence force for use against Uganda. These arms, donated by the Libyans, decimated the Ugandan tank corps and airforce. The Tanzanians backed Sibeko in a coup when Leballo was away from Tanzania. The coup failed and APLA killed Sibeko. The Tanzanians put forward Vus Make and shot dead nine APLA soldiers at Chunya, wounding over 40 more, on March 11th 1980 when APLA refused to accept Make, who had already met the Acting ANC leader Oliver Tambo and Bantustan puppet of American imperialism [Chief M. G.] Buthelezi in Nigeria and racist leader John Vorster in Liberia for discussions on turning the revolutionary PAC and APLA into a conference pawn.

The Tanzanians then brought John Nyathi Pokela up from Lesotho, thinking a Robben Island prisoner would be an ideal leader for acceptance, overlooking Pokela's elimination of PAC activists in the Western Cape during the Poqo Rising, murders which have still to be investigated. APLA refused to accept Pokela and attacked the PAC office in Dar es Salaam on the 14th April 1981 beating up Pokela's supporters and wrecking equipment. The Tanzanians brought Pokela to Zimbabwe to demand that Leballo, directing APLA and PAC in Salisbury [Harare], should be expelled. The Zimbabweans advised Leballo to leave, declaring that Nyerere's prestige as an elder statesman, and the Tanzanian manipulation of the OAU liberation committee and its funds, combining with the Tanzanian role as leader of the "front line states" made it almost impossible to resist.

The "London club" politicians in Zimbabwe, the Mercedes Benz, swimming pool, easy mortgage, tennis court set, also disliked Leballo's close relationship with Edgar Tekere, the ZANU (PF) Secretary-General, Flight-Lieutenant Jerry Rawlings of Ghana and the Libyan leader Colonel [Muammar] Gaddafy. Zimbabwe was under pressure from the Boers to limit Liberation armies' activities and Leballo was associated with those who criticised this craven acquiescence, saying that if the Boers were given "five years in which to change" they would not stay idle but would perfect methods of annihilation of human life north of the Limpopo and certainly give no chance to Black states to build up their strength for a confrontation. The "London Club" urged acceptance of the ANC strategy of conducting sabotage of installations and killing black collaborators, rather than white soldiers, in the hope that constant newspaper publicity and support for reform in "South Africa" would result in UN sanctions, moderate US support for limited change, constitutional talks and the imposition of the SACP-ANC as the "government" of "South Africa" totally reliant on the existing administration and its expertise, with wealth and power being given to those hacks that had gratefully played the game as black mouthpieces for Joe Slovo's SACP white activists, who can never be accepted at the ballot box.

The PAC should therefore have an emasculated leadership put on it which would talk of unity with the ANC and advocate detente and dialogue, polite words for the continued exploitation of Azanians under different faces. Happily the courage of APLA has weathered three years and three puppet leaders. APLA must never be disarmed. Give Azanians weapons and let them free themselves. Nyerere, we shall never accept your puppets. IZWE LETHU! [Our land!]

PAC Mission to UK and Eire
16 January 1982

Document 106. Excerpts from "South Africa's Impending Socialist Revolution: Perspective of the Marxist Workers' Tendency of the African National Congress," London, March 1982

[A] democratic society cannot arise and survive in South Africa on the foundations of capitalism. There can be no genuinely democratic state in our country unless the state of the racist and capitalist dictatorship is dismantled, shattered, "smashed"—to use the term of Marx—and the economic basis of society transformed. A "democratic state" in South Africa can be none other than a state in transition to socialism—*a state of workers' democracy*.

For all the efforts of middle-class theoreticians, the democratic aspirations of the working people cannot be accommodated in a separate historical "stage" of "national democracy", leaving the socialist tasks of the revolution unfulfilled. This reality of our struggle is inescapable and does not depend on the willingness of political leaders to recognise it. It follows from the inner laws of the productive system—capitalism in its epoch of senile decay. It rests on the class structure of our society and the relentless action of class forces upon each other, which can no more be ordered to halt than the wind and the waves. The general historical explanation for this reality has been most brilliantly set out, many years ago, in the works of Trotsky on the theory of permanent revolution. . . .

Because the two-stage idea is put forward today in the name of "Communism", it possesses an immense potential power to confuse and divide the working class. . . .

We must oppose any attempt to separate the struggle for democracy from the struggle for workers' power. It is the task of the working class to unite all the oppressed around its own organised strength and action. It is the task of all comrades of the ANC, and of all revolutionaries in the ranks of the trade unions and the youth and community organisations, to work to build the forces of the working class as the conscious basis of the democratic movement against the regime. . . .

The "alliance of democrats", much discussed in South Africa over the past year, is presented as a front of black workers, youth and middle class, together with democratic-minded whites. To such a combination of forces a number of workers' organisations have readily given support. . . . Nevertheless, it is not working-class organisations and leaders who *predominate* in the "democratic alliance", but leaders of the middle class. Aided by platforms provided by the Church, the press, etc., they define the aims of the movement solely in "democratic" terms. They assert the possibility of a negotiated settlement of the conflict in South Africa, and call for the support of the people solely to this end. . . .

Building the ANC

The central strategic and political task before us is summed up in the slogan advanced by [the MWT journal] *Inqaba ya Basebenzi*: *"Build a mass ANC on a socialist programme!"* It is only as a mass organisation, above all as an organisation of the black working class, that the ANC will be able to marshal the forces for the eventual armed overthrow of the racist and capitalist state. It is only on a clear socialist programme that the ANC will be able to maintain the unity of the working class and all the oppressed in action, and carry through the transformation of society on which our liberation depends.

In South Africa today there is a huge gravitation of popular support among the oppressed towards the ANC. Its flag is raised at mass meetings and funerals; its imprisoned and exiled leadership is publicly honoured; its programme is openly quoted and extolled. To understand the basis of this support, and to translate it into concrete organisation, we have first to confront an historical paradox.

In the re-awakening of the political movement of the 1970s, which was spear-headed by the youth, the ANC was not to the fore. In fact the youth were distinctly critical of the ANC at that time. They pointed to its origins as an organisation of conservative, middle-class Africans which devoted itself to petitioning for equal rights. Although the ANC had gained a mass following by the 1950s, the youth looked back on the decades of previous struggles and associated the ANC with the defeats suffered in those days. They also noted the absence of effective underground ANC organisation from the country since the mid-1960s. And when, in 1976, they marched into the teeth of gunfire from the police, they asked why the ANC, after 15 years of preparing armed struggle, was not able to provide arms for the defence of the movement.

Yet, in the course of the last five years, while the curve of the Black Consciousness movement has plummeted, the popular following of the ANC has shown a meteoric rise. While the inadequacies of all the middle-class leaders active within the movement in South Africa have been increasingly exposed in the mounting waves of mass action, the acclaim for leaders jailed and exiled by the regime has risen steadily.

There are a number of factors combining to produce support for the ANC. But at the root of it all is an historical law which is working itself out also in most, if not all, capitalist countries. This is that, when the mass of the workers turn to struggle, they turn first to the established, traditional organisations associated with their struggle in the past. The main reason for this is the need for the means of uniting their forces in action. In South Africa as much as anywhere, the workers understand that without unity they cannot conquer. The working people have need of *one political organisation* in which their forces may combine. It is not a sentimental but a practical matter. The black working people of South Africa have no alternative but to go to the ANC and make it their rallying point.

The ANC is chosen precisely because of its long history and because of the mass following it gained in the 1950s and early 1960s. It is chosen because, in the years since, in comparison with its rivals, it has maintained its cohesion and political continuity. It is chosen for the very reason that its leaders are jailed and exiled; that it is persecuted by the enemy; and that it has been seen to make no compromise with the oppressor. And it is chosen as the foremost of the organisations which have recognised the need to prepare armed force for the struggle against the regime. . . .

A careful consideration of the policies put forward by the ANC leadership indicates that they have not adequately come to grips with the objective character of the South African revolution, and do not put forward the task of overthrowing the bourgeoisie. A major influence in this regard has been the erroneous approach of the leadership of the South Africa CP. The programme of the Communist Party, adopted in 1962 and still its programme today, shows how deeply rooted the CP leadership has remained in the ideas of "two stages", despite all experience. . . .

In later writings, particularly by the more left-leaning of the CP leaders, we find formulations which on the surface may seem indistinguishable from the ideas of permanent revolution. Most influential of these writers has been Joe Slovo, whose approach is echoed from time to time in the pages of *The African Communist*. . . . But what is notable about comrade Slovo's article is that he refuses to put forward the concept of a *workers' state* and is not prepared to abandon the "national democratic state" formulation of the CP programme and other texts. . . .

Comrades in the South Africa CP ought to draw these questions to the attention of their fellows, and insist on clarification from the Party leadership. So far the leadership has shown itself completely unwilling to break with the two-stage theory and all its implications, because they have remained cemented within the international tradition of Stalinism. This is a problem which the rank-and-file of the South Africa CP will find themselves increasingly having to confront.

Any political approach which fails to come to terms with the need for workers' power unavoidably leaves a cover for attempts to compromise with the bourgeoisie. *The acute danger of this, especially in a country like South Africa, is that compromise with the bourgeoisie will also mean compromise with the bourgeois state machinery, and will leave the most dangerous forces of reaction undestroyed.* . . .

This is the epoch of world revolution. In every sector of the globe—in the advanced capitalist countries, in the ex-colonial world still in the grip of capitalism, and in the deformed workers' states of Stalinism—the great bulk of the population are moving or beginning to move on the road of revolution.

This is the epoch of transition from capitalism to socialism on a world scale, holding the prospect of the greatest advances in human history. Our revolution in South Africa is part and parcel of this wider process. . . . Let us rise consciously to the tasks posed by history, and with all our energies prepare.

Document 107. "Summary Report of the Discussion on Open Membership." Solomon Mahlangu Freedom College, Mazimbu, Tanzania, May 15, 1982

The discussants of this question first posed the questions: Why did the NEC [ANC National Executive Committee] decide to pose the question of Open Membership now? Is it time to consider the question of Open Membership now? Are there any changes of attitude in the white community towards our struggle?

Figure 22. Students at the ANC's Solomon Mahlangu Freedom College (SOMAFCO) in Mazimbu, Tanzania, studying for a test, mid-1980s. *UWC-Robben Island Museum Mayibuye Archives*

However, the necessity to discuss the question was recognized since, it was realised, the enemy is trying to win the Coloured and Indian populations over, a question that was discussed by COSAS [Congress of SA Students] as early as 1979. Also, there is a growing militancy at home of members of all national groups fighting side by side against the common enemy.

The common point of departure of the discussants was that it should be understood that if the ANC decides at any stage to opt for Open Membership and its top organs, say the NEC, become populated by members of various national groups, it should be understood that those members will not be representing the interests of their respective national groups; rather they are in those structures to protect the interests of, and advance the struggle of the struggling peoples of South Africa.

There were two dominating and opposed views on the topic, the view that membership should be open to all national groups and the view that membership should not be open to all. In both cases elaborate reasons were advanced. The other view was a minority view and was not elaborated on at any length. This was the view that membership should be open to all national groups, excepting the whites.

Reasons for Open Membership
1. A provision for Open Membership is made in the 1958 ANC Constitution, Clause One of which states that "membership shall be open to any person

above the age of 18, who accepts its principles, policy and program and is prepared to abide by its constitution and rules".
2. Open Membership does not automatically mean that whites will go to the NEC. This was brought to allay the fears of those who feared that Open Membership will ipso facto qualify white comrades for the NEC. People are elected into positions because of their capabilities.
3. Open Membership will show that people are united at home and abroad in their struggle against injustice. This is evidenced by the reaction of the people of all groups to the death of a white political activist, Dr Neil Aggett.
4. The military wing of the ANC, Umkhonto we Sizwe, has long opened its doors to all national groups.
5. Open Membership will offer the strategic advantage of enabling the ANC to explore other avenues and spheres of operation in areas hitherto exclusively meant for whites.
6. Collective political experience in the struggle will make it easy to build a non-racial society which the ANC will strive to inaugurate after our liberation. This is what the Freedom Charter advocates when it states, "South Africa belongs to all who live in it, Black and White."
7. Open Membership will accelerate the escalation of conflicts within the white community, and this will be to our advantage. Already this has happened when Wits [University of the Witwatersrand] and UCT [University of Cape Town] students publicly burned the South African flag and hoisted in its place the black, green and gold [ANC flag].
8. The paradox that whites can oppose the system but are not allowed to join the ANC can be used by the enemy to gain the confidence and support of those whites who oppose the system at home. Recently we have seen a number of conscientious objectors who refuse to take up arms against the so-called terrorists. All the whites who have adopted a similar stance against the enemy should be allowed, should they desire, to join the ANC.
9. The whites who join the ANC are not just sympathetic to the just black cause, they do so on the basis of a firm conviction. They looked at their long-term interests which are not protected by the present system and also realise that their short term interests are protected by the system for only a short time. In order to realise their long-term interests they have to fight side by side with the oppressed African majority.
10. The ANC enjoys support at home from all sectors of the South African society, black and white, and its aims are accepted. This can be seen from the public response to the anti-Republic campaign of 1981 which was called by the ANC. Further evidence is provided by the support of the Free-Mandela campaign started by the *Post*. This indicates that the people of South Africa recognise the ANC as their future government. Furthermore the statistics of the opinion poll which was conducted by the *Rand Daily Mail* as to the most popular organization in the South African Revolution, tell their own story. Revolutionaries of all national groups have a

role in our struggle and can contribute maximally in our struggle as full members of the ANC.

Consequences of Open Membership

Is Open Membership likely to cause a split within the ANC? Let us look at the splits that the organization has up to now suffered.

a) In 1959 some individuals broke away to form the PAC. This was caused by their opposition to the adoption of the Freedom Charter by the ANC as part of its program.

b) The Group of 8 broke away in [1975], rejecting the inclusion of all national groups in our ranks.

Both splits came about as a result of a narrow-minded and chauvinistic perspective of the nature of the South African struggle on the part of the individuals involved. They were rejecting the program of the ANC. By getting rid of them the ANC strengthened rather than weakened its position as it purged itself of reactionary elements.

Fears of division when membership is open to all should therefore not be entertained. Our sister organizations like SACTU [SA Congress of Trade Unions] and the SACP have open membership and history has assured us that such a step will not have disastrous consequences in the ANC.

Conclusion on this View

Open Membership will show that the ANC is developing with the times and is not a narrow minded and a conservative nationalistic organization.

The decision of the 1969 Morogoro Conference was arrived at after a sober assessment and analysis of the objective conditions. The situation has not remained static since 1969. Instead we have seen people of all groups coming together against the common enemy. This marks a qualitative change for the better in the political consciousness of the masses. Above all Open Membership does not contradict the fundamental policy of the ANC, rather it is towards the realisation of the Freedom Charter.

Reasons Against Open Membership

1. There has not been enough political mobilisation done on the masses. They are not yet ready for the inclusion of whites in our ranks and they identify oppression with a white skin rather than with the system.
2. The black and white workers of South Africa have not as yet recognized their common class interests. The death of Dr Neil Aggett should not be seen as a yardstick of heightened political consciousness on the part of the masses, though it is an indication of the level of political consciousness of the masses.
3. People in the rural areas have hardly been mobilised to a point where they can even consider the question of open membership.
4. It is recognised and accepted by the non-African members of the ANC that Africans, being in the majority of the oppressed people, should lead in the struggle. Africans should take the lead to liberate themselves.

Repercussions of open membership
1. Loss of support of present membership.
2. Open membership will confuse the masses at home.
3. May cause splits within our ranks.
4. The principles enshrined in the Freedom Charter will best be implemented after liberation. However this does not mean that the topic should be closed forever for discussion but more political work and mobilisation has to be done. The time has not yet come, conditions are not yet ripe for open membership.

Reasons for opening membership to Indians and Coloureds but not to whites

The activities of the Coloureds and Indians in the past years has shown that they are together with the Africans in the fight against oppression. Therefore membership should be open to them at all levels. This has not been observed in the white community.

Though membership should be open to other national groups, this has to be done with provisos: key positions in the higher organs of the organisation should be preserved for Africans only.

The President's position

The President symbolizes the nation and must be an African since the main content of our struggle is the liberation of the Africans. The people have not yet been mobilised to the extent where they can accept a white president.

Other key positions

Key positions like those of the Secretary General, Treasurer General and National Commissar should also be preserved for Africans only as they have a mobilising effect on the masses. Their preservation for Africans will reflect the African character of our struggle.

Document 108. Statement by Santo, 26-year-old ANC exile who survived Maseru raid of December 9, 1982

During 1980-81, I was detained for nine months. I had read *Sechaba* at home and had listened to Freedom Radio calling on workers to join the struggle. Knowing that my mother and my brother were going to be hurt by my activities, I decided to leave the country.

I knew several comrades when I arrived in Maseru on 11 September 1982, and within two days I was taken to Cuba House. Six comrades were already living there. I was quickly absorbed into the regular discussions that took place at Cuba. Vasta, one of those massacred, led discussions on our history, on topical subjects and on radio programmes. Those who could afford newspapers, shared them with us.

We were a happy family. When new comrades joined us, they brought news from home or an area we had heard of, but one story in common was the story of our oppression. Those from the Transkei spoke of the detentions there, from Soweto, the detentions of friends, and in Port Elizabeth, the manner in which industrial disputes between employer and employee become the arena for the police and the army. Each one taught us and we politicised each other. Those who joined the group would be shy in group discussions, but within a week we would see a big change.

I awoke when Vasta came in at 11.00 p.m. but went back to sleep. I woke suddenly when bullets were fired into our room. We took cover. The four on the bed—Santo [myself], Arrah, Vasta and Vido—jumped to the floor. After five minutes all was quiet. The door was not locked, there was no key. The door opened gently and when half opened, Arrah, who was closest, kicked it. But the soldier put his hand around and the shooting started.

We had no lights and the intruder came in with a torch. No grenades were thrown into the room, but explosions came from the kitchen, pantry and the bathroom. The first man shot me in the shoulder and his torch went off. I rolled into the corner under the window with my head under the bed and I covered myself with the clothes we had worn the previous day.

Arrah tried to get up and fight but he was shot and he fell. Two comrades had jumped out of the window but I was too afraid to move.

They picked up the bed to remove the suitcases. They threw the empty bags over me and some clothes while they were searching for documents. One searched while the other stood at the door shouting at us: 'Die, freedom fighters.' The fellow inside spoke in English while the fellow at the door had a Portuguese accent.

It seemed an age lying there. I knew my ear was exposed but I dared not lift my hand to cover it, as I would draw attention to myself. So I stayed there, not feeling the pain of my shoulder and breathing very gently. I wasn't sure when they left the room but there was a great fire and many explosions outside. I lay for about three hours in one spot.

At one stage I heard them dragging the comrades and counting them. It is possible that they photographed my comrades, as there was a bright light in the room. But that could have come from the explosions. I crept up to the door where my comrades were. I felt their bodies and they were cold and still. No-one breathed, there were no pulses, they lay there, their wounds gaping. Vasta and Arrah were there.

On peering outside, I saw a motor-car and ran back for cover. When all was still, I looked through the window and heard another blast. I took cover again. It was quiet for some time, no explosion, no raucous violent voices; English, Portuguese or Afrikaans. I went to the door. It was daylight. The shack, the car and the kitchen were burning.

I felt my comrades again, hoping in the pile at the door that one would be, like me, injured not dead. But no-one spoke when I called. "Vasta," I cried, "speak to me!" But they looked blankly. Softly, I called out their names, hoping one would answer. They were cold, all of them. I shook them and their hands, legs and heads fell clumsily around me. Arrah, Vasta, Samson, Vido, Dumi, Elso and Toto.

I was alone. I decided to run out as fast as I could in the direction of a comrade's place down the opposite road. I was in my underpants, cold and bleeding. When I reached the place, there was smoke and fire. I looked in and saw two comrades burning. I was scared and the fire was so intense that I could not remove their bodies from the fire.

I knocked on another comrade's door and he quietened me down and gingerly opened the door. They gave me no painkillers, only a blanket to lay on the floor. The pain was ghastly and I could not sleep.

At 6.00 a.m. a comrade arrived in a taxi, checking on all of us. He took me to the hospital, where I found Mandu from Cuba and Trinity.

DOCUMENT 109. Presentation by unidentified speaker to ANC seminar on women's political participation, Tanzania, 1982

This seminar was inspired by the speech the President of the African National Congress made at the closing of the first ANC Women's Section Conference in exile at Luanda, People's Republic of Angola, in September last year. That speech is available in the [ANC journal] *Sechaba* of December last year. In his speech at that occasion, the President cde [comrade] O.R. Tambo, had the following to say, and I quote:

> On the other hand, the women in the ANC should stop behaving as if there was no place for them above the level of certain categories of involvement. They have a duty to liberate us men from antique concepts and attitudes about the place and role of women in society and development and direction of our revolutionary struggle.

Inspired by these words, comrades, especially the words, "they have a duty to liberate us men from antique concepts and attitudes about the place and role of women in society and development", I would like to particularly address myself to the question of *attitudes* and in so doing I will talk about both men and women's attitudes.

It is a fact that tradition has made women think of themselves as inferior and less intelligent and therefore less competent than men in all spheres of life except those that women have been traditionally assigned to excel in. This concept of women's inferiority is still very strong amongst ANC women and it manifests itself in the following manner:

1. Lack of interest in attending political meetings such as those of the Women's Section general meetings, RPC [regional political committee] unit meetings, political and other seminars.
2. Inability and sometimes ability but lack of confidence in taking part in political and other discussions due to this complex and due to the lack of information on the various subjects.
3. Greater importance attached to personal interests than to demands of the present phase and even post independence phase of our struggle. This applies to men as well, but I will at this stage limit myself to women. What

I mean here is the fact that we have in the ANC a great need for qualified personnel in various fields—secretaries, primary secondary and nursery school teachers, catering officers, etc. etc. In fact all these needs of our struggle should be fulfilled by both men and women. The ANC gives large numbers of scholarships every six months or so to people of different levels of education and commitment but the tendency is to want to qualify or study in a certain field for personal fulfillment and not filling up the dire needs of our liberation movement.

4. Lastly, when discussing non-political attitudes of women I would like to mention the fact that there are those who will not pick up a *Sechaba* or a *News Briefing* because they are too busy with "other things". Those other things are usually washing, cooking, baking etc. How do we advance our kind i.e. the weaker sex if we do not develop the interest in finding out what is happening in the world? What is the direction of our liberation struggle and therefore where do we as women, as freedom-fighters, as revolutionaries, where do we fit in? How does one take a stand against anything or for anything if one is not at all informed about the very subject?

Having put forth the attitudes of women towards themselves, I would like to attempt to outline some of the attitudes of men, i.e. ANC men, towards women in regard to the women's place and their role in society and development and direction of our revolutionary struggle.

In most societies, and certainly ours, women far outnumber men. This therefore means a society whose women play only the secondary roles, are illiterate, ignorant and generally backwards, is a backward society for two reasons:

1) half the nation itself is backward i.e. if women form half the population
2) the women, as the people who are the first educators of children in their capacity as mothers transfer their backwardness and their ignorance to the children they bring up. This is regardless of whether the children will receive a good education at a later stage or not. After all, their parents, especially the mother will always have some influence on the child's upbringing.

This leads me to making the following points:

1. Men in the ANC are satisfied (except at the school, i.e. Somafco) with the non-involvement of women in the political arena. They seem to want us to be perpetually in the kitchen. Our relations with them are jeopardized if we attend first to the non-domestic affairs and are late or unable to perform to perfection the domestic work that awaits us.
2. In some instances, women suffer from starvation if they are down with malaria. This simply happens because male comrades believe that under no circumstances will they even fry an egg for a woman.
3. Some men refuse to accept the leadership and authority of women, i.e. it would appear they support that the lady comrade is senior to them in authority but in practice they would never take her instructions.
4. Women are always called to support men in the struggle and not to them-

selves advance. I believe that if our men were psychologically liberated from the old concepts about the role and place of women some of these attitudes would not be heard of. Just as it is the duty of women to liberate men from the old concepts of the rule and place of women in society so it is the duty of men i.e. progressive men to help and encourage women to shed off their complexes about their place being in the kitchen and to participate fully in the decision-making bodies of our movement, in the building of the kind of cadre that is worthy of our struggle and in the building up of our community for the seizure of power and later for reconstruction.

It is one of the tasks of the Women's Section to mobilise women politically. This is a task of both men and women but most of all of women. Without the support from our men, even in our personal dealing with them, women will find it harder and harder to turn back the clock of history and to advance the tasks set before us whether here or in South Africa, today or tomorrow.

Document 110. Minutes of meeting of South African Communist Party Unit 7, Lusaka, September 15, 1983 (abridged)

Present: GS [General Secretary Moses Mabhida], Goodie, Evie, Hal
Absent: [John] Nkadimeng; Cuthbert (on mission) 14.40 [hours]

Goodie welcomed GS. . . .

GS replied, expressing his own satisfaction. In every region visited he tried to exchange views with at least one unit such as this. The P [Party] began at the unit level; without units the Centre could not function.

He told us about the forthcoming meeting of the CC [central committee] and its proposed agenda. A major item was the changing situation at home.

Our activity as a P could have little meaning unless it reflected actual conditions inside. Efforts were being made to reconstruct the P at home. . . . Our P made a great contribution to the formation of African trade unions and has kept contact with the workers. We are now required to strengthen the links and make our presence felt in the rising tide of workers' resistance at home.

Our relations with the ANC have also stood the test of time but should be reviewed and reinforced at all times.

Comrade [USSR's Yuri] Andropov's statement of May 1983 drew attention to problems that had arisen in some fraternal parties notably in Poland. (GS recalled that similar weaknesses appeared in the parties of Hungary in 1956 and Czechoslovakia in 1968.) The weaknesses reflected unsound ideology and stressed the importance of a high level of theory.

Our P was in an even more difficult situation being surrounded by nationalism. If we fail to develop correct Marxist-Leninist outlook we shall be overcome by nationalist attitudes and values.

Our concern is with giving members a correct understanding of Marxist-Leninist theory. Few of us can go to a P school. We must acquire our knowledge within the units and classes organized by the Region committee.

We should take note of experiences in some African countries—Tanzania and Kenya are examples—which achieved independence with the assistance of the working class but had no working class party. This was a great weakness. As a result the workers benefited far less from independence than they deserved.

Our position is stronger; yet we cannot assume that ANC will always have a positive attitude to us. It is highly necessary to strengthen the P so that it can give correct leadership. In Vietnam Buddhist priests were mobilised by the resistance. SA could similarly produce a Christian nationalist party in opposition to ourselves; we should take note of the role of churches in the liberation movement.

The enemy is far from being strong politically. People's response to UDF [United Democratic Front] shows the direction of political trends. If change comes about, it must be on our terms. Steps are being taken towards this objective. The recent PB [politburo] meeting agreed that the P should take the lead in SACTU [South African Congress of Trade Unions].

It is time for the movement to go on the offensive. ANC must take the lead but this is not possible unless the Party is strong and united, ideologically and numerically.

There are complaints by young cadres in the West [Angola] of ill-treatment and injuries caused by carelessness. Yet P units in the region do not report such incidents. Why this failure? P members occupy key positions in the West but seem to forget their responsibilities to the P and movement. . . .

Evie: It is disturbing that the P fails to give direct lead to people at home on such issues as bread prices, bus fares, low wages. P fails to give a line or to issue pamphlets. If the idea is to give a lead through ANC some clarification should be given. Young generation may not see the P's influence.

Conditions in the camps mentioned by GS resemble those in [Kongwa] days when some comrades received SA prison treatment. Mashego's song reminds us of discrimination against recruits, failure to look after their well-being or correct bad treatment by seniors, including P member. All this is now being repeated in the West.

On the question of our relation with ANC there seems to be a feeling that its present leadership and policy will continue forever and can be relied on. P members however are unsure, and feel that the P is too much underground. It cannot operate efficiently with only one known functionary, the GS, who has in addition other important obligations. The goal of specialisation and distribution of responsibility is not being taken seriously. We ought to take note of emphasis in SU [Soviet Union] on specialisation.

Goodie: People at home are looking for Marxist literature. We fail to reply to attacks from BCM [black consciousness movement] and [Neville] Alexander group which get funds from Western sources. Pretoria regime fears UDF. Our material must go into the country on the many issues that arise—the bus boycott in Ciskei is a good example. Racist regime puts blame on communists and ANC—but we don't reply.

GS: *Inkululeko* was published in Island [Lesotho] and distributed inside with good results. Our printing press has been installed in Maputo and will soon operate. We hope that production of our material will then increase. Evie is correct in saying that we tend to work through ANC but this approach is wrong. P has good relations with ANC but also an independent role which we must never neglect. Only if P is strong can it influence ANC decisively.

Hal: Two sides to propaganda and education. One is to conduct polemics with opposition such as BCM; the other is to carry on struggle against capitalism which ANC cannot do, being a national movement representing all classes in the black population.

GS: P has not always made best use of personnel. It was a mistake to give members who are highly qualified the kind of work suitable for technicians—like distributing leaflets for which they received long jail sentences. All sections—the Party, SACTU and ANC should make strong efforts to establish themselves inside.

Evie: Guerrilla form of action is not the best for our purpose. Our political and military strategies require the development of armed struggle inside. Cadres ought to train and advise recruits inside. It is wrong to claim that ANC has a people's army now. MK is made up of individuals who came into exile for training.

GS: Enemy fears an internal armed force more than the infiltration into the country of individual cadres of MK.

Evie: There is similar weakness in the UDF. Its leaders do not possess a mass basis. . . .

Hal: . . . Immediate problem is [to] give policy orientation to UDF. Movement should consider whether this is not the time to mobilise people for struggle for political rights. Only by means of political power can oppressed rid themselves of pass laws and other forms of oppression, including deprivation of citizenship. An appropriate slogan is Votes for All!

GS expresses satisfaction with outcome of the meeting and receives a message of thanks by the unit chairman.

Ends 17.00 hours

Document 111. "The Constitutional Proposals and the UDF." ANC memorandum, Lusaka, October 26, 1983 (abridged)

INTRODUCTION

To a significant extent the two briefings we have provided so far on the UDF [United Democratic Front] show that we correctly assessed the basic directions and problems that have been associated with the development of the UDF.

It is now possible to look back and recognise that the movement for a united front at the level of overt mass mobilisation has been effectively launched despite the host of tactical and other problems associated with the process. At the same time, it is clear that there is a lot of work to be done to ensure that the potentials of the UDF are fully exploited, that the problems that arise are effectively resolved. . . .

THE NLM [national liberation movement] *AND THE UDF*

The question of the nature of a united front within the context of the specific situation obtaining in our country is still a matter on which our guidance is repeatedly sought by forces at home. Associated with this problem, there is also the need for us to refine the way in which we relate to the UDF. . . .

The GB [1979 Green Book] stated that it is by the calibre of the leadership and guidance that we offer that we shall come to occupy the leadership of the united front. This emphasises the fact that we do not see our relationship in terms of directives or control; it does not see us imposing our viewpoint and it takes into account that we are a banned organisation. More important, all levels of our movement need to recognise in practice that there is developing at home a leadership with which we have to work in a way that does not undermine that leadership's authority. It is a leadership that will mature as it comes to grips with practical problems, and we should encourage it to solve these problems on the ground as and when they arise. . . .

The calibre of our revolutionary leadership and guidance also requires that we find a balance between working quietly and behind the scenes to get people to understand our perspectives, and to understand how the programmes they are undertaking relate to our perspectives, as well as make our direct *political presence* felt amongst the masses. Our propaganda therefore needs to speak directly to our masses. . . . [W]ithout interfering or cutting across the efforts of the leadership of the broad popular front to solve the day to day problems, we cannot afford to slide into a position of saying that the leadership at home is quite capable of solving the problems within the country and that therefore there is no need for us to directly address the masses. . . . [W]e have to encourage the leadership that is developing at the mass level to gain greater confidence to solve the problems that confront it, whilst at the same time ensuring that that leadership increasingly recognises the need to consult us on the *major strategic and tactical problems* that confront it. To put the matter crudely, we must avoid a situation where we become simply a fund-raising mechanism for those involved in mass mobilisation.

We must keep in mind the high respect the forces at home give to the guidance of our organisation. There are many instances where the forces at home look to us for guidance; often the hesitancy that besets them in mapping out a course of action requires decisiveness from our movement. For example, in the early stages of the development of the UDF, the question of the Freedom Charter arose. Some of our activists at home and in the Forward Areas mistakenly saw the making of the acceptance of the Freedom Charter as a condition for membership to the UDF a means by which we could establish the leadership position of our movement. We were able to correct this tendency and, by and large, the forces at home recognised the correctness of our guidance; however, in the process of helping to bring about this correction, we have not sufficiently emphasised the distinction between not making the Freedom Charter a precondition for membership to the UDF and at the same time pushing more vigorously for the masses and members of individual organisations to publicly commit themselves to the Freedom Charter.

SOME CURRENT PROBLEMS OF THE UDF
The UDF and the Trade Unions. . . .

[T]here is much division within the unions (perhaps it is more correct to say union leadership) as to whether a union should or should not join the UDF. . . . [The UDF Declaration declares a belief in leadership by the working class, but more must be done by] the ANC, SACTU and our activists on the ground in order to persuade the unions to join the UDF. In some cases, as we shall see below, it seems necessary that we should engage in the debate, setting out our positions as to why the unions should pursue more rigorously the creation of a united TU [trade union] Federation, as well as join the UDF.

The strongest tendency which presents itself as an obstacle to the participation of unions in the UDF may be simplified and labelled as the "workerist" position. Inside the country it has been nurtured through academic research on SACTU, and SACTU's participation in the Congress Alliance during the 50's. Material based on some of these academic theses have been published in *Work in Progress* (possibly also in *Social Review*). This tendency also has been fed by the work of the [Rob] Petersen/[Martin] Legassick [Marxist Workers' Tendency] group dating from the time when they were functioning within SACTU. The Petersen/Legassick group have stepped up their work inside the country. This workerist tendency finds expression most strongly in the FOSATU [Federation of SA Trade unions] leadership as well as in GWU [General Workers' Union]. As a movement we have not taken up the substantive issues and dealt with them. We require a programme of propaganda by all sections of the NLM to place our view before the workers of our country. . . . The common strand uniting these diverse elements grouped under the workerist position is their opposition to the leadership of the ANC in the national liberation struggle, or what [Neville] Alexander has now taken to describing as "the hegemonic designs of the ANC".

Another focal point of resistance to joining the UDF emanates from circles who claim to support our movement. . . . The tendency we are referring to publicly expresses its position as supporting the UDF, pledging solidarity in action over the constitutional proposals etc, but stops short of making the unions concerned members of the UDF. The strongest case made out by this tendency, one with some limited validity, is that the specific unions involved need to be well organised before they take such a step as joining the UDF. Part of their case is that their joining the UDF at this stage may jeopardise the parallel process that is going on of uniting the TU's. Clear guidance is needed on this from the PMC [Politico-Military Council of ANC]. The position of this memo is that, despite the limited validity of their arguments, we need to overcome this tendency in the immediate future.

The above paragraphs refer to areas of work that our movement in its own name should be undertaking, some publicly, and some clandestinely. Let us turn briefly to some practical guidance that we need to put before our activists working in the UDF with regard to this problem. We have in mind here FOSATU, which is the best organized and largest of the existing federations among the progressive TU's. The UDF has already generated a powerful groundswell of support. It is estimated that the UDF commands the support of more than 1.5 million of our people at home. Positions being taken by various unions and groupings at home are another measure of the upsurge of support for the UDF. For example, CUSA [Council of Unions of SA] began with a balancing act of keeping its feet in both the UDF and NFC [National Forum Committee]. Since then, it has moved fully into the UDF. Joe Foster of FOSATU took up a public position that FOSATU could not associate itself with the UDF because FOSATU unions have a membership, some of whom belong to the UDF, and some of whom support Azapo and the NFC. Discussions have been going on between the UDF and FOSATU, but comrades on the ground who have been involved in the discussions, report that it is likely that FOSATU would soon express support for the campaigns being launched by the UDF though this would stop short of FOSATU joining the UDF. . . .

FOSATU has already condemned the constitutional proposals, the Koornhof Bills, etc and pledged to mobilize its membership to campaign against these proposals. FOSATU in the various areas maintains area and regional Shop Stewards Committees. Already in the Durban area, the UDF successfully approached the FOSATU Shop Stewards Committees to give them an opportunity to address the Shop Stewards Committees. Our information is that this was only attempted once. This process of going directly to the FOSATU Shop Stewards Committees and the union branches, needs to be made part of the UDF programme of action and given systematic attention both with regard to FOSATU unions as well as other unions. Similarly, workers who are members of TU's and also involved in the UDF through other community based organisations must be actively mobilised to campaign within their union structures. . . .

THE UDF AND THE RURAL POPULATION

To date the UDF is still largely urban based. . . . Our machineries need to constantly raise this area of work with activists functioning in the UDF and explore with them the ways in which the task of mobilizing the rural population receives high priority in the work of the UDF. . . .

THE UDF AND MOVES BY BANTUSTAN SO-CALLED LEADERS

The first meeting of the PMC held in April/May noted the discussions going on between [Cedric] Phatudi, [Chief M. G.] Buthelezi, the Matanzimas etc and the development in SABA [Buthelezi's SA Black Alliance]. Talk of united fronts and unity of our people has become fashionable. Nonetheless we should be monitoring these developments keenly and constantly ask ourselves whether certain developments cannot be exploited by the popular forces to make inroads into mobilizing the masses in the Bantustans. Inkatha has been consistent in condemning the sell-out of the [Allan] Hendrickses. It is already beginning to feel the sting generated by the momentum of the UDF. It is, typical of its muscling tactics, keeping up the pressure on the Indian Reform Party not to commit itself to participation in the PC [President's Council] and also putting pressure on [Amichand] Rajbansi and his National People's Party. . . .

In the meantime, the so-called leaders of the Bantustans, except for [Lucas] Mangope, have become louder in their rejection of the PC and calling for a national convention. Of course, typical of these forces' objectives of heading off the popular struggle, there are important qualifications to their positions eg in the statement of the 6 October, they state "political, social and economic reform in this country could proceed under the old constitution while we prepare for a national convention in which a constitution acceptable to all the people of SA could be negotiated". . . .

This grouping's rejection of the PC and calls for black unity and a national convention should alert us to the fact that they are feeling the rising mood amongst the people whom they would like to claim as their exclusive constituencies, of their alarm at the rise of the UDF and the growth of the NLM and that behind their populist rhetoric there is their greater fear of the masses of our people than of the regime. What is important for us is that the UDF reads the mood of the people in the Bantustans correctly and undertakes a vigorous programme to draw in the masses in the Bantustans into the mainstream of the united popular struggle. . . .

Document 112. "Dawn Breaks." Broadcast by ANC's Radio Freedom, Lusaka, November 24, 1983

Good evening fellow countrymen, mothers of the soil, combatants of Umkhonto we Sizwe throughout the country, comrades and friends. You are tuned to "Dawn Breaks", the revolutionary voice of the African National Congress Women's Section, the voice that calls on all women to stand up and fight for equality, peace and freedom. "Dawn Breaks" comes to you every Thursday evening at 9.30 p.m. South African time on short-wave 31, 9505 Kilohertz, from the External Service of Radio Zambia, Lusaka.

With you this evening is Karabo More and Nomsa Shange. Our programme stands as follows. First we bring you a commentary on puppet community council elections taking place as from November 26 until December 3. The commentary will be presented in English by Karabo More [portion missing]. Lastly in our programme we present a commentary on the indiscriminate violence unleashed by Gatsha [Buthelezi] and his impis [warrior brigades] on our sons and daughters [at the University of Zululand] in Ngoye and on our people in Durban townships. The commentary will be presented by Nomsa Shange in English, so stay tuned. Music — Fade out

INKATHA

Over the past weeks we have witnessed a rampage of violence unleashed on the oppressed people of our country by members of Inkatha Youth Brigade—a movement which has always claimed to be non-violent.

It is now evident that Inkatha is like a dog which does not want to bite the hand that feeds it—the apartheid regime, but becomes vicious when facing us—the oppressed. Inkatha's collaboration with the fascist regime was exposed by the racist prime minister immediately after the racist results of the so-called referendum when he said "he doesn't understand why Gatsha critisises him because he owes his position to the Nationalist Party." He further drew a comparison between Inkatha and the [Afrikaner] Broederbond saying Inkatha is the Broederbond of the Zulus.

Fellow mothers, Gatsha has declared war against those who are opposing his leadership and that of his masters—the racist regime. Using his impis and the Inkatha Youth Brigade, he has attacked and disrupted a solidarity meeting organised by the United Democratic Front in solidarity with the people of Lamontville, Chesterville and Klaarwater. The meeting was to discuss the intended incorporation of these Durban townships into KwaZulu. One member of Inkatha was quoted as saying "in fact we are after Reverend Mcebisi Xundu", leader of the Joint Rent Action Committee which is opposed to the incorporation of Durban townships into KwaZulu.

After the recent disturbances at Ngoye University which left five students dead, and the disruption of solidarity meetings, one wonders what Gatsha Buthelezi thinks about his non-violent Inkatha army.

It becomes necessary to ask the question—where does Gatsha draw the line between violence and non-violence? Can he still claim that Inkatha is a non-violent movement fighting for the liberation of South Africa? Certainly not! Inkatha has proved to the world that it is in fact a reserve brigade of the fascist Pretoria regime, fighting to preserve and protect the evil system of apartheid and to further oppress and exploit our people. Surprisingly enough, Gatsha has gone on record condemning the heroic actions of MK. It is indeed a sad day when a self declared fighter for freedom cries out loud when the apartheid regime is coming under heavy blows from the people's army. It is a further tragedy when this same self styled fighter for freedom mobilises his impis to disrupt attempts by the people to mobilise and consolidate their unity against the hated system of oppression. Indeed Gatsha's politics can be summed up as the politics of despair, the politics of collaboration. He has abandoned the path of struggle and now seeks his salvation in compromise and sellout solutions.

Inkatha's atrocious activities are not new, they are simply a continuation of the violence against the oppressed. We recall that in 1980 Inkatha unleashed a wave of terror against students demonstrating against Bantu education.

Mothers and sisters, Gatsha in his violent tactics is also using women like Mrs Ella Nxasana who is an official and a mouthpiece of Inkatha in Lamontville. We must help our sisters who are members of Inkatha Women's League. These women are our mothers, sisters and cousins who have been misled by the self serving policies of Inkatha ka [of] Gatsha. We must show them that they are waging a fruitless struggle. The only reward that Inkatha can expect for killing and maiming our husbands, sisters, brothers and children is continued oppression, suffering and poverty.

It is high time that we who are not members of Inkatha meet with our sisters and show them the correct path to freedom. The followers of Gatsha should know by now that their so-called chief of the Zulus has incorporated his impis into the racist army to fight the ANC, all peace loving and freedom loving people of our country. They must also know that he used them and made them believe that he is building the so-called impis and Inkatha so that they could fight the apartheid regime whereas deep down [in] his heart he knew that he is preparing them to fight the oppressed but struggling people of our country.

Have we mothers and sisters of Inkatha, especially we whose children and sisters are studying in Ngoye University, now turned into a battlefield of Inkatha, asked ourselves why our children protested against Gatsha's presence at the University? Mothers, the answer is simple. They have had enough of his monkey tricks and his sweet words. They have lost all the respect and confidence in him as a leader, and he could not take it. And so to release his tensions and depression he ordered his misdirected army to beat them up. Gatsha Buthelezi in his many reactionary speeches [has] always emphasised that Inkatha is fighting along the footsteps of the late Zulu King—Cetshwayo. But Cetshwayo fought [for] a just cause, knew his target and never deceived his followers. So Gatsha must be told in black and white to stop misrepresenting the brave and loyal Cetshwayo.

Mothers of the soil, let us intensify our campaigns against the incorporation of Lamontville, Chesterville and Klaarwater into KwaZulu.

Let us urge Inkatha Women's League and all members of Inkatha to join the rest of us—the oppressed, in our just struggle for freedom.

Let us not fight tribal wars because they will bear no fruits except that they will spill more of our blood.

Let us guard against elements such as Gatsha Buthelezi, [Patrick] Mphephu, [Lennox] Sebe, [Kaiser] Matanzima, [David] Thebehali, [Lucas] Mangope and many others who are against the demands of the oppressed.

Let us give massive support to the ANC and all MK cadres fighting in all corners of our country.

Away with Gatsha Buthelezi!
United we shall win!
Divided we fall!
The struggle continues and victory is certain!

Document 113. "Planning for People's War." Discussion document by Joe Slovo, Maputo, November 1983 (abridged)

The "Summarised Theses on our Strategic Line" contained in the Green Book and adopted by the NEC [ANC National Executive Committee] in August 1979 constitutes a starting point for the determination of our perspectives in the coming period. Those theses continue to guide us in the definition of the main content of the present phase of our revolution. . . .

On the specific question of the relationship between the political and military struggle, taking into consideration the then existing conditions, [we] came to the following conclusion which we summarised:

> The armed struggle is *secondary* and our priority task is to build up political revolutionary bases out of which its armed struggle (in the case of people's war) can be developed. In the meantime the purpose of armed activity is to keep alive the perspective of people's revolutionary violence as the ultimate weapon for the seizure of power and to *concentrate on armed propaganda* whose purpose is to stimulate political activity and organisation rather than to *hit* at the enemy.

This approach gave a definition to our activities since 1979 and more particularly, our military planning concentrated virtually exclusively on armed propaganda. The main questions which now arise are: Has the situation been so transformed and have we fulfilled enough of our objectives to move on to a new phase? In other words can we now move with greater purpose and begin to take concrete steps towards people's war? By people's war we mean war in which a liberation army becomes rooted amongst the people who progressively participate actively in the armed struggle both politically and militarily, including the possibility of engaging in partial or general insurrections.

What developments have taken place since 1979 which justify the search for such a new approach in our military planning and actions? It is true that in the *narrow sense* the objective we set ourselves for the creation of political revolutionary bases has so far not made significant headway. The policy of creating APCs [Area Political Committees] has been an almost complete failure.

But in the *broad sense* the political base in support of our revolutionary aims has widened immeasurably since 1979. The ANC and its allies stand virtually unchallenged (in the eyes of the overwhelming majority of the oppressed) as the guide of our revolution. The mass receptivity to violence as the only real answer is becoming more and more evident. Indeed the mood in support of our liberation movement has created several moments in which the people behave as if the ANC is a legal organisation, despite the threatening presence of armed police contingents. Every MK blow against the enemy, especially one involving life, is greeted by massive joy and celebration amongst the oppressed.

Of equal importance is the dramatic advance which has been made in the past few years in growth of mass organisations both at the regional and national level, [especially the rapid growth of trade unions and the creation of the United Democratic Front, together representing roughly 2 million people]. . . .

What does all this add up to in relation to our strategy in the coming period.

[We must learn from our past failures and continue engaging in armed propaganda]. But at the same time we cannot continue to confine ourselves to armed propaganda. If we do, then the promise which armed propaganda held out, that it is merely the first phase in the struggle for the violent overthrow of the regime, will sound less convincing and the credibility of our strategy of armed struggle will begin to fade, leading to political demoralization both within our ranks and among the people. Above all we believe that the objective situation favours preparations for the raising of our military struggles to a new level. The political and military activities of the past few years have helped to prepare the ground for the people's involvement in the armed struggle. not merely as sympathetic spectators but also as participants. . . .

[T]herefore . . . we must begin to create an armed presence within the country as a stage towards the building of a people's army which will survive and grow internally and will increasingly engage in people's war. What does this entail?

a) We must begin working immediately to prepare conditions for the creation of guerilla zones. A zone earmarked for this purpose must have the potential to safely accommodate (either on the terrain or among the people) trained and armed cadres which will constitute the nuclei for the internal recruiting, training, formation and survival of guerilla units.

b) Areas must be selected which have the potential over a period of time to be transformed into active guerilla zones. Initially this involves the injection of highly trained compact MK groups (defined as commando units) consisting of cadres each of which has the capacity to train and command local recruits. In other words, a group of, say, five MK cadres must aim to grow internally into five units of five. . . .

c) The commando unit must, in the initial period, concentrate on establishing itself in its area, relying increasingly on the local inhabitants for its survival and growth and choosing a suitable early moment to begin mixing with the local population with arms in hand. During the early stages of this process it will avoid military action or engagement with the enemy except when it is forced to defend itself or when it is engaged in specific action designed to facilitate its growth and entrench itself among the people, and not merely to hit at the enemy.

d) The selection of areas and their preparation as future guerilla zones must be made in the closest possible collaboration between the political and military implementation machineries. Such consultations must lead to a determination of which areas are ripe for early injection of a commando unit and the main emphasis of politico-military work in them, which areas need a prior period of sustained political work before we can be ready to inject armed cadres, and which areas should remain clear of overt military activity. The selective recruiting of cadres who come from areas earmarked for development into guerilla zones is obviously also a task requiring the closest possible collaboration between its political and military implementation machineries and this applies also to the main emphasis of political mobilisation and organisation of the areas in question.

e) In those areas selected for development as guerilla zones, immediate steps must be taken to build up the necessary arms and explosives caches which will meet the needs for the expansion of the commando units from among the local populace. Special procedures are required to ensure that until the contents of a cache are needed, its location should be known only to an external apparatus responsible for the creation of the caches.

f) The regions selected for development as future guerilla zones will, in general, be situated in rural areas. . . . But in the urban areas too, such supporting armed actions will only be sustained by a network of locally based cadres. The task of creating such a network is a priority and must be pursued even if it implies a scaling down of active armed blows for a short period. . . .

h) It of course remains an urgent objective that the local direction of military and political activity in a guerilla zone should be coordinated under an internally based leadership and it is our task to work towards the creation of organs capable of carrying out such functions. But we must see this as a process which, in the initial phase, will unavoidably demand specialisation by separate political and military machineries guided by our external leading political organs. . . .

Some Additional Specific factors
A) Rear Bases

The actual correlation of forces in Southern Africa creates special problems in relation to our external rear bases. Compared to the facilities which were available to [other liberation] movements . . . we are at a disadvantage when it comes to a more sustained external support base in terms of logistics and army reserves. Enemy pressure has already reduced our opportunities for using external bases even in relation to limited sabotage operations, and perhaps there is worse still to come.

Successful guerilla struggles (e.g. Cuba, Nicaragua etc) have been fought without this classical type of contiguous external rear base. In any case the only alternative to abandoning the armed struggle altogether is to find answers which compensate for this disadvantage. The main foundation of such answers is that we must create, as quickly as possible, a widespread internal presence which is not continually dependent on an external base. . . .

B) The Bantustans

The successful spread of people's war is inconceivable without the escalation of political and military struggles in the bantustans, in which over half of the African population is already forced to live. Perhaps the most important challenge we face is to activate the masses in the bantustans who in the recent period have shown few signs of mass resistance or organisation (the urban part of the Ciskei is an exception).

We have perhaps become victims of our own public propaganda that the bantustans are meaningless frauds and that very little has changed from the time when they were called "reserves". . . . The bantustans have transferred the old reserves into sub-centres of military and political power. Such power is underwritten and manipulated by the racist state but the local administration nevertheless wield a significant degree of legal sovereignty over legislation, the judiciary, the state bureaucracy and the armed police forces. . . .

C) The role of Partial and General Uprisings

The Green Book states that people's power will be won by revolutionary violence in a protracted armed struggle which must involve the whole people and *in which partial and general uprisings play a vital role*. This perspective remains valid. In this respect our struggle bears some resemblance to the Vietnam situation in which every key phase of the armed struggle was accompanied by such uprisings. Soweto-1976 was an example of a semi-spontaneous uprising which spread to other parts of the country and continued over a relatively long period of time. The event which started as a youth protest movement was reinforced by a number of effective solidarity general strikes by hundreds of thousands of workers. But despite the important contribution by the ANC stalwarts, our Movement was still too weak internally in '76 to give effective direction to the uprising, to combine it with organised armed blows and to make available the means which would have enabled the thousands of militants to confront the enemy more effectively. Despite persistent killings by the enemy, our youth showed a spontaneous readiness to sacrifice their lives (confronting guns with mere stones) over a period of many, many months. Imagine the potential if there had been an organised underground presence capable of giving direction and supplying a minimum of simple weaponry to quickly organised paramilitary units.

There can be no doubt that the situation today is much more favourable than in 1976 for the more effective combination of organized armed activity with insurrections of various degrees of intensity. The strength of the workers' movement, the proliferation of mass organisation and political resistance (one important expression of which is the emergence of the UDF), the dramatic impact of MK actions and, above all, the growing support for the ANC-led liberation front as the unchallenged leader of our revolutionary process, promote a new dimension to a perspective of combined political and military assault on the enemy. In this connection we should not under-estimate the crucial role of the political general strike *at the right moment*. We stress the need for proper timing because we will help discredit the political general strike as a revolutionary weapon if we do not approach it in a discriminating fashion.

If we are correct in saying that partial or general uprisings may well play a vital part in the unfolding of our revolutionary process, then it is necessary for certain steps to be taken *now* in order to be prepared for such an eventuality.

i) We must immediately begin to build up stores of simple basic equipment in the vicinity of all the major urban complexes which at the right moment

could be used to equip contingents which can be quickly trained and organised during emerging insurrection conditions.
ii) A study must be undertaken of the main nerve-centres of enemy pawns in every urban complex. Such a study must provide us with the knowledge of which forces should be concentrated at which points during an urban insurrection and should enable us to select priority targets.
iii) There must be special concentration on the creation and strengthening of mass organisation in the rural areas (especially the bantustans), so that urban and rural action can be drawn together at the crucial moments. . . .

Work in the Enemy armed forces

A fundamental transformation is taking place in the composition of the enemy's armed forces, a transformation which demands that we devote much greater energy than in the past to work within its ranks. [Blacks make up a growing proportion of the regime's army and police force. Thus] our people's army will increasingly be faced with black contingents. This is also intended by the enemy to give the struggle the appearance of a civil war in which blacks face blacks.

ARMING THE PEOPLE

A considerable amount of discussion has been taking place recently in our ranks on the concept of an armed people as the vital element in the pursuit of people's war. As a general proposition this concept is correct. But we have to be a little more clear about what exactly we mean in practice.

It is obvious that the policy of "arming the people" cannot mean that we begin *now* to distribute arms to whoever wishes to receive them among the oppressed. In the first place we have neither the capacity nor the means to do this on any meaningful scale. In the second place it would be completely wrong to engage in a policy of merely distributing weaponry to people and trusting to luck that they will use them on the side of the revolution.

The policy of "arming the people" has completely different meanings in the different phases of revolution. For example, once state power is achieved the *organised* distribution of arms amongst the people (under the general supervision of the Party and mass organisations) may be an imperative in order to defend the revolution against internal or external counter-revolutionary threats. As the struggle develops in the guerilla zones attention is always paid to creating armed paramilitary units and militia from among the people as part of the *organised support* for the revolutionary forces. We have also already referred above to the preparation that should be made now to ensure that we have the capacity to train and arm contingents which could suddenly swell our ranks during moments of partial or general uprisings. In addition we look forward to the time when large numbers of black troops will come to our side with arms in hand.

In other words if the concept of "arming the people" is to become anything more than a nice sounding cliché, it must become part of a policy to draw in more and more armed people as organised contingents in support of our struggle and acting under our leadership. Indeed the main burden of this whole discussion document has been to work precisely towards this aim.

CONCLUDING NOTE

If there is a short way of defining what the main emphasis of our strategic line should be, it is:

We must plan for a *protracted* armed struggle in which the foundation of people's war must be *urgently* organised and we must be ready to accept all the sacrifices and the patient dedication which such a perspective entails. At the same time the situation has within it the seeds of sudden transformation opening up the possibility of combined military and political assault on the enemy and leading to its overthrow by such combined insurrectionary forces. *We must prepare ourselves, and at all times be ready, for both these perspectives.*

Document 114. Excerpt from "Decisions and Suggestions from NEC/PMC Meeting." Notes from ANC leadership discussion about impending Nkomati Accord, Lusaka, January 25, 1984

1. The ANC must establish contact with the countries of the region like Tanzania, Zambia, Zimbabwe, Lesotho and Botswana. We need to know the thinking of these countries.
2. ANC cannot rescind its decision to engage in armed struggle.
3. We must indicate to Mozambique the implications of their decision and its likelihood to snowball. That this decision is tantamount to saying to us we must stop the armed struggle. We must find out from the Mozambican comrades whether they think that freedom is possible in South Africa without the armed struggle.
4. We must find out from the Mozambican comrades the implications of their decision that they will allow us only diplomatic presence in Mozambique. What does this mean in terms of people coming from home on transit to us. Will they be allowed. We must try to salvage whatever is possible in the interest of our struggle.
5. Without the armed struggle, our struggle is dead. ANC will not be a party to the destruction of our struggle.
6. The African National Congress has to review its decision on Lesotho in as far as military activities and on transit of men and materials in the light of the new situation.
7. Cadres selected for work in the frontline and forward countries must satisfy certain requirements like high political consciousness, discipline, and ability to work underground. They must be able to observe rules of underground existence.
8. The African National Congress must be able to deal with culprits promptly and firmly.

DOCUMENTS FOR CHAPTER 4   537

9. The meeting appreciated the problems of Mozambique but is of the opinion that those who want to destroy Mozambique will succeed as soon as they have succeeded in destroying the ANC.
10. If Mozambique capitulates, it will be no different from the so-called bantustans of South Africa. South Africa will be realising its dream of Constellation of Southern African States.
11. If the present trend of capitulation by Mozambique is not arrested, and if this trend is followed by the other countries of the region, then SADCC [Southern African Development Coordination Conference] will be dead because there would be no need for it.
12. ANC must be angry and aggressive. We must give Mozambique the benefit of our overall analysis of the situation and show that if the present trend in Mozambique continues to its logical conclusion it will represent capitulation to imperialism.
13. This trend is opposed to the progressive process that has been the dominant feature of the region and would be detrimental to the interest of the continent and the World.
14. To the African National Congress this [capitulation] would be the unkindest cut of all.
15. The African National Congress must turn the so-called diplomatic mission into underground whilst fulfilling the functions of political and diplomatic representation.
16. The African National Congress should undertake operations inside South Africa without consideration of the borders. The self imposed restriction should be considered non-existent.
17. MHQ [Military Headquarters] and PHQ [Political Headquarters] should begin to build reception bases for trained MK cadres. This means the building of a strong underground.
18. The African National Congress must begin to prepare contingency plans for VZ [Zimbabwe] and P [Botswana].
19. The African National Congress to embark on international Campaign.
20. The ANC to act from enlightened position of self interest, and to calculate implications in relation to the unfolding armed struggle. The self interest of ANC coincides with the interests of the countries in the region.
21. ANC must show Mozambique and the other countries why South Africa is acting in the manner it is doing now. We clear fallacy. And remove the arrogant inability to see the views of others.
22. ANC must remove the erroneous view that South Africa in the region has all the cards.
23. ANC must show Mozambique that South Africa wants to destroy the Mozambican revolution. That the starting point is the destruction of ANC, because it is in the way.
24. ANC must express its disappointment at the shabby treatment given us by Mozambique. Talks about ANC and South Africa [have] been going on for years without any official information from Mozambique.
25. ANC must not presume that the position of Frelimo is irreversible.

26. ANC must encourage direct and indirect pressures.
27. We must contact the solidarity groups who have been so appreciative of the romantic image of Frelimo and let them exert pressure even to the point of their publicly disassociating themselves from Frelimo.
28. ANC must put across the full meaning of the decision of Frelimo.
29. ANC must abandon self control and be guided by the interest of our struggle.
30. ANC must develop a new style of work and approach.
31. Socialist countries must do more than now. Imperialists too active. We must approach our friends and make them listen to us as people in the area. We must show that if the region is lost we all stand to lose.
32. We must inform our Mozambican friends that what is at stake now cannot be measured in economic statistics. It is the fate of the region affecting the world; it is social progress.
33. What would have happened if the countries that supported Mozambique had done the same?
34. The routes leading to the sea must be made not to function.
35. ANC must prepare to be inside.
36. ANC should adjust programmes to allow PHQ and MHQ to meet.
37. Women should be deployed into the country.
38. Discussions with Frelimo should also aim at gaining time for us to go underground.
39. ANC should remind Frelimo about the support ANC has given to her including rifles.
40. ANC should approach its friends to put pressure on Frelimo.
41. ANC must go underground everywhere. JS [Joe Slovo] is not the only one who is likely to be expelled.
42. The PHQ and MHQ should come together to work out means and ways of working underground. The control of the underground, coordination and ensuring that the numbers are correct and meet the requirements of the situation and the capacity of the machinery to maintain the cadres underground.
43. The entire leadership must be involved in working out strategy of overt and covert existence. Some of the leaders might have to disappear.
44. ANC must make it clear to the Mozambicans that ANC will not commit suicide.
45. ANC must prepare itself for a multi-facet strategy.
46. Comrades JS, TMb [Thabo Mbeki], C Hani and SM [Simon Makana], members of subcommittee, to prepare the ANC response to Mozambique.
47. Meeting agreed on how to report to our people on the current talks between Mozambique and South Africa.
    a). Start by mentioning the apartheid regime's counter-offensive.
    b). Start with the statement of DIP [Department of Information and Publicity] on the talks.
    c). Demands of the regime in the talks.
    d). Implications of these demands.

e). ANC has started talks with Frelimo on these demands. Talks continuing.
f). At some point our people shall be told about these talks.
g). ANC prepared.
h). Enemy trying to say ANC outside.
i). Demands coming from the enemy.
48. Statement to be prepared by DIP. . . .

DOCUMENT 115. "Report: Commission of Inquiry into Recent Developments in the People's Republic of Angola [Stuart Commission]." Lusaka, March 1984 (abridged)

Per its letter of the 13th February 1984, the Working Committee of the National Executive Committee of the African National Congress established a Special Commission to fully investigate the developments that have taken place within its ranks in the People's Republic of Angola.

Members of the Special Commission were: Comrade James Stuart (Convener), Comrade Anthony Mongalo, Comrade Sizakele Sigxashe, Comrade Aziz Pahad, Comrade Mtu Jwili [Daniel Oliphant].

The Terms of Reference of the Special Commission were to investigate and report on:
1. The root cause of the disturbances;
2. Nature and genuineness of the grievances;
3. Outside or enemy involvement, their aim and methods of work;
4. Connection in other areas;
5. Ring leaders and their motives. . . .

The Special Commission left for Luanda on the 13th February 1984, and started its work on the following day. During the next three weeks in Angola, the Special Commission visited and interviewed practically all the occupants of Viana Transit Camp, Pango, Quibaxe, Caxito and Caculama Military Training Camps. It interviewed all 33 cadres presently detained in the Luanda Maximum Security Prison as well as members of the Military High Command, the Regional Command and our Chief Representative in Angola. . . .

THE EVENTS: Background
The organisation is facing one of its most serious challenges since its inception. The disturbances that took place in our ranks in the People's Republic of Angola recently brought this into sharp focus.

The Commission's investigations show that to understand that situation, we must place the events in the context of the accumulation of problems in Angola in the last few years. It is clear that since 1979 there has been a gradual development of an explosive situation which finally erupted in December 1983. Why did this happen? . . .

[Camps in their early years were well organized and equipped. Senior leaders visited often.] However, after the destruction of Novo Catengue (1979) matters deteriorated sharply. Our interviews reflect that the [conditions] described below manifested themselves in one degree or another in all our camps.

ADMINISTRATION

Relations between administration and rank-and-file described as being of "master and servant". Elitism has developed. The administration's housing, cooking, eating and other facilities are practically cut off from others and this has increased their separation.

Special Privileges
a) *Food*: Administration have special logistics. They regularly slaughter live stock (pigs, ducks and chickens) for their consumption only, while the rank-and-file rarely eat meat.
b) *Cigarettes*: While cigarettes are not available to camps for long periods, administration always have adequate supplies.
c) *Liquor*: Administration drink regularly and if women comrades are around, they are invited to parties in administration section. However, drinking by cadres is severely punished.
d) *Womanising*: Widespread complaint that people in administration use their positions to seduce women comrades. . . .

MISMANAGEMENT
• Failure to show initiatives in solving various problems, e.g. food, shelter, etc.
• No attempt to discuss with rank-and-file to find solutions to problems;
• Strong belief that administration does not pass on cadres' comments and complaints to higher organs or that it "doctors" reports to suit its interests,
• Extremely limited organisation of political or cultural life;
• Criticisms by rank-and-file labeled as "anti-authority", "lack of confidence in leadership", "work of enemy agents", etc. There have been several cases of victimisation after criticism made in open meetings. This reached such a stage that even when some lower ranking staff units sensed growing discontent, they did not criticise the situation, because of fear of victimisation. Basically, channels of complaints and grievances have been closed down. . . .
• Mock attacks: Has resulted in many casualties. Appears that it is not properly planned to prevent casualties. . . .
• Improper deployment of personnel: There are many complaints that either through inefficiency or for other reasons, people are deployed wrongly, e.g. . . . [S]ome returning from Party School [in Soviet Union] are sent to work in the kitchen at times when there are shortages of commissars and instructors.
• Bureaucracy: Has reached alarming levels. In many cases autocratic centralism has replaced democratic centralism. Today cadres believe that it has

become impossible to see the leadership because of bureaucratic maneuverings.
- Nepotism: This leads to opportunism and corruption.

DISCIPLINARY MEASURES

From 1979 practically all disciplinary problems "resolved" by severe punishment and beatings. Destructive punishment as distinct from the earlier revolutionary constructive punishment became the order of the day. The tragic fact is that it was at its worst in the training camps. This has undoubtedly left a very bad impression on everybody. In fact some of those punished have been maimed and scarred for life, and there have even been deaths. . . .

CAMP CONDITIONS

Over the last few years the situation has deteriorated markedly. This affects almost all aspects of life in the camps and causes much resentment and anger. It also seriously affects morale and performance of every facet of living and training.

There is a belief that much of the logistical problems are man-created. It is clear that better organisation of administration and personnel can help minimise the acute problems. Planning, creativeness and initiative are sadly lacking.

[Food for cadres is poor, badly prepared, but better for administration. Health conditions are bad, malaria is rampant and bronchitis, asthma, kidney problems, TB, skin ailments and mental problems are common. Medical personnel are scarce, underqualified, and often unsympathetic. There are shortages of basic supplies such as clothing, soap, tents, etc.]

RECREATION

This has deteriorated sharply. In most camps the only facilities available are for volley-ball and soccer. There are practically no indoor games. There are no projectors or films or any other visual entertainment. No radios are available for comrades. Frankly speaking, we found no recreational facilities worth speaking of.

LIBRARY

Every camp has a great shortage of literature (political and general). We were surprised to learn that even our own material was in short supply. Many of the Movement's basic works are not available and have not been read by comrades. . . .

TRANSPORT

Most camps are without transport. This is a very serious problem because the camps are in remote areas, far from our stores and from hospitals, etc. Without transport, comrades cannot even attempt to solve their logistical problems by trying to obtain local supplies.

POLITICAL LIFE

The meeting of the regional commissariat (December 1983) confirmed that the political life of our comrades in the camps, especially in the Caculama training camp, has deteriorated.

There are many objective reasons, for example, good cadres have been deployed elsewhere and there is a shortage of experienced political instructors. Political instructors are short of current material and are not in dynamic touch with developments at home, and within the organisation.

However, many comrades feel that from the time we adopted the ZAPU [Zimbabwe African People's Union] methods (toyi toyi), the role of politics was consciously downgraded. The Commission strongly believes that the low level of political consciousness has contributed significantly to current problems. This was very evident in our meeting with trainees in Caculama. . . .

LONG STAY IN CAMPS

"Our lengthy stay and conditions in exile (i.e. camps) has made some of us to lose all sense of human feeling, lose complete touch with humanity, we do not have the same resistance".

These words of a cadre give some insight into the mood of depression and hopelessness that is widespread amongst those who have been in our camps for several years. For various reasons, many cadres have moved from one camp to another. They have not had the opportunity to go to the Front, abroad or even to Luanda. These constitute the most bitter section of our army. They remain in camps while others come and go.

Resentment builds up and anarchy sets in. They rationalise indiscipline, dagga [marijuana] smoking, drinking and rape by the fact of their being for so long in camps under abnormal conditions.

The Commission believes that the conditions in the camps, the total isolation from the outside world, the desperation and frustration of not being deployed make it practically impossible for cadres to survive (politically, morally and psychologically) in the camps for several years. . . .

GRIEVANCES AGAINST THE SECURITY DEPARTMENT

Interviews carried out by the Commission in all our camps reflect one unanimous response: that the security department carried out tasks which are not supposed to be theirs—the task of disciplining offenders.

Assumption of these duties at times without consultation or approval by other camp administration has sadly isolated the security department. The Department is said to have unlimited powers and to be immune from punishment, to an extent that some say that "it's an army within an army".

The harsh methods of enforcing discipline within the camps by some security department comrades have dangerously made it the most notorious and infamous department in the camps and perhaps in the whole movement. . . .

To the surprise of comrades, all this violence, harshness and brutality against them continues despite an order by Comrade Mashigo [Graham

Morodi], the then Regional Commander, prohibiting it. There seems to be no punishment for defiance of this order. . . .

CONCLUSION

The Security Department have become increasingly involved in deciding on and implementing disciplinary measures. Consequently, their major task of being the "eyes and the ears" of the Movement and helping to expose agents and protect our Movement has been seriously hampered. Some people remain suspects for years. . . . The majority of interviewees recognised the vital necessity of a security department. However, they questioned their methods of work which have resulted in almost universal fear and condemnation. . . .

Over the years visits to the camps by the leadership has decreased significantly. . . . [Even the] regional leadership . . . tend increasingly to spend more time in Luanda than in the camps. The cadres are beginning to feel that there is a growing gap between them and the leadership. Consequently they believe that their views and grievances are not known to the leadership. . . .

DEPLOYMENT OF CADRES

This aspect requires urgent and serious attention by the movement. It is a constant source of discussion in the camps.

Home Front:

The Commission found that cadres are deployed at the specific request of the [MK forward area] machineries concerned, that is, in most cases the machineries submitted names of specific individuals for deployment. The Regional Command or other relevant departments in the rear are not consulted.

This has given rise to a widespread belief that unless you have connections with the relevant machineries there is no hope for one to be deployed in the home front. The cadres experience has been that certain comrades who are deployed for the home front have a bad track record in the camps and yet [are] deployed because of their contacts. . . .

There are also cases where comrades have come for short courses but [been] "forgotten" and end up spending years in camps doing nothing until the relevant machinery or department "remembers" them. Some of the people affected were passport holders who could have returned to the country legally. . . .

Returnees:

Over the years comrades have been deployed into other areas, including the home front. Some of these comrades have been sent back to Angola for various reasons: unsuitable for tasks; indiscipline (i.e. womanising and drinking); cover blown; injured, etc.

In many cases no accompanying report has been sent on them. The Regional Command is therefore in the dark and unable to deploy these comrades most effectively. These comrades feel "dumped" and usually there is no further contact with their previous machineries. Most believe that they will never leave the camps again and a sense of frustration, desperation and anarchy sets in. These comrades have contributed [to] undermining confidence in the organisation. They relate stories about their experiences in the front; the shortcomings of front commanders. . . .

PACE OF THE ARMED STRUGGLE

There have been several discussions amongst the cadres about the pace of the armed struggle. There is a general acceptance that there is a "lull" in the armed struggle. The arguments basically were that since 1981 (a year of intensive action) nothing has been happening. They point to major political developments such as UDF, etc, Lamontville, Ciskei and Inkatha murders etc, and conclude that the masses are ready for the armed struggle and question why MK is not intensifying the armed struggle and not there to protect the masses. They argue that the front commanders are not up to the mark and that there might be sabotaging of the armed struggle. The President's call in 1982 to the MK cadres to analyse the situation and give their opinions on the state of the armed struggle and suggestions for its advancement was received enthusiastically. This was the first time that such a call had been made and [many] submitted their views. The fact that soon after that some camps were reprimanded by the National Commissar for the views expressed, strengthened the conviction that the views of the comrades, [if] it was frank and critical, did not reach the leadership. . . .

EVENTS

Events [of the mutiny] reflect the frightening situation into which our organisation, the ANC and MK, has sunk in the People's Republic of Angola—one of the most serious crises we have ever had to face. The nearly total collapse of the political, military and moral authority of our Organisation in Angola, the resultant confusion and fear and lawlessness, when aversion [toward] authority became paramount, are symptoms of a crisis which, in the opinion of the Commission, has deep-rooted causes and demands swift and decisive political action.

We wish to stress political action—as opposed to punitive security operations—to restore within the ranks of our organisation the necessary confidence, trust and political atmosphere without which we shall not move very far forward before the recurrence of the "Cangandala disturbances. . . ."

[MK's participation in Angola's war against UNITA led to opposition among cadres to fighting under Angolan commanders whose ability they questioned. As a result, discipline in MK sharply declined. In December 1983 an MK unit was sent to defend Cangandala, a village in Malange province. They resisted carrying out the duties assigned to them. The same occurred at Cacuso.]

Shooting started on December 16th, 1983. There was the traditional ceremony [marking Dingaan's Day] and then . . . some kind of a gun salute. When a cease-fire was ordered some sporadic shooting continued. By then UNITA was intensifying on mine warfare and ambushes.

One comrade was blown [up] by a mine near the defence position on the route to toilet. And when the news reached Cangandala that on 26th December five of our comrades were killed in an ambush—and that there is a trainee who died after being "punished" in Caculama training camp, the situation now became extremely tense and there was general demand to see the leadership. Then shooting in the air intensified around 12 or 13 January, 1984. Comrades were shooting in the camps as well as in the streets of villages, destroying the good relations that had developed between our comrades and the locals. At this stage the villagers fled their homes in fear of our comrades, who raised the demand: "We want to go home and fight there". At the height of the "shooting in the air", practically everybody in the camp, including some commanders and commissars were involved. The [Caculama] camp administration was then practically powerless to do anything to stop this lawlessness. It was supported by an insignificantly few comrades. When asked why they were "shooting in the air", comrades generally replied that they wanted to draw the attention of the leadership to them. This is what comrades told the villagers. . . . This behaviour finally led to the forced withdrawal of our men from Cangandala and Cacuso where they continued with their "shooting in the air". . . . The comrades from Musafa joined the others in Cacuso and together in two groups they travelled to Viana [transit camp] in Luanda.

About 40 trained comrades from Caculama Military Training Camp also defiantly left the camp and travelled by train to Luanda to join those already in Viana. Before their arrival in Viana, the occupants of this Transit Camp were moved to "The Plot", a few kilometers away.

On arrival in Viana, the first group of about 60 men were finally convinced to surrender their personal weapons. It was a general rule that comrades arriving in Viana surrender their weapons to the administration for the duration of their stay in Luanda. Fifteen men refused to surrender their arms on the grounds that they needed these arms "for their self-protection from the security department men". When the second, larger group arrived in Viana, they refused to hand in their weapons.

At about this stage, Solly Sibeko was detained in [an air freight] container in the camp (Viana). He was reported to have been mentally unstable and suffered from fits. After several days in the container, Solly Sibeko died. The death of Comrade Solly Sibeko in an already dangerously tense and confusing situation, in which rumors were spreading like wild-fire and in which the newly-appointed interim administration appeared to have been ineffective, further added fuel to the situation.

Dagga smoking and drinking was rife. Livestock was being slaughtered and consumed. Arms were being brandished openly. The situation was very volatile and the slightest spark could have triggered off major confrontation. It was a climate that could be easily exploited by enemy agents and lawless elements. The rumour that Solly's dead body was "riddled with bullets by the security men", further intensified the men's fear and hatred of this department.

On Sunday, the 5th February 1984, Cde Julius Mokoena (Regional Commander), Edwin Mabitse (Regional Commissar) and Comrade Captain, Regional Chief of Security, visited the Viana camp and told the comrades there to prepare an agenda for a meeting with the Regional leadership.

On Monday the 6th February, 1984 Khotso Morena [Mwezi Twala], Mompati and others called a meeting in the Plot under the pretext of ironing out irregularities in the Plot. . . . [but] instead the question of the comrades from Cangandala was raised and the decision reached was that they should all go to Viana to listen to the complaints of the comrades from Cangandala on the understanding that if they should agree with them they would join them but if they disagree with them they would criticise them. . . .

At Viana a "Committee of Ten" to work out the agenda and to "discuss with the Regional Command" was appointed. All camps as well as Amandla Cultural Ensemble, Women's Section and Propaganda unit were represented in the Committee of Ten. . . . The following agenda was adopted for the meeting with the Regional Command:
1. National Conference
2. Lies, distortions, etc.
3. Solly Sibeko to be buried by comrades
4. Vacillation of Regional Commissar
5. Security Department
6. Logistics
7. Medical situation
8. Contact with the leadership
9. Notification of all ANC centres about these events
10. Evacuees to be returned to Viana Camp

The atmosphere at the meeting was emotional and electric. The participants were armed with a variety of weapons and some individuals made provocative and inflammatory statements. However, it appears that these were controlled by the meeting.

The first meeting with the Regional Command was scheduled for Tuesday, 7th February, 1984 at 10h30 and a meeting to report back to the detachment for 14h00.

Both these meetings did not materialise as FAPLA [Angolan army troops] moved in on Tuesday 7/2/84 at 4h00 [a.m.] to disarm all comrades in the Viana camp.

At the moment when FAPLA appeared in the camp to disarm the Viana camp, some cadres had already formed a "circular defence" at the back of the camp. It was a very critical moment. Many claim that it was only the intervention of some of the members of the Committee of Ten that enabled the disarming to take place without serious fighting.

One comrade was killed in the crossfire during a brief exchange of fire at the beginning. One FAPLA [vehicle] was immobilised by a RPG shell. There were no casualties on the side of FAPLA units from the Presidential Regiment. Some of those in the "circular defence" positions surrendered their arms, others stored their weapons in the nearby bushes. . . .

ASSESSMENT AND CONCLUSION
A Plot?
In this part of our report, the first question we must address ourselves to is: Was there a plot, conspiracy by enemy agents within the ranks of our Movement to subvert the organisation, to seize power within MK and dictate to the leadership? If so, why was the movement not made aware of this conspiracy which involved the majority of our comrades in every camp? What was the role of the "Committee of Ten"?

This question remained uppermost in the minds of members of the Commission throughout the period of its work in Angola, especially after the Commission became fully aware of who, which type of person is to be found in Angola.

Despite the fact that Angola is generally regarded as reliable rear-base of our struggle, it has been used as a dumping ground for enemy agents, suspects, malcontents and undisciplined elements. . . .

The camps in Angola are riddled with those who are labelled as "suspects". Some have been in this category for as long as 8 years. For those amongst them who are innocent, life must be real hell, and it's sad commentary on the efficiency of the security department (and the internal structures of our movement) that this should be so. . . . Angola has also become the dumping ground for disciplinary offenders, even criminals, and the Commission strongly feels that Angola should be cleansed if it is to be a reliable rear-base.

The Commission has no doubt that enemy agents and other elements did exploit genuine grievances and fanned the disturbances at a certain stage. We have not uncovered any evidence that enemy agents organised the disturbances from the beginning.

Furthermore, the Commission was unable to find that the Committee of Ten was an organised conspiracy to take over the leadership or was instrumental in organising the disturbances . . . [although] some of the leading members of the Committee as well as those closely connected with them have a long record of dissension and anti-movement activities. . . . [O]ne comrade said that he sees a strong link between the enemy agents within our midst and those who created and prepared the ground for them. He was referring to the conditions and general life of comrades in camps. The Commission found conditions in some camps shocking, to say the least. Extremely poor quality of food, no fresh meat, vegetables or fruits for months; hardly any recreation facilities, low level of cultural activities, poor tents, uniforms, boots, sports shoes if any, no medicaments, corruption and fear is omnipresent. This is what we found. . . .

The Commission feels that these conditions in the camps coupled with the insensitivity and the open abuse of authority on the part of some officers, have prepared the grounds for these disturbances.

However, the Commission, while accepting that the cadres had many genuine grievances, strongly criticise the tactics adopted to solve these. Under no circumstances can we condone:

- the indiscriminate shooting and terrorising of the Angolan people;
- the total rejection and contempt of authority;
- the breakdown of military discipline;
- the orgy of drinking and dagga smoking.

The damage done to our reputation and relationship with the Angolan government, Army and people and with our allies in the socialist countries, and supporters internationally; the very dangerous opportunities created for our enemies to weaken and indeed destroy our organisation and the effect of these events on the unfolding revolution are very serious indeed. The cadres must be made fully [to] understand the consequences of their actions.

Links between regions: The Commission was not able to find any conspiratorial links between Luanda and other regions. . . . The demands for a national conference and the intensification of the armed struggle are common threads to be found in all regions.

The hitherto almost unrestricted contact between Angola and other regions and the gross violation of the "need to know rule" and the abundance of gossip rumors ("Radio Potato") constitutes a serious problem. Unfortunately many people in leadership positions are also responsible for this: urgent steps must be taken to remedy this. . . .

Finally, the Commission was struck by the fact that unlike the situation in most progressive countries, where priority attention in every respect is given towards moulding a strong reliable army, our People's Army is on the lowest or very nearly lowest rung of priorities. For the price of one of the motor-vehicles which are regularly smashed up in Lusaka without any apparent accountability, a number of problems could be solved in the camps. We wish to end our assessment by sounding a word of warning. The situation in Angola may be "under control", the fires of discontent may have been doused, [but] the fire has not been completely extinguished, and this can only be done by devoting more efforts, time, resources and political will towards the solution of the real problems in our camps in Angola.

RECOMMENDATIONS

[The Commission made 21 recommendations aimed at restoring confidence in the leadership. They recommended that preparations start immediately for an ANC national conference; National Commissar Andrew Masondo be "redeployed"; a general amnesty be granted to all mutineers; a reform of the security department be undertaken; army and camp administration, training, health and recreational facilities be improved and elite privileges abolished; and a report-back be made to the camps regarding the findings and decisions of the Commission.]

DOCUMENT 116. Notes on a visit to Nelson Mandela in Pollsmoor Prison, by Nicholas Bethell, January 27, 1985 (abridged)

I waited for Nelson Mandela in the Governor's office in the maximum security block of Cape Town's Pollsmoor Prison. Senior officers in yellow khaki uniforms with gold stars on their epaulettes, some with peaked caps pulled over their eyes like Guards sergeant majors, scurried in and out talking excitedly in Afrikaans. At last three men entered the room and one came towards me. . . . He was anxious to put me at my ease and he invited me to sit down at the desk where I was ready to make my notes. It was a second or two before I realised that this was the man I had come to see.

A 6 ft-tall lean figure with silvering hair, an impeccable olive-green shirt and well-creased navy blue trousers, he could almost have seemed like another general in the South African prison service. Indeed his manner was the most self-assured of them all and he stood out as obviously the senior man in the room. He was, however, black. And he was a prisoner, perhaps the most famous in the world, the man they write songs about in Europe and name streets after in London, the leader of the African National Congress, a body dedicated to the destruction of the Apartheid system, if necessary by force. He is the black man's folk hero, his fame made all the greater by the fact that he has been out of sight behind prison bars for nearly 22 years. . . .

Nelson Mandela says, "In my first ten years on Robben Island conditions were really very bad. We were physically assaulted. We were subjected to psychological persecution. We had to work every day in the lime quarry from 7 am to 4 pm with a one hour break, wearing shorts and sandals, with no socks or underwear and just a calico jacket. It was hard, boring, unproductive work and on rainy days in the winter it was very cold.

"The guards pushed us all the time to work harder, from dawn to sunset, and we could get solitary confinement if they thought we were slacking. The diet was maize porridge for breakfast with half a teaspoon of sugar, boiled grain for lunch with puzamadla, a drink made out of maize that is, to put it mildly, an acquired taste, and porridge with vegetables in the evening. There was a lot of tension between guards and prisoners."

Helen Suzman, who has campaigned for the black man's rights throughout 32 years in the South African parliament, remembers with horror her visits to Robben Island in the 1960s. 'Guards with alsatian dogs on leads and sometimes with swastikas tattooed on their wrists, would drive the men to work. I remember one prisoner complaining to me that he had been assaulted. I was noting down the details when the guard in question came running up saying "Ah, it was really nothing, Mrs Suzman, it was only a kick up the arse!"' Then around 1974 there were dramatic improvements especially in the treatment of "security prisoners". . . .

He says, . . "I am in good health. It is not true that I have cancer. It is not true that I had a toe amputated. I get up at 3.30 every morning, do two hours physical exercise, work up a good sweat. Then I read and study during the day. I get the South African newspapers as well as the *Guardian* weekly and

Time magazine. We have a radio in the cell,[but] can only get South African stations, not the BBC. I cultivate my garden. We grow vegetables in pots— tomatoes, broccoli, beans, cucumber and strawberries."

He gestured expansively to his right: "The major here has been tremendously helpful. He is really an excellent gardener." The major in question, Fritz van Sittert, who guards Mandela and his five cell mates and was detailed to supervise our meeting, did not react or even utter a word throughout the entire two hours. We spent the time just the three of us in the functional office with its G-plan furniture, dominated by a large glass-topped desk and overlooked by a picture of State President PW Botha wearing a silver order and an orange sash. The major was there not to censor the conversation, which was unhindered, but to make sure that no document or other object passed between us.

For instance, I was asked to obtain Mandela's signature on a paper authorising his name to go forward in the election of the rectorship of Edinburgh University. He was not allowed to sign the paper, but he agreed verbally to be a candidate: "I am very flattered. I am a politician and of course I like to win elections, but in this case it is such a kind gesture that I really don't mind if I win or lose."

Mandela had kind words too for Pollsmoor's Governor, Brigadier F. C. Munro. "The Brigadier does his best to solve our little problems. But, poor man, he has very little authority. Everything concerning the six of us he has to refer to Pretoria. For instance, a year ago my sister died and I wrote to my brother-in-law about her funeral. They blocked the letter. Why? I suppose because he is a policeman in Transkei and they don't want me to make contact with him. His name is Russell Piliso. They also blocked my letter to Bishop [Desmond] Tutu congratulating him on winning the Nobel Prize. A few days ago a friend of mine here received a letter completely cut to ribbons. It's not the poor Brigadier, it's the politicians. Still, conditions here are quite reasonable, better than on the Island. The food is good and there are no problems with the staff, racial or otherwise."

It was in order that I could confirm this that South African Minister HJ Coetsee authorised my visit, making it clear that I would not be allowed to bring press or television with me as Senator Edward Kennedy had wished. Mr Coetsee wanted the point to be made that Mandela was in good health and being well treated. And I can confirm that, generally speaking, that is the case. Even so, it was an unusual concession to a foreign parliamentarian.

Pollsmoor consists of a dozen long buildings built in the 1970s, each one a separate unit. It looks from the outside like a huge gloomy campus of a comprehensive school or red brick university. "This is the white women's section. This is the coloured men's section," explained Deputy Commissioner of Security, Major General "Bertie" Venter as we drove past the main barrier along roads lined with grass and flower beds, towards the Governor's dining room. Over lunch—steak and chips cooked and served by convicted men— Commissioner of Prisons, Lieutenant General "Willie" Willemse, presented his case that South African conditions are up to North American or West European standards. Each man, black or white, receives a minimum 10,571 kilojoule-per-day diet. Prisoners have decent clothes, family visits, recreation, and the possibility of parole. "If only people abroad knew the facts" he said, "we in South Africa would not be so harshly judged". . . .

The problem is, therefore, not one of brutal prison conditions. It is that Mandela and his friends . . . have spent 18 years on Robben Island and three in Pollsmoor all for no worse a crime than conniving at the destruction of property. It is a punishment that far exceeds the offence. . . .

The problem is that Mandela still supports the armed struggle. This is why some human rights bodies, for instance Amnesty International, will not campaign for his release. Also his case does not appeal to the Parole Board, since he shows no repentance for his past actions—rather the contrary—he makes no secret of his wish to return to the fray. This provides the authorities with the ideal pretext for not putting his name forward to State President Botha for clemency.

He says, "The armed struggle was forced on us by the government. And if they want us now to give it up, the ball is in their court. They must legalise us, treat us like a political party and negotiate with us. Until they do, we will have to live with the armed struggle. It is useless simply to carry on talking. The government has tightened the screws too far."

"Of course, if there were to be talks along these lines, we in the ANC would declare a truce. That is what SWAPO did in Namibia. But meanwhile we are forced to continue, though within certain limits. We go for hard targets only, military installations and the symbols of apartheid. Civilians must not be touched. This is why I deeply regret what happened in Pretoria on May 23rd 1983."

"A bomb went off and more than a dozen civilians were killed. Something must have gone wrong with the timing. It was a tragic accident. On the other hand the incident that took place in Vryheid (Natal) a few weeks ago when a South African lieutenant was killed, was quite justified. Some ANC members were in a house and the security forces came looking for them. We have reason to believe that their policy now is to shoot to kill rather than try to arrest our men. So they opened fire in self defence and the lieutenant was killed, as were several of our soldiers."

"We aim for buildings and property. So it may be that someone gets killed in a fight, in the heat of battle, but we do not believe in assassinations. I would not want our men to assassinate, for instance, the Major here. I would only justify this in the case of an informer who was a danger to our lives. And all this can end as soon as talks begin. It would be humiliating though for us simply to lay down our arms."

It is this "humiliating" condition that the South African government requires and which blocks any progress towards a political settlement and Mandela's release. Louis Le Grange, now Minister of Law and Order, says: "We are not so weak as to agree to talks with the ANC at the moment. But if they will forego the armed struggle and enter the political arena we will talk to them. As for Mandela, if you ask me whether I should recommend his release so that he can carry on where he left off, I say no. I can't give such advice unless he gives some assistance through his own attitude. Things are at a sensitive stage in South Africa. We have changed our constitution and are contemplating further changes. So we must have proper law and order. As things are Mandela's release would invite a lot of problems and trouble". . . .

Meanwhile, [Mandela] wants to see the ANC develop as a widely based national movement: "Personally, I am a socialist and I believe in a classless society. But I see no reason to belong to any political party at the moment. Businessmen and farmers, white or black, can also join our movement to fight against racial discrimination. It would be a blunder to narrow it."

"I appreciate the Soviet Union only because it was the one country that long ago condemned racialism and supported liberation movements. It does not mean that I approve of their internal policy. I was grateful, too, by the way, to Emperor Haile Selassie of Ethiopia who received me in 1962. He was a feudal ruler, but he supported our movement and I was grateful to him. Britain, too, has helped us, under Mrs Thatcher as well as under socialist governments, by condemning apartheid on principle. We may have different views about the methods that should be used, but the most important thing is to condemn apartheid outright. And this, as I understand it, is what your Prime Minister does."

Our talks drew to a close and Brigadier Munro invited me to visit Mandela's cell in the isolated wing of the long, low building. And so we walked in a slow procession up flights of stairs and around corners with Mandela leading the way as if showing me around his home. He did not open doors for me. This was done by sergeants with heavy keys after much saluting and clanking. Always, though, Mandela was the one who showed the way, inviting me to go first through every door and plying me with questions on Britain and the world, anxious, apparently, to supplement the information he gets from the radio and press he has in his cell.

Did I think that the Gorbachev visit would relax East-West tensions? What were my hopes for the Shultz-Gromyko talks? Would the Liberals at last make a break-through in British politics? What was Mrs Thatcher's secret of success? Who was now leader of the Labour Party?

And so we reached the "Mandela enclosure" on the third floor, a large room with six beds, plenty of books and adequate facilities for washing and toilet. The cell door is open almost all day. They have access to a long L-shaped yard surrounded by high white walls. As well as the vegetable pots there is a ping-pong table and even a small-scale tennis court, apparently unused.

Mandela proudly showed me his vegetables, like a landowner showing me his farm. As for the yard, he wished only that it was less monotonously black, white and grey. As a country man, he longed for green. And he understood, he said, what Oscar Wilde meant by "the little tent of blue that prisoners call the sky."

He showed me [a] damp patch on the cell wall, introduced me to his five cell mates, who apologised for being informally dressed. He explained who I was and briefly what we had been discussing. . . . And he joked as we prepared to leave, "Aren't there any other complaints? Doesn't anyone want to go home?"

And so we walked the last few yards towards the end of the enclosure and I prepared to say goodbye to this remarkable man whom I have begged the South African Government to release, on humanitarian grounds if for no other reason. A sergeant opened the grey, heavy steel door. Mandela said: "Well, Lord Bethell, this is my frontier and this is where I must leave you". . . . I walked through all the other steel doors, down the stone staircases, out through the front door into the fine Cape summer feeling poorer for being so suddenly deprived of this man's exhilarating company.

DOCUMENT 117. Speech by Zindzi Mandela at Jabulani Amphitheatre, Soweto, February 10, 1985

On Friday my mother and our attorney saw my father at Pollsmoor Prison to obtain his answer to Botha's offer of conditional release. The prison authorities attempted to stop this statement being made but he would have none of this and made it clear that he would make the statement to you, the people. Strangers like [Nicholas] Bethell from England and Professor [Sam] Dash from the United States have in recent weeks been authorised by Pretoria to see my father without restriction, yet Pretoria cannot allow you, the people, to hear what he has to say directly. He should be here himself to tell you what he thinks of this statement by Botha. He is not allowed to do so. My mother, who also heard his words, is also not allowed to speak to you today.

My father and his comrades at Pollsmoor Prison send their greetings to you, the freedom-loving people of this our tragic land, in the full confidence that you will carry on the struggle for freedom. He, with his comrades at Pollsmoor Prison send their very warmest greetings to Bishop [Desmond] Tutu. Bishop Tutu has made it clear to the world that the Nobel Peace Prize belongs to you who are the people. We salute him.

My father and his comrades at Pollsmoor Prison are grateful to the United Democratic Front who without hesitation made this venue available to them so that they could speak to you today. My father and his comrades wish to make this statement to you, the people, first. They are clear that they are accountable to you and to you alone. And that you should hear their views directly and not through others. My father speaks not only for himself and for his comrades at Pollsmoor Prison, but he hopes he also speaks for all those in jail for their opposition to apartheid, for all those who are banished, for all those who are in exile, for all those who suffer under apartheid, for all those who are opponents of apartheid and for all those who are oppressed and exploited.

Throughout our struggle there have been puppets who have claimed to speak for you. They have made this claim, both here and abroad. They are of no consequence. My father and his colleagues will not be like them.

My father says, "I am a member of the African National Congress. I have always been a member of the African National Congress and I will remain a member of the African National Congress until the day I die. Oliver Tambo is much more than a brother to me. He is my greatest friend and comrade for nearly fifty years. If there is anyone amongst you who cherishes my freedom, Oliver Tambo cherishes it more and I know that he would give his life to see me free. There is no difference between his views and mine."

My father says, "I am surprised at the conditions that the government wants to impose on me. I am not a violent man. My colleagues and I wrote in 1952 to [Prime Minister D.F.] Malan asking for a roundtable conference to find a solution to the problems of our country but that was ignored. When [J. G.] Strijdom was in power, we made the same offer. Again it was ignored. When [Hendrik] Verwoerd was in power we asked for a national convention for all the people in South Africa to decide on their future. This, too, was in vain. It was only then, when all other forms of resistance were no longer open to us that we turned to armed struggle.

"Let Botha show that he is different to Malan, Strijdom and Verwoerd. Let *him* renounce violence. Let him say that he will dismantle apartheid. Let him unban the people's organisation, the African National Congress. Let him free all who have been imprisoned, banished or exiled for their opposition to apartheid. Let him guarantee free political activity so that the people may decide who will govern them.

"I cherish my own freedom dearly but I care even more for *your* freedom. Too many have died since I went to prison. Too many have suffered for the love of freedom. I owe it to their widows, to their orphans, to their mothers and to their fathers who have grieved and wept for them. Not only I have suffered during these long, lonely, wasted years. I am not less life-loving than you are. But I cannot sell my birthright, nor am I prepared to sell the birthright of the people to be free. I am in prison as the representative of the people and of your organisation, the African National Congress, which was banned. What freedom am I being offered whilst the organisation of the people remains banned. What freedom am I being offered when I may be arrested on a pass offence. What freedom am I being offered to live my life as a family with my dear wife, who remains in banishment in Brandfort. What freedom am I being offered when I must ask for permission to live in an urban area. What freedom am I being offered when I need a stamp in my pass to seek work. What freedom am I being offered when my very South African citizenship is not respected.

"Only free men can negotiate. Prisoners cannot enter into contracts. Herman Toivo ja Toivo [of SWAPO], when freed, never gave any undertaking, nor was he called upon to do so."

My father says,

"I cannot and will not give any undertaking at a time when I and you, the people, are not free. Your freedom and mine cannot be separated. I *will* return."

DOCUMENT 118. "Sharpeville, Soweto and Sebokeng." Speech by John Nyati Pokela of PAC to the Special Committee Against Apartheid, United Nations, New York, March 22, 1985 (abridged)

Comrade Chairman, at the very outset allow me to most sincerely thank the Special Committee Against Apartheid for convening this Special Session to commemorate the twenty-fifth anniversary of the Sharpeville massacre. We of the Pan Africanist Congress of Azania are also in agreement with the theme of this Special Session, namely, "Sharpeville, Soweto and Sebokeng: Struggle for Liberation in South Africa and International Response".

The title of the theme, moreover, is not only suggestive but also objective. It is a recognition that the Sharpeville massacre of March 21, 1960, the Soweto Uprising of June 16, 1976 and the resistance of the people of Sebokeng to the imposition of the so-called new constitution constitute watersheds and milestones in the development of the just and legitimate struggle of our people for national liberation and self-determination.

Comrade Chairman, the three African townships specifically mentioned here have not been the only arena of African resistance, but they are very symbolic of the dominant political trend in occupied Azania. Allow me to elaborate.

The significance of Sharpeville does not lie only on the fact that the people there marched to the police station on March 21, 1960 in response to a call by the Pan Africanist Congress and offered themselves for arrest. This is because there were anti-pass campaigns before March 21, 1960. However, what highlights the March 21, 1960 anti-pass campaign was that it was qualitatively and quantitatively different from the past anti-pass campaigns. First and foremost, it was not a mere protest campaign, The slogan under which the PAC leadership launched the March 21, 1960 campaign was *"No Defence, No Bail And No Fine"*. This slogan itself reflected a new political approach and attitude; it reflected a conscious and principled rejection of the entire fascist-colonial status-quo in apartheid South Africa. Comrade Mangaliso Robert Sobukwe, the First President of the Pan Africanist Congress of Azania, was the first African political leader in modern times to tell the oppressors that the dispossessed people of Azania *did not recognise the status quo* and, therefore, would offer no defence and pay no fines.

This new political approach, Comrade Chairman, was introduced on the Azanian political scene by the Pan Africanist Congress of Azania. Comrade Sobukwe, from the very outset, maintained that two fundamental prerequisites must be realised, not through academic exercise but through struggle, before a successful revolution can be waged. First, to exorcise the African from feelings of inferiority inculcated into him for over three hundred years so that he will consciously choose "to starve in freedom rather than have plenty in bondage". Comrade Sobukwe firmly believed that "once the mind is free, the body will soon be free. Once white supremacy has become mentally untenable to our people, it will become physically untenable too—and will go". In pursuance of this the Pan Africanist Congress of Azania launched, in January 1960, the *Status Campaign*. The self-confidence that this campaign generated in the African masses paved the way for the March 21, 1960 Decisive, Final, Positive Action Against the Pass Laws.

The other important prerequisite was the conscious and total rejection of the oppressor's institutions and techniques of control. Comrade Sobukwe pointed out that "the white minority can maintain its continued domination *only* by perfecting the techniques of control in such a way as to enlist the active co-operation and goodwill of the oppressed". The rejection and destruction of these "techniques of control" is an important element in the struggle for national liberation.

Comrade Chairman, allow me to point out how the two prerequisites enunciated by Comrade Sobukwe have reflected themselves in events that have occurred in Sharpeville, Soweto and Sebokeng. At Sharpeville the trigger-happy forces of the illegal, racist minority regime resorted to the use of reactionary violence precisely because it was not a mere protest campaign. The mentally liberated and politically conscious African, following the PAC sponsored *Status Campaign*, did not plead for his inalienable rights *but demanded it!* In other words the PAC-led March 21, 1960 campaign unequivocally *challenged* the fascist-colonial status-quo in occupied Azania. Sharpeville, therefore, symbolises this qualitative transformation of the just struggle of the dispossessed people of Azania of one of mere protest to challenging the status-quo. Moreover, this qualitative transformation proved to be the political forerunner to the subsequent events that occurred in Soweto in 1976 and Sebokeng since September 1984.

Comrade Chairman, the emergence of Black Consciousness concept on the Azanian political scene in the 1970s, far from being a "primitive" concept, reflected the development of the ideas enunciated in the Status Campaign of the Pan Africanist Congress of Azania. The removal of the indoctrinated inferiority complex cannot be realised by integration or liberal sympathies, but rather by asserting the African right and dignity. It was this conscious rejection of the indoctrinated inferiority complex that sparked off the Soweto Uprising of 1976 when the students rejected the imposition of the oppressor's language. This struggle developed into a rejection of the entire inferior education system deliberately designed to keep our people in perpetual subjugation. Today that struggle has, understandably, developed to rejecting the entire apartheid system in occupied Azania. The Soweto Uprising of 1976, therefore, must be seen in its proper historical context—the conscious attempt by the Pan Africanist Congress of Azania to translate into practice what Comrade Sobukwe taught us, namely, we must consciously destroy the enemy's "techniques of control". Bantu Education is one of the key "techniques of control" devised by the fascist rulers in Pretoria. Since June 1976 students throughout the country have been on strike and as I speak here more than a quarter million Azanian students are striking inside occupied Azania.

Comrade Chairman, some self-styled experts who mistake phenomena for essence, have gone on record as describing the 1976 Soweto Uprising as "spontaneous". Actions may be spontaneous but political trends develop along certain declared lines. It will be recalled that Comrade Zephania Mothopeng, the veteran PAC leader and stalwart, was formally charged with 17 other PAC comrades for what the racist judge said, "for predicting and organising" the 1976 Soweto Uprising. Today Comrade Zephania Mothopeng is serving a 30 year jail sentence on Robben Island for his role in mobilising and organising the Soweto Uprising of 1976. . . .

Comrade Chairman, the emergence of the PAC on the Azanian political scene radically transformed the nature and tempo of the struggle. It was the PAC-led March 21, 1960 campaign that also ushered in the era of armed struggle. Armed struggle as a principal method of struggle emerged in the post-Sharpeville period. The Pan Africanist Congress of Azania was the first national liberation movement to form a military wing, which came to be known as *Poqo*. The initial combatants of *Poqo* were armed with home-made weapons, such as pangas [machetes] and home-made bombs, and whatever arms they could capture from the enemy. Even hostile academicians to the PAC have had to acknowledge that the most sustained and widespread armed struggle in modern times in South Africa was carried out by PAC/*Poqo*. It is also documented that over 120 *Poqo* militants were executed by the racist regime between 1961 and 1967. . . .

As regards the armed struggle, the PAC maintains, as a result of bitter experiences, that the struggle must be internally based. The classical methods used in Africa of waging armed struggle from neighbouring states cannot be wholly employed in the South African situation. Even this position of the PAC has been appreciated and accepted by the people inside the country. To demonstrate this truism, it will be recalled that after the Sharpeville massacre hundreds left the country to seek political asylum abroad; after the Soweto Uprising thousands left the country, but since the uprising following the imposition of the so-called new constitution, few, if any, left the country, not because oppression has lessened, but because the battle field is inside Azania. . . .

Comrade Chairman, this now brings me to the question of international response to our struggle. We of the PAC would like to take this opportunity to most sincerely thank the African, Non-Aligned and several Nordic countries for the principled assistance they have rendered to our struggle. We also thank the principled non-governmental organisations and support groups. However, we must also mention that the attitude of some Western countries, particularly the United States of America, has been to give overt and covert support to the racist regime through such disguised policies as "constructive engagement"... . In our candid opinion if the international community wants to seriously assist our struggle then it must immediately impose comprehensive and mandatory economic and military sanctions against the illegal Pretoria regime or fully support the armed struggle of the dispossessed people of Azania and the Pan Africanist Congress of Azania. There is no other principled path the international community can follow.

Comrade Chairman, the past 25 years has greatly enriched us as an organisation, both in experience and understanding. From Sharpeville to Soweto to Sebokeng our people, under the political leadership of the PAC, have increased their fighting capacity. We of the Pan Africanist Congress of Azania are proud that we have played a positive role in the awakening and politicisation of our people since Sharpeville. But we are even more proud that our people have entrusted us with the noble task of playing the pioneering role in the liberation of our country. That important appointment with history we are determined to keep!

DOCUMENT 119. "The Road to Freedom." Poem by Freddy Reddy, *Sechaba*, April 1985

Long is the road to freedom
Your impatience
Will not make it shorter comrade
I know heart
Is bursting with anger
Your brain burning
With the heat of vengeance

Waiting tortures
Waiting waiting waiting
Here there nowhere and everywhere
Longing
Lingering questions
Suspicion
Who is who isn't
I know your pain
Many have felt it from time began

Unpraised burial without lamentations
Many have trod on this road
Before you
Often bloody footprints
Landmarks
For you and me
To follow
The long uneasy road to freedom

Document 120. Memo from Moscow Camp detachment of Umkhonto we Sizwe, Angola, early 1985

PREPARATION OF THE NATIONAL CONSULTATIVE CONFERENCE

PRESENT: Moscow-Camp Detarchment.
AGENDA: Immediate problems of the revolution
CATEGORISATION: i) Individual
                  ii) Colective
                  iii) Regional
                  iv) National

Problems discussed at this meeting range from military, political, ideological, economic as well as social.

Our movement is today faced with many petty problems which, because of wrong solutions, have ended up uncontrolable. It is also a fact that most comrades returned from the front have in one way or another been creating problems to the movement there. But in most cases too, the solution to such problems was not the best possible one. Action was rush[ed]; spontenious and even apolitical in some cases. This has as a result created crisis and a series of complaints against the Security Department.

The Picture is further clarified by the points here-under noted, [verbatim] from the meeting

a) Age limit in the Security Department: Some operatives are too young and socially inexperienced to handle this task. Comrades sugest inclusion of older comrades to guide and assist them.
b) Its structures should be clearly outlined, i.e. Centralisation of Security; of Military Intelligence; and of personnel; interdependently.
c) The Security Department works independently as a supreme body, is very negligent and also relaxed. It also has too much power.
d) The department is isolated from the people thus rendering its work inefficient.
e) It should receive a sophisticated type of training so that its work can be geared towards home especially Military Intelligence. To infiltrate into the country so as to ensure survival of the fighters.
f) The manner in which they have conducted their work has resulted in humilation of comrades.
g) Proper criterion should be made in selecting operatives since most do not adhere to conspiracy norms, thus endangering the interests of the movement. Security Chiefs use classified information to woo female comrades.

There is also a problem as regards the general state of life here in Angola. Comrades have developed fear and other wrong concepts about our mission here in Angola. Issues raised [were] also raised and noted verbatism [in writing?].

a) The rights of MK-Soldiers should be outlined, moreso since they carry the brunt of this revolution.
b) Improved training facilities should be made available to the cadres.
c) Seperation of families for different tasks even where its not necessary, should be checked.
d) Comrades should be briefed on progress and retrogression in the front by reliable sources of the movement.
e) Training effects (i.e. track-suits, uniforms and boots) should not be hoarded for unspecified reasons.
f) Dying of comrades because of lack of transport in one area when they are sick should be averted e.g. comrades died in Caxito from malaria-fever, because of lack of transport when cars were roaming in Luanda.
g) The medical question, should be given deeper consideration. Comrades are delayed in treatment.
h) Advancement of cadres in all fields viz. Politics, military as well as academic should be implemented especially since some comrades have now stayed at least 7 years in Angola without further develop-ment.
i) The movement is still faced with the problem of proper administration in our offices as well as structurally.
j) The "Button Pressing" slogan comes as a result of actions taken viz a viz deployment of personnel. Angola is used as a [dumping?] privilage in the movement.
k) Viana-Camp Staff is marked for being notorious i.e. harsh punishments and beatings with serious end-results some of these comrades work.
l) Accountability in the usage of funds allocated to this region must be looked into.
m) Trained women are only deployed in offices, why never in the front as part of our trained personnel.
n) Who issued orders that comrades smoking dagga [marijuana] should be killed. At times agents participate in killing comrades e.g. (i) Beki (ii) Justice was condeming comrade in Maputo.
o) Some of the people who where beating dagga smokers were themselves smokers. The enemy agents proper are left free, some bred for better positions when comrades are being killed for triffles.
p) Allegations that the ANC is bankrupt by irresponsible people who want to hoard funds should be looked into especially since that is the life-line of our work.
q) Globe trotting while comrades who have wives in Tanzania are not able to visit their families should be curbed. Favoritism and double-standard treatment should be solved.
r) misuse of ANC funds e.g. Chief Representative buying expensive cars must not be done at the expence of the welfare in the region.
s) emulations should be restarted to emulate the comrade's efforts.
t) False allegations about comrades being agents be accounted for and not recurring in future.
u) Merit should open opportunities for able comrades to the front. Also vol-

unteers should be taken to the front since fighting entails death amongst other odds.

v) The long stay of comrades in Angola, thereby rendering them useless should be accounted for especially since Comrade Mzwai Piliso said it would be so (that certain comrades would rot in the camps) only to be later confirmed by the boers [Afrikaners].

This region also has a perculiar problem emanating from its military nature. Comrades problems of the front have thus been transfered to Angola.

i) Control and check should be applied to resolve the problem of embezzlement of funds by front commanders.
ii) Acountability on the death and arrests of comrades should be chanelled by front commanders until it reaches soldiers in the war.
iii) Certain machineries should not use too much money whilst there is no progress to justify it.
iv) The movement has been failing to infiltrate comrades to appreciable levels; at a correct time; using the same routes and personnel with the result that ambushes, arrests and even deaths have occurred.
v) Regionalism is so rife at some fronts that it hampers development. E.g. the Mozambican front was composed of people from Dube area [of Soweto] (friends at home) i.e. (Gebhuza [Siphiwe Nyanda], Moss, Mpanza, Kenny, Brick (little John) even the Army Commander [Joe Modise] himself.
vi) The Army Commander has failed in his work. He should infact account and if possible, be given another responsibility. Failure is mostly visible in the Botswana front.
vii) Front commanders should not use the idea of calibre when selecting front operatives with ill intensions.
viii) Comrades should not be sent to the front for personal whims of the comrades, commanders, e.g. Comrade Lefu was sent into the country to fetch the Army Commander's clothes, he was later paralised and died in Tanzania.

Some of the problems especially concerning logistics have now been cleared by the Treasure General, Comrade Thomas Titus Nkobi. It is hoped that other problems will be solved in this same spirit for the smooth running and advancement of our struggle.

AMANDLA!!! MATLA!!! [POWER]

DOCUMENT 121. "ANC Call to the Nation: the Future is Within Our Grasp!" Underground leaflet, April 1985

Events in our country are moving with astonishing speed. In our January 8th message we issued a call for the intensification of our liberation offensive on all fronts, the transformation of more and more localities into mass revolutionary bases, and the need to take further strides towards rendering the country ungovernable.

Only three months have passed since that call was made and already the surge of people's resistance and active defiance have reached new heights. The face of our country is changing before our very eyes.

- In the black ghettoes of the urban areas the legitimacy of authority of all types is not just under attack, it has been largely destroyed. Most of those who served white rule in so-called urban councils have suffered the wrath of the people. But many have respected the demands of the people by resigning.
- The tri-cameral parliament has exposed its complete impotence in the present crisis and continues to be shunned. The Bantustans are universally held in contempt.
- Well-organised stay-aways in localised areas have once again drawn attention to the potential of the organised workers to bring the ruling class to its knees.
- The people, by their actions, are teaching black police and soldiers that there is no place in our communities for those who wear the uniforms of apartheid and who carry out orders to kill, maim and torture their brothers and sisters.
- All attempts to tame our fighting students have failed and more and more schools and universities are becoming flashpoints for freedom.
- The continuing street confrontations with the enemy's armed forces show that our people, in massive numbers, not only want a new order in our country but are also prepared to sacrifice life, if need be, to bring it about.
- Fired by the heroic example of Umkhonto we Sizwe, more and more of our youth are searching for ways to organise themselves into effective combat units to defend the people, deal with the collaborators, and to hit back selectively at the enemy's armed personnel.
- The people, undaunted by massive state repression, are openly demonstrating over and over again that the ANC is their legitimate and overall leader on the road to People's Power.

On the side of the people the conditions for a revolutionary leap forward are beginning to mature. On the side of the ruling class the economic and political crisis has reached new heights.

It is clear that the racists cannot continue to rule in the old way. The bankrupt and dying regime is being kept alive by those who carry arms in its defence. All attempts by it to find alternative solutions have landed on the rocks. All Botha's reforms, designed to defuse the developing revolutionary assault, trigger off even more vigorous mass opposition. The promised alteration of the sex laws is the latest pathetic manoeuvre. It is another gesture to help the external allies of apartheid to stem the mounting international tide for the total isolation of South Africa. There will be real love across the colour line only when South Africa is completely free.

The growing ferment from below and the deepening crisis from above demand the urgent attention of our whole liberation front and all sectors of our struggling peoples.

The historic conditions which are necessary to ensure the collapse of the apartheid system and the creation by the people of a new social order are beginning to take shape in greater measure than ever before in our history. Yet much more remains to be done. It is the urgent task of our liberation movement and of all patriots to stimulate the further growth of those conditions which could bring the day of the people's seizure of power within our sight.

It is against this background that we once again call on all sections of our people to make the apartheid system more and more unworkable and the country less and less governable. At the same time we must work endlessly to strengthen all levels of mass and underground organisation and to create the beginnings of popular power.

More particularly:
- We call on our nationally oppressed working class to strengthen and unite the trade union movement and to sharpen the weapon of workers' power at the point of production in the struggle for national liberation. A long-lasting national work stoppage, backed by our oppressed communities and supported by armed activity, can break the backbone of the apartheid system and bring the regime to its knees. All patriots active in industrial organisation must examine the lesson of the recent successful stay-aways in the Transvaal and Eastern Cape and must set their sights on combining national stay-away action with countrywide mass popular actions.
- We call on our communities in the black ghettoes to replace the collapsing government stooge councils with people's committees in every block which could become the embryos of people's power.
- We call on our people and, more especially, our fighting youth in every black community, school and university to find ways of organising themselves into small mobile units which will protect the people against anti-social elements and act in an organised way in both white and black areas against the enemy and its agents. Every black area must become a "no go area" for any isolated individuals or pockets of the enemy's police or armed personnel. The people must find ways to obtain arms by whatever means from the enemy and from any other source. Appropriate forms of combat tactics must be developed for situations in which the enemy is on the rampage against the people. The proliferation of such units and their functioning in accordance with all the rules of underground secrecy will add inestimable power and strength to the armed wing of our liberation movement—Umkhonto we Sizwe.
- We call on all those among the black oppressed who serve in the machineries of apartheid to resign now. The Bantustans, the so-called parliaments for the Coloured and Indian people, the community councils and other organs of racist power must cease to function. They must find fewer and fewer participants as patriots join in the bitter struggle for power. At a time when so many have fallen and are falling to racist bullets, those who continue to sell their people's birthright will be shunned and made to feel the anger of the masses in both town and countryside.
- We call on the unemployed blacks now sitting in uniform to stop shooting their brothers and sisters in defence of white rule. They must refuse to carry out such orders. They must organise secretly to turn their guns against their masters.

- We call on those in the white community who have been conscripted into the army to refuse, in their own interests and those of their children, to be used as instruments of massacres and military domination over their black fellow citizens and over the people of Namibia, Angola and other parts of Southern Africa.
- We call on all social institutions, religious, cultural, civic and sporting, which retain a belief in the true brotherhood of man, to side even more vigorously with the cause of people's liberation and stand firm against racist intimidation.
- We call on the people everywhere to defy, in an organised way, the imposition of laws founded on race discrimination, to resist all attacks on their living conditions and to promote united resistance and action against the apartheid system and its agencies.
- We call on the white community in whose name racist barbarities are being perpetrated daily against the black majority, to move away from its support of apartheid and to increase the ranks of the growing number of democratic whites who are participating in our liberation struggle.
- We call, in this Year of the Cadre, on all political and military activists to work unceasingly to strengthen the ANC's underground presence and to reinforce our leadership core in every part of the country. The ANC-led liberation movement is the indispensable guide to the whole revolutionary process.
- We call on Umkhonto we Sizwe to intensify the armed struggle with all the means at its disposal and, more particularly, to concentrate more and more on actions against the enemy armed forces and police. We also call on our underground to help make such an intensification of armed activity possible by working day and night to create and strengthen our internal political revolutionary bases.

The period ahead presents all of us—whether in or out of the ANC—with an awe-inspiring challenge. Under the leadership of our liberation movement we can and must answer this call of history. Let the blood of our martyrs who are falling before the enemy bullets nourish our battle for freedom. Let our watchwords be: Unity in Mass Action! Confront the Enemy on all Fronts!

MAKE APARTHEID UNWORKABLE!
MAKE THE COUNTRY UNGOVERNABLE!
Forward to People's Power!
Long Live the ANC – the Vanguard of Our Revolution!

Document 122. "The Women's Question." Excerpt from report of Commission on Ideological and Political Work, ANC National Consultative Conference, Kabwe, Zambia, June 16–23, 1985

The commission noted that there is a world-wide movement aimed at eradicating the centuries-old oppression and subjugation of women. It is for this reason that the commission recommends that the movement lay out a

theoretical basis for the understanding and solution of the women's question within the liberation struggle. The commission noted that failure to address ourselves to this question has led to diverse and sometimes antagonistic contradictions on the understanding of the question. It therefore recommends that:
- The analysis of the women's question should be made, basing ourselves on the doctrine of the triple oppression of women in our country.
- The speech delivered by the President at the close of the Women's Conference in Luanda in 1981 should serve as a basis for the further development of the theory of women's emancipation within the liberation struggle.

Having noted that there is a general tendency to refer the question of women's emancipation to the Women's Section, the commission noted that the movement as a whole should begin to address itself to the problem. It therefore recommends that while working towards a common approach, units and branches of the movement must begin discussing the question.
- A national Seminar on the Women's Question must be organized.
- Such a seminar must work from the theoretical understanding that the liberation movement is committed to and must undertake the abolition of women's three-fold oppression as wage workers, as members of the oppressed nation and as of a lesser sex. Our policy is to liberate them from legal, economic and social disabilities. That liberation involves a radical change in male attitudes as well as females', including the eradication of chauvinism and male domination, [provision of] equal job opportunities and equal pay for equal work at all levels of employment, rights of inheritance, and monogamy for both wives and husbands.

The commission further noted that whereas the movement acknowledges that the relations between women and men are most durable and satisfactory when based on mutual respect and affection, there are cases in which men because of traditional attitudes, use their superior positions to take advantage of women. The commission considered that the condition is often open to abuse and calls on the movement to educate comrades who follow practices that are unethical and contrary to the high principles of the organisation; at the same time women in the movement should be educated to free themselves from the images projected by the mass media of women as slaves to fashion and sensuality.

Document 123. "Open Membership: Recommendations." ANC memorandum prepared for National Consultative Conference, Kabwe, Zambia, June 16–23, 1985

Historical Background
When the ANC was formed in 1912, it was an African organization. The task of the day was to unite the Africans across tribal lines, consequently to the closure of what is known as the first stage of our resistance i.e. armed re-

sistance to the colonial occupation and the 1910 marriage of the Boers and the British colonialism.

[The] 1947 pact of the three doctors (Xuma-Naicker-Dadoo Pact) heralded a new stage. Bold steps in search of unity of all the oppressed were being made, a process that culminated into the formation of the Congress Alliance in 1953. Perhaps this process was disrupted by the banning of the organisation in 1960, the repression of the early '60s and the forcing of the organisation into exile.

At the time of the [1969] Morogoro Conference it was agreed to open the membership of the ANC [in exile] to all nationalities because [otherwise we] would have the different Congresses (COD-SAIC-CPC) [white Congress of Democrats, SA Indian Congress, Coloured People's Congress] establishing a separate presence here outside. All congressites had to be brought under the umbrella of the ANC. As to the ANC membership inside the country, the feeling was that the masses at home were not ready. For the same reason, outside here [minority group members] could not be members of the NEC [National Executive Committee] which is the highest body of the ANC.

Present Conditions

Significant changes are visible during this decade. Two groups in particular, the so-called Coloureds and the Indians, have undoubtedly demonstrated their rejection of the Apartheid system and their commitment to the overthrowal of the regime. Glaring examples in support of their assertion are the 1980 school boycotts, the anti-SAIC [SA Indian Council] and the anti-CRC [Coloured Representative Council] campaigns. There has also been a visible growth of the white participation in the struggle, e.g. Neil Aggett, Barbara Hogan, Carl Niehaus, Jansie Lourens are shining examples out of the many.

As to the readiness of the masses inside the country and the legal organisations, the indications are very much positive. In their leadership structures you do find all the national groups. Though this should not be understood to be meaning that this process is completely free of friction and conflicts. Problems do arise from time to time; one group is accused of dominating or aspiring to. These problems fall back on us, they underline the pressing need for our presence.

As to the main content of our struggle, the [1969] *Strategy and Tactics* aptly puts it to be the liberation of the Africans, the most oppressed and the most downtrodden section of the SA population.

Comrade President OR Tambo in London, 1981, addressing the 60th anniversary of the SACP [SA Communist Party], defined the main content of our struggle as the liberation of the Blacks, [by which] he meant the Africans, Indians, and the Coloureds. This underlined a development from the line espoused in the *Strategy and Tactics*. But we find no contradictions between the two. Whether the content is defined as the liberation of the Blacks or the Africans, the Africans will always remain at the centre of our drive for liberation, given the SA situation. The Africans cannot be free without freeing all the oppressed sections of our population. Also the point cited above, i.e.

the total rejection of the apartheid system and their commitment to the overthrowal of this abhorrent system needs a special appreciation, [all the more so] given desperate attempts and manoeuvres by the enemy to win them to its side.

We agreed that the time has come for the opening of the doors of the ANC to all nationalities. But it should be our deliberate policy to promote Africans to positions of leadership. That is we should in all our structures reflect the SA reality, that the Africans are the most numerous and the most oppressed.

With regard to the [Freedom] Charter we failed to subscribe to the argument that since the document states that "SA belongs to all who live in it" and concludes by saying "These freedoms we shall fight for side by side throughout our lives until we have won our liberty", without specifying the affiliation to the nationalities, therefore ANC membership must be open to all. The question has been on the agenda of the ANC since the late '50s or rather [was] on the agenda of the ANC conference in 1958. Throughout these twenty-six years we have been very conscious of the Freedom Charter. It is our programme.

To conclude the question of the membership, it must be formally a principle of the Congress both inside and outside the country, in all the structures, without distorting the main content of our liberation struggle.

Document 124. ANC National Executive Committee report, presented by Oliver Tambo to the National Consultative Conference, Kabwe, Zambia, June 16, 1985 (abridged)

Comrade Chairman, Comrades, Delegates,

This day, the opening of the National Consultative Conference of the ANC, is a great and moving moment in the history of our struggle for national liberation. The days we will spend here will live forever in the records of that struggle as marking a turning point in the history of all the people of South Africa. Our Conference itself will be remembered by our people as a council-of-war that planned the seizure of power by these masses, the penultimate convention that gave the order for us to take our country through the terrible but cleansing fires of revolutionary war to a condition of peace, democracy and the fulfilment of our people who have already suffered far too much and far too long. . . .

Need for Maximum Unity . . .

Conference will . . . make the necessary assessment to ensure that . . . we enjoy maximum political and organisational unity within our own ranks and that all members are actually involved in activity which contributes to the advance of our struggle.

The question of open membership, as it has come to be called, is also on our agenda. In the period since the [1969] Morogoro Conference dealt with this issue, the National Executive Committee has raised it with the membership, at home and abroad, with a view to determine whether as a movement we still felt it was justified to keep the restrictions that were decided upon at Morogoro. There has been extensive discussion of this question. It should not be difficult for us to reach agreement and, building on what was decided at Morogoro, to take decisions that will take our movement and struggle further forward. . . .

[After 1969] two forces emerged—the "ANC (African Nationalists)" and the Black Consciousness Movement. The first was unsuccessful and the second had revolutionary potential until some began to see it as an alternative to the ANC. However, by building our relations with BCM activists, we frustrated the emergence of a Third Force. At the same time, our movement was confronted with strong pressure from within the OAU [Organisation of African Unity] to unite with the PAC. The leadership and the membership jointly resisted this pressure because we were convinced that such unity must grow in struggle among forces that are actually confronting the enemy. We were, further, not prepared to lend credibility to a group which, even then, had discredited itself as a divisive factor within our broad movement, whose complete collapse would help to limit the possibilities of the counter-revolution to plant its agents among the masses of our people.

In our discussions, we should take all these historical experiences into account because, as we shall show later, the idea of a Third Force did not disappear and is still with us today. Its creation will remain a strategic objective of the forces of counter-revolution.

In this regard, it is important to confront the matter objectively that within it, our broad movement for national liberation contains both a nationalist and a socialist tendency. Our national democratic revolution has both class and national tasks which influence one another. This is natural given the nature of our society and oppression and our historical experience. One of the outstanding features of the ANC is that it has been able to encompass both these tendencies within its ranks, on the basis of the common acceptance of the Freedom Charter as a programme that encapsulates the aspirations of our people, however varied their ideological positions might otherwise be.

The forces of counter-revolution continuously seek to separate these tendencies both politically and organisationally, set them at loggerheads, and thus divide the national liberation movement. That is why the enemy always speculates about divisions between "Marxists" and "nationalists" within our ranks. It is on this basis that the PAC was formed, as well as the group we have spoken of which called itself ANC (African Nationalist). Our enemies had entertained hopes that the BCM would emerge, survive and grow as the organised representative of the "nationalist tendency" within the national democratic revolution, independent of the ANC.

These issues are of relevance to this day particularly because certain elements within the country, which describe themselves as belonging to the black consciousness movement, have set themselves against the democratic movement. At the same time, significant numbers of democratic activists, particularly from among the youth, see the ANC as a socialist party and project it as such. Though it came into being later than the period up to 1974 that we have been talking about, it might be appropriate at this stage to refer also to the formation within the ANC of a "left"' faction which dubbed itself the "Marxist Tendency" within the ANC. This faction came out in opposition to our ally, the South African Communist Party, and sought to shift both SACTU [SA Congress of Trade Unions] and the ANC in a so-called left direction. Members of this group are no longer within our ranks. It is, however, true that some of their ideas have penetrated sections of the democratic movement inside our country. These need to be combated, once more, to ensure that this movement does not splinter into left and right factions.

We cannot over-emphasise the strategic importance of ensuring the unity of the ANC, the broad democratic movement and the masses of our struggling people on the basis of our programme, our strategy and tactics. . . .

We have already referred to the contribution that the BCM made to the activisation of our people into struggle. This is a positive contribution that we must recognise and to which we must pay tribute. We should also recognise the significant input that the BCM made towards further uniting the black oppressed masses of our country, by emphasising the commonness of their oppression and their shared destiny. These views were built on political positions that our movement had long canvassed and fought for. Nevertheless, we must still express our appreciation of the contribution that the BCM made in this regard while recognising the limitations of this movement which saw our struggle as racial, describing the entire white population of our country as "part of the problem". . . .

Buthelezi's Personal Power Base

[As part of our policy of encouraging resistance in the bantustans, the ANC encouraged Chief Buthelezi to form a mass democratic organisation]. Unfortunately, we failed to mobilise our own people to take on the task of resurrecting Inkatha as the kind of organisation that we wanted, owing to the understandable antipathy of many of our comrades towards what they considered as working within the bantustan system. The task of reconstituting Inkatha therefore fell on Gatsha Buthelezi himself, who then built Inkatha as a personal power base far removed from the kind of organisation we had visualised, as an instrument for the mobilisation of our people in the countryside into an active and conscious force for revolutionary change. In the first instance, Gatsha dressed Inkatha in the clothes of the ANC, exactly because he knew that the masses to whom he was appealing were loyal to the ANC and had for six decades adhered to our movement as their representative and their leader. Later, when he thought he had sufficient of a base, he also used coercive methods against the people to force them to support Inkatha. . . .

[A]lthough his efforts are doomed to fail, in a way [Buthelezi] is our fault. We have not done and are not doing sufficient political work among the millions of our people who have been condemned to the bantustans. The artificial boundaries purporting to fence them off from the rest of our country do not make them any less a vital and integral part of the popular masses fighting for national liberation and social emancipation in our country. . . .

Massive Involvement of the "Coloured" People . . .

[W]e should also mention that in 1980 we experienced the massive involvement of the "Coloured" people in the mass struggle. Of particular importance is the fact that this struggle took place in the Western Cape, the main area of concentration of these Black masses and, historically, the main stronghold of Trotskyism in our country. Furthermore, these "Coloured" masses acted together with their African brothers and sisters. The stay-at-home, called in the region for the days June 16 and 17 of that year, succeeded because both sections of the Black population supported it. Even when the fascist police shot down 40 patriots at the end of June that year, the only result was to weld the "Coloured" people even more firmly to the mass forces of our revolution, committed to the objectives spelt out in the Freedom Charter and loyal to the leadership of our movement.

This is the period when the Labour Party, with whom our movement had been in contact, responded to mass pressure to the extent of bringing about the downfall of the CRC [Coloured Representative Council], declaring its adherence to the Freedom Charter, supporting economic sanctions and announcing its intention to co-operate with the ANC. It is of course clear now that the leadership of this Party, even after it had changed with the demise of Sonny Leon, could not withstand the combination of enemy terror and bribes, and it abandoned these positions. By the time it deserted to the side of the enemy, it was clear that large sections of the "Coloured" population had come over to the side of the democratic revolution and that there was no significant organised political force in their midst capable of challenging the policy, strategy and tactics of our movement. . . .

Political Maturity: The UDF

The United Democratic Front, that outstanding example of the political maturity of our people, is a product of the years that our country's forces of progress have spent first to mobilise the masses of our people into action and to draw them into mass organisational formations, second to ensure that these masses adhere to a common political platform and, third, that this political unity finds expression in the kind of organisational unity which enables the people to move as one mass political army of revolution, under one command, focusing on the central question of all revolutions, whether peaceful or violent, the question of state power.

We take this opportunity to salute the countless patriots of our country who acted correctly and at the right moment, to make the UDF a reality, as a mass instrument of democratic change which inscribed on its banners the fundamental issue which we are about, namely the struggle for the birth of a united, democratic and non-racial South Africa. . . .

[Imperialist Offensive]

[Africans have long resisted imperialist efforts to dominate Southern Africa]. The difference between 1974 and 1984 was, of course, that the frontiers of freedom covered almost the entire border of South Africa. With the forces of reaction on the ascendancy in the greater part of the imperialist world, the same question was posed in circumstances in which it was difficult to answer in the forthright manner that Africa had replied a decade earlier.

And so the People's Republic of Mozambique signed the Accord on Nkomati in March 1984. At the height of the offensive of the revolutionary movement inside South Africa, externally the same movement had to retreat. . . . What had gone wrong? Why was it that in 1975 Africa could resolve that no matter how strong the enemy counter-offensive, we should not retreat and in 1984 be forced to accept retreat? The answer of course lies in the [policies of the American government].

Given the offensive posture of US imperialism, the Botha regime also felt that, for the first time in five years, the balance of forces was shifting in its favour. Consequently, it resolved that the opportunity had come for it also to go on the offensive, to shift that balance further in its own favour, in keeping with the global drive of its most powerful allies. . . .

The softening up process had started less than two weeks after [Ronald] Reagan was inaugurated as President of the United States. Our comrades were attacked and killed in Matola. Joe Gqabi was assassinated six months later. Griffiths Mxenge was murdered in Durban, the same city where Joseph "Mkhuthuzi" Mdluli had been killed five years before. Ruth First, the Nyawoses and other comrades were killed in cold blood. Our people, as well as nationals of Lesotho, were massacred in Maseru on December 9th, 1982. One after the other, patriots such as Neil Aggett, Mohammed Allie Razak, Bheki Zachariah Mvulane, Sipho Mutsi and Andries Raditsela, were to die in police custody, from attacks carried out by the bantustan administrations, from repressive measures carried out by the Pretoria regime, in ambushes laid by counter-revolutionaries in Angola and yet others, not necessarily members of the ANC, but opponents of apartheid such as Frikkie Conradie and Joe Mavi, in mysterious circumstances.

Puppet Forces on the Rampage

The South African army returned to Angola, where it remains to this day. The puppet forces went on the rampage throughout Southern Africa, in Lesotho, Angola, Mozambique and Zimbabwe. Where none could operate, as in the Seychelles, the Pretoria regime sent in its own forces, reinforced by mercenaries. Swaziland signed a secret agreement with Pretoria.

The countries of Southern Africa came under intense pressure to sign so-called non-aggression pacts, with the express aims of compromising the independence of these countries and recruiting them to join Pretoria in carrying out police activities against the ANC. The offensive spread wide with the bombing of our office in London and demands by Pretoria that the various governments of Western Europe should close down our offices. In the United States, [Jeremiah Denton], a veteran of genocidal war of aggression against the people of Vietnam, now turned Senator, chaired widely publicised hearings in the US Senate designed to stigmatise the ANC as a terrorist movement and an agent of the Soviet Union, exactly to justify a concerted imperialist offensive to destroy us.

Pretoria scuttled the cease-fire conference that it had agreed to hold with SWAPO [South West Africa People's Organisation], The implementation of [UN] Resolution 435 became impossible as the United States arrogantly sought to barter the independence of Namibia for the withdrawal of the internationalist Cuban troops in Angola.

Our Right to Fight

From the most unexpected quarters we heard that South Africa was an independent state and the ANC no more than a civil rights movement with no right to engage in armed struggle. We were told that we should wage struggle exclusively by political means and seek an alliance with the big capitalists of our country. At the same time, we should distance ourselves from the South African Communist Party and the Soviet Union and reorientate our international relations towards the imperialist countries. . . .

But fortunately, we had already alerted our people to what was likely to come and called on them to fight on. We had charged them with the task to make the country ungovernable and to defeat the cunning enemy manoeuvre represented by the amended apartheid constitution. And to that call and that challenge our people have responded with unequaled enthusiasm, persistence and courage. So we come to the perspectives that confront this historic Conference, our organisation and our people. . . .

The apartheid system is in a deep and permanent general crisis from which it cannot extricate itself. The apartheid regime cannot rule as before. It has therefore brought its military forces into the centre of its state structures and is ready to declare martial law when the need arises. The widespread and increasing use of the army in the effort to suppress the mass struggle in our country, even before martial law is invoked, reflects the depth of the crisis engulfing the racist regime.

Despite massacres and murders that are carried out daily by Botha's assassination squads, the masses of the people are engaged in a widespread struggle which the enemy cannot suppress and which is driving the enemy ever deeper into crisis. . . .

International Solidarity Grows

Internationally also, the movement of solidarity with our movement and our struggle is growing and increasing its effectiveness. Already, many countries consider the ANC virtually as a government and work with us as such. On the other hand, the process of the isolation of the racist regime is developing rapidly, especially and notably in the United States. In this respect, we should also mention the extensive political and material support that we enjoy from the Non-Aligned countries, the Nordic and other Western countries and the international anti-apartheid movement. . . .

The key to our further advance is organisation [because without a stronger] revolutionary organisation, we cannot take advantage of the uprisings we have spoken about and which are a reality of the mass offensive of our people. We have to discuss carefully the question why we are not as strong as we can and should be, review our experiences and draw the necessary conclusions. One thing that is clear is that we have to realise that we have in fact developed many cadres inside the country who understand our policy very well, who are in daily contact with the situation and our people and are committed to our organisation and struggle. It is vital that these cadres should be properly grounded in our strategy in its entirety, so that they can in fact advance all our strategic tasks.

Daily Contact with our People

It is very important that our leadership, by which we mean all those whom we consider the most mature among our ranks, must begin to involve itself directly in this work of internal organisation. We have to be in daily contact with our people . . . to tackle the tasks posed by our perspective of people's war. In this respect, we would like to mention in particular that we have to take the question of mass revolutionary bases very seriously. . . . What is missing is a strong underground ANC presence as well as a large contingent of units of Umkhonto we Sizwe.

We must correct this weakness in a determined and systematic manner because it is within these mass revolutionary bases that we will succeed to root our army. . . . We have to bear in mind the fact that the comrades we are training outside constitute the core of our army. They are the organisers and the leaders of the mass army that we have to build inside the country. They are our officer corps. We cannot deploy them forever as combat units. For obvious reasons, no army in the world fights with combat units composed of officers. Ours will be no exception. . . .

As Conference knows, of late there has been a fair amount of speculation about the ANC and the Pretoria regime getting together to negotiate a settlement of the South African question. This issue has arisen at this time exactly because of our strength inside the country, the level of our struggle and the crisis confronting the Botha regime. The NEC is however convinced that this regime is not interested in a just solution of the South African question.

Rather, it is interested to use the question of negotiations to divide our movement, demobilise the masses of our people by holding out the false promise that we can win our liberation other than through its overthrow. It also seeks to improve its image internationally. In any case, it is clear that no negotiations can take place or even be considered until all political prisoners are released.

However, the NEC is of the view that we cannot be seen to be rejecting a negotiated settlement in principle. In any case, no revolutionary movement can be against negotiations in principle. . . .

"Talks" Must not Impede our Struggle

The growing crisis of the apartheid system is, in any case, causing some sections of the White population to consider ways in which they can defuse the situation. Among these are elements from the big capitalists of our country, representatives of the mass media, intellectuals, politicians and even some individuals from the ruling fascist party. Increasingly these seek contact with the ANC and publicly put forward various proposals which they regard as steps that would, if implemented, signify that the racist regime is, as they say, moving away from apartheid.

This poses the possibility that our movement will therefore be in contact with levels of the ruling circles of our country that it has never dealt with before. It is absolutely vital that our organisation and the democratic movement as a whole should be of one mind about this development to ensure that any contact that may be established does not have any negative effects on the development of our struggle.

Yet another significant result of the growing strength of our movement is that many Western countries are also showing interest in establishing and maintaining relations with us. Our policy on this kind of question has of course always been clear. In principle we can have no objection to establishing such relations. However, there are important tactical questions to consider about the timing of these developments and the form that the relations we may establish should take. . . .

These events draw attention to the fact that we have to act in a manner that accords with the responsibilities that rest on our shoulders, with regard both to the short and the long term. If we seriously consider ourselves as the alternative government of our country, then we need to act and operate both as an insurrectionary force and a credible representative of a liberated South Africa.

With respect to the issues we have just raised, it is clear that we have to improve the quality of our diplomacy and therefore the training of our representatives and their staff. We need also to tap and utilise in a better way the intellectual cadres available to us, both inside and outside our country.

The scope, spread and intensity of our struggle has also thrown up a large leadership corps of our democratic movement. It is important that we pay close and continuous attention to the issue of maintaining close relations with these leaders, educate the masses of our people to understand and accept our own positions and at all times ensure that we are, as a movement, providing leadership on all major questions, in accordance with our position as the vanguard movement of our struggling people. . . .

Document 125. A delegate's impressions of the ANC National Consultative Conference, Kabwe, Zambia, June 1985, *Umsebenzi*, vol. 1, no. 2, mid-1985

In June this year, the ANC held its Second National Consultative Conference. The first Consultative Conference took place in 1969. Then I was a mere fledgling boy at Primary School, barely conscious of the nature of our oppression, let alone the ways and means of bringing it to an end. Now, 16 years later, a young communist and functionary of the ANC, I had the opportunity to take part in what could be called a South African people's parliament.

Many of the delegates were of my age group. Others were veterans of the Youth League, Volunteers of the Fighting Fifties and heroes of the 1967-69 battles in the then Rhodesia. There were 250 of us: commanders and commissars, trade unionists, political organisers, students and professional workers. All national groups—men and women—were there to thrash out the most burning question of the day—how to move forward and seize power.

The Conference was a culmination of a full year of discussion by all members of the movement. The overwhelming majority of the delegates were elected by the membership. The rest were selected on the basis of their work and experience.

A climax of months of discussion, the Conference was also an important beginning. The decisions taken have to be implemented. And the most important decision was expressed in the simple but far-reaching slogan: *"From the Venue of Conference to Victory!"*

Conscious of the challenges facing the movement, the delegates approached each and every issue with utmost seriousness. This mood was brilliantly captured in the message received just before Conference from our leaders in prison. It read in part: "We feel sure that all those delegates who will attend will go there with one central issue uppermost in their minds: that out of Conference the ANC will emerge far stronger than ever before".

Briefly, Conference took, among others, the following decisions:
- To strengthen the ANC underground
- To intensify armed struggle
- To further mobilise the people into decisive action and to strengthen the legal mass democratic movement
- To further adapt our structures to the demands of the present stage of struggle and ensure the broadest possible participation of the membership in the formulation and implementation of policy. Membership at all levels of the movement has been opened to all revolutionaries without regard to colour.
- To ensure the proper training and deployment of all cadres, and to constantly improve their education, health and cultural life.

We had a lively discussion on the issue of our Strategy and Tactics. Various concepts and categories were put under scrutiny: people's war, insurrection, the general strike, etc. All of these questions have been thrown up by the practical struggles inside the country. They have to be understood in context. Like in all other discussions, the deliberations on Strategy and Tactics showed a broad identity of approach among all members of the movement: on the Freedom Charter, forms of struggle and so on.

The historical unity of our fighting alliance was felt throughout the Conference. The delegates received with thunderous applause messages from the

SACP and SACTU. We also received messages from our friends and supporters all over the world.

In a Call to the people of South Africa, *"The ANC is With You!",* Conference outlined the major tasks facing us. The main one is to commit every patriot and everything for the seizure of power.

The ANC and the entire alliance have emerged from Conference very much stronger. The Conference was indeed a council-of-war to plan the final offensive for the seizure of power.

Victory is Within our Grasp!
From Conference to Victory!

DOCUMENT 126. "Summary of Discussions Between Certain Representatives of Big Business and Opinion-Makers in South Africa and the ANC." ANC memorandum, September 14, 1985

1. The meeting came about through the good offices of the President of the Republic of Zambia. President [Kenneth] Kaunda welcomed participants to the discussions [on September 13 at his private game lodge at Mfuwe in Zambia].

2. The visiting delegation consisted of Gavin Relly of Anglo American Corporation, Dr. Zach de Beer of Anglo American, Tony Bloom of Premier Group Holdings, Tertius Myburgh, editor of the *Sunday Times*, Harald Pakendorf, editor of *Die Vaderland*, J. de L. Peter Sordor, Director of South African Foundation and Hugh Murray, editor of *Leadership SA*. The ANC delegation was led by comrade President Oliver Tambo [and included Pallo Jordan, Mac Maharaj, Chris Hani, Thabo Mbeki and James Stuart].

3. The ANC and the visitors agreed that the discussions were not to be construed as negotiations, that the coming together of the two groups was not intended, whether directly or indirectly, to serve as talk about talks with the South African regime. The basic purpose was to come together as South Africans to enable the participants to get to know each other, and to look at the problems facing South Africa with a view towards understanding their different positions with due regard to the urgency with which the apartheid problem needs to be speedily resolved on the basis of the complete removal of apartheid which, beside being totally unacceptable to the people of South Africa, was a constant destabiliser in the whole Southern African region,

4. Although the discussion revealed certain fine distinctions in the views of the visitors their over-all position can be summarised as follows:

There is a general mood of change in South Africa on the part of the regime to move away from apartheid in favour of reform. In this regard, PW Botha was firmly committed to reforms and the visitors held forth the expectation that more reform was on the way. That is, PW Botha was sincere in his commitment to reform. At the same time, PW and his regime were uncertain about what they wanted to do and the direction in which they wanted to move.

Furthermore, the visitors were of the opinion that the more the Botha regime was put under pressure, the more they tended towards hardening into positions of intransigence. The visitors therefore represented a view that reform was a process undertaken by the regime and was already underway. They therefore saw the role of Big Business in terms of maintaining good relations with the regime in the expectation that they could continue to quietly nudge the Botha regime towards more reform (a view which could be characterised as the internal counterpart of Reagan's Constructive Engagement policy).

At the same time, Big Business is manifesting tendencies which accept the possibility that the Botha regime may not survive and therefore are simultaneously entertaining ideas which constitute a search for a "middle ground" in the South African body politic. The visitors tended to blur this concept in terms of, firstly, the building up of a grouping which would exert pressure on the Botha regime around certain specific demands such as the release of Nelson Mandela and political prisoners, an end to the State of Emergency etc., and secondly, in terms of a "middle ground" political grouping between the policy positions of the Nationalist regime on the one hand and the ANC on the other. They however pointed out that this search for "middle ground" was unable to generate any momentum because most of the forces were reluctant to become involved in the process because they wanted to be sure that their participation would have the approval of the ANC. Secondly, they felt that a gathering together of this "middle ground" would require the participation of Gatsha Buthelezi and that most of the other forces that were being canvassed in the country refused to join the process because they objected to his participation and, more important, because such forces were aware that the ANC did not look at Gatsha with any degree of favourable consideration.

Another variation of this search for a "middle ground" position they advanced ran as follows: They raised the view that sooner or later apartheid will go but that it would be too drastic a swing if the ANC were to take over power. However, no "middle ground" could take power without the approval of the ANC. It would be an act of statesmanship on the part of the ANC if the ANC could sanction such a development in order to ensure that SA does not become permanently ungovernable. This line of argument in our view tied up with the recent PFP-Buthelezi initiatives regarding the Convention Alliance.

5. Within this context of their reading of the situation they raised the Botha objections to negotiate with the ANC, viz
- The ANC commitment to the armed struggle.
- The ANC alliance with the SACP [SA Communist Party] and reliance on assistance from the Soviet Union and other socialist countries.

- They added to these question-marks their own concern about ANC economic policy with regard to a future South Africa.

6. The discussion noted the various positions that Big Business has been taking with regard to the current situation. The ANC viewpoint presented at this meeting was aimed firstly at disabusing them of some of the major misconceptions they had about the nature of the struggle and the positions of the ANC. Secondly, persuading Big Business and the opinion-makers that whilst we welcomed some of the positions that they were taking, we nonetheless were disquieted by the role that Big Business had been playing over the decades, as well as over the current crisis. Thirdly, to urge that as South Africans, there was an urgent need that Big Business take a more positive position.

7. In this context, and in direct relation to their perception of the problems, the ANC positions were outlined as follows:

A special characteristic of the crisis facing the Botha regime was the mass uprisings which were spreading throughout the country despite the State of Emergency and from which it was evident that the masses of our people found apartheid intolerable even if it meant sacrificing their lives to destroy it. That economic growth did not necessarily imply betterment of the conditions of life of our people and the removal of apartheid. On the contrary, the greatest industrial boom in our country (from the mid-sixties to the mid-seventies) led to the most profound entrenchment of apartheid and repressions.

That although the issue of change was in the air, the Botha regime had reached a point where it has no strategy except repression for handling the crisis and that we questioned even his sincerity with regard to his commitment to "reform". That the actions taken by the Botha regime had destroyed all his credibility with regards to his capacity both to initiate "reform" and his being accepted as presiding over the process of dismantling apartheid.

The ANC held a contrary view with regards to Botha's intransigence and did not accept the thesis that part of the problem was that the greater the all-round pressure applied to the Botha regime the more intransigent he became. The problem, rather, was his commitment to apartheid and white domination and that, whatever changes he is prepared to entertain, however insignificant they are, are precisely the results of the all-round pressure including economic sanctions and that our strategy was to escalate the struggle.

8. With regard to certain specific questions ANC policy was outlined around certain specific problems that they had raised. These included:

The armed struggle. It was explained that we do not relish violence, that it was state violence and the closing of all other meaningful avenues of change, which made the armed struggle necessary. Therefore to expect the ANC unilaterally to abandon the armed struggle was to ask us to abandon our people's aspirations. It is the ANC and its allies who have faith in the real democratic process.

It is the starting point of the ANC that we wish to create a political framework in which the will of the majority will express itself through normal democratic procedures based on one man one vote in a unitary South Africa. That our premise is that South Africa belongs to all who live in it and that our concept of democracy rests on the right of individuals; [not] perpetrating racist structures and a racist approach.

That our perspectives at the economic level were based on the Freedom Charter which requires the nationalisation of the monopoly industries, banks and the mines and required a re-distribution of the wealth of our country in contrast to the present economic order which is characterised by extremes of wealth co-existing with gross mass poverty. The precise ways in which such a policy would be implemented would depend on the democratic processes. Our conception recognised that there is a role in the transformations which we seek for various levels of private enterprise. At the same time, it was important to appreciate that the new State would need to be able to command the economy and control its resources in order to carry out our commitment to attend to the well-being of our people.

On the question of talks. It is Botha who is not willing to talk. His public criticism of Big Business coming to meet us emphasises this point. Talks assume that a state of war exists and that in our case the forces are the racist forces represented by the Botha regime and the democratic forces represented by the ANC. The ANC believes that we have not reached the stage where we can even talk about talks. The Botha regime has to take concrete steps in order to create the atmosphere where even talk about talks can be entertained. Such concrete actions would have to include

- First and foremost the release of Nelson Mandela and all political prisoners.
- The lifting of the State of Emergency, the release of all arrestees and detainees and the abandonment of the [Pietermaritzburg and Delmas] treason trials.
- Troops and police must be removed from the black townships and ghettoes.
- Lifting the ban on the ANC and removal of laws which would prevent us from organising the masses freely.

The above were cited as some of the principal changes which would have to take place before we reach the stage where negotiation can be seen as a practical possibility.

The question of the ANC's alliance with the SACP was explained as follows: Assertions regarding communist control and domination of the ANC would need to be substantiated if we are to adequately deal with these. However we offered an explanation in terms of the South African experience which led to the formation of the ANC in 1912 and the SACP in 1921. Our experience was concrete, namely,

- The Freedom Charter was adopted at Kliptown in 1955 and based on widespread canvassing of our people in all walks of life. It was then adopted by the ANC.

- The SACP has accepted the Freedom Charter as a policy guideline for the present phase of our struggle.
- Individual communists have always been members of the ANC, some of them serving in the highest organs of the ANC. Their conduct has always reflected commitment to the programme and policies of the ANC. As members of the ANC they have shown complete loyalty to the ANC.
- We explained the relationship between the ANC and the Socialist countries. We receive financial and material assistance from various countries in the west. The Socialist countries do not provide funds but have always willingly provided material assistance including arms. In all our dealing with the Socialist countries we have not once experienced a situation where they have tried to influence our views or tell us what to do.

9. Within this context, Big Business has a role to play, specifically:

They need to publicly increase and step-up the pressure on the regime especially with regard to the release of Nelson Mandela and all political prisoners and in relation to the steps which we have pointed to in paragraph 8 above. South Africa is in the grip of a permanent series of crises. Mass activity including strikes and other forms of industrial action by our workers is taking place and will increase. Certain voices in Big Business recognise that industrial action by workers will include political dimensions of action. Whatever the case, Big Business needs to visibly distance itself from the regime and handle such issues without calling in the army and police, without resorting to measures and institutions created by repressive legislation and without exploiting the special disabilities arising from the migrant labour system which is underpinned by the bantustans.

Hitherto, Big Business has actually played a role of reinforcing the apartheid state e.g. Armscor which has made South Africa self-sufficient in armaments has direct input by Big Business both in terms of personnel and production capacity. 60% of Armscor production comes from Armscor contracting out to private enterprise. Big Business therefore requires to begin to visibly detach itself in such cases.

10. The discussions were held in a cordial atmosphere. No definite positions were arrived at. No negotiations, whether direct or indirect, took place. The basic positions were such that participants gained a better understanding of each other's positions and participants on the side of Big Business and opinion-makers felt the need for greater contact with the ANC.

DOCUMENT 127. "The Situation in South Africa: Minutes of Evidence." Testimony of Oliver Tambo and Thabo Mbeki before the Foreign Affairs Committee of the British House of Commons, October 29, 1985 (abridged)

Sir Anthony Kershaw, Chairman: I welcome Mr Oliver Tambo and his friends, Mr Thabo Mbeki and Mr Aziz Pahad, and I am glad that they have been able to come. . . . Perhaps I could start by asking Mr Oliver Tambo if he would describe to us the structure of the African National Congress and its organisation.

Oliver Tambo: May I begin by thanking you very much indeed and by thanking the Committee for giving us this opportunity to appear before it. The African National Congress is headed by a National Executive Committee which is under present conditions established by what we call national consultative conferences. That takes into account the fact that we are largely operating outside South Africa and are illegal within South Africa itself. The National Consultative Conference appoints a National Executive Committee which then has various sub-committees under it. Between meetings of the National Executive Committee we have a National Working Committee which has the powers of the National Executive Committee. The National Working Committee has working immediately under it what is called the [Politico-Military] Council. This takes care of all problems relating to the internal situation in South Africa; it plans and . . . carries out decisions on all issues related to the internal struggle. Then for largely international work the National Working Committee has what is called the External Coordinating Committee. Then below these there are various sub-committees that constitute the executive arm of the African National Congress. We have, of course, to relate to the national leadership of the African National Congress which is at Robben Island, and we carry out as much contact as is possible in our circumstances. The ANC inside South Africa is, of course, illegal and we operate underground structures there. That is generally the structure of the ANC. I should mention that we have an armed wing in the African National Congress known as Umkhonto We Sizwe. This comes under the control of the Politico-Military Council. . . .

Jim Lester: We all feel a great repugnance for violence from whatever source, but it is especially unhelpful in terms of British public opinion, when we see violence of black against black. We understand that city councillors and town councillors have been murdered, and we see regularly on our television screens the real problems in some of the townships. Do you support and encourage that attitude—that people should turn on one another within a township—or is this something which you also agree is unhelpful to your cause?

Oliver Tambo: We think it is unavoidable, in a way. It is a product of the violent system in which we live. The councillors, some of whom have been killed, were collaborators with the regime at a very bad time, at a time when people were being killed for their resistance. Angers were aroused. Councillors were called upon to resign from these councils. Many of them did. Others were determined to operate structures which the people had always opposed. At a time when there was violence against the people, it was inevitable that their anger should vent itself against those who persisted in collaborating and sustaining these unwanted councils. . . .

The African National Congress was nonviolent for 50 years before it extended its struggle to embrace violence. . . . Throughout the past two decades our violence has been largely confined to attacking economic installations, pylons and so on—very few casualties, in comparison with the massive casualties that we have sustained from the apartheid system, including the Soweto massacre. This has been part of our life. After two decades, from 1961 through 1981 to the present, we met in June, we looked at this long history of violence from 1948 to the present, which has remained unabated, which has increased, which has mounted, and we said, "We have virtually been nonviolent now for about 30 years."

Peter Thomas: What do you mean by "nonviolent", because you had your military wing which was operating in Mozambique and various other places, did you not?

Oliver Tambo: Yes.

Peter Thomas: Then you had the agreement between Mozambique's President and South Africa, which meant that you were no longer able to operate. . . . What do you mean by the "new violence" which was agreed in June of this year at your ANC meeting? What do you mean by it? What do you mean by "the soft targets" and "the people's war"? Mr Lester mentioned the inter-black struggle which is going on, the policemen who are killed, the officials who are killed and their houses burnt, and that sort of thing. Is that something that you say is part of the ANC policy? Do you not condemn it?

Oliver Tambo: That, of course, was going on when we met in June. That had started a year earlier. No, what we decided in June was to intensify the struggle. We recognised that if the struggle is intensified beyond the levels that we had maintained for 20 fruitless years of selected sabotage—if it was to be intensified—it was inevitable that life would then be lost. Even in the course of attacking military establishments, the army, the police . . , that would involve bloodshed, and you would be reaching a level of conflict in which, as happens in all conflicts, the innocent would be hit, not deliberately but unavoidably. . . .

Peter Thomas: The children of black policemen and black officials have been killed and their houses have been burned. You say you do not condone it. Are you willing to condemn it?

Oliver Tambo: What I condemn with all the vehemence I can muster is the fact that for 70 years now—75 years this year, three-quarters of a century this year—we have been the victims of white minority rule which has progressively become more and more violent against us up to the point where it now assumes the forms that we are witnessing. It is that violence, that is where it all starts. I condemn that because, if the apartheid system stopped—and it is violent, it maintains itself by violence—if it stopped, all this would not be happening. No child would be shot dead, none would be killed even by a petrol bomb. All this is the precise result of what people, South African journalists and writers, reporters and editorial writers, have been warning the apartheid regime about. They have said during the 1970s already that unless the Pretoria regime changes there is trouble ahead, and the constant message was "Change before it is too late." They did not change before it was too late. We have had Soweto only in 1976, a few years ago, and we have had this persistent violence which we have witnessed ever since Botha came into power.

Now, all that must be taken into account before one condemns an individual act. I regret all these things, I regret them, but I would refuse to be asked to condemn individual acts when I know that those acts would not have been there in the first instance had there not been this criminal system, this crime against humanity. We think this is where we should focus. We should focus on the cause, not the symptom of the cause of all this, and the cause is the apartheid system.

Norman St John-Stevas: Mr Tambo, you have been very frank with us in stating your attitude to violence. I am sure it will be clear to you that this Committee totally condemns the use of violence to settle political disputes and that is the view . . . of the entire House of Commons. . . . In the event of a promise being made of a reform of the political framework with an election based on democratic suffrage, would the ANC come forward and contest the election as a democratic political party and renounce the use of force?

Oliver Tambo: We would. This is what we are fighting for. This is what we are insisting on. We say that the government must be the government of the people of South Africa, it should be an elected government, elected by the people of South Africa, not by a small white minority. . . .

Norman St John-Stevas: It is quite clear that you would like to see an end to apartheid—and indeed we all would—but is the ANC committed to a political philosophy that goes beyond the ending of apartheid? For instance, the Freedom Charter has some very definite views about nationalisation and land redistribution. Could you say something more about the attitude of the ANC to these matters?

Oliver Tambo: Well, the Freedom Charter is not formulated on the basis of any ideological positions. The Freedom Charter simply looks at our situation in which there is great wealth—immense—in the hands of a few while the vast majority of people are living in desperate poverty, and we say how do we adjust this position? How can this wealth be put at the service of the people as a whole? What are the mechanisms? And we start by accepting that it cannot go on, we cannot have a system which maintains this juxtaposition of immense wealth and immense poverty.

Norman St John-Stevas: Is it your intention to destroy the capitalist system as such, or to reform it?

Oliver Tambo: No, we do not want to destroy it. The Freedom Charter does not even purport to want to destroy the capitalist system. All that the Freedom Charter does is envisage a mixed economy in which part of the economy, some of the industries, would be controlled, owned, by the State (as happens in many countries), and the rest by private ownership—a mixed economy. The motive behind it is to ensure, if I may put it that way, a more equitable distribution of the wealth of the country. So we are looking at it purely from a pragmatic point of view. Can you have a government which sustains the present system of the distribution of the wealth of the country? We say that that government will not last in our country. . . .

Ivan Lawrence: Mr Tambo, it is not just what you hope for, but what you actually do, that people judge you by. I just want to go back, if I may, to the armed struggle, because it is very important that the world should not misunderstand your position. . . . [A bomb exploded] in a street in Pretoria, killing 19 people, and 217 people were injured, on 20 May 1983. The ANC claimed responsibility for that. . . . You told us that the violent attacks were confined to attacking economic installations . . . and presumably military installations. If that is so, will you disown all attacks in the ANC's name on African security policemen, community councillors, former ANC members who have turned State's witnesses, any bombing in city centres, shopping areas, public buildings and places of entertainment? Are any such future acts to be condemned by you and the ANC?

Oliver Tambo: Let me go back a little to the first part of this question. . . . In 1981 one of our most outstanding leaders [Joe Gqabi] was assassinated by South African agents. . . . In that year South Africa had raided our people—raided Mozambique—and massacred very brutally some 13 of our people who were simply living in houses in Mozambique. That was 1981. In 1982 the South African army invaded Lesotho and massacred not 19 people but 42 people, shot at point-blank range. 42. 12 of them nationals of Lesotho. So there was this mounting offensive against the ANC. I think your question fails to relate to this aspect: that we were victims of assassinations, of massacres, and in return for what? We were not killing anybody. . . . An armed struggle is an armed struggle. People die. It has been fortunate perhaps, in that time, that there have not been so many people dying on the other side of the conflict, but many on our side. They have been hanged, they have been sentenced to long terms of imprisonment, for exploding a bomb that destroyed a pylon; sentenced to life imprisonment. That is violence. This is what we are going through. As to these other people you are mentioning, we cannot condemn it. That is part of the struggle. The enemy is the enemy. . . .

[Britain] fought a war 45 years ago. How many children were . . . killed when the RAF [Royal Air Force] was bombing away in Germany and other places? How many? Why is this so strange with us? After all, we have got a fascist nazi regime that came into power in 1948 immediately after the defeat of Nazism in Germany. We are confronted with that. We have decided to fight and in fighting people will be killed. There must be no mistake, gentlemen, no mistake at all: we do not love violence, we dislike violence and we keep saying that this thing was thrust upon us, that we have rejected and resisted it for 10 long years. We never thought we would ever be violent for about half a century. We have restrained ourselves for a further 20 years, and it cannot go on like that. The other liberation movements have taken up arms and intensified their struggles and won their independence on our borders; while we are picking out pylons they were fighting a war. A war is a war. We have delayed it but we cannot delay it indefinitely. Apartheid is a crime against humanity and it is more a crime against us. We have suffered under it. We have got to fight it. We will fight it as resolutely as the British people fought Nazi Germany, as resolutely—and in the process we want to make no mistake about this. We are carrying on a struggle which others elsewhere have carried on, and it is an armed struggle, but it has been an armed struggle with so much restraint that we have tended to draw attention to the few acts of violence that we have carried out, diverting attention from the massive violence that comes from the operation of the apartheid system. . . .

Robert Harvey: Do you see any signs of progress towards change in the South African Government's current programme of political reform?

Thabo Mbeki: No, we do not see any change. The Botha regime is not addressing any of the substantive questions that our people want addressed. They are tinkering around with issues which they decide are important. For instance, there is a lot of noise which has been made about the restoration of common citizenship. It is not of much significance to us because even when they said "you have ceased to be citizens of South Africa" we did not think we had ceased to be citizens of South Africa. . . . I think it is significant that it is during the presidency of Botha, this great reformer, that you have got the levels of struggle that you have got today. It is because people are giving their response to what is supposed to be a process of reform and the people do not want that. . . .

Robert Harvey: . . . [W]ould you be prepared to renounce the use of violence in exchange for the release of political prisoners, and in particular Mandela?

Thabo Mbeki: No. . . . If Nelson Mandela was released . . . [he] is liable to be arrested because the ANC is banned. The release of the political prisoners on its own would never be a sufficient condition. . . . Many other things would have to be done; . . . the state of emergency must be lifted, the ban on the ANC must be lifted and on all other political organisations. And if the Botha regime has said "Okay, we are ready to dismantle apartheid and here are our actual practical measures to bring that about and we are ready to enter into negotiations as the Commonwealth said, negotiations which are going to lead to the formation of a nonracial and representative government," if all of that were seriously said by Botha, then of course there would be no need for violence . . . on our side.

Robert Harvey: Would you be prepared to engage in power-sharing? That is another of the subjects being talked about very much within the Botha Government at the moment.

Thabo Mbeki: It is an expression which we do not use. It suggests to us . . . a continued fragmentation of the population of our country, so that you would say, "Here is a white population, here is a Zulu population, here is a coloured population, and between them they constitute distinct groups and must share power amongst themselves". . . Certainly the perspective that the ANC has would not . . . be based on the continuation of these group distinctions (as they are called). We have said, talking to many of our own people—white people in South Africa—that, for instance, the ANC would be very much in favour of an entrenched bill of rights . . . but entrenching the rights of individuals, not the rights of groups, because those groups would get defined in the same way that the apartheid structure is defined today. . . .

Chairman: Mr Mbeki, does your last answer mean that you rule out a federal constitution such as many other countries have—for example, Yugoslavia?

Thabo Mbeki: We would not want to federate these constitutional units that the apartheid system has created. We cannot say we need a federal structure which must recognise the reality of the Bantustans. . . . We are against group areas. We are against a system which distinguishes whites—"Whites can stay there, Indians there." It is wrong. That has got to go. We cannot have a new system which entrenches exactly that arrangement. . . .

Ian Mikardo: Then in other words, you prefer the British system to the Yugoslav, is that it?. . .

Thabo Mbeki: . . . [We] are saying a united, democratic and nonracial South Africa. . . .

Dennis Canavan: To what extent do you think . . . sanctions would help to bring about peaceful democratic change in South Africa?

Oliver Tambo: The thing about sanctions is that it really aims to aid a peaceful resolution of the South African problem. That is the primary aim of sanctions: to make the process of transition through struggle as limited as possible in terms of the scale of the conflict. . . . What happens without sanctions is that we are confronted with the might of the regime and have to rely on our own struggle, on our own sacrifices. . . . [It] has got to become increasingly violent and escalate to very disastrous levels, involving a lot of destruction of property and life. That is what would happen if we had to do it unaided. . . . So sanctions are fundamentally aimed at limiting the escalation, limiting the scope of the conflict. . . .

Dennis Canavan: Critics of sanctions in this country and elsewhere sometimes claim that sanctions would hurt the black people of South Africa and . . . in neighbouring states such as Swaziland and Lesotho which have got close economic links with South Africa. What would you say to these critics?

Oliver Tambo: This has never been correct . . . because under apartheid people are suffering, and are suffering very badly, from this system, so much so that they would want to do anything they can to put an end to it. . . . There are three million unemployed already, without the use of sanctions. It is part of our life. . . . There have been opinion polls taken in South Africa recently which really confirm what I am saying, that the majority of the people are saying sanctions. . . . As far as the countries around South Africa are concerned, they have said they would not oppose sanctions because they agree that sanctions would bring a speedier end to the apartheid system than a struggle without the support of sanctions. They also recognise that the growing conflict is bound to spill over and affect them anyway and they would suffer more from such a conflict than from sanctions. . . .

Ivan Lawrence: Are you not saying this, Mr Tambo, that you concede that sanctions will lead to a large amount of additional unemployment to blacks and when unemployed blacks are running in the streets you will take them into your armed violent struggle against the state, this being thereby the end to the racist regime? Is that not what you are saying? If you are saying that, can you seriously expect the British people to support that?

Oliver Tambo: I am not saying we want our people to be in the streets. . . . If it is a matter of firms closing down because of the operation and effectiveness of sanctions, the white workers too will lose their jobs. Perhaps they would be concerned about this. . . . It is not that we want sanctions so that our people can be out of work: we say that we want our sanctions so that apartheid can end, this apartheid which everybody says must end. That is what must end and we are ready to make any sacrifice—it is not suffering, it is sacrifice—in order to see this system ended. . . .

Thabo Mbeki: I do not think they need to be unemployed to be mobilised. . . . If you take the last 12 months and take the involvement of employed workers in the struggle, two regional general strikes have been called in the last 12 months and the workers who were working said "We are going to stay at home because we are calling for an end of the state of emergency". They were working and you got 6,000 sacked because they went on political strike and they are ready to go on a political strike. They do not have to be unemployed in order to demand the vote. I do not think they need to be hungry to do that; they can think, look around and say "If the British workers can vote for themselves in the British House of Commons, why not us?" They do not have to be unemployed to reach that conclusion. . . .

Chairman: . . . I am afraid we must stop there. We are very grateful in the Committee to you and your colleagues for having come this afternoon and for the clearness with which you have put your views and answered our questions. Thank you very much.

DOCUMENT 128. Letter from Godfrey Motsepe, ANC representative in Brussels, to ANC headquarters, November 10, 1985

Cde. Nzo
Secretary General,
African National Congress (SA),
P.O. Box 31791, Lusaka

Dear Cde [Comrade] Nzo,

Due to immense pressure of work I have not been able to write to you sooner. Suddenly, like a bolt from the blue, it has dawned upon the ordinary person here that apartheid is truly akin to slavery. This transformation in the political understanding of the people here is due to the media generally, and to television in particular. People have seen the mindless brutality, callousness and barbarity of the fascist regime's security forces brought into their living rooms, night after night, in the recent period. We are simply flooded with requests for speakers, films, books etc about Apartheid. Organizations which ignored us formerly are now vying with one another to organize activities denouncing Apartheid. Above all, the heroic determination of our people to rid our land of the scourge of Apartheid colonialism has inspired and captured the imagination of millions of people.

Activities are flourishing all over the place. To cite only a few examples:

(a) The European Trade Union Federation organized a demonstration outside the S.A. embassy.
(b) Apartheid featured prominently, and was roundly condemned at this year's massive anti-nuclear missiles rally. See enclosed message of solidarity with us.
(c) The military attaché of the racists has been given his marching orders in conformity with one of the demands we drew up in conjunction with several organizations.
(d) A massive campaign is underway to boycott fruits, krugerrands [gold coins] etc from S.A.
(e) One of the mass movements of women, Socialistische Vooruitiende Vrouwen, has decided to bestow the honorary Presidency of their organisation to Winnie Mandela and they have requested us to invite one of the daughters of Nelson and Winnie Mandela to attend their annual congress on the 7th December here in Belgium. They are prepared to bear the costs as they are a very influential and important organisation. Do let me know as soon as possible.

Recently, I was invited to the Netherlands to meet two women from home who had requested to meet the ANC. They were on a tour organized by the Dutch churches. Their names were Vesta Smith and Virginia. Both very active in the Women's Federation, UDF and churches. Max Sisulu and I went to meet them in one of the suburbs of Amsterdam. It became quite clear that they were totally committed to the struggle for national and social emancipation of our people. Points raised during our discussion:

(1) They strongly wanted the ANC to know about the brutal counter-revolutionary role played by G. Buthelezi—virtually holding the people in the grip of fear: beatings, memberships of Inkatha under duress, people compelled to buy uniforms, buses for Inkatha by force; also to see him off and welcome him back from foreign jaunts. Assassinations of the late Mrs Victoria Mxenge, UDF leaders, Cosas et al. Prior to the burial of Mrs Mxenge, the cinema where the wake was held was attacked by Inkatha and the police and 36 mourners were brutally massacred. Expulsions of progressive priests, e.g. Rev. [Wesley] Mabuza and others, is now commonplace. They are sending me affidavits from the victims of Inkatha brutality, in the very near future. They stressed to us that the situation had reached crisis proportions with battle lines drawn between the communities opposed to Gatsha and the security forces. Mrs [Dorothy] Nyembe, who is sickly, lives on the run from Gatsha, and Aaron Mnisi's family too.

(2) They also asked constantly why there was no escalation of the armed struggle when the conditions at home were ripe. They asserted that the youth, including many other forces were willing and ready to participate ac-

tively if the skills and weapons were provided. We tried to explain, but I could see that they were not contented with our answers.

For the very first time since I arrived here, I was invited by the ICFTU [International Confederation of Free Trade Unions] to discuss with me and to introduce me to Mr. James Mndaweni, the President of CUSA [Council of Unions of SA]. Apparently the ICFTU were rebuffed by our people at home; in E. London, JHB [Johannesburg], Cape Town, Durban and P.E. [Port Elizabeth] the shop stewards and rank and file workers regaled them with strong words to the effect that they (the workers) are for sanctions and for the armed struggle. Now they are keen to meet with President Tambo. But they are not to be trusted as we all know that they work very closely with the bastion of all the reactionary forces in the entire world: the U.S. government.

Comrade Rose and I would want to be included amongst the Cdes [comrades] who would be going for a medical check-up in the GDR [German Democratic Republic]. We have been working at a feverish pace and now one can feel the strain and stress beginning to tell.

Comradely hugs to all and best regards. Forward to the seizure of power in the Year of the Cadre! Maatla ke a Rona! Amandla ngawethu! [Power is ours!]

Comradely yours,
Godfrey [Motsepe]

DOCUMENT 129. "A Submission on the Question of Negotiations." Internal ANC policy paper, Lusaka, November 27, 1985

This paper is an abbreviated version of a lengthier paper prepared for the sub-committee. The present version summarises the key points.

1. Talks with the enemy are, in and of themselves, not harmful. If negotiations are viewed as yet one more terrain of struggle, rather than as a means of drawing the struggle to a close, we have no reason to shun them. However, as has been demonstrated in the case of Namibia, the enemy may press for talks in order to employ them as a means to buy time and forcing the movement to wind down the struggle through a de facto moratorium. We must therefore approach talks as a means of winning at the conference table or consolidating what we have won on the battlefield. In other words we will enter into talks as a means of pursuing our political objectives employing other means, or to supplement our conventional means.

We must draw a sharp distinction between negotiations and a bargaining session. "Negotiations" is not a polite word for marketplace haggling, though they may sometimes assume this form. Negotiations and the shape they assume are largely determined by the relative strengths of the contending parties; which party is on the ascendant, and which one is in decline.

Should we go into talks, either voluntarily or through force of circumstance, we must enter into such dealings with the enemy with a view to extracting from the new situation the optimum conditions for the continuation of our struggle. Our strategic objective—people's power, as defined in the Freedom Charter—will remain the same, though the means we employ to arrive at it may have to change.

The enemy, like ourselves, will come to the conference table in order to secure his strategic objectives—the essentials of White domination. Each side will be seeking to gain tactical advantages from the very first session. The experience of SWAPO [South West Africa People's Organisation] and the [Zimbabwean] Patriotic Front are most instructive in this respect. Our first task will be to prevent the other side from emasculating us by surrounding and bracketing us with an array of dubious political forces within an "anti-apartheid spectrum". Secondly we shall be required to observe an iron-clad discipline to preserve a unified stand and single voice on all issues. Carelessly formulated pronouncements could unwittingly commit us to ends we had not intended.

2. What we would seek to achieve from such talks determines in large measure the terms under which we can agree to talk. We would seek to create conditions in which:
a) The mass democratic movement, led by the ANC, can continue to grow, with its influence and authority spreading so that it can visibly emerge as the chief determinant of the pace of events, able to intervene through mass action at any given moment;
b) the enemy's capacity to suppress the liberation forces, either militarily or judicially/administratively is neutralised;
c) The people's army is capable of wielding its military power in defence of the people's movement;
d) There is rapid movement towards a situation of dual power in which the mass democratic movement, under our avowed leadership, not only commands authority but can wield it in opposition to the enemy's power and can finally overthrow him; (1)
e) The seizure of power by the democratic forces becomes possible without the need to enter into armed combat or through a short sharp military operation (insurrection). (2)

We might also have to consider a situation in which we have to make do with a great deal less. The worst case scenario that could still be acceptable to us would entail:
a) conditions in which the racist state—executive, administration and judiciary—remains in place but its capacity to deploy its repressive forces against the democratic movement are seriously diminished—either by institutional constraints or the intercession of a neutral party;
b) the ANC has the legal right and political capacity to unite in common action all the pro-liberation forces (as distinct from anti-regime), while marginalising the forces of reform;
c) democratic elections are held and the ANC is realistically capable of chart-

ing a parliamentary road to victory by winning such elections and forming a government or leading a democratic coalition.

These define the assurances we will seek from the racists, before, during and after any negotiations. Our preconditions must seek to ensure that our movement—in its entirety—is capable of functioning legally, without fear of or hindrance from the enemy's repressive forces and to guarantee the integrity of the negotiating process itself. The preconditions we have agreed on are:
i) release of all political prisoners and detainees, all captured freedom fighters and prisoners of war;
ii) the lifting of the State of Emergency, the withdrawal of all SADF [SA Defence Force] and Police personnel from the townships and their confinement to barracks;
iii) the cessation of all political trials and/or trials arising from participation in the current uprisings, and the unconditional release of all those arrested and charged;
iv) the repeal of all politically repressive laws—the Riotous Assemblies Act, The Natives Administration Act of 1927, The Suppression of Communism Act/Internal Security Act, the General Laws Amendment Act of 1953, the Unlawful Organisations Act, the Terrorism Act, the General Laws Amendment Act of 1962, etc. and all other laws empowering the regime to proscribe freedom of assembly, speech and the press.

These preconditions could probably be added to and expanded to extend the area of political freedom which will be necessary for us to campaign effectively inside the country.

We must seek to minimise the possibilities of the forces of reformism shifting the focus of discussion to the centre and to the right by denying them an autonomous voice and status in any negotiations. The tactics SWAPO adopted during the Lusaka Conference of 1984 are most enlightening in this respect. SWANU [South West Africa National Union], the Namibian Democratic Front and even the German-settler Christian Democrats were separated from the MPC [Multiparty Conference] and polarised towards SWAPO. Earlier this year the idea of a Democratic Summit Conference was floated. Such a conference could provide the forum to reach a similar position even before any negotiations take place.

3. When we reach the conference table we should have our own set of concrete constitutional proposals (not merely the Freedom Charter), otherwise we will be forced to react to the other side's proposals. The NEC [National Executive Committee] must therefore immediately set up a constitutional think tank under the supervision of a sub-committee. Its task shall be to draft proposals to place before the NEC. The shortest time frame for such a task is three (3) months.

The proposed NEC subcommittee will also be responsible for studying and familiarising the leadership with the experience of our allies in this region and beyond who have either passed through or are engaged in negotiations in order to learn negotiating tactics and pick up tips on specific situations.

The Research Unit has already set in motion projects, in conjunction with the Economists' Unit, to examine the operationalisation of the Freedom Charter (i.e. its practical implementation). We had not anticipated the fleetfootedness of events. These will have to be speeded up and the time frame for their completion tightened.

Members of the Subcommittee:
Simon Makana
James Stuart
Z. Pallo Jordan.
Thabo Mbeki, owing to other commitments was unable to participate

NOTES

(1) The concept of dual power arose in the course of the revolutions in Europe during the 19th and 20th centuries. It describes a situation in which the revolutionary forces enjoy an unassailable and growing political authority over the overwhelming majority of the people, such that it renders the incumbent regime impotent in that it can no longer get anyone to do its bidding. Situations of dual power do not mean power sharing or seats in the cabinet. Classically, dual power implies an extra-parliamentary power exercised through leadership of alternative legislative organs, e.g. The Commune of Paris (1871); the Soviets in Russia (1905 and 1917); the Workers' Councils in Budapest (1919).

(2) Two possible scenarios could unfold in this instance. The first could entail a situation of dual power during which the masses intervene through peaceful demonstrations to drive an incumbent regime from the seats of power in favour of a revolutionary leadership. The classic example is the unseating of the Girondists by the Jacobins in 1792. The second entails the incumbent regime gradually losing its power to govern to alternative popular institutions but it cannot be dislodged except by force of arms; but precisely because it has lost legitimacy and power all that is required is a small scale military operation like that of November 7th in Petrograd, 1917.

DOCUMENT 130. "How to Master Secret Work." Article in *Umsebenzi*, vol. 1, no. 3, late 1985

SOME RULES OF SECRECY

Carelessness leads to arrests. Loose talk and strange behaviour attracts attention of police and izimpimpi [informers]. Secret work needs vigilance and care. *Rules of secrecy* help to mask our actions and overcome difficulties created by the enemy. But first let us study the following situation:

What Not To Do

X, a trade unionist, also leads a secret cell. He phones Y and Z, his cell members, and arranges to meet outside a cinema. X leaves his office and rushes to the meeting 30 minutes late. Y and Z have been anxiously checking the time and pacing up and down. The three decide to go to a nearby tea-room where they have often met before. They talk over tea in low tones. People from the cinema start coming in. One is a relative of X who greets him. Y and Z are nervous and abruptly leave. When X is asked who they were he hesitates and, wanting to impress his relative, replies: "They're good guys who like to hear from me what's going on." This opens the way for a long discussion on politics.

X has made many errors which would soon put the police on the trail of all three. These seem obvious but in practise many people behave just like X. They do not prepare properly; rush about attracting attention; fail to keep time; do not cover the activity with a legend (cover story); talk loosely etc. Others pick up the bad style of work. X should set a good example for Y and Z. To avoid such mistakes *rules of secrecy* must be studied and practised. They might seem obvious but should *never* be taken for granted.

Things to Remember
1. Always have a "believable" legend to cover your work! (X could have said Y and Z were workers he vaguely knew whom he had met by chance and had been encouraging to join the union).
2. Underground membership must be secret! (X had no need to refer to Y and Z as "good guys").
3. Behave naturally and do not draw attention to yourself! "Be like the people". Merge with them! (X, Y and Z behaved suspiciously).
4. No loose talk! Guard secrets with your life! Follow the saying: "Don't trust anyone and talk as little as possible." (X fails here).
5. Be vigilant against informers! They try to get close to you using militant talk to "test" and trap you. (Can X be so sure of his relative?)
6. Be disciplined, efficient, punctual (X was none of these). Only wait ten minutes at a meeting place. The latecomer may have been arrested.
7. Make all preparations beforehand! Avoid a regular pattern of behaviour which makes it easy for the enemy to check on you. (X made poor arrangements for the meeting; rushed there from a sensitive place and could have been followed; used the tea-room too often).
8. Do not try to discover what does not concern you! Know only what you have to know for carrying out your tasks.
9. Be careful what you say on the phone (which may be "bugged"), or in a public place (where you can be overheard)! Conceal sensitive information such as names etc by using simple codes!
10. Remove all traces of illegal work that can lead to you! Wipe fingerprints

off objects. Know that typewriters can be traced. Goods bought from shops can be checked.
11. Hide materials such as leaflets, weapons, etc. But not where you live. Memorise sensitive names, addresses etc. Don't write them down!
12. Carry reliable documents of identification!
13. Know your town, its streets, parks, shops etc. like the palm of your hand! This will help you find secret places and enable you to check whether you are being followed.
14. If you are arrested you must deny all secret work and never reveal the names of your comrades even to the point of death!
15. Finally, if any member of your underground cell is arrested, you must immediately act on the assumption that they will be forced to give information. This means taking precautions, such as going into hiding if necessary.

When the rules of secrecy are practised revolutionaries make good progress. Practise makes perfect and with discipline and vigilance, we will outwit the enemy and we will win!

Document 131. ANC press statement by Thabo Mbeki on resignation of Van Zyl Slabbert from Parliament, February 7, 1986

An act of vision has made this February day a moment of pride for all the people in South Africa. A solemn salute of honour is due to Dr Frederik Van Zyl Slabbert, who earlier today announced his resignation from the South African parliament.

Never in the history of our country has a white establishment political leader confronted the iniquity of the system of white minority domination as Dr Slabbert did today.

We salute his courage, his honesty and his loyalty to a common South African nationhood. These have led him to abandon a privileged and prestigious political position, an act which will be totally unacceptable to many of the people among whom he was born and bred.

Yet today millions of our people, of all races, will acclaim Dr Slabbert as a new *Voortrekker* [pioneer]. He has broken with a tradition of Afrikaner and white leadership which has sanctified racism and racial superiority.

He has aligned his being and his talent with the countless heroes and heroines who have perished in the struggle to assert the common humanity of the people of South Africa.

His refusal to remain in the racist tri-cameral parliament must serve as an example to all who consider themselves opponents of the apartheid system and yet continue to be part of the oppressive and repressive structures of the system of white minority rule. This includes all those who man the bantustans, sit in the tri-cameral parliament and others who might wish to serve in Botha's proposed National Statutory Council.

We take seriously Dr Slabbert's call for a negotiated settlement of the South African question. We would like to reiterate that we are always ready to negotiate for a South Africa which belongs to all who live in it, black and white.

But no negotiations are possible while the Botha regime refuses to recognise that our people must live together in one country, as equals and each with a right to vote for the political representatives of their choice.

Our task remains that of removing the apartheid system in its totality. Therefore the struggle must and will continue for the removal of the apartheid regime and the institution of a democratic system of government in a united South Africa. We look forward to Dr Slabbert's contribution towards the achievement of this goal.

Document 132. Letter from Stanley Mabizela, ANC representative in Tanzania, to ANC president and secretary general, Lusaka, March 7, 1986

Late yesterday I received a message requesting me to call without fail at the Norwegian Embassy [in Dar es Salaam] at 8.00 a.m. on the above-mentioned date. In the evening of 6th March I met Comrade Isco and I told him about this unusual request from the Norwegian Embassy. As he was in Arusha attending the conference on Peace and Security in Southern Africa he told me that on his return from Arusha to Dar es Salaam he had travelled with Professor [Hendrik W.] van der Merwe who was in the company of the Norwegians, and he knew for certain that the Norwegian Embassy 1st Secretary was going to put him up on Thursday, 6th March. He guessed that the Norwegians are possibly arranging a meeting between van der Merwe and myself. I then asked Isco to come along with me in the morning.

When we got to the Embassy this morning we, indeed, found Professor van der Merwe. He is short, really a small man, round face wearing glasses. The Norwegian 1st Secretary introduced us to each other, adding that he had invited me to join him and his Ambassador, Ola Dorum, in an informal discussion with Professor van der Merwe. I said it's O.K.

Professor van der Merwe began by saying he was in touch with our people in Lusaka, having had 2 or 3 meetings, from which meetings a number of other meetings followed. He told us who he is viz. a Quaker, an Afrikaner, and academician and that one of his greatest interests is to work as a bridge between antagonistic groups. He then explained that this was the aim when he first went to Lusaka to meet the A.N.C.

Professor van der Merwe, who had been participating in a Conference on Peace and Security in Southern Africa in Arusha, then said he was happy to meet me; that he had actually telexed from Johannesburg requesting to meet the Chief Representative of the A.N.C. [in Tanzania]; that he had requested for a similar meeting with the P.A.C. I told him that a telex message from him to P.A.C. was received by our Office and we did nothing about it. He blamed his Secretary for the error.

He told us that Comrade Winnie Mandela met him at Jan Smuts airport just before he left for Tanzania to discuss something with him, [and] at the end of their discussion Comrade Winnie had asked him to convey greetings to us in Tanzania and that the Comrades in Tanzania should send her something nice from Tanzania, preferably a kitenge [sarong]. We couldn't find a suitable kitenge but bought her a carving—Makonde warrior holding a spear!

Professor van der Merwe informed us that he was some kind of god-father to Zindzi Mandela. Comrade Nelson Mandela had requested him to visit him in jail and asked him if he could assist in Zindzi's education. In this regard he thinks he is succeeding as Zindzi was admitted into the University of Cape Town and now has passed her University 1st Year Courses. He told us that on the one occasion he met him, Comrade Nelson looked very well physically, and according to the latest report he received from Winnie, Comrade Nelson is in very good shape physically.

Professor van der Merwe told us that he is in touch with high Government people in South Africa including certain cabinet ministers. He told us that the issue of the release of Comrade Nelson has been on for the last 10 years. It is now well known that he has rejected all attempts to release him outside South Africa. But according to van der Merwe, Comrade Nelson is going to be released. Professor van der Merwe regrets that the media, almost without exception, distorted P.W. Botha's statement on the release of Comrade Nelson when he opened parliament this year. According to Professor van der Merwe, Botha did not make the release of Comrade Nelson conditional to the release of the two Soviet dissidents and soldier [Wynand] du Toit [captured] in Angola; he says Botha said he would release Comrade Nelson on humanitarian grounds and expressed the hope that his act of releasing Comrade Nelson would be reciprocated by the Soviet Union and Angola. He admits that Botha's statement coincided with a process that was going on vis-a-vis the release of the Soviet dissidents and that there had been consultation between South Africa, U.S.A., Israel etc. on this issue.

Van de Merwe says the cabinet is still divided on the release of Comrade Nelson. But up to about 10 Cabinet ministers are in favour of his unconditional release and over thirty Nationalist M.P.'s favour his release. One minister he cited as being in favour is Mr. Kotzee [Kobie Coetsee], the minister of Justice. But the Minister of Police, [Louis] Le Grange is opposed to this release.

Van der Merwe claims to know the Minister of Police and described him as a very conservative man. I quote, "he is a member of the Nationalist Party but his heart is in the Conservative Party". He went further to say P. W. Botha will release Comrade Nelson; that Botha desperately needs soldier du Toit in order to appease his right-wing.

One way in which Botha hopes to achieve this is that he is going to pressurise [Angolan rebel leader] Jonas Savimbi to release the 3 MPLA [Angolan army] soldiers that Savimbi captured. P. W. Botha says he is going to force Savimbi to yield to his demand. If that happened this would give him a good excuse to free Comrade Nelson as this is what the MPLA want before they release du Toit.

Van der Merwe says the Minister of Police is very conservative, and claims to have [access] to him. He claims that this minister is influential in Afrikanerdom. Van der Merwe says he recently got it second-hand from someone to whom P. W. Botha was confiding viz. that P. W. Botha is worried about the police force in South Africa. Van der Merwe claims that the police force in South Africa is supporting the Conservative Party of [Andries] Treurnicht; that the present Commissioner of Police, Johan Coetzee, is contemptuously referred to as "that academic" by the top brass of the South African police force, and so he has little influence on the brutal conduct of the police force. Professor van der Merwe said it pains him to hear people wherever he goes referring to South Africa as racist; he thinks this term is not very correct to use on South Africa except only in as far as the Police force part of the white population. He says the S.A.D.F. [South African Defence Force] is fast integrating with white soldiers saluting [a] Black Officer!!

Prof. van der Merwe, answering a question from Norwegian Ambassador on change in South Africa said he himself is convinced that there is going to be a change in South Africa. The regime has resigned itself to change. They think there is no point in hanging onto an outmoded Apartheid, in the process getting the country's economy destroyed and be defeated in the end. But he says it's not easy for P. W. Botha. The right-wing Afrikaner parties are growing in strength and so P. W. Botha is being forced to go slower than he would like. However, says Prof. van der Merwe, the Nats [National Party] Government is working on a new constitution in which South Africa will be divided into 8 regions or "states". The constitution envisages a federal South Africa. These regions or states will be carved with no consideration of race. In this regard, says van der Merwe, the Blacks, who outnumber whites, will automatically form the majority, both in the regions or "states" as well as in the Federal parliament. Therefore, he says, what [Foreign Minister] Pik Botha recently said about South Africa having a Black President is true except that P. W. Botha hated Pik's forwardness.

Van der Merwe says a referendum will be held. He is sure P. W. Botha will lose the white vote but Botha hopes to win the referendum through the Indian and Coloured vote. He assured us that the Nat Government is not going to create a 4th Chamber of Parliament to accommodate Africans because it would fail worse than it did with the Coloureds and Indians. According to van der Merwe the calculation of the Nats is that the new constitution will be rejected by such organisations as U.D.F, Cosatu etc. encouraged and supported by the A.N.C. which is not likely to be allowed to participate at this stage. The unbanning of the A.N.C. is still far away.

According to van der Merwe, Gatsha Buthelezi has already expressed willingness to participate in this federal scheme being worked out by the Nats government. But van der Merwe says Gatsha has problems; he is a tribal leader and not a national leader, and, therefore, whilst the Nats think that for a start they can get Gatsha to go along with them in the formation of a federal structure for South Africa they think that that can't be the end; that the majority support of groups like the A.N.C., U.D.F. and Cosatu will force even that federal structure to open up and unban the A.N.C. So, for him, it's a long process which is afoot.

Professor van der Merwe is certain that Comrade Nelson will be free soon. He told us of how many restrictions have been waived on him e.g. he now can talk leisurely with Comrade Winnie up to 2 hours if he likes with no interruption; that Comrade Nelson discusses the struggle freely with his wife, with no interruption from the listening warder.

He then turned on me and said the white people are afraid that the A.N.C. would nationalise the economy and bring about a communist state, and invited a response from me. The Norwegian Ambassador added his own views to the effect that they, too, in the West had fears that the A.N.C. would take South Africa to the East. I dismissed these fears as not founded on fact; that the A.N.C. has a very limited programme of nationalisation, and added [to] this that even the present regime has done a lot of nationalisation already.

Van der Merwe then said that whites of all shades in South Africa are concerned about the presence of the South African Communist Party in the ranks of the A.N.C. This factor, he said, strengthened the belief that the A.N.C. would go communist. He cited this that according to *Africa Confidential* almost half the members of the N.E.C. [National Executive Committee] were communists. The Norwegian Ambassador expressed the feeling that this mixture of the A.N.C.-cum-S.A.C.P. was something they felt concerned about.

I then asked if van der Merwe took the list as appears in *Africa Confidential* as authoritative. He said he didn't but that some people in the list were definitely members of the S.A.C.P. I then said I was not competent to evaluate the list as appears in *Africa Confidential*. I further pointed out that what I do know is that members of the S.A.C.P. were in the A.N.C. as A.N.C. members. I further pointed out that at this stage of our struggle the question of ideology in the A.N.C. enjoyed no priority; that we are looking for the broadest possible unity of the patriotic and progressive forces in our country in order to overthrow the apartheid regime. I further pointed out that we, in the A.N.C., are beginning to suspect that certain elements are focusing sharply on the presence of the S.A.C.P. within the ranks of the A.N.C. in order to bring about a division in the A.N.C. along ideological lines. At this point the Norwegian Ambassador rushed to say that that was not the intention except that he felt he should know as much as possible about the A.N.C. There are many other matters he said which are not important but meant really to assure me that they were on the side of the A.N.C.

After this point I indicated that I'd like to leave as I had other commitments. I thanked them for inviting us to the discussion. We shook hands with van der Merwe and I asked him to convey our greetings to Comrades at home and to take our greetings and present to Comrade Winnie Mandela.

In conclusion I want to express the view that this Prof. van der Merwe is a really peculiar person but I think he should be properly evaluated [or] researched so that he doesn't become an enigma.

DOCUMENT 133. "Yes to ANC Visit." *SRC News,* University of Cape Town, March 1986

On Wednesday more than 2000 students gathered in Jameson Hall to decide whether UCT should send representatives in a national NUSAS [National Union of SA Students] delegation to talk to the ANC. The proposal received overwhelming support with no votes against and only 16 abstentions.

This follows an initiative from the Wits SRC [University of the Witwatersrand Student Representative Council] that NUSAS should send a delegation to visit the ANC. On Wednesday last week our SRC voted unanimously in favour of the idea. A national executive meeting of NUSAS supported the proposal, but felt that consultation with students on the issue was crucial.

Speaking at the meeting in Jameson Hall, SRC President Glenn Goosen said, "For twenty-six years the African National Congress has been an enigma to white South Africans. Portrayed as an organisation of terrorist thugs, we have grown to fear, hate and despise anything associated with it. For many of us the mere mention of the ANC conjures visions of violence and death."

"Yet today, despite twenty-six years of relentless repression the ANC is the most powerful political force in the country."

"If we as concerned South Africans are going to contribute to our future, we cannot approach that future blind, we need to reckon with the ANC."

With a student mandate to send representatives to visit the ANC, the SRC will be collecting the questions and concerns that students wish to address to the ANC. Collection of these questions will be taking place on Monday & Tuesday next week and students are encouraged to participate.

The SRC will be making nominations of UCT students to the NUSAS National Council where a national delegation will be constituted. The SRC will make public the criteria on which nominations will be put forward.

YOUR QUESTIONS TO THE ANC WILL BE COLLECTED ON MONDAY & TUESDAY.
THIS CAMPAIGN IS *LEGAL.*

DOCUMENT 134. Report by Commonwealth Eminent Persons Group on meeting with ANC representatives in Lusaka, May 17, 1986

We travelled to Lusaka to brief the ANC leadership on progress and to share the negotiating concept with them. We reported that the concept had been with the Government for more than two months and that we had deliberately not revealed it to the ANC until this juncture because we had seen little point in discussing it with them prior to receiving positive indications from the Government. The Government, while indicating that it was considering it seriously, had not yet said either "yes" or "no". Its acceptance would involve the Government in doing a great deal to prove its sincerity and genuineness in wanting a negotiated solution. Our consultations with Nelson Mandela had been extensive but he had emphasized that in reacting favourably to the concept as a starting point he was speaking as an individual. He had stressed that, if there was to be a considered reaction from him, it would be necessary for him to consult with his ANC colleagues. We informed them that we had urged strongly upon the Government that Mr Mandela's proposal for consultations with fellow ANC prisoners and others inside the country be allowed.

Mr Tambo, ANC President, said it was not going to be possible to give a considered response straight away. He noted that the South African Government, after all these weeks, had still not given the Group a substantive answer. The ANC was in a far more difficult position than the Government. It was based in Lusaka in exile; the organization was spread out; it had responsibilities to many people, including leaders in jail and all those within South Africa who supported its endeavours and influenced its thinking.

By way of initial reaction, however, he was in a position to say that in so far as the concept corresponded to the principles and requirements of the Nassau Accord, it would command the support of the ANC.

Mr Tambo said the ANC had no objection to negotiations and would participate in them so long as they were proper and honest, and not just a device to quell internal demands and weaken external pressures. The ANC could never forget that they were dealing with a regime which did not honour its undertakings and was a master of prevarication. When the South African Government said it wanted negotiations the question arose whether it was honest in its intentions. Had Pretoria not negotiated with the South West Africa People's Organization (SWAPO) and the [Western] Contact Group for eight long years? Had it not negotiated with Mozambique and Angola and signed agreements which it had then proceeded to violate from the very outset?

There was thus a need for the South African Government to demonstrate its good faith, and for the Group to apply the acid test to satisfy itself that the Government was ready for negotiations. No negotiations could be fruitful if there were the slightest reservations in the mind of the Government about the dismantling of apartheid or "erecting the structures of democracy" as stated in the Nassau Accord.

Members of the ANC Executive sought a number of specific clarifications. For example, the concept could be interpreted as implying that the removal of the military from the townships would itself result in freedom of assembly and discussion. It would be helpful to know what the Group really meant. We clarified that these were separate thoughts: the Government was being asked both to remove the military from the townships and, additionally, to create conditions for freedom of assembly and discussion.

The ANC also wished to know what was meant by the phrase "power-sharing". If this were a code word for potential black participation in the racist Tricameral Constitution and its institutions, there would be no basis for a negotiation. We explained that the Government had given an assurance that the agenda would be an open one and that how the balance was struck on the question of power-sharing would be a matter for the negotiations themselves.

On the issue of violence, we clarified that the steps required of the Government would amount to a suspension of the violence of the apartheid system, and it was only in that context that a corresponding suspension of violence by the ANC was being sought. We had made it clear to the Government that it would be unrealistic and impracticable to expect the ANC to renounce violence for all time, regardless of the success or failure of negotiations, nor would we be prepared to endorse any such demand by the Government.

Mr Tambo affirmed the ANC and the Group had a common interest in reaching a point where all could say that apartheid was no more. The ANC appreciated that the concept contained within it the possibility of getting them to that position. He and his colleagues would want about ten days for consultations before giving a firm answer to the Group.

On this encouraging basis we returned to South Africa, having agreed to the possibility of a further round of talks with the ANC in Lusaka in the first week of June in the light of the Government's response.

DOCUMENT 135. "The South African Communist Party and the Current Political Situation in the Western Cape." Study document for underground SACP members, late 1986 (abridged)

Although during the second State of Emergency tens of thousands of activists have been detained, and although the work of our mass organisations has sometimes been disrupted, the struggle continues. The working class has mounted many militant strike actions even in the midst of the emergency. MK activity has taken shape—although many of its exploits, including some in the Western Cape, have not been reported. Our mass organisations, despite difficulties, function with great courage and ingenuity. In the underground, the ANC and the SACP continue to build and deepen their presence inside South Africa, and here in the Western Cape itself.

The struggle continues, but we must be under no illusions. As the day of victory approaches, so will the brutality of the enemy increase. After the failure of their first and second State of Emergency, the apartheid regime is now attempting to apply a more systematic, long-lasting and more brutal emergency. This time they are working more methodically. They have chosen to concentrate not only on leaders of our mass organisations, but also on our rudimentary organs of people's power—street committees, boycott committees, defence committees and people's courts. . . .

THE SACP-ANC ALLIANCE:

One of the outstanding achievements of our struggle over the last two years has been the firmer entrenchment of the ANC as the leading liberation force within our country. In the Western Cape, even within the Coloured sector (which in the past has not enjoyed deep-rooted Congress traditions), the ANC and its leadership has now won wide and popular support. As a result of these regional and national developments, the imperialists have been forced to realise they cannot bypass the ANC. Instead, they now try to "moderate" the ANC, they try to turn it into what it is not. A key aspect of this maneouvre is the imperialists' vain hope of breaking the fighting alliance between the ANC and the SACP. In this they will not succeed. . . .

PEOPLE'S WAR:

Attacks on police patrols and homes in Bonteheuwel and Guguletu; the burning of a train carriage in Woodstock; the harassment of Australian cricket mercenaries—all these are important examples of the beginning of people's war. Yet, our ability to hit back is still weak. We need to initiate and build smaller and highly clandestine combat groups whose main task is to harass the enemy, engage in revolutionary violence, economic sabotage and distribution of revolutionary propaganda. Members of these groups need to be politically conscious and disciplined. The groups should also be built in factories and industries so that when the bosses get arrogant—the workers can apply their own organised force. In due time, these people's combat forces will [raid?] the enemy police for weapons and use whatever they lay their hands on effectively. Work of our combat forces needs to be complemented by well planned and well organised mass political activity in the form of political and economic strikes, boycotts and so on.

PEOPLE'S POWER AND SOCIALISM:

The building of people's committees in our areas is an important and strategic task of our revolution. It is part of the struggle to build a people's army for people's war. Therefore, all mass organisations and trade unions should take this task very seriously. It is these very committees that we are building today, that will be the organs of the future people's government. It is these very committees that will also be organs of a future socialist revolution. This is why the active and practical involvement of the working class in building people's committees is crucial. Our communities should be able to govern themselves and also to defend themselves from enemy terror. An organised and disciplined system of defending our communities should be set up. It is in this context that the strengthening and consolidation of the civics in the African townships and the revival and rebuilding of CAHAC [Cape Areas Housing Action Committee] in the Coloured community should be understood.

THE PARTY AND THE DEMOCRATIC MOVEMENT:

The task of Communists in the mass democratic movement is to serve the masses, express their needs and to raise the level of the masses' consciousness. The masses require not only consciousness but also organisations. Communists are to help in this field too. The masses are the makers of history. For that reason, Communists respect them. They learn from them and move together with them towards national and social emancipation. Such is our strategy in the mass democratic movement.

It is therefore the duty of Communists and all those committed to socialism and freedom to work within the mass movement, to strengthen and broaden the alliance of classes within the movement and assert the leading role of the working class. The working class has to take its rightful place within the broad movement, but it will not do so automatically. It will win its leadership position only by practically taking part in the struggles waged by the masses. That is why our party campaigns ideologically against those ultra-leftists who dismiss the UDF as merely "populist" or petty bourgeois. At the same time, we insist on the right to propagate scientific socialism, not in a sectarian or divisive way, within the ranks of the UDF and its affiliates. Equally, we campaign against any attempt to inject workerist tendencies into the UDF and other mass democratic organisations. . . .

THE SACP AND THE TRADE UNIONS:

We in the SACP are proud to record that it was our party and its militants who, down the years, were in [the] forefront of developing progressive, nonracial trade unionism in South Africa. Our efforts in this field go back to the early 1920s. To this very day, there are underground Communist Party militants at work within the trade union movement.

For the SACP, the strengthening of COSATU and its affiliates is a major revolutionary task of the present time. A strong and a united trade union movement will contribute to working class participation and leadership within the broad liberation movement. However, it is important to realise that the working class needs more than a strong trade union movement. The history of all revolutions in our epoch confirms, in the hard theatre of struggle itself, that the working class requires also a revolutionary proletarian vanguard party. Such a vanguard communist party is made up of the most highly disciplined militants, guided by the principles of Marxism-Leninism, and it is linked organically to mass organisation and struggle. Only such a party is able to represent the *all-round*, short and long-term interests of the working class on every front—political, social, cultural, economic and military.

Despite their great importance, trade unions cannot replace nor be a substitute for a vanguard Marxist-Leninist party. Unions have neither the flexibility nor capacity to do so. But there are some, at present, who call for an "independent" trade union movement as the basis for a "socialist" party in South Africa (as if there is not already a socialist party in our country). There are, perhaps, some sincere but misguided activists who speak in this way. But there are also certain well known opportunists involved in these attempts.

Like the imperialists, these opportunists, who style themselves "socialists", are more concerned with building a third force alternative to the ANC-SACP alliance than with fighting the enemy. Having failed to construct a credible third force under the umbrella of the National Forum, they are now fishing about in the trade unions. . . .

But the "socialism" of these ultra-leftists opportunists is not just vague. It is also abstract. They cannot answer the basic strategic questions confronting South African revolutionaries: what are the material means in our concrete situation for destroying the power of the ruling bloc in order to lay the basis for building socialism in South Africa? A vague and abstract call for an "independent" "socialist" party based on the trade unions is not a serious answer to this question. It is also important to note that whilst the cadres of the ANC, MK, SACP, UDF and COSATU are hunted down and killed by the fascists, these gentlemen continue operating (attacking us) unfettered.

COMRADES, THIS IS NOT FOR YOUR PERSONAL USE ONLY. READ, DISCUSS AND PASS ON TO THOSE YOU TRUST. DO NOT DESTROY.

DOCUMENT 136. "A Few Points on the Current State of Struggle in S.A." ANC intelligence report, mid-1987

The last few years have seen many townships become ungovernable as township residents, spearheaded by the youth and students, have attacked the local authorities and security forces, the bantu education system, high rents and transport fares, removals, repression and bantustans.

The escalation of these struggles took the form of mass, popular uprisings, sometimes sustained for months and resembling a full scale civil war. They seldom planned or organised in advance, and relied more on informal networks than committee structures and procedures.

The trade union movement has been growing for 15 years, and has greater organised strength and experience than other sectors. The formation of COSATU has given it greater coherence and direction, and allowed it to develop in areas where it had been weak. For example, new offices have been established in the Eastern Transvaal at Nelspruit, Northern Transvaal at Pietersburg, and Orange Free State at Bloemfontein.

The shop steward locals have been central to the political thrust of the trade unions. They are loosely defined and non-bureaucratic structures which cover one township or industrial area and tackle any issue affecting workers, including rent, bantu education, bus fares etc. They have invited youth and students to attend their meetings and have played a coordinating and leadership role in some areas. They have continued to meet throughout the emergency and have filled some of the vacuum left by other organisations which have been smashed or hamstrung. So far they have consisted mostly of workers and not officials, and are less prone to the ideological and chauvinistic conflicts which plague regional and national structures like COSATU CEC [Central Executive Committee]. Locals can be relied on to take a militant, pro-ANC line on issues, and the worker leadership active at this level is often highly experienced and skilled.

There have been some ideological splits at local level, mainly as a result of the education/training work being done by ultra-left elements in CCAWUSA [Commercial, Catering and Allied Workers' Union], NUM [National Union of Mineworkers] and MAWU [Metal and Allied Workers' Union] (now NUMSA). Three groupings, working in direct contact with the Socialist Workers Party in Great Britain, are doing more than anyone else to politicise their members. Their mission is to drive a wedge between the trade unions and the ANC; and although it is ultimately hopeless, they can do a lot of damage. They have gained control of the Southern Transvaal region of COSATU and dominate the Johannesburg local which consists of about 150 shop stewards. The local is very active, meets once or twice a week, and innovative. An example is the initiative they took in forming street committees in Soweto. Other bases of opposition to the ANC exist in the leadership of NUTW [National Union of Textile Workers], CWIU [Chemical Workers' Industrial Union]. To date this has not penetrated very far into the membership, and probably never will. There is nonetheless an urgent need to step up education/training at shop-floor level.

The resistance flowing from the working class has been characterised by the traditions of the ANC and the Freedom Charter, and this will expand as the trade unions play a more and more central role in years to come. The occupation of the schools and the townships by security forces makes the workplace the best forum for discussion and decision making, and their crucial location in the economy gives workers a lot of leverage.

There are enormous regional differences within COSATU. The Transvaal and Eastern Cape are more militant and generally better organised than the others, although NUM organisation spreads across many regions and injects militancy into unlikely spots, like the Orange Free State. Natal organisation must be viewed in two parts, North and South. The Richards Bay area is very well organised and strong, with regular community based struggles in which trade unionists play a leading part. They have tackled Inkatha directly and helped promote progressive youth and student organisation. South Natal is well organised from a strict trade union point of view, but far less inclined to get involved in broader community and political issues. The Natal midlands, including Howick, Hammarsdale, Ladysmith and Newcastle are developing fast and will also be crucial in breaking the stranglehold of Inkatha.

COSATU, as a federation, faces many organisational and ideological problems, and there are times when it becomes counterproductive or seems ready to split. There are three main groupings made up of an ultra-left/syndicalist group around CCAWUSA, MAWU, CWIU, and parts of NUM; a UDF group around GAWU [General and Allied Workers' Union], Sarhwu [SA Railway and Harbours Workers' Union], ex-Macwusa [Motor Assembly and Component Workers' Union of SA], ex-Ummawusa [United Mining, Metal and Allied Workers' Union of SA], some Saawu [SA Allied Workers' Union] and Fawu [Food and Allied Workers' Union] branches; and a pro-ANC left wing group around Jay [Naidoo] and Cyril [Ramaphosa] which draws support from a wide range of unions. The splits and alliances between these groups usually revolve around community and political issues, relations to the ANC, UDF, Sayco [SA Youth Congress], Necc [National Education Crisis Committee], Nasco etc. Jay and Cyril are often caught in the middle between one group that wants little or nothing to do with Congress inspired political action, and another that sometimes advocates unstrategic and uncritical support for such action. Despite this, Jay and his group have managed to steer COSATU into leading roles on the abolition of passes, resolution of the education crisis, opposition to the SOE [state of emergency], development [of] youth and street committee structures, promotion of unemployed and farm worker organisation, and links to the ANC.

COSATU is due to adopt a political programme at its Congress in June, and this will include the FC [Freedom Charter]. They will also affirm their complete support for sanctions while taking steps to prepare workers for the effects of international pressure.

The communities have been the battle field on which student, youth, women's and residents' issues have been fought. We will look briefly at each one in turn.

Civics had been formed in so-called coloured and Indian areas in 1980-81, but had largely dissolved by the time of the Vaal uprisings in September '84. However, there were very few civics in African townships, and those that had been formed had little organisation and structure, few experienced organisers, no signed up membership or material resources. Nonetheless they enjoyed overwhelming support and could mobilise their constituency around pressing problems. But as struggle intensified, they faced extreme repression that neutralised many of their leading activists, and the lack of participative structures limited their ability to marshal their forces and manoeuvre strategically. They failed to define programmes of action and relied too heavily on spontaneous outbursts of popular anger. This means that resistance fluctuated, and it was difficult to consolidate mobilisation into organisation and to inject progressive political content into struggles. Many civics continued as self appointed committees of activists who had no regular contact with their base, although they were generally able to express the basic demands and aspirations of their constituency. In some cases however, notably Alexandra (Transvaal) and Soweto, the civic had nothing to do with the development of the street committees (SC's) and sometimes saw them as a threat.

The emergence of street committees has been a major development, and one that has the potential to take us beyond ungovernability towards people's power. Extreme repression however, has resulted in street committees either collapsing, going underground, or reverting to mundane domestic activities. They will have to find the right format according to local conditions, and will need to distinguish their role from that of other organisations such as the youth, the [RMC-Release Mandela Campaign], the student-parents committees etc. Much of this planning and definition was carried out by vanguard elements drawn mainly from the youth and the unions, many of whom are no longer around, and so the street committees are having a hard time organising themselves, formulating programmes of action, and withstanding repression. Many have collapsed, and very few are clear and focused, but the potential is still there.

The rent issue is a good example of the limits and possibilities of the struggle in the communities at the moment. Over fifty townships nationwide are not paying rent. This has spread since the rent hikes began in mid-84 and included such events as the Vaal uprisings in September 1984. However, very few townships actually planned a boycott of rents, discussed it door-to-door, and set up structures to coordinate and maintain the boycott. In most cases it took the form of an ever widening cycle of default which eventually involved the entire township and amounts that could never be paid. While it makes political sense to speak of a rent boycott, we must be careful not to fool ourselves into believing that it was a planned strategy.

The spread of street committees is very patchy. In the Transvaal it is mainly parts of Soweto, Mamelodi, Alexandra and some East Rand townships. The Vaal Civic no longer exists, and nor does ASRO [Atteridgeville-Saulsville Residents' Organisation]. In the Northern and Eastern Transvaal there are thousands of village committees, although many may not meet because of the reign of terror conducted by the army and vigilantes. The Durban and Cape Town townships generally have no street committees, although there have been some limited initiatives e.g. Khayelitsha. Eastern Cape and Boland towns tend to be much more organised than the major centres. Towns like Duncan Village, Mdantsane and Queenstown have been badly hit by detentions, assassinations and trials and local organisation has been unable to sustain itself.

The tactics of the security forces have been to eliminate activists and leaders through detention, murder and trials. Homes are attacked with grenades and petrol bombs, which makes it almost prohibitively dangerous to become involved. A web of informers tip them off as soon as activity stirs, and so street committees and youth and student structures have had to remain secret or anonymous. This seriously limits the role they are meant to play in organising, mobilising and politicising their constituency. A street committee is by definition a participative, interactive organ of People's Power. If its members and meetings cannot be known, how can it provide a vehicle for residents to deal with daily problems of oppression in the township?

Many activists, faced with the violence of an occupation force that shoots first and asks questions later, have been forced underground and now believe that without weapons their work is futile. This is obviously correct, in that defence is vital to their survival. But basic civic, youth and student issues still have to be taken up. These issues are above ground and generally reformist questions which require fairly open structures capable of working through legal channels to get rent reduced, houses built, students reinstated, evictions stopped etc. We need therefore to distinguish between the revolutionary underground and reformist, constituency based organisation. There is a need for all such organisations to take security precautions, to work clandestinely when necessary, and to employ tactics which contravene the emergency regulations e.g. stayaways, but they should remain distinct from the underground, revolutionary structures which deal with a qualitatively different type of work. Recruitment and training in the revolutionary underground and coordination of tasks will obviously intersect and overlap with civic, youth and student work, but it should not supplant it. This distinction is not very clear in practice and many frustrated, and sometimes inexperienced and untrained activists, may conclude that above ground, reformist work is no longer necessary or possible and substitute it with the revolutionary underground.

Most constituencies remain largely unorganised. Very few people have been signed up and allocated to structures through which they can contribute to struggle in a planned and systematic way. This weakens our ability to involve the mass of our people in strategic challenge to the system, and restricts the educative effects of such involvement in struggle. We have seen this clearly in areas which became ungovernable and then could move no further, and amongst people who have been involved in tumultuous and often traumatic events but still have a poor understanding and undeveloped consciousness. The lack of student organisation, and the confusion surrounding the concept of people's education, is an example of this shortcoming.

There is very little education and training work taking place, and information is in critically short supply. This makes for superficial understanding and action, and minimises the political content of those struggles in both the short and the longer term. Demands for the removal of troops, release of detainees, ending of the State of Emergency, scrapping of DET [government Department of Education and Training] etc. are relevant, but need to be situated or contextualised. What are we challenging? Why? What do we want? How can we get it? We need to move beyond slogans and propaganda and be clear about the society we are trying to build and how we will do it.

Document 137. "The Dakar Declaration." Statement by participants in IDASA conference, Dakar, July 12, 1987

1. A Conference organised by the Institute for a Democratic Alternative for South Africa (Idasa) took place in Dakar, Senegal, from 9th to 12th July, 1987. The participants comprised 61 South Africans, of whom the majority were Afrikaans-speaking persons who had come from South Africa, and a 17-person delegation from the African National Congress.
2. His Excellency President Abdou Diouf welcomed the participants and gave them exceptional hospitality.
3. The participants from South Africa took part in their individual capacities. They shared a common commitment of having rejected both the ideology and practice of the apartheid system. They were drawn from the academic, professional, cultural, religious and business fields.
4. Although the group represented no organised formation within South Africa, their place within—particularly—the Afrikaans-speaking communities and the fact that they were meeting with the ANC invested the Con-

ference with an overwhelming atmosphere that this was part of the process of the South African people making history. In similar manner the international community focused its attention on the Conference. Participants could not but be aware that some of the adherents of apartheid regarded the participation of the group as an act of betrayal, not only to the apartheid state, but also the community of Afrikanerdom.
5. The Conference was organised around four principal topics:
    - Strategies for bringing about fundamental change in South Africa;
    - The building of national unity;
    - Perspectives with regard to the structures of the government of a free South Africa, and;
    - Of the economy of a liberated South Africa.
6. The discussions took place in an atmosphere of cordiality and a unity of purpose arising from a shared commitment towards the removal of the apartheid system and the building of a united, democratic and non-racial South Africa.
7. The group listened to and closely questioned the perspectives, goals and strategies of the ANC. The main area of concern arose over the ANC's resolve to maintain and intensify the armed struggle. The group accepted the historical reality of the armed struggle and although not all could support it, everyone was deeply concerned over the proliferation of uncontrolled violence. However, all participants recognised that the source of violence in South Africa derives from the fact that the use of force is fundamental to the existence and practice of racial domination. The group developed an understanding of the conditions which have generated a widespread revolt by the black people as well as the importance of the ANC as a factor in resolving the conflict.
8. Conference unanimously expressed preference for a negotiated resolution of the South African question. Participants recognised that the attitude of those in power is the principal obstacle to progress in this regard. It was further accepted that the unconditional release of all political leaders in prison or detention and the unbanning of all organisations are fundamental prerequisites for such negotiations to take place.
9. Proceeding from the common basis that there is an urgent necessity to realise the goal of a non-racial democracy, participants agreed that they had an obligation to act for the achievement of this objective. They accepted that different strategies must be used in accordance with the possibilities available to the various forces opposed to the system of apartheid. They accepted that in its conduct this struggle must assist in the furtherance both of democratic practice and in the building of a nation of all South Africans—black and white.
10. It was accepted by the two delegations that further contacts were necessary. Equally, it was important that such contacts should involve more and wider sections of the South African people in order to dispel misunderstanding and fear, and to reinforce the broad democratic movement.
11. Conference expressed profound appreciation to His Excellency, President

Abdou Diouf, and the government and people of Senegal for the warm welcome extended to the delegates as well as the assistance afforded to them to assure the success of the Conference. It further expressed gratitude to Mrs Danielle Mitterrand for her assistance in organising the conference and extended thanks to all other governments and individuals who contributed material resources to make the Conference possible.

Document 138. Evaluation of Dakar conference by ANC participant, July 1987

1. The ANC delegation worked extremely well. Strategy and tactics were carefully planned and the major interventions under each of the four agenda items thoroughly discussed and well worked out. Tribute must be paid to Thabo [Mbeki's] fine handling of the delegation meetings and of the relations with the Idasa Group [Institute for a Democratic Alternative for SA] and Mac [Maharaj's] tactical flair.

The excellent interventions made early in the meeting by Thabo and Mac established the foundation for the exceptionally positive view of the ANC which virtually all of the Idasa Group (using this term to refer to the entire group which came to meet the ANC) formed during the course of the meeting. They repeatedly expressed their admiration for the political clarity of the ANC, the analytical and intellectual strength of the delegation and the openness of the ANC to discussion about its policies and approaches.

We could, however, have been better prepared had there been either earlier notice to the delegates or, more importantly, had steps been taken well in advance. For example, even without informing people of the actual purpose of the work, some of us could have been commissioned well before (whether we were to be delegates or not) to prepare briefings on the relevant materials and people, etc.

Generally, the meeting was successful and important. By the simple fact of its occurrence it has sharpened some divisions within the white bloc; it has helped solidify the disaffection with the regime of an important group of intellectuals some of whom were previously supporters of the Botha project and provided its ideological and intellectual support—after all, intellectuals have played a not unimportant role in the formulation of NP [National Party] reformist positions (Wiehahn, de Lange [Commissions], etc); it has established the basis for those who participated to carry forward their work among the middle strata of the whites and it has opened the way for further, more broadly based, similar meetings with the ANC.

Seen in the context of the weakening of the white bloc and the regime in the present and of developing white support for and participation in the transition in the future, the meeting was undoubtedly successful.

2. Although the members of the Idasa Group held many different, sometimes complementary, sometimes contradictory, views about political transforma-

tion and the national liberation movement, nonetheless it is possible to define three broad categories:
a. A radical group basically supporting the ANC, the Freedom Charter and the armed struggle and locating the masses, particularly the black working class, at the centre of political transformation.
b. A centre group which is less homogenous and more hesitant in its support for these fundamental aspects of the struggle. It is among this group that we find individuals worried about, but not necessarily hostile to, specific features of ANC policy and practice—ANC's position on "uncontrolled" violence, its preparedness to accept a range of strategies rather than insist upon conformity with its own strategies, guarantees about the future (multi-party state, judiciary, etc), the mixed economy and so on.
c. A third, "rightist" group which is pre-occupied with regional and compromise solutions, which is aimed not merely at reducing the level of violent conflict but is premised upon the belief that the political solution to the South African crisis rests with the white electorate. Interim solutions, therefore, are to be seen as providing the "space" and the conditions which would allow whites to be weaned away from apartheid to the gradual, and peaceful, development of a democratic, non-racial state. This group holds that the sine qua non of their strategy is that the ANC should renounce the armed struggle.

The importance of categorising the Idasa group in this way, particularly if it is assumed that these divisions are also replicated among the more progressive white intelligentsia generally, is that it suggests the need for the ANC to adopt different approaches to the different categories;
a. Little need be said about the first category since they really constitute part of the mass democratic movement and presumably would be related to in the same way.
b. What seems to be of paramount importance in relation to the middle group is that we should ensure in some way that they receive information about and explanations of ANC policy on as regular a basis as possible. They clearly stand in need of education and in this respect it is vital that the distorted accounts of ANC policies and practices which the regime propagates have, somehow, to be offset. It seems to me that many among these can be won over to the mass democratic movement, but to do this they have to be addressed by us.
c. The third group raises a different problem—here the issue is not education (although they also need this badly) but rather contestation since this group is influential and active in actually propagating regional solutions and in attempting to provide theoretical and historical justification of the political positions adopted. It is necessary here to engage publicly inside South Africa through the journals and papers (e.g. *Work in Progress*, *Suid Afrikaan*, etc) with these writers in order to demonstrate the theoretical and historical weakness of the analyses and the utter inadequacy of the political strategies.

3. The discussions at the formal meetings and also the virtually continuous informal discussions outside of the meetings suggested a number of points about our presentations which could, perhaps, be sharpened not only at future similar meetings but generally in our published material.

a. A frequent element in the positive assessment of the ANC related to its supposed pragmatism and its refusal to adhere to an ideological position. This comment came largely from members of the centre group, but not only. From my discussions it was not at all clear what was meant by the movement's pragmatism—sometimes it seems to refer to the acceptance of the mixed economy, at others the autonomy of the ANC from the SACP [SA Communist Party], at others the democratic character of the ANC and so on.

However, it seems to me that this is not a welcome characterisation of the ANC. The distinction between pragmatism and opportunism is very thin and confuses the issue. Our position is not pragmatic—the ANC has a definite ideology and objective coupled with tactical and strategic flexibility based on continuous analysis of the changing situation. The pragmatism label might be welcome to a section of the whites but would it be welcome to the masses, and does it not give a weapon to the ultra left. I don't want to make too much of this point but it might be useful to deal with this indirectly by the way in which we present our position.

b. Unfortunately, there was insufficient time to have a proper discussion on the economy and a number of points arose which need to be addressed by us in our research and in our writing. Among these points were:
  i. The [economist] Christo Nel type of approach, which stresses the need to abandon "isms" while at the same time a scenario of the economy which embodies capital*ism* is presented, is becoming very much the basis of the approach of the Anglo American Corporation. We had no opportunity to deal with this at the meeting but we need to address this in the South African literature especially as it will entail an elaboration of our position on the mixed economy.
  ii. This latter issue (the mixed economy) was only touched upon and this was, perhaps, fortunate because it is an issue which we deal with very weakly. Our stock response is that the "people will decide" after the defeat of apartheid what will be nationalised, when and with what priorities.

Obviously, it would be wrong for us to try to write blueprints of the economy in advance since so much will depend on the conditions at the moment of the transition and on the character of that transition (social forces involved, armed struggle, insurrection, etc). But surely we should be able to say more about the direction in which we want to go and why. This raises the whole question about the relationship of production and distribution and, at least in general, the type of controls and/or ownership that will be necessary to ensure both economic growth and massive redistribution. We obviously need directed research here (including comparative research) which would ground a much more coherent and definite position.

The point can be illustrated by reference to [businessman, Albert] Koopman's paper which we had no time to discuss. His paper dealt, albeit rather vaguely, with a re-organisation of management procedures and the labour process in his enterprises. He claimed that through consultation with the workers their creativity was released and, as a result, enormous wastages were ended, productivity increased and both profits and wages boosted. It was not clear what the position of the trade unions was in his enterprises.

What was of interest in his presentation is that it raised questions about how we might begin to think about the control of the private sector of the economy in the transition. After all, it is surely not sufficient to say we will have a mixed economy; we need to think about the kinds of controls which will have to be exercised over that sector of the economy and, undoubtedly, it will vary according to the internal differentiation of that sector (retail trade, wholesale trade, productive enterprises, etc). Koopman's paper raised the issue of workers' participation in management, the role of trade unions, limitations on profit and so on in the private manufacturing sector.

c. An important point which surfaced in both the formal meetings, in private discussions and most sharply in the informal meeting of those who remained behind in Dakar, related to the whole issue of the depoliticisation of ethnicity. Of course, the issue is pertinent to Inkatha but it came up in relation to the Afrikaner community.

Pallo [Jordan] dealt with this in part when he discussed the question of the continued recognition of Afrikaans. That is to say, a declaration of the right to language and culture (with racism, however, outlawed), including Afrikaans and Afrikaner culture, could contribute to depoliticising these issues and emphasising individual as against group rights.

But the point was developed also in a different direction and [PFP member of Parliament, Pierre] Cronje put it very strongly when he declared he was not prepared to participate in a politics which encouraged the continuity of the idea of the Afrikaner people as a political entity—he said that he had spent 20 years trying to break from that kind of politics and refused to return to it. This seems to raise an important issue about the whole question of ethnicity and our approach to it which needs to be spelt out much more rigorously and explicitly—here too we need research and writing.

d. In addressing the question of the armed struggle, a lot was, quite correctly, made of the historical commitment of the ANC to non-violence and to the conditions which led it to adopt the strategy of armed struggle. But little was said about the present politics of that struggle—for example, whether it was conceived of as the means of bringing the powerful South African army to the point of surrender and thereby the downfall of the regime or, alternatively, what its precise relationship is thought to be to the insurrectionary mass struggles (e.g. stretching the regime's resources to breaking point in conditions in which the army is unlikely to fragment, etc).

It was clear that most of the Idasa group had little understanding of the politics of the armed struggle and simply explained its emergence as due to "frustration" and then recognised its "historical existence". But they had no conception of the political strategy of the armed struggle and this should be made clear.

e. Although the ANC/SACP relationship was discussed on a number of occasions and the ANC position well presented, nonetheless there was considerable reliance on the historical role of the SACP and the fact that it was and had been nonracial. Again, it would have been useful to stress the convergence in the policies of the two organisations.

f. The question of negotiations was repeatedly raised and the conditions upon which the ANC insists made clear. However, one aspect which was not touched upon and which left our position somewhat unclear relates to the armed forces of the state. Is our position that if political prisoners are released, the ANC unbanned, politically restrictive laws repealed, we could then go to the negotiating table? Surely we need to say something about the army and police.

DOCUMENT 139. "The Question of Negotiations." Statement by ANC National Executive Committee, Lusaka, October 9, 1987

In the recent period, both the Pretoria regime and various Western powers have been raising the issue of a negotiated resolution of the South African question. Inspired by the deep-seated desire and unwavering commitment to end the apartheid system as soon as possible and with minimum loss of life and property, the National Executive Committee met and considered this matter with all due seriousness and attention.

We are convinced that the Botha regime has neither the desire nor the intention to engage in any meaningful negotiations. On the contrary, everything this regime does is directed at the destruction of the national liberation movement, the suppression of the democratic movement and the entrenchment and perpetuation of the apartheid system of white minority domination.

The racist regime has raised the issue of negotiations to achieve two major objectives. The first of these is *to defuse the struggle inside our country by holding out false hopes of a just political settlement which the Pretoria regime has every intention to block.* Secondly, this regime *hopes to defeat the continuing campaign for comprehensive and mandatory sanctions* by sending out bogus signals that it is ready to talk seriously to the genuine representatives of our people.

Fundamental to the understanding of the apartheid regime's concept of negotiations is the notion that it must impose its will on those it is talking to and force them to accept its dictates. In practice, the Botha regime is conducting a determined campaign of repression against the ANC and the mass democratic movement. This includes the assassination of leaders, mass detentions, military occupation of townships and a programme of pacification carried out by the so-called Joint Management Centres (JMCs).

The racists are out to terrorise our people into submission, crush their democratic organisations and force us to surrender.

All these efforts will fail. Rather than create a climate conducive to genuine negotiations, they will only serve further to sharpen the confrontation within our country and bring to the fore the prospect of the bloodiest conflict that our continent has ever seen.

Our struggle will not end until South Africa is transformed into a united, democratic and non-racial country. This is the only solution which would enable all our people, both black and white, to live as equals in conditions of peace and prosperity. The overwhelming majority of our people accept that the Freedom Charter provides a reasonable and viable framework for the construction of a new society.

We wish here to reiterate that the ANC has never been opposed to a negotiated settlement of the South African question. On various occasions in the past we have, in vain, called on the apartheid regime to talk to the genuine leaders of our people. Once more, we would like to reaffirm that the ANC and the masses of our people as a whole are ready and willing to enter into genuine negotiations provided they are aimed at the transformation of our country into a united and non-racial democracy. *This, and only this, should be the objective of any negotiating process.* Accordingly no meaningful negotiations can take place until all those concerned, and specifically the Pretoria regime, accept this perspective which we share with the whole of humanity.

We further wish to state again that the questions whether or not to negotiate, and on what conditions, should be put to our entire leadership, including those who are imprisoned and who should be released unconditionally. While considering these questions our leadership would have to be free to consult and discuss with the people without let or hindrance.

We reject unequivocally the cynical demand of the Pretoria regime that we should unilaterally abandon or suspend the armed struggle. The source of violence in our country is the apartheid system. It is that violence which must end. Any cessation of hostilities would have to be negotiated and entail agreed action by both sides as part of the process of the creation of a democratic South Africa.

Equally, we reject all efforts to dictate to us who our allies should or should not be, and how our membership should be composed. Specifically, we will not bow down to pressures intended to drive a wedge between the ANC and the South African Communist Party, a tried and tested ally in the struggle for a democratic South Africa. Neither shall we submit to attempts to divide and weaken our movement by carrying out a witch hunt against various members on the basis of their ideological beliefs.

The conflict in our country is between the forces of national liberation and democracy on the one hand and those of racism and reaction on the other. Any negotiations would have to be conducted by these two forces as represented by their various organisational formations.

We reject without qualification the proposed National Statutory Council (NSC) which the Botha regime seeks to establish through legislation to be enacted by the apartheid parliament. This can never be a genuine and acceptable mechanism to negotiate a democratic constitution for our country.

In practice, the National Statutory Council can never be anything more than an advisory body which would put its views to the apartheid parliament and the regime itself, which retains the right to accept or reject those views. What the Botha regime proposes as a constitution-making forum—the National Statutory Council—is therefore nothing but a device intended to enmesh all who sit on it in a bogus process of meaningless talk which has nothing to do with any genuine attempt to design a democratic constitution for our country.

In addition, this National Statutory Council seeks to entrench and legitimise the very structures of apartheid that our struggle, in all its forms, seeks to abolish. The unrepresentative organs of the apartheid structure of repression, such as the racist tri-cameral parliament and the bantustans, cannot be used as instruments for the liquidation of the very same system they have been established to maintain.

An essential part of the apartheid system is the definition and division of our people according to racial and ethnic groups, dominated by the white minority. To end apartheid means, among other things, to define and treat all our people as equal citizens of our country, without regard to race, colour or ethnicity. To guarantee this, the ANC accepts that a new constitution for South Africa could include an entrenched Bill of Rights to safeguard the rights of the individual. We are, however, opposed to any attempt to perpetuate the apartheid system by advancing the concept of so-called group and minority rights.

Our region is fully conversant with the treacherous and deceitful nature of the apartheid regime. There are more than enough examples of agreements which this regime has shamelessly dishonoured. Taking this experience into account, we insist that before any negotiations take place, the apartheid regime would have to demonstrate its seriousness by implementing various measures to create a climate conducive to such negotiations.

These would include the unconditional release of all political prisoners, detainees, all captured freedom fighters and prisoners of war as well as the cessation of all political trials. The state of emergency would have to be lifted, the army and the police withdrawn from the townships and confined to their barracks. Similarly, all repressive legislation and all laws empowering the regime to limit freedom of assembly, speech, the press and so on, would have to be repealed. Among these would be the Riotous Assemblies, the Native Administration, the General Laws Amendment, the Unlawful Organisations, the Internal Security and similar Acts and regulations.

We take this opportunity once more to reaffirm that *the African National Congress is opposed to any secret negotiations. We firmly believe that the people themselves must participate in shaping their destiny and would therefore have to be involved in any process of negotiations.*

Being fully conscious of the way the Pretoria regime has, in the past, deliberately dragged out negotiations to buy time for itself, we maintain that any negotiations would have to take place within a definite time-frame to meet the urgent necessity to end the apartheid system and lift the yoke of tyranny from the masses of our people who have already suffered for too long.

There is, as yet, no prospect for genuine negotiations because the Botha regime continues to believe that it can maintain the apartheid system through force and terror. We therefore have no choice but to intensify the mass political and armed struggle for the overthrow of the illegal apartheid regime and the transfer of power to the people.

We also call on all our people to reject and spurn Botha's so-called National Statutory Council and make certain that this apartheid council never sees the light of day.

We reiterate our appeal to the international community to join us in this noble struggle by imposing comprehensive and mandatory sanctions against racist South Africa to end the apartheid system and reduce the amount of blood that will otherwise have to be shed to achieve this goal.

Finally, we would like to express our gratitude to the Organisation of African Unity which, at its last Summit, adopted a Declaration on Southern Africa pledging Africa's support for the positions contained in the statement. We commend that Declaration to the rest of the world community as an important document laying the basis for concerted international action to banish apartheid racism, colonialism and war once and for all.

Document 140. "Briefing on Situation in P [Botswana]." ANC intelligence report, December 1987 (abridged)

Introduction

This paper is written as a briefing to the comrades who will be meeting the delegation from the P [Botswana] government. . . .

At present we have about 100 operatives in P. Of these, about 65 are full-time. We also have about 15 adults and 50 children who are "above-board" or non-operational. Apart from one or two exceptions, the vast majority of our full-time operatives are in P illegally.

We have the following structures in P:

-RPMC [Regional Politico-Military Council]
-Military
-Political
-NAT [ANC Department of Intelligence and Security]

-Cape Machinery
-OFS Machinery
-Special Ops
-National Ordinance
-Documentation Unit
-Finance and Logistics Unit

In terms of both structures and numbers our presence in P has increased significantly during this year. In January this year we had about 70 operatives in P, of whom about 50 to 55 were full-time. During this year the Cape and OFS machineries and the Documentation Unit were introduced into P.

The increase in numbers and structures in P are largely a result of the growing dependence of the Movement on P as a result of the problems experienced in other forward areas.

Our Activities and Methods of Work in P

Of particular importance here are three main factors. Firstly, the developing situation at home plus the increase in the number of areas at home for which P is responsible have led to an increase in the traffic between P and home. This is in terms of the servicing of internal contacts, the transit of internal contacts for training abroad etc.

Secondly, in the last few years, P has become a crucial area for the infiltration of comrades into the country. In fact, this has been the main focus of the P regional leadership for the past two and a half years. . . .

The third factor relates to our methods of work in P. Because of the pressure of the demands of the movement on our region, we have to some extent been forced to employ methods of work which are not satisfactory. Further, we are compelled to use methods which have long been known to the enemy, such as the pick-up.

Of particular significance here is the question of accommodation. The accommodation situation in P is very difficult, both for permanent comrades and transit cadres. We can no longer rely to any significant extent on assistance from locals and are forced to rely on rented accommodation and hotels. The vigilance of the local population and hotel employees in terms of reporting strangers has been a large cause of local arrests. Although the regional leadership has done its best to address this problem, the options are limited.

In the past, the P authorities have complained that they are forced to act against our people because of our bad style of work. Although this may be true in isolated instances, the vast majority of arrests of our people in P have not been due to this factor but to sustained attempts by the locals to track us down, coupled with the difficult accommodation situation in the area.

Nonetheless, in the last year or so we have developed resources and methods of work which have made it more difficult for the locals to track us down. This is borne out by information received from inside the P security organs. In addition, the RPMC has recently banned the attendance of comrades at discos, bars, music festivals and large social gatherings, thus eliminating this as an excuse by the locals for their actions against us.

It should be noted here that, while it is true that the RPMC recently noted a gradual deterioration in our style of work in the region, this deterioration was rarely responsible for local arrests. The RPMC has now addressed this situation and the improvement is already noticeable.

Security Situation in P

Over most of this year the security situation in P has shown a marked improvement after the dramatic deterioration which began in early 1985. However, in recent months, and especially in the last few weeks, the RPMC has noted a sudden and dramatic deterioration in the security situation. There are a number of factors involved here.

Firstly, there is the "end of year" factor. Every year at this time the enemy, in response to our own plans to celebrate December 16, launches a massive propaganda and security offensive against us. Last year and this year in particular this offensive has concentrated on P. . . .

Secondly, in recent months there have been a number of arrests inside the country of key comrades who had been serviced from P. Most notable here are the Cape Town arrests [of the Yengeni/Schreiner unit]. Further, parallel to our increasing infiltration of the country, there has been an increase in the number of comrades arrested at home on their way in. This has led to the enemy receiving in its hands a fairly large amount of fresh information about our presence, activities and methods of work in P. In our assessment the enemy has taken a clear decision recently to act on this information.

It is likely that the P delegation will raise the complaint that our comrades arrested inside the country talk too easily and freely, especially about their passage through P. This issue has been raised by the P SB [Special Branch police] during interrogation of comrades arrested in P on several occasions. . . .

Thirdly, there has been an increase in pressure by Pretoria on the P authorities. This has taken the form of propaganda accusing P of allowing increased use of its country by the ANC (including the accusations of a meeting between members of the MK High Command and the P authorities). It has taken the form of economic blackmail, such as the linking of the signing of the Soda Ash agreement between P and SA to the signing of a security pact. More recently it has taken the form of intensified searching at the main P/SA borders on the SA side.

There are now indications that the enemy is beginning a physical assault on the movement in P. Yesterday we received a report that the flat of one of our sympathisers (whose phone number had been given by HQ to a now arrested internal operative) was petrol-bombed.

Also recently, Thomas, a former NAT operative kidnapped from Swaziland and subsequently released inside the country without charge, has been spotted in P, at one stage in the vicinity of the house of one of our expatriate operatives (whose phone number was also given to internal operatives now arrested). . . .

Attitudes and Activities of the P Authorities

In the past year there has been a marked improvement in the attitude of the P authorities to us. Although our comrades are still being arrested, there is evidence that there has not been the same level of harassment as experienced from the middle of 1985.

Firstly, comrades recently arrested by the P authorities have noticed a more sympathetic approach to us by our interrogators, particularly the more junior ones. Secondly, there is information in our hands that the P government has been both doing its best to resist SA pressure for a security agreement, and has been seriously considering upgrading its relationship with the movement. The main sources of this information is contained in two enclosed documents—one the minutes of a meeting which took place between P and SA in June this year, and the other a memo from the P External Affairs Ministry recommending the re-opening of the ANC office in P.

Thirdly, in the latter half of this year we received a clandestine approach from the deputy commander of the BDF [Botswana Defence Force] (indirectly) suggesting on-the-ground liaison between their M.I. [Military Intelligence] and us. This liaison has been established and its form and content indicate a clear sympathy to us and willingness to co-operate. . . .

While it is true that there has been an improvement in the attitude of the P authorities to us in recent times, arrests and harassment of our comrades continues. In many cases the arrests are due to unavoidable situations where comrades fall into the hands of the local SB in the course of work. The normal procedure after arrest is relatively mild interrogation, followed by short detention and deportation. The repeated arrest of particular comrades in P does not affect their subsequent treatment. Also, the P authorities have now adopted the practice of returning captured documents to arrested comrades on their deportation. . . .

Prisoners

The writer of this briefing had the opportunity during his own recent arrest in P to spend some time with our sentenced comrades in prison in P. These are the three Transkei comrades (Majija etc) and Cde London Maputo—all of them sentenced for possession of arms.

Firstly, it is important to note that the morale of the comrades is inspiring, making representations on their behalf particularly necessary.

The over-riding complaint of the comrades is that, while they are prepared to suffer for the movement and the struggle, they find it very difficult to accept that they should be incarcerated in a country which is an ally of the movement. . . .

Representation and Liaison

The P RPMC has been suggesting for some time that attempts should be made by the movement to encourage the P authorities to agree to a higher level of representation of the Movement in P. Presently the comrade in charge of Dukwe [refugee camp] acts as an "unofficial" liaison between the P SB and the movement. This is useful at a practical level, but the comrade concerned is not himself suited to the job—he is untrained, inexperienced and lacks the maturity needed for such a task.

The information we have about the proposals of the P External Ministry for re-opening our office create an opening for us to raise this issue with the P authorities. It is highly unlikely, however, in the present climate, that they will agree to this. It may be possible, though, to raise the question of establishing a liaison person with more authority, so that liaison can take place at a higher level as well as at the lower levels. It may be suggested to them that such an arrangement can be organised in a totally non-public, "unofficial" manner.

The recently established clandestine liaison between the RPMC and their M.I. (Don't mention it to them!) indicates the possibility and desirability for the extension of such liaison (at an operational or "unofficial" level) between us and their main Security organ. The nature and content of such liaison will be determined by the extent of their willingness, but can include the exchange of information on enemy activities in and around P, the discussion of issues relating to their treatment of us or their complaints against us etc. . . .

Conclusion

While there has been a significant improvement in the relations between the Movement and the P authorities at a practical level in recent times, our increasing use of P and the enemy's response to that has created a situation in which the P authorities are once again faced with the difficult choice between us and Pretoria.

It is our guess that the present P delegation is here to ask for a significant let-up on the part of the Movement in our use of P. In particular they are likely to ask for specific comrades to be withdrawn.

DOCUMENT 141. "APLA selects white targets." Editorial in *Azania Combat*, no. 4, 1987

The Pan Africanist Congress of Azania is not an organisation that says one thing and does something else. The PAC has extended this fine tradition to its military wing, the Azanian People's Liberation Army.

At its formation on April 6, 1959, the PAC propounded what it called an "unfolding programme" to fight Pretoria, envisaging one campaign leading to another.

It is now a matter of record that the PAC-led Status Campaign (to free Africans mentally) in January 1960 had led to another PAC campaign, the Decisive Positive Action Campaign Against the Pass Laws, some 80 days later. And from there, the freedom road had led to the emergence of the PAC-inspired black consciousness movement and directly from that to Soweto on June 16, 1976.

The pattern has been "one campaign leading to another in a never ending stream", as promised by the PAC. When therefore we say the current situation in Racist South Africa (RSA) is not a spontaneous affair but a logical development of the sustained and principled struggle of the African masses, particularly since the PAC formation, we base ourselves on these undeniable historical facts.

Then the PAC is on record as having stated that it would not engage in any activity if that activity would not help increase the fighting capacity of the African masses. A look at the PAC's Status Campaign and the anti-pass campaign will show that these two PAC actions decisively increased the fighting capacity of the oppressed masses, both ideologically and organisationally, and the 1976 uprisings went a step further in this regard.

Now is 1987, which has been declared by the PAC as the year of Arming the African masses, particularly militarily, to increase basically their physical fighting capacity. To this point so far, the PAC has remained absolutely consistent.

Arming and training the African masses internally remains PAC's most important programme today, and hundreds of the oppressed masses of our country have so far benefited from this programme, which in actual fact began in earnest at the beginning of last year.

In its military programme, the PAC went further when the Chairman Johnson Mlambo ordered APLA combatants to strike the main blow at enemy soldiers and police because, in the words of his late predecessor Cde [Comrade] John Nyati Pokela, "the war must be fought at the level of mortals".

APLA forces, including the internally trained and armed African masses are doing exactly that, and Pretoria is already finding it extremely difficult to hide the fact that its security forces are direct targets of frequent PAC guerilla attacks, in which a number of enemy casualties are now known to have been sustained.

As we mark the 11th commemoration of the 1976 national uprisings, which began in Soweto, we pay tribute to the gallant APLA combatants, many of whom are direct products of those uprisings.

It is common cause that nowadays we throw bullets as opposed to stones in 1976 because now we are no longer just angry crowds of protesting students, but soldiers operating in well-organised military units against carefully selected strategic targets.

It is our express purpose to kill more and more South African security forces, particularly the boers [Afrikaners], because unless whites, who have been living in comparative peace since the Anglo-Boer war in 1902, are made to feel unsafe and until they are themselves killed, they will still feel safe to continue killing the Africans.

And in fact, although some whites are among the security forces known to have been killed by APLA men, time has almost come when for every African being killed by the racist security forces, a white person must be killed.

One Racist One Bullet!
Phambili Nomzabalazo Wabantu! [Forward with the People's Struggle!]
Viva PAC. Viva APLA! [Long Live PAC! Long Live APLA!]
Izwe Lethu [Our Land]
I-Africa.

DOCUMENT 142. Report by "General Tobetsa" on unsuccessful mission of Umkhonto we Sizwe unit, late 1980s

My unit was: James Khulu, M-Soviet(Commander), Tebello Matsatsa (Commissar), Kith Mosala and General Tobetsa.

Mission: was to go and eliminate the enemy agents based in Letlhabile and Vlakplaas. Specifically those who are from outside the country, who are now turning against us (ANC and MK).

The Commander went first with the Commissar to go to create bases for the unit. After sometime [he] came back to Botswana to collect me and Kith. Our infiltration was a success. We found a Commissar waiting for us inside in our base.

One day on a Friday, as a unit we decided to go to town to buy some blankets and food. But the unit said, since myself and M-Soviet go to town, we can start in the DLB [dead letter box, i.e. hiding place for weapons] first to check it, since [we] were going to remove it the same night. . . . [They got lost looking for a graveyard, and had to ask for directions. They returned at night with a car, but while they were digging they were surrounded.] We were attacked. Tebello ran away and I also tried to run away but they found us. They came back with us.

The way they were talking, we saw that they were having information. They also tried to dig but nothing was found and we went out with them. We found also those who were in the car had been arrested also. Whilst we were there, the police van came and took us to Phokeng Police Station. We did not stay a lot there and the Special Branch came and took us to Eerstekraal Police Station. There we were asked where were the others and the DLB and what was our mission.

Well, we told them that we were going to look for the DLB and Tebello said our mission was to attack Moroka Police Station. They asked us who was the Commander, I jumped in to say I was the Commander. They started directing their blows to me, they wanted to know the base but we said [we] were based in a mountain and that is when they started to separate us. They took me first to the DLB but we could not find anything. And at about 4 o'clock in the morning, we came back and others took Tebello to the DLB also.

I was tortured that time. What they wanted from me was the weapons and the others. But I was telling them different stories. They came with Tebello later and they told us that [we] were playing with them, we were not going to remove the DLB. [Now we] were going to do the DLB, but we refused. They took me to the place I had said was our base. When we reach the mountain there were signs that showed that people had been there before, and I was beaten and returned back to the police station [where] I was tortured again. . . .

We resisted until after two days, when I was shocked by electrical devices in my testicles. That is when I took them to the real base where we found nothing but blankets and food. The boers [Afrikaners] I was with [said] to me that this was a delaying tactic and [as] a commander I will suffer for it.

The torture was a daily process until [we] were transferred to Mafikeng. I was in Mmabatho Police Station and Tebello in Mafikeng Police Station. We were taken every morning to go for interrogation in the offices of those Special Branch and we were asked our real mission but we did not tell them.

Other boers came with a trunk full of photos [and] we were asked if we knew people who were in those photos, where had we first seen them, what were they doing, where they went for training, the type of training and where were they when we left. Each and every photo had a file, examples of these questions they were asking, what the boers did to them when arrested. . . .

One day, they came early in the morning, they told us that they had arrested M-Soviet and the person he was moving with escaped. They did not explain how. What made us to believe them was that they showed us the sketches of the place we were going to attack and they ordered us to draw sketches and to stop telling them lies. Well we drew sketches and since they were aware of the mission, we told them.

M-Soviet told them other targets which we were not aware of. He further told them that maybe we sold the weapons from the DLB. But later another chief came and told us that M-Soviet was co-operating and they had found ten (10) grenades he gave them. What he said was that whilst we were going to the DLB, he [was] standing watching us from some position.

They started giving us good food in the cells and that is when they told us that if and when arrested, we were no longer (no more) ANC. They said that your Commanders outside the country are working for them and they are getting money from them, they have big stomachs because they are eating monies, some of them are members of the special branches. They asked us to work for them and they would pay us. . . . We were given cigarettes every day in the cells and we were eating nice food and drinks so as to see and feel at home.

On the first (1) of August, we were taken out of the cells, we were welcomed with a braai [barbecue] by captains, colonels, majors and their subordinates. We were told that our monthly salary will [be] R700 and when we spot people we will get R2,500 [$1000]. In case we spot those planting bombs, we will get R3,500; and in case of identifying the one captured by them, it will be R300.

We were given a house in Tlabologo Village. We were staying with Tebello. One day at night, I asked Tebello when are we going to escape. He started saying we cannot escape for we might be killed by the ANC since it is dominated by Xhosas and we are not Xhosa speaking.

I saw that he was no longer prepared, but I agreed with him. And I added on what he was saying, so as to make him cool, until one day on a Friday when I decided to escape from there to Botswana. I surrendered myself and I [was] then deported to Zambia.

The boers have more than ten thousand (10 000) photos of comrades outside the country, with correct information on where they are. They once asked me who do I think Chris Hani is working for. I said for the people. They laughed. They then asked me about Bra [brother] A, I said something to answer. They said his name is Lombard [Lambert] Moloi, he is working for us, *maan*, and is giving the money to his wife in Lesotho. That is what they said.

They then asked me, since Mxolisi, Mzwakhe and Ronald went to Mozambique, from my observation (from the look of things), are they going to work there or are they to be infiltrated since Ronald and Mzwakhe are Natal Zulus. I was surprised how they knew that these comrades were there.

They told me not to be afraid, they are working with internal and external information. They said there is no struggle outside, but there is a game just because they are sending you knowing that we are going to kill you. They told me different structures of ANC and MK and other political structures, the heads, the deputies, secretaries and so on. But what I discovered, especially from the side of military, there is nothing they do not know.

I think that is what I remember, others will come up/out during the discussion.

Document 143. ANC National Working Committee minutes, Lusaka, February 22, 1988

Present: SG [Secretary General Alfred Nzo]; TG [Treasurer General Thomas Nkobi]; [Josiah] Jele; Mzwai [Piliso]; Tony [Mongalo]; Chris [Hani]; Dan Tloome; [Robert] Manci; Steve Dlamini; Sizakele Sigxashe; Joe Slovo; [Jacob] Zuma; [Joe] Nhlanhla; Ruth Mompati; Pallo [Jordan].

Agenda:
(i) Report from London.
(ii) PMC [Politico-Military Council] Proposals on Internal Propaganda and PASA [post-apartheid SA].
(iii) Agenda for the NEC [National Executive Committee] Meeting.

SG in the Chair. Chair suggested that the 1st item of the agenda be put off till Cde Thabo [Mbeki] returns from London, at which time a comprehensive report can be given covering all aspects of the [unpublicized] meetings.

Chris: On whose authority has Cde Thabo entered into discussion with these Afrikaner intellectuals [in Britain]? Does the NEC/NWC know anything of this?

Chair asked Cde Pallo to explain.

Cde Pallo explained that he had not known of this meeting until so advised by Cde Thabo when they met Gabriel Mokgoko of NAFCOC [National African Federated Chamber of Commerce] on Friday.

Chris: It is very disturbing that a member of the NEC leaves to hold discussions with Afrikaner intellectuals without prior consultations with NWC or at least PMC. I cannot understand why the NWC and PMC were not apprised. Anyone who goes to such a meeting should be delegated by the movement.

(There was a general acclamation of approval of these remarks.)

Nhlanhla: This is part of a bigger problem. There are lots of people who are meeting people from home without any consultation let alone coordination. There are more and more workshops being organised which involve people from home. There is a loss of control. The DPE [Department of Political Education] is for instance organising a workshop which entails participation from home. Where was that discussed? Even the character of the workshop needed prior discussion. For example, will one be permitted to disagree? DPE is not to blame; this is a symptom of a larger problem

Chris: One consequence of this uncontrolled contact is that people from home complain that we are saying different things to them.

Ruth M: There was also the PASA workshop here recently. What disturbs me is that the persons who are moving in and out [from home] are the activists. How long will they survive? What is more, all the women who were here were making assessments of the leadership based on the contributions at the meetings. Some were assessed as knowing nothing, others as PASA experts, and so on.

TG: I don't think now is the time to discuss this. We have already agreed to discuss the issue of organisation. I agree there is a general disintegration. We must discuss it thoroughly.

SG: I permitted discussion on this issue because comrades felt a need to react to the meeting which was mentioned. We should agree on how we are going to discuss the entire issue, not only in relation to meetings. It is important that there be consensus among us on how we deal with these when they crop up.

Jele: Comrade chairman I had thought that the report was not to be discussed because Cde Pallo told me that these matters will be deferred to a later date.

JS: Before we close discussion on this let us agree that between now and that meeting all delegations are appointed by the appropriate structures. There should be no exclusion of NEC members. When the women from home were here I was excluded. In general there should be appointment of delegations by the NWC.

S. Dlamini: All invitations should be forwarded to the Administrative Secretary. This is creating unnecessary contradictions in the movement.

SG: The Secretariat should be seized with the issue of the meetings that are planned and these should be brought to the NWC.

(There was a general consensus that these procedures should be adhered to.)

Nhlanhla: PASA should also be discussed by the NEC. There is no such ANC structure, yet it exists. How did it come into being?

Chris: Let the minutes record that we register our extreme displeasure that Cde Thabo has unilaterally gone to London without any consultation and without a mandate from the NWC.

JS: On PASA, Cde Chairman, I want to know and receive answers on it. Who controls it? Where do the finances come from? Who appointed the people who serve on it?

Pallo: There is a problem regarding this because sometimes the NEC takes decisions at the end of a meeting, when everyone is tired and not too attentive. PASA arose as a result of NEC decisions. I refer members of the NEC to a meeting at Green House in early 1986. There was a report from myself and Cde President drew the meeting's attention to the [US Secretary of State, George] Shultz Commission. It was that meeting that took a decision that the ANC needs to launch a comprehensive programme of research on a Post-Apartheid South Africa, if only because all sorts of other forces are engaged in it, and might end up writing our agenda. Subsequent to that meeting, the President attended the Swedish "People's Parliament", entered into discussion with the Swedes, who undertook to look into the possibilities of funding the project. They later agreed. All this too was reported to the NEC. During the last NEC meeting, October 5th to 9th 1987, I gave a lengthy report, again it was at the tail end of an NEC meeting. I recounted the setting up of the project, the meetings and workshops we had held in Harare and in Stockholm, involving people from home. I reported also that from these meetings there had emerged a consensus that PASA would be an autonomous structure in which ANC had an input but was not explicitly running it. This was to afford people from home a measure of protection. So Cde Nhlanhla is right, it's not there in the structures, it is not an ANC structure. I reported also that we had appointed a Secretariat which has taken charge of the administration—it was I that arranged for the meetings in Harare and Stockholm. Arising out of that report to the NEC it was agreed that we should pursue negotiations with either UNZA [University of Zambia] or Univ. of Zimbabwe to attach to them a South African Research Institute, under the control of PASA. I do not suggest that the secretariat is spending the moneys wisely or that it's doing a splendid job. But no one can claim the NEC was not kept informed on the developments.

(Interjection from Nhlanhla: Was there any decision on it?)

Pallo: No one disagreed with the issues that were raised and the reports were accepted.

Nhlanhla: I would say the issue must be placed on the agenda for the NEC. It's causing a great deal of problems with the general membership.

TG: There was a document on this circulated during the meeting in February last year.

SG: In fairness we must say that documents were circulated. We expected that they were read. We suggest that the documents be read in preparation for the NEC meeting. I was invited to a meeting of the PASA secretariat and it was decided at that meeting that it should fall under the President's Office.

Chris: It is true there was a document. But it was never said there would be a formal structure. If there is a structure, such a structure should be formally endorsed by the NWC and not by self-appointment. The principle of accountability must be maintained. Some of us will later ask what are our priorities? We might be opening up a can of worms.

Nhlanhla: The PASA idea was discussed. The issue here is did the NEC set up a structure? There was no structure set up by the NWC. Questions of who leads it, who are its personnel, where it reports to were never discussed.

JS: Who took the decision on the people who went to Sweden? Even if it's autonomous, PASA is using our personnel, our office space, our equipment. It is understandable that it is autonomous but we must appoint the personnel. We discuss it and set up the structures formally.

Pallo: Some of the decisions evolved almost naturally from previous decisions. Once it was decided that a project was necessary, we needed people to administer it, to convene meetings, etc. We can't expect the NWC to endorse every little decision.

SG: I suggest that we accept Joe N's proposal that the matter be discussed by the NEC. In preparation for that we can require the PASA Secretariat to prepare a report, plus a financial statement. In the meantime comrades had better look at the report that was placed before them. We can then take firm decisions, consciously taken decisions and not ones that just evolve.

(*The Chair* placed the proposed agenda before the NWC.)

Cde Pallo read the Agenda for NEC meeting:
i) State of Organisation - under the following headings:
   PMC Report
   ECC [External Coordinating Committee] Report
   NEC Secretariat Report
ii) Report of the Provisional Directorate of NAT [Department of Intelligence and Security]
iii) Report on TGO [Treasurer General's Office] from NEC Commission
iv) Any Other Business

The meeting is scheduled to commence 11th March until 15th March. Venue is here.

Nhlanhla: I would have been happier if the Secretariat looked at means to make this more compact. I don't see how the ECC Report will differ from the Secretariat Report.

SG: It was envisaged that the reports would encompass the state of organisation of the various departments of the PMC; the various departments under the ECC; then the work of the Secretariat.

Chris: We wanted to examine the state of organisation because we were worried about the absence of any thrust and priority. It is clear what you mean now. But we need to look at every department under a microscope.

Jele: Originally the secretariat had felt there was a need for a report on the internal situation because a crisis is approaching. The PMC on the other hand felt there was no need for that. If we are talking of an organisational report I think we can all agree.

Nhlanhla: What will be in the Secretariat Report?

SG: It was felt that the Secretariat must itself be subjected to scrutiny.

JS: Where does each department fall?

Zuma: Much as we have departments, there are some that are large and hence very complex. Could we not be flexible and have the Heads of the Departments, who would be very familiar with all aspects of their work, give the reports? We don't want superficial reports. The three Offices—President's Office, Secretary General's Office and Treasurer General's Office—could initiate the reports by the various departments falling under them.

JS: But at the meeting itself we want the report to be so subdivided that we can look at the SG—is he doing his work; how is his office functioning; what are the problems in that office, and so on. DIP [Department of Information and Publicity], all these should give reports.

SG: That's right. But remember when you talk of departments, each falls under one of the offices. So when you mention DIP that is not distinct from the President's Office because it falls under that office.

Chris: We should start at the top, with the NEC. The NEC must be looked at. It has already lost three members. Can we say there are sufficient numbers? Is it able to discharge its duties? Do we need to coopt? The main report must look at the NEC itself. From there we can go down to the NWC, the Secretariat, etc.

Nhlanhla: There are also the new departments that were set up. The Secretariat must come up with an approach that permits us to have an in-depth look at each of these too.

JS: The Secretariat should redraft the agenda and circulate it beforehand so that we can discuss it at next meeting.

(*Cde Pallo* drew the attention of the chair to two documents that had been circulated with the minutes which should be discussed.)

Nhlanhla: I suggest that we defer this to the next meeting. I am not casting aspersions but I would plead with those who record minutes to ensure that they are accurate. The other day I was shown a document purporting to be NWC decision regarding camp 32 [Quatro detention center]. There was no such a discussion and no such decision. I checked with a number of comrades, none of whom recall such a discussion.

Pallo: Cde Joe might not intend to cast aspersions but the impact of his remarks is that it does imply an aspersion. If the discussion never took place and the decision not taken, yet I have recorded one, the only implication is that I've forged it. There was such a discussion arising from a Report on Prisoner Exchange headed by Cde Chris. The report was written and distributed. From the discussion of that report there arose the decision in question. All this is on file and can be made available for Cde Nhlanhla's inspection.

JS: Cde Chair, the problem is that often decisions are recorded which were never properly adopted. There was the instance of Cde Jackie [Sedibe]. The NEC Decisions reflect that we decided that she has to be replaced as head of communications. There was a suggestion which was made and recorded but never formally adopted.

SG: There is also the complaint that the minutes are not read. At every meeting we should have the minutes.

JS: It is the job of the Chair to ensure that decisions are properly taken.

Jele: It should be our task too to remind the Chair.

Discussion concluded.

Decision: NEC Secretariat shall redraft Agenda and submit to NWC at the next meeting.

Jele: There are the CONTRALESA chiefs who are in town. We have proposed a delegation to meet them but any other NEC member who wishes to join the discussion may do so. The delegation we proposed is: Comrades Nzo; Jele; Chris; Nkadimeng; Nhlanhla; Nkobi.

(The proposed delegation was adopted.)

Ruth M: There is a delegation from Congo which is here and we need a delegation to meet them tomorrow evening.

(Proposals received: Ruth M; [James] Stuart; [Dan] Cindi; Adopted.)

SG: The Congo wants to set up a continental AA [anti-apartheid] movement. We have tried to impress on them that such a movement can succeed only if it is based on national AA movements.

Nhlanhla: If the SG cannot attend the meeting, let us ensure that time is allocated for him to receive a courtesy call from the Congo delegation.

Any Other Business:
(i) *Cde Pallo* reported on the meeting with Mokgoko of NAFCOC. NAFCOC would like a follow up meeting since 1986. It is tentatively agreed that a meeting will take place in mid-April. We have agreed on an agenda with them.
(ii) *Cde Zuma* reported that the Black Management Forum had met our people in London and are proposing a meeting with the ANC 19th to 20th March. Cde Pallo strenuously opposed such a speedy meeting. Reading their documents, he suggested, indicates that they are a very different kettle of fish from NAFCOC. We should gather more material, study it and meet them after we have met NAFCOC.
Proposal was accepted.
(iii) Letter from Mrs. Hashe (Dingo's wife)—a request for assistance to pay her rent which is in arrears as a result of rent strike. Sum of R500.00 requested. After brief discussion it was decided that we cannot entertain a request which will result in breaking of the rent boycott.
(iv) Letter from President of Botswana's Office to imprisoned comrades who had petitioned for amnesty, turning down their appeal was read. Cde Jele suggested that NEC delegation should go to Botswana to intervene.

Reported that he has written to President and will pursue the matter with him as soon as he comes back. He suggested that NEC members who are able to travel to Botswana should visit the comrades in jail.

Cde Chris suggested that we raise with Botswana the implications of their actions. We are quiet now but will not always be quiet.

[rest of document missing]

Document 144. "The Quiet Thunder: Report on the Amsterdam Cultural Conference." Article by Mandla Langa, *Sechaba*, March 1988

The conference and festival named Culture in Another South Africa (CASA) took place in Amsterdam from December 12th-19th 1987. The ANC Department of Arts and Culture in all its ramifications, the Dutch Anti-Apartheid Movement and, mainly, the CASA Foundation, made this event a staggering success.

Hundreds of cultural workers from inside and outside South Africa, notably from the UDF and COSATU, took part in strength; the outside world was represented by an impressive array of cultural workers—writers, graphic artists, film-makers, musicians, poets, dancers and clothes designers. The old and the vulnerably young shared platforms to give expression to one of the quintessential elements that bond a people into a nation: culture.

For many delegates, Amsterdam was intertwined with the notion of Afrikaners; Amsterdam is as different from Pretoria as day from night. Amsterdam houses people who still remember the ravages of Nazism; Pretoria still houses Nazis.

The opening night saw emotional performances from children whose everyday existence means facing Casspirs, bullets and punctured bodies that lie sprawled in the everyday streets. They sang, these children, and it was perhaps in their eyes that it became clear why apartheid, like Nazism, needs to be destroyed. The Jazz Pioneers, Abdullah Ibrahim, the *Amandla!* Cultural Ensemble, Mmabatho Nhlanhla and the hundreds of Dutch voices, gave all of themselves. There was electricity in the air, energy generated by South Africans meeting freely for the first time in years.

The conference grappled with all aspects of the arts, but in this instance within the framework of the struggle. There was no mincing of words: the arts are a weapon in the struggle for national liberation and democracy in our country. There is no way to separate culture from politics. These discussions were conducted in the most serious atmosphere; people could sing and dance, but it was borne in mind that all this expression of a people's value system could not thrive in a situation of racist domination and exploitation.

One question discussed at length was the position of women in the conditions of our country. The triple oppression of women was condemned. It was a moment for soul-searching for some of the participants, in that this question has always been glossed over; it was stressed that democratic culture should strive to "consciously promote the norms of equality between men and women."

A highlight in the evenings was poetry reading, chaired by Cosmo Pieterse. Poets such as Mavis Smallberg, Vernie February, Breyten Breytenbach, Baleka Kgositsile, Koerapetse Kgositsile, John Matshikiza, and this writer read from their works. Njabulo Ndebele started the trend by reading from one of his stories earlier in the day. The absence of Mongane Serote, one of the main organisers of CASA, was strongly felt.

The exhibitions made it painfully clear that South Africa is a potentially beautiful country with a people who, though surrounded by steel bars and barbed wire, can still let their imaginative creativity leap out and weave these tender images. We remembered gifted artists like Thami Mnyele, one of the 13 people butchered by the SADF in Gaborone on June 14th 1986.

In the smoky, crowded night club called "The Milky Way," Basil "Manenberg" Coetzee and his group, *Sebenza*, were to perform; standing in the wings were Jonas Gwangwa and Dudu Pukwana. When music started and the people were dancing and chanting freedom slogans, Thabo Mbeki, the ANC Director of Information and Publicity was given a chance to say a few words. And few they were. He spoke of the obscene anniversaries the regime is going to celebrate in 1988. He asked the gathering to remember what King Dingane said when faced with the enemy: "Bulala abathakathi!"—"Kill the sorcerers!" This became a battle-cry at the conference.

The main impulse in the discussion was the social responsibility of the cultural worker. This was outlined in the opening address by Barbara Masekela, the ANC Secretary for Culture. It became clear that cultural workers cannot divorce themselves from the preoccupations of a struggling community. This was reflected in all papers that were delivered. Delegates all agreed that the apartheid system must go. The media were enjoined to become a vehicle of this consciousness.

Journalists from home talked about their newspapers. The war against the *New Nation*, whose editor, Zwelakhe Sisulu, has been in detention for more than a year, was a case in point. The paper was represented by its deputy editor, Gabu Tugwana. It was made clear to all of us that South Africa had grabbed the tiger by the tail; the people of South Africa are in need of responsible reporting. They have the right to know.

The question of language was discussed. Writers such as Nadine Gordimer, Lewis Nkosi, Njabulo Ndebele, Jennifer Dunjwa Blaiberg—who came all the way from Brazil—sought ways to deal with this sensitive issue. The Freedom Charter states that all shall have equal right to use their own languages, and to develop their own folk culture. It was borne in mind that certain languages such as Afrikaans were regarded with contempt because of their association with the repressive regime. The duty of writers and academics was to appropriate this language and infuse it with democratic values. All of us had to be aware, though, of the way the regime has promoted languages, with the aim of legitimising and enforcing the bantustan system. The idiom of democratic culture must strive for authenticity, and be accessible to the mass of our people. The writer has a responsibility, too, to counter illiteracy.

The conference addressed the issue of the cultural boycott, and decided that:

> *"The struggle for the total isolation of the apartheid regime must continue. Among the tactics to be employed during this campaign, the academic and cultural boycott are crucial and must be maintained. However, in view of the growing significance of democratic culture as an alternative to the racist, colonialist culture of apartheid, the conference recommends that South African artists, individually or collectively, who seek to travel and work abroad, should consult beforehand with the mass democratic movement and the national liberation movement."*

The African National Congress was present, from the highest council to the membership. The Secretary-General and the Treasurer-General, Comrades Alfred Nzo and T.T. Nkobi, were there, and other NEC members present were Comrades Thabo Mbeki, Aziz Pahad and Pallo Jordan. Comrade Pallo delivered a paper on cultural policy, an invaluable contribution that helped steer the conference.

The CASA Foundation, Conny Braam and the Mayor of Amsterdam, Ed van Thijn, did much to make the occasion a success. Dutch people opened their hearts to South African people.

The last day was perhaps the most touching. Outside a church, metres and metres of the black, green and gold of the ANC billowed in the air. Inside, was the photographic exhibition, "The Hidden Camera." The images the photographers brought were a damning condemnation of the South African regime.

The hardest moment was the moment of parting. Here were South Africans from all over the world, including South Africa itself, who, for seven days had discussed, argued, resolved issues, moved using the same step, laughing, singing and sometimes crying. The moment of parting was laden with a mixture of sadness and hope; sadness that we should be separated by all these boundaries, hope because we all felt that the event had become another rock against the edifice of apartheid.

DOCUMENT 145. "Problems Faced by Women." Discussion notes in SACP *Inner Party Bulletin*, August 1989 (abridged)

There is probably not a woman in the movement who at some point has not felt she is being excluded from something she could very easily be part of, because she is a woman and because (a) either other comrades in her structures have not considered her for the particular task/course/unit etc because they simply do not take her seriously and are too busy trying to find suitable candidates among the available male comrades, or (b) they think secretly the work is not suitable for a woman.

It takes bloody-mindedness on the part of the individual woman to challenge this. Firstly, all women who raise gender questions in the movement are likely to be dubbed "western feminists", a tag that many women in the movement have come to fear because it has really come to mean in our ranks: "Politically questionable, divisive".

Secondly, there is always the nagging insecurity that comes with most women's socialisation that we might in fact not be good enough, that we might have been excluded because we are just not up to scratch. So mostly we keep quiet. Those who do try to challenge male attitudes are easy to discredit—as hysterical, ambitious, opportunistic beings.

We have all encountered sexist men in our areas; we have all known what it means to have unwelcome physical approaches or have been verbally abused simply because we are women. Most of us know cases of male comrades who have even raped or attempted rape of women and who have then been "rewarded" by a stint in Party school [in Moscow] or a "promotion" to another area of work, instead of being disciplined and severely punished.

The reason all of this goes on is that the prevailing attitude in the movement is ironically the same as that in the western world; that men rule, okay. . . .

Women in underground structures often find themselves in all-male units and therefore isolated from other women. This means that unless those male comrades are exceptionally liberated, there is no support structure for a woman who might have a range of problems from attitude problems of her comrades to a health problem which she feels embarrassed to discuss with male comrades. . . .

At what point is the Women's Section going to shed its charity organisation image, and stop the fetes and tea-making and realise that we have a serious problem in our movement; namely that although women constitute half the population of our country, much less than half the movement is female, and probably the same applies to the MDM [mass democratic movement] at home. Also that the women of the Women's Section are simply not representative of the women militants who are at home; nor are the Women's Section's activities exactly going to lure more women to our ranks.

The Women's Section is also making a fundamental mistake in not taking up issues of gender. In this it has been left behind by the women of COSATU at home, who have not been frightened to tackle these issues head-on.

At one point there was talk of a "discrimination committee" which would look into problems faced by women e.g. in a communal house, why do the male comrades pressurise the women into believing it is their responsibility to cook or clean? What has happened to this committee? Is it functioning? . . .

Because the movement tends to concentrate on its male comrades, it is often the case that a man in a relationship might have a much heavier work load than the woman. Which takes him out of the house more, and puts the housework burden on her shoulders, and hence creates a tension within the relationship. A relationship between two comrades should be stable and free of antagonistic contradictions, so that both comrades can concentrate whole-heartedly on their political work. Often because of the unequal development of comrades the "little woman at home" mentality is being perpetuated.

Many comrades might say that this is a personal matter between individual comrades within relationships. We would like to argue that it is a political matter, that all people's political work is affected by what happens in the home. That unless there is an attempt to tackle inequality in the home then we can forget about solving the issue in the broader society either. . . .

Hands up anyone who thinks "Vow" [the ANC's *Voice of Women*] is a good magazine. Most comrades are openly critical of this turgidly written, poorly presented publication which provides few fresh insights, items of news or issues which might inspire those who are not yet "initiated" into the movement.

"Vow" needs to get together with the editorial board of "Speak" [a UDF-oriented women's magazine] to find out what it's doing wrong. The answer will be that it is not writing what women want to read about. It is not enough to write, issue after issue, about the day in 1956 that 20,000 women marched on the Union Buildings and as one raised clenched fists. The point is, could we do that now? And if not, why not? Is it because "Vow" is still living in 1956?

We need articles on women's health and stimulating interviews with young women cadres in the underground, cartoons and record reviews and tips on raising kids to be non-sexist. We need to discuss our real problems and not be frightened to point fingers at the lameness of the Women's Section, or question the shortage of women guerrillas.

We need more time on Radio Freedom. We need women's issues to be raised as political issues every single day on every single broadcast. . . .

Recommendations:
1) Formation of a regional Woman's Committee at Party level which will have the following tasks:
    a) Drawing up a programme which can be incorporated into the general political training.
    b) Monitoring sexism within local Party ranks.
    c) Suggesting a system whereby health follow-ups can be done on women who have been to the west [Angola]; also providing suggestions for improvement of health care facilities for women in the west and in the movement generally. . . .
2) Individual units could make child-care arrangements for those comrades who have children, eg. Hire a child-minder who can look after children of the unit at various times.

3) There needs to be some sort of "social welfare" department to deal with emotional and psychological problems within our ranks. This would have to be staffed by professional people in whom comrades would not mind confiding. . . .

5. Breaking the Deadlock, 1988–1990

DOCUMENT 146. ANC report on a meeting held in Henley-on-Thames, England, with three Stellenbosch academics, October 31–November 1, 1987 (abridged)

Introduction

A meeting was held in Henley, England on the [31st October–1st November] 1987 between members of the ANC (Comrades Aziz Pahad, Wally Serote, Tony Trew and Harold Wolpe) and Willie Breytenbach, Willie Esterhuyse and Sampie Terreblanche. . . .

The meeting was organised on the initiative of Michael Young of Consolidated Goldfields who acted as chairman. He had previously discussed his interest of taking initiatives of this type with Comrades [Oliver] Tambo and [Thabo] Mbeki.

Although it was emphasised by us and reiterated by them that the meeting was *not* about negotiations, and although there was unclarity about who they represented and who they would report back to, we believe that Breytenbach and Esterhuyse and, perhaps, Terreblanche also, would be reporting back to people within the security establishment. . . .

[T]heir object was to obtain information about how the ANC would react to various possible moves by the state and especially the release of Govan Mbeki and, then, Nelson Mandela—aimed at opening, it was stated, the path to negotiations. [The political credentials of the three Afrikaners are summarized. All are professors at Stellenbosch University, well connected with the Broederbond and the security establishment. All signed a controversial March 1987 statement by 28 Stellenbosch academics critical of the slow pace of reform]. . . .

During the first session, WB gave what he called his analysis of the "perceptions" and position of the "securocrats". . . . In the last election the security question was the dominant issue. In the 2 years before the 6th May [1987] election, the mass struggles had raised doubts about the NP's [National Party's] ability and willingness to govern.

The relevance of the election lies only in the fact that the result was an endorsement of the NSMS [National Security Management System] and the role and policy of "securocrats." It had no importance in relation to parliament which has virtually become irrelevant. . . .

The "securocrat" establishment is made up of a secretariat of 120 people, 11 regional structures and 254 JMCs [Joint Management Centres]. The composition is approximately 60% civilian including the National Intelligence Department and 40% are police, security and army.

The approach of the "securocrats," other than the inner group of "controllers", is that political stability requires 20% coercion, 80% political solution. The political solution depends on the support of the mass of the blacks and in the short/middle term the question is whether this support can be won. Among this group, there are two different approaches: Cooption of the black population through reforms or recognise that the ANC is a principal actor and negotiate.

The possibility of negotiations with the ANC arises precisely because in the estimate of the "securocrats", the security measures have diminished two of the ANC's three options—mass mobilization and the creation of alternative structures have both been curbed. The ANC can still prosecute the armed struggle but in doing so it is deploying its weakest arm against the regime at *its* strongest point. Their perception is, therefore, that the ANC will *have* to negotiate.

On the other hand, the "securocrats" are much more amenable to negotiations than the politicians. The reason is that they do not have the "ideological emotionalism" of the politicians, they are ideology-blind; they are as "illiterate" as the ANC about economics and not aware of economic scarcity. They by-pass parliament. Their view of a solution is premised on the following:
- *The building blocks* from which the possibility of negotiations start:
    -Political stability has all but been accomplished.
    -The economy has begun to be regenerated.
- The *"bottom line"* of negotiation:
    -They accept that there must be a political system that "provides for all at the highest level" (that is the level of central state).
    -Given this acceptance, their question to the ANC is:

Will the ANC guarantee group (i.e. white) rights? Is the Freedom Charter open to this type of interpretation? Can the Freedom Charter concede ethnic "voluntary association" without domination? (Note: below it is made clear that this is simply the re-iteration of the claim for reserved rights for whites).

Secondly, can the Freedom Charter accommodate regional devolution of power. It is not clear what this means but, according to WB, it does *not* refer to ethnic states, nor does it involve the retention of Group Areas which the "securocrats" regard as unimportant as an instrument of policy. The central state, that is, will deal with "common affairs" and welfare functions, education etc will be devolved. . . .

At the final session of the meeting WB became more precise about actual initiatives and also there was further discussion on the "bottom line", but these are secondary issues which will only come into play once a negotiation path has been opened and the correct "atmosphere" established. The release of prisoners is, therefore, a prior matter.

Release of Political Prisoners

First, there are people on both sides who think that outright victory is possible. The question is whether this can be relinquished in order to open the path to negotiation?

Second, WB and WE state that it is *not* a condition of negotiation that the ANC relinquish violence. This *is* an issue for the electorate, but not for the "securocrats". They are interested in results and they have not and do not demand that the ANC abandon violence as a condition of negotiations. (But it is to be noted that, at a later point, WE stated that a response from the ANC which included something about the armed struggle would be necessary if the release was to be a step forward.)

Third, the crucial first step is the release of [Govan] Mbeki possibly followed by the release of Mandela and later, perhaps, the unbanning of the ANC although the "securocrats" regard the release of prisoners and the unbanning of the ANC as 2 quite distinct matters. The original conditional offer to release Mandela was designed to split the black population between those prepared to support violence and those not prepared to do so. This failed and a release into exile or on conditions is not on, according to the "securocrats".

A year ago the release of Mandela and other prisoners was not possible because it would have been interpreted as "violence paying off". Today, with the re-establishment of stability the position has changed and the regime is prepared to release Mbeki and Mandela. The regime wants to release prisoners because it wants to "settle" with urban blacks (for example, Inkatha will not go into the NSC [proposed National Statutory Council] without the release of prisoners.

Also, it may be argued that the purpose is to relieve international pressure on them in order to revive the economy. However, by responding positively the ANC will seize the initiative.

What is at issue now is for the regime to find a way of releasing prisoners without losing face, without stoking white fears about violence and without giving the CP [Conservative Party] the opportunity to make capital out of the release *and* what the response of the ANC will be:

- The first will be dealt with by granting the release on *humanitarian* grounds and it is for this reason that Mbeki will be released first.
- Second, what the "securocrats" want to know before any release is: what

will the response of the ANC be. If there is not some sort of positive response (in the sense of welcoming the release and treating it as a step towards negotiations) from the ANC, if the ANC downgrades the step and simply moves the goal posts, then there will be a blockage. Negotiations will lose, not the regime.

The ANC informed them that the ANC would obviously welcome the release of some prisoners, but would call for the release of all prisoners, would deal with the release in political and not humanitarian terms, etc etc.

A response of this kind was regarded by WB and WE as "positive".

It was then pointed out that so far the issue of release had been handled by lawyers and that it was necessary to shift it to the "political", that is to communication with the ANC. . . .

It is quite clear that this move is taken from what is believed to be a position of strength and in a situation in which it is believed that the ANC has little room for manouevre. (WB even posed the question of whether the ANC "was willing to be coopted".)

Although this view is held, the state is also acutely aware of the fact that without the release of prisoners further moves to stability are doomed (e.g. NSC [National Statutory Council] participation).

By releasing the prisoners, they believe the way will be opened to make viable the "reformist" political measures and in that way weaken the position of the ANC especially if it stays outside the "reformed" structures.

Document 147. "The NIC and the Three Plagues." Article by Yunus Carrim, *Weekly Mail,* February 12, 1988

Three major issues were raised by the controversy that has plagued the Natal Indian Congress (NIC) since its crucial conference late last year: how democratic is the NIC; is it going to participate in the House of Delegates when fresh elections are called; and how does the NIC see its relationship with its constituency?

It is precisely to ensure a greater degree of internal democracy that the conference was called [in November] last year. The decision to have the conference came out of two activist workshops held earlier in the year. The majority of those present had joined the ranks of NIC through the civic and political campaigns from the early 1980s, in particular the highly successful anti-tricameral parliament election campaign of 1984. They argued that the extent of organisational work they did was not matched by the degree of control they had over the organisation, particularly its executive. They pointed out that some of the executive members were not active; there was unnecessary factionalism; and there were accusations of domination by a "cabal".

Moreover, during the anti-election campaign, grassroots structures had sprung up, like the area committees, which did not have constitutional legitimacy, and whose relationship with the executive was not clear. It was necessary to formalise these structures. And for the executive and these structures to function more democratically and efficiently, branches based on individual membership had to be revived.

It was decided that an annual general meeting be held to do this. The constitution would be altered, an executive elected of people active at grassroots level, and the NIC would be put on a more democratic footing. In view of the State of Emergency conditions (several leading NIC members being on the run from police), it was decided that the conference would be open only to delegates and observers from fraternal organisations. A public report-back meeting was subsequently held to seek the community's approval for conference decisions.

It is a curious irony, then, that at a time when the NIC is moving towards greater democracy, it is coming under the most severe criticism for being undemocratic. Whatever its past failings, the NIC is committed to entrenching internal democracy. A new executive with greater grassroots activity has been elected. A working committee, comprising two representatives per branch and the executive members, will serve as the link between branches and the executive.

Further constitutional changes are in store to make the executive more accountable to the branches. Resolutions on "organising strategy" and "styles of work" stressed the need for maximum democracy and accountability within the organisation. Some of the criticisms of the NIC are, therefore, obsolete. Others are being dealt with by the creation of new structures. Yet others can only be resolved in practice. Democracy is not an abstract, given condition in any organisation. It has to be fought for concretely in struggle.

Will the NIC participate in the House of Delegates at the next election? Emphatically not! There has not been even a murmur of this at the workshops and conference. Indeed, the conference unanimously endorsed NIC's boycott policy—and even called for the more determined "social, political and international isolation of all members of the House of Delegates and all those who promote its existence". It was also decided to campaign against the October 1988 municipal elections.

There's no smoke without fire? There must be some substance to the claims of NIC participation? Sure, there are members who must feel that participation is tactically sound. They have a right to this view. But they have to raise it within the structures—and an organisational decision has to be taken on this. Insofar as individuals are representing their own views as that of the organisation and having discussions with House of Delegates MPs [members of Parliament] on this, they have to be disciplined. But at the last executive meeting all except three absent members signed an affidavit denying any such talks and agreeing on disciplinary measures, including possible expulsion, of anybody found guilty of this.

For the NIC, the boycott of the House of Delegates remains a tactic, rather than a principle—a tactic subordinate to wider strategy which stresses the need for maximum non-racial unity in action. Participation in the House of Delegates would seriously distract the NIC from this course. There is no way the NIC would participate without the support of the United Democratic Front as a whole—and that would clearly not be forthcoming.

In any case, the material conditions for participation simply do not exist at present. Despite the Emergency, all avenues for extra-parliamentary struggle have not been closed. There is no sign that the majority of the Indian people identify with the House of Delegates. There is no clear evidence that participation would secure significant material concessions for the people or open out useful organisational space. And of course the hostility of the African people to the tricameral parliament remains undaunted. It would, in short, be suicidal for the NIC to participate in the House of Delegates.

However, the NIC is trying to address its particular constituency creatively. It recognises the Indian community has significantly improved its material position since the heyday of the NIC in the 1940s and 1950s and is at present more difficult to mobilise for a non-racial democracy. Moreover, the entrenchment of the Group Areas Act and other aspects of social segregation has led to the alienation of the Indian from the African and other communities. In this context, the community has become uneasy about a non-racial democracy in which Africans will have the main say.

On the other hand, the community is clearly opposed to white domination—especially as it affects Indians. Even its most privileged strata have elements of discontent with the system. There is, moreover, a moral imperative in the community that cannot reconcile itself with the oppression that is intrinsic to apartheid. And the NIC, despite its present difficulties, continues to retain a certain credibility in the community, drawing people of considerably better quality and greater respectability than those who participate in apartheid institutions.

To the extent the NIC has a role to play, it must directly address the Indian community's anxieties and prepare it for a non-racial democracy.

Document 148. Church petition protesting restrictions on 17 organizations and COSATU, February 29, 1988

Dear Mr State President and Members of Parliament:

We, as leaders of a number of South African churches, have come to Parliament today to witness and pray in a time of crisis outside the buildings in which you make important decisions affecting the lives of millions of South Africans who belong to our churches. In terms of the principles of non-violent direct action, we informed the Government of our intentions before coming here. Once we have completed our act of worship outside where you work, we intend returning to St George's Cathedral.

We are deeply distressed at, and protest to you in the strongest of terms at, the restrictions which were placed last week on the activities of seventeen of our people's organisations, on the Congress of South African Trade Unions and on 18 of our leaders.

We believe that the Government, in its actions over recent years but especially by last week's action, has chosen a path for the future which will lead to violence, bloodshed and instability. By imposing such drastic restrictions on organisations which have campaigned peacefully for the end of apartheid, you have removed nearly all effective means open to our people to work for true change by non-violent means. Only yesterday one of our number pleaded publicly with our people not to react to your measures by resorting to violence, but if some of our people turn to violence you must take the responsibility.

We are particularly horrified at the restrictions you have placed on people and organisations who have been in the forefront of the struggle to bring peace to the strife-torn areas of Pietermaritzburg and KTC in Cape Town. Mr Archie Gumede, Mr Willie Hofmeyr and Mrs Albertina Sisulu are just a few of many people who are now banned from working for peace. Your actions indicate to us that those of you in government have decided that only violence will keep you in power; that you have chosen the "military option" for our country. It appears to us that you are encouraging the growth of black surrogate forces to split the black community and to smash effective opposition to apartheid, moreover that you are trying to ensure as far as possible that it is the blood of black people, and not of white people, that is spilled in your struggle to hold onto power.

We regard your restrictions not only as an attack on democratic activity in South Africa but as a blow directed at the heart of the Church's mission in South Africa. The activities which have been prohibited are central to the proclamation of the Gospel in our country and we must make it clear that, no matter what the consequences, we will explore every possible avenue for continuing the activities which you have prohibited other bodies from undertaking. We will not be stopped from campaigning for the release of prisoners, from calling for clemency for those under sentence of death, from calling for the unbanning of political organisations, from calling for the release of political leaders to negotiate the transfer of power to all the people of our country, from commemorating significant events in the life of our nation, from commemorating those who have died in what you call "riots" or from calling on the international community to apply pressure to force you to the negotiating table.

Last week many of us issued a statement in which we addressed primarily the oppressed people of our land, for we believe it is they who will decide in the final analysis when apartheid is going to be abolished. We urged them to intensify the struggle for justice and peace and we encouraged them not to lose hope, for victory against evil in this world is guaranteed by our Lord.

Our message applies also to you. Your position is becoming untenable.

Your fellow South Africans want nothing more than to live in a just and peaceful country and we urge you—without too much hope of being heard—to turn from the path you have chosen. If those of you in government persist with your current policies, then we urge those of you out of government to withdraw from white politics and to join the real struggle for democracy.

We urge you to take the following immediate action:
- Lift last week's restrictions, and end the State of Emergency.
- Unban political organisations, release and remove restrictions on our political leaders, allow exiles to return and free all detainees.
- Enter negotiations for a dispensation in which all of us can live together in peace, freedom and justice.

We have not undertaken this action lightly. We have no desire to be martyrs. However, the Gospel leaves us no choice but to seek ways of witnessing effectively and clearly to the values of our Lord and Saviour Jesus Christ and you give us virtually no other effective and peaceful means of doing so.

God Bless you.

Signed: Archbishop TW Ntongana (Apostolic Methodist Church of SA); Archbishop NH Ngada (United Independent Believers in Christ); The Rev Ron L Steel (Chairman, United Congregational Church of Southern Africa); The Rev James Gribble (Chairman, Good Hope District, Methodist Church of Southern Africa); The Rev Peter Storey (past President, SACC and Methodist Church); Bishop Lawrence Henry (Catholic Church, Cape Town); Pastor MD Assur (General Secretary, Evangelical Lutheran Church in Southern Africa); Bishop Olaf Theo Xulu (President of African Independent Churches); Pastor TM Chere (N. Tvl Council of Churches); Bishop Charles Albertyn (Anglican Church, Cape Town); Bishop George Swartz (Dean of the Anglican Province of Southern Africa and Bishop of Kimberley and Kuruman); The Rev Frank Chikane (General Secretary, SACC); Dr Allan Boesak (Moderator of the Ned Geref Sendingkerk); Bishop HB Senatle (African Methodist Episcopal Church); The Rev Dr Khoza Mgojo (President of the Methodist Church of Southern Africa); The Rev John P Scholtz (past President MCSA); Moulana Farid Esack (Call of Islam, Muslim Judicial Council); The Rev Canon Geoff Quinlan (Suffragan Bishop-elect, Anglican Church, Cape Town); The Ven Edward MacKenzie (Suffragan Bishop-elect, Anglican Church, Cape Town); The Rev Samson A Khumalo (Presbyterian Church of Africa, General Secretary); Archbishop Desmond Tutu (Metropolitan, Anglican Church); The Rev Paul Makhubu (General Secretary, CAIC); The Revd Edward King (Anglican Dean of Cape Town); The Revd Mmutlanyane Stanley Mogoba (General Secretary, MCSA); Archbishop Stephen Naidoo (Catholic Archbishop of Cape Town).

Document 149. "Fight for Your Rights." *CWIU Flame,* no. 12, March 1988

The government wants to take away many of the rights which workers have. It wants to change the Labour Relations Act. We cannot let them take us backwards to the 1960s.

Figure 23. Despite state repression and economic recession, the Congress of South African Trade Unions grew stronger throughout 1988 and 1989. Members of the National Union of Metalworkers (NUMSA), the confederation's fastest-growing affiliate, flex their muscles during a strike at Toyota in Durban, June 1989. *Rafs Mayet/africanpictures.net*

The campaign against the new Labour Bill has begun. The NEC [national executive committee] decided that urgent action was needed. We have to defend the working class against the new laws. The first step in the CWIU [Chemical Workers' Industrial Union] was to summon the shop stewards from all the companies to a meeting in working hours. The Transvaal Branch kicked off. Over 200 shop stewards attended from all over the Witwatersrand and the Highveld. Shop stewards were very angry. They decided to immediately take steps to fight for our rights.

The next step was to demand that the bosses take a strong stand against the Bill. They have been asked to sign a letter, which will be sent to the minister, rejecting the Bill. Other Branches are also having meetings at local levels. The third step will be to hold follow up meetings to assess the bosses' responses and discuss further action.

Workers are preparing for a big battle ahead. We need to mobilize all workers to face this attack in a united and disciplined way.

THE RIGHTS YOU WILL LOSE
A Direct attack on Factory Democracy
- It will be illegal for a majority union in a factory to demand the right to negotiate for the whole factory. Bosses will be able to have agreements with many unions in each factory. This crushes one union per factory and

attacks one union per industry. You will pay for lost production if you strike!
- Unions will be automatically guilty of inciting all strikes and can be made to pay for lost production during these strikes. So will workers and union officials.

The Bill will make striking more difficult and dangerous:
- Sympathy and solidarity strikes will be illegal.
- Workers will not be able to strike on the "same issue" in a period of 15 months.
- The steps to be taken before a legal strike are more complicated.
- The Bosses will be able to stop even legal strikes by going to the court.
- Bosses will be able to pick and choose whom they re-employ after a strike.

The new bill will make dismissals and retrenchments easier.
- Bosses will be able to fire a worker FOR ANY REASON without a hearing during the 1st twelve months of service.
- Bosses will not have to follow LIFO (last in, first out) when they retrench workers.

The Bill, if it becomes law, will weaken the unions and take away many of the rights which we have struggled for and won over the last ten years.

WE MUST FIGHT AND ORGANISE AGAINST THIS BILL!

DOCUMENT 150. "Azikwelwa! Stayaway! June 6, 7, 8—3 Days of United National Action." Anonymous flyer, June 1988

The workers have called for 3 days of national protest to be observed on June 6, 7, and 8 (Monday, Tuesday, Wednesday). We, the community, fully support this call and urge our people to observe these 3 days as a national stayaway. Let this message be spread to every corner of the country so that our people, wherever they are, strike together in one mighty action!

Let each and every person, whether a worker, a student, a businessman, or unemployed know clearly the reasons for this 3 day protest. Indeed the regime, big business and the international community must know why we are taking this action:

1. The boers [Afrikaners] have banned our organisation, the United Democratic Front (UDF) and many other mass organisations! They have also restricted Comrades [Govan] Mbeki, [Zwelakhe] Sisulu and many of our leaders.
2. They have restricted our mighty Federation, COSATU, and now they want

to use the Labour Bill to crush our trade unions and turn them into Useless Bosses Clubs.
3. At this very moment, they are planning to impose a third year of the hated State of Emergency on our people. Thousands of our leaders, and many scores of children, are still sitting in jail after 2 years of the regime's "Emergency"!
4. Every week, they are hanging our sons and daughters on Death Row!
5. They have silenced the people's newspapers, New Nation and South, and are threatening to silence more!
6. They want to celebrate 40 years of Nationalist Misrule by pushing more bodies of minority rule (Great Indabas and councils) down our throats.

ARE WE GOING TO CELEBRATE OUR OWN OPPRESSION? WE SAY NO! WE ARE NOT GOING TO TAKE THESE ATTACKS LYING DOWN. WE ARE GOING TO STRIKE BACK! LET THE BOERS AND THEIR SUPPORTERS KNOW THAT THEY HAVE STRUCK A ROCK AND WILL BE CRUSHED.

TO THE BOSSES WE SAY: You are making a serious mistake by siding with the Boers on these issues. You are wasting your time attacking COSATU. The workers expressed the feelings of the entire community by calling 3 days of national protest. Be careful that we do not redirect our anger away from the regime to focus on you. By threatening COSATU, you are challenging the entire oppressed community to treat you as the enemy.

TO THE PEOPLE WE SAY: On May 5 and 6 last year and on March 21 this year we showed our capacity for mass action on a scale which surprised even our supporters. The Boers and their supporters are doing everything they can to stop this action from going ahead because it is hitting them where it hurts most. These attempts will fail! Let us make sure that on June 6, 7, and 8 we stage an action which is more powerful than any mass action in the history of our struggle.

Guidelines
1. No one is to go to work on June 6, 7 and 8 (Monday. Tuesday and Wednesday). This applies to all areas of the country (national).
2. The reasons for this action must be clearly explained to everyone.
3. Let us continue our tradition of United Action which is carried out with discipline and unity.
4. Health workers and journalists may go to work. Health workers wear uniforms and journalists show ID cards.

END THE EMERGENCY!
UNBAN THE UDF!
SCRAP THE LABOUR BILL!

Document 151. "Municipal Elections." UDF policy paper by Titus Mafolo, June 1988 (abridged)

Before the banning of the UDF and other democratic organisations, speculations were rife about the possibility of UDF participation in the October municipal elections. The suggestions and discussions about this possible scenario have been raised by a whole range of people and groups: liberal press, academics, political groups, government supporters, and indeed comrades within our structures.

The mass democratic movement, pursuant to its tradition of free, open and democratic debate before deciding on any issue does not treat this matter lightly. It must be emphasised from the outset that no single democratic structure has until now proposed participation in the coming elections. What has happened, however, is that people have requested that we fully explain our position in relation to the October elections. . . .

Our approach to the municipal elections will in the first instance be determined by the state of our organisations, the mood of the masses and the strengths and weaknesses of the regime. Let us take a general look at our organisations.

State of our organisations and the mood of the masses . . .

Most of our mass organisations are facing the deepest crisis in the history of their existence. The state has reacted viciously to the proliferation of popular organisations and the emergence of grassroots structures like the street, block and area committees.

The attack on our organisations varies according to regions, areas and sectors. As far as regions are concerned the area most affected by repression is the Eastern Cape. We need not scratch our heads very hard to find out why.

Layer after layer of leadership in most parts of the country has disappeared into detentions. In some areas organisations have been rendered inoperative as the state desperately tries to break the people's resistance.

Cadres have to constantly duck and dive from the South African regime as well as the bantustan repressive forces. In some places like Northern Transvaal naked terrorism, and at times attacks by bandits from Renamo and Zimbabwe, became commonplace.

As a result many activists have to operate from outside their areas. This has had a negative impact on our organisations. But while it is difficult to freely and openly conduct the activities of the mass democratic organisations in most areas, this does not necessarily mean that organisations are dead.

A significant number of organisations have managed to adapt to the repressive conditions. This has been clearly demonstrated by the sustenance of rent boycotts, the success of the recent stayaways: the May 5th and 6th's last year in protest against all-white elections, the 21st March protest against the banning of the UDF and other organisations and the June 6 - 8th stayaway. . . .

The government

The government has to a large extent regained the confidence and support of its natural allies: big business, a section of the imperialists, the majority of whites and its stooges in the oppressed community. This is not surprising. The government has to a certain extent delivered the goods to its friends and supporters. Especially to the business community it liberally gave the privatisation, deregulation and now the Labour Relations Bill. To the imperialists it is still keeping their little ugly puppy, [Jonas] Savimbi, alive and kicking. It still destabilises the Frontline States thus making economic independence impossible. . . .

The state is grappling with many schemes and ideas as to how to contain the militancy of the masses. It has no long term political solutions to the crisis facing our country. It offers few houses, scattered upgrading schemes and a powerless National Council. But the people want full political power. It tries to promote spurious leaders and organisations but the people are not impressed. They want Mandela and his organisation.

The reasons behind the municipal elections

It is no accident that the state has called for municipal elections for all national groups on the same day. Firstly, the state wants to prove to the world that the policy of separate but equal is a viable option for the problems facing South Africa. If the polls are high, this will be concrete proof to this belief. . . .

[They hope elections will give puppet structures a new lease on life, but boycotts raise mass consciousness and disable apartheid institutions. We would gain nothing by joining ineffective councils. Our past rejection of dummy bodies has forced the government to keep changing its plans for reform.] [T]he boycott of dummy structures is not a limited ad hoc tactic to be used only in limited situations. Nor is it an inflexible principle. Rather it is a *strategy*, i.e. part of a general coherent approach to build united opposition and move towards one person one vote.

The way forward

For us to be able to move forward, we need to regroup the centre, reorganise our structures, strengthen our alliance with our fraternal organisations and broaden ourselves.

Regroup the centre

To challenge the coming elections effectively, we must have strong political centres at all levels of our movement. But what are political centres? To refresh our minds let's borrow *Isizwe*'s (vol 2 No 1, Sept 1987) description:

> "By 'political centres' we are referring to organisational collectives that are capable of providing political leadership, that are able to strategise, to lead. Political centres are collectives that do not simply react to one crisis after another. They are able to plan ahead, carrying the struggle to the enemy on the people's terms."

The main reason for the need to regroup the centre is because the political centres are the engine of our movement. The state is aware of this. That is why it always directs its repressive energies against the nucleus of our organisations whether at street, block and area level or at regional and national level. In regrouping our centre at all levels, the following are important:
- Revitalise activists. This is important because some of our activists have been demoralised by repression. . . .
- We must master the techniques of secret and underground work. This is imperative because more often than not large scale detentions break the nucleus of our organisations. Activists must learn to operate underground because the state of emergency will be with us for many years.
- Vigilance and discipline should guide our work.
- Rumour-mongering, unnecessary personal clashes etc should be done away with.
- Under the present conditions, the need for education and training increases.
- We should strive for more ideological unity. When the state is attacking us like now, we need each other more than ever before. We should therefore vigorously fight against factionalism, regionalism and individualism. . . .

Re-organise structures

Most of our structures are still in existence, though some of them are weak. One important reason for the weaknesses of our organisations is that they are unable to adapt to repressive conditions. This brings us to the point discussed earlier viz, that we must master secret and underground work. We must however be careful not to mistake our tactical adoption of underground work with the strategic adoption of underground work by the ANC.

We adopt underground methods so as to be able to continue with open, above board mass work. The most important task facing us is to re-organise and strengthen our grassroots structures like street committees. These structures are crucial for our campaign against municipal elections because in most parts of the country we will never be in a position to hold mass meetings and organise openly.

Civic organisations are the most important structures in our struggle against the municipal elections. All sectors should help rebuild and strengthen them. In areas where it is impossible to revive civics, other structures should be set up to oppose the municipal elections.

Strengthen alliances with fraternal organisations

With increasing repression, there is an urgent need for the mass democratic movement to plan, work and move forward as a solid block. The alliance between the UDF affiliates, Cosatu and the churches should be strengthened at all levels from national, regional and to the local level. . . . [I]t is important for Cosatu to play an active role in reviving community organisations where they have been smashed by repression. The fight against bodies of minority rule is not the concern of the UDF affiliates only. It is a challenge facing all democrats and oppressed people.

By strengthening our alliance with our natural allies we must be aware that we are helping to build our structures. For victories registered by Cosatu will always be celebrated by the entire democratic movement. Workers who belong to Cosatu unions also belong to our civics, youth and women structures. At the street, block and area levels Cosatu and UDF have worked together without any distinction between the two structures. What we need to do is to consolidate and co-ordinate this process.

We should also work very closely with the churches. Recently and particularly after the bannings, church leaders have shown their preparedness to confront the state. The mass democratic movement must guide and give lead to the progressive initiative taken by church leaders. . . .

Broaden the Front

Before the banning of the UDF, organisations in different parts of the country had dedicated themselves to work with structures outside the UDF and the broad democratic movement. This approach is more important now than before.

The government is trying to win over uncommitted sections of our community to join the collaborators. It is attempting to build a block of "moderate" leadership. The state will only succeed in this initiative if we fail to spread our moral and political influence to all sections of our community. . . . We need to draw taxi-owners, sports bodies, traders and religious groups closer to the mass democratic movement.

Position in the white areas

As we have already said, the mass democratic movement is calling for a boycott of the municipal elections. However we recognise that conditions in the white areas are different. Strategies and methods used in the enemy camp will always be different from those used in the people's camp.

White democrats should use the elections to strengthen the alliances forged in the white community and to win more whites to the mass democratic movement. We further call on all whites to continue to build anti-apartheid alliances and isolate the Nationalists and their allies. . . .

Conclusion

The campaign against the municipal elections is not the only one facing the mass democratic movement this year. It is, however, one of the most important ones. It is important because the state hopes to drag itself out of its political crisis especially in the oppressed communities. It is also important because, like in the past, our people should use this challenge to move to higher levels of organisation. . . .

Document 152. "Municipal Elections." Southern African Catholic Bishops' Conference flyer, July 1988

Why should Christians be concerned?

On June 29, South African Christian leaders made a statement about the October municipal elections. They said that Christians should not participate in their own oppression or in the oppression of others by standing as candidates or voting in the elections.

Why have our Christian leaders made this call? What is wrong with the elections? As Christians and South Africans, we need to know the truth behind the elections. We have a responsibility to our country and to our consciences to educate ourselves about the elections so that we can make an informed Christian decision about whether or not to participate.

Where do the municipal elections come from?

The municipal elections are part of the government's plan to implement its new constitution at a local level among all ethnic groups. It wants to make the constitution work at a grassroots level, especially among Africans. How has local government functioned in the past among Africans? Answering this question will help us to place the October municipal elections in their historical context.

The government has never provided popular and effective local government in the townships, although it has tried many different strategies. In the late 1970s and early 1980s, the government set up Community Councils and Black Local Authorities in the townships. These were meant to involve Africans in administering the townships after the 1976 Soweto Uprisings had exposed the unpopularity of the white-controlled Bantu Administration Boards.

However, township residents rejected these councils because they:
- Did not have real power to change things.
- Increased the hardship of residents through rent hikes and evictions.
- Often [were] used by corrupt councillors for personal gain.
- Could not do anything which did not have the approval of the government.

The people found effective ways to resist the councils. They forced councillors to resign. They set up structures such as street committees, people's courts and civic associations to run their own communities.

Repression and reform: the stick and the carrot

The government did not recognise the people's structures or concede to their demand for real power-sharing. Instead, in the period 1984-1988, they systematically crushed the people's structures and organisations.

They implemented a policy of repression by:
- Declaring successive States of Emergency which give the SADF [army] and SAP [police] wide-ranging security powers.

- Detaining, restricting or prosecuting thousands of anti-apartheid activists nationwide.
- Banning or restricting organisations including the United Democratic Front, the Congress of South African Trade Unions, the Azanian People's Organisation, civic associations and youth congresses.
- Severely restricting the media and controlling the flow of information.

Coupled with the strategy of repression, the government has tried to "win the hearts and minds" of the people through certain limited reforms. These include:
- Establishing the tricameral parliamentary system to incorporate "Coloureds" and Indians as junior partners in a system of white domination.
- Abolishing the Immorality Act, the Mixed Marriages act and the pass laws—but retaining the Group Areas Act, which has a detrimental effect on family life.
- Scrapping some forms of petty apartheid, for example desegregating trains.
- Upgrading some townships.

What does the government hope to achieve?

Through the October municipal elections, the government hopes to revive the Black Local Authorities. This will open the way to establishing the proposed "Great Indaba" or National Council for Africans at a central level—the government will have the "elected" black leaders to call on.

The recent reforms are designed to win legitimacy for the government's new constitutional dispensation both inside South Africa and internationally. By crushing anti-apartheid forces (the stick) while at the same time winning over collaborators with their reforms (the carrot), the government is bypassing the authentic leaders in a bid to show the world that its "separate but equal" policy can work.

In this way, the government hopes to win more time for white minority rule.

What is wrong with the elections?

None of the local authorities will have any real power. The government can overrule any decisions they make. They are also dependent on Regional Services Councils (RSCs) for the provision of services and the development of their areas.

The RSCs are made up of nominated representatives from the different racial municipalities.

These RSCs are not elected by the people. They are controlled by white municipalities, who buy more services and therefore have greater voting power.

The local authorities also do not have any control over the security forces in their areas. The government's secretive National Security Management System (NSMS) controls security through regional, sub- and mini-Joint Management Centres (JMCs). These JMCs gather information and intelligence about political activities in an area, target activists and organisations for repression and alert local authorities to the grievances of the people. Local councillors are sometimes co-opted to serve on these JMCs.

These problems and the limitations of local authorities arise from one fundamental flaw or weakness. The elections for local authorities are designed to help implement the government's new constitution at a local level. But this constitution is ethnically-defined. It categorises people according to race and preserves white minority rule.

The elections do not provide the voter with a choice between apartheid and non-racialism. They are nothing more than a modified form of apartheid, designed to prevent non-racial democracy.

How the state security network and JMCs form a shadow structure mirroring the government structures and relating at every level

NATIONAL SECURITY MANAGEMENT SYSTEM		OFFICIAL STATE STRUCTURES
State Security Council (SSC)	<--->	Cabinet
SSC Work Committee	<--->	Cabinet Committee Department heads
Interdepartmental Committees	<--->	Departments
Joint Management Committees (JMCs)	<--->	Provincial Executive Committees
Sub-JMCs	<--->	Regional Services Councils (RSCs)
Mini-JMCs	<--->	Local authorities

Conclusion

As Christians we have a responsibility to examine our consciences and choose between the values represented by the South African government and the values represented by the church. The church has declared the theological justification of apartheid a heresy. In order to remain faithful to the Gospel, we as Christians have to avoid sin or collaboration with sin.

To put this positively, God calls us to pursue truth and justice and to build his Kingdom. We can only begin to do this if we reject apartheid in all its forms and work towards a non-racial and democratic South Africa.

DOCUMENT 153. "Constitutional Guidelines for a Democratic South Africa." ANC policy paper, Lusaka, August 1988

The Freedom Charter, adopted in 1955 by the Congress of the People at Kliptown near Johannesburg, was the first systematic statement in the history of our country of the political and constitutional vision of a free, democratic and non-racial South Africa.

The Freedom Charter remains today unique as the only South African document of its kind that adheres firmly to democratic principles as accepted throughout the world. Amongst South Africans it has become by far the most widely accepted programme for a post-apartheid country. The stage is now approaching where the Freedom Charter must be converted from a vision for the future into a constitutional reality.

We in the African National Congress submit to the people of South Africa, and to all those throughout the world who wish to see an end to apartheid, our basic guidelines for the foundations of government in a post-apartheid South Africa. Extensive and democratic debate on these guidelines will mobilise the widest sections of our population to achieve agreement on how to put an end to the tyranny and oppression under which our people live, thus enabling them to lead normal and decent lives as free citizens in a free country.

The immediate aim is to create a just and democratic society that will sweep away the centuries-old legacy of colonial conquest and white domination, and abolish all laws imposing racial oppression and discrimination. The removal of discriminatory laws and eradication of all vestiges of the illegitimate regime are, however, not enough; the structures and the institutions of apartheid must be dismantled and be replaced by democratic ones. Steps must be taken to ensure that apartheid ideas and practices are not permitted to appear in old forms or new.

In addition, the effects of centuries of racial domination and inequality must be overcome by constitutional provisions for corrective action which guarantees a rapid and irreversible redistribution of wealth and opening up of facilities to all. The Constitution must also be such as to promote the habits of non-racial and non-sexist thinking, the practice of anti-racist behaviour and the acquisition of genuinely shared patriotic consciousness.

The Constitution must give firm protection to the fundamental human rights of all citizens. There shall be equal rights for all individuals, irrespective of race, colour, sex or creed. In addition, it requires the entrenching of equal cultural, linguistic and religious rights for all. Under the conditions of contemporary South Africa 87% of the land and 95% of the instruments of production of the country are in the hands of the ruling class, which is solely drawn from the white community. It follows, therefore, that constitutional protection for group rights would perpetuate the status quo and would mean that the mass of the people would continue to be constitutionally trapped in poverty and remain as outsiders in the land of their birth.

Finally, success of the constitution will be, to a large extent, determined by the degree to which it promotes conditions for the active involvement of all sectors of the population at all levels in government and in economic and cultural life. Bearing these fundamental objectives in mind, we declare that the elimination of apartheid and the creation of a truly just and democratic South Africa requires a constitution based on the following principles:

The State:
a) South Africa shall be an independent, unitary, democratic and non-racial state.
b) i. Sovereignty shall belong to the people as a whole and shall be exercised through one central legislature, executive and administration.
   ii. Provision shall be made for the delegation of the powers of the central authority to subordinate administrative units for purposes of more efficient administration and democratic participation.
c) The institution of hereditary rulers and chiefs shall be transformed to serve the interests of the people as a whole in conformity with the democratic principles embodied in the constitution.
d) All organs of government including justice, security and armed forces shall be representative of the people as a whole, democratic in their structure and functioning, and dedicated to defending the principles of the constitution.

Franchise
e) In the exercise of their sovereignty, the people shall have the right to vote under a system of universal suffrage based on the principle of one person, one vote.
f) Every voter shall have the right to stand for election and be elected to all legislative bodies.

National Identity
g) It shall be state policy to promote the growth of a single national identity and loyalty binding on all South Africans. At the same time, the state shall recognise the linguistic and cultural diversity of the people and provide facilities for free linguistic and cultural development.

A Bill of Rights and Affirmative Action
h) The constitution shall include a Bill of Rights based on the Freedom Charter. Such a Bill of Rights shall guarantee the fundamental human rights of all citizens irrespective of race, colour, sex or creed, and shall provide appropriate mechanisms for their enforcement.
i) The state and all social institutions shall be under a constitutional duty to eradicate race discrimination in all its forms.
j) The state and all social institutions shall be under a constitutional duty to take active steps to eradicate, speedily, the economic and social inequalities produced by racial discrimination.
k) The advocacy or practice of racism, fascism, nazism or the incitement of ethnic or regional exclusiveness or hatred shall be outlawed.
l) Subject to clauses (i) and (k) above, the democratic state shall guarantee the basic rights and freedoms, such as freedom of association, expression, thought, worship and the press. Furthermore, the state shall have the duty to protect the right to work, and guarantee education and social security.

m) All parties which conform to the provision of paragraphs (i) to (k) shall have the legal right to exist and take in part in the political life of the country.

Economy

n) The state shall ensure that the entire economy serves the interests and well-being of all sections of the population.
o) The state shall have the right to determine the general context in which economic life takes place and define and limit the rights and obligations attaching to the ownership and use of productive capacity.
p) The private sector of the economy shall be obliged to co-operate with the state in realising the objectives of the Freedom Charter in promoting social well-being.
q) The economy shall be a mixed one, with a public sector, a private sector, a co-operative sector and a small-scale family sector.
r) Co-operative forms of economic enterprise, village industries and small-scale family activities shall be supported by the state.
s) The state shall promote the acquisition of managerial, technical and scientific skills among all section of the population, especially the blacks.
t) Property for personal use and consumption shall be constitutionally protected.

Land

u) The state shall devise and implement a Land Reform Programme that will include and address the following issues:
   i. Abolition of all racial restrictions on ownership and use of land.
   ii. Implementation of land reforms in conformity with the principle of Affirmative Action, taking into account the status of victims of forced removals.

Workers

v) A charter protecting workers' trade union rights, especially the right to strike and collective bargaining shall be incorporated into the constitution.

Women

w) Women shall have equal rights in all spheres of public and private life and the state shall take affirmative action to eliminate inequalities and discrimination between the sexes.

The Family

x) The family, parenthood and children's rights shall be protected.

International

y) South Africa shall be a non-aligned state committed to the principles of the Charter of the Organisation of African Unity and the Charter of the

United Nations and to the achievements of national liberation, world peace and disarmament.

Document 154. Response to the ANC "Constitutional Guidelines" by Cassim Saloojee and Firoz Cachalia of the Transvaal Indian Congress, *Weekly Mail,* October 7, 1988

The Transvaal Indian Congress (TIC) shares a long history, a programmatic position and an ideology with the ANC, though their legal status differs. Our response to the ANC's Constitutional Guidelines will, therefore, be different in substance and in tenor from others because it comes from "within". However, our interpretation is not a representative statement of the internal congress movement as a whole. The guidelines have stimulated vigorous debate within our organisations and opinions will differ.

ANC has, for a long time, resisted pressures to formulate "blueprints". However, the old order in South Africa is disintegrating and we have entered a transition period, the outcome of which is uncertain. This has made it vital to visualise the nature of post-apartheid society more concretely and to advance practical proposals. In this context, we welcome the ANC's intervention. Its guidelines situate the organisation more clearly in the political spectrum, and provide a framework for debate.

The existing apartheid state is widely recognised as illegitimate and a basic source of political crisis and social strife. It is appropriate, therefore, that the guidelines begin with proposals for the radical re-ordering of the state. The strong element of centralism in the proposals is necessary to encourage the formation of a national identity. The apartheid state and the race politics of the National Party have perpetuated tribal and ethnic identities and encouraged racial chauvinism and division. A strong, non-racial state will be a creative instrument of national reconciliation.

At the same time, as the proposals recognise, the new post-apartheid South Africa can only be built on the basis of recognition of rights to cultural and linguistic expression. There is some confusion on this in the Left. It is sometimes wrongly assumed that differentiated cultural identifies are necessarily divisive, and a manifestation of "false consciousness". It is true that cultural identities have been manipulated by the NP for reactionary ends, but it does not necessarily follow that they are the unique product of separate development. Indeed, they have a separate existence and have positive elements.

The concept of group rights is rejected—implicitly, not explicitly—in the ANC proposals. Cultural forms do not "belong" to any ascriptively defined group. They are a universal human product. The rights to culture and linguistic expression are therefore an aspect of individual rights and the rights of freely associated individuals. They cannot and should not form the basis of claims to special privileges and powers.

This raises other important issues. Some may contend that the proposals are not sufficiently sensitive to the dangers that arise from the centralisation of authority. A closer examination of the guidelines shows that this is not so. The recognition of rights to free cultural and linguistic expression implies a separation between the state and civil society, a sphere in which churches, mosques, sports organisations, etc, may be constituted on a voluntary basis. Incidentally, we see no reason why Afrikaans churches, schools and cultural organisations should not continue to exist, provided only that access to them is not limited by racial criteria.

Similarly, we would argue that the strong emphasis on centralism in the guidelines is qualified by Clause D, which aims at enhancing popular participation in all levels of government; Clause B, which recommends a decentralisation of delegated powers to regional and local units; Clause M which commits the ANC to pluralism in the political sphere; and Clause X, which allows for the emergence of a legally-protected private sphere. In other words, the guidelines envisage a state which is both national and democratic.

The guidelines contain no detailed recommendations for a reordering of legal institutions, though the contents of the law will necessarily undergo detailed changes in a post-apartheid South Africa. The proposals do contain a Bill of Rights, and we welcome this. The Bill that has been proposed has a strong emphasis on "second generation rights", or economic and social rights, and on the duty of the state to eliminate race discrimination and social and economic inequalities.

Such a Bill could well serve as an important instrument for guaranteeing effective rights to the majority of the population while ensuring that necessary socio-economic changes take place in an orderly way and within a legal framework. It is not clear, however, whether the ANC sees the Bill as embodying "fundamental rights" or how such rights would be enforced. There is no mention also of "due-process" rights which should be included in a Bill of Rights.

The key challenge we are facing is to ensure that change takes place without destroying our productive infrastructure, indeed that it takes place in a way that facilitates further development. We must ensure, further, that through economic development, society as a whole advances and that we eliminate the crushing poverty and stifling ignorance so many are condemned to today. The current enthusiasm in ruling circles for privatisation and *laissez-faire* (mirrored in their equally strong fascination for the macabre achievements of the Chilean generals) promises only growing gloom for the majority.

We are hopeful that the forms of economic restructuring contemplated in the guidelines will make it possible for us to harness our national material and human resources effectively to achieve developmental political and ethical goals. The guidelines envisage a mixed economy combining planning and market mechanisms, with the state having an important role as economic regulator. There remains considerable scope for debate on the precise mix.

We believe, for instance, that market relations should be restricted for social services. Basic food, clothing, shelter and even cultural matter and information are goods and services which should not depend on market money relations. On the other hand, in the immediate post-apartheid period, market mechanisms could be expanded in the "small business" sector.

And here, as the proposals indicate, expansion need not occur exclusively on the basis of wage labour; cooperatives could play an important role, complementing state and private sector initiative. In sum, it is neither feasible nor desirable to attempt to subsume all economic activity under a central plan. On the other hand, the market is no panacea.

This raises another subject of intense debate within the democratic movement: worker rights. We fully endorse the ANC's express commitment to the concept of a Workers' Charter, protecting trade union rights and the right to strike. However, greater attention needs to be given to ways to expand the involvement of workers in decision making within the production process.

The proposals express some conflicting objectives, which may not be simultaneously realisable. We are not certain, for instance, whether it is possible to secure full employment within economies which permit private ownership of productive property and which distribute the social product through the market. The experience of the Nordic countries may provide valuable lessons in this regard.

The development of technology and science makes it possible to build a society free of poverty and class inequalities. We are suspicious of arguments critical of race discrimination, but which consider economic inequalities as rational or inevitable.

There should be no doubt that socialist ideas are pervasive within the democratic movement. But we are committed to working to achieve economic and social goals peacefully and pragmatically within the framework of a democratic constitution which allows all political forces with different economic programmes to organise and participate in regular elections.

The guidelines are essentially a programme for the establishment of a national democracy. This programme has been criticised within the broad extra-parliamentary movement by those advancing a more exclusivist nationalism (the "Africanists") and by "workerists" who claim to adopt a more purely socialist position.

However, it is not clear to us how their proposals for the political and economic restructuring of our society would differ in detail from those advanced in the guidelines. The PAC, for instance, has never committed itself to a denial of political rights for whites, and the "workerists" have never clarified whether they intend to abolish "commodity production" or private ownership.

South African liberalism is at best a selective appropriation of Western liberal/democratic traditions. While liberals have made a strong case for procedural rights, they have often been more than equivocal on the franchise issue. Attempts are continually being made to popularise constitutional mechanisms (minority vetoes, federation, etc) aimed at limiting the rights of the

African majority. The guidelines directly challenge liberals because they commit the ANC to a liberal/democratic constitution—with multi-party democracy, a Bill of Rights, equality before the law, etc.

The guidelines clarify the ANC position on a number of different issues, and as such must be welcome. They will no doubt appeal to a wide range of different constituencies. This is a source of strength. To the extent that they make the construction of viable compromises possible, they improve the prospects of peaceful transition to a non-racial democracy.

Document 155. "Joint Statement of the South African Rugby Board, the South African Rugby Union and the African National Congress." Harare, October 16, 1988

A meeting attended by representatives of the South African Rugby Board, the South African Rugby Union and the African National Congress was held in Harare on the 15th and 16th October, 1988. The meeting came about because of the common desire on the part of all the participating organisations to ensure that rugby in South Africa is organised according to non-racial principles.

The meeting confirmed this position and agreed that South African rugby should come under one non-racial controlling body. They agreed to work together to achieve these goals and called on all people of goodwill inside and outside South Africa to support this process. They also agreed that the accomplishment of the goals stated here is a necessity for South African rugby to take its rightful place in world rugby.

The leaders of the South African Rugby Board and the South Africa Rugby Union met with the ANC solely because of their belief that it can play a positive role to achieve the common objectives shared by the SARB and the SARU. These leaders are ready to meet at all times and shall meet any other parties or groups that may also play such a role.

The ANC accepted the good faith and sincerity of the rugby administrators at the meeting and undertook to use good offices to ensure that non-racial South African rugby takes the rightful place in African and world rugby to which we have referred.

Document 156. Letter from Mosiuoa Patrick Lekota to AZAPO leaders, handwritten, December 5, 1988

Palace of Justice, Pretoria
5 December 1988

Dear Coms Muntu [Myeza] and Pandelani [Nefolovhodwe],

Comrades Popo [Molefe], Moss [Chikane] and I have just had the privilege of a briefing on the exchanges you had with Com Tom [Manthata] on the need for coordinated and united responses to the impending release of some of our people's leaders. We are also informed of the positive responses you expressed on this issue. We are therefore writing to let you know that we share your sentiments on this matter. Yes, it is our fervent hope that both yourselves and those of our organisations' leaders who remain on the scene may forge an effective working relationship and format on the welcoming of our people's leaders. Such a relationship once firmly established could later be extended to other areas of our work and struggle, thus strengthening the strike force of the broad movement for freedom.

It is hardly necessary for us to lecture you on the necessity for unity in struggle. Your long experience has already familiarised you with what angles of the question we might explore in a note of this nature. All we wish to say here is that the present conjuncture suggests to us that the hour for united action has struck. Only determined steps and concrete deeds can produce that unity of which we have mused about for so long.

May we assure you at the same time that we have, in the past, also expressed similar sentiments to those [with whom] we are closely associated. And although we are presently speaking on our own account, we may say to you that as far as we are aware our shared views are generally accepted. Barring unavoidable personality problems then there ought not to be serious barricades on the road forward.

We add here that the earlier releases were on the whole surprise events. To that extent none of us may be blamed for failing to consult and prepare to receive the leaders. But we have taken too long to learn from that episode and we are still too slow in our response to the situation. By the time Comrades Zephania Mothopeng and Harry Gwala were released we should have been prepared for the eventuality. Everything had pointed to it for some months in advance. As a result our national leaders and heroes are returning to our communities and being received like any one of us. We all need to seriously think about and evaluate the national and international implications of our neglect. Certainly, if inadvertently, we [may] give credence to the theory of the government that our leaders do not enjoy popular support but that they were blown up and built by the media, that is, that their popularity is simply mythical.

In another few weeks or months another batch of significant leaders will be returned to us. Are we going to stand around divided and with folded arms again? We urge that everybody concern themselves with this question. Without pressuring to instruct those of you on the scene and, with the necessary circumspection, we recommend that interorganisational consultations be initiated in order to search for appropriate action. We believe that it can and should be done for the sake of our country's people.

Finally, we send you our warm regards and very best wishes in your operations. Amandla! Matla! [Power!]

Yours in the struggle,
M. Lekota and others

Document 157. "Keep South African Sports in Isolation." Op-ed article by Sam Ramsamy, *New York Times*, December 11, 1988

Sports have played a significant role in South Africa's search to gain international respectability for apartheid. Bringing American athletes like Carol Cady ("Why I Decided to Go to South Africa," *The Times*, Nov. 6) to the country is part of that search. The campaign to exclude South Africa from international sports is significant because it affects one of the major outlets for the aggrandizement of white supremacy.

Until isolation began to affect South African sports, there was a clear line of demarcation between black and white athletics. Then, desperate for reentry into international sports, white South Africa tried all sorts of formulas to appease international opinion. As was inevitable, all ended up being mere readjustments within the system of racial separation called apartheid.

First the changes were ad hoc dispensations that overlooked certain laws, so that blacks and whites could compete together or against each other in government-approved fixtures. During 1981 and 1982, the South African Government amended three laws within the mass of apartheid legislation to formalize the earlier dispensations. But the linchpin of apartheid sports legislation, the Separate Amenities Act, remains intact. The Separate Amenities Act determines the provision and use of sports facilities for the various race groups. The Government has now drawn a distinction between recreational and competitive sports. Mixing is allowed in competitive sports, but not in recreational sports.

Also the Government has very cleverly shifted the onus of permitting mixed-race sports events to municipal councils. Most municipal councils do not allow mixed-race sports events. The very few facilities that have been desegregated have virtually become black facilities, as whites have moved on to "'whites only" facilities.

Last July, the Johannesburg *Weekly Mail* revealed that in the province of Natal, 330,000 Africans who live in the townships of Umlazi and Lamontville share six soccer fields, seven tennis courts and two swimming pools. By contrast, the 212,000 whites living in the neighboring municipality of Durban have 146 soccer venues and 15 public swimming pools. (Tennis courts are in abundance.)

In Pietermaritzburg, 11,567 white school children share 32 cricket fields and 65 net practice facilities (for tennis, volleyball and netball). Some 13,000 "coloured" and Indian schoolchildren share one field and five nets. There are no cricket facilities for African children.

In 1979, the present Minister of Law and Order, A. K. Vlok, told the South African Parliament that less than 1 percent of all South African sports events included athletes of different races. The South African Government then commissioned the Human Sciences Research Council to investigate all aspects of sports. The council produced its final report in late 1982. A white South African newspaper, *The Star*, which supports the reinstatement of South Africa in international sports competition, said: "Statistics compiled by the H.S.R.C. tend to show that at all levels, multiracial sport is the exception rather than the rule. So much for the image of vanished colour bars so assiduously put out for overseas consumption." The position hasn't changed much since.

Sports are important both for apartheid's internal survival and for its international image. For this reason, South Africa spends astronomical sums of money to break out of its isolation. Unlimited financial resources are available to white South African national sports bodies to conscript blacks and to lure top sportsmen and women from overseas to compete in South Africa. Mediocre athletes from the United States have been easy prey for South African entrepreneurs, who offer these athletes twice, thrice, even 10 times the amount of money they can earn elsewhere. There is no doubt that financial rewards are the major—and, in most cases, only—consideration for overseas sports stars weighing whether to perform in South Africa. Therefore, it is not surprising to learn that golfers, tennis players and, more recently, track and field athletes have decided to venture there. Some of these athletes have tried to seek moral justification to mask the award of financial security.

Sports bodies obtain their finances largely from the apartheid regime. The South African Government provides undisclosed sums for so-called international liaison; this covers all-expenses-paid visits by international observers, and teams and individuals. Secondly, the Government provides generous tax rebates of nearly 90 percent for sports sponsors that lay out money to attract overseas competitors. In effect, the sponsors only need to provide about 10 percent of the total sponsorship sum.

South Africa has attempted to attract international sports bodies to visit the country and carry out inspections. But nearly all international bodies have rejected such invitations, saying the inspections would be meaningless since it is well known that apartheid legislation determines all aspects of life in South Africa, including sports. Only a few international organizations—right wing in outlook, or with strong South African sympathies—have carried out superficial investigations there. Even these organizations have been cautious of their support for South African sports.

There is now mixing in the major sports at the national level. And the South African Government has conferred "honorary white" status on its black sportsmen and women for the duration of a sports meeting in the hope that this will be a passport for white South Africa's international participation. South Africa's anti-apartheid sports organizations have refused to cooperate in this farce; after such events, blacks have to return to the humiliation of being treated worse than third class citizens in the country of their birth. Blacks demand equality every day of the week and every week of the year, not just during a sports event when white South Africa wishes to put on a display for the world.

Early this year, a black athlete, Matthews Temane, set a world best time for the half-marathon at an event organized under the aegis of the white South African Amateur Athletic Union. This did not make the lead story in a single major newspaper. When Zola Budd performed a similar feat in 1984,

South African newspapers insured that the news reverberated throughout the world. Worse still was the reaction after Temane's achievement. No one was remotely interested in who he was.

Was this because stories written about him and pictures taken of him relaxing at "home" would have revealed that "home" was a room shared with seven other miners? Was this because this black mineworker was forced to live in a single-sex compound? Was this because it was prohibited by law for his family to live with him? Of course, no white miner would have been subjected to such conditions.

Apartheid literally penalizes nearly all black athletes from birth. Much lower incomes, limited sports facilities, restrictions on travel, vastly inferior schools and equipment, frequent malnutrition, and the fact that whole sections of the black community are almost totally denied access to sports illustrate how apartheid shackles black athletes throughout their lives.

But faced with massive racial discrimination from cradle to grave in South African sports, supporters of South Africa require only that a few of apartheid's laws be suspended for an hour or two while their own sportsmen are present. And they accept at face value the white minority's claim that sport is "non-racial" and that selections are fair and open.

DOCUMENT 158. "Business in Post-Apartheid S.A." Article by Kay Makan in Transvaal Indian Congress leaflet, "Face to Face With the ANC," December 1988

Before Saturday morning of 8th October 1988 I had feelings of excitement and curiosity as to the reception and the type of people I would be meeting. The mixed feelings I express are the type one would feel prior to his first trip overseas in an airplane or a trip on a "bullet train" in Tokyo.

I was extremely impressed, and state that I found the members of the National Executive of the ANC most capable, highly intelligent and well informed on South African and world affairs. The dialogue and interaction that we were engaged in for two full days was very interesting and most educational.

We met the ANC as an entire group from within the country. But we also split up into various groups—such as religion, culture, education, business, labour, health, civics, youth, sport and so on. Each of these groups had people from our delegation as well as the appropriate representatives from the ANC.

I attended the discussion on the role of business. The ANC argued that businessmen definitely have a role to play in the ending of apartheid. They seemed to feel that it is in the interests of business that apartheid be done away with. The importance they attached to the role of business could be seen in the fact that they assigned treasurer-general Thomas Nkobi, Joe Slovo, and other senior members to represent the ANC at the discussion on business.

We discussed various issues, including the future of the free enterprise system, the extent of nationalisation, and the possibility of socialism, should the ANC come to power. Other issues discussed in the open session included sanctions and disinvestment, the armed struggle, and the cultural boycott of South Africa.

While we as businessmen did not necessarily agree with the views of the ANC, we were very impressed with the way they put their case across. They seemed to us to be very reasonable people who were also prepared to listen to our point of view. What was certainly very clear was that they are people one can talk to and exchange ideas with, even if one does not agree with their approach to issues.

The ANC argued that over 80% of the wealth in South Africa is controlled by a handful of people. They felt that there had to be a redistribution of wealth. But they felt that this could not happen overnight. They wanted some form of socialism, but without chaos. They referred to the failures of the socialist experiences of such countries as China, Hungary, Poland and Mozambique. They did not see a rapid move to socialism as the answer for South Africa.

They did feel though that the political liberation of Blacks without their economic liberation was totally inadequate. They committed themselves to eliminating social inequality based on race. They re-affirmed their commitment to the Freedom Charter, and said that they were committed to a mixed economy, with state, cooperative and private sectors.

They explained that they supported total sanctions and disinvestment against South Africa. We explained that as much as we could understand their point of view, as businessmen we could not agree with them. They saw sanctions and disinvestment as powerful non-violent means of opposing the South African government. They argued that the main target of sanctions was the South African state, and felt that it should serve to strengthen the movement against apartheid inside the country.

On the cultural boycott itself, it seemed as if they were moving in the direction of distinguishing between apartheid and anti-apartheid culture. While the former should be boycotted, the latter had to be encouraged. They called for greater consultation with the anti-apartheid movement inside the country to look into how this could be done. That is, that the cultural boycott should isolate apartheid culture without harming anti-apartheid culture.

We raised the matter of the armed struggle with them, and in particular the increasing attack on "soft targets". The ANC insisted that its policy remained to hit at "hard targets", and that they deeply regretted the death of innocent civilians in attacks on "soft targets". The ANC claimed that they were definitely not responsible for all of these attacks, and that some of them were clearly carried out by others in order to discredit the ANC. As far as those carried out by its own members were concerned, this was done against ANC policy, and attempts were being made to discipline the members concerned. The ANC had convened a special executive meeting to discuss the issue, and had called for a halt to such attacks. They hoped that this would happen. At the same time, however, they asked us to understand the frustrations of some of their members who were responsible for these attacks.

They also told us that because of the "government's intransigence and the persistence of state repression", they had "no choice but to escalate the armed struggle". We stressed to them that we were committed to non-violent means of bringing about change in South Africa. I firmly believe that all peaceful methods must be pursued to eradicate all forms of apartheid and the total abolishment of the Group Areas Act with an equal education system and equal opportunities for all South Africans irrespective of race, religion or creed.

Whatever our differences with the ANC, the most important point of our visit is that we are talking to each other and building bridges. This is the only way we can finally bring about a peaceful solution to the problems of our beloved country.

DOCUMENT 159. "Campaign for a Friendly City." Port Elizabeth Action Committee flyer, early 1989

PORT ELIZABETH is faced with a costly and potentially damaging referendum on open pools. In response to a positive move by the City Council declaring public pools open to all races, conservatives have forced a referendum on this issue.

The Port Elizabeth Action Committee is determined not to allow certain elements to drag us down the road of Boksburg and Carletonville. We cannot afford to become the Boksburg of the Cape.

In these times we should be doing all that we can to bring people together in order to work for a peaceful and non-racial future. We cannot allow our city to be destroyed by a minority which clings to racial prejudice,

Racism is unacceptable in any form. Those wishing to enforce racism on our city must be opposed at all costs. PE is looking to the future, not the past. We need to work together and to build together towards a FRIENDLY city of which we can all be proud.

What is the message we are going to send to our fellow citizens and the world? Will it be a message of racism and bigotry, or will it be a message of friendship and goodwill?

It's time to stand up and be counted. Turn the page and send a message of friendship.

PE cares. We share our facilities.

SIGN FOR A FRIENDLY CITY
We the undersigned residents of Port Elizabeth:
1. Believe that PE is a friendly city and that there is sufficient goodwill amongst PE residents upon which to build a peaceful and non-racial future.
2. We support the opening of all PE's facilities to all people.

[spaces for names, addresses and signatures]

INSTRUCTIONS:
1. The aim is to collect significantly more signatures in favour of open facilities than those who may vote against them. The results will be announced some time after the referendum,

2. Sign the petition and post to: PEAC, PO Box 2838, North End, 6056.
3. Please get your friends and family to sign as well.
4. Feel free to photostat this petition in order to collect more signatures.
5. Completed petition forms can also be delivered to the following collection points: Fogarty's Bookshop, Main Street; Lilia's Boutique, Allied Building, Main Street; Dulce Ice Cream, Rink Street; Niel's Men's Fashionwear, 35 Westbourne Road and 3 Grace Street; Tel-Aviv Israeli Grill, Parliament Street; Coimbra Cycles, 65 4th Avenue, Newton Park; Tivoli Italian Restaurant, Pamela Arcade, 2nd Avenue, Newton Park; Springbok Cycle & Hardware, 551 Main St., North End. More petition forms can be collected from these addresses.
6. Time is of the essence. Please return your petitions as soon as possible.

PE is a friendly city. We reject racism!

DOCUMENT 160. Press statement by hunger strikers at Johannesburg Prison, Diepkloof, January 23, 1989

We, the detainees at Johannesburg Prison, have decided to embark on a hunger strike on individual voluntary basis to protest our unjustified prolonged detention without trial and to demand our immediate unconditional release from detention. Many of us have spent more than 24 months in detention and every time we are redetained we are supplied with "new reasons", fabricated and [spun] out of the heads of our captors.

Our protest action stems from our painful experience and deep conviction that the regime intends to keep us here indefinitely. We are effectively sentenced to long prison terms without meaningful recourse to courts of law to prove our innocence. We also believe that our continued detention stems from the regime's malicious intentions to use us as scapegoats for their failure to address fundamental issues of the land and national grievances of our people. Our detention cannot stop the struggle for freedom.

We have tried everything in our power to persuade the regime to release us. We have sent memoranda, petitions and representations to both the Minister of Law and Order, Adriaan Vlok, and to the State President, P.W. Botha, exhorting them to address themselves to our situation, but to no avail. Some detainees sought several court interdicts as a last resort to secure their release. The regime showed no slightest concern, but instead proceeded to tighten up every knot and closed up whatever existing legal channel there was to secure our release. To add insult to injury, all campaigns and calls for the release of detainees were also declared illegal. All these inhuman measures have convinced us that the regime will not move on detentions. We are also convinced that we have exhausted all other means available to us. At the same time we insist that we have committed no crime and therefore do not deserve to be here. We shall go on with our hunger strike for as long as it takes to secure our release, whatever the consequences.

We see our action as the result of conscious, deliberate and voluntary personal choice. We hope it shall also reflect, to both the national and the international community, varying cases of painful experiences, stress, hardship and torture borne by detainees at their various points of detention. Some of us may never recuperate from the effects of this long unjustified detention. Our action should also disprove the regime's propaganda and distorted picture about detainees in South African prisons.

We are detainees from all walks of life: workers, students, youth, teachers, trade unionists, Christians, parents, etc. Amongst us there are breadwinners and children under age. We also have students whose future is deliberately wasted here. Schools have just re-opened whilst most students are still in detention, having already lost one to two years of study. A few of us in detention do not even belong to anti-Apartheid organisations and have never opposed Apartheid in a self-conscious way.

However, most of us are peace-loving democrats, respectable members of our democratic organisations, who throughout our opposition to unjust laws practised consistently our peaceful methods of opposition and protest to Apartheid. We are strongly committed to a democratic future of our country. We are fully aware of the risks and dangers involved in our action and the divisive tactics the regime might use to break our action, but we are determined to go on until everyone is released. We also demand the release of all other detainees held under the State of Emergency in SA prisons. Nothing save our total release shall dissuade us from our course of action.

Document 161. "A Different Kind of Bias is Behind White Support of the ANC." Op-ed article by Thami Mazwai, *Los Angeles Times*, February 21, 1989

As human-rights organizations throughout the world flex their muscles for another onslaught against apartheid in the new year, black South Africans hope that these groups will stop being partisan in their support for the liberation struggle. If the Western world is committed to the creation of a just society in South Africa, it should accept the democratic right of black Africans to decide which organization—the African National Congress (ANC), the Pan Africanist Congress (PAC) or the Black Consciousness Movement (BCM)—represents their aspirations. Several overseas organizations insist that the ANC should be the sole representative of South Africa's oppressed masses. Thus only its accredited representatives were given the platform at many meetings in Europe, Canada and the United States.

Financial assistance inside South Africa to anti-apartheid organizations has also been biased. Of at least $40 million given annually, less than 10% went to organizations supporting PAC or BCM policies. Among the many reasons why white supremacy has thrived were the government's policies of divide and rule. By favoring the ANC against the PAC and BCM, the overseas community must ask if it is not deepening the wedge in the black community and assisting the government in keeping blacks divided.

Various arguments as to why the ANC must be the only recipient of international support have been given, the major one being its stability over the years. The adoption of the Freedom Charter, the ANC's blueprint for a non-racial South Africa, by two of the largest organizations in the country, the United Democratic Front and the Congress of South African Trade Unions, reflects the wide support for the ANC, its backers argue. The two groups are not ANC affiliates, but they support many of its policies. It is also stressed that the admission of white members by the three organizations shows their commitment to a non-racial future. Conversely, since groups supporting PAC and BCM policies do not accept white members, their commitment to non-racialism cannot be trusted.

Supporters of PAC and BCM argue that downtrodden communities throughout the world and history have been bound together by their suffering and that therefore it is not wrong for blacks to be drawn to each other because of their oppression. "Also, we are as committed to a non-racial South Africa as the ANC is, but differ on strategies," one activist explained. "Zimbabwe is a classic example. Whites feared Robert Mugabe but have now found he is not the monster he was made out to be. The same will apply in Azania (South Africa). The PAC has even declared that 'in a liberated Azania the color of a man's skin shall be as irrelevant as the shape of his ears'."

Further, it is argued that the Azanian People's Organizations—Azanian National Youth Unity, African Women's Organization and Azanian Coordinating Committee—all opposed to the Freedom Charter, were just as active and had followings as large as the United Democratic Front and the trade-union congress.

"However, as our rivals enjoy millions of dollars in assistance they are able to bus members to meetings, organize conferences, print T-shirts and employ full-time workers. As these activities attracted the press and were reported on, it is assumed Freedom Charter organizations are stronger. But the question to be asked is, can they survive or get members to meetings without external funding? We have survived," the activist commented. He also pointed out that the adoption of the charter had split or created tensions in several organizations while others, including the United Democratic Front and the trade-union congress, had not adopted it.

If overseas organizations studied political trends in South Africa's townships more closely, they would note that support for the African National Congress or the Pan Africanist Congress varies from area to area and time to time. Recent trends show that the PAC has gained the upper hand, while between 1984 and 1986 the ANC rode the crest of a wave. The picture may be different tomorrow. Rivalry between the two dates back to 1958, when a faction of the ANC left to form the PAC.

Among the differences between the two is the ANC's assertion that "South Africa belongs to all who live in it, black and white," while its rivals say that occupation of the land by whites during colonialism does not entitle them to ownership. "When whites agree that the land belongs to us and accept majority rule, the contradictions between us shall have ceased," said a PAC spokesman. The two groups also differ on participation of whites in the liberation struggle. The ANC and its supporters accept them in their organizations while the PAC and allied groups believe that the presence of whites in black organizations neutralizes black militancy.

The case for nonsectarianism is strengthened by the cooperation of all groups in the country during the past four years when there were class and consumer boycotts in some townships, and there is an ongoing rent boycott. More than 2,000 people have died over the past two years, and more than 20,000 have been detained. It cannot be said that all of these victims were supporters of organizations that have adopted the Freedom Charter.

People in Europe and America rightfully reject President Pieter W. Botha's determination to control the lives of blacks. Why do they want to decide which of our political organizations is acceptable?

DOCUMENT 162. Letter from Ahmed Kathrada to friends, handwritten, February 25, 1989 (abridged)

> Pollsmoor Maximum Prison
> Tokai, 7966
> 25th February 1989

My Dear Navi and Daso,

Thanks for your letters of 15th and 20th December respectively. I also received your Xmas cards and Navi's card from Spain. And Daso, thank you for your *two* birthday cards! I don't want to ascribe motives but there is a lurking suspicion that you seem bent on exaggerating my age. You see I turned only 59 last year; yet on the one card you say "You are especially thought of on reaching your 60th!" Yet on the other you say "May your 60th birthday be…" Let me also correct one other wrong impression you may have gained. Twice in your letter you refer to "facilities" which we are supposed to be enjoying—as if we have recently been granted additional concessions or "facilities." No, our position is exactly the same as it has been for years.

The only person (as you've no doubt heard) whose status has significantly changed is Nelson. In the words of Government spokesmen, he now enjoys the category of a "special prisoner," of whom there is only one in South Africa. I suppose you know of our surprise "Xmas present"—on Friday 23rd December we were taken to Paarl (+ 30 miles) to visit Nelson in his luxury prison. And luxurious it is—make no mistake about that. Wall to wall carpeting, posh furniture, bedrooms with bathrooms en suite, a high-tech kitchen with gadgets I had never seen before, a white warrant-officer as his personal chef, swimming pool. We had breakfast and lunch with him, the latter in real style, with masses of cutlery, crockery and glassware. (After 26 years of metal containers I was nervous about handling all these fancy things, and when necessary, I resorted to the good old fingers, which in any case came long before knives and forks).

It was good to see Nelson almost completely recovered, and his old self again. We spent just over 7 hours together, and talked about all sorts of things. It was like old times again. However, I was sad when the time came to say goodbye—not because our temporary status as "special prisoners" had ended and we were returning to our "normal" prison, but because, stripped of all the fineries, we were leaving behind a prisoner, a lonely prisoner who has to serve his sentence with his books, newspapers, TV, radio, his letters, occasional visitors, and his thoughts. We are only 4 here, which is hard enough, but we are at least better off than he is. Nelson asked to convey his greetings to all the friends, and his thanks for the messages during his illness.

The recent developments around Winnie are distressing. One can only hope that by some miracle the dust settles soon, and brings an end all the pain, grief and suffering. . . .

Now for a word of criticism. In writing about the Harare concert you mention Bruce Springsteen and Sting; but how can you leave out Tracy Chapman? Apart from being Black, her simplicity, humility, sincerity, and social context of her songs should have penetrated that "classics-oriented" mind of yours. For this offence, you will have to make suitable atonement. Don't think that we have dropped Whitney [Houston]—she still remains our top favorite. But, and more so since Wembley, Tracy and Natalie Cole. No let me rather say we have developed quite a soft spot for them. . . .

In case media reports have reached London about Walter [Sisulu] going blind I must assure you that it is not true. He had an eye operation recently, and the Professor appears to be satisfied with the result. . . .

Nice to know that you are in touch with Mike (I call him "Varkie"). We haven't heard of him for years. My fondest wishes to him. Afraid his plans to "meet you in Fordsburg next year" are a bit on the optimistic side. . . .

This is all for now. Lots of love and best wishes to all of you.

from
AMK

Document 163. Memorandum from Nelson Mandela to P. W. Botha, March 1989 (abridged)

The deepening political crisis in our country has been a matter of grave concern to me for quite some time and I now consider it necessary in the national interest for the African National Congress and the government to meet urgently to negotiate an effective political settlement.

At the outset I must point out that I make this move without consultation with the ANC [of which] I am a loyal and disciplined member. . . . But in my current circumstances I cannot [consult the ANC], and this is the only reason why I am acting on my own initiative, in the hope that the organisation will, in due course, endorse my action.

I must stress that no prisoner, irrespective of his status or influence, can conduct negotiations of this nature from prison. . . . The step I am taking should, therefore, not be seen as the beginning of actual negotiations between the government and the ANC. My task is a very limited one, and that is to bring the country's two major political bodies to the negotiating table.

I must further point out that the question of my release from prison is not an issue, at least at this stage of discussions, and I am certainly not asking to be freed. But I do hope that the government will, as soon as possible, give me the opportunity from my present quarters to sound the views of my colleagues inside and outside the country on this move. Only if this initiative is formally endorsed by the ANC will it have any significance.

I will touch presently on some of the problems which seem to constitute an obstacle to a meeting between the ANC and the government. But I must emphasise right at this stage that this step is not a response to the call by the government on ANC leaders to declare whether or not they are nationalists and to renounce the South African Communist Party before there can be negotiations: no self-respecting freedom fighter will take orders from the government on how to wage the freedom struggle against that same government and on who his allies in the freedom struggle should be. . . .

Far from responding to that call, my intervention is influenced by purely domestic issues, by the civil strife and ruin into which the country is now sliding. . . . This is the crisis that has forced me to act. . . .

Obstacles to negotiation

I have already indicated that I propose to deal with some of the obstacles to a meeting between the government and the ANC. The government gives several reasons why it will not negotiate with us. . . .

Renunciation of violence

The position of the ANC on the question of violence is very simple. The organisation has no vested interest in violence. It abhors any action which may cause loss of life, destruction of property and misery to the people. It has worked long and patiently for a South Africa of common values and for an undivided and peaceful non-racial state. But we consider the armed struggle a legitimate form of self-defence against a morally repugnant system of government which will not allow even peaceful forms of protest. . . .

Right from the early days of its history, the organisation diligently sought peaceful solutions and, to that extent, it talked patiently to successive South African governments, a policy we tried to follow in dealing with the present government. Not only did the government ignore our demands for a meeting, instead it took advantage of our commitment to a non-violent struggle and unleashed the most violent form of racial oppression this country has ever seen.

It stripped us of all basic human rights, outlawed our organisations and barred all channels of peaceful resistance. It met our just demands with force and, despite the grave problems facing the country, it continues to refuse to talk to us. There can only be one answer to this challenge: violent forms of struggle. Down the years oppressed people have fought for their birthright by peaceful means, where that was possible, and through force where peaceful channels were closed. The history of this country also confirms this vital lesson. . . . [Both Africans and Afrikaners fought British imperialism.]

It is perfectly clear on the facts that the refusal of the ANC to renounce violence is not the real problem facing the government. The truth is that the government is not yet ready for negotiation and for the sharing of political power with blacks. It is still committed to white domination and, for that reason, it will only tolerate those blacks who are willing to serve on its apartheid structures. Its policy is to remove from the political scene blacks who refuse to conform, who reject white supremacy and its apartheid structures, and who will insist on equal rights with whites.

This is the reason for the government's refusal to talk to us, and for its demand that we disarm ourselves, while it continues to use violence against our people. This is the reason for its massive propaganda campaign to discredit the ANC, and present it to the public as a communist dominated organisation bent on murder and destruction. In this situation the reaction of the oppressed people is clearly predictable.

White South Africa must accept the plain fact that the ANC will not suspend, to say nothing of abandoning, the armed struggle until the government shows its willingness to surrender the monopoly of political power, and to negotiate directly and in good faith with the acknowledged black leaders. The renunciation of violence by either the government or the ANC should not be a pre-condition to but the result of negotiation. . . .

South African Communist Party

I have already pointed out that no self-respecting freedom fighter will allow the government to prescribe who his allies in the freedom struggle should be, and that to obey such instructions would be a betrayal of those who have suffered repression with us for so long.

We equally reject the charge that the ANC is dominated by the SACP and we regard the accusation as part of the smearing campaign the government is waging against us. . . . But since the allegation has become the focal point of government propaganda against the ANC, I propose to use this opportunity to give you the correct information, in the hope that this will help you to see the matter in its proper perspective, and to evaluate your strategy afresh.

Cooperation between the ANC and SACP goes back to the early twenties and has always been, and still is, strictly limited to the struggle against racial oppression and for a just society. At no time has the organisation ever adopted or cooperated with communism itself. Apart from the question of cooperation between the two organisations, members of the SACP have always been free to join the ANC. But once they do so, they become fully bound by the policy of the organisation set out in the Freedom Charter. As members of the ANC engaged in the anti-apartheid struggle, their Marxist ideology is not directly relevant. The SACP has throughout the years accepted the leading role of the ANC, a position which is respected by the SACP members who join the ANC. . . .

The government also accuses us of being agents of the Soviet Union. The truth is that the ANC is non-aligned, and we welcome support from the East and the West, from the socialist and capitalist countries. The only difference, as we have explained on countless occasions before, is that the socialist countries supply us with weapons, which the West refuses to give us. We have no intention whatsoever of changing our stand on this question.

The government's exaggerated hostility to the SACP, and its refusal to have any dealings with that party have a hollow ring. Such an attitude is not only out of step with the growing cooperation between the capitalist and socialist countries in different parts of the world, but it is also inconsistent with the policy of the government itself, when dealing with our neighbouring states. . . .

The reason for this inconsistency is obvious. As I have already said, the government is still too deeply committed to the principle of white domination and, despite lip-service to reform, it is deadly opposed to the sharing of political power with blacks, and the SACP is merely being used as a smokescreen to retain the monopoly of political power.

The smearing campaign against the ANC also helps the government to evade the real issue at stake, namely, the exclusion from political power of the black majority by a white minority, which is the source of all our troubles. . . .

Majority Rule

The government is equally vehement in condemning the principle of majority rule. The principle is rejected despite the fact that it is a pillar of democratic rule in many countries of the world. It is a principle which is fully accepted in the white politics of this country. Only now that the stark reality has dawned that apartheid has failed, and that blacks will one day have an effective voice in government, are we told by whites here, and by their Western friends, that majority rule is a disaster to be avoided at all costs. . . . If black political aspirations are to be accommodated, then some other formula must be found, provided that that formula does not raise blacks to a position of equality with whites.

Yet majority rule and internal peace are like the two sides of a single coin, and white South Africa simply has to accept that there will never be peace and stability in this country until the principle is fully applied. It is precisely because of its denial that the government has become the enemy of practically every black man. It is that denial that has sparked off the current civil strife.

Negotiated Political Settlement

By insisting on compliance with the abovementioned conditions before there can be talks, the government clearly confirms that it wants no peace in this country but turmoil, no strong and independent ANC, but a weak and servile organisation playing a supportive role to white minority rule, not a non-aligned ANC, but one which is a satellite of the West, and which is ready to serve the interests of capitalism.

No worthy leaders of a freedom movement will ever submit to conditions which are essentially terms of surrender dictated by a victorious commander to a beaten enemy, and which are really intended to weaken the organisation and to humiliate its leadership.

The key to the whole situation is a negotiated settlement, and a meeting between the government and the ANC will be the first major step towards lasting peace in the country, better relations with our neighbour states, admission to the Organisation of African Unity, re-admission to the United Nations and other world bodies, to international markets and improved international relations generally. An accord with the ANC, and the introduction of a non-racial society is the only way in which our rich and beautiful country will be saved from the stigma which repels the world.

Two political issues will have to be addressed at such a meeting; firstly, the demand for majority rule in a unitary state, secondly, the concern of white South Africa over this demand, as well as the insistence of whites on structural guarantees that majority rule will not mean domination of the white minority by blacks. The most crucial task which will face the government and the ANC will be to reconcile these two positions. Such reconciliation will be achieved only if both parties are willing to compromise. . . .

It may well be that this should be done at least in two stages. The first, where the organisation and the government will work out together the preconditions for a proper climate for negotiations. Up to now both parties have simply been broadcasting their conditions for negotiations without putting them directly to each other. The second stage would be the actual negotiations themselves when the climate is ripe for doing so. . . .

DOCUMENT 164. "Soweto Council Stalls Rent Negotiations." *Soweto People's Delegation NEWS*, April 5, 1989

Last year, on the 9 December 1988, the Soweto People's Delegation (S.P.D.) met the Soweto Council (SC) and presented the grievances of the people which led to the rent boycott. The Delegation then informed the council that it was going to commission a team of experts to undertake research into all matters related to the rent boycott and propose a way of resolving the problems.

The Soweto Council agreed to meet the Delegation by the end of January 1989 to discuss the proposals. The understanding of the Delegation was that the people of Greater Soweto (Soweto, Dobsonville and Diepmeadow) would only start paying service charges after an agreement satisfactory to the community shall have been reached between the Council and the Delegation. Once the research report was ready, the Soweto People's Delegation requested for a meeting with the Soweto Council in February 1989, [but] the Soweto Council informed the Delegation that they will only be able to consider a meeting with the Delegation sometime in March 1989.

March has come and gone and the Delegation has not heard from the Council. Instead the council has convened a public meeting to announce their own solution to the problem without talking to the Delegation as agreed at our last meeting with them on 9 December 1988.

The SPD has expressed serious concern and disappointment in the failure of the council to meet them. It is clear that the Council, like previous councils, has chosen to ignore the popular feelings of the people of Soweto. They have chosen to further their own personal interest and the politics of collaboration with [the] apartheid system rather than the interest of the majority of the people of Soweto.

This change of attitude of the Soweto Council was not surprising to the Delegation as we have information from reliable sources that the Joint Management Committee (JMC) held two meetings in December 1988 after the Delegation's meeting with the council, and in January 1989, to work out ways and means of stopping further negotiations between the SPD and the Soweto Council. In both meetings according to our source the JMC planned to devise a way of dealing with the problems of Soweto without talking to the SPD.

The Soweto Council [by] not responding to a request for a meeting with the SPD, and the calling of a mass meeting of mainly pensioners to announce their own solutions to the problems of the people of Soweto, without talking to the SPD, is a clear indication that the Soweto Council has decided to submit to the will of the JMCs. Submission to the will of the JMCs means that the Soweto Council is now just an instrument of the apartheid system to facilitate oppression and exploitation of the people of Soweto.

The Soweto Delegation thus hopes that the Soweto Council will see some light and free itself from the manipulations of the apartheid system and take the feelings of the majority of the people of Soweto seriously.

RESULTS OF THE RESEARCH COMMISSIONED BY THE SOWETO PEOPLE'S DELEGATION

The Soweto Delegation released the findings of the policy research on the Soweto Rent Crisis to the public in March 1989. Copies of the report will be available for R7.00 per copy as from the second week of April. A summary of the findings of the research teams are presented below.

CAUSES OF THE RENT BOYCOTT

What the Government Says: People are boycotting rent because of intimidation by revolutionary elements.

What the Research Report Says: The rent boycott was a direct response to the deteriorations of socio-economic conditions. Poor services by the government structures in the townships.

THE SIZE OF SOWETO DEBTS
1. Money owed because of Rent Boycott (excluding Dobsonville and Diepmeadow): R200 million
2. Loan for electricity upgrading programme (1979) and to finance the upgrading of roads, stormwater drainage, sewerage services and water supply (1980): R441 million
3. Budgeted deficit for 1988/89: R60 million.

TOTAL DEBTS: R701 million [about $250 million in a period of rapid fall in rand's value]

What the Government Says: The people of Soweto MUST PAY this debt OR THEY WILL LOSE THEIR HOUSES.

What The Mayor of Soweto Says: People must forget about arrears amounting to R701 million. The crucial question in this respect is who has authority to write off the arrears—is it the Mayor or the Government?

What The Report Says:

1. People of Soweto do not have money to pay the debt.
2. This debt is the result of the apartheid city, of separating Johannesburg from Soweto, and not the responsibility of Sowetans.
3. Soweto must find other resources (Public or Private) to finance itself.
4. There must be one tax-base for Johannesburg and Soweto.

HOUSING CRISIS

There is a backlog of 66 000 housing units in Soweto. The State has withdrawn from large scale provision of houses leaving it to the individual Sowetans and the private sector. But this only caters [for] 13% of Sowetans who to some extent can afford these highly priced houses.

This leaves about 87% of Sowetans on the waiting list living in squatters' shacks. The council and the government do not have a satisfactory solution to these problems, especially of squatters, who urgently need decent affordable houses.

SOLUTIONS:

1. Houses should be transferred to the people of Soweto. A mechanism for this should be properly and professionally worked out.
2. The government should provide large-scale housing schemes for the low income group mainly to help squatters.
3. That a COMMUNITY HOUSING TRUST FUND should be established, whose board of trustees must be persons of high esteem and shall have earned the community's respect and be accountable to it. To receive monies from sales of houses and reinvest it in building new houses for strictly the low income group.

SERVICE CHARGES

The research reveals that Sowetans are paying 11 cents per unit whilst Johannesburg whites pay 9 cents per unit for electricity charge. Even for water service Sowetans are paying more than their white neighbours.

An average Johannesburg rate payer pays R25.97 for (high) services whilst a Sowetan pays more service charges of R88.55 for poorer level of services. Here, the report shows clearly that the poor subsidise the wealthy, i.e. Sowetans are subsidising Johannesburg.

SUMMARY OF RECOMMENDATIONS

1. The arrears amounts must be written off.
2. The housing stock must be transferred to the ownership of the Soweto residents.

3. Soweto's infrastructural services must be upgraded to an acceptable standard.
4. An affordable service charge formula must be designed.
5. A single tax-base for Johannesburg and Soweto must be established.

In conclusion, what the report has done is simply to confirm what the people of Soweto and other areas throughout S.A. have been saying of their despicable conditions, that the main aim of apartheid is to keep them continuously in such inhuman conditions and where they will keep paying for their own oppression as they do.

	1980 %	1985 %
food	39.1	33.0
housing, electricity	8.7	15.1
transport	8.0	9.7
furniture and household equipment	6.4	8.6
clothing, footwear, accessories	11.3	7.1
insurance and funds	3.3	5.5
direct taxes	0.8	3.4
personal care	2.1	2.3
communication	0.6	2.2
medical and dental	1.2	2.1
fuel and light	4.9	1.7
washing and cleaning materials	1.9	1.6
alcoholic beverages	3.3	1.5

This table reveals that the percentage of income spent on housing and electricity costs were met by a decline in expenditure on essential items such as food and clothing.

Document 165. "The Path to Power: Programme of the South African Communist Party Adopted at the 7th Congress," Havana, April 1989 (abridged)

INTRODUCTION

The prospects of achieving a revolutionary break-through in South Africa are greater today than ever before in our history. The apartheid regime faces an all-round crisis which results from our broad revolutionary offensive, together with the internal contradictions among the rulers. The crisis of racial tyranny cannot be resolved, except by the revolutionary transformation of our country.

The national liberation offensive is led by the African National Congress in revolutionary alliance with the vanguard workers' party—the South African Communist Party—and the South African Congress of Trade Unions. It is a national liberation struggle that combines many mass democratic contingents—the youth, women, students, civic and others—and the trade union movement.

The mobilisation, organisation and unity in action of this large front of forces has swept into every corner of our country, into the factories, townships, schools, and rural villages. Our struggle is known through the world, stirring freedom-loving people in every country. The building of this broad front of forces inside and outside our country has been the greatest achievement of our struggle. . . .

In the decisive period ahead, the SACP has a crucial role to play in the mobilising, organising and ideological development of all contingents in our revolutionary struggle, and in particular the South African working class. The struggle for national liberation, the destruction of colonialism of a special type and the transition to socialism in South Africa require a vanguard Marxist-Leninist party capable of providing a highly disciplined organisation and the guiding light of a scientific socialist outlook grounded in South African realities. . . .

[Explanations follow of the World Revolutionary Process, the Revolutionary Process in Africa, and Colonialism of a Special Type.]

NATIONAL DEMOCRATIC REVOLUTION . . .

The foundation of the national democratic state will be popular representative institutions of government based on one-person, one-vote: universal and direct adult franchise without regard to race, sex, property and other discriminatory qualifications. These bodies will have to be accountable to the people and subject to popular control. For it to serve the people's interests, the new state machinery—the army, the police, the judiciary and the civil service—will be open to all South Africans loyal to democratic and non-racial principles. The state will guarantee the basic freedoms and rights of all citizens, such as the freedom of speech and thought, of the press and of organisation, of movement, of conscience and religion and full trade union rights for all workers including the right to strike. . . .

In the period after the seizure of power by the democratic forces, the working class will need to continue the struggle against capitalism. . . .

The fundamental question of any socialist revolution is the winning of political power by the working class, in alliance with other progressive elements among the people. The working class then sets out to eliminate exploitation by achieving public ownership and democratic control of the means of production. . . .

THE NATIONAL DEMOCRATIC MOVEMENT AND THE VANGUARD ROLE OF THE COMMUNIST PARTY . . .

Communists have never sought to transform the national democratic movement into a front for the Party. Participation by communists in the ANC, Umkhonto we Sizwe and other revolutionary organisations is based on our class appreciation of their distinct but complementary tasks. . . .

Millions of South Africans, including black workers, subscribe to various religious beliefs. The South African ruling class and its allies, like oppressors elsewhere in the world, have always tried to use religion as a tool to instill passivity and resignation among the working masses. With the development of the liberation struggle there has emerged an interpretation of religious doctrines which is in the interest of the struggling people. Moved by a profound rejection of oppression, countless religious leaders and believers have taken up the battle against the colonial system. Many are to be found within the ranks of the liberation movement and the people's army. The ideology of the South African Communist Party is based on scientific materialism. But we recognise the right of all people to adopt and practice religious beliefs of their choice. We work for the involvement of all antiapartheid forces in the common struggle for freedom and democracy. There is common ground between the immediate and long-term perspectives of the Party and a theology of liberation that identifies with the poor and oppressed. In actual struggle, this bond has grown and must be further strengthened. . . .

THE PATH TO POWER IN THE NATIONAL DEMOCRATIC REVOLUTION . . .
In what sense then can we talk of an insurrection as a possible path to power?

The crisis facing our ruling class will be aggravated still further by a combination of mass upsurge, in which working class action at the point of production will play a key role, mass defiance, escalating revolutionary combat activity, intensified international pressure, a situation of ungovernability, a deteriorating economy and growing demoralisation, division, vacillation and confusion within the power bloc. When all these elements converge in a sufficient measure, the immediate possibility of an insurrectionary breakthrough will present itself. *Such a situation will, of course, not simply ripen on its own; its fruition depends, in the first place, on the work of the revolutionary movement.* But we must also be prepared for a relatively sudden transformation of the situation. In the conditions of deepening crisis, "events triggered off by the tiniest conflicts, seemingly remote from the real breeding-ground of revolution", can, overnight, grow into a revolutionary turning point (Lenin). The regime's grip on its reins of power could be swiftly weakened and the stage set for a sustained national uprising leading to an insurrectionary seizure of power.

The subjective forces—both political and military—must be built up so that when these seeds of revolution begin to germinate, the vanguard will be able to seize the historic moment. *In this sense, all-round mass action, merging with organised armed activity, led by a well-organised underground, and international pressure*, are the keys to the build-up for the seizure of power. *Seizure of power will be a product of escalating and progressively merging mass political and military struggle with the likelihood of culminating in an insurrection.*

The revolutionary movement must place itself in the best position to plan for, and to lead, an insurrection at the right moment. This means, among other things, paying special attention to building factory, urban and rurally-based combat groups, popularising insurrectionary methods among the masses and winning over elements from the enemy's armed forces. The partial uprisings which have become a feature of our mass struggles must also be seen as a school for the accumulation of insurrectionary experience. The organisation of the industrial working class is of major importance; protracted national strikes and other industrial activity at the point of production will be a vital factor in the maturing of the "revolutionary moment". Above all, a political vanguard is needed to plan for, and lead, the insurrectionary assault at the crucial stage.

Prospects of a Negotiated Transfer of Power

There is no conflict between this insurrectionary perspective and the possibility of a negotiated transfer of power. There should be no confusion of the strategy needed to help create the conditions for the winning of power with the exact form of the ultimate breakthrough.

Armed struggle cannot be counterposed with dialogue, negotiation and justifiable compromises, as if they were mutually exclusive categories. Liberation struggles have rarely ended with the unconditional surrender of the enemy's military forces. Every such struggle in our continent has had its climax at the negotiating table, occasionally involving compromises judged to be in the interests of revolutionary advance. But whether there is an armed seizure of power or negotiated settlement, what is indisputable to both is the development of the political and military forces of the revolution.

We should be on our guard against the clear objective of our ruling class and their imperialist allies who see negotiation as a way of pre-empting a revolutionary transformation. The imperialists seek their own kind of transformation which goes beyond the reform limits of the present regime but which will, at the same time, frustrate the basic objectives of the struggling masses. *And they hope to achieve this by pushing the liberation movement into negotiation before it is strong enough to back its basic demands with sufficient power on the ground.*

Whatever prospects may arise in the future for a negotiated transition, they must not be allowed to infect the purpose and content of our present strategic approaches. *We are not engaged in a struggle whose objective is merely to generate sufficient pressure to bring the other side to the negotiating table.* If, as a result of a generalised crisis and a heightened revolutionary upsurge, the point should ever be reached when the enemy is prepared to talk, the liberation forces will, *at that point,* have to exercise their judgement, guided by the demands of revolutionary advance. But until then its sights must be clearly set on the perspectives of a seizure of power. . . .

The White Community and Armed Activity

In touching on these future possibilities, it is necessary to stress that one of the key factors influencing the ultimate responses of the army will be the work of our revolutionary alliance and the way its perspectives are understood by the white group as a whole. The opening declaration of the Freedom

Charter that "South Africa belongs to all its people, black and white" must unconditionally continue to guide what we say and do. It is necessary to intensify efforts to spread this message in the face of an unending enemy campaign of misinformation about our objectives of people's power. This message must also emerge from the nature of our organised combat actions and the targets selected. . . .

The Masses are the Key

The insurrectionary potential of our oppressed masses is growing. *While the "exact moment" of the seizure of power depends upon objective as well as subjective factors, there can be no doubt that what the masses do, led by the liberation alliance, influences the objective factors and hastens the arrival of that moment.* It is precisely this subjective factor which, in the last five years, has dramatically transformed the objective situation. The unique series of partial uprisings, the dramatic growth of the mass democratic movement, the emergence of giant trade union organisation, escalating armed actions and international mobilisation against the regime, are all inter-dependent processes which have changed the whole objective framework of struggle.

There is no aspect of the crisis facing the regime—whether it be the rapidly deteriorating economic situation or the divisions and vacillations within the power bloc—which has not got its primary roots in the soil of people's struggles. It is the all-round escalation of these struggles, combined with, and dependent upon, the consolidation and growth of mass and underground organisation, which will lead to the revolutionary breakthrough.

Our working class is the decisive force to bring about the collapse of racism and victory in the national democratic revolution as a stage towards building a socialist South Africa.

As always, we communists, together with our brothers, sisters and comrades in the liberation alliance, will remain at our posts however long the road to victory. The perspective of a protracted struggle can never be abandoned. *But, we are also convinced that the situation has within it the seeds of a sudden transformation.* We must prepare ourselves, and be ready. Our watch words are *unity, organisation and struggle.*

FOR A DEMOCRATIC VICTORY AND ADVANCE TO SOCIALISM! VICTORY IS CERTAIN!

Document 166. "Report of PC Meeting With BN." Minutes of meeting of ANC President's Committee with Beyers Naudé, Lusaka, April 25, 1989

Present: ORT [Oliver Tambo], SG [Secretary General Alfred Nzo], DTL [Dan Tloome],
By Invit: S.Tsh [Steve Tshwete], CH [Chris Hani], JJ [Josiah Jele], HM [Henry Makgothi]

President ORT welcomed BN [Beyers Naudé].

BN: I am deeply grateful. I am going to Malawi for a World Alliance of Churches meeting and have sought audience with you because of urgent matters arising from discussions in Parow and with Dullah Omar, and a message sent by NM [Nelson Mandela]. The message deals with the whole question of negotiations, Buthelezi, etc.

NM read what is in writing to Ismail Ayob [one of Mandela's lawyers]. One copy of the memo is with the Crisis Committee and the other is the one I have brought along. The distribution of copies is to be strictly controlled. (Meeting asked BN to read the document).

The following points made in document:
1) NM concerned by deep political crisis in country and desires negotiation of political settlement between ANC and government.
2) Expresses loyalty to ANC leadership in Lusaka.
3) Stresses that no prisoner can conduct negotiations from prison.
4) Negotiations are a matter of life and death for organisation and need to be handled through appointed representatives.
5) Steps he has taken should not be seen as beginning of actual negotiations, but as serving the limited task to bring country's major political bodies to negotiations table.
6) Question of his release is not an issue (in present discussions) but he does express hope that the government will give an opportunity for him to sound out his colleagues inside and outside.
7) Only if ANC endorses the initiative can it have meaning. No self-respecting organisation can take instructions from the government: to obey would be a violation of principles of the Movement and a betrayal.
8) Concerned by civil war into which the country is sliding with (prospects of) black and white slaughtering each other. The days ahead foreshadow more violent events.

(Beyond this point memo quotes NM speaking [to Ayob], i.e. not reading from notes).
9) "The reason I read is that the first time I met a government representative he said (the discussion was) confidential. I want my colleagues to know the government has announced they are talking to me. Everything I have done will (have to) be endorsed by my organisation."
10) Between May 1988, and 2 days ago, I have had 10 meetings with the government (side). Questions raised:
   a) Does ANC want to negotiate?
   b) How will I consult with ANC? 3 or 4 to come over? Ideally, I should go to entire leadership.
   c) Who do I want to consult with (internally)? Have given list of names, some in detention others in gaol. Government said they would go into the matter. List of names of people from W. Cape, Natal, EL [East London], PE [Port Elizabeth], OFS [Orange Free State], STvl [southern Transvaal], and Crisis Committee.

11) NM has impression that the government is in deep trouble and looking for a way out. Our people must carry on political work but make sure ANC and government do meet.
12) GM [Govan Mbeki]: His release was a test. The government says that his conduct had affected prospects of others, Walter [Sisulu] in particular. He could have gone about quietly and consulted. WS himself did not hope to come out. NM's point is that on release they would report to organisation and latter would say what they should do.
13) Buthelezi—there was a time when his Inkatha was regarded as the internal wing of ANC. NM had discussed with colleagues if he should reply his letters. All on [Robben] Island had said he ought to reply.

NM had discussed with colleagues if he should see Gatsha [Buthelezi]. Lusaka advised against seeing Gatsha, and Priscilla [Jana] had said Youth were unhappy with Gatsha.

Gatsha had written 2 letters: on NM's birthday, and while he was in Tygerberg [Hospital] on subject of his release. Walter had advised to acknowledge letters; Lusaka had said no reply. Archie [Gumede] and [Harry] Gwala had said he should reply. Lusaka advice came after NM had replied.

Meeting then discussed memo with view to obtain clarification. OR explained: He had met Ismail on 7th April. Ismail had said NM told him he had been talking to other side, and he would honour undertaking (of confidentiality). It may have been difficult to tell Ismail. But NM was working to bring ANC and regime to negotiating table, and that had been heard earlier. OR had said to Ismail: NM is in a difficult situation. If he told us, chances are that they (regime) would know. Whereas NM was observing confidentiality, they were not. They were discussing in a wide circle. It was even worrying that they were talking to him alone. On the other hand, if we replied, they would know. It is an advantage for them. Hence our demand that he should be released. It is untenable that they should be placed in a position where they can have information (from us) ahead of NM.

OR had said if we are going to negotiate end of this terrible system seriously, it was going to be a historic event. Negotiation represents the final stage (for us) when the regime is convinced that Apartheid must end. We have got to be certain and sure that when negotiations start they will be commensurate with gravity of situation we are trying to resolve.

NM had said we should decide who would represent (ANC). OR had said the entire leadership should be there, he himself included. If that position holds, we might feel we don't want to be flying hither and thither to CT [Cape Town]. If regime is serious about negotiations, it is unacceptable that some of the key players should be in gaol.

Followed a discussion on NM's correspondence with Gatsha Buthelezi.

BN: Ismail says he has impression there are things happening which would require an urgent response to Nelson:

i) Release of WS was imminent. Albertina [Sisulu] was not talking but an impression had been created they wanted to release him in next 2/3 weeks

(It was agreed to summon IA [Ayob] for Monday or Tuesday).

BN continued: 2 matters.
i) He, AB [Allen Boesak] & FC [Frank Chikane] had been invited by American Forum on Africa, the so-called Black Caucus. They urgently wanted guidance on how to tackle US visit.
ii) He had not seen WM [Winnie Mandela] in last 2 weeks, and was concerned about her situation. He had been approached with urgent request to convey the feeling of numerous people in Soweto that they were concerned by "aura of suspicion" around her, that her life may be in danger. Her irresponsible behaviour had raised suspicions that she may be cooperating with the enemy. In his (BN) view events had so disturbed her that she was prone to irrationality. Also the system may have a stake in spreading false rumours about her. The outcome of the tense situation in Soweto was a matter of concern.

Mandela Crisis Committee had tried to reassure WM and draw her out of her isolation, but her attitude had become hostile when she learnt of FC's letter which had got into enemy hands.

IA was of view that "Mandela Palace" should be sold immediately. There were problems surrounding ownership which would make sale problematic. NM was also of view that the property should be sold. He was furious about the amount which was being paid for Security Guards and had decided not to give authority for their payment after December.

OR: What gives rise to this suspicion of WM? Aren't people settling down to let bygones to be bygones? Can people seriously think she is working with system?

BN: There are 2 strains of thought in Soweto.
1. That she is cooperating with the system.
2. That WM does not want to be one with the Community and to be subject to collective discipline.

WM appears to have started an ANC Women's League consisting of a small disaffected Fedtraw [Federation of Transvaal Women] section. This is sort of thing that angers people.

OR: I heard about this and said the thing must be dissolved. It's exactly what we tried to prevent—division.

BN: reverted to the American invitation: It seems the US (group) wants us to present a new initiative, a new angle to pressurise (the regime). Randall [Robinson of TransAfrica] has stated that to continue preaching sanctions at this time is "a horse not worth riding." No impression will be made on Bush administration unless something new comes up. They (Randall) are simply breaking their heads (against a wall) in the US. He says at moment in US im-

pression is "law and order" has been restored, the government is running things in a reasonable and calm way and has been accommodating and helpful. Questions which they expect to face in US include:
i) Sanctions and loans.
ii) Possible release of NM. Where do we stand?
iii) What response to Namibia situation?
iv) What kind of pressure is possible in SA following Thatcher visit, rumours of negotiations, and rumours of new role of USSR.

They need guidance and did not wish to stray from ANC thinking. The meeting in Washington was to take place from Tuesday 16th May to 18th and this could be an important platform.

OR: We most certainly welcome the initiative because we stand or fall by what you will say. So we will review all these questions and try to arm you as far as possible. In general there is among our supporters a search for something new in strategies and tactics; it has been generated by the Namibia process; so we will do our best. (It was decided to await IA on NM document, and to await TMb [Thabo Mbeki] to discuss US questions. Also agreed that this matter is confidential to group).

OR thanked BN and meeting rose at 18.30 hours.

DOCUMENT 167. "The Role of Local Government." Excerpt from report of the Five Freedoms Forum-ANC conference, Lusaka, June 29–July 2, 1989

AIM:
The aim was to assess initiatives for change at a local government level and to consider the role local government will play in a future nonracial, democratic SA.

QUESTIONS DEBATED:
1. Assess the role of local government structures in desegregating South African society or in maintaining segregation.
2. Assess the effectiveness of current initiatives in opening the cities and improving the quality of life for all citizens.
3. What approaches can be adopted to further the process of opening our society and improving the quality of life.
4. Discuss the role local government should play in a future SA.

PARTICIPANTS
ANC members, extra-parliamentary organisation delegates and city and town councillors, including the mayors of East London (Mr Donald Card) and Midrand (Mr Ian Lourens).

PRESENTERS
Ilana Korber
Opening the cities will be a long process and will have to be done over and over again in other cities and towns to gain wider acceptance. The process was originally held up because it was seen to be a dilution of the national struggle. Also, originally the "open city" campaign was done quietly. These were later perceived to be incorrect strategies as local government was seen to be separate from national politics.

ANC
The ANC had little knowledge of "open city" campaigns but wanted to learn more about them and observe their effects. It was not aware that these campaigns held prospects for opening up dramatic avenues for breaking down apartheid structures.

However, as a result of the presentation ANC delegates felt the local government sphere may be more important and may present more challenges and opportunities than was realised within the ANC.

The ANC should consider building alliances in this area as well as formulating a common political culture around the role the ANC could play. The question was whether these structures would provide bridges to reach out to the grassroots structures in the townships? Also it recognised that these steps could be regarded as being part of a defiance campaign.

THE DISCUSSION
Much of the content of this commission was new to ANC members because they appeared to be unaware of the extent of grassroots activity being carried out by white organisations together with organisations within the MDM in trying to break down apartheid at local government level.

The city and town councillors in the FFF delegation said they experienced a credibility problem among blacks as they were seen as part of the "system" by many township activists. It was acknowledged that they should be seen to be in opposition to the National Party (NP) despite having actual control of a city or town council within the present structure of government. Councillors said they were also frustrated in attempts to introduce desegregation by opposition from the government, by the limited nature of the statutory avenues available to them and because there was little or no co-operation from black township organisations. They had to go through a learning process involving consultation and planning with these organisations to make progress. Their participation in regional services councils (RSCs) and joint management committees (JMCs)—structures seen as bolstering apartheid—are a major cause for their rejection.

Extra-parliamentary organisations and Democratic Party (DP) councillors in a number of cities were involved in "Open City" campaigns. However, it was recognised that different approaches and strategies were required for other towns where situations were very different. Single issue campaigns had considerable value for effectiveness and participation morale. All delegates said they gained by being part of the participation process and using campaigns as a method to change attitudes. It was noted that apartheid parameters should be challenged and not accepted as immovable. Constant creative thinking was needed.

The ANC accepted that local issue campaigns such as those for "Open Cities" should be endorsed by the MDM and participation in the campaigns should be broad. Councillors from every city and town expressed a real and urgent need for a bridging organisation to create contact with the MDM and the Five Freedoms Forum was frequently named as such an organisation. Without a bridging mechanism the councillors are unable to gain access to the MDM.

There was general acceptance that white opposition councillors should work for the ultimate elimination of their present apartheid structures and their replacement by single local bodies that democratically serve all the residents of the composite cities.

Document 168. "Jews for Social Justice." Excerpt from report of the Five Freedoms Forum-ANC conference, Lusaka, June 29–July 2, 1989

The meeting was requested by JSJ. Four people originally constituted the Jewish group, but as a result of the meeting appearing on the conference programme, several other Jews from the SA "home" group took the opportunity of attending.

Franz Auerbach was invited by the ANC delegates to act as chairperson of the meeting.

The ANC group consisted of five or six senior members. Discussion lasted about 80 minutes and was conducted throughout in a friendly spirit.

The Jewish delegation explained that as a minority group the SA Jewish community was inclined to be apprehensive about its future in a SA in which a black majority—including the ANC—controlled the government and it sought reassurance on several points.

The ANC replied that an ANC government would not discriminate against the Jewish Community in SA. Anti-Semitism is totally alien to the ethos of the ANC.

There was no problem in the Jewish community continuing to run its own day schools. The Jewish delegation explained that these schools were not exclusive and had some black pupils. The ANC stated it was not opposed to private schools, provided they did not practice racial exclusivity.

The ANC supports freedom of conscience, including freedom of religious observance.

South Africa-Israel relations:

The chairperson explained that for Jews the world over support for Zionism meant support for the State of Israel, though this did not necessarily mean support for particular actions for a particular Israeli government, but general support for the state and its welfare was universal among the Jewish communities in SA and elsewhere outside Israel.

The ANC explained that, in common with various member states of the Organisation of African Unity (OAU), the ANC would have a more positive position towards Israel if it improved its relations with Arab states in its region. As a liberation movement, the ANC naturally supported other liberation movements, including the PLO (Palestine Liberation Organisation). The ANC regarded Palestinians as an oppressed people.

The ANC hoped that relations between Israel and other states in the region would soon improve, and for this reason the ANC had warmly welcomed the PLO's recent recognition of the State of Israel. The ANC trusted the SA Jewish Community understood the ANC's position on this issue.

The Jewish delegation expressed the hope that since the ANC had expressed support for the PLO's recognition of Israel the ANC might possibly play some role in building a measure of trust between the PLO and Israel—a trust that was lacking.

The ANC expressed the view that if the SA Jewish community shared some of the widely expressed concern about the manner in which the Israeli government was handling the intifada [Palestinian uprising], it should publicly express such concern.

The delegation pointed out that in 1988 both Jews for Social Justice in Johannesburg and Jews for Justice in Cape Town had issued statements expressing concern over this issue. However it was also explained that many members of the SA Jewish community felt it was not proper for Jews to express public criticism of the Israeli government from outside the country. This was not dissimilar to the reluctance of blacks to express public criticism of the policies and shortcomings of particular governments in Africa, even where they disapproved of such policies and actions.

While the ANC understood this position it nevertheless hoped that progressive Jewish forces everywhere could exert influence on the Israeli authorities to hasten a resolution of the current regrettable conflict.

The ANC stated an ANC-led government would maintain friendly relations with all nations, including Israel, and hoped that by the time there was a change of government in SA the Middle East conflict would have been resolved. He said SA Jews would be free to support the State of Israel. This would only become a problem in the highly unlikely event of an ANC-led government breaking off relations with Israel.

The ANC asked the SA Jewish community to judge the ANC on its policies and proposals for SA which were the major concerns of the ANC. The relations between the ANC and the PLO and with Israel were relatively less important in the overall situation—only one of the many problems.

Thanking the ANC delegation for debating issues of concern to the SA Jewish community in a frank and friendly spirit, chairperson Auerbach gave an assurance on a matter not raised by the ANC that the JSJ and JFJ [Jews for Justice], as well as the Jewish individuals present, regretted any continuing military ties between Israel and the SADF [South African Defence Force]. The Jewish delegation also felt that the general trend of the discussions had been positive and had served to reassure the SA Jewish community.

DOCUMENT 169. "Wat die Besoek aan Lusaka vir my Beteken Het (What the Lusaka Experience Meant for Me)." Excerpt by Flip Potgieter from report of the Five Freedoms Forum-ANC conference, Lusaka, June 29–July 2, 1989, in Afrikaans and English

Ek is 'n doodgewone Suid-Afrikaner—lief vir my land en sy mense asook vir die wonderlike lewenswyse wat dit aan my bied. Oor die jare het dit egte meer en meer duidelik vir my geword dat die lewenswaardes wat ek as kosbaar beskou alleenlik kan voortbestaan indien dit beskikbaar is aan al die mense van ons land.

As opvoeder will ek sien dat gehalte opvoeding aan almal beskikbaar is. As stadsraadlid wil ek hê dat 'n goeie lewenstandaard binne die bereik van al ons mense is. As sportadministrateur is dit my begeerte dat al ons mense 'n gesonde lewenswyse kan ontwikkel.

Dit is al vir 'n geruime tyd aan teenstanders van die huidige regime duidelik dat dit slegs moontlik sal wees in 'n nie-rassige demokratiese Suid-Afrika, maar hoedat hierdie ideaal verwesentlik kon word was nie duidelik nie. As gevolg van die propagandaveldtog van die regering teen die ANC is 'n skewe, verwronge beeld geskep waardeur die ANC as deel van die probleem, eerder as 'n deel van die oplossing voorgestel is.

My besoek aan Lusaka as deel van die Five Freedoms Forum afvaardiging het hierdie opvatting vir ewig vernieting. Ek besef nou dat geen permanente oplossing vir Suid-Afrika beding kan word sonder die ANC nie en dat hulle, met hul nie-rassige beleid, inderdaad doel van die oplossing is en nie deel van die probleem nie.

Die leierskaphoedanighede van die ANC topbestuur het as 'n aangenome verrassing vir my gekom. Ons kan nie langer bekostig dat leiers soos Oliver Tambo, Thabo Mbeki, Pallo Jordan, Steve Tshwete—om maar enkeles te noem—nie binnelands beskikbaar is om ons mense te lei nie. Daarom is die ontbanning van die ANC van kardinale belang sodat die weg gebaan kan word vir onderhandelinge tussen alle partye in Suid-Afrika.

Deur gesprekke te fasiliteer oor aangeleenthede soos toekomstige ekonomiese stelsels, moontlike konstitusies, opvoeding, gesondheid—om maar enkele strydvrae te noem—berei instansies soos die Five Freedoms Forum ons op 'n verantwoordelike wyse voor vir die post-apartheid era. In die Afrikastate noord van ons het sodanige gesprekke nie plaasgevind nie, met tragiese gevolge. Dit en die ooglopende armoede van Zambia het dit weereens aan my tuis gebring dat suidelike Afrika alleenlik sal floreer indien stabiliteit in Suid-Afrika verlang kan word.

Op 'n meer persoonlike vlak was daar sekere ervaringe wat my vir altyd sal bybly. Die vriendskappe wat ek gesmee het met mede-Suid Afrikaners in die ANC was seker die uitstaande gebeurtenis. As Afrikaner het die feit dat ek Afrikaans met verskeie van die toplede van die ANC afvaardiging gepraat het van my die vrees ontneem dat my taal sal verdwyn in die toekomstige Suid-Afrika.

Alhoewel ek terdee daarvan bewus is dat die samesprekings en onderhandelinge tussen alle belangegroepe heelwaarskynlik uitgerek en uiters moeilik sal wees, is daar vir my vir die eerste keer waarlik hoop en sien ek uit na 'n opwindende tydvak in die geskiedenis van my land—miskien die mees opwindende periode ooit.

What the Lusaka experience meant for me
By Philip (Flip) Potgieter
Port Elizabeth City Councillor

I am an ordinary Afrikaner; I love my country and its people and also the wonderful way of life it gives me. Over the years it has become more and more clear to me that the values and standards that I treasure can only survive if they are made available to all the people of our country.

As an educationist I want to see that quality education is available to all. As a city councillor I want to ensure that a good standard of living is within the reach of all our people. As sports administrator it is my desire that all our people are able to develop a healthy way of life.

It has been clear for a considerable time to opponents of the present regime that this is possible only in a nonracial democratic SA, but it is not clear how this ideal can be achieved. As a result of the government's propaganda campaign against the ANC, a slanted, distorted picture has been created which depicts the ANC as part of the problem rather than part of the solution.

My visit to Lusaka as part of the FFF delegation has destroyed this view for ever. I now realise that no permanent solution can be achieved for SA without the ANC and that they with their nonracial policy are indeed part of the solution and not part of the problem.

The high qualities of leadership of the ANC's executive was a pleasant surprise. We can no longer afford not have leaders such as Oliver Tambo, Thabo Mbeki, Pallo Jordan, Steve Tshwete—to name but a few—available to lead people inside SA. It is therefore of cardinal importance that the ANC is unbanned so that the path can be opened for negotiation between all the parties in SA.

In facilitating discussions on such contentious subjects as future economic systems, a possible constitution, education, health—to mention but a few—institutions such as the FFF in a responsible way are preparing us for the post-apartheid era.

Such discussions did not take place in the African states north of our borders with tragic consequences. That and the conspicuous poverty of Zambia again brought home to me that southern Africa would only flourish if stability was desired in SA.

On a personal note, some of my experiences there will remain with me always. The friendships I made with fellow South Africans in the ANC was certainly the most outstanding happening. As an Afrikaner the fear that my language will disappear in a future SA evaporated as I spoke Afrikaans with several of the senior executive members of the ANC.

Although it is quite probable that discussions and negotiations between all the interest groups will be protracted and difficult, for the first time I have real hope and I look forward to an exciting period in the history of my country, perhaps the most exciting yet.

Document 170. "Negotiations for Political Settlement in SA." COSATU memorandum, June 1989

This report should be accurately given to all union structures and members. The purpose of the report is to get the views of members on the questions which are listed at the end of the report. From the discussion and decisions of our members, unions will be consolidating a national position on negotiations for our delegates to defend at the COSATU National Congress in July.

1. This is a report on discussion held between COSATU (1 delegate per affiliate) and our allies, and the NEC [National Executive Committee] of the ANC [in Lusaka, June 6]. The discussion concerned the process of negotiations, and was chaired by the GS [general secretary] of the ANC—A. Nzo.

2. It was stated that negotiations had already started. The ANC was being forced to negotiate by the combined power of imperialism (UK, USA, W. Germany), the eastern bloc (USSR, China), Africa and the Frontline States. The process of negotiation was inevitable and unstoppable, whether we liked it or not, and whether the time was right or not. Although the ANC and MDM agreed that we are not in a strong position for negotiations since the SOE [state of emergency] clampdown—we are being forced to establish our conditions for negotiations, whilst we try to build and strengthen organisation and campaigns on the ground.

3. *The pressure to negotiate is coming from the following countries:*
Imperialist Countries

USA: [President George H. W.] Bush says Botha must negotiate whilst the ANC is weak, but that the ANC must be included in any negotiated solution. The final result must be a government of 1 person 1 vote.

UK: [Prime Minister Margaret] Thatcher is the most reactionary and she must be regarded as a enemy. Her position is also for negotiated settlement but she wants to exclude the ANC as far as possible, and promote ethnic group rights. Also UK wants to divide MK from ANC by restricting MK and unbanning ANC.

W. Germany: Not very active on issue.

All these imperialist powers agree that:
(A) The Thatcher government must play the leading role in facilitating the process of negotiations.
(B) That Botha should negotiate whilst the MDM and the ANC are weak.
(C) If SA co-operates in the Namibian settlement then that will lay the basis for a negotiated settlement in SA.

Eastern Bloc Countries

Eastern bloc countries have agreed with imperialism on the need for a negotiated settlement to SA crisis. China has been saying to the SACP that apartheid must be removed through negotiations and thereafter the new government can gradually radicalise the economy. The Soviet Union also supports a negotiated solution to SA crisis, and has agreed that the Thatcher government must take the lead. It should be noted that these countries, who engaged in violent revolution to overthrow capitalism, now believe only in negotiations.

African Countries

The Frontline States (Angola, Botswana, Mozambique, Zimbabwe, Zambia): The key country here is Zambia who hosts the ANC. Zambia has been strongly pushing that ANC must find a negotiated settlement as Frontline States can no longer provide bases to ANC on their soil. They have said that if the ANC does not find a negotiated solution, then it will have to fight the war against apartheid from within the country. The Frontline States have said that after there is a settlement in Namibia, they will call a conference and lead in the settlement of SA. [President Kenneth] Kaunda has already indicated that he is willing to talk to F. W. de Klerk.

South Africa:
Nationalist government has:
(A) Had meetings with imperialist powers who told Botha to negotiate whilst ANC is weak.
(B) Had meetings with Inkatha where Gatsha [Buthelezi] told Botha that he will not participate in negotiations unless Botha releases all political prisoners who have done 15 years or more.
(C) Botha has also been putting pressure on Nelson Mandela to negotiate.
(D) Botha wants to break the revolutionary alliance of SACP/ANC before any negotiations.

4. The Thatcher government, with the backing of imperialism is trying to push their own plan for a negotiated settlement. They want Botha to release Mandela after the September 6 [1989] election, and then Thatcher will go to the Commonwealth Conference in October to push for the lifting of some economic sanctions against SA.

5. ANC and MDM need to respond to this process, because if we remain silent then Thatcher will pressure Frontline States to accept her proposal. Thus

a negotiation position must be formulated that can win the support of the Frontline States and the OAU [Organisation of African Unity] and so block Thatcher at the Commonwealth Conference. This negotiating position must be developed urgently by COSATU so that it can be communicated to the ANC, who in turn will take the position to the Frontline States before the OAU conference scheduled for July 20th.

6. Comrades need to urgently discuss the following questions:
- What further conditions for negotiations do we need? (for example, what kind of transitional government, multi-party or constituent assembly; when will we have ceasefire; what will be the position of SADF etc); what about group rights; what about Inkatha, Labour Party and all others in racist structures; what about black consciousness groups?)
- How do we as workers contribute our strength, ideas and direction to these negotiations?
- Why does USA think that UK must take lead in the negotiations? What will imperialism demand from us for their services and why are they doing this? How can we protect our interests against imperialism?
- The socialist countries believe in peaceful negotiation and that we do not have the power to take on the Botha regime militarily and/or through mass action. Why are they saying this? Do we agree or disagree with this? Can the armed struggle be stepped up?
- We believe in socialism. How can we force this to be on the agenda of any negotiations? How can we ensure that our interest in socialism is not forgotten by the negotiations?
- How are we going to change the balance of power in our favour during negotiations? How can we strengthen the working class forces so that the needs of workers are being attended to?

7. All shop stewards must be fully briefed on this report and must report/discuss with members. All the views of our members must be recorded and reported back for the locals, REC/RC [Regional and Regional Education Committees?] and nationally. Seminars will be arranged.

Document 171. "Preparing Ourselves for Freedom: Culture and the ANC Constitutional Guidelines." Discussion paper by Albie Sachs, Lusaka, July 1989 (abridged)

We all know where South Africa is, but we do not yet know what it is. Ours is the privileged generation that will make that discovery, if the apertures in our eyes are wide enough. The problem is whether we have sufficient cultural imagination to grasp the rich texture of the free and united South Africa that we have done so much to bring about; can we say that we have begun to grasp the full dimensions of the new country that is struggling to give birth to itself, or are we still trapped in the multiple ghettos of the apartheid imagination? Are we ready for freedom, or do we prefer to be angry victims?

The first proposition I make, and I do so fully aware of the fact that we are totally against censorship and for free speech, is that we should ban ourselves from saying that culture is a weapon of struggle. I suggest a period of, say, five years.

Allow me, as someone who has for many years been arguing precisely that art should be seen as an instrument of struggle, to explain why suddenly this affirmation seems not only banal and devoid of real content, but actually wrong and potentially harmful. It is not a question of separating art and politics, which no one can do, but of avoiding a shallow and forced relationship between the two.

In the first place, repeated incantation of the phrase results in an impoverishment of our art. Instead of getting real criticism, we get solidarity criticism. Our artists are not pushed to improve the quality of their work, it is enough that it be politically correct. The more fists and spears and guns, the better. The range of themes is narrowed down so much that all that is funny or curious or genuinely tragic in the world is extruded. Ambiguity and contradiction are completely shut out, and the only conflict permitted is that between the old and the new, as if there were only bad in the past and only good in the future. If one of us had the imagination of the Russian novelist Sholokhov, and wrote *And Quiet Flows the Tugela*, the central figure would not be a member of UDF or Cosatu, but would be aligned to Inkatha, resisting change, yet feeling oppression, thrown this way and that by conflicting emotions, and through his or her struggles and torments and moments of joy, the reader would be thrust into the whole drama of the struggle for a new South Africa. Instead, whether in poetry or painting or on the stage, we line up our good people on the one side and the bad ones on the other, occasionally permitting someone to pass from one column to the other, but never acknowledging that there is bad in the good, and, even more difficult, that there can be elements of good in the bad; you can tell who the good ones are, because in addition to being handsome of appearance, they can all recite sections of the Freedom Charter or passages of *Strategy and Tactics* at the drop of a beret.

In the case of a real instrument of struggle, there is no room for ambiguity: a gun is a gun is a gun, and if it were full of contradictions, it would fire in all sorts of directions and be useless for its purpose. But the power of art lies precisely in its capacity to expose contradictions and reveal hidden tensions—hence the danger of viewing it as if it were just another kind of missile-firing apparatus.

And what about love? We have published so many anthologies and journals and occasional poems and stories, and the number that deal with love do not make the fingers of a hand. Can it be that once we join the ANC we do not make love any more, that when the comrades go to bed they discuss the role of the white working class? Surely even those comrades whose tasks deny them the opportunity and direct possibilities of love, remember past love and dream of love to come. What are we fighting for, if not the right to express our humanity in all its forms, including our sense of fun and capacity for love and tenderness and our appreciation of the beauty of the world?

There is nothing that the apartheid rulers would like more than to convince us that because apartheid is ugly, the world is ugly. ANC members are full of fun and romanticism and dreams, we enjoy and wonder at the beauties of nature and the marvels of human creation, yet if you look at most of our art and literature you would think we are living in the greyest and most sombre of all worlds, completely shut in by apartheid. It is as though our rulers stalk every page and haunt every picture; everything is obsessed by the oppressors and the trauma they have imposed, little is about us and the new consciousness we are developing.

Listen in contrast to the music of Hugh Masekela, of Abdullah Ibrahim, of Jonas Gwangwa, of Miriam Makeba, and you are in a universe of wit and grace and vitality and intimacy, there is invention and modulation of mood, ecstasy and sadness; this is a cop-free world in which the emergent personality of our people manifests itself. Pick up a book of poems, or look at a woodcut or painting, and the solemnity is overwhelming. No one told Hugh or Abdullah to write their music in this or that way, to be progressive or committed, to introduce humour or gaiety, or a strong beat to denote optimism. Their music conveys genuine confidence because it rings from inside the personality and experience of each of them, from popular tradition and the sounds of contemporary life; we respond to it because it tells us something lovely and vivacious about ourselves, not because the lyrics are about how to win a strike or blow up a petrol dump. It bypasses, overwhelms, ignores apartheid, establishes its own space. So it could be with our writers and painters, if only they could shake off the gravity of their anguish and break free from the solemn formulas of commitment that people (like myself) have tried for so many years to impose upon them. Dumile [Feni], perhaps the greatest of our visual artists, was once asked why he did not draw scenes like one that was taking place in front of him: a crocodile of men being marched under arrest for not having their passes in order. At that moment a hearse drove slowly past and the men stood still and raised their hats. "That's what I want to draw," he said.

Yet damaging as a purely instrumental and non-dialectical view of culture is to artistic creation, far more serious is the way such a narrow view impoverishes the struggle itself. Culture is not something separate from the general struggle, an artefact that is brought in from time to time to mobilize the people or prove to the world that, after all, we are civilized. Culture is us, it is who we are, how we see ourselves and the vision we have of the world. In the course of participating in the culture of liberation, we constantly re-make ourselves. Organizations do not merely evince discipline and interaction between their members; our movement has developed a style of its own, a way of doing things and of expressing itself, a specific ANC personality. And what a rich mix it is—African tradition, church tradition, Gandhian tradition, revolutionary socialist tradition, liberal tradition, all the languages and ways and styles of the many communities in our country; we have black consciousness, and elements of red consciousness (some would say pink consciousness these days), even green consciousness (long before the Greens existed, we had green in our flag, representing the land). Now, with the dispersal of our members throughout the world, we also bring in aspects of the cultures of all humanity. . . .

This brings me to my second challenging proposition, namely, that the Constitutional Guidelines should not be applied to the sphere of culture. What?! . . . A member of the Department of Legal and Constitutional Affairs saying that the Guidelines should not be applied to culture? Precisely. It should be the other way round. Culture must make its input to the Guidelines. The whole point of the comprehensive consultations that are taking place around the Guidelines is that the membership, the people at large, should engage in constructive and concrete debate about the foundations of government in a post-apartheid South Africa. The Guidelines are more than a work-in-progress document, they set out well-deliberated views of the NEC [National Executive Committee] as enriched by an in-house seminar, but they are not presented as a final, cut-and-dried product, certainly not as a blueprint to be learnt off by heart and defended to the last misprint. Thus, the reasoning should not be: the Guidelines lay down the following for culture, therefore we must line up behind the Guidelines and become a conveyor belt for their implementation. On the contrary, what we need to do is analyse the Guidelines, see what implications they have for culture, and then say whether we agree and make whatever suggestions we have for their improvement. In part, we can say that the method is the message; the open debate the NEC wants on the Guidelines corresponds with the open society the Guidelines speak about. Apartheid has closed our society, stifled its voice, prevented people from speaking, and it is the historic mission of our organization to be the harbingers of freedom of conscience, debate, and opinion.

In my view, there are three aspects of the Guidelines that bear directly on the sphere of culture.

The first is the emphasis on building national unity and encouraging the development of a common patriotism, while fully recognizing the linguistic and cultural diversity of the country. . . .

The second aspect of the Guidelines with major implications for culture is the proposal for a Bill of Rights that guarantees freedom of expression and what is sometimes referred to as political pluralism. . . .

Finally, the Guidelines couple the guarantees of individual rights with the need to embark upon programmes of affirmative action. This too has clear implications for the sphere of culture. The South Africa in which individuals and groups can operate freely will be a South Africa in the process of transformation. A constitutional duty will be imposed upon the state, local authorities, and public and private institutions to take active steps to remove the massive inequalities created by centuries of colonial and racist domination. This gives concrete meaning to the statement that the doors of learning and culture shall be opened. We can envisage massive programmes of adult education and literacy, and extensive use of the media, to facilitate access by all to the cultural riches of our country and of the world. The challenge to our writers, musicians, painters, and dancers, to our dressmakers and potters and carpenters, to our broadcasters and journalists and publishers, to our teachers and sound specialists and film-makers, to all our cultural workers, is obvious.

DOCUMENT 172. "Negotiation—The Great Hoax." Editorial in *New Unity Movement Bulletin*, July 1989 (abridged)

In this year 1989, the ruling class and sections of the broad liberatory movement are paralysing political thinking with a kind of political drug: Negotiation. For the ruling class it means getting the rebellious masses to agree to accept some new forms of apartheid oppression and exploitation, by its bargaining with so-called "leaders" among the oppressed. For the opportunists, horse-dealers and plain sell-outs among the oppressed, generously helped by black liberals and white liberals, it means sitting down with the same rulers, bluffing themselves and deceiving the masses that liberation in all its senses can be got by "negotiating a settlement" with the oppressors. This is an act of treachery and deceit, no more, no less. What makes the act more deplorable is that it is now being taken up by all sorts of organisations within the "broad liberatory movement". It is not only the "Five Freedoms Forum" or the "Institute for a Democratic Alternative in South Africa" (IDASA) or the newly formed "Democratic Party"; or the born collaborators in the kitchens of the Tricameral Parliament (the House of Representatives and the House of Delegates) and the Homelands governments. From them we must expect this political deception and self-deception. But that the "negotiation" call should come from segments of the Trade Union Movement and the workers' leadership, from the exiled South African Communist Party and other movements in exile is far worse. . . .

For the idea that the fundamental rights of the masses can in the present circumstances be gained and protected by negotiation of any kind with the rulers is a disgraceful political hoax. The struggles of the masses have produced concessions. Some are vital: like the chance to organise Trade Unions on a non-racial basis. But, let us not forget, a Labour Relations Amendments Act has also been passed to cut off the political blood supply of the Unions and reduce them to voiceless, hamstrung bodies able to defend workers' rights in the workplace only. Then, some people may now swim at some beaches, but not at others; attend some theatres and cinemas, but not others; use some hotels and not others; get jobs as managers, personnel consultants and professionals in hospitals, courts and the civil service. But the fundamental citizen rights and the demands of the oppressed, the dismantling of homelands, locations and segregated schooling systems and the creation of a unified, non-racial democratic state have never been on the agenda of the ruling class. . . .

The political hoaxing is being backed up by the use of enormous funds poured into the country by world imperialism. Latest of these is some 1.7 billion rand from Tokyo, which monopolises the car, electronics, textile and much of the heavy industrial machinery business in Southern Africa. The heavily-funded trips overseas, to Lusaka and Harare by varieties of persons eminent, base and otherwise are another part of the exercise. So also is the heavily-funded operation of the National Sport Congress, the NSC, specially formed with the help of the Wits University "negotiators", certain trade union groups and sportspersons drawn by the awful scent of money into an operation to drag sportspersons to the "negotiation table". . . .

The weak, compromising, deceitful segments of the leadership of the masses have their fond illusions about negotiation. And they will join the ruling class in the conspiracy to crush those who oppose their dark, foul schemes to betray the masses. They will do this even as they claim to be advancing the interests of workers and the rural poor, the landless peasantry and the location-bound disfranchised masses!

Against this background we say the task of building national unity is not yet complete. The "negotiators" have never had national unity on their agenda. Unity has been an opportunistic threat, not a political task, with them. . . .

Non-collaboration is one of the most important weapons to secure the independent solutions which the oppressed seek. Their demands, their minimum demands, are contained in the [Unity Movement's] Ten-Point Programme. Their maximum demands are, in fact, much more. Negotiation cannot be the road to political democracy despite the tortured "logic" that seeks to draw the masses to the "negotiating table". It is in plain political language a cruel hoax.

DOCUMENT 173. Report to ANC on Women's Day meeting at Kaunda Square by Ronnie Kasrils, Lusaka, August 9, 1989

1. I was asked to brief the cdes [comrades] by the NEC [National Executive Committee] secretariat. Issues to be covered:
-situation at home
-Five Freedoms [Forum] visit to Lusaka
-negotiations
-Natal Peace initiative
-the Way Forward

The Commissar in charge of the meeting expected up to 40 cdes from 6 residences in the area.

2. The meeting was to commence at 9.30 am. Only 6 cdes were present. We began at 10 am with about 15 present. The Commissar who acted as Chairman asked for a report to be given but there was no Commander present so we commenced the meeting without any explanation concerning the absent cdes. Cdes continued to drift into the meeting. By 11 am there were 25 present.

3. I covered the points of the briefing at length and questions and discussion were then invited. The cdes scarcely related to the political issues. Their questions and statements were as follows:

i) They requested that their weapons be returned to them. They felt the leadership was not concerned about their security. If weapons were not returned, then leadership should at least provide security guards to protect them. They also complained that some cdes in Lusaka have weapons and asked why the residences were left defenceless. When I asked them if they knew why we had to disarm them, they stated that no reasons had been given. I explained the circumstances that had led to the decision and promised to report their request to the leadership.

ii) They asked why it had taken so long for them to receive a briefing on the issue of negotiations and the situation at home. They complained that briefings were few and far between.

iii) They enquired whether it was because the leadership was so busy meeting delegations from home, such as businessmen and the FFF that we were failing to visit them.

iv) They asked why they had to go on their own initiative to the RC [Regional Committee?] to look for the MK leaders and press for their deployment home (i.e. "Mchina"). They felt that if the leaders were serious about deploying them they would be coming to the residences to interview them.

v) They said they were told that the armed struggle is central to our efforts but that the leadership don't act in a practical way to organise the trained cadres, giving them the impression that we are in fact not serious. They say they have to go begging for Mchina at the RC, that the leaders don't seem to listen to what they are saying, that they are not given briefings, that they are not interviewed.

vi) Finally, they said that those in charge should stand aside if they can't do the job.

4. I answered their questions to the best of my ability and did what I could to raise their morale. I situated my remarks in the context of the defiance struggle taking place at home which needs to be reinforced by our own actions, struck an optimistic note, pointed out the realistic problems we face as a movement, called on them to maintain discipline and have faith in the leadership at this crucial time where change is imminent and promised to raise their questions and concerns with the leadership.

I must say that this was the most dispirited group of cdes I have met in a long time and that they seemed perfectly genuine in their complaints. These complaints need to be urgently addressed and this can be done by giving the cdes the attention they deserve which means increasing briefings and serious interviews regarding their deployment. The cdes did not waste time about their adverse conditions of life here. My own observation showed me that the poor conditions pertaining in their residence still prevail and that we do not seem to have taken any action to improve their standard of life here. If we are to carry the cdes with us at this complex stage of the struggle, particularly in regard to the question of negotiations, we must show them in deed and not simply in word, that we are serious about the importance of armed struggle. By this I mean not simply the question of increasing our actions but by paying them the respect due to them.

Ronnie Kasrils 9.8.89

Copy to: NEC Secretariat
           Army Commander
           Secretary of PMC [Politico-Military Council]

Document 174. "Declaration of the Organisation of African Unity Ad Hoc Committee on Southern Africa on the Question of South Africa" (The Harare Declaration), August 21, 1989 (abridged)

I. PREAMBLE

[The preamble declares that apartheid is an obstacle to peace and an affront to justice and human dignity, and must be abandoned. The Organisation of African Unity favors democratic rule and, consistent with the Lusaka Manifesto of two decades ago, prefers solutions arrived at by peaceful means. It therefore pledges to support the positions stated below.]

II. STATEMENT OF PRINCIPLES

14. We believe that a conjuncture of circumstances exists which, if there is a demonstrable readiness on the part of the Pretoria regime to engage in negotiations genuinely and seriously, could create the possibility to end apartheid through negotiations. Such an eventuality would be an expression of the long standing preference of the majority of the people of South Africa to arrive at a political settlement.

15. We would therefore encourage the people of South Africa, as part of their overall struggle, to get together to negotiate an end to the apartheid system and agree on all the measures that are necessary to transform their country into a non-racial democracy. We support the position held by the majority of the people of South Africa that these objectives, and not the amendment or reform of the apartheid system, should be the aims of the negotiations.

16. We are at one with them that the outcome of such a process should be a new constitutional order based on the following principles, among others:
• South Africa shall become a united, democratic and non-racial state.
• All its people shall enjoy common and equal citizenship and nationality, regardless of race, colour, sex or creed.
• All its people shall have the right to participate in the government and administration of the country on the basis of a universal suffrage, exercised through one person one vote, under a common voters' roll
• All shall have the right to form and join any political party of their choice, provided that this is not in furtherance of racism.

- All shall enjoy universally recognised human rights, freedoms and civil liberties, protected under an entrenched Bill of Rights.
- South Africa shall have a new legal system which shall guarantee equality of all before the law.
- South Africa shall have an independent and non-racial judiciary.
- There shall be created an economic order which shall promote and advance the well-being of all South Africans.
- A democratic South Africa shall respect the rights, sovereignty and territorial integrity of all countries and pursue a policy of peace, friendship, and mutually beneficial co-operation with all peoples.

17. We believe that agreement on the above principles shall constitute the foundation for an internationally acceptable solution which shall enable South Africa to take its rightful place as an equal partner among the African and world community of nations.

III. CLIMATE FOR NEGOTIATIONS

18. Together with the rest of the world, we believe that it is essential, before any negotiations can take place, that the necessary climate for negotiations be created. The apartheid regime has the urgent responsibility to respond positively to this universally acclaimed demand and thus create this climate.

19. Accordingly, the present regime should, at the very least:
- Release all political prisoners and detainees unconditionally and refrain from imposing any restrictions on them;
- Lift all bans and restrictions on all proscribed and restricted organisations and persons;
- Remove all troops from the townships;
- End the state of emergency and repeal all legislation, such as, and including the Internal Security Act, designed to circumscribe political activity; and,
- Cease all political trials and political executions.

20. These measures are necessary to produce the conditions in which free political discussion can take place—an essential condition to ensure that the people themselves participate in the process of remaking their country. The measures listed above should therefore precede negotiations.

IV. GUIDELINES TO THE PROCESS OF NEGOTIATION

21. We support the view of the South African liberation movement that upon the creation of this climate, the process of negotiations should commence along the following lines:
- Discussions should take place between the liberation movement and the South African regime to achieve the suspension of hostilities on both sides by agreeing to a mutually binding ceasefire.
- Negotiations should then proceed to establish the basis for the adoption of a new Constitution by agreeing on, among others, the Principles enunciated above.

- Having agreed on these principles, the parties should then negotiate the necessary mechanism for drawing up the new Constitution.
- The parties shall define and agree on the role to be played by the international community in ensuring a successful transition to a democratic order.
- The parties shall agree on the formation of an interim government to supervise the process of the drawing up and adoption of a new constitution; govern and administer the country, as well as effect the transition to a democratic order including the holding of elections.
- After the adoption of the new Constitution, all armed hostilities will be deemed to have formally terminated.
- For its part, the international community would lift the sanctions that have been imposed against apartheid South Africa.

22. The new South Africa shall qualify for membership of the Organisation of African Unity.

V. PROGRAMME OF ACTION

23. In pursuance of the objectives stated in this document, the Organisation of African Unity hereby commits itself to:
- Inform governments and inter-governmental organisations throughout the world, including the Non-Aligned Movement, the United Nations General Assembly, the Security Council, the Commonwealth and others of these perspectives, and solicit their support.
- Mandate the OAU Ad-Hoc Committee on Southern Africa, acting as the representative of the OAU and assisted by the Frontline States, to remain seized of the issue of a political resolution of the South African question.
- Step up all-round support for the South African liberation movement and campaign in the rest of the world in pursuance of this objective.
- Intensify the campaign for mandatory and comprehensive sanctions against apartheid South Africa; in this regard, immediately mobilise against the rescheduling of Pretoria's foreign debt; work for the imposition of a mandatory oil embargo and the full observance by all countries of the arms embargo.
- Ensure that the African continent does not relax existing measures for the total isolation of apartheid South Africa.
- Continue to monitor the situation in Namibia and extend all necessary support to SWAPO in its struggle for a genuinely independent Namibia.
- Extend such assistance as the Governments of Angola and Mozambique may request in order to secure peace for their peoples; and
- Render all possible assistance to the Frontline States to enable them to withstand Pretoria's campaign of aggression and destabilisation and enable them to continue to give their all-round support to the people of Namibia and South Africa.

24. We appeal to all people of goodwill throughout the world to support this Programme of Action as a necessary measure to secure the earliest liquidation of the apartheid system and the transformation of South Africa into a united, democratic and non-racial country.

Document 175. "Apartheid is Dying—Bury It Now." Natal Indian Congress and the Durban Municipal Employees Union flyer, August 1989

In the true spirit of non-racialism and unity our people are saying NO to apartheid laws and YES to a united non-racial democratic South Africa.

YES the majority of our people are involved in a campaign to bring about everlasting peace and justice in our country.

Are you part of this majority ?

- In Boksburg the supporters of apartheid are suffering because their votes led to a consumer boycott of white shops in their area.
- The National Party is confused and cannot rule anymore.
- [Allan] Hendrickse went for a swim in a white beach but later apologised to P. W. Botha for doing so.
- Ismail Omar of Solidarity planned to swim at the whites only beach but chickened out.
- The disgraced [Amichand] Rajbansi is now facing criminal charges.
- Candidates and their agents are using force and lies to get our people to vote for them.
- In Natal after 23 days of so-called special voting only 10% of our people have voted for HOD [House of Delegates]. It is clear that empty promises, lies, bribes, and violence will not force us to vote for these supporters of apartheid.

Join the majority who will not vote in an apartheid election.

DEFIANCE CAMPAIGN UPDATE:

- We launched a successful campaign against segregated hospitals. For the first time black patients without cards were treated in white hospitals throughout South Africa.
- Organisations of the people which were banned by the Government have begun to declare themselves unbanned.
- Our leaders who have been banned and prevented from working with their people are now openly and fearlessly defying their banning order.
- On 26 & 27 August workers throughout the country will meet to decide what action to take against the anti-worker Labour Relations Act.
- In Cape Town Archbishop [Desmond] Tutu led 800 people onto Blouberg Strand, a "whites only" beach. More than 2000 resisters were turned away.
- Over last weekend teachers of all races came together to form one teachers union. They have now started an "ALL SCHOOLS FOR ALL PEOPLE" CAMPAIGN.

ON SUNDAY 3 SEPTEMBER WE WILL BE GOING TO
ADDINGTON BEACH FOR A PICNIC.
ARE YOU COMING TOO???

JOIN THE MASS DEMOCRATIC MOVEMENT FOR A NON-RACIAL
DEMOCRATIC SOUTH AFRICA
DON'T VOTE DON'T VOTE

Document 176. Letter from ANC Department of Religious Affairs about visit by Zionist church leaders, Lusaka, October 5, 1989

The Administrative Secretary
IPC [Internal Political Committee]
P.O. Box 31791
LUSAKA

Dear Comrade

Re: Visit: Leaders of Zionist African Independent Churches

We hereby wish to bring to your attention that a delegation of the above-mentioned churches will be visiting Lusaka on the 17th November, 1989. There are some points we would like to highlight about this said delegation, namely:

(i) That they are conservative, and had been marginalised for a long time by the Main Line Churches. It is now that some progressive church groups have decided to bring them into the Mass Democratic Movement.
(ii) Their level of education is low, hence, they are not sophisticated.
(iii) They are vulnerable to the far right church groups which have their origin in America, e.g. [Jimmy] Swaggart, Rhema, etc. It is because of this factor that we feel they need to be protected by the movement.
(iv) Due to their still feudalistic church structure they are very sceptical about the leadership role of the youth and women in the struggle.

We therefore request your office to select a suitable matured delegation of the ANC which will meet them, considering the points highlighted above. We lay emphasis on the selection because among other things, our indigenous languages will be used during this important consultation, as indicated in (ii) above.

Some of the members of the delegation are: (i) Archbishop [N. H.] Ngada, (ii) Archbishop [Paul] Makhubu, (iii) Archbishop [T. W.] Ntongana and (iv) Archbishop [Z]. Reliable sources within the SACC [SA Council of Churches] hinted that Archbishop [Z] is suspected to be working with the enemy, but I have asked them to bring him along. I therefore request that precautionary measures should be taken. The delegation will be comprised of about 10 to 15 of them. Attached is the press cutting.

Sound Faith, Love and Endurance
F. F. Gqiba (Rev) ANC CHAPLAIN

Document 177. "Keeper of the Keys." Interview with Archbishop Desmond Tutu by Paul Bell, *Leadership SA*, October 1989 (abridged)

The peace marches through Cape Town and other cities have their origins in the churches' Standing for the Truth campaign and the Mass Democratic

Movement's defiance campaign. What was the background to the church campaign, and to what extent has it co-operated with the other?

The government's banning of organizations in February 1988 forced the churches to take a stand, starting with the march to Parliament, during which I and several other church leaders were arrested. The churches were being pushed into the vacuum created by government's action. This was a high water mark for interdenominational co-operation. After our release we said we hoped this was not going to be a flash in the pan, that we were now going to try and have a sustained movement. The Standing for the Truth campaign was born at a church convention later last year. We were saying we were going to have to put our bodies where our mouths were, in a manner of speaking. When restrictions and bannings escalated, people said it was important that the churches especially show they really mean business when they say they are non-violent. We showed that the non-violent option actually can work, especially to those who might be inclined to use the other option. There was a convergence with the MDM, which decided at about the same time that a defiance campaign should happen.

Central to this is a concept with its origins in passive resistance but which is now defined as non-violent direct action. How do you define it?

Part of the new nomenclature is an effort to underline the positive nature of what you're doing; that it is not a reactive, negative thing. It is not so much a defiance or disobedience. Rather it is something that is positive, an obedience of God's laws when these come into conflict with man's laws. It is not merely passively doing nothing. Certain things are direct action, but it is action meant to be non-violent. Like going onto the beaches. You wouldn't call that passive, but you accept the principle that, for example, you don't regard your adversary as an enemy but as a potential friend to be won over. You do not taunt people and you have a very profound respect for law, which is why you obey God's law.

Day to day, and event to event, how have you defined your personal role?

I think there was a buildup. We were all agreed as church leaders that we were now in an active phase, starting in February last year. The [September general] election gave us another point at which to highlight our concerns. And a number of things happened. We had fewer people under restrictions and were therefore able to make decisions fairly quickly. When the restricted persons "unrestricted" themselves, the churches offered to support them and to take appropriate action if anything happened to them. We were no longer just going to mouth pious resolutions.

I suppose it has been a help to have been the Archbishop of Cape Town, and to have been involved to some extent from 1976 until now. . . . I have been exceedingly fortunate in the calibre of people around me. And the Cathedral's support has been strategically quite crucial. . . . I have greater freedom of movement to some extent than a political leader. Church leaders do consult with the people, but they have recognised our autonomy as church persons, that our ultimate responsibility is to God, and they respect our understanding of the imperatives that God gives. Not that we are infallible. Not that we would ride roughshod. I hear the advice of community leaders, and I also have my own advisors, the senior persons in the diocese, the dean, archdeacons, and the other bishops. I often test things out against them, although I don't always take their advice. . . .

What, do you think, have been the effects of the march on the political atmosphere in the country?

It depends which side you are on. You could say: "Here is a government that is giving in," or: "Here is a government that is allowing peaceful protest to happen, and so it's a feather in the cap for that government." For me, it clearly demonstrated two very important things. First, that government had failed, despite all its repression, to knock the stuffing out of the people. It is remarkable. You stand up on a Friday in a church and say: "Let's march on Wednesday." You don't know how many people are going to pitch up. Then you get this incredible turnout. . . .

The second is that, despite all that has happened people actually care about a non-racial South Africa. It brings tears to your eyes. When you looked at the concourse that day and you said that people should hold hands, and you saw the kaleidoscope of colour and that people were just people, you saw it was actually for real. We are willing to be a country that, despite all that has conspired to work to the contrary, will be a country that counts. Because we are people.

It was a wonderful thing to be vindicated in the way that we were. And to be vindicated also in the matter of saying that, if you keep the police away, people will almost always be peaceful. When you look at the numbers of people involved in Johannesburg and Cape Town, it is overwhelming evidence that people are committed to peace and non-violence, even when they don't seem to have had any specific training. When Allan [Boesak] said to the people: "Brothers and sisters, this march is over," the [Cape Town] Parade, which had been chock-a-block, was clear within minutes. We went back to the Cathedral and said: "Let's sit down and just be quiet and just say thank you to God." We recognised that it could have gone so very badly wrong. And yet I myself am just thrilled at the vindication of the people.

It seems very unlikely that this could have happened in the PW Botha era. Is there, do you believe, anything different about FW de Klerk?

We've got to say yes. We have to remember, though, that it was under his Acting State Presidency that they used dogs and whips and tear gas and even threatened to use live ammunition, to stop people going onto beaches. We are seeing at the present time the fundamental schizophrenia that affects South Africa. Government spokespersons often say they really don't care what the world thinks, and then they behave in a way that demonstrates that they care very, very much.

I think there is a difference in style. I still want to see the evidence that there is a difference in substance. We still have people in detention; we've still got a state of emergency which has done nothing except to provide a screen behind which the police have been able to carry out their brutality.... We've had nearly four years of emergency and it has not helped to get rid of the root causes....

People have been urged to "give FW a chance". How do you respond to that notion?

I say I've heard this before. The business community said it after the [1979] Carlton conference, when they were dazzled by PW's nifty footwork. One heard it in the [1983] referendum campaign.... When others said, this constitution PW [Botha] is putting to you is fatally flawed, people said no, no, no, no! Give him a chance. We've never said we wanted everything. In 1980 we said all government need do was one or two things to demonstrate dramatically to the people that it was serious about change, not reform. We are not impressed by reformists. To talk about reform is to put us off right from the beginning. What we want is not reform, it is change.

Most of the white community do not actually want apartheid removed; it has brought them so many benefits. They want slight adjustments to remove the most horrendous aspect of it, which made the international community annoyed. But if they were able to produce something that made the international community say, "These guys are not so bad, and the loans can come again and it's business as usual," they wouldn't care two hoots about the rest.

A year or 18 months ago I spoke to three of the biggest business leaders at a private dinner. It was set up so we could try to find each other. It ended with me refusing to speak, sitting with my head in my hands, like this. They were saying they firmly believed most blacks wanted a full stomach and a roof over their head. I said: "Gentlemen, even for us there are some things that are slightly more important than that." That they could actually, to my face, have the capacity to insult our people.... Maybe they were not aware of it but it was a very deep hurt. We were speaking not just at cross purposes; we were speaking from different worlds.

Are you saying that, as far as you are concerned, whites still don't understand what blacks mean when they talk about change?

No; there are very many whites who certainly have been told now *ad nauseam* what the score is. Someone said it's impossible to wake up someone who is pretending to be asleep. No, many, many white people know what we are talking about and are as committed as anybody else to the ending of this system. I don't want to generalise, but I would say that many would prefer not to know.

Given the events of the last few weeks, there seems to be a greater lightness in the political atmosphere; a sense of greater manoeuvrability than there was at the beginning of this year. Do you accept that? You appear to be not as optimistic as one might have imagined.

I have always known that we are going to win. It doesn't depend on what white people think, you know. Really. And I'm not being arrogant either. I'm just saying that the moral imperatives are such that it actually doesn't matter, because there is no way that justice will not win out in the end, that repression will continue for ever and ever. The truth of the matter is that it's quite incredible that people can fly into Cape Town, over Crossroads and Khayelitsha, every day, and it doesn't sear them, it doesn't make them think, "How can we tolerate this obscene cheek-by-jowl existence with this sort of thing?" That they can accept the vilification of people like ourselves by the system. You hear Anglicans, Christians, who want to say to me, "Why do you advocate this, that and the other?" and think I am answerable to them. But I am no longer going to justify myself to white people. I will do what I believe is right. And those who find they cannot take it, tough luck.

But yes, there *is* a change in the sense that you have someone now, the State President, who does mind. You have someone who doesn't— That [wagging] finger! PW annoyed very many powerful people! We got some of them coming here after meeting with him and saying: "If anything helped to change our views about sanctions, it was our meeting with PW." And this from two powerful US senators who said to us: "We are from the conservative wing of the Democratic Party, but the way that guy treated us. . . . "

What, do you think, is the key possibility that FW de Klerk holds out?

It is possible that FW will realise that his way back into the world is going to be via us. It is only when the oppressed people and their leadership say things have changed, or are changing, that the world will sit up and take notice. The government can spend all the money it likes, but even simple things like whether he gets invited to the White House or not will depend on whether our friends think he ought to be. When the US president can talk to us and ask us: "Should I invite him? . . ."

You still have to say these chaps are extraordinary. In April this year there were 250,000 empty places in white schools which they say will not be taken by black children in overcrowded facilities. It's crazy! They are still saying group rights, group whatever. But no! To show we are reasonable creatures, we have said: "You've got six to nine months in which to begin to show that you really mean business."

How do you define the pressures on government, and what do you expect to happen in that time?

The parameters are the forthcoming meeting of Commonwealth heads of government in Kuala Lumpur—by which time Mr de Klerk will have to have done something to enable Mrs Thatcher to withstand the pressures there. Then there's the debt rescheduling in June next year. We realise he has a constituency that he has to nurse, but this constituency actually wants to be led. All its fears of a right-wing sweep have been disproved. I think this country wants boldness; it wants to see a president say: "We are scrapping Group Areas, and this and that and the other." Let him say: "We have to take people along. Here is my timetable. This is what I plan to do in this period to help to avoid chaotic change." He will be amazed at the number of people who would come to his support. And the world! How can one say to the world, "Don't reschedule these loans," when the man has said, "We are scrapping the acts. Detainees are out. Those who have been restricted are unrestricted."

When you met Mr de Klerk last week [on October 11], what impression did you gain of his commitment to change?

We had very earnest and intensive discussions. We came away impressed that there was an obvious concern regarding what we had to tell him, but we did not come away with specifics which would satisfy those we believe we represent. I must reiterate, however, that we went as facilitators, not negotiators. Our concern is that negotiations should get off the ground—genuine negotiations. We took the initiative to see Mr de Klerk because we seek a way out of the impasse.

Dr [Gerrit] Viljoen articulated the understanding that there was agreement on the issues we raised, that government wanted to normalise the security situation, i.e. lift the emergency; normalise the legislative situation, i.e. move away from discriminatory legislation; find an acceptable way of identifying those who would be regarded as authentic representatives of the various constituencies; and determine, by agreement, the mode in which negotiations would happen.

None of us would want further sanctions, even the present sanctions, if we could get the commitment we were seeking from Mr de Klerk in a specific timetable. We would be prepared to ask our friends to put their sanctions programmes on hold if we felt there was a commitment we could accept, that certain first actions had been taken which gave us to believe that a new dispensation was emerging. Mr de Klerk said that while we had real problems, so did he. We recognised that, but—without putting pistols to anybody's head—we are saying that if these things happened, we for our part would be able to say to our people: "Give them a chance, we think they are serious."

DOCUMENT 178. Affidavit of Butana Almond Nofomela, Pretoria, handwritten, October 19, 1989

I, the undersigned, Butana Almond Nofomela, do hereby make oath and state:

1. I am a thirty two year old male presently under sentence of death. My execution is scheduled for tomorrow morning, 20 October 1989, at 07 hours.
2. The contents hereof, unless [illegible] by the context, are true to the best of my personal knowledge and belief.
3. I did not commit the murder for which I stand condemned. I repeat my [illegible] at the trial which led to my death sentence. I confirm the contentions raised therein by myself and on my behalf by my Counsel.

4. I wish to hereby reveal facts about my past which, I respectfully contend, might very well have had a bearing on my conviction and/or sentence of death had they been known to the Trial Court, Appeal Court and the Honourable [illegible].
5. I was a member of the security branch stationed at headquarters in Pretoria from 1981 until my sentence of death on 2 September 1987.
6. During the period of my service in the security branch, I served under station commander Brig[adier Willem] Schoon. In 1981 I was appointed a member of the security branch's assassination squad, and I served under Capt. Johannes Dirk Coetzee, who was my commanding officer in the field.
7. Some time during late 1981 I was briefed by Brig. Schoon and Capt. Coetzee at Pretoria to eliminate a certain Durban attorney, Griffiths Mxenge. I was told by my superiors that Mxenge was to be eliminated for his activities within the African National Congress. They instructed me to travel to Durban in the company of Brian Justice Ngqulunga, David Tshikalange and Joseph Mamasela, colleagues of mine in the assassination squad. I was the leader of this group that was to eliminate Mxenge, and initially I was briefed alone. Thereafter, also in Pretoria, Coetzee briefed the four of us together.
8. Thereafter, Brian, David, Joseph and I travelled to Durban in one car—a Toyota bakkie [pick-up truck] with a canopy—where we met Coetzee at C.R. Swart Police Station. Coetzee had travelled to Durban separately.
9. Coetzee there gave us a photograph of Mxenge, and he furnished us with details as to Mxenge's whereabouts. Coetzee instructed us specifically not to shoot Mxenge, but to kill him with a knife. Coetzee also mentioned that there were vicious dogs where Mxenge lived, and he gave me a poison which he told me to mix with meat and to throw the meat into the yard for the dogs to eat and hopefully die.
10. That same day Brian, David, Joseph and I (Brian always drove as he knows Durban well) went to Mxenge's house in the early evening, after I had bought the meat and mixed it with the poison. On the way to Mxenge's home, Brian stopped the bakkie for me to get out and walk the rest of the way to the house. Brian and the others waited in the bakkie at a spot which was on the route that Mxenge normally took on his way home from work. The idea was that if he came past, they would attempt to stop him and kidnap him.
11. I in the meantime went to the house and threw the meat into the yard as planned. I returned to the others, but Mxenge had not yet appeared.
12. We then returned to the C.R. Swart Police Station, where we were barracked for the duration of our stay in Durban.
13. For the next few days we monitored Mxenge's movements. Then on a particular day, we parked our car in the middle of the road that he normally used to return home from work, very close to his home. It was late afternoon. We saw a white Audi approaching from a distance. We then opened the bonnet of the bakkie, pretending that the bakkie was stuck. Mxenge stopped behind the bakkie. He opened his window and asked

whether he could help us. I approached the car, and I said "yes please." He then switched off his ignition, and at the same time I produced my firearm, a Makarov pistol. I opened the door, and I ordered him to move across so that Brian could get in behind the wheel. Brian got in behind the wheel. Brian had also produced a firearm, and Joseph got into the back of Mxenge's car. I ordered David to follow us in our bakkie, and then I got into the back of Mxenge's car as well.

14. We had already decided previously that we would take Mxenge to the Umlazi Stadium, and that we would kill him there. At the stadium, more particularly outside the stadium, we all got out and ordered Mxenge to get out as well. We then started assaulting him with kicks and punches, until he fell to the ground. We then all stabbed him several times. He immediately died, and we commenced butchering his body. In accordance with our instructions from Capt. Coetzee, we removed Mxenge's items of value like money and a watch in order to simulate a robbery.

15. From the stadium, where we left Mxenge's body, we returned to the C.R. Swart Police Station with the bakkie and Mxenge's car. We parked both vehicles in a courtyard parking area at a Courthouse alongside the Police Station. Then I went into the Police Station to inform Capt. Coetzee that the mission had been completed. I then accompanied Coetzee to Mxenge's car, and Coetzee removed the number plates thereof and fixed false number plates to the car. He then dismissed the other three, and told me to accompany him to Piet Retief that night. He drove Mxenge's car, and I drove Coetzee's service bakkie.

16. In the early hours of the following morning we arrived at the Piet Retief Police Station, where we were met by certain men in plainclothes. They were expecting us. Coetzee drove Mxenge's car and I followed in the bakkie to the home of one of these men, and the car was parked in the garage. The garage was closed, and we all, the two men, Coetzee and I, set about stripping the car of the spare wheel, radio/tape, booster, sheepskins and [foil?] which we removed from the car and placed in Coetzee's car. Then Coetzee and one of the men in Mxenge's car, I in the bakkie and the other man in his own car drove towards the Swaziland border. We parked the cars in a plantation. Coetzee then ordered me to syphon petrol from the bakkie. I did so, and poured the petrol into a container that I had been carrying in the bakkie.

17. Coetzee then drove Mxenge's car a distance of some 500 metres into the plantation. He then beckoned me to come with the petrol in the car. He took the petrol and poured it all on the inside of Mxenge's car, and then the outside. He then poured a line of petrol outside the car leading up to the car, and lit the gas in this line. The flames reached the car, and explosive sounds were made as the car burnt. We waited until the fire burnt itself out. We then all returned to Piet Retief, leaving the burnt out shell of Mxenge's car in the plantation.

18. Coetzee and I immediately returned from Piet Retief to Durban in Coetzee's bakkie.

19. Some days thereafter, Brian, David, Joseph and I returned to Pretoria in

the service [vehicles] which we had travelled to Durban in, and Coetzee returned in his service bakkie. We drove in convoy.

20. The next day was month end. [Usually] at month's end we had a week off. Before going off, Coetzee handed Brian, David, Joseph and I R1000-00 [about $1000] each, which he said was from Brig. Schoon for successfully eliminating Mxenge.

21. Before we went off for our week, in fact, immediately after our return from Durban, all the items that had been removed from Mxenge's car and placed in Coetzee's service bakkie in Piet Retief were given to Sgt. Schutte by Capt. Coetzee in my presence, with the instruction that the radio/tape and booster were to be installed in Brig. Schoon's [illegible] vehicle. After my return from one week leave, Schutte remarked to me informally that the radio/tape had been installed into Brig. Schoon's [illegible] vehicle.

22. After my return from one week's leave, Capt. Coetzee informed me that Mxenge's wife is also active in the ANC's activities, and that he might require me to eliminate her as well at some future date. This was the last I heard of that.

23. I was involved in approximately eight other assassinations during my stint in the assassination squad, and also numerous kidnappings. At this stage, I do not recall the names of any of the victims. Some of the assassinations, four in fact, took place in Swaziland, one in Botswana, one in M[illegible], and one in Krugersdorp. The victims were all ANC members, except in Krugersdorp, where the victim was the brother of an ANC terrorist. This terrorist had allegedly shot and killed a policeman in De Weldt. The brother had been working in the United Building Society as a security guard (Krugersdorp branch).

24. All these missions were [prepared?] under different officers in the security branch. [Illegible] Capt. Coetzee, Maj. [Eugene] De Kock, Lt Vermeulen, [illegible] are their officers. Their superior was at all times Brig. Schoon, who was at all times aware of these matters.

25. I am instructed that due to the shortage of time, I cannot here furnish details of these other missions.

26. I now wish to explain why I have only revealed all this information at this stage. Maj. De Kock visited me with Capt. Naude after my sentence of death. De Kock told me that Brig. Schoon had asked him to convey to me that I was not to reveal anything about my activities as a member of the assassination squad, and he further promised that they will help me out of this problem. The visit by De Kock and Naude was in 1987. Thereafter other members of the security branch visited me at various intervals. They were Lt. Van Dyk, Lt. [illegible], Const[able] Mofalapetsa, Const. Khumalo, and some whose names I don't know. They all brought messages from Maj. De Kock that steps are being taken to get me out of the Maximum Prison.

27. Then on 12 October 1989 I received my notice of execution, and on 17 October 1989 a Capt. Khoza and a certain Lt., both members of the security branch, visited me and informed me that the instruction from

Maj. De Kock was that I should take the pain. I then realised that I had been betrayed by my superior officer, who had promised to assist me in getting out of the Maximum Prison.
28. It was at that stage that I decided to reveal all of the aforegoing; and I sent a message to the Lawyers For Human Rights to send someone to me to take a statement accordingly and to apply for a stay of my execution.

Signature: Butana Almond Nofomela

SIGNED AND SWORN TO BEFORE ME AT PRETORIA ON THIS THE 19TH DAY OF OCTOBER 1989, THE DEPONENT HAVING ACKNOWLEDGED THAT HE KNOWS AND UNDERSTANDS THE CONTENTS OF THIS AFFIDAVIT AND THAT HE CONSIDERS THE OATH TAKEN BY HIM TO BE BINDING ON HIS CONSCIENCE.

Seal and signature [illegible]

DOCUMENT 179. "Party Piece." Interview with Cyril Ramaphosa by Paul Bell, *Leadership SA,* November 1989 (abridged)

What is your general view of President de Klerk and his initiatives so far?
A new man, having come to power, is trying to show the people of South Africa and the world that he is a new broom, that he is committed to reforming South Africa. But he still has the legacy of the past. He is still part and parcel of the National Party machinery which is still committed to apartheid; although the rhetoric appears to be against apartheid and for its abolition. . . . If you go by de Klerk's formula, the white sector will remain intact as a group, whether it be Afrikaner, Jew or Portuguese. But black people will be subdivided into neat little ethnic compartments, so that ultimately the whites will retain power, irrespective of our wishes. . . .

We perceive some signs on government's part that it wants to move forward, but the problem is, they talk with forked tongues. They are not coming out clearly. . . . We say . . . there cannot be talks about talks until the climate for negotiation has been made conducive. Creating that climate means they have to unban organizations. We cannot talk to de Klerk about unbanning the ANC until he does it. We cannot talk to him about releasing political prisoners until he does it. He has to fulfill certain conditions before there can be any negotiation. If the ANC were to go to talks about talks, it would be doing so without a mandate from the people. The ANC has to obtain a very clear mandate from our people before it can enter into any form of talks.

Do you intend to begin gathering that mandate at your Conference for a Democratic Future planned for December?
No, it will not be mandate gathering; it will be to explain the views of our people as a whole on the question of negotiation. . . . We have been developing a strategy on the question of negotiations and how the necessary cli-

mate should be created. We are also discussing the OAU document [Harare Declaration]. As far as the MDM is concerned, the approach is that negotiations should be seen by our people as another arena of struggle.

Should that not be interpreted by the government as an indication that you do not intend to negotiate in good faith, that negotiations for you are simply part of the struggle rather than actually seeking agreement?

No, our strategic objective in negotiations is that they must in the end win us a free, non-racial, democratic South Africa. In proceeding to negotiations we have to take our people with us. We have to be accountable to all our people, through various structures from grassroots level upwards. We have to have representatives properly mandated to sit at the negotiating table. In other words, there must be mass approval, mass action, as we proceed to the negotiating table. Our people must understand fully what is being discussed. At a mass level they must be able to approve or disapprove the various proposals that may emanate from the negotiators they will have elected. Nor should anyone expect this process to be over quickly: negotiations will be protracted. . . . To us negotiation is not an end in itself. It is a process which will lead to a strategic objective. So we do not see the massive upsurge of our people stopping when negotiations commence.

[Government minister] *Gerrit Viljoen [foresees] a process in which black people would elect leaders to represent them in negotiations. Under what conditions would the MDM and the ANC be prepared to contemplate participation in that?*

I think the premise government is working on is misguided. To prescribe that we elect black representatives is unacceptable, in that it is premised on racism. We would not regard representatives elected in this way as authentic. The ANC and MDM have a number of white members and supporters. We will refuse to hold an election for Africans only. The ANC and MDM are composed of people of Indian origin, coloureds, Africans, as well as whites. We would be negating the true non-racial character of the MDM and indeed the ANC, if we were to participate in elections according to government's formula. This is another indication that the de Klerk government is not genuine about negotiations. It still wants to have representation at the negotiating table on a group basis, under white overlordship.

So, if government's premise is wrong, what would be the correct one in terms of putting together a negotiation structure and electing representatives to that structure?

I am sure that the ANC, when unbanned, will prove beyond doubt that it enjoys mass support. Support for the ANC, which already runs into millions, will immediately be seen to be overwhelming. Millions of people, including whites and people in the independent homelands, would immediately become card-carrying members. The release of the political prisoners has highlighted the profile of the ANC; it has shown, even to government, that the

ANC has to play centre stage at the negotiations. Once that has been arrived at, the ANC will be the key negotiator representing the people.

If the ANC discounts an electoral process in determining representatives and automatically accords to itself a pre-eminent role in negotiations, is it effectively saying that, if government won't negotiate with the ANC alone, the ANC won't negotiate at all?

Our view is that the ANC is central to negotiations. The matter of who else could be represented at such talks is under discussion by organisations of the people. If government says we need to go through an electoral process, it begs the question whether government itself is legitimate and should be able to call the shots. We would argue that it is not, because it does not have the moral support of all the people of South Africa. The best way of getting the negotiation machinery off the ground is to put together a constituent assembly. Then you have elections on a national basis. De Klerk appears to dismiss this out of hand because he fears the ANC will win overwhelming support.

But then there would be nothing left to negotiate. It would all be over.

No, it would not be all over. You would still have the National Party participating in the elections and they will have their own negotiating team. The ANC will also participate in negotiating a constitution.

It may make sense for you to say that the only basis on which to negotiate is on the basis of a transfer of power to the majority, and your constituent assembly idea immediately solves that. But that is the big sticking point. Government wouldn't let that get past first base.

It is a long road. The interesting thing is that government has shifted position, I do not know how many times, on the question of the ANC and negotiations. The ANC has remained consistent, and the OAU document crystallises discussions which have taken place over the years. The issues covered in that document do not deviate from the positions adopted and upheld by the ANC over the years. Government, on the other hand, shows it is confused and lacks direction. It has shifted its position to the point where it now accepts the need for a new constitution which will cover all people in South Africa. This is a definite shift. But they have not done it out of the kindness of their hearts. They have done it as a result of massive national and international pressure. But again and again, government wishes to prescribe how this constitution is to come about. . . .

Anyone who was out at the Sisulu home in Soweto in the week following the release of the Rivonia trialists cannot fail to have seen the National Reception Committee, which appears to constitute the effective leadership of the MDM, involved in meeting after meeting, obviously to decide on strategy. Can you outline where you are going in the next few months, as we move further into this pre-negotiation period?

Our strategy is guided by the goal of a non-racial and democratic South Africa, to be achieved through disciplined struggle involving the masses of our people. This strategy includes the strengthening of the structures of the MDM to meet the challenges that are beginning to unfold. The defiance campaign, which has been resoundingly successful, proved to government that it no longer has the initiative; this is in the hands of the people. We are now moving to the Conference for a Democratic Future where other strategies will be evolved. . . . The release of our leaders means that our people are going to be propelled into mass activity through the structures that are being resuscitated, rejuvenated, and rebuilt. These leaders are going to take their rightful place in our struggle. Some of the new tactics will be in response to the state's strategies which, as we see them now, are aimed at demobilising our people. Negotiations are being dangled as a carrot which the regime hopes our people will latch onto and think that government is serious and genuine and wants to come to terms with our demands. But we know that government wants to have a negotiated settlement on its own terms. As far as we are concerned they have not yet crossed the political threshold, and we are going to have to make them cross that political threshold. . . .

In terms of the overall leadership structure, what is the present relationship between those who have just been released, those who have led the struggle within the country, and those who remain abroad? Where is HQ?

Headquarters are still in Lusaka. [Walter] Sisulu has made that very clear. We are not going to have two ANCs. When the leaders were released, a number of people, government included, thought now would be the time to allow an above-ground, internal ANC. That is not on. It would divide the movement: it would be seen as the bad fellows outside and the good and moderate fellows inside.

You say HQ remains in Lusaka, but it's clear that strategy is being developed where it has to be—on site. Is it then ratified by Lusaka, or do they have a hands-off approach, as if to say that the leaders on the spot must handle it as they think best? How does the liaison work?

The ANC operates as a single entity. The leadership outside, the leadership that remains in prison, and the leadership in the country, all move in unison on virtually all issues. There are no contradictions. There may well be differences in emphasis but most of the things that have happened in recent weeks have arisen from joint decisions with the leadership at all levels, i.e., Nelson Mandela in Victor Verster prison, the leadership out here, and the leadership in Lusaka. . . .

You are not a member of the national executive, yet many would consider you, for example, as among the inner circle of leaders. Does the collective leadership extend beyond the executive?

I am not part of the ANC leadership, but the democratic culture that has evolved means decisions are arrived at with the input of the organisations of the people. A good example is the OAU document. Before its final draft, it was farmed out to these organisations, to the MDM leadership, to the leadership in prison, to Mandela himself. After views had been expressed, they were collected and synthesised by the National Executive Committee, and the final draft was put forward to the OAU. . . .

When Mr Mandela is released, what will his status within the struggle be?

Mandela is a member of the ANC, and his status is no different from the status of any other member of the ANC. However, his stature as a leader is such that his views have a lot of bearing on the leadership of the ANC. Once he is released and the processes start unfolding, he is one of those people who may have to be considered for a leadership position in the ANC.

Do you now, perhaps for the first time, have a real sense that your freedom is near?

I think many of us feel infused with hope that on our side things are beginning to come together. Because we have such great love for this country, we are prepared to ensure that there is as little rupture as possible in ushering in a new South Africa. I believe that the things we are doing are meaningful because our people are beginning to think and function in an effective political way. They are listening to what de Klerk is saying and not dismissing it out of hand, but considering it; they are critically analysing and interpreting events as they unfold. I am convinced that freedom is within our reach. Let me quote an Afrikaans saying: "Alles sal regkom as elkeen sy plig doen." [Everything will turn out well if everyone does his duty.]

Document 180. Interview with PAC chairman, Johnson Mlambo, Dar-es-Salaam, October 9, 1989, *SAPEM,* December 1989/January 1990 (abridged)

Should De Klerk be taken seriously?

I would agree that the international environment, the international action and the efforts of the people within racist South Africa itself, as well as the whole region, have made the South African regime take stock of the fact that the country-by-country approach of the OAU [Organisation of African Unity] has now finally reached the borders of racist South Africa. So the South African regime is forced to have a new navigator for South Africa, and that new navigator is De Klerk.

Even the Americans and the British have admitted that sanctions are biting. De Klerk has admitted that economic sanctions are effective and have led to the isolation of South Africa. His main aim is how to get South Africa back into the international community. But at the same time we must never forget that the racist regime is still a very violent creature. We still do not have peace in Angola or Mozambique, thanks to the South African regime. So we must be wary of the propaganda from South Africa and its friends.

Is the PAC involved in any of the talks concerning the dismantling of apartheid?

The position of the PAC has been well stated by our President [Zephania Mothopeng] who has said that there has been no genuine chance for peace in South Africa to date. And that the genuine conditions for peace can only come about by further continuation of our struggle. The very fact that the racist regime is continuing to arm itself is proof of the fact that the regime's public and international stance has been created merely to get some breathing space to arm itself and to acquire greater military technology.

Although there is talk of dismantling apartheid—that people like Bishop [Desmond] Tutu are trying to do this from within—the basic problems remain. Everybody wants peace, but everyone agrees with the PAC that the conditions for genuine negotiations have yet to be created. And this is what we are still trying to do.

What are the 'conditions'?

We want genuine democracy in our country, one person, one vote. And our struggle is a struggle to reclaim the land. One-seventh of the population owns 87% of the land in our country. Now the regime must redress that situation.

What would make the regime dismantle apartheid? What would be the precondition? How would you get them to do that?

The only thing that encourages the regime to make changes is continued pressure from the oppressed masses themselves. Therefore, we feel we must continue with our programmes, namely the intensification of the struggle, both the political and the armed struggle.

Don't you see the possibility of peace coming to South Africa without the preconditions you speak of? For example, a Lancaster House type of independence?

The struggle has taken a heavy toll on the lives of the oppressed people. So if there is a genuine opportunity for peace, we recognise that it would have to be taken. But you know as well as I that the British and Americans promised money for the people of Zimbabwe to acquire land and that the settlers' land was not to be expropriated. But has that money come? Today, even in a free Zimbabwe, the people are captive and their aspirations have not been fulfilled. So there are important preconditions we must secure for the people of South Africa before negotiations can take place. . . .

Don't you think that by holding on too strongly to your preconditions, the PAC might be outflanked by the ANC at the negotiating table?

The long and short of it is that the ANC has its own programme. The fact that the two organisations exist shows that we have a different outlook. As our President said, those who want to talk can go ahead and talk. We in the PAC still believe in our people's capacity to continue to struggle. However, we are aware of the pressure that can be brought to bear upon us by the Frontline States or the OAU to go to the negotiating table.

What about the white factor in South Africa if black majority rule comes to South Africa? What is the likely scenario?

When it comes to negotiation, you must realise that the Boers [Afrikaners] have been negotiating for some time with sections of the non-white community in South Africa, for example, Bantustans, the tricameral parliament etc. Now the South Africans want to co-opt some of us to give them more and more credibility and split the unity of the liberation movement. Something like the Namibian situation is what I envisage the South Africans trying to reproduce in South Africa—when even if the liberation forces win an election, they must be forced to make so many compromises, so that the genuine economic interests of the imperialists are left untouched. We will certainly do our best to thwart this.

Big business says . . . "leave it to the forces of supply and demand. Do not struggle against it because the economy will be damaged as a result. Hold onto economic power and that will allow for an economic apartheid for a long time in South Africa, even under black majority rule." Also there is the method of co-opting blacks into big business to divide the blacks by creating a black bourgeoisie.

The poor whites will remain in South Africa, the middle classes and professionals will try to leave, the white army will remain under a negotiated settlement. Our fears concern when we are to disarm and come in under international supervision, whilst their structures remain intact. They have a very large standing army which, unless disarmed, could be dangerous even after peace is agreed. . . .

There is also the possibility of a violent revolution in South Africa like in Mozambique, and in that case there would be a mass exodus of whites from South Africa.

Document 181. "Has Socialism Failed?" *Umsebenzi* discussion pamphlet by Joe Slovo, London, January 1990 (abridged)

INTRODUCTION

Socialism is undoubtedly in the throes of a crisis greater than at any time since 1917. The last half of 1989 saw the dramatic collapse of most of the communist party governments of Eastern Europe. Their downfall was brought about through massive upsurges which had the support not only of the majority of the working class but also a large slice of the membership of the ruling parties themselves. *These were popular revolts against unpopular regimes; if socialists are unable to come to terms with this reality, the future of socialism is indeed bleak.*

The mounting chronicle of crimes and distortions in the history of existing socialism, its economic failures and the divide which developed between socialism and democracy, have raised doubts in the minds of many former supporters of the socialist cause as to whether socialism can work at all. Indeed, we must expect that, for a time, many in the affected countries will be easy targets for those aiming to achieve a reversion to capitalism, including an embrace of its external policies.

Shock-waves of very necessary self-examination have also been triggered off amongst communists both inside and outside the socialist world. *For our part, we firmly believe in the future of socialism; nor do we dismiss its whole past as an unmitigated failure.* Socialism certainly produced a Stalin and a Ceausescu, but it also produced a Lenin and a Gorbachev. Despite the distortions at the top, the nobility of socialism's basic objectives inspired millions upon millions to devote themselves selflessly to building it on the ground. And no one can doubt that if humanity is today poised to enter an unprecedented era of peace and civilised international relations, it is in the first place due to the efforts of the socialist world.

But it is more vital than ever to subject the past of existing socialism to an unsparing critique in order to draw the necessary lessons. To do so openly is an assertion of justified confidence in the future of socialism and its inherent moral superiority. And we should not allow ourselves to be inhibited merely because an exposure of failures will inevitably provide ammunition to the traditional enemies of socialism. . . .

A LOOK AT OURSELVES

The commandist and bureaucratic approaches which took root during Stalin's time affected communist parties throughout the world, including our own. *We cannot disclaim our share of the responsibility for the spread of the personality cult and a mechanical embrace of Soviet domestic and foreign policies, some of which discredited the cause of socialism.* We kept silent for too long after the 1956 Khrushchev revelations.

It would, of course, be naive to imagine that a movement can, at a stroke, shed all the mental baggage it has carried from the past. And our 7th Congress emphasised the need for on-going vigilance. It noted some isolated reversions to the past, including attempts to engage in intrigue and factional activity in fraternal organisations, sectarian attitudes towards some nonparty colleagues, and sloganised dismissals of views which do not completely accord with ours. . . .

We do not pretend that our party's changing postures in the direction of democratic socialism are the results only of our own independent evolution. Our shift undoubtedly owes a prime debt to the process of perestroika and glasnost which was so courageously unleashed under Gorbachev's inspiration. Closer to home, the democratic spirit which dominated the re-emerged trade union movement from the early 1970s onwards, also made its impact.

But we can legitimately claim that in certain fundamental respects our indigenous revolutionary practice long ago ceased to be guided by Stalinist concepts. This is the case particularly in relation to the way the party performed its role as a working class vanguard, its relations with fraternal organisations and representatives of other social forces and, above all, its approach to the question of democracy in the post-apartheid state and in a future socialist South Africa.

The Party as a Vanguard and Inner-Party Democracy

We have always believed (and we continue to do so) that it is indispensable for the working class to have an independent political instrument which safeguards its role in the democratic revolution and which leads it towards an eventual classless society. But such leadership must be won rather than imposed. Our claim to represent the historic aspirations of the workers does not give us an absolute right to lead them or to exercise control over society as a whole in their name.

Our new programme asserts that a communist party does not earn the title of vanguard merely by proclaiming it. Nor does its claim to be the upholder of Marxism give it a monopoly of political wisdom or a natural right to exclusive control of the struggle. We can only earn our place as a vanguard force by superior efforts of leadership and devotion to the cause of liberation and socialism. And we can only win adherence to our ideology by demonstrating its superiority as a theoretical guide to revolutionary practice.

This approach to the vanguard concept has not, as we know, always been adhered to in world revolutionary practice and in an earlier period we too were infected by the distortion. *But, in our case, the shift which has taken place in our conception of "vanguard" is by no means a post-Gorbachev phenomenon.* The wording on this question in our new programme is taken almost verbatim from our Central Committee's 1970 report on organisation.

The 1970 document reiterated the need to safeguard, both in the letter and the spirit, the independence of the political expressions of other social forces whether economic or national. It rejected the old purist and domineering concept that all those who do not agree with the party are necessarily enemies of the working class. And it saw no conflict between our understanding of the concept of vanguard and the acceptance of the African National Congress as the head of the liberation alliance.

Despite the inevitable limitations which illegality imposed on our inner-party democratic processes, the principles of accountability and electivity of all higher organs were substantially adhered to. Seven underground Congresses of our party have been held since 1953. The delegates to Congress from the lower organs were elected without lists from above and always constituted a majority. The incoming Central Committees were elected by a secret ballot without any form of direct or indirect "guidance" to the delegates. *In other words, the Leninist concept of democratic centralism has not been abused to entrench authoritarian leadership practices.*

Our structures, down to the lowest units, have been increasingly encouraged to assess and question leadership pronouncements in a critical spirit and the views of the membership are invariably canvassed before finalising basic policy documents. Our 7th Congress, which adopted our new programme, *The Path to Power*, was a model of democratic consultation and spirited debate.

Special procedures designed to exclude suspected enemy agents as delegates to Congress limited complete free choice. But, in practice, these limitations affected a negligible percentage. Overall, despite the security risks involved in the clandestine conditions, the will of our membership finds democratic expression. *This spirit of democracy also informs our relationship with fraternal political forces and our approach to the political framework of a post-liberation South Africa.*

Relations with Fraternal Organisations . . .

We do not regard the trade union or the national movement as mere conduits for our policies. Nor do we attempt to advance our policy positions through intrigue or manipulation. Our relationship with these organisations is based on complete respect for their independence, integrity and inner-democracy. In so far as our influence is felt, it is the result of open submissions of policy positions and the impact of individual communists who win respect as among the most loyal, the most devoted and ideologically clear members of these organisations.

Old habits die hard and among the most pernicious of these is the purist concept that all those who do not agree with the party are necessarily enemies of socialism. This leads to a substitution of name-calling and jargon for healthy debate with non-party activists. As already mentioned, our 7th Congress noted some reversions along these lines and resolved to combat such tendencies. . . .

Democracy and the Future

Our party's programme holds firmly to a post-apartheid state which will guarantee all citizens the basic rights and freedoms of organisation, speech, thought, press, movement, residence, conscience and religion; full trade union rights for all workers including the right to strike, and one person one vote in free and democratic elections. *These freedoms constitute the very essence of our national liberation and socialist objectives and they clearly imply political pluralism.*

Both for these historical reasons and because experience has shown that an institutionalised one-party state has a strong propensity for authoritarianism, *a multi-party post-apartheid democracy, both in the national democratic and socialist phases, is desirable.*

We believe that post-apartheid state power must clearly vest in the elected representatives of the people and not, directly or indirectly, in the administrative command of a party. The relationship which evolves between political parties and state structures must not, in any way, undermine the sovereignty of elected bodies.

We also believe that if there is real democracy in the post-apartheid state, the way will be open for a peaceful progression towards our party's ultimate objective—a socialist South Africa. This approach is consistent with the Marxist view—not always adhered to in practice—that the working class must win the majority to its side: as long as no violence is used against the people there is no other road to power.

It follows that, in truly democratic conditions, it is perfectly legitimate and desirable for a party claiming to be the political instrument of the working class to attempt to lead its constituency *in democratic contest for political power* against other parties and groups representing other social forces. And if it wins, it must be constitutionally required, from time to time, to go back to the people for a renewed mandate. The alternative to this is self-perpetuating power with all its implications for corruption and dictatorship.

Conclusion

We dare not underestimate the damage that has been wrought to the cause of socialism by the distortions we have touched upon. We, however, continue to have complete faith that socialism represents the most rational, just and democratic way for human beings to relate to one another. . . .

The opponents of socialism are very vocal about what they call the failure of socialism in Africa. But they say little, if anything, about Africa's real failure: the failures of capitalism. *Over 90 percent of our continent's people live out their wretched and repressed lives in stagnating and declining capitalist-orientated economies.* International capital, to whom most of these countries are mortgaged, virtually regards cheap bread, free education and full employment as economic crimes. Western outcries against violations of human rights are muted when they occur in countries with a capitalist orientation.

The way forward for the whole of humanity lies within a socialist framework guided by genuine socialist humanitarianism and not within a capitalist system which entrenches economic and social inequalities as a way of life. Socialism can undoubtedly be made to work without the negative practices which have distorted many of its key objectives.

But mere faith in the future of socialism is not enough. The lessons of past failures have to be learnt. Above all, we have to ensure that its fundamental tenet—socialist democracy—occupies a rightful place in all future practice.

DOCUMENT 182. Speech by Nelson Mandela on the Grand Parade, Cape Town, February 11, 1990

Amandla! Amandla! i-Afrika Mayibuye! [Power! Power! Let Africa come back!]

My friends, comrades, and fellow South Africans, I greet you all in the name of peace, democracy and freedom for all. I stand here before you not as a prophet but as a humble servant of you, the people. Your tireless and heroic sacrifices have made it possible for me to be here today. I therefore place the remaining years of my life in your hands.

On this day of my release I extend my sincere and warmest gratitude to the millions of my compatriots and those in every corner of the globe who have campaigned tirelessly for my release. I extend special greetings to the people of Cape Town, the city which has been my home for three decades. Your mass marches and other forms of struggle have served as a constant source of strength to all political prisoners.

I salute the African National Congress. It has fulfilled our every expectation in its role as leader of the great march to freedom. I salute our president, Comrade Oliver Tambo, for leading the ANC even under the most difficult circumstances.

I salute the rank-and-file members of the ANC. You have sacrificed life and limb in the pursuit of the noble cause of our struggle. I salute combatants of Umkhonto we Sizwe, like Solomon Mahlangu and Ashley Kriel, who have paid the ultimate price for the freedom of all South Africans.

I salute the South African Communist Party for its steady contribution to the struggle for democracy. You have survived 40 years of unrelenting persecution. The memory of great communists like Moses Kotane, Yusuf Dadoo, Bram Fischer and Moses Mabhida will be cherished for generations to come. I salute General Secretary Joe Slovo, one of our finest patriots. We are heartened by the fact that the alliance between ourselves and the party remains as strong as it always was.

I salute the United Democratic Front, the National Education Crisis Committee, the South African Youth Congress, the Transvaal and Natal Indian Congresses. And COSATU. And the many other formations of the mass democratic movement.

I also salute the Black Sash and the National Union of South African Students. We note with pride that you have acted as the conscience of white South Africans. Even during the darkest days in the history of our struggle, you held the flag of liberty high.

The large-scale mass mobilisation of the past few years is one of the key factors which led to the opening of the final chapter of our struggle. I extend my greetings to the working class of our country. Your organised strength is the pride of our movement. You remain the most dependable force in the struggle to end exploitation and oppression.

I pay tribute to the many religious communities who carried the campaign for justice forward when the organisations of our people were silenced.

I greet the traditional leaders of our country. Many among you continue to walk in the foot-steps of great heroes like Hintsa and Sekhukhuni.

I pay tribute to the endless heroism of youth. You, the young lions, have energised our entire struggle. I pay tribute to the mothers and wives and sisters of our nation. You are the rock hard foundation of our struggle. Apartheid has inflicted more pain on you than on anyone else.

On this occasion we thank the world community for their great contribution to the anti-apartheid struggle. Without your support our struggle would not have reached this advanced stage. The sacrifice of the frontline states will be remembered by South Africans forever.

My salutations will be incomplete without expressing my deep appreciation for the strength given to me during my long and lonely years in prison by my beloved wife and family. I am convinced that your pain and suffering was far greater than my own.

Before I go any further, I wish to make the point that I intend making only a few preliminary comments at this stage. I will make a more complete statement only after I have had the opportunity to consult with my comrades.

Today the majority of South Africans, black and white, recognise that apartheid has no future. It has to be ended by our own decisive, mass action in order to build peace and security. The mass campaigns of defiance and other actions of our organisations and people can only culminate in the establishment of democracy. The apartheid destruction on our subcontinent is incalculable. The fabric of family life of millions of my people has been shattered. Millions are homeless and unemployed. Our economy lies in ruins and our people are embroiled in political strife.

Our resort to the armed struggle in 1960 with the formation of the military wing of the ANC, Umkhonto we Sizwe, was a purely defensive action against the violence of apartheid. The factors which necessitated the armed struggle still exist today. We have no option but to continue. We express the hope that a climate conducive to a negotiated settlement would be created soon so that there may no longer be the need for the armed struggle.

I am a loyal and disciplined member of the African National Congress. I am therefore in full agreement with all of its objectives, strategies and tactics. The need to unite the people of our country is as important a task now as it always has been. No individual leader is able to take [on] all these important tasks on his own. It is our task as leaders to place our views before our organisation and to allow the democratic structures to decide on the way forward. On the question of democratic practice, I feel duty bound to make the point that a leader of the movement is a person who has been democratically elected at a national conference. This is a principle which must be upheld without any exceptions.

Today I wish to report to you that my talks with the government have been aimed at normalising the political situation in the country. We have not as yet begun discussing the basic demands of the struggle. I wish to stress that I myself have at no time entered into negotiations about the future of our country, except to insist on a meeting between the ANC and the government.

Mr. de Klerk has gone further than any other Nationalist president in taking real steps to normalise the situation. However, there are further steps as outlined in the Harare Declaration that have to be met before negotiations on the basic demands of our people can begin. I reiterate our call for, *inter alia*, the immediate ending of the state of emergency and the freeing of all, and not only some, political prisoners. Only such a normalised situation which allows for free political activity can allow us to consult our people in order to obtain a mandate. The people need to be consulted on who will negotiate and on the content of such negotiations.

Negotiations cannot take place above the heads or behind the backs of our people. It is our belief that the future of our country can only be determined by a body which is democratically elected on a nonracial basis. Negotiations on the dismantling of apartheid will have to address the overwhelming demand of our people for a democratic, nonracial, and unitary South Africa. There must be an end to white monopoly on political power, and a fundamental restructuring of our political and economic systems to ensure that the inequalities of apartheid are addressed and our society thoroughly democratised.

It must be added that Mr. de Klerk himself is a man of integrity who is acutely aware of the dangers of a public figure not honouring his undertakings. But as an organisation we base our policy and strategy on the harsh reality we are faced with, and this reality is that we are still suffering under the policies of the Nationalist government. Our struggle has reached a decisive moment. We call on our people to seize this moment so that the process toward democracy is rapid and uninterrupted. We have waited too long for our freedom. We can no longer wait. Now is the time to intensify the struggle on all fronts. To relax our efforts now would be a mistake which generations to come will not be able to forgive. The sight of freedom looming on the horizon should encourage us to redouble our efforts. It is only through disciplined mass action that our victory can be assured.

We call on our white compatriots to join us in the shaping of a new South Africa. The freedom movement is the political home for you, too.

We call on the international community to continue the campaign to isolate the apartheid regime. To lift sanctions now would be to run the risk of aborting the process toward the complete eradication of apartheid. Our march to freedom is irreversible. We must not allow fear to stand in our way. Universal suffrage on a common voters roll in a united, democratic, and nonracial South Africa is the only way to peace and racial harmony.

In conclusion, I wish to go to my own words during my trial in 1964. They are as a true today as they were then. I wrote: "I have fought against white domination and I have fought against black domination. I have cherished the ideal of a democratic and free society in which all persons live together in harmony and with equal opportunities. It is an ideal which I hope to live for and to achieve. But if need be, it is an ideal for which I am prepared to die".

[In Xhosa] My friends, I have no words of eloquence to offer today except to say that the remaining days of my life are in your hands.

Amandla!

CHRONOLOGY

1980

Three MK guerrillas hold up Volkskas bank in Silverton, Pretoria; they and two hostages die when police storm bank (January)

Robert Mugabe and ZANU win Zimbabwe pre-independence election (February)

School boycotts start in western Cape (February), spread to include schools in other regions (March onward)

Sabotage attacks on SASOL oil-from-coal installations mark resurgence of ANC (June)

Major SADF incursion into southern Angola (June)

Defiance and township turmoil follow government ban on commemorations of Soweto uprising; over 40 die in western Cape (June)

Strikes and labor unrest spread in eastern Cape motor industry (June)

ANC-Inkatha rift publicized when Alfred Nzo attacks Chief Buthelezi on Radio Freedom (June)

Rent boycotts spread as township rents rise sharply (July)

Komani decision undermines pass laws (August)

Koornhof Bills introduced in Parliament (October)

Ronald Reagan's election brings conservatives to power in United States (November)

Labor unrest in Poland forces Communist government to recognize an independent trade union, Solidarity

1981

Eleven ANC exiles die in SADF raid in Matola suburb of Maputo (January)

PAC central committee elects John Nyati Pokela new chairman (February)

National Party wins general election by falling margin as white opinion swings rightward (April)

Protests mark 20th anniversary of Republic (May)

ANC's Joe Gqabi assassinated in Harare (July)

MK special operations unit stages rocket attack on Voortrekkerhoogte military base near Pretoria (August)

Rikhoto decision further erodes urban influx control regulations (October); Appellate Division upholds verdict (June 1983)

ANC's Griffiths Mxenge assassinated in Durban (November)

Ciskei homeland becomes "independent" (December)

ANC uncovers spies among its leading cadre in Angola; paranoia ensues

1982

White activist Neil Aggett dies in police custody; Johannesburg march by black mourners signals emerging non-racial alliance (February)

Andries Treurnicht forms Conservative Party (March)

Nelson Mandela and three other Rivonia men moved from Robben Island to Pollsmoor prison (March)

Government plan to cede Ingwavuma district to Swaziland ruled illegal by Natal Supreme Court (June); Appellate Division later upholds judgment (September)

Parcel bomb kills Ruth First in Maputo (August)

World Alliance of Reformed Churches suspends South Africa's Dutch Reformed churches; Allan Boesak elected WARC president (August)

Govender decision undermines Group Areas Act (November); inner city "grey areas" grow

Forty-two die in SADF raid on suspected ANC houses in Maseru; 12 of the dead are Lesotho citizens (December)

Four explosions set by MK saboteur damage unfinished Koeberg nuclear power station near Cape Town (December)

Economic downturn causes growing unemployment, inflation, widespread strikes; prolonged drought increases rural poverty

1983

Boesak and others call for "united democratic front" at Transvaal Anti-SAIC meeting (January)

Transvaal Indian Congress revived (May)

ANC car bomb outside Pretoria Air Force headquarters kills 19 (May)

AZAPO convenes National Forum at Hammanskraal to promote opposition unity (June)

United Democratic Front launched at Mitchell's Plain, Cape Town (August); it soon eclipses black consciousness oriented National Forum

Five die when Inkatha fighters invade University of Zululand at Ngoye to retaliate against Buthelezi's critics (October)

White referendum endorses new constitution (November)

Turnout low in 29 black local government elections (November–December)

1984

Mutinies begin, are crushed in ANC's Angolan camps (January–May)

UDF launches million signature campaign (January)

South Africa forces government of Samora Machel to sign Nkomati accord (March); MK expelled from Mozambique

School boycotts escalate (April)

Year-long Ciskei bus boycott winds down (July)

Low turnout in elections for new coloured and Indian houses of Parliament (August)

Promulgation of new constitution; Vaal uprising begins the same day (September 3)

Desmond Tutu wins Nobel Peace Prize (October)

Army deployed in Vaal Triangle; township violence spreads (October)

Largest political general strike in South Africa's history occurs as estimated 800,000 workers stay home for two days in Transvaal (November)

Reagan's re-election and TV coverage of mounting South African turmoil energize American anti-apartheid movement (November)

UDF leaders charged with treason (December)

1985

Violence over three days at Crossroads leaves 18 dead; township unrest continues (February)

Massacre of at least 19 funeral marchers by police in Langa township, Uitenhage, sparks wide protests; first perceived collaborators die in "necklace" killings as black local governments unravel (March)

Government repeals law against interracial marriage (April)

Pietermaritzburg treason trial of UDF and trade union leaders begins (May)

Consumer boycotts spread in eastern Cape (May–June)

Delmas trial begins; 22 face treason charges (June)

ANC holds consultative conference in Kabwe, Zambia (June)

Death squad murders Matthew Goniwe and three companions (June)

Johnson Mlambo elected chairman of PAC after Pokela's death (July)

Government declares state of emergency in eastern Cape and PWV area (July)

Political uncertainty causes American banks to call in South African debts, precipitating economic crisis (July)

P. W. Botha's hardline "Rubicon" speech offends business and foreign investors; rand value declines sharply (August)

COSAS banned (August)

Delegation of top South African business and media leaders meets ANC in Zambia, signaling crisis among white elites (September)

School boycotts widespread; Soweto Parents' Crisis Committee forms (October)

Kobie Coetsee visits Mandela in Cape Town hospital (November)

Natal Indaba proposes consociational multiracial government for province (November)

COSATU formed after long planning process (November–December)

Township violence and UDF-Inkatha clashes are ongoing; police shootings in Mamelodi result in mass funeral where ANC banners are displayed, Winnie Mandela is mobbed (December)

Government announces plan to introduce freehold tenure for blacks who have permanent urban rights (December)

Provocateurs fan ongoing AZAPO-UDF clashes in eastern Cape

Number of MK attacks in 1985 dramatically higher than in 1984

1986

Botha announces he will create advisory National Council for Africans; proposal is stillborn (January)

Van Zyl Slabbert and Alex Boraine resign from Parliament (February)

Security forces continue effort to quell township violence; dozens die in Alexandra township (February), 11 in Winterveld (March), at least 60 in Cape Town squatter areas (May), 20 in Soweto (August); lethal clashes between UDF, AZAPO, AZANYU, Inkatha supporters increase

Government lifts first state of emergency in bid to placate foreign lenders (March)

Natal Indaba proposes multiracial consociational government for province (March)

Addressing NECC conference in Durban, Zwelakhe Sisulu urges end of school boycotts, warns students that government's fall is not imminent (March)

Consumer boycotts, after period of suspension, resume in Port Elizabeth and a dozen other towns (April)

Massive national stayaway follows call by COSATU and NECC for May Day to be observed as public holiday (May)

Inkatha launches UWUSA (May)

Mandela meets Commonwealth Eminent Persons Group at Pollsmoor prison; SADF attacks ANC facilities in three frontline states three days later, aborting EPG mission (May)

Cape Town squatter areas around old Crossroads razed by vigilante action; estimated 70,000 made homeless (May)

Violent conflict in KwaNdebele homeland (May–August)

Government declares second state of emergency, imposes press curbs, begins vast wave of detentions (June)

COSATU, UDF, NECC, CUSA call successful national stayaway to commemorate Soweto uprising and protest state of emergency (June)

Pass laws repealed (June)

Rent boycotts ongoing in 48 townships (September)

Estimated 300,000 mineworkers stage work stoppage to observe day of mourning for accident victims at Kinross goldmine, signaling rising power of NUM (October)

U.S. Senate overrides Reagan veto of Comprehensive Anti-Apartheid Act, strongest Western sanctions measure yet (October)

Alarmed by international isolation and withdrawal of foreign companies, government imposes harsher media censorship, detains more critics and activists (December)

Political activism among Muslims increases during year

1987

Oliver Tambo meets with U.S. Secretary of State George Shultz in Washington, reflecting new ANC standing (January)

SAYCO formed at secret Cape Town meeting (March); township revolt being suppressed through thousands of detentions

Early general election returns National Party to power; Progressives lose ground; black workers and students stage national two-day election stayaway (May)

Bomb wrecks COSATU headquarters (May)

Three-month strike by SARHWU against state railways ends with concessions and union recognition (June)

IDASA takes delegation of Afrikaner notables to meet ANC in Dakar (July)

COSATU annual congress adopts Freedom Charter (July); UDF national conference follows suit (August)

Three-week strike by estimated 340,000 NUM members marked by violent intimidation; ends in standoff (August)

Contralesa formed (September)

ANC holds secret meeting with three Stellenbosch professors in Britain; discussion evolves into Mells Park "talks about talks" (October)

Open warfare between Inkatha and UDF supporters escalates, especially around Pietermaritzburg; police fan violence (October)

Major-General Bantu Holomisa, alleging corruption, seizes control of Transkei government from Stella Sigcau (December)

Security forces continue occupation of Turfloop campus throughout year

State-supported dirty tricks and vigilante activity increase throughout year

1988

Eighteen organizations including UDF, COSATU, AZAPO placed under restrictions in security crackdown; clergy stage Cape Town protest (February)

Mandela has first of many meetings with secret government team led by Niël Barnard (May)

State of emergency renewed for another year; press curbs widened; Inkatha-UDF violence wracks Natal (June)

Bomb wrecks Khotso House, headquarters of Council of Churches and other opposition groups (August)

Resistance to military conscription gathers momentum; ECC restricted (August)

Mac Maharaj and Siphiwe Nyanda enter South Africa to begin Operation Vula (August)

ANC releases Constitutional Guidelines for discussion (August)

Labour Relations Act threatens gains made by black trade unions (September)

Dissident Afrikaner journalists launch *Vrye Weekblad* (October)

Municipal elections demonstrate lack of black support for Botha reforms (October); rent boycotts ongoing throughout year

Mandela moved to warder's cottage at Victor Verster prison, allowed numerous visitors (December)

Angola, Cuba and South Africa sign agreement on Namibian independence (December)

Stompie Seipei and other youths beaten by Winnie Mandela's bodyguards at her Diepkloof house; Seipei dies (December)

UDF and COSATU representatives confer with ANC and SACTU in Harare (December); dozens of other "treks" to meet ANC occur during year

1989

Botha has mild stroke (January); caucus elects F. W. de Klerk National Party leader (February)

COSATU and MDM leaders in press conference criticize Winnie Mandela (February)

Detainee hunger strikes spread from Transvaal to eastern Cape; cabinet in Botha's absence authorizes releases (February–May)

ANC closes Angolan camps under terms of Namibian peace agreement, moves fighters to Uganda (February)

Moses Mayekiso treason trial ends in acquittal (April)

SACP congress in Cuba reaffirms "people's war" doctrine (April), but number of MK attacks declines during year

White activist David Webster assassinated; black mourners fill Johannesburg streets (May)

Economy severely strained by debt repayment burden, inflation, labor disruptions, trade sanctions, rising unemployment, falling gold price, and drought (May)

U.S. President George H. W. Bush receives MDM delegation at White House (June)

Death toll surges in Natal as government-trained Inkatha fighters are secretly absorbed into KwaZulu homeland police under Buthelezi's command (June)

Solidarity sweeps Polish elections, ending Communist rule (June); Beijing government massacres pro-democracy demonstrators in Tiananmen Square (June); Eastern Europe in turmoil

Mandela meets Botha at Tuynhuys (July)

Tambo has stroke in Lusaka; Nzo assumes acting ANC leadership (August)

MDM and churches launch defiance campaign against remaining segregation and restrictions (August)

OAU endorses Harare Declaration, ANC's position paper on negotiations (August)

De Klerk installed as president after general election (September)

National Intelligence Service representatives secretly meet Thabo Mbeki and

Jacob Zuma in Switzerland to start planning logistics of ANC's unbanning (September); Mells Park secret talks are ongoing

De Klerk allows major anti-apartheid marches in Cape Town, Johannesburg, Durban, East London, Port Elizabeth (September–November); similar demonstrations occur in Eastern Europe as Soviet power wanes

Sisulu, Kathrada, and other Rivonia trial prisoners released just prior to Commonwealth conference in Kuala Lumpur (October)

Death row prisoner Butana Almond Nofomela reveals existence of government hit squads and names commanders (October)

Erich Honecker forced from power in East Germany; demolition of Berlin wall follows, signaling implosion of Soviet bloc (October–November)

SWAPO wins Namibian pre-independence election (November)

Conference for a Democratic Future convenes in unity display among rival black organizations; most endorse Harare Declaration (December)

Mandela meets de Klerk at Tuynhuys (December)

Appellate Division in Bloemfontein overturns Delmas trial convictions (December)

1990

De Klerk announces unbanning of all proscribed organizations in speech opening Parliament (February 2)

Mandela freed, addresses huge crowd on Cape Town Grand Parade (February 11)

SOURCES

This section is a guide to materials used in producing this book. In addition to the secondary sources listed below and cited in endnotes, the major source has been the Karis-Gerhart Collection, an archive of interviews and approximately 10,000 South African political documents dating from the period 1964–1990. The hardcopy of the collection is in the Historical Papers division of the Cullen Library at the University of the Witwatersrand in Johannesburg. It is also available on microfilm from the Cooperative Africana Microform Project (CAMP) of the Center for Research Libraries, 5721 Cottage Grove Avenue, Chicago, Illinois 60637. A catalog of the collection is available online at www.crl.edu/areastudies/CAMP/collections/karisgerhart.htm. A duplicate set of many of the documents in the collection is in the Sterling Memorial Library at Yale University.

Archival Collections

Many of the documents reproduced in this book were first located in the following archival collections.

Inkatha Institute, Durban
International Defence and Aid Fund, London. IDAF collections were later moved to the Mayibuye Centre, University of the Western Cape, Bellville
SACHED (South African Committee for Higher Education) Library, Cape Town
Simons Papers, on microfilm. Originals are at the University of Cape Town Libraries, Manuscripts and Archives, www.lib.uct.ac.za/mss
South African History Archive (SAHA), Cullen Library, University of the Witwatersrand, Johannesburg, www.historicalpapers.wits.ac.za
South African Ministry of Justice, files on restricted persons. These files were later deposited in the National Archives, Pretoria, www.national.archives.gov.za
Star Library, Johannesburg

State Library, Pretoria, later called the National Library of South Africa, www.nlsa.ac.za
United Nations Centre Against Apartheid, New York
University of Cape Town Libraries, Manuscripts and Archives, www.lib.uct.ac.za/mss
University of Cape Town, Centre for Contemporary Islam
University of Fort Hare Library, Alice, www.liberation.org.za
University of London, Institute of Commonwealth Studies Library, http://commonwealth.sas.ac.uk
University of South Africa Library, Pretoria
University of the Western Cape, Mayibuye Centre, Bellville, later administered by the Robben Island Museum, www.robben-island.org.za
University of the Witwatersrand, Cullen Library, Historical Papers, Johannesburg, www.historicalpapers.wits.ac.za
University of York, England
Yale University, Sterling Memorial Library, New Haven

Trial Records

1984–1986 *State v. Ramgobin and others* (Pietermaritzburg treason trial)
1985–1988 *State v. Baleka and others* (Delmas treason trial)
1987–1989 *State v. Mayekiso and others*

Interviews

The following is a list of conversations and interviews cited in this volume. The Karis-Gerhart Collection includes approximately 900 interviews, many transcribed from tapes, and informal conversations conducted by Thomas Karis, Gail Gerhart, and other researchers. In footnotes, "conversation" has been used as a catch-all term for interviews and conversations conducted by Karis (K) and/or Gerhart (G), and the term "interview" has been used for transcripts and notes contributed to the collection by other researchers.

Akhalwaya, Ameen	New York, March 1988 (K)
Amabutho leaders in eastern Cape	Uitenhage, 1986? (Mark Swilling)
Axelsson, Roland	Lusaka, February 1988 (Victoria Butler)
Badsha, Omar	Johannesburg, August 2005 (G)
Beck, Karl	New York, January 1988 (K/G)
Bizos, George	New York, April 2006 (G)
Bizos, George	New York, October 1989 (K/G)
Boesak, Allan	New York, January 1990 (K/G)
Bolani, Thami	New York, August 1989 (K/G)
Breytenbach, Willie	Cape Town, November 1985 (K/G)
Brothers of Gugile Nkwinti	Port Alfred, October 1985 (K/G)
Chikane, Frank	Boston, telephone, June 1995 (K)
Cindi, Zithulele	Johannesburg, July 1989 (G)
Cooper, Saths	New York, October 1987 (G)
Cooper, Saths	Johannesburg, October 1985 (G)
Coovadia, Jerry	New York, June 1988 (G/Steve Mufson)
Dhlomo, Oscar	Durban, December 1989 (K)
Dhlomo, Oscar and Frank Mdlalose	New York, February 1987 (K/G)

SOURCES 739

Duncan, Sheena	New York, November 1987 (K/G)
Esterhuysen, Anriette	South Africa, December 1997 (G)
Evans, Gavin	Johannesburg, January 1991 (Howard Barrell)
Fazzie, Henry	Port Elizabeth, July 1989 (K/G)
Felgate, Walter	Johannesburg, February 1998 (G)
Filatova, Irina	New York, March 1991 (G)
Ganchin, Vladimir	New York, November 1987 (G)
Gasa, Nomboniso	Johannesburg, March 2004 (G)
Gastrow, Shelagh	Durban, July 1989 (G)
Gcina, Ivy	Port Elizabeth, July 1989 (G)
Geldenhuys, Deon	New York, July 1983 (K/G)
Gqobose, P. L. Mfanasekhaya	New York, April 1990 (K/G)
Green, Pippa	New York, January 1988 (Steven Robins)
Hani, Chris and Steve Tshwete	Lusaka, June 1988 (John Battersby)
Hunter, Roland	New York, October 1991 (K/G)
Ismail, Aboobaker	Johannesburg, telephone, July 2001 (G)
Issel, Johnny	Cape Town, December 1989 (K)
Jack, Mkhuseli and Stone Sizani	Port Elizabeth, July 1989 (G)
Jack, Mkhuseli	Uitenhage, March 1986 (Mark Swilling)
Jones, Larry	New York, May 1987 (notes on informal talk) (G)
Jordan, Pallo and Tom Sebina	Lusaka, August 1986 (K/G)
Kane-Berman, J. and Neo Mnumzana	New York, December 1985 (K)
Kasrils, Ronnie	Johannesburg, September and October 1990 (Howard Barrell)
Kasrils, Ronnie	Lusaka, August 1989 (Howard Barrell)
Kgokong, Jairus	Johannesburg, telephone, October 1997 (G)
Khoapa, Ben	Cleveland, telephone, October 1980 (K)
Khoapa, Ben	East Lansing, November 1986 (G)
Kuny, Denis	New York, September 1990 (G)
Kwadi, Amanda	Johannesburg, July 1989 (G)
Legwaila, Legwaila J.	New York, January 1988 (notes on informal talk)
Linda, Tamsanqa	Port Elizabeth, July 1988 (Rory Riordan)
Mabasa, Lybon	New York, April 1991 (G)
Macozoma, Saki	Johannesburg, December 1989 (K)
Made, Woza	November 1985, March 1986, and undated (Mark Swilling)
Maduna, Penuell	New York, early 1987
Mafole, Tebogo	New York, January 1990
Mafolo, Titus	South Africa, April 1986 (unidentified interviewer)
Maharaj, Mac	Johannesburg, February 1991 and November 30, 1990 (Howard Barrell)
Mahomed, Ismail	New York, December 1985 (K/G)
Mahomed, Yunus	Durban, November 1990 (D. R. Chetty)
Malan, Wynand and others	New York, December 1986 (K)
Maqina, Mzwandile	Port Elizabeth, January and November 1987 (Rory Riordan)
Maree, Johan and Helen Zille	Cape Town, November 1985 (K/G)
Masemola, Dikgang	Lusaka, February 1988 (Victoria Butler)

Masemola, Nathaniel	New York, March 1988 (K/G)
Mashinini, Mpho	New York, October 1991 (K/G)
Mateman, Don	Johannesburg, July 1980 (K/G)
Mati, Shepard and COSAS leaders	South Africa, 1986? (Tony Karon)
Matiso, Khaya	Port Elizabeth, July 1989 (G)
Matthews, Joe	Pretoria, June 1994 (K/G)
Mavi, Mxolisi Victor	New York, August 1991 (G)
Mayekiso, Moses	Johannesburg?, 1983? (Mark Swilling)
Mbeki, Thabo	New York, December 1985 (K)
Mbeki, Thabo	New York, May 1986 (G)
Midlands Chamber of Industry	Port Elizabeth, October 1985 (K/G)
Milne, John	New York, September 1986 (G)
Mirsky, George	New York, March 1990 (G)
Mkhatshwa, Smangaliso	New York, April 1989 (K)
Mndaweni, James	New York, November 1987 (K)
Mokoka, Geoffrey	Nairobi, May 1980 (G)
Molefe, Popo	Johannesburg, November 1990 (Howard Barrell)
Momoniat, Ismail	Johannesburg, December 1990 (Howard Barrell)
Moosa, Mohammed Valli	Johannesburg, early 1986 (Mark Swilling)
Moremi, Ntsizi	Nairobi, April 1980 (G)
Morobe, Murphy	Johannesburg, September 1995 (G)
Mothopeng, Zephania	Johannesburg, December 1989 (K)
Motlana, Nthato	New York, June 1987 (K/G)
Mtshali, Eric	Lusaka, February 1988 (Victoria Butler)
Nadison, Donovan	Port Elizabeth, July 1989 (G)
Netshitenzhe, Joel	Lusaka, February 1988 (Victoria Butler)
Ngubane, Don	Lusaka, February 1988 (Victoria Butler)
Nkondo, Curtis	New York, May 1989 (K/G)
Nkwinti, Gugile	Grahamstown, July 1989 (G)
Nonjeke, Johnson	Germiston, January 1983 (Mark Swilling)
Nxumalo, Jabulani ("Mzala")	New York, October 1990 (G)
Olivier, Gerrit	New York, February 1990 (notes on talk)
Omar, Dullah	Cape Town, July 1989 (G)
Patel, Quraish	Durban, July 1989 (G)
Pillay, Ivan	Lusaka, July 1989 (Howard Barrell)
Ramgobin, Mewa	Durban, July 1989 (G)
Ramphele, Mamphela	New York, October 1989 (G) (notes on talk)
Riordan, Rory	New York, February 1988 (K/G) (notes on talk)
Sachs, Albie	Johannesburg, late 1997 (G)
Saloojee, Cassim	Johannesburg, November 1990 (Howard Barrell)
Saloojee, Cassim	New York, October 1987 (G)
Santana, Aracelly	New York, December 1987 and January 1990 (K)
Schrire, Robert	Cape Town, November 1985 (K/G)
Sebidi, Lebamang John	Johannesburg, July 1989 (G)
Selebi, Jackie	Lusaka, February 1988 (Victoria Butler)
Slabbert, Frederik Van Zyl	Johannesburg, March 1998 (Rupert Taylor/ Adam Habib)
Slovo, Joe	Lusaka, August 1989 (Howard Barrell)
Sparg, Dallas and Mrs. Sparg	Port Alfred, October 1985 (K/G/Glenn Adler)
Stadler, Herman	Pretoria, October 1990 (Howard Barrell)

Stuart, James [pseud. Hermanus Loots]	Lusaka, April 1989 (K)
Terreblanche, Sampie	New York, June 1987 (K/G)
Thloloe, Joe	Johannesburg, December 1989 (K)
Thloloe, Joe	Johannesburg, June 1989 (G)
Thloloe, Joe	New York, September 1986 (K/G)
Thobejane, Senti	New York, August 1991 (K/G)
Thobejane, Senti and Thandeka Gqubule	New York, March 1991 (G)
Tini (former mayor)	Uitenhage, September 1987 (Mark Swilling)
Van der Merwe, Hendrik W.	Cape Town, November 1985 (K/G)
Van Heerden, Auret	New York, July 1987 (K)
Venkatrathnam, Sonny	New York, April 1985 and April 1988 (K)
Vigtel, Terge	Lusaka, March 1988 (Victoria Butler)
Waspe, Tom and Aneene Dawber	Johannesburg, July 1989 (G)

Unpublished Theses, Manuscripts, Papers, Reports, and Legal Briefings

Barrell, Howard, "Conscripts to Their Age: African National Congress Operational Strategy, 1976–1986," Ph.D. thesis, Oxford University, 1993 (Karis-Gerhart Collection, ANC).

Carrim, Yunus, "Changing Ethnic, Racial and National Identities of Indian South Africans in the Transition to a Post-Apartheid South Africa," paper presented at the University of the West Indies, Trinidad and Tobago, February 28–March 3, 1994.

Cherry, Janet, "Non-violent Direct Action and Civic Organisation in Port Elizabeth, 1980–1990," paper presented to Civics Project Workshop, Albert Einstein Institution and Witwatersrand University, 1993.

Emery, Alan Louis, "Insurgency and Democratization in South Africa: the Community Mobilization of Ideological, Military, and Political Power," Ph.D. thesis, University of California, Los Angeles, 2001.

Isaacs, Henry, "Reflections of a Black South African Exile," unpublished manuscript, 1986, 463 pp. (Karis-Gerhart Collection, PAC).

Isaacs, Henry, "South Africa's Pan African Congress in the 80's: Chronic Instability and Revolutionary Ineffectiveness," *Pambana: Journal on World Affairs and History,* August 1987, 71 pp. (Karis-Gerhart Collection, PAC).

Isaacs, Henry, "Struggles Within the Struggle: an Inside View of the PAC of South Africa," unpublished manuscript, 1985, 405 pp. (Karis-Gerhart Collection, PAC).

Kondlo, Kwandiwe Merriman, "In the Twilight of the Azanian Revolution: the Exile History of the Pan Africanist Congress (South Africa), 1960–1990," D. Litt Et Phil thesis, Rand Afrikaans University (University of Johannesburg), 2004 [http://etd.rau.ac.za/theses/available/etd-08182004–115716].

Kotze, Dirk, "Revisiting Colonialism of a Special Type," paper for the South African Political Science Association, Port Alfred, October 1989.

"Local-Level Negotiations: Case Studies and Implications," 1987, 63 pp. (defense briefing paper, *State v. Mayekiso*).

McKinley, Dale T., "The African National Congress in Exile: Strategy and Tactics, 1960–1993," Ph.D. thesis, University of North Carolina, 1995.

Naidoo, Kumaran [Kumi], "Class, Consciousness and Organisation: Indian Political Resistance in Durban, South Africa, 1979–1996," Ph.D. thesis, Oxford University, 1998.
Phillips, Merran, "The End Conscription Campaign 1983–1988: a Study of White Extra-Parliamentary Opposition to Apartheid," MA thesis, University of South Africa, 2002.
Ritchken, Edwin, "Leadership and Conflict in Bushbuckridge, 1978–1990," Ph.D. thesis, Witwatersrand University, 1995.
Shubane, Khehla, "The Soweto Rent Boycott," Honors thesis, Witwatersrand University, 1987.
Suttner, Raymond, "African National Congress (ANC): Attainment of Power, Post Liberation Phases and Current Crisis," unpublished draft paper, 2007, 46 pp.
Swilling, Mark, "Civic Associations in South Africa," draft paper, April 12, 1993, 21 pp.
Tetelman, Michael, "We Can: Black Politics in Cradock, South Africa, 1948–1985," Ph.D. thesis, Northwestern University, 1997.
Varney, Howard, "Truth and Reconciliation Commission Submission: The Caprivi Trainees," August 4, 1997, 35 pp.
Von den Steinen, Lynda, "Experiencing the Armed Struggle: The Soweto Generation and After," Ph.D. thesis, University of Cape Town, 2007.
Wolpe, Harold, "Aspects of the Present Situation in South Africa," Oxford University seminar paper, September 1988, 17 pp.

Selected Books and Articles on South Africa, 1980–1990

Abel, Richard, *Politics by Other Means: Law in the Struggle Against Apartheid, 1980–1994* (New York: Routledge, 1995).
Adam, Heribert and Kogila Moodley, *The Opening of the Apartheid Mind: Options for the New South Africa* (Berkeley: University of California Press, 1993).
Adler, Glenn and Jonny Steinberg, eds., *From Comrades to Citizens: the South African Civic Movement and the Transition to Democracy* (New York: St. Martin's Press, 2000).
Alden, Chris, *Apartheid's Last Stand: the Rise and Fall of the South African Security State* (New York: St. Martin's Press and London: Macmillan Press, 1996).
Alexander, Neville, "Non-collaboration in the Western Cape," in Wilmot James and Mary Simons, eds., *Class, Caste and Color: A Social and Economic History of the South African Western Cape* (New Brunswick: Transaction Publishers, 1992), pp. 180–91.
Annual Survey of South African Law (Cape Town: Juta, yearly).
Armstrong, Amanda, "'Hear No Evil, See No Evil, Speak No Evil:' Media Restrictions and the State of Emergency," in Glenn Moss and Ingrid Obery, eds., *South African Review 4* (Johannesburg: Ravan Press, 1987), pp. 199–214.
Barrell, Howard, *MK: The ANC's Armed Struggle* (London: Penguin, 1990).
———, "The Turn to the Masses: The African National Congress' Strategic Review of 1978–1979," *Journal of Southern African Studies,* vol. 18, no. 1, March 1991, pp. 64–92.
Baskin, Jeremy, *Striking Back: A History of Cosatu* (Johannesburg: Ravan Press, 1991).
Beaufre, Andre, *A Strategy of Action* (London: Faber and Faber, 1967).
———, *An Introduction to Strategy* (London: Faber and Faber, 1963).
Bennett, Mark, comp., "Stayaway Strikes in the 1980s (Part II), June 1986–June 1988," *Indicator SA,* vol. 5, no. 3, Autumn/Winter 1988.

Bernstein, Hilda, *The Rift: the Exile Experience of South Africans* (London: Jonathan Cape, 1994).
Boonzaier, Emile and John Sharp, eds., *South African Keywords: the Uses and Abuses of Political Concepts* (Cape Town: David Philip, 1988).
Bopela, Thula and Daluxolo Luthuli, *Umkhonto we Sizwe: Fighting for a Divided People* (Alberton: Galago, 2005).
Boraine, Andrew, "Security Management Upgrading in the Black Townships," *Transformation,* no. 8, 1989, pp. 24–46.
Borer, Tristan A., *Challenging the State: Churches as Political Actors in South Africa, 1980–1994* (Notre Dame: University of Notre Dame Press, 1998).
Botha, Roelof (Pik), "His South African Connection," in Hans d'Orville, ed., *Leadership for Africa: In Honor of Olusegun Obasanjo on the Occasion of his 60th Birthday* (New York: Africa Leadership Foundation, 1995), pp. 55–69.
Bozzoli, Belinda, *Theatres of Struggle and the End of Apartheid* (Johannesburg: Witwatersrand University Press, 2004).
Braam, Conny, *Operation Vula* (Jacana: Bellevue, 2004).
Brewer, John D., "Black Protest in South Africa's Crisis: a Comment on Legassick," *African Affairs,* vol. 85, April 1986, pp. 283–94.
Breytenbach, W. J., *The ANC: Future Prognosis* (Bellville: University of Stellenbosch Institute for Futures Research, 1989).
Brittain, Victoria and Abdul S. Minty, eds., *Children of Resistance: On Children, Repression, and the Law in Apartheid South Africa* (London: Kliptown Books, 1988).
Bundy, Colin, "'Action, Comrades, Action!' The Politics of Youth-Student Resistance in the Western Cape, 1985," in Wilmot James and Mary Simons, eds., *Class, Caste and Color: a Social and Economic History of the South African Western Cape* (New Brunswick: Transaction Publishers, 1992), pp. 206–17.
———, "Around Which Corner? Revolutionary Theory and Contemporary South Africa," *Transformation,* no. 8, 1989, pp. 1–23, and Jeremy Cronin's reply, "Inside Which Circle?" *Transformation,* no. 10, 1989, pp. 70–78.
———, "Street Sociology and Pavement Politics: Some Aspects of Student/Youth Consciousness During the 1985 Schools Crisis in Greater Cape Town," *Journal of Southern African Studies,* vol. 13, no. 3, April 1987.
Buntman, Fran, *Robben Island and Prisoner Resistance to Apartheid* (New York: Cambridge University Press, 2003).
Callinicos, Luli, *Oliver Tambo: Beyond the Engeli Mountains* (Cape Town: David Philip, 2004).
Carter, Charles, "'We are the Progressives': Alexandra Youth Congress Activists and the Freedom Charter, 1983–85," *Journal of Southern African Studies,* vol. 17, no. 2, June 1991, pp. 197–220.
———, "Community and Conflict: The Alexandra Rebellion of 1986," *Journal of Southern African Studies,* vol. 18, no. 1, March 1991, pp. 115–42.
Cassim, Fuad, "Growth, Crisis, and Change in the South African Economy," in John Suckling and Landeg White, eds., *After Apartheid: Renewal of the South African Economy* (London: James Currey, 1988), pp. 1–18.
Catholic Institute for International Relations, *War and Conscience in South Africa: The Churches and Conscientious Objection* (London: CIIR, 1982).
———, *Out of Step: War Resistance in South Africa, 1989* (London: CIIR, 1989).
Charlton, Michael, *The Last Colony in Africa: Diplomacy and the Independence of Rhodesia* (Oxford: Basil Blackwell, 1990).
Chaskalson, Matthew, Karen Jochelson and Jeremy Seekings, "Rent Boycotts and the

Urban Political Economy," in Glenn Moss and Ingrid Obery, eds., *South African Review 4* (Johannesburg: Ravan Press, 1987), pp. 53–74.

Chikane, Frank, *No Life of My Own: An Autobiography* (Maryknoll: Orbis Books, 1988).

Cobbett, William, and Robin Cohen, eds., *Popular Struggles in South Africa* (London: James Currey and Trenton: Africa World Press, 1988).

Cock, Jacklyn, *Colonels and Cadres: War and Gender in South Africa* (Cape Town: Oxford University Press, 1991).

Cole, Josette, *Crossroads: the Politics of Reform and Repression 1976–1986* (Johannesburg: Ravan Press, 1987).

Collinge, Jo-Anne, "The United Democratic Front," in South African Research Service, *South African Review 3* (Johannesburg: Ravan Press, 1986), pp. 248–66.

Commonwealth Group of Eminent Persons, *Mission to South Africa: The Commonwealth Report* (New York: Viking, 1986).

Crocker, Chester, *High Noon in Southern Africa: Making Peace in a Rough Neighborhood* (New York: W. W. Norton, 1992).

Davenport, Rodney and Christopher Saunders, *South Africa: a Modern History*, fifth edition, (Basingstoke: Macmillan, 2000).

Davidow, Jeffrey, *A Peace in Southern Africa: The Lancaster House Conference on Rhodesia, 1979* (Boulder: Westview, 1984).

Davies, Robert, Dan O'Meara, and Sipho Dlamini, *The Struggle for South Africa: a Reference Guide to Movements, Organizations and Institutions*, vols. 1 and 2 (London: Zed Books, 1984).

——— and Dan O'Meara, "Total Strategy in Southern Africa: an Analysis of South African Regional Policy Since 1978," *Journal of Southern African Studies*, vol. 11, no. 2, April 1985, pp. 183–211.

Davis, Stephen M., *Apartheid's Rebels: Inside South Africa's Hidden War* (New Haven: Yale University Press, 1987).

De Klerk, F. W. *The Last Trek—A New Beginning: the Autobiography* (London: Macmillan, 1998).

De Kock, Eugene, *A Long Night's Damage: Working for the Apartheid State* (Saxonwold: Contra Press, 1998).

De Kock, Wessel, *Usuthu! Cry Peace! Inkatha and the Fight for a Just South Africa* (Cape Town: Open Hand Press, 1986).

De Villiers, Les, *In Sight of Surrender: The U. S. Sanctions Campaign Against South Africa, 1946–1993* (Westport: Praeger, 1995).

Delius, Peter, *A Lion Amongst the Cattle: Reconstruction and Resistance in the Northern Transvaal* (Portsmouth: Heinemann and Johannesburg: Ravan Press, 1996).

Diar, Prakash, *The Sharpeville Six* (Toronto: McClelland and Stewart, 1990).

Du Preez, Max, *Pale Native: Memories of a Renegade Reporter* (Cape Town: Zebra Press, 2003).

Dugard, John, *Human Rights and the South African Legal Order* (Princeton: Princeton University Press, 1978).

———, Nicholas Haysom and Gilbert Marcus, *The Last Years of Apartheid: Civil Liberties in South Africa* (New York: Ford Foundation and Foreign Policy Association, 1991).

Ebrahim, Hassen, *The Soul of a Nation: Constitution-Making in South Africa* (Cape Town: Oxford University Press, 1998).

Ellis, Stephen, "Mbokodo: Security in ANC Camps, 1961–1990," *African Affairs*, vol. 93, no. 371, April 1994, pp. 279–98.

———, and Tsepo Sechaba [Oyama Mabandla], *Comrades Against Apartheid: the ANC and the Communist Party in Exile* (Bloomington: Indiana University Press and London: James Currey, 1992).
Ellmann, Stephen, *In a Time of Trouble: Law and Liberty in South Africa's State of Emergency* (Oxford: Clarendon Press, 1992).
———, "Law and Legitimacy in South Africa," *Law and Social Inquiry*, vol. 20, no. 2, 1995, pp. 407–80.
Esack, Farid, "Three Islamic Strands in the South African Struggle for Justice," *Third World Quarterly*, vol. 10, no. 2, April 1988, pp. 473–98.
Evans, Gavin, *Dancing Shoes is Dead: a Tale of Fighting Men in South Africa* (London: Black Swan, 2002).
Fine, Alan and Eddie Webster, "Transcending Traditions: Trade Unions and Political Unity," in Glenn Moss and Ingrid Obery, eds., *South African Review 5* (Johannesburg: Ravan Press, 1989), pp. 256–74.
Finnegan, William, *Crossing the Line: a Year in the Land of Apartheid* (Berkeley: University of California Press, 1986).
Frankel, Philip H., *Pretoria's Praetorians: Civil-Military Relations in South Africa* (Cambridge: Cambridge University Press, 1984).
———, Noam Pines and Mark Swilling, eds., *State, Resistance and Change in South Africa* (New York: Croon Helm and Johannesburg: Southern Book Publishers, 1988).
Frederikse, Julie, *The Unbreakable Thread: Non-Racialism in South Africa* (Bloomington: Indiana University Press, 1990).
Friedman, Steven, "The Power of Speech," *Leadership SA*, vol. 8, no. 3, 1989, pp. 101–104.
———, *Building Tomorrow Today: African Workers in Trade Unions, 1970–1984* (Johannesburg: Ravan Press, 1987).
———, ed., *The Long Journey: South Africa's Quest for a Negotiated Settlement* (Johannesburg: Ravan Press, 1993).
Gaddis, John Lewis, *The Cold War* (London: Penguin Books, 2005).
Gevisser, Mark, *Thabo Mbeki: the Dream Deferred* (Cape Town: Jonathan Ball, 2007), and *A Legacy of Liberation: Thabo Mbeki and the Future of the South African Dream* (New York: Palgrave Macmillan, 2009).
Gibson, Nigel, "Why is Participation a Dirty Word in South African Politics," *Africa Today*, vol. 37, no. 2, 1990, pp. 23–52.
Giliomee, Hermann and Lawrence Schlemmer, eds. *Negotiating South Africa's Future* (Johannesburg: Southern Book Publishers, 1989).
———, eds., *Up Against the Fences: Poverty, Passes and Privilege in South Africa* (Cape Town: David Philip, 1985).
Glaser, Daryl, "Behind the Indaba: the Making of the KwaNatal Option," *Transformation*, no. 2, 1986, pp. 4–30.
Golding, Marcel, "Black Consciousness and Trade Unions," *South African Labour Bulletin*, vol. 10, no. 2, October/November 1984, pp. 29–36.
Goodman, David, *Fault Lines: Journeys into the New South Africa* (Berkeley: University of California Press, 1999).
Goodwin, June, and Ben Schiff, *Heart of Whiteness: Afrikaners Face Black Rule in the New South Africa* (New York: Scribner, 1995).
Gouws, Amanda and Rhoda Kadalie, "Women in the Struggle: the Past and the Future," in Ian Liebenberg, Fiona Lortan, Bobby Nel, and Gert van der Westhuizen, eds., *The Long March: The Story of the Struggle for Liberation in South Africa* (Pretoria: HAUM, 1994), pp. 214–26.

Griffiths, Ieuan, and D. C. Funnell, "The Abortive Swazi Land Deal," *African Affairs*, vol. 90, no. 358, January 1991, pp. 51–64.

Hamann, Hilton, *Days of the Generals: the Untold Story of South Africa's Apartheid-Era Military Generals* (Cape Town: Zebra Press, 2001).

Hanlon, Joseph, ed., *South Africa: The Sanctions Report: Documents and Statistics* (London: James Currey, 1990).

Harris, Laurence, "South Africa's External Debt Crisis," in Bade Onimode, ed., *The IMF, The World Bank and African Debt: The Economic Impact* (London: Zed Books, 1989), pp. 172–91.

Harvey, Robert, *The Fall of Apartheid: the Inside Story from Smuts to Mbeki* (Basingstoke: Palgrave Macmillan, 2001).

Hassim, Shireen, *Women's Organizations and Democracy in South Africa: Contesting Authority* (Scottsville: University of KwaZulu-Natal Press, 2006).

Hauck, David, Meg Voorhes and Glenn Goldberg, *Two Decades of Debate: The Controversy Over United States Companies in South Africa* (Washington: Investor Responsibility Research Center, 1983).

Haysom, Nicholas, *Mabangalala: The Rise of Right-wing Vigilantes in South Africa* (Johannesburg: Centre for Applied Legal Studies, University of the Witwatersrand, 1986).

—— and Steven Kahanovitz, "Courts and the State of Emergency," in Glenn Moss and Ingrid Obery, eds., *South African Review 4* (Johannesburg: Ravan Press, 1987), pp. 187–98.

Helliker, Kirk, Andre Roux and Roland White, "'Asithengi': Recent Consumer Boycotts," in Glenn Moss and Ingrid Obery, eds., *South African Review 4* (Johannesburg: Ravan Press, 1987), pp. 33–52.

Hendler, Paul, *Urban Policy and Housing: Case Studies on Negotiation in PWV Townships* (Johannesburg: SAIRR, 1988).

Hendrickse, Allan, "The Constitution (3)," *Leadership SA*, vol. 2, no. 2, 1983, pp. 19–23.

Herbstein, Denis, *White Lies: Canon Collins and the Secret War Against Apartheid* (Oxford: James Currey and Cape Town: HSRC Press, 2004).

Hindson, Doug, *Pass Controls and the Urban African Proletariat in South Africa* (Johannesburg: Ravan Press, 1987).

Houston, Gregory, *The National Liberation Struggle in South Africa: a Case Study of the United Democratic Front, 1983–1987* (Aldershot: Ashgate and Cape Town: HSRC Press, 1999).

Hudson, Peter and Mike Sarakinsky, "Class Interests and Politics: the Case of the Urban African Bourgeoisie," in South African Research Service, *South African Review 3* (Johannesburg: Ravan Press, 1986), pp. 169–85.

Huntington, Samuel, "Reform and Stability in South Africa," *International Security*, vol. 6, no. 4, Spring 1982, pp. 3–25.

——, "The Trouble with Reform," *Financial Mail*, October 24, 1986, pp. 85–87.

Hyslop, Jonathan, "School Student Movements and State Education Policy: 1972–87," in William Cobbett and Robin Cohen, eds., *Popular Struggles in South Africa* (London: David Currey, 1988), pp. 183–209.

James, Wilmot G., ed., *The State of Apartheid* (Boulder: Lynne Rienner, 1987).

Jeffery, Anthea, *The Natal Story: Sixteen Years of Conflict* (Johannesburg: SAIRR, 1997).

Jenkin, Tim, "The Story of the Secret Underground Communications Network of Operation Vula," *Mayibuye*, vol. 6, nos. 1–6, May-October, 1995.

Jeppie, Shamil, "Amandla and Allahu Akbar: Muslims and Resistance in South Africa, c. 1970–1987," *Journal for the Study of Religion,* vol. 4, no. 1, March 1991, pp. 3–19.

Jochelson, Karen, "Reform, Repression and Resistance in South Africa: A Case Study of Alexandra Township, 1979–1989," *Journal of Southern African Studies,* vol. 16, no. 1, March 1990, pp. 1–32.

Johnson, Phyllis and David Martin, eds., *Frontline Southern Africa: Destructive Engagement* (New York: Four Walls Eight Windows, 1988).

Johnson, Shaun, ed., *South Africa: No Turning Back* (Bloomington: Indiana University Press, 1989).

Jordan, Z. Pallo, ed. *Oliver Tambo Remembered* (Johannesburg: Macmillan, 2007).

Joubert, Elsa, *The Long Journey of Poppie Nongena* (Johannesburg: Jonathan Ball, 1980).

Karis, Thomas G., "The Resurgent African National Congress: Competing for Hearts and Minds in South Africa," in Thomas M. Callaghy, ed., *South Africa in Southern Africa: The Intensifying Vortex of Violence* (New York: Praeger, 1983), pp. 191–236.

———, "Revolution in the Making: Black Politics in South Africa," *Foreign Affairs,* Winter 1983/84, pp. 378–406.

———, "South African Liberation: the Communist Factor," *Foreign Affairs,* Winter 1986/87, pp. 267–88.

Karis, Thomas G., and Gail M. Gerhart, *From Protest to Challenge: a Documentary History of African Politics in South Africa, 1882–1990,* volume 5, *Nadir and Resurgence, 1964–1979* (Bloomington: Indiana University Press and Pretoria: UNISA Press, 1997).

Kasrils, Ronnie, *"Armed and Dangerous": My Undercover Struggle Against Apartheid* (Oxford: Heinemann, 1993).

Kathrada, Ahmed, *Letters from Robben Island: a Selection of Ahmed Kathrada's Prison Correspondence, 1964–1989* (East Lansing: Michigan State University Press and Cape Town: Mayibuye Books, 1999).

———, *Memoirs* (Cape Town: Zebra Press, 2004).

Kentridge, Matthew, *An Unofficial War: Inside the Conflict in Pietermaritzburg* (Cape Town: David Philip, 1990).

Kibbe, Jennifer and David Hauck, *Leaving South Africa: the Impact of U.S. Corporate Disinvestment* (Washington: Investor Responsibility Research Center, 1988).

Kruss, Glenda, "The 1986 State of Emergency in the Western Cape," in Glenn Moss and Ingrid Obery, eds., *South Africa Review 4* (Johannesburg: Ravan Press, 1987), pp. 173–86.

Labour Monitoring Group, "The November Stay-Away," *South African Labour Bulletin,* vol. 10, no. 6, May 1985.

Laurence, Patrick, *Death Squads: Apartheid's Secret Weapon* (London: Penguin Books, 1990).

Legassick, Martin, *Armed Struggle and Democracy: The Case of South Africa* (Uppsala: Nordiska Afrikainstitutet, 2002).

Lewis, David, "Capital, the Trade Unions, and the National Liberation Struggle," *Monthly Review,* vol. 37, no. 11, April 1986, pp. 39–50.

Liebenberg, Ian, Fiona Lortan, Bobby Nel, and Gert van der Westhuizen, eds., *The Long March: The Story of the Struggle for Liberation in South Africa* (Pretoria: HAUM, 1994).

Lieberfeld, Daniel, *Talking with the Enemy: Negotiation and Threat Perception in South Africa and Israel/Palestine* (Westport: Praeger, 1999).

Lijphart, Arend, *Power-Sharing in South Africa* (Berkeley: University of California Press, 1985).

Lipton, Merle, *Sanctions and South Africa: The Dynamics of Economic Isolation* (London: Economist Intelligence Unit, 1988).

Lodge, Tom, *Politics in South Africa: From Mandela to Mbeki* (Bloomington: Indiana University Press, 2003).

——, "Soldiers of the Storm: a Profile of the Azanian People's Liberation Army," in Jakkie Cilliers and M. Reichardt, eds., *About Turn: the Transformation of the South African Military and Intelligence* (Midrand: Institute for Defence Policy, 1995), pp. 105–17.

——, "The African National Congress of South Africa, 1976–1983: Guerrilla War and Armed Propaganda," *Journal of Contemporary African Studies,* vol. 3, nos. 1 & 2, April 1984, pp. 153–80.

—— and Bill Nasson, *All, Here, and Now: Black Politics in South Africa in the 1980s* (New York: Ford Foundation and Foreign Policy Association, 1991).

—— and Mark Swilling, "The Year of the Amabuthu," *Africa Report,* March–April 1986, pp. 4–7.

Louw, Raymond, ed., *Four Days in Lusaka: Whites in a Changing Society* (Excom: Five Freedoms Forum, 1989).

Lowry, Donovan, *20 Years in The Labour Movement: the Urban Training Project and Change in South Africa 1971–1991* (Johannesburg: Wadmore Publishing, 1999).

Luckhardt, Ken and Brenda Wall, *Organize or Starve! A History of the South African Congress of Trade Unions* (London: Lawrence and Wishart, 1980).

Maaba, Brown and Seán Morrow, "Infiltration, Fear and Paranoia at Solomon Mahlangu Freedom College, 1978–1992," *War and Society,* vol. 23, no. 1, May 2005, pp. 107–24.

Malan, Rian, *My Traitor's Heart: A South African Exile Returns to Face His Country, His Tribe, And His Conscience* (New York: Atlantic Monthly Press, 1990).

Maloka, Eddy, *The South African Communist Party in Exile 1963–1990* (Pretoria: Africa Institute of South Africa, 2002).

Mandela, Nelson, *Long Walk to Freedom* (Boston: Little, Brown and Randburg: Macdonald Purnell, 1994), and later paperback editions.

Manganyi, N. Chabani and Andre du Toit, eds., *Political Violence and the Struggle in South Africa* (Halfway House: Southern Book Publishers, 1990).

Maphai, Vincent, "The Role of Black Consciousness in the Liberation Struggle," in Ian Liebenberg, Fiona Lortan, Bobby Nel, and Gert van der Westhuizen, eds., *The Long March: The Story of the Struggle for Liberation in South Africa* (Pretoria: HAUM, 1994), pp. 125–37.

Marais, Hein, *South Africa, Limits to Change: the Political Economy of Transition* (Cape Town: University of Cape Town Press, 1998).

Marcus, Tessa, "The Women's Question and National Liberation in South Africa," in Maria van Diepen, ed., *The National Question in South Africa* (London: Zed Books, 1988), pp. 96–109.

Marks, Monique, *Young Warriors: Youth Politics, Identity and Violence in South Africa* (Johannesburg: Witwatersrand University Press, 2001).

Martin, David and Phyllis Johnson, *The Struggle for Zimbabwe: the Chimurenga War* (Johannesburg: Ravan Press, 1981).

Marx, Anthony, *Lessons of Struggle: South African Internal Opposition, 1960–1990* (New York: Oxford University Press, 1992).

Mashabela, Harry, *Fragile Figures? The 1988 PWV Township Elections* (Johannesburg: SAIRR, 1988).

———— and Monty Narsoo, *The Boksburg Boycott* (Johannesburg: SAIRR, 1989).
Massie, Robert, *Loosing the Bonds: the United States and South Africa in the Apartheid Years* (New York: Nan A. Talese, 1997).
Matiwana, Mizana, Shirley Walters, and Zelda Groener, *The Struggle for Democracy: a Study of Community Organisations in Greater Cape Town from the 1960s to 1988* (Bellville: University of the Western Cape, 1989).
Mayekiso, Mzwanele, *Township Politics: Civic Struggles for a New South Africa* (New York: Monthly Review Press, 1996).
Mbeki, Govan, *Sunset at Midday: Latshon'ilang'emini!* (Braamfontein: Nolwazi Educational Publishers, 1996).
Mbeki, Thabo, "The Fatton Thesis: a Rejoinder," *Canadian Journal of African Studies,* vol. 18, no. 3, 1984, pp. 609–12.
McCuen, J. J., *The Art of Counter-revolutionary War: The Strategy of Counterinsurgency* (London: Faber and Faber, 1966).
McKinley, Dale, *The ANC and the Liberation Struggle: a Critical Political Biography* (London: Pluto, 1997).
Meer, Fatima, ed., *Treason Trial—1985* (Durban: Madiba Publications, 1989).
————, ed., *Unrest in Natal—August 1985* (Durban: Institute for Black Research, 1985).
Meredith, Martin, *Coming to Terms: South Africa's Search for Truth* (New York: Public Affairs, 1999).
Merrett, Christopher, *A Culture of Censorship: Secrecy and Intellectual Repression in South Africa* (Cape Town: David Philip, 1994).
Mills, Greg and David Williams, *Seven Battles that Shaped South Africa* (Cape Town: Tafelberg, 2006).
Minter, William, *Apartheid's Contras: an Inquiry into the Roots of War in Angola and Mozambique* (London: Zed Books and Johannesburg: Witwatersrand University Press, 1994).
Moodie, T. Dunbar, *Going for Gold: Men, Mines, and Migration* (Berkeley: University of California Press, 1994).
Morran, E. S. and Lawrence Schlemmer, *Faith for the Fearful? An Investigation into New Churches in the Greater Durban Area* (Durban: Centre for Applied Social Sciences, University of Natal, 1984).
Morrow, Seán, "Dakawa Development Centre: An African National Congress Settlement in Tanzania, 1982–1992," *African Affairs,* vol. 97, no. 389, October 1998, pp. 497–521.
————, Brown Maaba and Loyiso Pulumani, *Education in Exile: SOMAFCO, the ANC School in Tanzania, 1978 to 1992* (Cape Town: HSRC Press, 2004).
Moss, Glenn and Ingrid Obery, eds., *South African Review 4* (Johannesburg: Ravan Press, 1987).
————, eds., *South African Review 5* (Johannesburg: Ravan Press, 1989).
Moss, Rose, *Shouting at the Crocodile: Popo Molefe, Patrick Lekota, and the Freeing of South Africa* (Boston: Beacon Press, 1990).
Mufson, Steven, *Fighting Years: Black Resistance and the Struggle for a New South Africa* (Boston: Beacon Press, 1990).
Muller, Johan, "People's Education and the National Education Crisis Committee," in Glenn Moss and Ingrid Obery, eds., *South African Review 4* (Johannesburg: Ravan Press, 1987), pp. 18–32.
Murray, Christina and Catherine O'Regan, eds., *No Place to Rest: Forced Removals and the Law in South Africa* (Cape Town: Oxford University Press, 1990).
Murray, Hugh, "A Moment in History [Mfuwe meeting]," *Leadership SA,* vol. 4, no. 3, 1985.

Nasson, Bill, "The Unity Movement: its Legacy in Historical Consciousness," *Radical History Review,* vol. 46, no. 7, January 1990, pp. 189–212.
Nattrass, Nicoli, "Politics and Economics in ANC Economic Policy," *African Affairs,* vol. 93, no. 372, July 1994, pp. 343–59.
Nel, Philip, "The ANC and 'Communism'," in Willie Esterhuyse and Philip Nel, eds., *The ANC and its Leaders* (Cape Town: Tafelberg, 1990), pp. 42–65.
Nix, Jennifer, *Actions against Journalists in South Africa between 1960 and 1994* (Johannesburg: Freedom of Expression Institute, 1997).
O'Malley, Padraig, *Shades of Difference: Mac Maharaj and the Struggle for South Africa* (New York: Viking, 2007).
Orkin, Mark, *Disinvestment, the Struggle and the Future: What Black South Africans Really Think* (Johannesburg: Ravan Press, 1986).
———, ed., *Sanctions Against South Africa* (Cape Town: David Philip, 1989).
Padayachee, Vishnu, "Private International Banks, the Debt Crisis and the Apartheid State, 1982–1985," *African Affairs,* vol. 87, no. 348, July 1988, pp. 361–76.
Parker, Peter and Joyce Mokhesi-Parker, *In the Shadow of Sharpeville: Apartheid and Criminal Justice* (New York: New York University Press, 1998).
Pauw, Jacques, *In the Heart of the Whore: The Story of Apartheid's Death Squads* (Halfway House: Southern Book Publishers, 1991).
———, *Into the Heart of Darkness: Confessions of Apartheid's Assassins* (Johannesburg: Jonathan Ball, 1997).
Pickard-Cambridge, Claire, *The Greying of Johannesburg: Residential Desegregation in the Johannesburg Area* (Johannesburg: SAIRR, 1988).
Plaut, Martin, "Debates in a Shark Tank—the Politics of South Africa's Non-racial Trade Unions," *African Affairs,* vol. 91, no. 364, July 1992, pp. 389–403.
Pottinger, Brian, *The Imperial Presidency: PW Botha, the First Ten Years* (Johannesburg: Southern Book Publishers, 1988).
———, "The Eastern Cape Boycotts: Where Crisis has Become a Way of Life," *Frontline,* vol. 1, no. 8, March 1981.
"Pretoria's Masterplan: Cantons," *Front File,* August 1989, p. 6.
Price, Robert M., *The Apartheid State in Crisis: Political Transformation in South Africa, 1975–1990* (New York: Oxford University Press, 1991).
Reynolds, Andrew, ed., *Election '94 South Africa: the Campaigns, Results and Future Prospects* (New York: St. Martin's Press and Cape Town: David Philip, 1994).
Rosenthal, Richard, *Mission Improbable: a Piece of the South African Story* (Cape Town: David Philip, 1998).
Sampson, Anthony, *Black and Gold: Tycoons, Revolutionaries and Apartheid* (London: Hodder and Stoughton, 1987).
———, *Mandela: the Authorised Biography* (London: HarperCollins, 1999).
Sanders, James, *Apartheid's Friends: The Rise and Fall of South Africa's Secret Service* (London: John Murray, 2006).
Sapire, Hilary, "Politics and Protest in Shack Settlements of the Pretoria-Witwatersrand-Vereeniging Region, South Africa, 1980–1990," *Journal of Southern African Studies,* vol. 18, no. 3, September 1992, pp. 670–97.
Savage, Michael, "The Imposition of Pass Laws on the African Population in South Africa 1916–1984," *African Affairs,* vol. 85, no. 339, April 1986, pp. 181–205.
Scharf, Wilfried and Baba Ngcokoto, "Images of Punishment in the People's Courts of Cape Town, 1985–7: From Prefigurative Justice to Populist Violence," in N. Chabani Manganyi and Andre du Toit, eds., *Political Violence and the Struggle in South Africa* (Halfway House: Southern Book Publishers, 1990), pp. 341–72.

Schlemmer, Lawrence, "The October Municipal Elections: an Assessment," *South Africa Foundation Review,* December, 1988, pp. 2-3.
——, "South Africa's Futures: Probable Developments in the Medium Term," *South Africa International,* vol. 20, no. 2, October 1989, pp. 63-73.
Schuster, Lynda, *A Burning Hunger: One Family's Struggle Against Apartheid* (London: Jonathan Cape, 2004).
Seekings, Jeremy, "From 'Quiescence' to 'People's Power': Township Politics in Kagiso, 1985-1986," *Social Dynamics,* vol. 18, no. 1, June 1992, pp. 20-41.
——, *Heroes or Villains? Youth Politics in the 1980s* (Johannesburg: Ravan Press, 1993).
——, "People's Courts and Popular Politics," in Glenn Moss and Ingrid Obery, eds., *South African Review 5* (Johannesburg: Ravan Press, 1989), pp. 119-35.
——, "The Origins of Political Mobilisation in PWV Townships, 1980-84," in William Cobbett and Robin Cohen, eds., *Popular Struggles in South Africa* (London: James Currey, 1988), pp. 59-76.
——, *The UDF: A History of the United Democratic Front in South Africa, 1983-1991* (Cape Town: David Philip and Athens: Ohio University Press, 2000).
Seethal, Cecil, "Restructuring the Local State in South Africa: Regional Services Councils and Crisis Resolution," *Political Geography Quarterly,* vol. 10, no. 1, January 1991, pp. 8-25.
Sellström, Tor, *Sweden and National Liberation in Southern Africa,* volume 2 (Uppsala: Nordiska Afrikainstitutet, 2002).
Shaw, Mark, "Spy Meets Spy: Negotiating New Intelligence Structures," in Steven Friedman and Doreen Atkinson, eds., *South Africa Review 7: The Small Miracle—South Africa's Negotiated Settlement* (Johannesburg: Ravan Press, 1994), pp. 257-75.
Shubin, Vladimir, *ANC: a View from Moscow* (Bellville: Mayibuye Books, 1999).
Sibeko, Archie, with Joyce Leeson, *Freedom in Our Lifetime* (Durban: Indicator Press, 1996).
Sisulu, Elinor, *Walter & Albertina Sisulu: In Our Lifetime* (Cape Town: David Philip, 2002).
Slabbert, Frederik Van Zyl, *The Last White Parliament* (Johannesburg: Jonathan Ball and Hans Strydom, 1985).
Slovo, Gillian, *Every Secret Thing: My Family, My Country* (Boston: Little, Brown, 1997).
Slovo, Joe, *Slovo: The Unfinished Autobiography* (Johannesburg: Ravan Press, 1995).
South African Democracy Education Trust, *The Road to Democracy in South Africa, Volume 2 [1970-80]* (Pretoria: UNISA Press, 2006).
South African Institute of Race Relations, *Survey of Race Relations in South Africa* (Johannesburg: SAIRR, annual). Title changed in 1984 to *Race Relations Survey,* and after 1994 to *South African Survey.*
South African Research Service, *South African Review* (seven issues between 1983 and 1994, listed separately under editors).
Sparks, Allister, *Tomorrow is Another Country: the Inside Story of South Africa's Negotiated Revolution* (Johannesburg: Struik, 1994).
Stadler, Herman, *The Other Side of the Story* (Pretoria: Contact Publishers, 1997).
Stengel, Richard, *January Sun: One Day, Three Lives, A South African Town* (New York: Simon & Schuster, 1990).
Straker, Gill, *Faces in the Revolution: the Psychological Effects of Violence on Township Youth in South Africa* (Cape Town: David Philip and Athens: Ohio University Press, 1992).

Streek, Barry, "Illusion and Reality in South Africa's Sport Policy," *South Africa International,* vol. 16, no. 1, July 1985, pp. 29–41.

Surplus People Project, *Forced Removals in South Africa,* volume 1 (Cape Town: Surplus People Project, 1983).

Suttner, Raymond, *The ANC Underground in South Africa: a Social and Historical Study* (Johannesburg: Jacana Media, 2008).

Swilling, Mark, "Stayaways, Urban Protest and the State" in South African Research Service, *South African Review 3* (Johannesburg: Ravan Press, 1986), pp. 20–50.

———, "The Extra-Parliamentary Movement: Strategies and Prospects," in Hermann Giliomee and Lawrence Schlemmer, eds., *Negotiating South Africa's Future* (Johannesburg: Southern Book Publishers, 1989), pp. 63–68.

———, "The United Democratic Front and Township Revolt in South Africa," in William Cobbett and Robin Cohen, eds., *Popular Struggles in South Africa* (London: James Currey, 1988), pp. 90–113.

———, William Cobbett, and Roland Hunter, "Finance, electricity costs, and the rent boycott," in Mark Swilling, Richard Humphries, and Khehla Shubane, eds., *Apartheid City in Transition* (Cape Town: Oxford University Press, 1991), pp. 174–96.

——— and Khehla Shubane, "Negotiating Urban Transition: the Soweto Experience," in Robin Lee and Lawrence Schlemmer, eds., *Transition to Democracy: Policy Perspectives 1991* (Cape Town: Oxford University Press, 1991), pp. 223–58.

Switzer, Les and Mohamed Adhikari, eds., *South Africa's Resistance Press: Alternative Voices in the Last Generation Under Apartheid* (Athens: Ohio University Press, 2000).

Tambo, Oliver, *Preparing for Power: Oliver Tambo Speaks* (London: Heinemann, 1987).

"The Greater Soweto Accord," *History in the Making,* vol. 1, no. 2, November 1990, pp. 29–38.

Tomaselli, Keyan and P. Eric Louw, eds., *The Alternative Press in South Africa* (London: James Currey, 1991).

Transvaal Rural Action Committee, "KwaNdebele: The Struggle Against 'Independence'," in William Cobbett and Robin Cohen, eds., *Popular Struggles in South Africa* (London: James Currey, 1988), pp. 114–35.

Truth and Reconciliation Commission of South Africa Report, 7 volumes (Cape Town: Truth and Reconciliation Commission, 1998, 2002 and 2003).

Tsele, Molefe, "Education for Democracy—a Case Study: the National Education Coordinating [Crisis] Committee (NECC)," in Klaus Nurnberger, ed., *A Democratic Vision for South Africa: Political Realism and Christian Responsibility* (Pietermaritzburg: Encounter Publications, 1991), pp. 460–70.

Twala, Mwezi and Ed Benard, *Mbokodo: Inside MK—Mwezi Twala, a Soldier's Story* (Johannesburg: Jonathan Ball, 1994).

Uhlig, Mark, ed., *Apartheid in Crisis* (New York: Viking Penguin, 1986).

United Nations, *The United Nations and Apartheid 1948–1994* (New York: United Nations, 1994).

Unterhalter, Elaine, *Forced Removal: the Division, Segregation and Control of the People of South Africa* (London: International Defence and Aid Fund, 1987).

Van der Merwe, Hendrik W., *Peacemaking in South Africa: a Life in Conflict Resolution* (Cape Town: Tafelberg, 2000).

Van der Merwe, Stoffel, *And What About the Black People?* (Pretoria: National Party, May 1985).

Van der Ross, Richard, *The Rise and Decline of Apartheid: a Study of Political Movements Among the Coloured People of South Africa, 1880–1985* (Cape Town: Tafelberg, 1986).

Van Kessel, Ineke, *"Beyond Our Wildest Dreams": The United Democratic Front and the Transformation of South Africa* (Charlottesville: University of Virginia Press, 2000).
Van Staden, Gary, "Return of the Prodigal Son: Prospects for a Revival of the Pan Africanist Congress," *International Affairs Bulletin,* vol. 12, no. 3, 1988, pp. 35–64.
Viljoen, Gerrit, "Open for Business," *Leadership SA,* vol. 8, no. 8, 1989, pp. 71–74.
Villa-Vicencio, Charles, "The Church: Discordant and Divided," *Africa Report,* vol. 28, no. 4, July-August 1983, pp. 13–16.
——, *Trapped in Apartheid: a Socio-Theological History of the English-Speaking Churches* (Cape Town: David Philip and Maryknoll: Orbis, 1988).
Waldmeir, Patti, *Anatomy of a Miracle: the End of Apartheid and the Birth of the New South Africa* (New York: W. W. Norton, 1997).
Wentzel, Jill, "History of Attacks on Black Local Authorities," *Spotlight* no. 2 (Johannesburg: SAIRR, August 1991).
Wilson, Francis and Mamphela Ramphele, *Uprooting Poverty: the South African Challenge* (New York: W. W. Norton and Cape Town: David Philip, 1989).
Wolpe, Harold, *Race, Class and the Apartheid State* (London: James Currey, 1988).
Zartman, I. William, "Local Negotiations in South Africa," in Stephen John Stedman, ed., *South Africa: The Political Economy of Transformation* (Boulder: Lynne Rienner, 1994), pp. 65–84.

Periodicals

Africa Confidential
Africa News
Africa Perspective
Africa Report
African Affairs
African Communist*
Agenda
Al-Qalam
ANC News Briefing
Azania News
Cape Times
City Press
Clarion Call*
Crisis News*
Critical Health*
Dawn*
Democracy in Action*
Facts and Reports
Financial Mail
Frontline
Grassroots*
History in the Making
IDAF Focus
Ikwezi*
Indicator SA
Inqaba ya Basebenzi*
Isizwe*
Journal of Southern African Studies
Leadership SA
Mail and Guardian
Mayibuye*
Monitor
Muslim News
New Era
New Nation
New York Times
Rand Daily Mail
Reality
Resister
Rixaka*
SAIRR Spotlight
SASPU Focus*
SASPU National*
Searchlight South Africa*
Sechaba*
Social Dynamics
Social Review
South
South African Labour Bulletin
Southern African Political and Economic Monthly (SAPEM)
SouthScan
Sowetan
Speak*

Star
Sunday Independent
Sunday Times
*The Black Sash**
The Leader
Transformation
*Umsebenzi**
Upfront
VOW (Voice of Women)
Vrye Weekblad

Washington Post
Weekly Mail
*Work in Progress**

* indicates journals accessible on www.Aluka.org and http://disa.ukzn.ac.za

Published Sources of Documents in This Book

Chapter 1. Document 1: *Post,* March 21, 1980. Document 2: *Sunday Times,* April 6, 1980. Document 3: *Kwasa,* November 1980. Document 4: *Manchester Guardian Weekly,* October 4, 1981. Document 7: *Forced Removals in South Africa,* volume 4 (Natal) (Cape Town: Surplus People Project and Pietermaritzburg: AFRA, 1985). Document 13: *Rand Daily Mail,* April 8, 1983. Document 19: *Sash,* May 1985. Document 24: *Issues and Challenges: a Collection of Speeches by Enos J. Mabuza* (no publisher given, 1987?). Document 28: *Sechaba,* May 1987.

Chapter 2. Document 34: *NUSAS, Beyond Reform: the Challenge of Change,* July 1983. Document 50: Itumeleng J. Mosala and Buti Tlhagale, eds., *The Unquestionable Right to Be Free: Black Theology From South Africa* (Maryknoll: Orbis Books, 1986).

Chapter 3. Document 71: *South African Labour Bulletin,* January 1986. Document 78: *Issue,* vol. 15, 1987 (USA).

Chapter 4. Document 108: International Defence and Aid Fund, *Massacre at Maseru,* London, January 1985.

Chapter 5. Document 148: *Ecunews,* April 1988. Document 163: *South,* January 25–31, 1990. Document 165: *African Communist,* no. 118, 1989. Documents 167, 168, and 169: Raymond Louw, ed., *Four Days in Lusaka: Whites in a Changing Society* (Excom: Five Freedoms Forum, 1989). Document 182: *Southern Africa* Perspectives (New York: Africa Fund, 1990).

INDEX

Page numbers in italics refer to illustrations.

Action Youth, 56, 369–72
Actstop, 47, 294–97
affirmative action, 656, 698
Africa, Sandy, 389
African National Congress (ANC), 5–6, 13, 33, 42n, 50–52, 68, 112–14, 120–52, 156, 190, 194, 207–13, 411–13, 424, 425, 426, 427, 428, 437–46, 474, 506–509, 536–39, 561–64, 576–80, 594–95, 598, 604–608, 610–14, 625–31, 637–40, 658–61, 669, 670, 683–87, 725–28
    Amandla Cultural Ensemble, 546, 631. *See also* songs, singing and musicians
    appeals for non-African support, 137, 142–43, 172–73, 174, 441, 564, 565–67, 594–95, 608–10, 610–14, 687–93, 728
    armed struggle/violence and, 62, 137, 143, 148, 183, 185, 422–28, 455, 513, 588, 609, 611, 638, 666, 695, 701, 702, 727; ANC suspends, 209; calls to renounce, 140, 143, 146, 179, 181, 186, 488, 551–52, 577, 578, 585, 601, 611, 613, 615, 639, 673–74. *See also* Umkhonto we Sizwe
    as government-in-waiting, 147, 574, 654–58, 658–61
    conferences and meetings of: Morogoro conference (1969), 121, 159n, 517, 566, 567, 574; Kabwe conference (1985), 126, 129, 136–39, 150, 444, 559, 567–74; Mfuwe meeting with Relly group (1985), 142–44, 148, 161n, 576–80; Dakar meeting (1987), 143, *143*, 162n, 608–10, 610–14; Culture in Another South Africa conference (1988), 631–11; seminar on culture (1989), 695–99; Five Freedoms Forum conference (1989), 174, 687–93, 700, 701; meeting with National Intelligence Service (September 1989), 197; trek meetings with business, political groups, allies, 37, 99, 162n, 172, 173, 174, 183, 189, 191, 437–46, 463, 576–80, 595–99, 599, 599–601, 608–10, 610–14, 626, 661, 665–67, 683–87, 700. *See also* Mells Park talks
    Congress Alliance of 1950s, 9, 46, 105, 372, 397, 526, 566
    constitutional guidelines of, 145, 147, 152, 183, 591, 654–58, 695, 698
    coordination of political and military work, 121, 128, 129, 130, 138, 161n, 186
    cultural boycott and, 177, 633, 666
    Dakawa settlement of, 121, 203n, 507
    democracy: views regarding, 144, 150, 151, 152, 183, 441, 492, 493, 496, 578–79, 609, 615, 675; within organization itself, 134, 135, 159n, 162n, 208, 372, 540, 612, 727
    diplomacy of, 5, 121, 123, 133, 145–47, 148, 152, 189–90, 442–43, 509, 536, 574, 587–89, 693–95
    farm in Zambia, 121

African National Congress (ANC) (*continued*)
  financing of, 34, 121, 122, 123, 156n, 205n, 508, 560, 561, 580, 618, 627, 669
  Freedom Charter of, 50, 54, 56, 59, 60, 125, 149, 150, 162n, 183, 265, 375–76, 386, 424, 428, 440, 442, 456, 482, 492, 493, 495, 496, 516, 517, 518, 567, 568, 570, 575, 579–80, 590, 591, 592, 605, 606, 611, 615, 632, 638, 654, 656, 657, 666, 670, 674, 682–83, 696; critiques of, 56, 77n, 369–72; mixed economy implied in, 183, 583, 611, 612, 613, 657, 659; nationalization clause in, 50, 67, 126, 144, 146, 148, 149, 151, 209, 370, 438, 579, 583, 665. *See also* Congress of South African Trade Unions; National Union of Metalworkers of South Africa; political debates; United Democratic Front
  Green Book document of, 40n, 54, 76n, 525, 530, 534
  Harare Declaration, 189–90, 196, 197, 702–704, 716, 717, 719, 727
  ideology and policies of, 50, 105, 118n, 119n, 124–26, 131, 144, 147, 149, 151, 158n, 179, 181, 183, 198, 437–46, 492–98, 512–14, 514–18, 567–74, 576–80, 580–87, 611–14, 625–31, 654–58, 665–66, 670. *See also* political debates
  in frontline states ("forward areas"), 5–6, 33, 121, 123, 130–33, 140, 189, 441, 462, 463, 506, 536–39, 617–21, 693, 694, 694–95, 726
  in rural areas, 101, 130, 138
  Indians and coloureds and, 104, 118n, 128, 140, 496–97, 518, 566, 570, 602, 716
  Inkatha and. *See* Inkatha
  international support and prestige of, 114, 120, 123, 133, 139, 147, 172, 178, 580; damaged, 548
  Makiwane eight expulsion, 124, 149, 517, 568
  Marxist Workers' Tendency and, 119n, 126–27, 141, 511–14, 526; ANC expels leaders of, 137, 141, 149, 158n, 569; *Inqaba ya Basebenzi* journal of, 127, 512
  Mells Park talks (1987–1990), 181–82, 183, 185, 187, 211; at Henley, 625, 637–40
  military camps of. *See* Umkhonto we Sizwe
  necklacing and, 84, 115n, 439
  negotiation, views on, 4, 144, 145–48, 149, 181–83, 185, 187, 189–90, 197–98, 441, 573–74, 576, 580, 585, 589–92, 595, 600, 601, 615, 617, 637–40, 674, 675–76, 682, 683–85, 687, 693–95, 715–19; preconditions for, 146, 189, 197, 441, 579, 591, 600, 601, 614, 616, 637, 674, 676, 702–704, 715–16, 727–28

Nkomati Accord and. *See* Mozambique
open membership debate in, 125, 127, 136, 506, 514–18, 565–67, 568, 575
Operation Vula, 129, 162n, 186, 189, 204n, 204n, 538
organizational structures of, 121–22, 127, 128, 581, 617–18; department of arts and culture, 122, 140, 631; department of information and publicity (DIP), 122, 538, 539, 629; department of legal and constitutional affairs, 698; department of national intelligence and security (NAT) and complaints against, 122, 133–36, 508, 509, 542–43, 546, 547, 548, 559, 560, 561, 617, 619, 628; department of political education, 626; department of religious affairs, 95, 706
"people's power," principle and rhetoric of, 99, 174, 432, 434, 440, 562, 563, 590
post-apartheid South Africa (PASA), vision of, 125, 144–45, 150–51, 172, 182, 183, 438, 440, 441, 442, 577, 578, 590–91, 608–10, 612–14, 625, 626, 627, 628, 654–58, 665–67
propaganda inside South Africa, 139, 525, 526
Radio Freedom of, 125, 139, 509, 518, 528–30, 635
rank and file members of, 121, 123, 124, 127, 139, 147, 164n; demand for consultative conference, 134, 136, 546, 548. *See also* cadres *under* Umkhonto we Sizwe
religious leaders and groups and, 95, 127, 437–46, 508, 509
rivalry with other organizations, 124–25. *See also* Azanian People's Organisation; black consciousness movement; Inkatha; Pan Africanist Congress; United Democratic Front
sanctions and. *See* sanctions
Sechaba, journal of, 127, 518, 520, 521
"sole and authentic" claim, 147, 362, 509, 669
Solomon Mahlangu Freedom College (SOMAFCO), 121, 125, 154, 424, 507, 514–18, 521
South African Communist Party, alliance with. *See* South African Communist Party
Soviet Union and communist bloc, relations with ANC, Umkhonto we Sizwe, and South African Communist Party, 5, 67, 76n, 78n, 129, 131, 138, 149, 150, 151, 153, 159n, 161n, 194, 205n, 442–43, 473, 494, 523, 540, 552, 572, 577, 592, 674–75, 694, 722; collapse of communism in, 5, 151, 192 194, 208, 721; decline of commitment by, 95, 148, 185, 187, 208, 687

INDEX 757

strategies and tactics of, 126–30, 138, 142–45, 177, 198, 514–18, 531, 532, 566, 575, 591, 658–61, 683–87; fighters and talkers, 148, 149, 152, 185
Stuart Commission of, 135–36, 137, 160n, 539–48
supporters inside South Africa, 54, 75n, 127, 133, 142, 192–93, 232, 407, 430, 513, 531, 534, 573, 588, 601, 602
symbols and flag of, 76n, 83, 102, 224
trade unions and. *See* trade unions
trials of activists. *See* courts
tribalism in, 127, 157n, 507
Umkhonto we Sizwe. *See* Umkhonto we Sizwe
unbanning and transition period (1990–1994), 198, 207–13. *See also* transition period
underground of, 38, 50, 54, 72, 75n, 103–04, 121, 124, 127–30, 136, 138, 139, 140, 141, 185, 186, 189, 455, 456, 462, 463, 533, 536, 537, 538, 573, 575, 592–94, 601–604, 608, 650, 712, 714; leaflets, 561–64, 602. *See also* Operation Vula *under* ANC
United Democratic Front and. *See* United Democratic Front
Vietnam study tour (1978), 122, 127
Voice of Women (VOW), journal of, 635
weaknesses of, 103, 128–29, 138, 185, 186, 456, 463–64, 506–507, 531, 569, 572, 608, 612, 634–35; administrative, 123–24, 127, 183, 626
Western governments, relations with, 145–47, 151, 574, 580–87
whites in, 118n, 141, 161n, 349, 496–97, 566, 670–71, 716
women in, 121, 125–26, 508, 520–22, 528, 538, 564–65, 626, 633–36, 686
Youth League, 575
youth section of, 508
Zimbabwe political parties and, 159n, 542, 590
African People's Organisation (APO), 494
Africanists and Africanism, 33, 52, 54, 55, 67, 82, 88–89, 97, 105–06, 155–56, 163n, 173, 195–96, 207; *See also* Pan Africanist Congress; political debates
Afrikaners, 4–5, 37, 89, 94, 180, 181, 212–13, 223, 350–51, 376, 378, 440, 447, 608–10, 622, 624, 625, 674, 691–93, 715, 721; Afrikaner Weerstandsbeweging (AWB), 143, 439; attitudes of, 4, 7, 12–13, 37, 354, 439, 594, 613; Broederbond and, 529, 637; dissidents among, 78n, 166; elite, 4, 206n; political divisions among, 5, 245, 285, 597; use of Afrikaans, 162n, 448, 613, 632, 692, 693. *See also* churches; Herstigte Nasionale Party; Mells Park talks; National Party government
Aggett, Neil, 64, 128, 516, 517, 566, 571, 730

Alexander, Benny, 195, *195*
Alexander, Neville, 7, 51, 76n, 248–53, 458, 523, 526
Alexandra township, 13, 57, 58, 83, 91, 281, 435–37, 461, 606, 607; "six day war" in, 83, 92, 420–22; *See also* civic associations
Amnesty International, 551
Andropov, Yuri, 522
Angola, 443, 495, 694, 704; African National Congress in, 5–6, 121, 130, 131, 133–36, 137, 184, 185, 189, 194, 203n, 205n, 428, 520, 523, 539–48, 559–61, 635, 730, 731, 735; South African invasions of, 5–6, 184, 203n, 441, 564, 571, 596, 600, 729; UNITA (União Nacional para a Independência Total de Angola), 6–7, 131, 571, 596, 719; United States "linkage" policy toward, 6, 184, 572, 735
anti-Republic Day protests (1981), 67, 374, 516
apartheid
Boksburg and Carletonville as symbols of, 175, 667, 705
family life and, 304–305, 312, 315, 316, 727. *See also* Detainees' Parents Support Committee; intergenerational tensions *under* youth; Soweto Parents' Crisis Committee
opposition to: Artists Against Apartheid, 377; as crime against humanity, 384, 582–83, 584; as heresy, 402, 654; British Anti-Apartheid Movement and, 140, 393; Dutch Anti-Apartheid Movement, 631; Free South Africa Movement (USA) and, 81, 139, 393; international anti-apartheid movement and, 36–37, 81, 139, 145, 172, 390, 393, 572–73, 683. *See also* particular South African opposition organizations
system, 3, 13, 39, 41n, 207, 587–88, 597
apartheid laws, 67, 207, 94, 225–26, 262, 312, 699
African property rights under, 14, 16, 23, 25, 239–44, 281–85
African urban and "section 10" (Urban Areas Act) rights, 14, 17–21, 18, 20, 21, 38, 41n, 69, 239–44, 276, 278, 327. *See also* permanent urban residents
demand for repeal of all, 306, 591, 616, 655, 703
pass and influx control laws, 17–19, 20, 21, 41n, 222, 225, 256, 275–77, 280, 304, 360, 391, 416, 418, 435, 439, 554; repeal of, 21, 38, 90, 606, 652
security laws and regulations, 38, 39, 91, 209, 225, 226, 256, 285, 353, 354, 361, 391, 451, 453, 616, 703. *See also* National Security Management System and State Security Council *under* National Party government; specific laws and bills *under* apartheid laws

segregation of public amenities, 175, 705; beaches, 191, 236, 699, 705, 707, 708; *See also* Separate Amenities Act

specific laws and bills: Alteration of Boundaries of Self-Governing Territories Bill, 22, 28; Black Communities Development Act, 16; Black Local Authorities Act, 14, 16, 21, 306, 322–23, 391; Free Settlement Areas Act, 296, 297; General Laws Amendment Act (1953), 591, 616; General Laws Amendment Act (1962), 591, 616; Group Areas Act (1950) and evictions under, 45, 47, 225, 257, 263, 276, 282, 294–97, 312, 315, 316, 336, 338, 367, 391, 453, 586, 638–39, 642, 653, 667, 710; Immorality Act (1957), 348, 562, 653; Internal Security Act, 38, 44n, 56, 97, 226, 361, 591, 616; Labour Relations Amendment Act, 171–72, 482, 491, 644–46, 647, 699, 705; Natives Administration Act (1927), 591, 616; Orderly Movement and Settlement of Black Persons Bill, 17–18, 240, 251, 304; Population Registration [classification] Act (1950), 257, 367, 453; Prevention of Illegal Squatting Act, 276; Prohibition of Mixed Marriages Act (1949), 225, 348, 562, 653; Promotion of Orderly Internal Politics Bill, 166, 169; Riotous Assemblies Act, 591, 616; Separate Amenities Act, 297, 663; Suppression of Communism Act (1950), 591; Terrorism Act, 226, 372, 591; Unlawful Organisations Act (1960), 591, 616; Urban Areas Consolidation Act (1945), 282. *See also* land tenure

Asmal, Kader, 162n

Asvat, Abubakr, 358, 359

Atmore, Anthony, 344

Atteridgeville township, 60, 83, 363–64. *See also* civic associations

attitudes of blacks, 45, 82, 158n, 220, 222–23, 311; Africans, 16, 19, 41n, 75n, 104, 139, 144, 196–97, 249, 283–84; coloureds, 11–12, 25, 96, 246, 335, 356, 406–407; Indians, 25, 104, 246, 263–65, 335, 371–72, 642; to apartheid laws, 19, 21, 227, 311, 482; to black bourgeoisie, 284; to Botha reforms, 19, 74, 246–47, 268, 562; to capitalism, 483, 495; to homelands, 89, 289, 312, 562; to judges and rule of law, 21, 38, 227; to negotiation, 147, 220 (*see also* particular organizations); to violence, 82, 139, 144, 183, 220; to whites, 74, 232, 313. *See also* youth

Auerbach, Franz, 689, 690

Ayob, Ismail, 187, 684, 685, 686, 687

"Azania," use of term. *See* Pan Africanist Congress

Azanian People's Organisation (AZAPO), 46, 48–49, 50–52, 56, 67, 69, 75n, 76n, 82, 88–89, 114, 155, 156, 157n, 165, 186, 196, 200n, 205n, 248, 305–306, 358–63, 387, 527, 653, 661–62, 670; at United Nations, 383; clashes with rival organizations, 82, 397–98; court cases involving, 91, 360; *Frank Talk* journal of, 360, 361; health secretariat of, 358–59; students and, 58–59; trade unions and, 48, 61. *See also* Azanian National Youth Unity; National Forum; student organizations

banning, 13, 31, 35, 224, 225, 226, 230, 256, 316, 377; banned literature, 69, 81, 361; defiance of, 705, 707; demands to end, 68, 85, 90, 114, 144, 197, 219, 366, 391, 420, 450, 453, 475, 554, 579, 585, 643, 644, 703; house arrest and, 226; of meetings, 355, 393, 435, 436, 481; of political organizations, 45, 68, 90, 156, 311, 420, 566, 639, 653, 716; of trade unions, 156, 320. *See also* censorship *under* press

bantustans. *See* homelands

Bapela, Obed, 119n

Barayi, Elijah, 87, 435

Barnard, Niël, 180–82, 187

Barrell, Howard, 159n

beerhalls, 329, 339

Belgium, 587–88

Bernstein, Lionel, 203n

Bethell, Nicholas, 140, 549–53

Biko, Steve, 124, 346; death of, 169, 222, 361, 505

Bill, Francois, 93

Bishop, Di, 67, 269

Biyase, Manuset, 437, 441, 443, 445, 446

Bizos, George, 179, 202n

black consciousness movement, 10, 29, 33, 34, 45, 46, 47, 49–52, 54, 55–56, 59, 61, 67, 82, 96, 113, 124, 173, 196, 207, 220, 356, 513, 523, 556, 568, 569, 669–70, 697; African National Congress and, 124, 147, 173, 456, 496, 669; Black Consciousness Movement of Azania (BCMA), 124; Black People's Convention, 496; black theology, 117n; Pan Africanist Congress and, 154, 155, 156; South African Youth Revolutionary Council, 157n. *See also* Azanian People's Organisation

"black-on-black violence," 21, 33, 280, 438, 450, 480, 483, 581. *See also* police; vigilantes

Black Sash, 8, 17, 66, 67, 174, 239–44, 256–59, 268–70, 278, 329, 365–66, 366–69, 376, 378, 411, 412, 726

"black spot" removals and threatened removals, 23, 25, 26, 42n; Braklaagte, 25; Daggakraal, 253; Driefontein, 25, 253–54; Goshen, 25; Hekkel, 25; Kwelera,

25; Leeuwfontein, 25; Lesseyton, 25; Lusitania, 23, 233–35; Matiwane's Kop, 234; Mgwali, 25, 355; Mogopa, 25; Mooiplaas, 25, 355; Ngema/KwaNgema, 25, 253–54; Wartburg, 25
Blackburn, Molly, 67, 74, 268–70
Bloch, Graeme, 389
Bloom, Tony, 576
Boesak, Allan, 12, 52, 93, 95, 168, 170, 267, 310–15, 365, 399, 644, 686, 708
Boipatong township, 68, 69, 210, 211, 350–51
Bonhomme, Virgil, 325, 389
Bonteheuwel, 406, 602
Boraine, Alex, 142, 143, 161n
Boraine, Andrew, 463
Boraine, Nic, 399
Botha, Pieter Willem ("P. W."), 3, 4, 10, 13, 25, 32, 43n, 65, 78n, 80, 97, 165, 178, 179, 180–82, 190, 191, 219, 220, 222–24, 249, 250, 253–54, 266, 258, 259, 263, 275, 338, 410, 438, 439, 464, 550, 551, 576–77, 578, 596, 597, 668, 671, 693, 694, 705, 708, 709, 710; adoption of "total strategy" by, 25–31, 230; has stroke, 178, 187; meeting with Mandela (1989), 187, 188; Natal violence and, 113; resignation of, 190; "Rubicon" speech (1985) by, 36–37, 142, 198. See also National Party government
Botha, Roelof ("Pik"), 44n, 222, 235, 597
Botshabelo township, 20, 41n
Botswana, 5, 131, 238, 694, 714; African National Congress in, 121, 130–31, 139, 184, 441, 509, 536, 537, 562, 617–21, 623, 625, 630–31; Dukwe refugee camp, 621; Gaborone raid (1985), 146, 377, 632; Pan Africanist Congress in, 154
Braam, Connie, 633
Breytenbach, Breyten, 632
Breytenbach, Willie, 182, 202n, 637
Britain, 81, 132, 184, 268, 370, 371, 393, 674, 720; African National Congress and government of, 145–47, 197, 443, 552, 580–87; called imperialist power, 390, 393, 571, 572, 649, 682, 693, 694
Browde, Jules, 161n
Bruce, David, 78n
Budd, Zola, 664
Bunsee, Bennie, 153
Burton, Mary, 67
buses: attacked, 343, 373; boycotts of, 327, 352, 446; Mdantsane bus boycott, 26, 63, 254–56, 320, 355, 375, 394, 523; fare increases, 26, 65, 71, 170, 254, 325, 327, 336, 523, 604
Bush, George H. W., 184, 693
business
  black, 86, 371, 449, 651, 665–66, 721; Black Management Forum, 630; National African Federated Chamber of Commerce (NAFCOC), 13, 143, 626, 630; Western Cape Traders Association, 370
  white, 21, 29, 30, 95, 164, 481–85, 490–91; Anglo American corporation, 30, 37, 111, 142, 576, 612; political role of, 30, 36–37, 71, 84, 85, 86, 92, 110, 113, 142–43, 148, 176, 220–21, 285, 378, 481–85, 572, 574, 576–80, 649, 709, 721. See also consumer boycotts; negotiations, political
Buthelezi Commission and KwaZulu-Natal Indaba, 30–31, 191, 286–87, 483
Buthelezi, Mangosuthu Gatsha, 10–11, 13, 28–31, 33, 42n, 112–114, 142, 184, 190, 212, 219–21, 235–37, 285–86, 387–88, 394, 445, 488–90, 510, 527, 588, 597, 684, 685, 694; advocates non-violence, 489, 528, 529; African National Congress and, 30, 112, 125, 147, 285, 438, 488–90; as ally of big business, 142, 577; attacked by rivals, 87, 125, 221, 387–88, 486, 539–30, 569; attacks rivals, 30, 186, 321–22, 488–90, 528, 529, 530; called collaborator, 29, 321–22, 371–72, 390, 430, 450, 451, 529, 530; negotiations and, 30, 694; rejects independence, 28, 489; rejects sanctions, 30, 110. See also Inkatha
Buti, Sam, 13, 281

Cachalia, Azhar, 167, 184, 200n, 205n, 388, 389, 458
Cachalia, Firoz, 458, 658–61
Calata, Fort, 365
Calata, James, 508
Call of Islam. See Muslims
Camay, Phiroshaw, 88
Cape Action League, 47, 51, 55, 56, 317–20
Carolus, Cheryl, 50, 76n
Carrim, Yunus, 168, 640–42
Cassiem, Achmad, 97, 156
Castro, Fidel, 203n
Catholic church. See churches
Cato Manor, 325
Ceausescu, Nicolae, 722
Chatsworth, 325
Charterism and Charterists. See Freedom Charter under African National Congress; political debates
Chesterville, 327, 329, 529, 530
Chiba, Laloo, 458
chiefs and tribal authorities, 25, 26, 27, 29, 42n, 101–02, 283, 431, 452, 656, 726; Cetshwayo, 530; Congress of Traditional Leaders of South Africa (Contralesa), 27, 42n, 630; Dingane, 236–37, 632; Hintsa, 726; King Goodwill Zwelithini, 28, 237; Sekhukhuni, 726. See also homelands
Chikane, Frank, 32, 35, 50, 52, 93, 107, 110, 115n, 168, 170, 175, 187, 458, 644, 686
Chikane, Moss, 91, 206n, 661

children: in detention or prison, 32, 43n, 91, 98, 268–70, 272, 480, 647, 669; rights of, 657; violent deaths of, 311, 349–51, 373, 401, 420–22, 440, 582, 584
Chile, 659
China, People's Republic of, 153, 443, 666, 693, 694
Chinese minority, 8, 348
Christie, Renfrew, 159n
churches and Christians, 340, 726
 anti-communism and, 443, 444
 black church membership, 34
 black theology, 117n
 Kairos Document and, 94, 400–406, 451
 military chaplains and, 93, 401
 organizations of:
  Anglican church, 95, 142
  Catholic church, 117n, 228–32, 293, 341, 381, 382, 644; apartheid and, 228–32; leaders of, 31, 93, 94, 95, 143, 144, 169, 437–46; members of, 229; *New Nation* and, 58; non-racial schools of, 383; South African Catholic Bishops' Conference, 95, 169, 228–32, 359, 365, 381, 652–54
  Diakonia, 117n, 329, 411, 412–13, 445
  independent African churches, 706
  Institute for Contextual Theology, 94
  Koinonia, 117n
  Nederduitse Gereformeerde Kerk (NGK) (Dutch Reformed Church), 33–34, 94, 95, 142–43, 237–39; attack on Islam, 97, 464–66; black "daughter" churches, 34; Broederkring of, 237–38
  Rhema church, 706
  South African Council of Churches (SACC), 7, 34, 93, 94, 95, 110, 166, 168–69, 205n, 237–39, 260–63, 291, 365, 374, 461, 706; Eloff Commission and, 34–35, 93, 169, 260–63; funding of, 93, 260; Northern Transvaal Council of Churches, 238; Western Province Council of Churches, 94
  Standing for the Truth Campaign, 169, 191, 706–707
  World Alliance of Reformed, 52, 95, 684
  World Council of Churches, 87, 95, 96; aid to African National Congress and Pan Africanist Congress from, 34, 95, 117n, 205n
  Young Christian Students, 59, 117n, 365–66
  Young Christian Workers, 59, 117n
 political role of, 33–35, 82, 93–97, 168–70, 260–63, 291–92, 316, 331, 365, 374, 378, 394, 397, 398, 400–406, 412, 422, 437–46, 451, 523, 642–44, 650, 651, 652–54, 681
 right-wing, 35, 93, 706
 See also individual church leaders
Cindi, Dan (pseudonym of Tebogo Mafole), 630
Cindi, Zithulele, 77n, 358
citizenship rights, 219, 232, 239, 242, 244, 367, 368, 554, 585, 702; threats to African, 8, 12, 21, 22, 23, 222, 256, 312, 314
civic associations, 46–47, 52, 53, 57–58, 65, 71–72, 85, 113, 175, 307–10, 602, 606, 650, 652, 653
 coloured and Indian, 47, 52, 307–308, 325–26, 606
 demand for township upgrading made by, 20, 176, 277, 279, 290, 440, 653, 677
 democracy in, 55, 57, 58, 77n, 436–37, 606
 particular organizations: Alexandra Action Committee, 435–37; Alexandra Civic Association, 57; Alexandra Residents Association, 57; Atteridgeville-Saulsville Residents Organization, 57, 607; Bokmakierie, Bridgetown, Silvertown, and Kewtown Action Committee, 318; Brits Action Committee, 289–93; Cape Areas Housing Action Committee, 47, 318, 602; Cradock Residents Association, 71–72, 200n, 330–32; Diepkloof Civic Organisation, 307; Durban Housing Action Committee, 47, 324–29; East Rand People's Organisation, 336; Hambanati Residents Association, 327–28; Joint Rent Action Committee, 47, 112, 326–30, 529; Klaarwater Residents Association, 327; Krugersdorp Residents' Organisation, 307, 309; Lamontville Rent Action Committee, 328; Mgwali Residents' Association, 25; Newlands East Residents Association, 326; Organisation United Against Traitors, 379–80; Port Elizabeth Action Committee, 175, 200n, 667–68; Phoenix Rent Action Committee, 326; Port Elizabeth Black Civic Organisation (PEBCO), 72, 73, 395; Soweto Civic Association (*see* Soweto townships); Sydenham Heights Tenants Association, 326; Vaal Civic Association, 57, 68, 81, 200n, 338–39, 607; Western Cape Civic Association, 200n, 279
civil disobedience, 34, 94, 405, 707. *See also* conscription
Civil Rights League, 224–27
Coetsee, H. J. "Kobie," 179–80, 187, 550, 596
Coetzee, Dirk, 194, 712–14
Coetzee, Johann, 34, 395, 597
Cold War, 5, 480, 598

INDEX

Coleman, Audrey, 66, 67, 268–70
Coleman, Keith, 66
Coleman, Max, 66
collaborators, 8, 21, 46, 52, 69, 84, 101, 250–51, 281, 313, 337, 355, 371, 379–80, 396, 417, 418, 430, 435, 448, 449, 450, 451, 480, 529–30, 553–54, 562, 581, 699; violence against, 16, 58, 69, 122, 439, 511. *See also* informers and spies; necklacing; vigilantes
Coloured Persons' Representative Council, 10, 337, 566, 570
coloureds, 5, 31, 96, 220, 457, 566, 570, 602; coloured labor preference policy, 242; local councils for, 9, 17, 172; removed from common voters' roll (1956), 256; school boycotts by, 59–60, 406–409; South African Coloured People's Congress, 566; tricameral parliament and House of Representatives, 7, 8, 10, 11, 12, 28, 39, 56, 209, *266*, 296, 310, 336–37, 379, 563, 597, 699. *See also* attitudes of blacks; civic associations; Labour Party; workers
Commonwealth, the, 145, 189, 192, 694, 695, 710; Eminent Person's Group (EPG), 145–46, 179–80, 599–601
community councils (black local authorities), 14, 16–17, 33, 46, 56, 57, 65, 69, 72, 165, 176, 281, 309, 322–23, 327, 328, 336, 338–39, 343, 374, 417, 418, 435, 449, 450, 451, 649, 652–54; collapse of, 16, 58, 71, 114, 380, 396, 430, 434, 563, 652; corruption in, 16–17, 68, 278, 652; in Soweto, 16, 46, 56, 176, 222, 676–77; Lekoa, 68, 69; violence against councillors, 16, 69, 98, 101, 122, 329, 339–40, 562, 581. *See also* elections
Community Resource and Information Centre (CRIC), 67, 104–05, 459, 460
Concerned Citizens, 376, 378
Conco, Wilson, 372
Conference for a Democratic Future (1989), 173, 196, 715, 718
Congo, 630
Congress of South African Students (COSAS), 42n, 47, 50, 59, 60, 61, 67, 69, 72, 98–100, 117n, 363, 364, 366, 407, 515; African National Congress and, 50, 59; banned, 61, 82, 98, 394, 425; National Union of South African Students and, 59; United Democratic Front and, 60–61. *See also* student organizations
Congress of South African Trade Unions (COSATU), 90, 93, 100, 102, 106–11, 171, 173, 422, 452, 483–85, 469–74, 474–75, 477–79, 485–87, 597, 598, 603, 604, 605–606, 631, 650, 651, 726
    alliance with African National Congress and United Democratic Front, 87–88, *88*, 89, 107, 110, 141, 189, 191, 209, 431, 471, 473, 485–86, 606; Freedom Charter and, 110, 172, 482, 487, 606, 669
    campaigns: for May Day holiday, 89, 472, 490; Living Wage Campaign, 106, 467–68, 469, 477–79, 481; defiance campaign (1989) (*see* mass democratic movement *under* United Democratic Front)
    criticisms of, 485–86
    democracy in, 410, 468–69
    formation of, 86–89, 90, 141, 409–11, 431, 435, 485, 526
    government suppression of, 89, 468–69, 472; bombing of COSATU House, 89, 107, 469, 473; restrictions on (1988), 165, 166, 170, 171, 642, 646, 647, 653
    political negotiations and, 693–95, 699
    South African Congress of Trade Unions and, 87, 208
    whites in, 88, 670
    women in, 634
    See also stayaways; trade unions
conscription: conscientious objectors and, 66, 93, 381–84, 516; End Conscription Campaign (ECC), 66, 78n, 165, 174, 323–24, 365–66, 383, 441, 459; of Indians and coloureds threatened, 97, 265, 324, 336–37, 338; opposition to, 34, 66, 97, 127, *382*, 323–24, 564; South African Military Refugee Aid Fund (SAMRAF), 127, 509. *See also* South African Defence Force
Conservative Party, 7, 65, 165, 170, 175, 179, 190, 200n, 207, 259, 295, 439, 596, 597, 639
consociationalism, 30–31, 180, 251, 286–87
constitutions of South Africa: 1983 constitution, 9, 12, 37, 263–65, 317, 367, 572; 1993 interim constitution, 209, 212; bill of rights proposed, 190, 210, 245, 585, 616, 656, 659, 660, 698, 703; white referendum on 1983 constitution, 8, 65, 67, 256–59, 375, 709. *See also* National Party government
consumer boycotts, 58, 65, 71, 84–86, 90, 92, 98, 100, 112, 113, 175, 374, 411, 417, 418, 419–20, 427, 430, 434, 445, 446–47, 468, 475, 671, 705; Black Christmas, 84, 113, 416–18; OK Bazaars, 467–68
Cooper, Saths 75n, 358, 361
Coovadia, Jerry, 298, 389
courts
    death penalty, 193, 198, 647, 736
    judges, 37–38, 91, 210, 224–27, 703
    magistrates, 476
    political cases, 23, 25, 27, 37–39, 81, 112, 166, 175, 329, 332, 360, 372–73, 374, 607; against Inkatha warlords, 113, 483–84; Bethal trial, 154, 557; Cassiem and others, 97, 156; challenges to states of emergency, 91; Delmas (*State v. Baleka*), 79n, 81, 91, 148,

167, 173, 197, 206n, 579; demand for end to, 197, 591, 616, 703; *Komani* case, 38; labor cases, 359; of captured guerrillas, 122; Pietermaritzburg treason trial (*State v. Ramgobin*), 81, 394, 413–15, 460, 579; *Rikhoto* case, 38; Rivonia trial, 192, 717, 728; SASO Nine (*State v. Cooper*), 75n, 201n; *State v. Govender*, 39, 294, 295; *State v. Mayekiso*, 107, 119n; Sharpeville Six (*State v. Sefatsa*), 78n; treason trial of 1956–1961, 339, 442. *See also* apartheid laws; lawyers; people's courts

Cradock, 71, 363, 364, 396
crime, 83, 84, 283–84, 290, 385; "comtsotsis," 102. *See also* people's courts
Cronin, Jeremy, 158n, 389
Cronje, Pierre, 613
Crossroads, 20–21, 27, 241, 277, 278–81, 393, 448, 710; clinic in, 280–81
Cuba, 133, 148, 184, 187, 572
Cuito Cuanavale, 203n
cultural boycott. *See* African National Congress
Curry, David, 251

Dadoo, Yusuf, 54, 414, 415, 566, 726
David, Paul, 81, 458
de Beer, Zach, 576
de Klerk, Frederik Willem ("F. W."), 3–4, 166, 176, 182, 189, 190, 191, 192, *193*, 193, 194, 196–97, 198, 199, 249, 342, 694, 708, 710, 711, 715, 717, 719, 727, 728; after February 1990, 207–10; meeting with Mandela (1989), 197
de Klerk, Willem ("Wimpie"), 182
de Kock, Eugene, 714–15
de Lille, Patricia, 163n, 195
de Vlieg, Gille, 270
de Vries, I. D., 413–15
death squads. *See* police
democracy, 4, 8, 16, 18, 31, 112, 191, 210, 212, 258, 259, 265, 278, 383, 444, 468, 483–85, 488, 583, 723; as goal of opposition organizations, 3, 7, 53, 57–58, 59, 67, 99, 105, 126, 142, 173, 174, 177, 181, 199, 247, 252, 264, 267, 280, 286, 311, 312, 314, 315, 319, 321, 322, 333, 346, 355, 356, 365, 367, 369, 370, 371, 374, 386, 390, 391, 413–15, 428, 429, 434, 435, 436, 452, 453, 511–12, 632, 641, 658–61, 700, 702–703, 720, 728; demand for non-racial franchise, 337, 345, 368, 420, 475, 480, 486, 583, 587, 595, 656, 702, 720, 728; goal of "one city," 85, 174–75, 176, 284, 336, 678–79; "open city" campaigns, 175, 667–68, 687–89; in opposition organizations, 57–58, 77n, 104, 279, 307, 372, 377, 410, 433, 435, 436, 446, 504, 640–41, 723–24. *See also* African National Congress; trade unions

Democratic Party, 190, 209, 214n, 688, 699
Deng Xiaoping, 153
Denton, Jeremiah, 572
Desai, Barney, 163n
Desmond, Cosmas, 163n
detention without charge, 31, 32, 35, 45, 55, 80, 90–91, 98, 114, 128, 166, 178, 224, 225, 226, 230, 255–56, 293, 316, 355, 416, 417, 418, 420, 450, 463, 475–77, 519, 601, 615, 653, 668–69, 671; deaths in detention, 64, 102, 128, 222, 230, 311, 571; demands for end of, 85, 178, 366, 383, 469, 616, 644, 668–69, 703; Detainees' Parents Support Committee (DPSC), 46, 66, 174, 200n, 365–66, 374, 376, 475–77; Detainees Support Committee (Descom), 66, 200n, 254, 256, 365–66, 374; Detention Action Committee, 66; of trade unionists, 32, 89, 128, 469, 480; of women, 105. *See also* children; prisons and political prisoners
Dhlomo, Oscar, 235–37, 321
Didcott, John M., 227, 360
Diouf, Abdou, 608, 610
Dlamini, Chris, 87, *90*
Dlamini, Stephen, 160n, 161n, 625, 626
Doctors' Pact (1947), 566
Dos Santos, José Eduardo, 189
Douwes-Dekker, Loet, 61
drought, 67, 132, 303
Du Toit, Wynand, 596, 597
Dube, John (pseudonym of Adolphus Mvemve), 32
Dube, Msizi H., 112, 329
Dudley, Richard, 76n
Duduza township, 366
Dugard, John, 227
Duncan, Sheena, 67, 366–69
Durban City Council, 325, 326

Ebrahim, Ebrahim Ismail, 75n
Ebrahim, Gora, 163n, 196
economy, 4, 16, 18, 36–37, 68, 164, 248, 430, 431, 481, 495, 578, 597, 609, 638, 639, 679, 727; concentration of wealth in, 495; debt crisis (1985), 36–37, 90, 139, 164, 192, 687, 704, 709, 710–11; drought, 72; general sales tax (GST), 336, 338, 342, 396, 434; inflation, 89, 106, 164, 327, 337, 409, 420, 481; informal, 18; international assessments of, 36, 90; job reservation, 248, 263, 306; multinational corporations and, 36, 164, 224, 248, 381; National Party economic policies, 4–5, 36–37, 249; recession of early 1980s, 16, 21, 36, 57, 68, 72, 73, 89, 303, 407; skills shortage, 4, 36, 43n, 60, 247, 248; unemployment, 36, 68, 72, 73, 164, 240, 249, 292, 327, 336, 343, 396, 481, 586–87, 606, 727; urbanization, 17–21, 249 (*see also* Riekert Commission); white business attitudes and, 18, 36–37, 71, 84, 481–85 709; white workers and,

INDEX

4, 248. *See also* business; sanctions; trade unions
Edendale township, 113
education. *See* schools; universities
elections, 68, 230; 1981 white general, 223; 1983 black local authorities, 52, 56, 172, 322–23, 395, 528; 1984 tricameral Parliament and boycott of, 8, 12, 52, 56–57, 71, 98, 266, 264, 267–68, 333, 336–37, 356, 358, 360, 361, 394, 395, 457, 640; 1987 white general, 107, 174, 180, 638; 1988 municipal and boycott of, 97, 165, 169, 172, 174, 641, 648–51, 652–54; 1989 general, 190, 191–92, 202n, 694, 705, 707; 1994 first democratic, 189, 212–13
Eloff Commission. *See* churches
End Conscription Campaign. *See* conscription
Ensor, Paula, 158n
Esack, Farid, 95, 96, 97, 644
Esterhuyse, Willie, 182, 637
Ethiopia, 444, 552
Evans, Gavin, 78n
Evaton township, 68, 340, 342, 350–51
exiles: lives of, 50, 120, 134, 159n, 542, 701; demand for return of, 366, 383, 391, 644; return of, 207, 208, 209, 210

Fanti, Wilson, 25
Farisani, Simon, 35, 93
farm workers, 18, 23, 234, 239, 241, 282, 606; evictions of, 23, 26, 277, 283; Farm Workers Association, 359; sharecropping, 283
Fazzie, Henry, 50, 72, 79n, 271, 390, 427, 428
February, Vernon, 632
Federal Theological Seminary, 113
federalism, 11–12, 190, 212, 586, 597–98, 656, 660
Federation of South African Trade Unions. *See* trade union federations
Feni, Dumile, 697
Ferris, Hennie, 76n
Fihla, Benson, 50
First, Ruth, 32, 131, 571
Fischer, Bram, 157n, 726
Five Freedoms Forum, 174, 687–93, 699
forced removals, 19–21, 22, 23, 25, 26, 238–39, 241, 256, 265, 276–77, 283, 312, 316, 356, 382, 391, 604, 657; of Duncan Village, 355, 607; resistance to, 23, 25, 253–54, 289–93, 355, 393. *See also* "black spot" removals
Fort Beaufort, 355, 364
Foster, Joe, 63, 299–302, 371, 527
Freedom Charter. *See* African National Congress; Congress of South African Trade Unions; political debates; United Democratic Front
Freeway House. *See* United Democratic Front
frontline states. *See* particular countries

funerals, 69, 73, 74, 76n, 83, 97, 98, 100, 122, 151, 291, 329, 377, 420–22, 422–29, 443, 447, 461, 467, 731, 732

Gaetsewe, John, 161n
Galela, Champion, 79n
Galeng, Hoffman, 76n
Galeshewe township, 276, 372–74
Gandhi, Mohandas, and Gandhian tradition, 46, 697
Gazi (Gazides), Costa, 163n
George, Mluleki, 173
George, Vusumzi, 271–73
Germany, East, 589
Germany, West, 443, 693
Godolozi, Qaqawuli 79n
Goldstone, Richard, 39, 294; Goldstone Commission, 194;
Goniwe, Matthew, 33, 71–72, 83, 330–31, 365, 377, 390, 433, 461; funeral of 85, 271, 406
Goniwe, Mbulelo, 331–32
Goosen, Glenn, 78n, 599
Gorbachev, Mikhail, 151, 194, 552, 722
Gordhan, Pravin, 54, 103–04, 204n, 325, 457, 458
Gordimer, Nadine, 632
Gqabi, Joe, 33, 128, 131, 571, 584
Gqiba, F. F., 706
Gqubule, Simon, 200n
Gqweta, Sabelo "Phama," 155
Gqweta, Thozamile, 63, 115n, 255–56, 458
Gromyko, Andrei, 552
Group Areas Act (1950) and evictions under. *See* apartheid laws
Gugulethu township, 278, 399, 602
Gumede, Archie, 52, 55, 81, 167, 200n, 389, 394, 458, 643, 685
Gwala, Harry, 114, 126, 128, 158n, 202n, 209, 662, 685

Hanekom, Derek and Patricia, 159n
Hani, Chris, 40n, 137, 160n, 208, 508, 538, 625, 626, 627, 628, 629, 631, 683; murder of, 43n, 210, 212; negotiations and, 148, 185; Umkhonto we Sizwe and, 128, 134, 138, 185–86, 198, 625
Harare Declaration. *See* African National Congress
Harmel, Michael, 126
Haron, Abdullah, 464
Harvey, Robert, 202n, 585
Hashe, Sipho, 79n
health: infant mortality rates, 280; of blacks, 232, 280, 290, 358–59; of detainees, 476–77; services, 280, 306, 383; workplace safety and, 106, 453–55
Heard, Tony, 143
Hemson, David, 158n
Hendrickse, Allan, 10–11, 11, 251, 266, 268, 356, 371, 390, 527, 705
Herstigte Nasionale Party, 37, 259, 439
Hertzog bills of 1930s, 249

Heunis, Chris, 30, 172, 178, 249, 250, 290, 367
Hlapane, Bartholomew, 157n
Hofmeyr, Willie, 200n, 643
Hogan, Barbara, 159n, 566
Holiday, Anthony, 158n
Holomisa, Bantu, 204–205n
homelands ("bantustans"), 8, 12, 14, 21, 22–28, 40n, 46, 90, 111, 164, 191, 196, 209, 239–44, 249–50, 251, 256, 263, 283, 304, 306, 312, 314, 315, 336–37, 351, 391, 435, 527–28, 571, 604, 616, 633, 699, 721
  Bisho massacre, 210, 211
  consolidation of, 23, 30
  corruption in, 26, 101
  economies of, 247
  forced removals to, 19, 276–77. *See also* "black spot" removals; forced removals
  Moutse district and, 26–27, 42n, 275
  particular homelands: Bophuthatswana, 20, 21, 25, 26, 205n, 242, 245, 277, 289, 394; Ciskei, 21, 25–26, 63, 210, 242, 254–56, 320, 394, 533, 544; KaNgwane, 13, 16, 22, 42n, 143; KwaNdebele, 26–27, 274–75, 448, 450, 452; KwaZulu, 11, 13, 19, 22, 28–31, 112, 113, 114, 115, 235–37, 394, 488, 529, 700; Lebowa, 13, 26–27, 101–102; QwaQwa, 20, 29, 41n, 42n, 277; Transkei, 21, 25, 42n, 128, 204n, 242, 303, 394, 519, 550, 620; Venda, 21, 25, 238, 242
  political resistance in, 20–22, 27, 191, 274–75, 431–32, 452, 535, 569, 648
  poverty of, 18, 26, 396, 404
  redrawing borders of, 19–20, 25, 26–28, 112, 289, 529, 530
  trade unions in, 289
  See also citizenship rights; rural areas
hostels, 17, 33, 111, 209–10, 211, 304, 326, 328, 350, 352–53, 397, 434, 452
housing, 46, 80, 391; 99 year leases, 242–43, 283; bucket system, 290, 328; for Africans, 17–19, 80, 164, 232, 240–42, 276, 278–81, 304, 306, 308, 326–29, 383, 676–78; for Indians, 10, 39, 294–97, 325–26; freehold rights, 251, 283, 293; "grey areas," 39, 294–97; rates (property taxes), 325, 326, 337; site-and-service, 41n, 276–77; squatters, shacks and shack demolitions, 17–21, 41n, 58, 63, 72, 241, 278, 279, 283, 304, 327, 678; water and electricity costs, 176, 308, 322–23, 338–39, 343, 350–51, 678–79. *See also* civic associations; land tenure
Huhudi township, 276
Hungary, 592, 666
Hunter, Roland, 159n
Hurley, Denis, 93, 95, 117n, 169, 365, 413, 437, 438, 440, 443, 444, 445, 446

Indaba, *see* Buthelezi Commission
Indians, 5, 31, 39, 96, 220, 460, 566; businesses of, 411, 459; Inanda attacks on (1985), 372, 411–13; Local Affairs Committees for, 9, 17, 172, 326; school boycotts by, 60, 77n; South African Indian Congress (SAIC), 494, 566; South African Indian Council (SAIC) and anti-SAIC committees, 9–10, 46, 52, 263, 299, 337, 456, 566; South African Indian Council election of 1981, 9, 46, 298, 338; tricameral parliament and House of Delegates, 7, 8, 9, 28, 39, 56, 209, 245, 246, 263–65, 296, 308, 337, 563, 597, 640, 641, 699, 705. *See also* attitudes of blacks; housing; Natal Indian Congress; Transvaal Indian Congress; United Democratic Front
informers and spies, 31, 32, 84, 159n, 194, 281, 288–89, 330, 406, 427, 428, 439, 462–63, 593, 607, 706
Ingwavuma land deal, 22–23, 235–37, 286
Inkatha, 10, 28–31, 44n, 64, 75n, 87, 112–14, 221, 235–37, 252, 286, 321–22, 445, 459, 588, 639, 694, 695; ethnic nationalism of, 29, 125, 613; government support for, 33, 113, 114, 165, 178, 210, 211–12; Inkatha Freedom Party, 209–10, 211–13; negotiation, view of, 30; Operation Marion and, 113–14; rivalry with African National Congress, United Democratic Front, and Congress of South African Trade Unions, 29, 33, 54, 87, 88, *88*, 112–14, 117n, 125, 186, 190, 196, 335, 387–88, 411–13, 451, 483, 486, 527, 569, 605; South African Black Alliance of, 11, 29, 42n, 489, 527; threats made by, 29, 112, 221, 445; United Workers' Union of South Africa (UWUSA) and, 87–88, *88*, 451, 486; violent attacks against, 114; violent attacks by, 59, 113, 115n, 119n, 148, 186, 210, 321–22, 394, 411–13, 459, 483, 484, 528, 529, 530, 528, 529, 530, 544, 588, 731 (*see also* vigilantes); white business and, 29, 30, 87–88, 378, 483, 577; Women's League, 529, 530; Youth Brigade, 112, 528, 529. *See also* chiefs and tribal authorities; Mangosuthu Gatsha Buthelezi
Institute for a Democratic Alternative for South Africa (IDASA), 161n, 205n, 608–11, 614, 699, 734
Institute for Contextual Theology, 344
intellectuals, black, 7, 48, 50, 51, 163n, 195, 307, 344–49, 574
International Defence and Aid Fund (IDAF), 166, 278–81
Iran. *See* revolutions
Iraq, 153
Isaacs, Henry, 163n
Isandlwana, battle of (1879), 28
Ismail, Aboobaker "Rashid," 157n

Index

Israel, 40n, 596, 689–91
Issel, Johnny, 457

Jack, Mkhuseli, 72, 118n, 427, 428, 447–48
Jana, Priscilla, 373, 685
Jassat, Essop, 115n, 458, 461
Jele, Josiah, 137, 506, 509, 625, 626, 629, 630, 683
Jenkin, Tim, 158n
Jews for Social Justice, 377, 689–91
Jobodwana, Z. N., 162n
Joffe, Jonty, 463
Johannesburg Democratic Action Committee (JODAC), 67, 174, 365, 374–79, 459
Johnson, Lulu, 117n
Jones, Peter, 358, 361
Jordan, Pallo, 137, 160n, 204n, 576, 592, 613, 625, 626, 627, 628, 629, 630, 633, 691, 692
journalists, black, 7, 16, 196, 222
judges. *See* courts

Kagiso Trust, 166, 200n
Kasrils, Ronnie, 132, 148, 700–702
Kathrada, Ahmed, 126, 140, 192, 492–98, 671–72
Katlehong township, 302–305
Kaunda, Kenneth, 142, 174, 184, 509, 576, 694
Kearney, Paddy, 389
Kennedy, Edward, 51, 393, 550
Kentridge, Sydney, 227
Kenya, 523
Kgositsile, Baleka Mbete, 632
Kgositsile, Koerapetse, 632
Khayelitsha township, 20–21, 277, 278, 279, 607, 710
Khoapa, Ben, 124
Khrushchev, Nikita, 722
Kikine, Sam, 115n
Kinross mine disaster, 104, 453–55
Kistner, Wolfram, 34
Klaarwater, 327, 329, 529, 530
Kohl, Helmut, 390, 451
Koopman, Albert, 613
Koornhof bills, 14, 16, 17–18, 48, 52, 249, 251–52, 276, 306, 310, 315, 316, 317, 332, 333, 337, 375, 527; *See also* apartheid laws and bills
Koornhoff, Piet, 14, 16, 20, 23, 25, 221–22, 235–37, 240, 244, 253, 278, 279, 322–23, 327, 328, 329, 336
Korber, Ilana, 688–89
Kota, Zoliswa, 389
Kotane, Moses, 442, 726
Kriel, Ashley, 726
KTC township, 21, 643
Kuzwayo, Ellen, 46, 176
Kwadi, Amanda, 388
KwaMashu township, 19, 112, 411

KwaNobuhle township, 20, 269, 277, 466–67
KwaZulu. *See* homelands

Labour Party, 10–12, *11*, 29, 40n, 252, 267–68, 317, 695; African National Congress and, 10, 457, 570; August 1984 elections and, *11*, 12, 267–68, 337; opposition to communism 267
Lamontville township, 112, 327, 328, 329, 364, 387, 411, 412, 445, 529, 530, 544, 663
land tenure and land reform, 281–85, 371, 440, 583, 655, 657, 720; Bantu Trust and Land Act (1936), 282, 391, 453; Natives Land Act (1913), 23, 282, 391, 453. *See also* "black spot" removals; freehold rights *under* housing
Langa township (Cape Town), 278, 279, 416, 418
Langa township (Uitenhage), 20, 73, 277, 440; massacre in, 69, 73, *74,* 270, 375, 395, 396, 416, 418, 731
Langa, Mandla, 631–11
language and cultural rights, 299, 316, 372, 632, 655, 656, 658
Lapsley, Michael, 32
lawyers, role of, 20, 25, 38, 91, 113, 183, 187, 1933–94, 291, 293, 294, 307, 361, 473, 474, 509, 640, 684; Black Lawyers' Association (BLA), 56; in African National Congress, 145, 151, 654–58, 698; Lawyers for Human Rights, 174, 205n, 227, 715; National Association of Democratic Lawyers (NADEL), 56. *See also* courts
Le Grange, Louis, 342, 394, 396, 420, 451, 551, 596, 597
Leballo, Potlako, 152–53, 502–503, 504, 510–11
Lee, Stephen, 158n
Legal Resources Centre, 38
Legassick, Martin, 158n, 344, 526
Lekota, Mosiuoa Patrick, 50, 75n, 81, 91, 167, 173, 197, 201n, 388, 661–62
Lenasia township, 294
Lenin, Vladimir, 681, 722, 723
Leon, Sonny, 10, 570
Lesia, Mildred, 389
Lesotho, 5, 131, 153, 220, 236, 348, 586; African National Congress in, 121, 128, 508, 536, 625; Maseru raid (1982), 131, 440, 518–20, 571, 584, 730; Pan Africanist Congress in, 154; South African Communist Party in, 523
Letlhabile township, 289, 293, 623
Lewis, David, 161n
Liberia, 510
Libya, 97, 153, 154, 510, 511
Lourens, Jansie, 159n, 566
Loza, Elijah, 128
Luckett, Syd, 389

Lusaka Manifesto (1969), 702
Luthuli, Albert, 372, 441–442

Mabasa, Lybon, 49, 75n, 358
Mabhida, Moses, *151,* 160n, 426, 522–24, 726
Mabizela, Stanley, 595–99
Mabuza, Enos, 13, 16, 22, 29, 41n, 143, 161n, 281–85
Mabuza, Lindiwe, 157n
Mabuza, Wesley, 412, 588
Machel, Samora, 40n, 132, 133, *151,* 731
Madagascar, 509
Maduna, Penuell, 162n, 204n
Mafolo, Titus, 167, 174, 184, 200n, 388, 389, 648–51
Maharaj, Mac, 40n, 54, 75n, 104, 129, 136, 137, 142, 160n, 186, 189, 204n, 438–39, 440, 441, 443, 576, 610
Mahlangu, James, 27
Mahlangu, Solomon, 726. *See also* Solomon Mahlangu Freedom College *under* African National Congress
Mahomed, Ismail, 81, 413–15
Mahomed, Yunus, 103–04, 388, 389, 458
Makan, Kay, 665–67
Makana, Simon, 137, 160n, 508, 538, 592
Makatini, Johnny, 147, 160n, 509
Make, Cassius (pseudonym of Job Tlhabane), 33, 137, 160n
Make, Vus, 153, 510
Makgothi, Henry "Squire," 160n, 683
Makhubu, Paul, 644, 706
Makwetu, Clarence, 195
Malan, Daniel F., 554
Malan, Magnus, 113, 114, 249, 342
Malgas, Ernest, 50
Malindi, Gcina, 206n
Malindi, Zollie, 200n, 388, 389
Mamasela, Joseph, 712–14
Mamelodi township, 83, 91, 416, 418, 607
Manci, Robert, 160n, 625
Mandela, Nelson, 82, 87, 140, 145, 146, 154, 178–81, *188,* 192, 193, 197, 198, 202n, 204n, 207–208, 210, 213, 371, 407, 412, 423, 424, 425, 442, 549–53, 553–55, 585, 588, 596–97, 598, 600, 637, 639, 671–72, 694, 718, 719; after release, *199,* 207–13, 725–28; demand for release of, 122, 178, 217–19, 286, 393, 399, 450, 453, 516, 577, 579, 580, 596–97, 685; leadership style, 208; memo to P. W. Botha, 187–89, 672–76, 684–85, 687; moved to Pollsmoor prison, 140, 178, 179, *188;* moved to Victor Verster prison, 187; secret talks with government, 178–81, 187–89, *188,* 683–85, 727; visitors to, 140, 146, 189, 600, 671–72; Wembley tribute to, 178, 672
Mandela, Winnie, 104, 147, 163n, 194, 198, *199,* 205n, 460, 553, 554, 588, 596, 598, 672, 686, 727

Mandela, Zindzi, 140, 179, 553–55, 588, 596
Manenberg township, 406
Mangena, Mosibudi, 157n
Mangope, Lucas, 205n, 314, 528, 530
Manthata, Tom, 206n, 661
Manuel, Trevor, *53,* 388, 389
Mao Zedong, 153, 154
Maphumulo, Mhlabunzima, 42n
Mapoch, David, 27
Maqina, Mzwandile, 82
Marks, J. B., 159n
Marks, Joe, *53,* 200n
Marks, Shula, 344
Marxist Workers' Tendency. *See* African National Congress
Masekela, Barbara, 632
Masekela, Hugh, 697
Masemola, Jeff, 192
Mashatile, Paul, 388
Masondo, Amos, 458
Masondo, Andrew, 137, 544, 548
mass democratic movement (MDM). *See* United Democratic Front
Matanzima, Kaiser, 204n, 218, 314, 527, 530
Mathe, Deacon, 462
Mati, Joe, 128, 158n
Mati, Shepard, 117n
Matsaung, Lesiba, 237–39
Matshikiza, John, 632
Mavi, Joe, 349, 571
Mayekiso, Moses, 107, 119n, 141, 206n
Mayfair, 294–97
Mazwai, Thami, 669–71
Mbeki, Govan, 76n, 126, 179, 188–89, 202n, 637, 639, 646, 685
Mbeki, Thabo, 137, 142, 143, *143,* 148, 158n, 160n, 177, 182, 183, 187, 190, 196, 204n, 204n, 206n, 437, 441, 445, 508, 538, 576, 580, 585, 586, 587, 592, 610, 625, 627, 632, 633, 637, 687, 691, 692
Mbethe, Thanduxolo, 422–29
Mbuli, Mzwakhe, 388
Mcerwa, Thami, 361
Mdlalose, Frank, 235–37
Mdluli, Joseph, 571
Meer, Farouk, 458
Meli, Francis (pseudonym of Allan Madolwana), 127, 160n
Mells Park talks (1987–1990), 181–82, 183, 185, 187, 211; at Henley; 625, 637–40
Memani, Oliver, 278
Meyer, Lucille, 390
Meyer, Roelf, 211
Mgojo, Khoza, 644
Mhlaba, Raymond, 140, 192
Mhlawuli, Sicelo, 365
migrant workers. *See* workers
Milne, A. J., 413–15
Mitchell's Plain township, *53,* 406
Mitterrand, Danielle, 610
Mkhabela, Ishmael, 75n, 358

INDEX

Mkhatshwa, Smangaliso, 35, 93, 95, 437, 439, 443, 444, 446
Mkhize, Saul, 25, 253–54
Mkhonto, Sparrow, 365
Mkwayi, Wilton, 192
Mlambo, Johnson, 155–56, 163n, 479, 622, 719–21
Mlangeni, Andrew, 140, 192
Mndaweni, James, 88, 479, 589
Mntonga, Eric, 255
Mnyele, Thami, 632
Modise, Joe, 137, 160n, 507, 561
Mogale, Ephraim, 42n, 159n
Mogoba, Stanley, 644
Mohamed, Ismail, 115n, 388, 458
Mohapi, Mapetla, 505
Mohlakeng township, 309
Mokaba, Peter, 102, 107
Mokgabudi, Montso "Obadi," 131, 157n
Mokoena, Aubrey, 50, 104, 115n, 187, 458, 460
Mokoena, Isaac, 40n, 147
Mokoena, Timothy, 136, 203n
Molefe, Popo, 50, 52, 53, 75n, 81, 91, 129, 167, 197, 306–10, 337, 364–65, 388, 661
Molobi, Eric, 99, 458
Moloi, Lehlohonolo Lambert, 508
Moloise, Benjamin, 407
Molokoane, Barney, 157n
Momoniat, Ismail, 458
Mompati, Ruth, 157n, 160n, 437, 444–45, 625, 626, 630
Mongalo, Anthony, 160n, 539, 625
Montsitsi, Dan, 389, 462
Moonsamy, Kay, 75n
Moosa, Imrann, 358, 362
Moosa, Mohammed Valli, 50, 76n, 167, 388, 458, 461
Mopeli, T. Kenneth, 42n
Moposho, Florence, 157n, 160n, 506
Morobe, Murphy, 50, 75n, 76n, 107, 167, 205n, 388, 393, 458
Mosala, Letsatsi, 75n
Moselane, Geoffrey Tebogo, 343, 361
Mothopeng, Zephania, 154, 155, 163n, 195, 195, 286, 557, 662, 720
Motlana, Nthato, 46
Motlanthe, Kgalema, 158n
Motlatsi, James, 65
Motsepe, Godfrey, 587–89
Motshabi, John Pule, 507
Motsoaledi, Elias, 192
Motsuenyane, Sam, 13, 345
Mozambique, 5, 7, 22, 31, 130–33, 151, 152, 154, 238, 443, 444, 495, 666, 694, 704, 721; African National Congress in, 22, 95, 121, 123, 130–33, 184, 501, 508, 536–38, 561, 582, 584; FRELIMO, 131–32, 495, 496, 498, 501, 537–39; Matola raid, 131, 159n, 498, 571, 730; Nkomati Accord, 7, 40, 130–33, 184, 267, 571, 582, 600, 731;

Pan Africanist Congress in, 152, 154; RENAMO, 131–32, 571, 719; Soviet Union and, 131, 132
Mpanza, James "Sofasonke," 84
Mpetha, Oscar, 55, 159n, 167, 192, 460
Mphanga, Russell, 389
Mphephu, Patrick, 217, 218, 314, 530
Msimang, Selby, 508
Mthembu, Khehla, 75n, 196
Mufamadi, Sydney, 87, 187, 388
Mugabe, Robert, 7, 133, 159n, 219, 670, 729; suppresses opposition, 267;
Mulder, Connie, 239
Murray, Hugh, 576
Muslims, 95–97, 156, 316, 338, 437, 448–49, 464–66; Al-Qalam, 97, 464–66; Call of Islam, 97; Christians and, 464–66; in Parliament, 97; Muslim Students' Association, 96, 97; Muslim Youth Movement, 96, 97, 448–49; Qibla, 97, 156; Risalatuna, 448–49; United Democratic Front and, 97
Muzorewa, Abel, 7, 187, 217, 218, 367, 430, 451
Mxenge, Griffiths, 33, 128, 194, 571, 712–14
Mxenge, Nonyamezelo Victoria, 33, 113, 128, 389, 412, 588, 714
Myburgh, Tertius, 576
Myeza, Muntu, 75n, 196, 201n, 358, 361, 661

Naicker, G. Monty, 566
Naidoo, Jay, 87, 113, 171, 481–85, 605–606
Naidoo, Krish, 173
Naidoo, Mooroogiah J., 10, 81, 299, 337, 458
Naidoo, Stephen, 644
Nair, Billy, 50, 204n, 389, 458
Namibia (South West Africa), 95, 113, 147, 184, 194, 213n, 309, 495, 551, 589, 591, 687, 694, 704, 721, 735, 736; South African occupation of, 5–6, 130, 131, 247, 324, 381, 383, 391, 395, 564; South West Africa People's Organisation (SWAPO), 5–6, 133, 147, 184, 194, 203n, 213n, 381, 424, 496, 551, 554, 572, 590, 591, 600, 704, 736; United States "linkage" policy toward, 6, 183–84, 572
Napier, Wilfrid, 437, 439, 441, 443, 444, 445, 446
Natal Indian Congress (NIC), 9–10, 40n, 46–47, 50, 54, 103–04, 168, 208, 263–65, 298–99, 325, 457, 458, 459, 460, 462, 640–42, 705, 726; alleged cabal in (see United Democratic Front); boycott policy of, 9, 12, 641; democracy in, 640, 641; nonviolent policy of, 413–15; United Democratic Front and, 140, 168, 642
Nathan, Laurie, 78n
National Committee Against Removals, 19, 275–77
national convention: constituent assembly alternative, 56, 252, 319, 695, 717; demands for a, 56, 319, 366–69, 461, 462, 528, 554;

Lancaster House model, 141, 184, 367, 458, 461, 720; liberal whites' and promotion of Convention Alliance, 67–68, 142, 161n, 367–68, 378, 577
National Education Crisis Committee (NECC), 99, 102, 107, 117n, 200n, 429, 433, 435, 606, 726
National Education Union of South Africa, 200n, 427–28
National Forum, 48–49, 50–52, 55, 98, 155, 362, 527, 604
National Party government, 3–5, 12–14, 18, 114, 120, 131, 139, 142, 166–67, 169, 208–13, 220, 263, 366, 368, 394, 405, 401–402, 600, 610, 715
  anti-communism of, 5, 31, 95, 145, 178, 197, 230, 383, 443, 469, 481, 674
  Bureau of Information, 471, 472
  Bureau of State Security (BOSS), 220
  "constellation of states" plan of, 12, 39, 219–20, 249, 251, 489, 537
  constitutional changes and reforms proposed or made by, 7–8, 31, 48, 52, 74, 146, 222–23, 244–48, 249–52, 257, 306, 308, 310, 311, 312, 313, 315, 316, 317, 332, 334, 337, 527
  debates and indecision within, 5, 14, 120, 139, 180, 187, 430, 577, 597, 683, 705
  department of community development, 325, 326
  department of co-operation and development, 330
  department of education and training, 363–64, 365, 430
  department of information, 220
  diplomacy of, 184
  group rights principle of, and its critics, 13, 144, 180, 182, 190–91, 197, 212, 286–87, 372, 480, 585, 613, 616, 638, 655, 658, 695, 710, 716
  ideology of, 19, 95, 229–30, 710
  international criticism of, 22, 36, 80–81, 93, 120, 139–40, 145, 146, 169, 174, 190, 198, 246, 263, 430, 431, 562, 639, 663, 676, 708, 709, 717. See also sanctions
  Latin America influence on, 229, 438
  liberalization under, 4, 7–8, 19, 191, 368
  Mells Park talks. See African National Congress
  members' attitudes, 18, 27, 170, 222
  National Intelligence Service (NIS) of, 165, 178, 180, 197, 206n, 638
  National Security Management System, 32, 91, 190, 638, 653; Joint Management Centres (JMCs), 32, 176, 482, 615, 638, 653–54, 677, 688
  National Statutory Council, plan for, 13–14, 165, 181, 200n, 246, 286, 595, 639, 640; opposition to, 246, 450, 616, 617, 649, 653
  negotiation and, 4, 165, 176, 180, 181, 190, 196–97, 209–13, 600–601, 638–40, 716, 721. See also African National Congress
  "orderly urbanization" principle of, 19–20, 41n, 275–77
  "own affairs" principle of, 13, 14, 180, 191, 258
  peace song, 290
  plan to co-opt coloureds, Indians and African middle class, 10, 8, 11, 41n, 52, 74, 250–52, 312, 515, 638, 653, 721
  Port Natal Administration Board, 326–30
  repression by, 31–37, 80, 82–83, 114, 224, 225–26, 251, 367, 393, 483–84, 578, 614–15; crackdown of February 1988, 156, 165–68, 170, 171, 173, 642–44, 707; crackdown of October 1977, 45, 46; greater resistance provoked by, 82, 164, 425, 430; of early 1960s, 307; use of disinformation, 393, 471–72, 473, 478, 481, 683. See also banning; detention
  securocrats in, 176, 181, 197, 637–38, 639
  South African Broadcasting Corporation and, 29, 211, 217, 451, 469, 471, 472, 473
  State Security Council, 32, 113, 178, 190, 200n, 231, 482, 654
  "total strategy" of, 31–37, 229–30, 308
  Transvaal Provincial Administration, 176
  verligtes and *verkramptes*, 5, 7, 8, 12, 14, 190, 249
  Western support for, 8, 571
  "winning hearts and minds" program, 32, 91, 164, 653
  See also courts; police; South African Defence Force; individual party leaders
National People's Party, 9, 40n, 528
National Union of Metalworkers of South Africa (NUMSA), 106, 107, 110, 141, 171, 485–88, 490–91, 605; Freedom Charter and, 141; socialist ideology of, 110, 141, 486–87; strike in 1984, 65; strike in 1988, 490–91. See also trade unions
National Union of Mineworkers (NUM), 61, 64, 86, 87, 107, 193, 454, 605; strike in 1984, 61; strike in 1987, 110–12, 171, 407, 477–79, 482. See also trade unions
National Union of South African Students (NUSAS), 59, 66–67, 104, 105, 143, 306, 365, 376, 399, 440, 461, 462, 599, 726. See also student organizations
nationalization. See Freedom Charter
Naudé, Beyers, 91, 93, 95, 96, 127, 169, 174, 187–88, 205n, 366, 508, 683–87
Nazism, 225, 229, 281, 348, 505, 584, 631
Nchabeleng, Peter, 101, 102, 461
Ncube, Bernard, 176, 184, 187
Ndabeni, Thabo, 358
Ndebele, Njabulo, 631, 632

Ndebele, Sibusiso, 158n
Ndlovu, Curnick, 50, 184, 388
Ndou, Samson, 388
Ndzanga, Rita, 158n
necklacing, 84, 115n, 281, 398, 439, 472, 480
Neer, Dennis, 271–72
Nefolovhodwe, Pandelani, 75n, 201n, 661
negotiations, political: after February 1990, 207–13; as goal of church theology, 402; as goal of blacks and their allies, 224, 285, 383, 644, 675–76, 700–702, 711, 716–18 (see also particular organizations); rejection of, 699–700; speculation about, 144, 146, 218, 220, 247, 379, 512, 551, 573, 609; to deracialize sports, 173–74; white business view of, 36, 574
Nengwekhulu, Harry, 124
Netherlands, 145, 393, 442, 588, 631–33
Netshitenzhe, Joel, 437, 440, 445
Ngada, N. H., 644, 706
Ngcukana, Cunningham, 195
Ngoyi, Edgar, 50, 72, 79n, 388, 390
Ngwenya, Jabu, 104, 200n, 460
Ngxobongwana, Johnson, 21, 278–79, 281
Nhlanhla, Joe, 137, 160n, 182, 508, 509, 625, 626, 627, 628, 629, 630
Niehaus, Carl, 159n, 566
Nigeria, 153, 157n
Njikelana, Sisa, 63, 115n, 255
Nkadimeng, John, 160n, 161n, 437, 440, 522, 630
Nkoane, Simeon, 237
Nkobi, Thomas, 122, 137, 160n, 561, 625, 626, 627, 633, 665
Nkomati Accord. See Mozambique
Nkomo, Joshua, 130, 144, 185–86;
Nkondo, Curtis, 104, 115n, 458, 460
Nkondo, Ephraim, 136
Nkosi Sikilel' iAfrika (God Bless Africa), 314
Nkosi, Lewis, 632
Nofomela, Butana Almond, 193–94, 711–15
Nolan, Albert, 94
Non-Aligned Movement, 190, 704
Norway, 595–98
Ntantala, Templeton, 153, 154, 502
Ntloedibe, Elias, 153
Ntongana, T. W., 644, 706
Ntuli, Piet, 27, 42n, 274
Nuremberg trials, 225
Nyaka, Sefako, 358
Nyanda, Siphiwe, 186, 204n, 561
Nyanga township, 21, 278, 279
Nyembe, Dorothy, 50, 588
Nyerere, Julius, 189, 510, 511
Nzo, Alfred, 122, 132, 137, 145, 160n, 190, 496, 587, 625, 626, 627–28, 629, 630, 633, 683, 693

Oliphant, Daniel, 539
Omar, Dullah, 684
Onverwacht (Botshabelo) township, 20, 277
Oppenheimer, Harry, 30
Organisation of African Unity (OAU), 124, 147, 152, 189, 568, 617, 657, 676, 695, 702–704, 716, 719, 721; African Liberation Committee of, 153, 510, 511
Orr, Wendy, 38

Pageview, 294
Pahad, Aziz, 136, 160n, 182, 539, 580, 633, 637
Pakendorf, Harald, 576
Palestine Liberation Organization, 97, 690
Pan Africanist Congress (PAC), 75n, 97, 120, 124, 125, 152–56, 192, 195–96, 210, 214n, 502–504, 510–11, 517, 555–58, 595, 621–23, 719–21; African National Congress and, 124, 125, 147, 442, 496, 509, 568, 669–70, 720; *Azania Combat,* journal of, 155; Azanian National Youth Unity (AZANYU), 156, 195, 670; Azanian People's Liberation Army (APLA) and "cadre forces," 153, 155, 156, 163n, 502–503, 504, 510, 511, 621–23; China and, 153, 155, 159n; conflict and corruption in, 152, 153, 503–504; diplomacy of, 152, 153, 155, 167n, 196; financing of, 34, 152, 153, 154, 196, 503, 669–71; ideology and principles of, 52, 152, 154, 155, 156, 163n, 186, 195–96, 480, 505, 621–23, 660, 670–71, 719–21; *Ikwezi,* 153, 502–504; in frontline states, 152–54, 721; Indians and coloureds in, 156, 163n; military camps of, 153, 163n; National Council of Trade Unions and, 89, 195, 479–81; Pan Africanist Movement (PAM) and, 195–96, *195;* Pan Africanist Student Organisation, 195; patriotic front, 209; Poqo and, 155, 156, 511, 557; Qacha's Nek incident, 154–55; reintegration of African People's Revolutionary Party, 502; rejection of negotiation, 186, 720; support for, 670; trade unions and, 61, 88–89; unbanning of, 198; underground of, 152, 622; use of "Azania" by, 75n, 252–53, 305, 322, 361, 481, 505, 556, 670; weaknesses of, 120, 152–56, 163n, 214n, 503–504; whites in, 167n, 670–71. *See also* Africanism
Parliament and tricameral Parliament, 7–12, 28, 29, 63, 68, 142, 180, 198, 258, 263–65, 286, 336–37, 367, 391, 407, 449, 474, 483, 562, 616, 638, 640–42, 653, 699; sovereignty of, 37, 227. *See also* coloureds; Indians
pass laws. *See* apartheid laws
Passtoors, Helene, 159n
Patel, Ebrahim, 177
Patel, Haroon, 361
Patel, Quraish, 76n
pensions, 23, 391, 426
people's courts, 84, 119n, 601, 652; *makgotla,* 82

permanent urban residents (PURs), 242–43, 251. *See also* African urban and "section 10" rights *under* apartheid laws
Petersen, Rob, 158n, 526
Phatudi, Cedric, 13, 26, 527
Phoenix, 325, 326, 411
Pieterse, Cosmo, 632
Piliso, Mzwandile, 133, 160n, 506, 561, 625
Pityana, Barney, 124
Planact, 176, 440
Pokela, John Nyati, 153–56, 163n, 502, 511, 555–58, 622
Poland, 43n, 227, 370, 371, 522; Solidarity in, 78n, 227, 267, 370–71, 666
police, 18, 36, 48, 128, 226, 320, 341–42, 447–48, 597, 619, 652; behavior and methods of, 21, 27, 32, 33, 45, 60, 69, 72, 80, 81–82, 83, 86, 89, 92, 107, 111, 168, 171, 176, 230, 269–74, 278, 279, 288–89, 291, 292, 330–31, 351, 352, 353, 359, 360, 363–64, 373, 380, 382, 399, 408, 416, 417, 420–21, 430, 465, 466–67, 467–68, 471, 472, 597, 607, 623–25, 709, 711–15; blacks in, 40n, 122, 130, 247, 466–67, 535, 562, 564, 711–15; covert actions ("dirty tricks," "third force"), 32–33, 89, 107, 167, 169, 182, 194, 210, 292, 571; death squads and, 33, 72, 193–94, 209, 210, 365–66, 450, 571, 572, 614, 711–15; in Ciskei, 255, 394; in Lebowa, 102; in KwaZulu, 113, 114; Operation Katzen and, 42n; Operation Marion, 113, 114; torture, used by, 32, 35, 38, 91, 128, 226, 255, 272, 311, 394, 401, 416, 417, 420, 476–77, 623–24; Vlakplaas secret base, 623. *See also* vigilantes
political debates: 126, 460–61
 about Africanist, nationalist, black consciousness, multiracial, non-racial or "anti-racial" identities, 51, 52, 62, 88, 104, 126, 154, 195–96, 344–49, 371–72, 522, 660, 697
 about concept of "racial capitalism," 49, 248, 249, 252–53, 306, 459, 461
 about nationalization, 50, 126, 370, 438, 440, 598 (*see also* Freedom Charter)
 about socialism, 49–50, 53, 105, 110, 126–27, 144–45, 194, 305–306, 363, 369–72, 460, 486–88, 505, 511–14, 603, 660, 665–66, 695, 721–25
 about tactics, 45, 60, 73, 85–86, 103, 127, 536–39, 641–42, 649, 695 (*see also* "participation debate")
 about two-stage ("colonialism of a special type") thesis, 50, 105, 126, 150, 158n, 370, 372, 459, 494–97, 512, 514, 602, 680, 724–25
 Charterism versus its opponents, 47–52, 55–56, 59, 76n, 110, 141, 369–72
 externally-based guerrilla war versus internally-based insurrection, 45, 130, 138, 367, 459, 530–36, 575, 590, 613–14, 681–82

"participation debate," 8–11, 63, 167–68, 247–48, 335, 489, 640–42, 648, 652–54
race versus class perspective, 47–48, 49, 62, 102, 117n, 317–20, 344–49, 492, 493, 495
"workerists" versus "populists," 51, 62, 65, 89, 105, 110, 141, 170, 299–302, 318, 378, 526, 603–604, 660
working class versus elite leadership, 55–56, 64, 105, 369–70, 459, 485–86, 487, 512, 603
political violence, 16, 68–69, 72, 73, 80, 82, 191, 209–10, 211, 339–44; death tolls due to, 16, 73, 80, 82, 114, 119n, 191, 210, 213–14n, 340, 440; in Natal, 59, 88, 112–14, 119n, 209, 445, 483–84, 643; in western Cape, 97; "Lebanonization" of South Africa, 367. *See also* township uprising of 1984–1986
President's Council, 7–10, 21, 46, 223, 245–48, 250–51, 258, 264, 306, 310, 312, 319, 367, 451, 528; report on "orderly urbanization," 275–77
press, 20, 35, 81, 95, 97, 142, 198, 209
 alternative media, 58; *Azania Focus,* 166; *COSATU News,* 166; *Crisis News,* 166; *Grassroots,* 58, 166; *Isizwe,* 649; *Izwi Lase Rhini,* 58; *Izwilethu,* 166; *New Nation,* 58, 99, 166, 632, 647; *New Unity Movement Bulletin,* 699–700; *Saamstaan,* 58, 166; *Social Review,* 526; *South,* 58, 166, 647; *Speak,* 684; *Suid Afrikaan,* 611; *The Eye,* 58; *Ukusa,* 58, 328; *Vrye Weekblad,* 166, 194; *Work in Progress,* 166, 526, 611
 as opposition ally, 12, 25, 143, 166, 290, 361, 412, 582
 as state ally, 471, 474, 663
 censorship of, 31, 35, 36, 91, 97, 114, 119n, 143, 166, 198, 230, 379, 450, 451, 469, 480, 484, 647, 653, 695
 international media, 19, 20, 25, 34, 35, 37, 69, 93, 145, 191, 198, 209, 587
 particular newspapers and magazines: *Africa Confidential,* 444, 598; *Al-Qalam,* 166; *Cape Times,* 143; *Die Vaderland,* 576; *Financial Mail,* 94; *Ilanga,* 412; *Leadership SA,* 576, 706–11, 715–19; *Post,* 516; *Rand Daily Mail,* 261, 516; *Sunday Times,* 576; *Weekly Mail,* 36, 166, 468–69, 663
prisons and political prisoners, 46, 107, 140, 166, 417, 418, 458, 465
 demand for release of prisoners, 85, 90, 144, 181, 197, 366, 383, 391, 420, 453, 475, 573, 591, 615, 616, 639–40, 643, 668–69, 694, 703, 715, 727
 former prisoners, 50, 97, 102, 123, 128, 153, 155, 511
 hunger strikes and, 177–78, 191, 668–69
 march on Pollsmoor (1985), 82, 398–400, 408

particular prisons: Diepkloof, 177, 668–69; Modderbee (Modderfontein B), 178; Pollsmoor, 140, 178–81, 420, 483, 549–53; Robben Island, 42n, 50, 51, 113, 126, 140, 153, 155, 173, 178–79, 189, 197, 218, 426, 443, 483, 492–98, 549, 557, 581; Rooihell, 269; St. Alban's, 178, 271, 274; Victor Verster, 187, 189, 197, *199,* 671–72, 718
proposed prisoner exchange, 596, 629
release of prisoners, 173, 192–93, 194, 198, *199,* 207, 209, 210, 661–62, 716
See also detention without charge
Progressive Federal Party (PFP), 8, 12, 30, 142, 174, 190, 252, 376, 378, 613; and Inkatha, 24, 438, 577

Qaddafi, Muammar, 153, 511
Qibla. *See* Muslims
Qoboza, Percy, 7–8, 217–19
Qumbela, Mountain, 158n, 389
Qwanyashe, Miranda, 389
Qwelane, Jon, 221–22

Rabie, P. J., 38, 116n; Rabie Commission, 38
Rabkin, David and Sue, 158n
Rachidi, Hlaku Kenneth, 358
Raditsela, Andries, 86, 377, 571
Rajab, Mamoud, 9, 245–48
Rajbansi, Amichand, 9, 40n, 298–99, 356, 371–72, 390, 528, 705
Rala, Alex, 273–74
Ramaphosa, Cyril, 61, 65, 87, 107, 175, 187, 193, 198, 209, 211, 409–11, 605–606, 715–19
Ramatlhodi, Ngoako, 204n
Ramgobin, Mewa, 9, 81, 458
Ramokgadi, Martin, 128, 158n
Ramsamy, Sam, 663–65
Rand Revolt (1922), 250, 346
Rantete, Johannes, 69, 339–44
Rasool, Ebrahim, 97, 389
Reagan, Ronald, 5–6, 30, 37, 81, 145, 147, 184, 224, 347, 393, 451, 571, 733
Reddy, Freddy, 558
Reddy, Jagaram N., 40n
Reform Party, 11, 29, 337, 527–28
reforms. *See* National Party government
Regional Services Councils (RSCs), 16–17, 18, 175, 284, 450, 653, 654, 688
Release Mandela Campaign (RMC), 46, 50, 104–05, 200n, 386, 439, 456, 459, 460, 462, 606
Relly, Gavin, 142, 148, 576
RENAMO (Resistência Nacional Moçambicana), 7, 40n, 131–32, 648
Rensburg, Ihron, 272
rents, 10, 46, 85, 170, 308, 309, 330, 446, 604; boycotts, 16, 68, 91–92, 167, 175, 191, 284, 326, 327, 434, 452, 607, 630, 648, 671, 677; evictions, 47, 68, 91, 92, 175, 222, 276, 327, 339; increases, 16, 47, 57, 58, 65, 68,

69, 71, 80, 91, 112, 222, 276, 316, 322–23, 325, 326, 328, 329, 336, 338–39, 342, 343, 350–51. *See also* Soweto
Repression Monitoring Group, 66
revolutions: Chinese, 694; Cuban, 533; French, 268, 592; Iranian, 96–97, 158n, 185; Nicaraguan, 533; Paris Commune, 592; Russian, 129, 148, 161n, 494, 592, 694, 721; Vietnamese, 523, 534, 572
Rhodes, Wilfred, 389
Ribeiro, Fabian and Florence, 33
Riekert Commission (1979), 14, 17–18, 19, 251
Robben Island. *See* prisons and prisoners
Robinson, Randall, 686
Rockman, Gregory, 191
rugby. *See* sports
rural areas, 17, 18, 164, 233–35, 253–54, 396–97, 431–32, 452, 455, 495, 517, 527, 533, 535, 680; village committees, 431, 607. *See also* farm workers *and* migrants *under* workers
Russell, Philip, 142
Russia, 267, 444, 695

Sabelo, Winnington, 412
SACHED (South African Committee for Higher Education), 472
Sachs, Albie, 32, 162n, 177, 695–99
Sakukhuna, John, 274–75
Salojee, R. A. M., 200n, 388
Saloojee, Cassim, 54, 115n, 294, 295, 337, 393, 458, 658–61
sanctions, economic, 5, 11, 34–35, 36, 37, 94, 110, 139, 145, 146, 164, 165, 168, 169, 170, 189, 192, 197, 207, 224, 438, 439, 451, 480, 484, 511, 558, 586, 587, 588, 614, 617, 643, 666, 686–87, 694, 704, 710–11, 719, 728; arms embargo, 704; foreign divestment and disinvestment, 36, 44n, 110, 145, 164, 484, 666; oil embargo, 354, 704
Sankara, Thomas, *143*
SASOL, 351–54
Savimbi, Jonas, 131, 596, 649
schools, 234, 247, 290, 450, 705; black enrollment, 60; boycotts of black, 26, 27, 59–61, 65, 69, 71, 72, 77n, 80, 96, 98–99, 101, 102, 107, 161n, 343–44, 363–64, 364–65, 372–72, 406–409, 456, 566, 671; corporal punishment in, 71; demand for Education Charter, 60, 365, 434; independent school committees, 433, 452, 606; low quality of black, 59–60, 80, 164, 170, 232, 316, 383, 665, 667, 699; "people's education" and, 424, 432–34, 452, 608; private, 433, 689; rejection of Bantu education, 311, 433, 529, 604; sexual harassment of students by teachers, 60, 350, 374; teachers, 59, 99, 165, 250, 365, 406–409, 416, 418, 428, 433, 435, 452, 705; unrest in black, 95–97, 224, 343; white, 231–32, 296, 710
Schoon, Jeanette Curtis, 32

Schoon, Willem, 712, 714
Schreiner, Jennifer, 619
Seatlholo, Khotso, 157n
Sebe, Charles, 250
Sebe, Lennox, 26, 63, 218, 250, 255, 390, 394, 530
Sebidi, Lebamang, 176, 344–49
Sebokeng township, 68–69, 175, 339–44, 350–51, 361, 363–64, 555, 556. *See also* township uprising of 1984–1986
Sedibe, Jacqueline, 157n, 630
Sefanyetso, Shucks, 205n
Seipei, Stompie, 118n, 194
Sekhukhuneland, 101–02
Selassie, Haile, 552
Senegal, 608, 610
September, Dulcie, 33, 157n
September, Reg, 136, 160n
Serote, Mongane, 632, 637
Sewpersadh, George, 10, 81
Sexwale, Mosima "Tokyo," 158n
Seychelles, 571
Shakaville township, 328
Sharpeville township, 68–69, 340, 343, 350–51; massacre in (1960), 68, 73, 154, 171, 416, 418, 424, 505, 555–57
Shope, Gertrude, 157n, 160n, 508
Shubane, Khehla, 158n
Shubin, Vladimir, 151
Shultz, George, 146, 151, 552; Shultz Commission, 627
Sibeko, Archie, 161n
Sibeko, David, 153, 510
Sigxashe, Sizakele, 137, 160n, 508, 539, 625
Simons, Jack, 151, 162n, 507
Simons, Ray Alexander, 161n
Sisulu, Albertina, 55, 115n, 167, 176, 184, 200n, 388, 458, 460, 462, 643, 686
Sisulu, Max, 588
Sisulu, Walter, 140, 192, 197–98, 424, 672, 685, 686, 717, 718
Sisulu, Zwelakhe, 58, 99, 166, 429–35, 632, 646
Sizani, Stone, 390
Skosana, Simon, 26–27, 274–75
Skweyiya, Zola, 162n
Slabbert, Van Zyl, 43n, 142, 143, *143,* 367–68; resigns from Parliament, 142, 161n, 430, 594–95
Slovo, Joe, 132, *151,* 152, 194, 208, 443, 511, 514, 538, 625, 626, 627, 628, 629, 630, 665, 721–25, 726; joins ANC National Executive Committee, 136, 137, 160n; negotiations and, 148, 152, 682; Umkhonto we Sizwe and, 129–30, 134, 135, 138, 157n, 159n, 187, 204n, 530–36, 679–83. *See also* Operation Vula *under* African National Congress
Smallberg, Mavis, 632
Smith, Ian, 131, 367
Smith, Nico, 117n, 142–43, 439

Smith, Vesta, 588
Smuts, Jan, 443
Sobhuza II, King, 130, 235
Sobukwe, Robert, 153, 387, 502, 505, 510, 555, 556
Sofasonke party, 176
Soga, de Villiers Nteteleli, 271–72
songs, singing, and musicians, 52, 139, 291, 341, 407, 408, 422, 423, 424, 428, 523, 631–32; Abdullah Ibrahim, 631, 697; Basil "Manenberg" Coetzee, 632; Bruce Springsteen, 672; Dudu Pukwana, 632; Jazz Pioneers, 631; Jonas Gwangwa, 632, 697; Ladysmith Black Mambazo, 177; Miriam Makeba, 697; Mmabatho Nhlanhla, 631; Natalie Cole, 672; Paul Simon, 177; Stimela, 177; Sting, 672; Tracy Chapman, 672; Whitney Houston, 672
Sonto, Roseberry, 200n
Sotyelelwa, Peggy, 466–67
South African Broadcasting Corporation. *See* National Party government
South African Communist Party (SACP), 31, 50, 54, 76n, 101, 102, 141, 142, 149–50, 194, 208, 426, 427, 493, 494, 495, 496, 514, 522–24, 566, 601–604, 633–36, 679–83, 694, 699, 726; *African Communist,* journal of, 126, 514; African National Congress, alliance with, 31, 126, 142, 144, 149–52, 154, 179, 194, 208, 209, 438, 441–43, 446, 492–98, 517, 522–24, 569, 572, 576, 577, 579, 580, 598, 602, 612, 614, 615, 673, 674, 679–80, 694, 723; criticism of "workerists," 79n, 514; flag and symbols of, 83, 102, 443, 461; Havana congress, 187, 722, 723; ideology and principles, 126, 187, 522–24, 679–83, 723–25; *Inkululeko,* journal of, 523; *Inner Party Bulletin,* 633–36; members, characteristics of, 149–50, 162n, 194, 208; party school in Soviet Union, 522, 540, 634; post-apartheid goals of, 50, 151, 724–25; role in Umkhonto we Sizwe, 523; tactics and strategy of, 138, 141, 522–24, 679–83; two-stage ("colonialism of a special type") thesis (*see* political debates); *Umsebenzi,* journal of, 137, 139, 148, 574–76, 592–94, 721–25; unbanning of, 195, 198; underground, 72, 141, 150, 522, 524, 592–94, 601–604, 607–608, 634; United Democratic Front and, 208, 524, 603, 604; women in, 126, 633–36. *See also* South African Congress of Trade Unions; Soviet Union *under* African National Congress; trade unions
South African Congress of Democrats, 372, 375, 566
South African Council of Churches. *See* churches
South African Defence Force (SADF), 93, 137, 324, *382,* 381–84, 614, 682–83, 695,

721; atrocities in Namibia by, 381–82; attacks in frontline states, 5–7, 33, 131, 137, 146, 424, 440, 441, 518–20, 571, 584, 632, 649, 704, 719; blacks in, 130, 247, 562, 564, 597; deployed against strikers, 351, 352, 353, 467–68; deployed in townships and demands for troops' removal, 60, 66, 69, 71, 85, 91, 98, 113, 114, 171, 197, 278, 287–88, 373, 374, 383, 398, 411–12, 416, 417, 418, 420, 421, 430, 431, 432, 450, 453, 475, 579, 591, 600, 615, 616, 652, 703; in black schools, 60, 171, 424; in Lebowa, 103; military intelligence, 113, 182, 213n; ties with Israel, 691
South African Institute of Race Relations, 378
South African Law Commission, 191
South African Youth Congress (SAYCO). *See* youth organizations
South West Africa People's Organisation (SWAPO). *See* Namibia
Southern African Development Coordination Conference (SADCC), 537
Soweto townships (Johannesburg), 32, 69, 71, 83, 192–93, 287–89, 309, 350–51, 363–64, 458, 553, 606, 607; rent boycott in, 92, 175–76, 676–79; Soweto Civic Association, 46, 52, 92, 99, 175, 200n, 606; Soweto Parents' Crisis Committee, 99, 161n, 430, 431; Soweto People's Delegation (SPD), 175–76, 676–79. *See also* civic associations; community councils
Soweto uprising (1976–1977), 7, 19, 34, 45, 48, 59, 68, 74, 94, 96, 123, 130, 154, 169, 171, 186, 220, 222, 250, 284, 286, 307, 387, 416, 418, 464, 503, 505, 513, 534, 556, 557, 582, 652; commemorations of, 92, 360, 448–49, 451, 622
sports, 383; boycotts of visiting teams, 392, 416, 418, 602; international boycott of South African teams, 5, 173–74, 177, 207, 661, 663–65; National Sports Congress, 173, 700; non-racial, 316, 416, 418; organizations, 52, 651, 661; rugby, 177, 661; segregation in, 5, 223; South African Council on Sport (SACOS), 173, 195, 392
squatters. *See* housing
Stalin, Joseph, 514, 722
Starushenko, Gleb, 148
states of emergency, 102, 455, 652; demands for end of, 85, 197, 450, 475, 577, 579, 585, 591, 606, 616, 644, 703, 711, 727; first (1985–86), 32, 35, 36, 37, 82, 90–91, 97, 98, 376, 377, 379, 406, 416, 417, 421, 425, 430, 431, 435, 578; second (1986–90), 21, 32, 35, 36, 37, 43n, 86, 90–91, 92, 107, 114, 147–48, 165, 169, 170, 383, 398, 400, 467, 475, 479, 484–85, 601, 641, 647, 693. *See also* censorship *under* press
stayaways, 100, 434, 444–45, 448, 449, 534, 562, 607, 682; November 1984 Transvaal, 65, 69–71, 72, 73, 98, 349–51, 351, 392, 461, 563, 587; March 1985 eastern Cape, 72–73, 98, 392, 563, 587; March 1986, 427; May 1987, 107, 113, 474–75, 647, 648; June 1988, 171, 173, 646–47; September 1989, 191; June and August 1990, 211
Stofile, Makhenkesi Arnold, 76n, 159n, 354–57, 388, 390
Storey, Peter, 117n, 644
street and area committees. *See* United Democratic Front
Strijdom, J. G., 554
Strikes. *See* trade unions
Stuart, James (pseudonym of Hermanus Loots), 136, 137, 160n, 539, 576, 592, 630
students, 58–61, 72, 379, 406–408, 562
  demands of, 59–60, 71, 98, 99, 343–44, 350–51, 352, 363–64, 374, 424–25, 433, 446
  organizations of, 46, 52, 53, 71, 165; Azanian Students Congress (AZASCO), 394; Azanian Students' Movement (AZASM), 48, 49, 59, 321–22, 361, 362, 398; Azanian Students' Organisation (AZASO), 47, 48, 59, 67, 75n, 387; Black Students Society, 458; Muslim Students' Association (*see* Muslims); Pan Africanist Student Organisation, 195; South African National Students' Congress, 200n; Soweto Students' Congress, 288; Young Christian Students (*see* churches). *See also* Congress of South African Students; National Union of South African Students; schools; universities
Suttner, Raymond, 76n, 158n, 389, 458
Suzman, Helen, 549
Swaggart, Jimmy, 706
Swartz, Derrick, 388, 390
Swaziland, 5, 22, 131, 348, 489, 586, 714; African National Congress and Umkhonto we Sizwe in, 125, 130, 131, 132, 139, 159n, 184, 186, 499, 501, 508; Ingwavuma land deal and, 22, 235–37, 730; non-aggression pact with South Africa, 22, 132, 571; Pan Africanist Congress in, 152
Sweden, 153–54, 183, 184, 204n, 393, 442, 627, 628; Stockholm United Democratic Front-African National Congress meeting (1986), 463, 627
Swilling, Mark, 449

Tambo, Oliver, 96, 146, *151,* 152, 160n, 174, 177, 179, 193, 203n, 387–88, 423, 424, 425, 437–46, 488–90, 495, 496, 510, 520, 554, 565, 566, 567–74, 580–87, 589, 600, 601, 631, 637, 683, 685, 686, 687, 691, 692, 726; British parliament and, 146, 580–87; communist bloc and, 148, 151, 152; constitutional guidelines document and, 145, 152;

interchanges with Buthelezi, 112, 114; leadership of, 122, 123–24, 125, 132, 133, 134, 137–38, 144, 145, 146, 148, 151, 152, 157n, 181, 183–87, 189–90, 204n, 209, 544, 627; meets trek groups, 37, 142, 144, 148, 161n; policy statements, 40n, 137–38, 144, 151, 158n, 437–46, 567–74, 581–87; quoted in *Cape Times,* 143; Western diplomats and, 147, 151, 627

Tamboer, James Michael, 270–74

Tanzania, 121, 130, 133, 183, 189, 220, 523; African National Congress in, 203n, 424, 514, 515, 520, 560, 595, 596; Pan Africanist Congress in, 152–53, 163n, 479, 510–11, 595. *See also* Julius Nyerere

taxis, 18, 173, 175, 350, 651

teachers. *See* schools

Temane, Matthews, 664–65

Terre'blanche, Eugene, 143

Terreblanche, Sampie, 182, 637

Thatcher, Margaret, 5, 30, 145, 162n, 184, 189, 192, 206n, 552, 687, 693–95, 710

Thebehali, David, 16, 221–22, 530

Tinto, Christmas, 158n, 200n, 389

Tlhagale, Buti, 76n

Tloome, Dan, 160n, 625, 683

Toivo, Herman Toivo ja, 554

Toms, Ivan, 20, 78n, 278–81

torture. *See* police

township uprising of 1984–1986, 20, 26, 35, 128, 130, 136, 138, 145, 147, 155, 166, 172, 174, 179, 180, 186, 363–64, 375, 430, 578, 604, 671; Vaal uprising (1984), 68–71, 80, 81, 98, 112, 136, 155, 175, 338–39, 339–44, 361, 363–64, 430, 461. *See also* particular townships; political violence

toyi-toyi, 100, 118n, 447–48, 542

trade unions, 4, 26, 46, 58, 61–65, 73, 85, 92, 168, 170, 171, 194, 289, 452, 481–85, 604–606
  African National Congress and, 130, 209
  creating union federations, 64–65, 86–89, 301–302, 563
  democracy and, 62, 87, 103, 110, 208, 300, 301, 410, 468–69, 480, 482, 485, 487, 657
  education in, 175, 302, 362, 411
  financing of, 141
  Freedom Charter and. *See* Congress of South African Trade Unions; National Union of Metalworkers of South Africa
  health and safety standards and, 106, 453–55
  labor law and, 38–39
  political alliances of, 107, 110, 410, 531, 605, 606
  political goals of, 409–11, 485–88, 563
  registration debate in, 62–63
  repression of, 32, 63
  role in community struggles, 58, 65, 71, 72–73, 80, 85–86, 175, 300–301, 310, 320, 365, 410
  sanctions and, 110, 484, 606
  share options and, 482
  shop stewards in, 63, 170–71, 271, 300, 302–305, 353, 454, 472, 478, 490, 527, 589, 604, 605, 645, 695
  South African Communist Party and, 63, 141, 522, 603–604, 679–80
  strikes by, 63, 65, 80, 88, 89, 106, 107, 110–12, 164, 166, 171, 303, 359, 467–68, 469–74, 477–79, 490–91, 602; Durban 1973, 129; goal of general strike, 69, 138, 534, 563, 575, 682. *See also* particular trade unions; stayaways
  students and, 98
  United Democratic Front and. *See* United Democratic Front
  Urban Training Project and, 61
  violence against, 470, 471, 478
  whites in black, 64, 66, 374
  women in, 105
  See also workers

trade unions, particular
  African Food and Canning Workers Union (AFCWU), 64, 254, 256, 320, 392
  Black Allied General Workers Union, 359
  Black Allied Mining and Construction Workers Union, 359
  Black Allied Workers Union (BAWU), 61–62, 320
  Black Electrical and Electronics Workers Union, 359
  Cape Town Municipal Workers Association, 320, 392
  Chemical Workers Industrial Union, 171, 351–54, 605, 644–46
  Commercial, Catering and Allied Workers Union (CCAWUSA), 64, 73, 254, 256, 320, 467–68, 605
  Durban Municipal Employees Union, 705
  Food and Allied Workers' Union (FAWU), 90, 468, 605
  Food and Canning Workers Union, 90, 320
  General and Allied Workers Union (GAWU), 62, 87, 254, 256, 605
  General Workers' Union, 62–63, 64, 320, 392, 526
  Insurance and Assurance Workers Union of South Africa, 359
  Media Workers Association of South Africa (MWASA), 56, 320
  Metal and Allied Workers' Union (MAWU), 107, 369–72, 605. *See also* National Union of Metalworkers of South Africa
  Motor Assembly and Component Workers' Union (MACWUSA), 273, 320, 605

INDEX 775

National Automobile and Allied Workers' Union, 271
National Union of Textile Workers, 605
Orange Vaal General Workers Union, 254, 256, 320
Port Elizabeth Domestic Workers Union, 426
Retail and Allied Workers' Union, 90
South African Allied Workers' Union (SAAWU), 26, 52, 62, 63, 64, 254–56, 320, 394, 415, 605
South African Chemical Workers Union, (SACWU), 254
South African Laundry and Drycleaning Workers Union (SALDWU), 254, 256
South African Railway and Harbour Workers Union (SARHWU) and 1987 South African Transport Services (SATS) strike, 104–106, 107, 469–74, 605
South African Scooter Drivers Union (SASDU), 254
Sweet, Food and Allied Workers' Union, 87, 90
Transport and Allied Workers Union, 255
United Mining, Metal and Allied Workers' Union of South Africa, 605
United Workers' Union of South Africa (UWUSA). *See* Inkatha
See also National Union of Metalworkers of South Africa; National Union of Mineworkers
trade union federations
  Azanian Confederation of Trade Unions (AZACTU), 86, 88, 155
  Congress of South African Trade Unions (COSATU). *See* Congress of South African Trade Unions
  Council of Unions of South Africa (CUSA), 61, 62–63, 64, 65, 69, 86, 88, 254, 256, 320, 527, 589
  Federation of South African Trade Unions (FOSATU), 62–65, 69, 73, 86, 87, 141, 254, 256, 299–302, 302–305, 320, 352, 369, 371, 392, 411, 526, 527
  International Confederation of Free Trade Unions (ICFTU) and, 141, 589
  National Council of Trade Unions (NACTU), 88, 89, 155, 171, 173, 196, 479–81; principles of, 480, 481; negotiations and, 89. *See also* Pan Africanist Congress
  South African Congress of Trade Unions (SACTU), 61, 62, 64 87, 141, 161n, 370, 415, 508, 509, 523, 524, 526, 569; African National Congress and, 61, 62, 508, 517, 576; South African Communist Party and, 62, 141, 523, 524, 679–80
  Trade Union Council of South Africa (TUCSA), 61

transition period (1990–1994), 207–14; 1992 white referendum, 208; Bisho massacre, 210, 211; Boipatong massacre, 210, 211; constitutional negotiations, 209–13; Convention for a Democratic South Africa (CODESA) 1 and 2, 210, 211; Freedom Front, 213, 214n; Government of National Unity, 211, 212; sunset clauses, 212; *volkstaat,* 212, 213
Transvaal Indian Congress (TIC), 46, 50, 52, 56, 104, 208, 295, 296, 297, 337–38, 457, 458, 459, 460, 461, 462, 658, 665–67, 726; boycott policy of, 9–10, 12, 46, 337–38; non-violent policy of, 413–15
Trapido, Stanley, 344
Treurnicht, Andries, 7, 12, 65, 179, 218, 223, 597
Trew, Tony, 182, 637
trials, political. *See* courts
tribalism and regionalism, 125, 127, 157n, 421, 505, 530, 650. *See also* African National Congress; Inkatha
Trotsky and Trotskyism, 51, 54, 76n, 126, 512, 570. *See also* Unity Movement
Truth and Reconciliation Commission, 214n
Tsenoli, Lechesa, 389
Tshikalange, David, 712–14
Tshwete, Steve, 50, 75n, 185–86, 204n, 388, 389, 437, 444, 683, 691, 692
Tugwana, Gabu, 632
Tutu, Desmond, 7, 34–35, 74, 93, 95, 168, 170, 175, 178, 192, 205n, 222–24, 365, 644, 705, 706–11, 720; wins Nobel Peace Prize, 35, 93, 550, 553
Twala, Mwezi, 546
Tyacke, Eric, 61

Uganda, 184, 185, 335, 510
Umkhonto we Sizwe (MK), 46, 50, 121, 131–32, 138, 144, 154, 198, 203n, 288, 424, 425, 427, 428, 498–502, 528, 530, 563, 573, 581, 590, 601, 604, 617–21, 623–25, 726
  cadres, 132; attitudes and behavior of, 122, 123, 129, 131, 134–36, 137, 144, 148, 183, 184, 185, 197–98, 208–209, 501–502, 542, 558, 592–94, 700–702; camps for, 121, 130, 133–36, 137, 185, 508, 509, 523, 539–48, 559–61, 635; execution of, 103, 136, 194, 507; fighting against UNITA, 135, 544–45; health of, 541, 546, 548, 560, 575, 634, 635, 636; internal combat units, 46, 130, 138, 139, 148, 184, 439, 531, 532, 533, 535, 562, 573, 602, 681–82; recruitment of, 128, 184, 308; spies and agents among, 133, 136, 500, 508, 546, 547, 560, 619, 623; training of, 133, 149, 184, 442, 498–502, 535, 560, 575; transfer to Uganda of, 184; trials of, 122; undeployed, 185, 544, 560,

700–702; women, 126, 501, 540, 546, 559, 560
leaders, actions and accountability of, 134, 540–41, 544, 548, 561, 629
mutiny in (1984), 133–36, 137, 139, 185, 194, 205n
mystique of, 54, 132–33, 157n, 438
Nkomati Accord and. *See* Mozambique
policies and ideology of, 129, 498–502, 516, 700–702; goal of subverting security forces, 130, 138–39, 535, 563, 682; in frontline states, 139, 148, 184, 498–502, 533; "people's war" and, 129–30, 138, 148, 187, 461, 530–36, 573, 575, 582, 602; seizure of power as goal of, 138, 144, 146, 183, 185, 187, 210, 367, 368, 429, 531, 575, 576, 590, 681–82; soft targets debate in, 137, 186, 488, 551, 582, 666
Quatro detention center, 134, 136, 194, 629
sabotage and armed propaganda by, 50, 121, 122, 125, 129, 130, 139, 148, 154, 232, 440, 531, 532, 533, 581–82, 602, 729; Amanzimtoti bombing, 138, 376, 439, 440, 445; Pretoria car bomb (1983), 137, 551, 584; SASOL attack, 65, 122, 232, 729; special operations unit, 122, 131, 157n, 618; success rates, 122, 129, 157n
Soviet Union and. *See* African National Congress
Wankie campaign (1967–68) of, 575
weapons and arms caches, 139, 186, 533, 535, 563, 563, 580, 602, 623–24, 675, 701
See also African National Congress; particular frontline states; South African Communist Party
Umlazi township, 112, 113, 663, 713
United Democratic Front (UDF), 10, 12, 21, 27, 33, 52–57, 65–68, 73, 99, 101–03, 140, 142, 166, 168, 208, 252–53, 254, 265, 279, 281, 308, 310, 315–17, 322–23, 330, 354–57, 364–65, 369, 372–74, 388–97, 419–20, 425, 426, 445, 449–53, 455–64, 466, 474–75, 534, 544, 553, 597, 598, 603, 604, 650, 651, 670, 726
African National Congress and, 33, 54–55, 67, 72, 76n, 80–81, 82, 83, 99, 101, 103–06, 129–30, 140–41, 172, 191, 203n, 208, 455–64, 524–28, 531, 570, 718
alleged cabal within, 103–05, 140, 150, 168, 458–59, 460, 461, 462, 640
as "mass democratic movement" (MDM) (1988–1990), 172–74, 176, 177, 186, 189, 194, 196, 455–64, 575, 590, 602–603, 611, 633, 634, 650, 651, 683, 688, 689, 693, 694, 705, 706–707, 716, 717–18, 726; Crisis Committee of, 187, 684, 686; defiance campaign (1989) of, 191–92, 688, 701, 705, 707, 727; mass marches, 191–92, *192, 193,* 706–707, 708, 726; National Reception Committee of, 717
business and, 71, 450–51
coloureds and Indians and, 10, 12, 52, 56, 103–05, 168, 310, 356, 457, 460, 462
critics of, 55–56, 317–20, 356, 369–72
democracy in, 55, 57, 173, 208, 307, 357, 436, 456–63,
financing of, 57, 67, 166, 196, 205n, 461
founding and launch of, 52, *53,* 76n, 129, 191, 310–15, 319, 375
Freedom Charter and, 50, 54, 172, 369–72, 525, 670
Freeway House and, 102–03, 457, 459, 461, 462
government suppression of, 32, 38, 82–83, 90–92, 114, 148, 165, 167, 178, 377–78, 393–95, 449–50, 578, 604, 615, 646, 648, 651, 653; members and leaders detained, 55, 56, 58, 394, 399; trials of members and leaders. *See* courts; detention without charge
in homelands, 394
Inkatha and. *See* Inkatha
international contacts, 189, 392–93
leadership conflicts in, 103–06, 140–41, 456–63, 566
Million Signature Campaign of, 56, 265, 332–35, 356, 395
Muslims and. *See* Muslims
organization of, 54–55, 80–81, 90–91, 391–92
political education in, 53, 332–35
rivalry with other organizations, 33, 82, 186, 208, 397–98, 661–62
rural areas and, 527
South African Communist Party and, 603
strategies, goals and ideologies of member organizations, 52, 53, 56, 69, 82–86, 90, 99, 167–68, 267, 315–17, 357, 431, 435–37, 449–53
street and area committees ("people's power"), 83–84, 90, 91, 92, 100, 119n, 148, 167, 171, 290, 293, 421–22, 424, 427, 431, 432, 434, 436–37, 452, 563, 601, 606, 607, 638, 648, 650, 651, 652
trade unions and, 52, 53, 55, 62, 64, 81, 86, 89, 170, 392, 396, 426, 431, 434, 471, 526–27, 605–606
unbans itself, 191, 705
violence against, 147, 365–66
weaknesses of, 56–57, 58, 80–81, 356–57, 104, 395–96, 397, 436, 455–64
whites and, 55, 65–67, 90, 174, 175, 349, 435, 450, 651, 670–71, 688, 716
women and, 105–06

youth and, 386
See also civic associations; consumer boycotts; youth organizations
United Nations, 5, 124, 147, 152, 172, 190, 196, 197, 222, 236, 362, 391, 393, 657–58, 676, 704; High Commissioner for Refugees, 134; Special Committee Against Apartheid, 154, 362, 555
United States, 132, 393, 511, 572, 596, 664, 710, 720; African National Congress and government of, 146–47, 197, 589; called imperialist power, 51–52, 390, 393, 510, 571, 602, 603, 649, 682, 693, 694, 695, 699; Comprehensive Anti-Apartheid Act (1986), 37, 146, 197; Congressional black caucus, 686; constitution of, 245; "constructive engagement" policy, 347, 393, 557; Free South Africa Movement in, 79, 393; right-wing religious groups, 35, 706; TransAfrica lobby in, 178, 686. *See also* Ronald Reagan, Randall Robinson, George Shultz
Unity Movement and New Unity Movement, 10, 33, 47, 51, 55–56, 60, 64, 67, 76n, 119n, 173–74, 186, 196, 416–18, 458, 699–700; publication *Arise! Vukani!*, 390–94; Ten-Point Programme, 700; Trotskyism in, 51; *See also* Cape Action League
Universities, 32, 66, 166, 231, 484; "bush colleges," 59; Cape Town, 147, 152, 200n, 306, 398–400, 406, 407, 516, 596, 599; Fort Hare, 59, 153; Natal, 200n; North (Turfloop), 32, 59, 101; "open," 59; Rhodes, 200n; Stellenbosch, 66, 142, 181, 200n, 637; Western Cape, 59; Witwatersrand ("Wits"), 7, 105, 196, 200n, 217, 440, 458, 462, 516, 599, 700; Zambia, 627; Zimbabwe, 627; Zululand (Ngoye), 59, 321–22, 394, 528, 529, 530, 731
Urban Foundation, 279

Vaal uprising. *See* township uprising of 1984–1986
Van der Merwe, Hendrik, 147, 595–99
Van der Merwe, Stoffel, 40n, 244
Van Heerden, Auret, 67, 104–05, 457, 459
Van Niekerk, Barend, 227
Veriava, Joe, 359
verligtes and *verkramptes*. *See* National Party government
Verwoerd, Hendrik, 12, 190, 220, 249, 345, 554; and "grand apartheid," 8, 14, 18, 22, 25, 41n
vigilantes, 21, 26, 27, 33, 82, 89, 113, 167, 279, 280, 450, 643; A-Team, 448; Ama-Afrika, 82, 466–67; in Crossroads, 21, 27, 33, 448; KwaNdebele *Mbokodo, 27,* 274–75, 448. *See also* black-on-black violence; collaborators; Inkatha
Viljoen, Constand, 212–13

Viljoen, Gerrit, 25, 191, 342, 711, 716
Villa-Vicencio, Charles, 399
Vlakplaas secret base. *See* police
Vlok, Adriaan, 169, 178, 663, 668
Vorster, John, 4, 7, 9, 32, 169–70, 217, 218, 220, 222, 224, 368, 510
Vryburg, 57, 276, 309

Walus, Janusz, 43n
Wauchope, George, 358
Webster, David, 33, 43n, 735
whites: attitudes of, 16, 141–42, 196–97, 199, 232, 257–59, 375–79, 399, 439, 446, 481–85, 574, 594, 598, 610–11, 709–10; black reconciliation with, 181, 313, 315, 691–93; emigration of, 174; English-speaking, 170, 174, 259; farms and farmers, 18, 23, 27, 28, 137, 155, 440; immigration of, 31, 228–32; Jewish, 689–91, 715; leftist, 66, 376, 458; liberal, 20, 25, 65–68, 253, 259, 376, 378, 484–85, 660–61, 667–68; post-apartheid status of, 438; right-wing, 35, 37, 93, 143, 212, 251, 258, 439, 597; students, 67, 599; victimized for political role, 313; working class, 4, 49, 250, 587. *See also* African National Congress and; Afrikaners; Black Sash; business; Democratic Party; National Union of South African Students; Progressive Federal Party; United Democratic Front and
Wilkinson, Philip, 66, 78n, 381–84
Wilkinson, Rodney, 157n
Williamson, Craig, 159n, 506
witchcraft, belief in, 101–02, 363–64
Wolpe, Harold, 182, 202n, 637
women, 84, 293, 358, 376, 381, 428, 452–53, 520–22, 564–65, 631–32, 633–36, 657, 726; collective weakness of African, 105–06, 357; feminism and, 105, 126, 564–65, 634; multiple oppression of African, 306, 316, 426, 565, 631; patriarchal culture and African, 100, 105, 125, 520–22, 565, 634, 655; workers, 105, 360, 426, 565. *See also* African National Congress; South African Communist Party; United Democratic Front
women's organizations, 46–47, 53, 105–106, 310, 327, 458; African Women's Organization, 670; Federation of South African Women (FEDSAW), 46, 50, 105–06, 588; Federation of Transvaal Women (FEDTRAW), 106, 460, 686; Port Elizabeth Women's Organisation (PEWO), 395, 428; United Democratic Front Women's Congress, 106; United Women's Congress (UWCO), 106, 460; United Women's Organisation (UWO), 46, 105, 460; Women's Front, 105–06, 460
Woodstock, 379–80

workers: African, 48, 61–65, 249, 350, 369–72; call for leadership by, 102, 318, 370–72; coloured, 68–69, 72–73; commuter, 17, 18, 243, 251, 355; labour bureaus, 240, 276; migrant, 17–18, 33, 71, 101, 209–10, 242, 243, 249, 303, 306, 316, 351, 391, 397, 404, 448, 580. *See also* economy; farm workers; trade unions; whites

Xego, Michael, 273–74
Xhosas, 113, 159n, 159n, 625
Xuma, Alfred B., 565
Xundu, Mcebisi, 112, 388, 389, 412, 529

Yacoob, Zac, 77n, 298, 458
Yengeni, Tony, 619
Young, Michael, 181–82, 637
youth, black, 21, 267, 447–48, 452, 513, 534; "comrades"/*amabutho*/"young lions," 27, 69, 83, 84, 85, 86, 92, 100, 101–02, 112, 112–113n, 185, 203n, 208, 279, 281, 425, 726; female, 98; intergenerational tensions and, 21, 27, 33, 59, 69, 84, 100, 102, 185, 435; problems of, 185, 385; self-defense units and, 186, 209, 461, 563; unemployed, 58, 72, 73, 99–100, 195, 385, 586–87; "ungovernability" and, 83, 100, 185, 187, 284, 399, 431, 432, 455, 461, 561, 564, 572, 604, 606, 608
youth organizations, 46, 47, 53, 58, 60, 65, 73, 100, 208, 431, 462, 606, 653; Azanian National Youth Unity (AZANYU), 155, 195; Azanian Youth Organisation (AZANYO), 200n; Cape Youth Congress (CAYCO), 60, 100, 200n, 279; Cradock Youth Association (CRADOYA), 331; Halayo, 328; Port Elizabeth Youth Congress (PEYCO), 60, 72, 100, 426; Sekhukhuneland Youth Organisation (SEYO), 101; South African Youth Congress (SAYCO), 102–03, 107, 200n, 462, 606, 726; Soweto Youth Congress (SOYCO), 60, 69, 100, 200n, 385–86; Uitenhage Youth Congress (UYCO), 72, 73; Western Cape Youth League, 319; Young Christian Workers. *See also* churches
Yugoslavia, 586

Zaaiman, Andre, 205n, *382*
Zambia, 5, 37, 121, 126, 130, 136, 142, 152, 154, 184, 185, 197, 203n, 220, 528, 536, 576, 625, 691, 694, 732
Zani, Thami, 163n
Zihlangu, Dorothy, 200n
Zimbabwe (Rhodesia), 5, 118n, 131, 141, 144, 184, 187, 202n, 218–19, 238, 267, 571; 1980 election, 7, 217, 729; African National Congress in, 123, 130, 133, 139, 146, 423, 495, 496, 510, 536, 537, 542, 627, 694; Pan Africanist Congress in, 153, 154, 511, 670, 720
Zondo, Andrew, 445
Zulu, Alphaeus, 235–37
Zulu, Enoch, 156
Zulu, Thami (pseudonym of Muziwakhe Ngwenya), 194
Zulus, 112, 159n, 371–72, 448, 529, 530
Zuma, Jacob, 95, 160n, 182, 186, 206n, 629, 630

Gail M. Gerhart holds degrees from Harvard and Columbia universities. She has lived and worked in Africa for more than 25 years and has taught political science at the University of Nairobi, the University of Botswana, the American University in Cairo, Columbia University, and the University of the Witwatersrand, where she was a Fulbright visiting professor in 1994. She is the author of *Black Power in South Africa: The Evolution of an Ideology,* and the co-author of volumes 3, 4, and 5 of *From Protest to Challenge.*

Clive L. Glaser has degrees from the University of the Witwatersrand and Cambridge University. In 1995–96 he managed the Western Cape Oral History Project at the University of Cape Town. Since 1997 he has lectured in history at the University of the Witwatersrand. He is author of *Bo-Tsotsi: The Youth Gangs of Soweto, 1935–1976,* and has been editor of the journal *African Studies* since 2001.